# The *REDSKINS* Encyclopedia

## MICHAEL RICHMAN

TEMPLE UNIVERSITY PRESS
Philadelphia

# DEDICATION

To my wife, Cheryl Richman, who provided constant inspiration and support as I strived to complete this project. When the work appeared overwhelming, she often reminded me that on our first date, in April 1995, I talked about writing a book.

To my father, Ed Richman, who eagerly introduced me to the sports world when I was a kid and planted the seeds for my Redskins fanaticism.

Temple University Press
1601 North Broad Street
Philadelphia PA 19122
*www.temple.edu/tempress*

∞ The paper used in this publication meets the requirements of the American National Standard for Information Sciences—Permanence of Paper for Printed Library Materials, ANSI Z39.48-1992

The photo collage on the title page represents all eight decades of Redskins football: running back Cliff Battles (lower left) starred in the 1930s; quarterback Sammy Baugh (33) led the 1942 world championship squad, one of the Redskins' two NFL titles in their early years; running back Charlie "Choo Choo" Justice (22) provided excitement in the 1950s; quarterback Sonny Jurgensen (9), plus star receivers Charley Taylor (42) and Bobby Mitchell and tight end Jerry Smith (87), fueled an explosive offense in the 1960s; coach George Allen and quarterback Billy Kilmer (top row, second from left) led the team to five playoff appearances in the 1970s; defensive tackle Darryl Grant (77) made one of the most iconic plays in Redskins history by returning an interception for a touchdown in the 1982 NFC championship game; the Redskins followed with a win in Super Bowl XVII, after which NFL Commissioner Pete Rozelle presented the Vince Lombardi Trophy to Redskins owner Jack Kent Cooke (bottom row, third from left); the Hogs (top row, fourth from left) were key to the team's three Super Bowl titles in the 1980s and early 1990s; quarterback Brad Johnson (14) threw for more than 4,000 yards in 1999; receiver Santana Moss (bottom right) has made breathtaking plays in the 21st century.

A photo gallery of Redskins players through the years appears at the beginning of each chapter. Featured are (left to right) Hall of Fame quarterback-defensive back-punter Sammy Baugh (1937–52), running back Steve Bagarus (1945–46, 48), running back Johnny Olszewski (1958–60), Hall of Fame quarterback Sonny Jurgensen (1964–74), running back Larry Brown (1969–76), defensive end Dexter Manley (1981–89), receiver Charlie Brown (1982–84), receiver Art Monk (1980–93), cornerback Darrell Green (1983–2002), kick returner Brian Mitchell (1990–99), linebacker LaVar Arrington (2000–05), and current quarterback Jason Campbell.

This book is not sanctioned by the NFL or its teams.

Library of Congress Cataloging-in-Publication Data

Richman, Michael, 1961–
    The Redskins encyclopedia / Michael Richman ; foreword by Dexter Manley.
        p.  cm.
    ISBN-13: 978-1-59213-542-4 (cloth : alk. paper)
    ISBN-10: 1-59213-542-0 (cloth : alk. paper)
  1.  Washington Redskins (Football team)—History.  I. Title.
    GV956.W3R53 2008
    796.332'6409753—dc22
                                                    2007017378

2  4  6  8  9  7  5  3

# Contents

# Acknowledgments

WHEN I EMBARKED on this project in January 2000, never did I think that more than seven years would pass before it would see the light of day. During that period, many people cooperated with me to help make it a reality. I will be eternally grateful to all.

Let me start with my attorney and confidante, Phil Hochberg, the erstwhile Redskins public address and press box announcer of nearly four decades and a member of the panel that selected the 70 greatest Redskins in 2002. In addition to assisting with contractual issues and proofreading the manuscript, Phil encouraged me to forge ahead when things appeared murky as I was in the process of switching publishers. He remained optimistic that the project would one day succeed and showed unwavering patience in the face of my persistent expressions of panic. Phil's colleague, Karl Means, provided superb legal support.

Of those within the Redskins' organization, I must first extend a heartfelt thanks to the team's editorial director, Casey Husband. Since 1999, Casey has relied on me as his chief history writer, a role that assisted me enormously in my work on the book. Additional appreciation goes to Gary Fitzgerald, Karl Swanson, Jackie Gage, Larry Michael, Tim DeLaney, and the Redskins' public relations staff.

I am also indebted to the many former Redskins who granted me interviews and kindly shared their thoughts and recollections of the team. The list of players is long, but I must single out six who deserve special recognition: Redskins greats Charley Taylor, Sam Huff, Joe Theismann, Dexter Manley, Diron Talbert, and Vince Promuto. Each spent hours with me on the phone answering questions, offering insight impromptu, and never telling me that they had to leave to do something else. I know that athletes can feel nostalgic when reminiscing about their playing days, but it is still flattering to know how much of their time they gave. Many present-day Redskins were also accommodating, in particular Jon Jansen.

I can't forget three other former Redskins: Andre Collins, who provided valuable contact information in his role as the director of retired players for the NFLPA; Jim Ricca, the ex-president of the Washington Redskins Alumni Association; and Clyde Shugart. In addition to agreeing to interviews, Ricca and Shugart allowed me to sift through piles of old newspaper articles, game programs, and media guides. Jerry Olsen, the current director of the alumni association, was always at my beck and call for contact information, as was Laura Jacobs of the NFL Alumni Association.

Two other amazing helpers were former Redskins president John Kent Cooke of the Jack Kent Cooke Foundation, an organization named after the late Redskins owner that awards college scholarships to high-achieving students with financial needs, and Redskins fanatic Samu Quereshi. Both gave me access to photographs and other artwork from their treasure troves of Redskins memorabilia. Long-time Redskins fan Paul Herfurth and Terri Crane-Lamb of the Washington Redskins Cheerleaders Alumni Association also provided artwork, and Tom Riley of Eureka Van and Storage generously facilitated my researching of Redskins archive material.

Phil Hochberg is one of only two people never to play for the Redskins to be part of the Ring of Fame.

Several others deserve recognition:

- Steve Sabol of NFL Films and former Redskins radio play-by-play man Steve Gilmartin, both of whom graciously gave their time to review the manuscript.
- Pete Fierle, Saleem Choudhry, and Jason Aikens of the Pro Football Hall of Fame.
- Bob Carroll of the Pro Football Researchers Association, an organization dedicated to documenting and popularizing pro football history. Carroll co-authored *Total Football II: The Official Encyclopedia of the National Football League*, which was an excellent resource. T. J. Troupe of PFRA provided insightful analysis.
- The staff at Temple University Press and P. M. Gordon Associates, including Project Editor Linnea Hermanson.
- Dario Savarese of The Quarterback Club.
- John Labombarda of Elias Sports Bureau.
- Joseph White, the lead sportswriter for the Associated Press in the Washington area and my former boss with the AP.
- Long-time D.C. sportswriter and current *Washington Times* columnist Dick Heller, who offered editorial guidance, and Redskins beat reporter John Keim of the *Washington Examiner* and sports journalist Grant Paulsen of XM Satellite Radio and other media, both of whom provided research material.
- WTEM radio (Sports Talk 980) sports director Andy Pollin, for his research assistance.
- My researchers, who dug up vital information and compiled statistics: Bryan Greenberg, Danny Heller, Eric Nolle, Zack Klitzman, Michael Kaplan, Haywood Miller, Robert Brown, Sean Dunn, Buddy Sutton, Michael Karloff, and Alex Kaufman.

To those whom I failed to recognize for their contributions, please accept my apologies.

# Foreword

WHILE I WAS GROWING UP in Houston, my whole life was about football. I loved playing pickup games in the neighborhood and competing in school games. When the Dolphins and the Vikings came to Houston in 1974 to play in Super Bowl VIII, I walked several miles by myself just to watch players get off the bus. I saw Chuck Foreman, Sammy White, Jim Marshall, Fran Tarkenton, and other star players. That was the biggest thing in my life.

When the Redskins drafted me in 1981, I learned fast that I wasn't the only person who loved the game of football. People in Washington do, too, and they're so passionate about the team I played with for a decade, the Redskins. I wore the burgundy and gold at a time when Redskins wins were so common. I was honored to be part of such a great organization, and I feel like I'm still a part of it.

These days, I hear so many Redskins fans talk about the great players that stand out in the team's history going back to the days at Griffith Stadium: Sammy Baugh, Eddie LeBaron, Gene Brito. People also talk to me about Bobby Mitchell, Sonny Jurgensen, Charley Taylor, and Brig Owens. My name is mentioned in that same category, and I am proud to be part of such a hallowed group. There's a common denominator. People put their issues aside—black, white, rich, or poor, and they have a common admiration for the Redskins. That's all part of the team's loyal and fanatical fan base.

The Redskins have a rich history and have been a part of the fabric of the nation's capital for along time. As one of the NFL's original teams, they have also made a huge contribution to the league's storied history. All of that comes alive in *The Redskins Encyclopedia,* which tells the Redskins' story in a comprehensive and entertaining way. It's an information bonanza that makes you want to keep reading. Redskins fans are special, and they deserve a book like this.

Dexter Manley

# Introduction

WASHINGTON, D.C., as the popular belief goes, is not a true sports town in the mold of, say, New York, Philadelphia, Boston, or Chicago. The nation's capital is a four pro-sport city—football, baseball, basketball, and hockey—but there's something fascinating about the way one team dwarfs the others in popularity and is a local cultural phenomenon, to boot. That team has sold out all of its home games for the past four decades and has established such a grip on the National Capital Region that a win puts an extra skip in the community's step and fuels the sales of thousands of additional newspapers on Monday morning, but a loss triggers many long faces.

That team is the Washington Redskins.

The Redskins are a Washington icon along the lines of the White House, Congress, and the Supreme Court. The three most scrutinized people in the city are the president, the Redskins' coach, and the Redskins' quarterback—not necessarily in that order. "Hail to the Redskins," some would argue, is a more popular song in Washington today than the salute to the president, "Hail to the Chief." True, D.C. is not a sports town. But it is a Redskins town!

"The Redskins in this town are a unique property," said Rick "Doc" Walker, a local sports media personality who played tight end for the Redskins in the 1980s. "It's a tremendous relationship."

"The Redskins are a significant part of the history and spirit of the capital region community," said former Virginia senator George Allen, the son of famed Redskins coach George Allen. "The spirit of the song 'Fight on, Fight on, Til you have won, Sons of Washington'—that was the spirit of this whole region after the Pentagon was hit on September 11th."

The Redskins' reputation as the crown jewel of the local sports scene is a product of the team's status as the oldest and most storied sports franchise in town, in addition to having one of the richest traditions in the National Football League. In the 75 years since settling in Boston in 1932 (before moving to the nation's capital in 1937), the Redskins have won five NFL championships, including three Super Bowls, while making 21 postseason appearances. All three Super Bowl wins came during their glory days in the 1980s and early 1990s, when the Redskins were one of the league's elite teams season after season, a distinction that's still fresh in the minds of many Redskins fans. The Wizards, the Capitals, and the Nationals, by comparison, have one championship among them since they've been in Washington. (The Washington Senators won the World Series in 1924. They left the nation's capital in 1971, and the area was without a baseball team until the Nationals began play in 2005.)

There have been lean Redskins years, such as the post-World War II playoff drought, which lasted a quarter-century, and a stretch of mediocrity that has extended through most of the 1990s and into the early years of the 21st century. Throughout these down periods, however, the area's enthusiasm for its treasured football franchise has barely waned.

The regional phenomenon of this team and its supporters is the theme of *The Redskins Encyclopedia*. This book not only captures the history of the Redskins but explains why a city and a sports team came to be so intertwined, and why the identity of one would simply seem odd without the other.

In a metropolitan area that is diverse economically, racially, religiously, and culturally, the Redskins are the great unifier. The region is loaded with lawyers, lobbyists, and government bureaucrats and contractors, along with hosts of other white-collar employees, and so much of what happens revolves around politics, a hotbed of divisiveness.

"One of the things I loved about the Redskins is their fan base," said a Redskins great from the 1980s, colorful defensive end Dexter Manley. "There's such great tradition. We all seemed to come together for the same common denominator—to win. You could say in Washington everyone is so happy when the Redskins win. They would bring a Republican and Democrat together, and I bet they could settle a bill in a minute."

Diron Talbert, a Redskins defensive tackle in the 1970s, made this astute observation: "Washington really needs for that franchise to always be a winner because it is such a negative, negative town due to the politics. The city is much different than a lot of other cities to play in because everything is so negative. Yet, it really boosts the people and fans whenever the team is doing good. It's like it rejuvenates everybody."

Talbert told of an important detail that the city's mayor in the early 1970s, Walter Washington, shared during a visit to Redskin Park: "He said, 'On Sunday when you guys are playing, the crime rate is very low in the District.' He just laughed like hell, and so did we."

The Redskins captivated the area from the time they set foot in the nation's capital. They won the league championship in 1937 and stand as the only NFL team to do so in its inaugural season in a new city. Their coach at the time, Ray Flaherty, praised Redskins supporters after his squad beat the Bears in the 1937 championship game.

"It's not merely the contrast between Washington and Boston fans," Flaherty said in the *Washington Evening Star*. "It's the fact that the sentiment in Washington is a thing apart, something which couldn't be imagined. Believe you me, this has been the happiest football season of my life. Even if we had lost yesterday, the memory of those Washington fans would have been sufficient to cheer me through the next nine months until we return."

The Redskins' mystique was born. The team won two NFL titles and appeared in six championship games during that early golden era, which saw the emergence of the franchise's first perennial superstar, Sammy Baugh. Today, he's part of an esteemed list of Redskins who are indelibly linked with the franchise, players such as Sonny Jurgensen, Bobby Mitchell, Charley Taylor, Joe Theismann, John Riggins, Art Monk, and Darrell Green. Their biographies are in this book, as are the stories of many other players, season-by-season breakdowns, and scores of highlights and anecdotes that illuminate the team's history.

You'll also learn that the Redskins have built one of the most rabid fan bases in all of sports. Every Redskins home game has been sold out from 1966 to the present. Many people who bought Redskins season tickets in the franchise's early years have handed them down to members of their family like a treasured heirloom, and thousands of people are on the team's season ticket waiting list.

"One thing about the fans here in Washington, they've been there forever," Redskins coach Joe Gibbs said. "Those guys that have those tickets—it wasn't somebody who came in here late and grabbed one. We've got a fan base that really understands what the Redskins are all about. They've been there year in and year out. They know good football, they know bad football. They're going to let you know it when they don't like it, and they're also going to make that stadium a place that other teams will have a tough time in—if we're doing our part playing and coaching."

The Redskins' fan base actually spreads beyond the Washington area. They were the southernmost NFL team for many years and thus gained staunch supporters in Virginia, the Carolinas, and Georgia, among other parts of the region. That following has dissipated since other franchises have emerged in the South, but pockets of diehard Redskins fans still exist in the South Atlantic states. Large pro-Redskins contingents can also be found in cities such as Phoenix and St. Louis. There is even a Redskins fan club in England.

Supporters of other NFL teams, most notably the Cowboys and Giants, are scattered throughout the D.C. metro area, but

The Redskins have sold out all of their home games for the past four decades.

they are just flyspecks in a region that bleeds burgundy and gold. After the Redskins defeated Denver in Super Bowl XXII, 650,000 fans showed up for a parade in Washington to celebrate the win. Get this: Nearly 50,000 turned out to watch a *scrimmage* between the Redskins and the Ravens at FedExField in August 2006. Redskins receiver Brandon Lloyd said none of his *regular-season games* with the San Francisco 49ers the year before drew 50,000 fans.

Go to the parking lot at FedExField prior to a Redskins home game, and you'll see a sea of burgundy and gold. Thousands of ardent Redskins fans are wearing jerseys of their favorite players, and others are dressed in imaginative Redskins attire, such as Ian Godfrey, who wears a full Indian headdress with rubber shoulder pads, a burgundy Redskins jersey, white football pants, and Redskins shoes. His face is painted burgundy and gold. Then there's John Carter, whose license plate reads CB H8R—"Cowboy Hater"—and Jim and Vicki Brigman, who run a Redskins fan club in Atlanta and have driven to Washington for a Redskins-Cowboys game. Many vehicles in the lot are painted burgundy and gold, including a couple of school buses, one of which says "Redskins 12th man" on the side.

What makes a Redskins fan?

"It's for the love of the game," Carter said. "You've got to feel like you're a part of it, and the only way to feel like you're a part of it is to buy the stuff, wear their clothes, and support the Redskins even through good times and bad times."

Samu Quereshi, a native Washingtonian who maintains a vast collection of Redskins memorabilia in the basement of his house in Bethesda, Maryland, put it this way: "The Redskins were just ingrained in my heart and soul at a young age. I started to pay close attention to them in 1971, George Allen's first year, then in '72 they're in a Super Bowl. We've been really blessed to have all of these competitive years and all of the playoff years. There's a pride in the team and a real pride in the tradition for me."

Redskins fans are hungry for news about their team, and competition is fierce among media outlets in the Washington area, one of the largest media markets in the country, when reporting on the squad. The first item on the local television news after a Redskins game is often a report on the game and its implications. The area's two major broadsheet newspapers,

the *Washington Post* and the *Washington Times,* often run Redskins game coverage on the front page. Even the benching of quarterback Mark Brunell and the subsequent promotion of Jason Campbell to the starting role in 2006 was reflected on the front page of those two papers, along with the *Washington Examiner.* (The *Post* ran a letter from a disgruntled Washington-area resident on November 25, 2006, saying that there was too much Redskins coverage above the fold on the front page and that such news should be relegated to the sports section.) During the season, callers bombard the phone lines of the area's all-sports radio stations, WTEM and Triple X ESPN radio.

Perhaps Jim Murray, the late Pulitzer Prize–winning sports columnist for the *Los Angeles Times,* best described who the Redskins really are. The Cowboys have been known as "America's Team" since the early 1970s, but Murray was convinced that another team deserved that title. On the day the Redskins beat the Dolphins in Super Bowl XVII in Pasadena, California, on January 30, 1983, he wrote the following:

This team saw Slingin' Sammy Baugh, Sonny Jurgensen, Whiskey Kilmer.

Cliff Battles ranged behind its line long before John Riggins did, Frank Filchock passed here. Riley Smith blocked. Bobby Mitchell used to disappear here. Charley Taylor ran long, gorgeous pass routes and plucked the ball from an opponent's ear just as he crossed the goal line. Larry Brown, with a hearing aid in his helmet, crunched lines here. "Bullet Bill" Dudley caught punts here.

The Washington Redskins are a venerable team steeped in tradition. They're as much a part of Americana as Lee's horse or Sheridan's cavalry. They've got their own song, they were the first to have their own band and cheerleaders.

They should be "America's Team."

So Hail to the Redskins!
Hail Victory!
Braves on the Warpath,
Fight for old D.C.!

# The Franchise Is Born

THE ROARING '20s marked a decade of unbridled prosperity in the United States and an era when entertainment came into its own as a mainstay of American culture. Americans could choose from jazz, movies, theater, and radio offerings—and sports. In this golden age of sports, spectators forked out money in record amounts to see baseball games, college and pro football action, and boxing matches.

George Preston Marshall wanted some of the gate receipts. A wealthy entrepreneur who owned a Washington, D.C., business called the Palace Laundry, Marshall had diversified career interests. His business inclinations led him to collaborate with George Halas, owner of the NFL's Chicago Bears, and Cleveland department store tycoon Max Rosenblum to organize the American Basketball League (ABL). It was regarded as the first true national basketball circuit.

Marshall fielded an ABL team called the Palace Big Five, which began play in the 1925–26 season at the Arcadia, a 2,000-seat gym at 14th Street and Park Road in Washington. The franchise was a financial disaster, and Marshall sold it during the ABL's third season in 1928. But through his involvement in the league, he cultivated a strong relationship with Halas and ABL president Joe Carr, who was also the NFL's president. The two asked Marshall to invest in an NFL team.

The NFL was then in its infancy. Formed in 1920 as the American Professional Football Association, the league was renamed the National Football League after the 1921 season. By 1926, it had ballooned to 26 teams. Excitement surged along the way, mainly owing to the presence of stars such as Red Grange and Ernie Nevers, who electrified crowds with their offensive prowess. At one game in the 1925 season, 70,000 people turned out to see Grange's Chicago Bears host the New York Giants.

But the NFL began to struggle. Most teams were small-town franchises with limited financial backing and couldn't support pro football. Several clubs, including the Canton (Ohio) Bulldogs, the Hammond (Indiana) Pros, the Frankford (Pennsylvania) Yellow Jackets, and the Duluth (Minnesota) Eskimos, folded or suspended play.

Recognizing that business moguls like Marshall were needed to support franchises, Carr, Halas, and other NFL leaders made him an offer. With a goal of establishing teams in larger towns and cities, the league proposed to sell him the rights to the Newark (New Jersey) Tornadoes franchise, which had been forfeited to the league before the 1931 season. League officials mandated that Marshall locate the team in Boston starting in the 1932 season.

Marshall liked the idea and formed a syndicate that he led with three other investors. To minimize risk, the league offered the ownership group a reduced franchise fee. The syndicate agreed to pay $1,500 and to post another $1,500 as a guarantee that the Boston franchise would finish its first season. Years later, Marshall admitted that he never paid either fee. "The franchise didn't cost us a dime," he once said. "Just picked it up for the asking and the willingness to underwrite the losses."

On July 10, 1932, NFL owners voted in Atlantic City, New Jersey, to make Boston an official franchise in a league that had been whittled down to eight teams.

Said the Associated Press:

The National Professional Football League voted today to cut the player limit from 22 to 20. The league will open its season Sept. 18 when the Chicago Cardinals play in Green Bay, and will close Dec. 11 with a game between Green Bay and the Chicago Bears at Chicago.

The circuit will be composed of eight teams, equally divided between East and West. Boston is the only new team admitted to membership, replacing Providence, which was given the right to maintain an inactive franchise for a year. The Philadelphia franchise was forfeited.

Boston seemed like a logical choice to place a team. The hopping sports town supported two major league baseball clubs, the Red Sox in the American League and the Braves in the National League, and was enthusiastic about hockey, boxing, basketball, rowing, and even pro wrestling. College football was a hit at local schools such as Harvard, Boston University, Boston College, Amherst, Holy Cross, Dartmouth, and Tufts.

But Boston had never accepted pro football. In 1926, a team known as the Boston Bulldogs played in the first American Football League, which was founded to compete with the NFL. The league lasted only a year, and the Bulldogs reappeared in 1929 as an NFL franchise. A 4–4–0 season and failure to attract fans forced the team to fold.

Marshall faced an additional challenge: the nation was in the throes of the Great Depression. When people spent money, it was critical that the product provided the greatest possible return—a belief that applied equally to entertainment.

The businessman was optimistic that he could overcome those obstacles. One of his first moves was to sign a lease to play at Braves Field, the Braves' home stadium. He nicknamed his team the Braves. (In the NFL's early years, team owners sometimes copied the name of the city's baseball team to maintain identity with fans.)

To coach the squad, Marshall hired Lud Wray, a former player and coach at the University of Pennsylvania who had also played for the NFL's Buffalo All-Americans and Rochester Jeffersons. The owner gave Wray virtual carte blanche for recruiting players. No college draft existed, and the eight teams were free to sign anyone. Wray signed about 40 players, including a 260-pound tackle from Washington State, Albert Glen "Turk" Edwards, and West Virginia Wesleyan halfback Cliff Battles. Years later, the two were inducted into the Pro Football Hall of Fame.

Wray nabbed other promising rookies: guard George Hurley, a college teammate of Edwards; Southern California products in halfback Erny Pinckert and fullback Jim Musick; end Paul "Rip" Collins and tackle Jim MacMurdo out of Pittsburgh; quarterback Henry Thomas "Honolulu" Hughes and halfback Reggie Rust out of Oregon State; Wisconsin guard Joe Kresky; and Fordham center Tony Siano.

Wray also sought players with NFL experience and chose from an excellent pool. Three NFL teams had folded after the 1931 season, sending about 60 players scurrying. He acquired two ex-New York Giants, 235-pound tackle Corrie "Chang" Artman and back Tony Plansky; former Chicago Cardinals center Mickey Erickson; and end George Kenneally, who had played one of his five NFL seasons for the Boston Bulldogs.

The Braves opened their exhibition season by shutting out the semipro Quincy (Massachusetts) Trojans, 25–0, behind Musick's two touchdowns and one apiece by Plansky and Rust. The Providence Steam Roller, a team that consisted of many players once cut by the Braves, pulled off a 9–6 win. But with only a day's rest, the Braves bounced back to crush another semipro team 31–0. Next up: Boston's inaugural regular season game against the Brooklyn Dodgers.

# 2

# 1932–1936: Surviving in Beantown

LIFE WAS HECTIC for Boston Braves owner George Preston Marshall in the days preceding the debut of his NFL franchise. He crisscrossed the city to promote the Braves to sportswriters at myriad Boston newspapers. And unlike in the coming years, when he became irate at local media for what he perceived as skimpy coverage of his team, he had every reason to be excited on the morning of Saturday, October 1, 1932, when a big, bold headline streaked across the top of a *Boston Globe* sports page: "Boston Braves Open Pro Schedule Tomorrow Against Brooklyn."

The Braves faced a stiff test to stop one of the league's top passers, Benny Friedman, now a member of the Pro Football Hall of Fame. Friedman was no sensation against the new franchise but threw two touchdown passes to his favorite target, Jack Grossman, to lift the Dodgers to a 14–0 victory before 6,000 fans at Braves Field. The Braves earned their first win the next week, 14–6 over the New York Giants, although they couldn't produce another victory until four games later, when they beat Staten Island, 19–6. They struggled to a 4–4–2 record, fourth in the NFL behind the eventual champion Chicago Bears, the Green Bay Packers, and the Portsmouth (Ohio) Spartans.

It was also a struggle at the box office. Boston fans didn't embrace the Braves, contrary to what Marshall had first expected, and the team lost $46,000 in 1932. Marshall's three partners became skittish and quit, leaving him as the team's sole owner. After the 1932 season, the baseball Braves threatened to raise the rent for Marshall's use of Braves Field. He decided to move the team to Fenway Park, home of the Red Sox, and renamed it the Redskins, to suggest a kinship with the Red Sox. He also wanted to connect with an Indian theme similar to the Braves.

The hands-on Marshall fired Wray, too, and replaced him with William "Lone Star" Dietz, a part-blooded Native American. Dietz recruited six football stars from the Haskell Indian School in Kansas, where he had once played with the great Jim Thorpe and later coached for four years. The recruits included "Chief" Larry Johnson, Louis "Rabbit" Weller, and John Orien Crow. The charismatic coach told his players to pose with war paint, feathers, and full headdresses before the 1933 home opener against the Giants.

"During the game, the paint bothered some of the boys because it clogged their pores," Redskins halfback Cliff Battles said in Bob Curran's 1969 book, *Pro Football's Rag Days.* "The whole thing was so overdone it was embarrassing."

Battles and fullback Jim Musick gave the Redskins a one-two punch during the 1933 season. Musick led the NFL in rushing with 809 yards, and Battles collected 737, including 215 alone in a game against the Giants, the first time in NFL history a player had rushed for at least 200 yards in a game. The duo combined to score nine touchdowns. Tackle Turk Edwards was a rock on the front line, playing 710 of a possible 720 minutes.

But the mediocre Redskins finished 5–5–2, followed by a 6–6 mark in 1934. Marshall fired Dietz and hired Eddie Casey, an ex-college football star who had coached Harvard to a 20–11–1 record from 1931 to 1934. The Redskins lost seven straight games under Casey and finished 2–8–1 in 1935, the second-worst record in the league, behind Philadelphia.

Marshall then executed his third coaching change in four seasons. He showed Casey the door and replaced him with Ray "Red" Flaherty, a former All-NFL end and Giants assistant coach. At the same time, the NFL adopted a college football draft to give all teams a fair shot at competing. The Redskins selected Alabama star quarterback Riley Smith in the first round and Wayne Millner, a two-time All-American receiver from Notre Dame, in the eighth. Millner accounted for the third future Hall of Fame inductee on the team's 1936 roster, joining Battles and Edwards.

By then the NFL was stabilizing financially, although the Redskins were suffering at the turnstile. They were averaging about 5,000 fans at Fenway Park and incurring thousands of dollars in annual losses. Such college football teams as Harvard and Boston College were a huge attraction on Saturday, and many Bostonians occupied themselves on Sunday by going to church and the racetrack. To worsen matters, the Boston Shamrocks began play in 1936 in the upstart American Football League and won the championship.

With their first three games on the road that year, the Redskins lost to Pittsburgh, 10–0, but rebounded to beat Philadelphia, 26–3, and Brooklyn, 14–3. Battles was brilliant in both wins. He scored two touchdowns against the Eagles, one on a 67-yard run, and ran 68 yards for a touchdown against the Dodgers.

The 2–1 Redskins then hosted the Giants in their home opener, a game the *Globe* touted as "one of the bitterest rivalries in the National Football League, one that has more angles this year than ever before." For it, the Redskins unveiled new uniforms that consisted of jerseys with a deeper red color and large numbers on both sides, as well as gold pants.

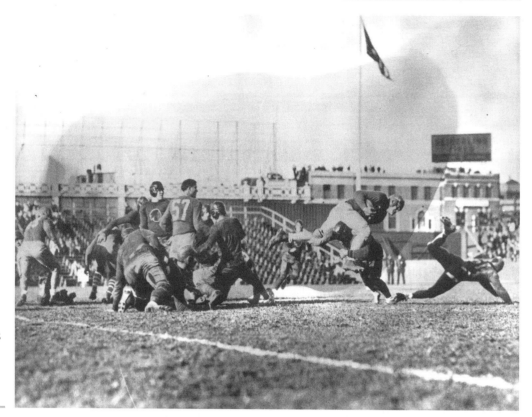

The Redskins battle the Portsmouth (Ohio) Spartans during the 1933 season, which marked the introduction of the Redskins' nickname.

Despite hard running by Battles and a solid effort by a stingy Redskins defense, New York won, 7–0. Giants back Alphonse "Tuffy" Leemans provided the only score with a second-quarter touchdown run. The game attracted a respectable crowd of nearly 18,000 fans, many of whom left in a sour mood—and not just because the Redskins lost.

Marshall noticed before the game that the crowd was growing and decided to raise the price of bleacher tickets at Fenway Park from 55 cents to $1.10 on the spot to help cover the team's mounting financial losses. The increase was a fortune for people in the Depression era, and his spontaneous decision irked those who were victimized.

"The new price arrangement found instant disfavor with the grandstand enthusiasts of 1935," the *Globe* wrote, " . . . they broke out with a [sarcastic] cheer right away. These 'fans' kept it up right through the ball game, rising to great heights at the end, when the announcer told when the Redskins would play at home again."

The price hike exacerbated Marshall's problems. After a 31–2 loss to the powerhouse Green Bay Packers on the road, the Redskins played six straight games at Fenway Park. A combined total of only 11,000 fans turned out to see Boston beat Philadelphia and the Chicago Cardinals, two of the league's lower-end teams, in consecutive weeks. After 11,220 people showed up for the Redskins' 7–3 loss to the Packers, Marshall's anger was palpable. He threatened to move his team to another city if attendance didn't increase markedly in the coming weeks, although he admitted that increasing ticket prices had perhaps alienated Boston fans.

"The nice thing about owning a pro football team is that all you have to do to move is pack your trunks," he said in the *Boston Herald* on November 9, 1936. "I can understand why no one came to see us play Philadelphia or the Cardinals, but when they are not even interested in seeing a team like the Packers, it is time to consider moving. Why, the Packers would draw more people in Paterson, N.J., than they did here today.

"There are five cities that would love to have us. Yes, Washington, my home town, has put a lot of pressure on me to move down there."

*Boston American* sportswriter Austen Lake responded to Marshall's tirade with a scathing column titled "George Marshall, or Portrait of Man in a Complaining Mood." He accused Marshall of expecting too much from fans, saying that they had a right to buy or not to buy tickets, and of being too demanding with reporters.

Marshall harbored a disdain for the Boston press. He lambasted the city's sportswriters for their scant coverage of the Redskins and accused them of devoting too much attention to the city's major college football teams, Harvard and Boston College, as well as to the Red Sox and Braves baseball teams. He was outraged when a leading Boston newspaper printed a six-column spread on a girls' field hockey game and nothing on the Redskins.

"The Boston sportswriters were loud in their dislike of pro football," Corinne Griffith, a one-time silent movie star who married Marshall in 1936, wrote in her 1947 book, *My Life with the Redskins*. "They didn't like the foreign ownership, and they didn't like George. At least that's what Mr. Austen Lake and Mr. Dave Egan of the *Boston American* said."

Amid the mudslinging, the 4–4 Redskins were in contention for the Eastern Division title. Their next game was at Fenway Park against the Chicago Bears, who were in a tight race with the Packers for first place in the Western Division. It was a must-win for both teams. The Bears crushed the Redskins, 26–0, before a crowd identical in size to that for the Packers game. The most entertaining scene for Redskin fans was when two peanut vendors engaged in a fight in the first-base pavilion.

But the Redskins were still alive. With wins in the last three games and losses by other teams, they could capture the Eastern Division and host the NFL championship game on December 13 at Fenway Park.

That's the way it looked on paper. Marshall had other ideas, especially after the Redskins routed Brooklyn, 30–6, and Pittsburgh, 30–0, before paltry crowds of 4,197 and 4,813 at home. "The city of Boston doesn't deserve this team," he barked. "We'll never play another game here."

Marshall immediately began seeking a site other than Boston should the Redskins, now dubbed the "lost tribe," qualify for the championship game. They did just that in their last regular season game against the Giants at the Polo Grounds in New York.

Nearly 20,000 people braved cold, wet, and foggy conditions to see the Redskins defeat the Giants, 14–0, and clinch the Eastern Division title. Don Irwin scored on a short run, and Battles returned a punt 75 yards in ankle-deep mud for the other score.

"I couldn't help being impressed by today's splendid turnout in the miserable weather," Marshall told reporters, needling Boston fans in the process.

The dedication of New Yorkers, plus Fenway Park's lack of floodlights to guard against fog or bad weather, prompted Marshall to urge NFL president Joe Carr to move the championship game from Boston to the Polo Grounds. After the Western Division champion Packers agreed to come to New York for the game, Carr approved the change.

Boston media scolded Marshall for orchestrating the move. "Regardless of conditions, a major league team should follow its schedule, and the 1936 playoff game was scheduled for the city represented by the Eastern Division winner," Paul V. Craigue of the *Globe* wrote on December 8, 1936. "Use your imagination a bit, George.

"Can you imagine the Red Sox winning the American League pennant and shifting their cud [portion] of the World Series to Yankee Stadium in the interest of the gate?"

Marshall defended his decision. Players were to receive 60 percent of the gate receipts, and he was certain the turnout at the Polo Grounds would overwhelm one at Fenway Park. He wanted his team to go where it would get the biggest returns.

"We have to be fair to the kids who won the divisional championship," he said in the *New York Times* on December 8. "If we meet Green Bay in Boston, they wouldn't get enough out of it to buy Christmas presents. But here in New York, they may get something substantial."

All the while, Marshall was eyeing another move, one that would allow his Redskins to leave Boston. He was considering three sites: Washington, the home of his laundry business; Philadelphia, where he could possibly merge the Redskins with the Eagles; and New York, a city large enough to support two football teams. Buffalo and Cleveland were also interested in the Redskins.

"I haven't decided what to do yet," Marshall said in the *Evening Star* in Washington on December 10. "And I won't be able to give it my undivided attention until I clean my fingers of some of the red ink I picked up in Massachusetts.

"We had 3,700 paying customers at the last game we played in Boston. That was a crucial game. It came close to deciding the title. The weather was perfect. My scouts tell me there are many, many more people in Boston than that. As a matter of fact, I have seen more people than that in the waiting room of the South Station on a Saturday night."

Marshall's immediate priority was selling tickets for the championship game, the first one in the NFL to be played at a neutral site. Nearly 30,000 spectators came to see the Packers, with the NFL's best offense, battle the Redskins, who sported the league's top defense.

Green Bay won, 21–6, behind three future Hall of Fame inductees who played important roles: quarterback Arnie Herber, end Don Hutson, and halfback Johnny "Blood" McNally. Herber threw two touchdown passes, the first one a 48-yarder to Hutson in the opening quarter. The Redskins responded with a 78-yard drive capped by Pug Rentner's 2-yard touchdown run. But Riley Smith missed the extra point, and Green Bay led, 7–6. On the opening drive of the second half, Herber hit Milt Gantenbein on an 8-yard scoring pass for a 14–6 game. The Packers put the game away in the fourth quarter after blocking their second punt and taking possession on Boston's 3-yard line. Bob Monnett scored on a short run.

The Redskins competed without much of their offensive firepower, as Battles injured his knee four minutes into the game and left for good. "That was akin to removing a spark plug from an automobile motor and expecting it to purr as efficiently as usual," Arthur J. Daley wrote in the *New York Times*.

What's more, Redskins center and defensive bulwark Frank Bausch got into a fight with Packers substitute Frank Butler in the third quarter. Both players were ejected, and Bausch's replacement, Larry Siemering, delivered hard-to-handle snaps that led to three fumbles.

Gross ticket receipts yielded $33,471. The Packers each received $250, compared with $180 for the Redskins. Three days later, Marshall announced the Redskins' departure from Boston. He chose Washington and negotiated with Clark Griffith, owner of the Washington Senators baseball squad, to lease Griffith Stadium for the 1937 season.

It had been a grueling ride for Marshall. He lost an estimated $100,000 over five seasons in Boston, where fans and sportswriters never fully embraced his franchise, although it suffered only one losing season. It may have been an unwinnable battle from the start. That's the way Corrine Griffith, who is credited with influencing Marshall to move the Redskins to Washington, described the situation in *My Life with the Redskins:* "No one in Boston actually cared whether they won or whether they lost; or whether they played their hearts out, out there on Fenway field; or whether they lived or whether they died."

The move to Washington became official on February 12, 1937. Was the nation's capital the right choice?

The Senators had long been the top sports attraction in town, having represented the sleepy southern city since 1901. They won the World Series in 1924 and captured the American League title in 1933 before becoming one of baseball's worst teams. On the gridiron, such local colleges as Maryland, Georgetown, George Washington, and Catholic University garnered modest fan support. The only other NFL team to ever play in the nation's capital, the Washington Senators, had

On a cold, wet, and muddy day at the Polo Grounds in New York on December 6, 1936, the Boston Redskins beat the Giants, 14–0, to win the Eastern Division and advance to the NFL championship game. Note the helmetless player in the thick of the pile.

folded after one season in 1921. One D.C. sports columnist believed the Redskins would suffer the same fate: "Some say it might be good to watch . . . once. But people won't go back week after week because the game is too imperfect. College football is more interesting."

Redskin Riley Smith told the *Sporting News* in 1997, "College football was still very popular all across the country, and Washington was still a baseball town. It was a big gamble on Mr. Marshall's part to bring us down to Washington."

It was a gamble he would win.

# 3

# 1937–1945: Redskins Transform Washington into a Championship City

**I**N THE YEARS just before and during World War II, Redskins mania consumed the nation's capital.

Democrats and Republicans alike bled burgundy and gold, and the fight song "Hail to the Redskins" became embedded in the city's culture. Anyone unable to speak intelligently on a Monday morning about a Redskins game, as *Washington Post* sportswriter Shirley Povich put it, was an "unbearable dolt."

The NFL was in its formative years, and the Redskins stood out as giants. From 1937, their inaugural year in Washington, until 1945, they amassed a magnificent 70–27–5 record. The nine-season span featured five NFL championship game appearances and two league titles. Think of a blockbuster hit.

Only one other perennial power, the Chicago Bears, matched the Redskins' dominance of that era. The two squads, in fact, carried on a classic rivalry, meeting four times in the NFL title game and each winning twice. The Redskins prevailed in 1937 and 1942, and the Bears won in 1940 and 1943. The Cleveland Rams eked out a victory in Washington's other championship game appearance in 1945.

In truth, the Redskins had a head start when they arrived in D.C. The squad, fresh off a championship game loss to Green Bay in 1936, was replete with outstanding players such as halfback Cliff Battles, end Wayne Millner, and tackle Turk Edwards, plus a shrewd coach in Ray Flaherty—all of whom were eventually enshrined in the Pro Football Hall of Fame.

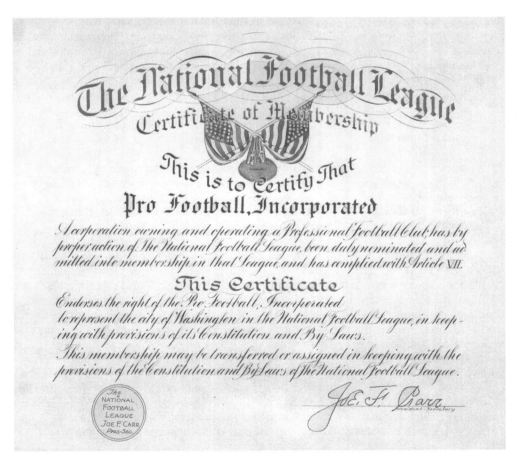

The Redskins' original NFL membership certificate

Together with Sammy Baugh, a supertalented rookie who showed up in 1937, they got the Redskins off to a rocking start in D.C.

Slingin' Sammy would be the team's main attraction for years to come. In addition to being the NFL's first great passer, he was a dangerous punter and defensive back in the days of single-platoon football, in which players on the same team competed on both sides of the ball, and evolved into one of the best all-around players ever. Other Redskins who stood out during those radiant years included quarterback Riley Smith; tackles Wilbur "Wee Willie" Wilken, Jim Barber, and John Adams; ends Charley Malone, Joe Aguirre, Ed Cifers, and Bob Masterson; guards Dick Farman, Les Olsson, Clyde Shugart, and Steve Slivinski; backs Andy Farkas, Dick Todd, Frankie Filchock, Ed Justice, Wilbur Moore, Erny Pinckert, and Steve Bagarus; and center Ki Aldrich.

The Redskins' glory coincided with an era of mixed news for the NFL. The addition of Cleveland in 1937 created a record 10 teams in a league that was becoming much more entertaining to sports fans. Single-season attendance topped one million for the first time in 1939, prompting Redskins owner George Preston Marshall, a master promoter and one of the league's most outspoken figures, to sing the NFL's praises in an interview with the *Los Angeles Times* that appeared on January 17, 1940:

> Football has become our national pastime. Football is both a game and a pageant. It can be played by any 22 men [on the field], no matter how good or how bad, and still have crowd appeal. That's why you get big crowds to high school games, to games between colleges.
>
> The National [Football] League played to a million and a quarter cash customers last year. It will play to a million and a half—maybe more—this season. Why? Because we give the public the greatest show on Earth.
>
> Now baseball, that's a commonplace game. You have one game every day, and one or more games doesn't mean anything. Besides, if it isn't played by the 18 best in the business, you are not interested. The same goes for a bum golf match or a couple of hams playing tennis. But if you saw two groups of youngsters playing touch football on a vacant lot, you would stop to see 'em. Why? Because the game has everything that appeals to Americans.
>
> And [football] has women appeal. Baseball hasn't got that. It has social background. The pageantry comes with the between-halves stunts. A big football game is an event. And of course, it follows that the National League plays the finest football in the world.

But the game Marshall was sensationalizing experienced a tenuous period in the early to mid-1940s. Players were marching off to fight for Uncle Sam in World War II, creating roster shortages that forced a number of franchise mergers. They included the Philadelphia Eagles and Pittsburgh Steelers in 1943, producing a team called the Steagles, and the Chicago Cardinals and Pittsburgh Steelers in 1944, producing a squad known as Card-Pitt. More than 600 players fought in the war; 19 lost their lives.

The war also forced many colleges to abandon football, creating a shallow pool of new talent. Rumors circulated that the NFL's 10 teams wouldn't be able to find enough capable players for the 1943 season and that the league was in jeopardy of folding.

Unlike some of his fellow owners, Marshall was more optimistic about the league's chances for survival. He said the war would eventually end and to fold would be detrimental to the NFL's future. Regarding his own squad, he said, "The Redskins won't quit. We'll continue even if it means playing [in] a four-team league."

Such drastic steps were never needed. The NFL, resuscitated by the return of many players following the war's end in 1945, quickly regained its footing on the sports landscape.

| EASTERN DIVISION | WESTERN DIVISION |
|---|---|
| Washington Redskins | Cleveland Rams |
| New York Giants | Chicago Bears |
| Philadelphia Eagles | Chicago Cardinals |
| Brooklyn Dodgers | Detroit Lions |
| Pittsburgh Pirates | Green Bay Packers |

## 1937: 8–3–0, 1ST PLACE— EASTERN DIVISION

### Head Coach: Ray Flaherty

What a sensational way for a sports team to debut in a new city! In their maiden season in Washington, the Redskins crafted an 8–3 mark to win the Eastern Division title before upending the Chicago Bears in the championship game, 28–21. To this day, the Redskins are one of only two teams in NFL history to capture a championship in the first season after relocating to another city. The Chicago Staleys won the title in 1921 after moving from Decatur, Illinois (they became the Bears in 1922).

The Redskins' performance captivated Washingtonians and extinguished doubts about whether the city had embraced its new team. At Griffith Stadium, expanded that year to seat about 34,000 people, the Redskins attracted crowds of more than 20,000 at four of six home games, including a turnout of 30,000 against the defending-champion Packers. Those numbers overwhelmed the Redskins' attendance figures in Boston.

"What really helped is we had a good team and won the championship the first year we were in Washington," Redskins halfback Sammy Baugh said years later. "I have no idea if we would have drawn fans or not if we had a real bad team. But we happened to have the best team in the league, and we proved that to be so. We got off to a good start. That got people coming to see the ball games."

Baugh himself attracted throngs of people to the ballpark. The dynamic rookie set an NFL record for pass completions with 91 in 218 attempts and threw for a league-high 1,127 yards. He also showed his versatility as a runner, a blocker, a punter, and a defensive back. He was named All-Pro, along with halfback Cliff Battles, who led the NFL in rushing yards (874) and rushing touchdowns (five), and tackle Turk Edwards, a dominant force on the line. End Charley Malone (28 catches, 419 yards) was one of the league's top receivers.

The Redskins used the sixth overall pick in the 1937 draft to select Baugh, an All-American from Texas Christian University. By the time the squad held its first-ever training camp at Anacostia Park in southeast Washington, curiosity about Baugh and the rest of the players sporting burgundy and gold was apparent. Sizable crowds flocked to watch practice, even to see players perform mundane conditioning exercises.

## Welcome, Sammy Baugh

George Preston Marshall, always the showman, immediately made 1937 first-round draft pick Sammy Baugh the focus of a publicity stunt. The owner told his prized pick, a country boy from Sweetwater, Texas, to dress in cowboy attire on his first flight to Washington. Baugh obliged and wore a ten-gallon Stetson hat, a Western-style shirt, chaps, and high-heeled cowboy boots.

In reality, Baugh was no cowboy, and he struggled to play the part. On exiting the plane in front of flashing cameras, he uttered, "Mah feet hurt."

"Mr. Marshall had his own reasons, I guess," Baugh said many years later. "I came from cowboy country, and he wanted me to dress a little cowboyish. I told him that I had some cowboy stuff but not much. I would never call myself a cowboy."

*Washington Evening Star* sportswriter Bill Dismer, Jr., described the fascination on August 29, 1937:

Definitely, the Redskins have "caught on." Whether it is the novelty of a major league professional eleven in Washington, the magic of All-America names, or the craving for football again after a long, hot summer, coach Ray Flaherty and his men have completely captured the fancy of all who have seen them during the past five days.

From the time their bus has brought the players each morning at 9:30 until they have been chased off the field some eight hours later, hundreds have followed their every move. Indeed, the only privacy the huskies have had during the day has come during their dressing in the locker room. Kids, the readiest of hero-worshippers, already have installed certain ones as their favorites and, as usual, have been the most persistent of hangers-on. Hardly has a Redskin been able to get up from a game of bridge or an easy chair in the Anacostia Field House without knocking over one of the tots.

Fans witnessed a talent-laden team. Besides Baugh and Battles, quarterback Riley Smith, halfbacks Dixie Howell and Ed Justice, and fullbacks Don Irwin and Erny Pinckert accounted for other weapons in a single-wing setup. Malone, like Wayne Millner, was among the league's best receivers, and 245-pound guard Les Olsson and 225-pound tackle Jim Barber helped Edwards anchor the front line.

Flaherty, back for his second season as the Redskins' coach, was monitoring the practice drills. His excellent work in 1936, when the Redskins lost in the championship game to Green Bay, prompted Marshall to extend his contract. While watching a practice, a confident Marshall acknowledged his team's potential: "They not only look good enough to repeat, but I think we'll beat the Green Bay Packers if we meet them in the playoffs again," he said as quoted by the *Evening Star*.

What he didn't want was a repeat of his bitter relationship with the city of Boston. He hoped Washingtonians would be much more enthusiastic about an NFL franchise than Bostonians were. To help generate interest in the Redskins, he

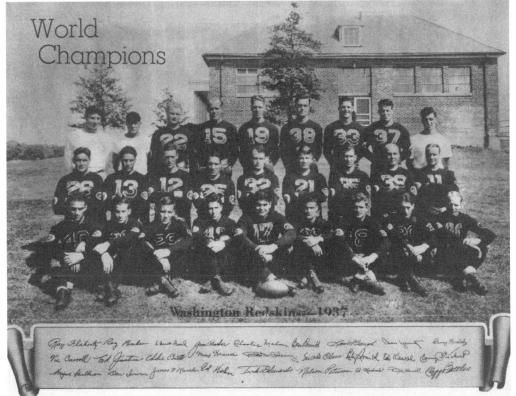

The Redskins' 1937 team championship photo

**Redskins vs. Giants --- 10 cents**

September 16, 1937

*Winners everytime*

**DODGE and PLYMOUTH**
America's Most Dependable and Economical Cars
**THE TREW MOTOR COMPANY**
ESTABLISHED 1914
1526 14TH STREET N.W.

The Redskins hosted the Giants in their inaugural game in Washington on September 16, 1937.

requested consistent coverage from sportswriters at Washington's top newspapers—the *Post,* the *Star,* the *Daily News,* and the *Times-Herald.* The *Star,* for one, ran a headline on September 11, 1937, that read, "Washington Gets Top-Notch Pro Football Team: George Marshall Gives Capital Classy Eleven Which Boston Didn't Appreciate."

"You boys have got to help me," the owner told the press. "I'm paying Sammy Baugh $5,000 to play quarterback, and I've got to put 12,000 fans in Griffith Stadium every game to break even."

On the field, the Redskins' 50–0 rout of an American Legion All-Star team served as a nice warm-up for the season opener on Thursday night, September 16, 1937, when a crowd of 24,492 appeared at Griffith Stadium to see the Redskins host the Giants. The New Yorkers were seeking revenge against a Redskins squad that prevailed when the teams last met to decide the 1936 Eastern Division champion. Riley Smith made sure that didn't happen.

Smith scored each Redskins point in their 13–3 victory. His 18-yard first-quarter field goal provided a 3–0 lead, and he kicked another 18-yarder in the final quarter to put the Redskins up, 6–3. The Giants resorted to an aerial attack to try to pull out a win, but Smith intercepted a pass, returned it 60 yards down the sideline for a touchdown, and kicked the extra point to account for the final score. As *Washington Daily News* sportswriter Dick McCann put it, "Reconstruction Finance

Chairman Jesse Jones threw out the first ball, and Riley Smith played with it all night."

Baugh was impressive, too, completing 6 of 11 passes for 115 yards. He also deflected throws and chased down runners for a Redskins defense that stifled the Giants, who once had a first-and-goal at the 2-yard line but couldn't score. Afterward, Giants star running back Tuffy Leemans said Baugh is "all they said he was."

Marshall even unveiled the wild entertainment that would mark his team's home games in coming decades. He arranged for "The Spirit of the Redskins," a pretty woman on a pinto pony, to ride the length of the field under a spotlight. A swing band played jazz and the rumba under a 40-by-50-foot mahogany stand. Irish tenor Joey Nash sang "When Irish Eyes Are Smiling" and "It Looks Like Rain in Cherry Blossom Lane" during time-outs. People dressed as Native Americans pounded on tom-toms all game.

The Redskins next hosted the Chicago Cardinals, who had upset the Packers two weeks earlier. The Cardinals also stung the Redskins, 21–14. End Gaynell Tinsley sparked Chicago's brilliant passing game with three touchdown catches.

The Redskins rebounded with an 11–7 win over Brooklyn that moved the 2–1 squad into a tie with the Giants and Pittsburgh for the Eastern Division lead, but they returned to .500 with a 14–0 loss to Philadelphia. The Eagles tallied first- and fourth-quarter touchdowns, while the Redskins blew multiple scoring chances. Washington came up empty despite penetrating the Eagles' 20-yard line four times.

The loss propelled the cantankerous Marshall into a tirade. He said the Redskins put forth a "disgraceful performance" in the "worst exhibition of professional football" he had seen in six years of owning the team. His players got the message and won six of their last seven games.

The Redskins first crafted three straight wins. They recovered from a 13–7 halftime deficit to beat the Pittsburgh Pirates, 34–20. Battles led the comeback with touchdown runs of 65, 60, and 71 yards and returned an interception 65 yards. Next came a 10–7 win over the Eagles on a cold, windy day at Philadelphia's Municipal Stadium; Smith kicked a game-winning 27-yard field goal with 1:40 left. The Redskins then blanked Brooklyn, 21–0.

The Pirates handed Washington a 21–13 loss, but the 5–3 Redskins bounced back with a 16–7 win over Cleveland to set up an important game against Green Bay at Griffith Stadium. The Packers led, 6–0, after star receiver Don Hutson caught a scoring pass in the first quarter. But in the second half, Battles's 1-yard run and Malone's leaping catch in the end zone accounted for Washington's 14–6 victory.

That win created a showdown between the 7–3 Redskins and 6–2–2 Giants to decide the division title. Although the Giants hosted the game at the Polo Grounds, the Redskins had a plethora of supporters.

On game day, a happy-go-lucky mob of some 16,000 Redskins fans boarded the largest number of chartered trains ever to leave Washington's Union Station and traveled to New York. Shortly after arriving at Penn Station, they marched through midtown Manhattan with Redskins band members who wore full, white-feathered Indian headdresses. Wearing a raccoon coat, Marshall led the contingent, which paraded to the tune of "Hail to the Redskins."

"At the head of a 150-piece brass band and 10,000 fans, George Preston Marshall slipped unobtrusively into New York today," Bill Corum of the *New York Journal-American* wrote.

By game time, the Polo Grounds resonated with a college atmosphere. Although Redskins supporters were a fragment of the crowd of 60,000—one of the largest turnouts in NFL history—it seemed that Indian feathers and burgundy and gold decorations were everywhere. Right before the game, two full-blooded Indian chiefs, Lone West and Tommy Hampton, did a war dance on the field.

The inspired Redskins destroyed the Giants, 49–14. Washington's point total was just 11 shy of what the Giants' defense had yielded all season.

The savvy Flaherty caught the Giants off-guard, altering 22 offensive plays and installing seven new ones. His boys darted to a 21–0 first half lead and never looked back. Baugh completed 11 of 15 passes and two touchdown passes to Millner. Battles rushed for 170 yards on 24 carries and with two touchdowns, one on a 76-yard interception return. Washington's defense held the Giants to 4 yards rushing.

When it was over, Redskins fans stormed the field and tore down both sets of goalposts, one of the first times such mayhem had occurred in NFL history. Those fans had reason to be ecstatic. Their team had engineered a stunning victory over a cocky opponent that had already packed its bags and left them on a train car in a New York rail yard. The train was destined for Chicago.

It was the Redskins who took the train to face the Western Division champion Bears—the "Monsters of the Midway."

## 1937 NFL CHAMPIONSHIP
**Washington 28, Chicago 21**
**December 12, 1937**
**Wrigley Field, Chicago**
**Attendance: 15,870**

### Baugh: "Everytime You Hit the Frozen Ground . . . You'd Be Bleeding"

If a football player lacked a thick skin, literally and figuratively, Chicago's Wrigley Field wasn't the place to be on December 12, 1937.

With the NFL championship at stake, the Redskins and Bears pounded each other in 15-degree temperatures on a frozen field draped with ice and snow. Although both teams wore rubber-soled basketball sneakers to combat the slippery surface, the brutal ground conditions left one player after another cut, bloodied, dazed, and staggering.

One such player was Redskins halfback Sammy Baugh, who could barely walk by the game's end. Even so, the rookie was nothing but spectacular. He completed 17 of 34 passes for 352 yards and three touchdowns—unfathomable numbers in those days—and single-handedly carried Washington to a 28–21 victory. An *Evening Star* headline read, "Baugh's Bewildering Passes Put Redskins Atop Pro Grid World."

"I never saw so much blood after a ball game in my life," Baugh said. "Everytime you hit the frozen ground, you landed on little pebbles, [and] you'd get scraped, and you'd be bleed-

ing. It was a terrible day to play. Your footwork was bad. You'd try to turn, and you'd slide and couldn't keep your balance very well on that icy ground. It was the worst game I ever played in terms of the conditions. They were bad."

*Washington Daily News* sportswriter Robert Ruark described the conditions this way: "It was colder than nine miles on an iceberg, slippery as a Vaselined eel, and wetter than a duck's spats."

Washington's win was all the more amazing given that the Bears had steamrolled over their 1937 opponents to clinch the Western Division with two games left, while the Redskins once appeared close to falling out of contention for the Eastern Division title. The Bears did nothing fancy along the way. Their offense revolved around a grind-it-out, power running game led by 6–2, 238-pound ironman fullback Bronko Nagurski and halfback Jack Manders, the NFL's leading scorer with 69 points. Washington's offense, in contrast, relied on versatility, quickness, and speed.

The two teams showed a disdain for each other in the championship game. Tempers flared repeatedly, and players took swipes at each other. On the first play, Riley Smith smashed his chin into an opponent and lost a tooth. Shortly after, the Bears' Bernie Masterson kneed the Redskins' Erny Pinckert on the ground and put him out of the game. Washington lost its starting guards, Les Olsson and Jim Karcher, to injury in the first 15 minutes.

The lead changed hands four times. The Redskins struck early when Cliff Battles scored on a 7-yard reverse for a 7–0 lead. Chicago responded with two touchdowns later in the first period. Bob Masterson passed 53 yards to Edgar "Eggs" Manske to help set up Manders's 10-yard scoring run. After Baugh threw an interception, Masterson tossed a 38-yard scoring pass to Manders, and Chicago led, 14–7.

With Chicago feeling the momentum, the Redskins were further jolted early in the second quarter when Baugh banged a knee and left the game. But the score hadn't changed when he returned just after halftime to enthusiastic cheers from the 3,000 Redskins fans who had braved the frigid temperatures.

Baugh didn't disappoint the Redskins' faithful. Like a surgeon, he began picking apart Chicago's defense, completing 7 of 9 passes with three touchdowns in what *Evening Star* sportswriter Francis Stann called "probably the greatest 15 minutes of play in history." Baugh found help on the receiving end from end Wayne Millner, "The Money Player." Millner caught nine balls for 179 yards and two touchdowns on the day, then the finest single-game receiving performance in NFL postseason history.

Millner's initial score came after Baugh, using the screen pass invented by Flaherty, found his favorite receiver in the flat. Millner raced into the end zone, outlasting Masterson and Ray Nolting, to complete a 55-yard play. Riley Smith converted for a 14–14 game.

Chicago drove 72 yards to regain the lead, 21–14, but seconds later, an off-balance Baugh whipped a pass 20 yards downfield to Millner, who again outran defenders and scored on a 78-yard play. Smith's extra point tied the game at 21 and, after the Redskins' defense held, Baugh and company took possession on their 20-yard line.

Washington soon faced a fourth-and-inches at midfield. Smith, the quarterback, disdained a punt and sent fullback Don Irwin on a plunge. In a collision of gladiators, Irwin met

Nagurski head on and made a first down by an inch. Two plays later, Baugh hit Ed Justice on a 35-yard scoring pass, and Smith converted for a 28–21 Redskins lead.

The Bears panicked in the final quarter, discarding their pet running game and throwing pass after pass with little luck. Frustration developed, and Chicago's 6–3, 210-pound Dick Plasman swung at Baugh's face on the sidelines. A wild melee erupted near Washington's bench, and several Redskins took shots at Plasman. One bloodied his mouth and nose with a direct punch. As the Bears raced across the field, police and fans rushed onto the scene, and a riot began growing. Redskins owner George Preston Marshall even left the stands to trade shots with his nemesis, Bears owner-coach George Halas. The altercation soon dissipated, and officials restored order.

When play resumed, the Redskins continued to withstand Chicago's aerial attack. Smith intercepted a pass with about a minute left to seal the win.

Stann of the *Evening Star* described the Redskins' fortitude as the clock wound down: "Ahead for the second time, they doggedly held this lead; tackles stepped into the breaches left by two injured guards, bruised and battered. Baugh was gone at the end, so was Erny Pinckert; Wayne Millner and Charley Malone were staggering as the final whistle sounded. But it was a case of they shall not pass."

| | | | | | | | |
|---|---|---|---|---|---|---|---|
| Washington— | 7 | 0 | 21 | 0 | — | 28 |
| Chicago— | 14 | 0 | 7 | 0 | — | 21 |

Wash —— Battles 7 run (R. Smith kick)
Chi —— Manders 10 run (Manders kick)
Chi —— Manders 37 pass from Masterson (Manders kick)
Wash —— Millner 55 pass from Baugh (R. Smith kick)
Chi —— Manske 4 pass from Masterson (Manders kick)
Wash —— Millner 78 pass from Baugh (R. Smith kick)
Wash —— Justice 35 pass from Baugh (R. Smith kick)

| Team Statistics | Wash | Chi |
|---|---|---|
| First Downs | 15 | 11 |
| Rushing Yards | 76 | 140 |
| Passing Yards | 388 | 203 |
| Passes | 21–41–3 | 8–25–3 |
| Punts–Average | 6–30.0 | 6–47.0 |
| Penalties | 1–5 | 1–15 |
| Fumbles–Lost | 3–3 | 3–2 |

## 1938: 6-3-2, 2ND PLACE— EASTERN DIVISION

### Head Coach: Ray Flaherty

Were the Redskins equipped to repeat as NFL champions? That was the big question on entering the 1938 season, and the early signs were poor. They were blown out of exhibition games in Dallas and Chicago against college all-star teams.

The Redskins were without a key figure from their 1937 championship team: Cliff Battles. The NFL's rushing champion had asked owner George Preston Marshall to raise his modest salary after Marshall upgraded the contract of the team's other backfield superstar, Sammy Baugh, who would earn a whopping $10,000 annually over the next three seasons.

Marshall refused, and Battles quit. He became an assistant football coach at Columbia University in New York City and never returned to the Redskins.

To compensate for his loss, the Redskins used their No. 1 draft pick to select Detroit University halfback Andy Farkas. Other new faces included 270-pound lineman Wilbur "Wee Willie" Wilkin, quarterback Frankie Filchock, end Bob Masterson, and backs Max "Bananas" Krause, George "Automatic" Karamatic, Ed "Chug" Justice, and Bill Hartman.

Krause shined in the season opener, a 26–23 win over Philadelphia. He scored on runs of 48 and 71 yards and on a 47-yard reception. On the touchdown catch, Baugh's twelfth completion in his first 13 throws, a wave of defensive linemen crushed the lanky passer, and he tore shoulder muscles. He was lost for a few weeks.

Hartman filled his shoes admirably when the Redskins hosted Brooklyn. The Dodgers jumped out to a 10–0 first-quarter lead, but Hartman threw 22- and 16-yard touchdown passes to Justice in the second period. Brooklyn kicked two fourth-quarter field goals to regain the lead, 16–13. But with 10 seconds left, Masterson, also a kicker, booted a field goal that hit the upright and bounced through to salvage a 16–16 tie.

Farkas was the key in week 3, a 37–13 Redskins rout of Cleveland, scoring on 1-, 7-, and 12-yard runs. After beating the Louisville Tanks in an exhibition game, 18–0, the Redskins fell 10–7 to the Giants before a record crowd of 35,000 at Griffith. Washington proceeded to upend Detroit and Philadelphia, and the 4–1–1 squad appeared headed for another Eastern Division title.

But Brooklyn again tied the Redskins, 6–6. The next week, Baugh, back in uniform, completed only 3 of 13 passes against Pittsburgh, but his 30-yard scoring pass to Karamatic with seven minutes left was enough in a 7–0 win.

Then came the much anticipated rematch of the 1937 championship game, although it failed to meet its billing, as the Bears coasted to a 31–7 win. Emotions ran high on both teams, and fists flew. Washington's postgame locker room resembled a hospital ward: six Redskins had noticeable injuries, including center Red Krause's black and bulging eye. "It was the toughest, meanest game I've ever played in my seven years in the pro league," Redskins tackle Turk Edwards told reporters. "But I think the Bears have got a few souvenirs, too."

Washington bounced back with a 51–6 exhibition win over the Richmond Arrows and blanked Pittsburgh for the second time that season, 15–0. The 6–2–1 squad would now meet the Giants for the third straight year in the season finale at the Polo Grounds to decide the division champion.

This time, New York spanked the Redskins, 36–0, their worst loss ever at the time. The mighty Giants defense shut down every phase of Washington's offense, which crossed midfield only three times and had seven fumbles. Baugh completed 4 of 12 passes and threw three interceptions. New York's offense was also dominant, outgaining the Redskins in yards, 346–211. For 54 minutes, the Giants controlled the ball or the Redskins were backed deep into their own territory. It was simple annihilation.

"Custer could have learned something at the Polo Grounds this afternoon," *Washington Post* columnist Shirley Povich wrote. "He could have seen how the Redskins could be taken

## PROFILE

### George Preston Marshall: Flamboyant, Controversial Redskins Owner Left Lasting Impact on NFL

For nearly four decades, George Preston Marshall was the chief owner of the Washington Redskins. He was known just as well as an NFL pioneer, showman, and marketing and promotional wizard. He was also no stranger to controversy: "He was very flamboyant, very aggressive, very outspoken and very difficult," said Jim Ricca, a Redskins middle guard in the 1950s.

Whatever his means, Marshall made an enormous impact on the NFL in its pre–World War II days. He also put the Redskins on track to becoming one of the most storied franchises in NFL history while molding them into an institution in the nation's capital.

He did so largely through his tremendous business acumen. It helped that the Redskins were an NFL powerhouse in their early years in Washington, reaching the championship game five times and winning two titles. But Marshall made them an even hotter attraction.

His key was entertainment. The colorful owner, who pushed the notion that pro football wasn't just a game but a spectacle, was adamant that Redskin fans should be entertained at home games from the time they entered the stadium until the time they left. He invested in extravagant halftime pageants other teams couldn't match. He brought in elephants, clowns, jugglers, singers, dancers, and the National Symphony Orchestra and arranged for vaudeville acts. Santa Claus would make surprise appearances at the season's final home game, arriving by parachute, helicopter, space ship, reindeer, or motorcycle.

The Redskins' owner also established the first team marching band and fight song on a grand scale. While the band played "Hail to the Redskins," smoke poured out of the big teepee on top of Griffith Stadium as a rhythmic tom-tom beat filled the air.

Marshall, described by one ex-Redskins player as a "carnival man," hoped his halftime shows would lure women to games. He thought that if they came, their men would follow. "For the women, football alone is not enough," he once said. "I always try to present halftime entertainment to give them something to look forward to—a little music, dancing, color, something they can

Entertainment was a centerpiece at Redskins home games while Marshall owned the team. Here, the National Symphony Orchestra performs on the field at halftime of a 1954 game at Griffith Stadium, while the Redskins' marching band waits its turn. Tepees signifying the Redskins' Native American theme line the top of the stands. The U.S. Capitol Building is in the background.

understand and enjoy. And the women add class to a sports gathering. They'll discourage a rowdy element."

The Marshall plan for color and pageantry left many in awe, even during the Redskins' lean years after World War II. "A Redskins game is something resembling a fast-moving revue with cues, settings, music, pace, tableaux and, hold your hats, boys—a ballet," *Washington Post* sportswriter Bob Considine once wrote. "Miraculously, the furbelows are never corny, never inappropriate, and charm rather than infuriate those hard-boiled fans who want their football raw. The amazing part of it all is that there's room left on the program for a football game."

Marshall set his eyes on entertainment early in life. Born in Grafton, West Virginia, on October 11, 1896, the son of a newspaper publisher, he launched an acting career in New York and dabbled in vaudeville, landing small parts in theater shows by his teens.

Eventually, Marshall inherited his father's Washington-based laundry business, which was struggling at the time. But he made the "Palace Laundry" a booming operation, as well as the source of a modest fortune, and glamorized it. He required employees to dress in blue and gold uniforms that matched the paint on the store's building at 9th and H streets in northwest Washington. He also

George Preston Marshall

## George Preston Marshall—*continued*

created the advertising slogan "Long Live Linen." He once paid for a full-page ad that was completely blank except for words at the bottom: "This page was cleaned by Palace Laundry." Marshall, known as the "Wetwash King," expanded the business into a 57-store chain. He sold it in 1948 for $800,000.

All the while, Marshall's ambitions took him beyond the laundry business. He participated in an ill-fated venture to promote auto racing at Roosevelt Raceway in Westbury, New York. He spent time in politics and became a delegate to the Democratic Party. He served as a director of the Greater Texas and Pan-American Exposition in Dallas in 1936, and he became the publisher of William Randolph Hearst's *Washington Times* newspaper in 1937, only to lose that job after a year.

Owning sports franchises fascinated him, too, and soon after locating the Braves (later the Redskins) in Boston in 1932, he established himself as one of the game's mavericks. He and other new NFL owners—Art Rooney (Pittsburgh Steelers), Bert Bell (Philadelphia Eagles), and Charles Bidwell (Chicago Cardinals)—joined the league's original pioneers—George Halas (Chicago Bears), Earl "Curly" Lambeau (Green Bay Packers), Tim Mara (New York Giants), and NFL Commissioner Joe Carr—to make

Marshall presided over a team that posted many "Famous Firsts."

### Marshall's Code of Conduct

George Preston Marshall demanded that his players show professionalism on and off the field and that they represent the Redskins in the best light possible. The owner thus implemented a "Code of Conduct" to enforce his standards for player behavior:

- You will be expected to conduct yourselves in such a manner as to always be a credit to the game, and to your club.
- Violation of publicly accepted and traditional training rules for athletes—rowdiness, boisterousness, and ungentlemanly conduct of any and every sort—will not be tolerated.
- In hotel lobbies, dining rooms, and other public rooms, and at all public functions where the team appears as a unit, shirts, ties, and coats are to be worn unless otherwise instructed.
- Night clubs, bars, cocktail lounges and gambling spots are definitely out of bounds.

"Marshall led a group of professional people, and he wanted us to be part of it," said Billy Cox, a Redskins tailback in the 1950s. "When you went with the Redskins, you were a step higher than players from other teams who came out in their old shirts."

new rules and improvements to the league that helped it grow exponentially.

Marshall was among most influential men in that group, often dominating meetings with his combustible personality. He pushed for innovative rule changes that would distinguish pro football from the more conservative college game and help transform the NFL into a fan-friendly sport that featured more passing and high-scoring games. He collaborated with Halas to promote a rule, for example, that permitted forward passing from anywhere behind the line of scrimmage. Before, the quarterback had to be at least 5 yards behind the line before throwing the ball. He also advocated placing the goalposts on the goal line, where they stayed until 1974.

Marshall was also the first team owner to propose splitting the teams into two divisions, with the winners competing in an NFL championship game. The first one was played in 1933. He also conceived of an all-star game, which pitted the NFL champion against a group of star college seniors, and helped initiate the Pro Bowl in its present form in 1950. Such foresight was a key reason Marshall was a charter member of the Pro Football Hall of Fame in 1963.

The Redskins' boss was bold and imaginative on other fronts, as well. He was the first NFL owner to sell season tickets and eventually packed 36,000-seat Griffith Stadium, the Redskins' home field for their first quarter-century, almost entirely with season-ticket holders. A sports broadcasting pioneer who gave the NFL advice that helped lead to the lucrative television revenue of

## George Preston Marshall—*continued*

today, in the late 1930s, Marshall formed a Redskins radio network that was considered the first of its kind in the NFL and was the first league owner to embrace the new medium of television in the 1950s. He launched networks that televised the Redskins locally and regionally.

Marshall is also credited with helping introduce the NFL to the West Coast, where the Redskins became the first team in league history to hold training camp. One of the team's West Coast training sites was at Occidental College in Los Angeles, a perfect location for a man who craved being a member of the popular and powerful. Case in point: He maintained a 15-year marriage to Ziegfield Follies performer Elizabeth Morton before divorcing her in 1935. He then married silent film star Corrine Griffith in 1936. Marshall and Griffith were married for 21 years.

"Marshall wanted to be at Occidental College so he could be close to all of his Hollywood friends," said Vince Promuto, a Redskins guard from 1960 to 1970. "He'd be in his tent having gin and tonics with them."

"Mr. Marshall was a very interesting guy to be around," said Eddie LeBaron, a Redskins quarterback in the 1950s. "I was going to law school in my last three years in Washington, and he invited me to his little lunch room, where he'd have senators and admirals and generals. It was one of the most scintillating places in Washington."

Like many of those he cozied up to, the egotistical man dubbed "Gorgeous George" yearned for publicity and made himself easily accessible to reporters.

Redskins Sammy Baugh, Bill Dudley, and Harry Gilmer (left to right) in the early 1950s with Corinne Griffith.

"Some say he's a show off and a blow-hard," Al Costello wrote in *The Quarterback* on October 5, 1946. "Others say he's merely publicity-conscious and promotion-minded for the benefit of his ball club. But at any rate, he's good copy for the newspapermen, and he does

---

### Corrine Griffith: "Orchid of the Screen"

George Preston Marshall didn't press all the buttons when it came to showing fans a good time. He had a sidekick, someone accustomed to entertaining the masses: one-time silent movie star Corrine Griffith.

Griffith, Marshall's wife for two decades, left her own lasting influence on the franchise. She was instrumental in organizing the extravagant halftime shows that became a franchise trademark. She also wrote the words to the Redskins' fight song, "Hail to the Redskins," and designed the team's burgundy and gold uniforms.

"If anybody is wondering what ever became of Corinne Griffith, one-time 'Orchid of the Screen,' she is here rapidly becoming the most influential woman in modern sports," *Washington Post* sportswriter Bob Considine once wrote. "The California girl whom Hollywood made into a kind of hothouse flower is, in truth, the main reason for the success of the burly Washington Redskins, whose verve, color and prosperity is influencing the whole picture of American football. The 'Orchid of the Screen' has become the 'Orchid of the Screen Pass.'

"From near bankruptcy, the Redskins now have come up to the eminence of drawing something in the neighborhood of 350,000 people in a single season, and they have so aroused this hard-to-please village that there is a move afoot to rename Griffith ballyard 'Corinne Griffith Stadium.'"

Griffith and Marshall married in 1936, when Marshall owned the financially struggling Boston Redskins. Griffith, enamored of the Washington area, encouraged her husband to move his team to the nation's capital, where he owned a thriving laundry business. (She was no relation to Clark Griffith, long-time owner of the Washington Senators baseball team.) In her 1947 book, *My Life with the Redskins,* she recounts a chat with famous journalist and short story writer Damon Runyon, a friend of the couple, on her desire to relocate: "You see, Damon, there are so many displaced citizens in Washington, from places such as Muleshoe, Texas; Ekalaka, Montana; and even Beverly Hills, California. Most of these [people] are alone in Washington with nothing to do on Sunday afternoon other than sit in parks and feed the squirrels and pigeons. I am convinced that if the team should move to Washington, it would give these same [people] an opportunity to expend some of their surplus energy."

Griffith started her career as a professional dancer before performing as a silent film actress from 1918 to 1931. Her first marriage, to movie producer Walter Mitchell Morosco, ended in divorce in 1934. She later met Marshall while performing in Washington in the play *Design for Living.* They divorced in 1957. Griffith died in 1979; her age at the time was unclear.

**George Preston Marshall—*continued***

know that every time he gets his name in the papers, or on radio, it means just that much more publicity for his football team and football in general."

Marshall had his faults, however, one being his insistence on running the Redskins with an iron-fisted, hands-on approach. Opinionated and bellicose, he told coaches which players to pick in the draft, set game strategy and challenged on-field decisions. From Griffith Stadium's press box, he phoned coaches on the sidelines with instructions. For example, before a game when the Redskins were still in Boston, he told his coach, William "Lone Star" Dietz, to kick off if he won the coin toss. On reaching the press box at the start of the game, Marshall saw the Redskins in receiving formation.

Marshall scolded Dietz: "I told you to kick off."

"We did," the coach replied. "They ran it back for a touchdown."

Not surprisingly, acrimony grew between Marshall and many of his coaches. The impatient owner hired 14 of them in the first 30 years of the franchise, sometimes applying the axe during the season. He had a stock explanation for handling coaches like a deck of cards: "Owners don't fire coaches, fans do."

"Marshall could promote the game, but he didn't know his ass from a hole in the ground about football, as far as I'm concerned," said Hall of Famer Bill Dudley,

who played in Washington in the 1950s. "He was just a big damn fan."

Players and business associates, too, found Marshall hard to deal with at times. "He was a unique human being," said Bernard Nordlinger, one of the Redskins' original attorneys. "On the plus side, he had the ability to attract loyalties in terms of understanding what people were trying to help him and those who weren't. On the minus side, he was an aggressive, domineering, cruel person. When he first knew me, he treated me like a total dog."

Marshall's failure to sign black players tainted his legacy. He refused for many years to integrate the Redskins, although all other NFL teams were doing so. Such ignorance sparked accusations of bigotry and propelled the Redskins' post–World War II downfall, which reached a nadir in the early 1960s.

By then, Marshall's failing health had caused him to relinquish control of the Redskins' daily operations. He died at age 72 on August 9, 1969.

Then–NFL Commissioner Pete Rozelle eulogized Marshall by describing him as a man of "imagination, style, zest, dedication, openness, dry humor, brashness, strength and courage. All of us who participate in some form of the game, and those millions who enjoy viewing it, are beneficiaries of what his dynamic personality helped shape over more than three decades."

---

apart, exposed as inept and beaten to a frazzle. The Giants did all these things today to win the Eastern professional championship and qualify as the team to meet the Green Bay Packers for the national title."

Anger swelled in the Redskins' locker room. Baugh tossed his helmet into a trunk, yanked off his shoulder pads, ripped the tape off his legs, and told reporters: "I'm mad, and don't let anybody tell you any different. . . . Hell, they played on the same field we did, didn't they? They played with the same football, and they were the same club we slapped down last year, weren't they? But everything went wrong. Nothing clicked."

At the farewell banquet for the 6–3–1 squad, George Preston Marshall reminded attendees that 12 Redskins in the 36–0 loss to the Giants were first-year players. He commended his team on its overall performance and predicted it would return to the championship game in 1939.

## 1939: 8–2–1, 2ND PLACE— EASTERN DIVISION

### Head Coach: Ray Flaherty

Redskins coach Ray Flaherty was an expert on the advantages of playing football in the cool environment of the Pacific Northwest. He grew up in Spokane, Washington, where he played at Gonzaga University.

Flaherty thus instructed his club to leave the hot, humid Washington area in the summer of 1939 and hold training camp more than 3,000 miles west at the Cheney Normal School

near Spokane. He was confident that the more comfortable climate 2,000 feet above sea level would prevent his players from being in poor physical condition, which he blamed for their inability to beat the Giants for the Eastern Division title in 1938. "I don't believe that will happen this year," Flaherty told reporters. "We're in much better shape for this campaign than we were last year."

The Redskins were well received after opening training camp in early August. Chief Black Spirit from the Spokane tribe in Cheney visited practices and gave Redskins captain Turk Edwards, who played at Washington State University in Pullman, the honorary title of "Chief Red Feathers."

"[The site] was perfect for football training," Flaherty said after training camp. "I don't know of any club with which I've been connected that had a more successful training season than the Redskins this year. We didn't have a serious injury, and the players are actually rarin' to go. Last year, they were worn out from the constant heat of Virginia, but it's a different story this year."

After opening the exhibition season in San Francisco by beating the Pacific Coast All-Stars, 20–7, the Redskins traveled down the coast and topped the semipro Los Angeles Bulldogs, 21–6. By the time they defeated the Eastern College All-Stars, 30–27, in their once hostile confines of Boston, the Redskins were being picked as one of the NFL's top teams. Their first test was in Philadelphia's Municipal Stadium before a crowd of 33,258, the largest turnout in Eagles' history.

The game was hyped as an aerial duel between the Redskins' Sammy Baugh and the Eagles' Dave O'Brien. But there was no score for three quarters. On the last play of the third period, Washington's Frankie Filchock returned a punt 28

## Payback Time in Boston

Redskins owner George Preston Marshall found retribution on the night of September 11, 1939, when his Redskins played an exhibition game in Boston, the town that barely supported his franchise from 1932 to 1936. About 28,000 fans, a turnout much larger than any from the Redskins' days in Boston, saw their former team defeat the Eastern College All-Stars, 30–27.

"Why it's wonderful," a giddy Marshall said afterward.

Boston media, once a target of Marshall's discontent, weren't so enthused. On game day, the *Boston Globe* mocked the owner in a cartoon on its sports page. It showed a dapper, seemingly smug Marshall and a Redskins player entering the stadium with bulging chests and their noses high, as if they were rubbing it in on Boston fans.

"Here you are, folks, just what you've been missing," Marshall said in the cartoon. One fan yelled, "Yea, well, he didn't look like that for us."

But *Boston Post* sportswriter Bill Cunningham wrote that Marshall had gotten a raw deal in the city: "I've always been a Marshall man, and it's always seemed to me that his record as a promoter here gleamed like a jeweler's window in comparison to some, even most, that could be cited. He filled the vacant Sabbath and brightened up the Monday sports pages. He paid all his bills and stuck not a soul. He made a lot of jobs for a lot of folks around here for five years, and there'd be more around now if his club were still here."

yards to the Eagles' 30-yard line. Baugh passed to end Charley Malone for the score, and the extra point accounted for a 7–0 Redskins victory.

The Redskins then tried to avenge their 1938 season-ending loss to the Giants. In the rain and mud at Griffith Stadium, Washington posted a 12–5 edge in first downs and a 206–74 edge in total yards. But the hosts botched repeated scoring chances, including Filchock's interception deep in Giants territory with less than five minutes left. The game ended in a scoreless tie, the only one of its kind to date in Redskins history.

Washington rebounded with a 41–13 win over the Brooklyn Dodgers. With Baugh out with a bum knee, Andy Farkas scored two touchdowns and Filchock, Dick Todd, Ed Justice, and Bo Russell added one apiece. Riding momentum, the Redskins defeated Pittsburgh in consecutive weeks, 44–14 and 21–14, to improve to 4–0–1 and stay tied with the Giants for the Eastern Division lead. Washington fell to Green Bay, 24–14, and the Giants grabbed first place with a 7–6 victory over Brooklyn.

But the Redskins reeled off four straight wins, the last three by an average margin of 29 points, while the Giants lost one game along the way. In the regular-season finale, the Redskins and Giants, both 8–1–1, met for the fourth straight year with the division title on the line.

Hysteria was at a fever pitch. About 15,000 Redskins supporters traveled to New York and, in a scene reminiscent of 1937, they paraded along Broadway behind the Redskins' band singing "Hail to the Redskins." An overflow crowd of 63,000 fans came to the Polo Grounds, and thousands more were turned away at the ticket windows.

Flaherty was confident the Redskins would win. "I never have believed that the Redskins would be able to run up a big score on the Giants, but I think we can lick them," he told reporters. "If it is by one point, I'll be satisfied. The only thing I can vouch for now, though, is that it is a tough game for either club to win."

It appeared that Washington was in position to win by a point after Redskins kicker Bo Russell, who was perfect all season, tried a 15-yard field goal with less than a minute left and the Giants leading, 9–7. The kick looked good, and the Redskins began celebrating, while Giants center Mel Hein and several teammates threw their helmets to the ground in disgust. But referee Bill Halloran called the kick wide right, and New York ran out the clock.

Pandemonium erupted. Irate Redskins fans, some intoxicated, stormed the field and chased a frightened Halloran. Flaherty and some of his players, clearly in disbelief, joined in pursuit. The coach berated the referee all the way to the dressing room and extracted an explanation on the ruling.

"Halloran told me he could have called it either way," Flaherty told the press. "He said it was like a close decision by an umpire on a ball or strike. I could argue, but it would do me no good. If that guy has got a conscience, he'll never have another good night's sleep as long as he lives."

That night at Washington's Union Station, 8,000 fans—men, women, children, newsboys, congressmen, judges, and others—welcomed the 8–2–1 Redskins home. They chanted in unity, "We wuz robbed." The team agreed but made no formal protest to the NFL, instead abiding by the rule that says the "referee shall be the sole authority for the score."

For the second straight year, the Giants had prevented the Redskins from reaching the postseason. But if it was any consolation, Marshall sounded like a prophet. He had said before the season the team that beat the Redskins would win the championship. Washington's two losses were to the squads that met in the championship game, the Giants and the Packers. Green Bay won, 27–0.

## 1940: 9–2–0, 1ST PLACE— EASTERN DIVISION

### Head Coach: Ray Flaherty

Talk about audacity! With a down yet to be played in the 1940 season, Redskins owner George Preston Marshall predicted that his team would soon be sporting championship rings: "I have surveyed the field and can earnestly say the Redskins will be the new champions," the Associated Press quoted him as

## Redskins Entertainment Firsts

George Preston Marshall's entertainment packages would have carried less zing if not for the creation of what evolved into Redskins icons: the team's marching band and its fight song, "Hail to the Redskins." The Pro Football Hall of Fame recognizes both as the first of their kind on a "grand scale."

The marching band is the most celebrated one in NFL history. Its origin is rooted in Marshall's idea to book a 19-member dance orchestra to perform at the Redskins' home opener in 1937, their first season in Washington. Members of the local Chestnut Farms Chevy Chase Dairy Band were in attendance and thought that they would like to perform, too. They approached the owner, who invited the 35-member band to play at the next home game.

Marshall was so impressed that he arranged for the band to play for the rest of the home schedule. He also fitted each band member with a burgundy-and-gold headdress to match the team's Native American theme. The band was so flashy and popular that Marshall invited the musicians to become charter members of the new, all-volunteer Washington Redskins Marching Band, which has since been the centerpiece of Redskins pregame and halftime performances.

The band's keynote song, "Hail to the Redskins," debuted around the same time. The fight song was the work of Corrine Griffith, Marshall's wife, and Barnee Breeskin, band director at the Shoreham Hotel in Washington. Griffith penned the lyrics and Breeskin wrote the music. They co-opted the melody from an old revival song, "Yes, Jesus Loves Me."

"Hail to the Redskins" has since become synonymous with the franchise and perhaps more popular than the other tune most identified with the nation's capital, "Hail to the Chief." The song is as revered as the great university fight songs of Notre Dame, Michigan, and Southern Cal. "Hail to the Redskins" has undergone revisions over the years. But one thing has been constant: It has been key to the pride of the Washington Redskins.

No other NFL team has ever matched the symbolism of the Redskins' marching band and fight song, and likely none ever will.

### Hail to the Redskins

| *Original Version* | *Current Version* |
|---|---|
| Hail to the Redskins, | Hail to the Redskins, |
| Hail Victory! | Hail Victory! |
| Braves on the warpath, | Braves on the warpath, |
| Fight for old D.C.! | Fight for old D.C.! |
| | |
| Scalp 'um, swamp 'um, | Run or pass and |
| we will | score |
| Take 'um big score. | We want a lot more. |
| Read 'um, Weep 'um, | Beat 'em, Swamp 'em, |
| touchdown | touchdown |
| We want heap more. | Let the points soar. |
| | |
| Fight on, fight on, 'till | Fight on, fight on, 'till |
| you have won, | you have won, |
| Sons of Washington. | Sons of Washington. |
| Rah! Rah! Rah! | Rah! Rah! Rah! |
| | |
| Hail to the Redskins, | Hail to the Redskins, |
| Hail Victory! | Hail Victory! |
| Braves on the warpath, | Braves on the warpath, |
| Fight for old D.C.! | Fight for old D.C.! |

saying. "This will be the greatest year in the history of football and the Washington Redskins."

*Washington Post* sportswriter Al Hailey shared Marshall's optimism, throwing in some fancy adjectives: "The outlook for the Redskins in 1940 is gigantic, colossal and stupendous," he wrote on September 15, 1940. "What's more, the Redskins will win the Eastern Division championship and then meet the Green Bay Packers in Washington in December for the world's championship, which the Redskins are a cinch to win."

The Redskins were equipped with a wealth of experienced players and promising rookies. All but two members of the 8–2–1 squad from 1939 were back. The top veterans were halfback Sammy Baugh and quarterback Frankie Filchock, the team's best passers, and running specialists Andy Farkas and Dick Todd.

The team also featured notable new faces: quarterback Roy Zimmerman and center Bob Titchenal, both from San Jose State, Ohio State center Steve Andrako, Gonzaga halfback Ray Hare, and Southern California halfback Bob Hoffman.

The Redskins had to settle a few personnel issues first. Wayne Millner was holding out, and Filchock and lineman "Wee" Willie Wilkin refused contracts offered by Marshall. Baugh's three-year deal at $10,000 per year was set to expire at the end of the 1940 season, and he and Marshall were jockeying for position.

Baugh announced that he planned to retire at season's end and become a college football coach, to which Marshall responded, "I think he will get out of football if he bumps into another spotty season. I think he will make a good coach. It's unfortunately true that the last two of Sammy's seasons here have been spotty."

Everything was settled by training camp at Gonzaga University. Unlike Marshall, Flaherty offered no grand predictions on the Redskins. He thought every NFL team was better than in 1939, singling out the Brooklyn Dodgers as the most

The Washington Redskins Marching Band

improved club. He also liked the Philadelphia Eagles and the renamed Pittsburgh Steelers in the Eastern Division and the Chicago Bears and Cleveland Rams in the Western Division. The Bears were also a preseason favorite of Eagles owner and future NFL commissioner Bert Bell, who predicted, "No one's going to beat the Bears this year. They're the greatest team ever assembled."

The Redskins were pretty good, too. After winning two exhibition games, 28–20 over the defending champion Packers and 35–12 over a college all-star team, they displayed their strengths in the season opener against the Dodgers.

Washington beat Brooklyn, 24–17, before 32,763 at Griffith Stadium. (Marshall increased the seating capacity at Griffith to about 36,000 before the season began.) The Redskins built a 17–0 first-half lead, but the Dodgers battled back to within seven points in the third quarter. Todd caught a fourth-quarter touchdown pass to account for Washington's final points.

Baugh returned to his sensational 1937 form, when he led the league in passing. He completed 11 of 14 passes, including a 41-yard touchdown pass to Ed Justice, and punted more than 50 yards three times, including a crucial 57-yard quick kick. "Never have I seen him play better than today," Brooklyn coach Jock Sutherland said afterward.

The Redskins followed by avenging their painful 9–7 loss to the Giants in the 1939 season finale. New York trailed, 14–7, in the third quarter and had a first-and-goal at the 3. But the

Redskins executed a goal-line stand. Todd later returned a punt 76 yards for a touchdown to account for a 21–7 victory.

The Redskins then beat Pittsburgh twice and the Chicago Cardinals, Philadelphia, and Detroit once each to post a 7–0 record. At that point they were the NFL's highest-scoring team, averaging nearly 30 points per game, and Marshall's brash preseason prediction seemed plausible.

But such explosiveness was nonexistent in the next game against Brooklyn at Ebbets Field. The Dodgers, behind the great all-around play of quarterback Ace Parker, took a 16–0 lead into the fourth quarter. The Redskins scored touchdowns on Baugh's pass to Bob Masterson and Bob Seymour's scoring run. But it wasn't enough in a 16–14 loss.

Next up, the 7–1 Redskins stood as underdogs to a powerful 6–2 Bears squad. But Washington's stingy defense and a fortunate decision by an official led to a 7–3 win before 35,231 fans at Griffith. Gate receipts of $51,783.76 accounted for the largest total to date at a Redskins game in Washington, according to press reports.

The Bears led, 3–0, in the second quarter when Dick Todd caught Filchock's pass and eluded two defenders to complete an 18-yard touchdown play. The Redskins maintained the 7–3 lead, but late in the final period, Chicago drove from midfield to just inches from the goal line. A penalty pushed the Bears back 5 yards, and two plays later Luckman threw a pass to All-Pro fullback Bill Osmanski in the end zone. Filchock separated Osmanski from the ball, and the final gun sounded.

## Marshall vs. Mara

As the Washington Redskins and New York Giants battled for NFL supremacy in the late 1930s and early 1940s, another fight between the teams raged in the front office. Their owners, the Redskins' George Preston Marshall and the Giants' Tim Mara, despised each other. Both men sported forceful personalities and wanted to run the league.

"The Mara-Marshall war is a lusty, ribald struggle for absolute control, rivaling in intensity the bitter clashes that featured the early days of baseball's National League when Barney Dreyfus, Charley Murphy and John McGraw were continuously at sword's point," Jack Singer wrote for the *New York Journal & American.*

The Marshall-Mara feud hit a boiling point after the Giants beat the Redskins 9–7 to win the Eastern Division title in 1939. After referee Bill Halloran ruled that Washington's late field goal attempt was no good, Marshall tried to convince other NFL owners that Halloran wasn't fit to officiate and demanded his suspension, according to press reports. Mara came to the referee's defense and helped him maintain his job, while Marshall persisted by reportedly asking his friend, U.S. Postmaster General Jim Farley, to have Halloran removed from his post office job in Providence, Rhode Island. The Redskins' owner also complained that "the Giants are running the league," Jack Miley of the *New York Post* wrote on April 12, 1940.

The M&M contentiousness surfaced again at a league meeting before the 1940 season. NFL president Carl Storck, who succeeded Joe Carr after his death in 1939, was up for reelection. Mara supported Storck, but Marshall, still peeved over Storck's refusal to punish Halloran, opposed the reelection.

Marshall even recommended *Chicago Tribune* sports editor Arch Ward for the job at $25,000 a year, then an enormous payment. Ward rejected the offer, and Storck signed a one-year contract for less than $8,000. It was "a distinct victory for Mara," Singer wrote.

The Bears screamed "interference," and their coach, George Halas, rushed onto the field to plead his case. That was enough for the loquacious Marshall to fire back. "The Bears are a bunch of cry-babies," he told the press. "They're front-runners. They're not a second-half team. The Bears are quitters. They fold up when the going gets tough." Todd chimed in, saying, "Who's afraid of the big bad Bear—I mean—the big bad wolf, big bad wolf."

The win positioned the Redskins to clinch the Eastern Division title, but they played their worst game of the year in losing to the Giants for the third straight time, 21–7, at the Polo Grounds. Washington rebounded with a 13–6 win over the Eagles to capture the division and qualify for the NFL championship game.

There, the 9–2 Redskins would face their nemesis, the 8–3 Western Division champion Bears, and hope that Slingin' Sammy's arm would shine one more time. The All-Pro completed 111 of 177 passes that year for a 62.7 completion percentage, 1,367 yards, and 12 touchdowns, all NFL highs. He also averaged a remarkable 51.4 yards per punt, an NFL single-season record to this day. Filchock threw for another 460 yards. Todd led the team in rushing with 408 (5.4-yard average) while subbing for Andy Farkas, who missed the season with a knee injury. Todd also tallied a team-high 402 receiving yards.

For the championship game, the Redskins would look to their threats on offense to overcome pro football's toughest defense. One team got the better of the other—by far.

## NFL CHAMPIONSHIP GAME
**Chicago 73, Washington 0**
**December 8, 1940**
**Griffith Stadium, Washington, D.C.**
**Attendance: 36,034**

### Marshall's Folly: Bears Hand Redskins Worst Whipping in NFL History

The most anticipated game in the NFL to date evolved into a watershed event for pro football.

The Redskins-Bears confrontation in the championship game on December 8, 1940, attracted an unprecedented amount of media coverage. It was carried on network radio, broadcast coast-to-coast to millions on 120 stations of the Mutual Broadcasting System. More than 150 sportswriters, the largest such contingent ever to cover a sports event besides the World Series, were on hand.

Internationally known figures in politics, military affairs, sports, entertainment, and society at large attended the game. They were part of a mortified overflow crowd at Griffith Stadium that witnessed the Bears' 73–0 humiliation of the Redskins. It stands as the widest single-game margin in NFL history.

Chicago was unmerciful, pounding the Redskins with a display of firepower that continues to leave football historians and trivia buffs in awe. The Bears scored 11 touchdowns, an NFL single-game record to this day. They unveiled their T-formation on offense and steamrolled with a potent ground attack that pounded out 372 yards and produced scoring runs of 68, 44, 42, and 23 yards. Chicago, which dominated Washington 492–232 in overall yardage, passed only eight times, while the befuddled Redskins had no choice but to air it out, throwing 49 passes. The Bears intercepted eight Redskins passes and returned three for touchdowns. Both figures also stand as NFL single-game records. New York Times sportswriter Arthur J. Dailey summed it up this way: "The weather was perfect. So were the Bears."

"Just seemed like it didn't make any difference what we did," Clyde Shugart, a Redskins guard at the time, said years later. "Everything backfired. We had more first downs than the Bears did. But of course, first downs don't count as touchdowns."

While putting on a clinic, the Bears made a fool of Redskins owner George Preston Marshall, who had called them "crybabies" and "quitters" after a 7–3 Redskins win over Chicago three weeks earlier. Then, a week before the title game, he sent the Bears a sarcastic congratulatory telegram for reaching the championship. It read, in part, "I hope I will have the pleasure of beating your ears off next Sunday and every year to come."

When Bears owner-coach George Halas, who carried on a love-hate relationship with Marshall, got wind of his inflammatory remarks, he wasted no time motivating his troops. Halas posted newspaper articles in the Bears' locker room, a move that was "like a shot in the arm for us," Bears lineman George Musso recalled.

The Bears focused not only on embarrassing Marshall but also on beating Washington—and they had the tools to do it. Chicago was equipped with six future Hall of Fame inductees in Musso, quarterback Sid Luckman, center Clyde "Bulldog" Turner, halfback George McAfee, guard Danny Fortmann, and tackle Joe Stydahar.

Chicago set the tone early. On the second play from scrimmage, Bears running back Bill Osmanski sprinted around left end and escaped down the sideline for a 68-yard touchdown run. Teammate George Wilson threw a crunching block that knocked two Redskins out of the play.

Washington's Max Krause returned the kickoff 56 yards, and the Redskins drove to the Bears' 25-yard line. Baugh threw to a wide-open Charley Malone at the 4, but the pass bounced off his hands on a play where he likely would have scored. Bob Masterson missed a 32-yard field goal attempt.

Chicago stormed back with an 80-yard scoring drive, and the rout was on. It was 21–0 at the end of the first quarter and 28–0 at halftime.

The Bears had used their revolutionary T-formation to stun Washington. Halas began to experiment with the scheme in 1932 and, in 1937, got help from football innovator Clark Shaughnessy, then the University of Chicago's coach. By 1940, the Bears were the only NFL team using the T, which replaced the single- and double-wing in the coming seasons as the basis for offensive backfield setups in pro football.

"They really worked on the T, and it was probably one of the primary things that gave them an advantage," Shugart said. "They sprung something on us we hadn't seen."

Meanwhile, Redskins coach Ray Flaherty, highly regarded for his motivational talks, assured his squad the game wasn't over. That was wishful thinking. The Bears returned three interceptions for touchdowns in a third quarter when they scored 26 more points. They added another 19 in the fourth period, prompting the game officials to ask both teams to run or pass for extra points due to a shortage of footballs. No net stood behind the goalposts, and the Bears had been booting kicks into the stands.

When the carnage ended, the Bears began to taunt. They targeted one man: Marshall.

"Who are the big cry babies now?" blared the Bears in their jubilant locker room. "So we fold and can't win the important games!" another player yelled. Someone else blurted out facetiously, "Well, at least Marshall was right about one thing. He said we'd have to win by a big score or not at all. I guess the score was big enough."

Marshall was irate. "Those guys out there today quit," he told reporters of his Redskins. Later he tried to smooth that over by saying, "They didn't lack courage, but they lost their heads."

Baugh was asked if the game would have been different if Malone hadn't dropped a sure touchdown pass in the first quarter. The Texan responded in his slow drawl: "I reckon it would have made the score 73–7."

Years later, Baugh theorized that the Redskins lost so badly possibly because they were mentally unprepared because of their win over Chicago three weeks earlier. "That's something about football—if you beat a team that's your equal, the next time you meet 'em you're not quite as high as you should be," he said in Myron Cope's 1970 book, *The Game That Was: The Early Days of Pro Football*. "And they're always higher than hell."

Baugh offered a much more outrageous opinion in a story first reported by Washington TV station WJLA in 2000. He accused the Redskins' linemen of trying to lose as a way to spite Marshall. He said the players were furious with their owner for taunting the Bears and that they let Chicago run up the score. The linemen already disliked Marshall because he was frugal with salaries, Baugh insinuated.

"I can't swear to it, but I heard a lot of grumbling from our linemen the week before the game," Baugh said in a separate interview. "[Marshall] said some terrible things and was putting stuff in the Chicago newspapers, running the Bears' players down. Maybe some of the Bears played with some of the Redskins in college. In other words, they knew these players pretty darn well, and some of them were close friends.

"Chicago didn't have to be dominant. If you're not going to play out there, anybody can run on you. We didn't play football."

Clyde Shugart said it was nonsense to believe the Redskins gift-wrapped the game: "Sammy is way off base on that. Those were stupid remarks for him to make. I don't recall anything like that. I didn't particularly like Marshall, but what the heck. I'm playing football, and I'm making more at the time than I could at something else. I don't remember any lineman making a remark to me about something like that."

Bears lineman George Musso also thought Baugh's comments were ridiculous: "That's just an excuse, just a lot of talk. Sammy had to say something. We outplayed them that day, that's all. It was a game where what we did was right and what they did was wrong."

Whatever the reason that the Bears destroyed the Redskins, the 1940 championship is etched in NFL lore as one of the league's all-time classics.

| | | | | | | |
|---|---|---|---|---|---|---|
| Chicago— | 21 | 7 | 26 | 19 | — | 73 |
| Washington— | 0 | 0 | 0 | 0 | — | 0 |

Chi —— Osmanski 68 run (Manders kick)
Chi —— Luckman 1 run (Snyder kick)
Chi —— Maniaci 42 run (Martinovich kick)
Chi —— Kavanaugh 30 pass from Luckman (Snyder kick)
Chi —— Pool 15 interception return (Plasman kick)
Chi —— Nolting 23 run (kick failed)
Chi —— McAfee 34 interception return (Stydahar kick)
Chi —— Turner 24 interception return (kick failed)
Chi —— Clark 44 run (kick failed)
Chi —— Famiglietti 2 run (Maniaci pass from Sherman)
Chi —— Clark 1 run (pass failed)

| Team Statistics | Wash | Chi |
|---|---|---|
| First Downs | 17 | 17 |
| Rushing Yards | 22 | 382 |
| Passing Yards | 223 | 120 |
| Passes | 20–51–8 | 7–10–0 |
| Punts–Average | 3–41.3 | 3–46.0 |
| Penalties | 8–70 | 3–25 |
| Fumbles–Lost | 4–1 | 2–1 |

## 1941: 6–5–0, 3RD PLACE—EASTERN DIVISION

### Head Coach: Ray Flaherty

A huge question loomed over the Redskins heading into the 1941 season. Would the team collapse due to its demoralizing 73–0 loss to the Chicago Bears in the 1940 championship game?

Their mental state aside, all signs indicated that the Redskins were well-prepared to bounce back and maintain their status as one of the NFL's powerhouses. They worked on eliminating their greatest weakness, line play, by acquiring veteran center Ki Aldrich and 240-pound rookie tackle Fred Davis, among other linemen, in the preseason. Plus, halfback Sammy Baugh, fresh off his best all-around season since entering the league in 1937, signed a new two-year contract.

"The 'Skins are a grim, hard-working, high potential of gridiron power that looms menacingly in the path of the world champion Chicago Bears," according to the *Washington Evening Star*. "If you can forget what the Bears did to them in that last game of 1940. But that was last year. This is another year."

The Redskins took care of a few administrative matters in the preseason. For one, owner George Preston Marshall set up training camp in San Diego after two years of camp in Spokane, Washington. The Redskins thus became the first team in NFL history to train in California, where the turnout for their exhibition games was big enough to encourage NFL franchises to locate there in future years.

After a short exhibition season that included a 30–0 win over the semipro Pacific Coast All-Stars, the Redskins hosted the Giants at Griffith Stadium in the season opener. Redskins back Frankie Filchock posted 68- and 51-yard runs, scoring a touchdown on the first one and setting up a field goal on the second. He got little support: Washington fumbled the ball five times and threw four interceptions, three by Baugh, in the 17–10 Giants victory.

## December 7, 1941: An Infamous Day

It's been called the most forgotten football game. When the Redskins defeated the Eagles, 20–14, at Griffith Stadium on December 7, 1941, the game meant nothing to either team, both of which were out of the postseason hunt. But the day it was played, as President Franklin D. Roosevelt proclaimed, would live in infamy.

Around game time at 2 P.M. (8 A.M. Pacific Standard Time), the Japanese bombed Pearl Harbor in Hawaii, the first time a foreign nation had attacked U.S. soil in nearly 130 years. Midway through the first quarter, the public address announcer began to send strange messages over the loudspeaker, urging military officers, government officials, and diplomats to leave the game and report to their offices in Washington, according to *Washington Post* columnist Shirley Povich, who was at the game:

"Admiral W. H. P. Bland is asked to report to his office at once!"

"The resident commissioner of the Philippines, Mr. Joaquim Eilzalde, is urged to report to his office immediately!"

"Joseph Umglumph of the Federal Bureau of Investigation is requested to report to the FBI office at once."

"Capt. R. X. Fenn of the United States Army is asked to report to his office at once."

As the announcements became more and more frequent, a curiosity grew among the 27,102 fans and players from both teams. Everyone was wondering what was happening but could only guess because Redskins management, which had learned about the Japanese attack through a telegraph message, refused to make an official announcement despite the horror of the moment and the inevitability of America going to war.

"I guess the Redskins didn't announce it because they didn't want to cause a panic," said Clyde Shugart, a Redskin lineman at the time who turned 25 that day. "We sensed that something happened, and everybody in the stands realized there was something wrong. But we didn't know what."

When George Preston Marshall was asked to explain his decision for withholding the information, the Redskins' entertainment-conscious owner said, "I didn't want to divert the fans' attention from the game."

By the third quarter, almost every news photographer had left the stadium, as had an estimated 3,000 spectators, and the game ended in almost complete silence. Redskins players reacted patriotically. That evening, a group of them protested the attack by marching on the Japanese embassy in Washington.

"We wanted to square the account if they were looking for a fistfight," Shugart said.

The Redskins' first loss in five season-opening games at home served as a wake-up call, and they took off on a five-game winning streak. First came a 3–0 victory over the Dodgers on a 37-yard field goal by rookie end Joe Aguirre. Aguirre's 39-yard field goal, along with Bob Masterson's three extra points, made the difference in the Redskins' 24–20 victory over Pittsburgh in week 2. Redskins back Dick Todd helped with two touchdowns, one on a 60-yard pass from Filchock.

Baugh then had his best game of the season. He threw two touchdowns, including a 32-yarder to Masterson with a little under three minutes left, to lift the Redskins to a 21–17 win over the Eagles. Baugh's 14-yard scoring pass to Bob McChesney and Todd's 71-yard punt return for another score propelled the Redskins to a 17–0 lead over Cleveland, and they held on for a 17–13 win.

Washington capped its streak with a 23–3 victory over Pittsburgh, acquiring first place in the Eastern Division by a half-game over the Giants. But the Redskins lost dangerous back Wilbur Moore for the season to a broken collarbone, and more bad news surfaced the next week on the injury front: Todd tore a ligament in his left leg against Brooklyn and was ruled out for at least three weeks. The Dodgers thumped the Redskins, 13–7, the start of a precipitous fall for the burgundy and gold.

In a much awaited rematch of the 73–0 classic, the Bears earned a 35–21 win before 30,095 fans at Wrigley Field. The Redskins topped their rivals in total yards (334–306) and first downs (18–9), prompting Flaherty and D.C. scribes to declare it a moral victory for the Redskins.

"If the Redskins can play the brand of ball they showed today, I believe they have an excellent chance of winning their remaining three games," Flaherty told reporters. "They might have been outscored today, but they were not out-gamed, and they displayed the kind of football I hope they will show the New York Giants next Sunday."

A 20–13 loss to the Giants knocked the 5–4 Redskins out of the playoff race before the final regular season game for the first time since 1936. After losing their fifth straight game, 22–17 to Green Bay, the Redskins closed with a 20–14 victory over the Eagles.

Washington's third-place finish in the Eastern Division left the 6–5 squad with no playoff money shares to split for the first time since moving to D.C. in 1937. But the mood was upbeat at a farewell luncheon.

"The general theme of the brief speechmaking was that the season was not the failure that many fans seemed to think," one sports reporter wrote. "They had played good ball in defeat, had held the respect of Washington's football public, and there were no regrets from management."

## 1942: 10–1–0, 1ST PLACE—EASTERN DIVISION

### Head Coach: Ray Flaherty

Although many NFL players were enlisting in the military and rosters were thinning out as American involvement in World War II hit full force, the Redskins escaped relatively unscathed.

The Redskins lost about five players—the least of any team—before the 1942 season. Their most notable departure was star back Frankie Filchock, who joined the U.S. Navy. Coach Ray Flaherty filed an application for commission in the navy, and rumors surfaced that Arthur "Dutch" Bergman, a former athletic director at Catholic University in Washington, might replace him. But Redskins owner George Preston Marshall denied negotiating with Bergman for such a position, and Flaherty coached the Redskins in 1942. Marshall hired Bergman as a scout.

When training camp kicked off in San Diego, the Redskins unveiled a squad stocked with "speed, brawn, power and experience," according to one newspaper report. The backfield was loaded. Sammy Baugh was back at passer, and Dick Todd and Andy Farkas were pegged to handle the running chores. Also in place were veterans Wilbur Moore, Ed Justice, Bob Seymour, and Roy Zimmerman and a list of promising rookies such as Canisius back Dick Poillon and Notre Dame back Steve Juzwik.

Marshall thought the Redskins featured their best line ever. It included veterans Wee Willie Wilkin, Dick Farman, Steve Slivinksi, Clyde Shugart, Ki Aldrich, and Clem Stralka, plus rookies Joe Zeno (Holy Cross) and George Watts (Appalachian State). Bob McChesney, Bob Masterson, Joe Aguirre, Ed Cifers, and Notre Dame rookie John Kovatch would man the ends.

"This is the greatest team we ever had—better than last year's or our championship team of 1937 or any of the rest," Marshall, as quoted by the *Washington Times-Herald,* boasted with his customary grandiloquence. "We won't be satisfied with anything less than the world's championship for 1942."

Flaherty gave his standard conservative outlook. "I don't know about winning the championship," the coach said in the *Times-Herald.* "That all depends upon how we make out on injuries. A lot of things can happen between now and December."

The Redskins were tested in the preseason. They defeated the Army All-Stars, a team comprised of the best NFL players, 26–7, before about 50,000 fans in the Los Angeles Coliseum. Then came a 28–7 win over the Packers and a 38–14 loss to the Bears.

The season opener pitted one of the NFL's strongest teams, Washington, against perhaps the weakest, Pittsburgh. For a while, though, it seemed that the Redskins were headed for an embarrassment. The Steelers trailed, 7–0, at halftime. But Bill Dudley, a rookie back from the University of Virginia and future Redskin and Hall of Fame inductee, returned the second-half kickoff 84 yards for a touchdown. Pittsburgh took a 14–7 lead late in the third period, and the 30,000 fans at Griffith Stadium were getting a bit restless.

The Steelers were prepared to pad it early in the final quarter when their kicker lined up for a 45-yard field goal attempt, but Aldrich blocked the kick. He retrieved the ball at the Steelers' 32 and raced in for the touchdown. Juzwik kicked the game-tying conversion and later scored his second touchdown on a 39-yard run to help lift the Redskins to a 28–14 win.

The Redskins followed with a freakish 14–7 loss to New York. Their defense was outstanding, holding the Giants to 51 yards and no first downs on a mud-caked field at Griffith. But 50 of those yards came on the Giants' first play from scrimmage, when Tuffy Leemans threw a touchdown pass to Will Walls.

Washington tied the game, 7–7, in the second quarter, but New York's O'Neale Adams intercepted Poillon's pass in the third period and returned it 66 yards for a touchdown. By the end, the Redskins had administered a 58-minute statistical beating to the Giants, who nevertheless again jinxed their Eastern Division rivals.

The Redskins spent the next month and a half gearing up for a rematch with the Giants by winning six straight games by an average of 13 points. The streak left the 7–1 Redskins comfortably in first place in the division.

More than 15,000 Redskins fans trekked to New York for the clash with the Giants, who were on their way to again bedeviling the boys from D.C. Washington drove deep into Giants territory six times in the first half, but four lost fumbles, an interception, and a stoppage on downs prevented any scoring.

Farkas, who coughed up two of those fumbles, redeemed himself on the second-half kickoff. He caught the ball on the 6, hesitated as a blocking wedge formed, and took off on a 94-yard run on the frozen turf for a 7–0 Redskins lead. He later capped a 70-yard drive with a 1-yard scoring plunge, and the extra point created a 14–0 edge. Baugh, who hit Masterson with a 32-yard pass on the drive, completed 19 of 26 passes for 211 yards on the day.

The Redskins held on for a 14–7 victory, snapping a four-game losing streak to New York. They won their final two games, 23–3 over Brooklyn and 15–3 over Detroit, to finish 10–1 and take the Eastern Division. (Their 10 wins stood as a franchise high until an 11–3 season in 1972). They would face their familiar foe from the West, the 11–0 Chicago Bears, in the NFL championship game at Griffith.

Washington seemed well equipped. Its defense had been phenomenal that season and was, in fact, one of the NFL's best of the 1940s. The unit held opponents to an average of eight points over the last nine games, and yielded only 13 in the last four combined.

Baugh was a sensation. He completed 132 of 225 passes for 1,524 yards and 16 touchdowns, with a league-high 58.7 completion percentage. His favorite receivers were Dick Todd (23 catches, 328 yards, five touchdowns) and Bob Masterson (22 catches, 308 yards, two touchdowns). Baugh also led the NFL in punting (48.2 average) and intercepted five passes.

Farkas also had an excellent all-around season. He posted a team-high 468 rushing yards with three touchdowns, caught 11 passes for 143 yards and two scores, returned 16 punts for 219 yards (13.7 average), and intercepted three passes. The man appropriately nicknamed "Handy Andy" was just that in the championship game.

# NFL CHAMPIONSHIP GAME
Washington 14, Chicago 6
December 13, 1942
Griffith Stadium, Washington, D.C.
Attendance: 36,006

## "Terrific" Redskins Avenge Humiliating Loss to Bears

More than two years had passed since the darkest day in Redskins history, a 73–0 loss to the Bears in the 1940 championship game. The catastrophic defeat left the Redskins bitter and starving for revenge. Their chance arrived in the 1942 NFL title game.

"We really wanted to get even with the Bears," said Clyde Shugart, a Redskins guard on the 1940 and 1942 squads. "We hated them because of that tremendous score they ran up. Of course, we never liked them anyhow."

The Redskins got even. Inspired by a suffocating defense that made the potent Bears offense look anemic, Washington prevailed, 14–6. Chicago's defense produced the Bears' only points.

The titanic win toppled Chicago's 18-game winning streak, which had included a 35–21 victory over the Redskins in 1941 and a 37–9 pasting of the Giants in the 1941 championship game. And it came against a Bears squad that finished the regular season undefeated at 11–0, the last team to do so until Miami went 14–0 in the 1972 regular season en route to a 17–0 mark.

But the "Monsters of the Midway" didn't only defeat their 1942 foes, they smashed them. The Bears accumulated a then-NFL-record 376 points and yielded a league-low 84. They allowed a measly 154 yards of offense per game and 12 touchdowns, led the NFL with 51 takeaways and posted four shutouts.

Plus, the Bears' innovative T-formation setup, which they had used to fool the Redskins in the 1940 championship game, was in high gear. But Washington was prepared to stop it this time. Scout Dutch Bergman evaluated the Bears at several of their games, while former end Wayne Millner, then an assistant coach at Notre Dame, and former Redskins tackle Jim Barber, a navy officer, helped with scouting. Redskins coach Ray Flaherty and assistant Turk Edwards traveled with Bergman to Chicago for the Bears' regular season finale, and Bergman pointed out ways to defuse their offense.

Were the Bears feeling cocky beforehand? A sign reportedly hung in their locker room at Wrigley Field saying, "Let's make it 74." Oddsmakers favored them by as many as 22 points.

The sellout crowd of 36,006 at Griffith Stadium, which included U.S. Army Chief of Staff George C. Marshall and other military officials on break from their wartime duties, was psyched for the showdown. The Bears deflated the crowd early in the second period. With the game scoreless, Chicago's Lee Artoe scooped up a Redskins fumble and ran 52 yards untouched into the end zone. His kick failed, but the Bears led, 6–0.

Later in the period, Redskins back Wilbur Moore intercepted a pass and returned it to the Bears' 42. Baugh decided to air it out. With "Bear-tight" pass protection, according to one reporter, he spotted Moore down the middle of the field. With a defender draped over his back, Moore made a breathtaking, over-the-helmet catch in stride while tumbling into the end zone. Bob Masterson's conversion made it 7–6 six minutes before halftime.

By the end of the half, Washington's defense had handcuffed the Bears' offense. Chicago gained minimal yardage and failed to cross the Redskins' 40. Baugh's booming punts—he averaged 53 yards on six kicks in the game—kept the visitors at bay, too.

In the third period, the Redskins pinned Chicago near the goal line, forced a punt, and took over on their 43. Enter Andy Farkas.

The Redskins' star back ran nine times on an 11-play drive. He tore through gaps in the Bears' line, biting off gains of 4 to 8 yards. He once ran six straight times, the last one a 1-yard plunge over right guard for a score. The ball popped out as

The Redskins are all smiles after gaining revenge on the Bears in the 1942 championship game.

he crossed the goal line, but officials had already ruled touchdown. Masterson's extra point made it 14–6 Washington with 7:35 left in the quarter.

Corrine Griffith, the wife of Redskins owner George Preston Marshall, dramatized the touchdown run in her 1947 book, *My Life with the Redskins:*

The ball was snapped. The Redskins charged with every ounce of strength they could muster. The Bears held with every ounce of strength they could muster. With neither side giving an inch, the result from Andy's point of view was a very-messy-looking pile of humanity. Andy couldn't see any way to cut through that sort of thing, so he just climbed up to the peak and slid down the other side head first to a touchdown, giving the Redskins a decided lead.

The Redskins weren't home free. Chicago drove from its 23 to Washington's 11 early in the fourth quarter. On first down, Bears back Frank Maznicki threw into the end zone, but the ubiquitous Baugh intercepted it to foil the threat.

Chicago later took over on its 20 with three minutes left. In the blink of an eye, Bears back Charlie O'Rourke completed three lengthy passes for a first down at the 2, and a penalty moved the ball to the 1. But Washington's defense again showed its championship form by executing a monumental goal line stand.

Bill Osmanski tried running it in, but Redskins linemen Dick Farman and Bill Young stuffed him. Hugh Gallarneau then ran over left guard for an apparent score, but the play was called back, as the Bears were penalized 5 yards to the 6 for illegal motion. Osmanski gained 3 yards, but Farman threw him for a yard loss on third down. On fourth down

from the 4, O'Rourke's pass bounced off Osmanski's fingertips in the end zone with 1:30 to play. The Redskins ran out the clock.

The fans at Griffith were ecstatic, and the Redskins' marching band played "Hail to the Redskins." In Washington's locker room, Ki Aldrich shouted, "We beat their pants off, we beat their pants off," as reported by the *Washington Post.*

"I knew all the time we could take these Bears," teammate Ed Justice told reporters. "I wasn't kidding when I offered to play them all or nothing. I knew we could stop their attack, and we did. Boy, oh, boy, what a line we had in there today."

Marshall, who "beamed like a child on Christmas morning," one reporter wrote, congratulated his players and called their performance "terrific." Even Bears linemen Joe Stydahar, Bulldog Turner and George Musso, vicious players in their own right, arrived to shake hands with their adversaries.

Flaherty praised the Redskins' defense, which held the Bears to 67 yards before their two long fourth-quarter drives. He singled out his linemen, crediting ends Masterson and Ed Cifers, tackles Young, Wee Willie Wilken, Eddie Beinor, and Fred Davis, and guards Shugart, Farman, Clem Stralka, and Steve Slivinski.

"Their vaunted T-formation never penetrated our 30," Flaherty said with exaggeration. "When the Bears got to the 1-yard line on their late drive and still couldn't score, they were completely defeated. No other team had halted them there in a couple of years."

The win was Flaherty's farewell gift, for he was off to serve as a navy lieutenant. He first gave a stirring speech to his squad. "Half of us are going into the service in a couple of weeks," he said as quoted by the *Post.* "Hit the enemy just as hard as you hit the Bears today. Do that, and this war won't take long to finish, and we can get back here pretty quick."

World War II ended two and a half years later—but it would be 40 years before the Redskins again ruled the NFL.

| | | | | | | |
|---|---|---|---|---|---|---|
| Chicago— | 0 | 6 | 0 | 0 | — | 6 |
| Washington— | 0 | 7 | 7 | 0 | — | 14 |

Chi —— Artoe 52 fumble return (kick failed)
Wash — Moore 39 pass from Baugh (Masterson kick)
Wash — Farkas 1 run (Masterson kick)

| Team Statistics | Wash | Chi |
|---|---|---|
| First Downs | 10 | 10 |
| Rushing Yards | 102 | 104 |
| Passing Yards | 119 | 66 |
| Passes | 8–18–3 | 5–13–2 |
| Return Yards, Kicks | 82 | 57 |
| Punts–Average | 6–42.0 | 1–52.5 |
| Penalties | 7–47 | 4–26 |
| Fumbles–Lost | 1–1 | 1–1 |

## 1943: 6-3-1, 1ST PLACE— EASTERN DIVISION

### Head Coach: Dutch Bergman

Not often does a team that loses its last three regular season games wind up in the NFL championship game—except if you're the 1943 Washington Redskins.

After winning six of their first seven games, the Redskins dropped their last three to finish tied with the Giants for first place in the Eastern Division at 6–3–1. But Washington routed the Giants in a playoff en route to reaching their fifth championship game in eight seasons, only to be blown out by their Western Division rival Bears, 41–21.

The Redskins nearly repeated as champions, although about half the team from their 1942 squad had departed to serve in World War II. Gone were such cornerstones as backs Ed Justice and Dick Todd, ends Ed Cifers and John Kovatch, and linemen Ki Aldrich, Clem Stralka, Bill Young, Fred Davis, and Ed Beinor. The Redskins were also without their long-time coaching icon, Ray Flaherty, who had enlisted in the U.S. Navy after the 1942 season. Redskins owner George Preston Marshall replaced him before the 1943 campaign with the team's top scout, Dutch Bergman.

Bergman had starred at running back on Notre Dame's great post–World War I teams. His roommate and backfield partner was George Gipp of "win one for the Gipper" fame. He later entered college coaching and became the head coach at Catholic University in Washington in 1930, leading the Cardinals to an Orange Bowl victory in 1936 and a Sun Bowl tie in 1940. Catholic finished 59–31–4 in his 11 seasons there.

"We are happy to announce the signing of Bergman," Marshall said at an introduction ceremony. "Bergman was one of the greatest halfbacks in Notre Dame football history. He has a record of outstanding achievement as coach at Catholic University and elsewhere. He is one of the keenest and soundest scouts, and we look forward with high confidence to successful years with him in command of the Redskins."

When the Redskins assembled for training camp in San Diego, Bergman faced the task of filling holes caused by the war. The team signed such promising rookies as tackle Lou Rymkus (Notre Dame), ends Al Piasecky (Duke) and Ted Lapka (St. Ambrose), and halfback Frank Akins (Washington State), and reacquired end Joe Aguirre, who had missed the 1942 season.

Although one sportswriter declared, "The Redskins can field a team which would rattle your teeth," it didn't appear that way during a tough exhibition season. Washington lost to the college all-stars, the Packers and the Bears. But in the exhibition finale, the Redskins beat the Chicago Cardinals, 43–21, to generate momentum heading into an opening-day meeting with the 0–2 Brooklyn Dodgers.

A record season-opening crowd of 35,540 at Griffith Stadium saw the Redskins win their 11th consecutive game by dismantling Brooklyn, 27–0. Redskins halfback Wilbur Moore scored three touchdowns, two on passes from Sammy Baugh and one on a 28-yard run. Baugh hit fullback Andy Farkas for another score. The Redskins dominated Brooklyn in yards, 431–164.

Washington then defeated Green Bay, 33–7, one of the worst beatings the Packers had endured in their 22 years in the NFL. Baugh threw four scoring passes to up his total to seven on the season.

The Redskins suffered a letdown the next week against the lowly Cardinals but managed to eke out a 13–7 win. They then demolished Brooklyn, 48–10, as Baugh tossed a team-record six touchdown passes. Moore, Farkas and Aguirre, who was proving to be a valuable addition at end, each scored two touchdowns for the 4–0 Redskins, the NFL's only unbeaten, untied team.

Washington's 14-game winning streak ended in a 14–14 tie with the Steagles, but the Redskins rebounded with a 42–10 win over the Detroit, as Baugh put on a spectacular all-around performance: four touchdown passes, four interceptions, and an 81-yard quick kick.

Such brilliance highlighted his superb season. He completed 133 of 239 passes for a 55.6 completion percentage, all league-high numbers, with 1,754 yards and 23 scoring passes. He also averaged 45.9 yards on 50 punts and intercepted an NFL-best 11 passes.

When the 7–0–1 Bears came to town the next week, Baugh played only five minutes due to injury, but he managed to throw a scoring pass to Farkas. His replacement, newly acquired George Cafego, tossed another one to Piasecky. Moore ran 20 yards for the third touchdown on a Statue of Liberty play in the Redskins' 21–7 victory, their 17th straight game without a loss.

The 6–0–1 Redskins, with a two and a half–game lead on the Steagles, seemed like a lock to win the Eastern Division. But matters turned bleak. They dropped their next three games, 27–14 to the Steagles and 14–10 and 31–7 to the Giants, to finish 6–3–1.

What caused the sudden collapse? According to *Washington Post* sportswriter Al Costello, Redskins players may have been burned out from "too much football": "Since July 20, the team has done nothing but practice, play, eat and sleep football," Costello wrote on December 13, 1943. "One week less than [five] months is too tough for any team to take and keep on winning, they declare almost in unanimity."

Whatever the reason, the Redskins and Giants, both 6–3–1, were deadlocked atop the Eastern Division. A playoff would decide which team meets the Western Division champion Bears in the NFL title game.

## Redskins and Gamblers, Any Ties?

The devastating news came at an already tenuous juncture for the Redskins. After two straight losses left them with a precarious hold on first place in the Eastern Division, the following headline appeared in the *Washington Evening Star* on December 8, 1943: "Rumors of Redskins' Gambling Being Probed by Club Leaders."

Redskins owner George Preston Marshall and coach Dutch Bergman were conducting independent investigations over rumors that Redskin players had been fixing some of the team's games in 1943. Marshall had reportedly asked D.C. Chief of Police Edward Kelly to order surveillance of key Redskins and see if they were associating with gamblers, or frequenting night clubs and liquor stores, actions that violated team rules. Bergman also tried to learn if the players had relationships with gamblers.

"If these reports have any basis of fact, I want to know about them," Marshall told the *Star.* "I have offered $5,000 to anyone who can prove a tie-up between the football club and the gamblers. If such a tie-up exists, I will take such action as the situation warrants. Gambling has no place in football, and I won't have any Redskin betting on any game in which he plays or [is] associating with gamblers."

Marshall, criticized in the press for betraying his players by ordering a witch hunt into their personal lives, later softened his position. "Anyone who says any Redskin player has been betting on professional football games is a liar," he told the press. "I am willing to pay $5,000 in cash for proof. That's how much confidence I have in my players."

The rumors first surfaced in late October and peaked in the days preceding the Redskins-Giants game on December 5, when whispers were circulating that the game was "in the bag" for New York, although the Redskins were 5–3 favorites. The Giants won, 14–10.

When the *Star* article appeared three days later, NFL public relations director George Strickler denied that the league was conducting a special investigation into the Redskins or players with other teams. He said that no evidence existed to substantiate the charges.

"Until something more than pool hall gossip and 'big shot' fancy is offered in evidence, no credence can be placed in the reports," Strickler said in the *Star.* "The fact that football games more often than not turn out differently than the oddsmakers anticipate proves only that the gamblers ought to go to work on an assembly line or on a section gang."

Redskins players were incredulous over the rumors. "I have never known of any gambling on football by any member of our team, and I don't believe a word of it," Bob Masterson, the team's player spokesman, said in the *Star.* "We don't have the gambling type on our club. Why, we haven't even got a horse player with us this year, and it's tough even getting up a gin rummy game on the trips."

The investigations by Marshall and Bergman turned up nothing.

## EASTERN DIVISION PLAYOFF GAME
Washington 28, New York 0
December 19, 1943
Polo Grounds, New York
Attendance: 42,800

### Dutch's Pep Talk, Baugh Spark Redskins Past Giants

Redskins coach Dutch Bergman, whether for motivational purposes or because he truly believed it, expressed doubts to his players that they could beat the Giants in an Eastern Division playoff game. The Redskins were riding a three-game losing streak at the time.

"Dutch charged us in the dressing room before the playoff," Redskins guard Al Fiorentino once told the *Washington Evening Star.* "He said that he made no plans to go to Chicago to play the Bears for the big title because he was confident the Redskins were ready to concede to the Giants. 'You've given up,' he told us, 'and I want no part of you.'"

A determined Redskins bunch proved their coach wrong. Before 42,800 mostly disgruntled fans at the Polo Grounds, the Redskins destroyed the Giants, 28–0. Washington controlled the whole game, with back Andy Farkas scoring on two 2-yard runs in the second period and a 1-yard plunge in the third quarter. Sammy Baugh was just about perfect, completing 16 of 21 passes for 299 yards, with an 11-yard scoring pass to rookie Ted Lapka for the final touchdown. He also intercepted two passes, returning one 40 yards to set up a score.

With Baugh picking apart the opposition, the Redskins appeared to be in good hands entering the NFL championship game.

| | | | | | | |
|---|---|---|---|---|---|---|
| Washington— | 0 | 14 | 0 | 14 | — | 28 |
| New York— | 0 | 0 | 0 | 0 | — | 0 |

Wash — Farkas 2 run (Masterson kick)
Wash — Farkas 2 run (Masterson kick)
Wash — Farkas 1 run (Masterson kick)
Wash — Lapka 11 pass from Baugh (Masterson kick)

# NFL CHAMPIONSHIP GAME
**Chicago Bears 41, Washington 21**
**December 26, 1943**
**Wrigley Field, Chicago**
**Attendance: 34,320**

## Sid Outshines Sammy in Bears' Convincing Win

December 26, 1943, the day the Redskins and Bears clashed for the fourth time in seven seasons to decide the NFL champion, could appropriately be named "Sid Luckman Day." Chicago's quarterback, defensive back, and punter was a one-man wrecking crew in the Bears' 41–21 victory at Wrigley Field.

In one of the most phenomenal postseason performances of all time, Luckman completed 14 of 24 passes for 286 yards and a championship-game-record five touchdowns that included two spectacular off-balance throws and two perfectly executed screen passes. He also ran for two sizable gains and rushed for 64 yards overall. He terrorized the Redskins on defense, too, intercepting two passes and returning each one 20 yards to set up touchdowns. His punting was also effective.

It was vindication for Luckman, a future Hall of Fame inductee who threw for 2 yards in Chicago's loss to the Redskins in the 1942 championship game and tossed four picks in Washington's 21–7 regular-season win in 1943. His Redskins counterpart had a rough day. Sammy Baugh suffered a slight concussion early in the game and was lost for 35 minutes. He returned in the second half and completed 7 of 11 passes for 110 yards and two touchdowns, but he didn't put his usual sizzle on the ball and threw passes behind receivers.

Entering the game, Bears supporters were concerned that Chicago's timing and coordination would be off because they hadn't played in about a month. The Redskins, in contrast, were coming off three straight pressure-packed games against the Giants, and rumors circulated that they would be burned out for the championship. The Bears were favored by seven points, although the underdog had prevailed in six of the seven meetings between the teams since 1937. The Redskins led the series, 4–3.

The Redskins suffered a setback early in the first period. After punting the ball, Baugh went to chase down the man returning the punt—Luckman. But Baugh's head slammed against the ground, causing the dazed man to see stars. As he was helped to the bench, Bears end George Wilson yelled, "What's the matter, Baugh, lost your guts?"

Still, the Redskins hung tough through a scoreless first period and, on the first play of the second quarter, Andy Farkas ran inches for a Redskins touchdown. Two completions by George Cafego, Baugh's replacement, to Wilbur Moore, plus a 21-yard pass interference penalty, set up the score.

Luckman retaliated three minutes later when he found Bears offensive workhorse Harry Clark with a 31-yard touchdown pass that tied the score at 7. He continued steering Chicago's T-formation on offense and led a drive to the 3. Fullback Bronko Nagurski, having returned to the Bears after a five-year break from football, carried it in for a 14–7 Chicago lead.

The seven-point margin held until halftime, when Redskins owner George Preston Marshall and Bears acting president Ralph Brizzolara created drama before the teams entered their

A sobbing Sammy Baugh is consoled by teammates after his head hit the turf early in the 1943 championship game. Dazed, Baugh asked, "What's the score? What's going on out there? Why won't they let me play?"

locker rooms. Marshall left his box seat and approached the field, and Brizzolara spotted him standing behind Chicago's bench. Thinking Marshall was trying to steal Bears signals, Brizzolara ordered him to step away and then sent a clubhouse attendant to escort him out by the arm. The Redskins' owner eventually talked his way out of the predicament.

Brizzolara later accused Marshall of unsportsmanlike conduct. Marshall reportedly answered by saying Brizzolara wasn't a gentleman and that he'd never speak to him again. The whole Bears' attitude was "very, very rude, to say the least," Marshall told the press. "It was a first-class bush-league trick."

Meanwhile, Chicago poured it on in the second half. Halfback Dante Magnani turned Luckman's screens into 36- and 66-yard touchdown passes for a 27–7 lead. Baugh returned after his 35-minute hiatus and threw a 17-yard scoring pass to Farkas. But Luckman answered with a 29-yard touchdown throw to Jim Benton with about 12 minutes left in the game.

The Bears, ahead 34–14, then executed a trick play. Bob Snyder lined up to kick off, but guard George Musso came from the side and made an on-side kick. The ball went 7 yards, a Redskins player touched and fumbled it, and the Bears recovered. Chicago held the ball for about nine minutes on a drive capped by Luckman's 16-yard touchdown pass to Clark for a 41–14 lead.

Washington was a battered team by game's end. Linemen Wee Willie Wilkin and Lou Rymkus had been useless after suffering early injuries. Back Bob Seymour, hurt in the first five minutes, played at half-speed for the rest of the game. Then there was Baugh's dinger. Redskins coach Dutch Bergman thought his team's injuries were critical to the outcome: "Luckman played a great ball game, he was magnificent," Bergman said in the *Washington Post*. "But I still think we could beat them again if everybody was in shape."

As in the 1937 championship game at Wrigley Field, the field conditions were treacherous. "It was a really bad day to be playing football," Redskins guard Clyde Shugart said years later. "Part of the field where the sun hit had thawed, and part of the field in the shade was hard as concrete. Some players used sneakers, and others used cleats. With cleated shoes, you fell down when running onto the frozen side, and with sneakers, you slipped and fell down when running onto the soft stuff, the mud."

Afterward, Bergman made a surprise announcement. He quit the Redskins, signing with a Washington radio station to broadcast a daily sports show.

| | | | | | | |
|---|---|---|---|---|---|---|
| Washington— | 0 | 7 | 7 | 7 | — | 21 |
| Chicago— | 0 | 14 | 13 | 14 | — | 41 |

Wash — Farkas 1 run (Masterson kick)
Chi —— Clark 31 pass from Luckman (Snyder kick)
Chi —— Nagurski 3 run (Snyder kick)
Chi —— Magnani 36 pass from Luckman (Snyder kick)
Chi —— Magnani 66 pass from Luckman (kick failed)
Wash — Farkas 17 pass from Baugh (Masterson kick)
Chi —— Benton 29 pass from Luckman (Snyder kick)
Chi —— Clark 16 pass from Luckman (Snyder kick)
Wash — Aguirre 25 pass from Baugh (Aguirre kick)

| Team Statistics | Wash | Chi |
|---|---|---|
| First Downs | 11 | 14 |
| Rushing Yards | 50 | 169 |
| Passing Yards | 199 | 276 |
| Passes | 11–24–4 | 15–27–0 |
| Return Yards, Kicks | 144 | 81 |
| Punts–Average | 5–40.8 | 5–32.0 |
| Penalties | 3–35 | 9–81 |
| Fumbles-Lost | 1–0 | 0–0 |

## 1944: 6-3-1, 3RD PLACE—EASTERN DIVISION

### Head Coach: Dudley DeGroot

The Redskins had seen enough. Victimized in the 1940 and 1943 championship games by a Bears team that ran the T-formation to perfection, they felt it was about time to incorporate the innovative offensive scheme into their system.

Redskins owner George Preston Marshall thus hired Clark Shaughnessy, father of the T-formation, as an advisory coach before the 1944 season. Shaughnessy had served in the same capacity when the Bears unveiled the T in the 1940 championship game and annihilated Washington, 73–0.

Shaughnessy taught the formation to Dudley DeGroot, who replaced Dutch Bergman as the Redskins' new coach. DeGroot had compiled a 24–6 coaching record over the prior four seasons at Rochester University and a 59–19–8 mark over eight seasons at San Jose State. He was also a one-time assistant to football legend Glenn "Pop" Warner at Stanford.

The Redskins began practicing the T in training camp in late July. Although only one player, second-year guard Al Fiorentino, had ever played in the formation, they appeared to acclimate themselves to the "tricky stuff remarkably well," one sports columnist wrote. "It looks like it was made for Baugh."

With former halfback, now quarterback, Sammy Baugh under center, the Redskins won their first five exhibition games, one of which came against one of the nation's best service teams. But World War II caught up with Sammy. The Texas draft board gave him a choice of working on his 3,000-acre ranch in Rotan, Texas, which was considered a "vital" occupation, and keeping a military deferred classification, or he could play football and automatically enter into a classification that meant a possible stint in the armed service. He chose to work on his ranch.

Baugh was conspicuous in his absence. The Redskins lost to Chicago, 28–0, in the last exhibition game, when they "were about as explosive as a bunch of Caspar Milquetoasts," according to the *Washington Post*.

The "footBaughless" Redskins were heavy underdogs to the Eagles in the season opener, a thriller before 32,549 fans in Philly. Washington trailed early but battled back behind the passing of Frankie Filchock, who was back after two years in the military, to tie the game at 24 in the third period. Filchock completed 25 of 33 passes for 291 yards overall.

Washington then crafted a 78-yard fourth-quarter touchdown drive that Filchock capped with a short pass to Wilbur Moore. Joe Aguirre, who had missed the previous four extra points, converted for a 31–24 lead with a few minutes left.

But a player who once vowed to get even with the Redskins did just that. Eagles halfback Joe Banta, traded by Washington to Philadelphia, caught a short touchdown pass with six seconds left. Another Redskins castoff, Roy Zimmerman, kicked the extra point to account for the final 31–31 score.

The Redskins were on the road again the next week in Boston, their former hometown, to face the Yanks. Back Bob Seymour carried Washington's offense, rushing for 2- and 20-yard touchdowns. Filchock's 45-yard scoring pass to end Ted Kapka gave the Redskins a 21–14 win.

It was the first of five straight victories. Baugh, who had received a deferral extension from his draft board, was in the lineup for the last four games of the streak, which left the 5–0–1 Redskins in first place in the Eastern Division.

The Redskins' chances for a third straight division title looked bright, for they would play three of their final four games at home. But a sellout crowd of 35,540 at Griffith Stadium saw the Eagles win in a runaway, 37–7. The Redskins couldn't execute out of the T and threw two interceptions that were returned for scores. The Eagles also converted a fumble into a touchdown.

Philadelphia now owned first place in the division. But the Bears clipped the Eagles, 28–7, and the Redskins upended the Yanks, 14–7, leaving the Redskins and Giants, both 6–1–1, in a first-place tie. New York left no doubt which team deserved to play in the championship game.

Washington lost two in a row to the Giants. In a 16–13 loss at the Polo Grounds, Aguirre kicked a 37-yard field goal with about a minute left to tie the game, but the Redskins' Al Fiorentino was called for holding. Aguirre's second attempt from 52 yards was short. The Redskins then departed quietly, losing 31–0 to the Giants in the season finale at Griffith.

Although the Redskins missed out on the postseason, their experiment with the T seemed to be working. Filchock and Baugh finished as the top two quarterbacks in the league. Filchock was named a second-team All-Pro after completing 84 of 147 passes for 1,139 yards and 13 touchdowns. His completions, touchdowns and completion percentage (57.1) were league-highs. Baugh connected on 82 of 146 passes for 849 yards and four touchdowns. The duo combined to set an NFL record for passing efficiency (.568 completion percentage), completing 170 of 299 throws. The Redskins' best receiver, Aguirre, was a consensus first-team All-Pro after catching 34 passes for 410 yards and four scores. Wilbur Moore caught 33 passes for 424 yards and five touchdowns.

Baugh had played his first eight seasons in the single wing. It took him several games to adapt to the T, but he eventually became comfortable in the formation. "[Clark] Shaughnessy told me, 'Don't worry about it, it'll come gradually where you love it," Baugh said in Myron Cope's 1970 book, *The Game That Was: The Early Days of Pro Football.* "Sure enough, after about half that season was gone, I wouldn't have gone back to [the] single wing for anything."

## 1945: 8–2–0, 1ST PLACE— EASTERN DIVISION

### Head Coach: Dudley DeGroot

The Redskins maintained their standard course of dominance in 1945, finishing 8–2 in a season that marked their sixth trip to the NFL championship game, where they fell by a point to Cleveland. The year also marked the end of a sustained period of glory for the franchise.

Washington's offensive firepower was again on display. Baugh, feeling at home in the T-formation, led the NFL in passing. He completed a league-high 128 throws in 182 attempts for 1,669 yards, with 11 touchdowns and four interceptions. His 70.3 completion percentage held as the league's all-time record until Cincinnati's Kenny Anderson posted a 70.55 percent mark in 1981. Baugh also led the league in punting average for the fourth time at 43.3 yards.

Plus, back Frank Akins finished second in the NFL in rushing with 797 yards, the second-highest total by a Redskin next to Cliff Battles's 897 yards in 1937. Rookie Steve Bagarus caught 35 passes, and Joe Aguirre kicked a league-high seven field goals. Washington's defense, not to be forgotten, allowed a league-low 121 points.

Prior to the season, NFL Commissioner Elmer Layden told all teams in the financially strapped league to cut traveling to a minimum. As a result, the Redskins didn't make their annual trek across country for training camp and held it at Georgetown University in Washington, where they were busy mastering the T-formation.

Team consultant Clark Shaughnessy said that quarterbacks Sammy Baugh and Frankie Filchock were both handling the ball under center as well as Chicago's Sid Luckman and Ray McLean, two of the NFL's most proficient T-formation quarterbacks. Shaughnessy also said that the entire Redskins backfield was hiding the ball and faking so much better than in the 1944 season. Baugh's initial assessment, as well, was that the Redskins were much better prepared for the T.

"We know that stuff now," the *Washington Evening Star* quoted Baugh as saying. "Last year . . . I was lost trying to call signals. I knew the plays I wanted to use, but doggone if I could think of the numbers. The T is complicated, and it was like trying to open a safe without knowing the combination. Half the time I was guessing and hoping it was the right number— sort of like praying for the jackpot. You can understand why we looked so bad at times, but it won't happen again. We've got it down now and we have more confidence in it."

Baugh and Filchock had a new receiver to target: Steve Bagarus. The tricky halfback from Notre Dame had returned after missing the 1944 season while serving in the army. Other new faces included center Al DeMao, a ninth-round Redskins pick out of Duquesne in 1942 who went on to serve in the military; 6–7½ tackle John "Tree" Adams, a second-round pick from Notre Dame; and Northwestern All-American back Bill DeCorrevont.

The Redskins played all five of their exhibition games against Western Division teams, finishing 3–1–1. In the season opener, though, they were upset by the Boston Yanks, 28–20,

before 25,000 fans at their old stomping ground, Fenway Park. Boston's line of Augie Lio, Tony Leon, Jim Magee, and former Redskins Al Fiorentino and Bob Masterson overwhelmed the Redskins, who had their "faces ground into the mud of Fenway Park," *Washington Post* sportswriter Al Costello wrote.

Washington responded with a six-game winning streak. The Redskins first topped the Steelers at Forbes Field, 14–0, behind 18-of-22 passing by Baugh, who by then was Washington's primary quarterback. Filchock had been relegated to a backup role.

The Redskins then gained first place in the Eastern Division with a 24–14 home win over Philly, which had been touted as the division's strongest team. Akins ran for two short touchdowns. In another 24–14 win, this time over the host Giants, Baugh was sensational. He completed 19 of 23 passes and intercepted two throws, returning one 80 yards. Bagarus caught seven passes for 80 yards.

Several Redskins returned from military stints by the start of November, including backs Dick Todd and Bob DeFruiter, and linemen Clem Stralka and Ki Aldrich. They joined a squad that beat the Cardinals, 24–21, on Joe Aguirre's 18-yard field goal with 38 seconds left; the Yanks, 34–7; and the Bears, 28–21.

The win over Chicago was nearly a carbon copy of the 1937 championship game. The Bears led, 7–0, 14–7, and 21–14, before some Redskins came up clutch in the fourth quarter. Baragus's 28-yard punt return set up Merlyn Condit's touchdown run for a 21–21 game, and Todd ran 30 yards and Akins ran 18 to set up Condit's second scoring run. Washington rushed for 210 yards to compensate for an unproductive passing game.

By then the 6–1 Redskins stood first in the division. They botched a golden opportunity to clinch it with a 16–0 loss to the Eagles, leaving both teams at 6–2. Philly subsequently did the Redskins a huge favor by losing to the Giants, while Washington routed Pittsburgh, 24–0. Baugh threw three touchdown passes, two to Bagarus.

Not done yet, Baugh completed 11 of 19 throws for 150 yards and a touchdown pass in the regular-season finale, a 17–0 whipping of the visiting Giants that secured the division title. Al Costello of the *Post* drooled over Baugh's performance: "If the Redskins were terrific yesterday, and they were, Sammy was something super. If he made a mistake all day, it wasn't apparent, and as the tall Texan nursed the team along slowly, carefully, one movement and daringly the next, but ever surely, it became more and more apparent he was the boss of the greensward beyond any lingering doubt."

The win set up a meeting on the road against the Western Division-champion Cleveland Rams for the NFL title.

## NFL CHAMPIONSHIP GAME
**Cleveland 15, Washington 14**
**December 16, 1945**
**Municipal Stadium, Cleveland**
**Attendance: 32,178**

### "Gentleman's Agreement," Goalposts Fuel Redskins Demise

Washington was stricken with bad luck in the 1945 championship game, while Cleveland played with what seemed like a ghostly twelfth man and profited from a boneheaded decision.

Such a confluence led to an infuriating day for one team. Final score: 15–14 Rams.

Cleveland found a friend in the goalposts, which were on the goal line at the time. A Sammy Baugh pass from his end zone hit a goalpost and landed in the end zone for an automatic safety. An extra point attempt by Cleveland's Bob Waterfield, tipped by a Redskin, hit the crossbar and fell over. Go figure.

Then came the brutal weather. With about six minutes left and Cleveland ahead, 15–14, the Redskins' Joe Aguirre tried a 31-yard field goal. Strong winds gusting into Cleveland's Municipal Stadium off adjacent Lake Erie wreaked havoc on the ball and sent it just wide of the goalpost. In her 1947 book, *My Life with the Redskins*, Corinne Griffith recounted the agonizing moments while the ball was in the air:

The ball rose high in the air, then headed hard and true toward the goalposts and three winning points. An icy wind, sweeping through the open end of the stadium, raced toward the goalposts, reached them just as the ball spiraled in between, caught it in its icy breath—and held it. The ball shivered, dropped, just a little, still well within the uprights and a world's championship, then drifted to the left. The ball staggered—the impetus behind it was dying.

The wind gave one last hard shove, drove the ball far to the left, six inches wide of the goalpost, and slapped it hard to the ice-coated ground below. Then, like an evil spirit bent on some ghoulish mission, the wind swept the full length of the field, screamed with delight at its freakish prank, leaped the grandstand and scuttled away, leaving in its wake a dizzy backwash of whirling snowflakes.

How cruel!

The Redskins could only blame themselves for the other major factor that tilted the game toward the Rams. On a bitterly cold day with temperatures barely above zero, the frozen field was as slippery as an ice skating rink. It had snowed the day before. Such conditions gave Washington, the only team to come equipped with sneakers for better traction, a distinct edge.

Rams coach Adam Walsh thus asked Redskins coach Dud DeGroot before the game if he would tell his players to remove their sneakers and wear cleats instead. DeGroot obliged.

His decision would haunt the Redskins, who were eyeing a 9–1 Rams team led by Waterfield, an electrifying rookie quarterback and the league MVP. Early on, his passing helped motor the Rams from their 21 to the Redskins' 5. But Cleveland was stopped on downs.

Baugh was then called for intentional grounding, putting the ball just inside the 3. Intent on getting the Redskins out of the precarious situation through the air, he aimed a quick crossing pattern to end Wayne Millner. But the pass hit the goalpost, giving Cleveland a 2–0 lead 9:20 into the first quarter. "I managed to get into the clear, I could almost taste the touchdown as Sam started to throw the ball," Millner said in Bob Curran's 1969 book, *Pro Football's Rag Days*. (The NFL ruled before the 1946 season that a pass hitting the goalposts is an incompletion.)

Shortly after, Baugh aggravated a month-old rib injury and departed for good, marking the second straight NFL championship game the Redskins had lost his services. Frankie Filchock filled in admirably. He tossed a 38-yard touchdown pass to Bagarus in the second quarter for a 7–2 Redskins lead.

Cleveland responded with a 70-yard scoring drive that ended on Waterfield's 37-yard pass to Jim Benton three and a half minutes before halftime. Redskin tackle John Koniszewski tipped Waterfield's conversion attempt, which wobbled toward the goalposts—but it slipped over the crossbar for a 9–7 Rams edge.

Throughout the first half, Redskins owner George Preston Marshall noticed that players on both teams were slip-sliding on the field. Unaware of the Walsh-DeGroot deal, he sought out Redskins equipment manager Kelly Miller in a halftime visit to the locker room.

"Why didn't you bring rubber-soled shoes for the team?" Marshall asked.

"I did, they're on top of the lockers, but the coaches didn't want them," Miller replied.

Marshall then demanded an explanation from DeGroot. "We're not allowed to get out the sneakers because I made a gentleman's agreement with Adam Walsh that we wouldn't use them," DeGroot said.

"Since when does it become a gentleman's game?" an irate Marshall replied. "You had no right to make any agreement with Walsh."

The quick-triggered Marshall essentially fired DeGroot on the spot, recalled Al DeMao, a Redskins center at the time, although DeGroot finished the game.

Back on the field, the Rams padded their lead early in the third period. Waterfield, who completed 14 of 27 passes for 192 yards on the day, threw his second touchdown, a 44-yarder to Jim Gillette, to end an 81-yard drive. Waterfield's conversion sailed wide right, and Cleveland led, 15–7.

Washington retaliated shortly after the Rams' touchdown. Filchock threw a 50-yard completion to Bagarus, a "dancing dervish [who] managed to keep his feet when opponents were slipping and slithering all over the field," Morris A. Bealle wrote in his book, *The Redskins: 1937–1958*. Cleveland's defense stiffened. But on fourth down from the 9, Filchock passed to a wide-open Jim Seymour in the end zone. Aguirre's conversion created a one-point game late in the third quarter.

Filchock wasn't done. His passing guided Washington into Rams territory twice in the fourth period to set up scoring opportunities. Shortly after Aguirre missed his 31-yard attempt, the Redskins took possession on their 42. With Filchock hitting short passes, they moved to the Rams' 39, but Aguirre's 46-yard attempt fell short with 2:10 to play. The Rams ran out the clock.

The *Washington Post* summed up the Redskins' afternoon: "Cold and defeat made it a miserable day for our heroes."

| | | | | | |
|---|---|---|---|---|---|
| Washington— | 0 | 7 | 7 | 0 — | 14 |
| Cleveland— | 2 | 7 | 6 | 0 — | 15 |

Cle —— Safety, Baugh's pass hit the goalpost
Wash — Bagarus 38 pass from Filchock (Aguirre kick)
Cle —— Benton 37 pass from Waterfield (Waterfield kick)
Cle —— Gillette 44 pass from Waterfield (kick failed)
Wash — Seymour 8 pass from Filchock (Aguirre kick)

| Team Statistics | Wash | Cle |
|---|---|---|
| First Downs | 8 | 14 |
| Rushing Yards | 35 | 180 |
| Passing Yards | 179 | 192 |
| Passes | 9–20–2 | 14–27–2 |
| Punts–Average | 6–36.0 | 8–38.0 |
| Penalty Yards | 34 | 60 |
| Fumbles–Lost | 1 | 1 |

# 1946–1961: Ominous Times for the Burgundy and Gold

**O**NCE A POWERHOUSE, the Washington Redskins took a precipitous fall from grace after World War II, sometimes resembling a franchise in disarray.

After winning 70 percent of the time in their first nine years in D.C., plus two NFL championships, the Redskins were mediocre to dreadful in the ensuing years. In the 16 seasons from 1946 to 1961, they won 39 percent of their games, with three years over .500 and no playoff appearances.

The final two seasons epitomized the Redskins' woes. They finished 1–9–2 in 1960 and 1–12–1 in 1961, the franchise's worst years ever, and went winless in 23 straight games during a stretch that consumed those two seasons. It was the most wrenching period in team history.

"They were the Washington Senators of the NFL," longtime Redskins public address announcer Phil Hochberg said, equating the Redskins of the early 1960s with one of the worst pro baseball teams of that era. "The Redskins were just atrocious, and they weren't even interesting to watch. It was frustrating."

In the nation's capital, where Redskin season-ticket sales plummeted, disgust with the NFL franchise was rampant, with lots of fingers pointed in anger at one man, Redskins owner George Preston Marshall. His problematic decision making, coupled with his micromanaging, iron-fisted approach, brought the team to its knees.

The coaching fiasco is one example. After promising to re-sign Ray Flaherty, who coached the Redskins during most of their early glory years before enlisting in the U.S. Navy during World War II, Marshall balked. He never again found a coach of Flaherty's skill. The impatient owner instead carried on a revolving-door policy that welcomed nine Redskins coaches—four alone in the first half of the 1950s—over the calamitous 16-year period.

The lack of coaching continuity was "very difficult," said Jim Ricca, a Redskins lineman from 1951 to '54 who played under Herman Ball, Dick Todd, Earl "Curly" Lambeau, and Joe Kuharich. "I started most of my career on defense, and I also had to go to the offensive meetings because I was a backup for both tackles," he said. "And when you get four different systems in four years, it's pretty hard to develop a winning offensive scheme. Everyone had different ways of calling signals and changing the play. We went to the colors, we went to the numbers."

Marshall, who once considered selling his team, also failed to acquire enough star players. When the All-American Foot-ball Conference, which debuted in 1946, tried luring big-name players and coaches from the NFL with lucrative salary offers, the owner refused to match those made to a host of Redskins, who opted to leave for greener pastures. The Redskins were consistently among the lowest-paid teams in the league, exemplifying how team management failed to focus on the essentials needed to create a winner.

"We didn't have much of a draft, no scouting, or anything else in those days," said Eddie LeBaron, an exciting Redskins quarterback in the 1950s. "We had good talent here and there but not a lot."

The Redskins' top talent included:

- LeBaron, a 5–7, 165-pounder who made the Pro Bowl three times and dazzled fans with his passing and ball-handling skills.
- Fellow quarterback Sammy Baugh, who enjoyed some of his greatest years after World War II before ending his Hall of Fame career in 1952.
- Undersized defensive end Gene Brito, a consensus first-team All-Pro in 1955, '56, '57, and '58.
- Guard Dick Stanfel, a consensus first-team All-Pro in 1956, '57, and '58 and a terrific run blocker.

Other Redskin stars from the era included linebacker Chuck Drazenovich and tackle Paul Lipscomb, both four-time Pro Bowlers; end Hugh "Bones" Taylor, a two-time Pro Bowler who set a slew of Redskin receiving records; and "Bullet" Bill Dudley, a Redskins running, passing, and kick returning threat in the early 1950s. Center Jim Schrader, linebacker LaVern "Torgy" Torgeson, safety Joe "Scooter" Scudero, running back Steve Bagarus, lineman John "Tree" Adams, fullback Don Bosseler, and kicker "Sugarfoot" Sam Baker were among those who also stood out.

But the Redskins simply couldn't keep pace with the dominant teams, and Marshall's racial policy did them no favors. When blacks began entering the NFL in large numbers after World War II, he insisted on signing only white players. The policy decimated his franchise: in the late 1940s and the 1950s, opposing teams acquired blacks who emerged as stars and even future Hall of Fame inductees. Marshall finally relented after the 1961 season by trading for Cleveland Browns running back Bobby Mitchell and a few other black players.

By then, the Redskins had languished through a decade—the 1950s—that renowned football historian Mickey Herskowitz called the "golden age" of pro football. The NFL experienced unprecedented growth, transforming itself from a league that once held a distant back seat in popularity to pro baseball to one that soared to new levels of prosperity and entered the modern age of sports on December 28, 1958.

That day in the NFL championship, the Baltimore Colts beat the New York Giants in overtime, 23–17. The game produced a marriage between television and pro football, as millions of viewers tuned in. When it ended, NFL Commissioner Bert Bell jumped from his box and shouted, "This is the greatest day in the history of pro football."

For the Redskins, it was just another day in an era of futility. "We weren't losing because of mistakes, we were always well-drilled," said Bosseler, a Redskin from 1957 to '64. "But the talent on the other side was a little better. It was very disheartening."

## 1946: 5–5–1, 3RD PLACE (TIE)— EASTERN DIVISION

### Head Coach: Turk Edwards

The Redskins' coaching door continued spinning in 1946. When the maligned Dud DeGroot quit to coach the Los Angeles Dons of the new All-America Football Conference, Redskins owner George Preston Marshall dipped into the team's family to select his third coach in four seasons.

Marshall named the great Redskins lineman Turk Edwards as head coach and another Redskins legend, receiver Wayne Millner, as Edwards's assistant. In the process, the owner took a page from his Midwestern rival, Chicago Bears owner-coach George Halas. "George Halas has the right system," Marshall told the press. "All his coaches come from the ranks of the Bears football team. Not a bad idea."

Edwards inherited a team that looked much different from the prior season. Backs Bob Seymour and Cecil Hare, end Joe Aguirre, and tackles Lou Rymkus, Wee Willie Wilkin, and Earl Audet had jumped to the AAFC. The Redskins traded backup quarterback Frankie Filchock to the Giants after he delivered a trade-me-or-else ultimatum, according to the *Washington Evening Star*.

Some key people—quarterback Sammy Baugh; backs Steve Bagarus, Dick Todd, Frank Akins, and Wilbur Moore; and linemen John Adams, Bill Young, and Ki Aldrich—were back. They and the rest of the team began holding training camp at Occidental College in Los Angeles, where the Redskins would train until 1962. The Cleveland Rams relocated to Los Angeles in 1946, and for many years Washington played a charity exhibition game against the Rams sponsored by the *Los Angeles Times*.

The Redskins opened the regular season by tying Pittsburgh, 14–14, at Griffith Stadium. They held a 14–0 lead late in the third period, but the underdog Steelers rallied and could have won. They barely missed a 25-yard field goal with 10 seconds left.

Washington's next opponent, Detroit, also missed a critical late field goal. This time the Redskins escaped with a 17–16 victory that triggered a three-game winning streak. Next came a 24–14 win over the Giants behind the "Bee-Bee" combo of Baugh and Bagarus. "Mr. Slinger slung and Mr. Snatcher

snatched twice for sensational touchdowns as the Redskins rose to their greatest performance of the yet young season to conquer the team experts freely predicted would give them (the) most trouble in defense of their Eastern Division championship," *Washington Post* sportswriter Al Costello wrote.

The Redskins improved to 3–0–1 with a 14–6 win over the Boston Yanks and then blew a 24–0 halftime lead over the Eagles en route to a 28–24 loss. The defeat, coupled with the Giants' 14–0 upset of Chicago, pushed the Redskins out of first place in the division. Turk Edwards made a crucial decision with his squad up, 24–21, and facing a fourth-and-1 on their own 40 with 2:55 to play. Instead of calling for a punt that likely would have pinned the Eagles deep in their territory, Edwards went for it. Philly stuffed ball-carrier Sal Rosato and proceeded to throw the winning touchdown pass.

The Steelers then handed the Redskins a 14–7 loss. Pittsburgh's Bill Dudley, the NFL's 1946 MVP, returned an interception 81 yards for a touchdown and ran a punt back 53 yards. After the loss, rumors surfaced that Edwards and advisory coach Clark Shaughnessy might be fired, although Marshall denied that was the case.

By then, the Redskins had a litany of key players hobbled by injuries, such as Baugh and Bagarus. Despite a charley horse and torn rib cartilage, Sammy came off the bench to spark his team to a 17–14 win over Boston.

The Redskins lost two of their next three games, leaving them 5–4–1 heading into the regular-season finale against the 6–3–1 Giants, holders of first place in the division. A win would give Washington the division title because of its victory over New York earlier in the season.

The game was billed as the Baugh-Filchock battle. Filchock dearly wanted to send his former team to defeat, and he got his wish before 60,337 fans at the Polo Grounds, completing 9 of 14 passes with two touchdowns to key a 31–0 Giants rout.

The Redskins' final 5–5–1 record, largely attributable to the rash of injures incurred throughout the year, marked their worst season to date in the nation's capital. The irascible Marshall issued a stern warning to his players at the team's annual farewell luncheon.

"The fans haven't lost faith in you despite a poor season," he said, as quoted by the *Star*. "The Washington public has been extremely loyal to the Redskins, and you have got to prove you haven't lost faith in yourselves. If your mind and heart [aren't into] playing football, don't come back next year. This is one game that can't be commercialized, and you've got to love it to play it well."

Marshall guaranteed that the Redskins would be a "fighting team" in 1947 or else. He stressed that one subpar year in no way meant his squad couldn't again become part of the NFL elite, reminding everyone of the Redskins' rise from a 6–5, nonplayoff team in 1941 to league champions the next season.

## 1947: 4–8–0, 4TH PLACE— EASTERN DIVISION

### Head Coach: Turk Edwards

For a quarterback near the twilight of his career, Sammy Baugh looked like he had never lost a step.

The 11th-year man crafted one of his best seasons, padding his vast collection of league records with single-season marks for completions (210), attempts (354), and passing yards (2,938). His yardage total was nearly 1,000 more than the prior league record. He also threw 25 touchdown passes. His aerial proficiency carried a Redskins offense that set NFL records for passing yards (3,336), pass completions (231), and attempts (416). The Redskins also posted 4,679 total yards, a number that topped the all-time mark but was second that year to the Bears (5,051).

Washington's defense, in contrast, was often out to lunch. The unit allowed the most points in the league by far (367, 31 per game) and the third-most passing yards (2,422). The unbalanced scenario paved the way for a 4–8 record, the Redskins' first losing season in D.C.

In preparing for the season, the Redskins began a youth movement that created the youngest team in franchise history. They acquired a solid group of rookies, the most prominent being pass receiving ends Hugh Taylor, a scrawny 6–4, 170-pounder from Oklahoma City University aptly nicknamed "Bones," and Syracuse's Joe Tereshinski, a key player in the college all-stars' smashing upset of the NFL champion-Bears. Promising Maryland quarterback Tommy Mont was set to compete for the No. 2 spot behind Baugh.

Baugh, halfback Dick Todd, and fullback Sal Rosato formed the foundation of the backfield, which had recently retired Redskins fullback Wilbur Moore as its new coach. But Steve Bagarus, the receiving end of the dangerous Baugh-Bagarus aerial combo, was traded before the season to the Los Angeles Rams in a deal unpopular with Redskins fans.

Slingin' Sammy delivered one of his best games ever in the season opener at Philly. He completed 21 of 34 passes for 364 yards and five touchdowns, connecting on his 1,000th career completion in the second period. Taylor was superb in his pro debut, catching 62-, 36-, and 18-yard scoring passes.

It was all for naught in the Redskins' 45–42 loss. The 87 total points accounted for one of the highest single-game scoring outputs in the NFL to date. In addition to their point production, the Eagles gained 401 yards.

Washington rebounded with a thrilling 27–26 win over the Steelers before an overflow crowd of 35,565 at Griffith Stadium. Baugh was again fantastic, completing 13 of 20 passes for 275 yards and three scores. Pittsburgh had a chance to win, but its 30-yard field goal attempt with 25 seconds left hit the goalpost.

Baugh then carried the Redskins again—literally. Never heralded for his rushing ability, he ran for two 1-yard scores in a 28–20 win over the Giants, tying his rushing touchdown total from his previous 10 seasons. The win left 2–1 Washington tied with the Eagles for the Eastern Division lead.

That was as bright as the 1946 season got for the Redskins, who suffered five straight losses. The last of those defeats—to a Detroit squad in the Western Division cellar—mathematically eliminated the 2–6 Redskins from the division race.

But Baugh wasn't done. When the Redskins hosted the Chicago Cardinals on November 23, 1947, under the banner of "Sammy Baugh Day," the legend delivered one of the most prolific games of his career. He completed 25 of 33 passes for 355 yards and six touchdowns in Washington's 45–21 victory. His performance came against the league's top defense and a team battling for the Western Division lead.

Sammy again sizzled the next week, completing 14 straight passes at one point in a 27–24 loss to Boston, and Washington split its last two games to finish 4–8. Other Redskins who had great seasons included end Bob Nussbaumer (47 catches, 597 yards) and kicker-back Dick Poillon (second in the league with 85 points).

At the team's farewell luncheon, Baugh apologized for his squad's eight losses. "I haven't got long to play," he said, as quoted by the *Washington Post*. "I'd like to play on at least one more championship team before I quit."

# 1948: 7–5–0, 2ND PLACE— EASTERN DIVISION

## Head Coach: Turk Edwards

At one point, the Redskins appeared quarterback-rich. They later made regrettable decisions on the quarterback front heading into the 1948 season.

Washington used its "bonus" draft choice to select Harry Gilmer, an outstanding passer at Alabama who had led the Crimson Tide to two Sugar Bowl appearances and one Rose Bowl. The Redskins also signed Charlie Conerly, a prolific passer at Mississippi who challenged Sammy Baugh's college records. Washington had drafted Conerly in 1945, when he was in the military; he returned to play at Mississippi before joining the Redskins in 1948.

Baugh hinted about retiring after the 1948 season, and the Redskins chose to groom Gilmer as Baugh's successor, thinking he was a better prospect than Conerly. They traded Conerly's draft rights to the Giants for Howie Livingston, one of the league's best defensive backs and the NFL leader in interceptions in 1944.

The trade led to one of the biggest gaffes in Redskins history. Gilmer never lived up to his billing. He suffered a severe leg injury in a 1948 preseason scrimmage that caused him to miss the entire campaign and was relegated mostly to kick returning in the three ensuing seasons. Conerly, meanwhile, crafted a solid 14-year career in New York, helping the Giants win the NFL championship in 1956 and division titles in 1958 and '59. Time after time, he tormented the club that let him go.

"We've been honoring Conerly since he broke into the league 11 years ago," Redskins General Manager Dick McCann told reporters in 1959. "He's thrown about 30 touchdown passes against us since he's been in the league. The guy has killed us."

The Redskins were wise, though, to draft Louisiana State back Dan Sandifer. He intercepted an NFL-record 13 passes in 1948—breaking Baugh's record of 11—and returned two of them for touchdowns. Washington was also equipped with a bunch of tested veterans in halfbacks Dick Todd and Dick Poillon, end Doug Turley, tackle John Adams, and center Al DeMao.

As usual, owner George Preston Marshall was beaming with optimism in his preseason outlook. He proclaimed that "this may be our year" and "we're a cinch for 1949," as reported by the *Washington Evening Star*. He said that where the Redskins finished in 1948 would depend on how well the rookies acquired the year before performed. "If they show

## Redskins Special Teams Excellence

- Eddie Saenz: NFL highs in kickoff returns (29) and kickoff return yards (797) in 1947
- Dan Sandifer: NFL highs in kickoff returns (26) and kickoff return yards (594) in 1948
- Saenz and Sandifer: Tied for NFL high in kickoff returns (24) in 1949
- Bill Dudley: NFL highs in FG percentage (76.9, 10–13) and X PT. percentage (95.5, 21–22) in 1951

the form we expect, we'll have a winner. Otherwise, we may have to wait a year. But the future looks pretty bright right now."

After a 1–3 exhibition season that included a 43–0 loss to the Packers, the Redskins beat the Steelers, 17–14, in the season opener. Turley returned a fumble 33 yards for a touchdown in the fourth quarter. Poillon converted for a 14–14 game and later kicked a 28-yard field goal with 20 seconds left. It was the third time in three years that a field goal had decided a game between the two teams.

Washington's offense shifted into high gear the next week, posting 485 yards and 24 first downs in a 41–10 shellacking of the Giants. Baugh completed 16 of 24 passes for 259 yards.

The Redskins and Steelers then engaged in another down-to-the-wire battle. This time, Pittsburgh's Joe Glamp kicked a 12-yard field goal with 33 seconds left to give the Steelers a 10–7 win. The Eagles subsequently dropped the Redskins to .500 with a 45–0 rout that Washington coach Turk Edwards, quoted in the *Washington Post,* called "the worst game a Redskin team has ever played," perhaps forgetting about a game he had played in, the 73–0 devastation at Chicago's hands in the 1940 championship.

Edwards's words may have inspired his troops, who won four straight. After beating Green Bay, 23–7, they massacred Boston, 59–21, setting a Redskins record for single-game points that has since been broken. Baugh completed 17 of 24 passes with four touchdowns and 447 yards, a league record at the time.

The Redskins followed with another win over the Yanks and a 46–21 drubbing of Detroit, leaving them 6–2 and a half-game behind Philly for first place in the Eastern Division. But the Eagles administered a 42–21 beating of the Redskins, who failed to contain quarterback Tommy Thompson, the league's top-rated passer in 1948, and future Hall of Fame running back Steve Van Buren.

After a 48–13 loss to Chicago eliminated Washington from the division title race, the Redskins suffered a 41–13 loss to a Rams team coached by ex-Redskins T-formation expert Clark Shaughnessy. Washington finished with a 28–21 win over the Giants, a game that featured an aerial circus involving Baugh (25 of 42, 350 yards, three touchdowns) and a name from the recent past: NFL Rookie of the Year Charlie Conerly (23 of 41, 225 yards, two touchdowns).

Unlike those two, Turk Edwards ended his third season coaching the Redskins on a sour note. With a 16–18–1 overall record, he resigned under pressure from Marshall,

who named him the team's executive vice president. The owner then began a search for another head coach, and a plethora of possible replacements, most of them coaching luminaries, circulated through the media: Notre Dame's Frank Leahy, Georgia's Wally Butts, Georgia Tech's Bobby Dodd, Texas's Blair Cherry, Kentucky's Paul "Bear" Bryant, Texas Christian's L. R. Meyer, and Paul Brown of the Cleveland Browns, three-time champions of the All-America Football Conference. Redskins backfield coach Wilbur Moore and Bears star quarterback Sid Luckman were other possibilities.

Marshall offered the job to Bryant, who accepted the position but had to back out when Kentucky refused to release him from a 10-year contract, according to the *Post*. The Redskins' boss made a decision that astounded many.

## 1949: 4–7–1, 4TH PLACE— EASTERN DIVISION

### Head Coach: John Whelchel (7 games), Herman Ball (5 games)

Redskins owner George Preston Marshall ended his tedious search for a new coach in February 1949 by naming John Whelchel as the head man. The standard response from people outside the organization was, "John who?"

John Esten Whelchel was a retired rear admiral who had last coached football in 1943 at the U.S. Naval Academy in Annapolis, Maryland, before spending six years at sea. The coaching layoff didn't seem to bother Marshall, who was convinced that Whelchel's military-born toughness would rub off on players that the owner considered undisciplined. The Redskins called Whelchel the "greatest thing ever to happen to pro football," according to the *Washington Post*.

Whelchel was the first native Washingtonian ever to coach the Redskins. He had directed Navy to a 13–5 overall record in 1942 and '43, his only two seasons at the academy. His Midshipmen used the single-wing formation, but Marshall required him to keep the T-formation in the Redskins' repertoire. The owner even commissioned Notre Dame coach Frank Leahy, who had led the Fighting Irish to three national titles, to teach Whelchel the T and help him polish other aspects of his coaching skills.

Not long into training camp, Whelchel had gained the admiration of many of his players. "He's using psychology on us, and I like it," tackle John Koniszewski told reporters. "Take that first day of camp, for example, when he let us play tough football and left us completely alone. We did more work than we would have done with routine stuff."

Once again, optimism oozed out of camp, and General Manager Dick McCann said he was anticipating a "record-breaking season" for the franchise. "We may have the best team we've ever had, especially with Harry Gilmer in the lineup," he said, as quoted by the *Washington Evening Star*.

Gilmer, the talented second-year quarterback out of Alabama, had missed the entire 1948 season due to a major leg injury. As for Sammy Baugh, back for his 13th year, newspaper reports out of his home state of Texas said this would be his last NFL season, the second straight year such

A changing of the guard: Redskins owner George Preston Marshall shakes hands with his new coach, Rear Admiral John Whelchel, in February 1949. Whelchel replaced Turk Edwards (left), who had just resigned after finishing 16–18–1 in three seasons at the helm (1946–48). Edwards was promoted to Redskins vice president.

rumors had surfaced. He dismissed the reports, calling them a publicity stunt choreographed by Redskins management, according to the *Star*. Gilmer and Baugh alternated at quarterback in the Redskins' 3–2 exhibition season, but Sammy ended up taking the taking the bulk of the snaps during the regular season.

The Chicago Cardinals, who had lost to the Eagles in the 1948 NFL championship game, were heavily favored over Washington on opening day and rolled to a 38–7 win before 24,136 fans at Comisky Park. Baugh's 5-yard scoring pass to end Dan Sandifer tied the game at 7 in the second quarter, before Chicago scored 31 straight points.

The Redskins responded with a 27–14 victory over Pittsburgh, breaking a three-game losing streak to the Steelers on the road. But in Washington's home opener, the Giants raced to a 45–35 win. Quarterback Charley Conerly, once discarded by the Redskins, threw three touchdown passes, two within minutes of each other in the third period to break the game open.

Baugh tossed 3 of his 4 scoring passes to end Hal Crisler in a 38–14 win over the New York Bulldogs that evened Washington's record at 2–2. Still, the defending-champion Eagles pounded the Redskins, 49–14. After a 14–14 tie with the Bulldogs, a game in which the Redskins were heavily favored, Washington held a 2–3–1 mark at midseason.

The Bulldogs' game had been touted as a must-win situation for Whelchel, whose coaching status was becoming more tenuous each week. Despite a 27–14 win over the Steelers, Marshall handed the admiral his walking papers to ensure the shortest Redskins coaching career at the time.

The owner replaced Whelchel with head line coach Herman Ball, who had joined the team in 1946 as chief scout and an assistant line coach. The switch was to no avail; the Redskins lost to the Eagles, Bears, and Giants. New York's Conerly completed 14 of 32 passes for 218 yards and "a pair

of the prettiest touchdown passes of the year," one reporter wrote.

The struggling Redskins routed Green Bay, 30–0, before 23,200 fans, the smallest crowd at Griffith Stadium since 1942, but a 53–27 loss to Los Angeles in the season finale left the 4–7–1 Redskins with their worst record in franchise history. Among the bright spots, the ageless Baugh posted a league-high 56.9 completion percentage (145 of 255 passing), with 1,903 yards and 18 touchdowns. End Bones Taylor caught 45 passes for team records of 781 yards and nine touchdowns. His touchdown total was also a league-high.

## 1950: 3–9–0, 6TH PLACE— AMERICAN CONFERENCE

### Head Coach: Herman Ball

Washington appeared to enter the 1950 season with more depth, power, and speed than any of its teams since the 1942 championship squad. So much for preseason hype: the Redskins posted the worst record in their 14-year history in the nation's capital: 3–9.

Washington had a solid draft, acquiring promising players such as North Carolina running back Charlie Justice, Oklahoma running back George Thomas, Penn State fullback Chuck Drazenovich, Kentucky center Harry Ulinski, Purdue tackle Lou Karras, and College of the Pacific quarterback Eddie LeBaron. The 5–7 LeBaron was seen as the successor to the aging Sammy Baugh but was called to serve in the Korean War.

Through trades, the Redskins also obtained the Lions' Bill Dudley, a versatile running back, receiver, defensive back, and kick returner—and a future Hall of Famer—and the Packers'

Paul Lipscomb, a 6–5, 245-pound tackle who Redskins coach Herman Ball was certain would be of immediate value.

The Redskins won all five of their exhibition games, including a sweep of the California teams, Los Angeles and San Francisco. (The 49ers, the Baltimore Colts, and the Cleveland Browns migrated to the NFL that season from the defunct All-America Football Conference.) With the regular season about to begin, Ball was optimistic that his team possessed the tools to become a championship squad, perhaps not in 1950 but at least by 1952. "Spirit and desire won five exhibition games for us, and it will win a good number of league games later on," Ball said in the *Washington Daily News* on September 14, 1950. "But it is only natural that the 20 first- and second-year men we have on the squad will make mistakes."

Eleven Redskin rookies started in the season opener against the neighboring Colts, and the Redskins posted a 38–14 victory behind sterling performances from two veterans: Baugh and end Bones Taylor. Baugh, who reportedly turned down the head coaching job at Baylor University in Waco, Texas, in the off-season, threw 31- and 27-yard touchdown passes to Taylor and a screen pass to second-year back Rob Goode that resulted in a 56-yard scoring play. Taylor also caught a 46-yarder from quarterback Harry Gilmer.

Such dominance influenced the press to peg the Redskins as the team with the best chance of beating Cleveland, four-time champions in the AAFC. The oddsmakers also thought highly enough of the Redskins to make them two-touchdown favorites over the Packers. Green Bay's 35–21 win left a bad taste in Ball's mouth: "It isn't good to lose any game," he told reporters when it was suggested that the loss might be a tonic for the team. "We've got to win and keep winning."

The loss kicked off an embarrassing Redskins collapse. In their home debut they fell to Pittsburgh, 26–7, the first time the Steelers had ever won in the nation's capital.

While Ball and his staff sought ways to stop the nosedive, the Redskins were suddenly being labeled the most inept team ever to wear the burgundy and gold. News that a chipped bone in Baugh's throwing arm might force him to miss the upcoming clash against the Giants and that Gilmer was ailing with a bad leg kept spirits down.

Gilmer, ready by game time, played impressively, leading the Redskins on 80- and 92-yard scoring drives that gave them a 14–7 second-quarter lead. But Washington was haunted by that former Redskin quarterback named Charlie Conerly, who baited defensive back Howie Livingston out of position and threw the game-winning scoring pass in the Giants' 21–17 victory.

The defeat knocked the Redskins virtually out of the league's title race, and they still had two games left against powerhouses Cleveland and Philadelphia. Another five straight losses, including 35–3 and 33–0 to the Eagles, left the 1–8 Redskins in the cellar of the newly renamed American Conference with three games left. Marshall gave no immediate public indication he was thinking of firing Ball, who was slated to handle the Redskins' draft choices in January.

Ball's boys salvaged some pride with wins over Baltimore and Pittsburgh. But a devastating aerial attack by future Hall of Fame inductee Otto Graham in the season finale lifted Cleveland—the eventual NFL champs—to a 45–21 rout that put the Redskins out of their misery.

## 1951: 5–7–0, 3RD PLACE— AMERICAN CONFERENCE

### Head Coach: Herman Ball (3 games), Dick Todd (9 games)

Once silent on the coaching future of Herman Ball, Redskins owner George Preston Marshall left no doubt early in the 1951 off-season that his patience was growing thin. "I'm not going to sit tight with a 3–9 team, you can bet on that," Marshall told the press.

Speculation swirled that the owner might move Ball into an executive post and hire a new coach. On January 10, 1951, the *Washington Evening Star* reported that Ball would be fired as coach but given the authority to name his successor. It was rumored that Clark Shaughnessy, father of the T-formation and a Redskins consultant in the 1940s, would return to D.C. as head coach.

Nothing materialized. Marshall retained Ball, who promised to deliver a winning team in 1951. The coach named defense as the Redskins' key theme and figured that an offense led by the passing of 14-year veteran Sammy Baugh and Harry Gilmer, the running of Rob Goode, the receiving of Bones Taylor, and the play of multithreat Bill Dudley would produce a lot of points.

But the defense looked anemic in a 58–14 loss to the Rams in the exhibition opener, and Marshall erupted with one of his customary tirades. "[The Redskins] looked like a school team, a school team that didn't believe in fighting," the owner said, as quoted by the *Star*. "Our boys act like one big happy family—and they played that way. Why, that [49-yard Rams touchdown] run of Tank Younger's was the worst I've ever seen. I could have run out on the field and stopped him myself. Our linemen stepped aside and let him go."

Washington was then blown out by San Francisco, 45–14, before beating the Lions, the Giants and the New York Yanks to close preseason play. A future Hall of Fame inductee, quarterback Bobby Layne, made sure Detroit gained revenge in the season opener. He completed 20 of 26 passes for 310 yards in a 35–17 win.

Ball tinkered with his lineup to little avail. The Giants crushed Washington, 35–14, in the home opener at Griffith Stadium. Next came a 45–0 spanking by the Browns that left the Redskins in last place in the American Conference and prompted the following assessment from *Evening Star* sportswriter Lewis F. Atchinson: "The once-proud Redskins have fallen to the low estate of whipping boys for the rest of the league. From end to end and back by back, they were woefully overmatched in personnel yesterday, and there is little hope for relief."

Meanwhile, a seething Marshall was about to dump Ball. "I don't intend to take this lying down," he said in the *Washington Daily News*. Names that surfaced as possible replacements included Redskins backfield and former Texas A&M coach Dick Todd; Ray Flaherty, who had coached the Redskins to championships in 1937 and 1942; and Heartley "Hunk" Anderson, who had co-coached the Bears with Luke Johnsos to a 24–12–2 mark, including an NFL championship, in the 1940s.

Media reports said Anderson was Marshall's first choice for the job, but Bears owner-coach George Halas blocked the deal by refusing to release him unless the Bears got Redskins standout tackle Paul Lipscomb in exchange. Marshall refused and named Todd as interim coach.

Todd's era began with a 7–3 win over the Cardinals. Baugh threw only seven passes, one a 46-yard scoring strike to back George Thomas. Washington then upset Philly, 27–23. Baugh completed 8 of 17 passes for 203 yards and a 53-yard scoring pass to Thomas, Dudley scored 15 points and Goode rushed for 123 yards and a touchdown en route to setting a Redskins single-season record of 951 yards on the ground. (Goode posted seven 100-yard rushing games that season, a Redskins record that stood for more than 50 years.)

The victories buoyed Todd's coaching status, although consecutive losses to the Bears and Giants virtually eliminated 2–5 Washington from playoff contention. But the Redskins didn't shelve their cleats for the season. Dudley's three second-half field goals helped lift them to a 22–7 win over Pittsburgh, and Dave Slattery of the *Washington Daily News* praised Todd: "In five weeks, Todd has transformed the Redskins from a listless doormat outfit into a hustling team that has won three of its last five games, and today is an even bet to end the season with its best won and lost record since 1948."

Slattery was on the mark. The Redskins' .500 finish over the final four games, which included a 31–21 upset of the eventual NFL-champion Los Angeles Rams, gave them five wins for the season, their most since 1948. Against the Rams, Washington posted 352 rushing yards and a team-record 64 carries that stands.

It was a refreshing way to end a year that once seemed headed for disaster, and it served as a building block for the 1952 campaign.

## No Pay for Exhibition Play

George Preston Marshall was known for being frugal when it came to paying his players. Sammy Baugh and center Al DeMao found out the hard way. When the pair asked Marshall during the 1951 exhibition season if the entire team could be paid for preseason games, Marshall responded in a belligerent tone. DeMao recalled the exchange:

We said, "The Bears are getting paid for it, other teams are getting it, why can't we get it?" Marshall said, "I don't know if the Bears are getting it, I don't know if anybody else is getting it, but I know you're not getting it!" Then he told us to get everyone together before practice because he wanted to talk to us. He said, "You're not going to get paid for exhibition games, so if anyone doesn't like that, feel free to leave right now." He pointed to the gate at the practice field, so that was the end of that.

## 1952: 4–8–0, 6TH PLACE— AMERICAN CONFERENCE

### Head Coach: Curly Lambeau

Redskins owner George Preston Marshall was so impressed with Dick Todd's 5–4 record in 1951 that he promoted him to head coach in the off-season. Todd was gone in almost the blink of an eye.

In a West Coast exhibition swing, the Redskins fell to San Francisco (35–0) and Los Angeles (45–23). Todd announced his immediate resignation after the Rams game, claiming that pressure from his business in Crowell, Texas, had forced him to step down, according to the *Washington Post*. The paper also reported that Todd and Marshall had exchanged words after the loss to the 49ers. "I told the players when I took over last year that either I would run the team my way or I wouldn't coach," the *Post* quoted Todd as saying. "I told the coaches the same thing this year. It was a choice between being a man or a mouse."

Marshall named several top candidates to replace Todd, including former Bears coach Heartley "Hunk" Anderson, the owner's top choice to replace Herman Ball in 1951, and Green Bay Packers coaching legend Earl "Curly" Lambeau. He ruled out the possibility that Sammy Baugh would become the Redskins' head coach, saying the Texas slinger would return for his 16th season as a player-coach. "It'll be a pro, that's certain," Marshall said, as quoted by the *Washington Evening Star*. "I'm tired of fooling around with these amateurs. I'm interested in getting a winner—and I don't care whose feet I step on to get it. I'm going to be cold-blooded about it."

Marshall hired one of the most celebrated coaches in NFL history in Lambeau, the fifth Redskins coach since the 1948 season. After founding the Packers in 1919, two years before they joined the NFL, Lambeau coached them to six championships before resigning after the 1949 season. He coached the Cardinals in 1950 and 1951 but quit with two games left in the latter season.

It was a surprising choice in a way, for one temperamental man, Lambeau, would be answering to a fiery, meddlesome owner. Controversy seemed inevitable. But Lambeau said he anticipated no problems even if Marshall interfered with the team's direction. "George's interference is constructive," Lambeau said in the *Star* on August 23, 1952. "For an owner to be interested in his team is a marvelous thing. From my experiences with George, I know I can talk to him and convince him of certain things. George will argue with you, but he'll go along with a coach who can convince him that his way is the right way."

Lambeau was optimistic that his troops would win at least seven games, a mark that appeared attainable on paper. Talented quarterback Eddie LeBaron, having missed the past two seasons, was back from his Marine Corps duties in the Korean War, and the Redskins traded for veterans who seemed capable of making immediate impacts, including running back Julie Rykovich, who had rushed for more than 1,100 yards over three seasons with the Bears. The Redskins also drafted players with strong potential, one being Northwestern defensive back Dick Alban.

After enduring three more exhibition-game beatings, Washington pulled an about-face in the season opener, defeating the heavily favored Cardinals, 23–7, under the lights in Chicago.

## Sammy Gets the Boot

In his first 15 seasons, Sammy Baugh was never ejected from a game. Then, in his 16th and final year, it happened.

In the Redskins' win over the Cardinals on September 28, 1952, the wiry Baugh got into a fight with 6-3, 250-pound Cardinals tackle Don Joyce. Joyce appeared to provoke the encounter when he barreled into Baugh as the quarterback released a pass and drove him into the ground. It looked like Baugh retaliated by swinging viciously at Joyce, but Sammy said he just grabbed his much beefier opponent. "I was afraid to let him go," the *Washington Evening Star* quoted Baugh as saying. "No tellin' what he would have done if I'd turned him loose."

Joyce was also tossed from the game.

Rookie quarterback Eddie LeBaron gets a tip from 16-year veteran Sammy Baugh in 1952. LeBaron was groomed that season to take over Baugh, who retired at the end of the year.

The 38-year-old Baugh was as sharp as ever, completing 11 straight passes in one sequence, with touchdown throws to Harry Dowda and Bones Taylor.

Virtually everything went south, as the Redskins lost eight of nine games. By the time they fell to 2–8 with a 48–24 pummeling at the hands of Cleveland, Lambeau was ripping into his squad, according to press reports. After one loss, he complained of what he called a "second-division" spirit, accusing certain players of refusing to work hard in practice and others of avoiding contact on the field. After another defeat, he carried on that many of his players' minds were unfocused leading up to the game, accusing them of thinking too much about parties.

At the same time, some players were disappointed in Lambeau. "He might have been a good coach when he was in Green Bay, but he suddenly forgot a lot of it," said Al DeMao, a Redskins center from 1945 to '53. "He wasn't much of a coach when he got here."

Marshall was nevertheless standing by him. "Curly will be back next year even if he doesn't win another game," the owner said, as quoted by the *Star* on November 4, 1952. "He's on his way with this team, but he'll need another year to finish the job—and we're going to finish it. The Redskins will be back on top in another year."

The Redskins won their last two games. LeBaron, who handled the quarterbacking duties most of the season, Baugh's last one, sparked the Redskins to a 27–17 win over the Giants with a breathtaking aerial performance. He completed 13 of 20 passes for 260 yards and four touchdowns, three of 65, 60 and 26 yards to Taylor. A *Washington Daily News* headline read, "LeBaron Arm Flays Giant Hopes."

The Redskins carried their momentum into a season-ending 27–21 upset of Philadelphia. The victory was sweet, for it ruined the Eagles' hopes of winning the American Conference. LeBaron completed only 8 of 24 passes but connected when it counted with touchdowns to Taylor and end Gene Brito. Taylor's catch, which marked a Redskins single-season record for touchdown receptions (12), tied the game at 21 with less than five minutes left. The Eagles needed a win to finish first in the conference but were stopped on downs. Soon after, LeBaron sneaked in from the 1 for the winning score. "I can remember one of the Eagles' players saying, 'Oh please don't score on us, you'll give [the conference title] to the Browns,'" LeBaron said.

Despite finishing 4–8, the Redskins earned accolades by showing resilience toward season's end. The day after the win over Philly, *Daily News* sportswriter Dave Slattery wrote, "In defeat, the Redskins this year had more color, more fight and more class than any Washington team since 1942."

## 1953: 6–5–1, 3RD PLACE— EASTERN CONFERENCE

### Head Coach: Curly Lambeau

The Redskins' surge toward the end of the 1952 season left many in the team's inner circle excited about the 1953 campaign—Curly Lambeau, for one.

The man entering his 35th season of pro coaching thought the Redskins would be stronger than the previous year. He made it known he wasn't aiming for a .500 finish but something closer to an NFL championship. "There are any number of reasons why I'm confident my team will be tougher," he told the *Los Angeles Times* just before the Redskins began training camp at Occidental College in Los Angeles. "One of them is the fact that [quarterback] Eddie LeBaron has a year's pro experience under his belt, and with Sammy Baugh gone, LeBaron is now the boss of the whole show. This kid just can't miss being a great quarterback."

The dashing and resourceful LeBaron wasn't the only talented quarterback at Lambeau's disposal. The Redskins used their No. 1 draft pick to select Maryland All-American Jack Scarbath, a runner-up for the 1952 Heisman Trophy. It was a Maryland All-American again in the second round, as the Redskins picked bruising 250-pound tackle Dick Modzelewski. Redskins owner George Preston Marshall reportedly sang the state song, "Maryland, My Maryland," to accompany "Hail to the Redskins."

The Redskins also drafted Michigan State All-American end Paul Dekker and 275-pound Nebraska tackle Don Boll and obtained rookie Oregon State back Sam Baker, who turned into an excellent kicker. They joined a solid cast of veterans that included Lauri Niemi and Paul Lipscomb, two of the league's best tackles and both Pro Bowlers in 1952; Bones Taylor, one of the game's premier receivers; backs Johnny Williams, a 1952 Pro Bowler, and Charlie Justice; center Harry Ulinski, who had spent the previous season in Canada; fullback Chuck Drazenovich; and ends Gene Brito and Joe Tereshinski.

As in recent seasons, though, frustration set in early; the Redskins posted a 1–5 record in exhibition games. If anything positive emerged from the preseason, it was the play of Scarbath, who took over as the signal caller after LeBaron injured his leg in a loss to the 49ers. Despite fracturing a finger on his throwing hand, Scarbath starred in a win over Green Bay and was impressive at other times.

Washington's two signal callers divided the action in the season opener, when the Redskins surprised the Cardinals, 24–13. Scarbath threw a 52-yard scoring pass to Justice in the first quarter, and touchdown runs by Drazenovich and Leon "Mule Train" Heath in the fourth period helped erase a 13–7 lead.

But it was a stingy defense—something Lambeau had built in training camp in order to prevent losses by embarrassing scores—that deserved the most credit for the win. The defense set up the three Redskin touchdowns and a field goal by forcing mistakes that gave them the ball 1, 20, 41, and 52 yards from Chicago's goal line.

The Redskins were again underdogs but battled to a 21–21 tie with Philly. Niemi recovered a fumble in the end zone, and Scarbath threw 24- and 61-yard touchdown passes to Taylor, the latter giving the Redskins a 21–14 lead in the fourth period. The Eagles drove 91 yards in 15 plays to even the score but missed a potential game-winning 27-yard field goal with less than a minute left.

A 13–9 win over the Giants ensured the 2–0–1 Redskins of their best start since 1946 and put them a half-game behind Cleveland for first place in the newly renamed Eastern Conference. An excited Lambeau credited his team's spirit for the victory. "They never quit trying," he told reporters. "Every man was up for this one. In beating the Giants, we beat a good

club. The Giants also were fired up and were better today than they were in their first two games. But we also played our best game of the year."

It appeared the Redskins might stay unbeaten, for they held a 14–13 lead over the mighty Browns in the fourth quarter. But Cleveland battled back, first with quarterback Otto Graham's 25-yard touchdown pass to his star receiver, Dante Lavelli, followed a few minutes later by the clinching touchdown.

From there, the injury-riddled Redskins lost by 10 points to the Colts and by 21 to Cleveland, which virtually clinched the conference title with its sixth straight win. Washington split its next two games and then won three in a row over the Giants, Steelers, and Eagles entering the season finale against Pittsburgh.

For the 6–4–1 Redskins, a win would mean a second-place finish in the conference, plus a nice Christmas gift for the 22,057 fans at Griffith Stadium. It wasn't to be. With Washington ahead 13–0 in the fourth quarter, the Steelers scored a touchdown and came close to another one before the Redskins crafted a goal-line stand and took possession on the 1-foot line with about eight minutes left. LeBaron, who had a miserable day with four interceptions, gambled to get the Redskins out of the jam, lobbing a short throw to Justice. But Pittsburgh's Jack Butler intercepted the pass and waltzed in for the tying score. The conversion gave the Steelers a 14–13 victory.

Marshall was upset in the postgame locker room, although his 6–5–1 Redskins had their first winning season since 1948. He said he was sorry his squad hadn't finished in a second-place tie with 7–4–1 Philadelphia, which closed with a 42–27 upset of the Browns. "Somebody was due to beat Cleveland," Marshall told reporters. "They'd had a lot of close squeaks this year. But we should certainly have beaten Pittsburgh."

## 1954: 3–9–0, 5TH PLACE— EASTERN CONFERENCE

### Head Coach: Joe Kuharich

From a head coaching change, to players bolting for Canada, to the death of a popular teammate, to a soft defense that essentially gave opposing offenses carte blanche—1954 evolved into one of those seasons of gloom for the Redskins. Their 3–9 mark matched the franchise's worst-ever won-lost record from 1950.

Frustrations began boiling in the off-season, when some Redskins stars bolted to the Canadian Football League, which was raiding NFL rosters with offers of higher salaries. Washington's biggest departures were quarterback Eddie LeBaron and Pro Bowl defensive end Gene Brito (formerly an offensive end), who both disliked Redskins coach Curly Lambeau. They signed with the Calgary Stampeders, reuniting with former Redskins offensive line coach and then-Calgary head coach Larry Siemering. LeBaron, who would likely have been Washington's starting quarterback in 1954, also played under Siemering at the University of the Pacific.

Redskins owner George Preston Marshall was furious with the CFL for infiltrating NFL territory, offering his classic hyperbole: "The British empire has dragged us into three wars, and it wouldn't surprise me if they got us into a fourth." Press reports said Marshall even threatened to sue tackle Lauri

Joe Kuharich took over as the Redskins' head coach in 1954. He posted a 26–32–2 mark, with one winning season, in five seasons in D.C.

Niemi, who left to play for the British Columbia Lions, over breach of contract. "A contract is a contract," the owner was known to say.

The Redskins started inauspiciously in exhibition play, getting pounded by the Rams and 49ers. After the loss to the 49ers, Marshall and Redskins coach Curly Lambeau engaged in a heated argument that included pushing by both of them in the lobby of a hotel in Sacramento, California, according to media reports.

The ruckus stemmed from Marshall's sighting of a few Redskins carrying packs of beer in the hotel, a practice he disallowed. The owner confronted the players (one of whom reportedly was end Bones Taylor) and later berated Lambeau, who saw no problem with players consuming a small quantity of beer after games. Marshall then made a familiar move: he fired Lambeau, who had compiled a 10–13–1 record over two seasons in Washington. "There was nothing I could do but let Lambeau go," Marshall said in the *Washington Post* on September 8, 1954. "It was impossible to keep him after a public demonstration like that. No president of a club can stand that sort of nonsense from a coach."

Marshall promoted Redskins offensive line coach Joe Kuharich to the team's head coaching role. Kuharich, a star guard at Notre Dame in the 1930s who later played three seasons for the Chicago Cardinals, had a successful four-year coaching stop at the University of San Francisco, where he directed what is regarded as one of the finest teams in college football history, the 9–0 Dons in 1951. He replaced Lambeau

for the first time as the Cardinals' head coach for the 1952 season, finishing 4–8, before coming to the Redskins.

The 37-year-old Kuharich, known as a strict disciplinarian, wasted no time applying his stamp. He implemented a much tougher training program and began to carve up the roster, cutting veterans who he felt were too complacent and acquiring young, hustling players. Half of the 33-man roster consisted of rookies by the start of the regular season, and only 12 players remained from the 1953 squad. The newcomers included offensive backs Billy Wells, Dale Atkeson, and Joe "Scooter" Scudero, a star on the 1951 San Francisco Dons; quarterback Al Dorow; and receiver Johnny Carson.

Defensive back Vic Janowicz, a Heisman Trophy winner drafted by the Redskins in 1952, signed after playing two years of pro baseball. Talented running back Rob Goode rejoined the team after spending two years in the Marines.

After an 0–6 exhibition season, the Redskins were thumped by the 49ers, 40–7, in the season opener. Washington's lone touchdown came on a 13-yard reception by Scudero from quarterback Jack Scarbath, who started the game after passing for 862 yards and nine touchdowns as a rookie in 1953. Scarbath and Dorow alternated as the season progressed.

The loss was a harbinger of things to come. The Redskins were routed by Pittsburgh (37–7), the New York Giants (51–21), Philadelphia (49–21), and the Giants (24–7). The defense was allowing touchdowns in astronomical numbers, and the offense was also pathetic. The Redskins gained 115 yards against the Eagles, then the team's lowest total ever.

Kuharich insisted he expected better things from his 0–5 squad, although not right away. "Either you take your lumps, or you cut your throat," he told the *Washington Evening Star*. "We're taking our lumps now. It's nothing new for me. I took over a high school team that hadn't won a game in two years, and that was tough. My first year at the University of San Francisco was just as bad as this, and yet, in both instances, we came out all right."

The Colts, who destroyed Washington in the preseason, then came to Griffith Stadium. The Redskins received stellar performances from two Michigan State boys, Dorow and Wells, in their 24–21 victory. Dorow completed 8 of 13 passes for 139 yards and a touchdown on a 48-yard pass to Wells, who totaled 95 yards receiving and 73 rushing. Atkeson bulled over for two scores.

Cleveland interrupted the Redskins' party, 62–3. The machine-like Browns, playing most of the game without star quarterback Otto Graham, amassed 515 yards against a defense that allowed the second-most points in Redskins history, a mark that still stands, as well as 33 first downs (15 rushing, 16 passing, two penalty). Washington's pitiful offense gained 64 yards (33 rushing, 31 passing), committed five turnovers, and averted a shutout only because of Janowicz's 37-yard field goal. "Redskins Grateful for Field Goal by Janowicz," read a *Washington Post* headline.

Questions began to surface about whether Marshall might fire his second coach in the same season. The owner remained supportive of Kuharich, however, even telling the press that his rookie-laden squad would be champions in two years.

The situation worsened. After beating the Steelers, 17–14, the Redskins lost to the Cardinals, Eagles, and Browns, to fall to 2–9. To compound their problems, 26-year-old tackle David Sparks suffered a heart attack a few hours after the second loss to Cleveland and dropped dead. The Redskins organization was stunned and dedicated the season finale to Sparks. But winning, even against the 2–9 Cardinals, would be a struggle: the crippled Redskins had only 25 players in uniform, and almost everyone was listed at two positions.

Nonetheless, Washington gave the Cardinals the dubious distinction as the NFL's worst team with a 37–20 win before a measly 18,107 fans at Griffith. Dorow posted an All-Pro performance by throwing four touchdown passes, three to Bones Taylor in the last game of the end's fabulous eight-year career in Washington.

In the process, Dorow showed much promise for 1955, as did Wells, who gained 516 yards rushing, 295 receiving, and 319 on kick returns. He was joined in the Pro Bowl by Rob Goode, who rushed for 462 yards; defensive back Dick Alban, who intercepted nine passes; and Taylor.

The overall returns on the season were horrible. The defense allowed 432 points and 57 touchdowns, team records that stand today despite the brevity of the 12-game season. The offense threw 32 interceptions, a team record at the time.

The embarrassment would end—albeit temporarily—in 1955.

## 1955: 8-4-0, 2ND PLACE— EASTERN CONFERENCE

### Head Coach: Joe Kuharich

Shortly after becoming the Redskins' coach in August 1954, Joe Kuharich stressed patience during the rebuilding process, saying it would probably take three seasons to mold the squad into a winner. He hit his mark earlier than expected.

Washington finished 8–4 in 1955, its best record since an 8–2 season in 1945, and placed second in the Eastern Conference. A key to the success was a defense that allowed 222 points and 25 touchdowns, compared with 432 points and 53 touchdowns in 1954.

Kuharich made smart personnel moves to fortify the defense. He helped talk standout end Gene Brito into returning from his one-year hiatus in the Canadian Football League and lured one of Brito's teammates, defensive back Norb Hecker. He also shipped middle guard Jim Ricca and defensive end Walt Yowarsky to Detroit for Pro Bowl linebacker LaVern "Torgy" Torgeson and traded for 49ers tackle J. D. Kimmel and Cardinals end Ralph Thomas. Around mid-season, the coach claimed hard-hitting defensive back Roy Barni, who had played for Kuharich at the University of San Francisco and with the Chicago Cardinals, off waivers.

Those players helped shape a formidable defense with existing Redskins such as tackle Volney Peters, linebackers Chuck Drazenovich and Nick Adduci, backs Scooter Scudero and Dick Alban, and end Chet Ostrowski.

Washington's offense was led by quarterback Eddie LeBaron, who also returned after one year in the CFL, and running back Vic Janowicz, the team's top rusher in 1955 with 397 yards. Washington benefited, too, from the addition of halfbacks Leo Elter and Bert Zagers, both of whom were acquired through trades, and rookie guard Lou "Red" Stephens, who proved to be an outstanding lineman.

Improvement was first evident in a 7–6 loss to San Francisco in the exhibition opener. The rejuvenated defense manhandled the 49ers' feared ground and air attacks, once stopping them on a goal-line stand.

"That's the best Redskin team I've ever seen so early in the season," 49ers' coach Red Strader told reporters afterward. "Their defense was terrific, and their coverage on passers was very sharp. Gene Brito, LaVern Torgeson, and J. D. Kimmel are going to make a big difference this year."

The Redskins then upset Los Angeles, 31–28, behind LeBaron's four touchdown passes, before going 0–2–1 to close out the exhibition season. In the season opener, Washington pulled off one of the biggest upsets in team history. The Redskins shocked Cleveland on the road, 27–17, after losing the first nine games in their all-time series against the Browns. LeBaron was outstanding, throwing 24- and 17-yard scoring passes to end John Carson and scampering 13 yards for the clinching touchdown. He also threw a 70-yard pass to Elter.

Two CFL transplants also produced big plays. Hecker intercepted two passes by quarterback Otto Graham, and Brito stole the ball from the Browns' other quarterback, George Ratterman, to set up a touchdown.

The Redskins then nipped Philadelphia, 31–30, after erasing a 16–0 deficit in one of the most bizarre sequences in NFL history. It began when Brito recovered a fumble on the Eagles' 32, and LeBaron threw a touchdown pass to Janowicz on the next play. Hecker's kickoff appeared headed out of bounds and, while the Eagles watched to see which way it would go, Thomas pounced on it at the 2 and slid into the end zone. Philadelphia fumbled the next kickoff, Torgeson recovered, and Janowicz ran for a score.

The 2–0 Redskins suddenly held first place in the Eastern Conference and were the surprise of the NFL. They dropped three of the next four, however, to nearly fall out of the title race with a 3–3 record.

But the Redskins did another about-face, winning four straight starting with a 34–21 victory over the Eagles. It was the first time since 1942 that the Redskins had beaten Philadelphia, preseason favorites to win the conference title, twice in one season. The Eagles fumbled six times, and the Redskins recovered each one.

Washington then took sole possession of second place in the conference with a 7–0 win over the 49ers. Several Redskins made key defensive plays, including Brito, who barreled into quarterback Y. A. Tittle late in the third quarter, knocked the ball loose, and recovered on the 49ers' 33. Three plays later, Zagers ran 13 yards to account for the game's only touchdown. The Redskins followed with their second straight shutout, 31–0 over the Cardinals. Janowicz produced 13 points on a touchdown, a field goal, and four conversions, and an unyielding defense held Chicago to 72 rushing yards.

In Washington's fourth straight win, 23–14 over the Steelers, Elter ran 33 and 20 yards for touchdowns, and Scudero returned a punt 49 yards for a score. Due to the Browns' 35–35 tie with the Giants, the Redskins trailed Cleveland by a half-game for first place in the conference.

The Giants subsequently ruined the Redskins' conference title hopes with a 27–20 win at Griffith Stadium, New York's fifth win in its last six games. The Redskins led, 20–17, at halftime, but a Giants' field goal and a touchdown pass by one-time Redskins castoff Charlie Conerly to Kyle Rote put New York up by seven. Later, with 1:03 to play, LeBaron threw a pass that was picked off in the end zone, sealing the Redskins' fate. Meanwhile, the Browns clinched the conference title by beating Pittsburgh en route to capturing the NFL championship.

The Redskins finished in second place in the conference with a 28–17 season-ending win over the Steelers. A then-record seven Redskins made the Pro Bowl—Brito, Drazenovich, LeBaron, Peters, Scudero (who gained 1,000 yards returning punts, kickoffs, and interceptions), Torgeson, and center Harry Ulinski. Kuharich was the consensus choice as NFL Coach of the Year, and Redskins owner George Preston Marshall signed him to a three-year contract.

Redskins great Sammy Baugh, then the head coach at Hardin-Simmons University in Texas, chimed in with some optimistic thoughts. "Merry Christmas to all," he said in the *Washington Post* on December 12, 1955. "I think the Redskins have one of the finest teams I've ever seen. I think you'll have a championship team here in two years."

## 1956: 6-6-0, 3RD PLACE— EASTERN CONFERENCE

### Head Coach: Joe Kuharich

The Redskins returned to familiar territory in 1956: mediocrity. They finished 6–6 after suffering a late-season collapse. Off the field, a tragic accident deprived them of vital offensive production.

Coach Joe Kuharich had hoped to build on the surprising success of his 8–4 squad from 1955. In the off-season, he traded star defensive back Dick Alban to Detroit for guard and two-time consensus first-team All-Pro Dick Stanfel, perhaps the best blocking guard in football. Stanfel had also starred when coached by Kuharich at the University of San Francisco.

Kuharich made draft picks, too, that paid off handsomely. The Redskins used their No. 2 choice to take Pittsburgh defensive end John Paluck, who went on to play eight solid seasons in Washington. With the No. 8 pick, the Redskins selected Oregon halfback Dickie James, an exciting player on offense and defense in his 10 seasons, eight with the Redskins. Plus, kicker-halfback Sam Baker, halfback Billy Wells, and receiver Steve Meilinger were all back after stints in the U.S. military.

A couple of off-the-field incidents, however, put a dagger in Kuharich's plans. The first happened shortly after Washington upset the Rams, 39–21, in the exhibition opener. Star halfback Vic Janowicz, the NFL's second-leading scorer in 1955 with 88 points (seven touchdowns, six field goals, 28 extra points), was in a car that spun out of control and hit a telephone pole. He suffered serious injuries, including brain damage, and never played another down in the NFL. Hours later, quarterback Al Dorow was in a car accident. His two broken ribs, plus kidney and back injuries, put him out of action for about a month.

Dorow's absence contributed to a dearth at quarterback. Eddie LeBaron injured his left knee in a training camp scrimmage and was on the sidelines. Ralph Guglielmi, the Notre Dame All-American who played sparingly as a rookie in 1955, entered the U.S. Air Force and would be gone for two years. The Redskins traded Jack Scarbath, who played the 1955

season in Canada, to Pittsburgh. Scarbath was Washington's leading passer in 1953.

Kuharich reacted by rotating two rookies in the first three exhibition games: West Virginia's Freddy Wyant, the team's No. 3 draft pick, and Don Bailey, who played in Canada in 1955 after being drafted by Washington. The Redskins went 1–2 during that span before LeBaron returned after a seven-week layoff. He and Wyant split time in the last two exhibition games, a loss to Baltimore and a win over Detroit.

A gimpy LeBaron started in the season opener at Pittsburgh, but the Redskins turned the ball over four times in a 30–13 loss. Then came a 13–9 loss to the Eagles, who won on quarterback Bobby Thomason's 1-yard run with less than four minutes left, and a 31–3 demolition at the hands of the Cardinals.

The 0–3 Redskins were the only winless team in the league, although Kuharich insisted that they were better than their record showed. The next week they beat Cleveland for the first time ever at Griffith Stadium, 20–9. Fullback Leo Elter rushed for 91 yards and one touchdown, James caught a 9-yard scoring pass from LeBaron, and Baker kicked two field goals, improving his season mark to 6 for 6. The Redskins' defense held the Browns to three field goals and no points in the second half.

LeBaron reinjured his knee in the game and didn't practice for a meeting against the 4–0 Cardinals. But Dorow, healed from his injuries, subbed masterfully in the Redskins' 17–14 upset. With his squad trailing by two touchdowns in the first period, Dorow threw a 34-yard touchdown pass to James and a 40-yarder to Meilinger. Baker's two conversions and his 23-yard field goal accounted for the remaining points.

Dorow started the next two games, two more shocking victories for Washington. Against 6–0 Detroit, the Redskins posted an 18–17 squeaker behind James's 41-yard touchdown run, Baker's three field goals and a safety on an intentional exit from the end zone by Detroit's punter. Then came a 33–7 romp over the Giants, winners of five straight. Dorow threw two scoring passes, a 7-yarder to John Carson and a 51-yarder to Meilinger, and Baker kicked two field goals, including a record 49-yarder at Griffith Stadium.

After four straight wins—three over teams that had been peaking—the 4–3 Redskins were pro football's hottest team.

"The Phoenix of legend that rose from its own ashes has been matched now by the Washington Redskins," *Washington Post* columnist Shirley Povich wrote on November 20, 1956. "They are positively resplendent as title contenders in the National Football League after burrowing from the wreckage of those three consecutive defeats at the start of the season."

Washington made it five in a row with a 20–17 victory over Cleveland, the first time the Redskins had beaten the Browns twice in one season. LeBaron, back from his injury, threw a 26-yard scoring pass to Carson with 91 seconds left to account for the win, which kept the 5–3 Redskins in the thick of the Eastern Conference championship race.

But they dropped three of their last four games. Halfback Frank Gifford scored three touchdowns to lift the conference-leading Giants to a 28–14 win, before the Redskins rebounded by beating Philly, 19–17, on Baker's 21-yard field goal with 25 seconds left, leaving them clinging to conference title hopes. But the Giants beat the Eagles to clinch the championship a day before Pittsburgh skunked the deflated Redskins, 23–0.

## Team of the South

Washington Redskins owner George Preston Marshall long regarded the southern United States as his team's natural territory. After all, from the year the Redskins moved to Washington in 1937 until 1960, when the Dallas Cowboys were formed, the Redskins were the southernmost team in the NFL. (The Dallas Texans played one season in 1952 before disbanding.)

Marshall, a shrewd promoter, seized the opportunity to attract southern fans, feeding them a steady diet of burgundy and gold in the 1940s, 1950s, and 1960s. Not long after the Redskins came to D.C., he launched a vast Redskins radio network that stretched from New England as far south as Florida. He later added television. He also arranged for the Redskins to play exhibition games in such cities as Mobile, Alabama; Norfolk, Virginia; Memphis, Tennessee; Shreveport, Louisiana; Winston-Salem, North Carolina; and Amarillo, Texas. The Redskins played an annual charity exhibition game, the Piedmont Bowl, in Winston-Salem.

Furthermore, Marshall required his players to make public appearances and sign autographs in the South. He even incorporated a few strains of "Dixie" into the team's fight song, "Hail to the Redskins."

The Redskins thus built a loyal following in the region and became known as the "Team of the South." Redskins booster clubs popped up in southern cit-ies, and caravans of Redskins fans from the Carolinas, Georgia, Virginia, and elsewhere traveled to see their team in the nation's capital and even journeyed to road games. Sportswriters from southern newspapers, including many in North Carolina, covered the Redskins like a home team. A reporter was once startled to find a small Redskins contingent from Winston-Salem in Chicago for a game against the Cardinals.

"We spent a lot of time in North Carolina, and there were a lot of Redskins fans down that way," said wide receiver Charley Taylor, who played for the Redskins from 1964 to '77. "In cities in North Carolina like Raleigh and Durham, they loved the Redskins, they grew up with the Redskins, they learned football through the Redskins. That's what was presented to them—the Washington Redskins."

Eddie LeBaron, a Redskins quarterback for much of the 1950s, also felt the Redskins fever in the South. "I used to speak at luncheons and quarterback clubs all over the South, and we were the 'Team of the South,'" he said. "The Redskins were in Atlanta and the Carolinas and southern Virginia. That whole area was just a hotbed of Redskins fans. They would come to Griffith Stadium by train. It would be South Carolina day and Virginia day and North Carolina day and Georgia day. It was a big thing."

Marshall's most powerful promotional tool was his radio and TV network. He contracted with the

---

A season-ending loss to Baltimore left the 6–6 Redskins in third place in the conference.

The Redskins nearly finished 7–5. They led the Colts, 17–12, with 15 seconds left, when a pass by quarterback Johnny Unitas bounced off defender Norb Hecker in the end zone and into the waiting arms of Baltimore's Jim Mutscheller. Redskins owner George Preston Marshall later scolded Hecker, who had been tied up the previous week in talks over the newly formed National Football League Players' Association. "It's strange that it should happen to Hecker," Marshall said in the *Washington Post*. "But when a player gets involved in other things, it's hard for him to keep his mind on football."

The dreary ending aside, seven Redskins made the Pro Bowl for the second straight year: "Sugarfoot" Sam Baker, one of the league's best kickers with 67 points; Elter, the NFL's 10th leading rusher with 544 yards; Dorow, who completed 55 of 112 passes for 730 yards and eight touchdowns; linebackers Chuck Drazenovich and Torgy Torgeson; Brito; and Stanfel.

## 1957: 5–6–1, 4TH PLACE— EASTERN CONFERENCE

### Head Coach: Joe Kuharich

Call it the year of the back. Mostly everything newsworthy about the Redskins in 1957 revolved around the offensive and defensive backfields.

Washington's coaches went backfield shopping in the off-season, drafting Miami fullback Don Bosseler and halfbacks Jim "Poodles" Podoley from Central Michigan and Ed Sutton from North Carolina. The trio was projected to add depth to an already solid backfield that featured quarterback Eddie LeBaron, halfbacks Dickie James and Scooter Scudero, and fullbacks Dale Atkeson and Leo Elter.

On the defensive side, hard-hitting back Roy Barni was shot to death in July 1957 by a truck driver whom Barni was trying to eject from his bar in San Francisco. This marked the third time in the past four seasons that a Redskins player had

American Oil Co., otherwise known as AMOCO, and Marlboro Cigarettes to sponsor the network. It consisted of about 40 TV and 100 radio stations at its peak and included a handful of stations in Northeastern states such as New York, Massachusetts, and Connecticut. The owner's slogan was "The Redskins every Sunday . . . in your living room or at the stadium."

Former Redskins coach Steve Spurrier, who grew up in Johnson City, Tennessee, received a healthy dose of burgundy and gold on the tube. "The only pro team we watched was basically the Redskins, so we sort of pulled for them," he said. "They were the only team on television on Sunday in the late '50s, early '60s. We didn't go crazy, but that was our pro football team for the South."

Meanwhile, Marshall made sure southern fans—whether those in the stands or others tuning in—connected with their regional brethren. He recruited standout players from the region such as North Carolina's Charlie "Choo Choo" Justice, a Redskins running back in the early 1950s. He called for "Dixie" to be played in pregame ceremonies at Redskins home games. The owner also coordinated extravagant halftime entertainment shows that reflected southern culture. He once invited a female band from Mississippi Southern College called the "Dixie Darlings" to perform. "Naturally, they will play southern-style music," Marshall said in the *Washington Daily News* on June 19, 1958. "Also for the

South, we've got the George Wythe Band coming in from Whytheville, Va. They're a corking good outfit, too."

Marshall was a true-blooded southerner. He was born in 1896 on a farm in Grafton, West Virginia, that had once belonged to a Confederate general, "Tiger John" MacCausland. In 1957, Bob Serling of United Press wrote, "Colonel Marshall, a man who insists that the South would have won the [Civil] war with a better defensive backfield, has gone out of his way to encourage Dixie acceptance of his Yankee team."

The Redskins' southern following has dissipated in recent decades due to the emergence of a host of teams in the region. Even so, the Redskins are still broadcast on a large radio network through the South. What's more, newspapers such as the *Richmond Times*, the *Virginian Pilot*, and the *Newport News* in southeastern Virginia continue to assign a beat reporter to the Redskins, an ongoing part of the sports fabric in the region.

"Oh yea, definitely," said Jim Ricca, a Redskins lineman for three seasons in the 1950s. "Even today, when I go to Arlington, Texas, to visit my cousins, I see die-hard Redskins fans, even though the Dallas Cowboys are nearby. People from the old school in the South are still Redskins fans."

been tragically lost. Barni's absence left a gaping hole in the defense.

Meanwhile, Kuharich implemented a new offensive alignment during training camp, a T-formation run out of an unbalanced line. The system was designed to grind out yardage in explosive bursts and compensate for the lack of a proven breakaway runner. It resembled the alignment Kuharich had deployed during his college coaching days at San Francisco, and some of the Redskins were impressed. "It's the most vicious attack I've faced since entering the National League [in 1951]," linebacker Torgy Torgeson told the *Washington Daily News*. "I can't say it's going to be a big hit on my own, but I can say that I'm positive it will be a linebacker's nightmare."

Washington's opponents didn't seem too concerned, for the Redskins finished 1–5 in the preseason. Kuharich was nevertheless upbeat about the season. "I think we've got our share of what is one of the finest rookie crops to enter the National Football League," he said, as quoted by the *Daily News*. "I can't tell how many games we'll win or lose, but I will say that this should be the most interesting Redskin team I have

coached. It has more depth and more offensive punch than a year ago."

The Redskins showed no "offensive punch" in a 28–7 season-opening loss to the Steelers, who clobbered Washington for the third straight time. Pittsburgh suffocated the heart of the Redskins' offense, a running game that produced 89 yards on 26 carries.

Kuharich adjusted by inserting Bosseler, Sutton, and Podoley into the starting lineup. They sparked an offense that gained 427 yards (247 rushing, 180 passing) in a 37–14 rout of the Cardinals. At the same time, the three rookies became affectionately known as the "Papoose" or "Lollypop" backfield. They carried Washington's offense for the rest of the season.

"I never really knew of three rookies starting in the same backfield," Bosseler said years later. "But Podoley and Sutton were both great halfbacks. Jim was like a rabbit, very agile. He ran track and was one of the fastest guys. Eddie was more of a power guy but had good speed."

The offense posted another big day with 346 yards against the defending NFL champion Giants. LeBaron threw for 229

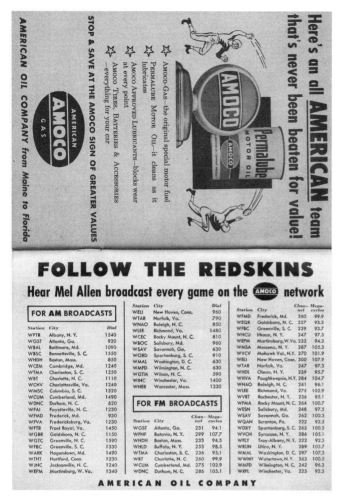
The Redskins broadcast network in 1952, sponsored by Amoco. That year, legendary sportscaster Mel Allen handled the play by play.

yards, 82 on a touchdown pass to Podoley. But New York countered with its own big plays, including a 66-yard scoring pass on a trick play from halfback Frank Gifford to end Bob Schnelker, to escape with a 24–20 victory.

Next, against the Cardinals, the Redskins gained more than 300 yards for the third straight game. Kuharich had only three words to explain what happened once the final gun sounded: "We got bombed." The Cardinals took a 21–0 lead and coasted to a 44–14 victory.

The unpredictable Redskins then fooled everyone, romping over the heavily favored Giants, 31–14. New York scored early with an 80-yard, 10-play touchdown drive. Washington responded with two quick scores on Sutton's 23-yard run and Bert Zagers's 76-yard punt return and dominated the rest of the game.

"This wasn't the same Redskins team that played indifferently against the Chicago Cardinals a week ago," Bus Ham wrote in the *Washington Post* on October 28, 1957. "Today, the men up in the front-line trenches, both on attack and defense, waded into the Giants and gave them a thumping that no champion likes to absorb."

Instead of capitalizing on the big win to jump into the Eastern Conference title race, the Redskins let their season

disintegrate fast with an 0–3–1 stretch that left them at 2–6–2. A leaky pass defense gave up big plays along the way.

One of the defeats during that stretch, 21–17 to the Western Conference-powerhouse Colts, was demoralizing. Washington was driving for the winning touchdown with time running out and reached the Colts' 20, but LeBaron fumbled the ball and the game away. In the postgame locker room, veterans Torgeson, Gene Brito, and Dick Stanfel were close to tears, according to the *Daily News*. Bosseler, who rushed for a touchdown and 81 yards, more than Baltimore's entire team, sat staring at his locker.

Washington finished its 5–6–1 season with a fight. The Redskins crushed the Bears, Eagles, and Steelers by a combined score of 66–13. In the season finale at Griffith Stadium, Pittsburgh gained 158 yards against a defense that received an outstanding performance from Brito, who earned his third straight Pro Bowl invitation. He was joined in the all-star game by Drazenovich, LeBaron, Stanfel, Podoley, and receiver John Carson.

Podoley was a centerpiece of one of the most amazing stories of the season in the NFL: the "Lollypop" backfield. He, Bosseler, and Podoley combined for more than 2,000 total yards. Bosseler led the team in rushing with 673, Podoley totaled 996 rushing and receiving and posted a league-high 20.5-yard reception average, and Sutton ran for 407. The "touchdown triplets" also combined for 20 touchdowns to give the Redskins one of their most consistent scoring punches in years.

"Those three kids have played every game and have carried 90 percent of our offense," Kuharich told the *Daily News* late in the season. "Except for a bump here and there, they haven't missed a minute's play."

## 1958: 4–7–1, 4TH PLACE— EASTERN CONFERENCE

### Head Coach: Joe Kuharich

Although Joe Kuharich had posted only a 22–25–1 record in four seasons coaching the Redskins, owner George Preston Marshall carried a genuine liking for the man. He even equated Kuharich with Ray Flaherty, who coached the Redskins during their early glory years.

Such admiration was surprising, for the Redskins' boss freely discarded coaches who failed to fulfill his strong passion for winning. He signed Kuharich to a five-year contract extension before the 1958 season.

The deal was short-lived. Kuharich wanted out after a frustrating 4–7–1 campaign, and Marshall obliged. Kuharch then accepted the head coaching position at Notre Dame, where he had been a standout guard in the 1930s, and Marshall promoted Redskins assistant Mike Nixon to the top job.

Another losing season was not what Kuharich envisioned when he signed the extension. He conducted his trademark wheeling and dealing on the player market, sending defensive tackle Volney Peters to the Eagles for offensive guard Menil Mavraides, receiver Steve Meilinger and defensive tackle J. D. Kimmel to Green Bay for defensive backs Doyle Nix and John Petitbon, and tackle Don Owens to the Eagles for tackle Jim Weatherall.

In perhaps his most intriguing acquisition, Kuharich traded a rookie lineman to the Cardinals for fullback Johnny Olszewski. The Redskins expected "Johnny O"—whom Kuharich had drafted with the No. 1 pick when he coached the Cardinals in 1953—to strengthen an already productive backfield and create an exciting one-two punch with fullback Don Bosseler.

On the quarterback front, Ralph Guglielmi, who shared playing time with Eddie LeBaron in 1955, rejoined the Redskins after a two-year stint in the U.S. Air Force. With LeBaron's deceptiveness and slick ball-handling style, plus Guglielmi's strong arm, Kuharich thought he had an ideal combination at quarterback.

LeBaron, Guglielmi, and third-stringer Rudy "The Rifle" Bukich split time in the preseason, when the Redskins finished 3–3 and looked like a squad with the potential to go far. Bears owner-coach George Halas liked what he saw in the Redskins after Chicago posted a 27–24 win in the last exhibition game. "This Redskins team is going to be right on the top of the heap," Halas said, as quoted by the *Washington Post*. "There's simply no question about it. They'll be in the race every week."

The most entertaining part of the preseason was a round of verbal punches between Marshall and perennial star quarterback Norm Van Brocklin, who was in his first season with the Eagles after nine great years in Los Angeles. Van Brocklin accused Marshall of cutting running back Leo Elter and linebacker Torgy Torgeson, who had three Pro Bowl appearances between them, just to save money. He also told the *Post* the best thing that could happen to the Redskins and the NFL would be for Marshall to "step in front of a cab."

Marshall fired back that Van Brocklin had a history of causing problems for coaches. The owner took the high road when it came to car collisions, though, saying he hoped only the Redskins would run over Van Brocklin.

Washington flattened the Eagles in the season opener, piling up 346 yards to 169 in a 24–14 victory. LeBaron completed 10 of 15 passes for 134 yards and a touchdown. Backs Dickie James and Scooter Scudero, who spent most of their time on defense, also made major contributions on offense after two teammates limped off with injuries. James made a sensational leap to deflect a Van Brocklin pass in the end zone at the end of the first half to preserve a 10–7 Redskins lead, and his 3-yard run served as the winning score.

The Redskins' defense was woebegone the next week, however, allowing 531 yards and 26 first downs in a 37–10 loss to the Cardinals. A headline in the *Washington Daily News* read, "The Redskins Resembled Cigar Store Indians." "Remember the old wooden Indians that used to stand guard outside cigar stores and watch the customers go by," Dave Slattery wrote in the *Daily News*. "That's exactly how the Redskins looked in Chicago when they flunked their first major test of the 1958 season miserably.

"They stood around Comiskey Park and watched and the Cardinals really went by—by air and by land. And it's a darn

---

## Redskins Alumni Band Together

In 1958, an organization was born to help "graduating" Redskins take their place in the community. Still alive today, it is called the Washington Redskins Alumni Association.

The group, believed to be the first of its kind in the NFL, was another in a series of innovations conceived by Redskins owner George Preston Marshall. He broached the idea in 1957 with three retired Redskins—Henry "Red" Krause, Jim Castiglia, and Al DeMao—who proceeded to round up other former teammates. They established an informal group, and the Redskins Alumni Association kicked off on October 15, 1958.

The original membership consisted of 23 ex-Redskins, including Castiglia, the president; DeMao, the vice president; secretary Andy Davis; treasurer Mike Micka; and Casimir "Slug" Witucki, chairman of the membership committee. The association outlined the following objectives in its constitution:

- To promote and conserve a continuing interest in the Washington Redskins football team and its players, past and present.
- To advance and serve the best interests of pro football in the Washington area.

- To create and maintain a spirit of good fellowship and harmony among members of the association.

Membership at first was limited to former Redskins. Retired players from other teams who live in the Washington area were later allowed to become honorary members.

"It was inevitable that some ivy should start clinging to the Redskins," *Washington Post* sports columnist Bob Addie wrote after the group was formed. "Like the New York Yankees of baseball, it's considered an honor to have been part of the Redskins. A group of Redskins alumni got together recently and decided to perpetuate that honor. We're a nation of 'joiners,' anyway, and what better group to join than one reliving the glorious deeds of the pro gridiron?"

The association served as a model for the NFL alumni movement, as more and more teams began forming their own alumni associations. The Redskins' association holds two annual fundraising events, including a golf tournament and a luncheon before the season starts to greet players on their return from training camp. The Redskins' outstanding offensive and defensive players from the prior season are honored at the luncheon.

Redskins coach George Allen speaks at the Welcome Home Luncheon on September 6, 1974. The Redskins Alumni Association hosts the annual event to welcome the team back from training camp.

good thing Lake Michigan was a mile off or they might have gone by sea, too."

Despite the whipping, more than 30,000 fans turned out for the Redskins' home opener against the Giants. LeBaron threw for 238 yards on 14 of 26 passing with one touchdown. But another signal caller, Charlie Conerly, again frustrated the team that traded him in 1948. He snapped a 14–14 fourth-quarter tie with a 10-yard scoring pass that gave the Giants the win.

In three games, a Redskins offense crippled with injuries had scored only 48 points. Guards Dick Stanfel and Red Stephens, perhaps the best blocking combo in the NFL in 1957, were fighting the effects of serious leg injuries. End Johnny Carson was also slowed by a leg ailment. The famed "Lollypop" backfield of Bosseler, Jim Podoley, and Ed Sutton, also banged up, had rushed for less than 200 yards. By the fourth game, Bosseler and running back Bert Zagers were injured and out of the lineup, and Sutton, Podoley, and newcomer Sid Watson were recovering from injuries.

Someone needed to step up. It was Olszewski, who rushed for 165 yards on 20 carries with one touchdown in a 34–0 shutout of Green Bay. Slattery of the *Washington Daily News* wrote the following of Olszewski: "Other backs through the years have gained a lot of yardage. But 'Johnny O' yesterday not only gained ground but literally challenged and smashed into the ground anyone who got in his way."

The win gave the 2–2 Redskins hope of possibly competing for the Eastern Conference title. But the injury-riddled squad lost five of its next six games, including embarrassing defeats of 35–10 to the Colts, the eventual NFL champs, and 30–0 to the Giants.

There was also a 20–10 loss to Cleveland, after which Marshall's loose lips again made for entertaining newspaper copy.

After the game, the Redskins waived Rudy Bukich, who told the *Washington Post* he felt he was let go because the team wanted to save one-third of his reported $16,000 a year salary. When told of Bukich's remarks, Marshall called him a "bum," according to the *Post*. The owner later said he was misquoted.

The season ended with a 14–14 tie against Pittsburgh and a 20–0 win over Philadelphia that secured Washington's fourth-place finish in the Eastern Conference.

## 1959: 3–9–0, 5TH PLACE— EASTERN CONFERENCE

### Head Coach: Mike Nixon

Conventional wisdom said the transfer of the Redskins' coaching baton from Joe Kuharich to Mike Nixon would be seamless. Nixon had been Kuharich's top assistant for five seasons with the Redskins, and the two were considered coaching twins with identical styles. Washington's offense and defense from recent seasons, and the schemes expected for use in 1959, were largely a joint product of both coaches.

But Nixon's real coaching influence—and the man from whom he derived the most ideas and theories—was the legendary Jock Sutherland. Nixon, nicknamed "Little Jock," had played for Sutherland when the coach molded the University of Pittsburgh into a national powerhouse in the mid-1930s and assisted him when Pitt won the national title in 1937. That year, Nixon helped develop Pitt's famed "Dream Backfield" of John Chickerneo, Harold Stebbins, Dick Cassiano, and Marshall Goldberg.

Nixon, who later assisted Sutherland with the Brooklyn Dodgers and Pittsburgh Steelers, had about 20 years of assistant coaching experience when handed the Redskins' reins. He inherited a squad without some impact players from recent years. Gene Brito, Washington's four-time All-Pro defensive end, who retired after the 1958 season, wanted to resume his career and was traded to the Rams for linebacker Larry Morris. (Morris never reported to the Redskins and was acquired by Chicago, where he helped anchor a defense that led the Bears to the 1963 championship.) Solid defensive tackle Jim Weatherall departed, and talented safety Scooter Scudero and consensus All-Pro offensive guard Dick Stanfel both left to become assistant coaches under Kuharich at Notre Dame. Nixon acquired six-year veteran Bob Toneff from San Francisco to help plug gaps on the defensive line.

The deepest unit was the offensive backfield featuring quarterbacks Eddie LeBaron, the NFL's top passer in 1958; up-and-coming Ralph Guglielmi; and rookie Eagle Day, who had spent two years in Canada, as well as backs Johnny Olszewski, Don Bosseler, Jim Podoley, and Ed Sutton. Acrobatic safety Dick James was expected to see much more playing time in the offensive backfield.

Ends Joe Walton and Bill Anderson, who combined for 50 catches, 928 yards, and seven touchdowns in 1958, were back, as was receiver Johnny Carson, who showed no signs of a severe back injury that had limited him to two full games the previous season.

"No one, from new head coach Mike Nixon on down, can predict whether the 'Skins are going to be terribly good or good and terrible," United Press International sportswriter Bob Serling wrote. "In many ways, they're loaded, particularly on offense. In other ways, they're merely loaded with question marks."

Nixon was succinct with his team outlook: "Great potential, no depth."

The Redskins showed little promise in a 1–5 preseason, their only victory a 23–21 squeaker over the Rams. LeBaron was sharp in that win, as well as in a 27–24 loss to San Francisco when he completed all 10 of his passes. Nixon started him in the season opener against the Cardinals at Soldier Field.

LeBaron completed 12 of 20 passes for 198 yards, but it was not enough to overcome a porous defense that allowed touchdown drives of 63, 64, 68, 80, 74, 78, and 77 yards in a 49–21 Cardinals romp. Those seven drives totaled 504 yards and consumed 41 plays, a jaw-dropping 12.3-yard average on each play. On the positive side, James scored three touchdowns and Bosseler rushed for 89 yards.

Nixon, a man with a pleasant, nice-guy personality, issued a tongue-lashing in the postgame locker room, according to press reports. "There are too many complacent players on this squad," he bellowed. "There are only 15 men on the team that can consider their jobs safe. The other 21 are playing football for us on a week-to-week basis." Nixon did not play favorites, though. Accusing some of his players of being out of shape, he increased practice time, called for risky full-contact scrimmages, and issued a weeklong curfew of 11 P.M.

The crackdown paid off, as the Redskins topped Pittsburgh, 23–17. Guglielmi, who alternated with LeBaron, threw a 70-yard scoring pass to Anderson and a 46-yarder to Walton, and kicking ace Sam Baker converted field goals of 25, 47, and 48 yards.

Tiny Redskins quarterback Eddie LeBaron unleashes a pass while being pressured by the Baltimore Colts at Griffith Stadium on November 8, 1959. In perhaps the greatest upset in team history, the Redskins beat the defending champion Colts, 27–24. Baltimore won its second straight NFL championship that season.

The Redskins made it two in a row with a 23–14 win over the Cardinals in the home opener. Bosseler and Sutton each ran a yard for touchdowns. Guglielmi, who completed 7 of 9 passes for 144 yards and hit Anderson with a 58-yard scoring pass, became the top-rated quarterback in the NFL, followed by LeBaron.

Nixon subsequently reverted to his soft side, giving his squad an extra day off from practice. That may have been one day too many. The Redskins lost three straight games heading into a meeting at Griffith Stadium against their neighbors, the defending champion Baltimore Colts.

The 2–4 Redskins looked like a punching bag for the 4–2 Colts, who featured six future Pro Football Hall of Fame inductees. Foremost among them was quarterback Johnny Unitas, whose golden passing arm had thrown for touchdowns in a record 31 straight games. Unitas threw two more scores against Washington to establish a league-high total of 19. But this day belonged to LeBaron and company. Washington rushed for only 54 yards, but LeBaron completed 16 of 32 passes for 208 yards and two touchdowns, including a 17-yarder to Anderson that gave the Redskins a 24–17 fourth-quarter lead.

Baltimore tied the game on halfback Lenny Moore's option pass to end Jerry Richardson, plus the conversion, and forced the Redskins to punt with time running out. But Unitas, the man credited with inventing the two-minute drill, threw a pass that defensive end Tom Braatz intercepted and returned to the Colts' 38. Baker came in with 12 seconds left and kicked a 46-yard field goal that sent the 32,773 fans into delirium as they celebrated one of the greatest upsets in Redskins' history.

Vice President Richard Nixon, a diehard Redskins fan who attended the game, bolted to the locker room to congratulate the Redskins players, owner George Preston Marshall and another Nixon, Mike. "I have never seen a game to surpass this one," the Associated Press quoted him as saying.

As memorable as the game was, the rest of the season may as well be forgotten. The Redskins lost their last five games by a combined score of 155–65. They finished 3–9 for the third time in the 1950s with a club that may have been the worst of the three. The 1959 squad scored the fewest points in the NFL, 185, and allowed a league-high 350.

The once-proud franchise would continue its fast descent as it turned the corner into the next decade.

## 1960: 1–9–2, 6TH PLACE— EASTERN CONFERENCE

### Head Coach: Mike Nixon

There are few other ways to say it: The Redskins were plain rotten in 1960.

Washington posted the worst record to date in franchise history, 1–9–2, its only victory coming over the winless, expansion Dallas Cowboys. The Redskins were a nonthreat on both sides of the ball. They scored 178 points, the lowest total in the NFL except for 177 by Dallas, and yielded 309 points, the second most behind Dallas (369).

The Redskins avoided suffering repeated blowouts, unlike in the previous season, but a rash of injuries, coupled with the offense's collapse at crucial times and a defense that allowed

Redskins coach Mike Nixon (right) looks on dejectedly as the Redskins fall to the Eagles, 38–28, to close their 1960 season at 1–9–2. Nixon was fired soon after, ending his dismal two-year stint in Washington. Defensive coach Torgy Torgeson is next to Nixon.

too many big plays, led to their demise. The infamous season included an eight-game losing streak that abruptly ended Mike Nixon's two-year coaching reign.

The final record was light years from the prediction made by halfback Jim Podoley, who delivered the annual preseason words of optimism normally orated by Redskins owner George Preston Marshall. "So we had a 3–9 season last year," Podoley said in the *Washington Post* on August 11, 1960. "Well, don't be surprised if we just reverse that this year. I won't go so far as to predict the championship for our club. But if it comes along, you can bet we won't run away from it. I honestly feel every trade we made has been a big help."

Nixon's most earth-shattering trade involved quarterback Eddie LeBaron, who had completed 539 of 1,104 passes for more than 8,000 yards and 59 touchdowns over seven seasons in Washington. The "Little General" had announced his retirement after the 1959 season, and, armed with a law degree, he joined a law firm in Texas. He later asked for a trade to the Dallas Cowboys. The Redskins obliged and, in return, received veteran Ray Krouse, an intimidating defensive lineman, plus the Cowboys' No. 1 and No. 6 draft choices for 1961.

LeBaron's departure elevated Ralph Guglielmi to starting quarterback. Guglielmi was supposed to have taken over as the starter in 1959 until a severe leg injury in an exhibition game left him with sporadic playing time during the season. This time, he faced no serious competition at the position, for the Redskins lost their No. 1 draft choice, Penn State All-American and Heisman Trophy runner-up Richie Lucas, to the Buffalo Bills of the American Football League, which debuted in 1960. Lucas was Washington's third No. 1 draft pick out of the past four to pass up playing in D.C., joining Boston College quarterback Don Allard (1959) and Maryland halfback Don Vereb (1956) both of whom went north to the Canadian Football League. Vereb signed with the Redskins in 1960.

Meanwhile, it was déjà vu for Guglielmi. He injured his right knee in the 31–7 exhibition opening loss to San Francisco and was projected to be out two to four weeks. Backup Eagle Day substituted in a 26–21 loss to Los Angeles, after which Nixon traded for St. Louis Cardinals third-year quarterback M. C. Reynolds. (The Cardinals moved to St. Louis in 1960 after playing in Chicago since 1920.)

Washington proceeded to lose its last four preseason games by a combined score of 112–20, poor preparation for the opening opponent: the NFL champion Baltimore Colts. Baltimore performed below par, but it was enough to post a 20–0 shutout. The closest the Redskins came to scoring was two missed field goals by Bob Khayat, a rookie guard-placekicking specialist. The *Washington Evening Star* was kind enough to call it a moral victory for Washington: "The Redskins have their hopes up again after holding the champion Colts to a 20–0 decision."

Guglielmi reappeared in the home opener against Dallas and gave the 21,142 fans at Griffith Stadium their money's worth. He completed 10 of 16 passes for 237 yards and a touchdown in a 26–14 Redskins victory. LeBaron battled his former team by connecting on 21 of 37 passes for 296 yards and two scores, but he also threw three picks. Khayat kicked four field goals. The win snapped Washington's six-game losing streak dating back to the prior season.

"Goog made the difference," a jubilant Marshall said, as quoted by the *Post*. "We can walk around town this week for a change. We won't have to duck into alleys. This one was it, great for the team, the town and everybody."

### Redskins Invade the Big Apple

New York City absorbed a healthy dose of burgundy and gold in 1960, the inaugural year of the American Football League. The owner of the New York Titans was former Redskins broadcaster and one-time minority owner Harry Wismer, who hired Redskins legend Sammy Baugh as head coach. Baugh's assistants were also ex-Redskins: Dick Todd (backfield coach), Bones Taylor (ends), and John Steber (line). Sammy posted two straight 7–7 seasons coaching the Titans. He, Todd, Taylor, and Steber were all gone by the time Wismer sold the Titans in 1963, when the franchise was renamed the Jets. Plus, quarterback Al Dorow, a Redskin from 1954 to 1956, played for the Titans in 1960 and 1961. He recorded league highs in passing both seasons.

Guglielmi then "came of pro football age," as one sportswriter put it, completing 16 of 23 passes for 141 yards in a 24–24 tie with the Giants. His 20-yard scoring pass to Podoley with 25 seconds left capped a pulsating comeback in the last two minutes from a 14-point deficit, one that left the 60,000-plus fans at Yankee Stadium chagrined. Guglielmi overcame 102-degree fever in the process.

He posted nearly identical numbers in a 27–27 tie with the Steelers, marking the only time the Redskins have played to two straight ties. Khayat kicked a 43-yard field goal to even the game with less than a minute left. Then, Bert Rechichar's 44-yard try for Pittsburgh with 22 seconds left hit the crossbar and bounced back. The Redskins took over on their 20 with 10 seconds left, but Nixon told Guglielmi to run out the clock. Signs of cynicism were evident in the postgame press conference, where Nixon was asked why he didn't call for a bomb and go for the win. "Are you kidding?" he retorted. "You can't gamble inside your 20. The Steelers had a timeout left, and an interception would have set them up for a field goal that would have beat us."

A win may have delayed the bleeding for Nixon, who began to endure regular cases of Marshall's wrath. At a press luncheon following a 31–10 loss to Cleveland that triggered an eight-game losing streak, Marshall told Nixon to deliver an alibi for the drubbing, according to the *Star*.

"I don't need anyone to alibi for me," Nixon replied angrily.

"Well, I do," Marshall shot back. "I'm in the ticket-selling business, and after you get beat 31–10, you need an alibi."

As the losses mounted, it became inevitable that the owner would hand Nixon his hat. Sure enough, Marshall fired the embattled coach after a season-ending 38–28 loss to Philadelphia, offering a contradictory yet comical explanation for his decision: "He was not fired. His contract was simply not renewed."

Marshall replaced Nixon, who went 4–18–2 in two years in Washington, with assistant defensive coach Bill McPeak. Amid the tumult of the season, there was a sentimental footnote: it was the last of 24 seasons for the Redskins at Griffith Stadium. They would move to a much larger stadium about four miles away along the Anacostia River in Washington.

## 1961: 1–12–1, 7TH PLACE— EASTERN CONFERENCE

### Head Coach: Bill McPeak

The 1961 season marked a momentous juncture in the Redskins' history. They celebrated their silver anniversary in the nation's capital and began playing in a brand-new, state-of-the-art home field: 50,000-seat D.C. Stadium.

The Redskins also sank to their lowest depths ever in 1961. They finished 1–12–1 in the debut of the 14-game season—the worst record percentage-wise in team annals (.107). It was a repeat of 1960, for opponents overwhelmed the Redskins in every phase of the game. Washington finished as the only team with less than 200 points at 174, an average of 12 per game. Even the expansion Minnesota Vikings scored better, at 285. The Redskins also suffered three shutouts and scored in single digits five times. The defense was just as anemic, as the Redskins placed next to last in points allowed with 392, barely better than Minnesota's 407.

The 1961 season marked the 25th anniversary of the Redskins' move to the nation's capital and the inaugural season of D.C. Stadium.

Losing, already a fact of life in Redskins land, reached epidemic proportions. Washington lost its first nine games, tied Dallas, and dropped its next three, to stand 0–12–1. Only a season-ending 34–24 victory over the Cowboys saved Washington from its only winless season ever. For further embarrassment, Minnesota won three games and the Cowboys won four in their second season of existence.

What was it like playing for the burgundy and gold at the time? "It was dismal," said Redskins guard Vince Promuto, who joined the team in 1960. "You couldn't enjoy having a great game if you didn't win. You just played."

Redskins highlights were so scarce that even the mundane play of kicker John Aveni stood out. He made 21 of 23 extra points and 5 of 28 field goals, including a team-record 52-yarder. He also caught a touchdown pass and finished as the Redskins' leading scorer with 42 points. Such feats made Aveni a household word. "The line they used was, 'Aveni put the excitement back into the kicking game,'" said long-time Redskins public address announcer Phil Hochberg. "This was so symptomatic of the kind of team the Redskins had."

It all took place under first-year coach Bill McPeak, who replaced Mike Nixon right after the 1960 season. McPeak had been an All-Pro defensive end during his nine-year career with the Steelers that ended in 1957. He was a player-coach his last two seasons and stayed another year to serve primarily as a talent scout. He joined the Redskins' staff in 1959 and was elevated to Nixon's No. 1 assistant in 1960, when he was in charge of the defense.

The youngest coach in the NFL at 35 and Washington's eighth coach in 13 years, McPeak inherited a squad with promising young players. With two No. 1 draft choices that season, the Redskins chose Wake Forest quarterback Norm Snead and Illinois defensive tackle Joe Rutgens, who would enjoy a solid nine-year career in Washington that included two Pro Bowl appearances.

As for the 6–4, 215-pound Snead, the Redskins felt he had the size and talent to excel after throwing for more than 4,000 yards at Wake Forest. He was sorely wanted by McPeak, who reportedly talked Redskins owner George Preston Marshall out

of selecting Georgia All-American quarterback Fran Tarkenton, a future Hall of Fame inductee. "The boy's intelligent and has ideal temperament for the quarterback position," McPeak said of Snead in the *Washington Post* on June 28, 1961. "Can he throw long? He can throw the ball a mile."

McPeak said the Redskins would not rely entirely on draft choices to rebuild, and he made a series of trades and cuts that shook up the roster. He dealt halfback Jim Podoley, one of the team's more exciting players in recent years, and fifth-year receiver Joe Walton to the Giants for Aveni and receiver Fred Dugan, among other players. The Redskins also lost veteran guard Red Stephens to the Vikings in the expansion draft, and 270-pound defensive tackle Ray Krouse retired after a notable 10-year career in D.C.

The biggest player transaction came at the quarterback position. Shortly before the season began, McPeak traded fifth-year quarterback Ralph Guglielmi to the St. Louis Cardinals for quarterback George Izo. Guglielmi had performed erratically in the preseason, throwing five interceptions in one game, as the Redskins went 0–5 and lost by a combined score of 144–61.

McPeak then handed the starting quarterback role to Snead, who by opening day was among the half of the 36-man roster with a year or less of NFL experience. Such rawness was palpable in a 35–3 loss to the 49ers, although Snead bounced back in week 2 against Philadelphia, completing 13 of 29 passes for 225 yards with an 80-yard scoring pass to Dugan that tied the score at 7 in the third period. But the opposing quarterback, a future Redskins superstar named Sonny Jurgensen, threw two scores in the Eagles' 14–7 win.

*Washington Post* columnist Shirley Povich lauded Snead's performance: "Redskin fans now can dream that they saw the making of a quarterback in the Eagles game, and perhaps they did. Young Norman Snead took a great leap forward yesterday, with a dramatic improvement over his first-game performance against San Francisco. In his second game, there was little of Snead's rookie-like behavior that marked his pro debut. He shed it in fat layers."

In the Redskins' debut at D.C. Stadium against the Giants, Snead tossed two touchdown passes, a 4-yarder to Don

## Marshall Buckles Under Pressure, Integrates Roster

After the 1961 season, the Redskins opened a new and critical chapter in their history by erasing a nagging stigma from the franchise.

Washington integrated its roster with black players, the last team in the NFL to do so. The Redskins traded for Browns running backs Bobby Mitchell and Leroy Jackson and Steelers guard John Nisby, and signed eighth-round draft pick Ron Hatcher, a running back. They also drafted Arizona wide receiver Joe Hernandez, who had spent two years in the Canadian Football League before playing one season in Washington in 1964.

The Redskins had disdained integration from the time racial barriers were toppled in the NFL after World War II. But the policy—implemented by owner George Preston Marshall—crippled the franchise, which gradually plunged to the depths of the league and finished with the worst record in team history in 1961 at 1–12–1.

"We were not pulling from the best talent, and if you don't pull from the best talent, which could be white or black, you can't win football games," said guard Vince Promuto, a Redskin from 1960 to 1970. "So they brought in Bobby Mitchell and John Nisby, and that was the beginning of us at least getting into championship position."

Over the years, Marshall rarely explained his refusal to integrate, except to sometimes make the ludicrous assertion, "We'll start signing Negroes when the Harlem Globetrotters start signing whites." He once wrote to NFL Commissioner Pete Rozelle saying it was not his policy to discriminate against black players: "The sole aim of this club has been, is, and will continue to be, to field a team that will best represent Washington in the NFL."

In addition to his racist beliefs, a common theory for Marshall's intransigence was his fear of alienating the Redskins' huge fan base in the South, where they were the most popular NFL team through the 1940s, 1950s, and 1960s. At the time, widespread segregation still existed in the region. Even Mitchell said the owner's position was grounded in business more than anything else: "Everything Mr. Marshall did was centered around marketing his team. He had this southern taste. Why jeopardize it if you don't have to?"

Al DeMao, a Redskins center from 1945 to 1953, agreed. "Marshall didn't dislike black people. It's just that he was thinking of the dollar. He figured he could compete without the blacks, but he was wrong. It hurt our attendance, and it hurt our ball club, too. There's no question about it."

By the late 1950s, as the civil rights movement was gaining momentum in the United States, fans, media, and the NFL were excoriating Marshall over his lily-white hiring practices. *Washington Post* sportswriter Shirley Povich, one of the owner's sharpest critics, once wrote that the Redskins' colors were "burgundy, gold and Caucasian." Referring to the great Cleveland Browns' running back, Jim Brown, Povich wrote, "Jim Brown, born ineligible to play for the Redskins, integrated their end zone three times yesterday."

Demonstrators massed outside stadiums hosting Redskins games at home and on the road, urging fans to boycott games. Picketers also blasted the *Los Angeles Times* for sponsoring a charity exhibition game between the Redskins and the Rams at the Los Angeles Coliseum. Famous Washington lawyer Edward Bennett Williams, interested in buying a small percentage of the team, tried to convince the owner to abandon his racial policy.

"I told him that from his point of view it was suicidal because it was just certain there would be an economic boycott on his two TV sponsors, Marlboro and Amoco," Williams once said. "And it was very clear to me that if he persisted in the racial policy, they'd drop him like a hot potato. I said, 'George, I can't come in unless there's a change. I can't come in for reasons other than I've articulated to you. I just can't be a part of an organization that's the last bastion of discrimination.'"

The pressure to integrate caught up with Marshall in 1961. U.S. Interior Secretary Stewart Udall repeatedly warned him that he would forfeit his lease to play in brand new D.C. Stadium, which was on federal property, unless he signed a black player. "The government actually stepped in and said, 'You want a stadium, do the right thing,'" Promuto said.

Marshall did. In December 1961, he instructed the Redskins to draft Heisman Trophy-winning running back Ernie Davis of Syracuse University with the first overall pick. Davis refused to sign with Marshall, saying "I won't play for that S.O.B.," so the Redskins traded him to Cleveland for Mitchell and Jackson. In a cruel twist to the story, Davis developed leukemia and died in 1963. He never played a down in the NFL, while Mitchell pursued a brilliant career that led to his Hall of Fame induction in 1983.

How did Marshall accept blacks on the Redskins? "He welcomed me with open arms," Mitchell said. "I never had any problems with him."

Bosseler and a 29-yarder to Dickie James. Those plays, plus a 48-yard interception return by recently acquired defensive back Dale Hackbart, erased a 7–0 Giants lead and put Washington up, 21–7, in the first quarter. The sharp turn of events had the crowd of 37,767 going wild.

Giants coach Allie Sherman then yanked 40-year-old quarterback Charlie Conerly—who was still functioning after the Redskins had traded him to New York 13 years earlier—for 35-year-old Y. A. Tittle. Tittle completed 24 of 41 passes for 315 yards to lead a comeback that resulted in a 24–21 victory. New York's tough defense handcuffed the Redskins after the first quarter and held them to only eight first downs and 145 yards on the day.

"The stadium was in better shape for the game than the Redskins," *Washington Evening Star* columnist Morrie Siegel wrote.

The 0–3 Redskins endured six more defeats, including a 53–0 stinker to the Giants, to account for the worst start to a season in team history at 0–9. A 28–28 tie against Dallas snapped a 17-game losing streak that began midway through the 1960 season, but losses to Baltimore, St. Louis, and Pittsburgh left the Redskins 0–12–1. One reporter wrote that they were playing the "worst brand of football in the l eague."

Teetering on a winless campaign, the Redskins received clutch play from their top all-around threat in the closer against the Cowboys. Speedy Dick James scored touchdowns on 3-, 5- and 39-yard runs, plus a 1-yard reception, in Washington's 34–24 win. His four touchdowns and 24 points held as single-game team records until Larry Brown tied him in both categories in 1973.

James was one of four Redskins to earn a trip to the Pro Bowl, joining offensive lineman Ray Lemek, center Jim Schrader, and defensive tackle Bob Toneff, who went for the third time. Snead emitted signs of being the Redskins' quarterback of the future. Under constant pressure from charging defenses all year and lacking a deep threat, he completed 172 of 375 passes for 2,337 yards, with 11 touchdowns and 22 interceptions. Such accomplishments, however, did little to soften the bone-chilling reality of a wretched season.

# 1962–1970: Perennial Doormat Sees Sonny Days

ON THE FACE of it, the Washington Redskins continued to resemble a wounded franchise, one still unable to emerge from the morass it had slipped into after World War II. The numbers from 1962 to 1970—a 50–69–7 record (43 percent success rate), one winning season, and no playoff appearances—were disconcerting.

But to call the Redskins unentertaining would be criminal. In fact, they displayed an electrifying offense that thrilled the masses in D.C. and led to sellout after sellout at home games. The offense was predicated on a potent aerial attack starring players who evolved into household names in the nation's capital: Jurgensen, Taylor, Mitchell, and Smith.

Quarterback Sonny Jurgensen was the trigger. The pot-bellied redhead, who became a Redskin before the 1964 season, used his graceful passing style to register astronomical numbers that consistently put him among the league leaders. His prime targets, wide receivers Charley Taylor and Bobby Mitchell and tight end Jerry Smith, were year after year among the best pass catchers in the NFL. The four-way threat was so lethal that in one season, 1967, Jurgensen finished No. 1 in passing, and his dangerous receiving trio placed a phenomenal first, second, and fourth in receptions.

One can safely argue that the Redskins' passing game of the era is among the greatest in NFL history. "I would put it right there at the top," said Mitchell, who, along with Jurgensen and Taylor, is in the Pro Football Hall of Fame. "There were teams that beat us with better players, but every one of them had a nucleus of players on offense and defense. We had no defense. But no team had an offense that played better than us."

The offense victimized powerhouses such as the Dallas Cowboys, who fell to Washington in some classic games in the 1960s that kicked off the famous Redskins-Cowboys rivalry. "They had a very, very explosive passing game," Cowboys Hall of Fame defensive tackle Bob Lilly said. "Sonny was always scary, he and all those guys. Bobby was fast. Taylor was always open. Smith was a very good receiver for a tight end. The running game wasn't that great, but with Sonny, you really didn't need a running game. If they'd have had a comparable defense, there's no telling what they would have done."

If only.

A defense that lacked a consistent crop of stars offered minimal resistance to opponents. The unit nonetheless featured some standouts, most notably outside linebacker Chris Hanburger, a four-time Pro Bowl selection in the 1960s; future Hall of Famers in safety Paul Krause and middle linebacker Sam Huff; cornerback Pat Fischer; safety Brig Owens; and linemen Joe Rutgens, Bob Toneff, and John Paluck.

At times the Redskins showed promise, but they failed to seriously threaten for a title. Starting in 1962, they posted six losing records and a .500 season until the legendary Vince Lombardi arrived as head coach in 1969. Under Lombardi, winner of five NFL titles in his days in Green Bay, the Redskins finished 7–5–2, their first winning season since 1955 and their fourth since 1945. As fate would have it, though, Lombardi died of cancer before the 1970 season, and the Redskins dipped back under .500 that year.

Meanwhile, the franchise underwent an evolution on the ownership end. Redskins owner and founder George Preston Marshall experienced serious health problems and handed control of the team's day-to-day operations to three members of his board of directors: acting president Leo DeOrsey and minority shareholders Milton King and Edward Bennett Williams. Williams, a famous criminal attorney, took complete control after DeOrsey died in April 1965.

The front-office transition came at a time when pro football was growing exponentially. Total regular-season attendance vaulted from 3.1 million in 1959 to nearly 9 million in 1969, a trend that hit home when the Redskins began to repeatedly sell out games in the mid-1960s. Concurrently, television revenue ballooned as a result of a series of handsome deals between the NFL and the networks. Although the influential Marshall once declared that the NFL would expand "over my dead body," the league increased to 16 teams by the mid-1960s and to 26 when the NFL merged with the American Football League in 1970.

"From the beginning of the '60s to 1970, the transition in football between a pure sport and entertainment was probably the greatest leap ever in any sport," said Vince Promuto, a standout Redskins guard in the 1960s. "We used to play exhibition games at a race track, and there'd be nobody there. By the time '66 or '67 came, the whole place was filled because of television, the big contracts. We were in a great time for football because it was undergoing a tremendous leap from being somewhat popular to being the world's number one game."

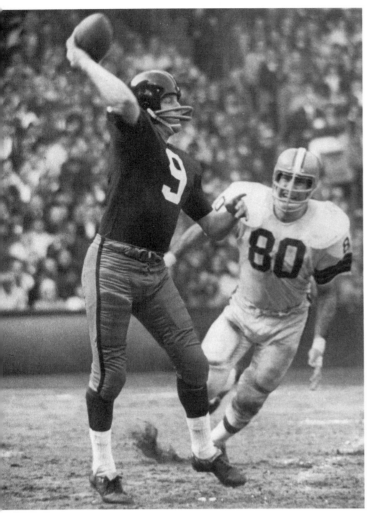

Sonny Jurgensen's golden right arm gave defenses fits and thrilled Redskins fans in the 1960s. From the time he arrived in D.C. in 1964 through the rest of the decade, the Redskins fielded one of the most explosive offensives in NFL history. He threw for more than 32,000 yards in his 18-season Hall of Fame career.

## 1962: 5–7–2, 4TH PLACE— EASTERN CONFERENCE

### Head Coach: Bill McPeak

When quarterback Sammy Baugh retired in 1952, the Redskins lost a player capable of electrifying crowds week after week. The well remained dry of that explosive highlight package until 1962.

The Redskins finished 5–7–2 that year, but newcomer Bobby Mitchell thrilled fans by catching 72 passes for 1,384 yards (19.2 average) and 11 touchdowns, all league highs. His reception and yardage totals were Redskin single-season records. He also led the team in scoring with 72 points, with one touchdown coming on a kickoff return. Fans anxious to see their new phenom began filling up 50,000-seat D.C. Stadium.

Mitchell wanted to be a superstar, and the Redskins badly needed one. They agreed before the draft in December 1961 to select Heisman Trophy-winning running back Ernie Davis with their No. 1 pick and trade him to Cleveland for Mitchell, who had spent his first four seasons with the Browns, and the rights to rookie halfback Leroy Jackson.

"We're not belittling Ernie Davis as a football player, but we were after the best breakaway-type back we could get," Redskins owner George Preston Marshall told the press. "We want to win some games in a hurry, and we think Mitchell can help us do it."

The Redskins were so high on Mitchell that they signed him to what may have been the most lucrative contract in team history at $18,000, according to the *Washington Post*. Other newcomers included four starters from the Eagles: running back Billy Barnes, defensive back Bob Freeman, linebacker Bob Pellegrini, and defensive tackle Ed Khayat, who had played in Washington in 1957. There were also trades for 49ers linebacker Gordon Kelley and 6–8 Packers defensive end Ben Davidson.

Mitchell was a running back in Cleveland, where he was overshadowed by the great Jim Brown. In training camp, Redskins coach Bill McPeak converted him to flanker to give second-year quarterback Norm Snead a prime target. Doing so was clever, for Snead and Mitchell became one of the most sensational passing-catching combos to hit the NFL in years.

After a 1–4 preseason, the Snead-Mitchell battery sparked the Redskins to a 4–0–2 start, generating a buzz in the nation's capital not seen for years. In the season opener against Dallas, Snead threw 81- and 6-yard scoring passes to Mitchell, who returned a kickoff 92 yards for a touchdown and helped set up the Redskins' other two scores, both 1-yard runs by Snead. But the Cowboys ran and passed at will, and the game was tied at 35 in the fourth quarter. Dallas quarterback and former Redskins star Eddie LeBaron passed the Cowboys into field goal range with seconds remaining, but kicker Sam Baker, another ex-Redskin, missed from 35 yards out.

The next week against Cleveland, a heavy favorite to win the Eastern Conference, the Redskins trailed, 16–10, late in the fourth quarter. But Mitchell spooked his former team. He took a short pass from Snead on the Browns' 40 and ran toward the Cleveland bench and coach Paul Brown, putting on a fake for the ages.

"It appeared that Mitchell was going to run out of bounds, but he turned a wicked corner and left two flabbergasted Browns while he went on to dazzle just about the rest of the Cleveland team," Jack Walsh of the *Post* wrote on September 24, 1962. "You can't make up things like this. It actually happened."

Mitchell sped the rest of the way for a touchdown, and Bob Khayat's conversion put the Redskins up, 17–16. The Browns drove into field goal position, but Redskins defensive back Dale Hackbart blocked Lou Groza's 35-yard attempt with seven seconds left. Cleveland recovered on the 44, and there was time for another play. This time, Groza's low kick bounced off the middle of the line.

Hundreds of elated fans greeted the Redskins at Washington National Airport. The cheering persisted courtesy of a 24–14 win over St. Louis before 37,419 fans at home. Mitchell caught 40- and 23-yard touchdown passes from Snead (13 of

The Redskins cheerleaders, the Redskinettes, debuted in 1962. Today they are known as "the first ladies of football."

22, 217 yards), and a headline in a Redskins' game program read, "Snead to Mitchell: Redskins Passing Combo Dazzles Fans and Foes." After beating the Rams to stand 3–0–1, the Redskins stayed unbeaten when Bob Khayat's 29-yard field goal with 14 seconds left clinched a 17–17 tie against St. Louis. The Redskins then topped Philadelphia, 27–21, as Mitchell caught eight throws for 147 yards, including two 28-yard scoring passes from Snead. Hackbart again came up clutch. He recovered two fumbles, and his end-zone interception in the last two minutes preserved the victory.

By then, the 4–0–2 Redskins held first place in the Eastern Conference, but the second-place Giants popped their bubble. Quarterback Y. A. Tittle passed the Redskins dizzy in a 49–34 Giants win at Yankee Stadium. His seven touchdown passes, three alone to former Redskins end Joe Walton, tied an NFL record and overshadowed a superb day for Snead (17 of 40, 346 yards, four touchdowns). Despite the loss, the Redskins remained the talk of the league. "The Redskins are real enough, all right," *New York Times* columnist Arthur J. Daley wrote. "In another year, their reality should be appalling. All they need is the time to consolidate what they have."

Other pundits considered Washington a freak team playing over its head, an assessment that seemed valid as the season progressed. Dallas routed the Redskins, 38–10, before 49,888 fans at D.C. Stadium, then the largest crowd to ever see a sports event in Washington, according to the *Post*. The loss, coupled with a Giants win, pushed the Redskins out of first place in the conference. But local enthusiasm remained high, for nearly 50,000 fans appeared at D.C. Stadium to see another upset of Cleveland, 17–9. Washington pounded the Browns on the ground, where backs Don Bosseler, Billy Barnes (the

Redskins' rushing leader that season with 492 yards), and Jim Cunningham combined for 142 yards. Bosseler also scored on two short touchdown runs.

But the 5–2–2 Redskins, firmly in control of second place in the conference, took a nosedive. With Snead losing much of his rhythm and unable to consistently get the ball to Mitchell, Washington dropped its final five games, including two losses by a total of five points to the Steelers. Contributing to the descent was a Redskins defense that allowed the third-most points in the league (367) by season's end.

Snead's season also came crashing down when he separated his shoulder in the final game. If not for the injury, he likely would have gone to the Pro Bowl after completing 184 of 354 passes for 2,926 yards, with 22 touchdowns and 22 interceptions. At least the Redskins knew a quarterback with much potential would be leading them in the future.

"That year, we had no personnel, but we kind of sneaked up on the league and caught people off-balance," Mitchell said. "They hadn't seen that type of offense. Then teams realized, 'Hey, they're still the Redskins,' and they started beating us up pretty good."

### 1963: 3–11–0, 6TH PLACE— EASTERN CONFERENCE

#### Head Coach: Bill McPeak

They were big teases for the second straight year, winning two of their first three games and holding the top spot in the

Eastern Conference for a time. The momentum fizzled fast. The Redskins lost 10 of their last 11 games to finish a lowly 3–11.

Washington's feeble defense yielded a league-high 398 points, but the offense was exciting at times, as flanker Bobby Mitchell posted another stellar season. After re-signing for $25,000 a year to become the team's highest-paid player ever, according to the *Washington Post,* he caught 69 passes for a league-high 1,436 yards and seven touchdowns. He was second in the NFL in receptions, and his yardage total snapped the team record of 1,384 he set in 1962.

Norm Snead, meanwhile, became the first Redskins passer to throw for more than 3,000 yards with 3,043, breaking Sammy Baugh's team record of 2,938 set in 1947. But Snead's touchdown passes dropped to 13 from 22 the season before, and his interceptions increased by five to 27. He was often benched in favor of backup George Izo.

Another of Snead's steady targets, rookie end Pat Richter, caught 27 passes for 383 yards and three touchdowns. He also handled punting chores, a position he held through the 1967 season. Veteran running back Don Bosseler led the team in rushing (384 yards) and caught 25 passes for 289 yards and two touchdowns.

The Redskins drafted Richter, a 6–5 All-American from Wisconsin, with their No. 1 choice. He signed for $20,000 to become the highest-priced rookie in team history, the *Post* reported. The Redskins used their next two picks on Michigan State defensive back Lonnie Sanders and Oregon defensive end Ron Snidow, both of whom played five seasons in Washington. Coach Bill McPeak also traded draft choices to bolster the defense, one to Pittsburgh for veteran defensive back Johnny Sample and one to San Francisco for Carl Kammerer, who played seven seasons in Washington, first as a linebacker and later as a defensive end.

At McPeak's request, the Redskins opened training camp at Dickinson College in Carlisle, Pennsylvania, ending a 16-year stay at Occidental College in Los Angeles. But the early exhibition results—a 28–26 loss to Chicago and a 41–13 loss to the Eagles—had McPeak on edge. "Disappointed?" the coach asked rhetorically in the *Post* after the loss to Philly. "That's the understatement of the night. We haven't played that bad a game since New York beat us, 53–0, two years ago. Before the game, I was hearing nonsense about teams needing victories. We need a victory more than anyone in the National Football League."

The Redskins closed out the preseason with two more losses. But McPeak, apparently over his earlier fit, predicted a win in the season opener on the road against the mighty Browns, even forecasting an Eastern Conference championship for his squad.

He ended up sounding foolish. Cleveland cruised to a 37–14 win, outgaining the Redskins 534 yards to 272. Bulldozing Browns fullback Jim Brown scored on 80- and 10-yard runs, and ran most of the way on an 83-yard pass-run scoring play. His former teammate, Bobby Mitchell, performed a similar feat on a 99-yard pass from Izo.

The Redskins regrouped to win two in a row, 37–14 over Los Angeles and 21–17 over Dallas. Washington trailed the Rams by one at halftime but scored 24 unanswered points in the second half. Courtesy of scrappy back Jim Steffen, Wash-

---

### Turnover Ignominy

The Redskins' 10 turnovers against the Giants on December 8, 1963 matched a franchise record set against the Giants on December 4, 1938. The infamous mark is also tied with a host of other teams for third-most in a single game in NFL history.

Now, tack on five turnovers by the Giants in the 1963 game, and the two-teams combined for the third-most in league history that day (15), a mark reached in three other games over the years.

---

ington's defense then made a surprise showing against Dallas. Claimed by the Redskins off waivers before the 1961 season, Steffen intercepted three passes by quarterback Don Meredith, returning one 78 yards for a touchdown. His third interception with 1:46 to play stifled the Cowboys' final threat and preserved Washington's 21–17 lead.

Things looked bright for the 2–1 Redskins, but they proceeded to experience one calamity after another. In a 21–7 loss to St. Louis that dropped them to 2–5, they posted six turnovers (three interceptions, three fumbles). McPeak told reporters the debacle was a "tragedy of errors, not a comedy." They followed with a seven-turnover fiasco that included three interceptions off of Snead in a 35–20 loss to Dallas. The loss put 2–6 Washington in a sixth-place conference tie with the Cowboys.

"Supposedly an up-and-down team, the Washington Redskins continued going one way today—down, down, down," Jack Walsh wrote in the *Post.* "The Redskins committed enough miscues to blow the fuse of the sturdiest IBM computer."

A seven-game Redskins losing streak ended with a 13–10 win over the Eagles before a sellout crowd of 60,671 at Philadelphia's Franklin Field. It was a sad time for the United States. President John F. Kennedy had been assassinated two days before, on November 22, 1963, and team officials had urged NFL Commissioner Pete Rozelle to postpone league games that weekend. He decided not to, a decision he later admitted regretting.

The Redskins dropped their final three games, the first one a 36–20 loss to the Colts. Afterward, Redskins acting president C. Leo DeOrsey—the team's main decision maker, in place of the ailing George Preston Marshall—said that the outcome of the last two games would affect any decision he would make regarding McPeak's coaching future, according to the *Post.* Those games were against squads bidding for the conference title, presenting a sort of redemption package for McPeak and his players. But teams that commit 10 turnovers rarely win, as the Redskins learned in a 44–14 loss to New York. Snead threw four interceptions and fumbled twice, and Izo had three passes picked off. McPeak was asked by the press how the defeat affected his coaching future: "I'm sure it won't help. It doesn't help anything."

The Redskins closed out the season with a 27–20 loss to Cleveland.

## 1964: 6–8–0, 4TH PLACE— EASTERN CONFERENCE

### Head Coach: Bill McPeak

The Redskins finished 6–8 in 1964, their eighth straight losing season. No surprises on that front. Still, this one was a landmark year.

Sonny and Sam came to Washington. That's Sonny and Sam as in quarterback Sonny Jurgensen (Jurgy) and linebacker Sam Huff, names that have since become synonymous with the Redskins franchise. They were joined by two other future Hall of Fame inductees, a Redskins icon himself in running back (and later receiver) Charley Taylor and safety Paul Krause.

The Redskins drafted Taylor, an Arizona State running back, with their No. 1 pick and Krause, an Iowa safety, at No. 2. That's the same order they placed in NFL Rookie of the Year voting. Taylor led the Redskins in rushing with 755 yards and caught 53 passes, an NFL receiving record for running backs, for another 814 yards. Krause intercepted a league-high 12 passes, one short of the NFL record set in 1948 by fellow Redskin Dan Sandifer, and picked off passes in seven straight games. He was the main reason the Redskins posted a league-high and team-single-season-record 34 interceptions in 1964.

The two others arrived through blockbuster trades. Coach Bill McPeak dealt quarterback Norm Snead, who had passed for 5,306 yards in three seasons in Washington but was low on McPeak's patience meter, for Eagles quarterback Sonny Jurgensen. McPeak considered Jurgensen, a consensus All-NFL selection in 1961, one of the league's top three passers, along with Baltimore's Johnny Unitas and New York's Y. A. Tittle. Defensive backs Claude Crabb of

the Redskins and Jimmy Carr of the Eagles also swapped teams in the deal.

Critics questioned why McPeak dealt the 24-year-old Snead for the 29-year-old Jurgensen—or young for old. The coach defended the deal by saying the seven-year-veteran Jurgensen was much more advanced and could win quicker. "If given the supporting cast, he can take the Redskins right to the top of the Eastern Division," McPeak said at the ceremony where Jurgensen reportedly signed a team-record $30,000 contract.

Snead believed that McPeak was under pressure to make a major move in light of the Redskins' 3–11 season in 1963, after which team management apparently gave the coach an ultimatum to win. "We gave Washington a taste of victory in 1962 when the Redskins won five games, lost seven and tied two after a fast start, and they expected big things last season," Snead told the Associated Press. "But a lot of things seemed to go wrong, including injuries to key players."

A few days later, McPeak traded versatile halfback Dick James, a Redskins icon for the past eight seasons and the NFL's top punt returner in 1963, plus defensive end Andy Stynchula and a fifth-round draft pick, for Giants middle linebacker Sam Huff and rookie defensive lineman George Seals. McPeak considered Huff, a two-time consensus All-Pro and four-time Pro Bowler, the best middle linebacker in the Eastern Conference.

"Despite the fact that we had to part with two of our most popular players, we feel we're taking a real step forward in trying to build a winner in Washington," McPeak told reporters. "I'm convinced that Huff is as good a football player as he ever was."

Meanwhile, McPeak took other steps to reshuffle the lineup in order to establish a high-powered offense and an improved defense geared around Huff. The coach acquired end Angelo Coia and four-time Pro Bowl defensive tackle Fred Williams

Linebacker Sam Huff (left) and quarterback Sonny Jurgensen, both future Hall of Famers, came to the Redskins through blockbuster trades in the spring of 1964. Here, Huff inks his deal with the Redskins as coach Bill McPeak looks on.

from the Bears in exchange for Washington's No. 1 draft choice in 1965. Other trades landed Colts fullback J. W. Lockett, nine-year veteran end Preston Carpenter and linebacker John Reger from the Steelers, and Browns defensive back Jim Shorter. By the time the season began, McPeak had traded away his No. 1, 4, 5, 6, and 7 draft choices for 1965. "We're very optimistic this year because of the trades we've made," he said, as quoted by the *Washington Post.*

Optimism quickly vanished. The Redskins lost their first four games, a stretch when the offense scored 58 points and Jurgensen was nonproductive. But the high-priced quarterback shifted into gear in week 5, spearheading a 35–20 win over the Eagles at D.C. Stadium. He completed 22 of 33 passes for 385 yards and five touchdowns against his former team, silencing the boo-birds who hounded him earlier that game. Snead, in contrast, hit on 12 of 35 passes for 126 yards and one score in his return to the nation's capital. Mitchell was sensational, catching a Redskins single-game record 12 passes and two touchdowns. Taylor caught two scoring passes and rushed for 61 yards.

After a 38–24 loss to St. Louis, the Redskins reeled off five wins in six games. First came a thrilling 27–20 victory over the defending-champion Bears, who were victimized by Jurgensen's four touchdown passes. His 15-yard scoring pass to Carpenter with a minute left provided the winning points. The Redskins followed with a 21–10 win over Philadelphia; Taylor scored on two 1-yard runs and Mitchell caught a scoring pass.

The eventual NFL champion Browns snapped Washington's two-game win streak with a 34–24 victory, but the Redskins responded with superb play on offense and defense in a 30–0 rout of Pittsburgh. Jurgy threw 80-yard touchdown passes to Taylor and Coia, while the defense picked off four throws—two by Johnny Sample and one each by Paul Krause and Jim Steffen. The defense repeated its four-interception effort the next week in a 28–16 win over the Cowboys. Of his two thefts, Krause returned one 35 yards for a touchdown in the final minutes to clinch the victory. Jurgensen then recorded another four-touchdown passing effort in a 36–21 win over the Giants, the first time the Redskins had beaten New York since 1957. Krause intercepted two more to increase his total to 12.

The win lifted the 6–6 Redskins into the conference's third-place slot, where they finished tied with the Eagles after losses to Pittsburgh and Baltimore. It was a disheartening climax to a season that otherwise generated promise for the future. In addition to the achievements of Taylor and Krause, Jurgensen finished as one of the NFL's top quarterbacks, completing 207 of 385 passes for 2,934 yards, with 24 touchdowns with 13 interceptions. Mitchell caught 60 passes for 904 yards and 10 touchdowns, and Preston Carpenter had 31 catches for 466 yards and three touchdowns.

No doubt, the offensive firepower was there. But would it lead to a winning season?

## 1965: 6–8–0, 4TH PLACE— EASTERN CONFERENCE

### Head Coach: Bill McPeak

Bill McPeak was at a crossroads. The coach hired in 1961 to revive a moribund franchise had produced four losing teams in four seasons. Impatience was building among Redskins management and fans for him to finish with a winning campaign and make the Redskins a championship-caliber squad.

It didn't take long for the verdict on McPeak—for all intents and purposes—to arrive. The Redskins lost their first five games to drop out of the Eastern Conference title race. Although they won six of their last nine, newly elected team president Edward Bennett Williams ended McPeak's coaching reign.

The 6–8 record fooled members of the local sports media who had made off-season predictions that the Redskins would win at least eight games. Middle linebacker Sam Huff, a de facto team spokesman in only his second season in D.C., envisioned an exciting squad capable of winning big. He stressed that the team's willingness to make bold trades similar to those of the perennial baseball power New York Yankees, such as the one that brought Bears fullback Rick Casares to Washington in 1965, would produce extra victories and an NFL title, according to the *Washington Daily News.*

Redskins coaches expected Casares, a 10-year veteran and the Bears' all-time leading ground-gainer at the time with 5,657 yards, to add to the impressive depth already entrenched on the offense. He was seen as a perfect complement to halfback Charley Taylor, who gained more than half of the Redskins' 1,237 rushing yards in 1964. Casares rushed for only 123 in 1964 due to a bad knee, but McPeak was confident that the injury had healed by the start of training camp. The trade also brought end-kicker Bob Jenks and sent offensive linemen Riley Mattson and Fred Hageman to Chicago. Other big deals produced Giants guard Darrell Dess, an All-NFL player in 1962, and Detroit running back Dan Lewis.

On defense, the Redskins returned a unit ranked fourth in the NFL in 1964. It featured an experienced linebacker corps in John Reger (11th season), Huff (10th), Jimmy Carr (ninth), and Bob Pellegrini (ninth), plus safety Paul Krause, the league's interception leader in 1964, and talented rookies in Arizona defensive back Rickie Harris and North Carolina linebacker Chris Hanburger.

"The team that wins the title nearly always is the one with the best defense," Huff told the press. "If [quarterback] Sonny Jurgensen can get us 30 points a game, our defense will take care of the opposition."

The Redskins opened with a 17–7 loss to the Browns. Jurgensen completed 9 of 21 passes for 124 yards and was yanked after three quarters for backup Dick Shiner. The running game (24 yards) was virtually nonexistent. Casares suffered bruised ribs that short-circuited his season—he rushed twice for 5 yards that year—and Taylor aggravated an ankle he broke during the preseason, an injury that stifled his running ability all year.

Jurgensen was again subpar in a 27–7 loss to the Cowboys, and McPeak labeled the upcoming game at Detroit a must-win. His players failed to see any urgency, committing eight turnovers in a 14–10 loss. Jurgensen completed 6 of 11 passes for 19 yards with four interceptions, and McPeak announced that Shiner would take over the starting role.

The switch was to no avail. Shiner, harassed constantly by the St. Louis defense, completed 13 of 32 passes for 193 yards in a 37–16 loss. Boos and jeers cascaded down all game from the record crowd of 50,205 at D.C. Stadium, where signs in the upper deck read "Week After Week We Suffer From McPeak" and "Bye, Bye, Bill." The maligned coach was seething in the postgame locker room. "Pathetic . . . disgusting," he grumbled to reporters. "I'm thoroughly ashamed of what went on out there today. It's pretty bad when half the people leave the stadium before the game is over."

A 38–7 shelling by the Baltimore Colts before another record crowd of 50,405 at D.C. Stadium stretched the losing streak to five. Jurgensen, back in the starting lineup, scored the Redskins' only touchdown on a 27-yard dash late in the first half, while flanker Bobby Mitchell had two scores called back because of penalties.

The ineptitude of a team outscored 133–47 in its first five games had reached crisis levels. A *Washington Evening Star* headline on October 18, 1965, read, "Redskins Headed for Record Depths of '61," a reference to their ignominious 1–12–1 campaign. Williams, who termed the season a "horrendous disappointment," declined to say how long he would tolerate the losing streak before shoving his coach out the door.

In hopes of rejuvenating his squad, Williams ordered a closed-door, players-only meeting where he spoke and listened to concerns. He refused to divulge specifics to the press from what he called a "give and take" session. Whatever was exchanged seemed to inspire his troops, for they pulled a Jekyll and Hyde similar to 1964.

Washington first posted a 24–20 upset of a 4–1 Cardinals squad. Jurgensen was sensational, completing 12 of 14 passes for 195 yards, with three touchdowns and no interceptions against the league's top defense. He presented Williams with the game ball. Jurgy delivered an encore performance in a 23–21 victory over Philadelphia. He connected on 23 of 35 passes for 293 yards, with touchdown passes to Taylor and Mitchell. Taylor also ran for a score. Tight end Preston Carpenter caught eight passes for 83 yards.

It was three in a row with a 23–7 win over the Giants. This time, safety Paul Krause produced the big plays by returning a fumble 31 yards for a touchdown and intercepting a pass in the end zone that ended a late Giants threat. Fullback Dan Lewis gained 85 yards on 19 carries and hit rookie split end Jerry Smith with a 26-yard scoring pass.

The winning streak had the Redskins on an emotional high. "We wonder why somebody didn't get Mr. Williams in after the first game instead of after five," punter-end Pat Richter said at the time. "That talk was the turning point for our team."

But the lowly Eagles, led by the sharp passing of former Redskins quarterback Norm Snead, topped the Redskins, 21–14. Washington rebounded with a 31–3 rout of Pittsburgh and then defeated the Cowboys, 34–31, in one of the greatest comebacks in Redskins history.

The Cowboys jumped out to a 21–0 lead, and Jurgensen, cold early on, was pelted with booming calls at D.C. Stadium of "WE WANT SHINER!" Unfazed, he orchestrated a jaw-dropping aerial show. He threw a 26-yard scoring pass to Taylor before halftime, and, after a Dallas field goal, he ran 1 yard for a score, to cut the lead to 24–13. The teams traded touchdowns, and Dallas led, 31–20, with less than six minutes left. But Jurgy was just gaining steam. Distributing the ball evenly among his receivers, he led a 64-yard drive that ended with his 10-yard scoring pass to Mitchell. Less than two minutes later, he capped an 80-yard march with a 5-yard pass to receiver Angelo Coia for the go-ahead score.

The crowd of 50,205 was in a frenzy, but it wasn't over. Dallas drove to the Redskins' 37 with seven seconds left, but Washington's Lonnie Sanders blocked Danny Villanueva's 44-yard field goal try as time expired. The one-time boo-birds

were now cheering incessantly for Jurgensen, who finished 26 of 42 for 411 yards and three touchdowns. "Dallas had a 21-point lead and was kicking our butt," Taylor told reporters. "But Sonny pulled off a miracle. We scored so fast it blew their minds."

"Twenty-eight years ago, the Redskins emigrated to Washington from Boston and since then have won 158 games in the National Football League," *Washington Post* columnist Shirley Povich wrote. "But for lingering glow there were few, if any, to compare with Sunday's 34–31 success against Dallas."

Although the Redskins lost two of their last three games, to finish 6–8, they had recovered from the depths of disaster to achieve what some would call respectability. But many question marks lingered heading into the off-season, one being who would coach the team after McPeak's inevitable departure.

## 1966: 7–7–0, 5TH PLACE— EASTERN CONFERENCE

### Head Coach: Otto Graham

It was no secret that after the 1965 season Redskins president Edward Bennett Williams was determined to lure a big-name coach to Washington.

Williams first fired Bill McPeak, who had tallied a 21–46–3 record over five seasons with the Redskins. According to the *Washington Post,* Williams tried to fill the post by contacting Notre Dame's Ara Parseghian, the college Coach of the Year in 1964, and Green Bay's Vince Lombardi, winner of three NFL championships up to then. He also touched base with Cleveland owner Art Modell about a possible interest in former Browns coach Paul Brown, who won four championships in the old All-America Football Conference and three NFL titles.

Williams outmaneuvered several other teams to indeed find a popular name, but a surprising one at that. He signed Otto Graham, Cleveland's famous quarterback, to a reported five-year, $60,000-a-year contract.

Graham had achieved the prodigious feat of leading the Browns to a league championship game in each of his 10 years as a pro, four when they played in the AAFC from 1946 to 1949, and another six after they entered the NFL in 1950. Seven of those appearances resulted in championships. One of the greatest pure passers in pro football history, he threw for nearly 24,000 yards and 174 touchdowns and was inducted into the Pro Football Hall of Fame in 1965.

But Graham's coaching resume was unspectacular. He had posted a 32–23–1 mark in a seven-year tenure at the U.S. Coast Guard Academy that included its first undefeated, untied team (1963) and its first bowl bid (the 1963 Tangerine Bowl). He also coached college all-star squads that defeated two NFL champions, the 1957 Lions and the 1963 Bears.

Williams liked Graham's tough-talking, no-nonsense approach. The coach vowed that there would be no loafers on the team and that he would never put his job in jeopardy by allowing even the highest-paid players to perform at less than 100 percent. "I did not fire a fine fellow like Bill McPeak to hire another pleasant man in his place," Williams said, as

### Redskins Fans:
### "Like Miss Wedgewood in a Tea Room"

NFL Films, the television production arm of the NFL, began to produce highlight films for every team when the outfit was in its embryonic stages in the mid-1960s. Steve Sabol, the son of NFL Films founder Ed Sabol and now the executive producer, described how he combined footage from Redskins-Bears games during that era—using imagination and trickery—in an effort to please Bears owner George Halas:

In the course of filming a Bears game, Chicago's Roger LeClair kicked a field goal into the stands at Wrigley Field. As a fan reached up to catch the ball, you see he's got a pistol stuck in his belt. George Halas saw it and was really upset that I'd put that in the highlight film. He said, "We don't have fans like that. I have to show this film to church groups, Kiwanis Clubs and Boy Scouts, and nobody's going to come to the games if they think there are fans like that with guns." Meanwhile, anybody who ever came to a game at Wrigley Field knew that the fans there made the infield at the Indianapolis 500 look like parliament. They wore the hoods with the leather jackets and had the box-car haircuts, and there was lots of beer throwing. Every fan who showed up at Wrigley Field looked like a thug. They had those little fedoras, the cigars, the black greasy hair. It was a really bad crowd. The next year, I sent a cameraman to a Redskins game. This was before NFL Properties, so you didn't have any pennants and sweatshirts. When Redskins fans came to a game, all the men wore the camel-haired coats, sport jackets and neckties, and the women wore the mohair sweaters, circle pins and scarfs. It was like Miss Wedgewood in a tea room—very, very well dressed. They applauded after a good play. So I inner-cut those fans into the Bears film. You'd see Chicago players like Mike Ditka catch a pass or Ronnie Bull score a touchdown, and then you'd cut to people applauding in the stands who were actually Redskins fans. So for five years, we had a special cameraman who was assigned to shoot Redskins fans for Bears highlight films. Halas never knew up to the day he died (in 1983) that those were Redskins fans cut into his highlight films.

---

quoted by the *Post*. "We are looking for a crack-down coach with a winning background."

Graham, who once had an adversarial relationship with Redskins owner George Preston Marshall, promised to field an exciting football squad. He said he would rather risk losing in high-scoring games that would propel fans from their seats than to win close, boring games by such scores as 3–0—a curious remark. He got his wish, sort of. The Redskins won seven games in 1966, the most victories for the franchise since an 8–4 season in 1955, while posting the league's third-highest per-game scoring average (25.1). They averaged 36 points in their seven wins.

Quarterback Sonny Jurgensen carried on with the aerial potency he showed toward the end of the 1965 season, finishing as the NFL's No. 2 passer (254 of 436, 3,209 yards, 28 touchdowns). His key targets were

- Receiver Charley Taylor—league-high 72 catches, 1,119 yards, 12 touchdowns
- Receiver Bobby Mitchell—58 catches, 905 yards, 9 touchdowns
- Split end-tight end Jerry Smith—54 catches, 686 yards, 6 touchdowns

But a leaky defense allowed the second-most points (355) and passing yards (3,237) and the fifth-most rushing yards (1,831) in the NFL. The Redskins had made some off-season acquisitions to help the unit, trading for Cowboys safety Brig Owens and veteran defensive tackle Stan Jones, a future Hall of Fame inductee. But the defense lacked overall experience and cohesiveness, operating with a different front line, for example, in the first six games.

"We didn't have great defensive talent in those days, and we struggled," Jurgensen said. "But we were exciting offensively. We'd go into a game thinking we'd have to score in the 30s to win. We went out and battled each week. We just weren't blessed with the best talent in the league."

After being outscored 124–57 in a 1–3 preseason, the Redskins were dismantled, 38–14, by Graham's old team, the Browns, in the season opener. Jurgensen threw five picks against the defending Eastern Conference champions.

Washington gift-wrapped another game, losing three fumbles to a St. Louis squad that turned two of them into touchdowns in a 23–7 victory. Graham then captured his first win in Washington, 33–27 over Pittsburgh. A solid all-around showing by the Redskins included 20 of 33 passing by Jurgy, eight sacks, and two interceptions, plus four field goals by kicker Charlie Gogolak.

Gogolak was an interesting story. That season, the Redskins made him the first placekicking specialist ever taken in the first round of an NFL draft. They signed the 165-pound Hungarian for $25,000 and insured his right foot for $1 million with Lloyd's of London, according to media reports. The investment paid off handsomely: "Gogo" finished as the league's third-leading scorer with a Redskins-record 105 points. (He and his brother Pete, who signed with the Giants in 1966 after two seasons in the AFL, were the NFL's first true soccer-style kickers.)

After no field goals in the first two games, Gogolak was asked if he and his million-dollar foot had been nervous against Pittsburgh. "Sure, I had butterflies in my stomach. I always do," he replied.

Meanwhile, in a rare back-to-back meeting between the same teams, the Redskins reached .500 with a 24–10 win over the Steelers. Jurgensen heaved scoring passes to the "touchdown

## "Roman Circus" Duel One for the Record Books

The NFL had never seen a scoring bombardment like it and is unlikely ever to see one like it again. The game gave the "proceedings of a Roman circus atmosphere," according to the *Washington Evening Star*. The *Washington Post* perceived it as an epic battle with both sides flinging shots, saying, "Little Big Horn was worse. There were no survivors among General Custer's troops." The description "wild and woolly Donnybrook" appeared in a 1966 Redskins game program.

Final score: Redskins 72, Giants 41.

The 113 combined points stands as an all-time NFL record, and the 72 by the Redskins is the best all-time tally in a regular-season game. Only the 73 points by the Bears when they shut out Washington in the 1940 championship game is greater.

The teams set a host of other league records before a boisterous crowd of 50,439 at D.C. Stadium on November 27, 1966. Among them was a combined touchdown total of 16 that remains first in NFL annals. The Redskins set an NFL-record 10 of those, seven on big plays when they scored every which way: A. D. Whitfield's 63-yard run; Brig Owens's 62-yard fumble and interception returns, Rickie Harris's 52-yard punt return, Bobby Mitchell's 45-yard run, and 74- and 32-yard catches by Charley Taylor from Sonny Jurgensen, who had a personal "subpar" day with 10 of 16 passing for 145 yards and three touchdowns. Whitfield also posted 5- and 1-yard scoring runs, and Joe Don Looney bulled in from 9 yards out. The Redskins led throughout and opened up a game-high 34-point cushion (62–28) in the fourth quarter.

Ironically, the Giants outgained Washington in total yards and first downs. They also posted six touchdowns, two on 41- and 50-yard passes. By game's end, the wild action had left many sore necks among those in attendance.

"D.C. Stadium was full of identifiable objects yesterday, most of them Redskins headed for touchdowns," *Washington Post* columnist Shirley Povich wrote. "There were moments when it appeared somebody had snuck a lively ball into the game. The two teams didn't grind out anything. They wound up playing soft-nosed football."

The scoring bonanza starred two teams dreadful on defense. New York yielded a league-high 501 points by season's end, 146 more than the second-place Redskins, and Washington middle linebacker Sam Huff had a premonition. "The Giants defense had gotten so bad under their coach, Allie Sherman, that I knew we were going to win the game big because we had Sonny Jurgensen, Bobby Mitchell, Charley Taylor, and a great offensive team," Huff said. "I predicted on the radio back in New York that we would score more than 60 points before the game was ever played. I said, 'This is the worst defense I've ever seen in the NFL.'"

Huff was clairvoyant. The Redskins led, 69–41, with seven seconds left and held a first down on the Giants'

22. What transpired next is up for debate. Huff, the defensive captain, insists to this day he called time out and told Redskins coach Otto Graham to send the field goal team into the game, saying, "Show no mercy, Otto. Promise me no mercy." Huff held a vendetta against Sherman, who traded the future Hall of Famer to the Redskins in 1964, when he was still in his prime.

"We were on the sidelines when the Redskins defense came off the field," said Steve Sabol, then an NFL Films cameraman and now its executive producer. "Otto Graham was saying, 'The game's over, the game's over.' But Huff said, 'No, Goddamit! Kick a field goal. Let's kill the son of a bitch!' Allie Sherman had cut him, and there was a lot of ill feeling between he and Allie."

Huff may have signaled a "T" to officials, but Redskins guard and offensive captain Vince Promuto said his word carried a lot more weight. With Washington's offense on the field, Promuto said he called time out and conferred with Graham about trying a field goal. Promuto held his own grudge against the Giants and wanted sorely to embarrass them.

"I've heard it 20,000 times that Sam Huff called that timeout," he said. "But playing in the '60s when Giants quarterback Y. A. Tittle was playing, and seeing him run up the score time after time when the Redskins were a lousy team, I thought, 'This is my opportunity.' I wanted to score one more time just for kicks. We could have let the clock run out, and we would have won, 69–41. But I wanted the field goal. I don't talk to Huff about it, let him have his fame."

Graham eventually called the number of kicker Charlie Gogolak, who booted a 29-yard field goal. The kick capped a performance that was lost in the frenetic pace of the afternoon. After his first extra point was blocked, Gogolak kicked nine straight to tie two players for the NFL single-game record for most extra points, a mark that stands. Graham was later asked why he sent Gogolak into the game.

"He needed the practice," the coach said.

A trite response on an otherwise captivating day.

| | | | | | | |
|---|---|---|---|---|---|---|
| New York— | 0 | 14 | 14 | 13 | — | 41 |
| Washington— | 13 | 21 | 14 | 24 | — | 72 |

Wash —— Whitfield 5 pass from Jurgensen (kick blocked)
Wash —— Whitfield 63 run (Charlie Gogolak kick)
Wash —— Brig Owens 62 fumble recovery (C. Gogolak kick)
NY —— Jacobs 6 run (Pete Gogolak kick)
Wash —— Whitfield 1 run (C. Gogolak kick)
Wash —— Looney 9 run (C. Gogolak kick)
NY —— Wood 1 run (P. Gogolak kick)
NY —— Morrison 41 pass from Wood (P. Gogolak kick)
Wash —— Taylor 32 pass from Jurgensen (C. Gogolak kick)
NY —— Jones 50 pass from Wood (P. Gogolak kick)
Wash —— Taylor 74 pass from Jurgensen (C. Gogolak kick)
Wash —— Harris 52 punt return (C. Gogolak kick)
Wash —— Owens 62 interception return (C. Gogolak kick)
NY —— Thomas 11 pass from Kennedy (kick failed)
NY —— Lewis 1 run (P. Gogolak kick)
Wash —— Mitchell 45 run (C. Gogolak kick)
Wash —— C. Gogolak 29 field goal

twins," a 60-yarder to Taylor and 51- and 70-yarders to Mitchell. The Redskins also intercepted three passes.

Washington made it three straight with a 33–20 victory over the expansion Atlanta Falcons. Taylor ran 12 yards for a score and caught an 86-yard scoring pass from a red-hot Jurgensen, who completed 17 of 26 passes for 286 yards and increased his four-game touchdown total to nine.

The steak ended with a 13–10 loss to the Giants, but the Redskins upset undefeated St. Louis, 26–20. Gogolak kicked four field goals to keep Washington within a point entering the fourth quarter, when Mitchell caught two touchdown passes to account for the win. Before the game, Graham made a move welcomed by Redskin fans: He shifted Taylor to wide receiver to better exploit his marvelous pass-catching skills and to make room for big, powerful runners in 230-pound Joe Don Looney, 222-pound Steve Thurlow, and 200-pound A. D. Whitfield. He also moved Jerry Smith from split end to tight end. "To get those running backs in there, he had to find a place for them," Taylor said. "That meant wide receiver was the place for me."

Looney ran for a score, Mitchell and Smith caught scoring passes, and Gogolak booted two field goals in a 27–13 win over the Eagles that put the 5–3 Redskins in the thick of the Eastern Conference title race. But the upcoming schedule was not friendly: Baltimore, the Western Conference's second-place team, and Dallas and Cleveland, two teams ahead of the Redskins in the East.

The Colts destroyed the Redskins, 37–10, and another scintillating Redskins-Cowboys showdown ended on a field goal with 15 seconds left that gave Dallas a 31–30 win. First, though, Jurgensen and Cowboys quarterback Don Meredith thrilled the record crowd of 50,927 at D.C. Stadium with a breathtaking passing duel. Jurgy completed 26 of 46 for 347 yards and three touchdowns, two to Taylor to accompany his 11 catches, and Meredith hit on 21 of 29 for 406 yards and two scores.

A 14–3 loss to Cleveland eliminated the Redskins from the conference title race. But they did not relax, humiliating the Giants, 72–41, in what stands as the highest-scoring game in NFL history. The offense stayed in high gear the next week in another cardiac affair with Dallas, this one ending with the Redskins winning, 34–31. Gogolak booted a game-winning 29-yard field goal with four seconds left.

The 7–6 Redskins needed a win or tie in the finale against the Eagles to post their first winning record since 1955. Washington led, 21–17, entering the fourth period, but Philly exploded for 20 points en route to a 37–28 victory. Jurgensen threw four scoring passes, two to Taylor, who tied the Redskins' single-season record of 12 touchdown catches set by Bones Taylor in 1952.

Normally, a .500 record does not justify breaking out the champagne. But for a team that had suffered nine straight losing seasons, it was encouraging in a way. Chalk up a respectable grade for the opening of the Graham era.

## 1967: 5–6–3, 3RD PLACE— CAPITOL DIVISION

### Head Coach: Otto Graham

The Redskins' 11th straight nonwinning season was discomforting in itself. The way they lost games in 1967 made the 5–6–3 campaign even more agonizing.

Blowing fourth-quarter leads cost the Redskins wins in five straight games and destroyed their playoff possibilities in the league's new four-division setup: Capitol, Century, Central, Coastal (the Redskins were in the Capitol Division). They self-destructed in myriad ways, among them defensive meltdowns, turnovers, and penalties. Some of their collapses came in the final seconds.

"We were out of the playoffs by about four minutes," defensive end Carl Kammerer recalled. "We lost about five games in two minutes, 40 seconds. We found ways to lose. A lot of successful teams find ways to win against all odds, but that year we just didn't get it done."

The frustration overshadowed a dazzling performance by the Redskins' prolific foursome: quarterback Sonny Jurgensen and his receiving trio of Charley Taylor, Jerry Smith, and Bobby Mitchell. Jurgensen finished as the NFL's No. 1 quarterback with 288 of 508 passing for 3,747 yards, all NFL records, plus 31 touchdowns and 16 interceptions. His touchdown total, which snapped the team record of 28 he set the year before, remains an all-time Redskins mark. (Joe Namath of the AFL's New York Jets passed for 4,007 yards that season; all AFL records were included in the NFL record book when the leagues merged in 1970.)

On the receiving end, Taylor was first in the league in receptions (70), Smith was second (67), and Bobby Mitchell was fourth (60), the first time three players from the same team had ever finished that high. Mitchell's total was all the more remarkable in that he was converted back to his old position of halfback early in the season. The trio accounted for 70 percent of the Redskins' league-high 3,887 passing yards and nearly 50 percent of the team's 347 points.

In Taylor's view, the Redskins offense did nothing tricky to baffle defenses: "We didn't know who the defenses were going to concentrate on, so we relied on a pact between ourselves and the coaches. No matter which player's number was called, we went all out. If it was called to Bobby, it wasn't like, 'You take the day off, Charley.' We all ran hard on every down, and Sonny read defenses to determine who they were double-teaming, then he'd throw to the other side. You had to be involved in every play."

Largely because the passing arsenal had meager support, the Redskins struggled to put teams away. They placed next-to-last in the NFL in rushing yards with 1,247, topping the expansion New Orleans Saints by only 55. The defense finished second in total yards allowed with 5,565 (438 more than the Saints), first in passing yards (3,713), and fourth in rushing yards (1,852). The Redskins also wallowed on special teams after record-setting kicker Charlie Gogolak aggravated a thigh muscle in the season opener and was lost for the year. An inability to find a suitable replacement cost Washington at least two wins.

The disjointed makeup caused coach Otto Graham to rethink the amateurish-sounding proclamation he made upon his hiring in 1966—that he'd prefer losing an exciting game instead of winning a boring one. "I had promised that I would bring exciting football to Washington, and I've kept my promise," the coach told reporters during the season. "But I'd rather have a dull victory."

Middle linebacker Sam Huff, who played in six NFL title games and won one championship with the Giants, thought that Graham's philosophy sounded ridiculous: "I said, 'You've got to be kidding. The name of this game is winning. A loss is a loss, a win is very gratifying.' That approach by Otto was one of the reasons I retired after the 1967 season. He just wasn't a great coach. He wasn't defensive-oriented at all."

Redskins President Edward Bennett Williams was thinking offense when he pushed for the selection of 6–4, 248-pound Idaho fullback Ray McDonald with the Redskins' top pick in the 1967 draft. The hope was that McDonald, the nation's leading rusher in 1966 with 1,329 yards, would improve a weak running game that had plagued the franchise for years.

Not since Rob Goode played for the Redskins in the late 1940s and 1950s had the team boasted such a huge runner. McDonald was much more powerful than Goode, and he possessed the speed, to boot. He ran 100 yards in 9.9 seconds, an impressive feat for someone his size. One NFL scout called him "a pro coach's dream . . . tough, hungry, big, powerful with speed." As early as training camp, Redskin defensive players were uttering, "Ray stings 'em when he hits."

McDonald was a bust. After rushing for 47 yards in a season-opening 35–24 loss to the Eagles and 98 plus three touchdowns in a 30–10 win over the Saints, he pulled a groin muscle in the fifth game and gained only 223 yards on the season. On the taxi squad for all but one game in 1968, he was cut before the 1969 season.

Early in the 1967 campaign, another Redskins rookie earned the spotlight. Seventh-round pick John Love, who returned a kickoff 96 yards against the Eagles for a touchdown the first time he ever touched the ball in the NFL, was Mr. Versatility in a 38–24 victory over the Giants that improved the Redskins to 2–1. The flanker-defensive back tallied 20 points on a 14-yard scoring pass from Jurgensen and a fumble recovered in the end zone, and by booting two field goals and two extra points while substituting for the injured Gogolak. He helped compensate for a Redskins defense that allowed 520 yards.

Fourth-quarter frustrations proceeded to set in. First came a 17–14 loss to Dallas, the fourth straight game between the rivals decided by three points or less. Jurgensen's 8-yard scoring pass to Taylor gave the Redskins a 14–10 lead with 70 seconds left. The Cowboys took over on their 29, and on fourth down from the Washington 36, quarterback Don Meredith threw a scoring pass to halfback Dan Reeves with 10 seconds left.

Next, with a 20–17 lead over Atlanta and 42 seconds showing, the Redskins were burned by substitute Falcons quarterback Terry Nofsinger, who completed four straight passes totaling 53 yards. Wade Traynham kicked a 31-yard field goal with two seconds left for the tie. Redskins defensive back Brig Owens, handling the kicking chores for an injured Love, missed two field goals and had an extra point blocked.

The story was nearly identical against Los Angeles. Tight end Jerry Smith caught his third touchdown pass, a 39-yarder from Jurgensen, for a 28–21 Redskins lead with two and a half minutes left. But the Rams engineered a 75-yard scoring drive that tied the game at 28 and left the Redskins at 2–2–2. Washington then surrendered a 13–7 fourth-quarter lead over the Colts and lost, 17–13, and St. Louis erased a 14–13 Redskins lead entering the final period to earn a 27–21 win, after which *Washington Post* columnist Shirley Povich issued a scathing analysis of the burgundy and gold:

The extent of the shoddy football played by the Redskins does not defy description. Sonny Jurgensen had his sorriest day as a passer within memory, and probably beyond. When they had the ball, the Redskins were their own worst

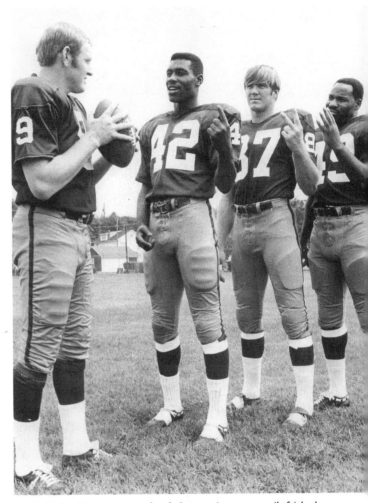

In 1967, Redskins quarterback Sonny Jurgensen (left) led the NFL in passing, while his superstar receiving trio of Charley Taylor, Jerry Smith, and Bobby Mitchell finished first, second, and fourth in receptions.

enemies. They squandered the heroic feats of their defensive unit, which five times forced the Cardinals to punt, and in the last six minutes, when they needed the ball desperately, they twice fumbled it away to the Cardinals.

Washington rebounded with a 31–28 win over San Francisco, followed by a 27–20 upset of Coastal Division-leading Dallas, a game the Redskins nearly gave away. They led 27–6 in the fourth quarter when Cowboys reserve quarterback Craig Morton threw two touchdowns to create a seven-point game. But safety Paul Krause intercepted Morton's pass with less than two minutes left to preserve the win, leaving the 4–4–2 Redskins in the division's No. 2 spot behind 7–3 Dallas.

The Redskins' playoff hopes disappeared due to a 42–37 loss to Cleveland and a 35–35 tie with the Eagles. George Mingo, Washington's fourth kicker of the year, missed a 36-yard field goal with seven seconds left against Philly. After beating Pittsburgh, 15–10, the Redskins closed with a 30–14 pounding at the hands of the heavy underdog Saints, part emblematic of the aggravating season.

Meanwhile, doubts were popping up about the future of Otto Graham, whose efforts to lift the Redskins out of

### Looney: As Crazy as They Come

The Washington Redskins have had their share of characters over the years, players whose behavior has ranged from entertaining to bizarre.

This player was bewildering, and his actions were perhaps befitted by his name: Joe Don Looney. The running back played in Washington for most of the 1966 season and all of 1967, a period when he solidified his reputation as the NFL's No. 1 problem child.

The 6–1, 230-pound Looney was a wonderful physical specimen with tremendous speed and size. But he was intractable and refused to accept discipline from coaches, who consequently lost patience with him; he played for five teams in his brief NFL career. He was drafted No. 1 in 1964 by the Giants, who traded him before the season to Baltimore, where he said he was an alien and was once arrested for kicking a neighbor's door. Before the 1965 season, the Colts traded him to Detroit, where, as the story goes, he once refused to carry coach Harry Gilmer's plays into the huddle, then disappeared at halftime. "If he wanted a messenger," Looney said of Gilmer, an ex-Redskins quarterback, "he should have called Western Union."

Detroit, anxious to jettison Looney, traded him to the Redskins for a draft choice early in the 1966 season. His abnormalities soon became known in D.C.

Guard Vince Promuto recalled a game that season against the Colts in Baltimore when Looney's teammates were yelling for him to enter the game. He was nowhere to be found at the time. Suddenly, Promuto said, Looney appeared from under a tall pile of parkas on the sidelines where he had been hiding. Receiver Bobby Mitchell, for his part, said Looney once vanished on a trip to a resort island after being told by coach Otto Graham he shouldn't practice because of injuries.

When Looney was around, Graham wanted him to keep his motor mouth shut. Once after a victory, the coach found him surrounded by reporters.

"Why don't you take a shower?" Graham asked.

"I've already had my shower," Looney responded.

"Then take another," Graham barked.

"He was a cuckoo guy," Promuto said. "He was such a nut. He said, 'People just misunderstand me.' There was definitely something wrong with him. He wasn't your run-of-the-mill football player."

Safety Brig Owens said of Looney, "Joe was in his own world. He came here with a history. He was a talent, but coaches were not sure how to work with him."

Looney, who shaved his head completely bald during his playing days, rushed for 178 yards and three touchdowns in 1966 but only 26 yards in his injury-plagued 1967 campaign, after which he was waived. He spent the next 14 months at war in Vietnam before finishing his career with New Orleans in 1969. But his enigmatic life continued. He was arrested for illegal possession of a submachine gun, and his interest in Buddhism led him to indulge in marijuana and psychedelic drugs, according to J. Brent Clark's 1993 book, *3rd Down and Forever: Joe Don Looney and the Rise and Fall of an American Hero*. He died in a 1988 motorcycle accident at age 45.

---

their annual doldrums were proving futile. "Otto must wonder if five years of this will be worth it, even at his salary," Lewis F. Atchison of the *Washington Evening Star* wrote late in the season. "He's patched here, traded there, picked up a player in the annual draft and, like his predecessors, discovered it isn't enough. The Redskins need massive first aid."

## 1968: 5–9–0, 3RD PLACE— CAPITOL DIVISION

### Head Coach: Otto Graham

Washington's 1968 season was nothing but a flop. Hurt by injuries to key players, plus mental breakdowns, poor personnel moves, and inconsistent execution, the Redskins fumbled and bumbled their way to a 5–9 record.

The year led to the dismissal of coach Otto Graham, who compiled a 17–22–3 mark over three seasons in D.C. He failed to validate the promise he had made on taking over the Redskins in January 1966 that they would be better than in previous years.

At first, Graham had refused to put a timetable on winning an NFL championship, although that goal became more defined in the months before the 1968 season. Knowing that his coaching clock was ticking, he urged his players to prepare for a run at the title. "Let's start the drive now to bring the championship to Washington," he wrote in a letter that appeared in the *Washington Post*. "It will not be easy, but the rewards are great and worth working for. We do have the people to win it. Our goal in 1968 is to have that winning ball club."

Before the season, however, Redskins management made some decisions that would add to the team's growing list of personnel blunders from recent seasons. Graham traded two-time consensus All-NFL safety Paul Krause to Minnesota for

Joe Don Looney

Otto Graham's prayers often went unanswered during his three-year tenure (1966–68) as Redskins coach. He finished 17–22–3.

reserve tight end Marlin McKeever and a draft choice. The move haunted the Redskins. McKeever never helped them at tight end, although he had a few good years at linebacker. Krause, on the other hand, played 12 more seasons, all in Minnesota, and retired as the league's all-time interception leader with 81, a record that still stands.

At the behest of team president Edward Bennett Williams, the Redskins traded their No. 1 pick in the 1969 draft to Los Angeles for Gary Beban, a UCLA quarterback who won the Heisman Trophy in 1967. Beban flopped at quarterback and played sparingly for the Redskins at running back, receiver, and defensive back before retiring from the NFL after two seasons.

There was sheer bad luck, too. The Redskins used their No. 1 draft pick that year on Oregon's Jim "Yazoo" Smith, one of the top college defensive backs. Graham said that he might also play some running back. Smith broke his neck late in the season and never played again.

On the plus side, Washington acquired two-time Pro Bowl cornerback Pat Fischer, who had played out his option with St. Louis. He spent the next 10 seasons in Washington, becoming one of the greatest cornerbacks in team history. The Redskins also used their No. 5 pick on Richmond punter Mike Bragg, who played 12 seasons with the squad, and No. 7 on Louisiana Tech running back Bob Brunet, who played nine years in Washington.

Star quarterback Sonny Jurgensen had off-season surgery on his golden right arm to remove calcium deposits. He showed no ill effects in the season-opener at Chicago, throwing four touchdown passes in a 38–28 win over a Bears

team that sported the NFL's best pass defense in 1967. Tight end Pat Richter caught three of them, and running back Gerry Allen converted a reception into a 99-yard scoring play.

But the Redskins came up lame against the Saints. They committed a bundle of errors, including a blocked punt, two fumbles, and an interception, that helped New Orleans coast to a 37–17 victory. "So consistently were the Redskins majoring in fumbles, bad snaps from center and untimely penalties, that it appeared they were going into a prevent offense," *Washington Post* columnist Shirley Povich wrote. The Giants then administered a 48–21 flogging of the Redskins, who at 1–2 needed a win in their home opener against the Eagles before the season began slipping away.

They got it. Jurgy completed 21 of 29 passes for 196 yards, throwing for one score and running for the other in a 17–14 victory. Running back Steve Thurlow carried 12 times for 64 yards and caught five passes for another 39. The Redskins then captured a 16–13 win over the Steelers that was bittersweet. Jurgensen suffered a rib injury that would hobble him for the rest of the season.

With Jurgy wearing a body cast that affected his throwing, the Redskins dropped three in a row, the last a 27–14 defeat to Minnesota. The Vikings' defense, led by a front line known as the "Purple People Eaters," sacked No. 9 seven times. He also threw an interception to a former teammate named Paul Krause. All the while, Jurgensen was operating behind an offensive line decimated by injuries. Guard Vince Promuto and tackle Mitch Johnson were out for the season, and guard Ray Schoenke had been sidelined after enjoying a tremendous year.

The Redskins redeemed themselves with a 16–10 victory over winless Philadelphia that improved their record to 4–5. Gerry Allen rushed for 86 yards and a touchdown, Bob Brunet added 59 more and Charlie Gogolak, back after missing nearly the entire 1967 season due to an injury, kicked three field goals. Backup quarterback Jim Ninowski, who replaced

Heisman Trophy-winning quarterback Gary Beban (right), with team president Edward Bennett Williams (left) and coach Otto Graham, signed with the Redskins in June 1968. Williams pushed for the trade, which sent a No. 1 pick to the Los Angeles Rams for Beban. Beban was a bust.

an ailing Jurgensen in the second quarter, completed 8 of 15 passes for 104 yards.

But four more losses, including a 44–24 stinker to a Dallas team that amassed 515 yards, left the Redskins 4–9 entering the final game against Detroit. They won, 14–3, in perhaps their greatest defensive effort under Graham, one of only 13 games in his three seasons in Washington that an opponent scored less than 20 points. But it might have ended differently if not for the clutch play of Redskins third-string quarterback Harry Theofiledes. Soon after replacing Ninowski with three minutes left, Theofiledes found Brunet on a swing pass that resulted in a 39-yard scoring play. After an interception, Theofiledes directed a touchdown drive that ended on Pete Larson's 2-yard run.

Afterward, Williams refused to discuss Graham's coaching status with the press, although the coach's departure seemed imminent. By then, many players had become disenchanted with Graham's coaching decisions and had lost respect for the once great quarterback. Some players had taken the pleasure of ridiculing him for his intense, humorless approach, calling him "Toot," the reverse of Otto, behind his back. In the overall player consensus, he was a super-nice guy but simply not NFL coaching material.

"He came from the Coast Guard Academy to coach an NFL team, which he couldn't do," said linebacker Sam Huff, who played under Graham in his first two seasons in Washington. "He was a quarterback, so he tried to change Sonny's style of throwing the football. It just didn't work for him. He didn't click with the team. He wasn't a motivating coach."

According to Promuto, "When Graham came in, the perception was the guy was really tough. But he made the biggest mistake in the world. He told us how good we are. People saw a different side of him, that he wasn't as tough as his persona, and players failed to put out for him."

Such apathy would end with the entrance of an esteemed coaching figure.

## 1969: 7–5–2, 2ND PLACE— CAPITOL DIVISION

### Head Coach: Vince Lombardi

The NFL's 50th anniversary season was epochal not only for the league but for one of its oldest franchises, too.

The Redskins finished 7–5–2, their first winning season since 1955 and only their fourth in nearly a quarter-century. What's more, the breakthrough took place under the direction of one of the NFL's all-time coaching greats, Vince Lombardi.

Team President Edward Bennett Williams pulled off a coup to sign Lombardi, a winner of two Super Bowls, five NFL titles, and 73 percent of his games as Green Bay's coach from 1959 to 1967. After buying out the last two years of Otto Graham's contract, Williams made an enticing offer that lured Lombardi to Washington over other interested teams, including Philadelphia, New Orleans, Los Angeles, Boston of the American Football League, and even the Naval Academy.

The press reported that Williams persuaded the widow of former Redskins acting president Leo DeOrsey to sell 130 of the team's shares to the Redskins' other owners for $10,000 each. He then offered Lombardi a package of 50 shares, or 5 percent ownership; the role of executive vice president; and a $110,000 salary. The Packers, for whom Lombardi had served as general manager in 1968, released him from his contract.

The hiring reverberated across the nation's capital. Yes, a consummate winner had been recruited to stop the Redskins' extended string of mediocrity. That St. Vince was so idolized amplified his arrival even more. The D.C. press dubbed it "the second coming."

"The biggest news to hit Washington since Secretary of State Seward bought Alaska for two cents an acre is that Vince Lombardi, former coach of the Green Bay Packers, is coming here to take over the coaching of the Washington Redskins," *Washington Post* columnist Art Buchwald wrote. "For those who don't know anything about professional football, the significance of this move is comparable only to [President] Charles de Gaulle leaving France to become president of Yemen."

Williams introduced his prized catch to a packed room of media at the Sheraton-Carlton Hotel in Washington on February 6, 1969, saying, "Gentlemen, this is the proudest moment in my life."

Lombardi, for his part, asked rhetorically, "Why did I choose Washington among offers from other cities? Because it is the capital of the world. And I have some plans to make it the football capital." He said he picked the Redskins over other teams because "I like him," pointing at Williams. "I would like to have a winner in my first year, if possible," Lombardi added. "But we have got to have the right people. We will have to be fortunate with injuries. There will have to be a charisma between the teaching and the receiving. I will demand a commitment to excellence and to victory."

Unlike the 1–10–1 Packers squad Lombardi inherited in 1959, his Redskins sported a strong nucleus. The offense, which in 1968 finished third in points and fifth in passing yards in the NFL, possessed the firepower of quarterback Sonny Jurgensen, receiver Charley Taylor, and tight end Jerry Smith. (Record-setting flanker Bobby Mitchell retired before the season.) Also in place was a solid offensive line consisting of guards Vince Promuto and Ray Schoenke, center Len Hauss, and tackles Walt Rock and Jim Snowden. A defense that had been pathetic in recent years nonetheless featured talent in safeties Brig Owens and Rickie Harris, cornerback Pat Fischer, linebackers Chris Hanburger and Marlin McKeever, and defensive end Carl Kammerer.

Lombardi knew that cast would be insufficient to make the Redskins champions, so he reshuffled the roster. He signed free agents in cornerbacks Mike Bass and Ted Vactor, as well as Charley Harraway, an underrated running back and excellent blocker who had played three seasons in Cleveland. He also signed 11-year veteran quarterback Frank Ryan to back up Jurgensen.

Lombardi also traded for several players he once coached in Green Bay, such as safety Tom Brown, defensive end Leo Carroll, and receiver Bob Long. By opening day, 19 of the 40 players who suited up for the Redskins' last game in 1968 were gone, including nine starters.

Lombardi reassembled the coaching staff, too. He hired ex-Steelers head coach Bill Austin to direct the offensive line and ex-Rams head coach Harland Svare as defensive coordinator. He also retained two of Otto Graham's assistants, switching Mike McCormick from offensive line to defensive line and keeping Don Doll as defensive backfield coach. His most interesting coaching move was luring middle linebacker Sam Huff out of retirement to become a player-coach.

Lombardi's first extended look at his squad came in training camp, where he decided to keep three of the team's 14 draft picks: Oregon State All-American center John Didion, Southern University linebacker Harold McLinton, and Kansas State running back Larry Brown. The 5–10, 190-pound Brown, a secondary ball-carrier in college and an eighth-round draft pick, beat out 1967 first-round pick Ray McDonald, who was cut, for the starting job. Brown's explosiveness made him a threat the Redskins hadn't seen for years: a bona fide weapon in the backfield who could balance the potent aerial attack.

The key to the passing proficiency rested with Jurgensen, who by training camp was delivering balls as crisply as ever after injuries hampered his release in 1968. Lombardi marveled at his right arm, and though a future Hall of Fame inductee, Bart Starr, had quarterbacked the Packers during their glory years in the 1960s, the coach knew Jurgy was in a different league in terms of sheer talent. Jurgensen "is the best I've seen, and he may be the best the league has ever seen," Lombardi once said. "He hangs in there under adverse conditions."

Jurgensen earned a "super" rating from Lombardi in the season opener at New Orleans. He completed 10 of 23 passes for 229 yards, with touchdown passes of 10 and 51 yards to Taylor and 13 yards to Smith, as the Redskins recovered from a 10–0 deficit to win, 26–20.

It looked like two in a row after Jurgensen's 13-yard scoring pass to Bob Long created a 23–20 lead over the defending Eastern Conference–champion Browns late in the fourth period. Cleveland took possession on its 15 with 1:24 left, when quarterback Bill Nelson hit receiver Gary Collins, whom Pat Fischer had shut out all game, for a touchdown. The conversion accounted for the Browns' 27–23 win. Larry Brown made his first major impact, rushing for 95 yards on 14 carries, including a 57-yard run.

The next week, Jurgensen completed 27 of 39 passes for 258 yards and a touchdown in a 17–17 tie with the 49ers that left the Redskins at 1–1–1. Redskins kicker Curt Knight, who beat out Charlie Gogolak in the preseason for the starting job, barely missed a 56-yard field goal with time running out.

Knight was 4 for 4 in a 33–17 victory over St. Louis before a sellout crowd of 50,481 in the home opener at RFK Stadium, where a banner read, "Welcome St. Vince." (D.C. Stadium was renamed RFK Stadium after the June 1969 assassination of U.S. Senator Robert F. Kennedy.) Jurgensen completed 19 of 34 throws for 238 yards, with scoring passes to Taylor and Smith, who had become known as the "Charlie and Jerry show" by combining for superb receiving week after week. Brown ran for 82 yards and fullback Charlie Harraway added 75 more, while the defense intercepted five passes, two by Fischer.

The Redskins then crafted a come-from-behind 20–14 win over the Giants. Down 14–0 late in the third quarter, Washington scored three touchdowns in a 7:42 span; two scoring runs by Harraway tied the score at 14, and an 86-yard punt return by Rickie Harris put the Redskins up, 20–14. Washington's defense prevented any late heroics, stopping New York on three straight plays inside the 3. Brown was fabulous, carrying 17 times for 105 yards and catching three passes for 21 more, emitting more signs of his potential to be Washington's back of the future.

"Until Larry Brown came in, we were strictly a passing team," guard Vince Promuto said. "That was kind of tough because there was no secret on third down or second and long that we were going to pass with a great quarterback like Jurgensen. It put a lot of stress on the offensive line to make sure our quarterback didn't get hit. A lot of times there were lookouts, which meant, 'Look out, Sonny.' Then Larry Brown came, and it was just great. We had a much better balance."

It appeared that another Lombardi powerhouse was in the making when a 14–7 win over Pittsburgh raised Washington's record to 4–1–1. But the Redskins captured only one of their next five games and struggled to keep pace with the Capitol Division–leading Cowboys.

After a 41–17 loss to the Colts and a 28–28 tie with Philadelphia, the Redskins battled Dallas in another of their classic encounters. Jurgensen was brilliant for three quarters, throwing four scoring passes that helped his squad erase a 17-point deficit and pull within 34–28 late in the third period. But he tossed three interceptions in the fourth quarter, as the Cowboys pulled away for a 41–28 victory. Jurgy was 24 of 35 for 338 yards, Taylor caught six passes for 155, and Smith hauled in seven passes for 98 yards, including 27-, 29-, and 11-yard touchdowns. In attendance was President Nixon, who made the first appearance by a U.S. president at a Redskins regular-season game, according to the *Post*.

"Without Jurgensen, it would have been a Dallas cakewalk," said a 1969 Redskins game program. "With Jurgensen, the game became an epic struggle for 53 minutes, 51 seconds."

The Redskins rebounded with a 27–20 win over Atlanta. Jurgensen gave another seemingly unconscionable performance, completing 26 of 32 passes for 300 yards. Harraway caught six throws for 110 yards, including a screen pass he

Cameras rolled and pens hit notepads during Vince Lombardi's introductory press conference on February 6, 1969. But St. Vince played down his mystique. "It is not true that I can walk across the Potomac," he said. "Not even when it is frozen."

turned into a 64-yard scoring play that gave Washington a 24–20 third-quarter lead. Long caught 10 passes for 108 yards, and Brown topped the 100-yard mark for the second time.

The 5–3–2 Redskins were now two games behind division-leading Dallas—but 10–0 Los Angeles and its famed "Fearsome Foursome" defensive line, featuring future Hall of Famers Merlin Olsen and Deacon Jones, were too much for Washington. Jurgy was sacked six times for 52 yards in losses in a 24–13 Rams victory.

Dallas clinched the division title the next week with a win over Pittsburgh, although the Redskins also had some celebrating to do. They took second place with a 34–29 victory over Philadelphia behind an All-Pro performance by Brown, who rushed for a season-high 138 yards on only 19 carries. The Eagles led, 16–13, at halftime, but Redskins end John Hoffman recovered a third-quarter fumble in the end zone and Knight converted for a four-point Redskins lead. Brown ran for a score to put the Redskins up, 34–22, in the fourth period.

The Redskins then secured their first winning season in 14 years with a 17–14 triumph over New Orleans, raising their record to 7–4–2. They bolted to a 17-point first-half lead on Harraway's 12-yard touchdown run, his 30-yard scoring catch and Knight's 19-yard field goal. The underdog Saints charged back in the second half. Led by backup quarterback Ed Hargett, they crafted a 53-yard third-period scoring drive and a 97-yarder in the fourth to pull to within three, springing the boo-birds from the 50,354 fans at RFK.

Later, the Saints regained possession on their 30 with 5:20 left and reached the Redskins' 43. But New Orleans lost the ball on downs, and the Redskins ran out the clock. Despite a 20–10 loss to Dallas in the season-finale, the Redskins were winners in their first season under Lombardi.

How did he do it?

"He basically took a great offense and used it to its fullest, and forced the defense to play well enough to keep the football in the offense's hands," said Bobby Mitchell, who became a Redskins scout that year. "He said many times to our faces, 'God, if I'd have had this offense [in Green Bay].' He had Starr and all those guys, yet he couldn't believe that a team with the

## PROFILE

### Lombardi Injected Redskins with Winning Fever

"There's only one place in my game, and that's first place. There is a second place bowl game, but it is a game for losers played by losers. It is and always has been an American zeal to be first in anything we do, and to win, and to win, and to win."

Such words personified the flaming determination of Vince Lombardi, whose fierce desire to be victorious became infectious among his Redskins players. Many of them had never played on a winning team before his arrival in 1969. After one season under the coaching mastermind, many of those same players walked with a swagger.

"When we got Lombardi, that was the first time we could distinguish great coaches from coaches," said guard Vince Promuto, who played under three coaches in Washington before Lombardi. "He started us moving in the right direction."

The Redskins' first true taste of Lombardi came during minicamp and training camp before the 1969 season. The squad became acquainted with everything from "Lombardi Time," which required players to arrive at least 10 minutes early to a meeting, to his gruff demeanor, to his disdain for player cliques, to his emphasis on not only wanting to win but knowing *how* to win.

The latter point was critical, for the Redskins had folded in so many winnable games in recent years. Lombardi pointed them in the right direction by relying on key themes he had used so masterfully in Green Bay, one being his insistence on teamwork.

"He brought everyone together as a team and said you couldn't win it individually, but as a team you could succeed at almost anything," safety Brig Owens said. "He taught us that everyone had a responsibility, you couldn't afford to make mistakes, and that if everyone did their job properly that would be the creation of success on a particular play."

Lombardi believed in doing easy things with consistent excellence rather than complicated things poorly. A perfectionist, he required the Redskins to practice the same plays over and over again until executing them flawlessly, a strategy integral to making his celebrated power sweep so dominant in Green Bay. His practices were concise but intense, an hour and a half at the most, packed with a lot of repetition. "You don't do things right once in a while, you do them right all the time," he was known to say. He also remarked: "They call it coaching, but it is teaching. You do not just tell them it is so, you show them the reasons why it is so, and you repeat and repeat and repeat until they are convinced, until they know."

"You had to enroll in the way he was going to approach the game," cornerback Pat Fischer said. "We had to practice hard, and he wanted total concentration. He sometimes used a violent method of assailing someone. But it was almost by design, just to remind people it was possible that if you don't concentrate 100 percent, this is what's going to happen. He would say, 'We're going to practice for an hour and 30 minutes, now give me 100 percent. I want to practice as close to perfect as we can.'"

Lombardi was such a stickler for simplicity that he devoted time to teaching the Redskins basic fundamentals, something the previous regime of coach Otto Graham had mostly shunned. "It's all about blocking and tackling, gentlemen," he would say. "If you execute your job assignment, we'll win." Case in point: he showed his offensive linemen that firing off the ball faster and being more aggressive with blocking assignments gave them an edge on defenders.

"All you had to do was hit a defender right in the middle of the chest and push him backward while you stayed parallel to the line," Promuto said. "That way, the runner could pick a hole and didn't have to focus on a hole that was designated for the play. You didn't have to take crazy positions where if the guy was inside you, you had to block him to the outside, which was impossible to do."

Jurgensen said that the way Lombardi drew up and designed plays made them appear uncomplicated: "He'd say, 'They can't stop this play,' and you're thinking, 'This is a great football play, they can't stop it.' He would leave the room and an assistant coach would explain the same play, and you'd say, 'That play can't work.' It was because he had great teaching skills."

Lombardi also relied on psychological ploys he'd used in Green Bay. With his strong, commanding voice, he gave dynamic pep talks and confronted players nose to nose before games urging them to perform vigorously. He also elevated people beyond their mental breaking points to where they continued performing at peak level. For example, his "up-and-down" exercise—which called for running in place, hitting the ground, bouncing up, and moving forward, backward, and sideways—led players to extreme exhaustion, but they developed the intestinal fortitude to block it out. According to Promuto, someone may have been fatigued after 25 repetitions when the season began but could do perhaps 80 by season's end, thus preparing him for the stamina-testing fourth quarter of a football game.

Lombardi's bombastic, militaristic approach had little, if anything, to do with his intention to belittle anyone. He was just playing with their psyche, said receiver Bobby Mitchell, who retired just before the 1969 season but was kept on by Lombardi to serve as a Redskins scout. "He would earn respect by pushing you right to the breaking point where you said, 'If I get a club, I'll kill the old man,'" Mitchell said. "But he knew just when to pull you over and hug you and say, 'I'm starting you in the game, I expect you to do this.' He'd release you from your anger, and he knew when to give you back your manhood so you'd play your heart out for him."

Defensive end Carl Kammerer said of the coach, "Vince Lombardi was the greatest, and it probably took us six weeks to figure it out. He got in your face, and everybody would hear him say, 'Mister.' His voice would

## Lombardi Injected Redskins with Winning Fever—*continued*

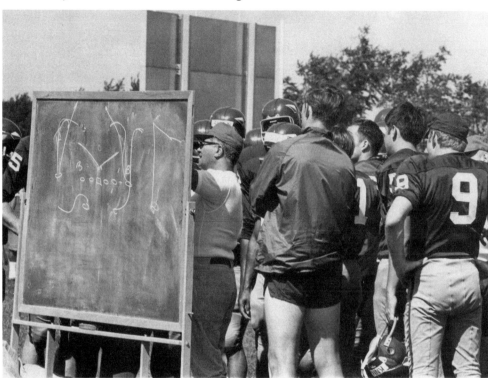

Lombardi goes over Xs and Os with his troops during training camp in 1969. The coach had "great teaching skills" and made everything seem uncomplicated, said quarterback Sonny Jurgensen (9).

ring everywhere. But you realized that all he was trying to do was get you to play at a level above where you were satisfied at playing. He knew there was more in you, and, by golly, he was going to get it out. He had that kind of spirit, fire and desire."

But not everybody appreciated Lombardi's law-and-order platform. Running back Bob Brunet quit before the 1969 season mostly because of the coach's constant yelling. Larry Brown said the old saying that Lombardi treated everyone like dogs was true. Center Len Hauss had reservations about him, too.

"The Lombardi year was the worst year I can ever recall in football for myself," said Hauss, who played for 14 seasons. "Mentally, it almost broke me. One day after practice, Sonny asked me, 'Isn't Lombardi great? He kicks you in the rear and screams at you and makes you give

100 percent.' I said, 'Sonny, that's great for you because you've got to have somebody do that. I give 100 percent, and I don't need that, and I really don't appreciate it.' If you thought you were giving 100 percent anyway, you didn't really like to have somebody call you a dirty rotten lazy dog and kick you in the rear to make you do better when you thought you were already doing the best you could."

Jurgensen speaks for most of his teammates, though, when saying Lombardi's no-nonsense philosophy, coupled with his gifted football mind and dynamic leadership skills, were welcomed: "We were in awe of him. He had won, and he knew what it took to win. It didn't take me any time to understand why Green Bay was so successful. He was by far the best coach I ever played for—the best coach anyone ever played for."

offense we had hadn't been winning like Green Bay. But Green Bay also had a hell of a defense."

Jurgensen steered the offense with one of his yeoman seasons, posting league highs in completions (274), attempts (442), and passing yards (3,102), plus 15 touchdown passes. Brown rushed for 888 yards, fourth best in the NFL, and just missed Rookie of the Year honors. Harraway's 55 catches were the most by an NFL running back. Taylor caught 71 passes, second most in the NFL, for 883 yards and eight touchdowns. His sidekick, Smith, caught 54 for 682 yards and nine scores. Jurgensen, Brown, and Smith made the Pro Bowl, as did Fischer, center Len Hauss, and linebacker Chris Hanburger.

Meanwhile, speculation was rampant that the Redskins were on track to becoming a contender under Lombardi. Their five losses came against teams with a 40–13–3 overall mark, and their seven wins equaled the number Green Bay posted in Vince's first season there in 1959. The nation's capital couldn't wait for the 1970 season to begin.

"We never thought in terms of the Green Bay Packers, we just knew how good we could be as a team," safety Brig Owens said. "We were thinking we could win a lot of games and be in the race for the championship. There was no play where the offense felt anybody could stop them. That's a lot of confidence."

## 1970: 6–8, 4TH PLACE— NFC EAST

### Head Coach: Bill Austin

The 1970 season was an emotional roller-coaster for the Redskins. The death of Vince Lombardi to cancer just before the season began deflated a team excited about building on its 7–5–2 record from 1969. Instead of making strides toward an NFL championship, the demoralized Redskins fell to 6–8.

"What a disaster," said Steve Gilmartin, the Redskins' radio voice at the time. "It was a real downer all the way around. The feeling was like, 'Oh boy, we're going to regress terribly.'"

Lombardi's health began to deteriorate months before the season started. He underwent exploratory surgery in June 1970, when doctors detected a tumor in his colon they believed to be benign. But his body continued to break down, forcing him to miss the start of training camp, and he tapped offensive coordinator Bill Austin as interim coach. Meanwhile, doctors discovered the tumor was malignant, and Lombardi's players knew that without a miracle, he was unlikely to return. "We knew something was seriously wrong because he wasn't at training camp," running back Larry Brown said.

Lombardi died at age 57 on September 3, 1970, about two weeks before the season opener. His loss was "devastating," Redskins safety Brig Owens told WRC-TV in Washington in 1999. "I don't think there was a guy on our team who didn't shed a tear. We knew we had the privilege of being in the presence of someone really great, and that we had the privilege of being coached by him."

Team president Edward Bennett Williams eulogized Lombardi by saying, "He had a covenant with greatness, more than any man I've ever known. He was committed to excellence in everything he attempted. Our country has lost one of its great men. The world of sport has lost its first citizen. The Redskins have lost their leader. I personally have lost a beloved friend."

The immortal coach was inducted into the Pro Football Hall of Fame in 1971. His .750 winning percentage (105–35–6 overall record) stands as the best ever for an NFL head coach with at least 100 career victories.

With little time to search for a replacement, Williams kept Austin in his interim role. Despite Austin's dubious head coaching record of 11–28–3 from 1966 to '68 in Pittsburgh, Williams liked that he was a disciple of Lombardi. After playing guard in the 1950s for the Giants when Lombardi coached the team's offense, Austin served as an offensive assistant under Lombardi in Green Bay from 1959 to '64. After his coaching stint in Pittsburgh, he joined Lombardi's staff in Washington in 1969.

Austin inherited a squad that Lombardi had predicted would be much improved from 1969, mostly because it had acquired a year of seasoning under one of the greatest coaches of all time. The Redskins were returning their landmark offensive sparkplugs in quarterback Sonny Jurgensen, wide receiver Charley Taylor, and tight end Jerry Smith, plus Larry Brown.

Brown was the Redskins' bright spot in the trying 1970 campaign. The second-year back became the first Redskin to rush for at least 1,000 yards in a season with 1,125, an NFL-high mark that earned him consensus All-Pro honors and his second straight Pro Bowl invitation. His yardage total also broke the squad's single-season rushing record of 951 set by Rob Goode in 1951.

The Redskins, playing with a sort of "win one for the Gipper" spirit in honor of Lombardi, finished 5–1 in an exhibition season that included a 17–14 win over Baltimore, the eventual Super Bowl champions. At the team's annual Welcome Home Luncheon, Williams predicted that the Redskins would post their best season since 1945, the last time they played in an NFL championship game.

"The loss of Vince Lombardi is an opportunity for greatness disguised as an insolvable problem," he told the audience. "This team is going to become addicted to succeed in his name. He has left us a fine football team and a fine coaching staff." Looking at Austin, Williams asked, "What higher accolade could come to any football coach than to be selected to succeed Vince Lombardi by Vince Lombardi?"

The season opened not as Williams envisioned. The 49ers rolled to a 26–17 victory behind a defense that sacked Jurgensen six times for 56 yards in losses and swatted away pass after pass. Brown, who ran 75 yards for a touchdown, pounded out 114 the next week in St. Louis, the first of six games that season he reached the century mark. But Jurgensen had another rough outing, throwing two interceptions that were returned for touchdowns in a 27–17 loss. Austin later scolded the perennial All-Pro. "It was the worst day of throwing I've ever seen Sonny have," the coach told reporters. "He didn't see the defenses."

Jurgy and the offense clicked in a 33–21 victory over the Eagles. He completed 14 of 28 passes for 139 yards and two scores, and Brown's 110-yard rushing day made him the NFL's top ground-gainer. The workhorse running back would battle such players as the Giants' Ron Johnson and Denver's Floyd Little for the league's No. 1 spot as the season progressed. Then came a 31–10 romp over Detroit in the home opener at RFK Stadium. Brown ran for 101 yards, while Jurgy completed 14 of 20 passes for 255 yards and three scores. The win was against an undefeated Lions team featuring the NFL's top-ranked defense.

The 2–2 Redskins had a chance to make it three straight before a national television audience in their first appearance on ABC's *Monday Night Football*, which was in its inaugural season. But their defense took the night off in a 34–20 loss at Oakland, Washington's first regular-season game ever against a former American Football League team. The Raiders amassed 458 yards, and quarterback Daryle Lamonica toyed with the Redskins' secondary (19 of 27, 232 yards, three scores).

Brown gained only 34 yards against Oakland, but he pounded out 110 to regain the NFC rushing lead in a 20–0 victory over Cincinnati at RFK, the Redskins' first shutout since 1964. Then came a 19–3 romp of the Broncos in a high-altitude game at Denver's Mile High Stadium, giving the Redskins nine straight quarters without allowing a touchdown—plus a 4–3 record. Washington's defense was so stifling that the Broncos entered Redskins territory only four times.

Austin had said that if the Redskins could reach the halfway mark at 4–3, they would be in solid shape down the stretch, for five of the squad's last seven games were at home. At the same time, the next five games were against teams contending for their division leads. Washington, plagued by injuries, mental mistakes, a defense that ultimately allowed the second-most rushing yards in the NFL, and perhaps an emotional hangover from the death of Lombardi, dropped all five.

The Redskins first lost 19–10 to a Minnesota squad sporting the NFL's best offense and defense, after which Austin still declared his 4–4 team should win the NFC East. But the Redskins relinquished a 19-point fourth-quarter lead to the Giants in a 35–33 loss, then fell to Dallas (45–21), the Giants (27–24), and Dallas (34–0). The season was essentially over for the 4–8 Redskins.

"The Redskins seem to have lost their spirit," *Washington Post* columnist Bob Addie wrote. "It has been a traumatic year starting with the death in September of Vince Lombardi. It was too much to ask that Bill Austin assemble the stunned elements and mold them into a winning ball club."

According to Larry Brown, "A lot of people were disappointed with [Lombardi's] passing, and it had somewhat of a negative impact on the team to the extent we didn't have a very good year. I'm not sure if the final record was solely related to his death or that we didn't make any deals to get new personnel. But it caught everyone by surprise that he wasn't going to be there."

Drama was still in order for the star running back. In missing the 34–0 loss to Dallas because of a knee injury, he lost the NFC's top rushing spot to Ron Johnson. He returned in the next game, a 24–6 victory over Philadelphia, with an 85-yard performance that vaulted him above the 1,000-yard barrier and back to the top of the NFL charts with 1,081. After surpassing 1,000 yards about eight minutes into the game, Brown walked off the field with the ball he had just carried, flashing a "V" sign as the 45,000 fans at RFK gave him a standing ovation.

After the game, someone near the Redskins' locker room told Edward Bennett Williams that the team's performance against the lowly Eagles was "a little better" than that during the five-game losing streak, the *Washington Evening Star* reported.

"I don't think so," Williams snapped.

It was no secret that Williams was disgusted with the erosion of the 1970 season and the booing that rained down from fans at RFK. But he had been quiet about whether Austin would continue in his post, a silence some interpreted to mean that he would be seeking another big-name coach. Candidates named in the press included Notre Dame coach Ara

Larry Brown walks to the sideline with the "1,000-yard" ball after becoming the first Redskin to top the coveted mark against the Eagles on December 13, 1970. He finished with 1,125 yards that season and 5,875 in his eight-year Redskins career, today the second-best mark in team history.

Parseghian and Los Angeles Rams coach George Allen, both of whom Williams had pursued in the past, plus Penn State coach Joe Paterno and former Oklahoma coach and then-ABC Sports analyst Bud Wilkinson.

Williams would make a decision that ignited a seminal period in Redskins history.

# 6

# 1971–1980: Long Drought Ends, Redskins Regain Winning Flair

IN REFLECTING on the NFL of the 1970s, the sheer dominance of a handful of teams stands out: the Pittsburgh Steelers, undefeated in four Super Bowls in the decade; the Dallas Cowboys, who reached the Super Bowl five times and won twice; and the Miami Dolphins, two-time Super Bowl winners who also posted the only undefeated season in NFL history.

The Washington Redskins sat on the next tier. The franchise with four winning seasons and no postseason appearances over a quarter-century came alive to record eight winning years in the 1970s.

The chief architect of that feat was the colorful George Allen, who coached the Redskins to a 69–35–1 overall record from 1971 to '77, a seven-year stretch that featured five playoff appearances and an NFC championship in 1972. The Redskins lost that year to Miami in Super Bowl VII and bowed out in the first round of the playoffs in the other four seasons.

"George Allen put the Washington Redskins' franchise on the map as far as I'm concerned," said defensive tackle Diron Talbert, a Redskin from 1971 to '80. "They'd been off the map for so many years. Then all of a sudden to turn it around and have seven consistent seasons of pretty good football. No Super Bowl wins, but we were in the playoffs a lot. We were just a hair short."

"The Redskins hadn't won in so long when I came here in '71," said Billy Kilmer, another key player in the Allen era. "That was kind of a new experience for everybody. We were the first team in so many years to make Washington a winning town."

Such success galvanized a championship-starved city where there was little else to root for on the pro sports front. The city's baseball franchise, the Washington Senators, jumped town right before the 1971 NFL season began and became the Texas Rangers. The basketball team, the Washington Capitals of the old American Basketball Association, moved to southern Virginia in 1970.

The football squad injected the nation's capital with a dose of Redskins mania far exceeding that of the franchise's early glory years. Burgundy and gold became the city's unofficial colors, and regular home sellouts continued at RFK Stadium, as the waiting list for Redskins season tickets became longer and longer. News from the team's new practice facility, Redskin Park, garnered a flood of local interest. Redskins merchandise sales skyrocketed, too. A banner at RFK encapsulated the city's infatuation with its football team: "Redskins: Love'M or Leave Town."

"The word 'Redskins' became in," said Steve Gilmartin, the team's radio play-by-play voice from 1964 to '73.

Case in point: After the Redskins shocked the Cowboys in 1971 to open the Allen regime at 3–0, Kilmer recalled a scene on the team's return to Dulles Airport in Virginia where the players couldn't leave because of a traffic jam that stretched 13 miles to the Capital Beltway: "The people were jam-packed, they came out there trying to see us. I knew then that we'd unlocked something here that's unbelievable, and that I'd never seen being in the league for 10 years. We got the fans enthused and really brought them alive. It just kept snowballing."

Kilmer was among a litany of Redskins who helped propel the Redskins to success. The list included fellow Allen acquisitions in Talbert, defensive end Ron McDole, safety Kenny Houston, wide receiver Roy Jefferson, linebacker Brad Dusek, and running back Mike Thomas. They and other newcomers teamed with existing Redskins standouts in quarterback Sonny Jurgensen, wide receiver Charley Taylor, running back Larry Brown, tight end Jerry Smith, center Len Hauss, cornerback Pat Fischer, safety Brig Owens, and linebacker Chris Hanburger. The wily veteran-laden squad took on almost a folk image, operating through most of the 1970s under the moniker of the "Over the Hill Gang."

"For the first time, they firmly believed they could win," Gilmartin said. "When Vince Lombardi was there for just the 1969 season, some of the veterans bought into it, but they didn't feel as though they were going to be contenders. They figured they would be respectable. When they looked at the talent that, say, the Dallas Cowboys had, and they knew they'd have to play them twice in one season, realistically they said, 'We're not going to beat the Cowboys, the Cowboys are going to beat us.' In 1971, they became a very confident football team."

The Redskins' winning ways made them a hit with TV networks. They were among the top teams in national television appearances in the 1970s, including 16 games on ABC's *Monday Night Football*, which became a national spectacle as the NFL took on a prime-time image. Fascination in the Redskins even consumed members of Congress, some of whom disliked not being able to see the Redskins play at home because of the NFL's television blackout rule and threatened legislative action against the league, according to *Total Football II: The Official Encyclopedia of the National Football League.* The NFL eventually adopted a rule in 1973 allowing the blackout to be lifted if a game is sold out 72 hours in advance.

It didn't take long for Redskins mania to swell during the George Allen era. Here, some 10,000 Redskins fans welcome their team home following a 20–16 upset of the Cowboys in 1971.

Plus, the Redskins helped position the NFC East as one of the most feared divisions in the league. The division, one of six formed through the merger of the NFL and American Football League in 1970, consisted of the Redskins and Cowboys, whose rivalry reached a fever pitch in 1970s, plus the Giants, Philadelphia, and St. Louis.

"George Allen raised the bar in our division, no doubt about it," Cowboys Hall of Fame defensive tackle Bob Lilly said. "When we improved, the Redskins would improve, and pretty soon the Giants and Eagles were improving, and soon our division was much stronger. We won a Super Bowl, and the Redskins went to the Super Bowl."

The Redskins never had a losing season under Allen. But Redskins president Edward Bennett Williams lost patience with the intractable coach and dismissed him after his second nonplayoff season, 1977. His departure ended an era that the coach's son, also named George Allen, described as a period of "Camelot."

"I don't know if you'll ever have another team that had all those characters," said Redskins Hall of Fame safety Kenny Houston, who played five seasons under Allen. "That team had so many characters that will be remembered for a long, long time. All the older people related to that particular group. The team kind of took on a national appearance. It was very, very special."

The torch was passed to Allen disciple Jack Pardee, who registered a .500 mark over three seasons in Washington without making the playoffs. He was fired after his final year, 1980.

## 1971: 9–4–1, 2ND PLACE—NFC EAST

### Head Coach: George Allen

The Future Is Now. The Over the Hill Gang. The Ramskins. Sonny vs. Billy. George Allen. The Redskins-Cowboys rivalry.

Each one evolved as a subtheme to the Redskins' joyous 1971 campaign, when the squad posted a 9–4–1 mark good enough for its first playoff appearance and only its fifth winning year since 1945. The Redskins lost in the first round of the playoffs to San Francisco—a blip in an otherwise unforgettable season in team history.

The turnaround from a 6–8 season in 1970 can be explained in two words: George Allen. The Redskins' new coach rejuvenated the squad with a brazen style that led to his selection as NFL Coach of the Year by the Associated Press, *Pro Football Weekly,* and the *Sporting News.* He was also named NFC Coach of the Year by United Press International.

This was the second time Allen had transformed a struggling franchise. After taking over a Los Angeles Rams team in 1966 with seven straight losing seasons, he compiled a 49–17–4 record over five winning years that included two playoff appearances. His sweetest year was 1967, when the Rams finished with the best record in team history at 11–1–2. He earned NFL Coach of the Year honors from UPI and *Sporting News* and shared the AP award.

Allen didn't get along with Rams owner Dan Reeves, though, and was fired after the 1970 season. Redskins president Edward Bennett Williams, intrigued by Allen since the

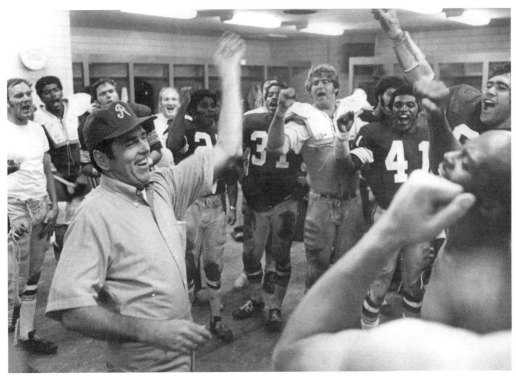

With the animated George Allen as their coach, the Redskins often showed the enthusiasm of high school kids. "Let's have three cheers for the Washington Redskins," he'd say after a big win. "Hip, hip, hooray. Hip, hip, hooray. Hip, hip, hooray." But the postgame atmosphere was vastly different following losses in the Allen era. "If we lost . . . it was like a funeral," said his son, George Allen.

two met at a league meeting several years back, proceeded to snatch the coach with help from Redskins minority owner Jack Kent Cooke, who came to know Allen when he owned the NBA's Los Angeles Lakers and the NHL's Los Angeles Kings.

After firing beleaguered Redskins coach Bill Austin in early 1971, Williams made Allen the highest-paid coach in NFL history at the time, with a reported seven-year contract carrying an annual salary of $125,000. The contract included benefits such as the home of Allen's choice worth up to $150,000, a car and chauffeur, and hefty bonuses for reaching the playoffs. Allen also received an option to buy 5 percent of the Redskins' stock and the authority of a general manager, allowing him to sign, cut, and trade players and negotiate their contracts.

Williams introduced Allen to the media at the Redskins' D.C., office on January 6, 1971, calling him the finest football coach in the business. "We have had a losing syndrome for 15 seasons with one exception," Williams said. "The fans are impatient. I think we are obliged to get the best possible coach and personnel. I think we have taken a dramatic step in signing George Allen." He added, "I am saying unequivocally, unqualifiedly and unambiguously, that this is the last coach I will ever hire."

Allen's arrival kicked off a wave of breaking off-season news. The period was highlighted by his rapid-fire trades and his desire to swap future draft picks for grizzled veterans who he felt would bring immediate success. In the process, the coach promised not to make the fans wait several years for a winner and issued his self-proclaimed motto, "The Future Is Now!"

In his first move, he obtained Saints quarterback Billy Kilmer for reserve linebacker Tom Roussel and a pair of mid-level draft choices. Kilmer, a 10-year veteran with average passing skills but a competitive fire that made him a leader, was projected as the backup to long-time superstar Sonny Jurgensen.

Later on draft day, Allen pulled off an audacious deal with his former team. He sent seven draft choices and linebacker Marlin McKeever for six Rams, including the starting linebacker corps of Jack Pardee, Myron Pottios, and Maxie Baughan; defensive tackle Diron Talbert; guard John Wilbur; special teams star Jeff Jordan, and a fifth-round draft choice. They and other acquisitions from L. A. would become known as the "Ramskins."

The addition of Pardee, Pottios, and Baughan, each of whom was at least 30 years old and contributed to a trio with 34 years of NFL experience, met Allen's penchant for coaching seasoned veterans over untested rookies, who he thought made too many mistakes. Those three, plus the 6–5, 255-pound Talbert—the key newcomer in the transaction, in Allen's view—helped satisfy the coach's goal of upgrading one of the worst defenses in the league in 1970. The deal would also help meet Allen's philosophy of relying on a tough, opportunistic defense that put his traditionally unexciting, mistake-free offense in position to score.

"This is great, terrific for the Redskins," Allen told reporters. "We've upgraded our defense at least 25 percent. It's worth at least two victories. Our goal now is nine or ten wins."

The trade also excited Allen's friend, President Nixon, who responded enthusiastically in a letter to the coach: "Great trade. I'm predicting the Redskins for a championship in '71 or '72."

The deal mystified those who thought Allen's swap of young for old would handcuff the team's ability to win. But it was hard to doubt Allen's keen eye for talent or lack thereof, an attribute he once used to sucker the Redskins into one of their most embarrassing trades ever.

In Los Angeles before the 1968 season, Allen sent Heisman Trophy-winning quarterback Gary Beban to Washington for a first-round draft choice, although many NFL experts believed that the rookie was worth no more than a second-round pick. Edward Bennett Williams, who took the bait from Allen, signed Beban to a three-year, no-cut contract worth a reported $350,000. But Beban was a flop, and the Redskins cut him after the 1970 season. Allen nearly manipulated former Redskins coach Otto Graham, too, into trading future Hall of Fame receiver Charley Taylor.

Meanwhile, Allen continued dealing draft choices like a deck of cards for solid veteran players, some of whom had become disgruntled with their teams. He further bolstered the defense by acquiring three ends, including Verlon Biggs, a three-time all-American Football League selection with the Jets, and fellow AFL star Ron McDole of the Bills.

"We had an unusual group of guys," safety Brig Owens said. "They were renegades, guys whose careers had been washed up. George brought guys in to play a specific role and nothing else."

Allen considered special teams tantamount to the defense as the most critical phases of football. He thus obtained San Diego's Leslie "Speedy" Duncan, who had tallied more than 5,000 yards in punt and kickoff returns in his career. Allen was counting on Duncan to improve the team's dismal punt return average of less than 2 yards in 1970. And in another acquisition of a big-time player, Allen obtained Colts flanker Roy Jefferson for receiver Cotton Speyrer, the Redskins' top draft choice in 1971.

On the coaching front, Allen brought in five of his Rams assistants: Ted Marchibroda (offensive coordinator); LaVern "Torgy" Torgeson (defensive coordinator), a Redskins linebacker in the mid-1950s; Boyd Dowler (receivers); Joe Sullivan (assistant coach); and Marv Levy (special teams).

The Redskins came to look drastically different from their 1970 team. In wheeling and dealing, Allen had swapped seven players and 24 draft picks for 19 new veterans on the 40-man roster, which featured 10 new starters, mostly on defense. They would team with established members of that unit such as Brig Owens, linebacker Chris Hanburger, and cornerback Pat Fischer.

Moreover, 11 players were 30 years of age or older, giving the popular inscription on the Statue of Liberty—"Give Me Your Old, Your Tired, Your Weak, Your Infirmed"—sort of a Redskins flavor. The squad's geriatric image prompted *Washington Evening Star* sportswriter Steve Guback to conceive of a moniker, the "Over the Hill Gang." "Allen has overhauled the Redskins' scene more than anybody since [Redskins founder] George Marshall marched the whole club down here from Boston in 1937," Guback wrote on July 4, 1971.

The remodeled Redskins split their first four exhibition games and then suffered a setback in a 27–10 loss at Miami. Quarterback Sonny Jurgensen fractured a bone in his left shoulder while making a tackle on an interception return, sidelining him for at least six weeks. Allen, who had touted Jurgy as one of the greatest quarterbacks in football, called the injury a "severe blow." In stepped veteran backup Billy Kilmer, who completed 15 of 24 passes for 175 yards and two touchdowns in a 17–17 tie with Cincinnati in the preseason finale.

Another of the graybeards, or "old geezers" as Allen called them, starred in the season opener at St. Louis. Thirty-three-year-old safety Richie Petitbon, one of the "Ramskins," intercepted a career-high three passes, one of which set up the Redskins' first touchdown and another of which sealed a 24–17 win over the Cardinals. Washington's tenacious defense forced seven turnovers, one being a fumble that Hanburger returned 16 yards for a touchdown. The win improved Allen's opening-day coaching record to 6–0.

Kilmer completed only six passes in Allen's ball-control offense. But he connected on 23 of 32 for 309 yards and two touchdowns the next week in a 30–3 flogging of the Giants at Yankee Stadium. The offense amassed 427 yards, while the defense was again masterful, holding the Giants to 156.

Suddenly, a town so accustomed to Redskins' mediocrity began asking if their 2–0 start was a fluke or a sign of things to come. That question was answered unequivocally against

George Allen's imports from Los Angeles, the Ramskins: (back, left to right) John Wilbur, Diron Talbert, Allen, Maxie Baughan, Myron Pottios; (front, left to right) Tommy Mason, Boyd Dowler, Jack Pardee, Jeff Jordan

## Allen: "Tell Alex Karras I Said Hello"

Alex Karras made a name for himself as a pro football star, a television actor, and a comedian. There's an asterisk beside his name in Redskin lore.

As part of his quest to stock the Redskins with seasoned veterans, George Allen wanted to acquire the 36-year-old defensive tackle off waivers a few days before the 1971 season began. The four-time All-Pro, recently released by Detroit, refused to go to Washington. He said he wanted to play on a contending team and insinuated that the Redskins couldn't win without quarterback Sonny Jurgensen, who was sidelined for a few weeks with an injured shoulder.

Allen ridiculed the stubborn Karras. "A blow to us? Heck no," the coach told the *Evening Star*. "He's been a great pro, and now they put him on waivers. I know what it's like to get hurt like that, mentally." The coach had another pointed message for Karras after the Redskins' 24–17 season-opening win over St. Louis: "Tell Alex Karras I said hello."

- "Hail to the Over the Hill Gang"
- "Deadskins Come Alive"
- "Life Begins at 30"
- "Kill 'em Kilmer"
- "Like a Fine Wine, the Redskins Have Come of Age"
- "There Is Never a Blue Monday when the Redskins Play on Sunday. We're No. 1."

Washington's defense took over from there in a 22–13 victory, compensating for a sputtering offense that failed to score a touchdown on four possessions inside the Oilers' 20. Defensive end Ron McDole intercepted a pass and returned it 18 yards for the Redskins' only touchdown, while the defense held Houston to 62 yards and three points in the second half. Curt Knight kicked a Redskins-record five field goals.

The oldest of the newly acquired "old-geezers," 35-year-old linebacker Jack Pardee, then stole the show. A cancer survivor, Pardee intercepted three passes and forced a fumble to key a 20–0 victory over St. Louis at RFK Stadium that lifted the Redskins to 5–0. The crowd chanted, "Par-DEE, Par-DEE, Par-DEE" for the man who was named AP Defensive Player of the Week. The Redskins offense piled up 349 yards, and Larry Brown ran for a career-high 150.

The Redskins' fifth win, their first 5–0 start since 1940, coincided with a Dallas loss, leaving Washington two games ahead of the Cowboys in the NFC East. All the while, the football landscape was captivated by the surprising squad. Allen was pictured on the cover of *Newsweek* magazine, which ran an article titled, "Pro Football's Red-Hot Redskins." A *Sports Illustrated* article was headlined, "Ice Cream Man Cometh: George Allen, Coach of the Redskins," in reference to Allen's proclivity for ice cream.

"Washington, D.C., was going absolutely nuts," defensive tackle Bill Brundige said. "You walk into a restaurant, I couldn't buy a drink or something to eat because of the fans. It was just crazy."

The party ended temporarily, as the Redskins stumbled against a Kansas City team two seasons removed from winning Super Bowl IV. Washington built a 17–6 halftime lead largely due to the outstanding play of Charley Taylor, who caught seven passes for 125 yards and two touchdowns. But his second touchdown was costly. In crossing the goal line to complete a 36-yard pass from Kilmer, he broke his ankle while being tackled from behind, ending his season. Washington's offense collapsed in the second half, when the Chiefs rolled up 237 yards and another Taylor, Otis, caught five passes for 105 yards and two touchdowns, including a one-handed grab in the end zone for the winning score in a 27–20 Chiefs win.

Allen and the Redskins were despondent afterward. (The coach later said that the Redskins would have at least won the NFC East title with a healthy Taylor.) Even so, 10,000 maniacal fans braved the rain and fog to offer cheers and support upon the team's return to Dulles Airport, another sign of the city's emotional outpouring for its favorite sports franchise. The crowd sang "Hail to the Redskins" and shouted "We're still number one!"

The Redskins rebounded with a 24–14 win over New Orleans that, coupled with the Cowboys' loss to Chicago, again put Washington two games ahead in the NFC East. Kilmer completed 13 of 22 passes for 204 yards against his former team. He also ran 2 yards for a touchdown and passed 36

the 2–0 Cowboys, the defending NFC champs and winners of 15 of their last 16 games. "This is the team to beat for the championship," Kilmer told the press. "We're ready, we're eager. This will make our whole season if we beat them in Dallas."

The Redskins did just that before 70,000 fans in the rain-soaked Cotton Bowl. Fullback Charley Harraway ran 57 yards into the end zone on the third play from scrimmage, and Kilmer threw a 50-yard touchdown pass to Roy Jefferson on a play-action pass—the offense's new secret weapon—for a 14–0 lead. The Redskins maintained the lead with the help of a defense that stifled a dangerous Dallas offense and held the NFC's top rushing team to 82 yards in a 20–16 Redskins win. The defense's performance, in fact, exemplified the whole 1971 season, when the Redskins allowed about 100 yards rushing per game, intercepted a league-high 29 passes and yielded 13.6 points per game.

Washington's postgame locker room was a sea of jubilation led by the gleeful Allen. "Men, I know this is an overworked word, but it was a great, great victory, a complete team victory," he said. "Nobody gave us a chance, but we thought we could win if we played our game and didn't make mistakes."

Back home, a city starving for a winning sports franchise was in a frenzy over the 3–0 Redskins, the only undefeated, untied team in the NFL. An estimated 10,000 fans greeted the Redskins upon their return to Dulles Airport in Virginia, while an *Evening Star* headline asked, "What Hath George Allen Wrought?"

Fan appreciation was rampant in the home opener against Houston. A record RFK Stadium crowd of 53,041 gave a three-minute standing ovation before the game, as the Redskins were introduced one by one. Banners hung all around:

yards for another score to Brown, who rushed for 113. Fischer returned an interception 53 yards for the final touchdown.

Kilmer also threw two picks on an offense that looked inept at times, a harbinger of the mighty struggles it would endure. Taylor's season-ending injury and leg ailments incurred by Brown, who gained only 110 yards over the next four weeks, ground the offense to a virtual halt. The Redskins would score only one touchdown in a span of 15 quarters, at the same time losing their hold on first place in the NFC East.

First came a 7–7 tie with lowly Philadelphia, a game the Redskins nearly lost until Kilmer hit Clifton McNeil, a one-time NFL receiving champ acquired by Allen to replace Taylor, on a 32-yard scoring pass with four minutes left. The Eagles failed to get off a 35-yard field goal attempt as time expired. But Kilmer was booed by an RFK Stadium crowd disenchanted with his four interceptions and excessive conservative rushing calls. For the first time, there were signs of a quarterback controversy pitting Kilmer against Jurgensen, whom Allen had reactivated before the game.

Allen, who had declared himself a "one quarterback man," was later adamant with reporters about his starter: "Kilmer's my quarterback. At no time did I consider replacing Kilmer with Sonny Jurgensen." He relented, but not before the Redskins were hurt by a bizarre play. Washington led the Bears, 15–9, early in the fourth quarter, thanks to Knight's five field goals, until a Chicago touchdown tied the game at 15. The snap was high on the conversion, and holder and quarterback Bobby Douglass chased after it. From about the 35, he unleashed a wobbly, floating pass to 250-pound linebacker Dick Butkus, who had lined up as a backfield blocker and was eligible as a receiver. Butkus lunged into the end zone and cradled the ball for a 16–15 lead.

Allen called on Jurgensen with about two minutes left. The redhead shook off his rust and led a 41-yard drive that set up a 45-yard field goal try by Knight with seconds remaining. The kick, caught in a strong crosswind, just missed.

Afterward, Allen spoke incredulously of the Redskins' bad luck, from Butkus's catch, which the coach called a "10,000 to one play," to Knight's missed field goal. He also affirmed that Kilmer, who completed 20 of 30 mostly dump-off passes for 163 yards, would remain his starting quarterback for the upcoming showdown against Dallas at RFK.

In what players from both teams were calling a "championship" game, the Redskins fell quietly, 13–0, and lost their NFC East lead. Dallas got all the points it needed on a 29-yard first-quarter touchdown run by quarterback Roger Staubach. Washington's feeble offense rushed for 65 yards, while Kilmer completed 10 of 16 passes for 118 yards and no interceptions. By halftime, the crowd of 53,041 at RFK was incessantly booing his unspectacular performance and chanting, "We Want SONNY! We Want SONNY!" Allen summoned No. 9 late in the third quarter, but he threw two interceptions.

With four games left, the 6–3–1 Redskins needed resuscitation. President Nixon and D.C. Mayor Walter Washington offered their help. At the team's new training facility, Redskin Park, both men gave emotional speeches in which they told the players how important the Redskins were to the community and that the fans were proud of their team. Nixon also predicted that the Redskins would probably win three of their last four games and make the playoffs.

That's exactly what happened, beginning with a 20–13 win over the Eagles. Jurgensen started but suffered another shoulder injury that forced him to the sidelines early in the second quarter. Kilmer stepped in and threw a 28-yard score to Jefferson just before halftime, the offense's first touchdown in three games. Cornerback Mike Bass returned an interception 38 yards for a 20–6 Redskins lead in the fourth quarter.

Allen and his buddy, President Richard Nixon, lead practice drills at Redskin Park in 1971. With the 6–3–1 Redskins winless in three straight games, Nixon visited Redskin Park to give his favorite football team a pep talk. The Redskins proceeded to win three of their last four games and make the playoffs for the first time in a quarter-century.

Nixon and Allen were similar in various ways, including their passionate disdain for the press. They were also industrious men who yearned to win. Allen was thus dubbed "Nixon with a whistle." "My father loved the competitiveness of President Nixon," the younger George Allen said.

"Geez, I'm glad to get that seventh victory," Kilmer told the press. "It's been a long time coming. Number seven is harder to come by than rolling one in Las Vegas."

With Kilmer back in the starting role, the Redskins recorded a 23–7 win over the Giants, marking the first time Washington had beaten New York twice in one season since 1953. Oft-injured Larry Brown returned to his old form, gaining 129 yards on 25 carries, while the Redskins' defense intercepted five passes. The 8–3–1 squad was now entering its biggest game of the season and the most monumental one of Allen's career against the 7–4–1 Rams—his former team.

Dubbed the "George Allen Bowl," the game featured elements of a heavyweight title fight: a record Monday night television audience of 66 million and a crowd of 80,000 at the Los Angeles Coliseum, playoff implications for both squads, and a bevy of pregame jawing. Rams quarterback Roman Gabriel vowed to jam the ball down Allen's mouth, and Rams defensive end Deacon Jones said L. A., listed as seven-point favorites, would "blow" Washington off the field. Allen said his defense would shut down the Rams "gadget" offense, and Redskins defensive tackle Diron Talbert declared Los Angeles would make enough mistakes for Washington to win. To add to the drama, eight Redskin players, including Talbert, and five coaches were ex-Rams. "I remember before playing that game the tension in the locker room . . . you could cut it with a knife," Kilmer said.

The classic opened not to the Redskins' liking. Four minutes into the game, the Rams took a 7–0 lead on Kermit Alexander's 82-yard interception return. An unruffled Kilmer retaliated with a bomb to Jefferson, who caught the ball between two defenders and ran into the end zone to complete a 70-yard scoring play. After an exchange of field goals, Kilmer threw a 32-yard scoring pass to Clifton McNeal for a 17–10 Redskins' lead two minutes before halftime.

Then came what Allen called the turning point in the game. The Rams fumbled on the ensuing kickoff, and the Redskins recovered at the 8. A penalty moved the ball to the 2, but Brown couldn't punch it through on three straight runs. Not known for taking risks, Allen chose to go for it on fourth down. Brown, sweeping wide to the right, cut behind Charley Harraway's devastating block on Alexander and scored.

Washington scored again to take a 31–10 lead early in the third quarter, though the Rams closed the gap to seven late in the game and had one last chance with 35 seconds left. But Speedy Duncan intercepted Gabriel's pass and returned it 46 yards for a score that clinched a wild card playoff spot for the burgundy and gold.

The Redskins' postgame locker room was euphoric. Allen received a game ball, as did Jefferson (eight catches, 137 yards, two touchdowns) and Kilmer (14 of 19, 246 yards, two scores). The ecstatic coach led his customary "hip-hip-hooray" cheer after a Redskins win and told his team: "This is a great, great victory. It's the best win of our lives. Men, let's just go on from here."

"It was 15 minutes of crazy bedlam in the locker room, and George was leading it all, jumping up and down," Jefferson recalled. "He looked like a toy that you'd just wound up, jumping and clapping. It was truly exciting."

Talbert said, "We were really charged up for the game. You can imagine, all of us being let go, traded. The Redskins needed that win to make it all work for them. It was a victory we would not be denied. We whipped them from top to bottom the whole game."

With no chance to win the NFC East, the Redskins were flat in the season finale against playoff-bound Cleveland, losing 20–13 to finish 9–4–1. It was the most Redskins victories since 1942, when they finished 10–1 before winning the NFL championship game.

In the week preceding the playoffs, the Redskins got news that four players made the Pro Bowl: Larry Brown, who was stopped 52 yards short of his second straight 1,000-yard season; center Len Hauss; Jefferson, who caught 47 passes for 701 yards and four touchdowns; and Curt Knight, the NFC's leading scorer with 114 points. Brown was also named to the UPI All-NFC team, as was linebacker Jack Pardee. Hauss, Jefferson, and safety Richie Petitbon made the second team, while Kilmer, defensive end Ron McDole, and cornerback Mike Bass received honorable mention recognition.

It was on to San Francisco to face the NFC West champion 49ers, a team well familiar to Allen from his coaching days down the coast in Los Angeles.

## NFC DIVISIONAL PLAYOFF GAME
### San Francisco 24, Washington 20
### December 26, 1971
### Candlestick Park, San Francisco
### Attendance: 45,364

## Uncharacteristic Mistakes Doom Redskins

It sounds so simplistic, but it was vintage George Allen. The Redskins' coach emphasized that the key to beating San Francisco in an opening-round playoff game would rest with his squad avoiding mental errors. Washington's pregame motto was "hit and no mistakes."

Allen was prophetic. Two uncharacteristic letdowns by his beloved special teams, a blocked field goal and a bungled snap on a punt, led to a 10-point swing in San Francisco's favor. Toss in an interception that helped set up a 49ers touchdown, plus an unsuccessful fourth-down conversion attempt that gave San Francisco momentum en route to another touchdown—and the 49ers exited with a 24–20 victory.

"I'm only going to say this once," Allen abruptly told reporters afterward. "I'm very proud of our football team. We had a great season. We overcame a great deal of adversity to get this far. We made too many mistakes, and they didn't make any, that's why we lost. I said before the team making the fewest mistakes would win."

The loss was tough for Allen to swallow. Falling to a team he held a 6–3–1 record against from his days in Los Angeles left his career playoff record at 0–3. Redskins players were also dejected, knowing they came up short against a team they matched up well with on paper.

Moreover, the 49ers lost twice to NFC West rival Los Angeles, which Washington had routed two weeks prior. If not for that Redskins win, in fact, the 49ers would have missed the playoffs. "Our players would rather play the 49ers than the Rams," Allen said beforehand. "It's difficult to beat a team twice and do it in three weeks. Even though they lost to the Rams twice, I think the 49ers are a better football team."

## PROFILE

### A State-of-the-Art Practice Facility: Redskin Park

George Allen was flabbergasted. On bringing his Los Angeles Rams to D.C. to play the Redskins in 1969, he told then-Redskins coach Vince Lombardi it was inconceivable how Lombardi prepared his team for games in such an antiquated system.

The Redskins worked out at a practice field near RFK Stadium. Players carried their uniforms and gear to and from the field. There was no security, and onlookers often interrupted training sessions. The Redskins sometimes traveled to sandlot and high school practice fields because their regular field was under water, frozen, or unplayable. Even the meeting rooms at the team's downtown D.C. office were in poor condition.

Allen tried to remedy the situation after becoming Redskins coach, and he wouldn't tolerate a stopgap measure; it had to be something bold and futuristic in nature. The man known as a pro football visionary thus called for the creation of a state-of-the-art training and administrative complex—one that outdistanced the practice facility of any other NFL team by the time it opened just before the 1971 season. It was called Redskin Park.

Built on seven acres of land near Dulles Airport in Northern Virginia, Redskin Park featured a full-length grass practice field and a smaller artificial turf surface. Next to the fields was a two-story, 22,500-square-foot building consisting of every amenity a football team would want: large and small meeting rooms, carpeted locker rooms, training rooms, weight rooms, equipment storage rooms and film rooms; a whirlpool, sauna, handball courts, and basketball area; and offices for a doctor and a dentist. Each coach and scout had a private office

with his own projector, and a 70-car parking lot sat in front of the building. The structure "contained more treasures than King Tut's tomb," Bill Gildea and Kenneth Turan wrote in their 1972 book, *The Future Is Now.*

The innovation met Allen's goal of establishing "everything under one roof" at a complex for year-round use. "The Redskin players will no longer be a bunch of gypsies," he proclaimed upon the opening of Redskin Park. "Redskin Park is like everything else we do, have done and will continue to do. It will help us win. We are not interested in anything that won't help us win."

The facility's isolation was also critical to Allen. It sat about 35 miles way from the hustle and bustle of downtown Washington, nestled in a remote, forested area called Dulles Industrial Aerospace Park. Nothing could conceivably distract the team during meetings and practice sessions. The location was similar to how Allen's Rams practiced at a facility about a half-hour from Los Angeles.

"George knew he had to have a practice field away from the city so our minds would be directed at football," Redskins quarterback Billy Kilmer said. "There was nothing out there at the time. It was just farm fields and practice fields. The nearest bar was about five miles away. We were isolated. But it was a fine facility."

*Evening Star* sportswriter Steve Guback said, "I remember when I saw it for the first time, kids were riding horses out there. It was nature and the law."

Allen enforced the law in what became his own little kingdom. To maintain privacy, he closed all practices to the public and surrounded the grounds with a fence. Tall trees, another sort of security blanket, flanked all sides

Redskin Park: "Everything under one roof."

## A State-of-the-Art Practice Facility: Redskin Park—*continued*

of the fields; Allen gave the trees such names as "Pignut Hickory" and "Virginia Pine." The often suspicious coach also hired a security man, retired California policeman Ed "Double-0" Boynton, to scrupulously patrol the grounds with a keen eye for trespassers and spies. The media came to mock Redskin Park as "Camp Paranoia," "The Bunkers," and "Fort Allen." "Redskin Park had the secrecy of the CIA with the aura of a mental institution," Jennifer Allen, the coach's daughter, wrote in her 2000 memoir, *Fifth Quarter: The Scrimmage of a Football Coach's Daughter.*

Redskin Park also gave Allen a reputation as a free spender. The coach, never hesitant about dishing out big bucks if he thought it would satisfy his bottom line—winning—requested a half-million dollars for the facility, a figure approved by team president Edward

Bennett Williams and the Redskins' board. Williams, who had given Allen an open-ended expense account, nevertheless voiced his concern that the investment was steep. "When Coach Allen came to Washington, we agreed he had an unlimited budget," Williams said at the team's 1971 Welcome Home Luncheon. "He has already exceeded it."

The coach was perturbed by that remark, according to Redskins Hall of Fame linebacker Sam Huff, who was at the luncheon. "George Allen got right up to the microphone and lashed at him," Huff said. "He said, 'You want to win or not? You brought me in here to win, this is what it takes. Don't be counting the money.'"

The Redskins remained at the facility for the next two decades.

---

San Francisco was slightly favored in the Redskins' first postseason game in 26 years, but the 49ers committed the first big mistake in the wet, windy conditions. Redskin Jon Jaqua blocked a punt and fell on it at the 49ers' 28. A few plays later, quarterback Billy Kilmer's 5-yard scoring pass to tight end Jerry Smith put the Redskins up, 7–0.

After an exchange of field goals, the Redskins threatened again late in the first half. Speedy Duncan, the NFL's top punt returner, ran one back 47 yards to the 49ers' 12 with about 30 seconds to play, setting up a perfect opportunity to take

momentum into the locker room. The ultraconservative Allen then tried a gimmick play. Kilmer called an end around to receiver Roy Jefferson, who was thrown for a 13-yard loss. (Redskins defensive end Bill Brundige later told reporters that President Nixon had called Allen before the game saying he'd like him to run a flanker reverse with Jefferson, a statement that the coach's son, George Allen, refuted years later.) With time running out, Washington was forced to try a field goal. George Berman's snap was low, and Curt Knight's attempt was blocked.

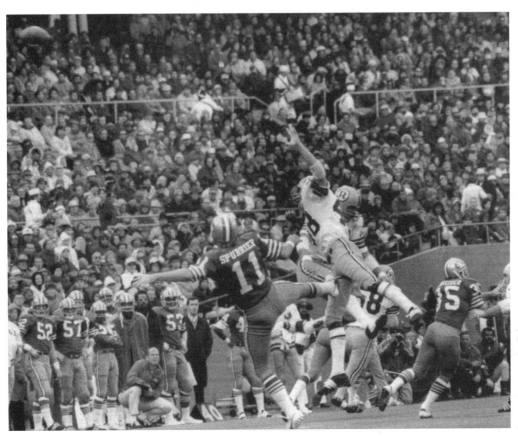

Redskins special teams star Jon Jaqua blocks a punt by the 49ers' Steve Spurrier in the first quarter, setting up a short drive that gave Washington a 7–0 lead. Spurrier was the Redskins' head coach in 2002 and 2003.

Another Redskins gamble backfired after Duncan returned the second-half kickoff 66 yards to the 49ers' 34. Allen opted to go for it on fourth-and-inches from the 11, but running back Larry Brown was caught for a 2-yard loss on a sweep to the left. "It was just inches," Allen said later. "The percentages were in our favor to pick it up."

It was a major turning point: Three plays later, 49ers quarterback John Brodie hit receiver Gene Washington on a 78-yard touchdown pass. Kilmer threw an interception that set up another touchdown, Brodie's 2-yard pass to tight end Bob Windsor, and San Francisco was up, 17–10, late in the third quarter.

Knight's 36-yard field goal closed the gap to four. But another huge error by the normally accurate Berman spelled doom for the burgundy and gold. His snap went through the legs of punter Mike Bragg and skidded into the end zone on the slick Astroturf, and the 49ers' Bob Hoskins landed on it for a touchdown. The conversion created a 24–13 game with a little more than three minutes left. "George Allen brought in George Berman from the Rams just to snap, but his snaps really cost us in that game," Redskins defensive end Ron McDole recalled.

The Redskins retaliated quickly on Kilmer's 16-yard scoring pass to Brown, then got the ball back and moved close to midfield with the clock ticking down. But the 49ers sacked Kilmer as time expired.

Despite the loss, the game was momentous for the Redskins in the eyes of *Washington Evening Star* columnist Morrie Siegel. "Mark down December 26, 1971, as an epochal day in the history of Washington," he wrote. "It is to be remembered as the first time the Redskins' season ever lasted that long. Normally, football interest died before Halloween. Never before have the Redskins been extended to 15 games. It is over now, 24–20 San Francisco, and please, no flowers. The guys died a valiant team, but they died gloriously."

| | | | | | | |
|---|---|---|---|---|---|---|
| Washington— | 7 | 3 | 3 | 7 | — | 20 |
| San Francisco— | 0 | 3 | 14 | 7 | — | 24 |

Wash — Smith 5 pass from Kilmer (Knight kick)
SF —— FG Gossett 23
Wash — FG Knight 40
SF —— G. Washington 78 pass from Brodie (Gossett kick)
SF —— Windsor 2 pass from Brodie (Gossett kick)
Wash — FG Knight 36
SF —— Hoskins, fumble recovery in end zone (Gossett kick)
Wash — Brown 16 pass from Kilmer (Knight kick)

## 1972: 11–3–0, 1ST PLACE—NFC EAST

### Head Coach: George Allen

The "Over the Hill Gang" proved that an aging squad with a plethora of castoff players can finish on the brink of an NFL championship.

Defying the expectations of many, the oldest team in the league gelled masterfully and marched through the regular season to finish 11–3. The Redskins then annihilated Green Bay and Dallas in the playoffs by a combined score of 42–6 to qualify for Super Bowl VII, where their dramatic run ended.

The Miami Dolphins beat Washington, 14–7, to finish 17–0 in the only undefeated, untied season in NFL history.

The season marked the first time since 1945 that the Redskins had played in an NFL championship game. It also represented another giant stride toward the creation of a powerhouse under George Allen.

"We had a year to be together, one year under our belt," defensive tackle Diron Talbert said. "The players got used to each other. The Redskins and Ramskins got used to each other. Mostly, we had some pretty good talent, and we used it well, with Larry Brown and Billy Kilmer and Sonny Jurgensen working together, and great receivers. We also had a great defense that was always rated number one or two in the league, and we had great special teams. Our trip to the Super Bowl didn't just accidentally happen. It happened because everybody worked together."

All three phases of the team—offense, defense, and special teams—clicked. Kilmer enjoyed his finest season ever. He completed 120 of 225 throws for 1,648 yards, with 19 touchdowns and 11 interceptions, earning the first and only Pro Bowl appearance in his 16-year career. The fiery competitor also proved to be a genuine leader, again filling in admirably when Jurgensen, the better passer of the two, was lost midway through the season with an injury. Brown was named NFL MVP after rushing for 1,216 yards, the NFC's top mark, and the offense scored 336 points, second in the conference.

The defense, for its part, yielded an NFC-low 218 points and recorded 33 turnovers and 35 sacks. Linebacker Chris Hanburger was named NFC Defensive Player of the Year after intercepting a career-high four passes. Special teams blocked five field goals and four punts.

Early signs pointed toward 1972 as being the Redskins year. Virtually an entire defense that placed as one of the top units in the NFL in 1971 was intact. What's more, key players on offense were back and healthy, namely Brown, Jurgensen, wide receiver Charley Taylor, and tight end Jerry Smith. The latter three had missed nearly the entire 1971 season with injuries. The receiving trio of Taylor, Smith, and Roy Jefferson promised to provide tremendous aerial striking power even in Allen's conservative offense. In the backfield, Brown would again have fullback Charley Harraway, a devastating blocker, to lead his convoy.

Allen pulled off a handful of off-season roster moves, including a trade for 49ers free safety Roosevelt Taylor, who played in Chicago in the early 1960s when Allen was the Bears' defensive coordinator. The coach's disdain for rookies, coupled with his wheeling and dealing in the player market, had left the Redskins with no draft picks in the first seven rounds of the 1972 draft. In their two most notable picks, they drafted 29-year-old running back Moses Denson, who had played the last two seasons in the Canadian Football League, and Southern Colorado State wide receiver Frank Grant.

Unlike the previous season, the Redskins had two healthy quarterbacks heading into opening day: Kilmer and Jurgensen. In fact, the Redskins seemed to have the strongest one-two quarterback punch in the league, even better than Roger Staubach and Craig Morton in Dallas.

The two split time in the six exhibition games, with Kilmer playing the first half and Jurgensen the second. Jurgy, who had shed about 30 pounds to fall under 200 for the first time in ages, outshined his teammate statistically—but Kilmer also played well in a 4–1–1 preseason that included wins over heavyweights Miami and Baltimore. Allen favored Kilmer and named him the starter while also ruling out rotating his two veteran quarterbacks during the regular season. "That's the only way it can be," Allen told reporters of his decision to start Kilmer. "We won with Billy, and he's our quarterback. He did an excellent job last year."

Allen also predicted at least 10 victories but muted his optimism. "Right now, we're only as good as our last game, and we lost that game to San Francisco in the playoffs. What we did the rest of last year is history. Our success will be determined not by how well we play our defenses or the kicking game, but how well we work together as a 40-man team. Togetherness, that's the phrase."

Special teams determined the Redskins' fate in a season-opening, 24–21 Monday night victory at Minnesota. The primary hero was a player reactivated by Allen five days before the game after going unclaimed on waivers: reserve wide receiver Bill Malinchak. With the game less than three minutes old, he blocked a punt, scooped up the loose ball, and ran 16 yards into the end zone. But Washington's offense was sluggish, and the Redskins trailed, 14–10, early in the fourth quarter.

Kilmer, who completed only 5 of his first 13 passes, then led a 58-yard scoring drive capped by Brown's 3-yard run. Minnesota fumbled the ensuing kickoff, and Malinchak again made the highlight reels by recovering the ball deep in Vikings territory. The play set up a 9-yard scoring run by Harraway with about three minutes left that sealed the victory. After beating Minnesota for the first time ever, the Redskins charged up the Metropolitan Stadium ramp and shouted, "We're on our way."

They took another step with a 24–10 win over the Cardinals. Brown, who rushed for 105 yards against the Vikings, piled up 148 to become Washington's all-time leading running back with 3,214 yards. Jerry Smith, who caught only 21 throws in the season but seven for touchdowns, to earn the nickname "Home Run," snared two scoring passes. Special teams produced another big play, a blocked field goal by defensive end Verlon Biggs that cornerback Mike Bass picked up and ran 32 yards for a score. The defense intercepted two passes that also led to touchdowns.

Despite the 2–0 mark, some Redskins fans were annoyed with Allen's strategy, which relied on defense and special teams, coupled with a run-oriented offense that made the fewest mistakes possible. In fact, some of the 53,000 fans at RFK

## Sonny vs. Billy Duel Captivates Washington Area

"I LIKE SONNY!" "I LIKE BILLY!" The bumper stickers were everywhere in the Washington metro area, as fans took sides in the Redskins' first legitimate quarterback controversy of the modern era.

The choices, Sonny Jurgensen and Billy Kilmer, starred in a captivating duel over four seasons from 1971 to 1974. They alternated starting roles and subbed for one another when injuries sidelined their aging bodies.

Both competitors carried a fierce desire to play, but they never let the rivalry become acrimonious, supporting each other on the field and hanging out together away from the game. Their friendship lasts to this day.

"We've been friends for years and years," said Jurgensen, about five years older than Kilmer. "We realized there wasn't a good body between us, so the only way we were going to be successful was to help each other."

Said Kilmer, "We knew that we were playing on a winning team, and we didn't want to split the team down the middle. We wanted to keep everything going."

Kilmer, who lacked Jurgensen's grace, strong arm, and accuracy, credited No. 9 for helping mold him into a better quarterback. "Sonny helped me funda-mentally, he really changed the way I threw the ball. I used to get a lot of sore arms. I watched him and saw how he'd get his hips in there. I tried to copy his delivery a little bit."

Kilmer played by far the most in the four seasons they were together. He was Allen's preferred choice, for his conservative, no-risk approach mirrored the coach's philosophy. But Jurgensen was the apparent favorite in the community, where the aerial wizardry he used to bedevil defenses in the pre-Allen years was vivid in the minds of Redskins fans. A 1972 survey conducted for local television station WTTG found that 45 percent of respondents preferred Jurgensen as the starter, compared with 42 percent for Kilmer. Fans implored Allen to play Jurgy, one banner at RFK Stadium exclaiming, "Allen: Keep Your Sonny Side Up!" Another banner read, "No More Sonny Days," referring to Jurgensen's retirement before the 1975 season.

Redskins center Len Hauss said that the rivalry was good for the team but was hard getting used to at first: "It was pretty tough on those of us who were here because it almost made you choose between one of two quarterbacks. I'd played with Sonny for seven years already, and it didn't take you but a couple of hours to get to know Billy pretty well. Soon you discovered that both of these guys were great quarterbacks and great leaders. Both of them wanted to play really bad. But it was a good, honest competition."

Billy Kilmer called the Redskins' signals at quarterback for most of the George Allen era. Allen preferred Kilmer's conservative, no-risk approach over Sonny Jurgensen's more daring style.

Stadium against St. Louis booed Kilmer for his pedestrian passing approach and shouted, "WE WANT SONNY!" The disenchanted folks remembered Jurgensen from his prolific passing days of the 1960s and thought he would lead the team to exciting wins now that he had the support of an excellent defense.

"The Redskins are a boring team to watch," *Washington Star* columnist Tom Dowling wrote on September 26, 1972. "Not just wearisome or mildly dull, but debilitatingly and crashingly boring, like a three-hour Sunday afternoon sermon on the importance of plotting good works in attaining the blessings of Life Hereafter, the celestial Super Bowl itself."

There was nothing boring about the final minutes of the Redskins' next game at New England. Washington's Curt Knight kicked a 33-yard field goal to tie the game at 24 with just under two minutes left. But the Patriots were called for roughing the kicker, and Allen opted to wipe the points off the board and take the first down on the 21. After the Redskins went 1 yard in three plays, Knight missed a 27-yard field goal with 1:22 left, but it wasn't over.

New England ran the ball three times with little success. On fourth down, that one-time reject Malinchak stormed through to block the punt. The ball rolled into the end zone, where he laid a hand on it just before the end line. His momentum carried him out of bounds while he apparently controlled the ball, but the referee ruled he didn't have possession in the end zone and called a safety, making the score 24–23 with 57 seconds left. After a free kick, the Redskins took the ball on the Patriots' 48 and positioned Knight for a 50-yard field goal try. His kick was wide.

It was one of the most agonizing losses in Redskins history. In addition to the controversial call involving Malinchak, officials ruled that Roy Jefferson didn't have both feet down in the end zone and negated an apparent touchdown catch with about two minutes left—although films later showed otherwise. The Redskins also had themselves to blame. Their

defense allowed the Patriots to recover from a 14–0 first-half deficit. Second-year quarterback Jim Plunkett threw for two touchdowns and 255 yards, and rookie running back Josh Ashton ran for 108 more.

"I don't recall ever losing a more frustrating game," Allen wrote in a note to the press afterward. "I went for the win rather than the tie. I'd do the same again. We had our opportunities, but we didn't take advantage. Minnesota was a team victory. Today was a team loss."

From the final gun, rumors swirled that Kilmer—who threw three touchdowns but missed seven of eight throws in the last two minutes—might take a back seat to Jurgensen for the upcoming game against the 0–2 Eagles. Indeed, Jurgy led most first-team practice drills at Redskin Park, and reporters became inquisitive about whether a change was in the works. The questioning made Allen testy, and he barred the press from practice. He also announced no quarterback switch.

On game day, however, old No. 9 was introduced at RFK as the starter, prompting a roaring ovation from the sellout crowd. Looking rusty, he threw three interceptions in a scoreless first half when many fickle fans hooted and jeered. But in the third quarter he led an eight-play, 75-yard scoring drive featuring completions of 25 yards to Smith and 35 to Taylor. He later connected with Jefferson on a 36-yard scoring pass that accounted for a 14–0 Redskins victory. Jurgy was 7 of 7 in the second half and 14 of 24 overall for 237 yards.

"I was very tight in the first half," Jurgensen told reporters. "I was really guiding the ball. Then I connected on my first pass of the second half to Jerry Smith, and that really felt good."

Washington's defense, which held the Eagles to 60 yards rushing and posted four sacks in the second half, turned in another demonstrative performance in a 33–3 trouncing of the Cardinals. The unit held St. Louis to 151 yards and forced four turnovers, and along with a special teams gang that partially blocked a punt, it helped set up 23 Redskins points. Jurgy hit his first six passes and completed 13 of 18 overall for 203 yards, Brown had his fourth straight 100-yard rushing game, and Knight was 4 of 4 on field goals.

The victory set up a showdown at RFK between the 4–1 Redskins and 4–1 Cowboys, teams tied for first in the NFC East. Allen billed the pivotal match-up as a "championship" outing with "Super Bowl" written on it, although it seemed Dallas would claim the bragging rights upon taking a 20–7 lead midway through the third quarter. No so fast, said Jurgensen. Recording key completions, he led two 80-yard touchdown drives that ended with runs of 34 yards by Brown and 13 by Harraway. Knight kicked a 42-yard field goal, and the Redskins won, 24–20.

Jurgensen completed 11 of 16 passes for 180 yards, and a banner at RFK read, "Four More Years of Nixon and Sonny," a reference to President Nixon's pending victory in November 1972 that reelected him to the White House for four more years. Brown, for his part, played the game of his career, rushing for 95 yards and catching seven passes for another 100, with two touchdowns. He was named NFL Offensive Player of the Week.

But just as Jurgy was peaking, he was gone. During a scoreless first quarter against the Giants, he threw a 13-yard completion to Jefferson. Although no defenders were near him, his leg gave way. The 38-year-old hobbled off the field and gave way to Kilmer, whom Jurgensen had replaced three weeks before. Kilmer took a while to find a groove but ended up completing 8 of 16 passes for 114 yards, with two touchdowns and an interception in a hard-fought, 23–16 victory that lifted the Redskins to 6–1.

Despite his clutch performance, Kilmer said later he was thankful to have Brown, who was even more sensational than against Dallas. Displaying a remarkable resilience that left him battered and exhausted, he ran 29 times for 191 mostly grind-it-out yards. His longest gain was a 38-yard touchdown run in the third quarter that snapped a 9–9 tie and put the Redskins up for good. He tallied another 42 yards on two catches, including a 7-yard scoring reception, and was named NFL Offensive Player of the Week for the second straight week.

But unruly fans among the 63,000 at Yankee Stadium pelted Brown with oranges. One dumped a can of beer over his head as he exited the field, and an intruder in the postgame locker room pushed forward and taunted the Redskins' star. After police corralled the guy and pulled him away, Brown voiced his anger at members of the New York media. "I'm on top in New York, and you resent it," he charged as his teammates egged him on. "They threw beer and oranges at me. I love to win in New York."

For Jurgensen, who was diagnosed with a torn left Achilles tendon, the season was over. The ball now rested solely with Kilmer. Protected by an offensive line that allowed only 11 sacks on the year, he resembled an All-Pro in leading the Redskins to five more victories to clinch the NFC East title. The stretch included another heated victory over the Giants in which opposing players threw punches on the field, and opposing assistant coaches slugged it out afterward. *Washington Star* columnist Morrie Siegel called the teams the "NFL's Hatfield's and McCoys."

Another win was telling. In a game billed as a possible preview to an opening-round playoff matchup, the Redskins knocked off the Central Division-leading Packers, 21–16, at RFK. They followed with their ninth straight victory, a 23–7 win over the Eagles, to clinch the NFC East.

"This is just one step," Allen told the press afterward. "Last year, our goal was to make the playoffs. This year, our goal was to win the Eastern Division title and go on from there."

---

## An Enduring Logo

In the early 1970s, Walter "Blackie" Wetzel, president of the National Congress of American Indians and chairman of the Blackfoot tribe, urged the Redskins to replace the "R" logo on their helmets with the head of an Indian chief. From photos he presented to Redskins officials of Indian chiefs in full headdress, a composite was developed that gave birth to a new logo on Redskins helmets in the 1972 season. It exists to this day.

I said, 'I'd like to see an Indian on your helmets,'" Wetzel said in the *Washington Post* on January 26, 2002. "It made us all so proud to have an Indian on a big-time team. . . . It's only a small group of radicals who oppose those names. Indians are proud of Indians."

---

With the division title secured and two games left, the coach was asked if he planned to rest any of his starters to avoid injuries before the playoffs. "Rest some of my starters?" he retorted. "We'll make that decision later in the week. We can't afford to lose too much momentum. We did it with the (11–0) Rams in 1969 and lost our final three games, plus the playoffs."

Allen resorted to common sense. In addition to other key players, he rested Brown, who was hobbling on a bruised right knee and a bruised left heel after carrying the ball 285 times, for the upcoming game at Dallas. The Redskins fell behind, 28–3, and lost, 34–24.

Brown also missed a 24–17 loss to Buffalo, allowing Bills running back O. J. Simpson to win the NFL rushing title with 1,251 yards. The back-to-back losses left the 11–3 Redskins with the most regular-season wins in franchise history. They also triggered concern that the squad might be physically and emotionally spent, or just lacking confidence, heading into the postseason. "We didn't lose any confidence at all," Kilmer said years later. "They were meaningless games to us. We were getting ready to win those playoff games."

## NFC DIVISIONAL PLAYOFF GAME
**Washington 16, Green Bay 3**
**December 24, 1972**
**RFK Stadium, Washington, D.C.**
**Attendance: 53,140**

### Allen's Nifty Defensive Switch Trips Up Packers

Manny Sistrunk was sort of a forgotten man. Replaced as the starting left tackle on defense early in the season by Bill Brundige, he'd been relegated mostly to spot duty.

That changed in the opening round of the playoffs against Green Bay. Redskins coach George Allen pulled his middle linebacker and inserted Sistrunk as a fifth lineman to help stymie the Packers' John Brockington and MacArthur Lane, a powerful running duo comparable with the Rams' famed "Bull Elephant" backfield of the 1950s. Allen's clever maneuver, called the "quarter defense," worked to perfection in a 16–3 Redskins victory.

Brockington and Lane, who rushed for a combined 1,848 yards in the regular season, gained a measly 65 yards on the day, nine for Brockington and 56 for Lane. The 265-pound Sistrunk, lined up over center, repeatedly stuffed holes and prevented the Packers from generating any meaningful offensive production. The rest of the defensive line—ends Ron McDole and Verlon Biggs, and tackles Brundige and Diron Talbert—also played superbly.

"Manny had a hell of a game," McDole said. "He jammed them. Manny was big and strong, and he could push people around. He was manhandling their center all day, and they couldn't block him. I'm sure they weren't prepared for it."

According to Talbert, "We had five big defensive guys just charging upfield knocking people around, and the offense is wondering, 'What in the hell do they have going on here?' It was a hell of a defense because you can hardly block it. We caught them by surprise. We whipped the hell out of them."

Redskins quarterback Billy Kilmer was knocked silly early on. With the game scoreless in the first period, he took a

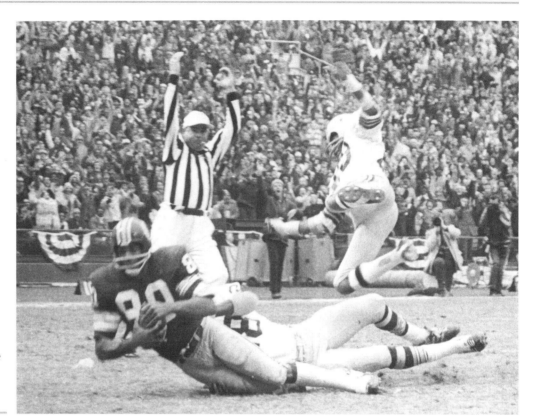

Roy Jefferson's gorgeous 32-yard touchdown catch against the Packers gave the Redskins a 7–3 lead in the second quarter. They never looked back.

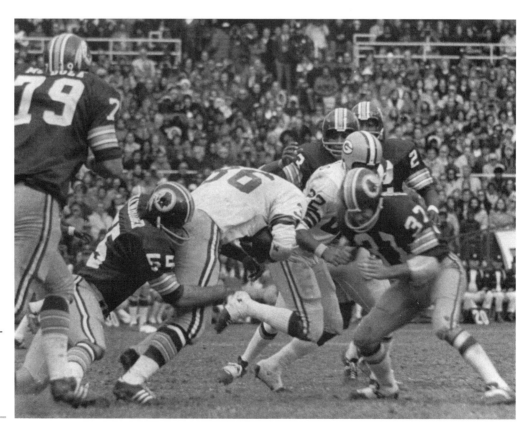

Defensive end Ron McDole (79), linebacker Chris Hanburger (55), and safety Pat Fischer (37) were part of a swarming Redskins defense that stifled Green Bay's powerful running game in the playoffs. Here, Hanburger drags down star running back MacArthur Lane, who gained 56 yards on the day.

vicious blindside shot to the chin that sent him to the ground like a bowling pin. As he was helped to the bench, an eerie hush swept through the crowd of 53,140 at RFK Stadium. Seldom used backup quarterback Sam Wyche, activated from the taxi squad at midseason, began warming up on the sidelines.

"I was really wobbly," Kilmer recalled. "In fact, I still have a lump where the guy got me. I'm on the bench, and they're giving me smelling salts. The doctor is telling me to read the scoreboard, and I can't even see it. [Safety] Richie Petitbon runs up to me and says, 'Billy, Billy, you've got to get back in the game.' I said, 'Why?' He said, 'Sam Wyche is warming up, and he's already thrown two interceptions.' I started laughing. That just brought me out of nearly passing out. I ran back in the huddle and never missed a play."

Green Bay took a 3–0 lead on Chester Marcol's 17-yard field goal 5:31 before halftime, but rookie Herb Mul-Key sparked the Redskins by returning the ball 42 yards to their own 40. A revived Kilmer then led a six-play, 60-yard touchdown drive that ended with his picture-perfect 32-yard strike to receiver Roy Jefferson, who faked out his man on a post pattern and caught the pass in stride at the goal line. (Jefferson had five receptions on the day.) Later, a short punt gave the Redskins possession on the Packers' 41, and Curt Knight booted a 42-yard field goal to create a 10–3 game just before halftime.

Washington's defense and Knight's foot applied the finishing touches. The defense continued handcuffing Brockington and Lane and kept quarterback Scott Hunter, an average passer at best, from exploiting voids in the secondary left by the five-man front. He completed 12 of 24 passes for 150 yards. Knight connected on two more field goals to go 3 for 3 in the game, snapping out of a regular-season slump when he made only 14 of 30 tries. Larry Brown, back in action after sitting out the last two regular-season games, paced the Redskins' ball-control offense with 101 yards on 25 carries. Punter Mike Bragg boomed kicks that pinned the Packers deep in their own territory.

Knight's last field goal, a 46-yarder with less than three minutes left, sealed the win—the Redskins' first postseason victory in nearly 30 years and George Allen's first playoff win in four tries.

| | | | | | | |
|---|---|---|---|---|---|---|
| Green Bay— | 0 | 3 | 0 | 0 | — | 3 |
| Washington— | 0 | 10 | 0 | 6 | — | 16 |

GB —— FG Marcol 17
Wash —— Jefferson 32 pass from Kilmer (Knight kick)
Wash —— FG Knight 42
Wash —— FG Knight 35
Wash —— FG Knight 46

## NFC CHAMPIONSHIP GAME
## Washington 26, Dallas 3
## December 31, 1972
## RFK Stadium, Washington, D.C.
## Attendance: 53,129

### "Near Perfect" Redskins Whip Dallas, Gain Super Bowl Berth

The front-page headlines in Washington's two major newspapers were in harmony on January 1, 1973: "How Sweet It Is . . . Champs at Last," read the *Washington Star-Daily News.* "Happy 1973! We're a Winner at Last," exclaimed the *Washington Post.*

How true. The Redskins' 30-year drought of winning a championship of any kind ended on New Year's Eve with a 26–3 rout of the Cowboys in the NFC title game. The colossal win dethroned the defending Super Bowl champions and earned the Redskins a once unfathomable achievement—a trip to the Super Bowl. It also served as the crowning moment in the 12-year NFL coaching career of George Allen, who called the win a "near-perfect" performance by his veteran-laden squad.

"I said all along, give me a bunch of older men who have taken care of themselves, and I can go all the way," the jubilant coach told reporters after the rout. "A lot of people wrote us off as too old, too slow and too heavy. Nobody wanted them. I just want to say they're a great group. The 'Over the Hill Gang' is a beautiful name."

The Redskins embarrassed their fierce rivals while playing like champions. They piled up 316 yards of offense in a mostly methodical fashion to wear down the Cowboys' famed "Doomsday Defense." Quarterback Billy Kilmer played the game of his life, completing 14 of 18 passes (.778 completion percentage) for 194 yards and two touchdowns to receiver Charley Taylor (seven catches, 146 yards). Larry Brown rushed 30 times for 88 yards. And Curt Knight set a playoff record by hitting all four of his field goal attempts, punctuating his amazing 7 for 7 performance in the first two playoff games.

Washington's defense stifled the Cowboys' offense and prevented a touchdown for the second straight playoff game. Dallas gained only 169 yards, and quarterback Roger Staubach, a future Hall of Famer, completed 9 of 20 throws for 98 yards. Unable to find receivers open, he scrambled five times for 59 yards but endured three sacks for 29 yards in losses. Running backs Calvin Hill and Walt Garrison combined for 37 yards on 16 carries.

"It was a huge game for us, just to get to the Super Bowl the way we did," said Kilmer, whose offensive line provided airtight protection. "And the way we won the game so decisively. Everybody played so good that day."

Cowboys cornerback Mel Renfro said that the Redskins caught Dallas flat after its 30–28 playoff win over the 49ers that featured a comeback from a 15-point fourth-quarter deficit: "We had just come off a very emotional win in San Francisco the week before, and it was right after Christmas. We came to Washington thinking we'd just float by the Redskins, but they had something for us. They beat us soundly, and we deserved it. Anything can happen on any given Sunday, and it was one of those Sundays where it was the Redskins' day and not the Cowboys."

The one-sided affair followed mud-slinging that consumed both teams before the game. Emotions began boiling after the Cowboys' 34–24 victory over the Redskins on December 9, when Allen accused Dallas receiver Lance Alworth of making dirty, crack-back blocks aimed at the knees of linebacker Jack Pardee. Alworth vehemently denied ever making such blocks and charged Pardee with trying to knee him in the head. Pardee admitted doing so, but only after he blamed Alworth for trying to take out his knees.

Redskins defensive tackle Diron Talbert, for his part, said that Cowboys coach Tom Landry should start Craig Morton at quarterback in the championship game. Staubach had missed the entire season with a shoulder injury until returning to

Redskins' receiver Charley Taylor, here beating Dallas cornerback Charlie Waters, caught seven passes for 146 yards in the NFL Championship game, including 15- and 45-yard touchdowns.

lead the miracle comeback against San Francisco. "There's no way they can start Staubach," Talbert told reporters. "Morton has been number one all year and has brought the Cowboys this far. If Landry doesn't start him, all those guys will start wondering about their jobs. It could break the team apart." Landry opted to start Staubach and tossed a needling remark at Kilmer, saying that the Cowboys had an edge on the Redskins because the mobile Staubach was a better athlete than old No. 17.

"When I saw that statement in the paper on Sunday morning, I was pissed," Kilmer said years later. "That fired me up. I could have gone and played right then."

Under gray skies and in unusually high 60-degree temperatures, the teams played to a scoreless tie in the first quarter. But the Redskins pieced together a 37-yard drive that Knight capped with an 18-yard field goal about 10 minutes before halftime. Soon after, Kilmer tested Dallas left cornerback Charlie Waters, whom Taylor beat for a 51-yard reception to the Dallas 21. Minutes later, Taylor cut inside Waters and caught a 15-yard scoring pass. Knight's conversion put the Redskins up, 10–0, with 5:33 left in the half.

Dallas threatened later when Staubach ran 29 yards to the Washington 39. But the Redskins held on downs, and Toni Fritsch's 35-yard field goal hit the left upright and bounced through for a 10–3 game. Fritsch missed a 23-yarder right before halftime.

In the third period, Washington made a rare mistake that could have led to a tie game. Kilmer fumbled a center snap,

and the ball bounced toward the Redskins' goal line. Two Cowboys made desperate lunges, but tight end Jerry Smith recovered it at the 18.

Later in the quarter, Washington crafted an 11-play, 78-yard scoring drive. Kilmer mixed runs mostly by Larry Brown and a few passes to move the ball into Dallas territory, where the Redskins faced a third-and-10 on the 45. Kilmer again tried to exploit the Cowboys' left cornerback, which this time was third-year man Mark Washington. In one of the prettiest throws ever by the self-proclaimed "wobbly" passer, Kilmer launched a bomb down the sideline to Taylor, who caught the pass in full stride past the diving Washington and strode into the end zone.

"Dallas was forever bracing Kilmer with that third down and long-yardage situation, forcing him to pass," Blackie Sherrod of the *Dallas Times-Herald* wrote. "But it was like whopping a tiger across the face with a stock of Polish sausage. Kilmer simply ate it up."

It was good Knight from then on. The kicker booted field goals of 39, 46, and 45 yards, after each of which the roar from the 53,129 fans at a rocking RFK Stadium became louder. The band started playing "California, Here We Come," in reference to the Redskins' pending trip to Los Angeles to face Miami in Super Bowl VII, and the fans chanted "Amen" and "We're Number One." When the final gun sounded, thousands of delirious fans stormed the field, while Redskin players hoisted Allen onto their shoulders and carried him through the mob.

"We were all on top of the world after that game," defensive end Ron McDole said years later. "That was kind of like our Super Bowl."

| Dallas— | 0 | 3 | 0 | 0 | — | 3 |
|---|---|---|---|---|---|---|
| Washington— | 0 | 10 | 0 | 16 | — | 26 |

Wash — FG Knight 18
Wash — Taylor 15 pass from Kilmer (Knight kick)
Dallas — FG Fritsch 35
Wash — Taylor 45 pass from Kilmer (Knight kick)
Wash — FG Knight 39
Wash — FG Knight 46
Wash — FG Knight 45

## SUPER BOWL VII
**Miami 14, Washington 7**
**January 14, 1973**
**Los Angeles Coliseum**
**Attendance: 90,182**

### Undefeated Dolphins Pull Plug on Redskins' Historic Season

It was an exercise in futility for the Redskins, while the Dolphins, no models of excellence themselves, did just enough to stay a few steps ahead. That confluence brought the Red-skins' remarkable journey through the 1972 season to a somber end.

On an afternoon when their only points came courtesy of a ridiculous decision by a place kicker, the Redskins succumbed to Miami, 14–7, in Super Bowl VII. With the win, the 17–0 Dolphins became the only NFL team ever to finish a regular season plus playoffs undefeated and untied, a feat that stands.

"We lost to a great football team," Redskins linebacker Chris Hanburger said years later. "Granted, we didn't play that well offensively or defensively, yet we had a chance to win that football game and just couldn't do it. They were by far the best team that day and throughout the season."

The Dolphins weren't dominant statistically, outgaining the Redskins by 27 yards and recording four fewer first downs. The game came down to making big plays, which Miami did and the Redskins didn't. In what seemed like a cruel joke but a vivid example of Washington's painful day, quarterback Billy Kilmer's fourth-quarter pass to a wide-open Jerry Smith in the end zone hit the goal posts, which then paralleled the goal line, and bounced incomplete. His next pass was intercepted in the end zone, as Miami preserved its 14–0 lead.

Two weeks after playing the best game of his career in the NFC championship, Kilmer struggled. He tossed three interceptions to accompany 14 of 28 passing for 104 yards. The Redskins were also unproductive on the ground. Larry Brown (72 yards, 22 carries) was manhandled by Miami's swarming "No Name Defense," which zeroed in on him all game while counting on a bad day from Kilmer. "The

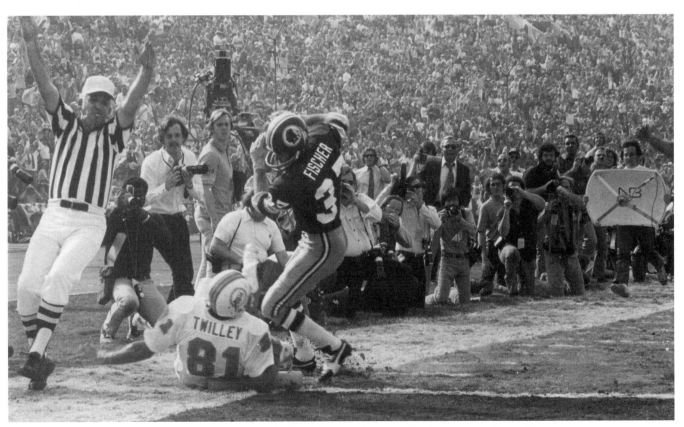

Miami's Howard Twilley falls over the goal line in front of the Redskins' Pat Fischer to complete a 28-yard scoring catch that gave the Dolphins a 7–0 lead in Super Bowl VII.

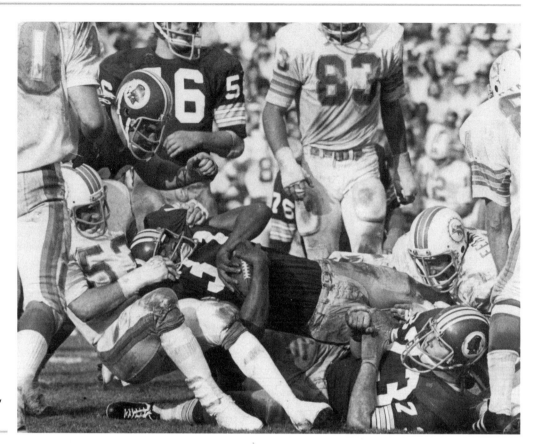

Redskins ball carriers such as fullback Charley Harraway found it tough going against the Dolphins' "no-name defense."

Dolphins had a perfect defense, and we didn't adjust to it quick enough offensively," Kilmer recalled. "They stopped our running game cold. We came out in the second half and went up and down the field, but our offense couldn't get into the end zone."

That the Redskins appeared out of sync perhaps stemmed from their coach, George Allen, being so uptight in the days preceding the game. The coach made his players feel stressed out by confining them to meeting after meeting. "The guys never really had a chance to relax," safety Brig Owens recalled. "We had a group of guys who were pretty wild. You can't corral the types of guys we had and keep them in meetings. So we went into the game flat."

Allen also had trouble handling the pregame Super Bowl hype in Southern California. He voiced displeasure that print and broadcast media, which numbered more than 1,000, were demanding so much of his players' time during Super Bowl week. He called it a "circus atmosphere" and repeatedly complained of distractions. "If I had my selfish way, I'd have come out here on Friday [two days before the game]," he growled.

Once, the NFL required Allen and Miami coach Don Shula to be in Newport Beach for a mass media interview, causing Allen to seethe. "Do you realize that I'm missing my first meeting with my team in 23 years?" he asked the press. "I hope you have some questions of value. Let's get going, so I can get to practice." Concerned about further distractions, he prevented his players' wives from joining their husbands until after the Super Bowl. "I wish they'd stop in Chicago and stay there," he said. "They have the rest of their lives to be together, but there's only one Super Bowl."

The Dolphins, losers to Dallas in Super Bowl VI, at least had experience confronting pregame Super Bowl tension. But they had no edge on paper, where the teams were relatively even. Both squads were run-oriented, the Redskins with 1,216-yard man Larry Brown, and the Dolphins with a trio that helped establish an all-time NFL rushing record of 2,960 yards: Larry Csonka (1,117), Mercury Morris (1,000), and Jim Kiick (521). The three backs ran behind the best offensive line in the league.

Both teams also featured powerful defenses—the Redskins yielded the fewest points in the NFC (218) and Miami allowed the fewest in the league (171)—and two future Hall of Fame coaches, Allen and Miami's Don Shula. The two had built a rivalry in the 1960s, when Allen coached the Rams and Shula the Colts in the old NFL Western Conference. Shula held a 4–3–1 edge. Ironically, Miami's last loss of any kind was by three points to the Redskins in the 1972 preseason.

The oddsmakers favored Washington by one, but Allen would have no part of it. "There isn't a weakness on the team," he said of the Dolphins. "We've never faced a team that has set so many impressive records, and we haven't played a team with a 16–0 record."

Before 90,182 fans at the Los Angeles Coliseum, Allen's old stomping ground, and a Super Bowl-record 75 million television viewers, the Redskins seemed to get the first big break by recovering a botched snap on a punt on the Dolphins' 20. But an official ruled that Redskin Harold McLinton interfered with the snap before the ball left the hand of center Howard Kindig, and Miami retained possession. "Kindig would lift the ball up when he snapped it, so we planned to have Harold hit his hands in order to misdirect the ball," Redskins defensive end Ron McDole said. "But Harold did such a good job, that the ball hit the side of Kindig's thigh and fell down underneath him. Normally, it goes as a bad snap, and nobody knows what happened."

Later in the quarter, the Dolphins sidestepped another dart when Miami's Dick Anderson recovered a fumbled punt by his own man at the Dolphins' 37. They drove to the Redskins' 28 in six plays. Quarterback Bob Griese, who started the game although backup Earl Morrall had led the Dolphins to 10 straight wins while subbing during the year for Griese, then connected with receiver Howard Twilley in the end zone. Garo Yepremian's conversion created a 7–0 game.

The Dolphins dominated the rest of the half, as their tenacious defense bottled up Brown and harassed Kilmer in the pocket. Two sparkplugs were end Manny Fernandez (11 unassisted tackles) and middle linebacker Nick Buoniconti, who intercepted a pass in the quarter and returned it 32 yards to the Redskins' 27. The Dolphins moved to the 2, and Kiick ran it in for a touchdown. The extra point gave Miami a 14–0 halftime lead. The margin could have been larger, but Griese's 47-yard touchdown pass to receiver Paul Warfield was called back due to a trivial penalty.

By halftime, Miami's defense had limited the Redskins' conservative offense to a 49 yards rushing, and Allen, seeking some type of a spark, gave one of his typical exhortations just before the second half: "Every damn guy in here now. Everybody listen to this. We've got 30 minutes to live."

The inspired Redskins, airing it out more, moved the ball on 45-, 33-, and 79-yard drives into Miami territory but couldn't buy a break. One drive put them on the Dolphins' 10 with five minutes left, but Kilmer's pass was intercepted in the end zone by safety Jake Scott, who returned the ball 55 yards to the Dolphins' 48. Scott, who picked off two passes on the day, was named Super Bowl MVP.

The Dolphins moved to the Redskins' 35 with time running out, and Yepremian set up for a 42-yard field goal to ice the game. But his low kick hit the helmet of 6–6 Dolphins lineman Bob Heinz. (It appeared that Redskins lineman Bill Brundige, who had his hand in the air, blocked the kick, but Brundige said the ball hit Heinz's helmet.) Yepremian scooped up the ball and made a feeble attempt to throw a pass, batting it upward like a volleyball. Redskins cornerback Mike Bass grabbed it and sprinted 49 yards down the sideline for a score. The conversion made it 14–7, with 2:07 left.

The 6–5, 270-pound Brundige remembers closing in on Yepremian, a diminutive Cypriot: "The ball is flipping around on the ground, and I'm chasing Yepremian, it's the end of the fourth quarter, 85 degrees out, I'm exhausted, my tongue's hanging out. When Yepremian looked at me bearing down on me, he must have thought I was trying to kill him, and all I was trying to do was get my breath. He was scared because I looked so mean, when I was actually just tired as hell. The ball slipped out of his hand, and Bass caught it in mid-air and started running."

"I had a place kicker who wanted to be Walter Mitty," said Don Shula, referring to the fictional character who dreamed of doing heroic acts. "When he kicked a field goal, he'd come off the field, and we'd high-five each other. This time, he ran into the end zone. He didn't want to come close to me."

Washington was suddenly back in the game. When its defense held Miami to one first down and forced a punt, the

The Redskins' defense couldn't stop Dolphins hard-nosed fullback Larry Csonka, who rushed for 112 yards and a touchdown on only 15 carries.

Redskins were 70 yards from the tying touchdown with 1:14 to play. But Kilmer threw two incompletions and dumped one off to Brown for a loss of four. On fourth down, defensive ends Bill Stanfill and Vern Den Herder smothered Kilmer, ending the game.

Shula received a victory ride on the shoulders of his players, who each earned $15,000 to $7,500 for the Redskins. A despondent Allen muttered to reporters, "We'll be back."

| | | | | | | |
|---|---|---|---|---|---|---|
| Miami— | 7 | 7 | 0 | 0 | — | 14 |
| Washington— | 0 | 0 | 0 | 7 | — | 7 |

Miami – Twilley 28 pass from Griese (Yepremian kick)
Miami – Kiick 1 run (Yepremian kick)
Wash — Bass 49 fumble return (Knight kick)

| Team Statistics | Mia | Wash |
|---|---|---|
| First Downs | 12 | 16 |
| Rushing Yards | 184 | 141 |
| Passing Yards | 88 | 104 |
| Total Yards | 272 | 245 |
| Passes | 8–11–1 | 14–28–3 |
| Return Yards, Kick | 33 | 45 |
| Punts, Average | 7–43.0 | 5–31.2 |
| Penalties | 3–35 | 3–25 |
| Fumbles–Lost | 2–0 | 1–0 |

## RUSHING

Miami—Csonka 15–112 1TD; Kiick 12–38; Morris 10–34.
Washington—Brown 22–72; Harraway 10–37; Kilmer 2–18; C. Taylor 1–8; Smith 1–6

## PASSING

Miami—Griese 8–11–88, 1 TD, 1 INT
Washington—Kilmer 14–28–104, 3 INT

## RECEIVING

Miami—Warfield 3–36; Kiick 2–6; Twilley 1–28, 1 TD; Mandich 1–19; Csonka 1-minus-1
Washington—Jefferson 5–50; Brown 5–26; C. Taylor 2–20; Smith 1–11; Harraway 1-minus–3

# 1973: 10–4–0, 2ND PLACE—NFC EAST

## Head Coach: George Allen

The Redskins' key theme in 1973 was loud and clear: a return trip to the Super Bowl. Losing to the Dolphins in Super Bowl VII had deflated the entire team, but the loss made everyone hungrier to go back to the grand stage of pro football. And many preseason polls predicted that the squad would repeat as NFC champions.

It wasn't to be.

The Redskins cruised through a 10–4 season to tie Dallas for the NFC East title and earn a wild card playoff spot. They bowed out in the opening round with a 27–20 loss to Minnesota.

"When we lost in the Super Bowl, everyone on that team believed that the next year we're coming back and winning it," defensive tackle Bill Brundige said. "Nobody dreamed that that was the only Super Bowl we'd play in."

Safety Brig Owens (left) intercepts a pass in front of Cowboys tight end Billy Joe Dupree in a Monday night game in 1973, then returns it 26 yards for a touchdown that provided the winning points in a 14–7 Redskins victory. Owens picked off 36 passes as a Redskin, today the second most in team history.

Duke Zeibert (front row, center), legendary owner of the popular D.C. restaurant that bore his name, brought cake and ice cream to Redskin Park every Thursday after a win during the George Allen era. This visit was on Thursday, October 18, 1973, four days after the Redskins beat the Giants and three days before they hosted the Cardinals. Allen is preparing to stick a knife into the last name of Cardinals quarterback Jim Hart in the middle of the cake. The Redskins won, 31–13. Mel Krupin, general manager at the time at Duke Zeibert's, is on the far left, and defensive end Verlon Biggs is on the far right. Linebacker Dave Robinson and defensive linemen Manny Sistrunk, Diron Talbert, and Ron McDole (left to right) are in the back.

The 1973 Redskins sported one of the most talented teams in franchise history—on paper, at least. In addition to the return of nearly every player from a squad with one of the league's best offenses and defenses in 1972, coach George Allen stockpiled more talent in the offseason. By opening day, the roster consisted of some 20 players who'd earned Pro Bowl honors. As long as the "Over the Hill Gang" didn't give way to old age, the Redskins seemed headed for greatness.

Allen first acquired superstar safety Kenny Houston from the Houston Oilers in exchange for five solid players, including offensive tackle Jim Snowden, tight end Mack Alston, and wide receiver Clifton McNeil. The Redskins also obtained former All-Pro tight end Alvin Reed in the deal. Allen later traded for former All-Pro linebacker Dave Robinson from the Packers.

The coach made his most shocking deal during training camp. With Larry Brown holding out, Allen acquired controversial Chargers running back Duane Thomas for a first-round draft choice in 1975 and a second in 1976. Thomas rushed for 1,596 yards in his first two seasons in the league with Dallas, but the Cowboys traded the moody and enigmatic player to San Diego, where he missed every down in 1972. Allen, however, took a chance on him, as he had with other disgruntled players who later evolved into contributing members of the Redskins. The acquisition upgraded a backfield that also consisted of Larry Brown, Charley Harraway, Moses Denson, and Herb Mul-Key.

At quarterback, Sonny Jurgensen, fully recovered from the Achilles tendon injury that sidelined him for the last half of the 1972 season, was still the best pure passer in the NFL. But Allen named Billy Kilmer his starter in training camp.

"Kilmer is number one," Allen told reporters. "There's no question about that. He took us to the playoffs two straight years and to the Super Bowl last season. We're pleased with Sonny's progress and expect him to be 100 percent. You need two good quarterbacks to go all the way. Miami proved it last season."

Kilmer and Jurgensen split time in the exhibition season, when the Redskins dropped their first game by three points before reeling off five straight wins. Each quarterback was hot at times, and Duane Thomas and all-everything Herb Mul-Key, who returned a kickoff 102 yards for a touchdown, looked solid.

A record crowd of 54,316 at RFK Stadium (1,000 seats were added to RFK in the off-season) on opening day saw an old nemesis. Quarterback Johnny Unitas, who had led Baltimore to 12 wins in 13 career games against the Redskins, was now wearing the uniform of the San Diego Chargers, an odd scene. San Diego had also acquired Deacon Jones, a pillar on Allen's "Fearsome Foursome" defensive line in Los Angeles, as part of a sweeping team overhaul.

But the 40-year-old Unitas was no match for the Redskins' opportunistic defense, which scored or set up 31 points, intercepted four passes, recovered three fumbles, and posted eight sacks in a 38–0 wipeout. The sack total contributed to a team-record 53 that year, a mark since broken. Allen said before the season that the defense, which had lost only outside linebacker Jack Pardee to retirement, had a chance to be better than in 1972.

In week 2, however, Cardinals quarterback Jim Hart passed for 286 yards and led scoring drives of 76, 71, 68, and 53 yards in a 34–27 St. Louis victory. Kilmer was 14 of 22 for 161 yards and one touchdown, nothing embarrassing at all, but Allen yanked him for Jurgensen in the third quarter.

The coach refused to name his starter for the upcoming game at Philadelphia, but a sign at Veteran's Stadium spelled it out: "Sonny Days Are Here Again." Jurgy completed 16 of 29 passes for 195 yards and two touchdowns, both to Charley Taylor, in a 28–7 victory. Like a Jekyll and Hyde, Washington's defense held the Eagles to 70 yards, with eight sacks and two interceptions, and served as a great source of offensive production. Linebacker Chris Hanburger returned an interception 45 yards to set up Larry Brown's short scoring run, and safety Ted Vactor returned an interception 34 yards for a touchdown.

The win set up a showdown between the 2–1 Redskins and the 3–0 Cowboys, holders of first place in the NFC East. Washington's defense, again needing to come up big against one of the NFL's most powerful offenses, responded beautifully before a Monday night football audience.

With the score tied at 7 late in the fourth quarter, Redskins safety Brig Owens returned an interception 26 yards for a touchdown. The conversion created a 14–7 game. The Redskins forced Dallas to punt with about two minutes left, but the ball took a funny bounce and hit Redskins tight end Jerry Smith. Dallas recovered on the Redskins' 31 and drove to the 4, and quarterback Craig Morton threw three incompletions, setting the stage for one of the most spectacular defensive plays in Redskins history. On fourth down, Morton dumped a pass off to fullback Walt Garrison around the 1, but Kenny Houston was right there to upend Garrison before the goal line. Ball game.

Houston proceeded to pick off two passes in a 21–3 victory over the Giants that put the 4–1 Redskins in first place in the NFC East over 3–2 Dallas. They followed with a 31–13 win over the Cardinals; the Redskins' defense contributed to 24 of Washington's points and scored its sixth touchdown of the season.

If only the sluggish offense, beset by one of the most inept running attacks in the NFL, could function properly. Against a Saints team with one of the league's worst defenses, the Redskins gained 179 yards and never crossed the opponent's 20 in a 19–3 loss. Kilmer started the game after Jurgensen suffered torn cartilage in his left leg against St. Louis. The offense followed with an equally dismal 190-yard, five-turnover performance in a 21–16 loss to Pittsburgh, the Redskins' first defeat in five Monday night games in the Allen era.

Having fallen into a first-place tie with Dallas, and possibly sensing that the season was slipping away, the Redskins held an emotional players-only meeting. They responded with a 33–9 blowout of San Francisco, as the offense came to life with 343 yards. Kilmer completed 22 of 39 passes for 267 yards and, when he was knocked woozy for one play, Jurgensen entered and threw an 18-yard touchdown pass to Brown.

After a 22–14 win against the Colts, the Redskins posted a 20–0 Thanksgiving Day shutout of the Lions at Tiger Stadium. They took a one-game lead in the NFC East after the Cowboys lost to Miami a few days later. Washington then made it four wins in a row with a 27–24 victory over the Giants that featured a wild fourth-quarter comeback and another chapter in the Billy-Sonny "hobble and wobble" show. Kilmer twisted his left ankle early in the third quarter, and Jurgy saw his first extended action in five weeks, completing 12 of 15 passes for 135 yards. He completed 11 straight during 77- and 66-yard fourth-quarter touchdown drives that helped Washington recover from a 21–3 deficit.

Jurgy started in the next game at Dallas but limped off the field toward the end with a gimpy knee. It was a bad day for the Redskins all around, as the Cowboys romped to a 27–7 victory, creating a tie for the division lead between the two 9–4 teams. "We're going to have to beat the Eagles, that's all there is to it," Allen told the press, referring to his squad's playoff hopes.

In reality, there were all kinds of playoff possibilities, one being that a win over the Eagles in the season finale and a loss by Dallas would give the Redskins the division title, while a Redskins' loss and an Atlanta win would give the Falcons the NFC wild card spot. The Redskins beat the Eagles, 38–20, to qualify for the playoffs for the third straight year, this time as a wild card entry. Washington and Dallas both finished 10–4, but the Cowboys won the division because they beat the Redskins by more points in head-to-head competition.

Kilmer returned to the starting lineup against the Eagles, but Larry Brown stole the show. The workhorse posted his best single-game performance ever, racking up 150 rushing yards and 105 receiving yards in the snow at RFK. He also scored four touchdowns, tying team single-game records for points (24) and touchdowns (four) set by Dickie James in 1964. A *Washington Star* headline on December 17, 1973, appropriately read: "Brown: One-Horse Sleigh."

The 10–4 Redskins were now heading to the upper reaches of the Midwest to face the 12–2 Minnesota Vikings, winners of the Central Division.

## NFC DIVISIONAL PLAYOFF GAME
**Minnesota 27, Washington 20**
**Metropolitan Stadium, Bloomington, Minn.**
**December 22, 1973**
**Attendance: 45,475**

### Gutsy Kilmer Not Enough to Rescue Redskins

Billy Kilmer was uncomfortable—to put it lightly—in the week preceding the Redskins' opening-round playoff clash against Minnesota.

Washington's quarterback had gone to the hospital three times during the season due to an intestinal blockage. This time, he spent more than three days in the hospital and relied on intravenous feeding with the playoff game only a few days away. He was no doubt weak.

"I had these violent pains," Kilmer recalled. "The hospital people put a tube down my throat and into my stomach to try to get all the bad stuff out. It was like a vacuum cleaner."

Still, the ironman played gallantly. He was 13 of 24 for 159 yards and one touchdown, a 28-yarder to receiver Roy Jefferson in the fourth period that cut the Vikings' lead to four, 24–20. It wasn't enough, as Minnesota held on for a 27–20 victory.

The game, played on a frozen field in bitter cold weather, was very close statistically. There were also four lead changes, the first one largely due to the Redskins' special teams, which wreaked havoc on the Vikings. With the Vikings up, 3–0, in the second quarter, Washington's Bob Brunet recovered a fumbled punt on the Minnesota 21, setting up Larry Brown's 3-yard scoring run. Curt Knight's conversion gave the Redskins a

## Allen Made Special Teams Special

George Allen loved his special teams, and he believed that players on those units were special, although they were seldom treated that way. He once had his special teams introduced as the starting lineup at a Monday night game.

He liked to depend on his special teams for at least two wins per season. Year after year, Allen's Redskins influenced games with blocked kicks, clutch kick returns, and forced turnovers, elevating the once anonymous sector of football to new levels of respect.

"We would dominate special teams in every phase," said perhaps the most famous of Allen's Redskin special teamers, Bill Malinchak, who blocked four punts in the 1970s. "People recognized that we were really making a difference in games, if not just outright winning them."

Allen knew that special teams were crucial back when he coached the Rams. In a 1967 game against the Packers, a blocked punt late in the fourth quarter set up the Rams' winning touchdown in a dramatic 27–24 victory. In 1969, Allen hired one of the NFL's first two official special teams coaches, Dick Vermeil. (The same year, Marv Levy served as the Eagles' special teams coach and came to Washington with Allen in 1971.)

As Vermeil remembers it:

George told me he had lost a game because of a kickoff return and missed a playoff spot. Then when they evaluated all the kickoff films during the year they found out that a few guys on kickoff coverage didn't make a tackle the entire season. So he felt the whole process of coaching the kicking game had to be better detailed and put into the hands of one man.

George was always looking for an edge. He was a fanatic in terms of detail. He felt there were details not being taken care of within the kicking game, and that the only way to do it would be to hire a special teams coach.

When Allen came to D.C., special teams began entering the limelight, largely because of his crop of special teams stars: kamikazes Jon Jaqua, Rusty Tillman, Bob Brunet, and Pete Wysocki; kick returners Speedy Duncan, Ted Vactor, and Eddie Brown; kicker Mark Moseley; punter Mike Bragg, and Malinchak. Even defensive end Ron McDole figured into the mix with his uncanny ability to block kicks.

"At the time, special teams were just becoming recognized," Malinchak said. "They were always kind of a filler between possessions. It was like, 'Send a bunch of guys in, let's get this over with.' George Allen with special teams coaches Marv Levy and Paul Lanham said, 'Here's an opportunity.'"

The rest of the football world took notice.

7–3 edge that held until halftime, an encouraging sign in that Washington had won every game that season when leading after the first 30 minutes.

But the Vikings took the second-half kickoff and drove 79 yards, regaining the lead on a short touchdown run. Washington then received a kick from an inconsistent source. Knight, who had made only 22 of 42 field goals in the regular season and missed a 17-yard chip shot in the first quarter, hit from 52 yards out. He followed with a 42-yarder that put the Redskins up, 13–7, early in the final period.

Vikings quarterback Fran Tarkenton, who completed 16 of 28 passes for 222 yards with two touchdowns, subsequently led a 71-yard touchdown drive that ended with his 28-yard scoring pass in the corner of the end zone to receiver John Gilliam. Gilliam beat Speedy Duncan, who was seeing his first cornerback duty in a long time because starter Pat Fischer had suffered two broken ribs in the second quarter. Kilmer immediately tossed an interception that was returned to the Redskins' 7, and Tarkenton hit Gilliam for another touchdown and a 24–13 lead.

"Speedy hadn't played corner all year, he was more like a safety," Kilmer said. "John Gilliam ran behind him for two touchdowns. Nobody could cover him. We had them right up until the fourth quarter."

The Redskins appeared knocked out, until their special teams made another clutch play. Ken Stone blocked a punt—the Redskins' ninth blocked punt or field goal on the year—and Washington took over on the Vikings' 28. Kilmer immediately threw a scoring pass to Jefferson with 5:38 left.

But Tarkenton, who completed 7 of 9 passes in the fourth quarter, led a 43-yard drive that set up Fred Cox's 30-yard field goal for a 27–20 Minnesota lead with about two minutes left. Working with one time-out, the Redskins moved to the Vikings' 42, but Kilmer threw four straight incomplete passes, and the Redskins' season was over.

| | | | | | |
|---|---|---|---|---|---|
| Washington— | 0 | 7 | 3 | 10 | — | 20 |
| Minnesota— | 0 | 3 | 7 | 17 | — | 27 |

Minn — FG Cox 19
Wash — L. Brown 3 run (Knight kick)
Minn — B. Brown 2 run (Cox kick)
Wash — FG Knight 52
Wash — FG Knight 42
Minn — Gilliam 28 pass from Tarkenton (Cox kick)
Minn — Gilliam 8 pass from Tarkenton (Cox kick)
Wash — Jefferson 28 pass from Kilmer (Knight kick)
Minn — FG Cox 30

# 1974: 10–4–0, 1ST PLACE (TIE)— NFC EAST

## Head Coach: George Allen

One of the knocks on George Allen's teams is that they were fast starters and, for the most part, slow finishers that lost momentum heading into the playoffs. The 1974 squad defied that theory.

Midway through the campaign, the 4–3 Redskins were sputtering and the outlook was bleak that they'd reach the playoffs for the fourth straight year. Trailing the Cardinals by three games in the NFC East, the squad was simply fighting to stay afloat.

But the Redskins clawed back into the division title race by winning six of their last seven games, the capper a 42–0 devastation of Chicago. In fact, they came within a desperation bomb by a rookie quarterback playing his first minutes in the NFL of making it seven in a row. They ended up tying the Cardinals atop the NFC East at 10–4 and claimed another wild card playoff spot. St. Louis won the division due to its two wins over Washington.

*Washington Star* sportswriter Steve Guback gave Allen his due for the turnaround. "If there was one thing Allen maintained all season long it was the Redskins' emotion and drive," Guback wrote on December 21, 1974, just before the playoffs began. "He called every game a 'championship game' and has his team believing it. His intensity at practice, his restlessness during a game, his exuberance after victory infected the Redskins almost to the point where they seemed possessed. They played the way Allen wanted them to play, always fired up."

But it was a familiar story in the playoffs, as the Redskins were eliminated in the first round for the third time in the first four seasons of the Allen era. "Allen's first four seasons were great because we made the playoffs each year," Redskins quarterback Billy Kilmer said. "It was disappointing because we won in only one of those seasons."

Not known for offensive explosiveness in the early years under Allen, the Redskins compiled amazing numbers in 1974 that left many Washingtonians and NFL insiders in awe. Kilmer and Sonny Jurgensen finished as two of the league's best passers. The 40-year-old Jurgensen, bruised and battered most of the year, placed No. 1 in the NFC in completion percentage (64.1) after connecting on 107 of 167 passes for 1,185 yards, with 11 touchdowns and five interceptions. The 35-year-old Kilmer was close behind, completing 137 of 234 passes for 1,632 yards (58.5 completion percentage), plus 10 touchdowns and six interceptions. They aimed for Charley Taylor (54 catches), a Pro Bowl selection; Jerry Smith (44); Roy Jefferson (43); and Larry Brown (37).

The passing game, which was largely responsible for the Redskins' NFC-high 320 points, compensated for a virtually nonexistent running attack. Brown, playing with frail knees, posted a team-high 430 yards rushing, followed by Moses Denson (391). Duane Thomas had the Redskins' only 100-yard rushing game.

The defense was like an Allen defense usually is: imposing. The unit yielded 196 points, fourth lowest in the NFL, and allowed single-digit points in four games, not including the shutout of the Bears. The Redskins also led the NFC in interceptions (25) and allowed yardage totals in rushing and passing that were among the best in the conference. Linebacker

Chris Hanburger, defensive tackle Diron Talbert, and safety Ken Houston made the Pro Bowl.

The season also saw the appearance of two players who would make seismic impacts on the franchise in years to come. Early in the off-season, Allen traded the Redskins' No. 1 draft choice in 1976 to Miami for the rights to quarterback Joe Theismann, who had excelled for three seasons in the Canadian Football League after finishing as the Heisman Trophy runner-up at Notre Dame in 1970. Allen also acquired free agent kicker Mark Moseley, a three-year veteran who was out of football in 1973 after losing his job with Houston. He beat out veteran Curt Knight, who displayed a torrent of inconsistency in 1972 and '73, to become the Redskins' starter.

Theismann saw action at quarterback in the first two exhibition games while the veterans were on strike against the owners. During the 42-day walkout, Allen worked hard to keep his team from being fractured, according to Redskins offensive tackle George Starke. "It always amazed me that we had a practice schedule," Starke said. "I know George was meeting behind the scenes with his generals (team captains), which was against league rules at the time, and giving them practice stuff to do so we had something to officially work with as a team. He wanted the team to stay together because at some point the strike was going to be over. Other coaches and owners were trying to split their teams because they were trying to get their players to come in. George knew those teams would not fare well when the strike was over."

After the strike ended, the Redskins wrapped up a 1–5 preseason, not a good way to prepare for a brutal regular-season schedule. In addition to their traditional home-and-away games against NFC East foes, the Redskins would face back-to-back Super Bowl champion Miami, AFC Central division champ Cincinnati, and NFC West division-winner Los Angeles. There were two Monday night games.

The season opener seemed like déjà vu from 1973, as the defense accounted for or set up almost all of the Redskins' points in a 13–10 win over the Giants. Cornerback Mike Bass returned an interception 28 yards for a touchdown, and his fumble recovery in Giants territory set up another score.

The Redskins' offensive came alive in week 2 against St. Louis, crafting drives of 51, 61, 69, 78, and 47 yards. It was for naught in a 17–10 loss. The Cardinals, who scored on a 71-yard fumble return and a 75-yard run from scrimmage, improved to 2–0 and moved into first place in the NFC East, a spot they held all season.

The Redskins bounced back with a 30–3 rout of the Broncos in a Monday night game but dropped a 28–17 decision to Cincinnati after falling behind by 25 points. Washington beat the Bengals statistically but surrendered more big-play scores on a 90-yard punt return and a 47-yard fumble return, both by cornerback (and future Redskin) Lemar Parrish.

The 2–2 Redskins now trailed St. Louis by two games and second-place Philadelphia by one. A loss in week 5 to Miami would damage playoff hopes. Sonny Jurgensen's golden arm kept the Redskins in contention.

Jurgensen, who started the game in place of Kilmer, completed 26 of 39 passes for 303 yards and two touchdowns. He threw three interceptions in the first half but put on a clinic in the last two minutes. With Miami up, 17–13, he completed 6 of 7 passes on a 60-yard drive, the last one a 6-yard toss to fullback Larry Smith, a preseason acquisition who replaced veteran Charley Harraway. (Harraway had bolted for the new

World Football League, which signed a number of NFL players to lucrative contracts.) Moseley's conversion gave the Redskins a stunning 20–17 win in the first rematch of Super Bowl VII.

"Sonny responded with the dash and élan of a 20-year-old," according to the Redskins edition of *Pro! Magazine* on October 20, 1974. "There may have been other days in Sonny's long and distinguished career when he was as good as last Sunday, a few even when he may have been better, but none was ever more important."

Next, Jurgensen completed 17 of 30 passes with three touchdowns, and the defense intercepted five passes, in a 24–3 win over the Giants. The win set up a collision in St. Louis between the 4–2 Redskins and 6–0 Cardinals, who squeaked by, 23–20, to pull three games in front of Washington in the NFC East.

Jurgy gave another solid performance: 20 of 29 for 201 yards and two scores. But he was hobbling by game's end, and Allen tapped Kilmer to start at Green Bay in a 17–6 Redskins victory. Kilmer started again the next week at Philadelphia, but Allen called on No. 9 with the Redskins trailing 20–7 early in the third period. The redhead crafted another extraordinary comeback, completing 14 of 23 passes for 172 yards and one touchdown, a 30-yard game-winning pass to Charley Taylor late in the fourth period. It capped a 72-yard drive in which he completed 6 of 7 passes for 69 yards. Taylor caught nine passes for 155 yards.

With St. Louis having lost two straight, the 6–3 Redskins were suddenly back in the thick of the NFC East race. They'd try to build on their momentum in a 12-day period that included three games, two against their top rivals, the Cowboys.

The Redskins first ran up a 28–0 halftime lead on Dallas at RFK. But they got conservative in the second half and nervously watched the Cowboys close the gap to seven. Dallas later had a first-and-goal at the 7 with about four minutes left but failed to score.

A 26–7 rout of the Eagles preceded another clash with the Cowboys on Thanksgiving Day at Texas Stadium. When the Redskins led, 23–17, and Dallas faced a second down at midfield with 28 seconds to play and no time-outs left, it appeared Washington was set to sweep the Cowboys for the first time ever. But rookie quarterback Clint Longley, summoned earlier in the game to replace an injured Roger Staubach, hit Drew Pearson on a late 50-yard touchdown pass. The conversion gave Dallas a 24–23 victory in one of the most thrilling games in the history of the Redskins-Cowboys rivalry.

But the Redskins kept marching to the playoffs and clinched at least a wild card berth with a Monday night win over the Rams. The Redskins fell behind, 10–0, to the Western Division leaders but Kilmer threw three touchdown passes in the second quarter to spark his squad to a 23–17 win that put the 9–4 Redskins in an NFC East tie with 9–4 St. Louis. A win over the Bears in the season finale, coupled with a St. Louis loss to the Giants, meant the Redskins would win the division, once a distant thought.

Both Washington and St. Louis won, forcing the Redskins to settle for a wild card spot. In their 42–0 dismantling of the Bears, the Redskins piled up 511 yards in perhaps the most overpowering display of offense in the Allen era. All three of their quarterbacks, Kilmer, Jurgy, and Joe Theismann, took part in the show; Theismann, seeing his first extended action of the season, completed 6 of 7 passes for 123 yards and a touchdown. Washington's defense had four interceptions and four sacks and allowed 126 yards.

By punctuating their regular season with such a convincing performance, the 10–4 Redskins looked red-hot heading into their opening-round playoff game against the 10–4 Rams.

## NFC DIVISIONAL PLAYOFF GAME
**Los Angeles 19, Washington 10**
**Los Angeles Coliseum**
**December 22, 1974**
**Attendance: 80,118**

### Turnovers, Second-Half Collapse
### Send Weary Redskins Packing

The Redskins must have felt like Lewis and Clark. Two weeks after flying to Los Angeles and topping the Rams to clinch a playoff berth, they took part in another 3,000-mile, cross-country trip to confront L.A. in the playoffs.

This time, the travel-weary Redskins looked flat, turning the ball over six times and doing little on offense in a 19–10 loss. "It's kind of tough to play a team twice in two weeks at their park and win, traveling across the country like that," Redskins quarterback Billy Kilmer said years later. "But in the first half, we played pretty good, we kept it close."

But the Redskins, ahead 10–7 at halftime, collapsed like dominoes in the second half. Fumbles early in the third period by running back Larry Brown and kick returner Doug Cunningham set up field goals that put the Rams up, 13–10. Quarterback Sonny Jurgensen replaced Kilmer for his first true playoff action as a Redskin. This time the miracle comeback specialist failed to rescue his team.

Early in the fourth period, Jurgy was hit hard by Rams defensive tackle Merlin Olsen, and his pass wobbled into the hands of linebacker Isiah Robertson. Robertson, with help from a devastating block on Jurgensen, returned the interception 59 yards for a touchdown to account for the final score. The Rams' defense, one of the best in the league, preserved the lead by intercepting Jurgensen twice more in what would be the final game of his 18-year Hall of Fame career.

The Redskins, who posted one of the lowest turnover totals in the NFL in the regular season, picked a bad time to play their sloppiest game of the year. But a Rams turnover, cornerback Pat Fischer's interception, set up the Redskins' go-ahead touchdown in the first half, fullback Moses Densen's 1-yard run. Punter Mike Bragg, subbing for an injured Mark Moseley, converted, sending the Redskins into the locker room up, 10–7.

Washington's offense didn't have to do much from that point on, for the Rams mustered only 182 yards in the game. But turnovers spelled defeat for the burgundy and gold.

| | | | | | | |
|---|---|---|---|---|---|---|
| Washington— | 3 | 7 | 0 | 0 | — | 10 |
| Los Angeles— | 7 | 0 | 3 | 9 | — | 19 |

LA —— Klein 10 pass from Harris (Ray kick)
Wash — FG Bragg 35
Wash — Denson 1 run (Bragg kick)
LA —— FG Ray 37
LA —— FG Ray 26
LA —— Robertson 59 interception return (pass failed)

# 1975: 8–6, 3RD PLACE—NFC EAST

## Head Coach: George Allen

It's conceivable that Redskins fans with heart problems were advised to find healthier things to do than follow their team religiously in 1975.

The cardiac squad battled for its life in three sudden death games, a record for a 14-game season, and competed in five games overall that came down to the final play. (The NFL had implemented overtime in 1974.) The final two overtime games, back-to-back losses to St. Louis and Oakland late in the season, crippled the Redskins' playoff hopes. They failed to reach the playoffs for the first time in five years under George Allen and finished 8–6.

"The Over the Hill Gang didn't just quietly fade away; but went down with all guns blazing in the same storybook style that marked them as champions from 1971 to 1974," according to the Redskins' edition of *Pro!* magazine on December 21, 1975.

That was the flowery way of looking at it. Realistically, the Redskins' role as postseason spectators triggered questions about the future of the franchise, namely, whether Allen's philosophy of trading draft choices for seasoned veterans was starting to haunt the aging squad. The age factor seemed to mostly affect Allen's cherished defense, which allowed 4,761 yards and 276 points, high totals to date in his tenure in Washington and far beyond the prior season's numbers. The injury-riddled unit yielded chunks of yards and points down the stretch, when the Redskins lost four of their last six games and failed to keep pace with St. Louis and Dallas, younger teams that defeated Washington with the playoffs in doubt and finished higher in the NFC East.

The offense, on the other hand, racked up one of the highest yardage totals in the Allen regime (4,844) despite suffering its own stream of injuries. Thirty-six-year-old quarterback Billy Kilmer posted another superb year, finishing as one of the NFC's top quarterbacks with 178 of 346 passing (51.4 completion percentage) for 2,440 yards, plus 23 touchdowns and 16 interceptions. And contrary to the Allen doctrine that rookies were secondary to his team's fortunes, first-year running back Mike Thomas, a fifth-round pick from UNLV, ran for 919 yards and was named NFL Rookie of the Year.

Another off-season acquisition, eight-year veteran quarterback Randy Johnson, created a four-quarterback alignment that included Kilmer, Joe Theismann, and Sonny Jurgensen. Someone was bound to go. The one who departed was the most popular of the four in the eyes of Redskin fans and a favorite of local sportswriters, too.

Allen made the controversial decision of pushing Jurgensen, one of the most prolific passers in NFL history, into retirement. After Jurgy became a free agent on May 1, Allen refused to renew his $120,000 contract and named Kilmer his No. 1 man, followed by Theismann and Johnson. Jurgensen, who never saw eye-to-eye with the defensive-minded Allen, was upset about hanging up the burgundy and gold uniform he'd worn for 11 seasons in the nation's capital.

"That was a very sad moment," Jurgensen, nearly 41 at the time, said in looking back. "I felt I could still contribute. I felt I would have enough intelligence to know when to get out.

"The way it came down was George and I met at the Dulles [Airport] Marriott. Billy had a desire to be traded at the time,

## Allen Considers Gigantic Investment

George Allen had a history of making dramatic acquisitions. This one would have been really big.

With thoughts of patching holes on the defensive line before training camp began in July 1975, Allen and his top assistant, Tim Temerario, pursued help in 7–5, 445-pound pro wrestler "Andre The Giant." The behemoth turned down a contract offer reported to be about $100,000, preferring to use his colossal size on the mat.

"That was more of an off-season stunt than anything else," *Washington Star* sportswriter Steve Guback said years later. "Andre couldn't play football for crying out loud. He didn't know how to rush a passer or shed a blocker. It made for a nice off-season story."

Andre the Giant gives Redskins quarterback Joe Theismann a lift on July 8, 1975, at Duke Zeibert's restaurant in Washington.

Quarterback Billy Kilmer sneaks into the end zone for the winning score in a 30–24 overtime thriller against Dallas on November 2, 1975, one of three overtime games the Redskins played that season. Two weeks later, it appeared they had another win locked up when Redskins cornerback Pat Fischer (bent over) jarred the ball from Cardinals receiver Mel Gray (lying down) in the end zone at the end of regulation. But the officials ruled it a catch, and the conversion tied the game at 17. St. Louis won on a field goal in overtime.

but George was trying to talk Billy out of that. He said they would want me to come back if Billy demanded a trade, but not to come back if they could talk Billy into staying. That was hurtful. It didn't sit well. It made me decide that if you don't think I can help you, then thank you very much."

Kilmer looked sharp in the preseason, completing 53 of 93 passes for 834 yards and 10 touchdowns. Mike Thomas and another rookie running back, Ralph Nelson, rushed for a combined 522 yards.

The season opened with great promise. The Redskins annihilated the Saints and Giants in back-to-back games at RFK Stadium by a combined score of 90–16. After the latter win,

the *Washington Star* ran a headline that read, "49–13—Are They the New Redskins?"

The Redskins came back to Earth in losing to the Eagles, 26–10, but rebounded with a 27–17 win over the Cardinals in a Monday night game. Kilmer was hot, Thomas rushed for 100 yards, the defense intercepted three passes and recovered two fumbles, and the special teams offered some trickery. With the score tied at 10 in the second half, the Redskins lined up for a 37-yard field goal. Theismann, the holder, rolled out with the ball and passed to linebacker John Pergine, who rumbled in for the score to give the Redskins the lead for good.

The Redskins subsequently fell to Houston, 13–10, but continued on their roller-coaster ride with a 23–7 victory over the Browns, as Thomas rushed for 124 yards.

Then came the first overtime thriller, a 30–24 win over the Cowboys that lifted the 5–2 Redskins into a first place tie with Dallas. With the score tied at 24, the Cowboys had a chance to win it in regulation, but the Redskins' Bryant Salter blocked a 28-yard field goal try with 13 seconds left.

In overtime, Redskins safety Ken Houston intercepted a pass by quarterback Roger Staubach and returned it to midfield. A personal foul on Staubach, who took a swing at cornerback Pat Fischer, moved the ball to the 35. Kilmer completed two passes to Charley Taylor, and the Redskins ran for a first down to the 1. An offside call on Dallas moved the ball six inches from the goal line, where in the huddle Kilmer had a message for guard Walt Sweeney: "I said I'm going to quarterback sneak it right behind you, Sweeney," Kilmer recalled.

Booed relentlessly for throwing four interceptions earlier in the game, Kilmer sneaked into the end zone, and the 55,000 fans at RFK erupted.

Washington followed with a 21–13 victory over the Giants. Thomas rushed for 123 yards, and Randy Johnson, in for Kilmer after the starter injured his shoulder in the first half, brought the Redskins back from a 13–7 deficit by completing 11 of 16 passes for 138 yards and directing 87- and 62-yard scoring drives.

Meanwhile, injuries were decimating the starting lineup, sapping the Redskins of their consistency and depth. But *Washington Star* columnist David Israel wrote that the resourceful squad was somehow hanging on:

For the Washington Redskins, the ephemeral quality of heroic NFL existence has been so graphically illustrated this season. The injuries continue to occur unimpeded. Weekly, there are more names on the roster that are probable or doubtful than there are names playing guard.

Kilmer was the star last week against Dallas, yesterday he was sent to the X-ray machine in the second quarter of the Redskins' 21–13 victory over the New York Giants. The left side of the offensive line has been wiped out, the defensive backfield corps has been depleted, as has the receiving corps. There is, each week, a paucity of healthy running backs. Now a starting linebacker has been injured.

In the standings, the 6–2 Redskins were tied with St. Louis for first in the NFC East, although a brutal schedule was ahead consisting of the Cardinals, Oakland, and Minnesota, all division winners by season's end. The Redskins first fell to St. Louis on a maddening day. Trailing 17–10 with time running out, the Cardinals had a first down on the Redskins' 6. Quarterback Jim Hart threw three incompletions, and on fourth down, he hit leaping receiver Mel Gray in the end zone. Cornerback Pat Fischer collided with Gray simultaneously, and the ball fell to the turf.

Confusion ensued. One official ruled touchdown, another signaled incompletion. After about a 10-minute huddle, the officials emerged, calling it a touchdown.

"The evidence is clear he didn't catch the ball," Fischer said in hindsight. "Just as it hit his shoulder, I made contact. I doubt if he would have ever caught it, but they said he had it that fraction in the end zone and called it a touchdown. Gray immediately knew he didn't catch it because he put his hands on his helmet in frustration."

Jim Bakken's extra point tied the game at 17, and his 37-yard overtime field goal gave St. Louis a 20–17 win and first place in the division. The next week, the Redskins saw an instant replay when 48-year-old George Blanda kicked a 37-yarder in overtime to give the Raiders a 26–23 win.

Although the 6–4 Redskins were in third place in the division, Allen told reporters his squad would make the playoffs. Washington pulled out victories in two straight breathtaking games, first a 31–30 victory at RFK over an undefeated Vikings squad. Defensive end Ron McDole preserved the win by blocking a 45-yard field goal on the game's last play. Then came a 30–27 win over the Falcons on Mark Moseley's 39-yard field goal with two seconds left. Kilmer, playing with a broken bone in his foot and a separated shoulder, had one of his greatest days as a pro, completing 25 of 38 passes for 320 yards and three touchdowns.

Now, a Redskins win over Dallas would put them in the playoffs. A loss, and the season was over. The Cowboys determined Washington's fate with a 31–10 pounding at Texas Stadium. Toss in a 26–3 loss to the Eagles in the finale—when Randy Johnson and Joe Theismann combined for seven interceptions and the RFK crowd repeatedly booed its team—and the 1975 season was over.

# 1976: 10–4, 2ND PLACE—NFC EAST

## Head Coach: George Allen

By 1976, it appeared "The Future Is Now" philosophy of Redskins coach George Allen had mortgaged not only the team's future but also its present.

Since arriving in 1971, "Trader George" had dealt an abundance of early-round draft picks for players, mostly seasoned veterans who he envisioned could help the squad win immediately. The Redskins picked no earlier than the fifth round in their first five drafts in the Allen regime. Allen also zapped the Redskins of valuable draft picks through the rest of the 1970s.

The coach had to improvise. His tool: a new era of player free agency. In late 1975, the courts overturned a rule that had established "fair and equitable" compensation when a team lost a free agent to another team. Franchises were now more inclined to sign free agents who had completed their contract-option seasons because no compensation was required.

Allen grabbed the fat wallet of team president Edward Bennett Williams, who gave the coach carte blanche, and formed what was then the most expensive Redskins squad ever, one with a $2 million to $4 million payroll. The coach signed running back Calvin Hill, a one-time Cowboys star who had played in 1975 in the World Football League, for an estimated $135,000 per year. Hill had two 1,000-yard seasons to his name and was NFL Rookie of the Year in 1969. Allen also signed Jets fullback John Riggins, a 1,000-yard rusher and Pro Bowl player in 1975, to a multiyear contract worth a reported $1.5 million.

Two other free agents also agreed to hefty contracts: Cowboys tight end Jean Fugett, a four-year veteran coming off his biggest season with 38 catches for 488 yards, and Falcons quarterback Pat Sullivan, a former Heisman Trophy winner.

## PROFILE

### Edward Bennett Williams: In Defense of the Washington Redskins

Edward Bennett Williams was a towering figure in the legal profession. The celebrated trial attorney defended people such as Teamsters' boss Jimmy Hoffa, "Godfather" Frank Costello, singer Frank Sinatra, billionaire oilman Armand Hammer, Greek shipping magnate Aristotle Onassis, baseball great Joe DiMaggio, boxing champ Sugar Ray Robinson, and Wisconsin senator Joseph McCarthy of "McCarthyism" infamy. The rich and powerful flocked to him like he was a "miracle worker who could make the guilty go free," Evan Thomas wrote in his 1991 biography of Williams, *The Man to See.* He was tightly connected in political circles, a confidant to some of the most famous people in Washington.

Williams's enormous influence was also palpable in the NFL. As the Redskins' president from 1965 to 1979, a period when he owned a small percentage of the franchise, Williams attracted gargantuan names to the organization.

In his biggest move, he talked legendary coach Vince Lombardi out of retirement in 1969. He lured another brilliant coach, George Allen, to Washington in 1971. In 1978, he hired Bobby Beathard, who became arguably the finest general manager in NFL history. Essentially, Williams laid much of the groundwork for the Redskins to stand as one of the NFL's most successful franchises from the early 1970s to the early 1990s.

"He pulled all the triggers," Redskins cornerback Pat Fischer said. "No one else could have gone and persuaded Lombardi to come and coach. No one could have made a

better or stronger commitment to use the tools that were out there and get the people to achieve what everybody wanted: winning. Then what does he do? He brings in George Allen. Is that a strong commitment to having a successful organization? It's unparalleled, really."

Redskins linebacker Sam Huff said of Williams, "He was a great salesman. He knew how to bring the big names in."

Williams's ties to the Redskins began in the late 1950s, when he was a lawyer for Redskins owner George Preston Marshall. He bought 5 percent of the franchise in March 1962. Three years later, when Marshall turned seriously ill, he became team president and took control of its daily operations.

Williams, who proclaimed his love for "contest living . . . in which every effort ends up a victory or defeat," saw his squad open 0–5 in 1965, prompting him to share his frustration with reporters: "I'm accustomed to winning or losing because of something I do. Here, I don't even know what's wrong. I wake up nights trying to figure out what's wrong."

One problem Williams tried to fix was the Redskins' dubious status as one of the lowest-paid teams in the league. He called for compensating the squad's coaches and star players with top-of-the-line salaries.

"There is this to say about Edward Bennett Williams— when he hires a Redskin coach it's no nickel-and-dime deal," Francis Stann wrote in the *Evening Star* on January 8, 1971. "He guaranteed Otto Graham $60,000 a year for

Williams enjoys a laugh with Redskins radio play-by-play man Steve Gilmartin (far left) and Redskins Hall of Fame receiver Wayne Millner, a long-time team scout, during a mini-camp at Georgetown University in June 1969. Williams didn't meddle in team affairs but enjoyed "being around the guys" at practice, Gilmartin said.

## Edward Bennett Williams: In Defense of the Washington Redskins—*continued*

five years. He gave Vince Lombardi everything but RFK Stadium. Today, he's got George Allen on the payroll for seven years. Plus fringe benefits."

As Williams once said, "If you want something good, you've got to pay for it. I never got anything for nothing. Certainly nothing worthwhile."

Williams graduated summa cum laude from Holy Cross College in Massachusetts and earned his J. D. degree from prestigious Georgetown University Law School in Washington. After taking control of the Redskins, he influenced several players, including guard Vince Promuto, tight end Pat Richter, and safety Brig Owens, to attend law school.

"He cared beyond winning and losing," Promuto said. "He actually talked to all the players and told them he was concerned about their afterlife because the normal career of a football player is only three-and-a-half to four years. He said we have to do something with the rest of our lives like getting into universities and getting job interviews. He was an extremely good guy for being the owner of a football team."

"He was a very, very powerful guy," Promuto added. "People like me would go to court for his summation during a criminal case. You couldn't get a seat in the courtroom. Everyone talks about (legendary American criminal lawyer) Clarence Darrow being a great attorney. Yet in my era with the Redskins, Williams was the Clarence Darrow of the country, for sure."

Williams relinquished control of the team's day-to-day operations in 1980 to Redskins majority owner Jack Kent Cooke. By then, the famed counselor had realized his dream of buying a Major League baseball team, the Baltimore Orioles. In 1983, when the Orioles won the World Series and the Redskins captured Super Bowl XVII, he became the only owner in pro sports history believed to have won a Super Bowl and World Series in the same year.

Williams sold his 5 percent interest in the Redskins to Cooke in 1985. He died of cancer at age 68 on August 13, 1988.

"Ed was a non-playing jock," Redskins flanker-running back Bobby Mitchell said. "He really loved sports, football and baseball. His tenure as president was very good. We didn't win any championships, but he had ways of talking to us and keeping us from giving up. He was a great speaker, anyway."

As Brig Owens put it, "Edward Bennett Williams was a winner."

---

Sullivan, who had languished on Atlanta's bench the prior four seasons, was cut before the season started.

The arrival of Hill and Riggins created sort of a dream backfield. They joined with two-time 1,000-yard rusher Larry Brown, the all-time leading ground gainer in Redskins history, and halfback Mike Thomas, the 1975 NFL Rookie of the Year. The Redskins also had reliable reserve fullbacks Moses Denson and Bob Brunet. Allen refused to re-sign Duane Thomas, who'd rushed for 442 yards in two seasons in Washington.

The Redskins were thin at other positions, such as cornerback, so Allen traded defensive tackle Manny Sistrunk and three draft picks to the Eagles for rookie cornerback Joe Lavender. The coach also acquired a former nemesis in Dolphins safety Jake Scott, the MVP of Super Bowl VII.

Edward Bennett Williams voiced high hopes for his 1976 squad, promising at the Redskins' annual Welcome Home Luncheon, that this season would be the best one in team history. The Redskins responded with a 3–0 start, though not everything was a cinch.

Washington trailed the Giants, 17–12, with about two minutes left in the season opener at RFK, when kick return specialist and backup safety Eddie Brown, a lightning bolt all season who led the NFL with 646 punt return yards, ran one back 45 yards to the Giants' 42. Quarterback Billy Kilmer, dazed from a blow that left him with a bloody nose and with ribs hurting from a hit in the preseason, then delivered one of his patented gutsy performances. He connected with Larry Brown and Roy Jefferson on fourth down plays, before throwing a 5-yard scoring pass to Mike Thomas with 53 seconds left in the Redskins' 19–17 win.

The Redskins followed with a 31–7 rout of the expansion Seattle Seahawks and then met the Eagles in a Monday night game. In the "Bedtime Story" that lasted nearly four hours, the Redskins, inept on offense and defense, allowed the lowly Eagles to hang around and score a late touchdown that sent the game into overtime tied at 17. In overtime, Eddie Brown intercepted a pass that gave the Redskins possession at the Eagles' 23. Mark Moseley kicked a game-winning 29-yard field goal with 2:11 left in overtime.

The 3–0 Redskins were now tied with Dallas atop the NFC East. But Chicago's 33–7 spanking of the Redskins and a Cowboys victory snapped the tie. Washington gained only 119 yards against the Bears and appeared headed for its first shutout defeat since 1971, until quarterback Joe Theismann threw a 1-yard scoring pass to tight end Jerry Smith in the waning minutes.

Theismann, who entered the game after Kilmer bruised his throwing arm and shoulder, earned his first career start the next week against 0–4 Kansas City, the first of a four-game home stand. He passed for 270 yards and two scores, and electrified the crowd with his scrambling. But with a minute left, the Chiefs used a three-handoff flea-flicker and scored on a 37-yard touchdown pass to shock the Redskins, 33–30. Washington rolled up 438 yards, but its defense remained in question. The unit, with 11 interceptions and 10 sacks in the first three games, had no picks and one sack against the Bears and Chiefs. The Redskins had also allowed an average of 418 yards in their past three games.

The defense looked like its old self in a 20–7 win over the Lions, as cornerbacks Pat Fischer and Joe Lavender intercepted passes that led to scores, and the pass rush posted five sacks.

The 4–2 Redskins proceeded to trip up the Cardinals, 20–10, in the "mud bowl." The rivals struggled in a steady downpour on a sloppy, beaten-up field at RFK before a Monday night TV audience that saw the Cardinals fumble the ball nine times and lose eight of them.

Despite their butterfingers, the Cardinals led, 10–6, in the fourth quarter. But Mike Thomas ran for a touchdown to create a 13–10 game, and Eddie Brown took a punt and sloshed 71 yards through the mud for the clinching score in one of the most thrilling plays of the Redskins' season. Theismann, who started his fourth straight game, was sacked seven times. On the last one, he took a vicious shot to the kidneys that forced him to the sidelines, and Allen started Kilmer in a pivotal upcoming game against Dallas. At the time, the Redskins and Cardinals were tied for second in the NFC East at 5–2, a game behind the 6–1 Cowboys.

Kilmer was booed mercilessly at RFK during an unproductive performance in the Cowboys' 20–7 victory. In what resembled the quarterback flip-flopping from the Sonny vs. Billy days, Theismann replaced Kilmer in the fourth period and went on to start in a 24–21 win at San Francisco, completing 20 of 32 passes for 302 yards and three touchdowns, all to tight end Jean Fugett.

But the Giants snapped an 11-game losing streak to the Redskins with a 12–9 win, leaving Washington two games behind St. Louis in the wild card race. Allen's bunch was being written off. "The Redskins now have about the same chance of making the playoffs as Jerry Ford has of being president on the morning of Jan. 21 [1977]," *Washington Star* columnist David Israel wrote on November 15, 1976, playing on the fact that Ford had just been voted out of office and would not be inaugurated.

No so fast, for the Redskins crafted four straight wins. After a 16–10 win over St. Louis in which Thomas rushed for 195 yards, Washington blanked the Eagles, 24–0. The Redskins' defense had five sacks, two fumble recoveries, and two interceptions against Philly, and Thomas gained 49 yards to join Larry Brown as the only Redskins to ever top the 1,000-yard rushing mark.

Two of the Redskins' heralded free agents, relatively silent all season, proceeded to show their worth. In a 37–16 victory over the Jets, John Riggins ran for 104 yards against his former team, and Calvin Hill added 73. Kilmer, who returned to the starting lineup against St. Louis, was sensational with 13 of 17 passing and three touchdowns. The defense again was sharp with six sacks, two fumble recoveries, and two interceptions.

Washington and St. Louis were now both tied at 9–4, lending drama to the final day. A Redskins win over Dallas would give them the wild card spot, owing to their two victories against St. Louis. They could not win the NFC East title, which the Cowboys had secured. But in Texas Stadium, where the Redskins had never won, they showed the Cowboys which team was better on December 12, 1976.

The three expensive free agents—Riggins, Hill, and Fugett—scored touchdowns on a Redskin offense that amassed 358 yards. Riggins ran for 95 alone. Hill showed up his former team with a 15-yard scoring run with less than five minutes to play that put the Redskins ahead for good, 20–14. Shortly after, Redskin lineman Dennis Johnson intercepted a tipped pass, setting up Riggins's 3-yard scoring run. A fired-up Redskin defense sacked quarterback Roger Staubach five times, intercepted two passes and recovered two fumbles.

With the victory, the Redskins earned their fourth season of at least 10 wins and fifth playoff appearance in the Allen era. They also embarrassed skeptics who had buried them when times were tough earlier in the year. On his way off the field and into the Redskins' locker room, Allen ripped down a banner that read, "LOSERS." And why not? It was his turn to laugh it up.

## NFC DIVISIONAL PLAYOFF GAME
**Minnesota 35, Washington 20**
**Metropolitan Stadium, Bloomington, Minn.**
**December 18, 1976**
**Attendance: 47,221**

### Déjà vu: Vikings, Tarkenton Derail Redskins in Playoffs

The "Purple People Eaters" and the rest of the squad dressed in purple devoured the Redskins on a balmy 40-degree December afternoon in Minneapolis.

The Central Division champs were in control from nearly start to finish in a 35–20 victory that wasn't nearly that close. It was the second time in four seasons the Vikings had eliminated the visiting Redskins in the opening round of the playoffs.

"It was very frustrating," Redskins receiver Roy Jefferson said. "You knew you were going to be in the playoffs, and that doggone Minnesota beat us two times. It was up there. We never played them at home."

The Vikings set the tone on the first play from scrimmage with a 41-yard run. They led 21–3 at halftime and 35–3 late in the third period, before the Redskins scored two touchdowns in the fourth quarter. Vikings running backs Chuck Foreman and Brent McClanahan each rushed for more than 100 yards, and quarterback Fran Tarkenton gave a yeoman performance similar to his 1973 playoff dismantling of the Redskins with 12 of 21 passing for 170 yards and three touchdowns.

To Vikings Hall of Fame offensive tackle Ron Yary, Tarkenton was the difference in both playoff games: "When you get into the playoffs, you're really at the mercy of your quarterback. Fran had big days. Everything else was probably even."

The Redskins' quarterback, Billy Kilmer, completed 26 of 49 passes for 298 yards and two touchdowns, as his squad abandoned its running game. But some of his passes were dropped while a win was achievable, including one in the end zone by Frank Grant, the team's top receiver for the season with 50 catches, that would have cut the lead to 21–10 at halftime and given the Redskins crucial momentum.

The loss marked a dubious distinction for Redskins coach George Allen. It was his seventh defeat in as many playoff games on the road, including those from his days in Los Angeles. It was also the fourth time his Redskins had lost in the opening round as a wild card team, a statistic that puzzles Redskins from the Allen era.

"In those playoff games, I never felt like we lost, we were just never in sync for some reason," special teams star Bill Malinchak said. "We were just a half-step off for some reason. We never clicked in those games."

After the loss to the Vikings, media peppered Allen and his players with questions about the Redskins' future—which was suddenly blurry despite their amazing regular-season finish. Allen said he had one more season on his seven-year Redskins contract and that he planned to honor it.

| Washington— | 3 | 0 | 3 | 14 | — | 20 |
|---|---|---|---|---|---|---|
| Minnesota— | 14 | 7 | 14 | 0 | — | 35 |

Minn — Voigt 18 pass from Tarkenton (Cox kick)
Wash — FG Moseley 47
Minn — White 27 pass from Tarkenton (Cox kick)
Minn — Foreman 2 run (Cox kick)
Minn — Foreman 30 run (Cox kick)
Wash — FG Moseley 35
Minn — White 9 pass from Tarkenton (Cox kick)
Wash — Grant 12 pass from Kilmer (Moseley kick)
Wash — Jefferson 3 pass from Kilmer (Moseley kick)

# 1977: 9–5, 2ND PLACE—NFC EAST

## Head Coach: George Allen

Preeminent trial lawyer Edward Bennett Williams, so accustomed to winning big in the courtroom, also wanted monumental successes from his football team. The Redskins' president saw five playoff appearances in the 1970s but no NFL championships as insufficient. He thus issued a forceful challenge before the 1977 season: "Last year, we had 10 wins and four losses, a creditable showing in any sports endeavor," he wrote through the Redskins' alumni association. "But it wasn't good enough. This year, we must be better."

Record-wise, the Redskins were worse. They finished 9–5 and missed the playoffs for the second time in seven seasons under George Allen. His defense allowed 189 points, the team's lowest total in the 17-year history of the 14-game season. The unit also recorded two shutouts and held two other teams to single-digit point totals. But the offense was nonexistent. The Redskins scored 196 points, the lowest total by far in the Allen regime and nearly 100 points less than the prior year.

Were Redskin fans losing patience with Allen because of he relied on his defense to win games and settled for a conservative snore and bore offense? "I don't think the fans ever turned on Allen," said Steve Guback, the Redskins' beat writer at the time for the *Washington Star*. "They were winning, and when you're winning, people are enthusiastic. A lot of fans were willing to accept George's thinking because he'd been successful."

Williams would disagree with Allen, however, especially when it came to the quarterback position. Allen's constant favorite was Billy Kilmer, the steady but unspectacular player who mirrored the coach's philosophy of a no-frills offense. Williams preferred Sonny Jurgensen, and then Joe Theismann, over Kilmer. Guback once quoted Allen as saying that Williams called the coach at 11 o'clock one night during the 1977 season and ordered him to bench Kilmer for Theismann or else the coach's contract would not be renewed for the 1978 season.

"I knew Ed Williams, he never liked me as a quarterback," Kilmer said. "He'd get drunk and call George in the middle of the night and say, 'You've got to bench Billy for Sonny or Theismann.' But he didn't know anything about football."

Allen started the 38-year-old Kilmer in the first six games, which the Redskins split. They first lost to the Giants, 20–17, the only season-opening defeat in Allen's 12-year NFL coaching career. The game was tied at 17, but Giants linebacker Harry Carson recovered a fumble by halfback Mike Thomas on the Redskins' 19 with 1:48 to play, setting up a 30-yard field goal that provided the winning points. Thomas's fumble typified the Redskins' propensity for making an abundance of mental mistakes that season in the form of turnovers and penalties, uncharacteristic for an Allen-coached team.

Washington rebounded with three straight wins. First came a 10–6 victory over Atlanta at RFK Stadium, where the crowd ferociously booed Kilmer, who threw two interceptions in the fourth quarter, and chanted, "WE WANT JOE!" But Kilmer stuck it to his detractors with 12 of 21 passing for 206 yards, three touchdowns, and no interceptions in a 24–14 win over the Cardinals. The Redskins then slipped past Tampa Bay, 10–0.

Washington's defense looked sharp through the first four games. But with first place on the line in the NFC East, the unit allowed 34 points in an 18-point loss to the Cowboys, followed by a 17–6 loss to the Giants that left the Redskins at 3–3.

All the while, injuries were piling up. Fullback John Riggins, once projected for a possible 1,000-yard season, was out for the year with torn knee ligaments. That left Thomas, Clarence Harmon, and Calvin Hill to handle the bulk of the rushing. (Larry Brown, the Redskins' all-time leading rusher at the time with 5,875 yards, retired before the season due to his brittle knees.)

Injuries had also sidelined two veteran icons, cornerback Pat Fischer and linebacker Chris Hanburger, plus offensive linemen Terry Hermeling and Ron Saul and special teams star Eddie Brown. Tight end Jean Fugett, safety Jake Scott, receiver Charley Taylor, and defensive linemen Diron Talbert, Ron McDole, and Bill Brundige were also banged up.

According to the Redskins edition of *Pro!* Magazine on October 30, 1977, " . . . the Redskins are sporting enough braces, casts, splints and bandages to outfit an emergency room during the rush season. Remember the railroad scene in *Gone with the Wind* where the camera slowly pulls back to show row after row after row of wounded soldiers writhing in agony? Tuesday mornings at Redskins Park look remarkably like that pageant of pain."

Although the Redskins had scored only two touchdowns in the past 12 quarters, Allen delivered a vote of confidence for Kilmer to continue leading the offense. But the coach did an about-face and tapped Theismann to start in the upcoming game at Philadelphia, even though Theismann had publicly criticized Allen for benching him.

Theismann completed 16 of 34 passes for 218 yards with two touchdowns and an interception in a 23–17 victory over the Eagles. Then came a 10–3 Monday night loss to Baltimore. With the ball deep in Colts territory and time running out, Theismann threw a scoring pass to Calvin Hill. But the officials ruled that the clock had run out before the snap, leaving the 4–4 Redskins four games behind first-place Dallas.

After a 17–14 win over Philly on Mark Moseley's 54-yard field goal late in the game, Washington topped the Packers, 10–9, on Monday night. The playoffs were in sight, but the 6–4 Redskins needed to win their last four games to be assured of a wild card spot.

Despite losing, 14–7, to the Cowboys, the Redskins continued to fight, beating Buffalo in another 10–0 sleeper. Allen then benched Theismann, who had won four of the previous six games as the starter, and inserted the quarterback who he felt was the better clutch-performer: Kilmer. Old Billy started in a 26–20 win over the Cardinals and a 17–14 season-ending win over the Rams.

The latter victory left Redskins clinging to playoff hopes. But the next day, Chicago beat the Giants on a field goal with nine seconds left in overtime to earn the NFC's wild card spot. The Redskins and Bears each finished with 9–5 records and were tied with 8–4 conference marks, the first possible tiebreaker. In the second tiebreaker, the Bears outscored their NFC opponents by 48 points, the Redskins by only four, giving Chicago the playoff spot.

A measly nine seconds separated the Redskins from going to the playoffs for the sixth time in seven seasons. Plus, the depleted squad had scraped and clawed its way back into the playoff picture in winning five of its last six games, displaying its usual determination under Allen while relying on a blocked kick, an intercepted pass, or a great return to generate a spark. Did the Redskins thus have room for a moral victory in 1977?

"As long as I continue to coach, there won't be a season where a team has shown much more character, class and leadership, coaching and togetherness," Allen said, as quoted by the *Washington Star*. "This was probably our best year ever, from all standpoints, overcoming adversity and all, whether we made the playoffs or not. It still was a great season. I'm just proud of our team, coaches and organization."

## A War of Words

The Redskins' 10–0 win at Tampa Bay on October 9, 1977—the Buccaneers' 18th straight loss since entering the NFL one year prior—was as exciting as a weed. But there were fireworks afterward.

Redskins defensive tackle Bill Brundige told a *Tampa Tribune* reporter that he admired the Bucs' defense, but he noted that Tampa Bay coach John McKay was going to learn that his I-formation setup on offense wouldn't work in the NFL. "He isn't at Southern Cal any more playing Stanford," Brundige reasoned. McKay won four national championships at USC before jumping to the NFL in 1976 to coach the Bucs.

McKay fired back at a news conference: "Anybody in his right mind who says the I-formation won't work is a dumb ass idiot. A tackle down on all fours probably doesn't know the offensive set."

Brundige, a math major at Colorado with a high IQ, took exception to having his intelligence questioned and mocked McKay in the process: "I probably know more about his offense than he does," he told the press. "He's the worst coach in the NFL, and please quote me on that."

## 1978: 8–8, 3RD PLACE—NFC EAST

### Head Coach: Jack Pardee

Out with the old, in with the new. That theme embodied the Redskins' 1978 campaign, a topsy-turvy season in which they finished 8–8.

The Redskins exploded to win their first six games, but fizzled even more dramatically to lose eight of their last 10 in the inaugural year of the 16-game season. Remnants of the Over the Hill Gang were around for the collapse, as the veteran-laden squad gave way to a much younger team with many new faces. The makeover was part of a sweeping team overhaul that triggered some banner headlines.

Phase one involved the January 1978 departure of George Allen, the most successful coach in Redskins history at the time. His exit stemmed from his antagonistic relationship with Edward Bennett Williams, the team's sometimes overbearing president. The two strong-minded men rarely saw eye-to-eye on personnel decisions and became entangled in a power struggle. There was animosity within the ranks.

"Ed had a panic button," said Steve Guback, the Redskins' beat writer at the time for the *Washington Star*. "The minute the Redskins lost, he'd want a change. But George would just do his own thing and ignore him. Ed was not the kind of guy who would be ignored. That triggered a lot of friction."

Their central point of dispute was Allen's seven-year contract, which was set to expire in March 1978. Before the 1977 season, Williams and Allen had tentatively agreed to a new contract calling for a four-year extension and a doubling of Allen's annual salary to a reported $250,000. The deal also allowed Allen to retain his roles as coach, general manager, and team vice president. Allen never signed the extension, apparently because it failed to renew an option for him to buy 5 percent of the organization's stock, which was then valued at $20 million.

Williams and Allen reinitiated contract talks once the 1977 season ended, but negotiations bogged down over the same sticking point, Allen's part ownership of the team. At the same time, Allen was rumored to be investigating other coaching opportunities, namely with his former team, the Rams. Williams became fed up with Allen's stalling and fired him, telling the *Washington Post* he gave George Allen "unlimited patience, and he exhausted it." Asked about the remark he first uttered in 1971 that Allen would be the last coach he would ever hire, Williams retorted, "Well, I was wrong."

Williams's decision provoked the coach into making vitriolic comments. "The only reason I haven't signed another contract is because of one man—and that's Williams," Allen told the *Star*. "I haven't applied or approached anyone about another job since I've been here. I've given the Redskins, the organization, the players and the community everything I have—my heart and soul and even my health, and this is what you get?"

The bitter Allen continued with his tirade: "Williams is a Jekyll and Hyde, anybody who deals with him knows that. One day he calls you up, and he's ranting and raving. The next day he's as meek as a kitten. That's his training. He's an actor." Allen further castigated his boss by calling him "deceitful" and a "cold-blooded fish."

Jack Pardee

Allen was hired by the Rams and coached two exhibition games in 1978 before being let go. He never coached again in the NFL. It has been said that his venomous remarks about Williams alienated other owners and got him blackballed from the league.

Williams, for his part, proceeded to consider the sort of big-name coach he had previously hired for the Redskins in Otto Graham, Vince Lombardi, and Allen. His list of possible successors included former Notre Dame coach Ara Parseghian, winner of two national championships, and St. Louis coach Don Coryell. There was also Chicago coach Jack Pardee, whom Williams had admired since Pardee played linebacker for the Redskins in 1971 and '72.

Pardee, a two-time All-Pro in 15 NFL seasons, had called the signals in Allen's complicated defensive systems in Los Angeles and Washington. Considered an Allen protégé, he served as an assistant on his staff in 1973 before coaching the Florida Blazers of the World Football League to the championship game in 1974. He later coached the Bears to a 20–22 record over three seasons that included a 9–5 record and a playoff appearance in 1977.

Williams signed the 41-year-old Pardee to a three-year contract that, unlike Allen's, limited him strictly to coaching duties. Williams also hired Dolphins player personnel director Bobby Beathard, considered one of the most clever front-office minds in the game, to become the Redskins' first true general manager in nearly two decades.

Meanwhile, Pardee rebuilt a coaching staff that had lost several members as a result of Allen's departure. He promoted Redskins backfield coach Joe Walton to offensive coordinator and signed Richard "Doc" Ulrich as defensive coordinator. He also tapped former Redskins safety Richie Petitbon as defensive secondary coach.

For the draft, the Redskins lacked a pick until the ninth round because of Allen's habit of dealing draft picks for veterans. Beathard, however, traded up to select Florida running back Tony Green in the sixth round. The general manager also dealt the team's No. 1 pick in 1979 to Cincinnati for cornerback Lemar Parrish and defensive end Coy Bacon, both former All-Pros. Other acquisitions included Colts wide receiver Ricky Thompson and Dolphins halfback Benny Malone.

Beathard and Pardee also weeded out icons from the Allen regime. Charley Taylor, the NFL's all-time leading receiver with 649 catches, safety Pat Fischer, tight end Jerry Smith, center Len Hauss, and special teams specialists Bob Brunet and Rusty Tillman all retired or were cut. "Pardee was openly trying to get rid of the old guys," Hauss said. Also gone was All-Pro kick return specialist Eddie Brown, who was traded to Los Angeles. The Redskins also traded Larry Jones, holder of the team's kickoff return record that still stands (102 yards).

A familiar face was still hanging around in 39-year-old Billy Kilmer, the oldest quarterback in the league. He signed a two-year contract, but Pardee assigned him to the bench and named fifth-year-man Joe Theismann as the undisputed starter, the nod Theismann had anxiously been awaiting.

After a 2–2 preseason, the Redskins ushered in the Pardee era by shocking New England, 16–14. The Patriots had the ball late in the game and led by five, but Redskins defensive tackle Dave Butz caused a fumble that linebacker Brad Dusek picked up and ran 31 yards for the winning score.

Washington made it two in a row with a 35–30 win over the Eagles in the home opener at RFK Stadium. The Redskins' offense racked up 403 yards, and Theismann connected on 14 of 29 passes for 228 yards and three scores, including a 37-yarder to receiver Danny Buggs on a flea-flicker that gave Washington a 35–16 fourth-quarter lead. Greater use of the flea-flicker was part of Joe Walton's bid to make the offense much more exciting than in 1977, when the Redskins averaged only 14 points per game. The former Redskins receiver designed a system with more multiple sets and formations, more men in motion, and more gimmick plays. After the win over the Eagles, the *Washington Star* ran a headline saying, "These Days It's Hail to the Thrillskins."

"These are no longer the Redskins," *Star* columnist Morrie Siegel wrote on September 11, 1978. "They are born again with a new coach, a new quarterback and a new name."

Next came a 28–10 smashing of the Cardinals in St. Louis. Tony Green, showing that the loss of Eddie Brown and Larry Jones mattered little, scored on a 99-yard kickoff return after posting an 80-yard punt return for a TD the week before. The Redskins rushed for 255 yards, including 108 from John Riggins, who came into his own as a Redskin back in 1978, rushing for 1,014 yards after being used mainly as a blocking back in his first two seasons in D.C.

While the offense was earning rave reviews, the defense also contributed mightily. The stout unit silenced a high-powered Jets offense in a 23–3 win, setting up a Monday night showdown between the 4–0 Redskins and 3–1 Cowboys at RFK.

With President Carter watching from Williams's box, the Redskins outmuscled Dallas, the defending Super Bowl champions, 9–5. The president saw another sterling performance by the defense, which stopped the Cowboys' potent offense from scoring a touchdown on four possessions inside the 20. Dallas once failed to score on six straight plays inside the Redskins' 7. Kicker Mark Moseley accounted for Washington's points on 52-, 42-, and 27-yard field goals.

The 5–0 Redskins were now two games up on Dallas, Philadelphia, and the Giants in the NFC East, a lead they maintained with a 21–19 squeaker over Detroit. The 6–0 record marked the first time the Redskins had won their first six games since the days of Sammy Baugh. They were also winners of nine straight, counting the last three games in 1977.

## Theismann's Antics Infuriate Cowboys

On the last play of the Redskins' 9–5 win over Dallas on October 2, 1978, Redskins quarterback Joe Theismann took a safety by running out of the back of the end zone. With several Cowboys in pursuit, he circled in the end zone waving the ball dangerously high before running out of bounds. That stunt enraged Cowboys president and general manager Tex Schramm, according to the Redskins' press box announcer at the time, Phil Hochberg:

Joe Theismann was dancing in the end zone toward the end of the game, and Tex Schramm was the angriest I've ever seen one man because of the way the game evolved and Theismann's antics in the end zone. It was such a frustrating night for Dallas, and I remember Schramm stormed out of the press box. You could see the steam coming out of his ears.

The Cowboys had the last laugh. They walloped the Redskins, 37–10, en route to winning the NFC East and earning their second straight trip to the Super Bowl.

Everything was pointing not only to an NFC East title but also to home field advantage through the playoffs. With 10 scoring passes and five interceptions, Theismann seemed comfortable in his new leadership role. The Redskins' offense, looking solid as a whole, had scored almost all of the team's 132 points through the first six games; Washington tallied 83 in the same period in 1977. Yardage was up, too.

Just as quickly, the Redskins took a nosedive. Theismann played horribly in consecutive losses to the Eagles and Giants and was yanked for Kilmer. The 16-year veteran completed 12 of 23 passes for 185 yards and two scores in a 38–20 win over San Francisco. Then he went 2 of 11 in a Monday night game against the Colts before being yanked in the third quarter for Theismann. Theismann couldn't rescue his squad in a 21–17 loss that dropped the Redskins to 7–3.

Theismann returned to the starting lineup in a 16–13 win over the Giants that Moseley clinched with a 45-yard field goal in overtime. With five games to go, the 8–3 Redskins were still in the driver's seat, a game ahead of Dallas in the NFC East.

They plummeted to 8–7 with losses to St. Louis, Dallas, Miami, and Atlanta. Because there were now two wild card berths per conference instead of one, the Redskins were clinging to long-shot playoff hopes entering the season finale against the Bears at RFK. Washington trailed 14–3 after three quarters when Pardee sent Kilmer into the game. He led a 51-yard scoring drive that ended on his 17-yard pass to tight end Jean Fugett with about two minutes left. But Kilmer mustered no more in a 14–10 loss that signaled his final NFL game.

The game also marked a calamitous end to a once promising season. The Redskins' offense was anemic in the final 10 games, averaging 14 points. That figure was inflated due to the team's 38-point outburst against the 49ers. Bobby Beathard told the press that too many Redskins didn't care about the team's fate. One reporter simply described the 1978 Redskins as a "very poor football team."

Theismann blamed injuries for the collapse. Halfback Mike Thomas, for one, missed three games due to a mysterious sprained ankle while the Redskins were slumping.

"In football, if you can't stay healthy, you can't win," said Theismann. "That's what caught up to that '78 ball club. We had a few people nicked, and we didn't get the ball bouncing the way we wanted. We got off to a great start. Everything went our way in the early part of the season. The back end of that, a lot of things didn't go our way."

## 1979: 10–6, 3RD PLACE—NFC EAST

### Head Coach: Jack Pardee

For most of the 1970s, the quarterback situation in the nation's capital resembled a game of musical chairs, whether it was Sonny vs. Billy or Billy vs. Joe. Not any more in 1979.

After Kilmer was waived prior to the season, the Redskins became Joe Theismann's team. The sixth-year man responded by putting forth his best season to date, a season that established him as one of the NFL's top quarterbacks. He posted then-career highs in completions (233), attempts (395), completion percentage (59.0), yards (2,797), touchdowns (20), and quarterback rating (83.9). One could also see solid leadership skills in the one-time Heisman Trophy runner-up and Canadian Football League star.

Theismann's growth keyed a 10–6 Redskins season that surprised many league-wide experts, who expected another average year in Washington during the rebuilding process of coach Jack Pardee and general manager Bobby Beathard. The Redskins went so far as to secure—or so it seemed—at least a wild card playoff spot heading into the final weekend. But a wicked series of events, top among them a one-point loss to Dallas, eliminated Washington from playoff contention.

Even so, Pardee was honored for his splendid job as Associated Press Coach of the Year. Running back John Riggins posted his second straight 1,000-yard season with a then-career-high 1,153, and Mark Moseley's bull's-eye kicking left him tied for second in NFL scoring, one below the league leader. "Mr. Consistency" converted a league-high 25 field goals and by season's end had set a new Redskins' kicking record with 546 points.

Washington's offense was complemented by a defense that allowed one of the lowest point totals in the NFL (295). Led by players such as cornerback Lemar Parrish, who picked off a career-high nine passes, and defensive end Coy Bacon, who posted 15 sacks and recovered four fumbles, the stingy unit held eight opponents to 14 points or less.

Prior to the season, the Pardee-Beathard "de-Allenizing" was still in process. The Redskins said goodbye to Kilmer, defensive end Ron McDole, safety Jake Scott, and nine-time Pro Bowl linebacker Chris Hanburger, leaving defensive tackle Diron Talbert as the only charter member of the Over the Hill Gang. The team also released linebackers Harold McLinton and Mike Curtis, other George Allen-era veterans, and All-Pro kick returner Tony Green. Mike Thomas, who gained 3,360 yards in the past four seasons in Washington, was not re-signed.

Pardee and Beathard also acquired players who would play monster roles in the Redskins' upcoming glory years. They drafted San Diego State tight end Don Warren (fourth round), Penn State linebacker Rich Milot (seventh), and Central Arkansas linebacker Monte Coleman (11th), and signed Maryland linebacker Neal Olkewicz through free agency. Trades landed defensive end Joe "Turkey" Jones and safety Tony Peters.

Milot, Coleman, and Olkewicz saw significant playing time at linebacker and became known as "the Three Musketeers." On opening day, though, the defense couldn't contain Houston running back Earl Campbell, the 1978 NFL rushing leader. He rumbled for 166 yards on 32 carries with two touchdowns, and his 3-yard run with two minutes left accounted for the winning points in a 29–27 thriller at RFK Stadium. The Redskins were up, 27–13, early in the fourth quarter, but their defense, which yielded 365 yards that day, let the lead slip away.

The Redskins won six of their next seven games. After the defense blew another large lead, this time a 21-point edge over Detroit, Moseley's 41-yard field goal with 13 seconds left accounted for a 27–24 win. The defense then yielded single-digit point totals in five more victories, including a 27–0 shutout of the Giants in a Monday night game. Washington also split with the powerful Eagles, first losing 28–17 before posting a 17–7 victory that saw the defense record seven sacks, two interceptions and two fumble recoveries.

At 6–2, the Redskins were one of the NFL surprises. They stood tied with the Eagles for second place in the NFC East, a game behind the Cowboys. Washington's defense had surrendered only 111 points, the best in the NFL, and Theismann was looking sharp with a 62 percent completion rate to accompany his 1,250 yards and eight touchdowns.

The Redskins stumbled with losses to the Saints and Steelers but remained tied with the Eagles for second in the division at 6–4; Washington and Philly led in the race for the NFC's two wild card spots, and the Redskins were playing four of their last six games at RFK.

First came two victories at home, 30–28 over St. Louis on Moseley's 39-yard field goal in the waning seconds and 34–20 over Dallas, a convincing win. "In the final nine seconds, with the crowd roaring, Mark Moseley booted a 45-yard field goal [against Dallas]," *Washington Star* sportswriter Steve Guback wrote on November 19, 1979. "It had absolutely no bearing on the game but showed the Dallas Cowboys and maybe, just maybe, the entire National Football League who's boss. It was like a period under a big, bold exclamation point."

The Redskins won two of their next three, leaving them 10–5 entering a critical season-ending game against the Cowboys. Sitting in a three-way tie with Dallas and Philadelphia for first place in the NFC East, the Redskins, amazingly, were still uncertain whether they would even be in the playoffs. The Cowboys and Eagles were at least assured of wild card bids.

The good news was the Redskins were mostly in control of their own destiny. A win over Dallas sounded sweet: The franchise's first NFC East title since 1972 and homefield advantage through the playoffs. A loss and the Redskins would still be in the driver's seat for a wild card spot, for the 9–6 Bears, also pushing for a wild card berth, trailed Washington in net points to date by 33—the next tiebreaker.

The intensity was swirling in Texas Stadium on December 16, 1979. "Even though the game was not a playoff game, it certainly had the feel of a playoff game because everything was on the line for both teams," said safety Mark Murphy, the Redskins' leading tackler that season.

It was a seesaw battle. The Redskins built a 17–0 lead in the second quarter on Moseley's field goal, plus Theismann's short touchdown run and his 55-yard scoring pass to halfback Benny Malone. Dallas fought back to take a 21–17 lead in the third period. But Moseley kicked another field goal, and Riggins scored on a 1-yard run and a 66-yard dash around the right side.

With a 34–21 lead and eight minutes to play, it appeared that the Redskins were en route to a division title. "I remember some of my teammates celebrating during the game and thinking to myself, 'It's too early to start celebrating,'" Murphy said.

He was right, for one could never dismiss the Cowboys as long as the master of miracle finishes, quarterback Roger Staubach, was in control. The future Hall of Famer completed three passes covering 59 yards, the finale a 26-yarder to tailback Ron Springs (the father of current Redskins cornerback Shawn Springs) that cut the lead to six. After Dallas regained possession, Staubach picked apart the Redskins' defense with completions of 20, 22, and 25 yards to put the ball on the 7. He then hit receiver Tony Hill for a touchdown in the end zone, and the conversion gave the Cowboys a 35–34 lead with 39 seconds left. Washington moved the ball close to the Dallas 40, but time ran out before Moseley could try a field goal.

The Redskins exited the field with their heads down, incredulous over the cruel ending. But what about the wild card spot? Chicago, which averaged only 18 points per game entering the final week, had beaten St. Louis, 42–6, to outdistance the Redskins by four net points. Washington's once promising season was over.

Pardee, near tears in his postgame press briefing, gave a spiritual explanation: "The Lord giveth, and the Lord taketh away." To rub it in, Cowboys defensive end Harvey Martin threw a funeral wreath into the Redskins' locker room, an unprofessional act he later apologized for.

"It was an almost unbelievable circumstance not to make it," linebacker Neal Olkewicz said years later. "It was very disappointing."

## 1980: 6–10, 3RD PLACE—NFC EAST

### Head Coach: Jack Pardee

John Riggins demanded more money. The Redskins balked, only to pay a steep price nevertheless.

The Redskins' star running back, coming off two straight 1,000-yard seasons, sat out the 1980 campaign over a contract dispute, essentially retiring from a league where he stood as one of its all-time leading rushers. His absence left a mammoth void that derailed the Redskins' offense and sent the squad tumbling to a 6–10 mark, its first losing season since 1970.

"John Riggins retired, that's all you need to know," Redskins quarterback Joe Theismann said in summarizing the team's collapse. "Our offense was built around two things, my ability to be a high-percentage, accurate passer and John's ability to run the football. When Riggo retired, we weren't built to be able to handle the adjustment. We struggled."

That's putting it mildly. The Redskins lost nine of 11 games during one stretch and stood 3–10 late in the season, jeopardizing the job of beleaguered coach Jack Pardee. Sure enough, Redskins owner Jack Kent Cooke, who had just moved to the D.C. area to take control of the team's daily operations from Edward Bennett Williams, fired Pardee right after the 1980 campaign.

"I loved Jack Pardee," Redskins linebacker Neal Olkewicz said. "He was an old linebacker, and he basically spent most of the time with us. Riggins sat out one year, and Pardee paid the price for it."

Firing Pardee, who pieced together a 24–24 mark over three seasons in D.C. and came within seconds of winning the NFC East title in 1979, was an "extremely difficult thing to do, but dad did it primarily because he simply couldn't communicate with Pardee," said John Kent Cooke, the son of Jack Kent Cooke and the Redskins' executive vice president at the time.

The gloomy season contrasted with the buoyancy resonating through the organization when training camp opened in July 1980. The Redskins were confident that they had added more firepower to one of the NFC's highest-scoring offenses from 1979 by signing Art Monk, a record-setting wide receiver-running back at Syracuse. Redskins coaches planned to position the 6–2, 209-pound Monk, the team's first first-round pick in 12 years, at wide receiver, where over time he became one of the greatest in NFL history.

Plus, Theismann was fresh off his best year to date. The Redskins were also returning a defense that subdued opponents in 1979 with perhaps the best secondary in the league. The backfield featured safety Ken Houston and cornerback Lemar Parrish, perennial Pro Bowlers, and cornerback Joe Lavender.

Riggins threw a wrench into the team's hopes. He mysteriously walked out early in training camp and returned to his home in Kansas. Then in the final season of a five-year contract with an annual salary of $300,000, he reportedly was seeking a raise and an extension. General manager Bobby Beathard, with a nod from Cooke, refused to renegotiate. Riggins admitted in later years that the season-ending 35–34 loss to Dallas in 1979 that knocked the Redskins out of playoff contention largely influenced his decision to quit, saying that he thought he would never reach the Super Bowl.

The Redskins began the preseason using fullback Clarence Harmon, who rushed for 267 yards in 1979, as Riggins's replacement. When it seemed more apparent that Riggins would not return, the Redskins traded two No. 2 draft picks to the 49ers for fullback Wilbur Jackson, who had rushed for nearly 3,000 yards over five seasons. Jackson also caught a career-high 53 passes in 1979. Beathard also signed free agent fullback Rickey Claitt.

Riggins's exit failed to stop Jack Kent Cooke from predicting a Redskins Super Bowl-winning season in 1980 barring major injuries. He didn't envision the horrifying 1–5 start that began with a 17–3 loss to Dallas in a Monday night game at RFK Stadium. Riggins's absence was noticeable. The Redskins rushed for 58 yards, 39 by Harman and 11 by halfback Buddy Hardeman, and their lone points came on a 45-yard field goal by Mark Moseley, who missed two other tries.

In week 2 against the Giants, Moseley hit another 45-yarder with two minutes left to account for a 23–21 win. This time the Redskins rushed for 208 yards, with a team-high 77 by Claitt.

Washington dropped games to Oakland, Seattle, Philadelphia, and Denver while enduring a rash of major injuries; five starters missed the Oakland game, for example. The running game

continued to sputter, and the Redskins also evolved into their own worst enemy by committing a plethora of penalties, many at crucial times. Officials whistled the Redskins for a total of 31 penalties in the losses to Seattle, Philadelphia, and Denver.

"We look like a little league team that hasn't quite learned how to play the game yet," Pardee told reporters after his squad committed 12 penalties, five alone by veteran offensive tackle Terry Hermeling, in the loss to Seattle. The Redskins would finish as one of the league's most penalized teams.

Washington regained momentum with a 23–0 shutout of the Cardinals and a 22–14 victory over the Saints. The Redskins' offense, becoming healthier, racked up 453 yards against St. Louis, as Theismann completed 21 of 37 passes for a then-career-high 307 yards with two touchdowns, while the defense recorded six sacks and two interceptions.

But the 3–5 Redskins, apparently starting to mesh, lost five straight games in a slide that seemed uglier than the first one, as penalties, mental mistakes, and big plays allowed by the defense became the norm. Mediocre teams handed the Redskins two of those losses in embarrassing fashion. Washington fell behind 23–0 in the first half of a 39–14 loss to the Vikings and then allowed Chicago to take a 35-point first-half lead in an eventual 35–21 loss. The Redskins dropped to 3–10 with losses to the Eagles, who eventually reached Super Bowl XV; the Cowboys; and the Falcons.

By then, alarm bells were sounding in the nation's capital. The Redskins had won their last three games, but team officials knew that a lengthy rebuilding process was mandatory for the franchise, which still had a nice nucleus. Theismann passed for nearly 3,600 yards. Monk emerged into a bona fide big-play threat and led the team in catches with 58 for 797 yards and three touchdowns. He made the All-NFL rookie team. Clarence Harmon proved to be a threat out of the backfield with 54 receptions. Mike Nelms, obtained in the off-season after starring in the Canadian Football League, posted nearly 1,300 kick return yards to spark the Redskins' "Wild Bunch" special teams and earn Pro Bowl honors. Wilbur Jackson chalked up more than 1,000 yards, 708 on the ground.

On defense, safety Mark Murphy led the team in tackles for the second straight year, followed by second-year linebacker Monte Coleman, who was starting to terrorize offenses. Parrish intercepted seven passes and made the Pro Bowl for the eighth time.

But Pardee's future was tenuous at best. He took much of the blame for the disappointing season, and local media reported that he was in a philosophical dispute with Beathard over how to run the team. A *Washington Post* headline on November 22, 1980, read, "Pardee's Split with Beathard Heart of Issue." It seemed one of them would be axed, but who?

"The handwriting was on the wall that Pardee would not survive," *Washington Star* sportswriter Steve Guback said.

Jack Kent Cooke refused to say publicly if Pardee would not return—and the coach said he wouldn't quit—but the team already started searching for a new coach. The press reported that the Redskins had contacted Southern California coach John Robinson, whose Trojans had won the national championship in 1978. Former Redskins coach George Allen and former Raiders coach John Madden, two of the most successful coaches in NFL history, were also rumored as possible replacements.

The Redskins eventually hired an ingenious football mind who led the franchise through its most successful period ever.

# Redskins-Cowboys: A Rivalry Ingrained in NFL Lore

THE DALLAS COWBOYS. No opponent in the modern era of the Washington Redskins has sparked as much resentment among players and fans in the nation's capital.

Maybe it's those stars on the helmets, or that sacrosanct image of the self-dubbed "America's Team," or that myth about the hole in the roof at Texas Stadium "so God can watch his favorite team play"—all elements that have fueled an abhorrence of the snooty Cowboys. As Redskins guard Mark May eloquently put it after a 41–14 rout of Dallas in 1986, "There are three great things in life. Winning the lottery, having a baby, and beating the Cowboys this badly."

The NFC East foes have carried on an emotional rivalry in recent decades, one of the best, in fact, that the NFL has had to offer. The rivalry has starred an assortment of characters, from quarterbacks Sonny Jurgensen and Don Meredith in the 1960s, to coaches George Allen and Tom Landry in the 1970s, to Redskins defensive end Dexter Manley, the Hogs, and the Cowboys' Whites, Danny and Randy, in the 1980s, to Dallas's big three of Troy Aikman, Emmitt Smith, and Michael Irvin in the 1990s, and to the recent clashes between teams coached by Joe Gibbs and Bill Parcells, long-time rivals in their own right.

Through it all, there has been no shortage of drama in games pitting the burgundy and gold against the dreaded blue and silver.

"The intensity when we played Dallas was unbelievable," said Kenny Houston, a Redskins safety who clashed with the Cowboys when the rivalry intensified to new heights in the 1970s. "If you came out of the game, and you weren't bleeding or could barely walk, you hadn't played. They really felt like that. I wish we could have played them every game during the year. We just loved to play them. It was always the perfect setting: Monday night, Thanksgiving Day, a 4 o'clock start, RFK. Those kinds of games still give you [goose] bumps."

Cowboys quarterback Roger Staubach, who played during the same era, agreed: "It was a bitter rivalry, and both teams were really intense. We didn't like them, they didn't like us. But there was a lot of respect."

In the series, Dallas holds a sizable 55–37–2 edge through the 2006 season, largely because the Cowboys have won 16 of the past 22 games against Washington. It has been all Redskins when the stakes have been highest, though. They've won both times the rivals have collided in the playoffs: the NFC championship games in the 1972 and 1982 seasons.

The franchises harbored bitterness toward one another even before the Cowboys stepped on the field. It was the late 1950s, and the 12-team NFL was considering expanding to as many as 16 teams. Redskins owner George Preston Marshall placed a key vote opposing the entry of a Dallas franchise for fear it would upset fan interest in his Redskins in the South. The Redskins were the NFL's southernmost franchise at the time, and they played exhibition games through the South and as far west as Texas.

Dallas oilman Clint Murchison, the franchise's prospective owner, plotted to retaliate against Marshall, who had earlier rejected an offer from Murchison to buy the Redskins and keep them in D.C., according to the *Washington Evening Star*. Murchison negotiated with Barnee Breeskin, who wrote the music to "Hail to the Redskins" in 1937, to purchase the composer's rights to Marshall's beloved song. Murchison then gave the Redskins' owner an ultimatum: Either allow a Dallas franchise into the league or you can't play the song.

Marshall capitulated, and the Cowboys were born. After the Redskins won the first meeting between the teams in 1960, the Cowboys moved to the Eastern Conference in 1961, the first season of a home-and-home series between the rivals that has existed ever since. By the time they collided in the final game that year, the 0–12–1 Redskins were winless in 23 straight games—the worst slump in team history.

The Redskins topped Dallas to avoid what would stand as their only winless season ever, but not before Cowboys fans tried to antagonize their adversary—Marshall. Pranksters smuggled crates containing about 100 live chickens into D.C. Stadium (later RFK Stadium) with the idea of spreading chicken feed and releasing the chickens all over the field at halftime, when Santa Claus was supposed to make a guest appearance. Stadium guards, however, caught wind of the "chicken incident" just before it was unleashed and confiscated the crates.

Over the next half-dozen seasons, as the Cowboys rose to prominence and the Redskins remained mired in mediocrity, neither team recorded a season sweep of the other. Between 1965 and 1967, they engaged in some wild battles that resembled shootouts at the OK Corral: 34–31 Redskins, 31–30 Cowboys, 34–31 Redskins, 17–14 Cowboys, 27–20 Redskins.

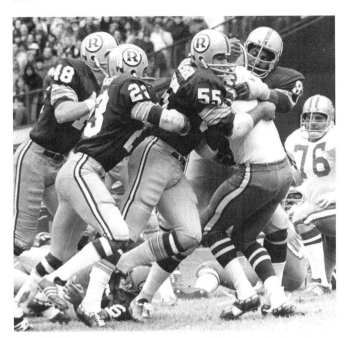

The Redskins have never gone out of their way to treat the Cowboys hospitably. Here, linebacker Chris Hanburger (55) and defensive end Jimmie Jones, with help from defensive backs Brig Owens (23) and Jon Jaqua, rough up a Dallas ball carrier in 1971.

In four of those five games, the winning points came in the final two minutes.

Washington's strength was a potent aerial attack led by Sonny Jurgensen. The Cowboys, who lost in the NFL title games in 1966 and 1967, featured Don Meredith and wide receiver and Olympic gold medal sprinter Bob Hayes, along with a star-studded defense.

"Playing the Cowboys was a tremendous challenge for us," Jurgensen said. "The rivalry grew because they were a class organization, a very good football team. For us, we were struggling and trying to get better, and anytime we played them, we knew we had to be at our best. We had to score a lot of points to beat them, we couldn't stop them defensively. They lined up and said, 'Hey, this is what we're going to do, see if you can beat us.'"

The Cowboys did so six straight times from 1968 to 1970, before the arrival of someone who would intensify the rivalry severalfold: George Allen.

Formerly the coach of the Los Angeles Rams, Allen knew all about the Cowboys from when the teams scrimmaged during training camp in Southern California. He detested Dallas coach Tom Landry, general manager Tex Schramm, and others in the organization and was giddy over the chance to face the Cowboys again in Washington.

"We always hated the Dallas Cowboys," Jennifer Allen, George Allen's daughter, wrote in her 2000 book, *Fifth Quarter: The Scrimmage of a Football Coach's Daughter.* "And now, with the Cowboys in the Redskins' division, we hated them even more."

In their first meeting in the Allen era, the Redskins shocked the Cowboys, winners of Super Bowl V the year before, en route to qualifying for the playoffs for the first time in a quarter-century. The eventual Super Bowl champion Cowboys won the rematch at RFK Stadium, and the teams split in the regular season in 1972 before playing each other again in the NFC championship game at RFK Stadium.

All the while, Allen was whipping his players into a fury by stressing his antipathy for the Cowboys and their pompous reputation. The Cowboys, for their part, accused Allen and his staff of spying on practices. There were charges of dirty play. The result was a mutual feeling of animosity. "The Cowboys promoted themselves at the time as America's team," Redskins safety Brig Owens said. "But we were in the nation's capital. We were the true America's team as far as George was concerned."

In a surreptitious move, Allen tapped one of his treasured veterans, defensive tackle Diron Talbert, to make comments to the press intended to rattle Roger Staubach, a Naval Academy graduate with a goody-goody image. Talbert, a Texas native, obliged by saying the Cowboys' quarterback "wears skirts" and "can't read defenses."

"Those things kind of worked," Staubach said. "George believed you distract the other team by saying things, and Landry wouldn't allow us to say anything."

The Redskins overwhelmed Dallas in the championship game, 26–3. As the win became more apparent, Redskins reserve quarterback Sam Wyche was heard on the sidelines sharing his love for the Cowboys: "Die you dogs, Die you Dallas dogs."

No Herculean win would stop Allen from loathing the Cowboys. The animated coach once took karate lessons with martial arts expert Jhoon Rhee and chopped boards in a team meeting to show what he could do to the stone-faced Landry if the two met at midfield during a game. Allen's real goal was to motivate his troops.

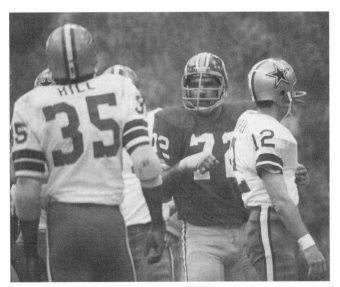

Defensive tackle Diron Talbert (72) was George Allen's right-hand man in the 1970s when it came to stoking anti-Cowboys sentiment. Talbert made outrageous remarks in hopes of unnerving Roger Staubach (12), saying the Cowboys' quarterback "wears skirts" or "can't read defenses."

## Indelible Moments
## in Redskins-Cowboys Rivalry

- 1966: Redskins quarterback Sonny Jurgensen and his Dallas counterpart, Don Meredith, light the skies for 753 passing yards and five touchdowns in a 31–30 Cowboys win.

- 1973: Redskins safety Ken Houston tackles fullback Walt Garrison at the goal line to preserve a Redskins Monday night victory.

- 1974: Obscure Cowboys rookie quarterback Clint Longley throws a 50-yard scoring pass in the last seconds to bite the Redskins on Thanksgiving Day in 1974.

- 1975: Redskins quarterback Billy Kilmer sneaks into the end zone from inches out for the game-winning score in a 30–24 overtime win.

- 1979: Cowboys receiver Tony Hill catches a 7-yard scoring pass in the final seconds of a 35–34 season-ending Dallas win that helped prevent the Redskins from making the playoffs.

- 1982: In one of the most famous plays in Redskins history, defensive tackle Darryl Grant intercepts a tipped pass and high-steps into the end zone to secure a 31–17 win in the NFC championship game. The win catapults the Redskins to Super Bowl XVII, where they win their first NFL championship in 40 years.

- 1987: The Redskins win a replacement game against a Cowboys team featuring some of its regular players, 13–7.

- 1989: The 0–8 Cowboys pull off a 13–3 upset for their only win that season.

- 1992: Redskins defensive end Jason Buck strips Cowboys quarterback Troy Aikman of the ball in the end zone, and teammate Danny Copeland recovers for the winning points in a 20–17 win over a Dallas team that goes on to win Super Bowl XXVII.

- 1999: Aikman passes 76 yards to receiver Rocket Ismail in overtime to account for a 41–35 win by the Cowboys, who had trailed by 21 points in the fourth quarter.

- 2005: Receiver Santana Moss catches 39- and 71-yard scoring passes in the final minutes to lift the Redskins to a shocking 14–13 win.

- 2006: Kicker Nick Novak boots a 47-yard field goal with no time on the clock to give the Redskins a 22–19 victory.

"Everything [Allen] did focused on beating the Cowboys," NFL Films president Steve Sabol said. "He'd crumple a piece of paper and say, 'If I can get this piece of paper in the waste basket, we're going to beat the Cowboys.' Or he'd pick up a stone and say, 'If I can throw this stone and hit the tree, we're going to beat the Cowboys.' He was obsessed with Dallas. We picked up some sound from him when the Redskins beat the Cowboys in Texas Stadium in 1976. He turned to our camera when he knew the game was over and said, 'Tom Landry, hah, hah, hah. Tex Schramm, hah, hah, hah. Roger Staubach, hah, hah, hah.'"

Said Redskins quarterback Joe Theismann, "George's whole thing about playing the Cowboys was they were prima donnas, and we were bullies, let's get them in a street fight, and we can kick their rear ends. It was all about us getting physical with the Cowboys. At the time, the Cowboys used the shotgun on offense and had the flex defense, and so much about them seemed cerebral. It wasn't that they were better than you, it was that they could outsmart you. We felt we needed to take it into the gutter."

The rivals continued vying for supremacy in the NFC East and split each year during Allen's reign until his final season, 1977, when Dallas swept the series before appearing in the Super Bowl for the fourth of five times in the 1970s.

Between the late 1970s and the early 1980s, the Cowboys enjoyed a six-game winning streak over the Redskins, but it ended on a cold gray day in Washington on January 22, 1983. In the NFC championship game, Redskins running back John Riggins gained 140 yards and defensive tackle Darryl Grant returned an interception for a touchdown that sealed a 31–17 victory over Dallas.

Creaky RFK Stadium rocked that day. "I remember standing on the sidelines at the end of the game, and people were just banging their feet against those aluminum seats," Theismann said. "I felt the ground shake beneath my feet, literally. That's all part of the Redskins-Cowboys rivalry."

At the time, Redskins coach Joe Gibbs was shaping a dynasty that would win three Super Bowls over the next decade. Unlike Allen, the tight-lipped coach kept Cowboys-related matters to a monotone. Redskin fans were a different story. They vocalized their hatred for the Cowboys during a phenomenon called "Dallas Week," when a buzz circulated through the nation's capital in anticipation of a clash between the rivals. Redskin fans were also fanatical at RFK Stadium, where they were no gracious hosts to the blue and silver. Just ask Cowboys quarterback Danny White:

These were the most despicable, obnoxious people I had ever seen in my life. They'd come down to the rail before the game and at halftime, anytime we were running on and off the field. I remember coach Landry telling us, "Whether you're sitting on the bench, on the field, going into the locker room, don't take your helmet off." They'd throw stuff at you and make obscene comments. It was like walking into a dungeon of thieves or something. These fans wanted to have an impact on the game. The greatest feeling in the world for a Cowboy in those days was to go to RFK Stadium and do something on the field to shut them up.

The Cowboys did so in the 1983 season opener, when they recovered from a 20-point halftime deficit to eke out a 31–30 Monday night win. "That was one of the greatest games in my

## BOMBS AWAY IN BIG D

### Redskins Victimized by Rookie Quarterback

Clint Longley enjoyed less than 30 minutes of fame in his NFL career. It came at the Redskins' expense.

On November 28, 1974, Thanksgiving Day, the Dallas quarterback delivered one of the most astonishing performances in the history of the Redskins-Cowboys rivalry. Longley directed three second-half touchdown drives and threw two scoring passes, including a 50-yarder to receiver Drew Pearson with 28 seconds left that hoisted the Cowboys to a 24–23 victory.

Here's the irony: The rookie had never thrown a pass in the NFL. A one-time small college All-American at Abilene Christian in Texas, he warmed the bench behind future Hall of Fame inductee Roger Staubach for the first 11 games of the 1974 campaign.

Defensive tackle Diron Talbert, a master at making controversial remarks about the Cowboys, thought he knew of a way for his Redskins to win their fifth straight game. "If you knock [Staubach] out, you've got that rookie facing you," Talbert told the press. "That's one of our goals. If we do that, it's great. He's all they have."

Talbert got his wish. With the Redskins leading, 16–3, early in the third period, linebacker Dave Robinson knocked Staubach out of the game. Enter Longley, who had moved up to second string a few weeks earlier after Dallas traded veteran Craig Morton. Longley quickly threw a 35-yard scoring pass to tight end Billy Joe Dupree. He later steered a four-play, 64-yard drive that ended on fullback Walt Garrison's 1-yard touchdown run. The Redskins regained the lead, 23–17, on running back Duane Thomas's 19-yard run early in the fourth quarter.

On recovering Pearson's fumble with 2:29 left, the Redskins seemed en route to a joyous Thanksgiving dinner. "We could smell the turkey," Redskins receiver Charley Taylor said.

But Longley was calm and in control when Dallas regained possession on their 40 with 1:45 to play and no timeouts. He even told Garrison to "shut up" after the fullback brought a play into the huddle and began explaining it. On fourth-and-6, Longley completed a pass to receiver Bob Hayes just past the first-down marker. Two plays later at midfield, the quarterback, nicknamed the "Mad Bomber" for his tendency to go for broke in practice, went for it all. With good protection, he spotted an open Pearson racing downfield past rookie nickel back Ken Stone. Pearson hauled in Longley's perfect strike inside the 5 and scored.

The conversion put the Cowboys up, 24–23. Redskins quarterback Billy Kilmer fumbled on the next possession, and Dallas ran out the clock before 63,000 delirious fans at Texas Stadium.

The postgame cameras were glued to Longley, who completed 11 of 20 passes for 203 yards and two touchdowns. "I wasn't nervous, but I sure was excited," he said at the time. He said he was aware of the inflammatory comments by Talbert, who also was the focus of media curiosity.

"Reporters came up to Diron and said, 'What did you think of that Longley kid?'" Redskins defensive end Ron McDole recalled. "He said, 'Who in the hell is Longley?' We didn't know who he was, we didn't know his name or anything. They said, 'The guy who just beat you.' He said, 'Pretty good.'"

Said Talbert, "I don't think Longley caught us by surprise. The worst thing about it is that Staubach was having a bad day. We said we were going to knock him

Clint Longley

## BOMBS AWAY IN BIG D—continued

out and, sure enough, we did. We just made a mistake or two in being lined up in the wrong defenses. Could have been we didn't know [Longley] had an arm that strong, but if you're a good defensive team it doesn't make any difference who the quarterback is."

Longley turned out to be a one-game wonder. He returned to the bench and stayed there through the 1975 season before being traded to San Diego, where he played one year as a backup and retired from the NFL. One of the nine career games he played in, though, will forever haunt the Redskins.

### Turkey Day Feast

The Cowboys have a 6–0 record against the Redskins on Thanksgiving Day. Each game has been played in Dallas:

* 29–20, November 28, 1968
* 24–23, November 28, 1974
* 37–10, November 23, 1978
* 27–17, November 22, 1990
* 21–10, November 28, 1996
* 27–20, November 28, 2002

### "Monday Night Miracle"

Improbable. Spectacular. Exhilarating. Take your pick. The Redskins' 14–13 victory over the Cowboys at Texas Stadium on Monday night, September 19, 2005, was all of the above.

Consider: Washington's offense, plagued by turnovers and penalties, was anemic for the first 55 minutes against a swarming Dallas defense, and Redskins punter Andy Groom was getting lots of reps. Dallas led, 13–0, and Cowboys coach Bill Parcells was 77–0 when leading by at least 13 points in the fourth quarter. The Redskin faced a third-and-27 deep in their territory. You could safely chalk up a W for Dallas.

Then came one of the most unbelievable sequences in Redskins history. Redskins quarterback Mark Brunell, resorting to the running ability that helped define his game in the 1990s in Jacksonville, scrambled 25 yards, and then completed a 20-yard pass to receiver James Thrash on fourth down. Soon came a fourth-and-15 on the Dallas 39 with 3:46 left.

Brunell stayed composed and threw a perfect scoring pass to receiver Santana Moss in the back of the end zone to cut the lead to 13–7, Washington's first touchdown in nearly eight quarters of play in 2005. The Redskins forced a punt and took over on the Cowboys' 20. After a 10-yard completion to running back Clinton Portis, Brunell launched a gorgeous bomb that hit Moss in stride behind the secondary, and he took it the rest of the way to tie the game at 13 with 2:35 left. Nick Novak's conversion put the Redskins up by one.

The breathtaking display of explosiveness—the touchdowns came in a span of 71 seconds—altered the game's complexion and silenced the rabid Cowboys fans at Texas Stadium. Dallas had two more possessions, once starting on Washington's 48. But the Redskins' defense hung tough, and the burgundy and gold escaped with a win dubbed the "Monday Night Miracle."

Redskins coach Joe Gibbs, kneeling on the sideline as the clock ticked down, leaped into the arms of his players when the final gun sounded and was doused with a bucket of cold water. The 65-year-old Hall of Fame coach, looking and sounding emotionally spent, described the win as "one of the great moments for me in sports."

"I don't know what to say," Gibbs said in his postgame press conference. "I was proud of the way [the Redskins] fought. The defense just hung in there and kept slugging. Their crowd was really into it and hurt us a bunch of times. In the end, just unbelievable plays. Kind of takes your breath away. I'll appreciate it forever. I'm just thrilled . . .

"It's a rare moment for all Redskins fans because we all know how many times we've been beat by Dallas," Gibbs added. "I just know everybody back home really enjoyed it."

The win was even sweeter because it came on a night when the Cowboys inducted their legendary 1990s-era trio of quarterback Troy Aikman, receiver Michael Irvin, and running back Emmitt Smith into the team's Ring of Fame. But not everyone stayed up to watch the stirring comeback, Redskins and Cowboys supporters alike. Cowboys quarterback Drew Bledsoe told reporters of how he had voice mails and e-mails from people offering congratulations before they went to bed, unaware, of course, that the Redskins would pull out the stunning victory.

Those who snoozed missed a classic.

Redskins receiver Santana Moss was electrifying in the "Monday Night Miracle." Here, he hauls in a bomb from Mark Brunell before coasting into the end zone to complete a 70-yard play that tied the game at 13 with about two minutes left. The conversion put the Redskins up by one.

career because of the fans," White said. "They were stomping and screaming and yelling and pretty proud of themselves. At the end of the game, you could hear a pin drop."

But with characters such as Riggins, Theismann, and Dexter Manley, Washington's No. 1 anti-Cowboys propaganda man at the time, the Redskins proceeded to win three straight games over Dallas, their first winning streak ever in the series. They later crafted a four-game win streak that included a 13–7 victory using only replacement players during the strike-shortened 1987 season. Some Cowboys starters, including White and future Hall of Fame defensive lineman Randy White, played in that game.

The Cowboys, struggling at the time, slipped precipitously in 1989 by finishing 1–15 under first-year coach Jimmy Johnson. That one win came over—you guessed it—the Redskins, proving that a victory over Dallas is never a certainty. Then, when the Redskins began the 1991 season 11–0, Dallas snapped the streak with a 24–21 victory. The Cowboys, improving rapidly at the time, won three Super Bowls through the 1995 season. In all three of those seasons, the Redskins beat Dallas at least once.

The Cowboys began dominating the series, constructing a 10-game winning streak that ended on the last day of the 2002 season. That stretch included a series of horrifying moments

and heartbreaking losses for the Redskins, including when they relinquished a 21-point fourth-quarter lead on opening day in 1999 and lost 41–35 in overtime on Aikman's 76-yard pass to receiver Rocket Ismail, and when Cowboys defensive end Ebenezer Ekuban took the liberty to drag quarterback Jeff George backward by his shoulder pads across the Texas Stadium turf in a Dallas win in 2000.

The rivalry had become so one-sided that it no longer seemed like a rivalry—but when Joe Gibbs returned to D.C. in 2004, all signs indicated that the old Redskins-Cowboys magic would resurface. Gibbs and Cowboys coach Bill Parcells had staged a fierce rivalry of their own when Parcells coached the two-time Super Bowl champion Giants during Gibbs's first stint in Washington.

"I'm sure the rivalry will be back," Parcells said at the time. "I don't think there's any doubt. It will be great. It's good for the league and, hopefully, it will be good for both Joe and I. It will be great to see him over on the other side. It will be like déjà vu."

The two teams have split in the three seasons since. Parcells got the better of Gibbs in 2004, winning both games by three points. In 2005, the Redskins beat Dallas twice in one season for the first time in a decade, starting with a dramatic 14–13 victory behind quarterback Mark Brunell's two long touchdown passes to receiver Santana Moss in the final minutes. The win marked the Redskins' first one at Texas Stadium since 1995, and Gibbs beat Parcells for the first time since 1987. Later that season, the Redskins spanked Dallas by 28 points for their most lopsided win ever in the series.

In 2006, the Redskins and Cowboys each won once, and their second game produced one of the wildest endings in NFL history—and proved that *anything* is possible when the two teams meet. With the game tied at 19 and 31 seconds left, Redskins kicker Nick Novak missed a 49-yard field goal, and the Cowboys drove downfield and positioned themselves for a 35-yard attempt by Mike Vanderjagt, the most accurate kicker in NFL history. Redskin Troy Vincent blocked the kick, and teammate Sean Taylor recovered the ball and ran to the Dallas 45. A 15-yard penalty on Taylor's return gave the Redskins the ball on the Dallas 30. A game can't end on a defensive penalty, and with no time on the clock, Novak booted a 47-yard field goal for a 22–19 Redskins win.

After that one, a lot of people were asking if what they had seen was real or fiction. It was just one of those classic Redskins-Cowboys moments. "It's always the Dallas rivalry where we always seem to have these big, crazy endings where we come up with the win," Redskins defensive lineman Renaldo Wynn said afterward. "It's unbelievable."

Redskins offensive tackle Jon Jansen, with an incredulous look on his face, was equally amazed: "I don't know why it is, but ever since I've been here our games against Dallas have had their quirks and funny things. This definitely tops them all. I can't think of anything that's been wilder than this. Last year in Dallas when we scored those two late touchdowns, that was not something that has been repeated very often. But this one was a little crazier."

# 7

# 1981–1992: An Icon Among the NFL Elite

**T**HEY WERE THE TOAST of Washington, kings riding high through what resembled a football dreamland. To the delight of every Redskins fan in D.C., across the nation and abroad, they were models of excellence.

From 1981 to 1992, the Redskins appeared in four Super Bowls and won three times, captured five NFC East titles, and made the playoffs in eight seasons. Their 140–65–0 record, which included a 16–5 postseason mark, equals a .680 winning percentage that was among the NFL's best during the 12-season span.

Such achievements spelled one word—D-Y-N-A-S-T-Y—and came on the watch of a coach named Joe Gibbs, who steered the Redskins through the entire period. At his departure after the 1992 season, he was regarded as one of the greatest to ever coach the game and earned induction into the Pro Football Hall of Fame in 1996.

During his stay, the nation's capital was in a state of delirium as Redskins fever swelled to new heights. A love affair existed between the town and its burgundy-and-gold sports team, which continued to sell out RFK Stadium game after game and even built an international following. Redskins supporters, described by Canadian-born team owner Jack Kent Cooke as the "best bloody fans," were more rabid than ever.

They didn't just hope for championships. They expected them.

"The fans fed off of us," said linebacker Monte Coleman, one of the Redskins' stars of the era. "The more we started to win and go to Super Bowls, we were the talk of the town. Everybody was behind us. Redskins fever went from being good to being great. It rose about two to three notches."

The hub of the pandemonium was 55,000-seat RFK Stadium, one of the smallest but arguably the most intimate venue in the league. Ace kick returner Mike Nelms remembered how raucous the fans were at RFK, which he called "a shot in the arm, a 12th man on the field": "That stadium actually took on a life of its own," he said. "You could look over and see everything going up and down. People would scream, 'WE WANT DALLAS!' If you were playing Dallas, it gave you chill bumps, and if you weren't playing Dallas, it gave you chill bumps in anticipation. When you see those fans, they come to life."

"I don't use the word cozy very often, but RFK was pretty tight," said long-time TV network pro football analyst John Madden, who broadcast many games at RFK during the era. "You could literally feel the fans because when they would start to yell or get excited, the whole stadium would bounce, our broadcast booth would bounce, you could feel yourself going up and down, then the cameras were going up and down."

He added, "I loved that band and the fight song, 'Hail to the Redskins.' That whole thing gives you chills. The kind of stadium, the team, Joe Gibbs, all the players, the fans, Riggo running off tackle with the Hogs. The whole thing was a pretty doggone good package."

Gibbs, the glue for the package, enjoyed solid support in the front office. Cooke was lenient with his checkbook when it came to player signings and gave Gibbs and general managers Bobby Beathard (1978–89) and Charley Casserly (1989–99) a lot of room to operate. Plus, Gibbs's assistant coaching staff was stable in the otherwise volatile world of football coaching.

On the player front, myriad Redskins evolved into household names. They included 1970s-era holdovers in Coleman, quarterback Joe Theismann, running back John Riggins, kicker Mark Moseley, tight end Don Warren, wide receiver Art Monk, and defensive tackle Dave Butz, as well as Gibbs-era finds in wide receivers Gary Clark and Ricky Sanders, defensive linemen Dexter Manley and Charles Mann, cornerback Darrell Green, quarterbacks Doug Williams and Mark Rypien, and offensive linemen Joe Jacoby, Russ Grimm, and Jeff Bostic.

It was a cohesive group, sort of like a family, that featured true characters in Theismann, Riggins, Manley, and Clark, to name a few, who helped shaped the team's image. Nicknames like "the Hogs" and the "Fun Bunch," running plays called "50 Gut" and "70 Chip," and terms like "Counter-Trey" became ingrained in the lexicon of Redskins fans.

Why did the team have so much personality? "Because the individuals had personality, and we were allowed to show it," Theismann said. "You talk about the genius of Joe Gibbs—he allowed every one of us to be whoever we were. He didn't try to stifle our personality, but yet he was able to mix them all together."

The Redskins consisted of more than stars, for obscure names who became solid role players in Gibbs's system factored in with the squad's overachieving persona. Such players as wingback Nick Giaquinto, special teamers Greg Williams and Pete Cronan, and linebacker Larry Kubin, all on the Redskins' Super Bowl team in 1982, fit that bill. Plus, the Redskins signed low-round draft picks, free agents, and refugees from other leagues perhaps more than any other team in that era.

Joe Gibbs's coaching staff remained amazingly intact through his first coaching stint in Washington, a key reason for the Redskins' consistent success. This photo of his 1982 staff shows (back L-R) LaVern "Torgy" Torgeson (defensive line), Wayne Sevier (special teams), Dan Henning (assistant head coach), Charley Taylor (wide receivers), Don Breaux (running backs), and Warren "Rennie" Simmons (tight ends); and (front L-R) Dan Riley (strength coach), Larry Peccatiello (linebackers), Richie Petitbon (defensive coordinator), Gibbs, Joe Bugel (offensive coordinator), and Bill Hickman (defensive scout).

"We used every resource we had," Gibbs said. "That's what you need to do. There's no set way of building a team. You try to get talent every single way you can get it, through the draft, through signing free agents out of college, through free agency. Any way you can acquire talent, you need to be on top of your game and be ready to do that. We did that, Bobby Beathard did that, Charley Casserly did that. They really helped me in trying to get good talent. You've got to be willing to move mountains to get whatever you've got to get."

Offensive line coach Joe Bugel said, "We always went out and made sure we got smart, tough people. We had a premium on tough guys. We didn't want prima donnas. We wanted snot blowers who liked to practice, liked to hit. We had guys like that, the Theismanns, the Riggins. We had great personalities. The Grimms, the Jacobys—those guys liked to work. They just came around here and hung out here. This was their place, their platform."

According to Grimm, "A lot of it was the chemistry on that football team. The one thing that sticks in my mind is that coach Gibbs said his toughest job is not the Xs and Os but making sure he picks the right 53. Those are the guys who have to go 17 weeks and even longer into the playoffs."

During the 12-year glory period, San Francisco was the only team to top the Redskins in winning percentage at .738. The 49ers captured four Super Bowls during the era. Denver made the Super Bowl three times but lost all three, including Super Bowl XXII to the Redskins.

Gibbs's departure coincided with the start of an unfettered form of free agency and salary cap provisions that would make it very difficult for teams to enjoy the stability the Redskins experienced during that era, when many of the same faces adorned the roster year after year.

"Free agency hit, and the team went in different routes," said Rypien, a Redskin from 1987 to 1993. "We were probably the last of the dinosaurs. We did everything as a team. It was a unique group."

## 1981: 8–8, 4TH PLACE—NFC EAST

### Head Coach: Joe Gibbs

On the face of it, an 8–8 record spells mediocrity. But the Redskins' 8–8 record in 1981 was oh so special.

After dropping their first five games and appearing headed for a disastrous season, the Redskins won eight of the last 11—the three losses coming to playoff-bound teams—and remained in the playoff race through the last week. The rebound laid much of the groundwork for their upcoming Super Bowl-winning season and beyond.

"When we came out of that 0–5 start, nobody wanted to go back to it," said Joe Gibbs, who made his Redskin coaching debut that year. "We were highly motivated, and we learned a lot. That drove us for the first two or three years."

An offensive specialist, Gibbs implemented a well-oiled system that racked up yards and points that year, reminiscent of the Redskins' offensive machine from the 1960s. He also made the squad more entertaining to watch after years of frequent offensive stagnation under coaches George Allen and Jack Pardee.

"All the way around, it was a lot more fun to play," said Art Monk, one of the Redskins' top receivers that year. "The offense was much more flexible and wide open than under Pardee, and more exciting."

In Pardee's final season, 1980, the Redskins sported one of the NFL's least productive offenses, and team owner Jack Kent Cooke sought a coach who could inject pizzazz into the system. Armed with a recommendation from general manager Bobby Beathard, he hired the 40-year-old Gibbs on January

Joe Gibbs addresses the media at his opening press conference on Jan. 13, 1981. At the time, Redskins owner Jack Kent Cooke called him a "pioneer in the game."

13, 1981, and signed him to a three-year contract starting at $115,000 annually.

Gibbs arrived with 17 years of assistant coaching experience, most of it in the pros and a lot of it under Don Coryell, architect of the pass-happy "Air Coryell" system. Gibbs's most recent stint had been with the San Diego Chargers, where he served for two seasons as offensive coordinator under Coryell and called plays for an explosive San Diego offense. The Chargers averaged 400 yards per game and scored 418 points in 1980, when they finished 11–5 and lost in the AFC championship game.

"Joe appeals to me because of his obvious dedication to the game," Cooke said at the time. "And I believe his abilities match his ambitions. He's a pioneer in the game inasmuch as he recognized before others the perceptible change in the character of the game."

"When Joe Gibbs came, I was excited," Redskins quarterback Joe Theismann said. "He's bringing a system that [Hall of Fame quarterback] Dan Fouts had used to post big numbers in San Diego. I was ecstatic."

Gibbs and Beathard immediately focused on weeding out the team's aging veterans. They influenced some of the last vestiges of the George Allen administration to retire, including defensive tackle Diron Talbert, safety Kenny Houston, offensive tackle Terry Hermeling, and special teams standout Pete Wysocki, and worked to create a younger squad through the draft, free-agent signings, and trades.

No one knew it at the time, but Draft Day 1981 would evolve into a treasure trove of picks for the burgundy and gold, players who made substantial impacts for the franchise in the coming years. The top acquisitions were

- Pittsburgh offensive tackle Mark May (first round)
- Pittsburgh center Russ Grimm (third)
- Oklahoma State defensive end Dexter Manley (fifth)
- South Carolina State wide receiver Charlie Brown (eighth)
- Rice guard Darryl Grant (ninth)
- Portland State wide receiver Clint Didier (12th)

"That was the greatest draft in the history of the Washington Redskins," then-scout and later general manager Charley Casserly said. "It was a cornerstone, a foundation for a number of years."

On the trade market, the Redskins dealt a second-round choice to Baltimore for Joe Washington, a speedy halfback who caught a league-high 82 passes in 1979. Free-agent signings included Terry Metcalf, a one-time flashy runner with the St. Louis Cardinals who had played his past three seasons in the Canadian Football League, Cal-Poly San Luis Obispo linebacker Mel Kaufman, and 6–7, 300-pound Louisville offensive tackle Joe Jacoby.

Gibbs also hired an assistant coaching staff that served as a key piece of the Redskins' foundation in the coming years. He brought in Dan Henning (assistant head coach), Joe Bugel (offensive line), Don Breaux (running backs), Wayne Sevier (special teams), Larry Peccatiello (linebackers), Warren "Rennie" Simmons (tight ends), and LaVern "Torgy" Torgeson, who had two prior coaching stints with the Redskins. Richie Petitbon, the Redskins' secondary coach in recent seasons, was promoted to defensive coordinator.

By training camp, someone made a surprise appearance. Low and behold, it was long-lost superstar running back John Riggins, who pronounced to the media in his comical way, "I'm bored, I'm broke, and I'm back."

"I didn't have any apprehension about coming back," Riggins, who sat out the 1980 season, told reporters. "A lot of the guys welcomed me back. I learned a lot not playing last year. I kept up with what the Redskins were doing. I think they were a lot better than their 6–10 record. But I'm not looking back on last year. I want to look ahead and make the most of the upcoming year."

"This might be my last year," he added. "I don't know. We'll have to see what happens. I'm taking it one year at a time. My last game was against Dallas [in December 1979], and it doesn't seem like I've been out a whole year. There are a lot of people out here, and I have to work to get my old job back."

Not everyone greeted Riggins with open arms. "Get rid of him," *Washington Post* columnist Dave Kindred wrote on June 12, 1981. "He deserted the team last year and doesn't deserve to be welcomed back."

After a 3–1 exhibition season, the Redskins, looking drastically different following an off-season overhaul, kicked off the Gibbs era against the Cowboys at RFK Stadium. Theismann threw a career-high 48 passes and completed 22 for 281 yards. But Dallas destroyed drives with interceptions, picking off four in all, and exited with a 26–10 victory. The Redskins also lost two fumbles.

Washington followed with four turnovers and punted the ball 10 times in a 17–7 loss to the Giants, spoiling another career-high performance by Theismann: 318 yards passing. The Redskins then amassed 521 yards against St. Louis, with Theismann passing for 388 plus four touchdowns. Sounded like enough for a win, but Washington's special teams yielded a 50-yard punt return for a touchdown and mishandled a snap on a punt that led to another score in a 40–30 loss. Then came a 36–13 loss to the Eagles, who reeled off 22 straight points in the last 10 minutes, and a 30–17 loss to San Francisco before a legion of disgruntled fans at RFK.

Holy debacle.

A season that began with so much hope was fading fast for the 0–5 Redskins. The offensive looked much more explosive than the previous season, averaging 345 yards through the first five games—but sacks, penalties, and turnovers were crippling the team. The 49ers, for example, scored on an 80-yard fumble return and a 32-yard interception return. Compounding the problem was a rash of injuries that prevented the Redskins from developing consistency. "We were just dropping like

## Down on Riggins's Farm

Joe Gibbs may have been key to developing a potent passing attack as an assistant in San Diego, but he also understood the importance of a strong running game. Hence, in one of his first moves after being hired as Redskins coach, Gibbs flew to Lawrence, Kansas, to coax John Riggins, one of the league's all-time leading rushers, out of retirement.

After missing Riggins on his first visit to his farm, Gibbs returned the next morning and spotted a man who had been out hunting dressed in camouflage and carrying a gun and a beer. He knew it was Riggins, but he didn't know what to expect from the inimitable figure:

> When I talk about people, I say don't go off résumés. When you pick people, you've got to try to understand people. But that meeting was a big shock for me, because it's not what I expected being a young coach and going in there trying to sell John on the deal. I told him how important it was for him to play for the Redskins, and that he should get back into football while he was still in his prime. I said, too, that we'd arrange to trade him if he didn't feel he could play for the Redskins.
>
> Now, I didn't expect a couple of things he said, and I kind of came out of there thinking I probably missed evaluating him. He said if I got him back to Washington, he'll make me famous. I was going, "Goodness, gracious. Man, this is going to be a nightmare trying to coach this guy."

Days later, the phone rang at Redskin Park. It was Riggins, who agreed to play again only if it was with the Redskins, according to general manager Bobby Beathard. (Riggins already had a no-trade clause in his contract.) The next season, Riggins literally carried the Redskins to a Super Bowl victory, fulfilling the initial promise he made to Gibbs.

"The bottom line on that deal is, we signed John Riggins, and he made me famous," Gibbs said. "Exactly what he said came true."

Redskins 315-pound defensive tackle Dave Butz rumbles with an interception to set up a touchdown in a 24–7 win over the Bears that ended Washington's five-game losing skid and gave Joe Gibbs his first win as the Redskins' coach.

Hey, if I don't win, so what. I've had the opportunity,'" he told NFL Films.

Cooke summoned Gibbs to his office to discuss the crisis, but the tough-minded owner remained confident that his rookie coach could turn things around. "Dad was concerned because he had chosen Gibbs on a recommendation from Bobby [Beathard] and on an interview that he had with Gibbs," said the owner's son, John Kent Cooke, the Redskins' executive vice president at the time. "He was aware that he had given up a great deal in Jack Pardee [the NFL Coach of the Year in 1979] over the strenuous objection of his minority partner, Edward Bennett Williams."

Theismann also found it imperative to meet with Gibbs. He made a surprise late-night visit to the coach's home out of concern that his ties to Gibbs were strained. Gibbs had benched Theismann in the third quarter of the loss to the 49ers for backup Tom Flick, and Theismann was the subject of trade talks with Detroit and the Los Angeles Rams, according to the *Washington Post*.

"I've heard people say I wasn't a Joe Gibbs guy, and I don't think Joe was convinced I was committed to football because I had all these other things going on," said Theismann, one of the top passers in the league at the time. "I owned restaurants and did television and radio shows. He and I would sit in meetings where I was his quarterback, he was my coach, but there really wasn't that intangible connection you have to have for a successful working relationship.

"I explained to him how important football was to me, and that I would give everything else up if he wanted me to just prove to him that football was the single most important thing in my life."

Gibbs remained loyal to Theismann and tried to balance his offensive attack by putting greater emphasis on the running game. He implemented a one-back, two-tight end setup with Riggins, underutilized through the first five games, and

flies," said Joe Washington, who missed four games that season due to injury.

Plus, dissension was everywhere in D.C., and Cooke and Gibbs were feeling the heat. "I remember Mr. Cooke came over to me one time and said, 'Joe, you won't believe what they're calling me when we leave RFK Stadium,' Gibbs said in a 1996 interview with NFL Films. "I said, 'Yes sir, I will Mr. Cooke, because they're calling me the same thing.'"

Gibbs was concerned his days were numbered as the Redskins' coach. "I thought, 'Man, I've reached it. This is great.

Joe Washington alternating as the featured backs. Many of Gibbs's skeptics welcomed the move, including Redskins Hall of Fame linebacker and radio analyst Sam Huff: "We were very critical of Gibbs during that 0–5 period. I kept saying, 'What do you have John Riggins for? John Riggins has to run the football. Run the ball, run the ball!'"

Said offensive line coach Joe Bugel, "We went from a two-back setup after John Riggins and Joe Washington came up to Joe [Gibbs]. Riggo said, 'Joe, I'm not a blocker, and I like to run the ball. Little Joe said, 'I'm too little to block, and I'd like to be a pass receiver and run the ball.' So we said, 'Nickel back, first down back.' Riggins and Joe Washington were perfect. With the one back . . . we'd run it down their throats."

And what happened? The Redskins rushed for 227 yards, 126 by Riggins and 88 by Washington, in a 24–7 win over the Bears at Soldier Field. They threw 25 passes, their lowest total by far at that point. And for a change, the opposition committed the big blunders, as Bears quarterback Vince Evans threw four interceptions. Middle linebacker Neal Olkewicz returned one 10 yards for a touchdown in the first quarter, and 6–7, 315-pound defensive tackle Dave Butz rumbled 26 yards with one in the second quarter, coming inches from the goal line. Riggins scored to put the Redskins up, 17–0, his first of two touchdowns.

The win was colossal. "That was really the turnaround in all of our careers, but for Gibbs especially because he was feeling the heat," Olkewicz said. "A lot of people thought we weren't going to win a game. But we won, and everything kind of switched around."

The Redskins fell to 1–6 with a 13–10 loss to Miami and then crafted a four-game winning streak with the help of "Go-Go," Joe Washington. He ran 15 times for 47 yards and caught nine passes for 97 more with a touchdown in a 24–22 win over New England. He then rushed 23 times for 93 yards and caught four passes for 22 in a 42–21 win over St. Louis. Riggins showed his power around the goal line by running for three short scores.

Next came a 33–31 win over Detroit on Mark Moseley's 44-yard field goal with 43 seconds left, his fourth of the game. "Go-Go" ran 27 times for 144 yards and two touchdowns and caught three passes for 20 yards. One week later, Moseley's double dose of clutch kicking, his 49-yarder with seconds left in regulation and a 48-yarder in overtime, gave the Redskins a 30–27 win over the Giants.

Suddenly, the 5–6 Redskins were in contention for a wild card playoff spot, and what had once seemed like a calamity had shaped into a salvageable season. Gibbs apparently sensed an evolution taking place.

"I remember Gibbs coming over to me in probably the only time he ever talked to me straight up," Butz said. "He said, 'Dave, I don't want you to get discouraged, but I want to tell you we're on the verge of doing great things. I want you to keep doing what you're doing, but do not get discouraged.'"

The Redskins slipped with losses to Dallas and Buffalo but went on another winning streak—three games—starting with a 15–13 upset of the Eagles, who were battling Dallas for first place in the NFC East. Philly appeared ready to win when kicker Tony Franklin set up for a 24-yard field goal with under a minute left. But the snap was bad, and the 1981 Redskins won for the first time over a team with a winning record.

The Redskins then demolished the Colts, 38–14. Theismann completed 23 of 36 passes for 339 yards and two touchdowns, Joe Washington ran for 73 yards, and Riggins gained 50 with

two scores. The Redskins amassed 486 yards before piling up 502 in a 30–7 win over the Rams in the season finale.

By then, the Redskins' offense was like a Sherman tank obliterating defenses at will. The yardage against Baltimore and Los Angeles added to a season total of 5,623, more than 600 better than the Redskins' prior record and one of the best marks in the league. The Redskins also set team records for most total plays (1,081) and first downs (334), and scored 347 points, four short of the team record at the time.

"Once we got going in the latter part of the season, there wasn't a question of whether we would win," Theismann said. "The only question in our mind was how many points we'd score."

Theismann chalked up his best year to date. He set a team record with 293 completions and threw for 3,568 yards, less than 200 behind Sonny Jurgensen's all-time Redskins high. His completion percentage rose, too, after the Redskins switched to the single-back offense. Joe Washington caught 70 passes, two shy of the Redskins' all-time record, and had a team-high 916 yards rushing. Riggins pounded out 714 more. Mike Nelms, the only Redskin chosen for the Pro Bowl, set records for most yards on combined kick returns (1,591) and the highest kickoff return average (29.7). He also returned two punts for touchdowns.

"After starting 0–5, we were winning left and right like gangbusters, so we knew then we were a good football team," Joe Washington said. "Our strong finish was an indication of what we really had. Going into the [1982 season], we really felt we had something grand to build on."

# 1982: 8–1, 1ST PLACE—NFC

## Head Coach: Joe Gibbs

It was a turbulent season in the NFL, one that saw a two-month gap without football because of a maddening player strike. For the Redskins, it was a season of sheer elation.

The Redskins finished 8–1 in the truncated regular season and followed with playoff romps over Detroit, Minnesota, and Dallas to gain a ticket to Super Bowl XVII. There, they won their first NFL championship in 40 years with a 27–17 victory over Miami, a win that signaled the Redskins' emergence among the NFL elite.

"It was a Cinderella year, a storybook year," said Redskins kicker Mark Moseley, one of the team's superstars that season. He became the first kicker ever to be named league MVP after converting 20 of 21 field goals (.952 percentage) and hitting a record 23 straight dating back to the 1981 season. He also hit a field goal that clinched the Redskins' first playoff berth since 1976.

Running back John Riggins, for his part, crafted one of the most spectacular performances in NFL postseason history, rushing for 610 yards over four playoff games. Quarterback Joe Theismann finished as the NFC's top passer with a 91.3 rating and was named NFL Player of the Year by the Maxwell Football Club. His favorite targets were receivers Art Monk and Charlie Brown, who tallied 67 catches and more than 1,100 yards between them. Brown also caught eight touchdowns.

The defense yielded a league-low 128 points and was among the least charitable units in rushing and receiving yards.

The clever minds that assembled the machine received their just recognition. Joe Gibbs earned consensus NFL Coach of the Year honors, and general manager Bobby Beathard was named NFL Executive of the Year.

"There was such a whirlwind that year because we were on strike for nine weeks and came back," said Redskins safety Mark Murphy, the squad's leading tackler for the fourth straight season. "It was one of those years when everything fell into place. It was just really exciting to be a part of it."

Perhaps the season would have been just a dream if a rookie kicker had capitalized on his shot to make the team. The Redskins used their 11th-round pick to draft talented Miami (Florida) kicker Dan Miller, who challenged Moseley, a 34-year-old entering his 12th season, for most of the preseason. Moseley, fresh off an injury-plagued year when he made 19 of 30 field goals, remembers nearly being discarded by the team he had rescued many times with his right foot.

"I was told that all Miller had to do was perform and the job was his," Moseley said. "I was also told I didn't even need to come back to camp if I wanted to go somewhere else. That was because of Bobby Beathard. He had been trying to replace me ever since he came to Washington [in 1978]."

In what now seems serendipitous, Miller missed two field goals in the last exhibition game, a 28–21 loss to Cincinnati, and was cut from the squad. Moseley proceeded to construct his momentous season.

Meanwhile, Gibbs and Beathard made decisions to fortify their burgeoning squad. After trading disgruntled cornerback Lemar Parrish, they used the team's second-round pick on San Diego State cornerback Vernon Dean, who replaced veteran Joe Lavender during the season and earned *Football Digest* Defensive Rookie of the Year honors. Patriots defensive end Tony McGee was acquired in a trade. The Redskins also signed rookie free-agent punter Jeff Hayes and assigned him to handle kickoff duties, shielding Moseley from reinjuring himself on kickoffs.

Who would have envisioned a Super Bowl year after the Redskins finished 0–4 in the preseason? Exhibition games are rarely an exact barometer, though, as evidenced by the Redskins' 37–34 season-opening victory on the road over Philadelphia, 10–6 the year before and two seasons removed from a Super Bowl appearance. Theismann was as sharp as ever, completing 28 of 39 passes for 382 yards, with three touchdowns and no interceptions. He repeatedly brought the Redskins back from the brink of defeat, while Moseley displayed his golden right foot that was so prominent in 1982. When the Eagles took a 34–31 lead with a minute left, the Theismann-Moseley duo was instrumental in pulling out the victory.

Theismann first guided the Redskins 32 yards in five plays to set up Moseley's 48-yard game-tying field goal as time expired. After winning the overtime coin toss, the Redskins drove 62 yards in eight plays, and Moseley provided the winning points from 26 yards out.

Redskin players and coaches erupted as if they had won the Super Bowl. An elated Gibbs leaped into Theismann's arms, a sign that their once chilly relationship was on the mend.

"It was an incredible moment," Theismann recalled. "I was on an unbelievable emotional high. It guess you could call that the beginning for both Gibbs and I. The 8–3 finish in 1981 set a real foundation of what type of team we could be, and then to come out and beat the Eagles in their place at Veterans Stadium. The Eagles are always a tough, tough, tough game for us."

Said Gibbs, "That was one of the biggest games we ever played. It kind of got us started in the right direction."

The Redskins built on their momentum with a 21–13 win over the Buccaneers in monsoon-like conditions in Tampa. It was so slippery that Bucs quarterback Doug Williams fumbled the ball four times on center exchanges. The Redskins had no turnovers, and Moseley defied the weather conditions by

With the snow falling on December 19, 1982, Mark Moseley boots a 42-yard field goal that gave the Redskins a 15–14 win over the Giants and put them in the playoffs. In doing so, Moseley set an NFL record with his 21st straight field goal. "I never had any doubts at all," he said about making the kick. Moseley kicked a slew of game winners for the Redskins and today stands as the team's all-time leading scorer (1,206 points).

kicking three more field goals, although he missed two extra points. In addition, the Redskins' offense gave a sneak preview of the "Riggo Drill" that became so famous in the playoffs. With his squad up, 21–13, Riggins carried the ball eight straight times for 51 yards over the last 3:36 to run out the clock, part of his workman-like 136-yard, 34-carry performance. The latter figure tied a 45-year-old team record.

Two games. Two wins over 1981 playoff teams. But with the National Football League Players Association (NFLPA) and team owners locked in a dispute over terms of the collective bargaining agreement, a player strike seemed imminent. After the win over the Bucs, Gibbs told his players not to walk off the job, so they could build on their success. "We're hot, let's not strike now," he said.

But the NFL players carried out the first regular-season walkout in league history, citing interest in acquiring more shares of television revenues, among other issues. Few could have imagined at the time that there would be no football games for 62 days. "Those were difficult times, but we all felt some changes were necessary," said Murphy, the team's player representative to the NFLPA.

All the while, Gibbs's players followed his advice to stick together and not cross the picket line in bits and pieces. They lifted weights in unison and gathered for sandlot drills. Doing so gave them an edge on opposing teams, most of which scattered during the break.

"They weren't normal coach-monitored practices, but we spent time going over old game plans just to keep ourselves sharp," Theismann said. "We really worked on relationships off the field, which made us a better football team."

"A lot of teams got fractured. Gibbs was a part of us remaining as a unit," said Redskins linebacker Neal Olkewicz. "He kind of understood that it was more important for the team to stay together than for everybody to voice their opinion on everything going on. We knew it was going to be over at some point, and we felt we'd have a good chance if we stayed together as a team."

The Redskins appeared to be in excellent shape—physically and mentally—when the strike ended after eight weeks of cancelled games. The union and owners agreed to restart the season on November 21 and play seven more regular-season games, plus a 16-team, four-week playoff, or the Super Bowl Tournament. The eight playoff spots from each conference would be based on how well the teams finished in the entire conference, not in their divisions.

Back in action, the Redskins improved to 3–0 with a 27–17 win over the Giants in the Meadowlands. Theismann completed 16 of 24 passes for 185 yards and two touchdowns in a game the Redskins led all the way. Then came a 13–9 victory over the Eagles on November 28, remarkably the Redskins' first home game of the season. Redskin cornerback Jeris White picked off two passes, one of which stopped a late Eagles drive deep in Redskins territory.

The 4–0 Redskins were now one of only two undefeated teams, along with Miami. But the Cowboys sent them to their first defeat on a frustrating day at RFK. Dallas built a 17–0 lead after three quarters, but the Redskins came within seven in the fourth quarter on Moseley's 38-yard field goal and Theismann's 17-yard touchdown pass to Charlie Brown. Washington appeared to be ready to drive for a tie, but Cowboys quarterback-punter Danny White ran 20 yards for a first down on a fake punt. Dallas later recovered two of its own fumbles and sealed the win on a 46-yard run by Ron Springs.

Theismann completed 19 of 29 passes for 234 yards with one touchdown but also had three interceptions.

Despite the loss, the 4–1 Redskins were tied with Dallas and Green Bay for first place in the NFC. They rebounded to win by the score of Moseley 12, Cardinals 7. The kicker, maneuvering delicately on frozen artificial turf in St. Louis, was 4 for 4 on field goals to reach 18 in a row. He missed his first kick from 37 yards out. But the Cardinals were offside, and his second try was good.

Moseley was now three kicks from breaking Garo Yepremian's NFL record of 20 straight field goals set over the 1978–79 seasons. The drama started to build. "Every reporter suddenly came out of the woodwork," he recalled. "It wasn't like now where every television station has somebody there, but for that time it was a pretty big affair."

Plus, the Redskins were one win from clinching a playoff berth. But they were the antithesis of a playoff team in the first half against the Giants at RFK. They committed five turnovers, four on interceptions by Theismann, and trailed, 14–3, at halftime. Joe Washington's 22-yard run closed the gap to five points, but Moseley missed the conversion. He later kicked a 31-yard field goal in the fourth period to tie Yepremian's record and create a 14–12 game with 8:23 left. After regaining possession, the Redskins drove 46 yards to the Giants' 25 and called time out with nine seconds left.

Moseley entered the game amid elements of a Hollywood script:

- A playoff berth at stake
- The NFL kicking record on the line
- Snow falling steadily on the beaten-up turf at RFK

The unflappable kicker said he felt at the time there was no way he would miss: "Going into the game, I felt good about it. I actually had a dream that week of kicking a game-winning field goal against the Giants to set the record. I never had any doubts at all. It wasn't like I was nervous or uneasy about it."

## Rigginomics 101

John Riggins played sparingly in the final two games because of a pulled thigh muscle but decided to put the Redskins on his back entering the playoffs. He approached offensive line coach Joe Bugel with a demand to carry the ball a lot more.

"I was kind of Riggins's guy to go to Joe [Gibbs]," Bugel said. "Riggins said, 'Go tell coach Gibbs I'd like to run the ball 35 times this game.' So I said, 'Joe, Riggo wants to run it 35.' He went, 'Okay, we'll give it to him 38 times.'"

Hence, the introduction of "Rigginomics," a take on President Reagan's economic theories at the time known as "Reaganomics." The course consisted of Riggo right, Riggo left, and Riggo up the middle with his battering ram runs. Opposing defenses would be sorry they enrolled.

The snap and Theismann's hold were perfect, and Moseley met the ball true and hard. Giants linebacker Byron Hunt got a hand on the ball, but it stayed straight and split the uprights with plenty of room to spare. Theismann jumped into Moseley's arms, and RFK Stadium shook in a scene resembling a winter wonderland.

The playoff bid was now in hand. But Moseley's kicking had disguised the fact that the Redskins had scored three touchdowns over the past 16 quarters. The offense, however, began to click.

The Redskins racked up 448 yards against New Orleans—250 through the air and 198 on the ground—in a 27–10 victory. Theismann threw 58- and 57-yard touchdown passes to Charlie Brown, and Moseley kicked two more field goals to run his streak to 23. The defense held the Saints to 197 yards and sacked quarterback Guido Merkens five times.

Then came a 28–0 shellacking of St. Louis that improved the Redskins to 8–1 and clinched home-field advantage through the playoffs. (Dallas lost its final two games to finish in second place in the NFC at 6–3.) Washington was again clicking on all cylinders. Theismann threw scoring passes to Joe Washington and tight ends Rick Walker and Clint Didier. The Redskins held an opponent to less than 200 yards for the second straight week and forced five turnovers.

"It seemed that after the Giants game, our offense started to gel," recalled Moseley, who missed a field goal against the Cardinals to end his streak. "We went down to New Orleans and kicked their tails, you couldn't stop our offense. Our offense was really rolling when we went into the playoffs. Nobody could slow us down."

Said defensive tackle Darryl Grant, "Coach Gibbs said, and it always came true, teams that get hot maybe the third, fourth, fifth game before the end of the season usually go all the way. You have to get hot and continue the momentum."

The Redskins did just that on the road to Super Bowl XVII.

## NFC PLAYOFF GAME
**Washington 31, Detroit 7**
**January 8, 1983**
**RFK Stadium, Washington, D.C.**
**Attendance: 55,045**

### Smurf Takes Big Bite out of Lions in Redskins Win

An obscure receiver named Alvin Garrett took center stage at a most critical time for the Redskins.

With starter Art Monk out after breaking his foot in the season finale against St. Louis, and with reserve Virgil Seay hobbling, the Redskins' receiver corps was decimated heading into the first round of the Super Bowl Tournament against Detroit. Enter the 5–7, 178-pound Garrett, who had one catch for 6 yards in the regular season while playing mostly on special teams.

But Garrett, then in his second season, hauled in six passes for 110 yards and three touchdowns against Detroit, inspiring the Redskins to a 31–7 victory. Suddenly, everyone knew about Alvin Garrett.

"Alvin was a tough guy, a special teams guy," said Charley Taylor, the Redskins' receivers coach at the time. "You get guys with great hearts and good skills, and they'll play. They'll catch the ball. That's what he did."

Against a 4–5 squad that entered the postseason in last place among the eight NFC playoff teams, the Redskins took a 10–0 lead in the first quarter on cornerback Jeris White's 77-yard interception return and Mark Moseley's 26-yard field goal. Garrett began tormenting the Lions in the second period.

On a third-and-19 from the Detroit 21, Redskins quarterback Joe Theismann spotted Garrett running on the left side past first-year cornerback Bruce McNorton. Garrett caught the perfect pass around the 2 and scored. Garrett again victimized Norton before halftime with another 21-yard scoring catch in the same spot. "It looked like an instant replay," Lions coach Monte Clark told reporters later. Moseley's conversion put the Redskins up, 24–0.

Detroit drove deep into Redskins territory twice in the first half but lost fumbles both times. The Lions turned the ball over five times on the day.

The Redskins iced the victory early in the third quarter. They drove 73 yards in five plays, the finale a 27-yard touchdown catch by Garrett, who beat rookie cornerback Bobby Watkins. John Riggins rushed for 25 yards on the drive as part of his 25-carry, 119-yard day against one of the league's best defenses against the run. Theismann was sharp, completing 14 of 19 passes for 210 yards and three touchdowns.

When the Lions averted a shutout on David Hill's 15-yard scoring catch in the third quarter, it marked the second touchdown yielded by the Redskins' defense over the past 11 quarters. Detroit rolled up 365 yards of offense, but only 95 came on the ground, where Washington held dangerous running back Billy Sims to 19 yards.

In the end, Monte Clark was eating his words. The Lions' coach had said prior to the game that he didn't think the Redskins were a great team.

"We always used to hear a lot of remarks like that from other teams, especially in the early years of Gibbs," Redskins linebacker Neal Olkewicz said. "But those words motivated us. We were the kind of guys who liked to fight. If somebody said you can't do it, then you fight harder."

| | | | | | | |
|---|---|---|---|---|---|---|
| Detroit— | 0 | 0 | 7 | 0 | — | 7 |
| Washington— | 10 | 14 | 7 | 0 | — | 31 |

Wash — White 77 interception return (Moseley kick)
Wash — G Moseley 26
Wash — Garrett 21 pass from Theismann (Moseley kick)
Wash — Garrett 21 pass from Theismann (Moseley kick)
Wash — Garrett 27 pass from Theismann (Moseley kick)
Det —— Hill 15 pass from Hipple (Murray kick)

## NFC DIVISIONAL PLAYOFF GAME
**Washington 21, Minnesota 7**
**January 15, 1983**
**RFK Stadium, Washington, D.C.**
**Attendance: 54,592**

### Riggins a la Carte Too Much for Vikings

Riggins, Riggins, and more Riggins.

The Vikings were served that meal in the second round of the Super Bowl Tournament but found it far from appetizing.

The bulldozing back rumbled through the Vikings' seemingly helpless defense, carrying the ball 37 times for 185 yards, both personal highs. His total carries were also a team record.

He repeatedly ran off-tackle on standard Redskin plays called "40 Gut" and "50 Gut," just bearing down with smash-mouth football while leading his troops to a 21–7 win that put them in the NFC championship game.

"Every time we looked up, he was in our secondary," Vikings linebacker Matt Blair remembered. "We always had to catch up to him."

Riggins's indestructible offensive line, newly nicknamed the Hogs, was sensational in its own right. The line knocked over Minnesota's smaller defensive line like bowling pins and created gaping holes for the 6–2, 240-pound Riggins.

"It was just Hogs stuff," Redskins right tackle George Starke recalled. "We were knocking people down, and John was running through the holes. Our style of blocking and his style of running went together perfectly. The Vikings did a lot of bizarre stunts on the line to try to disrupt our line and confuse us. But the Hogs were so sophisticated by that point that it didn't matter what the defense did."

Said Blair, "That line was just destroying our defensive line and linebackers."

Washington wasted no time showcasing Riggins against a Vikings squad that finished 5–4 in the regular season and topped Atlanta, 30–24, in the playoff opener. He carried the ball seven times for 34 yards on the Redskins' first possession, a 66-yard drive that ended on quarterback Joe Theismann's 3-yard scoring pass to tight end Don Warren. Theismann, who had an exceptional day of his own with 17 of 23 passing for 213 yards and two touchdowns, completed a 46-yard flea-flicker to one-time-reserve-turned-star Alvin Garrett later in the quarter. It fueled a seven-play, 71-yard march that ended with Riggins's 2-yard scoring run on fourth down. Mark Moseley's conversion put the Redskins up, 14–0.

Vikings quarterback Tommy Kramer responded in the second period with a 46-yard bomb to receiver Terry LeCount. Running back Ted Brown ran 18 yards for a score to cut the lead in half. But Theismann countered later in the quarter with an 18-yard touchdown pass to Garrett to cap a 70-yard, eight-play drive.

There was no scoring in the second half, when Moseley missed two field goals. Minnesota failed twice on fourth downs deep in Redskins territory, and receiver Sammy White dropped three passes, one in the end zone. All the while, Riggo kept chugging along, rushing 18 times for 110 yards in the final 30 minutes.

As Riggins left the field for the last time with about a minute left, the packed house at RFK Stadium acknowledged his awe-inspiring performance with a standing ovation. He

## How the Super Bowl XVII-Champion Redskins Were Built

| Year | Draft (15) | Trades (8) | Free Agents (24) Waivers (2) |
|---|---|---|---|
| 1972 | | | T George Starke (W) |
| 1973 | | | |
| 1974 | | QB Joe Theismann (from Miami) | K Mark Moseley (FA) |
| 1975 | | | DT Dave Butz (FA) |
| 1976 | | CB Joe Lavender (from Philadelphia) | RB John Riggins (FA) |
| 1977 | | | DT Perry Brooks (FA) RB Clarence Harmon (FA) S Mark Murphy (FA) |
| 1978 | | | G Fred Dean (FA) |
| 1979 | TE Don Warren (4) LB Rich Milot (7) LB Monte Coleman (11) | S Tony Peters (from Cleveland) | LB Neal Olkewicz (FA) |
| 1980 | LB Mat Mendenhall (2) | RB Wilbur Jackson (from San Fran) CB Jeris White (from Tampa Bay) | C Jeff Bostic (FA) S-KR Mike Nelms (FA) TE Rick Walker (FA) |
| 1981 | G Mark May (1) C-G Russ Grimm (3) DE Dexter Manley (5) LB Larry Kubin (6) WR Charlie Brown (8) DT Darryl Grant (9) TE Clint Didier (12) | RB Joe Washington (from Baltimore) | TE Rich Caster (FA) LB Pete Cronan (FA) WR Alvin Garrett (W) RB Nick Giaquinto (FA) T Joe Jacoby (FA) S Curtis Jordan (FA) LB Mel Kaufman (FA) LB Quentin Lowry (FA) CB LeCharls McDaniel (FA) WR Virgil Seay (FA) RB Otis Wonsley (FA) |
| 1982 | CB Vernon Dean (2) DE Todd Liebenstein (4) QB Bob Holly (11B) T Donald Laster (12) | DE Tony McGee (from N. England) QB Tom Owen (from N. England) | P Jeff Hayes (FA) T Garry Puetz (FA) S Greg Williams (FA) |

## Unique Subgroups Give Redskins Fun-Loving Identity

The Hogs. The Smurfs. The Fun Bunch. Sounds like a lineup of cartoon characters.

The Redskins spawned those unique subgroups during the 1982 season. The Hogs was a nickname bestowed on the offensive linemen for their portly image and blue-collar demeanor; the Fun Bunch consisted of players who slapped high fives in the end zone after touchdowns; and the Smurfs featured three pint-sized receivers.

Their existence led to a strong sense of camaraderie among the players and gave the Redskins a fun-loving personality that helped endear them to their fans.

"Guys took pride in giving themselves those names," said offensive tackle Joe Jacoby, a charter member of the Hogs. "They fed off of it. Those names were kind of funny, but they kept the team together. It was something where the players went out and had to live up to that reputation every week."

The Hogs were by far the most popular subgroup and the earliest one to gain fame. Offensive line coach Joe Bugel coined the term while directing his troops during training camp at Dickinson College in Carlisle, Pennsylvania, before the 1982 season.

"I was looking around one day, and I saw a lot of big, fat bellies," Bugel said. " 'I said, okay you Hogs, let's go down to the bullpen and hit those sleds.' It caught on and everybody started laughing. The team rallied around them, and the more the opponents talked about them, the more they had to back it up."

Said Redskins guard Ron Saul, "Bugel said, 'Guys, we've got to take control of the situation. In the NFL, you've got the Purple People Eaters, the Dallas Doomsday Defense, the Fearsome Foursome, the Steel Curtain. But nobody's named an offensive line. We're going to become the Hogs.' I thought, 'That's great. I can't wait to go home and tell my wife.'"

As the Redskins piled up wins in the regular season and romped through the playoffs, the nickname mushroomed in prominence and charter members of the group evolved into household names—something special for normally obscure offensive linemen. Members included the starting five on the line, tackles Jacoby and George Starke, guards Russ Grimm and Mark May, as well as center Jeff Bostic, reserve guard Fred Dean, and tight ends Rick Walker and Don Warren. (Saul spent the 1982 season on injured reserve.) Running back John Riggins was an honorary member.

Bugel, known as "Boss Hog," sought ways to keep the Hogs tight as a unit. "His comment was, 'For the next six months, you two on the left side of the line are married. Know each other better than you would your wife,'" Jacoby said. "We knew each other so well that we didn't have to make line calls and stuff like that. He wanted to create sort of a college atmosphere, so he made us wear a Hogs T-shirt once a week. If we didn't, we were fined. The money went into a pool, and we used it for a party

The original Hogs at a black-tie pork feast. (Left to right) Russ Grimm, Fred Dean, George Starke, Mark May, Joe Jacoby, Don Warren, and Jeff Bostic. Rick Walker is seated.

The Fun Bunch specialized in slapping high fives in the end zone after Redskin touchdowns. The group, including members Otis Wonsley (39), Art Monk (81), and Charlie Brown (87), had much to celebrate during this 51–7 playoff win over the Los Angeles Rams on January 1, 1984.

at the end of the year. That's how he built togetherness among us on the line."

All the while, a case of Hogmania consumed the nation's capital. There were Hog reports on the radio and commercial sales of Hog hats and Hog T-shirts. Starke, known as "Head Hog" because of his seniority in the group, even trademarked the nickname and formed Super Hogs Inc., which sold Hogs merchandise. The Hogs were featured in national publications such as the Sporting News. They even had their own male cheerleaders in the Hogettes, who debuted in 1983 and have appeared at every Redskins home game since clad in brightly colored wigs, polka dot and checkered dresses, and plastic hog snouts.

The nickname stayed intact through the Gibbs era, when the Hogs dwarfed most defensive linemen in size and established themselves as a model for the 300-pound-plus offensive lines of today. They were a pillar on Redskin teams that reached four Super Bowls and won three NFL titles during the original Gibbs era, and Jacoby and Grimm formed perhaps the best left side in NFL history. New Hogs emerged over the years, such as tackles Jim Lachey and Ed Simmons, guards R. C. Thielemann and Mark Schlereth, and the multidimensional Raleigh McKenzie.

"It remained a unifying body that primarily does dirty work, that's unselfish, that does it for John Riggins and [quarterback] Joe Theismann and [wingback] Joe Washington, whoever reaps the benefit from it," Walker said of the Hogs.

The Fun Bunch was Walker's brainchild. His goal was to unite everyone who caught passes after star receiver Art Monk suffered a season-ending injury in the final 1982 regular season game. As a result, Walker and Warren; receivers Charlie Brown, Virgil Seay, and Alvin Garrett; wingback Nick Giaquinto; and H-backs Clarence Harmon and Otis Wonsley jumped in a choreographed high five in the end zone after a Redskins touchdown catch. The Fun Bunch debuted in the first-round playoff win over Detroit and existed through the 1983 season until being banned because of the perception of taunting.

"Art's injury was very depressing because he was a primary go-to guy," Walker said. "So you've got to do something to get yourself out of it. That group had a ton of fun."

Three members of the Fun Bunch—5–7 Alvin Garrett, 5–8 Virgil Seay, and 5–10 Charlie Brown—were also Smurfs. The nickname was derived from a children's cartoon show called The Smurfs.

The outstanding play of Garrett in the 1982 postseason, when he caught 15 passes for 244 yards and five touchdowns, lifted the Smurfs into the limelight. During Super Bowl week in Pasadena, California, the trio went to Disneyland and posed for pictures with the real Smurfs, tiny blue-skinned characters dressed in white trousers and a cap who lived in mushroom-shaped houses in Smurf Village.

That week, "I felt more like the ringmaster of a circus than the quarterback of a football team," Theismann remembered. "My wide receivers were called the Smurfs, my offensive line was called the Hogs. John Riggins on a Friday night before the Super Bowl attended a party in a tuxedo, a top hat, and tails. The linebackers dressed up in Army fatigues. It was fun, everything was new."

Seldom-used receiver Alvin Garrett came out of nowhere to catch five touchdown passes in the Super Bowl Tournament. Here, he heads to the end zone in the second-round win over the Vikings.

responded by stopping near midfield, taking off his helmet, and bowing to the crowd, first on the Redskins' side of the field, then on the Vikings' side. He gave an appreciative wave before heading to the bench.

"That was classic Riggins," Redskins linebacker Neal Olkewicz said in retrospect. "For a lot of other people, it would have been corny or fake, but for Riggins it was perfect."

The Redskins' defense deserved kudos, too. The Vikings rushed for only 79 yards against a unit that was becoming more dominant each week.

"Everyone knew we had a high-powered offense, but no one knew this defense could stand up and play well," defensive end Tony McGee recalled. "[Defensive coordinator] Richie Petitbon and other coaches put us in the right positions, and we took pride in everything we did."

With the clock winding down, chants of "WE WANT DALLAS! WE WANT DALLAS!" reverberated through the stadium, a reference to a preferred matchup against the Cowboys in the NFC championship game. The fans got their wish. With a 37–26 win over Green Bay, the silver-and-blue folks would be coming to the nation's capital to face the red-hot Redskins.

| | | | | | | |
|---|---|---|---|---|---|---|
| Minnesota | 0 | 7 | 0 | 0 | — | 7 |
| Washington | 14 | 7 | 0 | 0 | — | 21 |

Wash — Warren 3 pass from Theismann (Moseley kick)
Wash — Riggins 2 run (Moseley kick)
Minn — T. Brown 18 run (Danmeier kick)
Wash — Garrett 18 pass from Theismann (Moseley kick)

## NFC CHAMPIONSHIP GAME
**Washington 31, Dallas 17**
**January 22, 1983**
**RFK Stadium, Washington, D.C.**
**Attendance: 55,045**

### Redskins Beat Cowboys Again
### with Super Bowl Trip at Stake

In the annals of the storied Redskins-Cowboys rivalry, this win ranks with the best of them all for the boys from D.C.

The Redskins manhandled the so-called "America's Team" on a frigid, gray day in the nation's capital, 31–17, to advance to Super Bowl XVII. They led from nearly start to finish and again showed that when it came to the biggest game possible between the rivals, the Redskins had the Cowboys corralled. Ten years before, Washington had beat Dallas in the NFC championship game to advance to Super Bowl VII.

"I wanted to beat them so badly," said Redskins defensive end Dexter Manley, who'd voiced "I hate Dallas" rhetoric all week. "I grew up watching the Cowboys. They had this attitude that they're bigger than life, that they're supreme, that they're prima donnas. If it wasn't for two plays, I didn't have a good game that day."

Those two plays were huge. The pass-rushing specialist plowed into Dallas quarterback Danny White in the second quarter and knocked him out. He also tipped a screen pass in

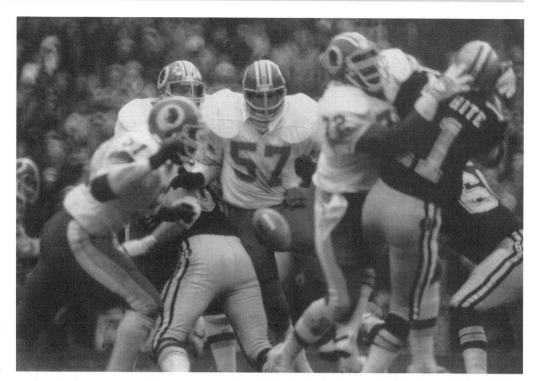

Redskins defensive end Dexter Manley plows into Cowboys quarterback Danny White in the second quarter, knocking him out of the game.

the fourth quarter that defensive tackle Darryl Grant intercepted and returned 10 yards for the touchdown to secure the victory.

Quarterback Joe Theismann turned in another solid game, completing 12 of 20 passes for 150 yards and a touchdown with no interceptions. Running back John Riggins continued his superb play, grinding out 140 yards on 36 carries with two scoring runs. He flourished behind the Hogs, who pummeled the Cowboys' famed Flex defense.

"We were crushing them running the ball," offensive tackle George Starke recalled. "The Hogs were pretty mean-spirited. We ran only a few plays, and we would tell the Cowboys' linemen when (we) were coming. We'd say, 'Randy White, this one is coming over you.' He'd get pissed off, but the play would come over him. The next play would come over John Dutton. We'd say, 'Dutton, this one is coming over you.' We'd just knock them out of there."

Entering the Super Bowl Tournament, conventional wisdom was that the NFC championship game would come down to these two teams. Unlike the Redskins' strong showings against the Lions and Vikings, Dallas was erratic in its two wins, 30–17 over Tampa Bay and 37–26 over Green Bay. The Cowboys, winners of six straight over the Redskins, were slight favorites.

Dallas took the opening kickoff and marched 75 yards in 14 plays, settling for Rafael Septien's 27-yard field goal. The Redskins immediately went to their bread and butter: Riggo. He carried five times for 30 yards on an 84-yard drive that ended on Theismann's 19-yard scoring pass to receiver Charlie Brown in the back of the end zone.

Washington later muffed two chances to score after setting up near midfield. But the Cowboys fumbled the ball on a punt and Redskins linebacker Monte Coleman recovered it deep in Dallas territory. Riggins carried three times, the last a 1-yard scoring run for a 14–3 lead.

Manley grabbed his first headline late in the half. He bowled into White in the backfield and forced the quarterback's head

to hit the ground. White was seeing stars. "It was probably the next morning before I knew where I was," White recalled. "Watching the tape, it didn't look like he hit my head at all, it wasn't a violent hit. The only thing I can think of is that when I hit the ground, I must have gotten knocked out. I never did regain any memory of that game, from the trip up there, to warm-ups, to the first quarter, second quarter, third or fourth."

Gary Hogeboom took over and threw a 6-yard scoring pass to receiver Drew Pearson early in the third quarter to cut the margin to four. But Redskin Pro Bowler Mike Nelms returned the ensuing kickoff 76 yards. After Theismann's 22-yard pass to Brown, Riggins bulled into the end zone for another score and a 21–10 lead.

The Cowboys retaliated again with an 84-yard drive capped by Hogeboom's 23-yard pass to receiver Butch Johnson. They regained possession and began a drive on the Redskins' 32. But linebacker Mel Kaufman intercepted a Hogeboom pass, and Mark Moseley's field goal created a 24–17 game with 7:12 left.

Then came the clincher: On first down from the Cowboys' 20, Manley tipped a Hogeboom screen pass intended for running back Tony Dorsett. The ball floated for a few seconds while Grant waited for it to fall back to Earth. "Everything went in slow motion, and it just looked like time had stopped," Grant remembered. "It took forever for the ball to come down. I just wanted to get in position, get underneath the ball, catch it, and run as fast as I could."

Once the ball settled into his arms, the 6–1, 275-pound Grant rumbled toward the end zone, avoided an arm tackle by the diving Dorsett and high-stepped his Redskins into Super Bowl XVII. The 55,000-plus fans at RFK Stadium lapsed into delirium as the stands rocked. "The stadium was unbelievable," Redskins coach Joe Gibbs said. "Those stands were moving about three feet, they were going up and down."

Redskins defensive tackle Darryl Grant intercepts a pass tipped by Dexter Manley and returns it 10 yards for a fourth-quarter touchdown that gave the Redskins a 31–17 lead. The play punched the Redskins' ticket to Super Bowl XVII and stands as one of the most indelible moments in team history. "It just never goes away," Grant said of the play. "It still sends chills down my spine."

Said Coleman, "To look over and see 50,000 people cheering for you, we're playing our rival team and to go out and play the way we played, the crowd played a big part in it."

With 12 seconds left, Gibbs was carried off the field on his players' shoulders, while fans rushed the field and tore down the goalposts. Players from both teams, thinking the game was over, began heading to their locker rooms. But there was time for one more play, although some of the Cowboys were reluctant to again take the field knowing they were about to lose their third straight NFC championship game.

"They were totally demoralized, they were so pissed," Starke said. "The officials had to drag them out of the locker room, they wouldn't come out. The quarterback wouldn't come out."

A wide receiver, Pearson, took the final snap and put his Cowboys out of their misery.

| | | | | | | |
|---|---|---|---|---|---|---|
| Dallas— | 3 | 0 | 14 | 0 | — | 17 |
| Washington— | 7 | 7 | 7 | 10 | — | 31 |

Dallas — FG Septien 27
Wash — Brown 19 pass from Theismann (Moseley kick)
Wash — Riggins 1 run (Moseley kick)
Dallas — Pearson 6 pass from Hogeboom (Septien kick)
Wash — Riggins 4 run (Moseley kick)
Dallas — Johnson 23 pass from Hogeboom (Septien kick)
Wash — FG Moseley 29
Wash — Grant 10 interception return (Moseley kick)

## SUPER BOWL XVII
### Washington 27, Miami 17
### January 30, 1983
### Rose Bowl, Pasadena, Calif.
### Attendance: 103,667

### Day of the Diesel: Riggins Carries Redskins to First Super Bowl Win

John Riggins had carried the Redskins this far, but he wasn't about to stop churning his powerful legs. In the process, he carved a spot in football immortality.

His venue was Super Bowl XVII. The beefy running back knocked the Dolphins' defense silly by rushing 38 times for a Super Bowl-record 166 yards in a prime-time production of the Riggo drill. Forty-three of his yards came on a touchdown run that stands as the most famous play in Redskins history and is indelibly engraved in Super Bowl lore.

The run, executed when Riggins grandly took his cue on a fourth-and-1 play in the fourth quarter, erased a 17–13 Dolphins lead. The Redskins proceeded to win, 27–17, and Riggins was unanimously named the game's MVP. "John was basically an unstoppable force through the whole game," Redskins quarterback Joe Theismann said.

Dolphins defensive end Doug Betters agreed: "We just couldn't stop him. He seemed to get stronger as the game progressed and was relentlessly running on us. We were kind of grinding down. He wasn't going to be denied."

Riggins's performance punctuated his near superhuman exploits in the four-game Super Bowl Tournament. The workhorse ran 136 times for 610 yards and four touchdowns, becoming the first player to rush for 100 or more yards in four

straight playoff games: 119 against Detroit, 185 against Minnesota, 140 against Dallas, and 166 against Miami. "I was just a foot soldier waiting for my next command," Riggins once said of his yeoman display.

Truth be told, Riggins was not the only Redskin standout on that incandescent day. Theismann completed 15 of 23 passes for 143 yards with two touchdowns and two interceptions, wrapping up a superb postseason of his own when he posted a phenomenal 110.8 quarterback rating and a 68.2 completion percentage.

And the Redskins' defense was sensational. The swarming unit suffocated the Dolphins by holding them to 176 yards and nine first downs. Miami rushed for 96 yards, the fifth straight game and sixth in the last seven the Redskins had held a team to less than 100 on the ground. Quarterbacks David Woodley and Don Strock, who subbed for Woodley on the last series of the game, completed 4 of 17 passes and missed on all 12 of his throws in the second half, when the Dolphins posted 34 yards, two first downs, and no completions.

"It was just one of those games where you catch stride," Redskins linebacker Monte Coleman said in looking back. "We put lots of pressure on [Woodley] in the second half. We came out with a blitzing scheme and sent safeties, linebackers at him trying to keep him off balance as much as possible. We were sending guys from all over the place."

Miami's defense, in contrast, yielded 400 yards, 276 on the ground, after showing its stinginess earlier in the playoffs. In a 14–0 AFC championship game win over the Jets, for example, the Dolphins intercepted five passes and allowed 139 yards, including only 46 by NFL rushing champ Freeman McNeal. For the Super Bowl, the Dolphins believed that by controlling the bulwark of the Redskins' offense, Riggins, they would have an excellent shot at winning. But the Redskins had no plans to deemphasize Riggo. "We'd be dumb to do anything else but to get on that wagon and let Riggins hitch up and pull us along," Redskins offensive line coach Joe Bugel said leading up to the game.

"With a guy like Riggins, a Hall of Fame running back, you knew you had to stop him," Miami defensive end Kim Bokamper said in retrospect. "He wasn't our sole focus, but we knew first and foremost Riggins was going to be the key."

The Dolphins, one of only four teams to beat Washington in the last 22 games, scored on their fifth play from scrimmage. Wide receiver Jimmy Cefalo outran cornerback Tony Peters down the right sideline, and Woodley hit him with a 76-yard touchdown pass.

Miami's defense stopped Washington on two subsequent drives. But late in the first quarter, Redskin defensive end Dexter Manley sacked Woodley and forced a fumble, and defensive tackle Dave Butz recovered on the Dolphins' 46. The turnover set up Mark Moseley's 31-yard field goal.

Miami answered with Fulton Walker's 42-yard kickoff return and a 14-play, 50-yard march that chewed up nearly nine minutes until it stalled on the Redskins' 3. Uwe von Schamann's 20-yard field goal put Miami up, 10–3, six minutes before halftime. Woodley's three completions on the drive were, amazingly, his last ones of the game.

The Redskins responded with an 11-play, 80-yard march that ended with the tying score, Theismann's 4-yard touchdown pass to Alvin Garrett in the corner of the end zone, a play similar to the fade patterns Garrett had run earlier in the playoffs that resulted in touchdowns. It was the fifth touchdown catch for the once obscure receiver in the Super

Bowl Tournament. Moseley's conversion tied the game at 10.

Walker victimized the Redskins again by running the kickoff back 98 yards for a score, the first time a Super Bowl kickoff had been returned for a touchdown, to put Miami up at halftime, 17–10. Only three teams had rebounded from halftime deficits in the Super Bowl to win, but the Redskins were not in panic mode.

"[Defensive coordinator] Richie Petitbon was a master at making halftime adjustments," Coleman said. "We made the necessary adjustments and carried them out."

On offense, the Redskins planned to continue with the heart of their game plan: running Riggins in a smash-mouth system behind the Hogs and overpowering Miami's smaller but faster defensive front known as the "Killer B's." The Redskins, who dominated time of possession by more than 12 minutes, ran mostly to the side where 6–7, 300-pound left tackle Joe Jacoby outweighed Bokamper, a right defensive end, by about 50 pounds.

"They relied on quickness and flying to the football, and we were methodical and more of a slug-it-out team," Jacoby said. "We didn't want to get into a sprinting contest with them. We wanted to just keep the ball on the ground and march up and down the field. We pretty much stayed with our whole game plan and used our size to just slowly, methodically wear them down."

Case in point: On the opening drive of the second half, the Redskins chewed up nearly seven minutes and moved 63 yards in 18 plays before settling for Moseley's 20-yard field goal. Both offenses failed to threaten for the rest of the third quarter, although the Dolphins came inches from taking perhaps an insurmountable 24–13 lead.

From his own 18, Theismann threw a pass that was tipped by Bokamper, who looked up at the fluttering ball and appeared ready to catch it unimpeded from the goal line. The ball hit Bokamper's hands, but quarterback-turned-defensive-back Theismann reached in to knock it down. The Redskins breathed a huge sigh of relief, while Bokamper agonized over coming so close. "It was a pretty heads-up play by Theismann," Bokamper said. "A lot of quarterbacks would stand there and just watch the ball come down. He had the wherewithal to go make a play. It ended up making the difference."

Said Theismann, "Suddenly, the ball goes up in the air, and time almost stopped for me. It's like my whole world went into slow motion. My legs felt like they were in quicksand. I kept moving toward where I thought the ball was going to be and just figured if I could dive and maybe get my hands in between Kim's, I could strip the ball away. In almost a desperate effort, I just sort of lurched and leaned forward and managed to knock it down." Otherwise, "He would have had a touchdown, and we would have lost the football game."

Theismann was intercepted on the drive. Then Miami went three-and-out for the third time in the half, and Washington took possession on its 48 early in the fourth quarter.

By then, Riggins had pounded the Dolphins' defense with runs of 4 to 6 yards, having totaled 93 on 27 carries. But the Diesel was only warming up. He ran twice for 8 yards, and H-back Clarence Harmon gained 1. It was judgment time, for Washington faced fourth-and-inches on the Miami 43 with a little more than 10 minutes left and the Dolphins leading, 17–13. Although failure may have meant ultimate defeat for the Redskins, plus a chance at avenging the franchise's loss to Miami in Super Bowl VII, Gibbs opted to go for it.

The Dolphins' defense stacked the line, expecting the same scenario as the 103,667 fans at the Rose Bowl and the 100 million television viewers around the world: a run by big No. 44. "We basically knew the Redskins so well that you could call when John Riggins was going to get the ball," said Sam Huff, one of the Redskins radio color analysts at the game. "So did the Miami Dolphins. Stopping him was another thing."

Theismann called the play in the huddle: "Goal line, goal line. I-left, tight wing, 70 chip on white." Tight end Clint Didier went in motion and circled back. Dolphins cornerback Don McNeal, who was following Didier, slipped momentarily. At that moment, Theismann handed off to Riggins, who headed for a huge hole on the left side created by H-back Otis Wonsley, Jacoby, and another Hog, left guard Russ Grimm.

Redskin blockers accounted for every defender except McNeal, who stepped up and aimed to stop Riggins short of the first down. "I said, 'Man, I'm going to make this tackle. This is going to be great,'" McNeal remembered. The 5–11, 185-pounder, slightly off-balance, hit Riggins on the side around the numbers and slid down, holding onto his jersey

John Riggins breaks away from the Dolphins' Don McNeal on his famous 43-yard scoring run that provided the Redskins' winning points in Super Bowl XVII. Riggins put the Redskins on his shoulders that season in the playoffs. The workhorse ran 136 times for 610 yards and four touchdowns, including 166 in his MVP performance in the Super Bowl. "I was just a foot soldier waiting for my next command," he said.

Charlie Brown (87) scores on a 7-yard pass from Joe Theismann that sealed the Redskins' win over Miami. Alvin Garrett (89) scored earlier on a Theismann pass.

around the waistline. Riggo unceremoniously shook McNeal off and steamrolled through with only daylight ahead. With his face exuding determination, he raced untouched down the left sideline into the Southern California sunset and crossed the goal line for the longest touchdown run in Super Bowl history at the time. "That shot is one of our classics," NFL Films Executive Director Steve Sabol said. "Just his face so contorted with how intense he was, and the expression of his face pinched under his helmet." Riggins was mobbed in the end zone by his convoy, the Hogs, who at the same time hoisted themselves into the global football conscience.

To Sabol, the run featured elements of a classic moment: "It was a game-deciding play in the fourth quarter of a close game by a Hall of Fame player. There were no penalties and no controversies on the play. It was, in a way, symbolic of the Redskins, the Joe Gibbs offense and the Riggo drill. It was fourth-and-1, and Riggins just ran over Don McNeal. As much of a finesse coach as Gibbs was, he was also a guy who would look you in the eye and say, 'Here we come, our best against your best, see if you can stop us.' It was also the crowning moment for the Hogs."

Theismann said the touchdown was the nadir for the Dolphins: "I think when John basically ran over the defensive back, they probably had to say to themselves, 'How in God's name are we going to stop this guy?'"

Said Doug Betters, "I don't think we folded our tent and went home, but we were definitely demoralized by that. It was the whole concept of having a diesel truck just running over you and not being able to stop him."

Miami went nowhere in four plays. And with who else but Riggins carrying on 8 of 12 plays, the Redskins drove 41 yards for another touchdown, Theismann's 7-yard pass to Charlie Brown with 1:55 left. Soon after, ecstatic Redskins hoisted

Gibbs onto their shoulders and carried the NFL's newest coaching phenom off the field.

"It's hard to put in words what it's like to win a Super Bowl, but it was like a dream come true," said Coleman, part of a Redskins roster that earned $70,000 per player for winning the Super Bowl Tournament.

In the euphoric Redskins locker room, President Reagan called to offer congratulations to Gibbs. The president also asked if he could change the spelling of his last name by putting an "i" and another "g" in it so it would sound like Riggins. The game's MVP, meanwhile, chimed in with one of his outrageous remarks: "At least for tonight, Ron's the president, and I'm the king."

Everyone associated with the Redskins had a right to feel like royalty. At least 500,000 fans flooded the streets of Washington and braved a torrential downpour to pay tribute to their new champions, as the Redskins rode through town with the shiny Vince Lombardi trophy. "Each one of you has a small piece of this trophy today," Gibbs said.

There would be more Super Bowl trophies to come.

| | | | | | | |
|---|---|---|---|---|---|---|
| Miami— | 7 | 10 | 0 | 0 | — | 17 |
| Washington— | 0 | 10 | 3 | 14 | — | 27 |

Miami — Cefalo 76 pass from Woodley (von Schamann kick)
Wash —— FG Moseley 31
Miami — FG von Schamann 20
Wash —— Garrett 4 pass from Theismann (Moseley kick)
Miami — Walker 98 kickoff return (von Schamann kick)
Wash —— FG Moseley 20
Wash —— Riggins 43 run (Moseley kick)
Wash —— Brown 6 pass from Theismann (Moseley kick)

NFL Commissioner Pete Rozelle presents the Vince Lombardi trophy to Redskins owner Jack Kent Cooke in his team's jubilant locker room. NBC's Mike Adamle holds the microphone, as coach Joe Gibbs (far right) looks on.

| Team Statistics | Miami | Wash |
|---|---|---|
| First Downs | 9 | 24 |
| Total Yards | 176 | 400 |
| Rushing Yards | 96 | 276 |
| Passing Yards | 80 | 124 |
| Passes | 4–17–1 | 15–23–2 |
| Sacks Allowed | 1–17 | 3–19 |
| Return Yards | 244 | 109 |
| Punts–Average | 6–37.8 | 3–45.7 |
| Penalties | 4–55 | 5–36 |
| Fumbles–Lost | 2–1 | 0–0 |
| Time of Possession | 23:45 | 36:15 |

## RUSHING

Miami—Franklin 16–49; Nathan 7–26; Woodley 4–16; Vigorito 1–4; Harris 1–1
Washington—Riggins 38–166, 1 TD; Garrett 1–44; Harmon 9–40; Theismann 3–20; Walker 1–6

## PASSING

Miami—Woodley 4–14–97, 1 TD, 1 INT; Strock 0–3
Washington—Theismann 15–23–143, 2 TD, 2 INT

## RECEIVING

Miami—Cefalo 2–82, 1 TD; Harris 2–15
Washington—Brown 6–60, 1 TD; Warren 5–28; Garrett 2–13, 1 TD; Walker 1–27; Riggins 1–15

## 1983: 14–2, 1ST PLACE—NFC EAST

### Head Coach: Joe Gibbs

What do you call a team that scores an NFL-record 541 points, posts a remarkable plus-43 turnover ratio, loses a total of two regular season games by one point each, and annihilates oppo-nent after opponent en route to reaching its second straight Super Bowl?

A juggernaut, perhaps.

The 1983 Redskins ran roughshod over their NFL brethren, literally and figuratively, and operated with a dominance rarely seen before in pro football history. Mercy was not in the Redskins' lexicon, for in addition to rewriting the league's record books, they set new all-time team marks such as total yards (6,139), points scored (541), and regular season wins (14).

The awesome demonstration propelled the Redskins to an NFC East title, followed by a 44-point annihilation of the Rams in the playoff opener and a win over the 49ers in the NFC championship game. Next was Super Bowl XVIII, but that's where the Redskins met their match. The Los Angeles Raiders treated the burgundy and gold like paperweights in a 38–9 wipeout. The defeat, compounded by the largest losing margin at the time in Super Bowl history, 29 points, tainted a historic Redskins season.

"We were the best team in the history of football," said Redskins quarterback Joe Theismann, the league MVP that season. "That will never be known because we didn't win a Super Bowl."

Guard Russ Grimm rated the 1983 team above the Redskins' 1991 squad that finished 14–2 and advanced to win Super Bowl XXVI, but he shared Theismann's frustrating sentiment. "The best team I played on was the 1983 team. We lost two games that year by one point. We averaged nearly 35 points a game. But we didn't win the big one."

The Redskins had several league leaders that year. Joe Gibbs was named NFL Coach of the Year for the second straight season. Theismann enjoyed the best season of his 12-year NFL career, completing 60.1 percent of his passes with career highs of 3,714 yards and 29 touchdowns and a career-low 11 interceptions. His 97.0 quarterback rating was second in the NFL, behind Atlanta's Steve Bartkowski (97.6). His favorite target was receiver Charlie Brown, who caught a team-record 78 passes.

John Riggins, running behind the Hogs, rushed for a career-high 1,347 yards. His 24 rushing touchdowns set an NFL record for most touchdowns in a season. Kicker Mark Moseley's 161 points broke the league's single-season record for most points without touchdowns.

Theismann, Brown, and three of the Hogs—Grimm, tackle Joe Jacoby, and center Jeff Bostic—made the Pro Bowl. Jacoby, Grimm, Theismann, and Riggins earned consensus All-Pro honors.

The defense, meanwhile, finished No. 1 in the league against the run, yielding 81 yards per game, with middle linebacker Neal Olkewicz leading the team in tackles and defensive tackle Dave Butz posting team highs in sacks (11.5) and fumble recoveries (five). An indomitable rushing defense forced teams to pass so often that the Redskins' secondary earned the moniker of the "Pearl Harbor Crew." (The defense allowed the most passing yards in the NFL.)

"Our run defense was great, and a lot of games we'd be ahead 21–0 early in the first quarter, so teams abandoned their game plans and just started throwing," said Redskin safety Mark Murphy, who intercepted a team-high nine passes and finished second in tackles. He and Butz made the Pro Bowl and were named consensus All-Pros.

"We were under attack all the time," Murphy said. "We gave up a lot of yardage, but we had an awful lot of turnovers. You just didn't want to give up the long bombs."

With 34 interceptions and 27 fumble recoveries, the defense often put the offense in position to ring up points, reserve receiver Virgil Seay said. "We took advantage of every opportunity the defense gave us. We didn't squander opportunities to score, whether by touchdown or field goal. And if we didn't score and had to punt the ball back, we won the field position game."

Before the season, the Redskins drafted two players who soon became standouts in the NFL. One was Darrell Green, a 5–8, 170-pound cornerback out of tiny Texas A&I who possessed world-class speed, and the other was Nevada–Reno defensive end Charles Mann. Green ended up playing 20 years for the franchise, the longest career in team history. The Redskins also chose North Carolina running back Kelvin Bryant, who played in the United States Football League before signing with Washington in 1986.

After a 2–2 exhibition season, the Redskins began tackling a schedule that featured three West Coast trips and three Monday night games, including one against the Cowboys in the season opener. That game was a rematch of the previous season's NFC championship game, a decisive Redskins win. It looked like it would be two in a row when they held a 23–3 lead at halftime, to the delight of a rambunctious crowd at RFK Stadium. Mark Moseley's three field goals, Riggins's short touchdown run, and Theismann's 41-yard pass to Brown accounted for the Redskins' scoring. But Dallas retaliated in the second half with three touchdown passes by quarterback Danny White, who also ran for a score, and escaped with a 31–30 win.

The loss was deflating, but Gibbs had a postgame warning for his troops: "We better forget Dallas in a hurry. Philadelphia's off to a fast start, and we've got them looking right down our throats."

The Redskins took heed and went back to business. They reeled off wins over the Eagles, Chiefs, and Seahawks behind solid performances from their offensive workhorse, Riggins,

and their defense, before hosting the undefeated Raiders at RFK, a game that became "one for the record books," according to Theismann.

The Redskins led, 17–7, at halftime, but Raiders quarterback Jim Plunkett fired three scoring passes in the second half, and a 97-yard punt return gave Los Angeles a 35–20 lead with 7:31 to play.

That's when the fun began. Theismann, who had a spectacular day (23 of 39, career-high 417 yards, three touchdowns, no interceptions), tossed a screen pass to elusive wingback Joe Washington, who skirted down the sideline after a vicious block by Bostic for a 67-yard gain to the Raiders' 21. Three plays later, Charlie Brown hauled in an 11-yard touchdown reception, one of his career-high 11 catches in the game.

The conversion cut the lead to eight with 6:15 left, and the Redskins regained possession when special teams standout Greg Williams recovered an onside kick at the Raiders' 32. After Moseley's 34-yard field goal made it 35–30, Los Angeles went nowhere in three plays, and the Redskins took over on their 31 with just under two minutes left. Theismann completed three passes to Brown for 63 yards. After an incompletion, Washington circled out of the backfield and dove in the end zone to catch a 6-yard pass for the winning points in the 37–35 classic.

The crowd of 54,016 erupted, having seen what was touted as a possible preview to the Super Bowl. "I wouldn't be surprised if we met them again in January," Redskins guard Mark May told *Sports Illustrated*. The teams totaled 890 yards of offense in a game the *New York Times* described as one of the most entertaining in NFL history. And the Redskins proved they could win without Riggins, who missed a chunk of the action with the flu.

"That game probably solidified the fact that we could win football games in different ways like coming from behind," Joe Washington said in hindsight. "We weren't a team that needed to just grind the ball out on the ground. We had a lot of weapons that we would move around and do a lot of different things."

The Redskins, 4–1 at the time, won eight of their next nine games—the only loss coming in a 48–47 decision to the Packers—heading into hostile territory, Dallas. The 12–2 teams were tied for first place in the NFC East and owned the best records in the league, ingredients for a heavyweight duel. The Redskins tried to outpsych their foes early on.

A few days before the game, Redskin players purchased military fatigues at a D.C. store. They wore them on the plane flight to Dallas and on the bus to the hotel, aiming to prove that they were on a mission in the "Invasion of Dallas." The media caught wind of their outlandish attire. "The press was going nuts, they wanted one of us to talk about this," offensive tackle George Starke remembered. "Our spokesman was Neal Olkewicz. Olky told reporters, 'We're just going to war, we want the Cowboys to understand this.' It freaked the Cowboys out and got into their heads."

The Redskins raced to a 14–0 first quarter lead on Riggins's short scoring run and Theismann's 40-yard pass to tight end Clint Didier. But the Cowboys scored on their last two possessions of the half to create a 14–10 game, leaving one to wonder if Dallas would pull off a comeback similar to the season opener. This time the Redskins stayed in control, as Theismann threw a 43-yard pass to Monk, Riggins ran for another short touchdown, and the defense intercepted quarterback Danny

## Redskins, Packers Engage in High-Scoring "Ping-Pong" Match

More than 55,000 fans came to Lambeau Field in Green Bay on October 17, 1983, to see a Monday night football game. They saw a dazzling show of offensive fireworks in one of the wildest games ever played.

The Redskins and Packers amassed staggering totals of 95 points, 1,025 yards, 56 first downs, and 138 offensive plays. The frenetic pace included 21 plays of 20 yards or more, 15 of those coming on pass receptions. There were 17 scoring plays, five lead changes, and three ties. The contest resembled a "ping-pong match," said Redskins kicker Mark Moseley, who just missed a 39-yard field goal on the game's last play, allowing the Packers to eke out a 48–47 victory.

"It was remarkable," said Moseley, who had hit four field goals earlier. "I don't think I ever took my kicking shoe off in that game because I couldn't tell from one second to the next whether I might be back out there kicking another field goal or extra point."

Both pass defenses took the night off, for the teams piled up 771 yards through the air. Packers quarterback Lynn Dickey shredded the Redskins' secondary with 22 of 30 passing for 387 yards and three touchdowns, distributing the ball among seven receivers. Redskins quarterback Joe Theismann was 27 of 39 for 390 yards and two touchdowns, hitting six receivers in all. His top target was wingback Joe Washington, who caught nine passes and two touchdowns.

"It wasn't a good game to be in the secondary," Redskins safety Mark Murphy said. "They were a pretty explosive offense."

Said Redskins linebacker Monte Coleman, "Whatever we tried on defense, it didn't stop them. They also couldn't stop us. It was touchdown after touchdown. I can't say the best team won. We were saying all we have to do is just hold, and they would drive down the field."

The 95-point total stands as the second highest in a game in Redskins history, behind the NFL-record 113 in Washington's 72–41 win over the Giants in 1966.

---

Dallas came unglued mentally in the second half. Cowboys coach Tom Landry could be seen on the sidelines yelling "No, no, no, Danny" before a fourth-down audible by his quarterback that failed. Dorsett threw the ball at the head of Redskins defensive tackle Darryl Grant. Two frustrated Cowboys tried to break up a celebration by the Fun Bunch, as the group slapped high fives in the end zone after a touchdown, and the Cowboys lined up only 10 players for a Redskins extra point try.

"Anytime you can get into a player's head and get them out of their game plan, that's a big plus for you," Redskins linebacker Monte Coleman said. "That's what happened in that game. The things we were doing were working, the things they were doing were not."

The Redskins proceeded to capture the NFC East with a 31–22 comeback win over the Giants in the season finale. The victory gave the Redskins 14 wins, something no other NFC team had ever done, and secured home-field advantage through the playoffs. As the game wound down, Redskin fans hoping to meet the Cowboys in the conference championship game resorted to their customary chant of "WE WANT DALLAS! WE WANT DALLAS!"

This time, they wouldn't get their wish.

## NFC DIVISIONAL PLAYOFF GAME
**Washington 51, Los Angeles Rams 7**
**January 1, 1984**
**RFK Stadium, Washington, D.C.**
**Attendance: 55,363**

### Redskins Devour Rams in New Year's Day Massacre

It was a display of force never before seen in Redskins' postseason history, and one that may never happen again.

On January 1, 1984, the Redskins welcomed the Los Angeles Rams into the New Year by pummeling them as a heavyweight would a flyweight. The 51–7 final score was only one indication of Washington's dominance that day and of the bloodbath endured by the Rams.

"I've had enough of the Redskins," Rams coach John Robinson groused afterward, factoring in the 42–20 spanking Washington dealt to his squad late in the season.

The rematch was over before Rams coaches could adjust their headsets. Executing with surgical precision, the Redskins scored on their first five possessions to take a 38–0 second-quarter lead, an NFL playoff record at the time for first-half scoring by one team. Although the Rams scored a touchdown before the end of the half, the game was a formality from then on. The Redskins scored 13 unanswered points in the second half to pad their rout.

Washington was an offensive machine that day, amassing 455 yards behind the stellar play of

- Quarterback Joe Theismann—18 of 23, 302 yards, two touchdowns
- Running back John Riggins—119 yards and three short scores
- Receiver Art Monk—two touchdown catches
- Receiver Charlie Brown—six receptions, 171 yards

---

White for the third time and held future Hall of Fame halfback Tony Dorsett to 34 yards rushing. The resounding 31–10 win marked the Redskins' first season sweep ever against their long-time nemesis.

"They just beat the stink out of us," Cowboys cornerback Ron Fellows told reporters.

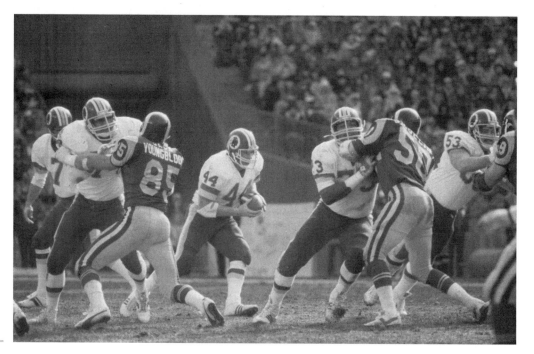

John Riggins looks for running room behind Hogs (left to right) George Starke, Mark May, and Jeff Bostic in the Redskins' 51–7 rout of the Rams. Riggo ran for 119 yards and three TDs that day.

"We beat the Rams in the next-to-last game of the season, 42–20, and I remember John Robinson saying he didn't think we were a very good football team," Theismann said. "Then we beat them 51–7, and he came back and said, 'I'm still not convinced they're a very good football team.' I'm like, 'Okay, what do you need to see now?'"

Robinson saw a flawless defense. The Rams gained 204 yards and just 51 on the ground. Rookie running back Eric Dickerson, who led the NFL with 1,808 yards rushing, was held to 16.

Rams quarterback Vince Ferragamo threw three interceptions, the last of which rookie cornerback Darrell Green returned 72 yards for a touchdown to account for the final score. Green caught the ball after it was tipped by Dickerson, and the man with sprinter speed needed only to reach midfield before raising his fist to signify touchdown.

"I want to credit everything to the coaching staff," Redskins defensive end Dexter Manley said in looking back. "For one reason or another, they put us in the right position. We studied film, and we were very prepared."

The Redskins had had two weeks since the end of the regular season to prepare for the game, while the Rams were playing their third road game in three weeks. Los Angeles won the first two of those contests, including a 24–17 upset of Dallas in a wild card playoff game. But their visit to D.C. was another story.

"It was just one of those days," Redskins coach Joe Gibbs said afterward.

| LA Rams— | 0 | 7 | 0 | 0 | — | 7 |
|---|---|---|---|---|---|---|
| Washington— | 17 | 21 | 6 | 7 | — | 51 |

Wash — Riggins 3 run (Moseley kick)
Wash — Monk 40 pass from Theismann (Moseley kick)
Wash — FG Moseley 42
Wash — Riggins 1 run (Moseley kick)
LA —— Dennard 32 pass from Ferragamo (Lansford kick)
Wash — Monk 21 pass from Theismann (Moseley kick)
Wash — Riggins 1 run (Moseley kick)
Wash — FG Moseley 36

Wash — FG Moseley 41
Wash — Green 72 interception return (Moseley kick)

## NFC CHAMPIONSHIP GAME
**Washington 24, San Francisco 21**
**January 8, 1984**
**RFK Stadium, Washington, D.C.**
**Attendance: 55,363**

### Moseley, Friendly Officials Help Redskins Slip Past 49ers

This was a day the Redskins needed somebody to rescue them, or else there may have been no return to the Super Bowl. Thank heaven for those anonymous guys wearing black and white.

Reeling from three quick fourth-quarter touchdowns by the 49ers that tied the NFC championship game at 21 and left the Redskins on life support, Washington drove 78 yards to set up a 25-yard field goal that accounted for a 24–21 win and a trip to Super Bowl XVIII.

Who knows what would have happened on that drive, though, without two questionable pass interference calls.

After the Redskins reached the San Francisco 45, quarterback Joe Theismann overthrew receiver Art Monk by a few feet. But cornerback Eric Wright was called for interference, a 27-yard penalty that put the ball on the 18. The 49ers argued that the pass was not catchable and, thus, the flag shouldn't have been thrown. Two plays later, Theismann missed receiver Alvin Garrett in the end zone, but safety Ronnie Lott was whistled for holding receiver Charlie Brown at the 8, where the ball was placed. Lott argued that Brown was nowhere near the play.

Afterward, 49ers coach Bill Walsh told reporters he was "bitter" about both calls and argued that his squad was robbed.

"Today, the penalty against Wright wouldn't have been called because [the officials] interpret the rules differently," Walsh said. "Looking at the tape, there really wasn't any foul at all" on the play by Lott.

Lott's penalty set up Mark Moseley's 25-yard field goal try with 40 seconds left. But given that he'd already missed from 45, 41, 38, and 34 yards, the ordinary chip shot seemed far from automatic. On top of that, Moseley would be kicking from a slippery turf at RFK Stadium that had tormented him and 49ers kicker Ray Wersching, who missed both of his field goal attempts.

"All day long, neither he nor I could do anything," Moseley recalled. "We couldn't even stand up. Receivers were falling down all day."

So Moseley tried something different. "I didn't even take any steps to the ball," he said. "I just had Joe [Theismann] mark where he was going to put it. I put my plant foot down and just stood there waiting for the snap. I just wanted to make sure I could keep my feet under me. When the ball came, I swung my leg out and kicked it through."

San Francisco was out of time-outs. With the RFK Stadium crowd chanting "DEFENSE! DEFENSE!" 49ers quarterback Joe Montana threw four straight incompletions, ending the game and allowing the Redskins to breathe a sigh of relief.

It was expected to be much easier. The Redskins, fresh off a 44-point trashing of the Rams for their 10th straight win, were heavy favorites over the 49ers, winners of four straight. Experts surmised that Washington's power running game, led by Riggins and the Hogs, would overpower the 49ers' much lighter defensive front, which relied on speed and finesse.

Riggins pounded out 136 yards, his sixth straight 100-plus postseason rushing output, on 36 carries. His two short scoring runs, and Theismann's 70-yard touchdown pass to Brown late in the third quarter, created a 21–0 game. But Montana, who was neutralized through the first three quarters, showed signs of why he would one day enter the Pro Football Hall of Fame. As part of his 347-yard passing day, he tossed scoring passes on three straight possessions: 5 yards to Mike Wilson, 76 yards to Freddie Solomon, and a 12-yarder to Wilson to knot the game at 21 with seven minutes left.

The Redskins and their normally raucous fans were stunned. "We caught the Redskins' defense with some really big pass plays, and the whole stadium went quiet," Walsh recalled. "We really had the momentum."

But the sellout crowd exploded on Moseley's game-winning kick. The victory wasn't aesthetically pleasing, but with it the Redskins became the first team since the 1978 and '79 Steelers to make a repeat trip to the Super Bowl.

| | | | | | | |
|---|---|---|---|---|---|---|
| San Francisco— | 0 | 0 | 0 | 21 | — | 21 |
| Washington— | 0 | 7 | 14 | 3 | — | 24 |

Wash — Riggins 4 run (Moseley kick)
Wash — Riggins 1 run (Moseley kick)
Wash — Brown 70 pass from Theismann (Moseley kick)
SF —— Wilson 5 pass from Montana (Wersching kick)
SF —— Solomon 76 pass from Montana (Wersching kick)
SF —— Wilson 12 pass from Montana (Wersching kick)
Wash — FG Moseley 25

## SUPER BOWL XVIII
**Los Angeles Raiders 38, Washington 9**
**January 22, 1984**
**Tampa Stadium**
**Attendance: 72,920**

### Black Sunday: Peaking Raiders Embarrass Listless Redskins

"We laid an egg."

That's how Redskins linebacker Neal Olkewicz summed up his team's ghastly performance in Super Bowl XVIII, when the Los Angeles Raiders played a near-flawless game and toyed with Washington in a 38–9 shellacking.

Simply put, the Redskins stunk that day, for each facet of the team—offense, defense, and special teams—was dysfunctional. The Redskins gained only 90 yards rushing, their bread and butter all season; threw an interception that was returned for a score; relinquished nearly 400 yards of offense, including 191 on the ground to the game's MVP, Marcus Allen; and gave up a blocked extra point and a blocked punt, the latter of which resulted in a Raiders touchdown.

The Raiders exploited such ineptitude to chalk up their second Super Bowl win in the past four seasons.

"They had their 'A' game on," Redskins tight end Rick Walker said. "In the Super Bowl, you can't dig yourself in a hole against an excellent team that makes plays, plays great defense, and can run the ball."

Said Olkewicz, "We just seemed to be running out of gas for some reason. That year, I thought we had one of our most dominant teams, but we just barely got by the 49ers in the playoffs. The Raiders had a lot of talent, and they just kind of hit their stride in the playoffs and basically had a great day in the Super Bowl."

The AFC West champion Raiders routed their two previous playoff opponents, Pittsburgh and Seattle. Allen ran for 121 yards against the Steelers and 154 against the Seahawks, against whom the Raiders held AFC Rookie of the Year Curt Warner to 26 yards rushing.

Los Angeles appeared primed for the NFL's big show, a game billed as a beauty for a Super Bowl. It pitted the 16–2 Redskins, winners of 11 straight and 31 of their last 34, against the 14–4 Raiders. The two teams had already slugged it out in arguably the most exciting NFL game of the 1983 season, Washington's 37–35 comeback win on October 2.

They matched up well on paper, two big, physical squads with excellent defenses against the rush and a strong reliance on running the ball, the Redskins with 1,347-yard-man John Riggins and the Raiders with 1,014-yard Marcus Allen. Los Angeles had also added a new wrinkle since the regular-season encounter that would handcuff the Redskins' passing game and ultimately their entire offense. The Raiders acquired Patriots All-Pro cornerback Mike Haynes (a current Hall of Famer), who, along with the other cornerback, All-Pro Lester Hayes, allowed Los Angeles to play tight man-to-man coverage on dangerous receivers Art Monk and Charlie Brown.

Meanwhile, two teams that engaged in repeated post-whistle skirmishes in the regular-season game fought a war of words during Super Bowl week. Loquacious defensive end Dexter

The Redskins got off on the wrong foot in Super Bowl XVIII when the Raiders' Derrick Jensen blocked this Jeff Hayes punt in the first quarter and recovered it in the end zone.

Manley guaranteed his Redskins would give the "Raiders to the gators" in the Florida swamps, and that he'd break the neck of the player across from him, left tackle Bruce Davis. Mercurial defensive end Lyle Alzado, who epitomized the Raiders of the nasty silver-and-black tradition, promised to tear off the heads of several Redskins, including 6–7, 310-pound All-Pro offensive tackle Joe Jacoby.

Redskins heads were hanging early on. After Mark Moseley missed a 44-yard field goal, the Raiders' Derrick Jensen blocked a punt and recovered the ball in the end zone. Matt Bahr converted for a 7–0 first quarter lead. The Raiders went up, 14–0, in the second period on quarterback Jim Plunkett's 12-yard pass to receiver Cliff Branch, a play set up by a 50-yard connection between the two. Moseley converted a 24-yard field goal, but Los Angeles applied a devastating blow right before halftime.

The Redskins had a first down on their 12 with 12 seconds left, and quarterback Joe Theismann went to the sidelines to confer with coach Joe Gibbs about the next play. Gibbs, said Theismann, wanted to call the same "rocket screen" pass to Joe Washington that had gained 67 yards in the regular-season game against the Raiders.

"I didn't want to call that play, I tried to talk him out of it," Theismann said. "We were a long way from the Raiders' end zone, and I said to him I don't like putting the ball in the air. He said, 'It worked the last time against them.' I said, 'You don't think they know that?' I walked onto the field but turned around and started to walk back to make an argument. He looked at me and said in a very stern way, 'Run it!'"

From the end zone, Theismann aimed a screen pass at Washington in the flat. But reserve linebacker Jack Squirek,

playing Washington man-to-man while the rest of the pass defense was in a zone, stepped in front of him, picked off the throw, and ran 5 yards for a score. Gibbs later told the media that he thought 23 seconds remained in the half at the time, not 12. Either way, the Raiders took a 21–3 lead into the locker room.

"When we went in at halftime, we were pretty well licked," Olkewicz said. "They had pretty much dominated from the beginning. It was their day, not ours."

In the first half, the Raiders' defense rendered Washington's offense useless. With the luxury of knowing that Hayes and Haynes were blanketing Brown and Monk, the Raiders, from a 3–4 alignment, constantly moved their linebackers onto the line of scrimmage to give the appearance of a goal-line defense, manhandling the Hogs in the process. Nose tackle Reggie Kinlaw, considered by Theismann today as the game's MVP, not Allen, did a superb job clogging up the middle. Afterward, Raiders defensive end Howie Long touted the seven players in the 3–4 defense as the "Slaughterhouse Seven."

The result: the Redskins were choked off on the ground and through the air. Riggins ran for 64 yards on 20 carries; Theismann completed 16 of 35 passes for 243 yards, with no touchdowns and two interceptions, and endured six sacks; and Monk and Brown caught four passes in all, none in the first half.

"When they pulled their guards and tackles, we really stuffed the gaps," Raiders coach Tom Flores recalled. "We dared them to throw the ball. We took away their slants and made them throw fades, and we were right on them."

The Redskins showed some life when they took the second-half kickoff and drove 70 yards in nine plays for a touchdown.

The Raiders' swarming defense had Joe Theismann constantly on the run. The Redskins' quarterback never found a rhythm, completing 16 of 35 passes for 243 yards with two interceptions.

Theismann completed three passes for 50 yards, and Riggins rushed for the other 20, pounding it over from the 1. In a sign of the Redskins' frustrating day, however, 6–7 Don Hasselbeck (the father of former Redskins quarterback Tim Hasselbeck) blocked the extra point. The score remained 21–9.

The misery continued when the Raiders orchestrated their own 70-yard march that Allen capped with a 5-yard run. He later closed the curtain on the Redskins' season. The slashing back ran left, escaped the reach of safety Ken Coffey, then reversed field and darted through a huge gap en route to a 74-yard touchdown run, the longest of its kind in Super Bowl history. By game's end, Allen had broken John Riggins's Super Bowl-record 166 yards rushing from the year before.

Although a full quarter remained, the game was essentially over. "When the game got out of hand, there was no chance of them coming back because we shut down their running game," Raiders Hall of Fame linebacker Ted Hendricks said. "They got so far behind that they had to pass, and our corners smothered their receivers. They couldn't do anything."

Bahr's fourth-quarter field goal put the Raiders up, 38–9, and set a Super Bowl record at the time for most points by one team.

"It was one of the toughest losses I've ever faced," Gibbs said. "For all of us, it was an earth-shattering experience. I never realized you can feel that bad about coming in second. It was awful. We just met a really good football team on a bad day."

The Redskins' postgame locker room was like a morgue, with coaches and players distraught. Riggins sat on a table with his head down searching for answers to questions from the same reporters who during Super Bowl week had pumped up the Redskins as an invincible squad.

"Before the game, the media were talking about the Redskins as the greatest thing since sliced bread, a dynasty, scored more points than anybody in the history of the game, more takeaways, and this and that," Redskins defensive tackle Darryl Grant said in looking back. "You're listening to everybody tell you how great you are, and everything's rolled out for us on a red carpet. The Raiders had to eat all that and got tired of hearing it. They weren't happy campers. That's not to say they weren't a good team."

The Raiders were more than good on that dark day in Redskins history. They proved resoundingly to be the best.

| | | | | | | |
|---|---|---|---|---|---|---|
| Washington— | 0 | 3 | 6 | 0 | — | 9 |
| LA Raiders— | 7 | 14 | 14 | 3 | — | 38 |

LA —— Jensen recovered blocked punt in end zone (Bahr kick)
LA —— Branch 12 pass from Plunkett (Bahr kick)
Wash — FG Moseley 24
LA —— Squirek 5 interception return (Bahr kick)
Wash — Riggins 1 run (kick blocked)
LA —— Allen 5 run (Bahr kick)
LA —— Allen 74 run (Bahr kick)
LA —— FG Bahr 21

| Team Statistics | Wash | LA |
|---|---|---|
| First Downs | 19 | 18 |
| Total Yards | 283 | 385 |
| Rushing Yards | 90 | 231 |
| Passing Yards | 193 | 154 |
| Passes | 16–35–2 | 16–25–0 |
| Sacks Allowed | 6–50 | 2–18 |
| Return Yards | 167 | 30 |
| Punts–Average | 8–32.4 | 7–42.7 |
| Penalties | 4–62 | 7–56 |
| Fumbles–Lost | 1–1 | 3–2 |
| Time of Possession | 30:38 | 29:22 |

## RUSHING

Washington—Riggins 26–64, 1 TD; Theismann 3–18; J. Washington 3–8
LA—Allen 20–191, 2 TDs; Pruitt 5–17; King 3–12; Hawkins 3–6; Willis 1–7; Plunkett 1–2

Raiders defensive end Lyle Alzado engaged in a pregame war of words, promising to tear off the heads of some Redskins. He had the last laugh.

## PASSING

Washington—Theismann 16–35–243, 2 INT
L. A.—Plunkett 16–25–172, 1 TD

## RECEIVING

Washington—Didier 5–65; Brown 3–93; J. Washington 3–20; Giaquinto 2–21; Monk 1–26; Garrett 1–17; Riggins 1–1
L. A.—Branch 6–94 1 TD; Christensen 4–32; Hawkins 2–20; Allen 2–18; King 2–8

## 1984: 11–5, 1ST PLACE—NFC EAST

### Head Coach: Joe Gibbs

The Redskins had to dig deep—literally and figuratively—to overcome what was a "year of agony," in the words of the *Washington Post*.

Placing 30 players on injured reserve, including four Pro Bowlers and myriad starters, and fielding a different starting lineup week after week created serious hardships for the 1984 Redskins. Managing the roster was a juggling act for general manager Bobby Beathard and coach Joe Gibbs. Moreover, the Redskins opened 0–2; another two straight losses left them 5–4 and one game out of first place in the NFC East, but only one game above last place, as well.

Yet the resilient bunch posted a 6–1 finish that ended with back-to-back two-point victories over Dallas and St. Louis, the latter of which wrapped up the division title. Those hard-fought wins typified how the 1984 Redskins had to claw and scrape every step of the way.

"We did have lots of injuries, but we still found ways to win," Redskins quarterback Joe Theismann said.

The Redskins needed great performances to persevere. Wide receiver Art Monk had a fabulous season with an NFL-record 106 catches for 1,372 yards and seven touchdowns. He made his first Pro Bowl and was a unanimous All-Pro selection. The defense set a team record with 66 sacks, smashing the prior mark by 13.

In the end, the Redskins came within five points of reaching the NFC championship game, falling to the Bears in the first round of the playoffs. The defeat spoiled Washington's bid to become the first team since the 1971–73 Miami Dolphins to appear in three straight Super Bowls.

The injury list began growing during Washington's 2–2 preseason, a troubling sign heading into the Redskins' opening game against Miami at RFK Stadium. It was a rematch of Super Bowl XVII, but this time the Dolphins came armed with a future Hall of Fame quarterback named Dan Marino.

The second-year wonder shredded the Redskins' secondary in Miami's 35–17 win, going 21 of 28 for 311 yards and five touchdowns. His 26- and 74-yard scoring passes to receiver Mark Duper gave Miami a 14–10 halftime lead, and he threw two scores to tight end Jim Jensen and one to receiver Mark Clayton in the third quarter. The inability of the Redskins' defense to contain Marino elicited boos from fans at RFK.

The next week, another future Hall of Fame quarterback picked apart the Redskins' defense. On a Monday night in San Francisco, Joe Montana completed 24 of 40 passes for 381 yards and two touchdowns in a 37–31 49ers victory. San Francisco built a 27–0 lead and then withstood a frenetic second-half comeback to avenge its loss to the Redskins in the NFC championship game the prior season.

"We really came out roaring after losing the playoff game," 49ers coach Bill Walsh remembered. "That game was really important to us. We went way ahead, and they nearly caught us at the end. Those are the kinds of great, epic games we had against the Redskins."

Two weeks, two losses, and a team that had been to back-to-back Super Bowls was suddenly eyeing major problems. Falling behind in both losses by such large margins had prevented Washington from relying on a ball-control game centered on John Riggins's pounding runs and Theismann's short passes. The defense had allowed nearly 700 yards of passing with no interceptions. Plus, more Redskins, such as Pro Bowl receiver Charlie Brown and defensive end Todd Liebenstein, had joined the injury parade.

Washington was staring at 0–3 when the Giants led, 14–13, after three quarters. But the Redskins rallied behind two players from their much-maligned secondary: Cornerback Vernon Dean returned an interception 36 yards for a score, and safety Curtis Jordan scooped up a fumble and ran 29 yards into the end zone in a 30–14 Redskins win.

It was the first of five straight victories by the rejuvenated Redskins, who won by an average of 20 points during that span. Riggins averaged 126 yards in the last four wins en route to a 1,200-yard season.

Meanwhile, trades and free-agent signings had become regular occurrences at Redskin Park, where players were being activated and cut with rapid-fire speed to stabilize a roster decimated by injuries in multiple positions. One player traded for was Raiders wide receiver Calvin Muhammad, who caught an 80-yard touchdown pass in a 34–14 victory over Dallas that capped the five-game winning streak.

The 5–2 Redskins sat in first place in the NFC East and were headed toward six straight wins with a 21–10 lead over the Cardinals in the third quarter. But St. Louis battled back on two scoring passes by quarterback Neil Lomax, who threw for 361 yards overall. Cardinals kicker Neil O'Donoghue missed an extra point and a field goal in the fourth quarter, but he made up for it with a game-winning 21-yard field goal in his squad's 26–24 victory.

Another loss, 37–13 to the Giants in the Meadowlands, put the 5–4 Redskins in a second-place tie with New York in the NFC East. Giants quarterback Phil Simms riddled the Redskins' secondary with 339 yards and two touchdown passes.

Luckily for Washington, an easier part of the schedule was approaching. And with a 27–14 win over the Falcons on a Monday night at RFK, the Redskins returned to first place, this time as part of a four-way tie with New York, Dallas, and St. Louis. Riggins bulled his way for 100 yards on 32 carries, plus two short touchdowns, but he aggravated his sore back and sat out the next game against the Lions. No sweat, for 5–8 rookie Keith Griffin rushed for 114 yards on 32 carries, and H-back Otis Wonsley ran for three short scores in a 28–14 Redskins win.

Riggins reappeared the next week against the Eagles and gained 92 yards on 26 carries. But he fumbled three times, and Theismann threw three interceptions in a 16–10 Eagles win. Washington rebounded with back-to-back wins, 41–14 over Buffalo and 31–17 over the Vikings on Thanksgiving Day. The latter triumph contributed to another convoluted picture in the NFC East with the Redskins, Giants, and Cowboys tied atop the division at 9–5 entering the final two weeks.

A 30–28 victory over the Cowboys in Texas Stadium, plus a Giants' loss to the Cardinals, gave the Redskins sole possession of first place. But things appeared bleak for them at halftime, when a 21–6 Cowboys lead prompted a tirade by Gibbs. "I was sitting in the back," linebacker Monte Coleman told the press. "I heard a racket up there. I guess it might have been coach Gibbs."

His message hit a nerve, for the Redskins erupted for 17 unanswered points in the third quarter. Cornerback Darrell Green returned an interception 32 yards for a touchdown and on the ensuing kickoff, special teams ace Otis Wonsley caused a fumble that teammate Anthony Washington recovered. Theismann hit Calvin Muhammad with a 22-yard scoring pass that cut the lead to one, and Moseley's field goal put the Redskins up, 23–21.

Dallas took a five-point lead in the fourth quarter, but a 55-yard drive by the Redskins ended on Riggins's 1-yard touchdown plunge with 6:34 to play. Washington's defense held Dallas twice, and the Redskins exited the field in jubilation.

It was a gritty triumph, as exemplified by the pounding taken by a Redskins offensive line that relinquished eight sacks. Guard Russ Grimm had to leave the game after being poked in the eye. Tackle Joe Jacoby persisted despite a sorely

bruised shoulder, and hobbling tackle George Starke, a 12-year vet, played like a trouper. "Those guys were dropping like flies, and I had to go out and play," Starke remembered. "That's how it was. We had to win. I was on the end of the bench, and I was going to take the day off. But I went out there on one leg."

For the 10–5 Redskins, the divisional race now stretched into the final week against the 9–6 Cardinals at RFK. The stakes were high: The winner would take the NFC East, get a bye in the first playoff week, and host a divisional playoff game. If the Redskins lost, they would host a wild card game. If the Cardinals lost, they would empty their lockers for the season.

Art Monk also had a lot riding on the game. He had 95 catches through the first 15 games and needed seven more to break the single-season record set by the Houston Oilers' Charlie Hennigan in 1964.

Monk's 23- and 12-yard scoring catches, Riggins's 5-yard run, and Moseley's field goal gave the Redskins a 23–7 halftime lead. But the Cardinals fought back in what evolved into a wild affair with 766 yards of passing. Neil Lomax, who again victimized the Redskins' secondary with 468 passing yards, tossed 75- and 18-yard touchdown passes to Roy Green, helping the Cardinals take a 27–26 lead.

The Redskins, who took over on their 27 with about six minutes left, constructed a drive for the ages. Theismann scrambled for a first down and then came on a third-and-19 on the Cardinals' 47. But he stayed cool and spotted his money receiver, Monk, who had already broken Hennigan's record and would catch 11 passes on the day, for a 20-yard reception amid a crowd of defenders. Soon after, Moseley booted a 37-yard field goal for a 29–27 Redskins lead.

St. Louis had one last chance. Lomax completed five passes to move the ball to the Redskins' 33. But with the Cardinals out of time-outs and the final seconds ticking off, Neil O'Donoghue rushed a 51-yard field goal try that missed.

The Redskins and their 55,000 supporters at RFK celebrated, while the Cardinals left the field dejected. "We came within a foot of pulling it off, but that's how the game of football goes," Cardinals Coach Jim Hanifan said years later.

## NFC DIVISIONAL PLAYOFF GAME
**Chicago 23, Washington 19**
**December 30, 1984**
**RFK Stadium, Washington, D.C.**
**Attendance: 55,431**

### Bears Defense, Trickery Too Much for Redskins

Unlike the last two weeks of the regular season, this game featured no Redskins fourth-quarter heroics. The NFL's No. 1 defense guaranteed that.

Washington began three drives in Bears territory in the final period but produced a scant number of yards and no points. The end result was a stunning 23–19 loss to Chicago, a burgeoning team one year away from winning a Super Bowl. The loss marked the only home playoff defeat in Redskins coach Joe Gibbs's first stint in Washington.

The Redskins finished ahead in total yards (336–310), first downs (22–13), and total plays (76–57). But the Bears' intimidating 46 defense, designed by defensive coordinator Buddy Ryan, suffocated Washington's offense when it counted. Chicago, which set an NFL record for single-season sacks (72), downed quarterback Joe Theismann seven times and held running back John Riggins to 50 yards on 21 carries. The Bears' defense also compensated for an offense operating without starting quarterback Jim McMahon.

"That game was the first sign that the Bears' team was pretty special," Redskins safety Mark Murphy said. "Their defense was unbelievable."

Said Theismann, "When Buddy Ryan first put the 46 defense in with the Bears, nobody could block it. Their front seven had athletes out the guzoo."

Walter Payton led the Bears on offense. The Hall of Fame running back ground out 104 yards on 24 carries and threw a 19-yard touchdown pass on an option play that gave Chicago a 10–3 lead just before halftime.

The Bears stretched their lead early in the third quarter. Quarterback Steve Fuller threw a short pass to receiver Willie Gault, and the one-time Olympic sprinter completed a 75-yard touchdown play. The conversion failed, and the Redskins followed with a 74-yard drive that ended on Riggins's 1-yard run for a 16–10 game.

But the Bears exploited a questionable roughing the punter call to go up, 23–10, on Fuller's 16-yard pass to wide receiver Dennis McKinnon. They lost a fumble on their next possession, and the Redskins drove 36 yards for another 1-yard scoring plunge by Riggins at the end of the quarter.

Riggins ran the ball only once more, as Gibbs resorted to an aerial attack to try to beat Chicago's constant blitzing. "I didn't have confidence in John at that point," the coach said in his postgame press conference. "I felt our passing game gave us our best shot."

Said Bears Coach Mike Ditka, "I always thank Joe. He says, 'What are you thanking me for?' I say, 'Because you quit running the ball. As soon as you quit running Riggins, we had a chance to beat you.' I'm sure he wishes he would have run Riggins another 30 times, and they probably would have beaten us."

The Redskins began drives on the Bears' 36, 40, and 45 in the fourth period. But the closest they came to scoring was Mark Moseley misfiring on a 41-yard field goal. Meanwhile, Theismann, operating behind a beleaguered offensive line that had lost guard Ken Huff to a broken ankle in the first half, was a marked man in the pocket, where he was sacked four times in the final quarter. The Redskins closed the game with 17 straight passes.

"We had chances to win that game," Theismann said in retrospect. "We were inside their 50-yard line repeatedly in the second half and got no points out of it."

| Chicago— | 0 | 10 | 13 | 0 | — | 23 |
| Washington— | 3 | 0 | 14 | 2 | — | 19 |

Wash — FG Moseley 25
Chi —— FG Thomas 34
Chi —— Dunsmore 19 pass from Payton (Thomas kick)
Chi —— Gault 75 pass from Fuller (kick failed)
Wash — Riggins 1 run (Moseley kick)
Chi —— McKinnon 16 pass from Fuller (Thomas kick)
Wash — Riggins 1 run (Moseley kick)
Chi —— Finzer takes safety

# 1985: 10–6, 1ST PLACE—NFC EAST (3-WAY TIE)

## Head Coach: Joe Gibbs

Call it a transition year, a remodeling, an overhaul. The Redskins added all kinds of new faces to what was one of the league's oldest rosters in 1984 and bid good-bye to others long synonymous with the burgundy and gold.

Such cornerstones as safety Mark Murphy, offensive tackle George Starke, wide receiver Charlie Brown, running back Joe Washington, and special teams ace Mike Nelms departed before the season began. They were part of a package of nearly 25 players from the Redskins' 1982 Super Bowl team not around to kick off the year. Plus, two iconic names with roots from the George Allen era—quarterback Joe Theismann and running back John Riggins—finished their careers in 1985.

By season's end, quarterback Jay Schroeder, wide receiver Gary Clark, and running back George Rogers had surfaced as the new faces of the Redskins. They paced a 10–6 squad that finished in a three-way tie for first in the NFC East but missed the playoffs for the first time in four seasons.

But the Redskins were so close. They won five of their last six games and stayed in playoff contention until being eliminated on the final weekend.

"There were a lot of questions early in the year about how good we were because [at one point] we were 5–5 and people were wondering how the team was going to shake out," Schroeder said. "But we had a lot of great, what I'd call professional football players. They weren't about to give up. They just did their job, and they knew if they stuck with it long enough, good things were going to happen, and they did."

Rogers's entrance into the Redskins' neighborhood was their first major move in the 1985 off-season. They traded their No. 1 pick in the 1985 draft to New Orleans for Rogers, who had rushed for 4,267 yards over four seasons with the Saints after winning the Heisman Trophy in college. The Redskins also received the Saints' fifth-, 10th-, and 11th-round draft picks.

The Redskins drafted a player who would prove valuable in the coming years as a mainstay on the Hogs: Tennessee guard Raleigh McKenzie (11th round). Mississippi safety Barry Wilburn (eighth); Texas running back Terry Orr (10th), who evolved into a solid tight end; and Tulsa defensive tackle Dean Hamel (12th) also enjoyed nice stints in Washington.

McKenzie joined an offensive line riddled with injuries in 1984, and one that yielded 21 sacks in the final three games. To further stabilize the line, the Redskins acquired three-time Pro Bowl offensive tackle R. C. Theilmann from Atlanta for former Redskins Pro Bowl receiver Charlie Brown. On the receiving end, the Redskins signed wide receiver Gary Clark, one of a slew of United States Football League imports to land in the NFL. Clark made an immediate impact, catching 72 passes for 926 yards and five touchdowns in 1985 while en route to becoming one of the top receivers in Redskins history.

Workhorse running back John Riggins agreed to a one-year contract and returned for his 14th season. He would compete with the 6–2, 230-pound Rogers for time in the Redskins' single-back setup.

Washington finished 4–0 in a preseason highlighted by battles at two key positions. Ancient kicker Mark Moseley withstood a challenge by former USFL star Tony Zendejas, while

## Babe Lights Preseason Fireworks

It's hard to build a legacy based on preseason accomplishments. But if anyone has done it in Washington, it's The Babe.

Babe Laufenberg is perhaps the most beloved preseason player in Redskins history—and one of the unluckiest, too. A quarterback drafted by the Redskins in the sixth round in 1983, he participated in four straight training camps and exhibition seasons (1983–86), never to set foot in a real game. He also joined the Redskins during the 1987 season and stayed for two games before being cut, missing out on a Super Bowl share by one game.

Nevertheless, Laufenberg made a habit of thrilling the crowds at RFK Stadium in the dog days of summer. They called him "Mr. August."

- Against the Dolphins in 1983, he completed 9 of 17 passes for 86 yards to earn the third-string job.
- Against the Patriots in 1984, he completed 10 of 17 passes for 154 yards with a 36-yard scoring pass, all in the fourth quarter, to nearly rally the Redskins to victory.
- Against the Patriots in 1985, he threw two touchdown passes in the final seven minutes, including a 25-yarder with four seconds left, to lift the Redskins to a 37–36 win.
- Against the Steelers in 1986, he orchestrated a come-from-behind 27–24 win by hitting on 13 of 20 passes with a 30-yard touchdown pass.

Despite his feats, the 6–2, 195-pounder with the rock star hair length and an unorthodox release just couldn't beat out quarterbacks like Joe Theismann, Jay Schroeder, Doug Williams, and Mark Rypien. When Laufenberg was cut before regular-season play began in 1985, general manager Bobby Beathard told the press, "It's just terrible that a guy like Babe Laufenberg can't be on this team."

Laufenberg got a chance elsewhere. He played in regular-season games in New Orleans (1986), San Diego (1988), and Dallas (1989 and `90). His best year was with San Diego; he appeared in eight games and completed 69 of 144 passes for 778 yards, with four touchdowns and five interceptions.

Schroeder got the nod over Babe Laufenberg in the competition for the No. 2 quarterback spot behind Theismann.

Theismann turned 36 on opening day, a Monday night game against the Cowboys at Texas Stadium, but the 12-year veteran had no reason to celebrate. He threw a career-high five interceptions that led to a host of points in a 44–14 Dallas rout. Theismann was benched late in the fourth period for Schroeder and then experienced more humiliation.

The subject of verbal attacks all game by Cowboys players and fans steaming from the way he knelt at the end of the Redskins' 30–28 victory over Dallas in 1984 and then ran around to kill more time, Theismann heard the crowd sarcastically sing a tailored rendition of "Happy Birthday." The game thus became known as the "Happy Birthday" game.

"It was the cruelest moment I've ever been through," he said. "We were getting our ass handed to us, and I sat on the bench and all of Texas Stadium was singing 'Happy Birthday' to me. If it had been natural turf, I would have been able to crawl under a blade of grass."

The Redskins pulled even with a 16–13 win over Houston but needed help from the zebras. Penalties nullified two Oilers touchdowns, and a 50-yard catch to the Redskins' 9 was called back due to a penalty. Then came a 19–6 loss to the visiting Eagles, who had no touchdowns in their first two games, and a 45–10 drubbing at the hands of the eventual Super Bowl-champion Bears, dropping the Redskins to 1–3. The 35-point margin marked the Redskins' worst loss in nearly a quarter century.

An inauspicious start, no doubt. The Redskins had been outscored, 121–46, Theismann was one of the lowest-rated passers in the NFL, and special teams had yielded an average of 37.3 yards on kick returns, plus a 99-yard touchdown by Chicago's Willie Gault. Leadership also seemed to be lacking as a result of the loss of such key veterans as Murphy and Starke.

But the Redskins still had one of the best running games in the NFL and put it to good use when the 3–1 Cardinals came to town on Monday night. With Riggins and Rogers both rushing for more than 100 yards—the first time in Redskins history two players had topped the century mark in the same game—and the defense picking off five passes, Washington cruised to a 27–10 win. Riggins then tallied 114 yards and three touchdowns in a 24–3 win over the Lions, lifting the Redskins to 3–3.

The Giants, in sacking Theismann seven times the next week, also sacked the Redskins' momentum with a 17–3 win. But Washington rebounded with a 14–7 win over the Browns, against whom Riggins had a 112-yard day, and devoured Atlanta by 34 points, as two Redskins again topped 100 yards rushing: second-year man Keith Griffin (164) and Rogers (124). The 5–4 Redskins were back in the playoff picture, but a 13–7 loss to Dallas returned them to .500.

Now at a crossroads, the Redskins desperately needed a win against a Giants squad coming to RFK for a Monday night clash. "Somehow, some way, we've got to make it happen," Theismann said at the time. "And I think with everyone pulling for us, we still can."

The Redskins pulled it out, but not on Theismann's watch. With the score tied at 7 early in the second period, he took a lateral from Riggins on a flea-flicker and looked to pass in the pocket. Then came one of the grisliest scenes in sports history.

Giants all-world linebacker Lawrence Taylor led a trio of players who converged on Theismann and dropped him for a sack. At the same time, the quarterback's leg bent at an extreme angle and snapped. As Theismann lay sprawled on the field writhing in pain, Taylor frantically signaled to the Redskins' medical staff to get on the field. The stadium went silent.

"I remember turning to my spotter and saying, 'His career's over,' said Phil Hochberg, the Redskins' public address announcer at the time. "That's without even knowing what happened to him."

In came Schroeder, a former catcher and outfielder in the Toronto Blue Jays' farm system who had thrown eight passes in nearly two seasons in the NFL. He wasn't taking snaps in practice, for that matter. Was he nervous? "Not really," he said. "I just wanted to relax and do the things I was taught to do. I tried to focus, take each play for what it was and try to do the best we could."

On his first pass against the NFL's No. 1 defense, the 6–4, 220-pound Schroeder hit diving Redskins receiver Art Monk for a 44-yard completion. The play typified Schroeder's poise through the evening before an awe-stricken crowd of 53,371 and millions more watching on TV.

Schroeder hit Monk again early in the third quarter, this time for 50 yards, on a four-play drive capped by Riggins's 1-yard run that put the Redskins up, 14–7. The Giants retaliated with two touchdowns for a 21–14 lead, but Moseley's 28-yard field goal on a 65-yard drive cut the lead to four early in the final period. The Redskins recovered an onside kick for the second time that evening, and Schroeder led a march that ended with his 14-yard scoring pass to tight end Clint Didier, climaxing his unflappable performance in the 23–21 Redskins win.

Hochberg remembers the crowd getting more behind Schroeder, who completed 13 of 20 passes for 221 yards, as the game progressed: "It was a truly emotional experience to see a team leader go down, then to see a novice step in and lead the Redskins to victory that night."

Next up, Schroeder completed 15 of 28 passes for 164 yards and one touchdown in a 30–23 victory over the Steelers. Plus, he wasn't intercepted or sacked for the second straight game. He then threw a team-record 58 passes for 348 yards against a 49ers squad vying for a wild card playoff spot of its own. San Francisco won, 35–8.

The loss proved too much for the 7–6 Redskins to overcome. They captured their final three games, the latter of which featured a team-record 206 rushing yards by Rogers, who finished with 1,093. But their wild card hopes died on the final day when the 49ers beat Dallas and the Giants beat Pittsburgh, leaving San Francisco and New York, both 10–6, as the NFC's wild card teams. Dallas, which also finished 10–6, won the NFC East. (The 10–6 Redskins finished behind the Cowboys and Giants because of a poor divisional record and lost out to San Francisco in head-to-head competition.)

Nevertheless, there was a silver lining to the roller-coaster season, according to Schroeder, who completed 112 of 209 passes for 1,458 yards, with five touchdowns and five interceptions. "Winning five out of the last six games was definitely a building block for the next year," he said.

## 1986: 12–4, 2ND PLACE—NFC EAST

### Head Coach: Joe Gibbs

What team wears blue-and-white uniforms, plays in the NFC East, has a Hall of Fame-caliber coach, sports a ferocious defense led by perhaps the greatest linebacker in NFL history, and—not to be forgotten—torments the Redskins?

Answer: The 1986 New York Giants.

The Giants beat the Redskins all three times they collided that year, and by wider margins each time. From scores of 27–20 and 24–14 in the regular season to a 17–0 shutout in the NFC championship game, the Giants were a thorn in the Redskins' side. Led by coach Bill Parcells and outside linebacker and league MVP Lawrence Taylor, New York finished 14–2 in the regular season en route to winning Super Bowl XXI.

New York's dominance tainted an impressive campaign for the Redskins, who finished 12–4 and earned a wild card playoff berth. The Redskins topped the Rams and upset the Bears in the first two rounds of the playoffs before meeting those dreaded Giants.

"It's frustrating any time you lose to a team three times, but also understand they ended up being the Super Bowl champions," said Redskins quarterback Jay Schroeder, who was sacked 12 times and threw nine interceptions against the Giants in 1986. "They were a very good football team. Unfortunately, we couldn't get over the hump of beating them."

Schroeder was one of a number of new stars to emerge for the Redskins in 1986, their 50th season in the nation's capital. In his first full year as a starter, he became the first Redskins quarterback to throw for more than 4,000 yards (4,109) and made the Pro Bowl. A low-percentage passer with a powerful arm, he completed 276 passes out of a team-record 541 attempts, with 22 touchdowns and 22 interceptions.

Schroeder aimed many of his passes at the one-two punch of Gary Clark (74 catches, 1,265 yards, seven touchdowns) and Art Monk (73 catches, 1,068 yards, four touchdowns). Clark and Monk made the Pro Bowl, along with cornerback Darrell Green (team-high five interceptions), defensive end Dexter Manley (team-record 18.5 sacks), and two Hogs who went for the fourth straight year: Russ Grimm and Joe Jacoby.

Schroeder's starting role marked a changing of the guard in the nation's capital. He quarterbacked a Redskins team that for the first time in more than two decades wasn't led under center by Sonny Jurgensen, Billy Kilmer, or Joe Theismann, who was unable to rehabilitate himself from the horrific injury that ended his 1985 season and retired. Another famous Redskin, John Riggins, retired as the fourth leading rusher in NFL history at the time with 11,352 yards.

The departure of Theismann and Riggins, along with tight end Rick Walker, safety Tony Peters, and others, was part of a youth movement orchestrated by general manager Bobby Beathard and Gibbs. They wanted to dispose of decaying veterans from one of the league's oldest teams in 1985 (average age 27.2 years) and drafted a series of players who would contribute, some mightily, in the coming years. Rookies included Boise State defensive end Marcus Koch (second round), Kansas cornerback Alvin Walton (third), Arkansas linebacker Ravin Caldwell (fifth), Washington State quarterback Mark Rypien (sixth), and Brigham Young linebacker Kurt Gouveia (eighth).

The Redskins also raided the United States Football League (USFL), which folded in the summer of 1986 after three years of play. The most promising acquisition was Kelvin Bryant, a speedy running back with nifty moves who finished as one of the top rushers in USFL history with 4,055 yards. He also caught 141 passes for 1,270 yards. The Redskins had the rights to Bryant because they picked him in the 1983 draft. The Redskins also signed USFL refugees including quarterback Doug Williams, wide receivers Ricky Sanders and Derek Holloway, and wide receiver–kick returner Clarence Verdin.

Williams, who played two seasons with the USFL's Oklahoma Outlaws after starring for five years with Tampa Bay in the NFL, was brought in strictly as a backup to Schroeder.

Gibbs was well aware of what Williams could do, for the coach had served as Williams's offensive coordinator in Tampa Bay in 1978. "We're very fortunate to have gotten Doug," Gibbs said at the time. "He took Tampa Bay to three playoffs in five years, so that's saying something."

In town for opening day was a refocused Eagles squad led by first-year coach Buddy Ryan, architect of the famed 46 defense that served as the backbone of Chicago's Super Bowl-winning season in 1985. The bombastic Ryan bragged about his Eagles version of the 46 defense in the days preceding the game. But with the Redskins en route to shredding Philadelphia's defense for 433 yards in a 41–14 victory, RFK Stadium fans did the talking with mocking chants of "BUDDY, BUDDY, BUDDY!"

The Redskins displayed a host of weapons on offense. Schroeder completed 19 of 38 passes for 289 yards and two touchdowns. Bryant provided a new dimension, catching four passes for 76 yards and one touchdown, and running 16 yards for a touchdown as part of a 21-point burst in the second half. He and George Rogers, who gained 104 yards on 20 carries, gave the Redskins an inside-outside threat reminiscent of the early 1980s with John Riggins and Joe Washington.

Punter Steve Cox, who also had the power to hit long field goals, booted a Redskins-record 55-yarder, and Clark caught seven passes for 100 yards.

"The first win means a lot," Gibbs told the press afterward. "I was uptight before the game. We all needed this."

The Redskins improved to 2–0 with a 10–6 win over the Raiders in a rematch of Super Bowl XVIII. Washington trailed 6–3 entering the final period. But Schroeder hit tight end Clint Didier, a big-play threat all year, on a 59-yard pass midway through the quarter, setting up Rogers's 3-yard run. The news was not all great, as Bryant suffered knee and ankle injuries that sidelined him for a few weeks, and linebacker Mel Kaufman, who had two sacks that day, was lost for the season with a ruptured Achilles tendon.

Comebacks were common for the Redskins in '86. The next week, they trailed San Diego by 18 points in the first half on the road. But Schroeder, who threw for 341 yards and hit bomb after bomb, connected with Clark on a 14-yard scoring pass with about a minute left to pull out a 30–27 win. Washington followed with a 19–14 victory over undefeated Seattle (Cox's 57-yard field goal topped his team record set three games earlier), then posted a 14–6 win over the Saints. Rogers ran for 110 yards on 31 carries against his former team, and the Redskins allowed 14 or fewer points for the fourth time in five games.

The 5–0 Redskins then dropped a 30–6 decision to the Cowboys in Dallas. They rebounded with a win over St. Louis, but a 27–20 loss to the Giants, along with a Cowboys win, created a tie for first in the NFC East between Washington, Dallas, and New York, all 6–2.

The Redskins trailed 20–3 against the Giants but battled back to tie the game on a field goal early in the fourth quarter by rookie Max Zendejas, a free agent who was signed after Mark Moseley was cut earlier in the year. Giants running back Joe Morris, who trampled over the Redskins' defense for 181 yards, ran 13 yards for a touchdown with 1:31 left. With time running out, Schroeder completed passes to Clark that moved the ball to about the Giants' 30. But Clark, who tallied a team-record 241 receiving yards, slipped on a pass intended for him on fourth down. Schroeder threw for 420 yards against the

Giants' defense, though the Redskins were ineffective on the ground.

Washington subsequently won five straight games, including a 38–32 overtime victory over Minnesota in which the teams combined for 1,013 yards and seven lead changes. There was also a 41–14 rout of the Cowboys and a 20–17 win over St. Louis that guaranteed a home-field wild card playoff spot.

Finally, the showdown everyone was waiting for: the 11–2 Redskins versus the 11–2 Giants for first place in the NFC East, a game that Redskins defensive end Dexter Manley described as a "Super Bowl" matchup. The Redskins were no match for the Giants, particularly their vaunted defense, before 55,642 at RFK. Schroeder was intercepted six times, and Taylor made life miserable for the Redskins' quarterback by sacking him three times. New York's 24–14 victory wasn't that close.

The Redskins then fell 31–30 to Denver, where a missed extra point by Zendejas made the difference, before yielding a 14–0 halftime lead to the lowly Eagles at Veterans Stadium. The deficit prompted Gibbs to unravel in the locker room.

"Gibbs ran in the locker room and started having a fit and a temper tantrum," Manley recalled. "He threw everything over. He threw chairs, turned the tables over, punched tables. It was so out of character for him. But I'll tell you what, it was very effective because it got everyone's attention because we knew Joe Gibbs was serious. We went out and played football."

The Redskins trailed by the same score entering the fourth period. But Schroeder completed 9 of 12 passes for 142 yards and two touchdowns, part of a 21-point barrage that lifted Washington to a 21–14 win. It marked the seventh time in 12 games that the Redskins had pulled out a win when trailing heading into the final quarter.

## NFC WILD CARD GAME
## Washington 19, Los Angeles Rams 7
## December 28, 1986
## RFK Stadium, Washington, D.C.
## Attendance: 54,180

## Methodical Redskins Overcome Self-Destructing Rams

There was nothing spectacular about it. No offensive explosiveness like that on display during the regular season, no aerial fireworks shooting off quarterback Jay Schroeder's rocket arm. The Redskins played it conservatively and by doing so earned a 19–7 wild card victory over the Rams.

"People always say, 'You didn't score that many points, you didn't do this or that,'" Schroeder said. "We did what we needed to do to win the football game."

Schroeder completed 13 of 23 passes for 90 yards, with one short touchdown pass and no interceptions. George Rogers rushed 29 times for 115 yards after gaining more than 1,000 yards in the regular season. Kicker Jess Atkinson, signed late in the season to replace the struggling Max Zendejas, booted four field goals.

"That was the highlight of my short career," said Atkinson, who played in only 11 games over four seasons. "To be able to kick four field goals in a playoff game at RFK Stadium, in my first game there, was as good as it got for me."

The Rams outgained the Redskins, 324 yards to 228, and league-leading rusher Eric Dickerson churned out 158 alone. In the game's deciding factor, however, Los Angeles committed six turnovers, the Redskins none.

Dickerson fumbled the ball three times, once on the game's fifth play. Redskins safety Alvin Walton returned it 21 yards to the Rams' 44 to set up Atkinson's 25-yard field goal. Later, the Redskins drove 60 yards in seven plays, aided by some major penalties, and Schroeder connected with running back Kelvin Bryant for a 14-yard touchdown pass to put the Redskins up by 10.

After the Rams lost another fumble, this one in the second period, the Redskins drove 53 yards in 14 plays to set up Atkinson's 20-yard field goal for a 13–0 halftime lead. The methodical drive exemplified how the Redskins remained content to take "what the Rams were going to give us," as Schroeder put it.

"They came out playing a lot of three-deep zone," he said. "They wanted to challenge us and say, 'Okay, we're going to take away the deep ball, are you going to be patient enough to make the little throw underneath and move the ball down the field? See if you can beat us that way.' We made the adjustment. We knew going in that that was probably going to be their philosophy, so we were satisfied with taking the stuff underneath and moving the ball down the field."

Atkinson was true on a 38-yarder in the third quarter, but the Rams rallied. Dickerson broke free for a 65-yard run, setting up quarterback Jim Everett's 12-yard scoring pass to Kevin House for a 16–7 game early in the fourth quarter. Soon after, the Rams moved to the Redskins' 39 and faced a fourth-and-1. But Dickerson fumbled the ball away for the third time, and Atkinson booted a 19-yard field goal with less than a minute left.

The victory earned the Redskins a date with the "Big, Bad Bears," NFC Central Division champions and a 14–2 squad seeking its second straight Super Bowl win. "The good news is we won," Redskins coach Joe Gibbs told media after beating the Rams. "The bad news is we have to go to Chicago."

| LA Rams— | 0 | 0 | 0 | 7 | — | 7 |
| Washington— | 10 | 3 | 3 | 3 | — | 19 |

Wash — FG Atkinson 25
Wash — Bryant 14 pass from Schroeder (Atkinson kick)
Wash — FG Atkinson 20
Wash — FG Atkinson 38
LA —— House 12 pass from Everett (Lansford kick)
Wash — FG Atkinson 19

# NFC DIVISIONAL PLAYOFF GAME
## Washington 27, Chicago 13
## January 3, 1987
## Soldier Field, Chicago
## Attendance: 65,141

## Resourceful Redskins Put Muzzle on Ditka, Bears

From the way they were mouthing off, the Bears seemed to have reserved a spot for the NFC championship game. Coach Mike Ditka predicted it would be "tough" for the Redskins to beat his squad. Team president Mike McCaskey said his heavily favored Bears had no plans to lose. Some of Chicago's players were also busy making gaudy music videos showing their Super Bowl Shuffle.

By sundown at Soldier Field, the Bears were preparing to get out their golf clubs: Washington 27, Chicago 13.

"It was pretty inspiring to pull off that win," Redskins offensive tackle Joe Jacoby said. "They were reading their press clippings and doing their Bear dance. They were going in overconfident, and I don't think they looked at us as any big threat. They thought they were moving on to play in the championship game and hopefully the Super Bowl. We took it personally.

"We had quite a few guys who were banged up playing that game," added Jacoby, who played with an oversized cast on his right hand. "But we slugged it out after falling behind early and came back and won."

It was a gritty victory, considering the circumstances:

- The Bears were playing after 13 days' rest, compared with five for the bruised-and-battered Redskins.
- Chicago's first-ranked defense allowed only 187 points in the regular season.
- The Bears won the league rushing title for the fourth straight year.
- Chicago had lost only three times over its past 35 games, a stretch that included a 23–19 win over the Redskins in the 1984 playoffs and a 45–10 demolition of the Redskins in 1985.

But the 14–2 Bears had played an incredibly soft schedule in 1986, and the Redskins exploited their weaknesses. Quarterback Jay Schroeder and receiver Art Monk hooked up for two touchdowns, and a steady Redskins offense controlled time of possession by more than seven minutes. The defense held the Bears to 93 yards rushing and 220 overall, putting forth a goal line stand in the second period. The great Walter Payton, who gained 1,353 yards in the season, tallied only 38 on 14 carries, and Chicago self-destructed in the second half by committing three turnovers that preceded 17 Redskins points.

"It was a very good win because the year before we scored first against them, then they ran back a kickoff for a touchdown, and it just kind of snowballed on us," Schroeder said. "We were a much better team [in 1986] and were more prepared to go in and face them."

The Bears led, 13–7, at halftime on a 50-yard touchdown pass from quarterback Doug Flutie to receiver Willie Gault, and two field goals by Kevin Butler. Flutie, a rookie who had seen scant playing time during the regular season, was filling in for injured starter Jim McMahon.

On his scoring catch, Gault faked out Redskins cornerback Darrell Green, who had beaten Gault to win the NFL's "Fastest Man" competition that season. Green atoned for his lapse in the third quarter, intercepting a pass and returning it 17 yards to the Bears' 26. Three plays later, Schroeder threw his second scoring pass to Monk, this one a 23-yarder on a perfectly timed out-and-up pattern. Jess Atkinson's conversion gave the Redskins the lead for good, 14–13.

After Chicago's Dennis Gentry returned the ensuing kickoff 48 yards, the Bears moved deep into Redskins territory. But safety Alvin Walton recovered Payton's fumble on the 17, and the Redskins crafted an 11-play, 83-yard drive that ended on Rogers's 1-yard touchdown run in the fourth quarter. Atkinson later hit 25- and 35-yard field goals, one of which was set up when Redskins linebacker Monte Coleman recovered a fumbled punt on the Bears' 4-yard line.

By game's end, Da Bears had nothing more to brag about.

| | | | | | | |
|---|---|---|---|---|---|---|
| Washington— | 7 | 0 | 7 | 13 | — | 27 |
| Chicago— | 0 | 13 | 0 | 0 | — | 13 |

Wash — Monk 28 pass from Schroeder (Atkinson kick)
Chi —— Gault 50 pass from Flutie (Butler kick)
Chi —— FG Butler 23
Chi —— FG Butler 41
Wash — Monk 23 pass from Schroeder (Atkinson kick)
Wash — Rogers 1 run (Atkinson kick)
Wash — FG Atkinson 35
Wash — FG Atkinson 25

## NFC CHAMPIONSHIP GAME
**New York Giants 17, Washington 0**
**January 11, 1987**
**Giants Stadium, East Rutherford, N.J.**
**Attendance: 76,633**

### Redskins Blown Away by Giants, "Vicious" Wind

Giants Stadium was a house of horrors for the Washington Redskins on January 11, 1987.

With winds gusting at up to 35 miles per hour, plus biting-cold temperatures, Washington's pass-oriented offense was unable to get untracked. Erratic quarterback Jay Schroeder, misfiring on passes that were redirected by the wind, completed 20 of 50 with one interception. The Redskins ran only 16 times for 40 yards.

The Giants, meanwhile, built a 17–0 first-half lead and let their A-plus defense do the rest to capture the NFC championship game and advance to Super Bowl XXI. It was the only time the Redskins were shut out in Joe Gibbs's first coaching stint in Washington.

"The wind was vicious," Giants coach Bill Parcells remembered. "Neither team was going to do much offensively going into that wind."

Agreed Redskins kicker Jess Atkinson, "The wind was as bad as any game I ever played in, college or pro. The farthest field goal I made in warm-ups was 27 yards, and that was going into the wind."

The Giants won the coin toss but elected to kick off with the wind at their backs. It was a deft choice that immediately handcuffed the Redskins, who gained 4 yards in three plays. Steve Cox's 23-yard punt into the swirling wind gave the Giants the ball on their 47, and they moved into position for Raul Allegre's 47-yard field goal for a 3–0 lead.

After sure-handed Redskins receiver Gary Clark dropped a bomb that looked like a touchdown, Cox's second feeble punt gave the Giants the ball on their 38. They drove nearly 40 yards, and quarterback Phil Simms threw an incompletion on third-and-10. The Giants were called for holding on the play, but in a curious decision, Gibbs accepted the 10-yard penalty instead of forcing Allegre to try a 43-yard field goal with the wind at his back.

Simms completed a 25-yard pass to receiver Lionel Manuel and, three plays later, tossed an 11-yard touchdown pass to Manuel for a 10–0 Giants lead.

In the second period, the Redskins set up to try a 51-yard field goal with the wind at their backs. But Jeff Bostic's snap

Redskins quarterback Jay Schroeder is seeing stars as he's helped off the field at the end of the NFC Championship game. Schroeder, who suffered a concussion in the third period, had a miserable day against the Giants after throwing for a Redskins-record 4,109 yards in the regular season.

was low, and Giants linebacker Carl Banks recovered the ball on the Redskins' 49. Simms hit tight end Mark Bavaro for 30 yards, and running back Joe Morris took it in from the 1 to put the Giants up by 17.

Ball game.

New York played keep-away from then on. Equipped with the NFL's second-leading rusher in Morris (29 carries, 87 yards), they ran 46 times overall and controlled time of possession by more than six minutes. The Redskins ran only once in the second half and threw 34 times, as New York's defense prevented them from whittling away at the lead. Consider this telling statistic: Washington was 0–14 on third down and 0–4 on fourth down.

Another key statistic stemmed from the punting game. On kicks into the wind, Giants Pro Bowler Sean Landeta averaged 42 yards, compared with 29 for Cox, giving New York a sizable edge in field position. The punt return game was crucial, too, according to Parcells.

"What turned that game in our favor is our punt returner didn't let any punts hit the ground, and the ball hit the ground on their punt returner a few times," he said. "I think the net difference there was over 100 yards. That helped us get better field position, and in that kind of game that's what you need."

As for Schroeder, it was a brutal day. The Pro Bowl quarterback was sacked four times and suffered a concussion in the third quarter when his head slammed against the artificial turf. Giants linebacker Lawrence Taylor wrote in his 1987 book, *LT: Living on the Edge,* that Schroeder became "shell-shocked," saying that he kept looking over his shoulder just before releasing the ball to see if defenders were bearing down on him. Schroeder denied the charge.

"It was a tough evening," Schroeder said. "We just didn't make the plays when we had opportunities, and they did."

| | | | | | | |
|---|---|---|---|---|---|---|
| Washington— | 0 | 0 | 0 | 0 | — | 0 |
| New York— | 10 | 7 | 0 | 0 | — | 17 |

NY — FG Allegre 47
NY — Manuel 11 pass from Simms (Allegre kick)
NY — Morris 1 run (Allegre kick)

# 1987: 11–4, 1ST PLACE—NFC EAST

### Head Coach: Joe Gibbs

He was nearly traded in the preseason. He rotated in and out of the starting lineup during the season, officially noted as a backup to quarterback Jay Schroeder. Many in NFL circles thought the best days of the 10-year veteran had passed.

By the end, Doug Williams was royalty to the Redskins.

After replacing Schroeder in the season finale at Minnesota and steering the Redskins to an overtime victory, Williams became the undisputed starter and exhibited clutch performances in playoff wins over the Bears and Vikings. The latter victory sent the Redskins to Super Bowl XXII, where Williams threw for a Super Bowl-record 340 yards and four touchdowns to earn MVP honors in the Redskins' 42–10 demolition of the Denver Broncos.

The Super Bowl climaxed a whirlwind season for Williams, whose career had taken several turns that left him eyeing an uncertain future.

"Doug wound up being the right man in the right place," Redskins Coach Joe Gibbs said. "You've got a guy who played great when he first came out of college, went and starred in the [United States Football League], turned around and became a backup, then comes all the way back and is MVP in the Super Bowl. That's one of the great stories in sports history."

The Super Bowl victory served as the Redskins' second NFL championship in seven seasons under Gibbs, and solidified their position as one of the premier teams of the 1980s. They met and some would argue exceeded the great preseason expectations placed on a squad that reached the NFC championship game in 1986. Their four losses were by a total of 11 points. "There are certain times when you have a team you know is special," Redskins receiver Gary Clark said. "We knew that season was special."

As with their first Super Bowl win in the '82 season, the Redskins prevailed after weathering the turmoil of a strike-shortened year in which three games involved replacement players and one week of play was cancelled. Talk of a possible strike mushroomed during the exhibition season, when players and owners traded serious threats. The National Football League Players Association (NFLPA), upset over terms of the collective bargaining agreement, set a strike deadline of September 22. The owners voted to play with anyone who would cross the picket line in case of a strike.

"The players association thought they had the upper hand in negotiations, and their mantra was that they are the game," said John Kent Cooke, the Redskins' executive vice president at the time. "We decided to have replacement squads just to show the [regular players] they were not the game, but an integral part of the game, and that the league would go on no matter who the players were."

Meanwhile, the Redskins pursued talks with the Raiders about a trade for Williams, who, at 32, was about to enter his 10th season of pro football, including two years in the USFL. The Raiders offered a second-round draft choice for him, but the Redskins wanted a first-round pick.

"I was pissed off [in Washington] because I wanted the opportunity to play, and the Raiders were going to afford me that opportunity," said Williams, who threw only one pass in '86. "Being a backup wasn't really what I wanted to be."

## The Replacements

In 2000, a Hollywood movie based on the remarkable run by the Redskins' 1987 replacement team hit the screens. Its name: none other than "The Replacements." The football comedy starred Gene Hackman as the coach (Jimmy McGinty) and Keanu Reeves as the quarterback (Shane Falco) of the Washington Sentinels, a motley squad of scabs that went 3–1 while the regular players were on strike. The final game, a 20–17 win over Dallas, ended the regular season and put the Sentinels in the playoffs. Interestingly, action scenes in the film were shot at the Baltimore Ravens' home field, then known as PSI Net Stadium.

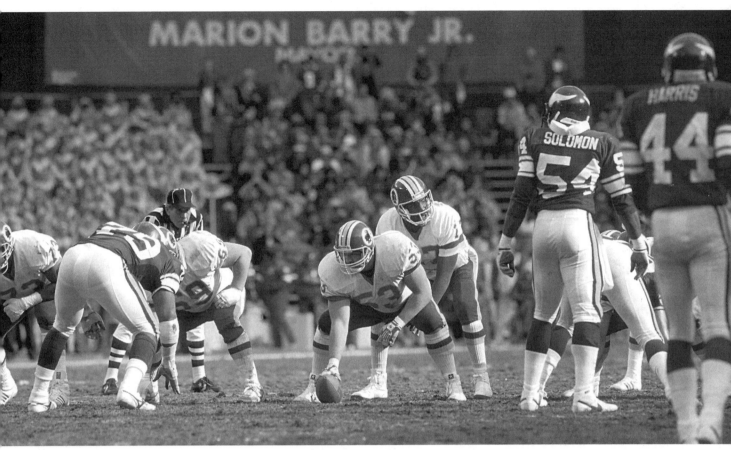

Doug Williams took over the signal-calling duties late in the 1987 season. He quarterbacked the Redskins to three post-season wins, including one here against the Vikings in the NFC championship game and a rout of the Broncos in Super Bowl XXII. Williams's rise to become MVP of the Super Bowl after once warming the bench is "one of the great stories in sports history," Redskins coach Joe Gibbs said.

No deal was consummated, however, leaving Williams relegated to the bench and the Redskins holding on to his $475,000 contract.

"Joe Gibbs told me he decided not to make the trade because he had a feeling I was going to be more important to them than I was to the Raiders," Williams recalled. "He actually told me in his office that we were going to find a way to win a championship with me being a part of the team. I didn't see it at the time because I was a little 'teed,' and I didn't care. I wasn't looking that far."

Williams proved his value in the season opener against the Eagles at RFK Stadium. Schroeder, mediocre in the Redskins' 3–1 exhibition season, sprained his shoulder early in the first quarter and left the game. Williams proceeded to complete all four of his passes on a short drive that ended with a 6-yard touchdown toss to receiver Art Monk. Kicker Jess Atkinson converted for a 10–0 Redskins lead but dislocated his ankle upon being hit by the Eagles' Andre "Dirty" Waters, who was known for taking late shots.

Philadelphia tied the game in the second period, but Williams hit lengthy completions on two scoring drives that put the Redskins up, 24–10. The Eagles again tied the game, only to see Williams respond with a 39-yard touchdown pass to Monk and a 46-yarder to Clark on a drive that ended with a

field goal by punter Steve Cox, Atkinson's replacement, for the final points in a 34–24 victory.

Williams was outstanding despite his long layoff, completing 17 of 27 passes for 272 yards and two scores. Plus, the starting job was now his, for Schroeder was projected to be out at least three weeks. The Redskins signed a name from the past to back up Williams, preseason marvel Babe Laufenberg. Free-agent kicker Ali Haji-Scheikh, who had struggled since setting an NFL record for most field goals (35) in his 1983 rookie season with the Giants, was also signed.

Haji-Scheikh's inability to try an extra point, due to a low snap by Jeff Bostic, made the difference in a 21–20 loss to the Falcons. Williams had another solid game, hitting on 18 of 30 passes for 198 yards and three touchdowns.

The frustration of the loss was compounded by the imminence of the strike. Sure enough, the players walked off the job, hoping to pressure the owners into paying higher salaries and approving a more player-friendly form of free agency. The owners set their plan in motion to use replacement players for games that would count in the standings, unlike the 57-day strike in 1982, when play just stopped.

Redskins management was prepared. General manager Bobby Beathard and his scouting staff led efforts to assemble a makeshift squad consisting mostly of unsigned rookies and former NFL rejects. "That was almost like another draft," Beathard said. "It was a lot of fun."

Suddenly, such names as quarterbacks Ed Rubbert and Tony Robinson, wide receiver Anthony Allen, running backs Lionel Vital and Wayne Wilson, tight end Craig McEwen, punt returner Derrick Shepard, and defensive linemen Dan Benish and Steve Martin represented the burgundy and gold. Washington's replacements won their first two games, 28–21 over St. Louis at RFK, where Allen amassed a team-record 255 receiving yards, and 38–12 over the Giants in the Meadowlands.

A few days later, Redskins regulars and disgruntled union players throughout the league decided they'd seen enough. They returned to work after a 24-day layoff without any of their demands being met. (The Redskins ended up being the only team where no players crossed the picket line.) The major networks were televising the games, many of which were drawing modest crowds, circumstances that "broke our backs," said Redskins linebacker Neal Olkewicz, the team's player representative to the NFLPA. He said the regulars resented the replacement players, who were mockingly called "scabs."

"They basically hurt our cause, so we weren't happy about that," Olkewicz said. "We understood that they were marginal guys who were just trying to make a living. It wasn't a fun time. We caved in."

Former Redskin safety Mark Murphy, then an executive with the union, said of the owners, "They learned from the '82 experience. They had to come up with something to negate the effectiveness of the strike. We felt at the time [the replacements] would risk the credibility of the NFL, but they were effective in the sense that they allowed the owners to continue to have the games on TV. It put a lot of pressure on us, and players started crossing the picket line."

Although the regulars returned to work on October 15, three days before another Sunday of football games, the NFL ruled they had to sit out one more week. With another game to display their talents, the "Scabskins" pulled off an emotional 13–7 win over the Cowboys on Monday night at Texas Stadium. Dallas played with a host of regulars who had crossed the picket line, including future Hall of Famers in running back Tony Dorsett and defensive tackle Randy White. When Rubbert went down in the first quarter with an injured shoulder, things looked bleak for the Redskins. Tony Robinson, a Heisman Trophy candidate during his days at Tennessee who was on a work furlough from prison after a cocaine conviction, filled in with 11 of 18 passing for 152 yards and two interceptions.

The win left the 4–1 Redskins—one of only three teams to finish 3–0 in the replacement series—in first place in the NFC East, one game ahead of Dallas. Washington's toughest divisional foes, New York and Philadelphia, lost all three of their replacement games.

The full-time Redskins who took the field against the Jets at RFK were a much healthier squad, compared with before the strike, and Schroeder was back starting at quarterback. A crowd of 53,497 showed up for the return, and one sign read, "BOY, ARE WE GLAD YOU'RE BACK!" But the appreciation turned to a loud chorus of boos when the Redskins' offense proved to be flooded with cobwebs. Dropped pass after dropped pass, Schroeder's ineptness, a smattering of penalties, and the Jets' 16–7 lead with less than 10 minutes left prompted fans to scream for a return of the scabs.

But Schroeder rebounded from a 9-of-28 start to hit six of his last 10 passes for 111 yards. He found Kelvin Bryant for completions of 15 and 59 yards, before throwing a 2-yard scoring pass to the elusive running back with about six minutes left. After the defense held, the Redskins drove 61 yards with the help of a 39-yard pass to receiver Ricky Sanders, to set up Haji-Sheikh's 28-yard game-winning field goal with 54 seconds left.

While the offense was lifeless for most of the game, the defense earned kudos for holding the Jets to less than 200 yards and twice preventing scores after they moved inside the 5-yard line.

The Redskins played a much better all-around game the next week in a 27–7 win over Buffalo. Bryant was again key, catching two touchdown passes from Schroeder, who scored on a 13-yard bootleg. The Bills gained only 21 yards rushing. The Eagles later handed Washington a 31–27 loss, however. Quarterback Randall Cunningham's 40-yard touchdown pass with a minute to go provided the winning points, and Schroeder completed only 16 of 46 passes with two interceptions, triggering talk of a quarterback controversy.

Schroeder continued misfiring the next week against the Lions and was benched in the second quarter. Williams entered and threw a 16-yard touchdown pass to Bryant and a 42-yarder to Gary Clark for a 17–3 Redskin lead. The defense did the rest in Washington's 20–13 victory, holding the Lions scoreless after they began three fourth-quarter drives in enemy territory.

Williams was 11 of 18 for 161 yards with two scores, and Gibbs named him the starter for a Monday night game at RFK against the 2–7 Rams. Los Angeles took a 23–9 lead after producing touchdowns on a 35-yard fumble return, a 95-yard kickoff return, and a 1-yard run following a blocked punt. Williams (24 of 46, 308 yards) led a comeback that put the Redskins in position to win. Two of his passes in the final seconds bounced off Monk's hands, and the Rams exited as 30–26 winners.

Welcome to a new chapter in the quarterback saga. Williams strained his back in practice, allowing Schroeder to return as the starter against the defending Super Bowl champion Giants, 3–7 at the time. The Redskins failed to score in the first half despite four drives into Giants territory, and New York held a 19–3 lead late in the third quarter.

Schroeder, horrible up to that point, then put on one of the clutch comeback performances so emblematic of his 1986 season. Over an 11:21 stretch of the third and fourth quarters, he threw scoring passes of 34 yards to Clark, 6 to running back Keith Griffin, and 28 to Sanders as part of his 17 of 25, 217-yard work of art in the second half. The Giants, trailing 23–19, had one last chance to win, but running back Tony Galbreath was stopped 2 yards short of the end zone on the game's final play.

As the 8–3 Redskins prepared to play at St. Louis, where a win would clinch the NFC East title, Williams's back seemed healed. Gibbs opted to start Schroeder, instead. Williams, having stepped aside for what he thought was the good of the team, became choked up while speaking to the press.

"Joe Gibbs made a statement that starting quarterbacks don't lose their job unless they get hurt, and then they come back, which was fine with me," Williams said in reflecting back. "I understood it. But when I become the starter, and if I get hurt, I shouldn't lose my job. But I did. But that's some-

## In A Rush

The Redskins won 36 straight games in the 1980s when at least one of their running backs rushed for 100 or more yards in a game. The streak ended in 1987.

| Opponent | Year | Score | 100-Yd Rusher | Yards |
|---|---|---|---|---|
| Chicago | '81 | 24–7 | John Riggins | 126 |
| Detroit | '81 | 33–31 | Joe Washington | 144 |
| Tampa Bay | '82 | 21–13 | Riggins | 136 |
| Detroit* | '82 | 31–7 | Riggins | 119 |
| Minnesota* | '82 | 21–7 | Riggins | 185 |
| Dallas* | '82 | 31–17 | Riggins | 140 |
| Miami* | '82 | 27–17 | Riggins | 166 |
| Philadelphia | '83 | 23–13 | Riggins | 100 |
| St. Louis | '83 | 38–14 | Riggins | 115 |
| Detroit | '83 | 38–17 | Washington | 147 |
| N.Y. Giants | '83 | 31–22 | Riggins | 122 |
| L.A. Rams* | '83 | 51–7 | Riggins | 119 |
| San Francisco* | '83 | 24–21 | Riggins | 123 |
| New England | '84 | 26–10 | Riggins | 140 |
| Philadelphia | '84 | 20–0 | Riggins | 104 |
| Dallas | '84 | 34–14 | Riggins | 165 |
| Atlanta | '84 | 27–14 | Riggins | 100 |
| Detroit | '84 | 28–14 | Keith Griffin | 114 |
| Dallas | '84 | 30–28 | Riggins | 111 |
| St. Louis | '85 | 27–10 | George Rogers | 104 |
| St. Louis | '85 | 27–10 | Riggins | 103 |
| Detroit | '85 | 24–3 | Riggins | 114 |
| Cleveland | '85 | 14–7 | Riggins | 112 |
| Atlanta | '85 | 44–10 | Griffin | 164 |
| Atlanta | '85 | 44–10 | Rogers | 124 |
| Philadelphia | '85 | 17–12 | Rogers | 150 |
| St. Louis | '85 | 27–16 | Rogers | 206 |
| Philadelphia | '86 | 41–14 | Rogers | 114 |
| Seattle | '86 | 19–14 | Rogers | 115 |
| New Orleans | '86 | 14–6 | Rogers | 110 |
| St. Louis | '86 | 28–21 | Rogers | 118 |
| San Francisco | '86 | 14–6 | Rogers | 104 |
| L.A. Rams* | '86 | 19–7 | Rogers | 115 |
| N.Y. Giants† | '87 | 38–12 | Lionel Vital | 128 |
| Dallas‡ | '87 | 13–7 | Vital | 136 |
| Buffalo | '87 | 27–7 | Rogers | 125 |
| St. Louis | '87 | 34–17 | Rogers | 133 |
| Denver‡ | '87 | 42–10 | Timmy Smith | 204 |

*Playoff
†Super Bowl XXII
‡Replacement game

thing we all had to deal with. Everybody in my family was an athlete, and they always told me that cream rises to the top if it sets long enough. The door opened. It might not be wide. But you've got to squeeze in there."

Schroeder thought the starting job was his: "I had to think that. That's what makes you a player in the NFL. I was just unfortunate in that I was battling an injury and wasn't able to perform like I thought I should. I separated my shoulder in the first game, and I tried to come back right after the strike. My shoulder was never at full strength that year, and I had trouble with accuracy."

Schroeder played respectably in wins over St. Louis and Dallas and a loss to Miami. By then, the 10–4 Redskins were firmly in control of first place in the NFC East heading into the season finale at Minnesota.

But Schroeder struggled against the Vikings, having thrown two interceptions on 9 of 17 passing with the game tied at 7 early in the third quarter. The Redskins' only score had come on safety Barry Wilburn's 100-yard interception return, which stands as a team record. Gibbs thus tapped Williams, who had told reporters a few days before he thought he would never return to the starting lineup.

Williams tossed a 46-yard touchdown pass to Sanders and then threw two interceptions that helped the Vikings score 17 straight points to go up, 24–14. But the Redskins scored 10 in the last five minutes on Haji-Sheikh's 37-yard field goal and Williams's 51-yard pass to Sanders that tied the game at 24. Haji-Sheikh missed a field goal at the end of regulation but redeemed himself with a 26-yarder on the first possession in overtime for a 27–24 win, Washington's second straight over the Vikings in overtime.

The game marked the third time that Williams—who completed 11 of 22 passes for 217 yards, with two touchdowns and two interceptions—entered in relief to lead the Redskins to victory. So who would start in the opening round of the playoffs on the road against the Bears?

"It eventually became obvious that Doug was the guy who should be starting," Gibbs said.

The coach's instincts proved right.

## NFC DIVISIONAL PLAYOFF GAME
**Washington 21, Chicago 17**
**January 10, 1988**
**Soldier Field, Chicago**
**Attendance: 65,268**

### Instant Replay: Redskins Bedevil Bears in Windy City

For the second straight year, the Redskins entered the Bears' house in the postseason and showed the hosts the door.

With a clutch performance by quarterback Doug Williams, an acrobatic punt return by cornerback Darrell Green, and an intimidating display by their defense, the Redskins stunned the Bears at Soldier Field, 21–17.

The sweet victory on a frigid day clarified how good the Redskins really were after a regular season when their replacement players won three games and their regulars had only one solid performance. The Bears, for their part, failed for the second season in a row to win a Super Bowl after their breathtaking display as NFL champions in 1985.

"The Redskins played extremely well in both games," Bears safety Dave Duerson said of Washington's back-to-back playoff wins over Chicago. "But quite frankly, we were just snakebitten. Both in '86 and '87, we were not playing with our full boat of starters. We should have won three Super Bowls in a row, but we simply didn't get it done."

As in 1986, the Bears and their grandiloquent coach, Mike Ditka, were talking before the 1987 playoff game. Ditka said that Redskins defensive end Dexter Manley had the "I. Q. of a grapefruit" after Manley allegedly called the coach a "bum" for spitting gum at a fan. The Bears also voiced their urge to exact revenge on the team that toppled them in the playoffs the year before. "I'd love to play them," Duerson told reporters. "We have a score to settle."

Redskins coach Joe Gibbs said the Vikings did his squad no favors by upsetting the Saints in the wild card game, a win that matched the Redskins against the 11–4 Bears in Chicago. "Last year's game is going to make it tremendously tough on us because we went in there and beat [the Bears]," he told the press. "They have their quarterback this year, and last year they didn't."

He was referring to Jim McMahon, who missed the 1986 playoff game due to a shoulder injury and sat out the last three regular-season games in 1987 with a torn hamstring. The Bears lost two of those three games and barely won the other. But McMahon, a winner in 28 of his last 29 starts, was back, and the Bears took a 14–0 lead on a 2-yard scoring run by Calvin Thomas in the first period and a 14-yard touchdown catch by Ron Morris eight minutes before halftime. The latter score capped a drive that spanned more than nine minutes.

Despite the deficit, the Redskins tried to stay focused. "Being on a team with a bunch of veterans and Joe Gibbs as the coach, you don't panic even being down 14 points," Williams said. "You just do what you've got to do. We knew what was at hand."

Indeed, the Redskins went 72 yards in seven plays for a touchdown. Williams spotted receiver Ricky Sanders for 32 yards on third-and-9, then found tight end Clint Didier for 14 yards to the Bears' 3. Running back George Rogers took it in.

After the Bears missed a field goal, Williams moved the Redskins 69 yards in less than a minute, hitting Didier with an 18-yard strike down the middle for a 14–14 game. The score remained tied until early in the third quarter, when Gibbs tapped Green to return a punt with the Bears pinned deep in their own territory. Although the Redskins' fastest and most versatile athlete was a proven threat at returning punts, Gibbs knew of the risks.

"You put him back there, and he gets hurt, now you lose your top cover guy," Gibbs said in looking back. "But when we got to the playoffs, particularly that year, we said if it was a crucial part of the game, we'd put Darrell back there and run the risk."

Ditka remembers challenging his punter, Tommy Barnhardt, to kick it to Green despite his athleticism. "I was probably stupid enough to do that," Ditka said. "You have an ego, you trust your team so much and say, 'We can stop the guy.' We probably should have punted away from Green, but we didn't. Every game is made by one or two plays. He made a play that made that game."

It stands as one of the most memorable plays in Redskins history. Green caught the ball on his 48 and headed through a seam on the right side. Around the 35, Bears tight end Cap Boso came up and tried to undercut Green, who vaulted Boso, made an immediate cut toward midfield, and began clutching his rib cage—an enduring image in Redskins lore. Green then shifted into cruise control and, with interference from teammates, outran everyone into the end zone.

With the Redskins ahead, 21–14, their defense did the rest. The unit held the Bears to 92 yards in the second half and picked off three passes by McMahon, who hurt his left shoulder on his scoring pass to Morris. Safety Barry Wilburn intercepted one of the passes in the end zone to halt Chicago's last serious threat with 9:20 to play. The Redskins sacked McMahon five times on the day, three alone by defensive end Charles Mann.

As the clock wound down, TV cameras caught Bears running back Walter Payton, who played the last game of a 13-year career in which he finished as the NFL's all-time leading rusher, sitting dejectedly on the bench. The Redskins, on the other hand, were elated to be in the NFC championship game for the second straight year.

"For us to come back after being down 14–0 said a lot about the character of that football team," said Williams, who completed 14 of 29 passes for 207 yards, with a touchdown and an interception. "Darrell Green's punt return, and Ricky Sanders' [32-yard] catch across the middle were two plays that really turned the game around."

| | | | | | | |
|---|---|---|---|---|---|---|
| Washington— | 0 | 14 | 7 | 0 | — | 21 |
| Chicago— | 7 | 7 | 3 | 0 | — | 17 |

Chi —— Thomas 2 run (Butler kick)
Chi —— Morris 14 pass from McMahon (Butler kick)
Wash — Rogers 3 run (Haji-Sheikh kick)
Wash — Didier 18 pass from Williams (Haji-Sheikh kick)
Wash — Green 52 punt return (Haji-Sheikh kick)
Chi —— FG Butler 25

# NFC CHAMPIONSHIP GAME
**Washington 17, Minnesota 10**
**January 17, 1988**
**RFK Stadium, Washington, D.C.**
**Attendance: 55,212**

## Resilient Green Assures Redskins Another Trip to Super Bowl

Will he or won't he play?

That question dominated the news in the nation's capital in the days leading up to the Redskins-Vikings NFC championship game at RFK Stadium.

The person in question was Redskins All-Pro cornerback Darrell Green, who damaged rib cartilage on his dramatic

---

## Green's Theatrics

NFL Films President Steve Sabol compared Darrell Green's dramatic punt return to a play in 1962 when hobbling Green Bay Packers linebacker Ray Nitschke intercepted a pass against Detroit and limped across the goal line to score.

"It's an example of the resolute spirit, determination and courage of a single player, a Hall of Fame player," Sabol said of Green's return. "A play like that is a blend of so many things, of historical relevance, of romance, of drama. It's a moment you hand down from generation to generation, sort of a precious heirloom."

punt return for a touchdown in Washington's playoff win over Chicago. He would be sorely needed to shut down the Vikings' dangerous wide receiver, Anthony Carter, who led the NFL in 1987 with a league-high 24.3-yard reception average.

Not only did Green play, but he produced his second straight clutch performance. Carter caught seven passes for 85 yards, but Green, having taken a pain-killing shot just before kickoff, held Carter in check by preventing any game-breakers. The cornerback with world-class speed also broke up a fourth-down pass at the goal line with less than a minute left, a memorable play that preserved the Redskins' 17–10 lead and sent them to Super Bowl XXII.

The entire Redskins defense played superbly: two goal-line stands that held the Vikings to three points, eight sacks, and 76 yards rushing. The unit also compensated for an offense that struggled.

"We ran the ball very efficiently that day," Redskins offensive tackle Joe Jacoby recalled. "We were going up and down the field and getting inside the 20s, but we couldn't punch it in. But our defense hung in there and gave us big plays, especially the one at the end that preserved the victory."

The Vikings had been the surprise of the playoffs. Despite entering the postseason with the worst record among all playoff teams at 8–7, they upset the Saints, 44–10, and the 49ers, 36–24. Carter caught 16 passes for 306 yards in the two wins. He also returned a punt 84 yards for a touchdown against New Orleans. (Minnesota's win over the 49ers allowed the Redskins to host the championship game.)

Knowing that Green would be lining up against Carter and that he'd been injured the week before, the Vikings planned to pick on him, according to Minnesota quarterback Wade Wilson. "We wanted some plays where we'd run at him, and he'd have to make tackles, and we'd get him beat up a little bit," Wilson said. "We also wanted to let Anthony work on him one-on-one."

The Vikings opened by holding the ball for eight minutes and moving to the Redskins' 33 before being forced to punt. The Redskins immediately drove 98 yards in eight plays, and quarterback Doug Williams hit running back Kelvin Bryant for a 42-yard scoring pass.

While the Vikings failed to generate any offense against a swarming and blitzing defense, the Redskins' offense also sputtered. Kicker Ali Haji-Sheikh missed 38- and 47-yard field goals, and Williams had trouble connecting with receivers; he was 4 of 14 in the first half. Such inconsistency allowed the Vikings to hang around, and Wilson's 23-yard scoring pass to wide-out Leo Lewis tied the game at 7 just before halftime.

Williams continued to misfire in the second half on an offense that produced one three-and-out series after another, prompting boos from the home crowd of 55,212. Gibbs said later that he never considered replacing Williams with Jay Schroeder.

Meanwhile, the Redskins' defense forced the game's only turnover. Linebacker Mel Kaufmann intercepted a tipped pass to set up Haji-Sheikh's 28-yard field goal for a 10–7 Redskins lead with 4:30 left in the third period. The Vikings responded by driving to a first-and-goal at the 3. But that reliable defense stiffened and on third down from the 1, linebacker Neal Olkewicz stopped running back D. J. Dozier for no gain. The Vikings decided not to go for it, and Chuck Nelson's 18-yard field goal created a 10–10 game.

Williams then found his mark on a 70-yard, eight-play march. He hit receiver Gary Clark for 43 yards to set up his 7-yard touchdown pass to Clark that put Washington ahead, 17–10, with five minutes left.

But the Vikings drove 60 yards to the Redskins' 6, where two straight incomplete passes created a fourth-and-4 with less than a minute left. The boisterous RFK crowd, which had been drowning out Wilson's signals, rose to a fever pitch. As for the defense, "We weren't doing a lot of talking," Green remembered. "This was our season to go to the Super Bowl, and we didn't want overtime. I expected the ball to go to Carter. I'm thinking, 'You ride the horse that brought you here.'"

Wilson dropped back to pass and fired the ball to running back Darrin Nelson, an excellent receiver, on the far left around the goal line. The pass hit Nelson in the chest, but Green arrived simultaneously and pounded Nelson in the back. Nelson looked like he was losing control of the pass, but Green's hit disrupted the ball enough to where it hit the ground.

An ecstatic Green bolted upfield holding his hand high in triumph. The Redskins bench and the delirious home crowd erupted. Gibbs, kneeling on the sidelines just before the snap with his head down, said Green answered his prayers.

The win assured that Williams would become the first black quarterback to start in a Super Bowl—but the veteran, who completed 9 of 24 passes for 119 yards, felt dejected.

"I was sitting in the locker room with my head hung down, and [offensive assistant] Dan Henning came to me and said, 'Remember, Doug, I'm up in the stands, I'm watching you,'" Williams recalled. "He said he saw how many balls I threw away and how many times I avoided a sack. He remarked that I had no interceptions and two touchdown passes, and we won."

Williams had every reason to hold his head high two weeks later.

| | | | | | |
|---|---|---|---|---|---|
| Minnesota— | 0 | 7 | 0 | 3 | — | 10 |
| Washington— | 7 | 0 | 3 | 7 | — | 17 |

Wash — Bryant 42 pass from Williams (Haji-Sheikh kick)
Minn — Lewis 23 pass from Wilson (C. Nelson kick)
Wash — FG Haji-Sheikh 28
Minn — FG C. Nelson 18
Wash — Clark 7 pass from Williams (Haji-Sheikh kick)

## SUPER BOWL XXII
**Washington 42, Denver 10**
**January 31, 1988**
**Jack Murphy Stadium, San Diego**
**Attendance: 73,302**

### Redskins Crush Broncos with Spectacular Offensive Show

Lightning struck in the form of burgundy and gold on January 31, 1988. Those who witnessed it saw a remarkable chapter in football history.

In the most breathtaking display of offensive firepower in Super Bowl history, the Redskins erupted for 35 points and 356 yards in less than six minutes in the second quarter. The onslaught obliterated a 10-point Denver lead and catapulted the Redskins to a 42–10 rout in Super Bowl XXII—Washington's second Super Bowl victory in the 1980s.

"They looked like a juggernaut, a machine," said Frank Herzog, the Redskins' radio play-by-play man at the time. "It was just a field day, it was like a scrimmage. The precision was unbelievable. They were so stunned by the Broncos in the first quarter, then everybody got nervous and went to work and, boom, it was over. It was like checkmate, and we had a half to play."

Washington's triggerman was quarterback Doug Williams, who orchestrated one of the greatest individual feats in NFL championship-game history. He threw for a Super Bowl–record 340 yards and four touchdowns and walked away as the unanimous choice as MVP.

But it was no one-man show. On an offense that posted a Super Bowl–record 602 yards, rookie running back Timmy Smith ran for 204 alone, another all-time Super Bowl high. Smith, making his first career start, averaged a whopping 9.3 yards per carry, time after time running through enormous holes opened by the Hogs, who toyed with the Broncos' much smaller defensive front and gave Williams airtight pass protection. Second-year Redskins receiver Ricky Sanders caught nine passes for a Super Bowl–record 193 yards, including 80- and 50-yard touchdown throws from Williams. Ironically, Williams, Smith, and Sanders weren't starters when the season began.

Plus, a stellar defense bewildered Broncos star quarterback John Elway, who had a forgettable game. The future Hall of Famer completed 14 of 38 passes for 257 yards with three interceptions. Denver rushed for 97 yards.

Elway's subpar performance ran counter to the media's portrayal of him during Super Bowl week. The quarterback with a history of pulling off dramatic wins such as the 1986 AFC championship game, when he brought the Broncos from behind and made himself famous with "The Drive," was described by media as the second coming. A headline in the *Washington Times* asked, "Are there any flaws in Elway's game?"

The focus on the less celebrated Williams centered on his being the first black quarterback to start in a Super Bowl. A media contingent in the thousands fed off the storyline like sharks and asked him repeatedly about how it felt to have the unique opportunity. One reporter even asked whether he had always been a black quarterback, though, thinking back, Williams said that reporter was probably referring to how long he had been known as a black quarterback.

Herzog compared Williams's situation to being in a "pressure cooker." But Williams handled the questions with grace and dignity, stressing his role as the Redskins' quarterback, not as a black quarterback. "Everything before the game was black," he said. "But when the game came, it was time to strap it on and do what we came to do. I was there for the game, and I had finally made it."

The drastic size difference between the teams was another popular pregame topic. The Redskins' starting offensive line, which averaged about 6–4, 280 pounds and stood as the heart of their power running game, dwarfed the Broncos' defensive front, which relied on finesse, speed, and a lot of shifting. The scenario resembled the Hogs' huge size advantage over the Dolphins' defensive line in Super Bowl XVII. The Redskins felt they could simply outmuscle the Broncos, who were keenly aware of the size discrepancy.

## Entering the Record Books

The Redskins set 19 Super Bowl records and tied 10 others in Super Bowl XXII. Almost all of them were connected in some way to their 35-point second quarter. Among the records set:

- Most total yards (602)
- Most yards passing (Doug Williams, 340)
- Most yards rushing (Timmy Smith, 204)
- Most yards receiving (Ricky Sanders, 193)
- Most yards gained in one quarter (356)
- Most points scored in one quarter (35)
- Most yards passing in one quarter (Doug Williams, 228)

Records tied:

- Most touchdown passes (Doug Williams, four)
- Most touchdowns receiving (Ricky Sanders, two)
- Longest pass completion and longest reception (80 yards, Williams to Sanders)
- Most rushing touchdowns (Timmy Smith, two)

"I had my family out to dinner, and I remember seeing one of the Redskins' offensive linemen that night," Broncos safety Tony Lilly said. "I went, 'My God, we have nobody even close to that size, and he's enormous.'"

The Broncos came roaring out before 73,302 fans at Jack Murphy Stadium in San Diego and the worldwide TV audience. On the first play from scrimmage, Elway tossed a 56-yard touchdown pass to rookie Ricky Nattiel, one of the Broncos' talented receiving trio dubbed the "Three Amigos." On a trick play on Denver's next drive, running back Steve Sewell threw a 23-yard pass to Elway to the Redskins' 13, setting up a field goal that created a 10–0 game.

If that wasn't enough of a scare for the Redskins, Sanders fumbled the ensuing kickoff, igniting a mad scramble for the ball deep in his own territory. The Broncos claimed to have it, but officials ruled that Redskins linebacker Ravin Caldwell made the recovery. "I felt like we recovered the ball, but we were overruled," Broncos coach Dan Reeves said years later.

Despite the reprieve, Washington still trailed by 10 points to a team sporting the AFC's top-ranked offense, which possessed quick-strike capability in Elway and company. The Redskins had faced a similar deficit a few weeks earlier against Chicago in frigid conditions but fought back to win. What were they thinking this time?

"When we got down, 10–0, there was no real panic on our faces," Redskins receiver Gary Clark said. "It was like, 'Let's go buckle up and play.'"

Said Williams, "We felt as long as we didn't make any mistakes, we were going to come back. And if you can come back in 13 below, there's no reason you can't come back in 85 degrees."

The Redskins first had to deal with the loss of Williams, who suffered a hyperflexed left knee late in the first quarter

Redskins receiver Ricky Sanders set Super Bowl records for receiving yards (193) and touchdown catches (two). Here, he races to the end zone to complete an 80-yard touchdown reception that ignited the Redskins' 35-point explosion in the second quarter.

while setting up in the pocket. He limped off the field writhing in pain, and backup Jay Schroeder came in for two uneventful plays. After a quick Denver possession, the Redskins took over on the Broncos' 20 with Williams back calling the signals.

Williams had been anxious to return, partly owing to his disdain for Schroeder stemming from the NFC championship game the year before. "I remember that game like it was yesterday," Williams said. "Schroeder got hit, he was woozy, and [Redskins coach] Joe Gibbs was sending me on the field. Schroeder waved me off. We got beat, 17–0, but we still had a quarter to go. There was no telling what could have happened."

What happened next in Super Bowl XXII transformed the Broncos and their sea of orange-clad fans into one despondent group. On the Redskins' first play of the second period, Williams executed a play-action pass to freeze Denver's defense and aimed the ball down the right sideline to Sanders, who caught it around midfield and outraced Lilly and cornerback Mark Haynes into the end zone to complete an 80-yard play. Williams struck again four minutes later with a 27-yard scoring pass to a diving Clark in the end zone. After Smith found a

monstrous hole off-tackle on the Redskins' popular Counter-Trey play and ran 58 yards for a touchdown, Williams found Sanders for another score, this time on a 50-yard bomb. He closed the quarter with an 8-yard touchdown pass to tight end Clint Didier.

In less than six minutes of possession, the Redskins had gone from 10 points down to 25 points ahead. Smith ran the ball five times in the quarter for 122 yards, an unbelievable 24.2-yard average. Williams set a single-quarter Super Bowl record with 227 passing yards and tied Super Bowl marks with his four touchdown passes and 80-yard pass to Sanders. His surgical accuracy left many in awe, including Redskins Hall of Fame quarterback Sonny Jurgensen, who provided radio color analysis on the game.

"Nobody goes into a game realizing you're going to be that hot with the ball," Jurgensen said. "He was just in one of those grooves where everything he threw was on the button and everybody was playing well around him. He got into a zone where he couldn't miss anything."

Lilly agrees. He remembers Williams' precision on his 50-yard scoring pass to Sanders, a play preceded by the

Previously unknown running back Timmy Smith ran through the Broncos' defense for a Super Bowl-record 204 yards.

quarterback's gorgeous fake to Smith on the Counter-Trey, which befuddled the Broncos all game. "I bit on it hard," Lilly said. "I was 5 yards from the line of scrimmage when I realized, 'Man, [Smith] doesn't have the ball.' I just remember running down the field in pursuit of Sanders, and I knew Doug hadn't thrown the ball yet. All I remember thinking is, 'Overthrow him, overthrow him, overthrow him.' Then I was like, 'Unbelievable, he put it right on the dime.'"

To Redskins offensive tackle Joe Jacoby, a rock on an offensive line that blew the Broncos off the ball, the Redskins' second quarter consisted of "magical moments when things happen perfectly."

"Eighteen plays, five touchdowns, 356 yards total offense in a quarter," Jacoby said in amazement. "Some teams don't even do that in one game. We did it in one quarter. It's just hitting the right plays against the right defense, one after another. It was uncanny."

With the halftime margin at 25 and the Broncos demoralized, the game was over for all intents and purposes. Washing-

As the Redskins' offense built a huge lead over Denver, the defense went wild on John Elway. Here, linebacker Monte Coleman harasses the Broncos' quarterback.

ton stuck to a ball-control offense in an anticlimactic second half, when Williams threw only eight passes and Smith capped the scoring with a 4-yard touchdown run early in the fourth quarter. The Redskins' defense unloaded on Elway, who scrambled for cover play after play and was sacked five times that day. Any remaining juice in the Broncos was squeezed out, and they went down in their second Super Bowl defeat in two years.

"We were just better," Clark said in a matter-of-fact tone. "Quite frankly, we knew it, they knew it, everybody should have known it."

A few days later, more than 600,000 Redskins fans jammed Pennsylvania Avenue in D.C. to honor their heroes in a victory parade. Redskins coaches and players also appeared at a White House ceremony hosted by President Reagan, who had some flattering words for his hometown football team.

"The Redskins didn't simply enter the history books Sunday night, they re-wrote them," the president proclaimed. "Fellows, what else is there to say but hail to the Redskins."

| | | | | | | |
|---|---|---|---|---|---|---|
| Washington— | 0 | 35 | 0 | 7 | — | 42 |
| Denver— | 10 | 0 | 0 | 0 | — | 10 |

Den —— Nattiel 56 pass from Elway (Karlis kick)
Den —— FG Karlis 24
Wash — Sanders 80 pass from Williams (Haji-Sheikh kick)
Wash — Clark 27 pass from Williams (Haji-Sheikh kick)
Wash — Smith 58 run (Haji-Sheikh kick)
Wash — Sanders 50 pass from Williams (Haji-Sheikh kick)
Wash — Didier 8 pass from Williams (Haji-Sheikh kick)
Wash — Smith 4 run (Haji-Sheikh kick)

| Team Statistics | Wash | Den |
|---|---|---|
| First Downs | 25 | 18 |
| Total Yards | 602 | 327 |
| Rushing Yards | 280 | 97 |
| Passing Yards | 322 | 230 |
| Passes | 18–30–1 | 15–39–3 |
| Sacks Allowed | 2–18 | 5–50 |
| Return Yards | 57 | 106 |
| Punts–Average | 4–37.5 | 7–36.1 |
| Penalties | 6–65 | 5–26 |
| Fumbles–Lost | 1–0 | 0–0 |
| Time of Possession | 35:15 | 24:45 |

## RUSHING

Washington—Smith 22–204, 2 TDs; Bryant 8–38; Rogers 5–17; Clark 1–25; Griffin 1–2; Williams 2–2; Sanders 1–4
Denver—Lang 5–38; Elway 3–32; Winder 8–30; Sewell 1–3

## PASSING

Washington—Williams 18–29–340, 4 TDs, 1 INT; Schroeder 0–1
Denver—Elway 14–38–257, 1 TD, 3 INTs; Sewell 1–1–23

## RECEIVING

Washington—Sanders 9–193, 2 TDs; Clark 3–55, 1 TD; Warren 2–15; Monk 1–40; Bryant 1–20; Smith 1–9; Didier 1–8, 1 TD
Denver—Jackson 4–76; Sewell 4–41; Nattiel 2–69, 1 TD; Kay 2–38; Winder 1–26; Elway 1–23; Lang 1–7

## PROFILE

### Jack Kent Cooke: Shrewd Redskins Owner Made Major Impact on the Sports World

Jack Kent Cooke often prevailed when he met a business challenge. The dynamic entrepreneur epitomized a winner.

When he died in 1997 at age 84, Cooke held a spot in America's highest brackets of wealth, with estimated holdings of $1 billion. His fortune stemmed from success with radio and cable TV stations, newspapers, real estate interests, and pro sports teams such as the NBA's Los Angeles Lakers, the NHL's Los Angeles Kings, and the Washington Redskins.

The Redskins created the most enduring piece of his sports legacy. He served as the franchise's majority owner from 1974 to 1997, a period when the Redskins reached the playoffs 10 times and won Super Bowls in the 1982, 1987, and 1991 seasons.

During Cooke's tenure, the Redskins had great coaches in George Allen and Joe Gibbs and a host of talented players. But without the owner's fierce desire to win and marvelous business and leadership traits, huge success might have been unattainable. The Redskins lost money while playing at RFK Stadium, one of the NFL's smallest venues, but Cooke showed a willingness to shell out huge contracts for a team that often carried one of the league's highest payrolls—if he thought doing so would produce victories.

Case in point: Cooke paid Doug Williams nearly $1 million for a two-year contract in the mid-1980s, then a jaw-dropping sum for a backup quarterback. Williams reciprocated by leading the Redskins to a win in Super Bowl XXII. In 1988, Cooke paid Bears free-agent linebacker Wilber Marshall $6 million over five years, making him the highest-paid defensive player in NFL history at the time. Marshall helped key a dominant defensive performance in the Redskins' win in Super Bowl XXVI.

"There will always be a certain group of NFL owners more dedicated to winning than being a financial success," Gibbs said. "Mr. Cooke was more dedicated to winning. If you convinced him that this player is what it would take to win a Super Bowl, he was going to get him, because I don't think he wanted you to have any excuses. He was going to give you every single thing that he felt made good sense that you requested."

Cooke was also happy to let Gibbs and general managers Bobby Beathard and Charley Casserly run the team. "Mr. Cooke was a really tough guy to work for but a great owner," Beathard said. "I liked him, Joe liked him, and we got along with him. We said, 'Mr. Cooke, let us do it our way. If it works, great, if it doesn't work, fire us.' That was the only thing we asked, and he always did that. He was terrific."

Cooke showed a special touch when motivating his coaches, players, and extension staff, emphasizing the positive during tough periods.

"He was at his best when times were at their worst," Gibbs said.

The Squire

"He'd come to me, and I'd be thinking, 'I'm going to get myself chewed out here.' Instead, he'd say to me, 'We're going to bounce back from this. I know what happened.' His encouragement in those situations made me feel great.

"He understood people, and he understood how to motivate people. He was one of the best analyzers of people I've ever been around. You handle people differently ways to get the most out of them. He was very good at that. He knew what made me tick, and he knew what made Bobby Beathard and Charley Casserly tick. He knew how to motivate and hit on the right subjects at the right time."

Cooke's people skills helped make him a fabulous salesman, and he radiated with an entrepreneurial spirit starting in his childhood. Born on October 25, 1912, in Hamilton, Ontario, he grew up in an upper-middle-class home. But when the Great Depression hit in 1929, his family encountered tough financial times. He dropped out of high school to work and vowed to make lots of money.

"That he had the nerve to believe this possible . . . when fear and a 'give-up' mood had struck most North Americans, and when 25 percent of all Canadians were unemployed, is a testament to the spirit of optimism

---

### Cooke Not Short on Words

Jack Kent Cooke, a voracious reader, was an urbane speaker who articulated pithy quotes. Case in point: After the Redskins beat the Dolphins in Super Bowl XVII, he proclaimed, "I am in a state of ecstasy. Never mind that nonsense about euphoria and so on. It is sheer, unadulterated, uncompromising ecstasy."

## Jack Kent Cooke: Shrewd Redskins Owner Made Major Impact on the Sports World—*continued*

Cooke's box at RFK Stadium regularly featured a Who's Who from high society. In the front row here is Cooke's wife, Marlena Cooke (farthest to right), Vice President Dan Quayle (next to Marlena Cooke), and Sen. George Mitchell (fifth from left). In the second row is U.S. federal judge Stanley Sporkin (second from left), author Larry L. King (third from left), Marriott International CEO Bill Marriott (third from right), and Redskins general manager Charley Casserly (second from right).

he had always shown," Adrian Havill wrote in his 1992 book, *The Last Mogul: The Unauthorized Biography of Jack Kent Cooke.*

Cooke became a self-made success. He went from hustling money at a Toronto racetrack to selling encyclopedias and soap. He was also fascinated with the radio business and, on a sales trip, he met the owner of a tiny radio station in Ontario, Roy Thomson, who hired him in 1937 to manage a sister station for $25 a week. Through ingenuity and perseverance, Cook made the station profitable. "Dad fell in love with the station because he loved the attention and glamour of the entertainment industry," said his son, John Kent Cooke, a long-time Redskins executive under the elder Cooke. "He realized that radio in those days was the be and end all."

Cooke and Thomson invested in stations together, and Cooke went out on his own and bought a Toronto station that became a broadcasting powerhouse. He was a millionaire by age 30.

Meanwhile, Cooke expanded his business empire through the sports industry, which had always intrigued him. In 1951, he bought the Toronto Maple Leafs, a minor league baseball team that went on to win four International League pennants. The *Sporting News* once named him Minor League Executive of the Year. After gaining U.S. citizenship in 1960 and moving to Los Angeles, he bought a 25 percent interest in the Redskins for $350,000 and gradually increased his stock in the team. "I like the sport, I like the city, I like everything about the Redskins," Cooke once said.

Cooke's main concentration was on the West Coast. He paid $5.2 million for the Lakers in 1965, then the highest price ever for an NBA team, and bought the expansion Kings a year later. He insisted that both

teams play in a modern sports palace and, despite resistance from city officials, he privately financed a $16 million arena in Inglewood, California, called the Forum. It opened in 1967. Back East, he promoted the first blockbuster fight between Muhammad Ali and Joe Frazier in 1971 at Madison Square Garden, paying each boxer $2.5 million, an outrageous figure at the time.

Cooke became the Redskins' majority owner in 1974 after buying enough stock in the organization. But NFL cross-ownership rules barred him from managing the team because of his interests in the Lakers, who won an NBA championship in 1972, and the Kings. After selling both teams and the Forum, Cooke bought a 51-acre estate in the picturesque, rolling hills of Upperville, Virginia, about 45 minutes outside Washington, and took full control of the Redskins' day-to-day operations from team president Edward Bennett Williams.

Cooke was then an obscure figure in the nation's capital. But the flamboyant tycoon soon became synonymous with money and power in a city with lots of it. A workaholic who admired the saying by legendary baseball executive Branch Rickey that "luck is the residue of design," he made investments that elevated his wealth to meteoric levels. He bought Elmendorf Farms, the famous thoroughbred horse racing and breeding farm in Kentucky; the Los Angeles *Daily News;* and a chunk of land in downtown Manhattan. He paid $1.155 billion to buy cable television stations. His returns on those investments were huge, and he reached a reported value of as high as $1.2 billion. *Forbes* magazine once rated him 170th among the 400 richest Americans.

His professional endeavors, combined with a stormy personal life featuring five marriages to four

## Jack Kent Cooke: Shrewd Redskins Owner Made Major Impact on the Sports World—*continued*

different women, including one who spent time in jail for conspiring to import cocaine into the United States, made Cooke a source of curiosity. Nattily attired and sporting his trademark wraparound sunglasses, he could be seen observing his Redskins from the owner's box at RFK Stadium.

The box featured a cross-section of politicians, military officers and renowned journalists, among other celebrities who yearned to be in the company of Cooke, a social icon. Names like political columnist George Will, Reagan administration official Bob Bennett, Senator Eugene McCarthy, CIA director Richard Helms, CBS reporter Leslie Stahl, General Colin Powell, and author Larry L. King frequented the box. An occasional invitee was Maryland Senate president Thomas "Mike" Miller, Jr., who once flattered Cooke by telling him, "There's probably 40,000 people who look up at you in the box."

"No, all 58,000 look up," Cooke responded with his customary vanity. "I'm part of the show."

As Miller put it, "Jack Kent Cooke had a flair about him, very cosmopolitan in terms of his dress, in terms of his speech, his homes in D.C. and Virginia. The Redskins had suffered for decades under [owner] George Preston Marshall's tight fistedness or absentee ownership. So when [Cooke] took over the Redskins and opened his wallet and put a quality team on the field, he became a hero to Redskins fans, who suffered for many years."

Cooke, a nominee for entry into the Pro Football Hall of Fame in 1996, was an eternal optimist and workaholic who loved life. He would say, "This is the greatest day in the history of the world, even better than yesterday, though yesterday seemed an impossibility." He said in his latter years that he didn't plan to die.

Age caught up with him, though, and he passed away from heart failure at age 84 in the library of his D.C. home on April 6, 1997.

"Jack Kent Cooke will be remembered as one of the premier owners in NFL history and one of the great sportsmen and entrepreneurs of American business," NFL Commissioner Paul Tagliabue said at the time. "A self-made man of wide-ranging talents, Jack Kent Cooke loved the game, loved to win, and knew how to field a winner."

## 1988: 7–9, 3RD PLACE (TIE)—NFC EAST

### Head Coach: Joe Gibbs

After winning a Super Bowl in such a devastating fashion, after making a bold move to acquire a big-time impact linebacker in the off-season, and after opening the year with what seemed like their running back of the future, the 1988 Redskins did what few could have imagined: They flopped.

The Redskins finished 7–9, the only losing record in Joe Gibbs's first coaching stint in Washington. Contributing to the fall was a rash of injuries that affected virtually every position on the team, the league's worst turnover ratio at minus 24, and an unbalanced offense with an inept running game.

"We had our worst season the year after a Super Bowl-winning season," Gibbs said. "I had no indication anything was going to happen other than a return trip to the Super Bowl."

Super Bowl XXII hero Doug Williams said that the Redskins entered the season aiming for another Super Bowl ring: "You've got to be. When you go to camp with that ring on, you want another one at the end of the year. But things happen where you get derailed. Everybody's gunning for you once you get to the top; it's hard."

Williams and second-year man Mark Rypien alternated at quarterback, with Williams starting 10 games and Rypien 6. They combined to set team records for passing yards (4,136), attempts (592), completions (327), passing first downs (202), and touchdown passes (33).

If only the running game were that productive! No Redskin rushed for more than 500 yards, and of the team's 289 nonpenalty first downs, only 87 were on the ground. The bruising, grinding running game—a trademark of Gibbs's early Redskin teams—no longer existed. Second-year man

Timmy Smith, who exploded onto the scene with 204 yards in Super Bowl XXII, proved to be a one-game wonder. He gained 470 yards on 155 carries (3.0 average) with three touchdowns. Such low numbers stemmed from injuries and his questionable work ethic, and the Redskins left him unprotected after the season under the new Plan B free agency system.

Heading into the season, in contrast, the Redskin were eyeing Smith as the team's next great running back. They also acquired what seemed to be their next great linebacker in a blockbuster deal, offering Bears free agent Wilber Marshall—a consensus All-Pro in 1986 and an intimidator in the mold of the Giants' Lawrence Taylor—an astounding five-year, $6 million contract. The Bears didn't match the offer and received Washington's No. 1 draft choices for '88 and '89 as compensation.

The transaction, which made the Redskins the first team since 1977 to lure a veteran free agent from another squad, marked a new chapter in the NFL free-agent bidding war that would escalate in a few years. At the time, Redskins general manager Bobby Beathard was concerned about the league-wide ramifications of the deal. "We certainly wanted Wilber, but we didn't want to upset the league and start something that was wrong," Beathard said in retrospect. "But it was inevitable that [current-day] free agency was coming."

On the quarterback front, the aging Williams underwent surgery to repair a bum left knee and also battled a bad back, but Cooke rewarded him for his performance in Super Bowl XXII with a three-year contract worth more than $3 million, and Gibbs tapped him as the starter over the disgruntled Jay Schroeder, who threw for more than 4,000 yards in 1986 but took a back seat to Williams at the end of the 1987 campaign.

## PROFILE

### Bobby Beathard: "The Standard of GMs"

He didn't fit the portrait of an NFL general manager. That blond, pageboy haircut, that playful smile, that California surfer-boy image, that laid-back, soft-spoken demeanor, and work attire that often consisted of short-sleeved shirts, shorts, and jogging shoes.

That innocent appearance belied the real Bobby Beathard, a magician when it came to making player personnel decisions and uncovering talent, some of it in the most obscure places. It's no stretch to say he was perhaps the best ever at his craft. In a career that spanned four decades, he was a player personnel executive on teams that made seven Super Bowl appearances.

His era of greatest fame was as the Redskins' general manager from 1978 to 1989, a stretch when they played in three Super Bowls and won twice, XVII and XXII. The *Sporting News* named Beathard NFL Executive of the Year in those two Super Bowl-winning seasons. The Redskins also captured Super Bowl XXVI with a squad heavily assembled on Beathard's watch. "In the NFL, there's no Midas, just Beathard," the Redskins once wrote of their astute personnel man.

"He's the best general manager in the history of the National Football League," said former Redskins general manager Charley Casserly, who was on Beathard's staff for 11 seasons in Washington. "I was lucky enough to work for people like him. Bobby was a great human being, excellent eye for talent, very easy to get along with, would listen to you, encouraged you to have your own opinion. He would think outside the box and was very aggressive in his way of doing things."

Said former Redskins star receiver Gary Clark, "He's the standard of GMs. If every other GM could have the type of illustrious career Bobby Beathard had, you'd be talking about them."

Clark, who played for a Division I-AA college football program and was not picked in the primary NFL draft in 1984, was one of the diamonds in the rough unearthed by Beathard. He helped find many others in low-round draft picks, unheralded free agents, and USFL refugees. He also located talent in Canada. (In those days, free agents were mostly undrafted players discarded by other teams.) In essence, Beathard loved to take chances and gamble.

"Certain scouts and people who go out looking at talent just have a certain knack," said Joe Jacoby, an obscure free agent who signed with the Redskins in 1981 and went on to a star-studded career at right tackle on offense. "It doesn't mean he was always right. But he was more right than wrong in picking up those diamonds in the rough who panned out. He would go to obscure places and look for players and find them. I was one of them. Bobby was just uncanny how he could pick out those players."

Beathard's key strategies included swapping a high draft pick for several on the lower end. "If there were a lot of good players in the draft, we felt we could afford to trade down a little and take a lower pick in the second round, or give up a first rounder to get more picks," Beathard said. "There were some years when we'd do it, and things didn't fall the way we anticipated, and it didn't work out. It was a calculated risk, and for the most part it worked."

Among Beathard's acquisitions that didn't work out were wide receiver Malcolm Barnwell, obtained in a 1985 trade from the Raiders for a No. 2 pick, and San Diego State cornerback Tory Nixon, the team's top draft pick that year.

In his remarkable NFL journey, Beathard also worked in the front office in Kansas City, Miami, San Diego, and Atlanta. He was a scout for a Chiefs team that lost to Green Bay in Super Bowl I; the player personnel director for a Dolphins squad that captured two Super Bowls in the early 1970s, including a win over the Redskins in Super Bowl VII; and the general manager for a Chargers team that lost to San Francisco in Super Bowl XXIX.

The El Segundo, California, native once aspired to play pro football. After quarterbacking Cal Poly-San Luis Obispo to 9–1 records in 1957 and 1958 while rooming with John Madden, now a long-time NFL television color analyst and former Oakland Raiders coach, Beathard signed with the Redskins in 1959. Ralph Guglielmi and 5–7 Eddie LeBaron were the top quarterbacks on the roster. "Eddie LeBaron was shorter than I was," said Beathard, who stands about 5–9. "He helped me, and then they moved me to safety, which I liked better."

Beathard didn't make the team but signed in 1960 with the Los Angeles (now San Diego) Chargers of the new American Football League. He was cut again but benefited from his experience. "I loved it," he said. "I was there for six preseason games, got to play a lot, then got cut. [Long-time Oakland Raiders owner] Al Davis was our receivers coach, [pro football legend] Sid Gillman was the head coach, so I met a lot of people in football who enabled me later on to have an opportunity to get into it."

Beathard began his front-office career as a part-time scout for the Chiefs in 1963. He joined the Falcons in 1968 as a scout, and the Dolphins in 1972.

In Miami, Beathard made personnel decisions that helped elevate the Dolphins to preeminence. In becoming Washington's general manager in 1978, he already had a reputation as one of the best personnel men in the business. "He has compiled a record that is without equal in the NFL for finding and signing talent," Redskins President Edward Bennett Williams said at the time.

Beathard put his stamp on the Redskins. Of the 49 players on the Redskins squad that won Super Bowl XVII in January 1983, 35 arrived over the three most

## Bobby Beathard: The Standard of GMs—*continued*

Beathard, with coach Joe Gibbs (left) and other members of the Redskins' staff, works his magic on April 26, 1983, draft day. In the first round, the Redskins chose a little cornerback out of Texas A&I, Darrell Green, who ended up playing 20 seasons in Washington.

recent seasons. That team consisted of 26 free agents, and 11 Redskins were drafted in the fifth round or lower. Moreover, of the Redskins on their Super Bowl-winning roster in 1987, only defensive tackle Dave Butz wasn't a Beathard acquisition.

"It was fun working for Bobby Beathard," said Kirk Mee, a player personnel expert and scout on Beathard's staff. "He was the same personality every day, whether we won or lost. He made our meetings enjoyable and created a very positive atmosphere. He had that façade of being nice, but underneath if he didn't think a player,

assistant coach, or scout was doing his job, he'd get him out of there. Everybody worked hard because they wanted to please Bobby."

Beathard left the Redskins in May 1989. Most recently, he served as a consultant to the Falcons and retired after the 2003 campaign at age 67.

"It's been a lot of fun," Beathard said of his career as an NFL executive. "I've been really fortunate to be able to be in the right spot a lot of times where we've enjoyed a lot of success. I've been around a lot of great people."

---

Schroeder said he wanted to be traded before the 1988 season: "Yes, because coach Gibbs decided after the Super Bowl that he was going to go with Doug. In the beginning, he said he was going to give me a shot in training camp, but that didn't come true, and I wanted a chance to play and continue my career, so I asked to be traded. I was frustrated, the coaching staff was frustrated with me."

The press circulated all kinds of rumors of a pending trade, with the quarterback-hungry Raiders leading the list of takers. Schroeder hung on through the exhibition season and backed up Williams, but he was booed at RFK Stadium by Redskins fans, who disliked how he pouted after he was benched and considered him a pariah. A *Washington Post* headline read, "Before the Infection spreads, release or quarantine Schroeder."

"We agreed we wanted to trade him," Beathard said. "He was very talented but didn't seem to fit in people-wise. The guys never hung around him. We knew he had talent, but there was no charisma."

A deal was made on opening day. The Redskins traded Schroeder and some conditional draft picks to the Raiders for All-Pro offensive tackle Jim Lachey. Rypien, who played well in Washington's 3–1 exhibition season, was now Williams's backup.

The Redskins looked like Super Bowl champions in the first half of their Monday night season opener against the Giants in the Meadowlands. Dominant on both sides of the ball, they took a 13–0 lead on two field goals by Chip Lohmiller, the team's top draft choice in 1988 (second round), and Williams's 29-yard touchdown pass to receiver Ricky Sanders.

The Giants tied the game at 13 in the third period, and Redskins' miscues decided the game in the final quarter. New York blocked a punt and ran the ball in for a touchdown with about 10 minutes to play. Later, Giants linebacker Pepper Johnson sacked Williams and forced a fumble that lineman Jim Burt recovered and ran with for a touchdown to secure the 27–20 win.

## PROFILE

### Charley Casserly: Living Your Dream

If you're looking for a Horatio Alger story in the NFL, look no further than Charley Casserly.

It was 1977, and Casserly was a teacher and the head football coach at Minnechaug High School in Massachusetts. Eager to move up in coaching, he sought a college position, with no success. He also wrote to each of the 28 NFL teams hoping to obtain a low-level coaching position, thinking that doing so would create a bridge to a college job.

Two teams offered interviews: the Patriots and the Redskins.

"I ended up coming to the Redskins with [coach] George Allen," Casserly said. "The deal was work for a year for nothing and, after a year, get hired for $10,000. They had done this with other people before, some they hired, some they didn't. I just looked at it as the opportunity of a lifetime."

Casserly started before the 1977 season as a gofer, answering phones and breaking down tapes, among other tasks. All the while, his survival skills were tested."To put things in perspective," Casserly said, "I lived in the YMCA in Alexandria [Virginia] for $8 a night. I'm 28, not married, I've got $500 in the bank, I've got a car with 120,000 miles on it. Two years before that, I was renting the third floor in a three-family house. The house burned down, and I lost everything I owned. Had no insurance."

Casserly persevered. He eventually became a full-time scout, then assistant general manager. He earned the grand prize—promotion to the Redskins' GM slot—when Bobby Beathard stepped down before the 1989 season.

Casserly served as general manager for the next 10 seasons, overseeing personnel decisions in the Redskins' 1991 Super Bowl-winning year. He began as general manager of the expansion Dallas Texans in 2002 and stayed with them through the 2005 season.

Now, that's one rags-to-riches story.

Casserly (center) watches practice with Redskins owner Jack Kent Cooke (left) and general manager Bobby Beathard.

The Redskins rebounded with two wins at RFK, 30–29 over the Steelers on Lohmiller's 19-yard kick with 12 seconds left and 17–10 over the Eagles. After throwing 102 passes in total against the Giants and Steelers, Williams toned things down against Philadelphia, when Smith posted his second 100-yard rushing game.

Williams subsequently underwent emergency appendectomy surgery, clearing the way for Rypien to start. The Redskins dropped two in a row—the latter a heartbreaking 24–23 loss to the Giants in which Lohmiller missed an extra point and shanked a 36-yard field goal with less than two minutes left—to fall to 2–3. By then, Washington's running game was

## Bugel and Petitbon: Cream of the Redskins' Assistant Crop

They were icons on Joe Gibbs's coaching staff, two assistants who were so instrumental to the Redskins' rise to glory: Joe Bugel and Richie Petitbon.

Bugel, the Redskins' offensive line coach from 1981 to 1989, is most famous for molding the Hogs into the most dominant offensive line of the era. He helped make legendary Redskins running plays such as "50 Gut" and "70 Chip" work to perfection. Animated and vocal, he ran intense practices and taught exceptional run- and pass-blocking techniques.

He was an "outstanding coach," said offensive tackle Joe Jacoby, one of the original Hogs. "Great motivator, a very thorough technician. It was almost like being on the Radio City Rockettes because all of us had to step with the right foot on whatever play was called. That's how meticulous he was in going through the films and grading us."

Petitbon was the brains behind the Redskins' defense for all 12 years of Gibbs's first coaching regime in D.C., holding titles ranging from defensive coordinator to assistant head coach–defense. While Gibbs concentrated on running the offense, Petitbon called the shots for defenses that normally ranked among the best in the league and pulled out a host of critical games.

"Richie Petitbon was a very good guy," defensive tackle Dave Butz said. "Very creative, very knowledgeable, very dedicated to the game. He did an outstanding job."

Said defensive end Dexter Manley, "You have to give credit to Richie Petitbon. He was the defensive man."

Joe Bugel (right) and head coach Joe Gibbs are all smiles after the Redskins sealed a critical 30–28 win over Dallas late in the 1984 season. Bugel was one of Gibbs's top lieutenants in the 1980s.

Bugel and Petitbon advanced to become head coaches. Bugel was head coach of the Phoenix Cardinals for four seasons (1990–94), finishing 20–44. After two years as an assistant with the Raiders, he served as Oakland's head coach for one season and went 4–12. He returned to Gibbs's staff in Washington in 2004 and is on it today. Petitbon, a four-time All-Pro safety who played 14 seasons, the last two with Washington in the early 1970s, was named Redskins head coach after Gibbs retired in March 1993. He went 4–12 that season and was fired.

Other assistants on Gibbs's staff for all of most of his first stint in Washington included

1. Don Breaux (running backs)
2. Warren "Rennie" Simmons (primarily tight ends)
3. Charley Taylor (wide receivers)
4. Larry Peccatiello (linebackers)
5. LaVern "Torgy" Torgeson (defensive line)
6. Wayne Sevier (special teams)

Petitbon, holding the game ball after a Redskins win over the Giants that clinched the NFC East title in 1983, was integral to the Redskins' stretch of dominance in the 1980s and early 1990s.

not producing, so Smith was yanked as the featured back and replaced by the elusive Kelvin Bryant, who proved to be the quintessential all-purpose threat:

- 118 yards rushing, 82 receiving, and three touchdowns in a 35–17 win over Dallas
- 73 yards rushing, 68 receiving in a 33–17 win over Phoenix
- 140 yards rushing, 70 receiving in a 20–17 win over Green Bay

In four games as the starter, the 6–4, 232-pound Rypien had looked like the next Johnny Unitas. He completed 70 of 116 passes (60.3 completion percentage) for 1,075 yards, with 12 touchdowns and four interceptions. He injured his ribs late in the Phoenix game, and Williams returned to start against the Packers.

Beating Green Bay left the 5–3 Redskins tied atop the NFC East with New York. But they lost six of their last eight games starting with a 41–14 pounding at the hands of the Oilers. They rebounded by beating New Orleans on a late field goal but suffered a major loss when their offensive machine—Bryant—experienced a season-ending knee injury. Then came a three-game losing streak that crippled the Redskins' playoff chances.

Meanwhile, the injury bug was everywhere. The defensive ends, cornerbacks, linebackers, and offensive line had all been hit hard. Guard Mark May was the only Hog to start every game, and he and defensive end Charles Mann were the only Redskins to make the Pro Bowl. Washington was also committing turnovers and making mental mistakes at an alarming rate.

Williams and Rypien, for their part, were playing musical chairs under center, but there was no open controversy or feuding. A T-shirt depicted the quarterbacks as cartoon characters, with Rypien saying "I'm for Mark" and Williams saying "I'm for Doug." The words "United We Stand" surrounded the cartoons.

The Redskins remained on life support for a playoff berth with a 20–19 win over the Eagles. After Rypien tossed three interceptions, Williams entered and completed 20 of 32 passes for 206 yards and a touchdown. Lohmiller's 44-yard field goal with one second left clinched the victory, his third game-winner of the season. But the Cowboys, riding a 10-game losing streak, killed any playoff hopes with a 24–17 win.

In a 20–17 loss to Cincinnati in the season finale, Lohmiller's 29-yard field goal try in the closing seconds hit the upright—a fitting end to a frustrating year. "When teams don't gel, you don't win, and we didn't gel well," Williams said.

## 1989: 10–6, 3RD PLACE—NFC EAST

### Head Coach: Joe Gibbs

"Discouraging" is too soft a term to describe the Redskins' losses in their first two games in 1989. They were backbreakers.

After a 52-yard field goal on the final play accounted for a 27–24 loss to the Giants, the Redskins blew an 11-point lead in the fourth quarter and were victimized by a freak play that lifted the Eagles to a 42–37 victory.

The defeats staggered the Redskins, who struggled for two-thirds of the season and stood 5–6 at one point. Despite winning their last five games and finishing as one of the hottest teams, they were eliminated from playoff contention in the next-to-last week. It was the second straight year the Redskins missed the playoffs.

"Anytime you open with the Eagles and Giants in the NFC East and lose, you're behind the eight ball," Redskins quarterback Mark Rypien said. "No matter what you do at the end, you're still going to be in a situation where if it's down to a tie or something like that, then they have the upper hand. Those were tough losses to open the season."

The Redskins still put an exciting product on the field. They sported the NFL's No. 1 passing offense and set a team record for total yards (6,253) that stands. The leader of the powerful attack was Rypien, who matured into one of the league's top quarterbacks in his first full year as a bona fide starter and earned his first invitation to the Pro Bowl. He passed for 3,768 yards, the Redskins' second-highest total ever at the time, completing 280 of 476 throws (59 completion percentage), with 22 touchdowns and 13 interceptions.

On the receiving end, Art Monk, Gary Clark, and Ricky Sanders each totaled more than 1,000 yards in catches, the second time in NFL history three players on the same team accomplished that feat. The receiving trio, newly nicknamed the "Posse," caught 245 passes and 21 touchdowns. Running back Earnest Byner hauled in an extra 54 balls.

Byner and fellow running back Gerald Riggs arrived in a major off-season deal intended to resuscitate one of the league's worst rushing games. On draft day, general manager Bobby Beathard gave Atlanta the Redskins' second-round pick in 1989 and first-round pick in '90 for Riggs, a 6–1, 230-pound battering ram who had posted three 1,000-yard seasons, including a 1,719-yarder. His ability to wear defenses down gave the Redskins a weapon they had lacked since John Riggins retired after the 1985 season. Beathard also traded running back and kick returner Mike Oliphant, Washington's third-round pick in 1988, to Cleveland for Byner, a one-time 1,000-yard rusher. A *Washington Post* headline read, "Redskins Get a Run for Their Money."

Beathard pulled off another shocker a few weeks later by announcing his resignation after 11 seasons as the Redskins' GM. Media reported that he stepped down because he was at odds with coach Joe Gibbs over player personnel decisions. Beathard denied it at the time, saying he wanted to move to his native Southern California with his wife, Christine.

At one point, Redskins owner Jack Kent Cooke tried to entice him to stay, Beathard remembers. "I guess Mr. Cooke didn't want me to leave. He gave me an envelope and said go home and show Christine. I guess it was an offer I couldn't refuse. But I never opened the envelope. I'd already decided I was leaving, and I gave it back to him unopened." Assistant general manager Charley Casserly was tapped to replace Beathard.

By the start of training camp, the Redskins' quarterback position was in for a shakeup. Doug Williams, soon to turn 34, could not participate because of a lower back injury. (He later had surgery for a herniated disk.) Rypien thus earned the top job and started four games in Washington's 4–1 exhibition season. Second-year man Stan Humphries, the Redskins' sixth-round pick in 1988, started the other game and looked erratic.

## NFC East: The Real Black-and-Blue Division

The NFC East was by far the best division in football from 1986 to 1990, a period when the Redskins, Giants, and Eagles took turns beating up on each other at the same time they were threats to win the division. Something was often at stake when the I-95 foes collided, making for one intriguing Sunday after another. Toss in the Cowboys, who were under .500 each season during the period but rarely made it easy for the Big Three.

"Coming out of the Eastern Division, you had us, the Giants, Dallas, and Philadelphia. Those were some bruising people," Redskins defensive tackle Dave Butz said. "They didn't just like to play football, they liked to play a physical game of football."

New York won two Super Bowls and the Redskins won one during the five-season stretch. But the Giants, then led by one of the all-time coaching greats in Bill Parcells and equipped with a ferocious defense, beat Washington nine of 11 times; the Redskins' only two wins were in the 1987 strike-shortened season. Even more puzzling, the Giants won one nail-biting game after another by scores of 24–23, 27–20, 27–24, 20–17, and 24–20. The Redskins seemed jinxed.

"They had great teams, and we had very good teams," Joe Gibbs said. "We seemed to play some of our absolute best games against them and still lose. It seemed that no matter how hard or how good we played, it came down to some really close finishes, and we lost a bunch of them. They were tough on everybody. It was hard to beat them."

Said Redskins defensive end Dexter Manley, "The Giants had our number. The 'tuna' [Parcells] wasn't doing anything special, I can guarantee you that. It's just that they were a better football team than we were personnel-wise. We were staying with some guys for too long."

In contrast, New York split 10 games with the Eagles, who matched up well with the Giants because of a nasty and intimidating defense of their own shaped by coach Buddy Ryan. That same defense took no mercy on the Redskins, but Gibbs beat Ryan 8 of 11 games in the five-year period, including once in the playoffs.

"It was very unsound what Buddy did," long-time *Sports Illustrated* NFL writer Paul Zimmerman said of Ryan's defense. "[Opponents] would be shaking their heads while they're getting oxygen or an iron lung because he wanted to hurt people. Parcells called it Neanderthal football."

Like the previous season, the Redskins opened on a Monday night against the Giants, this time at RFK. New York held a 14–3 lead at the half, but the Redskins climbed back, and linebacker Monte Coleman's interception and 24-yard return for a touchdown gave Washington a 24–21 lead in the fourth quarter. But Giants kicker Raul Allegre booted two late field goals, including a 52-yarder on the last play to account for the Giants' 27–24 victory.

Washington amassed 457 yards of offense, 111 on the ground by Riggs. But the man reputed to be a nonfumbler put the ball on the ground twice. His fumble the next week against the Eagles resulted in a catastrophe at RFK. The Redskins built a 20–0 first-quarter lead. But Philly chipped away behind an All-Pro performance by quarterback Randall Cunningham, who posted team records in completions (34) and passing yards (447) to go with five touchdown passes, one of which cut the lead to 37–35 with 1:48 left.

Riggs, who rushed for a team-record 221 yards that day, ran 58 yards to the Eagles' 22 on the next possession, apparently icing the win. But he fumbled a few plays later after bumping into center Raleigh McKenzie. Linebacker Al Harris picked up the ball, and, while being pulled down, shoved it to defensive back Wes Hopkins, who raced 77 yards down the sideline to the Redskins' 7. Cunningham then found tight end Keith Jackson alone in the back of the end zone for the winning score in what *Philadelphia Daily News* sportswriter Ray Didinger described as a "ridiculous, amazing, preposterous comeback win."

The Redskins committed six turnovers in all.

"We were just icing it at the end of the game, and Gerald Riggs fumbled the ball," said Gibbs, sounding mystified even years later. "That ball was one foot from going out of bounds, and they picked it up. It's unbelievable. That was one of the toughest losses I've ever had. We had more than 400 yards of offense and lost the game."

Washington won four of its next five to improve to 4–3, only to suffer two demoralizing losses. In a 37–24 loss to the Raiders, the Redskins committed eight turnovers, drew 135 yards on 12 penalties, rushed for 21 yards, and yielded seven sacks. Rypien fumbled on four of those sacks as part of his tendency to show butterfingers after being hit in the pocket.

The next week against the 0–8 Cowboys at RFK, Williams, who started in place of Rypien, completed 28 of 52 passes for 296 yards. But he threw two picks and couldn't engineer a touchdown drive in a 13–3 loss. Dallas running back Paul Palmer, a graduate of nearby Winston Churchill High School in Potomac, Maryland, rushed for 110 yards and scored the game's only touchdown on a 2-yard run.

While the Cowboys celebrated what would be their only win of the season under first-year coach Jimmy Johnson, Gibbs was steaming, according to Redskins radio color analyst Sam Huff. "I can remember only one time when Gibbs lost his temper during an interview," Huff said. "I said, 'Coach, you just lost to an 0–8 team.' Holy cow, when you say the coach blew one he should have won. Oh man, he just let it all out. He said, 'I told everybody, I told everybody that Dallas was a good team. I told you, Sam, Dallas was a good team. You didn't believe me, I told you.'

"I said in a very calm voice, 'Joe, they were 0–8 coming in here against you, how good could they be?'"

The 4–5 Redskins rebounded with a 10–3 upset of the Eagles. Williams's back pain resurfaced, however, and Rypien

In 1989, Redskins receivers Ricky Sanders (83), Gary Clark (84), and Art Monk (81), a.k.a. "The Posse," each totaled more than 1,000 receiving yards.

returned to start a Monday night game against the Broncos, who dealt Washington another maddening defeat. Denver, playing without superstar quarterback John Elway, exited with a 14–10 victory. Career backup Gary Kubiak threw two scoring passes, and rookie Bobby Humphrey rushed for 110 yards.

The loss left the 5–6 Redskins lunging for answers to the incredibly inconsistent play that had plagued them through the first 11 games. Of the Redskins' six losses, four were by three points or less and two were decided in the last minute. Injuries were piling up, and such starters as guard Mark May and cornerback Darrell Green were out for the season. Riggs had been hobbled by injuries after rushing for 332 yards in the first two games. (Cornerback Barry Wilburn and defensive end Dexter Manley missed time because of drug-related suspensions.) The playoffs were a remote possibility.

"You have to understand the high standards that Joe Gibbs and Redskins football had," Rypien said. "At that point, the frustration level was very high because a lot was expected of us. When you win Super Bowls and championships, anything less is unacceptable."

Looking for a spark, Gibbs called The Posse into his office and asked them to step up. They did, and the passing game ran like a machine over the final five games, when Monk, Clark, and Sanders caught 89 balls for 1,334 yards and eight touchdowns. "There's no doubt, those guys in their prime were as good as anyone," said Rypien, who sizzled during the five-game winning streak by completing 65 percent of his passes for 1,430 yards, with eight touchdowns and four interceptions.

The defense contributed to the streak, too, by allowing an average of 15 points. The season ended with a 29–0 win over a Seattle team in playoff contention, the Redskins' first shutout since 1984.

## 1990: 10–6, 3RD PLACE—NFC EAST

### Head Coach: Joe Gibbs

The scenario was disconcerting: three straight seasons without the playoffs, three straight years of organizing vacations instead of vying for another Super Bowl victory.

The Redskins were eyeing that possibility after a loss to Dallas left them at 6–5 with five games left in the 1990 campaign. They could perhaps sneak in at 8–8, given that the NFL had added a third wild card team per conference that season. Before even thinking that far, though, they needed to balance out their inconsistent offensive attack.

Consider this: Washington rushed 14 times for 36 yards against the Cowboys, while quarterback Mark Rypien threw passes as if his life depended on them—a career-high 54 to be exact. The one-dimensional approach touched a nerve in Redskins coach Joe Gibbs, according to offensive line coach Jim Hanifan.

"I remember on the plane [home], Joe says to me, 'I'm going to guarantee you one thing. We're going back to Redskins football,'" Hanifan said. "He had gotten caught in that atmosphere of throwing the ball every down, and that nothing's good unless it's a 20-, 25-yard gain. True as it was, that next week when we played a really good Dolphins team, it was back to the Redskins' style of football that Joe had put in there a long time ago with John Riggins. We pounded the living heck out of Miami, and we started becoming a little more of a balanced team."

The "John Riggins" that day and in the coming weeks was Earnest Byner, who averaged 121 yards and 28 carries in the last five regular-season games. The Redskins captured four of those, including victories over playoff-bound Miami, Chicago, and Buffalo, which eventually reached Super Bowl XXV.

The inspiring finish earned the 10–6 Redskins a playoff berth. They defeated NFC East-rival Philadelphia in the wild card game before losing to San Francisco in the second round. Despite the loss, the foundation was set for what would be a Super Bowl-winning season in 1991.

"I think 1990 was a big year for us because all of a sudden we had a great running back in there in Earnest Byner," Hanifan said.

Byner, who rushed for a career-high 1,219 yards to finish second in the NFC behind Detroit's Barry Sanders, made the Pro Bowl in 1990, as did Redskins left tackle Jim Lachey, wide receiver Gary Clark (team-high 75 catches, 1,112 yards, eight touchdowns), and cornerback Darrell Green.

Rypien, who recorded respectable numbers despite missing six games due to injury (166 of 304, 2,070 yards, 16 touchdowns, 11 interceptions), entered the season as the starter after Gibbs did some reshuffling at the position. In the off-season, the coach named the up-and-coming Stan Humphries as Rypien's backup and signed a relic off the Plan B free-agency system as the third-stringer, 33-year-old career journeyman Jeff Rutledge.

But Gibbs refused to protect Doug Williams, who missed nearly the entire '89 season due to back problems, and placed him on Plan B. No team signed the 34-year-old Williams, and the Redskins opted not to renew the third and final season of his $1.2 million annual contract, ending his four-year stint in Washington.

Williams said the dismissal was the only time he felt a strain in his relationship with Gibbs since the two first worked together in Tampa Bay in 1978. "[Gibbs] said he was going in a new direction with the young quarterbacks, which I had no problem with," Williams recalled. "But he brought in Jeff Rutledge, who was a year younger than me. I could have been third string. So is he going young? Let Mark compete, let Stan Humphries play, but keep Doug Williams in case they can't play."

On the coaching front, Redskins offensive line coach Joe Bugel, famous for coining the term "Hogs," bid farewell to become head coach of the Phoenix Cardinals. The Redskins hired Hanifan, an assistant coaching colleague of Gibbs with St. Louis in the 1970s and another master offensive line coach, to replace Bugel.

The Redskins gave Bugel a nasty homecoming reception in the season opener at RFK Stadium—as in 31–0. Rypien threw three touchdowns as part of his 17 of 31, 240-yard day, and the defense forced five turnovers, including safety Alvin Walton's 57-yard interception return for a touchdown.

But the Redskins began sputtering. In addition to a 26–13 spanking at the hands of the defending Super Bowl champion 49ers, who gained nearly 500 yards, the Redskins endured their fifth and sixth straight losses to the Giants, as late turnovers spoiled excellent winning opportunities. New York improved to 7–0 with its second victory over the Redskins, who fell to 4–3.

The Redskins were staring at .500 when they trailed Detroit, 35–14, in the third quarter at the Silverdome. Gibbs tapped Rutledge to replace Humphries, who had been under center since Rypien suffered a knee injury in a win over Dallas in week 3. Humphries had looked dreadful at times, throwing three interceptions in both losses to the Giants and three against the Lions before being yanked.

Rutledge crafted the game of his life. He completed his first eight passes as part of a 30-of-42, 363-yard performance. His 34-yard scoring pass to Gary Clark on a fourth-and-6 with 5:48 left cut the Lions' lead to 38–31. Not known for his running ability, he scooted 12 yards for a touchdown on a quarterback draw with 18 seconds left. Lohmiller's conversion tied the game at 38.

In overtime, Rutledge's 40-yard pass to Art Monk on a third-and-15 from the Redskins' 5 sparked a 73-yard drive that ended on Lohmiller's 34-yard field goal. It climaxed a marathon contest that left both sides physically and emotionally spent—one in which the Redskins impacted the record books:

- They tied the NFL record for first downs (39).
- They set a team record for yards (674) and completions (43), and tied the team record for passing attempts (63).
- Their 21-point deficit tied the greatest comeback in Redskins history set against the Cowboys in 1965.
- Receiver Art Monk tied his team record for receptions (13).

Rutledge was chosen NFC Offensive Player of the Week. With the Redskins back on track at 5–3, Gibbs named him

to start for a Monday night game against the 4–4 Eagles in Philly. This time he played like a true career backup: erratically. In his defense, he was under constant harassment from a fierce Eagles defense. In the third quarter he fumbled after being hit hard, and defensive lineman Clyde Simmons returned the ball 18 yards for a touchdown to put the Eagles up, 21–7.

Rutledge injured his thumb on the play and left the game, one of the Redskins' many headaches on a night when the Eagles' defense pounded them into submission. Nine Redskins, most of them on offense, were forced out with injuries. "I remember the crowd going crazy and several of our guys getting wiped out and pulled off the field, and the Eagles' fans just loving it," Hanifan said.

Rutledge's replacement, Humphries, left the game with an injured knee, and rookie running back Brian Mitchell, an option quarterback in college, finished the game under center. He scored on a 1-yard run late in the fourth quarter, but it wasn't enough in a 28–14 loss that left the Redskins black and blue. A *Philadelphia Daily News* headline the next day read, "Skins Out Cold."

"It was a horrendous day," Redskins head trainer Bubba Tyer recalled. "We were out on the field at least 10 times to attend to somebody. You can go a whole game and never go out on the field."

Tyer remembers receiving advice from Eagles safety Andre "Dirty" Waters: "He told me as I was standing over somebody, 'You'd better get some body bags, you'd better get these guys off the field, you'd better get more buses to get them back home.' He's cussing and hollering and using foul language at us, and all of a sudden another Eagle is kneeling next to us and praying and putting his hands on one of my players trying to heal him. I look over and it's [superstar defensive end] Reggie White," an ordained minister.

The evening thus became known as the "body bag" game. "Body bag was big," Gibbs said. "We got whipped about as solidly that day as any good football team I've been a part of. That was a very, very one-sided game. It was not good, it was not a happy deal."

The Redskins, tied for second in the NFC East with Philly at 5–4, remained solidly in the running for a wild card spot, but they were still being written off. A *Washington Times* headline read: "Redskins Have Become Lost Cause." Gibbs, for his part, administered a private butt-kicking to his troops and challenged them to play better with New Orleans coming to RFK.

Rypien returned to start and showed no signs of rustiness despite his six-game layoff. He completed 26 of 38 passes for 311 yards with four touchdowns in a 31–17 victory over the Saints. Byner rushed for 166 yards to become the first Redskins back to top the 100-yard mark that season.

Then came the extreme offensive lopsidedness in the 27–17 loss to the Cowboys, and Washington was 6–5 with five games to play. The situation was similar to the year before, when the 5–6 Redskins teetered on the brink of playoff elimination before winning their last five games.

This time, they held a players-only meeting the night before the next game against the 9–2 Dolphins, and Byner approached Gibbs requesting a heavier rushing load. Washington's other key running back, Gerald Riggs, was out with a nagging arch injury. "I listened and agreed with Earnest," Gibbs said in the Redskins' 1991 yearbook. "In truth, if Earnest didn't get it done, there was no one else to turn to."

The 5–10, 215-pound Byner was the *man*. He rushed

- 32 times for 157 yards and three touchdowns in a 42–20 rout of a Dolphins team with the league's No. 1 defense
- 28 times for 121 yards in a 10–9 win over the Bears
- 39 times for 149 yards in a 25–10 win over New England
- 31 times for 154 yards in a 35–28 loss to Indianapolis

The loss to the Colts, coupled with an Eagles victory, left Washington and Philly tied at 9–6 while they jockeyed for the top two wild card spots. A first-round playoff clash appeared inevitable. They won their season-ending games, the Redskins 29–14 over Buffalo and the Eagles 23–21 over Phoenix, but Philadelphia was assured home-field advantage by virtue of a better division record than Washington.

Even so, the Redskins had a chance to gain revenge against those big, bad Eagles, who had rubbed it in a few weeks prior. Is it just the matchup the Redskins wanted? "Absolutely," Redskins safety Brad Edwards recalled. "It's hard to beat a good team twice, so we felt like the odds certainly were in our favor. Philadelphia had an absolutely phenomenal defense, but we felt like we could scheme well enough to score enough points. I felt ultimately we could stop their offense."

## NFC WILD CARD GAME
**Washington 20, Philadelphia 6**
**January 4, 1991**
**Veterans Stadium, Philadelphia**
**Attendance: 65,287**

### Redskins Avenge Bitter Loss to Eagles, Embarrass Buddy

Super Bowls, conference and division championships, and many other epochal moments were produced by the Joe Gibbs-coached Redskins.

In terms of the most emotional victories of the era, Washington's 20–6 first-round playoff win over the Eagles on their home turf ranks right up there. The triumphant Redskins exorcised their demons from that horrific night nearly two months before, when the Eagles pummeled them in the infamous "body bag" game.

"That's about as excited as our football team had been in a while," Gibbs said. "It stemmed more from having your rear end kicked. When you get your clock cleaned like that, all we had to do was show the film. Probably the biggest motivating factor is to whip somebody really good, and they'll remember it."

The 20–6 shocker wasn't even that close. Redskins defensive coordinator Richie Petitbon devised a scheme that befuddled the Eagles' offense and its magician-on-feet, quarterback Randall Cunningham, who was sacked five times. Redskins quarterback Mark Rypien, not sacked at all, picked apart Philly's ferocious defense at just the right times. The Redskins' workhorse in the latter part of the regular season, running back Earnest Byner, accounted for 126 total yards.

The Eagles did their share of chest-thumping in the days prior, thinking they would obliterate the Redskins for the second straight time. Brash and bombastic Eagles coach Buddy

Ryan mouthed off. He predicted that Byner, whose late fumble had likely cost the Browns the 1987 AFC title game against Denver, would cough up the ball three times. When informed by the press at Redskin Park of Ryan's comment, the dignified Gibbs refused to respond.

"That was the big difference between Buddy and Gibbs," said Ray Didinger, a *Philadelphia Daily News* sportswriter who was there at the time. "Buddy tried to win the game from Monday to Friday, as much as he tried to win it on game day, and Joe understood better than anybody that what you said [during the week] didn't matter."

The Redskins' players also kept quiet and waited to strike while the Eagles' mouths were hot. In the early minutes, Cunningham hit tight end Keith Jackson for a 66-yard gain to the Redskins' 11. Washington's defense stiffened, and linebacker Monte Coleman sacked Cunningham for a 10-yard loss on third down, forcing Philly to settle for a field goal. In the second period, the Eagles recovered a fumble by running back Gerald Riggs and took possession on the Redskins' 25. Philadelphia moved to the 2, but the defense again held. Another field goal made it 6–0.

Rypien subsequently shifted into gear. He hit receiver Art Monk on a third-and-9 for 28 yards to the Eagles' 39. After connecting with Byner for 23 yards, Ryp found Monk for a 16-yard touchdown. Lohmiller's conversion put Washington up, 7–6, about six minutes before halftime.

After regaining possession, the Redskins drove deep into Eagles territory, where Rypien connected with Byner in the flat for about 10 yards. When Philly cornerback Ben Smith flipped Byner over, he fumbled upon hitting the ground, and Smith picked up the ball and ran 94 yards for a touchdown. Suddenly, Buddy looked like a genius.

But wait. The officials reviewed the play on tape and ruled that Byner's knee had hit the ground before he fumbled, sending the Eagles and their fans into a rage. Lohmiller hit another field goal to make it 10–6 at halftime.

"That's one of those momentum things where you think, 'Oh, no, this is the play they've been looking for,' Redskins offensive tackle Jim Lachey said. "You didn't want those guys to get hot all of a sudden and start feeling good about themselves. If that would have gone the other way, it would have been much more of a dogfight the rest of the game."

In the third quarter, Lohmiller was true again from close range to put the Redskins up, 13–6, while Cunningham continued to struggle against Petitbon's defensive scheme that swarmed him with blitzing and shut down his receivers, prompting Ryan to make a controversial move. The coach benched Cunningham and put in veteran Jim McMahon, who threw three incomplete passes. Rypien iced the victory on the Redskins' next possession with a 3-yard scoring pass to Gary Clark for a 20–6 lead.

Cunningham returned in the fourth quarter, but the defense kept up the pressure. And although retribution was nearly at hand, the Redskins refused to taunt. Offensive line coach Jim Hanifan remembers a few players, including guard Russ Grimm, walking on the sidelines saying, "Nobody say anything bad. Let's not even talk about it."

In the postgame locker room, NFL Films caught Gibbs imploring his troops to "win with style." His adversary, Ryan, a loser of three straight opening-round playoff games, was fired a few days later.

| Washington— | 0 | 10 | 10 | 0 | — | 20 |
| Philadelphia— | 3 | 3 | 0 | 0 | — | 6 |

Phil —— FG Ruzek 37
Phil —— FG Ruzek 28
Wash — Monk 16 pass from Rypien (Lohmiller kick)
Wash — FG Lohmiller 20
Wash — FG Lohmiller 19
Wash — Clark 3 pass from Rypien (Lohmiller kick)

## NFC DIVISIONAL PLAYOFF GAME
## San Francisco 28, Washington 10
## January 12, 1991
## Candlestick Park, San Francisco
## Attendance: 65,292

### Redskins Fall in Day of Missed Opportunities

For one quarterback, it resembled a typical day at the office. For another, it was a day of cruel disappointment.

Displaying surgical precision, San Francisco's Joe Montana completed 11 of 13 passes for 192 yards on three first-half touchdown drives. The Redskins' Mark Rypien, on the other hand, was intercepted three times in the second half—twice in the end zone—with his team in possession inside the 49ers' 20.

Final score: 49ers 28, Redskins 10.

"When you're playing against a great offensive team, and you get some opportunities to score and you don't, you know it's going to come back and haunt you," Redskins offensive tackle Jim Lachey said. "You get 14, 17 points out of that, it's a different ball game. When you don't take advantage of them, the defense gets momentum, the offense and the fans are back into it, and you don't win."

With the win, the 49ers beat Washington for the fifth time in the last six games that the two teams had met. Their most recent victory was a 26–13 thumping early in the 1990 season, when Montana passed for 390 yards and two touchdowns. By season's end, he was named league MVP for the second straight year.

But word had it that this Redskins team, victorious in five of its last six games, including an emotionally charged win over the Eagles in the wild card game, was better prepared to face the 49ers. A *Los Angeles Times* headline read, "It's No Shoo-In for 49ers," while *USA Today* announced, "More intense Redskins team ready for formidable 49ers."

The Redskins scored a touchdown on their first drive, a 74-yard, eight-play march capped by Rypien's 31-yard touchdown pass to receiver Art Monk (10 catches, 163 yards). The 49ers responded with their own eight-play, 74-yard scoring drive that ended on fullback Tom Rathman's 1-yard run.

Chip Lohmiller's 44-yard field goal put the Redskins up, 10–7, but Montana, who had picked apart the Redskins' secondary on his first drive, did it again on an 80-yard march capped by his 10-yard scoring pass to receiver Jerry Rice. The Redskins went nowhere, but a punt pinned the 49ers on their 11. Not a problem for Montana, who directed an 89-yard, five-play drive. He threw completions of 47 and 32 yards, plus an 8-yard scoring pass to receiver Mike Sherrard.

By then, Montana had tormented the Redskins with his coolness in the pocket and pinpoint accuracy. His touchdown

pass to Rice, for example, barely missed the outstretched arm of Redskins cornerback Darrell Green, the four-time NFL's Fastest Man. Afterward, Redskins coach Joe Gibbs told reporters that if the future Hall of Famer had thrown some balls "three inches" either way, Redskins defenders could have made the play.

Washington's defense held Montana to 74 yards passing in the second half and sacked him twice. But the Redskins failed to capitalize on gorgeous scoring opportunities with the ball on the 49ers' 7, 15, and 19. On the first two, Rypien's passes were picked off in the end zone. Redskins linebacker Monte Coleman set up the third opportunity when he intercepted a pass with 10:28 to play and returned it to the 19. Rypien threw four incompletions. On his final pass, 49ers cornerback Eric Davis appeared to interfere with receiver Gary Clark in the end zone but no flag was thrown.

San Francisco nose guard Michael Carter later intercepted a tipped pass and rumbled 61 yards to secure the win.

Did the Redskins have a mental letdown after beating the Eagles?

"My feeling is no, we just played a better football team," Redskins safety Brad Edwards said. "San Francisco had just a phenomenal offensive scheme. They had the right people running the right system, and we were outplayed. They also had an extra week to prepare. It's just tough when you've got to win an extra ball game."

| Washington— | 10 | 0 | 0 | 0 | — | 10 |
| San Francisco— | 7 | 14 | 0 | 7 | — | 28 |

Wash — Monk 31 pass from Rypien (Lohmiller kick)
SF —— Rathman 1 run (Cofer kick)
Wash — FG Lohmiller 44
SF —— Rice 10 pass from Montana (Cofer kick)
SF —— Sherrard 8 pass from Montana (Cofer kick)
SF —— M. Carter 61 interception return (Cofer kick)

## 1991: 14–2, 1ST PLACE—NFC EAST

### Head Coach: Joe Gibbs

Call it the epitome of a dream season, a year when the Redskins could seemingly do no wrong. So flawless in their execution and sporting the team chemistry of champions, they romped through the 1991 campaign en route to winning their third Super Bowl under coach Joe Gibbs.

From opening day, when the Redskins devoured the Lions by 45 points, until their 37–24 pasting of Buffalo in Super Bowl XXVI, Washington barely skipped a beat in a way that was excruciating for opponents. The Redskins captured their first 11 games and finished 14–2 to tie the 1983 squad for the franchise's most regular-season victories ever. They recorded shutouts of 45–0, 34–0, and 23–0, and captured other games by 39, 31, 27, 25, and 21 points.

The bulldozing continued in a postseason when Washington posted three victories by an average of 20 points. The word "awesome" took on a new meaning in the nation's capital, which again reveled in the success of its favorite pro sports franchise, a perfect blend of old, young, athletically gifted and intelligent players, as well as journeymen who filled a specific role.

Safety Brad Edwards (27), outside linebacker Andre Collins (55), and running back Ricky Ervins (32) were three of the more unsung impact players on the Redskins' 1991 Super Bowl-winning team.

"That season was like a dream," Redskins running back Earnest Byner said. "Everything fell into place. Ryp had the great year, the defense was playing great, special teams. It was just there. It was like being on a joy ride."

Ryp—as in sixth-year quarterback Mark Rypien—enjoyed a breakout season. Steady throughout, brilliant at times, and with a beautiful touch on the long ball, he connected on 249 of 421 passes (59.1 completion percentage) for 3,564 yards and 28 touchdowns, with only 11 interceptions. His passer rating, 97.9, was one of the league's best. He was one of a record eight Redskins to make the Pro Bowl.

"I remember [former Redskins] offensive line coach Joe Bugel always saying that our offense is like a Cadillac, and we need somebody to drive that Cadillac," offensive tackle Jim Lachey said. "That's what Mark Rypien was. He distributed the ball, put us offensively in the right situations, and he was smart, being one of 11 instead of trying to carry the team. Don't get me wrong. He was hot and threw some balls like I'd never seen, especially the long ball."

In all fairness, Rypien was protected by a lot of pork that provided airtight pass protection and masked his huge lack of mobility. The Hogs yielded a league-low nine sacks, the fewest in team history, and would have set an all-time NFL record if not for allowing three in a meaningless regular-season finale against the Eagles. Pro Bowlers Lachey and right guard Mark Schlereth, plus the multidimensional Raleigh McKenzie and original Hogs Joe Jacoby, Russ Grimm, Jeff Bostic, and Don Warren, formed an impenetrable wall.

Often, the running backs and tight ends stayed back to protect Rypien, who targeted his throws to the most dangerous wide receiver trio in the NFL—The Posse:

- Art Monk, 71 catches, 1,049 yards, 8 touchdowns
- Gary Clark, 70 catches, 1,340 yards, 10 touchdowns
- Ricky Sanders, 45 catches, 580 yards, 5 touchdowns

"Joe (Gibbs) did a great job of distributing the ball," Clark said. "One week it would be Art, one week it would be Ricky, one week it would be me. It worked out well."

As proficient as the passing game was, the Redskins were much more of a running team. Their strategy was elementary: wear down opponents with a punishing running game that finished among the NFL's best and then cripple them with the pass. Byner led Washington with 1,048 yards, followed by rookie sparkplug Ricky Ervins with 680, most in the second half of the year. Gerald Riggs gained 248 yards and tormented defenses around the goal line with 11 scores. The Redskins posted a league-high 21 rushing touchdowns.

With such a litany of weapons, the Redskins scored a league-high 485 points. Of those, an NFL-best 149 came off the foot of Pro Bowl kicker Chip Lohmiller, who outscored one team all by himself. Second-year man Brian Mitchell, another special teams star, returned two punts for touchdowns.

And how about that "Capital Defense"! The hard-hitting, swarming, opportunistic unit permitted 224 points, second-lowest in the league, and only 41 in the three playoff games. Only five opponents scored more than 20. Cornerback Darrell Green turned in his fifth Pro Bowl season and defensive end Charles Mann his fourth, while second-year linebacker Andre Collins led the team in tackles with 151. Right behind him were linebacker Wilber Marshall and safety Brad Edwards, both with 135.

Then-*Washington Post* Redskins beat writer Richard Justice said that the 1991 Redskins were far from being one of the greatest NFL teams he had ever seen, but there was something special about them. "They probably had one superstar, Gary Clark, and a whole bunch of other guys who did their job," Justice said. "Wilber Marshall was close to being a superstar on defense, and for what Joe asked, Mark Rypien was terrific. They simply functioned as a unit, got going and rolled over people. They had a lot of older guys who were totally committed to the system and to doing what Joe [Gibbs] asked. I think they had three guys all year late for their weight-room appointments. That team had guys like Monte Coleman, Joe Jacoby, Donnie Warren, and Art Monk. Those were classic Gibbs guys."

Those Redskins were components of a solid team that had existed for a decade. The web just needed to be tightened. The off-season saw the arrival of two defensive lineman through trades who would prove valuable—Lions tackle Eric Williams and Steelers end Tim Johnson—and such Plan B free agents as Eagles safety Terry Hoage, Chiefs safety Danny Copeland, and 49ers middle linebacker Matt Millen, an 11-year veteran with three Super Bowl rings. Other newcomers included Michigan State defensive tackle Bobby Wilson, the Redskins' first No. 1 draft pick since 1983, and the third-round pick, Ricky Ervins. The squatty 5–7, 200-pound running back had missed most of his senior year at Southern Cal due to an ankle injury after leading the PAC 10 in rushing as a junior with 1,385 yards.

For the Redskins to be a true Super Bowl contender, however, they needed Rypien to elevate his game. Rypien failed to report to training camp due to a contract dispute, however, prompting team owner Jack Kent Cooke to call him a "bloody idiot."

Ryp was demanding the average annual salary for a starting NFL quarterback of about $1.4 million. The Redskins came in at $2.4 million over three years. After a 10-day holdout, he settled for a base salary and incentives that equaled the going rate—but it was only a one-year contract, meaning he was gambling on having a big season or else.

"It was also an educated guess as far as, 'I feel good, I feel comfortable in this offense,'" Rypien said. " 'Unless something happens injury-wise, let's role the dice and see what happens. If not, it's going to happen somewhere else.' There was no [current-day] free agency then, so I didn't have any bargaining power except to sit out."

After entering camp about 15 points lighter, Rypien played solidly for most of the exhibition season, but the team as a whole was a different story. While the Redskins posted a 1–3 mark that included a 24–21 overtime loss to Cleveland in which they blew leads of 14–0 and 21–14, Gibbs railed over his squad's ineptness. It sounded like his typical paranoia, for the last time Washington had a losing preseason record, 1982, they crafted a Super Bowl–winning season.

This time, were Gibbs's instincts right? You be the judge: The Redskins won their first 11 games.

They debuted with a 45–0 rout of Detroit at RFK Stadium. Everything was clicking. Rypien completed 15 of 19 passes for 183 yards and two touchdowns. Byner ran 16 times for 83 yards and a score, and even completed an 18-yard touchdown pass to Sanders. Clark caught six passes for 107 yards and a touchdown. Green intercepted two passes and the defense held the Lions to 154 yards. Mitchell returned a punt 69 yards for

## *Playboy* Picks the Redskins

*Playboy* magazine is not on the tip of everyone's tongue when predicting which teams will reach the Super Bowl. WTTG-TV-5 sports director Steve Buckhantz referred to the racy magazine, though, while interviewing Redskins coach Joe Gibbs after a 24–21 overtime loss to Cleveland that dropped the Redskins to 1–2 in the preseason. What ensued embarrassed one person and infuriated another. As Buckhantz tells it:

Before the game, I had interviewed [Redskins owner] Jack Kent Cooke in his booth live, and he told me, "This is the best team we've had, I expect them to go to the Super Bowl." So we get into the locker room, and I'm live with Gibbs, and I say to him, "You know, with two weeks to go until the regular season, I'd be concerned if I were the head coach with the way the team has played, especially since everyone is saying this is the best team you've ever had." Well, obviously, you get guys in an emotional state after a game like that, and he wasn't happy.

He said, "Now, wait a minute. Who is everybody?" I said, "A lot of people." He said, "Who's a lot of people?" Not thinking that I had just interviewed his boss three hours before who said he thought they had the best team ever, all I could think about was that I had read *Playboy*'s Pigskin Preview, and they had picked the Redskins to go to the Super Bowl.

I said, "*Playboy*."

He said, "*Playboy, Playboy, Playboy* picking football, take that for what it's worth, Steve. We haven't won a division around here in four years, and I think you have to look at the source. I'm not taking that as a knock on our team. Anybody who wants to say it, they can go ahead and say it. But certainly nobody around here has said it. Right now, we've got real problems." He was as animated as anybody has ever seen him, and his veins were standing out of his neck, and he was mad. Then, he just looked at me, and I finished by saying, "Gotcha."

Of course, they won the Super Bowl in Minneapolis, and I got him after the game and stuck a mike in front of him. He had this grin on his face from ear to ear.

I said, "I hate to say I told you so." He said, "Well, they were right. For the first time, *Playboy* was right. I feel pretty stupid about that [incident]. I was mad at somebody. It might have been anybody I attacked that day. I'll never do that again."

a score, the Redskins' first punt return for a touchdown since 1981.

Washington led, 21–0, at the end of the first quarter, 35–0 at the half, and 42–0 after three periods. The 45 points stands as the largest margin of victory in Redskins history, and it could have easily been more. Gibbs told backup quarterback Jeff Rutledge to take a knee four times when the Redskins had the ball on the Lions' 1 in the game's waning minutes.

"When we came out of that 1–3 preseason, I can remember thinking this might be the worst team I've played on since I've been in the league," said Brad Edwards, then in his fourth season. "We just did not look that great. After we beat Detroit, 45–0, I kind of went, 'Wow, we might be pretty good. Where were these guys for the last six weeks?'"

Then came an early season test on the road against a fast-improving Cowboys team that would finish 11–5 and make the playoffs for the first time since 1985. The Redskins prevailed, 33–31, because Chip Lohmiller converted long field goals like chip shots. He hit 53-, 52-, 46-, and 45-yarders, made three extra points, and boomed kicks out of the end zone in his best game ever as a pro.

The Cowboys took a 21–10 lead with touchdown drives of 80, 80, and 84 yards. But Rypien's 37-yard scoring pass to Monk, plus Lohmiller's 52-yard field goal with eight seconds left in the half, created a 21–20 game. After the teams traded field goals, Mitchell ran 3 yards on a fake punt, keeping an 85-yard touchdown drive alive that put the Redskins up for good, 30–24.

"Gibbs always said there's a moment early in a season when teams either come together or continue to struggle," Justice said. "For that team, I believe it was that win at Dallas that got things going."

Next, the Redskins disposed of Phoenix, 34–0, followed by a 34–27 win over the Bengals, against whom Mitchell returned a punt 66 yards for a touchdown to stake the Redskins to a 24–10 halftime lead. The Bengals clawed back to tie the game at 27, before Riggs ended a late 53-yard drive with his third short scoring run of the day.

The Redskins improved to 5–0 with a remarkable third shutout at RFK, 23–0 over the Eagles. By then, a fortuitous pattern had formed in Washington's favor. All championship teams need luck, and the Redskins were finding it by playing teams without their key players:

- Lions All-Pro running back Barry Sanders missed the game due to injuries.
- Cowboys star running back Emmitt Smith gained 104 yards on his first five carries, including a 75-yard scoring run. But he became dehydrated late in the first quarter and was ineffective for the rest of the game.
- Cardinals starting quarterback Timm Rosenbach missed the game due to injury.
- Eagles starting quarterback Randall Cunningham was out with an injury and his replacement, Jim McMahon, was injured late in the first quarter and lost for the game. Third-stringer Pat Ryan finished under center.

Meanwhile, victories over Chicago and Cleveland lifted the Redskins to 7–0, their best start since 1940. The offense scored on 6 of 11 possessions against the Browns, and Ricky Ervins erupted onto the scene. After replacing the injured Byner in the second half, he gained 133 yards on 13 carries, including a 65-yard scoring run.

The Redskins entered their bye week firmly in control of the NFC East with the season not half over. Gibbs, though, was professing caution. "We'll probably get in trouble if we start thinking that we're a better team than we are," the worrywart told reporters. "Any team can beat us, and we can probably beat any team."

Next up were the defending Super Bowl–champion Giants, who were 4–3 and fighting for a wild card playoff spot. New York had won six straight games over the Redskins, who needed a win if for nothing other than to prove they were legit. Beating the Giants was "definitely one of the litmus tests in the NFC East at the time," Lachey said. "If you wanted to win anything, you had to take care of the Giants, which we weren't doing. Coach Gibbs put a big emphasis on that game. It was tight and hard fought."

New York led at the half, 13–0. Clark dropped a bomb in the second quarter that looked like a sure touchdown and another likely touchdown pass in the end zone in the third period. But he redeemed himself with a 7-yard scoring reception that capped a 20-play, 84-yard drive over 7:55, then a 54-yard scoring catch with 12:50 to play for a 14–13 Redskins lead—one of Rypien's many completions of more than 40 yards on the season. Lohmiller's 35-yard field goal with 51 seconds left ended another beautiful drive—62 yards, 14 plays in 7:43—and accounted for the four-point win.

The Giants' jinx was over. "It was a breath of relief for us to get that monkey off our back and work toward what we wanted: a Super Bowl win," Rypien said.

Now 8–0 for the first time in their 69-year history, the Redskins faced another major hurdle against the 7–1 Oilers led by former Redskins coach Jack Pardee, who returned to RFK for the first time since being fired at the end of the 1980 season. The game was billed as a possible Super Bowl preview.

Washington's impeccable mark appeared in jeopardy when Houston's Ian Howfield lined up for a 33-yard field goal with four seconds to play and the game tied at 13. In another sign of Redskins luck, his kick went wide left. Darrell Green's diving interception of a Warren Moon pass early in overtime set up Lohmiller's game-winning 41-yard field goal.

The Redskins seemed out of sync by committing eight penalties for 69 yards and fumbling three times. But they gained 349 yards against one of the league's best defenses, with Byner rushing for 112 and Rypien completing 21 of 34 passes for 195 yards. Houston gained 267 yards, far below its season average.

Ryp then orchestrated a Tchaikovsky-like performance. He torched a Falcons secondary missing superstar cornerback Deion Sanders with six touchdown passes and 442 yards in a 56–17 demolition. His six touchdowns tied the team record set by Redskins legend Sammy Baugh in 1943 and 1947, and he was 4 yards short of Baugh's record for total yards. Clark caught scoring passes of 61, 19, and 82 yards, and Monk caught 19- and 84-yarders for touchdowns. Washington amassed 559 yards overall.

Next up, Rypien completed 21 of 28 passes for 325 yards and two touchdowns in a 41–14 win over the Steelers that clinched a playoff berth for the 11–0 Redskins. Gibbs said at the time he felt like being on a "dream ride." Were the coach and his players dreaming of a 16–0 mark, which would make them the first team since the 1972 Dolphins with an undefeated regular season?

"There was not a prevalent thought of, 'Hey, we're 11–0, do you know how close we are?'" Edwards said. "It was certainly not talked about inside the locker room."

Dallas put any such thoughts to rest with a 24–21 shocker at RFK in a game that wasn't that close. The Cowboys beat Washington in every phase. They controlled the ball for almost 40 minutes and led 21–7 on backup quarterback Steve Beurlein's 23-yard fourth-quarter touchdown pass to receiver Michael Irvin. By then, Dallas had outgained the Redskins 357 to 107 in yardage.

The Redskins responded with a 92-yard drive that ended on Riggs's 1-yard run, but Dallas drove 58 yards while milking another seven minutes off the clock and clinched the win with a field goal. Emmitt Smith rushed for 132 yards on 34 carries. Irvin caught nine passes for 130 yards while running the Redskins' top cover man, Darrell Green, ragged. Dallas also had its share of luck, converting a successful onside kick and a 34-yard Hail Mary touchdown pass at the end of the first half from quarterback Troy Aikman to receiver Alvin Harper.

The loss "stung," Lachey said. "Eye-opener, a little bit. After winning 11 in a row, you kind of get a feeling of invincibility. After that, we knew that anything can happen in football. It brought us down to earth a little bit knowing that our work is not finished, that we can't just walk out on the field and win."

Such was the case the next week against the 3–9 Rams, who led 7–6 at halftime against a flat Redskins squad. But Gibbs performed his obligatory chair-kicking ritual in the locker room, and his boys got moving en route to a 27–6 win that clinched the NFC East title.

New Orleans was upset the following week, giving the Redskins home-field advantage through the playoffs. They proceeded to trail lowly Phoenix, 14–0, at the half. This time, linebacker Matt Millen did the screaming in the locker room, and Washington woke up for a 20–14 win, followed by a 34–17 victory over the Giants at home, the first time the Redskins had beaten their NFC East rival two times in a nonstrike season since 1983.

Rypien threw three touchdown passes against New York but scared the nation's capital early in the fourth period. Upon delivering a 50-yard scoring pass to Clark, his throwing hand appeared to hit the helmet of Giants lineman Leonard Marshall. Rypien split the nail on his middle finger but X-rays found no break.

Ryp played until early in the second half of the season finale against the Eagles but Gibbs yanked him and many of the other starters for fear of injury. The Redskins nearly pulled this one out, but a 38-yard field goal with 13 seconds left gave Philly a 24–22 victory and ruined the Redskins' shot at joining the 1984 49ers and '85 Bears as the only teams to ever go 15–1 in a 16-game season.

"Quite frankly, we should have been 16–0," said Clark, who made the Pro Bowl for the fourth time. "We were the best team in the league. Of all teams to lose to, it was the Cowboys. We should have won that game. We also lost to Philadelphia. But we'd already lost to Dallas, and the mentality of being 16–0 was already over. Joe wanted to protect some of our players versus the Eagles."

## NFC DIVISIONAL PLAYOFF GAME
**Washington 24, Atlanta 7**
**January 4, 1992**
**RFK Stadium, Washington, D.C.**
**Attendance: 55,181**

### Businesslike Redskins
### "Hammer" Brash Falcons

The Falcons did a lot of pregame trash talking. Cocky and boisterous, they made it clear they were out to avenge their 39-point loss to Washington in November. They sang "To Hell with the Redskins," a twisted version of the Redskins' fabled fight song, "Hail to the Redskins." They sent 47 players out to midfield for the opening coin toss to rattle their opponent.

The Redskins did their talking when it counted, during a 24–7 playoff victory that sent Washington to the NFC championship game.

"I never heard anybody say they were bothered or that we had to pay them back for that," Redskins linebacker Andre Collins said of the Falcons' intimidation tactics. "We were a great team. We had won 14 regular-season ball games, and the two we lost were by a total of five points. We just wanted to take care of business and finish out the season the right way."

In cold, wet, and brutally windy conditions that favored Washington and its versatile running game, the Redskins slashed and slopped through the mud at RFK Stadium for 162 yards. All-Rookie selection Ricky Ervins maneuvered for 104 alone and a scoring run. Gerald Riggs plowed through for two touchdowns. With the Hogs subduing the Falcons' much smaller defensive front, the Redskins methodically controlled the clock for more than 36 minutes while not turning the ball over.

"For an offensive lineman and a Hog, it was perfect weather," Redskins offensive tackle Jim Lachey said.

Atlanta, on the other hand, was handicapped by its run-and-shoot offense, a pass-oriented system difficult to execute in treacherous field conditions. Quarterback Chris Miller threw four interceptions, while the Redskins shut down star receivers Andre Rison and Michael Haynes. The Falcons, who fumbled twice, rushed 14 times for 43 yards and gained only 193 yards of offense. Their loquacious cornerback, Deion Sanders, compared the squad's struggles with the run-and-shoot to having a "gun with one bullet."

The Falcons had promised that this one would be much different from their 56–17 loss to the Redskins on November 10, when Rypien shredded Atlanta's secondary for six touchdowns and 446 yards. Miller missed that game, as did two consensus All-Pros on the Falcons, Sanders and offensive tackle Mike Kenn. Atlanta proceeded to win five of its next six games, including a 27–20 upset of the Saints in the NFC wild card game.

The 12–5 Falcons marched into RFK to the tune of their new theme song, "2 Legit 2 Quit," sung by their No. 1 cheerleader, rapper M. C. Hammer. As Hammer looked on with his buddy, heavyweight boxing champ Evander Holyfield, the first quarter went scoreless. Early in the second period, Ervins ran 17 yards for a touchdown to end an 11-play, 81-yard drive.

Redskins defensive tackle James "Jumpy" Geathers later recovered a fumble on the Falcons' 39, and Riggs rammed into the end zone from 2 yards out for a 14–0 edge.

Atlanta cut the lead to 7 before halftime. The margin could have been wider, but Redskins kicker Chip Lohmiller missed three field goals largely because he couldn't get his footing in the mud. He was true, however, from 24 yards out in the third period, and Riggs's 1-yard run in the fourth behind a convoy of Hogs secured the win.

Suddenly, a seat cushion came flying out of the upper deck of RFK, and before anyone knew it, cushions were raining down on the field in what looked like "huge confetti," Lachey said. The Redskins had given away the seat cushions as part of a promotion.

"The crowd was in a very festive mood, and all it took was one seat cushion coming from the upper deck," Redskins public address announcer Phil Hochberg recalled. "The whole field was littered with them."

Said Lachey, "It was just one of those scenes in your athletic career that you'll never forget."

| Atlanta—    | 0  | 7  | 0  | 0  | —  | 7  |
| Washington— | 0  | 14 | 3  | 7  | —  | 24 |

Wash — Ervins 17 run (Lohmiller kick)
Wash — Riggs 2 run (Lohmiller kick)
Atl —— T. Johnson 1 run (Johnson kick)
Wash — FG Lohmiller 24
Wash — Riggs 1 run (Lohmiller kick)

## NFC CHAMPIONSHIP GAME
**Washington 41, Detroit 10**
**January 12, 1992**
**RFK Stadium, Washington, D.C.**
**Attendance: 55,585**

## Redskins Rout Lions to Advance to Super Bowl XXVI

Emotion can carry a team only so far. The adrenaline-packed Lions had won seven straight games since guard Mike Utley went down with a freak injury that left him paralyzed. Their mantra was, "Thumbs up for Ut."

In the NFC championship game at RFK Stadium, though, the Lions collided with a burgundy-and-gold squad playing near-perfect football. Adios, Detroit. The Redskins deflated their foes, 41–10, to advance to Super Bowl XXVI. It was the second straight week the Redskins annihilated a playoff opponent they had scorched in the regular season.

"We looked at them the same way as Atlanta," Redskins quarterback Mark Rypien said. "We said, 'Hey, we thumped these guys before [45–0], but you see what they did after we thumped them? They came back and played as good as anyone.' The ironic thing was we probably played our best football game when it counted in the NFC championship game."

Rypien completed 12 of 17 passes for 228 yards, with two second-half touchdown passes that broke the game open. The backfield combo of Ricky Ervins and Earnest Byner rushed for 117 yards, and the Redskins' defense subdued the Lions' "Silver Stretch" run-and-shoot offense, the second straight week

defensive coordinator Richie Petitbon had derailed the gimmicky system. Lions quarterback Erik Kramer completed 21 of 33 passes for 249 yards and a touchdown but was harassed and sacked four times, three by linebacker Wilber Marshall. Kramer also fumbled thrice and threw two interceptions. Barry Sanders, the league's No. 2 rusher with 1,548 yards, gained 44.

Kramer was hot entering the game. He completed 28 of 39 passes for 341 yards and three touchdowns in Detroit's 38–6 divisional playoff win over the Cowboys, who had handed the Redskins one of their two losses that season.

"I remember watching that game and saying to myself, 'I really hope we get the Lions,'" Redskins linebacker Andre Collins said. "Even though Kramer was hot and they had some big receivers and Barry Sanders, I thought defensively we matched up better against the Lions than Dallas."

Kramer was welcomed rudely on the game's first play. Redskin Charles Mann barreled into him and forced a fumble that fellow defensive end Fred Stokes recovered on the Lions' 11. Two plays later, Gerald Riggs plowed in from 2 yards out for a 7–0 Redskins lead. On the next series, Redskins linebacker Kurt Gouveia intercepted a pass and returned it 38 yards to the Detroit 10. Chip Lohmiller's 20-yard field goal made it 10–0 with 4:01 gone.

The Lions stayed alive with a touchdown and a field goal in the second period and trailed 17–10 at halftime. The score was a slight surprise, for the Redskins had entered as two-touchdown favorites. The Lions also led in total yards, 209 to 112—but it was just a matter of time before things got out of hand.

"Earnest [Byner] was saying, 'Hey, it's going to come, it's going to come,'" Redskins offensive lineman Raleigh McKenzie remembered. "We knew the running game was going to take off, and we were going to give ourselves a chance to win. We knew if we scored one or two more times, our defense would stop those guys."

That's what happened.

Ryp hit two 45-yard passes in the third quarter, one to tight end Terry Orr that set up a Lohmiller field goal and another to Gary Clark for a touchdown that put the Redskins up, 27–10. Meanwhile, Washington's defense suffocated Detroit, which gained 95 yards in the second half, and the Redskins added touchdowns in the fourth quarter on Rypien's 21-yard pass to receiver Art Monk and cornerback Darrell Green's 32-yard interception return.

"Did that look like a rerun of the last time or what?" Lions coach Wayne Fontes asked afterward. "There's no doubt they outplayed us. They beat us up. No excuses."

Said Redskins offensive tackle Jim Lachey, "We were just really whipping up on the Lions, it wasn't even a close game. It's fun when you can sit there in the second half and enjoy it a little bit, knowing your next stop is going to be in the Super Bowl."

Destination: Minneapolis.

| Detroit—    | 0  | 10 | 0  | 0  | —  | 10 |
| Washington— | 10 | 7  | 10 | 14 | —  | 41 |

Wash — Riggs 2 run (Lohmiller kick)
Wash — FG Lohmiller 20
Det —— W. Green 18 pass from Kramer (Murray kick)
Wash — Riggs 3 run (Lohmiller kick)

Det —— FG Murray 30
Wash — FG Lohmiller 28
Wash — Clark 45 pass from Rypien (Lohmiller kick)
Wash — Monk 21 pass from Rypien (Lohmiller kick)
Wash — D. Green 32 INT return (Lohmiller kick)

## SUPER BOWL XXVI
**Washington 37, Buffalo 24**
**January 26, 1992**
**Hubert H. Humphrey Metrodome, Minneapolis**
**Attendance: 63,130**

### On the Mark: Redskins' Ryp Bills for Third NFL Title in Gibbs Era

If this were a popularity contest, Redskins quarterback Mark Rypien would have lost.

During Super Bowl week, one advertising executive described him as having non-Madison Avenue looks and a lack of charisma. Essentially, he was labeled in the press as boring, stiff, and unattractive, unlike his more flamboyant and media savvy counterpart, Bills quarterback Jim Kelly.

"I never got caught up in that," Rypien said. "I thought it was kind of funny and distasteful, but it had nothing to do with football outside of giving me an edge to say, 'Hey, listen, as great a player as Jim Kelly is, I don't want to see him walking around here with a Super Bowl ring.' To tell you the truth, it might have given me a psychological edge."

Rypien used that edge to apply his final imprint on an outstanding season. In the crowning moment of his 12-year NFL career, he completed 18 of 33 passes for 292 yards and two touchdowns to earn MVP honors in the Redskins' 37–24 victory over Buffalo in Super Bowl XXVI at the Metrodome in Minneapolis.

Ryp was just one of many standouts on a Redskin squad that looked synchronized that day. Gary Clark and Art Monk each caught seven passes for 114 and 113 yards, respectively, and Clark caught a touchdown pass. Gerald Riggs bulled in for two short touchdowns. Earnest Byner tallied 49 yards rushing and 24 receiving with a touchdown catch, and the Hogs manhandled the Bills' 3–4 defensive front led by end Bruce Smith, now the all-time NFL sack leader.

"Against Buffalo, we knew we had a special team that year that would be hard to beat if we played up to our standards," Clark said.

The Redskins' defense, for its part, made mulch of Buffalo's offense. Kelly, now in the Hall of Fame, threw four interceptions as part of a 28 of 58, 275-yard day and was flustered all game by blitzes. He never found his rhythm, and his 58 pass attempts, many in desperation, set a Super Bowl record. Safety Brad Edwards picked off two passes, made a legion of bone-jarring hits, and received votes for MVP. Linebacker Wilber Marshall was utterly devastating with a team-high 11 tackles and two forced fumbles. Buffalo rushed for 43 yards, with star running back Thurman Thomas gaining 13 on 10 carries.

The final 13-point margin failed to magnify the Redskins' dominance. Washington led 24–0 in the third period and 37–10 in the fourth until Kelly threw two late scoring passes.

"The bottom line was, we just hit them at their peak," Kelly said in retrospect. "There was nothing we could do to slow them down. We had a ton of dropped passes, I missed some reads. I guess we found ourselves pressing a little bit too much. We knew the Redskins had one of those teams . . . you almost had to play a perfect game to beat them."

The game featured the league's two most potent offenses. The Bills, with their quick-strike, no-huddle attack, scored 458 points in the regular season, second only to the Redskins' 485. Kelly completed 304 of 474 passes for 3,844 yards with 33 touchdowns—all league highs. His favorite target was Andre Reed, one of the NFL's top receivers with 81 catches for 1,113 yards and 10 touchdowns. Thomas, the AFC rushing leader with 1,403 yards and the NFL leader in yards from scrimmage with 2,038, was named NFL MVP. The weapons were in place for Buffalo to make up for their 20–19 loss to the Giants in Super Bowl XXV.

Thomas was too self-absorbed during Super Bowl week. He touted himself as the "Michael Jordan" of his team in response to a remark by Buffalo's offensive coordinator Ted Marchibroda that Kelly was the "Michael Jordan" of the Bills' offense. He also complained of not getting enough respect from the media and skipped a mandatory news conference.

Gary Clark, who caught seven passes for 114 yards and a touchdown in Super Bowl XXVI, shows which team is No. 1.

For Redskins quarterback Mark Rypien, here handing off to Earnest Byner, Super Bowl XXVI was the high-water mark in his 12-year NFL career. He completed 18 of 33 passes for 292 yards and two touchdowns and was named the game's MVP.

His actions fired up the Redskins. "There were rumors that they were debating or fussing about who would be MVP of the game between Bruce Smith and Thurman Thomas," linebacker Monte Coleman said. "We were very low key. We were on a mission to go out and win a football game."

Thomas looked like an airhead when the game began. He couldn't find his helmet and missed the first two plays from scrimmage. The Bills went nowhere, and the Redskins took over and drove 89 yards for a first-and-goal at the 2. Three plays later, Rypien hit Monk in the back of the end zone for a touchdown, but instant replay found that Monk's foot had stepped on the end line, and the play was nullified in the first touchdown reversal in Super Bowl history. Holder Jeff Rutledge mishandled the snap on a 19-yard field goal attempt, and the game stayed scoreless.

The teams then traded interceptions. Edwards's first pick gave the Redskins a first down on the Bills' 12. Three plays later, Rypien's pass was tipped and intercepted. It was an inauspicious start for both teams.

"Usually in a Super Bowl, there's a little bit of a sparring going on, everybody's checking out personnel and finding where matchups can be found in certain formations," Redskins offensive tackle Jim Lachey said. "We had a pretty good grasp of them, we just weren't finishing stuff off."

Washington engineered back-to-back scoring drives in the second quarter. Rypien's 41-yard pass to Ricky Sanders set up Lohmiller's 34-yard field goal 13:02 before halftime. The Bills went three plays and out, and a short punt gave Washington possession on its 49. The Redskins moved to the Bills' 10, when Byner took Rypien's pass in the flat and dove into the corner of the end zone for a score.

The Bills' offense again sputtered, as cornerback Darrell Green intercepted Kelly on the Bills' 45. Rypien hit Clark for 34 yards, and Ervins's 14-yard run gave Washington a first down at the 1. Riggs waltzed in for a 17–0 lead. In less than six minutes, the Redskins had scored 17 points.

The rest of the half was scoreless, although toward the end of the quarter, the Bills, who by then had abandoned their running game, moved to the Redskins' 20. On third down, Kelly misfired on a pass to Reed in the end zone. It appeared that Edwards had climbed Reed's back, and when no flag was thrown, Reed slammed his helmet to the turf and was whistled for a 15-yard unsportsmanlike conduct penalty.

"That is a real sign of desperation and frustration," Edwards said. "You could tell that they collectively were frustrated, not only being down by 17 points and having an opportunity not realized at that point, but also not exactly knowing what they were up against."

The onslaught continued in the third quarter. Redskins linebacker Kurt Gouveia intercepted his third pass of the playoffs and returned it 23 yards to the Buffalo 2. Riggs rumbled in for another touchdown and a 24–0 lead.

The Bills trimmed the margin to 14 points on a field goal and Thomas' 1-yard scoring run. But the Redskins, with the Hogs keeping the Bills' defense off balance, responded with an 11-play, 79-yard scoring march that broke Buffalo's back. Rypien completed four passes to Clark on the drive, including a 30-yarder on a play in which Clark faked out his man on a post-corner route and caught the ball in stride for a touchdown that put the Redskins up, 31–10.

"That was the icing on the cake," Rypien said. "Gary was so good at making the post corner fake. I just laid the ball out there."

The Redskins' defense frustrated Bills quarterback Jim Kelly, who threw four interceptions. Here, Redskins linebacker Kurt Gouveia returns one of them to the 2, from where Gerald Riggs ran it in for a 24–0 lead early in the third quarter. Fellow linebacker Wilber Marshall (58) had an outstanding game with a team-high 11 tackles and two forced fumbles.

After two Lohmiller field goals made it 37–10 with 11:36 to play, Kelly led two long scoring drives that ended on his short touchdown passes to cut the lead to 13. But the Redskins held on and exited the field as champions.

Kelly, who was knocked woozy in the final period and had to leave the game for a play, sounded a bit forgetful in the postgame press conference. "Forgive me if I don't remember everything that happened," he said. "I don't think I want to."

### Three Rings

The win over Buffalo marked the fourth Super Bowl appearance and third Super Bowl ring for six Redskins standouts from the first coaching era of Joe Gibbs: wide receiver Art Monk and linebacker Monte Coleman, plus four Hogs—tight end Don Warren, center Jeff Bostic, guard Russ Grimm, and tackle Joe Jacoby.

"We probably did something that we hope can be repeated by the modern-era Redskins," Coleman said. "You can put on one of your rings and just go back and marvel at the years that you had with the Redskins, the things you were able to accomplish. It's a good feeling."

| | 1 | 2 | 3 | 4 | | |
|---|---|---|---|---|---|---|
| Washington— | 0 | 17 | 14 | 6 | — | 37 |
| Buffalo— | 0 | 0 | 10 | 14 | — | 24 |

Wash — FG Lohmiller 34
Wash — Byner 10 pass from Rypien (Lohmiller kick)
Wash — Riggs 1 run (Lohmiller kick)
Wash — Riggs 2 run (Lohmiller kick)
Buff — FG Norwood 21
Buff — Thomas 1 run (Norwood kick)
Wash — Clark 30 pass from Rypien (Lohmiller kick)
Wash — FG Lohmiller 25
Wash — FG Lohmiller 39
Buff — Metzelaars 2 pass from Kelly (Norwood kick)
Buff — Beebe 4 pass from Kelly (Norwood kick)

| Team Statistics | Wash | Buff |
|---|---|---|
| First Downs | 24 | 25 |
| Total Yards | 417 | 283 |
| Rushing Yards | 125 | 43 |
| Passing Yards | 292 | 240 |
| Passes | 18–33–1 | 28–58–4 |
| Sacks Allowed | 0–0 | 6–35 |
| Punts–Average | 4–37.5 | 3–47.0 |
| Penalties | 5–82 | 6–50 |
| Fumbles–Lost | 1–0 | 6–1 |
| Time of Possession | 33:43 | 26:17 |

## RUSHING

Washington—Ervins 13–72; Byner 14–49; Riggs 5–7, 2 TDs; Sanders 1–1; Rutledge 1–0; Rypien 6–4
Buffalo—K. Davis 4–17; Kelly 3–16; Thomas 10–13, 1 TD; Lofton 1–3

## PASSING

Washington—Rypien 18–33–292, 2 TDs, 1 INT
Buffalo—Kelly 28–58–275, 2 TDs, 4 INT; Reich 1–1–11

## RECEIVING

Washington—Clark 7–114, 1 TD; Monk 7–113; Byner 3–24, 1 TD, Sanders 1–41
Buffalo—Lofton 7–92; Reed 5–34; Beebe 4–61, 1 TD; K. Davis 4–38; Thomas 4–27; McKeller 2–29; Edwards 1–11; Metzelaars 1–2, 1 TD; Kelly 1–8

# 1992: 9–7, 3RD PLACE— NFC EAST

## Head Coach: Joe Gibbs

How the Redskins managed to sneak into the playoffs in 1992 is anybody's guess. Call it a minor miracle.

It was a year when

- Redskins starters missed 69 games due to injuries.
- An inconsistent offense showed none of the magic from the 1991 Super Bowl-winning season.
- Turnovers and missed opportunities were plentiful.
- Washington played one of the league's toughest schedules.
- The Redskins' last two regular-season games were losses.

Through it all, the Redskins persevered to stay in playoff contention, although they needed help getting in. The Vikings came through on the final Sunday by beating the Packers, assuring 9–7 Washington its eighth and final playoff appearance under coach Joe Gibbs. The Redskins beat the Vikings in the first round before falling to the 49ers.

"Maybe from a statistical standpoint we didn't do as much," quarterback Mark Rypien said. "It wasn't a banner year like the year before. But we put ourselves in a position again to go to another Super Bowl. We just didn't get it done."

Rypien wasn't all-world like the year before. He threw for nearly 3,300 yards but had more interceptions (17) than touchdowns (13). His passer rating (71.7) was a shadow of his 1991 figure. The offense scored 300 points, compared with 485 the prior season, and was often forced to settle for field goals in the opponent's red zone.

The offense struggled amid constant shuffling on the offensive line, which used at least eight different starting combinations because of injuries. Only guard Mark Schlereth and the multidimensional Raleigh McKenzie started every game. Ryp was sacked 23 times, compared with nine in 1991.

"It was tough," McKenzie said. "Everybody had to bounce around, the running backs, defense. We also showed our age on some occasions. But we came back and, like always, the guys who could play a little nicked up, they did. That was just one of those years that coaches dread."

Only four players started every game on defense, but the resourceful unit bailed the Redskins out time after time, registering six second-half shutouts. Middle linebacker Kurt Gouveia led the team with 169 tackles, and fellow linebacker Wilber Marshall, the only Redskin to make the Pro Bowl, had a monster year with 138 tackles, a team-high six sacks, and three forced fumbles. Safety Brad Edwards posted a team-high six interceptions.

The injury bug hit early in training camp, as starting defensive tackle Eric Williams was ruled out for the first 10 weeks of the regular season. Turmoil also surfaced with contract negotiations. Three 1991 Pro Bowlers—Rypien, left tackle Jim Lachey, and cornerback Darrell Green—staged holdouts, as did receiver-kick returner Desmond Howard, the Heisman Trophy winner out of Michigan whom the Redskins had moved up to select that year with the fourth overall pick.

Rypien was absent for the second straight year. He demanded a raise that would earn him nearly $4.5 million per year, the top salary range in the NFL. When the Redskins came in much lower, at about $3 million per year, he thought about possibly playing in the Canadian Football League.

With Ryp out, third-year man Cary Conklin started the first two exhibition games, both Redskins losses, and looked sharp. Rypien then acquiesced and accepted a four-year, $12 million incentive-loaded package just in time for the Redskins-49ers meeting in the American Bowl in London. He looked rusty in a 17–15 loss and a 27–23 win over the Raiders and then learned that Redskins fans can have amnesia. In a 30–0 loss to the Vikings at RFK Stadium, he threw three interceptions and was rewarded with a lusty booing.

The misery persisted in a 23–10 season-opening loss to Dallas on a Monday night at Texas Stadium. The Cowboys dominated both sides of the ball, while the Redskins appeared lifeless in a continuation of their 1–4 preseason. Rypien, sacked for an 11-yard loss on the game's first play and harassed all night, completed 20 of 38 passes and one touchdown but was way off target on several throws.

"I didn't play very well," Rypien said in reflecting back. "They just handed it to us."

Two of the Redskins' other holdouts—Green and Lachey— also struggled. Green was beaten on a 26-yard scoring pass to receiver Alvin Harper, and Lachey had difficulty controlling dangerous defensive end Charles Haley.

The Redskins rebounded with back-to-back wins at RFK, 24–17 over Atlanta and 13–10 over Detroit. Despite being obliterated statistically, the Falcons stayed alive with big plays such as Deion Sanders's 99-yard kickoff return for a touchdown. Desmond Howard, expected by the Redskins to be an impact player, returned a punt 55 yards for a touchdown but was relatively useless for the rest of the year.

Rypien threw three interceptions against the Lions, who blew a chance to send the game into overtime. Rookie Jason Hansen shanked a 49-yard field goal with 1:46 to play, leaving the Redskins 2–1. "There's no need to panic," Redskins tight end Terry Orr said afterward of his team's shaky start. "If we were 0–3, then there'd be reason to panic. As long as we're winning, we're headed in the right direction."

The squad regressed against the winless Cardinals. With the Redskins up by 18 points early in the fourth period, Rypien tossed two interceptions that were returned for touchdowns, and the Cardinals went on to win, 27–24. The self-destructing loss magnified the struggles of Ryp, who was playing with pain in his throwing arm.

Prior to the 1992 season, the Redskins moved into a new 162-acre training and practice site in Ashburn, Virginia, called Redskins Park. The facility, much more elaborate than the team's former site a few miles away in Chantilly, features a 65,000-square-foot, two-story building and four football fields.

"I'm not making excuses for myself," Rypien said in looking back. "But when you have a detached biceps tendon and you're not feeling as strong as you once did, you're now throwing footballs that are 2 yards short of a receiver."

Still, Rypien posted his best game yet. He completed 16 of 26 for 245 yards and a touchdown in a 34–3 Monday night romp over Denver at RFK. He also sneaked in for two scores. Seven of his completions went to receiver Art Monk, who broke Steve Largent's all-time record for catches and finished the night with 820. The defense, led by Wilber Marshall, held the Broncos to a season-low 128 yards.

Two more victories, 16–12 over Philly and 15–13 over the Vikings, lifted Washington to 5–2. Redskins kicker Chip Lohmiller, who finished tied with the Saints' Morten Anderson for leading scorer in the NFC (120 points), booted eight field goals in those two games, including a game-winning 49-yarder with 1:09 left against Minnesota.

But the Redskins fell, 24–7, to the Giants, whose ball-control offense maintained possession for two-thirds of the game and gained 389 yards. "We got whipped," Gibbs said afterward. "There's nothing more you can say."

Now at the midway point, the 5–3 Redskins were tied with the Eagles for second place in the NFC East (Dallas was in first at 7–1), with three road games ahead on the schedule. Washington knocked off the Seahawks, 16–3, before being blown out by the Chiefs and Saints.

The loss to New Orleans ended a miserable stretch for the 6–5 Redskins, who had scored only four touchdowns, including one by the defense, in six games. The Posse—Monk, Gary Clark, Ricky Sanders—wasn't producing the way it did in 1991, the running game was ineffective, and Rypien was out of sync. The injury list was getting longer by the minute: center Jeff Bostic was out for the year, and Green and Lachey had missed play since early in the season.

The Redskins, a.k.a. the walking wounded, were digging deep into their reserves.

But one constant—the defense—came up big in a 41–3 smashing of the Cardinals. The Redskins intercepted five passes, three by Edwards, and recovered one fumble. Five of the Cardinals' turnovers were converted into points. Byner and Ricky Ervins, who combined for 113 rushing yards, then ran for 168 in a 28–10 rout of the Giants. The Redskins' offense was clicking with a season-high 393 yards, and Rypien completed 15 of 18 passes for 216 yards and two touchdowns.

The two-game streak appeared in jeopardy when the Cowboys led, 17–13, with 3:14 left in the fourth quarter at RFK. Then came "The Play." Dallas quarterback Troy Aikman dropped back to pass in his own end zone, but defensive end Jason Buck collapsed the pocket and forced a fumble. Running back Emmitt Smith recovered the ball and tried to throw it out of the end zone, but he lost control and a pileup ensued. While the referees searched for the ball, Redskins safety Danny Copeland emerged with it for a touchdown to account for a 20–17 win.

"The Play" was the coup de grâce in the Redskins' superb defensive performance. The unit forced four turnovers and held the eventual Super Bowl-champion Cowboys scoreless in the second half, when Washington tallied 13 unanswered points.

The 9–5 Redskins were now sitting comfortably in playoff position, although a spot was yet to be secured. So what did they do? They lost their last two games, 17–13 to the Eagles in Philly and 21–20 to the Raiders at RFK. The Redskins led the Raiders, 20–14, with less than two minutes left. Then 37-year-old quarterback Vince Evans, in for an injured Jay Schroeder, completed a 50-yard pass to speedster Willie Gault on an 80-yard drive that ended on Evans's 3-yard scoring pass to Tim Brown in the closing seconds. There was an eerie silence among the incredulous crowd at RFK.

"This is very disappointing for us, it's a heartbreaker," Jason Buck said afterward. "We come back, play a home game with the playoffs on the line against a team that was really out of it. It's terrible to drop one like that."

Now, the only way the Redskins could make the playoffs is if the Vikings beat the Packers the next day. The Redskins got lucky. Minnesota won, 27–7, leaving Washington and Green Bay tied for the final NFC wild card spot. The Redskins got the nod based on a better record against common opponents—although it wasn't the most graceful way to make the playoffs.

"After being so magnificent the year before, there were probably a lot of people on the outside saying, 'This team doesn't belong here,'" Redskins linebacker Andre Collins said. "But we felt, hey, we have as good a shot as anyone to win this thing if we can get fired up."

## NFC WILD CARD GAME
**Washington 24, Minnesota 7**
**January 2, 1993**
**Hubert H. Humphrey Metrodome, Minneapolis**
**Attendance: 57,353**

### Mitchell, Redskins Defense Lead
### Upset Win over Vikings

The defending Super Bowl champs were sick of hearing it. They were sick of hearing from media and others that they didn't deserve to be in the playoffs because they had backed in. By the end of a 24–7 playoff win over the Vikings, the cynics had gone silent.

The Redskins embarrassed the Central Division champions with what one would call an old-fashioned butt-kicking. They prevailed in total yards (358–148), first downs (24–9), and time of possession (42:43–17:17). Redskins return man Brian Mitchell was phenomenal, with 209 all-purpose yards, 109 on the ground on 16 carries (nearly 7 yards per carry). He also returned a punt 54 yards and ran 38 yards on a fake punt to set up his 8-yard scoring run.

The Redskins' defense was also super, holding the Vikings to 69 yards after they gained 79 on the game's opening drive. The unit blitzed and harassed quarterback Sean Salisbury, who was starting only his fifth career game. He completed 6 of 20 passes, threw two interceptions, and was sacked four times, three by defensive end Fred Stokes.

"Honest to God, we went limping into that game," Redskins linebacker Andre Collins recalled. "I remember a lot of guys being hurt. But you just have to give credit to our veterans like Monte Coleman, Art Monk, Charles Mann. All those guys had been there so many times in these big games, and it was just business as usual. And we beat them pretty good. It was a pretty easy win."

The Redskins traveled to Minneapolis physically and mentally drained from a long regular season. Coach Joe Gibbs tried to psyche his squad up the night before the game by showing the opening scene from the 1970 movie *Patton*. In the scene, pugnacious World War II American general George Patton said, "No bastard ever won a war by dying for his country. He won it by making the other poor dumb bastard die for his country."

The Redskins relinquished a touchdown on the game's opening drive—a 79-yard march that ended on Terry Allen's 1-yard run—before getting untracked. Redskins cornerback Martin Mayhew picked off a pass by Salisbury and returned it to the Vikings' 33, setting up Chip Lohmiller's 44-yard field goal. Safety Brad Edwards intercepted Salisbury again in the second quarter in Vikings territory, and a few plays later, Earnest Byner ran 3 yards to put the Redskins up, 10–7.

"We had an excellent game plan and keeping Salisbury bottled up in the pocket was the biggest thing we were doing," Edwards said. "We didn't want to give him passing lanes where he'd have clear vision downfield. Our guys did that well."

Mitchell, a spark all season on special teams, then pulled off the play of the game. On fourth-and-3 at the Redskins' 44, he lined up as the upback in punt formation. The one-time option quarterback in college took the snap and ran around right end for 38 yards. Soon after, he ran 8 yards for a touchdown for a 17–7 game.

Before the half ended, the mercurial Gary Clark, the Redskins' top receiver in 1992, threw a temper tantrum on the sidelines because he thought Rypien wasn't throwing enough balls his way. Gibbs stepped in, and the two exchanged words that looked like anything but pleasantries.

Clark's turn would come. On a time-consuming 71-yard drive, he caught a 29-yard pass on a third-and-16 and a 24-yard touchdown pass with 17 seconds left in the third quarter. Mitchell rushed five times on the drive and, with Ricky Ervins out with a bad ankle and Byner struggling with a bad back, he carried the load in the entire second half, when the Redskins put on a clinic. They maintained possession for 25:22 and outgained the Vikings 190 yards to 9. The new-look Hogs of Jim Lachey, Ray Brown, Raleigh McKenzie, Mark Schlereth, and Ed Simmons, plus 270-pound tight end Ron Middleton, pounded away at the Vikings' much smaller defensive front.

Lachey, who subdued sack artist Chris Doleman, remembers the running play "70 Outside" being called about seven times in a row. "We were just going off tackle," Lachey said. "We just kept throwing it down and throwing it down and throwing it down. It was like, 'Hey, if something's working, don't stop it, keep going until they find a way to stop it.'"

| | | | | | |
|---|---|---|---|---|---|
| Washington— | 3 | 14 | 7 | 0 | — 24 |
| Minnesota— | 7 | 0 | 0 | 0 | — 7 |

Minn — Allen 1 run (Reveiz kick)
Wash — FG Lohmiller 44
Wash — Byner 3 run (Lohmiller kick)
Wash — Mitchell 8 run (Lohmiller kick)
Wash — Clark 24 pass from Rypien (Lohmiller kick)

## NFC DIVISIONAL PLAYOFF GAME
**San Francisco 20, Washington 13**
**January 9, 1993**
**Candlestick Park, San Francisco**
**Attendance: 64,991**

### Mistakes, Bad Luck Seal Redskins' Fate
### in San Francisco

It was a cruel ending, but one so indicative of the rocky road traveled by the Redskins in 1992.

Trailing 17–3, the Redskins crept back into their playoff game against San Francisco by scoring 10 straight points. With momentum on their side and a first down on the 49ers' 23 with 9:30 to play, they were eyeing the go-ahead touchdown—and possibly the knockout punch.

Quarterback Mark Rypien tried to hand off to running back Brian Mitchell, who was presented with a hole big enough for a Mack truck. But Ryp and Mitchell misconnected on the exchange, and the ball settled onto the muddy turf. San Francisco recovered it and went on to win, 20–13.

"I didn't secure the ball that well," Rypien recalled. "So when I handed it to Brian, it was a little bit loose, and the exchange wasn't very good. It was my fault more than anything. We had a chance going in there to win."

Mistakes, missed opportunities, and just plain bad luck spelled defeat for the defending Super Bowl champs. In addition to the fourth-quarter fumble, Mitchell fumbled late in the second quarter, helping set up a 49ers touchdown. Rypien threw two interceptions and missed receiver Gary Clark for a potential touchdown in what seemed like a repeat of his 1990 playoff performance against San Francisco, when he threw three interceptions that squandered golden scoring opportunities. "I left my heart in San Francisco," as Rypien put it. Washington's running game produced only 73 yards on a Candlestick Park field that was downright treacherous after being soaked with rain.

"The field was horrible," Redskins offensive tackle Jim Lachey said. "Take one step onto the field and you're sinking into water. The running game was a big part of our attack, and

## Gibbs Delivers a Shock, Calls It Quits

One of the characteristics that made Joe Gibbs a great coach—his unwavering commitment to labor all night several days a week at Redskin Park, where he slept on his office couch—curtailed his career. Struggling mentally and physically from 100-hour work weeks, he quit coaching after the 1992 season.

Gibbs, 52 at the time, publicly announced his resignation before a slew of reporters and TV cameras at Redskin Park on March 5, 1993. He admitted not feeling well during the last half of the 1992 season as a result of what he called a "migraine equivalence," a condition that had made it difficult for him to sleep. He denied being a victim of "burnout," the term popularized by Eagles coach Dick Vermeil to describe his resignation a decade before, but said he needed more than just the off-season to recuperate.

Gibbs also voiced his desire to spend more time with his wife, Pat, and his sons, J. D. and Coy. Gibbs was then in his second year of owning Joe Gibbs Racing, which was fresh off a win in the Daytona 500, the Super Bowl of stock car racing, but he said he wasn't retiring to focus on NASCAR. He left open the possibility of some day returning to coaching.

"It's not burnout with me," Gibbs said during the news conference. "People may argue that case. I love football, I love the competition, I love being in here, I love the meetings, and I feel I can still do that. I'm not in a situation where something has been used up inside of me."

His resignation stunned many Redskins players and coaches.

"It was a shock when he left because everybody was getting prepared to come back to play the next season," wide receiver Gary Clark said. "We reached the second round of the playoffs the previous sea-

son but lost to San Francisco in a game we probably should have won. So we felt we had a good opportunity to make another run at it."

Said offensive line coach Jim Hanifan, "I don't think any of us had an inkling he was going to retire. The only thing I knew was that he looked tired, haggard. Of course, we always looked tired and haggard. All of the offensive guys pulled overnighters, not the defensive fellows."

Redskins owner Jack Kent Cooke immediately named long-time Redskins defensive coordinator Richie Petitbon as Gibbs's replacement. Petitbon, 55 at the time, had been a candidate for the top job in Chicago, which was left vacant when Mike Ditka was fired after the 1992 season. Petitbon interviewed with the Bears, but Cowboys defensive assistant Dave Wannstedt got the job.

"I've often said that I'd rather be lucky than good," Petitbon said at the news conference. "I really think somebody was looking after me with that Chicago situation because, right now, you'd have a suicide on your hands."

In hindsight, Redskins General Manager Charley Casserly said he would have recommended former Giants coach Bill Parcells, a two-time Super Bowl winner, if Gibbs had resigned right after the Redskins' season-ending playoff loss to San Francisco in January 1993. "I can't tell you what Parcells would have done, but Cooke would have offered him the job," Casserly said. Former Broncos coach Dan Reeves, who had taken Denver to three Super Bowls, was also available at the time.

Parcells and Reeves signed on to coach the Patriots and the Giants, respectively. So by the time Gibbs stepped down, Cooke opted to tap Petitbon as his new coach.

we never really got it cranked up the way we needed to. The 49ers were able to take care of business and win."

The 49ers, who entered the game after a bye week with the NFL's best record at 14–2, didn't coast to victory. Quarterback Steve Young, the league MVP, completed 20 of 30 passes for 227 yards and scrambled through the slush for 73 more. But he lost three fumbles and threw an interception to single-handedly keep the Redskins in the game.

The 49ers drove 83 yards in six plays to score on the game's opening drive. Young threw a 5-yard touchdown pass that bounced through the hands of cornerback A. J. Johnson and into the arms of receiver John Taylor—the first sign the Redskins were snakebitten.

Young fumbled later in the quarter, and the Redskins marched 61 yards for Chip Lohmiller's 19-yard field goal. But another long 49ers drive, 76 yards, set up a field goal that made it 10–3. It appeared there would be no other scoring before halftime, but Mitchell's fumble late in the second quarter gave the 49ers the ball on the Redskins' 35, and Young completed a 16-yard touchdown pass to tight end Brent Jones. Jones fumbled at the three, but the ball bounced perfectly into his arms as he crossed the goal line for a 17–3 lead.

The Redskins looked jinxed.

Mistakes by Young swung the momentum after halftime. He fumbled deep in Redskins territory, and Lohmiller booted a 32-yard field goal to cut the margin to 11. Late in the third quarter, Young fumbled in the pocket, and Redskins defensive end Charles Mann recovered at the 49ers' 15. Three plays later, Rypien snuck into the end zone for a 17–13 game.

One of the league's best offenses went nowhere in three plays, and Washington regained possession with 12:58 left. Rypien completed three passes, and Byner ran twice to create a first down on the 49ers' 23. Then came the infamous fumble, and San Francisco chewed up seven minutes and kicked a field goal for a seven-point edge with 2:22 left.

Washington got the ball back with 78 yards to go for the tying score, but Rypien was sacked three times and threw an incomplete pass, sealing the Redskins' fate for 1992.

"I just remember never getting on track that game," Redskins linebacker Andre Collins said. "I just remember feeling like our team was desperate, like we were trying all kinds of things to light a spark, and it just never happened. It was just a long day in San Francisco."

| | | | | | |
|---|---|---|---|---|---|
| Washington— | 3 | 0 | 3 | 7 | — | 13 |
| San Francisco— | 7 | 10 | 0 | 3 | — | 20 |

SF —— Taylor 5 pass from Young (Cofer kick)
Wash — FG Lohmiller 19
SF —— FG Cofer 23
SF —— Jones 16 pass from Young (Cofer kick)
Wash — FG Lohmiller 32
Wash — Rypien 1 run (Lohmiller kick)
SF —— FG Cofer 33

# 1993–2006: Mediocrity, Redskins Style

THE PERIOD BEGAN with a steep fall from glory, then plateaued into a long stretch of mediocrity that forced Washington Redskins fans to awaken to many blue Mondays. Two second-round playoff appearances triggered waves of excitement, but those moments were ephemeral. On the whole, the Redskins failed to establish a consistent winning footing in the 14-year period from 1993 to 2006.

The Redskins posted a 95–128–1 mark (.426) that included only three winning seasons. They scraped and clawed in hopes of regaining their elite status of the 1980s and early 1990s, a period that featured three Super Bowl wins, and constantly tried to rebuild. But that old Redskins magic was gone. Their fate was sealed by poor coaching, a tendency to misfire on free agent acquisitions and high draft picks, a frequent inability to pull off wins in close games, a propensity for beating themselves, and plain bad luck. You'd be hard pressed to find the ingredients of a perennial winner.

Toss in instability at the most important position on the field. Seventeen quarterbacks started for the Redskins during the 14-year period. Two whom they gave up on—Rich Gannon and Brad Johnson—later started on teams that reached the Super Bowl, with Johnson winning a ring. Another one, Trent Green, took his squad to the AFC championship game. Redskins quarterbacks, we hardly knew ye. In comparison, the Packers enjoyed 13 straight nonlosing seasons beginning in 1992, plus two Super Bowl appearances and one Super Bowl win, using just one quarterback, Brett Favre.

The era began with the departure of a Redskins coaching legend, Joe Gibbs, and ended with Gibbs concluding the third season of his comeback in the nation's capital. In between, former Redskins defensive coordinator turned head coach Richie Petitbon finished 4–12 in 1993 and was fired after one season. In came Cowboys offensive coordinator Norv Turner, who went 49–59–1 through nearly seven seasons of coaching Redskins teams often tagged as underachievers until he was fired with three games left in the 2000 campaign.

Thus began a chaotic sequence that resembled the days in the 1940s and 1950s of trigger-happy Redskins owner George Preston Marshall, only this time it happened under Dan Snyder, a local business phenom who bought the Redskins for $800 million before the 1999 season. Terry Robiskie, the Redskins' receivers coach, lost two of the last three games in 2000 in an interim head coaching role and was let go. Marty Schottenheimer, one of the most successful coaches in NFL history,

mustered an 8–8 mark in 2001 but was fired after one season. Much ballyhooed University of Florida coach Steve Spurrier finished 12–20 over the next two seasons and departed.

The coaching parade resulted in a glut of new assistant coaches and new philosophies on offense and defense. Players shuffled in and out of Redskins Park like a deck of cards. One who weathered the volatility and remained a Redskin, offensive tackle Jon Jansen, became the longest-tenured player on the team in the 2004 off-season despite having played only five NFL seasons. He felt like a senior citizen at the time.

"In terms of the organization, yea, I am," Jansen said with an incredulous chuckle in May 2004. "I've seen everybody change. It's amazing how fast it happens. To be with one team for only six years, and you're the longest-standing guy. That's the way it's gone here." He added, "It's been tough because you don't know if your style is going to fit with the next coach that comes in. You just don't know if you're going to be the next one out the door. Everybody, every position, all my friends are gone."

When Gibbs returned to the Redskins in January 2004, hopes soared that the franchise would recapture the dominance it had displayed during his first coaching stint, from 1981 to 1992. It wasn't to be. Gibbs's 2005 squad was arguably a dropped interception away from reaching the NFC championship game, but his other two teams posted losing records. His three-year mark entering the 2007 season was 21–27.

All along, the Redskins have struggled to exploit the modern era of unfettered free agency, which kicked off in the 1993 off-season. Around that time, they began signing free agents who never panned out, including linebacker Carl Banks, defensive linemen Leonard Marshall and Al Noga, tight end Ethan Horton, receivers Tim McGee and Alvin Harper, and defensive back James Washington.

Several first-round draft picks in the 1990s were also busts, namely quarterback Heath Shuler (1994), receiver Michael Westbrook (1995), and offensive tackle Andre Johnson (1996). Wide receiver Desmond Howard, a Heisman Trophy-winning receiver drafted by the Redskins in the first round in 1992, was a disaster, too. "We made a couple of draft mistakes, with Shuler being one," said Charley Casserly, the Redskins' general manager at the time.

Casserly departed before the 1999 season, and his position has not been filled, a scenario that has taken a toll on the 21st-century Redskins. Without a true GM on board, they have

Redskins first-round draft busts of the 1990s: Heisman Trophy-winning wide receiver Desmond Howard (1992, fourth overall pick), quarterback Heath Shuler (1994, third overall), and often injured wide receiver Michael Westbrook (1995, fourth overall)

made some dubious moves through free agency and trades, acquiring players who exhibited much promise on arriving in D.C. but fell short of expectations, names like cornerback Deion Sanders, running back Trung Canidate, linebacker Michael Barrow, quarterback Mark Brunell, safety Adam Archuleta, and wide receiver Brandon Lloyd.

In addition, management has parted ways with players who went on to excel with other teams, including Brad Johnson, running back Stephen Davis, linebacker Antonio Pierce, cornerback Champ Bailey, and kicker David Akers. After the 2005 season, the Redskins refused to re-sign veteran cornerback Walt Harris. Picked up by the 49ers, he finished tied as the NFC leader in interceptions with eight in 2006, while the Redskins forced an NFL record-low 12 turnovers that season.

Gibbs, who as team president is in charge of player personnel decisions, has acknowledged that the front office has let some players leave who should have been re-signed. "That was my responsibility, and I shouldn't have let it happen," he said.

The Redskins have also deemphasized building from within, a critical component to winning consistently. Of the 53 players on their active 2006 roster, for example, only 14 were drafted by the club. The rest were traded for or signed through free agency. The Patriots' 2006 roster, by comparison, consisted of 29 players that the team drafted, 17 of whom were starters. New England, by the way, has won three Super Bowls in the 21st century.

Despite the turmoil, Redskins superstars have emerged. Linebacker Ken Harvey went to four straight Pro Bowls in the 1990s, when kick returner-running back Brian Mitchell smashed NFL special teams records. Cornerback Darrell Green was named to the NFL 1990s All-Decade Team. Brad Johnson threw for 4,000 yards in 1999, and wide receiver Santana Moss set a Redskins single-season record for receiving yards in 2005. Running backs Terry Allen, Stephen Davis, Clinton Portis, and Ladell Betts have ground out 1,000-yard seasons.

## 1993: 4–12, 5TH PLACE—NFC EAST

### Head Coach: Richie Petitbon

From optimism to disbelief to sheer disgust: the Redskins' 1993 season went up in flames.

The Redskins finished 4–12, the franchise's worst winning percentage (.250) in three decades. The squad won its season opener over the defending Super Bowl champion Cowboys but lost its next six, as the season slipped away rapidly from first-year coach Richie Petitbon, who had taken over for the legendary Joe Gibbs. Petitbon was fired at the end of the campaign.

Who would have expected such an alarming fall?

After all, with Petitbon, a long-time defensive coordinator on Gibbs's staff and a coach respected for his clever strategies that outwitted the best offenses, the sentiment around town was that the coaching transition would be seamless. True, Petitbon inherited an aging team, and was promoted at a time when the NFL was undergoing a paradigm shift that allowed players to test their value in a new, unfettered free-agent market, in return for a yearly cap on the amount of salaries teams could offer. Yet even Gibbs said at his parting press conference that the Redskins would handle the changes "maturely" and "better than anyone else."

"The Redskins' organization has always been the best when things are at their worst, or when there's a change, or when there's a strike, or when there's a USFL or something like that on the scene," Gibbs said. "Just like now, there's a big change going on in the league. This'll be the team that does it better than anyone else."

With their payroll at about $50 million and the salary cap anticipated to be a little more than $30 million for the 1994 season, when the cap would come into effect, the Redskins opted not to re-sign such free agents as long-time standout receiver Gary Clark, defensive linemen James "Jumpy" Geathers and Fred Stokes, and cornerback Martin Mayhew. Washington also lost linebacker Wilber Marshall, the team's lone Pro Bowler in 1992, after designating him their "franchise player." Marshall signed with the Oilers for more money than was offered by the Redskins, who received two mid-round draft choices in return.

At the same time, Redskins owner Jack Kent Cooke refused to pay signing bonuses for any big-time free agents, such as Reggie White, the premier pass rusher in the NFL, who continued his Hall of Fame career with his new team, the Packers. Washington instead signed one-time impact players who had reached the twilight of their careers in Vikings pass rushing specialist Al Noga, Giants linebacker Carl Banks, and Bengals receiver Tim McGee.

"We had to drastically cut our payroll for the 1994 season because you had to be under the cap," said Charley Casserly, the Redskins' general manager at the time. "We could have had Reggie White and chose not to do it."

In the draft, the Redskins selected two stars from Notre Dame: cornerback Tom Carter (first round) and running back Reggie Brooks (second). Brooks, one of Washington's only bright spots in 1993, with 1,063 rushing yards, plus 85- and 78-yard touchdown runs, and made the Pro Football Writers Association's All-Rookie team. Other picks included Florida State defensive end Sterling Palmer and Maryland tight end Frank Wycheck.

The preseason brought a mixed bag of news. Perennial Pro Bowl offensive tackle Jim Lachey suffered a major knee injury in an exhibition-opening win over the Browns and was lost for the year. Quarterback Mark Rypien, however, looked sharp after undergoing surgery to repair a detached biceps tendon that had hampered him in 1992, when he was one of the league's lowest-rated passers. He was now mixing in a lot more short throws in a system directed by new offensive coordinator Rod Dowhower. "[The surgery] made a world of difference because I came out firing," Rypien said.

The Redskins as a whole came out smoking in a season-opening Monday night game against Dallas before 56,345 fans at RFK Stadium. In a 35–16 Redskins win, Rypien threw three scoring passes and all-everything Brian Mitchell ran for 116 yards and two touchdowns. The Redskins crafted drives of 99, 80, 78, and 65 yards against the NFL's No. 1 defense from 1992. Dallas appeared out of sync playing without two-time league rushing champ Emmitt Smith, who was holding out due to a contract dispute.

"We rocked Dallas in the opener, we looked strong and good," offensive lineman Raleigh McKenzie said in retrospect. "We just looked like the regular old Washington Redskins."

They took on a new identity from then on. Against the Cardinals at RFK, Rypien was yanked down while scrambling in the second period and tore ligaments in his knee. Seldom used backup Cary Conklin came on in relief and completed 16 of 29 passes for 169 yards, with a touchdown and an interception. The Redskins looked ragged all around, though, and Phoenix exited with a 17–10 win to break a 14-game losing streak at RFK.

With Rypien projected to be out at least three weeks, Conklin stayed in the starting role. The Redskins dropped five more in a row, including a 34-point loss to the Giants at RFK and a 30-point loss to the Cardinals on the road. Conklin, inconsistent in the eyes of Petitbon, was benched at one point during the streak for Rich Gannon, a veteran acquired by the Redskins

in the preseason. He played briefly before Ryp returned after a two-game layoff on October 10.

He looked nothing like the preinjury Mark Rypien, throwing four interceptions in one game, a 24–10 loss to Buffalo that gave the 1–6 Redskins their first six-game losing streak since 1963. "I wasn't even ready to come back, but I saw my guys struggling," Rypien said. "But on one leg, I was ineffective."

Rypien was one of many banged-up Redskins. Injuries decimated the offensive line, as starters Moe Elewonibi, Mark Schlereth, Ed Simmons, and Joe Jacoby all missed playing time. They were replaced by players foreign to Redskins fans, names like Vernice Smith, Darryl Moore, and Greg Huntington. "We were playing with offensive linemen and didn't even know their names," O-line coach Jim Hanifan recalled. There was virtually no continuity on offense, which was guilty of lots of mental errors and turnovers, while the defense, hobbled by its own set of serious injuries to such players as veteran defensive linemen Charles Mann and Eric Williams, was allowing streams of big plays.

Were the Redskins ready to call it a season?

"We were saying publicly, 'Hey, we can turn it around, we can go on a run,'" said Redskins linebacker Andre Collins, who missed the first few games due to injury. "But the reality of it was by the end of that seventh week, we weren't a very good football team. It just was never going to happen that year."

The Redskins lost six of their last nine games, including ugly losses of 3–0 to the Jets at RFK, the first time Washington had been shut out at home since 1980; 10–6 to the lowly Los Angeles Rams; and 38–3 to Dallas at Texas Stadium. All the while, Petitbon's job security came into question, but Cooke refused to say publicly which way he was leaning. Redskins radio analysts Sam Huff and Sonny Jurgensen tried to alert Petitbon to the crisis at hand.

"Richie was a great friend of Sonny and Sam," Huff said. "We went to him at different times and said, 'Richie, you've got to kick ass and take names in this game. You've got to do it here, or you're going to get fired.' He said, 'Everything's okay, babe, everything's okay.' I don't know what it was. He should have been a great coach. But to follow Joe Gibbs was pretty tough."

Then-Redskins executive vice president John Kent Cooke, the son of the team's owner, said that Casserly was never told to look for a new coach during the season. "We had hoped with each game, things would turn around," Cooke said, "and even if we didn't win it, at least we may start to play well and have something to look forward to. But for some reason, Richie couldn't persuade Dad that he could turn it around. And Richie became quite defensive and blamed Charley Casserly for not bringing players in and so on. That was not a good situation. Joe Gibbs never complained about the quality of our players when we didn't win our first five games in '81."

Some players questioned decisions by Petitbon and his staff to give priority to unproven talent over veterans such as 14th-year receiver Art Monk and 10th-year running back Earnest Byner. "They self-appointed [second-year receiver] Desmond Howard the heir apparent to Art Monk," Rypien said. "He didn't even have to compete for it."

The Redskins closed by falling to Minnesota, 14–9, before some 13,000 no-shows at RFK, one of seven losses within a touchdown that year. The offense scored 230 points, fourth fewest in the league. Petitbon was fired a few days later. According to Casserly, though, it is not fair to evaluate him as a head coach because of the environment in which he took the job. The free agents signed by the Redskins made little or no impact. "We ended up having to gut the team and start over from scratch in '93," Casserly said. "Petitbon was in the wrong spot at the wrong time."

Redskins linebacker Monte Coleman agreed: "I thought Richie was a great coach that one year. It was very unfortunate that he got fired. Free agency came in, we lost a lot of players."

# 1994: 3–13, 5TH PLACE—NFC EAST

## Head Coach: Norv Turner

They entered the year with a new, young, energetic coach who had been a top assistant on back-to-back Super Bowl winners in Dallas. Also new was a player projected to be their quarterback of the future, plus one of the best outside linebackers in the game.

The result: a season more calamitous in many ways than the 1993 campaign.

The 3–13 Redskins set a franchise record for losses, and their ignominious winning percentage, .188, exceeded only the two single-win seasons in franchise history, 1960 and 1961. The 1994 squad was also the first Redskins team ever to lose every home game and the sixth team in NFL history to do so in a 16-game season. The year was nothing but a fiasco.

"On paper and in practice, you wouldn't have thought that that was a 3–13 team," Redskins guard Raleigh McKenzie said in hindsight. "We came to play strong. That was the year that a bunch of our older guys who were the main focus of the team were let go, or they weren't signed back or retired. Many times when you lose some of your continuity, you either try to overcompensate for what you missed or assume that the next guy will be the same. It just didn't fall into place the way we hoped."

Many of the icons from the great Joe Gibbs teams, popular names such as Joe Jacoby, Jeff Bostic, Charles Mann, Mark Rypien, Earnest Byner, Art Monk, and Ricky Sanders, were indeed gone by the start of the season. The housecleaning was mostly the work of general manager Charley Casserly and the Redskins' new coach, Norv Turner.

Shortly after firing Richie Petitbon in early January 1994, Redskins owner Jack Kent Cooke signed Turner to a five-year contract worth about $3 million. Turner had been the Los Angeles Rams' receivers coach from 1985 to 1990 before taking over in 1991 as the offensive coordinator of a Cowboys team that placed last in the league offensively the year prior. In the coming seasons, as the Cowboys' offense became one of the NFL's best and Troy Aikman established himself as one of the league's top quarterbacks, Turner gained a reputation as an offensive brain.

By the time Dallas defeated Buffalo for its second straight Super Bowl victory in January 1994, Turner was a hot item on the head coaching market. His arrival in Washington on February 2, 1994, triggered memories of another imaginative offensive coordinator who later became famous as the Redskins' head coach: Joe Gibbs.

"Norv had his own qualities that were very appealing," former Redskins executive vice president John Kent Cooke said. "He was highly recommended by a number of people,

especially Charley Casserly. He was knowledgeable about the sport and anxious to become a head coach."

Redskins radio analyst Sam Huff said Turner was the wrong pick. "Charley Casserly and [Jack Kent Cooke] made the mistake of going with an arch enemy, the Cowboys. He wasn't welcome here. If you're an enemy, you're an enemy. When he came here, the Redskins' fans didn't welcome him. They didn't need a Dallas Cowboy to come here and tell them they're messed up."

Turner inherited an aging team that was about $20 million over the newly implemented salary cap. Redskins management thus had to cut long-time veterans and renegotiate contracts in hopes of meeting the $34 million cap. The most contentious parting involved 15th-year receiver Art Monk. Team officials offered Monk $600,000, down from his request of $1.15 million. Monk, then the NFL's all-time leading receiver with 888 catches, refused the offer and departed acrimoniously. He signed with the Jets, catching 46 passes for 581 yards and three touchdowns in 1994.

"[Monk] figured he could still play at a high level, but we didn't think he could," Casserly said. "But probably if we didn't have the salary cap, we would have paid him a million bucks, a million one, a million two, whatever he was making to keep him in D.C. for another year. The new system came, and we couldn't do that."

The Redskins also released quarterback Mark Rypien, whose career had taken a turn for the worse after his spectacular 1991 season, as well as backup quarterbacks Rich Gannon and Cary Conklin. In 1993, the trio threw for 2,764 yards—the second-lowest total in the NFL—and combined for 11 touchdowns and 21 interceptions.

With Washington owning the No. 3 draft pick and the passing game in need of major repairs, Casserly and Turner eyed the top two blue-chip quarterbacks, Tennessee's Heath Shuler and Fresno State's Trent Dilfer. The 6–2, 221-pound Shuler, noted for his tremendous all-around athletic ability, threw for more than 4,000 yards in college with 36 touchdowns and 12 interceptions. He entered the draft after his junior season. The 6–4, 235-pound Dilfer, more of a pro-style quarterback, amassed nearly 7,000 yards with 51 touchdowns and 21 interceptions. Both ballyhooed players had been showered with conference and national honors.

The universal feeling was that Casserly favored Dilfer and Turner wanted Shuler. The Redskins chose Shuler, a decision that was "completely unanimous, from the owner, to the GM, to all the people involved in the evaluation," Turner said years later. According to Casserly, Dilfer would have been the choice if Joe Gibbs were still coaching in Washington. Other picks included 6–3, 315-pound Temple offensive tackle Tre' Johnson (second round) and Tulsa quarterback Gus Frerotte (seventh).

"The thing that put Heath over Trent was probably his mobility," Turner said. "People put a lot of weight on Heath playing at Tennessee, compared with Trent playing at Fresno State. Reflecting on it, most people will tell you that neither deserved to be picked that high."

Through free agency, the Redskins signed one of the best outside linebackers in the game, Arizona's Ken Harvey. Also signed was Cowboys guard John Gesek, Giants defensive end Leonard Marshall, Chargers quarterback John Friesz, and Rams receiver Henry Ellard, one of the leading pass catchers in NFL history. In addition, Turner restructured the assistant coaching staff to compensate for the departure of Gibbs's right-hand men Charley Taylor, Larry Peccatiello, Rennie Simmons, Wayne Sevier, Don Breaux, and Torgy Torgeson.

When training camp opened, the Redskins' quarterback of the future was nowhere to be found. After a 13-day holdout, Shuler signed an eight-year, $19.25 million contract, then the richest deal in team history. The rookie looked spotty through the first three exhibition games—all losses—before completing 19 of 30 passes for 206 yards in a 22–21 win over the Steelers.

Friesz, a fourth-year player who started every exhibition game, opened under center in the season opener against the Seahawks at RFK Stadium. He looked sharp on the game's first drive, an eight-play, 82-yard march that ended with his 27-yard scoring pass to Desmond Howard, the first touchdown catch in the three-year career of the former Heisman Trophy winner.

Hello, Norv Turner era!

Things went downhill from there. Brian Mitchell's fumbled punt set up a Seahawks touchdown that tied the game, and a Friesz interception was returned 69 yards for a score. Two more Seattle touchdowns in the second half accounted for a 28–7 win. Friesz completed 17 of 32 passes for 210 yards, with two interceptions, while Shuler (3 of 8, 14 yards) saw spot duty.

Friesz started again against the Saints and looked like an All-Pro, throwing four touchdown passes in a 38–24 win at the Superdome, the first victory in the Turner era. Two of his scores went to Ellard. The Friesz-Ellard combo struck again on the road against the Giants. Friesz (32 of 50, 381 yards, two touchdowns) threw 10 completions to his favorite receiver and could have had more, but the Redskins dropped seven passes. They also committed a flurry of penalties in a 31–23 loss.

Friesz then went cold in a 27–20 loss to Atlanta at RFK, tossing three interceptions. Shuler entered in the fourth period and was tapped to start the next week against the visiting Cowboys.

It was rocky period for the high-priced rookie. He went 11 of 30 for 96 yards while facing constant harassment in a 34–7 loss to Dallas. And after showing modest improvement in a 21–17 loss to the Eagles in Philly, he threw five interceptions in a 19–16 overtime loss at RFK to the Arizona (formerly Phoenix) Cardinals and was booed mercilessly by Redskins fans seemingly bitter over his lengthy contract holdout.

With the season disintegrating for the 1–6 Redskins, Turner tapped Gus Frerotte to start at quarterback. The 197th pick in the draft had shown sparks in preseason mop-up duty, but nobody expected much against Indianapolis at the RCA Dome. But Frerotte gave a jaw-dropping performance, completing 17 of 32 passes for 226 yards with two touchdowns and no interceptions in a 41–27 Redskins win. His completions and yards were Redskin records for a quarterback making his first start, and he was named NFC Offensive Player of the Week.

"He missed his first couple of throws and fumbled a snap, and if he didn't do that, I would have thought there was something wrong with him," Turner said in a press conference afterward. "He was exceptional. He's going to continue to get better. He's a talented guy."

Frerotte's performance transfixed the nation's capital. A *Washington Post* headline read, "Gus! Rookie Frerotte Gets Started With Win," while the *Washington Times* mockingly asked, "Heath Who?" Frerotte became an instant fan favorite, as everyone began climbing on the "Gus bus." Fans felt a

Norv Turner, fresh off a Gatorade shower, was all smiles after his first win as the Redskins' head coach, 38–24 over the Saints on September 11, 1994.

kinship to the unheralded quarterback with a $140,000 salary, compared with Shuler's millions. In the ensuing weeks, however, Frerotte experienced rookie woes similar to Shuler's and was yanked early in a 31–7 loss at Dallas that left the Redskins 2–9.

Shuler returned and started the final five games. He improved dramatically, posting an 84.4 passer rating in a four-game stretch in December, about double his mark from earlier in the year. The Redskins, however, continued losing and stood 2–13 with a seven-game losing streak heading into the season finale at the Rams. A 24–21 win stopped the bleeding but failed to mask the misery of a season for which Jack Kent Cooke had originally predicted his squad would finish 9–7, possibly 10–6.

"That football team was going to struggle through a period of time no matter who the coach was," Turner said in hindsight. "I knew that coming in.

Even so, it hurt that the Redskins simply didn't know how to win. They lost eight games after taking a lead into the second half, four when the deciding points were scored in the last minute and two on the final play. Seven of their defeats came by a total of 21 points. After a 26–21 loss on December 4, when Tampa Bay scored the winning touchdown in the last minute, Turner said to reporters: "Five weeks ago, I told the team we hit bottom. We didn't. This is as low as you can get."

Who was to blame for such ineptitude? An article in *Washingtonian* magazine in December 1994, said that Casserly would be the "likely fall guy," noting that the general manager "has had four mostly lousy drafts since taking over from Bobby Beathard. Most of Casserly's free agent signings—overpriced older players such as Tim McGee, Carl Banks, and Leonard Marshall—have been busts." The article said that the GM's likely successor would be assistant Cardinals general manager Bob Ackles, a friend of Turner.

"That's completely unfounded," John Kent Cooke said years later. "Pure, unadulterated, nonsense."

## 1995: 6–10, 3RD PLACE—NFC EAST

### Head Coach: Norv Turner

The Redskins' 1995 season provided a snapshot of the good, the bad, and the ugly.

The good: Gus Frerotte blossomed into a solid NFL quarterback, and three of the Redskins' six wins came against teams en route to the playoffs, including two upsets of the eventual Super Bowl champions, the Cowboys.

The bad: Washington posted its third straight season of double-digit losses, the first and only time the franchise has experienced such a stretch, while its $19-million-man, quarterback Heath Shuler, gave little indication that he deserved to be picked No. 3 in the 1994 draft.

The ugly: In a carbon copy of their futility from 1994, the Redskins lost four games decided in the last two minutes, plus two games on the final play. Another loss came when Washington, trailing 14–6 with the ball 1 yard from the end zone and seconds remaining, failed to punch it in. Plus, the Redskins sometimes dominated teams on paper, to no avail. Case in point: they topped the Giants in yards (306–160), first downs (21–9), and time of possession (38:40–21:20) but still lost when New York scored the winning points with 1:12 to play.

Redskins return man extraordinaire Brian Mitchell said the inability to put opponents away was a reflection of coach Norv Turner, who went 9–21–1 in seven seasons with the Redskins in games decided by three points or less.

"Many times people say the team's personality comes from the coach," Mitchell said years later. "Our team's personality as far as not having a killer instinct or being a closing team came from our coach. If we were up by two touchdowns, [the players] felt that if we'd get another touchdown, we'd put ourselves in a better position. Unfortunately, our coach felt, 'Let's try to close this game out without embarrassing anybody.' Then somebody goes and gets a touchdown and a two-point conversion, and we lose by one point."

Shuler voiced a different theory on why the Redskins were losing an abundance of heartbreakers: "It was the youth on our team," he said. "We were so, so young. Norv struggled as a head coach because we didn't have a lot of personnel. I think we started four rookies in my first year [1994]. It's difficult to win in that league with so many rookies."

One rookie who joined the Redskins in 1995 was Colorado wide receiver Michael Westbrook, the No. 4 pick in the draft. The Redskins passed up Joey Galloway and Miami defensive tackle Warren Sapp to pick Westbrook, a 6–3, 215-pound physical specimen whom they considered a bigger and faster version of Redskins famed receiver Art Monk. Westbrook told Washington all-sports radio station WTEM that he was "like Michael Jordan with a football." But like Shuler the year before, he played hooky during training camp because of a contract dispute. After holding out for 26 days, he missed much playing time during the season and caught only 34 passes.

The Redskins drafted Westbrook to complement veteran receiver Henry Ellard, who was coming off a 74-reception season. Redskin officials parted ways with receiver Desmond Howard, the former Heisman Trophy winner who had evolved into a bust. After catching only 66 passes with five touchdowns in three Redskin seasons, Howard entered the expansion draft and two years later shocked the world by becoming MVP of Super Bowl XXXI. He piled up 244 return yards, including a 99-yard kickoff return for a touchdown, in Green Bay's 35–21 victory over New England.

Why didn't Howard make it in Washington? "He wasn't good enough," then-Redskins general manager Charley Casserly said. "His size at receiver was really limiting for him. The guy was a top return guy and one of the best in the NFL, but we had probably the best one in Brian Mitchell. So the return thing was never going to work for us."

In the free agent market, the Redskins signed Vikings running back Terry Allen, a two-time 1,000-yard rusher, in hopes of improving a running game that averaged only 88 yards per game in 1994. The Redskins also looked to free agency to shore up their defense, one of the worst in the league in 1994, by signing linebackers Rod Stephens and Marvcus Patton, along with safeties Stanley "The Sheriff" Richard and James Washington.

Meanwhile, cornerstones from Joe Gibbs's era continued to depart. Offensive linemen Raleigh McKenzie and Mark Schlereth left via free agency, linebacker Andre Collins and running back Ricky Ervins were released, and linebacker Monte Coleman, who wore the burgundy and gold for 16 seasons, retired.

The Redskins were considerably younger than in past seasons (average age 26.4) at the start of training camp at Frostburg State University in Frostburg, Maryland, their new summer location after 32 years in Carlisle, Pennsylvania. With veteran John Friesz gone via free agency, Turner designated Shuler as the starting quarterback over fellow second-year-man Frerotte, who nonetheless outplayed Shuler during a 1–3 preseason. But Shuler, who threw three interceptions that were returned for touchdowns, got the starting nod for the season opener against the Cardinals at RFK Stadium.

The Redskins opened as they did in 1994—magnificently—as Westbrook ran 58 yards with a reverse for a 7–0 first-quarter lead. But in the second period, Shuler took a hard hit from Arizona's Clyde Simmons and went to the sidelines.

Frerotte finished up and completed 9 of 15 passes for 157 yards, including a 2-yard scoring pass to newly signed tight end Scott Galbraith and a 73-yarder to receiver Leslie Shepherd in a 27–7 Redskins win. Washington's machine-like offense amassed 456 yards, 259 on the ground. Allen rushed for 131 on 26 carries.

Shuler, diagnosed with a sprained right shoulder, was ruled out for a few weeks, thrusting Frerotte into the starting role. Would Shuler regain his starting job when he's healthy? "That's obviously an impossible question to answer," Turner told reporters. "When Heath's ready to play, we'll deal with that."

Shuler told reporters that it is an "unwritten rule" that a player doesn't lose his job due to injury. "But if Gus has the team on a roll, then it's Norv's decision," he said at the time.

Thus a quarterback controversy was triggered. Although the Redskins dropped their next three games, including a 38–31 defeat to Denver when Broncos quarterback John Elway threw a 43-yard touchdown pass on the game's final play, Frerotte posted nice statistics and earned the admiration of his teammates, who nicknamed him "the sniper" because of his accuracy.

"He could make some plays, and at that level, you've got to show the ability to make plays," Redskins tackle Jim Lachey said. "When he got his opportunity in games, he did some things."

"Gus played really well," Shuler said. "You can't fault the way he played. The thing was everybody tried to make Gus and I like we were enemies, and we were great, great friends. That was what was so ironic about it. It was a very, very difficult situation."

Then came the biggest win to date in the Turner era. The Redskins stunned the 4–0 Cowboys, 27–23, before 55,489 delirious fans at RFK Stadium. Frerotte completed 13 of 24 passes for 192 yards and two touchdowns, and threw a pass that was returned for a touchdown. Allen, who rushed for 121 yards with one touchdown and caught a scoring pass, was named NFC Offensive Player of the Week.

The Redskins built a 27–10 lead in the third quarter, but the Cowboys rallied without superstar quarterback Troy Aikman, who had left the game owing to an injury in the first quarter. Redskins cornerback Tom Carter intercepted a pass on the game's final play to seal their first win over a division opponent since the 1993 season opener against the Cowboys, who had mauled the Redskins by an average of 29 points in three games since then. "The rivalry wasn't great in the last three games," Turner told reporters, "but it is a great rivalry, and it was today."

The Redskins lost six of their next seven games, starting with a familiar sight: a 37–34 loss to the Eagles on a field goal in overtime. Then came another heartbreaker, a 24–20 loss to Arizona on a 1-yard scoring pass with 1:16 left. Washington finally pulled out a nail-biter against the Lions at RFK. Kicker Eddie Murray, signed in the preseason to take over for a struggling Chip Lohmiller, booted a 39-yard field goal with four seconds to play to tie the game, 30–30. In overtime, cornerback Darrell Green intercepted a pass and returned it 7 yards for a 36–30 win, as the Redskins improved to 3–5.

Frerotte, effective up to that point, began to slip. He threw four picks in a loss to the Giants and also looked abysmal in losses to the Chiefs and Seahawks. When Shuler entered in the fourth quarter with the Redskins trailing the Seahawks, 17–10, RFK fans showered him with boos. He threw two interceptions but later completed eight straight passes on a 68-yard drive capped by his 5-yard touchdown pass to Westbrook.

With the season a wash, Turner named Shuler the starter, and the Redskins again shocked the Cowboys, 24–17, before losing to the Giants, 20–13. In the next-to-last game against the St. Louis Rams, Shuler completed 10 of 13 passes for 103 yards with one touchdown in a little more than a quarter of play, but he suffered another setback, breaking a finger on his throwing hand. Frerotte went the rest of the way in a 35–23 Redskins win and then started in a 20–17 win over Carolina.

To Turner, three wins in the last four games represented a strong building block heading into the 1996 season. "No question," the coach said in looking back. "We felt we had done enough things well in a lot of different phases, so we thought we could build on that and become a good team."

## 1996: 9–7, 3RD PLACE—NFC EAST

### Head Coach: Norv Turner

Gus or Heath? Such was the million-dollar question facing Redskins coach Norv Turner: whom to choose as his starting quarterback.

Of the two, Gus Frerotte had made a much stronger impact since he and Shuler entered the NFL in 1994. After becoming an instant celebrity with his smashing debut that year against the Colts, Frerotte started 11 games in 1995, throwing for 2,751 yards, with 13 touchdowns and 13 interceptions. Despite stretches of inconsistency, the classic drop back passer looked more poised and confident than Shuler, a running quarterback in college who had struggled reading pro defenses and suffered injuries that slowed his progression.

Frerotte was also the unequivocal favorite among Redskins fans, who saw the meekly paid quarterback as an underdog to the $19.25 million Shuler, the boyish-looking athlete referred to by media as the "bonus baby." Fans admired the hard-working, take-charge image of Frerotte, a native of the blue-collar town of Ford Cliff in western Pennsylvania, the breeding ground for other great quarterbacks named Montana, Unitas, Marino, Namath, and Kelly. "In Gus We Trust" T-shirts were in vogue. Frerotte was also a favorite of Redskins radio analyst and Hall of Fame quarterback Sonny Jurgensen, who had been in his corner since day one and even tutored him.

Meanwhile, Shuler's 13-day contract holdout from his rookie season continued to reverberate negatively among Redskins fans, who were quick to shower him with boos when he stepped on the field.

"It was a very, very tough place to play. Gosh, it was tough," Shuler, who grew up in Bryson City, North Carolina, rooting for the Redskins, said years later. "It almost seemed like everybody hated me in Washington. The hard part about it was the expectations were so high. The fans weren't going to wait and see what happens three or four years down the road. They wanted to see what happens now because the team has such a rich tradition."

In training camp that year, Turner opened the competition for the starting quarterback job. Frerotte and Shuler looked sharp in the first two exhibition games. But in the third game, a 28–7 loss to the Bengals, Shuler fumbled the ball and threw an interception, prompting Turner to name a starter for the season opener against the Eagles at RFK Stadium.

It was Gus.

"Obviously, a lot of things go to into making a decision like that, but from a coaching standpoint we felt we had a better chance to win with Gus," Turner said. "Gus was more ready to play than Heath at the time."

Looking back, Frerotte said he was very surprised by the move: "You want it to happen, but you're never quite sure that it will. If it didn't, I would have just kept doing what I had been doing all along, working hard and studying, and if I got my shot I'd be ready to play."

Looking like the Redskins' quarterback of the future, Gus Frerotte started every game in 1996, as well as the first two-thirds of 1997. But his career in Washington fizzled out.

Frerotte was ready then. In 1996, he completed 270 of 470 passes for 3,453 yards (57.4 completion percentage), with 12 touchdowns and 11 interceptions, and was chosen as a Pro Bowl alternate. Shuler took only one snap all year.

Teamwise, Washington won seven of its first eight games, albeit against a featherweight schedule consisting of opponents with a 27–37 record, and held first place in the NFC East at the midway point. But the Redskins lost six of their last eight, including some when displaying their embarrassing habit of blowing late leads, and tied Minnesota for the final NFC wild card playoff spot. Due to an inferior conference record, the 9–7 Redskins missed the playoffs for the fourth straight year.

What factored into the 7–1 start?

Frerotte was unspectacular but steady. Running back Terry Allen had an NFC-high 803 yards rushing by the midway point and was named NFC Offensive Player of the Month for October, when he rushed for three touchdowns apiece in back-to-back wins over the Giants and Colts. A bend-but-don't-break defense preserved several victories, a welcome change from past years when the Redskins were unable to seal Ws in crunch time:

- In a 10–3 win over Chicago, the Bears had three shots at the end zone from the 13-yard line in the final minute but failed to score. It was the first time Washington held a team to no

touchdowns since a 3–0 loss to the Jets in 1993, and Turner gave everyone on defense a game ball. Redskins defensive tackle Sean Gilbert, a free agent acquired in the off-season, was named NFC Defensive Player of the Week after posting seven tackles, one sack, and three quarterback hurries.
- Washington intercepted three passes in a 17–10 win over St. Louis. The Rams had the ball on the Redskins' 23 with less than three minutes left, but an interception by cornerback Tom Carter preserved the win.
- In a 27–22 win over New England, the Patriots scored with 5:33 left to close the gap to 24–22. But the defense stopped running back Curtis Martin (164 rushing yards) on a two-point conversion attempt, before driving 74 yards for a field goal by Scott Blanton.
- Carter had another clutch interception in a 31–16 win over the Jets after wrestling the ball away from receiver Key-shawn Johnson in the end zone to preserve a Redskins' fourth-quarter lead.

The seven-game winning streak was the Redskins' longest since their 1991 Super Bowl-winning season, and Redskins fans could taste an NFC East title and possible home-field advantage in the playoffs. But Redskins cornerback Darrell Green tried to put matters in perspective, telling Washington all-sports radio station WTEM "we're not that good."

He was right, not to mention that much tougher opponents lay ahead. First came a 38–13 loss to Buffalo on the road that foretold future doom. Allen gained 49 yards on 15 carries, and the Redskins' defense yielded 476 yards and 31 first downs.

The defense was even more pitiful in a 37–34 overtime loss to the visiting Cardinals, who gained 615 yards, a Redskins single-game record. Most of the yardage came from the arm of 35-year-old quarterback Boomer Esiason. Benched earlier in the year, the former University of Maryland star threw for 522 yards, the third most in NFL history at the time and the most against the Redskins since Y. A. Tittle's 505 in 1961. He completed 35 of 59 passes, with three touchdowns and four interceptions.

Esiason, who rallied the Cardinals from a 27–13 deficit to a 34–34 tie at the end of regulation, was unconscious in the fourth quarter and overtime, when he connected on 23 of 35 passes for 351 yards and two touchdowns. The overtime period was bizarre. Arizona won the coin toss and drove to the Redskins' 15, but kicker Kevin Butler missed a 32-yard field goal. The Cardinals regained possession but fumbled, setting up a 38-yard try by Blanton. His kick was good with 3:18 left, but Scott Galbraith was called for holding, a penalty Turner later called "inexcusable." Blanton missed from 48 yards out, and Arizona drove to the Redskins' 19, but Butler's field goal hit the goalpost with 37 seconds left. However, Redskins safety Darryl Morrison was ruled offsides, and Butler was true from 32 yards out, ending a heart-wrenching game for the Redskins and their fans.

"We got to the point where we were beating them, and we figured that we had the game won before it was over," Redskins linebacker Ken Harvey, a former Cardinal, said years later. "There's no such thing."

Washington rebounded with a 26–21 win over Philly on the road to regain sole possession of first place in the NFC East. Blanton was 4 of 4 on field goals, as the Redskins snapped an eight-game losing streak to the Eagles.

The final Redskins game at RFK Stadium, a 37–10 win over Dallas on December 22, 1996

But Washington's defense continued to yield a lot of yards, and so went the Redskins' playoff hopes. They dropped four straight games, including a 24–10 loss to Tampa Bay; the Redskins allowed more than 200 yards rushing for the second straight week. Afterward, Redskins linebacker Marvcus Patton told the press that the unit "played like babies. We didn't tackle." The next week, a 27–26 loss to those irritating Cardinals on a field goal with four seconds left eliminated the Redskins from playoff contention. Washington's offense scored only one touchdown in each of those four losses.

The Redskins closed the year by routing the Cowboys, 37–10, on a historic and emotional day at RFK Stadium. It was the Redskins' final game in the 36-year history of RFK, where they went 173–102–3, including 11–1 in the playoffs.

Frerotte completed 22 of 31 passes for 346 yards, while Allen rushed for 87 yards to break John Riggins's single-season team record of 1,353 and ran for three touchdowns to finish with a league-high 21.

It was too little, too late.

"We got complacent," said Harvey, who made his third straight Pro Bowl. "It was like saying if we play at that same level every game, we're going to win. But every game is different. Sometimes you have to raise the level to make that extra catch. Sometimes, you have to be so scared of losing that you're going to stretch out that extra inch and get that extra yard. We just kind of lost focus."

Then-Redskins' offensive line coach Jim Hanifan said the 7–1 start was a "farce": "We were not a 7–1 football team. We were probably at the most a 4–4 if not a 3–5. We lucked out, and we won games by a point or two. All of a sudden, reality

came to bear in the second half of the season. All of a sudden, we were exactly what we were. That happens a lot of times with teams because they win a game here, and they luck out over here, then the media jump on it and all of a sudden hell breaks loose, and they have a poor year."

## 1997: 8–7–1, 2ND PLACE—NFC EAST

### Head Coach: Norv Turner

How much of a tease can one team be?

A year after opening 7–1 but losing six of their last eight games to fall out of the playoff picture, the Redskins led or straddled the top of the NFC East for most of the 1997 season before going 2–3–1 down the stretch, missing the playoffs by half a game.

It came down to the final weekend. The Redskins beat the Eagles to finish 8–7–1, but the Vikings and Lions also won that day to go 9–7 and secure the final two NFC Wild Card spots. Given that the Redskins had beaten Detroit earlier in the season and would have clinched a playoff spot by finishing 9–7 based on head-to-head competition, that half-game difference loomed humongous.

It would have been a nonfactor had the Redskins won games they should have won and not lost games that slipped away, troubling trends so common during the era of coach Norv Turner. Take, for instance, a 17–14 loss to a Cowboys squad that scored 11 points in the final two minutes and won on a field goal with four seconds left; or a 23–20 loss to a dreadful St. Louis team also on a field goal in the closing seconds.

Maddening, indeed, although the real killer came in a pivotal late-season matchup against the Giants. With first place in the NFC East on the line, Redskins quarterback Gus Frerotte did a lousy job of using his head.

After scrambling for a touchdown late in the first half to put the Redskins up, 7–0, Frerotte celebrated by ramming his head into a padded, concrete wall at the Redskins' new home, Jack Kent Cooke Stadium. He sprained his neck and stayed in for two more plays. Recently acquired backup Jeff Hostetler, unfamiliar with the offense, played the rest of the game, throwing three interceptions and losing a fumble.

With the score 7–7 in overtime, receiver Michael Westbrook, who had attacked and beaten up running back Stephen Davis on the sidelines during a preseason practice, again let his mercurial personality get the best of him. Angry over an official's ruling, he ripped off his helmet, slammed it to the turf, and was whistled for unsportsmanlike conduct. The 15-yard penalty forced kicker Scott Blanton to try a 54-yard field goal that fell short with seconds remaining, marking Washington's first tie since the regular-season overtime session was implemented in 1974.

"That was the most frustrating, boring game," Redskins return man Brian Mitchell said in looking back. "It was kind of a combination of what went on through the year. We never disciplined Michael Westbrook for a lot of stuff, and it cost us in certain situations. I used to always say that in practice, he'd

mess up and nobody would say anything to him. In Mike, I saw a guy with all the potential in the world. But when I went into battle with him, I didn't see a guy with that desire, that fight to become the best."

Frerotte's head-slamming stunt, meantime, was beyond explanation and left many people shaking their own heads. "It's not as if he put his head down like a bull charging," said Phil Hochberg, the Redskins' public address announcer at the time. "He ran over to the wall, but we weren't sure what the hell he was doing. I don't think people really realized what was happening. Only in retrospect did it take on a great significance."

Turner said he didn't see the head-banging but was "dumbfounded" when Redskins trainer Bubba Tyer shared the bizarre news about Frerotte's injury. "If he'd gone up to high-five the wall or jumped up and hit his back on the wall in excitement, it's a sign of emotion," Turner said. "But he head-butted it and later they told me he head-butted it where the enforcement pole was. Gus was a young player and was going through some frustration in terms of the fans getting on him. They booed him early in that half. It was kind of his way of saying, 'Hey, screw you.'

"There's no question in my mind if Gus plays the whole game we win, and we're a playoff team."

The brain lapse was the nadir of Frerotte's subpar season. His numbers were down nearly across the board from his banner 1996 campaign, and he ranked among the NFL's worst passers. He completed 204 of 402 passes (50.7 completion per-

## Cooke's Dream for a New Stadium Becomes Reality

Jack Kent Cooke's quest to build a new stadium for his Washington Redskins evolved into a 10-year soap opera.

Starting in 1987, the Redskins owner negotiated with D.C., Virginia, and Maryland officials for a stadium site, but talks became contentious and broke down. D.C. Mayor Sharon Pratt Kelly once called him a "billionaire bully" because of what she perceived as his demanding negotiating tactics. A letter of intent that he signed with Virginia governor Douglas Wilder for a stadium at Potomac Yards, a tract of land in Alexandria, Virginia, fell through, as did Cooke's plan to build a stadium in Laurel, Maryland.

With all of the trouble he had finding a new site, he never threatened to move the team out of Washington.

"He would never do that because he was well aware Bob Short's name was mud, the same way Walter O'Malley's name in Brooklyn was mud," said his son, long-time Redskins executive John Kent Cooke. "Short was the guy who moved the Senators baseball club out of Washington [in 1971], and O'Malley disap-

pointed so many people in Brooklyn when he moved the Dodgers to L.A."

Cooke's patience paid off. In 1995, he reached a favorable deal to build a 78,600-seat, football-only stadium near Landover, Maryland, a Washington suburb. He pumped $360 million of his money into the stadium and named the area Raljon, after John Kent Cooke and his other son, Ralph Kent Cooke. The venue was built with amazing speed, and after the Redskins ended a 35-year stay at RFK Stadium in 1996, they debuted in their new, state-of-the-art home with a 19–13 win over Arizona on September 14, 1997.

Jack Kent Cooke missed the spectacular opening. He died from heart failure at age 84 on April 6, 1997. At a memorial ceremony, John Kent Cooke announced that the new stadium would be called Jack Kent Cooke Stadium (it's now called FedExField).

"I was extremely proud to name the stadium after my father then, and I still am today," Cooke said. "My father spent 10 years trying to build that stadium, and he had all kinds of trouble. The politicians were involved, the press was skeptical. Yet, he overcame all those things, and it was one of the satisfying things in my life to be able to complete the stadium for my father and put his name on it."

centage) for 2,682 yards, with 12 interceptions and a career-high 17 touchdown passes. His season was cut short when he broke his hip with three games left.

Prior to the season, Gus had been picked by readers of *Washingtonian* magazine as the "best-loved Redskin" and had signed a four-year, $18 million contract that rewarded him for his solid play in his first three years. Around the same time, the Redskins' brass parted ways with Heath Shuler, once considered the franchise's quarterback of the future. After opting not to renew their contract option on Shuler, they traded him to the Saints for a fifth-round draft choice in 1997 and a third-rounder in 1998. Shuler threw two touchdown passes and 14 interceptions for New Orleans in 1997, before suffering a foot injury that ended his NFL career. Today, he is paralyzed in the left foot.

Why did Shuler struggle in D.C.? "When you're coming to a team that's 4–12, you're going to have to handle some real adversity," Turner said in hindsight. "That was hard on Heath. He also had a tough time getting comfortable with the NFL game, which was much different for him than what he'd done in college. The thing that's forgotten is Heath got hurt a number of times. It seemed like every time he was getting a comfort level and started to play a little bit, he had a setback. In the 1995 season, he went through a [late-season] stretch where he was doing some things pretty good, but he broke his finger."

With Shuler gone, the Redskins signed Jeff Hostetler as a backup. The 12-year veteran, who had replaced injured starter Phil Simms late in the 1990 season and quarterbacked the Giants to a win in Super Bowl XXV, threw for a career-high 23 touchdowns with the Raiders in 1996.

For the defense, the preseason focus was on revamping a unit ranked 28th overall and 30th against the run in 1996. (Defensive coordinator Ron Lynn was fired at the end of the '96 season.) The Redskins took six defensive players in the draft, including Miami defensive end Kenard Lang (first round), Colorado linebacker Greg Jones (second), and Arizona State linebacker Derek Smith (third). They also signed free agents in cornerback Cris Dishman, defensive tackle Chris Mims, and Giants safety Jesse Campbell.

The Redskins designated 6–5, 320-pound defensive tackle Sean Gilbert as their "franchise" player, meaning that he couldn't negotiate with another team as a free agent. But Gilbert failed to report to training camp due to a contract dispute. The Redskins offered about $4 million per season, while Gilbert, who had only three sacks in 1996, at one point wanted $5 million. Gilbert's agent said he was making his demand based on a "revelation from God." No deal was reached, and Gilbert sat out the year.

"When we traded for Gilbert, I said the biggest reason why not to make the trade was that he had only one year left on his contract," Turner said. "I said if we're not going to re-sign him, we shouldn't make the trade. One of the big things that hurt us [in 1997] is we were short a defensive lineman, and we struggled through a number of injuries. We let our best defensive player sit out, and unfortunately, we could have signed Sean for under $4 million."

With Gilbert gone, coupled with injuries to the line, Washington's defense suffered. The soft interior failed to shut down big, bruising runners such as Pittsburgh's Jerome Bettis, Tennessee's Eddie George, and Baltimore's Bam Morris. The 250-pound Bettis, for example, trampled on the Redskins for 134 yards in a 14–13 Steelers win that evened the Redskins' record at 1–1.

Washington won three of its next four games, although the one loss came to a mediocre Eagles squad that controlled the ball for almost 40 minutes and racked up 449 yards—203 on the ground—and 26 first downs. Then came a 21–16 victory over Dallas in a Monday night game that lifted the 4–2 Redskins into first place in the NFC East. Running back Terry Allen sprained his knee and was replaced by Stephen Davis, who rushed for 94 yards and two touchdowns. After some shaky performances, Frerotte was a solid 12 of 23 for 155 yards and a touchdown, with no interceptions.

A 28–24 loss to Tennessee (George rushed for 125 yards) and a 20–17 loss to Baltimore (Morris rushed for 176) returned the Redskins to .500. They routed the Bears, 31–8, behind 125 rushing yards from Allen, who'd returned after a two game layoff, followed by a 30–7 demolition of the Lions. The Redskins' offense, one of the NFL's best, gained 388 yards in both games.

The Redskins and Giants, both 6–4, held first place in the NFC East. But a 2–3–1 slide, which included the infamous 7–7 tie with the Giants and the 23–20 loss to the Rams, left Washington and Philly tied for second in the division at 6–6–1 behind the 7–5–1 Giants. Frerotte fractured his hip in the fourth quarter of the loss to the Rams and was lost for the year.

In came Hostetler, who threw three touchdown passes in a 38–28 win over the Cardinals on the road. In need of two wins in the final two games and a Giants loss to win the division, the Redskins laid an egg, committing six turnovers and fumbling a snap that led to 20 points, the difference in a 30–10 loss to the Giants in the Meadowlands.

On the final weekend, Washington topped the visiting Eagles, 35–32. Minnesota also won, so the Jets had to beat Detroit for the Redskins to enter the playoffs through the backdoor. New York led by 10 points but the Lions fought back to win, 13–10. The Jets reached the Detroit 9 late in the fourth quarter, but the Redskins watched in frustration as Detroit stopped the threat with a controversial interception.

The bottom line, in Mitchell's view, is that the Redskins shouldn't have depended on other teams to control their destiny. "I always said if we don't make it to the playoffs, it's our fault," he said. "So many times we got ourselves into a situation where we'll make the playoffs if this happens, or if that happens. If we would have just gone out and won two or three more games, we would have taken care of our business. But we got into too many games where we either didn't close it out or made stupid mistakes at a crucial point and lost, and then we expect another team to do our job."

## 1998: 6–10, 4TH PLACE—NFC EAST

### Head Coach: Norv Turner

One scene said it all: 16th-year cornerback Darrell Green, a fixture on the Redskins' glory teams in the 1980s and early 1990s, vented his frustration during a 34-point loss to the Vikings that dropped the Redskins to 0–7. He broke into tears on the sidelines.

"That's really the way everybody felt," Redskins quarterback Trent Green said in retrospect. "It was bad."

The 0–7 record made for an agonizing period when the squad could do no right. Penalties, turnovers, injuries and a simple case of the ball bouncing the wrong way added up to self-destruction and sent the Redskins to their worst start since 1961, when they opened 0–9 en route to a 1–12–1 mark.

Although by then the season was essentially a wash, the Redskins rebounded to win six of their last nine games, including three wins over teams battling for playoff spots. Sparking the comeback was Trent Green, a long-time Redskins backup quarterback who finally got his shot in 1998. Then in his sixth year, he started 14 games, including the last 9, and posted some nice numbers: 278 of 509 for 3,441 yards with 23 touchdowns and 11 interceptions (81.8 passer rating).

But the dreadful start was too much to overcome, and the playoffs were a no-go for the sixth straight season. "We had a lot of things go wrong that year in terms of injuries, we had a lot of injuries on the offensive line," Trent Green said. "It was just a very frustrating start and an unbelievably frustrating year as a team. We just couldn't get anything going."

The Redskins envisioned a much grander scenario after making some eye-opening personnel moves in the 1998 off-season. General Manager Charley Casserly added about 630 pounds of beef to the interior of the defensive line—part of one of the league's worst defenses against the run in recent seasons—and dished out $57 million in contracts in doing so.

The Redskins signed free agent and three-time Pro Bowl tackle Dana Stubblefield, the 1997 NFL Defensive Player of the Year. He had played his first five seasons for the 49ers. Next to arrive was tackle Dan "Big Daddy" Wilkinson, the league's No. 1 draft pick in 1994. The Redskins traded their first- and third-round picks in the 1998 draft for Wilkinson, widely considered an underachiever in his four seasons with the Bengals. (The Redskins also traded disgruntled defensive tackle Sean Gilbert, who had sat out the 1997 season because of a contract dispute, and received two first-round picks, 1999 and 2000, from the Panthers.)

"We were very excited to get Stubby and Wilkinson," Casserly said. "We didn't think Stubblefield was [future Hall of Fame defensive end] Reggie White, but we thought he was a good football player, and we thought Wilkinson was underappreciated in Cincinnati. I thought they would make a major difference in the play of the defensive line."

The trade for Wilkinson deprived the Redskins of a No. 1 pick for the first time since 1990. In the second round, they chose Oklahoma tight end Stephen Alexander, who caught 104 passes for 1,591 yards and six touchdowns for the Sooners. Other picks included UCLA running back Skip Hicks (third round), Richmond linebacker Shawn Barber (fourth), Purdue center Mark Fischer (fifth), and Texas–El Paso cornerback David Terrell (seventh).

Expectations for a dynamite season were peaking by the time training camp started, and pundits were touting the squad as a veritable force in the NFC. But the Redskins showed no signs during their 1–3 preseason that they were about to dominate. The first-team offense, which generated a paltry number of points, looked hideous. Quarterback Gus Frerotte was erratic and connected on one of eight throws for 21 yards in the last exhibition game, a 27–17 loss to Buffalo.

Frerotte, then in his fifth year, was coming off a mediocre 1997 season. "Gus had played well at times but had never had the consistency you need to win enough games to be a playoff team," Turner said in hindsight. "He went to the Pro Bowl in '96 and had quite a year, but there were a number of situations and plays where you looked at it and said, 'Hey, this is stuff that you do good in three or four games but all of a sudden you don't do well here.' If he was going to have some consistency, he had to have a sense of urgency about the way he prepared all the time."

Frerotte looked sharp early in the season opener against the Giants in the Meadowlands. His 17-yard scoring pass to receiver Leslie Shepherd, plus Scott Blanton's 46-yard field goal, had the Redskins up, 10–3. Frerotte also threw a 31-yard touchdown pass to receiver Michael Westbrook, but a holding call nullified the play.

Gus went into a funk early in the third period. With the Redskins on their own 5, he tossed a pick that was returned to the 2, setting up a Giants touchdown. Frerotte, who sprained his shoulder on the play, threw another interception on the next series that was returned 24 yards for a score that created a 24–10 game.

Friction erupted on the Redskins' sideline, where TV cameras caught linebacker Marvcus Patton, one of the team's top tacklers from recent seasons, giving Frerotte a verbal scolding. The quarterback stayed in for a few more plays before being shaken up again.

Unable to call on veteran backup Jeff Hostetler, who was inactive after spraining his knee in the preseason, Turner tapped Trent Green. He looked nothing like a quarterback who had thrown only one pass in his four previous seasons, completing 17 of 25 for 208 yards, plus two touchdowns and a 62-yard throw to Westbrook. He hit 15 of 16 at one point, but the Redskins fell, 31–24.

Afterward, Turner called one of Frerotte's interceptions "just a horrible decision" and named Green the starter for a Monday night game against the 49ers at Jack Kent Cooke Stadium. "Trent made a bunch of plays, he gave the offense a lift," the coach said at the time. "The things he did in the game warrant a chance for him to start."

Green completed his first three passes against San Francisco, the last one a 9-yard touchdown pass to Shepherd for a 7–0 Redskins lead. It was lights out from then on. The 49ers piled up 504 yards, and quarterback Steve Young completed 21 of 32 passes for 303 yards and three touchdowns in a 45–10 rout of the Redskins, their worst home loss in exactly 50 years.

"This was about as embarrassing as the Clinton affair," Stubblefield said as quoted by the *Baltimore Sun*, referring to the ongoing sex scandal involving President Clinton and White House intern Monica Lewinsky. "We got embarrassed in front of the entire nation."

The humiliation continued with losses to Seattle, Denver, Dallas, and the Eagles, who, like the Redskins, were 0–5 entering the game. Green posted respectable passing stats in the first six games but threw seven interceptions and fumbled the ball four times. He was benched in favor of Frerotte in the third quarter of the loss to the Eagles.

Turner named Gus the starter against the 5–0 Vikings in the Metrodome, where the Redskins were 4–0 all-time. This time, they got spanked, 41–7. Their offense totaled 177 yards and nine first downs, and their lone touchdown came after a fumbled punt was recovered on the Vikings' 2. Frerotte (10 of 26, 117 yards, one interception) was sacked five times. (The Redskins O-line yielded a team-record 61 sacks on the year.)

Turner chastised his squad in a postgame press conference: "That's as poor a performance as I've ever been involved with. We're totally inept on offense. We can't snap two plays in a row and not jump offsides. When a guy's open, we can't get him the ball. When we get him the ball, he doesn't catch it. We've got guys going the wrong way."

The upcoming bye week was no consolation for what had been a treacherous stretch. Against a brutal schedule that included the defending Super Bowl champion Broncos and the soon-to-be NFC champion Vikings, the Redskins were outscored 227 to 93 and 114 to 36 at Jack Kent Cooke Stadium, where disgusted home fans wore bags over their heads and mocked Turner with chants such as "Norv Must Go." "Impeach Norv" was also a familiar refrain. Then-Redskins president John Kent Cooke, preoccupied with efforts to purchase the team, recalled that he had no intention of firing Turner or Casserly at that point.

The much advertised interior defense, for its part, had been soft on the run, as five different players rushed for more than 100 yards, including two in the loss to Dallas: Emmitt Smith and Chris Warren. The defensive line was playing without end Rich Owens, who suffered a preseason injury that sidelined him for the year. Pass rushing specialist N. D. Kalu was signed in his place. Stubblefield was lost for the season after reinjuring his knee during the bye week.

To add to the tumult, the Redskins released two unproductive kickers, Scott Blanton and David Akers, and signed former Colts Pro Bowl kicker Cary Blanchard. (Akers later signed with the Eagles and is today one of the most dependable kickers in the NFL.) Hostetler, unhappy about warming the bench, decided to undergo season-ending surgery after saying he was accidentally hit on the sideline during the loss to Seattle.

At quarterback, Turner again named Green the starter. The *Washington Post* reported that sources at Redskin Park were saying Turner was upset with Frerotte for allegedly criticizing the coach in private with reporters. Casserly remembered a "clash" between the two, but Turner said years later that there was nothing personal in his decision to bench Frerotte.

Meanwhile, the Redskins split their first four games after the bye week. They opened with a 21–14 win over the Giants at Jack Kent Cooke Stadium, where Green completed 21 of 31 passes for 225 yards and one touchdown, and ran for another. The Redskins committed no turnovers, compared with 17 in the first seven games, and the defense held the Giants to 86 yards.

In the next three games, the Redskins beat the Eagles handily but lost twice to the Cardinals, once by two points and once by three points, marking seven losses to Arizona in the Turner era by a total of 18 points. Green had a monster outing in the second game against Arizona, completing 30 of 49 passes for 382 yards with four touchdowns. He led the Redskins back from a 31–0 halftime deficit before they fell, 45–42, to drop to 2–9.

Then came a four-game winning streak during which the ball bounced the Redskins' way, unlike in the first seven weeks of the season. After a 29–19 victory over Oakland, when Leslie Shepherd caught a tipped pass for a touchdown, the Redskins topped the Chargers, 24–20, when Green hit Shepherd in the right corner of the end zone with 1:54 left.

The Redskins then disposed of Carolina before knocking off the Buccaneers with another fourth-quarter comeback. Green hit Stephen Alexander on a 15-yard touchdown pass for the game winner with 5:49 left, one play after the Redskins had recovered a fumbled kickoff return. The streak and season ended with a 23–7 loss to the Cowboys.

The second half of the season was sort of a moral victory. Washington was five points away from winning eight of its last nine games, given the two losses to Arizona. The Redskins played the role of spoiler by beating the Giants, Raiders, and Bucs, all of whom finished 8–8 and missed the postseason.

Trent Green, who had considered quitting the NFL after being cut by the Chargers after his rookie year, 1993, found it "very rewarding" to get the chance to play nearly the entire season after holding a clipboard for so long. "I was at the point in my career where I was 28 years old, I had no playing experience and at some point in time it catches up to you," he said. "I felt that if I didn't get some significant playing time in '98, my career might very well be over."

Personnel decisions made during and after the bye week keyed the turnaround, according to Green and Turner. "You had a lot of young guys getting an opportunity to play for the first time," Green said, "players like Stephen Davis, Stephen Alexander, myself, Skip Hicks, James Thrash, Chris Thomas, Brad Badger. We were just trying to make the most of the opportunity and didn't get too caught up in what was going on in terms of the 0–7 record. We really got on a roll in the second half of the season."

"We kind of regrouped," Turner remembered. "The thing that was good about that football team, and the thing that made the difference for us next year in '99, was we came back and made changes in terms of who we were going to play and how we were going to approach things."

# 1999: 10–6, 1ST PLACE—NFC EAST

## Head Coach: Norv Turner

Wild—bizarre—historic—exciting—and even soap opera-like. It was all of the above for the Redskins in 1999.

The 10–6 Redskins won the NFC East and made the playoffs for the first time in seven seasons. Once there, they made a nice run to the Super Bowl, beating Detroit in the opening round and battling Tampa Bay down to the wire before succumbing.

But that's just the skinny on a year dominated by a change in team ownership that brought a man who set rigid standards for achievement and injected the organization with a fresh attitude by refusing to tolerate half-hearted efforts. Such was the approach of 34-year-old Dan Snyder, a native of nearby Montgomery County, Maryland, who officially took control of the team in July 1999. He arrived knowing a thing or two about winning, having molded his company, Snyder Communications, in Bethesda, Maryland, into a billion-dollar firm.

"Without question, Snyder brought an energy level, an accountability, that I haven't seen in past years," Redskins Hall of Fame quarterback and long-time radio analyst Sonny Jurgensen, who became a close advisor to the new owner, said during the season. "It's different now. Everybody's accountable, coaches, players. They have to be accountable for what they do, how they conduct themselves and how successful they are. This is something that since [Joe] Gibbs left has been steadily going downhill."

Snyder was a central figure in a whirlwind off-season. Before owner Jack Kent Cooke died in April 1997, he created a will that left most of his nearly $1 billion estate with a foundation to give scholarships to college students. He also instructed trustees of his estate to auction off the Redskins to the highest bidder, a deal that included Jack Kent Cooke Stadium.

In a bid to purchase the Redskins, team president John Kent Cooke (left) lost out to Maryland businessman Dan Snyder, who bought the franchise for $800 million, a record price at the time for an American sports team.

In January 1999, a group led by New York real estate mogul Howard Milstein; his brother, Edward; and Snyder won the auction after submitting the highest bid at $800 million, a record price at the time for an American sports team. The group outbid Redskins president John Kent Cooke, the son of Jack Kent Cooke, among other prospective owners.

The sale was subject to NFL approval, and the Milstein-Snyder group, sensing opposition by NFL owners concerned that Howard Milstein's financing was too leveraged, withdrew its offer. Cooke again bid for the team, but Snyder, a minority partner in the Milstein-Snyder team, led another investment group that submitted an equity-heavy $800 million bid. League owners unanimously approved the proposal in May 1999, ending nearly four decades of the Cooke family's ties to the Redskins.

"I had the desire and the will—even the ingenuity—but not enough money to keep the Redskins in my family," John Kent Cooke said in a statement. "In the end, my family could not pay the price of our success, and others could in these affluent times."

What the Redskins—namely, general manager Charley Casserly—accomplished personnel-wise during the extended ownership bidding process set the platform for a winning season. The first big personnel move was at quarterback. The Redskins cut sixth-year-man Gus Frerotte, whose career had taken a turn for the worse. He started only two games in 1998, while taking a back seat to Trent Green, who started the other 14.

Green, an unrestricted free agent, said he would have re-signed with the Redskins if not for the confusion regarding the sale of the team. But he turned down a contract offer from Washington and returned to his hometown, St. Louis, by signing with the Rams. A few hours later, Casserly sent three draft picks to the Vikings—first- and third-rounders in 1999 and a second-rounder in 2000—for 6–5, 225-pound quarterback Brad Johnson.

A ninth-round draft choice out of Florida State in 1992, Johnson saw little action in his first four seasons before posting outstanding passing ratings in 1996 and 1997. In the latter season, he threw for 3,036 yards and 20 touchdowns. But he was injured twice in 1998, when NFL Player of the Year Randall Cunningham quarterbacked the 15–1 Vikings to the NFC championship game.

Media skeptics argued that the Redskins paid too much for Johnson, saying he was injury prone and had started only 23 games in his career. They said management should have kept the draft picks in order to continue rebuilding. A *Washington Post* headline read, "Questionable Move for Team in Question," and the *Washington Times* wrote, "Paying through facemask, avoiding egg on the face."

Casserly defended the acquisition of Johnson, who had a 62 percent career completion mark. "If you took a vote in the NFL about the best quarterback available, it would be 31–0 for Brad Johnson," the general manager told reporters. "So do you want to win or do you want to punt? We want to win. That's why we made this trade."

On draft day, Casserly shuffled his cards. The Redskins made two trades involving 11 players in the first 90 minutes, enabling them to take coveted Georgia cornerback Champ

Bailey with the No. 7 pick and acquire an extra first-round draft choice for a total of three in 2000. The 6–1, 184-pound Bailey, who entered the draft after his junior season, was college football's premier cornerback in 1998. He also was a solid wide receiver, having caught 59 passes for 978 yards and five touchdowns at Georgia.

Washington also traded to move up three spots in the second round to No. 37, where they drafted Michigan offensive tackle Jon Jansen. The Redskins hoped he would help fortify one of the team's sore spots from 1998, an offensive line that allowed a franchise-record 61 sacks.

In other personnel moves, the Redskins acquired free agents in Bengals strong safety Sam Shade, Chargers defensive end Marco Coleman, Bears offensive tackle Andy Heck, and Cardinals fullback Larry Centers, a two-time Pro Bowler and a superb receiver out of the backfield. Centers set a league record for catches by running backs with 101 in 1995.

These days, Casserly speaks with pride about how he maneuvered personnel-wise through a tenuous period leading up to Snyder's official takeover of the team in July 1999. It was no secret that the general manager and coach Norv Turner were likely lame ducks. Plus, Casserly and John Kent Cooke were sued by Howard Milstein, who alleged that the two had tried to damage his bid to buy the team.

"That spring, the situation I was put in was an awkward one, but the organization and I responded dramatically because we all knew we were being fired by Milstein," Casserly said. "Number two, when Milstein drops out, Snyder takes over, then the next day I'm getting sued by Milstein for everything I owned. Under those conditions, we went through that off-season and still got Brad Johnson, Champ Bailey, Jon Jansen, Larry Centers, Marco Coleman, Andy Heck, Sam Shade, and negotiated trades to get three number ones. I also left them with $15 million in cap room. It was a difficult spring, to say the least, but we held everything together and got it going in the right direction."

All the while, rumors were rampant that Casserly and Turner were feuding. Snyder kept Turner but fired Casserly, who had spent 22 seasons with the organization. Former 49ers director of player personnel Vinny Cerrato, originally hired by Howard Milstein, assumed many of Casserly's duties, and Casserly stayed on as a consultant to the owner. Snyder fired about 25 front-office and stadium employees at the time.

"Basically, Dan Snyder and I just didn't see eye to eye," Casserly recalled. "No hard feelings. It wasn't going to be comfortable for me to stay anyway because I had backed Cooke in the sale of the team. No axes to grind. There are a lot of people who would have some animosity there. I never did. I understood the situation. I went to him and said, 'Listen, this isn't working. Just let me go, and you get on with your life, and I'll get on with mine.'"

Despite giving Turner a greater say in personnel decisions, Snyder didn't let the coach with a five-year record of 32–47–1 and no playoff appearances off the hook. The rookie owner wanted immediate results and issued an ultimatum to Turner: Make the playoffs or you're fired.

In statements to the media, Snyder also delivered tough talk to his players, saying that he had no desire for anyone who failed to work hard or stayed in shape. He is believed to have forced the training camp release of fifth-year offensive lineman Joe Patton after Patton missed a block that led to a sack of Brad Johnson in the first exhibition game.

"In the world I come from there's pressure every minute to perform," Snyder told *Sports Illustrated* in an article that appeared on November 15, 1999. "So on this team, those who don't want to play, like Joe Patton, we'll pack up all their (baggage) and throw it out in the parking lot."

The Redskins barely missed going 4–0 in the preseason, as Tampa Bay scored in the waning seconds of the last exhibition game for a 16–13 victory. The Snyder era officially kicked off when the Redskins hosted the Cowboys in the season-opener at newly renamed Redskins Stadium—formerly Jack Kent Cooke Stadium—on September 12, 1999.

Dallas led 14–3 early, but the Redskins exploded with 32 straight points for a 35–14 lead entering the fourth quarter. But in a typical Redskins collapse under Turner, the Cowboys tied it up with three straight touchdowns. Washington had a chance to win it at the end of regulation, but a poor snap prevented kicker Brett Conway from trying a 41-yard field goal.

On the Cowboys' first possession in overtime, quarterback Troy Aikman faked a handoff, safety Matt Stevens bit and receiver Raghib "Rocket" Ismail was all alone for a 76-yard touchdown catch, leaving nearly 80,000 fans gasping in horror at the cruel turn of events.

The loss spoiled a spectacular debut by Brad Johnson (20 of 33, 382 yards, two touchdowns). Michael Westbrook caught five passes for 159 yards, and fellow receiver Albert Connell had four catches for 137 yards. Fourth-year running back Stephen Davis, who had assumed the lead role in the backfield, rushed for 109 yards and two touchdowns. Overall, the Redskins' offense churned out 504 yards, but in a sign of things to come, the defense allowed 541.

The offense remained explosive, as the Redskins posted wild wins of 50–21 over the Giants, 27–20 over the Jets and 38–36 over Carolina to improve to 3–1. The 50-point output against the Giants marked the first time Washington had scored that many since 1991. Johnson remained blistering hot. He was named NFC Offensive Player of the Week after a 20 of 28, 231-yard, three-touchdown performance against the Giants and a 20 of 33, 337-yard, four-touchdown display against Carolina. Through the first four games, he completed 62 of 90 passes for 894 yards and a league-high nine touchdowns with no interceptions. His 119.9 quarterback rating was second to the Rams' Kurt Warner.

That's not all. The veteran quarterback was showing poise and leadership skills that had been missing for most of the Turner era.

"He's made all the difference in the world," Sonny Jurgensen said at the time. "He has experience, he understands the offense, he's playing as well as anybody who can play the position. And he's got everyone else playing well. Michael Westbrook's having his best year. Albert Connell. Last year, the line gave up 61 sacks. They're not doing that now because they believe in the quarterback, and they believe that he's going to make plays for them. The Redskins haven't had an offensive leader in years. Now they have one."

The defense was another story. A unit with six No. 1 draft picks yielded NFL highs of 433.5 yards and 29.5 points per game through the first four weeks. The Redskins thus hired 72-year-old Bill Arnsparger, architect of the "No Name Defense" from Miami's 17–0 season in 1972, to assist beleaguered defensive coordinator Mike Nolan, a move Snyder reportedly influenced.

The Redskins improved to 4–1 with a 24–10 win over Arizona, but with first place in the NFC East on the line, they fell, 38–20, to the Cowboys at Texas Stadium. They rebounded with a 48–22 rout of the Bears at home, where Stephen Davis rushed for 143 yards and 320-pound defensive tackle Dan Wilkinson returned an interception 88 yards for a score. As for Johnson, his 14 scoring passes and two interceptions through seven games appeared to make him a strong candidate for league MVP. But his numbers began to dip, as the Redskins suffered a 34–17 loss to Buffalo, which posted 413 yards and 24 first downs and controlled the clock for 41 minutes, and a 35–28 loss to the Eagles, against whom Washington committed six turnovers, including three interceptions by Johnson.

"People are seeing that our season is slipping away and that our playoff chances could be gone if we don't start getting things done," Connell said of his 5–4 squad. "We can't wait."

Fullback Mike Sellers concurred: "Our patience is wearing thin. Everybody wants to win, but it's getting close to the end of the season, and we have plans to reach the playoffs."

The Redskins reacted by posting two straight wins at newly renamed FedExField (Snyder sold the naming rights to the delivery company), keeping the 7–4 squad in first place in the NFC East. In one of the wins, 23–13 over the Giants, Davis rushed for 183 yards and an improved Redskins defense had four sacks, two fumble recoveries, and three interceptions, and yielded 72 yards rushing.

Washington still hadn't beaten a winning team, though, and losses to the Lions and Colts, sandwiched around a win over the Cardinals, left the Redskins at 8–6. Still, they were on top in the feeble NFC East, a game over the Cowboys and Giants.

Meanwhile, media reports were saying that Turner was considering quitting, playoffs or not, because he had grown weary of the impetuous Snyder. The owner had reportedly given Turner a stern 40-minute lecture in the Redskins' locker room after the 38–20 loss to Dallas and had met privately with five players before the 28–3 win over the Cardinals. On December 21, the *Washington Times* reported that Turner would consider a buyout of his $1 million-a-year contract and resign after the season.

Snyder had gained a reputation for being meddlesome, although some people supported his micromanaging approach. "Mr. Snyder is very aggressive with the things he wants to do, and the players are feeding off of that, too," kick returner Brian Mitchell said at the time. "He has a lot of energy and tries to carry that energy over to the team. It's a whole new change, a whole new era."

"Mr. Snyder has injected new life into this football team," long-time Redskins radio analyst Sam Huff said. "From the beginning, he's been very, very active, and he's done wonders. When you move as fast as he moves, you're going to make mistakes. But his accomplishments have greatly overcome the few errors he's made."

The suspense of whether Turner would meet Snyder's pre-season ultimatum fizzled before the Redskins played the 49ers in a Sunday night game on December 26. Losses that day by Green Bay and Carolina allowed the Redskins to seize a wild card playoff spot. But an even bigger prize—the NFC East title—was there for the taking with a road win against 4–10 San Francisco.

The Redskins seemed oblivious to what was at stake, for the 49ers led, 20–10, early in the fourth period. But an interception by Redskins safety Matt Stevens set up Brett Conway's 34-yard field goal, and Johnson's 1-yard sneak tied the game at 20

In his first season in Washington, quarterback Brad Johnson passed for 4,005 yards, the second-best total in Redskins history. He made the Pro Bowl.

with 3:28 left. The 49ers, who piled up 418 yards and 24 first downs, drove to the Redskins' 22. In perhaps the biggest play of the season, linebacker Shawn Barber stripped the ball and defensive end Anthony Cook recovered, forcing overtime.

The Redskins needed four plays to go 78 yards. Johnson passed twice to running back Skip Hicks, and wingback Larry Centers ran 12 yards to the 49ers' 33. Johnson then found Centers wide open in the right flat, and the veteran scooted into the end zone untouched for the game winner.

In a giddy Redskins' postgame locker room, Snyder handed the game ball to Turner. Two days later, team officials confirmed that Snyder wanted his coach back for the 2000 season. "Dan probably did the right thing," Turner said in looking back. "When he came out and said, 'If we don't make the playoffs, I'm not keeping him,' it took a little bit of the edge off for everyone, and we didn't have to deal with it all year. If he hadn't done that, every time we were preparing to play someone, every time a reporter would cover a game, we'd have spent half an hour talking about that subject. It just became a foregone conclusion and probably helped us in the long run."

Snyder, whom *Sport Magazine* named the 1999 NFL "Owner of the Year," agreed that his demanding style had a positive influence on Turner. "Jack Kent Cooke was a great owner because everyone knew they were going to win," Snyder

## Happy Halloween

One week after being called into a meeting with Dan Snyder after a disappointing loss to Dallas, Norv Turner had a surprise for reporters.

"This was a gift from Larry Centers for Halloween," the Redskins' coach said of his fake tooth after a 48–22 win over the Bears on November 1. "Sorry I was a little late. I was in a meeting with Mr. Snyder."

said in February 2000. "It all starts at the ownership level. With me there, I added the emphasis, 'Let's win now, let's go get the other team.' It goes a long way, and it played well for Norv. It created an opportunity for him that he didn't have before with a low-keyed type of owner."

A banner was raised at Redskin Park saying, "1999 NFC Eastern Division Champions," and the Redskins closed the regular season and entered the new millennium with a 21–10 win over Miami at FedExField on January 2, 2000, their only victory all season over a team with a winning record. Brad Johnson played about a half and passed for 75 yards to finish with 4,005, a career high and the second-best total in Redskins history. He also posted the league's fifth-highest quarterback rating (90.0) and earned his first Pro Bowl invitation.

It was off to the playoffs, where the Redskins would host the Lions in the first round in a bid to return to the Super Bowl for the first time since the 1991 season. "It's been too long," Brian Mitchell, who played on that Super Bowl team, said at the time. "It's time to get something going. It's time to let others watch. We don't need to be watching."

## NFC DIVISIONAL PLAYOFF GAME
## Washington 27, Detroit 13
## January 8, 2000
## FedExField, Landover, Md.
## Attendance: 79,411

### Redskins Feast on Lions, Frerotte in Playoff Win

After a year hiatus, the "Gus Bus" rolled back into town. The Redskins cooled its engines and captured something that had eluded them since the 1992 season: a playoff victory.

While holding former Redskins quarterback Gus Frerotte to 7 of 17 passing for 111 yards in the first half, with 58 of those coming on a Hail Mary, the Redskins cruised to a 27–0 halftime lead en route to a 27–13 win over Detroit. Washington's much-improved defense, aggressive and swarming, allowed only 258 yards and one rushing first down, sacking Frerotte five times and intercepting him twice.

Running back Stephen Davis, who set an all-time Redskins rushing record in 1999 with 1,405 yards despite missing the last two regular season games with a sprained ankle, started and served as a huge inspiration. He rushed for 119 yards on 15 carries with two touchdowns, before a sprained knee late in

the first half sidelined him for the rest of the game. Quarterback Brad Johnson had a solid outing, throwing for 174 yards and a touchdown pass that made the score 27–0 late in the first half.

The final margin could have been bigger, but Redskins tight end Stephen Alexander dropped a touchdown pass, and Washington missed out on a relatively easy scoring opportunity in the second half.

"At that point, I thought we were as close as we could possibly be to being a championship team," Redskins return man Brian Mitchell said in looking back. "We had finally arrived, put ourselves in a position."

The Lions committed 12 penalties while suffering their 20th loss in 20 games in Washington, including three playoff games. The 8–8 squad entered the game limping with four straight losses. Their last win had come in Detroit against the Redskins on December 5, an ugly day for the burgundy and gold. The Redskins, rattled by the crowd noise at the Pontiac Silverdome, were penalized 14 times for 122 yards. Johnson was sacked five times and coughed up a fumble that was returned for a touchdown.

This time, the Redskins would be playing before nearly 80,000 maniacal supporters at FedExField and a crowd hostile to Frerotte, who was subbing for injured starter Charlie Batch. An indisputable fan favorite before being released after the 1998 season, Frerotte was mocked by the crowd for head-butting a concrete wall at the stadium during a crucial game in 1997. A sign in the area where Frerotte rammed his head read, "This X Marks Gus's Spot." Frerotte said he expected the hostile crowd reaction but that he was displeased when a fan threw beer in his face after the game.

The Redskins welcomed Frerotte on the game's first play. Linebacker Greg Jones came off the corner and sacked him for a 7-yard loss, leaving Gus with a dislocated a finger on his nonthrowing hand. "We wanted to get pressure on [Frerotte] early," Redskins coach Norv Turner recalled.

After the Redskins held, Detroit began self-destructing. The Lions were called for running into the punter, giving the Redskins a first down. A few plays later, a 41-yard pass interference penalty set up a 1-yard scoring run by Davis.

On the Redskins' next possession, Davis raced 58 yards to the Detroit 29, a run that "kind of got everyone fired up big," Turner remembered. Davis later took it in from the 4 for a 14–0 lead. Cornerback Champ Bailey's interception and a roughing the passer penalty then set up Brett Conway's 33-yard field goal, and Davis's 32-yard run put Conway in position for a 23-yard kick and a 20–0 lead. Johnson's 30-yard scoring pass to Connell with 1:46 left in the half capped an 82-yard Redskins drive.

In an otherwise uneventful second half, fireworks erupted early in the third period. After throwing an interception, Johnson was blocked by Lions defensive end Robert Porcher. The two began scuffling and exchanging punches, and players from both sides charged in. Redskins guard Tre' Johnson, trying to defend his quarterback, took a swing that inadvertently struck referee Bill Leavy on the head. The NFL later issued a then-record $154,000 in fines to 23 players. Tre' Johnson, who had been ejected from the game, received the harshest punishment, a $50,000 fine and suspension for the first game of the 2000 season.

Detroit's offense finally managed a score with about nine minutes left when safety Ron Rice returned a blocked field goal 94 yards for a touchdown.

While Stephen Davis rushed for 119 yards and two touchdowns on a bad ankle, former Redskins quarterback Gus Frerotte had a rough day in his return to FedExField.

| Detroit— | 0 | 0 | 0 | 13 | — | 13 |
|---|---|---|---|---|---|---|
| Washington— | 14 | 13 | 0 | 0 | — | 27 |

Wash — Davis 1 run (Conway kick)
Wash — Davis 4 run (Conway kick)
Wash — FG Conway 33
Wash — FG Conway 23
Wash — Connell 30 pass from Johnson (Conway kick)
Det —— Rice 94 blocked FG return (pass failed)
Det —— Rivers 5 pass from Frerotte (Hanson kick)

## NFC DIVISIONAL PLAYOFF GAME
**Tampa Bay 14, Washington 13**
**January 15, 2000**
**Raymond James Stadium, Tampa, Fla.**
**Attendance: 65,835**

### Ball Bounces Bucs' Way in Win over Luckless Redskins

Credit this win to the Buccaneers' defense—and a boatload of luck.

The third-ranked unit in the NFL reduced one of the league's top offenses to rubble in the second half, holding the Redskins to 26 yards while producing two turnovers that led to 14 points. Monster breaks, ones cruel to the Redskins and their faithful, were also pivotal in lifting Tampa Bay to a 14–13 victory that ended the Redskins' playoff ride.

The last of those breaks was the most telling. With 1:17 to play, the wind at his back, and the Bucs up by one, Redskins kicker Brett Conway lined up to try a 52-yard field goal. It was a little out of his range, but he had easily drilled a 48-yarder earlier. Conway never attempted the kick. Dan Turk's snap bounced several times on the ground, and holder and quarterback Brad Johnson failed to get a pass off.

"It was really disappointing because I thought we'd make the field goal," Redskins coach Norv Turner said years later. "[Turk] just lost his grip on the ball as he snapped it. You never take anything for granted in this league." (On a sad note, Turk died of cancer less than a year later at age 38.)

The Bucs, winners of the NFC Central at 11–5 and coming off a bye, were solid favorites entering the game. Washington faced a daunting challenge against Tampa Bay's defense, for 1,405-yard rusher Stephen Davis was hurting and left offensive tackle Andy Heck was ruled out after straining a hamstring against Detroit.

Davis, playing on a bad ankle and knee, ran for 35 yards in the first half, when Conway's 28-yard field goal with 5:37 left accounted for the only score. Washington's rejuvenated defense held the Bucs' offense to 69 yards and only 24 on the ground, where the duo of fullback Mike Alstott and tailback Warrick Dunn had combined for 1,565 yards in the regular season. Bucs rookie quarterback Shaun King was also ineffective.

When Redskin Brian Mitchell returned the opening kickoff of the second half 100 yards for a touchdown, followed by Conway's 48-yard field goal midway through the third period for a 13–0 lead, it looked like a visit to the NFC championship was in sight for the burgundy and gold. "I thought at that point we had won the game," Mitchell recalled.

All the Redskins had to do was stop the Bucs' anemic offense and play smart. But a mistake by the normally cool-headed Brad Johnson gave Tampa Bay much-needed momentum. With the ball at midfield, he tried to force a pass that safety John Lynch intercepted at the 27. King connected on throws of 16 and 17 yards, before safety Leomont Evans was called for a 31-yard pass interference penalty. Soon after, Alstott bounced off several tacklers and ran 2 yards for a score.

Early in the fourth period, Johnson fumbled while being sacked, and Bucs defensive tackle Warren Sapp, the NFL Defensive Player of the Year, recovered at the Redskins' 32 with 13:21 to play. Two plays later, the Bucs faced a third-and-3, and it looked like the Redskins had held when King was sacked by linebacker Shawn Barber and fumbled.

But Dunn picked up the loose ball on the 30 and ran 13 yards for a first down. Alstott ran 5 yards on a fourth-and-1 to give Tampa Bay a first down at the 3, and King, about to be sacked by defensive end Ndukwe Kalu, flipped a scoring pass to tight end John Davis. Martin Gramatica's extra point created a 14–13 game.

"If we had found a way to fall on the ball or just found a way to stop Dunn short of the first down, I don't think they ever get back in the ball game," Turner said in hindsight.

After the teams traded punts, the Redskins took over on their 38 with 3:05 to play. Two passes to Skip Hicks, subbing for Davis, and a pass and a run by Larry Centers moved the ball to the Bucs' 33 with two minutes left. But Johnson overthrew a receiver and Hicks was stopped for no gain, and Conway, the NFC's second-leading scorer that season (115 points), entered to try the game-winner.

The rest is history.

"We fought so hard to get in position to have an opportunity to win the game," Centers recalled. "Not being able to see the field goal at least fly toward the uprights made it that much more disappointing."

| | | | | | | |
|---|---|---|---|---|---|---|
| Washington — | 0 | 3 | 10 | 0 | — | 13 |
| Tampa Bay — | 0 | 0 | 7 | 7 | — | 14 |

Wash — FG Conway 28
Wash — Mitchell 100 kickoff return (Conway kick)
Wash — FG Conway 48
TB —— Alstott 2 run (Gramatica kick)
TB —— Davis 1 pass from King (Gramatica kick)

## 2000: 8–8, 3RD PLACE—NFC EAST

### Head Coach: Norv Turner (13 games), Terry Robiskie (3 games)

When you pay an NFL-record $100 million in player salaries , you expect big results. The Redskins gave results in 2000. They just weren't the ones owner Dan Snyder and the Redskins' faithful hoped to see.

The Redskins evolved into one of the most expensive flops in the history of pro sports. After opening the year with the apparent makings of a Super Bowl contender, then posting a 6–2 mark by the midway point, they stumbled to finish 8–8 and fell short of the playoffs. Missing out on the Super Bowl and the whole postseason was the climax of a rough stretch and showed that spending money for the sake of obtaining marquee names does not guarantee championships in the free-agency, salary-cap era of the NFL.

Those names were veteran stars from other teams who suddenly arrived at Redskins Park: future Hall of Famers in cornerback Deion Sanders and defensive end Bruce Smith, rifle-armed quarterback Jeff George, and hard-hitting safety Mark Carrier. Snyder and company hoped that they would help thrust a Redskins squad that was a field goal away from reaching the NFC championship game in 1999 to loftier heights.

The experiment failed, and late in the season Snyder did what everyone expected him to do if the team missed its goals. He fired seventh-year coach Norv Turner.

"Norv got the rawest deal," Redskins defensive end Marco Coleman said. "All the guys liked him, and he should have at least had an opportunity to bring the guys back that he had and see if they could have got it going again. I don't think we needed as many guys as they brought in to get us over the hump."

Inability to meet their preseason hype made the Redskins the butt of media and fan criticism. It would have been muted if they only had a decent field goal kicker. The Redskins used *five* kickers and lost three games largely because of missed field goals. "We were 7–6 when I left the team," Turner said in 2005. "Had we had a competent field goal kicker, that team easily could have had 10 wins at the time."

The immediate focus in the 2000 off-season was on revamping a defense ranked 30th in the league in 1999. Although the unit had improved as the season progressed and yielded 14.2 points on average in the last six games, Snyder fired defensive coordinator Mike Nolan and replaced him with former Eagles and Packers head coach Ray Rhodes, known for his aggressive, attacking defenses.

The owner then began his audacious spending spree. He shelled out megabucks for Smith ($25 million, five years), the No. 2 sack leader in NFL history with 171; Carrier ($16 million, five years), a three-time Pro Bowler; and George ($18.25 million, four years). The Redskins also signed Cardinals running back Adrian Murrell, who had three straight 1,000-yard rushing seasons on his résumé.

The acquisition of George, who was assigned to back up Johnson, mystified many. Although the remarkably accurate passer had amassed more than 26,000 passing yards in 10 NFL seasons, he had traveled a bumpy road with five teams and his hot-headedness had gotten the best of him. His reputation had been stained by a 1996 shouting match with Falcons coach June Jones, after which George was suspended for four games and released from the team. He later played two seasons in Oakland and in 1999 in Minnesota, where he was 9–3 as a starter and threw for 2,816 yards and 23 touchdowns.

In 1999, George was the NFL's third-rated passer (94.2) and Johnson was fifth (90.0), giving the Redskins perhaps the best one-two quarterback combination in the league. With his quirky sidearm release, George could throw the ball longer and harder than Johnson, but Turner objected to the signing of George.

"I personally never thought Jeff George was the type of player who would fit our situation," Turner said. "I just didn't think it was in the best interest of our football team from the standpoint of chemistry. I thought our quarterback situation was good. I thought Brad was a guy that could get done the things we wanted to do like winning a Super Bowl. I made that clear."

The most monumental signing was yet to come. In June 2000, the Cowboys cut flashy and celebrated cornerback Deion Sanders, known as "Prime Time" or "Neon Deion." The Redskins immediately released long-time return man Brian Mitchell and signed Sanders, a seven-time Pro Bowler, for $56 million over seven seasons with an $8 million signing bonus. Legendary cornerback Darrell Green, who helped lure Sanders to Washington, approved of the deal, although it meant that Green, a regular starter about to enter his 18th season, would back him up.

The acquisition of so many big-name free agents irked others on the team, according to Mitchell, who signed with the Eagles:

You had guys like [tailback] Stephen Davis, Brad Johnson and [fullback] Larry Centers who had busted their butts to take us to the playoffs [in 1999], and we could have easily ended up in the championship game and then all of a sudden you bring in Bruce Smith and Deion Sanders and Jeff George, and they become your poster children. You open up a press guide, those guys are there. The guys who had done everything to get you in a position of notoriety, you just came in and washed them away. I talked to many guys during that time who were basically pissed. What had Bruce Smith done for the Redskins, nothing? Deion Sanders, nothing. They'd done a lot for other teams. It began to be basically a trust issue with the players and management.

Centers said he felt no disrespect: "I looked at it from an optimistic point of view that we're bringing in more soldiers, people to help us get done what we wanted to get done, to win a championship. I saw it as a challenge that I needed to step my game up to be one of the bright spots on the team, not one of the weak links."

For the 2000 draft, the Redskins initially had three No. 1 picks. They traded two of them, the 12th and 24th choices, to the 49ers for the third overall pick, giving Washington the second and third picks. The Redskins used the No. 2 pick on Penn State linebacker LaVar Arrington and No. 3 on Alabama offensive tackle Chris Samuels.

Arrington, an amazing package of power, quickness, and agility, had earned the Bednarik Award as the nation's top defensive player and the Butkus Award as the premier linebacker in college football, both in 1999, his junior season. Samuels finished his college career by going 47 games without yielding a sack and won the Outland Trophy as the nation's best lineman as a senior.

After a 3–1 preseason, uneventful except that center Cory Raymer tore ligaments in his knee and was lost for a few weeks, the remodeled Redskins were ready to debut. They were the No. 1 topic of conversation in pro football circles, a curiosity everyone wanted to see, and their schedule included eight games on national TV. Las Vegas bookies pegged them as solid favorites to go all the way, and Snyder ordered a banner to

be hung at Redskins Park proclaiming "The Future Is Now." The late, great Redskins coach George Allen had coined that phrase in 1971.

"Our goal is simple. Win the Super Bowl, now, this year, let's go get it!" Snyder said during the 2000 off-season. If the players can't understand it, they shouldn't be with us. We will not stop until we win one Super Bowl, then two, then three, then four. This town will understand that we are very driven on one goal, and it's winning the Super Bowl every year.

"Last year was a great year, it was a good beginning. But we're not satisfied. We're more fired up than ever to bring that trophy home."

The Redskins got off to a roaring start by beating Carolina, 20–17, at FedExField. Stephen Davis ran 23 times for 133 yards, and Brad Johnson was 25 of 36 for 234 yards. But credit went mostly to the retooled defense, which featured three former NFL Defensive Players of the Year in Bruce Smith, Deion Sanders, and defensive tackle Dana Stubblefield, as well as eight first-round draft picks. The unit allowed 236 yards and sacked Panthers quarterback Steve Beuerlein six times. Smith (1.5 sacks) drew double teams at right end, giving left end Marco Coleman (2.5 sacks) a wide path to Beuerlein.

"Having Bruce Smith on the other side sure helps," Coleman said at the time. "Seems like the whole offensive line is on him. I'm going to do everything I can to take advantage of that."

The defense was stingy the next week at Detroit, although Sanders was picked on repeatedly and acknowledged playing the worst game of his career. Washington's offense gained 333 yards, but Johnson threw a career-high four interceptions, including three in the fourth quarter, and Detroit won, 15–10.

To worsen matters, the Redskins' best receiver and big-play threat, Michael Westbrook, damaged ligaments in his knee and was lost for the season. That week in practice, kicker Brett Conway aggravated a right quad muscle and was unable to play. The Redskins signed former Raiders and Buccaneers kicker Michael Husted.

Things got worse. Before a record franchise crowd of 84,431 on Monday night against 0–2 Dallas, the Redskins

## FREE AGENT FRENZY

Mark Carrier

Jeff George

Deion Sanders

Bruce Smith

were embarrassed, 27–21. They committed six penalties for 82 yards, including a pass interference call against Darrell Green that helped the Cowboys get in the end zone, and a personal foul on the sideline against offensive tackle Andy Heck that killed a fourth-quarter drive.

Johnson (30 of 48, 241 yards) was unable to throw down-field without Westbrook. The quarterback's second-quarter fumble led to a Cowboys touchdown, and for the second straight game, he threw a late interception as the Redskins were mounting a potential go-ahead drive. Boos rained down at FedExField, and fans demanded that Turner replace Johnson with Jeff George. But the coach said later he was sticking with Johnson.

With the NFC East-leading 3–0 Giants coming up and all four of the 1999 conference finalists on the schedule within a span of seven games—Tampa Bay, Jacksonville, Tennessee and St. Louis—the Redskins needed a fast turnaround to make the playoffs and meet their preseason billing. Was it now or never?

"I don't think it's now or never, it's now," offensive tackle Jon Jansen said at the time. "We're not looking past the Giants game."

Distractions were everywhere. Guard Tre' Johnson had served a suspension in the season opener for inadvertently hitting a referee in the 1999 playoffs, and Mark Carrier, who applied a helmet-to-helmet hit in the season opener, had been suspended for the Detroit game. Safety Sam Shade was fined $7,500 for an illegal hit, and Stubblefield had been arrested and charged with assaulting his wife. Conway was let go in a questionable release after the loss to Dallas. Toss in the quarterback controversy and the injuries to Westbrook and Raymer, who was also ruled out for the year.

The Redskins held a players-only meeting where such veterans as Bruce Smith and defensive tackle Dan Wilkinson spoke. "A lot of the old guys wanted to voice their concerns to some of the young guys," Jansen said. "We said everything we needed to say. We just need to go out and play."

The Redskins won five straight games, starting with a 16–6 win over the Giants on the road. Johnson, in resembling his old self, hit 14 of 20 passes for 289 yards and two touchdowns. "Brad just showed he was the old Brad," receiver Albert Connell said at the time. "He had a slow start, but we always knew he would come on eventually. It wasn't anything different. Brad really stepped up in the pocket and made his plays."

The Redskins followed with a 20–17 win over Tampa Bay, as Sanders dazzled the FedEx crowd of 83,532 by returning a punt 57 yards in overtime to set up Husted's 20-yard game-winning field goal. Next, Husted kicked a 24-yard game-winner with two seconds left in a hard-fought 17–14 win over the Eagles at the Vet. Then came a 10–3 win over the Ravens at FedEx, as Stephen Davis ran for 91 yards, including a 33-yard touchdown run in the fourth quarter, and a 35–16 win over the Jaguars in Jacksonville, where Johnson turned in another yeoman effort. He completed 16 of 24 passes for 269 yards, with scoring passes of 11, 49 and 77 yards to Connell.

But the 6–2 Redskins dropped another Monday night game to a Tennessee team that scored on a 69-yard punt return and an 80-yard interception return. Johnson completed 21 of 40 passes for 202 yards with two touchdowns but three interceptions. He also sprained his knee, and George was named the starter for the upcoming game at Arizona.

George completed 20 of 39 passes for 276 yards with two interceptions, and the Redskins dominated in total yardage (431–178). But Redskins kicker Kris Heppner, who had replaced Husted, missed two field goals, including a 33-yarder with 5:01 left, in a 16–15 loss. Goodbye Heppner.

Two kickers were signed, 44-year-old ex-Redskin Eddie Murray for field goals and extra points, and Scott Bentley for kickoffs. In a 33–20 Monday night win at St. Louis, Murray was 4 of 4 on field goals, and Bentley recovered his onside kick to set up a field goal. Washington's defense, one of the top-ranked units in the NFL, held the most explosive offense in football to its lowest point total since 1998 and almost 75 yards below its season average. Quarterback Trent Green was sacked six times. "That's what Mr. Snyder spent all the money for, to revamp the defense," Deion Sanders said at the time. "We've done just that."

The 7–4 Redskins were now tied with the Giants for second place in the division behind the 8–4 Eagles. The next two games at FedExField were telling.

Unable to stop a one-man show named Donovan McNabb, the Redskins dropped a 23–20 decision to Philly. The Eagles' superstar rushed for 125 yards, the highest total for an NFL quarterback in almost three decades. He scored on a 21-yard bootleg and scrambled 54 yards to set up the winning field goal. He also completed passes to 10 different receivers for 118 yards. When asked how big a headache McNabb was that day, Marco Coleman replied: "I don't think they make Tylenol that big."

Murray had a chance to send the game into overtime, but his 44-yard field goal with 1:21 left was wide right. George completed 25 of 43 passes for 288 yards and two touchdowns. But Turner, having promised Johnson his starting job back once he was 100 percent healthy, kept his word for a game against the Giants.

Washington's offense looked anemic, going possession after possession without a first down. Johnson threw two critical interceptions and was benched with the Redskins trailing 9–0 in the fourth quarter. George rallied his squad with a 10-play, 97-yard touchdown drive that created a 9–7 game. Later, his completion to receiver James Thrash with time running out appeared to have Murray in good position for a winning field goal. But the play was overturned after an instant-replay review.

Forced to set up farther back, Murray was a few yards short on a 49-yard try, marking the sixth time that year the Redskins had the ball with less than two minutes left and lost. Their playoff chances were crippled, and the firing of Turner appeared imminent.

It happened the next day, and passing game coordinator Terry Robiskie was promoted to interim head coach. (After the season, Snyder told all-sports D.C. radio station WTEM that Ray Rhodes was at the top of his list to replace Turner but didn't want the job.) The Redskins also reportedly considered hiring the colorful former Kansas, UCLA, and Georgia Tech coach Pepper Rodgers, but he was named vice president of football operations.

"I appreciate the opportunity Dan Snyder gave me," Turner said at his parting news conference. "I don't think anyone can question his passion, how badly he wants to win. He put me in good position to have an opportunity to win. We went to the playoffs last year with a 10–6 record and won the division. With the schedule the way it is, this team still has a chance to

Flamboyant cornerback Deion Sanders was welcomed enthusiastically at FedExField as a Redskin in 2000, but he had one of the worst seasons in his 14-year career.

be 10–6. That's the disappointing thing for me. There's part of me that would like to be a part of it, but there's a part of me that understands why it's important and it's necessary to make a head coaching change right now."

The Redskins hoped that the no-nonsense Robiskie, who gained attention earlier in the season due to a sideline shouting match with Connell, would spark the 7–6 squad, which was alive for a wild card playoff spot. But the Redskins suffered a 32–13 roasting at the hands of the Cowboys and a 24–3 loss to the Steelers that eliminated them from playoff contention. George started both games, and Johnson started the season finale, a 20–3 win over Arizona that ended with Robiskie getting a Gatorade shower.

The interim coach voiced his desire for Snyder to promote him. "You hate to sit down and say that as a head coach I coached three games and that I lost all three of them," Robiskie told the press. "If this is my last opportunity ever in my life to be a head coach, I might be one of the few guys who can say I won the last game I coached as a head coach. That's an honor in itself. In terms of how elated I was, I kept turning around

looking for a TV camera to say I was going to Disneyland." But the front office sidestepped Robiskie to seek a proven head coach who could reassemble the pieces from a once promising season that had deteriorated fast.

"I thought because of what we had done the year before, we would be a very, very competitive team, I thought we'd be a good football team," Turner said. "But you never know in terms of chemistry, and then there were some issues that we didn't address. The year before we kept the offensive line together with Band-Aids, tape and glue. That group was getting up in age, and some of our problems during the 2000 season were directly related to that. We had a number of injuries on the offensive line."

Larry Centers echoed Turner on the issue of chemistry, or lack thereof: "We had a lot of individuals out there playing to shine and to look good, but from a team standpoint we never established the mentality where we would go out and play for each other. I don't think our number one focus as a team was to win ball games. Our number one focus was to watch different players perform. We missed the point that it's a team effort, and you just can't win it with one or two guys making plays and everybody else sitting back and watching. That hurt us down the stretch."

## 2001: 8–8, 2ND PLACE—NFC EAST

### Head Coach: Marty Schottenheimer

It was a chaotic season, to say the least. After opening the year with a five-game losing streak during which they looked lifeless at times, the Redskins showed spurts of dominance as they won their next five and got back in the playoff race. They were the first team in NFL history to make that five-and-five turnaround—but they soon fell out of playoff contention and finished 8–8 for the second straight year.

Oh, and a Redskins head coach was fired for the second straight season. Marty Schottenheimer was shown the door shortly after the last game when he and owner Dan Snyder reportedly failed to agree on who had authority over player personnel decisions.

Schottenheimer had been a surprise pick in the first place. With the embarrassment from the 2000 season hovering over the Redskins, Snyder wasted no time searching for a coach to revive his wounded franchise. His list of candidates included former Redskins coach Joe Gibbs, two-time Super Bowl–winning coach Bill Parcells, former St. Louis Rams coach Dick Vermeil, and Florida coach Steve Spurrier. In January 2001, however, the Redskins announced their choice to be

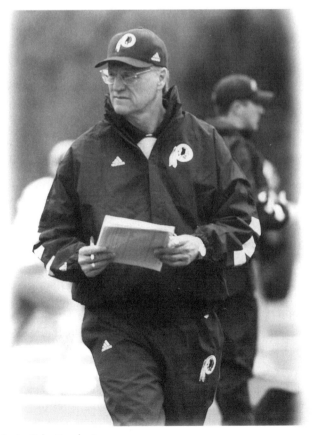

Marty Schottenheimer

Schottenheimer, the 12th-winningest coach in NFL history at the time.

Are you kidding? Schottenheimer, working as an ESPN analyst while on a coaching hiatus, had lambasted Snyder on national TV after the firing of Norv Turner late in the 2000 season. Schottenheimer said he might coach again but had no interest in working for Snyder, saying he didn't think the two could coexist. He implied that the owner had too much influence in player personnel moves.

But by the time Schottenheimer was introduced as the 24th head coach in Redskins history, he had formed a brighter picture of his new boss. "It became very obvious to me that Dan Snyder has been after the same thing that Marty Schottenheimer has been after his entire career, and that's to win a world championship," said Schottenheimer, who signed a four-year, $10 million deal and was given full control of player personnel decisions. "It begins today in a partnership in which two individuals have to begin the process of developing the kind of trust and interaction that I have no doubt Dan Snyder and I will achieve."

In Schottenheimer, Snyder hired a man with the best winning percentage at the time among active coaches with at least 100 wins (.609). He sported a 150–96–1 record after going 46–31–0 in Cleveland (1984–88) and 104–65–1 in Kansas City (1989–98). He had gone to the postseason in 11 of his 15 coaching years, including trips to three AFC championship games, but had failed to reach the Super Bowl.

"Marty Schottenheimer is a first-class coach, a winning coach who comes close to the ultimate mountain but still needs to stake a claim and put the flag up there," Snyder told Washington all-sports radio station WTEM. "That's what he's going to do, and it'll be a Washington Redskins flag."

The old-school, no-frills Schottenheimer stripped the Redskins of their glitz and glamour from the year before and refitted them with a blue-collar image. In his first major move, he dismissed player personnel director Vinny Cerrato and a bevy of assistant coaches, including Terry Robiskie, the Redskins' interim head coach for the last three games of the 2000 season. He assembled a staff with six primary coaches who had worked under him in Kansas City.

It was a family reunion. Schottenheimer, a defensive specialist, named his brother, Kurt, the Redskins' defensive coordinator. Kurt's predecessor, Ray Rhodes, who had molded the Redskins into the league's No. 4 defense in 2000, had been allowed to speak with other teams. Brian Schottenheimer, Marty's son, became quarterbacks coach. Marty also hired Bill Arnsparger, architect of the famous "No Name Defense" on Miami's 17–0 team in 1972, as a defensive assistant.

Schottenheimer released about two dozen players from the 2000 squad, including starters Dana Stubblefield, Keith Sims, Irving Fryar, Tre' Johnson, Mark Carrier, and Larry Centers. The cuts were mainly to slash the Redskins' inflated payroll and get them under the $67.4 million salary cap. Such players as Centers failed to respond well to Schottenheimer's preseason workout regimen, hastening their exit.

The Redskins lost key players to free agency, namely quarterback Brad Johnson, middle linebacker Derek Smith, defensive end N. D. Kalu, and wide receivers James Thrash and Albert Connell. (Johnson signed with Tampa Bay and quarterbacked the Bucs to a win in Super Bowl XXXVII in January 2003.) But Schottenheimer remained conservative in paying newcomers, nothing like the wild spending spree from the year before. He signed players whom he had coached in Kansas City, including receiver Kevin Lockett, running back Donnell Bennett, and guard Dave Szott. Also new were veteran offensive linemen Matt Campbell and Ben Coleman, tight end Walter Rasby, kick returner Michael Bates, and running back Ki-Jana Cater, the first overall pick in the 1995 draft.

Washington's top two draft picks were wide receiver Rod Gardner (first round), one of the leading pass catchers in Clemson history, and Mississippi State cornerback Fred Smoot (second), a finalist in 2000 for the Jim Thorpe Award that goes annually to the nation's best defensive back. (Veteran cornerback Deion Sanders, critical of the Redskins and Schottenheimer in the off-season, returned to play pro baseball for the Cincinnati Reds and retired from the NFL.)

Schottenheimer went the whole off-season without signing an experienced backup to Jeff George, however. The coach had named George the starter, although his tendency to air it out clashed with Schottenheimer's modified West Coast offense, which called for quick, short passes. Not until George was sidelined by tendonitis in his throwing shoulder early in training camp at Dickinson College in Carlisle, Pennsylvania, where the Redskins had returned after holding camp in 2000 at Redskins Park, did Schottenheimer get the message.

The Redskins considered signing Trent Dilfer, who they passed up in the 1994 draft for Heath Shuler and who had just quarterbacked the Ravens to a win in Super Bowl XXXV before being cut. Schottenheimer balked, but after a 20–0 loss to Kansas City in the first exhibition game, when second-year man Todd Husak and rookie Sage Rosenfels combined for three interceptions, the coach signed sixth-year quarterback Tony Banks.

George started the last two preseason games but looked rusty in the finale, throwing an interception and fumbling twice in a 33–13 loss to New England. By then, the 1–3 Redskins had been outscored 105–40 overall and 80–13 in the three losses, and their starters had been seriously outplayed. Alarm bells were sounding, yet Schottenheimer spoke of winning a Super Bowl.

"In establishing a goal, the worst error you can make is to arbitrarily set a standard that might well be beneath what you're actually capable of achieving," he said at the Redskins' Welcome Home Luncheon. "With that in mind, we set one standard, one goal, and we're in the process of pursuing that goal, and that's to become champions of the National Football League—and to do it this year."

The Redskins resembled anything but a championship team early on, showing sheer ineptitude on offense, defense, and special teams. Losses to San Diego (30–3) and Green Bay (37–3) on the road and to Kansas City at FedexField (45–13) accounted for one of the worst stretches in franchise history.

George engaged in a heated sideline exchange with Schottenheimer against the Chargers and was benched in the third quarter after being largely ineffective (8 of 18, 66 yards, two picks). He went the distance against the Packers (15 of 24, 102 yards, one interception), but Schottenheimer, annoyed that the irascible quarterback wasn't responding to his plays, cut him, named Banks the starter, and signed veteran journeyman Kent Graham as the backup. (Arizona was scheduled to visit FedExField in week 2, but the NFL cancelled play that weekend because of the September 11 terrorist attacks on New York and Washington.)

"I reached the point where I didn't feel the Washington Redskins could win with Jeff George as the starting quarterback," the coach said at the time. "When I reached that point, I had to try to evaluate whether it would serve our purpose to have him as a backup. I didn't think he could come off the bench and help us win."

George told WRC-TV-4 in Washington that he was "shocked" by the move. "I didn't expect it," he said. "We're going through some tough times. It's a team thing."

Against Kansas City, the Redskins yielded 546 yards of offense, and boos rained down early and often at FedEx. Afterward, first-year Chiefs coach Dick Vermeil, who had encouraged Schottenheimer to speak with Snyder about the Redskins' opening, offered a defense for his maligned friend: "They don't have enough good players. They've got a bunch of old guys who like to bitch and moan. Now, they have to go work for a living. I've been through that before."

Schottenheimer responded that he did have enough good players, despite his first 0–3 coaching start ever, three losses by an average of 32 points, and offensive and defensive units that were among the league's worst. In addition, player confidence in the coach was vanishing fast.

Marty's iron-fisted, my-way-or-the-highway approach had rubbed many players, including veteran defensive end Bruce Smith, the wrong way, as did his militaristic style of coaching. In training camp, which tight end Stephen Alexander described as "three-and-a-half weeks of boot-slashing camp," Schottenheimer had called for the dreaded "Oklahoma Drill," in which a running back lines up behind a blocker who is man-on-man with a defender, and the back has to gain a certain amount of yards. Camp Marty also consisted of two-a-day practices in sometimes oppressive heat.

The coach also lost supporters by telling 19th-year cornerback Darrell Green he had to compete with Fred Smoot for a starting job. Green subsequently announced plans to retire at season's end.

With a mutiny brewing, Schottenheimer called for a team meeting and allowed players to air their views. "Marty just sat back in that meeting," defensive end Marco Coleman recalled "and said, 'We're all men here. Express what the problem is. Let's get it out of the way so everybody doesn't need to talk behind each other's backs. Let's be clear so everybody can be on the same page, so we can get rid of it and move on.' Guys just stood up and expressed their opinion about a lot of things going on within the team. For instance, Darrell Green, who had seen several Redskins coaching changes and had been with the team for a long time, voiced his opinion. It was pretty healthy because we started to win really soon after that."

The Redskins showed signs of life and stood tied with the Giants, the defending NFC champs, 9–9 in the fourth quarter. But Banks threw two costly interceptions, one of which was returned 34 yards for a touchdown in a 23–9 loss. Then, in a battle of 0–4 teams, the Redskins lost 9–7 to the Cowboys at Texas Stadium after appearing to have a win locked up. With 2:40 left and Washington up, 7–3, the Cowboys recovered a Stephen Davis fumble and drove 58 yards for the winning field goal.

Near wins were no consolation for an 0–5 start, and rumors surfaced that Schottenheimer might be gone after the season unless his troops made a dramatic turnaround. They were eyeing an 0–6 record when Carolina led 14–0 with 10 minutes left at FedExField.

Then came a play that reversed the team's fortunes. Linebacker LaVar Arrington, knocked woozy earlier in the game, intercepted a tipped pass and returned it 67 yards for a touchdown. The Redskins went on to win, 17–14, on a 23-yard overtime field goal by Brett Conway, signed in the off-season after being cut by the Redskins in the 2000 campaign.

"I didn't think it would take this long, but it did," Schottenheimer told reporters. "I'm more delighted for the players than for myself. They didn't give up."

Four more weeks brought four more wins. In convincing wins over the Giants (35–21) and the Seahawks (27–14) at FedExField, Banks, who had needed time to learn the offense, looked sharp, and Davis rushed for more than 100 yards. Next, the Redskins and Broncos combined for 12 fumbles, five of which were lost, and 12 dropped passes in sloppy conditions at Invesco Field at Mile High Stadium. But the Redskins found a way to win. Graham replaced Banks, who suffered a concussion late in the first half, and threw two scoring passes in the fourth quarter, including the game-winner with 2:48 left.

The 4–5 Redskins were now set for a showdown at Veterans Stadium against 6–3 Philly, holders of first place in the NFC East. Could the red-hot Redskins pull off the big upset?

Final score: 13–3 Washington.

The Redskins' much improved defense neutralized Eagles all-everything quarterback Donovan McNabb, who passed for 92 yards and rushed for 39. Washington's defense, wracked by injuries earlier in the season, also stopped Philly twice on fourth downs in the second half. On offense, Ki-Jana Carter, subbing for an injured Davis, scored on a 5-yard run in the first half, while Conway kicked 43- and 32-yard field goals.

Wonder of wonders, the 5–5 Redskins were suddenly a game behind the 6–4 Eagles in the NFC East, an unfathomable scenario a few weeks prior. The Redskins were the talk of the league, and *Sports Illustrated* put them on the cover of its magazine. Arrington compared the resurgence to the awakening of a "sleeping giant." At the same time, players were buying into Schottenheimer's system.

"At first, it was a shock to everybody what Marty wanted," Coleman recalled. "Then once that was clear, we got into a groove of knowing exactly what was expected. As professionals, at some point everyone just realized that we're going to have to play this season regardless, so we might as well do the best we possibly can to adapt to what's going on. Guys just sucked it up and moved forward."

The surprising Redskins could smell six straight victories when they hosted the 2–8 Cowboys. But Dallas's rushing game piled up 215 yards, and Washington lost to the Cowboys for the ninth straight time, 20–14. The Redskins rebounded with a 20–10 win over the Cardinals at FedEx to revive their playoff hopes.

Consecutive home losses to the Eagles and Bears, however, eliminated Washington from playoff contention. Banks failed to produce in crucial moments, and the Redskins' offense, which averaged only 14 points through the first 14 games, experienced a serious drought in the red zone.

The Redskins had the ball on or inside the Eagles' 30 seven times and exited with two field goals. Banks threw critical interceptions, one in the end zone and one at the 3, and misfired on a fourth down pass. Against Chicago, the Redskins trailed, 20–13, with a second-and-1 from the Bears' 3 late in the game. Davis was stopped for no gain, and Banks threw two incomplete passes. It seemed surprising that the ball didn't go

on all three plays to the beefy Davis, who was en route to a team-record 1,432 rushing yards.

The bottom line: No playoffs for the Redskins for the second straight year.

"It's disappointing," Arrington, who evolved into one of the league's most feared outside linebackers and earned his first Pro Bowl invitation, said at the time. "It's a hurtful feeling because we've come so far. But at the same time, it's reality, and we've got to get over it. We have to approach every game as equally important. Even though there may be a false pot of gold out there under the rainbow, there's a sense of satisfaction to go out and play as hard as you can every Sunday."

"8–8 looks and sounds a lot better than 7–9," Banks said. "There's only a one-game difference, but there's a huge difference in the preparation you take into the off-season."

In the final weeks, as the Redskins beat New Orleans and Arizona to finish 8–8, Schottenheimer's job status in D.C. dominated the news. His future hinged on Snyder's desire to hire a general manager and whether the coach would agree to relinquish his player personnel duties. The owner was apparently satisfied with Schottenheimer's coaching performance, although he wasn't pleased with the off-season release of fullback Larry Centers, who went on to have a Pro Bowl year in Buffalo, and with Marty's decision to gamble on Jeff George and then cut him two games into the season.

The *Washington Post* reported that Schottenheimer's contract included a clause that allowed Snyder to hire a front-office executive with general manger-type responsibilities. Snyder reportedly was interested in hiring former Redskins general manager Bobby Beathard or former Packers general manager Ron Wolf. But Schottenheimer, despite wanting to retain the job, would not acquiesce to the point of giving up full control of roster moves.

"Would I like to come back? You bet your tail," Schottenheimer told reporters. "I love coaching. And you know what? If this is arrogant, so be it. I'm pretty damn good at it."

The owner and coach remained at loggerheads, and Schottenheimer was fired in mid-January 2002. At the same time, the Redskins were finalizing a blockbuster deal with pass-happy coach Steve Spurrier, who had resigned at the University of Florida a few days earlier.

The Fun 'N' Gun was about to debut in D.C.

## 2002: 7–9, 3RD PLACE—NFC EAST

### Head Coach: Steve Spurrier

Welcome to the NFL, Steve Spurrier. Pro football, as you learned, is worlds apart from the college game you dominated for years.

Spurrier arrived in Washington after winning 82 percent of his games in 12 seasons at the University of Florida, where his Fun 'N' Gun offense, a high-flying aerial attack, had made him a legend. A 4–1 preseason in which the Redskins scored a team-record 164 points, plus an opening-day victory when they cranked out 442 yards, sparked early optimism that the Fun 'N' Gun could work against the big boys.

It proved to be false hope. Spurrier struggled implementing his offense against defenses faster, stronger, and savvier than in the college ranks. The self-dubbed "ball coach" seemed out of his element, often looking and sounding flummoxed, and was unable to "pitch and catch" with the incredible efficiency he once showed. On an offense that posted nice overall statistics but struggled for consistency, he played musical chairs with his quarterbacks, former Florida Gators Shane Matthews and Danny Wuerffel and rookie Patrick Ramsey, and was indecisive about whether to focus on the pass or the run. One week the Redskins barely ran the ball and threw 51 passes, another week they finished with two 100-yard rushers.

Five of the Redskins' seven wins came when they ran the ball more, but their star running back, three-time 1,000-yard rusher Stephen Davis, was saddled with injuries and gained only 820 yards. He became unhappy in Spurrier's offense and publicly complained about his lack of carries, while the press questioned why Spurrier was ignoring arguably his top offensive threat. By season's end, Davis's days in D.C. were numbered.

Moreover, ragged play, mental breakdowns, and shoddy special teams play fueled the team's mediocrity. The Redskins committed 116 penalties for 968 yards, the sixth-highest figures in the league, and turned the ball over in waves at inopportune times (i.e., five turnovers in a 27–21 late-season loss to the Giants that ended the squad's playoff hopes). The Redskins lost a league-high 20 fumbles.

"Turning the ball over was the most consistent thing we did all year long," defensive end Bruce Smith, part of a defense that finished fifth in the league and kept the squad in a number of games, said at the end of the season. "The effort was there by each and every individual. But when you don't protect and take care of the football, you lose. That's a simple formula."

For Spurrier, who suffered his most losses since finishing 5–6 at Duke in 1987, his only losing season as a head coach, the jury remained out on whether he could succeed in the NFL. He vowed at season's end to invest several more years in the pros before stepping away.

Was Spurrier ill-prepared for his NFL coaching introduction?

"I think he underestimated the NFL," Redskins offensive tackle Chris Samuels said. "He thought it would be easier, just to come and do the same things he did in college."

Spurrier, the Redskins' fourth head coach in 13 months, had been known for his innovative, imaginative, and prolific offenses at Florida (1990–2001). His teams averaged about 35 points a game, 460 yards, and 310 passing yards. He compiled a 122–27–1 record, with seven Southeastern Conference titles and a national championship, and posted 10 or more wins in nine seasons, including a 10–2 mark in 2001 that ended with a 56–23 win over Maryland in the Orange Bowl.

Spurrier had once played quarterback at Florida, where he won the Heisman Trophy in 1966 and earned the nickname Steve "Superior." He spent 10 seasons in the NFL, nine as a backup quarterback with the 49ers and one with the Buccaneers, and later had head coaching jobs in the pros. With the Tampa Bay Bandits of the United States football League (1983–85), he went 35–19 with two straight playoff appearances. His 1984 team was the first in pro football history to produce a 4,000-yard passer and two 1,000-yard rushers in the same season. He later produced a 20–13–1 record in three seasons at Duke and led the school to its first Atlantic Coast Conference championship in a quarter-century.

Spurrier, who signed a five-year, $25 million contract with the Redskins, said at his introductory press conference on January 15, 2002, that he left Florida to "see if my style of coaching can win in the NFL." He credited Redskins owner Dan Snyder with triggering his migration out of the Sunshine State.

"I really believe I am here today because Dan Snyder convinced me that this is the best opportunity," he said. "He said, 'Steve, you want a challenge, you want to coach at the highest level, you want to coach in a big ballpark, you want to coach where we have the best fans in the country. I'm giving you that challenge right now.' He convinced me that he wanted me to be his coach. I told him he's a good recruiter."

The folksy Spurrier, a native of Johnson City, Tennessee, said he wasn't sure which approach he would use on offense. He said he might run the ball 45 times and "pitch" it 20 times, or vice versa, but he promised to use Stephen Davis regularly. "I want Stephen Davis to know that we're going to run the ball. He's a big part of our offense."

The rookie coach laid out bold goals: "Each year they will be the division championship, the playoffs, the Super Bowl, the Lombardi Trophy.

"I was telling Mr. Snyder that the sunshine followed the Gators and maybe the sunshine follows the Redskins, too," he said. "We're going to have some good fortune. We have a lot of good players and have a team that is very capable of having a big year next year. How big we're going to find out."

Spurrier dipped into his Gator past. He selected three assistant coaches from his Florida staff and signed former Gator quarterbacks Danny Wuerffel and Shane Matthews, both NFL journeymen. Wuerffel, the Heisman Trophy winner in Spurrier's national championship year (1996), had played for three other NFL teams and had not thrown a pass since 1999. Matthews, a nine-year veteran who played for Spurrier in the early 1990s, had started only 15 games in nine NFL seasons. When asked why he settled on Matthews and Wuerffel over more seasoned quarterbacks, Spurrier said they were "cheap and available." (Tony Banks, who started 14 games for Washington in 2001, was released.)

The Redskins added another quarterback in Tulane's Patrick Ramsey, the last draft pick in the first round. The 6–2, 220-pound Ramsey set many school records at Tulane, completing 798 of 1,355 throws for 9,205 yards and 72 touchdowns.

Spurrier also signed three former wide receivers who had played for him at Florida: Chris Doering, Reidel Anthony, and Jacquez Green. Anthony was cut before the season started.

The biggest off-season acquisitions were on defense. Spurrier hired Marvin Lewis, one of the top defensive minds in the game, as defensive coordinator. Lewis had previously coached in Baltimore, where his Ravens defense had finished second in the NFL for three straight seasons and in 2000, a Super Bowl-winning year for Baltimore, set a league record for fewest points allowed in a 16-game season (165).

Through free agency, the Redskins signed linebacker Jesse Armstead, a five-time Pro Bowler with the Giants, and two-time Pro Bowler Jeremiah Trotter of the Eagles. Armstead and Trotter, plus LaVar Arrington, The Quarterback Club Redskins Player of the Year in 2001 and a Pro Bowl selection, created a formidable linebacking trio. The Redskins also signed free agent defensive linemen Daryl Gardener and Renaldo Wynn to team with future Hall of Famer Bruce Smith and Dan Wilkinson on what looked like a strong front four. Two-time Pro Bowl cornerback Champ Bailey and up-and-coming cornerback Fred Smoot highlighted the defensive backfield.

It was a Florida reunion when new Redskins coach Steve Spurrier brought two of his former Gators quarterbacks, Shane Matthews (left) and Danny Wuerffel (right), along for the ride. Former Florida wide receivers Chris Doering and Jacquez Green also played for the Redskins in 2002.

The offense, however, remained the talk of the town, with everyone asking the question, Would Spurrier's Fun 'N' Gun work in the NFL?

The Fun 'N' Gun was in full view in a 4–1 exhibition season, when the Redskins racked up a ton of passing yards and tallied 35 or more points in the first four games, all victories. At quarterback, Spurrier alternated among Wuerffel, Matthews, Ramsey, and second-year-man Sage Rosenfels, who was later traded to Miami. After a 28–24 loss to New England in the exhibition finale, Spurrier tapped Matthews to start in the season opener against Arizona at FedExField.

"It's going to be an exciting offense," Redskins offensive tackle Jon Jansen said at the time. "It's going to be wide open, it's going to be high-powered, it's going to be probably something that this area has never seen before. I'm sure there will be more passing than in the past couple of years. But we'll still get Stephen Davis the ball a couple of times."

With 442 yards, Washington's offense looked Spurrieresque in a 31–23 win over Arizona. Matthews completed 28 of 40 passes for 327 yards, with three touchdowns to three different receivers. Davis rushed for 104 yards and a second-half touchdown that put the Redskins ahead for good.

Matthews was named NFC Offensive Player of the Week, but his recognition was short-lived. He completed 10 of 22 passes for 62 yards against the Eagles at FedExField on *Monday Night Football* before leaving the game in the second quarter with a sprained shoulder. By then, Philly was en route to a 31–7 rout. Wuerffel finished the game but was ineffective, as well.

Washington yielded 451 yards of offense and gained 179, while Eagles quarterback Donovan McNabb applied his customary whupping on the Redskins by completing 26 of 38 passes for 292 yards and two touchdowns. He rushed for 36 yards and a score. The Redskins' only touchdown came on Jacquez Green's 90-yard punt return.

The Redskins again looked inept in a 20–10 loss to the 49ers on the road. The defense allowed 252 rushing yards, and the offense mustered only 217 total yards. Matthews struggled

and was benched in the fourth quarter for Wuerffel, who was named the starter against the 1–3 Titans in Tennessee.

Wuerffel injured his shoulder on the first series, and with Matthews also ailing, Spurrier tapped Patrick Ramsey, who had missed the first 16 days of training camp owing to a contract dispute and was inactive for the first three games. Even so, the rookie gave a performance reminiscent of quarterback Gus Frerotte's spectacular rookie debut in a 1994 win over the Colts. He completed 20 of 34 passes for 268 yards with two touchdowns and no interceptions in a 31–14 win. He connected with eight different receivers and directed four touchdown drives in succession.

The offense totaled 442 yards, and Stephen Davis, seldom used in recent weeks, rushed for 90 despite seriously spraining his knee in the first quarter. He ran 1 yard for a touchdown and caught a 14-yard touchdown pass on a trick play. The Redskins' defense also played well, intercepting three passes and holding the Titans to 59 yards rushing.

Spurrier said he was happy with Ramsey's toughness and named him the starter for a game against the Saints at FedExField. But the rookie threw four interceptions—three on the team's first four possessions—in a 43–27 Saints win. Davis fumbled on the other possession, and the Saints converted those four turnovers into 20 points.

In addition to Ramsey's struggles, the Redskins' O-line gave up seven sacks, the defense surrendered two touchdown passes in third-and-long situations, and the Saints' Michael Lewis returned a kickoff and a punt for touchdowns. The Redskins committed 11 penalties.

Spurrier went into a tirade afterward: "As a team, we looked like we didn't care if we win the game or not," he told the press. "It's pitiful watching us play right now. We'll try to make some corrections. We'll try to find out guys that want to bust their tail and play their assignments. Those that don't, we've got to make changes if we can't get them to play disciplined. Obviously, we looked like a poorly coached team, offense, defense and special teams.

"I can't watch this. Redskins' fans can't watch this. They're not going to pay good money to watch a bunch of guys play like we did."

The Redskins were again pathetic in a 30–9 loss to the Packers. Ramsey was sacked six times and missed a number of throws. He also fumbled the ball repeatedly and was charged with losing three of them. The offense penetrated Green Bay's red zone three times but exited with only two field goals. On the Redskins' penalty front, the magic number again was 11.

In his two starts, Ramsey had operated behind a banged-up offensive line. Guard Brenden Stai and tackle Chris Samuels were ailing, and former Redskins guard Tre' Johnson was re-signed.

The 2–4 Redskins then crafted back-to-back wins to pull to .500. Six–2, 250-pound kicker James Tuthill, who had replaced the injured Brett Conway earlier in the season, kicked his fourth field goal of the game, a 22-yarder with 18 seconds left, in a 26–21 win over the Colts at FedEx. Shane Matthews started in place of Ramsey and was sacked once.

Then, with the Redskins starting a three-game road trip in Seattle, Spurrier called for more runs than passes for the third straight game in a 14–3 win over the Seahawks. Rookie Kenny Watson led the way, with 110 yards on 23 carries. The Redskins did all of their scoring in the first half, when Matthews completed touchdown passes to Darnerian McCants and Rod Gardner. In the second half, the Seahawks penetrated the Redskins' 40 four times but were held scoreless by Washington's improved defense.

A *Washington Post* headline read, "This Team Was Born to Run." And surely, in facing the 26th-ranked defense in the league in the Jaguars, losers of four straight, Spurrier would continue pounding the ball away on the ground in his return to Florida.

After using a balanced attack on the Redskins' opening drive, a 77-yard march that ended on Matthews's 20-yard touchdown pass to Gardner, Spurrier went into his "pitch and catch" mode. He called for 41 passes against nine runs in the last 50 minutes, but the Redskins' offense remained stuck in neutral and failed to overcome poor field position. The Jaguars, meanwhile, scored 26 unanswered points in their 26–7 win.

Spurrier shouldered the blame for the loss. "I was dumb enough to think we could throw it up and down the field," he told the media. "We ran a little bit here and there and had a little success, but I got away from it too much. So looking back, I called a lousy game."

"It's disappointing," Matthews said at the time. "We had a chance to get over the .500 mark. We had our chances and let them slip away."

Next up against a Giants defense ranked 24th against the run but fifth against the pass, the Redskins passed on 60 percent of their plays in wet, blustery conditions in the Meadowlands. Final score: 19–17 Giants. Spurrier, who was being criticized in the media for his play-calling, said the loss was "disappointing and frustrating" and that he had no answers to his game plan that called for 21 runs and 37 passes. Stephen Davis had an answer. "What we do best is run the football," he told reporters. "We have to do more of that."

Spurrier got the message, calling for 39 runs to 24 passes in a 20–17 win over the Rams at FedExField. Davis carried 31 times for 88 yards and pounded into the end zone on three short touchdown runs. Danny Wuerffel, named the starter after Spurrier benched Matthews, played his best game as a

pro, completing 16 of 23 passes for 235 yards. The offense tallied 362 yards and 21 first downs against a tough St. Louis defense.

The Rams, trailing 20–17, drove to the Redskins' 6 and used their last time out to stop the clock with 17 seconds left. On first-and-goal, quarterback Kurt Warner dropped back to pass, but Redskins linebacker LaVar Arrington penetrated the backfield, hit Warner, and stripped him of the ball. Defensive tackle Daryl Gardener recovered to preserve the win.

The playoff light was flickering for the 5–6 Redskins, but losses to Dallas and the Giants eliminated them from playoff contention. Ramsey, who had replaced Wuerffel during the Giants game and led two late scoring drives, was tapped to start against the Eagles on the road. He was sharp in a 34–21 loss (23 of 35, 213 yards, three touchdowns, no interceptions) and followed with another commendable showing in a 26–10 win over Houston at FedEx. Then came a 17 of 31, 209-yard showing in a season-ending 20–14 victory over Dallas at FedExField that snapped a 10-game losing streak to the Cowboys.

Afterward, Spurrier named Ramsey the starter for the 2003 season. "I will say I have been really pleased with Patrick Ramsey these last three games," the coach said in a news conference. "He made a few bad plays, but he has made more good plays. Patrick has learned a lot and has a lot of potential. He can make all the throws, and he's a tough guy who can stand in the pocket. We have a quarterback with tremendous potential."

Arrington, who was picked for his second straight Pro Bowl, singled out coaching stability as a key to the team's future. "If we can keep people in place, we can build toward a good future," he said at the time. "We have the talent. But when you keep bringing in new people, a piece of the puzzle here, a piece of the puzzle there, we're talking mass movement, you're all out, you're all in, it's hard. You've got to try to figure out ways to overcome it. That's what we were faced with this year. Hopefully, we can be under a system for two years and see what happens."

## 2003: 5–11, 3RD PLACE—NFC EAST

### Head Coach: Steve Spurrier

The Redskins and turmoil were one and the same in 2003.

You name it, there were distractions, and they snowballed as the season progressed: shoddy and sometimes boneheaded play on the field, incessant rumors that coach Steve Spurrier would resign or be fired at season's end, an outright lack of discipline by some players, ridicule of owner Dan Snyder. The hits just kept on coming.

The miserable season ended when the Redskins were routed 31–7 by the NFC East champion Eagles and finished 5–11, their worst record in nearly a decade. Spurrier quit three days later, taking with him a dubious 12–20 record in two seasons in Washington. The one-time coaching genius at Florida had failed to meet the hype and expectations that overflowed when he arrived in D.C. and signed a five-year, $25 million deal.

"The [2003] season was the low point of my NFL career for a lot of reasons," Redskins offensive tackle Jon Jansen said after the season, his fifth in the league. "It was extremely frustrating just to be a part of it. It was embarrassing to see a team as storied and with the great history of the Redskins to have to go through what it did the last couple of years."

The season was humiliating to say the least. The squad broke a 55-year-old franchise record for penalties in one season with 124 for 1,038 yards, and player apathy seemed to permeate the roster. Media reported players' cell phones going off during team meetings, players being late for meetings, and players refusing to practice late in the season. *Washington Post* sports columnist Thomas Boswell documented seeing Redskins players joking around in the locker room after a hard-fought 27–25 loss to the Eagles, and Redskins star linebacker LaVar Arrington lashed out at teammates for doing likewise after a 24–7 loss to Buffalo.

Both defeats contributed to a freefall when the Redskins lost 10 of their last 12 games, after opening the season 3–1.

"There was an incredible amount of a lack of discipline from day one," said Brandon Noble, a Redskins defensive tackle at the time. "There were guys walking five minutes late into team meetings, guys playing video games in meetings. Guys would walk in late and there would constantly be a chatter, like a whisper of people talking even while the head coach was talking."

Noble came to D.C. as part of a busy off-season signing period when the Redskins were again was one of the league's most active teams in the free agent market. The front office looked to fill specific needs, and mostly one team was affected by the deep pockets of Redskins owner Dan Snyder—the New York Jets.

Four Jets standouts, guard Randy Thomas, wide receiver Laveranues Coles, kicker John Hall, and kick returner Chad Morton, all discarded the green and white for the burgundy and gold. They didn't come cheap:

- Coles—$35 million over seven years, including a franchise-record $13 million signing bonus
- Thomas—$28 million over seven years
- Morton—$8 million over five years
- Hall—$7 million over five years

Jets General Manager Terry Bradway reportedly said the Redskins paid too much for Coles, who snagged 89 passes for 1,264 yards and five touchdowns in 2002. But Coles's speed is exactly what Spurrier wanted so he could mold his offense into more of a wide-open scheme similar to his famed Fun 'N' Gun at Florida. The Redskins also signed speedy Rams running back Trung Canidate.

Spurrier and company also felt that the third-leading rusher in team history, bruising back Stephen Davis, was no asset to the coach's "pitch and catch" system. The Redskins didn't renegotiate the contract of Davis, an unrestricted free agent who left and signed with Carolina. He reacquainted himself with his old team later in the season.

The backfield lacked a true threat all season, and the Redskins were also bereft of a legitimate run stopper. Defensive tackle Darryl Gardner, The Quarterback Club Redskins Player of the Year in 2002, left via free agency. Noble suffered a season-ending knee injury in the second exhibition game, and tackle Dan "Big Daddy" Wilkinson, who posted only 17 tackles in 2002 and had been an overall disappointment in his five seasons in D.C., refused to take a pay cut from his base salary of $3.5 million and was released in training camp.

"I said prior to [Wilkinson's release] that he was one of the guys we couldn't afford to lose," Redskins defensive end Bruce Smith told reporters at the time.

There was also controversy on the quarterback front. Veteran Rob Johnson, the backup to former Redskins quarterback Brad Johnson on Tampa Bay's Super Bowl-winning team in 2002, was signed to back up second-year man Patrick Ramsey. Rob Johnson struggled in the preseason, though, and the Redskins re-signed Danny Wuerffel, the one-time Heisman Trophy winner from Florida who had played for Spurrier.

After a 1–3 preseason, however, Spurrier told the press that Snyder had influenced the release of Wuerffel, as well as Kenny Watson, the team's second-leading rusher in 2002 with 534 yards. The Redskins thus rolled the dice by entering the season with only two quarterbacks on the active roster: Ramsey and Rob Johnson.

Through it all, "cautious optimism" was the theme at Redskin Park. And the air was electric when the Redskins hosted the Jets in the season opener before 85,420 fans at FedExField.

The "Jetskins" were worth every penny against their former team. Hall was 3 of 3 on field goals, including a 33-yarder with five seconds left that gave the Redskins a 16–13 win. Coles caught five passes for 105 yards. Thomas opened holes for a rushing attack that gained 160 yards, 77 by second-year man Ladell Betts. Chad Morton had some nice returns.

"You couldn't write it up any better," Redskins cornerback Champ Bailey said afterward of the debut by the ex-Jets. "You've got a guy who kicks three field goals and the game-winner."

Ramsey had an outstanding first half, going 12 of 13 for 156 yards with a 4-yard scoring pass to receiver Darnerien McCants. But he struggled in the second half, and the Jets converted an interception and fumble into field goals to tie the game at 13. Ramsey also did something he wasn't noted for, scrambling 24 yards to the Jets' 31-yard line with 1:30 left in the game. The run helped set up Hall's game-winner.

Unlike some of his one-sided play calling in 2002, Spurrier used a balanced attack with 34 rushes and 23 passes. Washington's defense held the Jets to 158 yards and 11 first downs. "Now, can I coach in the NFL?" the cocksure coach, flashing a smirk, asked rhetorically as he walked past reporters after the game.

The Redskins improved to 2–0 with a 33–31 win over the Falcons in Atlanta. Ramsey posted career highs in completions (25) and yards (356), and Coles had career highs in catches (11) and yards (180). Receiver Rod Gardner caught nine passes for 115 yards, and Canidate gained 89 on 15 carries. The defense turned in the decisive play, however: Redskins linebacker Jesse Armstead sacked Falcons quarterback Doug Johnson in the end zone late in the third quarter for a 26–24 Redskins lead. They held on for the win.

One negative statistic stood out. Ramsey was sacked six times and fumbled twice; he suffered a bruised shoulder but stayed in the game.

The offensive explosiveness continued against the Giants at FedExField, as the Redskins amassed 456 yards, only to lose 24–21 on a field goal in overtime. The loss was compounded by Washington's 17 penalties, which tied a 1948 single-game franchise record. The penalties, which LaVar Arrington called "self-inflicted wounds," included a holding call on offensive tackle Chris Samuels that nullified a touchdown and a personal foul on linebacker Jeremiah Trotter on a third-and-24 that allowed the Giants to continue a drive and score a touchdown.

Redskins quarterback Patrick Ramsey and coach Steve Spurrier confer during a 16–13 win over the Jets on opening day. By the end of the season, Ramsey was on the bench and Spurrier was on his way out of Washington.

Washington then gained sole possession of first place in the NFC East with a 20–17 win over the eventual Super Bowl–champion Patriots. New England fought back from a 20–3 deficit and appeared headed toward spoiling the upset, driving into Redskins territory with about a minute left. Then safety Ifeanyi Ohalete broke up a fourth-down pass by quarterback Tom Brady to seal the win.

The 3–1 Redskins had benefited from some unforeseen breaks: The Jets and Falcons played without starting quarterbacks Chad Pennington and Michael Vick, respectively, and the Patriots were missing nine starters. At the same time, though, the Redskins were piling up penalties. They were flagged for nine against New England and 11 more with seven false starts in a 27–25 loss to the Eagles on the road. Ramsey rallied the Redskins from an 11-point deficit in the waning minutes against Philly but overthrew Coles on a two-point conversion pass that would have tied the game with seconds remaining.

"I'm frustrated with all of these guys, and they're probably frustrated with me," the coach, visibly distraught, said afterward.

Then came a 35–13 rout at the hands of the Buccaneers. While former Redskin quarterback Brad Johnson had a spectacular day on his return to FedExField (22 of 30, 268 yards, four touchdowns), Ramsey continued getting bounced around like a Ping-Pong ball. Sacked four times—all by superstar defensive end Simeon Rice—he was replaced in the fourth quarter by Rob Johnson, who was sacked twice.

Ramsey, who was taking some vicious hits in the pocket, had been sacked 21 times through six games. As a result, Spurrier was being pilloried in the media over the squad's anemic pass protection.

"I don't think protecting the quarterback was a very high priority," Jansen said in hindsight. "There were other things the coaches were concerned about."

"There wasn't any one person you could blame it on," Ramsey said after the season. "You can't blame it on the offensive line, you can't blame it on the receivers. There was plenty of blame to go around." The quarterback suffered a bruised hip and a hand injury in a 24–7 loss at Buffalo. The Bills, with the NFL's last-ranked offense, outgained the Redskins 432 to 169 and rushed for nearly 200 yards. Spurrier later questioned the desire of his team.

"We have to regroup and find out who really wants to play," he told the press. "I don't know how much fight we had in our team. It was embarrassing the way we played. It seems like we lost our fight, lost our drive."

The Redskins tried to regroup during a turbulent bye week. They brought in Joe Bugel, coach of the Redskins' legendary "Hogs" offensive line from the 1980s and early 1990s, as a consultant, as well as former Redskins linebacker coach Foge Fazio. They cut quarterback Rob Johnson and tried re-signing Danny Wuerffel, but he refused to come back in light of the preseason fiasco. Tim Hasselbeck, a second-year pro who had thrown two passes since leaving Boston College, was signed. Also signed was two-time Pro Bowl defensive tackle Darrell Russell, who was previously suspended for violating the NFL's drug rules, to help shore up a defense allowing globs of yards.

The defense looked inept in a 21–14 loss at Texas Stadium to the Cowboys, who outgained the Redskins, 400 yards to 213, and sacked Ramsey four times, forcing him to leave the game twice due to injuries. With the 3–5 Redskins having suffered four straight losses and their season fast unraveling, speculation turned rampant about Spurrier's fate. Comcast SportsNet said that the coach had resigned but was talked out of it two days before the season opener. CBS SportsLine.com reported that Spurrier was considering quitting, and *New York Post* gossip columnist Cindy Adams wrote shortly after the loss to the Cowboys that Snyder had fired Spurrier and chosen a successor.

Snyder had fueled the gossip about his coach by phoning former Cowboys coach and two-time Super Bowl winner Jimmy Johnson before the Dallas game. Johnson said on *Fox NFL Sunday,* where he was an analyst, that Snyder had called to discuss the challenges a college coach faces going to the pros. Johnson transitioned to the NFL after coaching the University of Miami to a national championship in 1988.

Spurrier denied rumors of an imminent departure and said he was sticking to his plan to coach at least through the 2004 season. Redskins management said through the media that they remained supportive of Spurrier.

To add to the chaos, defensive end Bruce Smith publicly questioned why Spurrier had relegated him to a backup role against Dallas while the defensive end was so close to breaking Reggie White's all-time sack record of 198. "I have team goals and individual goals," the self-serving Smith said to the press. "At some point in time in your career, you have to take a stance and be a little selfish." (Smith broke the record late in the season.)

A 27–20 win over Seattle at FedExField stopped the bleeding. But the Redskins dropped six of their last seven games, including a 20–17 loss at Carolina that left them at 4–6. A face from the past, Stephen Davis, scored the winning touchdown on a controversial 3-yard run and later said the game was "personal, very personal." He rushed for a career-high 1,444 yards that season, a lot of which the Redskins could have used. Canidate led the Redskins in rushing with 600 yards.

The next week at Miami, Ramsey, still getting pounded while battling a bruised bone in his foot, suffered a concussion and gave way to Hasselbeck, who completed 15 of 30 passes for 150 yards and a touchdown in the Redskins' one-point loss. Hasselbeck, the brother of Seattle quarterback Matt Hasselbeck and the husband of Elisabeth Hasselbeck, a finalist from the reality TV show *Survivor: The Australian Outback* and a current co-host on ABC's *The View,* stayed under center the rest of the year, throwing for 1,012 yards and five touchdowns.

As the losses mounted, Spurrier sounded as if he had simply run out of answers. "This is new for a lot of us—trying to win the close ones," he said after a 24–20 loss to the Saints left the Redskins 4–8. "We've not done very well at it, the last three weeks especially. We're a play or two away now, it seems like."

"You could just kind of tell from the look on his face that he was not having a good time," Brandon Noble said in reflecting back. "He seemed to age rapidly. You could see the writing on the wall. There were obviously whispers that he might leave, but it was never from a credible enough source."

After the season-ending loss to Philly, Spurrier remained coy about his future but promised changes to his staff. He resigned on December 30 with three years left on his contract. "This is a very demanding job," he said in a statement. "It's a long grind, and I feel that after 20 years as a head coach, there are other things I need to do."

Spurrier's Fun 'N' Gun offense—the centerpiece of everyone's curiosity when he jumped to the NFL—had simply failed in the pros. The unit fell from No. 1 in the league early in the 2003 season to 23rd overall. In addition, repeated breakdowns on the offensive front led to 42 sacks; Ramsey took 30 alone. Why didn't the Fun 'N' Gun offense click? "Maybe it just wasn't the right time, the right players, the right coaches," Jansen said.

Jansen implied that Spurrier was handicapped by not understanding how to deal with NFL players: "It wasn't a football matter, it was a people matter," Jansen said. "Pro football's a lot different than in college because in college, the guys don't have opinions. Coaches are the ones who run the show. But you give a guy some money, and all of a sudden he has an opinion. You got 53 guys with opinions, and the head coach has got to be the one who kind of lassos those opinions and says, 'Hey, you can have an opinion, but mine's the only one that matters.' It was just a matter of learning to deal with NFL players."

On Spurrier's resignation, Snyder and Redskins personnel executive Vinny Cerrato began searching for a successor. They interviewed former Giants coach Jim Fassel, former Vikings coach Dennis Green, and Seahawks defensive coordinator Ray Rhodes, who had held the same position with the Redskins in 2000. At the same time, clandestine negotiations were under way with perhaps the most popular figure in Redskins history.

His return would flip the nation's capital upside down.

## 2004: 6–10, 2ND PLACE—NFC EAST (3-WAY TIE)

### Head Coach: Joe Gibbs

He didn't win another Super Bowl; nor did he at least take the Redskins back to the playoffs, as many had anticipated. In fact, he finished 6–10, his worst head coaching mark in 13 seasons in the NFL.

So went the reintroduction to coaching for Joe Gibbs, who showed that he had accumulated a lot of rust during his 11-season layoff. His 2004 squad was victimized by mental breakdowns, shoddy play, poor clock management, and the second-most penalty yards in Redskins' history (1,045)—all characteristics so foreign to the Redskins during Gibbs's first stint in Washington.

Gibbs, who had made his name as an offensive mastermind, also put forth an offense that lacked a pulse for much of the season and scored only 240 points, the Redskins' second-lowest total in the history of the 16-game season, not including the 1982 strike-shortened year. The offense, led during the first half of the year by inefficient quarterback Mark Brunell, finished 30th in the league.

Even so, the Redskins were never blown out of a game, and of their 10 losses, seven were by seven points or less. They stood 3–8 at one point, but Gibbs remained resolute that things would turn for the better, sounding the call for his troops to "stick together" and "hang tough." Sure enough, they won three of their last five games, including an upset of the playoff-bound Vikings in the season finale, and came about two and a half minutes from possibly winning all five.

Gibbs remained emotionally steady throughout the season, said Redskins middle linebacker Antonio Pierce. But when it was all over, the coach said his return to the NFL had been "very hard." "We lost games every way you could lose them," he said after the Vikings game, "but our guys just kept coming back. It's a tribute to them and their character. I'm proud of that, and I told them that I was proud to be with them."

"This team has to get used to Joe Gibbs," said Redskins radio analyst and Hall of Fame linebacker Sam Huff. "You have to get rid of people who are making mental mistakes. This is pro football, you don't make those mistakes. But Gibbs knows what he's doing, and he's kind of working his way through all of this. He hasn't coached in 12 years, so he's getting used to the system."

Although the offense struggled, the defense was spectacular, finishing first in the NFC and third in the NFL with 4,281 yards allowed (267.5 per game). The unit was fifth in the NFL in points allowed (260). The brains behind the defense, one of the most dominant in Redskins history, belonged to first-year assistant head coach–defense Gregg Williams. Williams, who came to Washington after his firing as Buffalo's head coach following the 2003 season, had once served as an assistant on the same staff in Houston with Buddy Ryan, one of the greatest defensive minds in NFL history.

The defense, a swarming, blitzing, and attacking system, kept the Redskins alive in many games. The unit excelled using mostly unheralded "no-name" players such as Antonio Pierce (team-high 160 tackles), defensive tackle Cornelius Griffin (six sacks), outside linebacker Marcus Washington (130 tackles, 4.5 sacks), cornerback Shawn Springs (six sacks, five intercep-

## He's Back!

A city starving for a winner in its beloved Redskins received divine intervention in the early days of 2004.

Joe Gibbs was back.

The three-time Super Bowl winner returned to the job he had surprisingly walked away from 11 years earlier. His comeback was perhaps even more stunning, for he had repeatedly said he no longer wanted to coach in the NFL, despite briefly entertaining the possibility of coaching the expansion Carolina Panthers in 1995.

The second coming of Gibbs shook the national capital region and became the talk of the city. The two major newspapers, the *Washington Post* and the *Washington Times,* splattered his return across the front page of their entire paper. Local TV stations cut into normal programming to announce the blockbuster story. National media also swallowed it up. A *New York Times* headline read, "Coach Embraced as Hopes Soar in Washington." Requests for Redskins season tickets shot up by the thousands.

The story dwarfed Washington's biggest pro sports news of recent years: the arrivals of Michael Jordan

"There is no net," Gibbs declared during his return press conference, despite winning three Super Bowls in his prior coaching stint with the Redskins. "There's nothing going to catch us."

tions), and rookie safety Sean Taylor (four interceptions), the team's first-round draft pick in 2004 (No. 5 overall). Marcus Washington was the only Redskin to make the Pro Bowl.

"He brought a mentality of aggressiveness," Redskins defensive tackle Joe Salave'a said of Williams. "He adopted a Buddy Ryan scheme. Most of the concepts are still true. He just added wrinkles to it. He put players in position to make plays."

On returning to the Redskins, Gibbs vowed to "dive" into his new job, and he restructured the team with the speed of a racecar. He assembled a new coaching staff that included four members of his original staff in offensive line aficionado Joe Bugel, Don Breaux, Jack Burns, and Warren "Rennie" Simmons. The former three came out of retirement, as did longtime NFL offensive coordinator Ernie Zampese.

"I came back because of Gibbs, only him," Bugel said in May 2004. "And for the Redskins. That old saying is true for us: once a Redskin, always a Redskin. When we left here, the program was in pretty good shape, then it started declining.

That affected a lot of people. To see what's happened with the team in recent years, that hurts a lot of people."

Among others, Gibbs also lured Gregg Williams, Bears defensive coordinator Greg Blache, whose unit finished fifth in the NFC in 2003, and former Redskins star running back Earnest Byner, previously the Ravens' director of player development. Byner would coach the Redskins' running backs.

On the player front, Gibbs orchestrated the acquisition of Jacksonville quarterback Mark Brunell, an 11-year veteran and the 11th-rated passer in NFL history at the time (85.2). The Redskins traded a third-round draft pick to the Jaguars for Brunell, who signed a $43 million, seven-year deal with an $8.6 million signing bonus. He had lost his starting job in 2003 to rookie Byron Leftwich.

The Redskins also dealt four-time Pro Bowl cornerback Champ Bailey to the Broncos for running back Clinton Portis, who rushed for more than 1,500 yards in 2002 and 2003, his first two seasons in the league. Portis gave the Redskins a slip-as the Washington Wizards' team president, Jaromir Jagr as the Washington Capitals' supposed savior, and the Redskins' prior coaches, Marty Schottenheimer and Steve Spurrier. Jordan's decision to return to the court was also huge, but not since the iconic Vince Lombardi in 1969 had the entrance of a sports figure so excited the nation's capital.

The shock was at meteoric levels on January 8, 2004, the day Gibbs was introduced at Redskins Park as the team's new coach. He arrived with Redskins owner Daniel Snyder—who doled out $28 million over five years for the 63-year-old Gibbs—in a procession of limousines. Gibbs exited with his wife, Pat, to the delight of dozens of delirious fans who sang "Hail to the Redskins" and waved such signs as "Joe Gibbs = God, Mr. Snyder = Genius, Being a Redskins Fan = Priceless." A banner in burgundy and gold proclaimed, "Welcome Home, Coach Gibbs!" The coach shook hands with fans hoping to catch a glimpse of him.

Some 500 people packed the Redskins Park auditorium for Gibbs's introductory press conference. The throng included local and national media, and a Who's Who of stars from the first Gibbs era including Art Monk, Gary Clark, Darryl Grant, Joe Jacoby, Neal Olkewicz, Darrell Green, Mark Moseley, Don Warren, and Charles Mann. Also in attendance were three assistant coaches from the original Gibbs regime who were joining his new staff: Joe Bugel, Don Breaux, and Jack Burns.

Gibbs addressed the audience in front of the three shining Super Bowl trophies captured by his Redskins teams. But he downplayed his glory days in Washington, refusing to wear his Super Bowl rings, and zeroed in on the issue at hand: resurrecting a team that had posted four straight nonwinning seasons.

"I come here with the most humble spirit," he said, sounding a bit nervous. "I really truly believe my part is a small part. I'm anxious to be a part of this. I'm coming into this with my eyes wide open. This is all new, this is different for us. We're trying to go forward with our players and a whole new group of people. From this point on, the past doesn't buy us much, other than relationships."

In returning to the Redskins, Gibbs sold his 5 percent ownership stake in the Atlanta Falcons but maintained ownership of Joe Gibbs Racing. His NASCAR team, which he launched in the early 1990s, had posted two championships in the premier year-long NASCAR series and a win in the Daytona 500, the Super Bowl of stock car racing. He had been part of an ownership group that had unsuccessfully bid for the Redskins in 1998.

Gibbs made no guarantees of what he would achieve in a game where the players were bigger, stronger, and faster than in his first go-round. He admitted to be eyeing a steep learning curve much like the one Dick Vermeil faced in 1997 when he returned from a 14-season pro coaching hiatus. Vermeil proved that he could shake off the cobwebs by coaching the St. Louis Rams to a win in Super Bowl XXXIV in the 1999 season.

Gibbs acknowledged that he couldn't lean on his legacy to shield him from possible failure: "There is no net. I am hanging. There is nothing down there. There's nothing going to catch us. And that may be the biggest thrill. Knowing how hard it is, but getting a chance to do something that is super hard."

---

pery runner with a quick first step, unlike the big, burly backs on Gibbs's prior Redskin teams, such as John Riggins, George Rogers, and Gerald Riggs.

Through free agency, the Redskins beefed up the defense. They acquired end Phillip Daniels and linebacker Michael Barrow, plus Cornelius Griffin, Marcus Washington, and Shawn Springs. Released from the defense were relics in 19-year end Bruce Smith, the NFL's all-time sack leader, and 11-year linebacker Jesse Armstead, as well as linebacker Jeremiah Trotter, a disappointment in his two seasons in D.C.

Given the presence of Gibbs, would the Redskins recapture the glory that his teams had achieved in the 1980s and early 1990s, as so many optimists envisioned, and perhaps even make a trip to Super Bowl XXXIX? Two popular Redskins called for patience as training camp approached.

"It's easy to say everything is good now because there are no live bullets yet," linebacker LaVar Arrington said. "We've got to wait until we're playing, and it gets to crunch time."

"It's a wait and see for me just because it's my fifth coaching staff in six years," offensive tackle Jon Jansen said. "I've been excited about things before and they haven't worked out." Yet, he added, "[Gibbs] didn't just leave football and completely stop competing in something. There's a certain way he goes about doing things, and that's obviously bred success in football and NASCAR. Now that he's back here, why should it stop?"

Jansen's season was over before it started. Early in the Redskins' exhibition opener, he ruptured an Achilles' tendon and was lost for the season. The Redskins signed 19th-year offensive lineman Ray Brown, who had played in Washington from 1989 to 1995, but the loss of Jansen was big.

In the quarterback situation, Brunell and third-year man Patrick Ramsey alternated through the first four exhibition games. Brunell was the more productive of the two, and Gibbs named him the regular-season starter before the final preseason game, a 27–0 win over Atlanta that gave the Redskins a 3–2 mark.

The Gibbs-II era opened with a bang when Clinton Portis ran 64 yards for a score early in the first quarter of the season-opening game against Tampa Bay.

The Gibbs-II era kicked off with a 16–10 win before more than 90,000 fans at FedExField—the 500th victory in franchise history. The new Clinton administration made a splendid debut of its own. Early in the game, Portis found an opening on the right side and exploded for a 64-yard scoring run on his first carry as a Redskin. The conversion made it 7–0.

The Redskins took a grind-it-out approach from then on, with Portis carrying 29 times for 148 yards and John Hall kicking three field goals. The Redskins' defense yielded only 169 yards and 10 first downs and forced two turnovers that were converted into scores.

The Redskins then visited the Giants and scored on their first drive, a 53-yard march that ended with Brunell's 2-yard pass to rookie tight end Chris Cooley, a third-round draft pick that year out of Utah State. But the offense went into a shell, committing seven turnovers before the game was over. The normally sure-handed Portis fumbled twice, and Ramsey, who replaced Brunell after he aggravated a hamstring early in the second half, threw three interceptions. The Giants converted turnovers into 17 points in their 20–14 win.

Brunell returned to start on Monday night against the Cowboys at FedExField, a game pitting Gibbs against Cowboys coach Bill Parcells, two gladiators and old-time rivals who were meeting for the first time in 14 years. Parcells again managed to outwit Gibbs, as he had so many times in the past.

Dallas took a 21–10 lead with 13 minutes left when running back Richie Anderson threw an option pass to receiver Terry Glenn for a touchdown. Brunell (25 of 43, 325 yards, two touchdowns) then found a rhythm after a rough first three quarters and hit receiver Rod Gardner with a 15-yard touchdown pass and receiver Taylor Jacobs with a two-point conversion with 4:30 left. With the Redskins out of timeouts, Dallas milked almost the entire clock and left Washington with only 13 seconds to operate. Brunell threw a 47-yard pass to Gardner (10 catches, 167 yards, two touchdowns), who caught it at the Dallas 21 but was unable to get out of bounds. The clock expired.

Washington lost its third straight, 17–13 at Cleveland, as the offense posted less than 100 yards rushing for the second straight game. The Redskins committed seven penalties, including three personal fouls, and had to burn two timeouts in the fourth quarter to make sure they were in the right offensive formation; they lost a third when challenging a call (replay challenges would be troubling for Gibbs all season). Plus, a headset problem hampered communication between Gibbs and his players for part of the game.

When it rains, it pours.

"We need improvement," Gibbs told reporters afterward. "We turned the ball over seven times against the Giants, then we come back against Dallas and go turnover free. Then we turn around and against the Browns we turn the ball over a couple of times. You can't do that and expect to win at this level."

Meanwhile, media were questioning the effectiveness of Brunell, who during the first three weeks had looked like anything but the 11th-rated passer in NFL history. A *Washington Times* headline read, "This QB doesn't fit the system," while the *Washington Post* wrote that "Quarterback Is a Question Mark." But Gibbs showed gave no indication he might bench Brunell.

Brunell looked putrid in a 17–10 loss to Baltimore at FedExField, completing 13 of 29 passes for 83 yards, with a touchdown and a pick. The Redskins' offense took the game off with 107 yards, their lowest total since 1961.

The Redskins broke their four-game losing streak with a 13–10 win over the host Bears, as Portis rushed for 171 yards. Swedish kicker Ola Kimrin, signed after John Hall had suffered a groin injury, booted two field goals, and Brunell threw a touchdown pass to Gardner. But Brunell's woes continued, for he completed 8 of 22 passes for 95 yards with an interception that was returned 70 yards for a touchdown. The Redskins' defense again looked superb, holding the Bears to 160 yards and receiving excellent performances from tackle Cornelius Griffin, cornerback Fred Smoot, and safety Sean Taylor.

"Our defense just played great," Gibbs told the press. "That's been the story these first six weeks."

With the bye week on them, the 2–4 Redskins were eyeing some serious problems. Brunell, the team's $43 million man, had completed only 51.2 percent of his passes and had a 69.8 quarterback rating. Plus, the offense was yet to score more than 18 points in a game and was averaging only 14.

Gibbs appeared determined to stick with Brunell, although his explanation for doing so sounded puzzling. "My focus is, if Mark wasn't playing the way we wanted him to play, or if I felt Mark was the main reason why we couldn't get something done on offense, I would talk to him," Gibbs told the press. "Mark would understand, and we would do something. But that's not the case."

Redskins fans showed their disgust for Brunell when the Packers came to town on Halloween. Boos rained down on the quarterback, who was pathetic in the first half, while fans yelled in unison, "RAM-SEY! RAM-SEY!"

With the Redskins trailing 20–7 in the fourth quarter, Brunell threw a 12-yard touchdown pass to Rod Gardner. He later completed a short pass to Portis, who ran the rest of the way for a 43-yard touchdown that tied the game at 20 with 2:43 left. But Redskins receiver James Thrash was called for illegal motion, and the score was nullified. Brunell was intercepted on the next play, and the Packers went on to win, 28–14.

Brunell followed with a 58-yard performance, the third time in the last four games he had tallied less than 100 yards, in a 17–3 win at Detroit. He threw only two passes in the second half, when Portis picked up the slack by tossing a 15-yard score to receiver Laveranues Coles for a 10–3 Redskins lead. The other touchdown came when Walt Harris returned a blocked punt 13 yards. "I told Coles I needed this for my quarterback rating," Portis joked of his scoring pass.

Brunell hit rock bottom in a 17–10 loss to the Bengals at FedExField. He was 1 of 8 for 6 yards with an interception on the Redskins' first four drives (0.0 passer rating), and Gibbs finally yanked him. His completion rate was 49.8 percent at the time. Ramsey entered and lit a spark under the Redskins' offense, going 18 of 37 for 210 yards and leading two drives of more than 65 yards, a welcomed sign given the Redskins' past

futility in moving the ball. He also threw a 9-yard touchdown pass to Cooley, plus two interceptions.

"Brunell is one of the highest-rated quarterbacks in the history of the game, so Gibbs was giving him the benefit of the doubt," Sam Huff said regarding the coach's decision to stick with the veteran quarterback. "It just didn't work."

Ramsey was solid in road losses to the Eagles and Steelers that dropped the Redskins to 3–8, then looked sharp in a 31–7 win over the Giants at FedExField, the first game in which the Redskins scored more than 20 points all season and their best all-around performance to date. He completed 19 of 22 passes for 174 yards and three touchdowns, while Portis rushed for 148 yards to top 1,000 for the third straight season. The defense held the Giants to 145 yards and shut down rookie quarterback Eli Manning, the No. 1 pick in the 2004 draft.

After a tough 17–14 loss to the Eagles at FedEx, Washington topped the 49ers on the road, 26–16. With the NFC fielding so many weak teams, the 5–9 Redskins, bunched in with a slew of other sub-.500 teams, were amazingly alive for a wild card playoff spot. But a 13–10 loss to Dallas at Texas Stadium killed their faint postseason hopes.

Leading 10–6 with time running out, the Redskins couldn't put the game away. Dallas took over on its 25 with 1:25 left and faced a fourth-and-10. But 41-year-old quarterback Vinny Testaverde hit receiver Patrick Crayton for 15 yards and found him three plays later down the right sideline for a 39-yard scoring pass with 30 seconds left. Ramsey's completion to Coles allowed Jeff Chandler, the Redskins' third kicker in 2004, to try a 57-yard field goal. The kick was on target but a few yards short.

"It was a microcosm of the season," Redskins defensive tackle Brandon Noble said of the loss. "We played them for 59 minutes, and that last minute just snuck away. It was just a good play by them and a bad play by us."

With one game left, the Redskins salvaged some pride with a 21–18 win at FedExField over the Vikings, who fell to 8–8 but snuck into the playoffs. In a solid all-around effort:

- Ramsey, already named by Gibbs as the starter for the 2005 season, went 17 of 26 for 216 yards, with two touchdowns and an interception.
- Running back Ladell Betts, subbing for the injured Portis, carried 26 times for 118 yards, career highs at the time.
- Washington's defense held the NFL's third-ranked offense in check and sacked 6–4, 265-pound quarterback Daunte Culpepper four times.
- The Redskins had three penalties for a season-low 13 yards.

"The win over the Vikings is huge because it's the last game we'll play for a while," Noble said at the time. "It's a taste in your mouth we'll live with for the next six months. All you remember is usually the last game."

## A Political Peculiarity

Why would a game between the 3–4 Packers and 2–4 Redskins on October 31, 2004, at FedExField spark an avalanche of national media attention? Because since 1936, the outcome of the Redskins' last home game before the U.S. presidential election had predicted the winner 17 out of 17 times. The formula was simple. If the Redskins won, the incumbent won. If the Redskins lost, the challenger won.

After the Packers beat the Redskins, 28–14, Democratic challenger John Kerry must have been smelling victory over Republican incumbent George W. Bush. Bush broke the string on November 2, however, to win his second term in the White House.

## 2005: 10–6, 2ND PLACE—NFC EAST

### Head Coach: Joe Gibbs

They were all but buried, written off by many in the sports media with five games remaining. Having suffered three straight maddening losses, the 5–6 Redskins appeared destined for another round of off-season contemplation.

But these Redskins proved to be special. They showed heart and character, two intangibles that their three-time Super Bowl-winning coach, Joe Gibbs, mentions so often but that get overlooked when things aren't going well.

The Redskins won their last five games. After topping St. Louis and Arizona, they knocked off NFC East rivals Dallas, New York, and Philadelphia by an average of 19 points. A season-ending win over the Eagles hoisted the 10–6 Redskins to wild card status in the playoffs, where they beat Tampa Bay but lost to Seattle in the second round.

"We played our butts off," offensive tackle Chris Samuels told reporters after the Redskins were eliminated by the Seahawks. "I'm proud of this team, proud of this coaching staff, Joe Gibbs. A lot of people, they counted him out. They talked bad about him, said he was outdated, this and that, this and that. He showed them he's one of the best coaches in the league if not the best. We're on the right track. Next year, we'll come back and get 'em."

Gibbs applied a touch of his old magic, defying skeptics who said the game had passed him by during the Redskins' 6–10 season in 2004, his comeback year. The Hall of Famer built a winning atmosphere among his troops in 2005 and restored pride to a franchise that had weathered a series of calamitous seasons since last reaching the playoffs in 1999.

Gibbs and his staff also transformed an offense ranked 30th in his first year back to 11th in 2005, a year that produced two franchise record setters: explosive wide receiver Santana Moss (1,483 receiving yards, Pro Bowl) and running back Clinton Portis (1,516 rushing yards). Second-year tight end–H-back Chris Cooley had an outstanding season with 71 catches, and 278-pound H-back–fullback Mike Sellers caught seven touchdown passes.

Thirteenth-year quarterback Mark Brunell enjoyed a renaissance after a horrid year in 2004. The lefty posted an 85.9 passer rating with 3,050 passing yards, 23 touchdowns, and 10 interceptions and was once a candidate for NFL Comeback Player of the Year until cooling off toward the end of the season. His touchdown-interception ratio was one of the best in Redskins history.

In fairness, none of those playmakers would have thrived without a stout offensive line featuring left tackle Samuels, who made the Pro Bowl for the third time; guard Randy Thomas, who was having a Pro Bowl-caliber year until a season-ending injury in the 14th game against Dallas; and right tackle Jon Jansen, who played the entire season with two broken thumbs. Center Casey Rabach and much improved guard Derrick Dockery also made key contributions.

The defense was much the same superaggressive attack from the year before. The unit, which came alive during the five-game winning streak to produce 17 sacks and 17 turnovers, offsetting a dearth in both categories, finished ninth in the league. A host of players gave stellar performances, including linebackers Marcus Washington (125 tackles, team-high 7.5 sacks) and Lemar Marshall (team-highs of 132 tackles and four interceptions); defensive linemen Phillip Daniels (eight sacks), Cornelius Griffin, and Joe Salave'a; cornerback Shawn Springs; and Sean Taylor, who emerged as one of the most feared safeties in the NFL in his second season and made bone-rattling hits that were heard miles away.

The defense thrived despite losing two key players to free agency during the 2005 off-season, linebacker Antonio Pierce and cornerback Fred Smoot. No big-time players were signed to replace them. Instead, the focus was mostly on the opposite side of the ball. Gibbs had insisted that he wanted his offense to be much more explosive than in 2004, one consistently able to complete long passes, move the chains, and keep defenses honest. To do that, he acquired two speedy 5–10, 190-pound wide receivers with impressive per-catch yardage averages in Santana Moss and David Patten.

Moss came in a trade with the Jets for disgruntled receiver Laveranues Coles, who in 2004 had caught 90 passes but for only 950 yards and one touchdown. In his four seasons, Moss had 151 catches for 2,416 yards and 19 touchdowns, with a 16-yard receiving average. Patten, coming off his eighth season, signed as a free agent. In 2004 in New England, he had 44 catches for 800 yards, with career highs of seven touchdowns and an 18.2-yard average.

"We got some guys with some real explosion," Gibbs told reporters. "We need to be a better downfield passing team. We need to jump in the end zone. Last year, it got to the point where we couldn't make the big play."

The Redskins also pulled off a big deal with Denver for the second straight year, sending three draft picks, including their No. 1 in 2006, for the Broncos' No. 1 pick (25th overall) in 2005. That gave the Redskins two first-round choices. At No. 9, they picked Auburn cornerback Carlos Rogers, the 2004 Jim Thorpe Award winner as the nation's top cornerback. At No. 25, it was 6–4, 223-pound Auburn quarterback Jason Campbell, the Southeastern Conference Player of the Year in 2004 and the MVP of the Sugar Bowl, in which the Tigers beat Virginia Tech to cap a 13–0 season.

Despite picking Campbell, Gibbs dispelled any myths about a quarterback controversy. He reiterated that fourth-year man Patrick Ramsey was still the Redskins' starter, noting that Ramsey looked much more confident and relaxed with the offense than in 2004, when he started the last seven games. For Ramsey, it was his turn to seize the moment and prove himself to be a bona fide NFL starter.

He was erratic in the preseason, though, throwing four interceptions and two touchdown passes and looking confused at times. After Ramsey threw two picks in a 24–17 loss to the Bengals, a perturbed-sounding Gibbs told reporters that Ramsey "knows we can't" turn the ball over like he did. For his part, Brunell played better than Ramsey during the 1–3 preseason.

Ramsey was intercepted on the Redskins' first possession in the season opener against the Bears at FedExField, but he subsequently reeled off some completions, including a 52-yarder to Moss that put the Redskins on the Chicago 28. A few plays later, Bears linebacker Lance Briggs sacked Ramsey using a vicious clothesline forearm, causing a fumble that the Bears recovered.

Ramsey hurt his neck on the play and left the game. In came Brunell, who led three drives that set up field goals by John Hall, with the third one creating a 9–7 game late in the third period. The Redskins' defense held the Bears to 166 total yards, and Cornelius Griffin's sack and fumble recovery ended Chicago's last possession.

The next day, Gibbs named Brunell to start in the upcoming game at Dallas. Ramsey told Comcast SportsNet he didn't agree with the decision, and ESPN reported that Ramsey had requested a trade after being told of his benching. Gibbs and Ramsey denied the ESPN report in interviews with the media, and Ramsey said, "I'm a Redskin right now."

After Patrick Ramsey went down with an injury on opening day against the Bears, 13-year veteran Mark Brunell called the signals for nearly the rest of the 2005 season. Brunell threw 23 touchdowns and 10 interceptions, and was once a candidate for NFL Comeback Player of the Year.

Back on the field, the Redskins pulled off one of the most dramatic sequences in Redskins' and *Monday Night Football* history. After their offense sputtered for the first 55 minutes against the Cowboys at Texas Stadium, Brunell threw 39- and 70-yard scoring passes to Moss within a 71-second span to erase a 13–0 Dallas lead and give the Redskins a 14–13 victory—and an enormous dose of confidence.

"It's one game, and we're going to enjoy it right now," Brunell said during a postgame news conference. "The offense has had a rough go the last 18 months or so, so this is big for us."

After savoring the stunner during a bye week, the Redskins hosted the tough 2–1 Seahawks and led nearly the whole way. But Seattle tied the game at 17 in the final quarter and had a chance to win it with one second left. A 47-yard field goal try hit the upright.

After winning the overtime coin toss, the Redskins drove 55 yards to position themselves for a game-winning field goal. Two third-and-long conversions, Brunell's 18-yard scramble and his 30-yard pass to Moss, kept the drive moving. Rookie Nick Novak, a University of Maryland product and the all-time leading scorer in Atlantic Coast Conference history, drilled a 39-yarder 5:31 into the extra period for the game-winner. The Redskins had signed Novak after Hall injured his quad against the Bears.

Yes, sir. Washington was 3–0 for the first time since 1991 and held first place in the NFC East. The offense, which converted 13 of 18 third downs against Seattle, was much more explosive than the previous season, meeting Gibbs's wish. The defense resembled Gregg Williams's well-oiled machine from 2004, having allowed only 12 points a game.

But the Redskins were living dangerously. Their three wins were by a total of six points, and they had lost the turnover battle in each game and were minus-four overall.

"It's kind of like we've got the luck on our side a little bit," cornerback Shawn Springs said after the win over Seattle.

"That's what you need when you talk about having great seasons and good seasons. Dallas might have been the game that kick-started us, then Santana and Mark hooked up for a big play at the end of today's game. You need some breaks to go your way."

## Redskins Honored

- Receiver Santana Moss was named NFC Offensive Player of the Week twice, once after his two-touchdown performance against Dallas on September 19 and once after catching five passes for 160 yards and three touchdowns against the Giants on December 24.
- Antonio Brown won NFC Special Teams Player of the Week after returning a kickoff 91 yards for the game-winning touchdown against Arizona on December 11.
- Defensive end Phillip Daniels was named NFC Defensive Player of the Week after his four-sack game against Dallas on December 18.
- Linebacker Marcus Washington was named NFC Defensive Player of the Month for December. He had 35 tackles, four sacks, one interception, two forced fumbles, and two fumble recoveries in a five-game span.
- H-back-fullback Mike Sellers won NFC Special Teams Player of the Week for his performance against the Eagles in the season finale.

In the same breath, Springs cautioned against overconfidence: "We haven't won a Super Bowl or gone to the playoffs yet. I tell my teammates, 'Don't start counting how many wins we've got.'"

The Redskins took to the road for games against supertough AFC West foes Denver and Kansas City, but they were a hair short in both games. In a 21–19 loss to the Broncos, Brunell's two-point conversion pass to David Patten was tipped away. His fourth-down pass to Moss was on target but deflected in the end zone in the waning seconds of a 28–21 loss to the Chiefs. (The Redskins were 0–4 against AFC teams.)

The Redskins got back on track with a 52–17 rout of one of the league's worst teams, the 49ers. Washington scored 50 points for the first time since 1999 and its most points ever at FedExField. Two of Brunell's scores went to H-back Mike Sellers, who had turned into a receiving threat around the goal line after dropping off the NFL radar screen for a few seasons; of his five catches to date, four were for touchdowns. Portis rushed for 101 yards with three short scores, breaking his touchdown drought that dated back to the latter part of the 2004 season. Washington's defense, sparked by the return of linebacker LaVar Arrington, held San Francisco to 194 yards.

At that point, the Redskins' offense was averaging 387 yards. Brunell, who was performing beyond anyone's expectations, and Moss, who was proving to be worth every penny, were on a torrid pace. Through the first six games, Moss averaged a whopping 20 yards on 38 receptions with five touchdowns. Brunell's passing stats following the Bears game were as such:

- 20 of 34, 291 yards, two touchdowns, interception against Dallas
- 20 of 36, 226 yards, two touchdowns, interception against Seattle
- 30 of 53, 332 yards, two touchdowns against Denver
- 25 of 41, 331 yards, three touchdowns against Kansas City
- 13 of 20, 252 yards, three touchdowns against San Francisco

Meanwhile, the 4–2 Redskins sat in a three-way tie for first place with Philly and New York in the NFC East. They went north to face the Giants in their biggest regular season game in recent memory. With the stakes so high, they forgot to show up: 36–0.

The Giants, playing on an emotional current due to the death of long-time owner Wellington Mara a few days prior, toyed with the Redskins. Giants running back Tiki Barber romped for 206 yards (8.6 average) against the NFL's fourth-ranked defense, and Washington was outgained, 386 to 125; committed four turnovers; and posted seven first downs against the 31st-ranked defense. New York controlled the ball for 40 minutes.

The loss also marked only the second time that Gibbs's Redskins had been shut out (the other one was against the Giants in the NFC championship game in January 1987). Former Redskins quarterback Joe Theismann, at the time an ESPN analyst on NFL games, said the loss was "embarrassing."

"It looked like the Giants wanted a street fight, and the Redskins didn't want any part of it," he said in an interview. "That was as close to a butt-kicking as I have seen in a football game in a long time and very, very uncharacteristic of what

---

## "How 'Bout Those Redskins!"

Shortly after Washington's 35–7 rout of the Cowboys on December 18, a long-time Redskins fan voiced his pleasure. In a pregame ceremony, Dallas Mavericks guard Darrell Armstrong wished the crowd at American Airlines Center in Dallas a happy holiday season and then shouted, "How 'bout those Redskins!"—a take on the popular line, "How 'bout them Cowboys!" The Mavericks fined Armstrong $1,000 for the comment.

---

the Redskins have been under Joe Gibbs. If I was a member of the Redskins, and I played a game like that, I couldn't wait to get my uniform on for the next game to prove that what everyone saw was an aberration."

The loss dropped the Redskins into a tie for last place in the division with the Eagles, who were heading to town riding a seven-game winning streak over Washington. Philly was without superstar receiver Terrell Owens, who had been suspended for "conduct detrimental to the team" after making inflammatory comments in an interview with ESPN.com, and All-Pro quarterback Donovan McNabb was playing with a sports hernia. Still, the Eagles were in position to win the game with the Redskins leading, 17–10, and 1:32 to play. On fourth-and-4 from the Redskins' 7, McNabb tried to thread a pass into the end zone, but safety Ryan Clark picked it off to secure the win.

Against the Eagles, Brunell (21 of 29, 224 yards, one touchdown) regained his passing touch after a woeful effort against the Giants, and the Redskins' defense held its opponent to 45 yards rushing.

"Philadelphia's been on top of our division," Redskins tackle Joe Salave'a said after the game. "In order to right the ship, we had to come out and give them a good run for their money. I thought we did, and we'll see them again. It was a great feeling. I want to enjoy this one for 24 hours and get ready for the next ball game."

The 5–3 Redskins were now positioned nicely for a playoff run heading into the second half of the season. But a stretch of three straight excruciating losses left them teetering on the edge of playoff elimination:

- 36–35 to Tampa Bay on a controversial two-point conversion run in the final minute
- 16–13 to a Raiders team coached by former Redskins coach Norv Turner on a field goal with less than two minutes left
- 23–17 in overtime to a Chargers team coached by former Redskins coach Marty Schottenheimer

The loss to the Chargers marked the third straight game that the Redskins had led in the fourth quarter, and frustration was everywhere in a somber postgame locker room.

"For me personally, this is about the toughest stretch I've been through," Gibbs said. "They were very close and very hard fought. When you go through something like that it is a measure for all of us. You get measured during adversity. We are going to have to see how we fight back. So far our guys have been unbelievable."

"You couldn't tell me we'd be 5–6 at this point," guard Randy Thomas said. "I'd probably beat your ass. It's kind of hard to even think about the way it's happened. Early on, we found ways to win. I guess we're finding ways to lose."

When asked if the Redskins were hoping for losses by other NFC teams with playoff possibilities, linebacker LaVar Arrington snapped back: "We've got to win. Forget if. There's no reason to look at everybody else if we can't win a game. We've got to take care of our home first."

One more loss and the Redskins were out of the playoff race, so someone needed to step up. Enter Clinton Portis. The Redskins' star running back said he approached Gibbs and demanded to carry the ball more as part of an offensive attack based on smash-mouth football.

"That was a team decision," Portis said in June 2006. "We knew our bread and butter. Let's stop trying to fool people and trick people and hold onto a lead. Let's run it down their throat. That's what we did."

Indeed, Portis put the team on his shoulders, rushing for more than 100 yards in each of the last five regular-season games behind the Redskins' talented O-line and wearing defenses down. When it was all over, he had set a team record for single-season rushing yards (1,516) and 100-yard rushing games (nine). He also tied the team mark for consecutive 100-yard games (five).

As a team, the Redskins crafted a stretch reminiscent of the strong season finishes so common during Gibbs-I. They first knocked off St. Louis (24–9) and Arizona (17–13) on the road, before steamrolling over the Cowboys at home, 35–7, Washington's most lopsided win ever over its most despised rival.

The Redskins clicked on all fronts. Coming off a pitiful performance against Arizona, Brunell threw four touchdown passes. With defenses keying on Moss and with the Redskins without a legitimate No. 2 receiver (David Patten had been put on injured reserve and James Thrash was out with an injury), Chris Cooley had a career day, catching three scoring passes as sounds of "COOOOOOLEY!" reverberated around FedExField. The Redskins scored 21 points off turnovers.

Washington's defense made mincemeat out of the Cowboys' offense. Immobile Dallas quarterback Drew Bledsoe was sacked seven times and threw three picks. Defensive end Phillip Daniels had four of those sacks, tying a Redskins' all-time mark. He also recovered a fumble and tipped a pass that Cornelius Griffin intercepted. Marcus Washington was all over the place with two sacks, one of which forced a fumble that set up a Redskins touchdown. He also intercepted a pass that led to seven points.

Cowboys coach Bill Parcells, who wore a scowl as his team was bamboozled, was succinct in his press conference: "We were awful."

Suddenly, the Redskins had gone from being buried to one of the hottest and most dangerous teams in the NFL. They had gained control of the sixth and final NFC playoff spot, holding tiebreakers over fellow 8–6 squads Dallas, Minnesota, and Atlanta.

The Redskins then spanked the Giants, 35–17. Moss, single-covered for most of the game, made New York pay. He

hauled in two scoring passes from Brunell in the first quarter, a 17-yard screen pass and a 59-yard bomb. He also caught a 72-yarder from forgotten quarterback Patrick Ramsey, who entered the game after Brunell sprained a knee ligament with the Redskins clinging to a 21–17 lead in the third quarter. Ramsey went 5 of 7 for 104 yards and a touchdown (153.3 passer rating).

The mood in the Redskins' postgame locker room was festive. Kicker John Hall dressed as Santa Claus and called himself "Santana Claus."

Speaking of the clutch performance by Ramsey, Redskins offensive tackle Jon Jansen said, "I told him a long time ago, sooner or later we're going to need him to step in and play big. He was ready when the time came."

Jansen added, "We're just playing a great brand of ball right now at the right time. Offensively, defensively, special teams, we've got everything clicking. The coaches are putting together good game plans, and we're executing them."

Moss said focus would be imperative heading into the season finale on New Year's Day against the Eagles at Lincoln Financial Field: "We know what we have at stake, and we'll just try to go out and do what we've been doing. Stay fresh and get us another win. We've been through a lot this year, good and bad, and we've tried to learn from it and move on."

On December 31, the Giants beat Oakland to clinch the NFC East, so the only thing the Redskins could hope for was a wild card spot. The 6–9 Eagles had experienced a tumultuous season, a year after losing in Super Bowl XXXIX. But playing in black-and-blue Philadelphia is never easy, particularly for an NFC East rival, and Redskins fans had to sweat this one out.

Gibbs named Brunell to start the game. Brunell, who passed for fewer than 200 yards in each of the final seven regular season games and was limping as a result of a knee injury from the Giants game, hit a wall against Philly (9 of 25, 141 yards, touchdown, interception). The inspired Eagles led 20–17 heading into the fourth period, but Washington's defense rose to the occasion, forcing turnovers that led to 14 points.

First, Redskins middle linebacker Lemar Marshall intercepted a pass by backup quarterback Mike McMahon, subbing for the injured Donovan McNabb, and returned it to the 22. On the next play, Portis burst up the middle and then shifted toward the left side and into the end zone for a 24–20 lead, his second score of the day. Later, Daniels's sack of new Eagles quarterback Koy Detmer forced a fumble. Safety Sean Taylor scooped it up and ran 39 yards for a score to seal a 31–20 Redskins victory.

Playoffs, here we come!

"I knew we could do it," Arrington said in the jubilant locker room. "I knew as a team the Eagles weren't going to lay down. I knew they were going to come out here and fight. It made the victory that much better because they fought their tails off."

With a new season upon them, the 10–6 Redskins, the NFC's No. 6 playoff seed, would be heading south to play the No. 5 seed, 11–5 Tampa Bay, the conference's other wild card team.

"Right now, we're in a one-game season," Jansen told reporters. "Our backs have been up against the wall for a long time, which isn't the case for a lot of playoff teams.

When your back's up against a wall, you have to do certain things to make sure you win, and you have to be able to fight through certain things. We've been able to do that. So going into the playoffs we have maybe a slight advantage in that regard, especially having to win our last one on the road."

## NFC WILD CARD PLAYOFF GAME
**Washington 17, Tampa Bay 10**
**January 7, 2006**
**Raymond James Stadium, Tampa, Fla.**
**Attendance: 65,514**

### Redskins Defense Spectacular in Win over Bucs

When Washington and Tampa Bay met in the playoffs in January 2000, and when they collided in the 2005 regular season, the Redskins were bedeviled by bad luck. This time, they were showered with good fortune.

The Redskins fumbled the ball three times and recovered each one. They received a favorable call off instant replay that prevented a touchdown near the end of the game. They overcame the third-quarter ejection of their star safety, Sean Taylor, who was accused of spitting on an opponent.

The defense was in the right place at the right time. Linebacker LaVar Arrington's interception of a tipped pass set up a short touchdown run, and Taylor returned a fumble 51 yards for another touchdown. Both first-quarter scores were all the points the Redskins needed in a 17–10 playoff win over the Buccaneers.

Washington's defense also forced three turnovers and registered three sacks, and held Tampa Bay to 243 yards. The defense's superb performance compensated for an offense that

posted the least number of yards ever by a winning team in a playoff game: 120. Quarterback Mark Brunell threw for 41 yards and tossed what could have been a backbreaking interception, and running back Clinton Portis rushed for 53 yards, ending his streak of five straight 100-yard outings. Washington's longest drive was 40 yards.

Granted, the Redskins were facing the league's No. 1 defense, but Washington's offense redefined the meaning of ineptness. Brunell joked in his postgame press conference that he would gladly accept the Offensive Player of the Week award. "Our defense was incredible," Brunell said. "They won this game for us. They came up with big plays."

The defense struck early. On Tampa Bay's second possession, tackle Joe Salave'a tipped a pass by quarterback Chris Simms, and the ball floated into the arms of Arrington, who returned it 21 yards to the Bucs' 6. On the next play, Portis found a hole off left tackle and scored for a 7–0 lead.

Tampa Bay drove to the Redskins' 34 on its next possession when running back Cadillac Williams, the NFL Offensive Rookie of the Year, fumbled. Linebacker Marcus Washington picked it up and started to run until he, too, coughed up the ball. Taylor scooped it up and ran 51 yards for the touchdown, his second in two weeks. Just like that, the Redskins led by 14 points only 10 minutes into the game.

Taylor's play triggered a flashback to the January 2000 playoff encounter. During a critical sequence in the fourth quarter, Bucs quarterback Sean King fumbled, but teammate Warrick Dunn recovered it and ran 13 yards for a first down. A few plays later, Tampa Bay scored the winning points in its 14–13 victory.

Meanwhile, the Redskins' offense remained stagnant, and the Bucs crept back into the game. The teams traded field goals before the end of the half, and Simms capped a 51-yard Tampa Bay drive in the third period with a 2-yard touchdown run, creating a 17–10 game with 9:40 left in the quarter.

Tampa Bay was now riding tsunami-like momentum, and when the Bucs drove to the Redskins' 19 with 7:41 left in the final quarter, one could sense them cutting into the lead even more. But the Redskins' resolute defense stuffed 250-pound fullback Mike Alstott on a third-and-1 and forced Simms into an incompletion on fourth down.

Shortly after, Brunell threw an interception that gave the Bucs possession at the Redskins' 35. Tampa Bay went nowhere, and again, Simms threw incomplete on fourth down. His third-down pass had sailed perfectly into the arms of receiver Edell Shepherd in the end zone, and for a second it appeared the Bucs had the game-tying score. But officials ruled that Shepherd lost control of the ball as he came down, a call supported by instant replay. (In the regular-season game, instant replay upheld a controversial call allowing Alstott's run on a two-point conversion that gave Tampa Bay a 36–35 win.)

The Redskins' offense, still stuck in neutral, punted once again, and the Bucs took over on Washington's 46. Simms, neutralized all game after throwing for 279 yards and three touchdowns against the Redskins in the regular season, tossed a pass that was tipped by tackle Cornelius Griffin and intercepted with 1:05 left by Marcus Washington.

Game over.

"We were pretty fortunate to get out of here with a win against this type of football team, especially with the way our

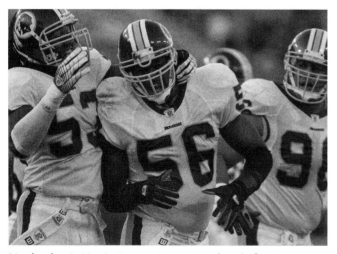

Linebacker LaVar Arrington is congratulated after intercepting a pass that set up a 6-yard scoring run by Clinton Portis. The Redskins' defense held the Bucs to 243 yards on the day.

offense performed," Redskins guard Ray Brown told reporters. "We didn't get it done offensively."

Asked if he knew beforehand that he would pass for only 25 net yards, Brunell responded, "I would have told you our season was over. [But] to get a W in the playoffs, particularly on the road, you don't really care about the numbers. You don't care how pretty it is or how effective you were on offense. You're in the playoffs against a very good defense. We'll take it."

Arrington, who won his first playoff game since being drafted by the Redskins in 2000, looked like he was in another world while speaking with the press. "It feels good, but it just doesn't seem like this is really happening," he said. "Maybe that's what it feels like, like it's not really happening. If this is really real, this is cool."

| | | | | | | |
|---|---|---|---|---|---|---|
| Washington— | 14 | 3 | 0 | 0 | — | 17 |
| Tampa Bay— | 0 | 3 | 7 | 0 | — | 10 |

Wash — Portis 6 run (Hall kick)
Wash — Taylor 51 fumble recovery (Hall kick)
TB —— FG Bryant 43
Wash — FG Hall 47
TB —— Simms 2 run (Bryant kick)

# NFC DIVISIONAL PLAYOFF GAME
## Seattle 20, Washington 10
## January 14, 2006
## Qwest Field, Seattle
## Attendance: 67,551

## Sluggish in Seattle: Redskins' Offense Looks Miserable in Defeat

The Redskins' anemic offense finally proved too much for the squad to overcome.

Washington gained 289 yards against Seattle, but more than half of those came in the fourth quarter, when the Redskins were playing catch-up. At the same time, the Redskins' defense couldn't bail out the team for the third straight game, despite holding the NFL's No. 1 scoring offense to eight points below its average.

The result was a 20–10 playoff loss that ended the Redskins' winning streak at six and closed the chapter on their entertaining season.

"That's my responsibility," Redskins coach Joe Gibbs, speaking in a press conference, said of his offense that converted 5 of 19 third downs against Seattle and scored two touchdowns in two playoff games. "Obviously, we wanted to be much more productive than we were in the playoffs. That'll be one of the things we look hard at, how offensively can we do a better job."

The Redskins' ground game, their bread and butter during a late-season surge that put them into the playoffs, produced a measly 59 yards. Running back Clinton Portis, bothered by banged-up shoulders, was ineffective for the second straight game (41 yards, 17 carries). In the first three quarters, quarterback Mark Brunell was just as dreadful as he was against Tampa Bay the previous week. "They were bringing extra peo-

ple, they stuffed us," Brunell told the press. "We did not run the ball the way we wanted to. That's kind of our M. O."

Despite those shortcomings, the game was winnable for the Redskins against a 13–3 Seattle squad that had a week off after the regular season. Washington captured the turnover battle, three to one, but failed to capitalize on some delicious scoring opportunities, as well as the fact that running back and league MVP Shaun Alexander (NFL-high 1,880 yards) was sidelined nearly the whole game with a concussion.

The 5–11, 225-pound Alexander left the game for good in the first quarter after being popped by defensive tackle Cornelius Griffin and linebacker LaVar Arrington. He had gained only 9 yards on six carries, and the Redskins had to be feeling giddy.

Both the Redskins, who opened the game with five straight three-and-outs, and the Seahawks failed to generate any offense in what became a punting show in the steady rainfall. But the Redskins got a big break when Pierson Prioleau recovered a fumbled punt on the Seattle 39. A few plays later, John Hall's 26-yard field goal gave Washington a 3–0 lead with 8:59 left in the second period.

Suddenly, the deafening crowd at Qwest Field, where the Seahawks were 8–0 in the regular season, fell silent. On the next drive, cornerback Carlos Rogers had daylight in front of him when he stepped in front of a receiver near the sideline and began to cradle a pass from quarterback Matt Hasselbeck. The Redskins were eyeing a 10–0 lead that, given the stinginess of their defense, could provide a possible trip to the NFC championship game.

Rogers dropped the pass, though, and Hasselbeck, who posted an NFC-high 98.2 passer rating that season, led a 12-play, 76-yard drive that ended with his 29-yard scoring pass to receiver Darrell Jackson (nine catches, 143 yards) for a 7–3 Seahawks halftime lead. Early in the second half, Hasselbeck capped a 10-play, 81-yard march by running 6 yards into the end zone for a 14–3 edge.

Seattle took a 17–3 lead early in the fourth period, but the Redskins' offense finally came to life. Brunell, who was 22 of 37 for 242 yards but unable to produce much in the first three quarters, found a wide-open Chris Cooley for a 52-yard catch and run. Two plays later, Brunell's pass bounced off Seattle cornerback Andre Dyson and into the arms of receiver Santana Moss in the end zone. Hall converted for 17–10 game.

Return man Josh Scobey fumbled the ensuing kickoff, and Hall recovered at the Seattle 40. The Redskins failed to capitalize on the opportunity, as Hall's 36-yard field goal try went wide left. Seattle then chewed up more than five minutes while driving for a field goal that clinched its first playoff win since 1984.

"That was a tough assignment here," said Gibbs, who lost for the first time in five games coaching against Seattle. "It kind of tells you the reason why people fight so hard for home-field advantage. That's the way it's supposed to be when you go on the road."

"We need to get more offense than we had, we need to get more points than we had," offensive tackle Jon Jansen told reporters. "We're happy to be part of the top eight. But obviously we want to be the top one, and that's not going to happen. We'll go back to the drawing board and see if we can win the division, get home field advantage and do it next year."

| Washington— | 0 | 3 | 0 | 7 | — | 10 |
|---|---|---|---|---|---|---|
| Seattle— | 0 | 7 | 7 | 6 | — | 20 |

Wash — FG Hall 26
Sea —— Jackson 29 pass from Hasselbeck (Brown kick)
Sea —— Hasselbeck 6 run (Brown kick)
Sea —— FG Brown 33
Wash — Moss 20 pass from Brunell (Hall kick)
Sea —— FG Brown 31

## 2006: 5–11, 4TH PLACE—NFC EAST

### Head Coach: Joe Gibbs

Joe Gibbs called it the most disappointing season in his 15 years as the Redskins' head coach. One could argue that 2006 was also the most disappointing season in franchise history.

Consider this: In the off-season, all signs pointed to the Redskins' spirited finish in 2005, when they won six straight games to reach the second round of the playoffs, as a springboard to a season that would possibly end with confetti raining down on the victorious squad in Miami in Super Bowl XLI. In training camp, quarterback Mark Brunell fueled the optimism by saying "anything short of going all the way would be a disappointment." And the front office made what seemed like savvy personnel moves to fine-tune an already talented squad, while Gibbs brought in an assistant coach with a track record of devising explosive offenses.

So much for preseason hype. The Redskins floundered, finishing 5–11 and in last place in the NFC East while establishing themselves as the NFL's biggest flop.

Gibbs has said many times that the past doesn't buy you anything, and his words rang true in 2006. He took responsibility for the precipitous fall and called the season a "big step back."

"I was brought here to win football games, and certainly going 5–11, that's not getting it done," he said at the conclusion of the third season of his much publicized comeback. "The responsibility for that is with me. To all of our fans, the way you've supported us here all the way down through the years and during my time with the Redskins, I feel awful when we don't win football games. You guys deserve a winner. There are a lot of players here who bust their butts to get you a winner. But it's been my responsibility to get wins, and anytime you go 5–11, I got to step up and say I didn't get the job done."

As the season spiraled out of control, incredulous looks became more palpable on the faces of Redskins players, many of whom were at a loss for words. After the season-ending loss to the Giants, defensive end Phillip Daniels vented his frustrations when asked if the preseason Super Bowl chatter had become a distraction for him and his teammates.

"It doesn't matter what the talk is," he said. "But you can't just roll out on the field and expect to win. Everybody looks at paper and says, 'Oh, yea, we're going to the Super Bowl.' You've got to play the game. That's why the game is played between those lines. If you don't come with it, then another team's going to get you.

"When I came into this season, I expected home field advantage in the playoffs," he added. "I can't sit here and lie to you."

The wretched season was reminiscent of the Redskins' superhyped team in 2000 that underachieved, finished 8–8,

After producing defenses that finished No. 3 in the league in 2004 and No. 9 in 2005, Gregg Williams saw his unit plummet to 31st in 2006. Players like Adam Archuleta (40), signed before the season to the most lucrative contract for a safety in NFL history, came up short.

and failed to reach the playoffs. Expectations for that team had swelled largely due to the off-season signings of high-priced free agents such as future Hall of Famers Deion Sanders and Bruce Smith, as did the hopes for the 2006 squad following a series of ballyhooed off-season acquisitions. The 2006 crew was mostly a disappointment.

The Redskins, sorely in need of a No. 2 receiver behind superstar Santana Moss, acquired the exciting Antwaan Randle El through free agency and traded two mid-round draft picks to the 49ers for Brandon Lloyd. Although Randle El was thrilling at times, he finished as only the team's fourth-leading receiver, with 32 catches for 351 yards and three touchdowns. Lloyd, invisible for stretches, caught 23 passes with no touchdowns, and his playing time diminished down the stretch. He was also a problem child, once throwing his helmet on the field in disgust, a 15-yard penalty, and engaging in what looked like an argument on the sidelines with Randle El.

Free agent defensive end Andre Carter, for his part, struggled through the first half of the season but ended up leading the team in sacks (six). Then there was the saga of free agent Adam Archuleta, who signed the most lucrative contract for a safety in NFL history ($35 million, seven years). Archuleta was a bust. Asked to play more of a coverage role than in his previous five years in the league, he was repeatedly victimized on pass plays and was relegated to special teams for the last half of the season. Speaking to reporters late in the season, he called his first year in Washington "extremely bizarre."

Carter and Archuleta were part of a defense that took a serious nosedive after posting league rankings of ninth (2005) and third (2004) under defensive guru Gregg Williams. In 2006, his unit was 31st and exited with some ominous statistics:

- 5,688 yards allowed, 35 short of the Redskins' all-time mark of 5,723
- 12 turnovers, the fewest in league history for a 16-game season
- 19 sacks, a league low and franchise record low
- 30 touchdown passes and 55 pass plays of 20 yards or more, both first in the league, and 15 pass plays of 40 yards or more, the No. 2 mark
- A third-down conversion clip of 43.7 percent, one of the league's highest marks

What happened? While the defensive line and linebackers looked futile at times in stopping the run and harassing quarterbacks, a secondary that lacked depth took a fierce beating. Surgery in mid-August kept starting cornerback Shawn Springs out for two months, and cornerback Carlos Rogers, forced into the No. 1 cover position in Springs's absence, was beaten regularly and dropped a host of possible interceptions. Newly acquired veteran cornerbacks Mike Rumph and Kenny Wright were burned too often in pass coverage, as was hard-hitting safety Sean Taylor, although he was a late Pro Bowl selection.

The Redskins could have used eighth-year safety Pierson Prioleau, who suffered a season-ending injury on the first play of the regular season, as well as 11th-year cornerback Walt Harris and fifth-year safety Ryan Clark. The latter two were not re-signed in the off-season. Harris signed with the 49ers and finished tied in 2006 as the NFC leader in interceptions (eight). Management discarded Clark, a solid player and leader in the locker room, for Archuleta.

To add to the turmoil, an ESPN.com article in late November quoted an anonymous Redskins player who called Gregg Williams "arrogant" and accused him of recklessly letting players leave the team. Former *Washington Post* Redskins beat reporter Tom Friend, who wrote the article, suggested that such decisions by Williams were responsible for the defense's demise in 2006. Gibbs refused to directly address the article.

The offense, meanwhile, sputtered in the first half of the season and often struggled in the red zone as it tried to adapt to the system of new associate head coach–offense Al Saunders. Brunell, in his 14th season, started the first nine games and threw only four interceptions. But he failed to move the team consistently, looking dreadful at times. Gibbs benched him and tapped second-year quarterback Jason Campbell, who proved that investing two No. 1 draft picks in him was worth it. He completed 110 of 207 passes for 1,297 yards, with 10 touchdowns and six interceptions, displaying his rocket arm, mobility, poise, and toughness. Gibbs named him the Redskins' starting quarterback for 2007.

The offensive line of bookend tackles Jon Jansen and Chris Samuels (Pro Bowl), center Casey Rabach, and guards Derrick Dockery and Randy Thomas had a terrific year. The Redskins yielded 19 sacks, the third-best mark in the league, while the line opened holes for the league's fourth-leading rushing team (2,216 yards, 138.5 per game). Star running back Clinton Portis was injury riddled and went on IR midway through the season, but fifth-year man Ladell Betts filled his shoes and crafted a 1,154-yard season.

The performance of special teams reminded everyone of the days of special teams genius George Allen in the 1970s. Rock Cartwright set a team record for kickoff return yards (1,541), including a 100-yard return for a touchdown. Randle El returned a punt 87 yards for a score. There were also two blocked punts and a blocked field goal. And the Redskins appeared to find a kicker in Shaun Suisham, who hit 8 of 9 field goals after signing in early December. Suisham became the 16th Redskins kicker since Chip Lohmiller was cut before the 1995 season.

Bright spots were few and far between, however. The following moments were emblematic of the Redskins' woes:

- After returning a punt 87 yards for a touchdown against the Colts, Randle El celebrated by running into the goal post, a 15-yard penalty for unsportsmanlike conduct. Sean Taylor was offside on the kickoff, putting the ball on the 10. Punter Derrick Frost booted it as officials were blowing whistles to delay his kick, and he yanked off his helmet in anger, a penalty that pushed the ball back to the 5. Indianapolis ended up taking over on its 47 and drove for a field goal that cut the lead to one at halftime and destroyed the Redskins' momentum in an eventual 36–22 Colts win.
- The Redskins had a first-and-goal on the 7 against Dallas at FedExField but couldn't score in six plays. (A Cowboys penalty provided another first down on the 2.) From the 1, Portis was stopped twice and Betts once. For some mystifying reason, two beefy Redskin backs, 254-pound T. J. Duckett and 280-pound Mike Sellers, didn't touch the ball in that sequence.
- Eagles quarterback Donovan McNabb completed a 20-yard pass against the Redskins in Philly, but Springs, standing behind the receiver, knocked the ball up in the air. The Eagles' Correll Buckhalter, running the other way, caught

Second-year-man Jason Campbell started the last seven games in 2006 and emitted signs of being the Redskins' quarterback of the future. He completed 110 of 207 passes for 1,297 yards, with 10 touchdowns and six interceptions.

it and ran 37 yards for a score. "That's the way things have been going around here," Springs said. "Work hard, work hard, and then just still fall short."

- In a 24–14 loss to Atlanta, the Redskins relinquished a 14–0 lead and showed poor clock management after taking possession on the Falcons' 27 with 2:03 to play. Campbell's passing moved the ball to the 2, and a spike and incompletion created a third-and-1 with 51 seconds left. Campbell, looking confused about what to do, handed off to Betts, who was stopped for a 2-yard loss. An incompletion on the next play ended the game.

- With the Redskins driving for a score on their first possession of the season finale against the Giants, Betts fumbled deep in Giants territory, and New York's Fred Robbins recovered and ran 67 yards to set up a field goal. Redskins safety Vernon Fox later dropped an interception in the end zone, and the Giants scored a touchdown on the same possession to take a 10–7 lead. Those two turnover-related plays cost the Redskins 10 points in their 34–28 loss.

Months prior, no one in Redskins land could have envisioned such a struggle. A deal in the off-season between the owners and players increased the salary cap to $102 million and allowed the Redskins to do what they love to do: dip into the free agency market. They lured Archuleta, Carter, and Randle El, and traded for Lloyd.

The most stunning arrival was Al Saunders, who had guided Kansas City's offense to the NFL's No. 1 ranking in the two previous seasons. Prior to his five years with the Chiefs, he spent two seasons as the wide receivers coach for the "Greatest Show on Turf," the explosive, pass-happy offense of the Rams. The hope was that Saunders would incorporate such sizzle into the Redskins' offense. Gibbs assigned Saunders to call plays, a job that the head coach had played a key role in since his first season in Washington in 1981. But Gibbs said his self-demotion wasn't a big deal.

Preseason publications predicted that the Redskins would be in the thick of the NFC East, which seemed like a toss-up among Washington, Dallas, New York, and Philadelphia. *Sports Illustrated* picked the Redskins to finish first in the division.

But an 0–4 exhibition season in which the Redskins were outscored, 104–27, triggered cause for alarm. Their point total was the least in an exhibition season in the 46 years that the franchise has listed preseason results.

Sure, Gibbs went 0–4 and 1–3 in exhibition games in two of his Super Bowl–winning seasons in Washington, and the preseason is often a poor measurement of exactly how a team will fare in the regular season. But something smelled rotten about this go-round. The defense relinquished big play after big play, and the first-team offense failed to score a point. The buzz line was that the Redskins had resorted to a vanilla offense by using only 2 percent of Saunders' 700-page playbook.

"There's definitely a reason to be concerned," Chris Samuels said after a 27–14 loss to the Jets. "You want to win every game. But I don't think it's a point where we need to panic. There's nothing counting against us at this point. We're still evaluating talent. We're holding a lot of plays back. But at the same time we're losing."

Gibbs sounded peeved after the Jets game: "As far as I'm concerned, I'm concerned. We need to all take a real serious hard look at this."

It hurt that the offense had been thrown out of whack when Portis separated his shoulder in the exhibition opener against the Bengals. Soon after, the Redskins traded a draft pick in a three-way deal that landed the Falcons' T. J. Duckett, a former first-round draft choice. But in one of the season's biggest mysteries, Duckett was barely used. (Instead of parting with a draft pick, the Redskins could have spent virtually nothing to sign free agent Stephen Davis, the third-leading rusher in Redskins history. Davis signed with St. Louis and scored a touchdown in the Rams' win over the Redskins on December 24.)

Portis returned when the Redskins, the oldest team in the league, took the field for the season opener on Monday night, September 11, against the Vikings at FedExField. Before a franchise-record crowd of 90,608 on the fifth anniversary of the September 11 terrorist attacks on the United States, the Redskins fell, 19–16. Redskin John Hall kicked three field goals but was wide on a 49-yarder in the closing seconds.

The following week at Dallas, Washington's offense looked miserable and Brunell was erratic. But the Redskins hung around and threatened in the third quarter while trailing, 17–10. Brunell lobbed a pass for tight end Chris Cooley that was picked off at the 1, however, and the Cowboys drove 99 yards for a game-clinching touchdown in their 27–10 win.

During the telecast, NBC analyst John Madden questioned whether Brunell was the right quarterback to lead the Redskins' offense. Others in the media expressed concern about Brunell's play, and there were calls for Campbell, who had moved up in the depth chart after the off-season trade of Patrick Ramsey. Brunell had resorted to a dink-and-dunk passing game, and there was confusion as to why he was not exploiting the Redskins' primary receiving corps of Moss, Randle El, Lloyd, and Cooley.

"Why have a Ferrari if you're not going to drive it," Brian Mitchell, the ex-Redskins special teams star, reasoned while giving his Redskins analysis on Comcast SportsNet.

With the 0–2 Redskins in a must-win situation, Brunell silenced his critics against the Texans in Houston—and then some. The lefty completed 22 straight passes, a league record, in a 31–15 Redskins victory. His 89 percent completion percentage (24 of 27) broke Sammy Baugh's team record set in 1940. While again resorting to a mostly horizontal passing game, he distributed the ball much better to his receivers. Portis, who had sat out the Dallas game because of his sore shoulder, rushed for 86 yards and two touchdowns and caught two passes for 78 yards.

In an encore performance, Brunell completed 18 of 30 passes for 329 yards and three touchdowns against a stout Jacksonville defense at FedExField. All three of his scoring passes went to Moss, who had one of his amazing games. Early in overtime, Brunell completed a pass around midfield to Moss, who turned it into a 68-yard catch-and-run that accounted for a 36–30 win. Moss was named NFC Offensive Player of the Week.

Portis rushed for 112 yards, and the Redskins gained nearly 500 for the second straight week. Samuels described the game as a "statement" win. "It is a statement around the league," he said. "Jacksonville's one of the top defenses. They've been shutting people down. Nobody thought we could run on those guys, and for us to go out there and put up what we put up, made plays all day throwing the ball, it says a lot that we're coming and we're a good group of guys."

Now on a roll, the 2–2 Redskins would face the 1–2 Giants, who were one overtime pass away from losing their first three games but stood fresh off a bye week. For the second straight year, the Redskins took the day off in the Meadowlands.

In a 19–3 loss, the offense gained 164 yards and the defense allowed 411, including 123 rushing to Tiki Barber. Then came a demoralizing 25–22 loss at FedExField to Tennessee. The Titans, 0–5 entering the game, overcame a double-digit deficit behind the play of rookie quarterback Vince Young and Travis Henry, who rushed for a career-high 178 yards. Brunell's poorly thrown last-minute interception sealed his team's fate.

As the Redskins' lead disappeared, the boos at FedExField became louder and louder. "That was disheartening to hear our fans boo," defensive lineman Renaldo Wynn said. "I've never heard it since I've been here in five years. I don't blame them. The expectations that we have for this team are the expectations that they have for us."

Redskins tight end Chris Cooley snags a pass from quarterback Jason Campbell late in a game against Carolina on November 26. He broke a couple of tackles, escaped into the open field and raced down the sideline and into the end zone to provide the winning points in a 17–13 Redskins victory. The play was one of the few dramatic highlights for the Redskins in 2006.

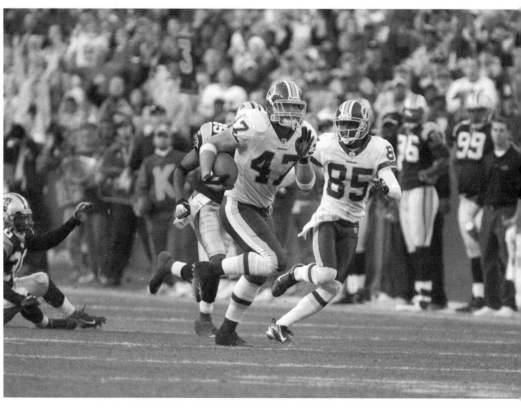

Gibbs wouldn't budge when it came to Brunell. "I'm not afraid to change anything, and I don't think I would hesitate to change something if it's best for our football team," he said. "Right now, changing Mark—I don't think that's the answer."

But Brunell was again ineffective in a 36–22 loss to the eventual Super Bowl-champion Colts at the RCA Dome that left the Redskins 2–5 entering their bye week. But in an NFC that resembled a sea of mediocrity, a couple of wins could lift them back into the playoff race.

## Redskins: A Money-Making Machine

Since Dan Snyder bought the Redskins in 1999, his team has showed scant signs of being a powerhouse. Things have been vastly different off the field, where Snyder has hit the jackpot.

The wily businessman and long-time Redskins fan has built his team into a money-making machine in the 21st century. *Forbes* has rated the Redskins as the most valuable NFL team for seven straight years through the magazine's annual rankings as of August 2006. In 2006, the Redskins were worth more than $1.4 billion, an increase of 13 percent from the previous year and nearly $250 million more than the second-ranked Patriots, according to *Forbes*. The magazine said the Redskins had an operating income in 2006 exceeding $108 million, more than double every other NFL team except for Houston and Tampa Bay.

With Snyder in command, *Forbes* has also singled out the Redskins as the first American team ever to clear the billion-dollar mark in value and one of the richest sports franchises in the world.

How has Snyder done it?

In his first season with the Redskins, Snyder sold the naming rights of the Redskins' stadium in Landover, Maryland, to delivery company FedEx for $207 million, then the biggest naming rights deal in sports history. The stadium's seating capacity at the time was 78,600, but Snyder has since expanded it into the largest venue in pro football at nearly 92,000 seats. Many of the additions have been expensive premium seats.

In addition to plastering ads all over the stadium, Snyder has increased ticket prices to among the highest in the NFL. He has also opened Redskins retail stores throughout the Washington area and launched Triple X ESPN Radio, three local all-sports radio stations with trimulcast programming and strong Redskins coverage. *Forbes* looks primarily at sponsorship, advertising and premium-seating revenue to determine its rankings.

"In terms of franchise value, the Redskins are miles ahead of any other team in the United States," said Kurt Badenhausen, an associate editor at *Forbes*. "Daniel Snyder has done an unbelievable job of squeezing every single bit of revenue out of that stadium. The Redskins are way ahead of anyone else in sponsorship revenue and premium-seating revenue."

---

With 35 seconds left in a Redskins-Cowboys duel at FedEx, that much-needed shot of momentum was looming. But Redskins kicker Nick Novak, who had replaced an injured John Hall a few weeks prior, was wide right on a 49-yard field goal, and the Cowboys drove the other way. Quarterback Tony Romo's 28-yard completion to tight end Jason Witten, who beat Archuleta, put the ball on the Redskins' 6 with 17 seconds left, setting up a chip-shot 35-yard field attempt with six seconds left for one of the most prolific kickers in NFL history, Mike Vanderjagt.

Then appeared what seemed like a hand from God. Troy Vincent, a 15th-year safety acquired only a few days before, blocked the kick, the first of his career. Sean Taylor recovered the ball and ran 30 yards to the Dallas 44, and another 15 yards were tacked on for a face mask penalty.

This time, Novak's 47-yard kick with no time left on the clock initially sailed right but hooked left and just inside the goal post for an improbable 22–19 Redskins victory. Streams of Redskins, including Vincent, who would be named NFC Special Teams Player of the Week, mobbed Novak, as Renaldo Wynn yelled, "You gotta believe! You gotta believe!"

Afterward, Wynn said it was the type of victory that could turn the Redskins' season around: "Things happen for a reason, man. We're 1–0. Next, we try to go 2–0. We feel it's how you finish that you're measured. November and December. That's when teams make it to the next show, which is the playoffs."

A 27–3 loss in Philly returned the Redskins to Earth. The Eagles bullied their NFC East rivals, and Brunell had a rough day that included an interception that was returned 70 yards for a touchdown. Redskins quarterback Todd Collins warmed up in the fourth quarter but didn't get in the game.

The Redskins' postgame locker room was as silent as a morgue, unlike the joyous atmosphere a week prior. Redskins guard Randy Thomas questioned why a quarterback change would do anything for the team at that point, calling Brunell "our leader and our quarterback," while defensive tackle Cornelius Griffin urged his teammates to keep fighting. "No matter how bad it gets, we're never going to give up," Griffin said. "If we get hit in the mouth a couple of times, we're going to swing back with all we've got. We may not rock them, but we'll hit them with something. That's how we've got to be."

The next day, Gibbs relented on the quarterback front and named Campbell the starter for the upcoming game at Tampa Bay. (Gibbs said earlier in the season that in the case of a quarterback change, Collins would go in during a game and Campbell during the practice week in preparation for the next game.)

Campbell looked cool and confident in his debut, completing 19 of 34 passes for 196 yards and two touchdowns, a 3-yarder to Chris Cooley to cap a 76-yard drive and a 4-yarder to tight end Todd Yoder to cap an 80-yard march. But the Redskins fell, 20–17. With Portis gone for the season after breaking his hand against Philly, they gained a season-low 64 rushing yards, while the Bucs piled up 181 on the ground.

Gibbs had seen enough. In his postgame press conference, he called for a return to the "principles" of Redskins football.

## A Q&A With Dan Snyder

- What has it been like owning a pro sports team you grew up rooting for? "Owning the Redskins is the high point of my life, as it would be for any die-hard fan."

- You made millions before buying the Redskins and have since turned them into the richest NFL team year after year. Have you taken the same approach with the Redskins, such as aggressiveness in making potentially lucrative deals, as with your previous business endeavors? "There's no secret to our success. We work hard and keep moving forward with all of our efforts. Hard work produces great results. I am passionate about everything I do."

- Since buying the team, you have taken a lot of criticism in the press and have even described yourself as a "lightning rod" for criticism. Has it been justified? "Some, yes; many times, no. When you hear something awfully negative and person- ally hurtful from someone you've never met, you realize the lack of homework and thoroughness today's 'instant news' cycles have perpetuated."

- You have also been criticized for spending too much money on free agents and for not hiring a true general manager, among other front-office decisions. Are there moves with the Redskins you would have done differently? "Absolutely. There are moves I would not have made, and there are moves I regret not having made. But they've all helped me be a better owner."

- You're obviously hungry to win a Super Bowl. Do you have the patience to wait until it happens? "All of my biggest successes have come from being patient. We'll succeed in adding another Super Bowl, and more than just one."

- Will you be able to bring the Super Bowl to the nation's capital? "I hope to eventually bring the Super Bowl game itself to Washington so all of us can share in the greatest single game in the world."

"We have to run, we have to stop the run," he said. "When we get back to those [principles], we will start winning football games." There had been a feeling around town that Gibbs was at odds with Saunders over the latter's tendency to focus on the passing game and his desire to call too many trick plays. Against the Bucs, the Redskins ran the ball 21 times, compared with at least 40 in the wins over Jacksonville and Houston.

Somebody got the message, for the Redskins began playing smash-mouth football. Over the last six games, they ran an average of 35 times for 166 yards. The 5–10, 223-pound Betts was a workhorse, and he showed that T. J. Duckett wasn't needed in the first place. Starting on November 26 against Carolina, Betts had five straight 100-yard games, tying the team record held by Portis and Rob Goode.

Meanwhile, Campbell showed flashes of excellence and of being the Redskins' quarterback of the future. With the Redskins trailing Carolina by three points in the final minutes, he found Cooley over the middle on a crossing pattern. Cooley (team-high 57 catches) ran the rest of the way on a 66-yard catch-and-run that gave the Redskins a 17–13 victory. Campbell also experienced growing pains, as when Falcons defensive end Chauncey Davis intercepted his ill-advised pass and returned it 41 yards.

The Redskins' powder-puff defense didn't give Campbell much help at the end, allowing 579 yards in a 37–31 loss to St. Louis in the next-to-last game and a career-high 234 rushing yards to Tiki Barber in the 34–28 season-ending loss to the Giants. Barber, playing the last regular-season game of his 10-year career, ran for 55-, 50-, and 15-yard touchdowns.

In the locker room, Redskin players reflected on the fact that the season had deteriorated before their eyes. Brunell was asked if he regretted saying in training camp that the year would be a disappointment if the Redskins didn't go all the way. "Not at all," he said. "I don't understand. Every quarterback in the NFL should be saying the same thing, that not going to the Super Bowl is a disappointment. That is why we are here. We are here to win championships. It wasn't a prediction. I wasn't bragging about anything. I was just saying that needs to be our goal. Unfortunately, we were far short from that."

Gibbs, who stressed late in the season that he planned to fulfill the five-year contract he signed upon his return in 2004, said his team got off to an "awful start" but praised its hard work down the stretch. "There were a number of players who made real statements about their future," he said. "We have some key ingredients to build on."

# 9

# Washington Monuments

FROM THE TIME the Pro Football Hall of Fame opened its doors in 1963 through today, the Washington Redskins have received just representation. Twenty busts in the prestigious institution in Canton, Ohio, are of people who made "primary" or "minor" contributions in the NFL to the burgundy and gold. The list includes 14 players, five head coaches, and Redskins founder and long-time owner George Preston Marshall, who is featured elsewhere in *The Redskins Encyclopedia*.

In addition, three Redskins beat writers are recipients of the Dick McCann Award, which is presented annually to a journalist for "long and distinguished reporting on professional football." The three honorees are *Washington Post* sportswriters Dave Brady (1973) and Len Shapiro (2001) and Lewis F. Atchison of the *Washington Star* (1972). McCann, the Redskins' general manager from 1946 to 1962, served as the Hall of Fame's first director until his death in 1967. Furthermore, the special fans section of the Hall of Fame features Michael Torbert, founder of the popular Redskins cheerleading group known as the Hogettes, and Zema Williams, or "Chief Zee,"

who has cheered on the Redskins at games for nearly three decades while dressed as an Indian chief.

Players featured in this chapter must have spent at least three seasons with the Redskins. Two defensive linemen, Deacon Jones and Stan Jones, both played one year in Washington after achieving fame elsewhere and are not included. The same holds true for Earl "Curly" Lambeau and Vince Lombardi, who coached the Redskins for a total of three seasons but won their place in Canton for coaching the Packers to 11 NFL titles, and Otto Graham, who was honored for his outstanding play in Cleveland, not his three seasons coaching the Redskins in the 1960s. Lombardi, who led the Redskins to their first winning season in 14 years in 1969, is featured elsewhere in *The Redskins Encyclopedia*.

Also not featured are Marv Levy, who coached Redskins special teams in 1971 and 1972 but was inducted for coaching Buffalo to four Super Bowls in the 1990s, and Don Shula, a Redskin defensive back in 1957 who was honored for winning the most NFL games of all time in his 33 years of coaching, most of them with the Dolphins.

| Name | Position | Redskin Years | Inducted | Status |
|------|----------|---------------|----------|--------|
| George Allen | Coach | 1971–77 | 2002 | Primary |
| Cliff Battles | RB/DB | 1932–37 | 1968 | Primary |
| Sammy Baugh | HB/QB/DB/P | 1937–52 | 1963* | Primary |
| Bill Dudley | RB/DB/K | 1950–51, 53 | 1966 | Primary |
| Turk Edwards | T | 1932–40 | 1969 | Primary |
| Ray Flaherty | Coach | 1937–42 | 1976 | Primary |
| Joe Gibbs | Coach | 1981–92 | 1996 | Primary |
| Ken Houston | S | 1973–80 | 1986 | Primary |
| Sam Huff | LB | 1964–67, 69 | 1982 | Primary |
| Deacon Jones | DE | 1974 | 1980 | Minor |
| Stan Jones | DT | 1966 | 1991 | Minor |
| Sonny Jurgensen | QB | 1964–74 | 1983 | Primary |
| Paul Krause | S | 1964–67 | 1998 | Minor |
| Curly Lambeau | Coach | 1952–53 | 1963* | Minor |
| Vince Lombardi | Coach | 1969 | 1971 | Minor |
| George Preston Marshall | Founder/Owner | 1932–69 | 1963* | Primary |
| Wayne Millner | E | 1936–41, 45 | 1968 | Primary |
| Bobby Mitchell | RB/WR | 1962–68 | 1983 | Primary |
| John Riggins | RB | 1976–79, 81–85 | 1992 | Primary |
| Charley Taylor | RB/WR | 1964–77 | 1984 | Primary |

*Charter member

The Hogettes

Zema Williams, a.k.a. Chief Zee

## GEORGE ALLEN

### Eccentric, Passionate Coach
### Left Legacy as NFL Pioneer

Head Coach, Marquette; Michigan • **NFL Career:** 1966–77 (12 seasons) • **Redskins Years:** 1971–77 (7) • **HOF Induction:** 2002 • **Born:** April 29, 1918 (Grosse Point Wood, Mich.) • **Died:** December 31, 1990 (Rancho Palos Verdes, Calif.)

George Allen is one of the greatest coaches in pro football history. His 118–54–5 record over 12 NFL seasons equals a .686 winning percentage, No. 3 all-time for coaches with at least 100 victories. He made the playoffs seven times and transformed perpetual losing squads, the Los Angeles Rams and the Washington Redskins, into title contenders.

Those are prodigious feats in themselves. But it's *how* he ascended so high that makes his story compelling. It starts with this fact: George Allen lived to win football games. He compared losing to "death."

"True," George Allen, the coach's son, said emphatically. "If it was a home game and we won, we'd go to [popular D.C. restaurant] Duke Zeibert's after the game. It would be a great celebration. If we lost, the heck if we're going out. It was like a funeral. You'd get in the car and drive home and everyone would be quiet and glum. It truly was like a wake."

Allen channeled almost every minute of his waking hours into winning, whether it was by watching game films or preparing players. He saw sleep as leisure time. He even confined his diet to peanut butter and jelly sandwiches, milk and ice cream (hence his nickname, "Ice Cream") so he wouldn't have to waste time chewing. He looked for any edge he could find to topple an opponent, as in when he charted the sun prior to Super Bowl VII so it wouldn't be in his players' eyes. He

The master motivator addresses his Redskins during a 1972 pregame huddle. Allen "had a way of making every guy feel like they were the most important guy on the team," one of his players said.

was so intense on the sidelines, tugging his cap and licking his fingers.

Such neurotic behavior was common for the eccentric coach. In fact, he wanted his assistants and players to know of his obsession with the game so they would adopt the same approach.

"He reveled in having that reputation," said Marv Levy, the Redskins' special teams coach under Allen for two seasons in the early 1970s. "If you went home at 11:30 at night and were done with your work, you could count on there being a note on your desk the next morning: 'Marv, could you get me the film of so on and so forth,' signed by George Allen at 12 midnight. He worked hard to let you know he was that way."

Allen was also a master psychologist who relied on the power of positive thinking, never cursing to motivate. He lived by inspiring slogans and quotes, such as this one on his desk at Redskin Park: "Is what I am doing, or about to do, getting us closer to our objective . . . winning?" Fastidious, he'd point to a picture hanging crooked on the wall, shake his head, and say, "Sometimes, I wonder if the organization knows what winning is all about."

"We once lost a couple of games in a row, and he was very upset," long-time Redskins scout Kirk Mee said. "He called all the secretaries in the building and talked to them. He said players are going to come, and they're going to deal with you, and you've got to be up, you can't be down. He didn't want the secretaries to have their morale down and be talking behind the players' backs and criticizing."

Allen's passion to win lit a fire under his players, many of whom gave every ounce of energy for their idiosyncratic leader. Often speaking in clichés, he exhorted players with

inspirational tactics and phrases that seemed silly but worked most of the time. He instilled a high school atmosphere in the process. "Forty men together can't lose," he'd preach in the pregame huddle. "Let's have three cheers for the Washington Redskins," he'd say in the locker room after a win, his players responding with a "hip, hip, hooray" three times over. He loved the ribald song his players chanted following a victory:

> Three cheers for Allen,
> Three cheers for George,
> Hooray for George,
> He's a horse's ass.

"George was childish in a lot of ways," said Steve Guback, who covered the Redskins for the *Washington Star* during the Allen era. "That stomping around on the field after a victory and that cheer with the horse's ass, all that was high school stuff. But the players enjoyed it, and George enjoyed it and got a lot out of them with it."

"He was just plain corny about a lot of things he said and did, but you couldn't help but get caught up in it," Redskins linebacker Chris Hanburger said.

Consider this outlandish stunt: As part of the legendary Redskins-Cowboys rivalry, which Allen intensified during his stay in Washington, the coach held a personal feud with his Dallas counterpart, Tom Landry. Allen took karate lessons with martial arts expert Jhoon Rhee and later positioned himself in stances in a team meeting to show what he could do to Landry during a Redskins-Cowboys game.

"That was just his way of saying to us, 'Get ready,'" Redskins safety Brig Owens said. "If it came between the two of us at the

## Allen's Wisdom

- "Every time you win, you're reborn. When you lose, you die a little."

- "Close games are won by attitude . . . winning attitude. If we convince ourselves we'll accept only winning today, we'll win."

- "Winning is the science of being totally prepared. There is no detail too small."

- "If you're not being tested, you're not living. It's a test that challenges your character. The tougher the job, the greater the reward."

- "The greatest moment in sports is when you've got a victory, and you give away game balls."

- "How many times, out of meekness or inertia, do we talk ourselves out of a reward easily attained?"

- "People of mediocre ability sometimes achieve outstanding success because they don't know when to quit. Most men succeed because they are determined to."

50-yard line, I'd be a little older but in better shape. He was saying it was all about preparation. If you work harder, and you're prepared, and you're better prepared than your opponent, then you can win."

All the while, Allen's ingenious football mind paved the way to many victories. He revolutionized the game on defense, introducing innovative schemes such as the "nickel" alignment with five players in the secondary and the "quarter" defense, a five-man defensive line designed to stop the run. He also helped pioneer the blitz. Redskins defensive tackle Bill Brundige said Allen used 160 different defensive audibles, noting that "we were prepared for anything." Allen exploited special teams, too, priming those units more than any previous NFL coach to make big plays.

To execute his strategies, Allen relied mostly on seasoned veterans, and he loved to wheel and deal to acquire proven talent. He made some 120 trades in his 12-year NFL coaching career, including about 80 with the Redskins.

Allen also was widely regarded as a "player's coach." He fought for comfortable player salaries and the best practice facilities, as was the case with brand new state-of-the-art Redskin Park, and gave special recognition for on-field feats. He promoted player camaraderie by encouraging team parties and arranged for Duke Zeibert, owner of the D.C. restaurant, to bring ice cream and cake to practice after victories. He also welcomed the "5 O'Clock Club," a group of players who gathered after practice in a shed at Redskin Park to drink beer and tell stories.

"George Allen was a very interesting cat," Redskins offensive tackle George Starke said. "He didn't drink or anything like that, but he knew team bonding was very important. So the Redskins had a party every Friday. It was all this food, all this booze and all these chicks. I'm sure George paid for it."

The story of Bill Malinchak speaks to the players' admiration for Allen. A Redskins punt blocking specialist, Malinchak retired after the 1974 season to pursue a career on Wall Street.

Allen asked Malinchak to return for a late-season playoff run in 1976, wanting him especially for the final game against the Cowboys. Allen had watched enough films to know he could possibly squeeze a big play out of him. Sure enough, Malinchak blocked a punt in the Redskins' 27–14 victory over Dallas that clinched a playoff spot.

Why did Malinchak suspend his white-collar career to return to the Redskins? "George was certainly the greatest coach I ever played for," he said. "He really prepared ball players for games probably as good or better than anybody ever, not only with execution, but mentally, too. When you went into that game, you felt like the game rested on your shoulders, whether you were a special teams player or if you're name was Billy Kilmer or Charley Taylor. He made you feel that every player needed to make a big play. That's a special quality. If you wanted to play football, you'd want to play for George Allen."

That sentiment existed long before Allen came to the Redskins. After spending nine seasons as head coach at Morningside College in Iowa and then Whittier College in California, he began his pro career as an assistant with the Rams in 1957. The next year, he became an assistant with the Bears, where Clark Shaughnessy, one of the most imaginative coaches in NFL history, was the defensive coach.

In addition to learning from Shaughnessy, Allen incorporated ideas on running defenses from the master's thesis he wrote in the late 1940s at the University of Michigan titled "A Study of Outstanding Football Coaches' Attitudes and Practices in Scouting." He took over as Chicago's defensive coordinator in 1963 and helped shape perhaps the greatest defense in NFL history, one that forced five turnovers in the Bears' 14–10 win over the Giants in the 1963 NFL title game. Afterward, Bears players carried him off the field on their shoulders.

After his successful head coaching stint in Los Angeles from 1966 to 1970, Allen arrived in the nation's capital in January 1971.

"When he came in, you felt a winning atmosphere came with him," Redskins Hall of Fame receiver Charley Taylor said. "He understood people very well, and he had a way of relating to the game of life. Those two things go hand in hand, and we had a complete team. He surrounded himself with people who love to play the game and preached that you win as a team and lose as a team."

Not every player loved Allen. Redskins Hall of Fame quarterback Sonny Jurgensen had a sour relationship with the coach primarily because of his dogged focus on defense. "George Allen wanted to win defensively," Jurgensen said. "He said, 'If we don't make mistakes offensively, we can win.' That wasn't the way I had played before he came. He changed our offense. He wouldn't let us do whatever we were doing under Vince Lombardi [in 1969]. He changed the keys in the passing scheme, which didn't make sense to me. I said, 'Why are we throwing here when this linebacker is over here, and we've got the tight end, Jerry Smith, standing there wide open?' He said, 'You're not going along with the program, you're supposed to throw here.' It was always that way and, offensively, it hurt us."

The press also viewed Allen with cynicism, and vice versa. He believed that the media's job was to serve as a cheerleader for his squad, not to report anything negative or controversial that could give "intelligence" to opponents or embarrass the Redskins. He pleaded with journalists to understand that philosophy. "When you write about who should be quarter-

## The Allen Years

### NFL

| Year | Team | Record | % | Postseason |
|------|------|--------|---|------------|
| 1966 | LA Rams | 8–6-0 | .571 | 0–0 |
| 1967 | LA Rams | 11–1-2 | .917 | 0–1 |
| 1968 | LA Rams | 10–3-1 | .769 | 0–0 |
| 1969 | LA Rams | 11–3-0 | .786 | 0–1 |
| 1970 | LA Rams | 9–4-1 | .692 | 0–0 |
| 1971 | Wash | 9–4-1 | .692 | 0–1 |
| 1972 | Wash | 11–3-0 | .786 | 2–1 (Lost in Super Bowl VII) |
| 1973 | Wash | 10–4-0 | .714 | 0–1 |
| 1974 | Wash | 10–4-0 | .714 | 0–1 |
| 1975 | Wash | 8–6-0 | .571 | 0–0 |
| 1976 | Wash | 10–4-0 | .714 | 0–1 |
| 1977 | Wash | 9–5-0 | .643 | 0–0 |
| **Totals** | | **116–47–5** | **.705** | **2–7** |

### USFL

| Year | Team | Record | % | Postseason |
|------|------|--------|---|------------|
| 1983 | Chicago | 12–6-0 | .666 | 0–1 |
| 1984 | Arizona | 10–8-0 | .555 | 2–1 (Lost in USFL championship game) |
| **Totals** | | **22–14–0** | **.611** | **2–2** |

back," he told the press, "you're hurting the fans in Washington, you're hurting the football team."

Allen's suspicions about the media earned him comparisons to President Nixon, who was in office during the coach's early years in D.C. Reporters dubbed Allen "Nixon with a whistle" because, like the president, he believed that the press was attacking him in a game of "gotcha." They both withheld as much information as possible. "Nixon was secretive, and George followed the same line," Guback of the *Washington Star* said.

The media also gave Allen the dubious title of the "Flim-Flam Man," a reference to his deviousness and apparent lack of ethics. The NFL fined him for such infractions as trading the same draft picks and not informing referees that he was activating a player. Guback described another of the coach's shady habits: "I can recall a few times when a team put a player on waivers about a week before the Redskins would be playing that team, and George would sign him. The only apparent reason he would get him was to pump him for information. That enhanced his reputation of trying to be within the rules but yet sort of bending them."

After leaving the Redskins in January 1978, Allen had a brief and unceremonious head coaching stint back in Los Angeles (he was fired in the preseason) before continuing his triumphant ways in the new United States Football League. He recorded two winning seasons, including a 12–9 mark in 1984

Allen implored the press to write positive things about his Redskins.

that ended with his Arizona Wranglers losing in the championship game. Remarkably, he never suffered a losing season in 14 years of pro coaching.

Allen, an exercise fanatic, chaired the President's Council on Physical Fitness and Sports under Ronald Reagan from 1981 to 1988. Shortly thereafter, he returned to his lifelong passion, becoming the head coach at Long Beach State in California in 1990. Critics said that he would be crazy to take the position given that he was 71 at the time, but Allen shrugged them off and coached the 49ers to a 6–5 record, their first winning season since 1986.

Allen died a few weeks after the season. In 2002, he received the ultimate honor in pro football: a Hall of Fame induction.

"He'd say, 'God, it's a great day to be alive,'" the younger George Allen said at the induction ceremony. "He'd be excited and charged up. He'd love it, and he'd say it's a team victory. With him, every success was always a team success."

## CLIFF BATTLES

### "The High-Stepping Phantom in Moleskins"

RB, DB, No. 20, West Virginia Wesleyan • 6–1, 195 • **NFL Career:** 1932–37 (6 seasons) • **Redskins Years:** 1932–37 (6) • **HOF Induction:** 1968 • NFL 1930s All-Decade Team • **Born:** May 1, 1910 (Akron, Ohio) • **Died:** April 28, 1981 (Clearwater, Fla.)

He was the Redskins' first true offensive superstar and one of the NFL's first great running backs.

From the time the franchise settled in Boston in 1932 through its first season in D.C. in 1937, Cliff Battles dazzled crowds with his nifty moves and amazing breakaway speed. He rushed for 3,542 yards over six seasons, nearly a 600-yard average that was big at the time in the nascent NFL, and became the first player to rush for more than 200 yards in a game. He won two league rushing titles, received All-Pro honors three times and helped anchor the Redskins' 1937 team that won an NFL championship.

"Cliff Battles was a superstar," Giants Hall of Fame center Mel Hein said in Bob Curran's 1969 book, *Pro Football's Rag Days.* "He had great speed and all the moves any back would need. He could run like a deer, and once he got past the line of scrimmage, you could say goodbye to him. He was gone for a touchdown."

In addition to the Pro Football Hall of Fame, Battles is enshrined in the College Football Hall of Fame. The Kenmore, Ohio, native played for tiny West Virginia Wesleyan from 1928 to 1931. A triple threat with amazing breakaway speed, he was named to several All-America teams and was also a Phi Beta Kappa scholar. He acquired the nickname "Gip" (sometimes spelled "Gipp") that apparently stemmed from his admiration for Notre Dame All-American back George Gipp, the subject of Knute Rockne's famous "win just one for the Gipper" speech.

"In 1931, the East produced not only one of the best players of the year but of all time in Cliff Battles of West Virginia Wesleyan," Allison Danzig wrote in his 1956 book, *The History of American Football.*

Art Bachtel, a college teammate of Battles, remembered him this way: "He was the greatest open-field runner I ever

Cliff Battles

saw," Bachtel said in the *Akron-Beacon Journal* on December 13, 1999. "He didn't run but seemed to lope along. It was his natural way of running. Whenever we broke him through the line, it was almost certain to be a touchdown."

Battles fascinated George Preston Marshall, who tracked athletic pursuits of players from his home state, West Virginia, after founding an NFL franchise and locating it in Boston in 1932. His interest in Battles grew when seeing him play against Washington-area schools like Navy and Georgetown.

After Battles finished at West Virginia Wesleyan, Marshall dispatched a talent scout, Jerry Corcoran, to sign him. Battles signed with the expansion team for $175 per game, spurning offers from such teams as the New York Giants and Portsmouth (Ohio) Spartans.

"I chose the Braves because they were the only team to send a personal representative to see me," Battles said in *Pro Football's Rag Days.* "Mr. Marshall was from West Virginia, and he told [Corcoran], 'Sign Battles or keep right on going south and don't come back.'"

Battles was an immediate star. He rushed 148 times for a league-high 576 yards for the Boston Braves in 1932 and tacked on 737 the following year for the Redskins, the franchise's new nickname. In 1933, Battles gained 215 yards alone in a game against the Giants, a Redskins single-game record for nearly 60 years until Gerald Riggs broke it in 1989 with 221.

After two seasons of less than 500 yards, Battles rushed for 614 and five touchdowns in 1936. After he raced 67 yards for a touchdown in a game against the Eagles, the *Boston Herald* dubbed him "the high-stepping phantom in moleskins." And in a 14–0 win over the Giants that secured the Eastern Division title that year for the Redskins, Battles sloshed 80 yards through the mud and rain at New York's Polo Grounds.

In 1937, the year the Redskins relocated to Washington, Battles enjoyed his greatest season statistically, rushing for league highs of 874 yards and five touchdowns. He posted runs of 71, 65, and 60 yards in one game and ran 73 yards for one score and returned an interception 76 yards for another in a 49–14 Eastern Division title-clinching win over the Giants. One week later, Battles starred again in a 28–21 win over the Bears in the NFL championship game. He scored the Redskins' first touchdown on a 7-yard reverse and, after catching a screen pass from Baugh, he ran 55 yards on frozen Soldier Field for another score.

Battles was in the prime of his career but never played another down for the Redskins. It was because of money. After being named a first-team All-Pro in 1937, Battles asked Marshall for a salary increase. Stories vary as to how much money Battles made, and how much more he requested. In Myron Cope's 1970 book, *The Game That Was: The Early Days of Pro Football,* Battles said he earned $4,000 and wanted a raise of about $1,000. It's also been reported he was paid $3,000 and requested a modest raise or that he wanted his $2,500 salary increased to $4,000. Baugh said that Battles made $2,750 and wanted a $250 raise.

The bottom line is Battles didn't get a raise, and he quit and became an assistant football coach at Columbia University in New York City. In *Pro Football's Rag Days,* he said that Marshall balked because Baugh was going to leave the Redskins to play baseball for the St. Louis Cardinals if he didn't get the hefty raise he had requested. (Baugh was the NFL's highest-paid player at the time at $8,000.) Marshall, however, told the *Washington Times-Herald* on February 15, 1940, that he offered Battles $5,000, a $1,200 increase from his prior salary.

Sixty years later, Baugh sounded incredulous over the way Marshall handled the situation: "He let the best damn back in the league at the time, Cliff Battles, get away over 250 damn dollars. When I found out about that, I couldn't believe it. Hell, if I had known at the time, I would have given him the money."

Battles left Columbia in 1942 and joined the U.S. Marines during World War II. He coached a Marine football team and later coached the Brooklyn Dodgers in the newly formed All-America Football Conference in 1946 and 1947.

"Cliff was a great running back, the best we had," Baugh said. "He was also a fine person and one of the nicest people I've ever been around."

# SAMMY BAUGH

## Texas Slinger Revolutionized Pro Football with His Amazing Arm

HB, QB, DB, P, No. 33, Texas Christian • 6–2, 182 • **NFL Career:** 1937–52 (16 seasons) • **Redskins Years:** 1937–52 (16) • **HOF Induction:** 1963 (Charter Member) • NFL 1940s All-Decade Team and NFL 75th Anniversary Team • **Born:** March 17, 1914 (Temple, Tex.)

To remain buoyant in its early years, the NFL welcomed all of the attractions it could find, players who could lure streams

Sammy Baugh, the Texas slinger

of fans to the ballpark. One of the league's premier draws at the time was a tall, wiry Texan named Sammy Adrian Baugh.

Baugh was the top passer of his day. With the ability to whip them long and short, Slingin' Sammy lit the skies in his 16 seasons with the Redskins and helped revolutionize the pro offense, which was run-based before his rookie year in 1937. In setting a host of passing records, the immortal one threw for some 22,000 yards and led the league in passing six times, the most of anyone during his career. His completion percentage (56.7) was an all-time NFL best when he retired.

Fans witnessed more than a passer in Baugh, an outstanding multidimensional athlete in the days of single-platoon football. In fact, you'll get a lot of support for him as the greatest all-around player ever. As a safety, he intercepted 31 passes, an NFL record that has since been broken, and once picked off four in one game. Also a master of the quick kick, he posted a 45.1-yard career punting average that stood as an NFL record for many years and still holds the all-time mark for the best single-season average (51.4). In one year, 1943, Baugh led the league in passing, interceptions, and punting.

They just don't make them anymore like Sammy Baugh, a charter member of the Pro Football Hall of Fame in 1963. The six-time All-NFL player was one of four quarterbacks named to the NFL's 75th anniversary team in 1994—along with Joe Montana, Johnny Unitas, and Otto Graham—and was honored as a member of the all-time two-way team. He was No. 11 on the *Sporting News* list of the 100 greatest players of all time, announced in 1999.

How good was Sammy Baugh? "He was the best passer I ever saw," said Ace Parker, one of Baugh's contemporaries at quarterback and a fellow Hall of Famer. "He could do everything. He could pass, he could play defense, he was the best kicker, and he still holds the single-season punting record [51.4]."

Another Hall of Famer and triple threat, Bill Dudley, concurred. "He was the best, as far as I'm concerned," said Dudley, who teamed with Baugh for two seasons in the early 1950s. "He could not only throw the ball. He could play defense, he could punt the football, he ran it when he had to. He and I roomed together, and he was a football man. He knew football, played it, and everybody had a lot of confidence in him."

Baugh had the charisma, to boot. He carried an allure with fans, who mobbed the friendly fellow from Sweetwater, Texas, at home and on the road for autographs. In D.C., his magnetism helped pack Griffith Stadium starting in 1937, when the squad won an NFL championship in its maiden season in Washington. Baugh played on Redskin teams that won another championship in 1942 and made five title game appearances by 1945.

Bernard Nordlinger, a D.C. lawyer who helped incorporate the Redskins when they moved from Boston to Washington, explained the area's fascination with the team in two words: "Sammy Baugh. He was a colorful character, and he was a magnificent athlete, dramatic, totally different than football players today. He was like the Babe Ruth of football. He was an incomparable attraction."

Bucko Kilroy, an Eagles tackle from 1943 to 1955 and former Redskins assistant coach, told NFL Films: "He had the charisma to attract fans. I remember in Philadelphia at Shibe Park, that when we played the Redskins in those days and Sammy Baugh was playing, we turned down 15,000 people at the game, [they] couldn't get in. He was an attraction."

Baugh's celebrity-like appeal opened doors for him in Hollywood. Part Cherokee, he starred in the early 1940s as cowboy Tom King, Jr., in the serial *King of the Texas Rangers.* A newspaper photo showed him in cowboy attire standing next to actor Duncan Renaldo, later of "Cisco Kid" fame. Both men have their guns drawn, and the caption read: "Yassuh, Sammy's a rootin', tootin' cowboy already."

Prior to his pro career, Baugh captivated fans at Texas Christian University, where the two-time All-American established himself as the greatest passer in college football history at the time. He helped propel the Horned Frogs to Cotton Bowl and Sugar Bowl wins, and a 1935 national championship. Today, Joe Namath and Joe Montana are the only other quarterbacks who have claimed both college and pro championships.

Baugh's college coach was Dutch Meyer, who unveiled a wide-open offense that resembled today's shotgun spread. "Everything I learned about the passing game I learned from coach Meyer at TCU," Baugh said in an interview in 2000. "We had a good passing game."

Redskins owner George Preston Marshall, who drooled over Baugh's talents, swiped him with the sixth overall pick in the 1937 draft. Others such as Bears owner and coach George Halas and celebrated sportswriter Grantland Rice thought the 6–3, 185-pound Baugh was too frail to play pro football. Rice once told Marshall: "You better insure that right arm for a million dollars. The tough guys in this league will tear it off him. He just isn't big enough to take the pounding he's going

Baugh starred as Ranger Tom King Jr., in the 12-part 1941 series, *King of the Texas Rangers.* Here, he is acting out a scene with actress Pauline Moore (Sally Crane) and actor Duncan Renaldo (Lt. Pedro Garcia).

to get. I have my doubts that a skinny kid like that can last more than a season or two."

Baugh would defy the pessimists. After throwing a touchdown pass in a 6–0 victory by the college all-stars over the defending champion Green Bay Packers, he signed with the Redskins for an NFL-high $8,000. And from the first day of training camp in September 1937, Baugh was cool and confident. He was tossing passes when Redskins coach Ray Flaherty told him that it's easier for receivers to catch a ball thrown around their face, and that he should target the eye. As the mythical story goes, the brash rookie nodded before asking, "Which eye, coach?"

Slingin' Sammy found his mark. Playing tailback in the old single-wing formation, he completed 91 of 218 passes for 1,127 yards as a rookie, all league-highs, and was named a first-team All-Pro. His 91 completions were an NFL record. He broke with tradition that the pass was a desperation tactic reserved for third-and-long and boldly threw on first and second down, and from punt formation.

Baugh showed how great he was in the 1937 NFL championship game. He completed 17 of 34 passes for 352 yards and three touchdowns while willing his squad to a 28–21 win over the Bears. In for every offensive and defensive play, he was crippled by game's end after taking a beating on Wrigley Field's frozen tundra. He received a standing ovation from Redskins and Bears fans alike upon leaving the field for the last time. At that point, "Baugh slipped into football immortality," *Washington Evening Star* sportswriter Francis Stan wrote on December 13, 1937. "Eckersal and Thorpe, Cagle and Grange, Nagurski and the Four Horsemen, Oliphant and Hefflefinger . . . they moved over, these burly ghosts of the past, and made room for Slingin' Sammy."

Just like that, Baugh considered leaving football to play baseball, which he had starred in at TCU. Nicknamed Slingin'

Sammy for his rifle arm while playing third base and shortstop, he signed with the St. Louis Cardinals in the spring of 1938 and played with two of their farm teams in hopes of making the majors.

"I did think I was going to play baseball instead of football," Baugh once told the *Washington Post.* "I only promised Mr. Marshall I would play football for one year. Had a good arm playing shortstop and third base. But after the same job I wanted was a fellow named Marty Marion [one of the game's best shortstops in the 1940s], and I went back to football. Anyway, I had problems with the curveball."

Redskin fans will be forever grateful he remained a Redskin, for the "Texas tornado" remained the foundation of their dominance in the ensuing years. The dangerous all-around threat was everywhere in the 1942 NFL title game, a 14–6 win over the Bears. He threw a 39-yard touchdown pass, intercepted a pass that ruined a Chicago scoring threat, and averaged 53 yards on six kicks, one of which he boomed 85 yards.

The following year, when Baugh pulled off his hat trick in league bests, his numbers read as such:

- 133 of 239 passing (55.6 completion percentage)
- 11 interceptions
- 50 punts for 2,295 yards (45.9 average)

Aside from being multidimensional, Baugh possessed football smarts and superb leadership skills, said Clyde Shugart, a Redskins lineman who played five seasons with Sammy: "There was no question he knew what he was doing in football," Shugart said. "Sam didn't hesitate about changing plays on the field if he could see where we could take advantage of somebody because of a vacant space or something. He'd call

timeout and sketch something on the ground about changing a play to a degree. His life revolved around football. Playing guard, I just felt like this is our number one bread and butter. He treated everyone so great, you just wanted to go out and do your best for him."

Baugh played in the single- and double-wing formation before becoming a true "quarterback" when the Redskins' switched to the T-formation in 1944. A year later, he connected on 128 of 182 passes for a phenomenal 70.33 completion percentage, an NFL record that stood until Cincinnati's Ken Anderson broke it in 1982 (70.55).

"I hated the T when we went to it in 1944, but my body loved it," Baugh said in Robert Peterson's 1997 book, *Pigskin.* "I probably could have lasted a year or two more as a single-wing tailback, my body was so beat up, but the T gave me nine more seasons."

The 1945 season marked the end of the Redskins' early glory years and the beginning of many disappointing ones, but Baugh continued slingin'. When a sellout crowd turned out at Griffith Stadium on November 23, 1947, on "Sammy Baugh Day" and the legend received a new station wagon with the words "Slingin' Sam" on it, he reciprocated with a jaw-dropping performance: 25 of 33 passing for 355 yards and six touchdowns in a 45–21 victory over the Chicago Cardinals. His touchdown total tied his Redskin record set in a 1943 game against Brooklyn.

Baugh remained high atop the NFL charts in passing in the late 1940s. In 1952 he gave way to Eddie LeBaron as the team's starting quarterback. Although the Redskins finished 4–8 that year, the season finale on December 14, 1952, was a historic day in team annals: It was the last game in Baugh's career. A *Washington Post* headline noted the gravity of his departure:

Baugh's uniform sits by the fireplace at the end of the 1952 season, his last of 16 years in the NFL.

## Baugh's NFL Records on His 1952 Retirement (Partial List)

- Most seasons played—16
- Most career passes attempted—3,016
- Most career passes completed—1,709
- Most career passing yards—22,085
- Most career interceptions thrown—205
- Most career touchdown passes—187
- Most seasons leading the league in passing—6*
- Best single-season completion percentage—70.33 (1945)
- Best career completion percentage—56.7 (500 or more attempts)
- Best single-game average passing gain—18.58 (at least 20 attempts)†
- Most single-season passing yards—2,938 (1947)
- Most single-season passes completed—210 (1947)
- Most pass interceptions—31
- Best career punting average—45.1 (at least 250 punts)
- Best single-season punting average—51.4 (1940)†
- Most punts in one game—14 (vs. Eagles, November 5, 1939)

*Tied with Steve Young
†Still stands

## Baugh's Current Redskins Records

- Best single-season completion percentage—70.33 (1945)
- Best single-season quarterback rating—109.7 (1945)
- Most career touchdown passes—187
- Most touchdown passes in one game—6 (vs. Cardinals, November 23, 1947; and vs. Brooklyn, October 31, 1943)*
- Most career interceptions thrown—205
- Most interceptions thrown in one game—6 (vs. Giants, November 11, 1951)†
- Most punts in one game—14 (vs. Eagles, November 5, 1939)
- Longest punt—85 yards (vs. Eagles, December 1, 1940)
- Best career punting average 45.1 (at least 250 punts)
- Best single-season punting average 51.4 (1940)

*Mark Rypien also threw six touchdown passes in one game.
†Jay Schroeder also threw six interceptions in one game.

"Washington Loses an Institution When Baugh Makes Farewell Appearance as Redskin Today: Lean Texan Has Been Mr. Football Around Here for 16 Years."

The legend started the game but stayed in for only three plays in a 27–21 win over the Eagles before 22,468 fans at Griffith Stadium. When the final gun sounded, his teammates hoisted him on their shoulders and carried him off the field, where he was mobbed by fans and stayed until dark to sign autographs—just as he had done so graciously during his career.

"I enjoyed my years in Washington," he said. "I didn't care much for a big city, that's all there was to it. I was a country boy, and I was always happy going back home in the off-season."

After retirement, Baugh coached Hardin-Simmons University in Texas to a 23–28 mark over five seasons (1955–59), before coaching the New York Titans (now the Jets) of the American Football League to a 14–14 mark over two seasons in the early 1960s. His Houston Oilers of the AFL finished 4–10 in 1964.

Today, Baugh's number, 33, is the only one to be retired by the Redskins. Few players in team history have been as admired or worshipped as Sammy Baugh.

# BILL DUDLEY

## "Virginia Gentleman" a Model of Football Versatility

RB, DB, K, No. 35, Virginia • 5–10, 182 • **NFL Career:** 1942, 1945–51, '53 (9 seasons) • **Redskins Years:** 1950–51, '53 (3) • **HOF Induction:** 1966 • NFL 1940s All-Decade Team • **Born:** December 24, 1919 (Bluefield, Va.)

So much about Bill Dudley was unconventional. He threw sidearm. He placekicked without stepping into the ball, swinging his leg like a pendulum. And at 5–10 and 176 pounds, he was small and slow, with an unorthodox running style, although his nickname, "Bullet Bill," suggested otherwise.

Dudley compensated for his lack of finesse and other deficiencies with a toughness and savvy that made him one of the greatest all-around players in NFL history. In nine seasons—three each with the Steelers, Lions, and Redskins—Mr. Versatility did almost everything you could ask of one player. He rushed, caught passes, returned punts and kickoffs, intercepted passes, punted and place kicked, and played safety fearlessly. Consider his numbers:

- 3,057 yards rushing, 1,383 receiving, 985 passing
- 1,743 yards on kickoff returns, 1,515 on punt returns, 193 punts
- 23 interceptions
- 484 points scored on touchdowns, field goals, and extra points

Dudley's best season was in 1946. Playing for the Steelers, he finished No. 1 in the NFL in rushing (604 yards), interceptions (10,242 yards), and punt returns (27,385 yards, 14.3-yard average). He also posted 452 passing yards and 48 points on five touchdowns, 12 extra points, and two field goals. He was named the league's MVP and a consensus first-team All-Pro.

How did Dudley, a 1966 inductee into the Pro Football Hall of Fame, outperform opponents who were more athletically gifted? "I don't know," he said. "I always felt I wasn't nearly as fast or as big as my opponents, but I felt there was only one way to compensate and that was to know as much as I could. I studied the game from the time that I was a little kid. I loved the game of football. I didn't even think about being good, bad or indifferent. I never concerned myself with whether I was the leading ground gainer or pass interception leader, or anything else like that. I just played to try to win a ball game."

He didn't win a lot—his best team was a 7–4 Steelers' squad in 1942—but he always exerted 100 percent effort until the final gun sounded. Part of the single-platoon era when players went both ways, he averaged 50 minutes per game one season. He drew kudos for his fierceness and dedication. "Dudley is rated by rival coaches and players as one of the league's most versatile backs," according to a Redskins 1951 game program. "But first and foremost is his competitive spirit, the hallmark of a true champion."

Early on, Dudley's size hurt his chances of making it as a football player. A native of the small town of Bluefield, Virginia, he was once denied a football tryout because his high school didn't have a uniform small enough for him. He eventually made the team, but many recruiters thought he was too small to play in the college ranks. Virginia Tech's football program rejected him because of his size.

Virginia coach Frank Murray took a chance on Dudley, who began his college career in 1939 as a 150-pound tailback and defensive back. By 1941, after growing to 175 pounds, he was one of the nation's most exciting players. He led the major colleges in yards that season with 2,441, including rushing, receptions, interceptions returned, and punt and kickoff returns. He also scored 134 points, nearly half the point production for the 8–1 Cavaliers. He completed 57 passes for 856 yards. Dudley became the school's first football All-American and was named the consensus college Player of the Year.

After the Steelers drafted him in 1942, Dudley excelled in the old single-wing formation. He ran for a 55-yard touchdown in his first game and led the league in rushing yards (696) and punt return yards (271). He was named All-NFL. His career was interrupted by World War II, and he spent three years in the Army Air Corps as a B-29 pilot. In between his bombing runs, he played service football and was named MVP in his league. He returned to the Steelers late in the 1945 season.

Despite his amazing 1946 season, Dudley had differences with Pittsburgh coach Jock Sutherland and was traded to Detroit. But he kept pace as one of the league's top all-around players, scoring 13 touchdowns for the Lions in 1947, seven on catches, four on rushes, one on a punt return, and one on a kickoff return. He also threw two touchdown passes.

Dudley was traded again before the 1950 season to the Redskins and played a variety of positions. That year, he returned a punt 96 yards for a touchdown to set a team record that stands. In 1951, he finished with league-high percentages in field goal kicking (76.9 on 10 of 13) and conversions (95.5 on 21 of 22). Overall, he converted 77 of 78 extra points in his three seasons in Washington. In regard to his unorthodox "rocking chair" style of placekicking, "He never took a step except the swing foot," said Bill Walsh, a center for the Steelers from 1949 to 1954.

Bill Dudley

Dudley made the Pro Bowl in 1950 and 1951. The Redskins honored him with "Bill Dudley Day" on October 21, 1951, when they beat the Chicago Cardinals, 7–3, before 22,960 at Griffith Stadium.

Said a 1951 Redskins game program, "A day in his honor isn't necessary to get the best out of Bullet Bill. "One of the game's most consistent performers, the Virginia gentleman already has earned a niche in football's Hall of Fame by his all-around play. Dudley's gridiron qualities are matched by his manners off the field. Without question, he is one of the game's most popular stars—a player's player.

"No individual is more worthy of the honors that will be paid Bill on this day, and none will be more appreciative.... a feller, an old pro like him, puts everything he has into every play, day or no day."

Dudley sat out the 1952 season with arthritis and bursitis in his knee and spent time as the backfield coach at Yale. He returned to the Redskins in 1953 as a player-coach, and hit clutch field goals that helped lift the Redskins to a 6–5–1 mark, their first winning record since 1948. In one game, his fourth-quarter field goal provided the winning points in a 24–21 victory over the Giants.

He retired from football after the 1953 season.

"He was just a real good, smart football player and a hell of a good runner," Walsh said. "He wasn't fast, but he could really pick out where his blockers were and then would find the hole. He was noted for that change of direction."

# TURK EDWARDS

## Immovable Lineman Made "Big" Impact in NFL's Early Years

T, No. 17, Washington State • 6–2, 265 **NFL Career:** 1932–40 (9 seasons) • **Redskins Years:** 1932–40 (9) • **HOF Induction:** 1969 • NFL 1930s All-Decade Team • **Born:** September 28, 1907 (Mold, Wash.) • **Died:** January 12, 1973 (Seattle, Wash.)

He was dubbed the "Rock of Gibraltar." At 6–2, 265-pounds, Redskins lineman Turk Edwards was a mountain of a man for his day.

Edwards, who played for the Boston Braves–Boston Redskins–Washington Redskins for nine seasons, was one of the NFL's first "big" tackles. A devastating blocker and tackler at a time when many single-platoon players stayed on the field for 60 minutes, he toyed with opponents using overwhelming strength and power, yet he had the speed and agility to chase down ball-carriers. He was also a smart player and possessed excellent leadership skills. He claimed All-NFL honors in 1932, 1933, 1936, and 1937, and was a cornerstone on the 1937 Redskins team that won the NFL championship.

Edwards was inducted in 1969 into the Pro Football Hall of Fame, which described him as a "steamrolling blocker and smothering tackler." He "played with such immovable and impregnable tendencies and, thus, became the best of his era. Like many of the pros of that period, Edwards was an iron man. In one 15-game season in Boston, Turk played all but 10 minutes of the entire season."

"Turk was the biggest man on the field and the fastest lineman on the field," said Clyde Shugart, a Redskins guard from 1939 to 1943. "He kicked off, too. I always said that's one man the opposition got out of the way of. He'd run right into a man and knock him over. He was a really good leader. He was captain of the team."

Albert Glen Edwards also overwhelmed opponents on the college level. A native of Washington State, he played at Washington State University, becoming a first-team All-American tackle as a junior. That season, he blocked a punt and returned it for a touchdown, helping the Cougars preserve an unbeaten season and gain a trip to the 1931 Rose Bowl. Cougars coach Babe Hollinbery gave Edwards his curious nickname by saying one day when the tackle was late for practice, "I wonder where that big turk is."

When Edwards finished playing college ball, no draft existed in the upstart NFL. He received offers in 1932 to play for the New York Giants, Portsmouth (Ohio) Spartans, and the expansion Boston Braves, and chose the Braves, who submitted the highest offer: $1,500 for the season. From Washington State, he chauffeured a busload of fellow rookies to training camp near Boston.

Edwards proved to be one of the prize catches for Braves owner George Preston Marshall, anchoring the offensive and defensive lines. With his gargantuan frame, he opened holes in 1932 for rookie Cliff Battles, who gained a league-high 576 yards rushing. The following year, he played 710 of a pos-

Edwards (right) with his coach at Washington State, Babe Hollingbery. Hollingbery gave Edwards his nickname, "Turk."

sible 720 minutes for the newly renamed Redskins. He was key to fullback Jim Musick gaining an NFL-high 809 yards and Battles 737.

In a 14–0 win over the Giants that secured the Eastern Division title for the Redskins in 1936, Edwards used his oversized hands to block two punts, made tackles all along the line, and opened huge holes for Redskin runners. In the Redskins' inaugural game in Washington on September 17, 1937, a 13–3 win over the Giants, he made an emphatic introduction before his new home fans with New York behind by seven points in the third period and a few yards from the end zone.

According to one newspaper account, "Three times, [future Hall of Fame running back] Tuffy Leemans and company smashed their way at the Redskin line but didn't gain an inch." "On fourth down, Tuffy crashed directly at Turk's position. The crowd was in a constant uproar, and as Tuffy headed for what appeared to be the tying touchdown, a huge red-shirted figure, with a golden number '17' on his back, collided fearfully with the Giant ace. When the ball was placed down, it belonged to the Redskins on the 3-yard line."

"Turk Edwards and his brilliant line, more than any other single incident, sold professional football to Washington that night."

On that 1937 Redskins squad, which finished as NFL champions, Edwards opened holes for Battles (NFL-high 874 yards rushing) and provided a shield for tailback Sammy Baugh (NFL-high 1,127 yards passing). He bowled opponents over with what *Washington Times-Herald* sportswriter Vincent X. Flaherty called his "exceptional tonnage."

Before the 1940 season, Edwards was named the Redskins' top assistant to coach Ray Flaherty and also intended to continue as a player. Despite being bruised and battered after eight seasons, he was confident about his effectiveness on the field.

"I feel as good as ever," he said in the *Washington Star* on August 16, 1940. "Can I stand up throughout the season? Well, you know that because of our two-team system, a Redskin hardly ever plays a full game and, although I can't move as fast as I did, I think my legs will carry me through. Until we started training, I played 36 holes of golf every day since July 10, and my legs are in good shape. All in all, I'm as anxious to get started again as I've ever been."

Edwards played well in the season opener, but his career ended in a bizarre incident before the second game against the Giants. After shaking hands at midfield with Giants center Mel Hein, a future Hall of Famer and Edwards's former teammate at Washington State, he turned to jog to the sideline and his spikes got stuck in the turf. His often injured knee gave way, and the once indestructible man never played another down in the NFL.

Edwards maintained his ties to the burgundy and gold. He was a full-time assistant from 1940 to 1945, when the Redskins remained an elite team, and took over as head coach before the 1946 campaign. His tenure was uneventful. He went 5–5–1 in 1946, 4–8 in 1947, and 7–5 in 1948, and left football after spending 17 seasons with the Redskins. Corrine Griffith, Marshall's wife, praised Edwards for his commitment to the organization in her 1947 book, *My Life with the Redskins.* "Nice, big, loyal, Turk, [17] years with the Redskins," she wrote. "He had always been nice and loyal, but he hadn't always been as big; the longer he stayed with the Redskins, the more he expanded. Most people think Turk's big body is full of flesh and bones, but they're wrong; his body has to be that big to carry around all that loyalty."

Ray Flaherty

## RAY FLAHERTY

### Brilliant Innovator, Motivator Coached the Redskins to Greatness

Head Coach, Gonzaga • **NFL Career:** 1936–42 (7 seasons) • **Redskins Years:** 1936–42 (7) • **HOF Induction:** 1976 • **Born:** September 1, 1903 (Spokane, Wash.) • **Died:** July 19, 1994 (Coeur d'Alene, Ida.)

He displayed the swagger of a championship coach, the intellect of an innovative genius, and the oratorical skills of a shrewd motivator. Ray "Red" Flaherty packaged those qualities to mold the Redskins into a juggernaut in the franchise's early years.

Flaherty won four Eastern Division titles and two NFL championships in seven seasons as the Redskins' coach (1936–42). His overall record, 56–23–3, equals a .701 winning percentage that is No. 1 in the Redskins' record books. (Dudley DeGroot's winning percentage is .725, but he coached only 19 games.) Flaherty was inducted into the Pro Football Hall of Fame in 1976.

"He was an excellent coach, a hard driving coach," said Clyde Shugart, a Redskins guard who played four seasons for the freckle-faced redhead. "He kept everybody on the ball and under control. He wasn't soft. He kept our noses to the grindstone."

Redskins Hall of Fame quarterback Sammy Baugh, who played his first six seasons under Flaherty, said, "He did a hell of a job. He was a good man for us, a good football man. Our boys had a lot of hope when Flaherty was there."

His coaching achievements aside, Flaherty is best remembered in NFL lore for his famous suggestion in the 1934 NFL championship game. The 6-foot, 206-pounder then played end for the Giants, who were hosting the Bears on a bitterly cold day at the Polo Grounds in New York. The field was frozen solid.

With the Giants trailing, 10–3, at halftime, Flaherty suggested they switch from cleats to basketball sneakers to gain better traction on the field. New York proceeded to craft a comeback and won, 30–13, and Flaherty became known as the hero of the storied "Sneakers Game."

Flaherty spent the next two seasons as a Giants player-coach, before Boston Redskins owner George Preston Marshall signed him as his head coach in 1936. Although the Redskins were coming off a 2–8–1 campaign, Flaherty stated boldly he'd resign if he didn't win the NFL championship. He came so close, leading the Redskins to their first-ever winning mark, 7–5, an Eastern Division title, and a spot in the championship game against Green Bay. The Packers won, but not before Flaherty had been showered with praise.

"If the improvement of the Redskins since the start of the season is a fair sample of [Flaherty's] work, he's just about the best coach in the business," *Boston Globe* sportswriter Paul V. Craigue wrote after the Redskins destroyed Pittsburgh, 30–0, late in the season. "Boston may well be the capital of the pro football world in the near future."

After Marshall moved the Redskins to Washington in 1937, Flaherty continued working his magic. In the Redskins' 28–21 win over the Bears in the 1937 championship game, he introduced the behind-the-line screen pass, which Baugh used as part of his 18 of 33, 354-yard, three-touchdown performance.

"They were breaking their necks trying to rack up Baugh," Flaherty once said. "That's what made the screen pass go. It had been nullified downfield, but we put it in behind the line of scrimmage, and the Bears didn't know how to stop it."

In a 14–6 win over the Bears in the 1942 championship game, Flaherty implemented a novel two-platoon system on offense. One unit featured Baugh's passing from the single-wing formation and the other unit, with Frankie Filchock at tailback, was predicated on a pounding running game. Defenses were bewildered.

Flaherty was more than an Xs and Os man. He was adroit at motivating his players, using words and psychological tactics to round their minds into game shape. Depending on the situation, he would berate, cajole, or flatter just like the great motivator he was often compared with, Notre Dame coach Knute Rockne. Like Rockne, Flaherty was known for his tough pregame pep talks.

"We've seen him whip a laggard into a fury with a verbal lashing that might have fetched another coach a punch in the nose," *Washington Post* sportswriter Shirley Povich wrote on October 12, 1940. "We've seen him play on his players' personal pride to get the same effect that on another day he would gain by threats. We've heard him, on occasion, tell his squad of pros bluntly that they're getting good wages for only 60 minutes of football a week and, dammit, to give him that 60 minutes this afternoon."

Flaherty could also be a man of a few words that carried considerable weight. Case in point: Prior to the 1942 championship game, the coach wrote on the locker-room chalkboard a subtle reminder of Washington's loss to the Bears in the 1940

Flaherty (right) and Redskins owner George Preston Marshall are all smiles on December 8, 1939, as the coach inks a new five-year contract reportedly worth $10,000 a year.

title game: "73–0." He also made a rousing speech that had his players in a frenzy by kickoff.

"Flaherty told us he didn't care whether we won the game or not but to just beat the living [expletive] out of them," Shugart said. "He kind of got choked up, and [assistant coach] Turk Edwards started to say something, and the same thing happened. I always said that if somebody hadn't opened the door, we would have run right through it to get out onto the field."

Flaherty left the Redskins after the 1942 season to serve as a U.S. Navy lieutenant during World War II. He'd made a deal with Marshall that he could return to the Redskins once the war was over, but that didn't happen. Instead, he became the first "name coach" from the NFL to join the new All-America Football Conference, where he coached the New York Yankees for three seasons and the Chicago Rockets for one. His Yankees reached two championship games, both losses to the Cleveland Browns. He retired from coaching in 1949 with a career record of 80–39–5 (.679 winning percentage).

"He was a good motivator and disciplinarian, and he was strictly a fundamentals man," said Ace Parker, a Hall of Fame quarterback for the old Brooklyn Dodgers from 1937 to 1941. "That's why he had good teams. He stressed fundamentals and wanted them carried out. It wasn't just the haphazard way of doing it."

## JOE GIBBS

### Most Celebrated Coach in Redskins History

Head Coach, San Diego State • **NFL Career:** 1981–92, 2004–06 (15 seasons) • **Redskins Years:** 1981–92, 2004–06 (15) • **HOF Induction:** 1996 • **Born:** November 25, 1940 (Mocksville, N.C.)

His name is synonymous with the Washington Redskins like that of no other coach in team history: Joe Jackson Gibbs.

## The Flaherty Years

| NFL | | | | |
| --- | --- | --- | --- | --- |
| Year | Team | Record | % | Postseason |
| 1936 | Boston | 7–5 | .583 | 0–1 (Lost in NFL championship game) |
| 1937 | Wash | 8–3 | .727 | 1–0 (NFL champions) |
| 1938 | Wash | 6–3–2 | .636 | 0–0 |
| 1939 | Wash | 8–2–1 | .772 | 0–0 |
| 1940 | Wash | 9–2 | .818 | 0–1 (Lost in NFL championship game) |
| 1941 | Wash | 6–5 | .545 | 0–0 |
| 1942 | Wash | 10–1 | .909 | 1–0 (NFL champions) |
| Totals | | 54–21–3 | .711 | 2–2 |

| AAFC | | | | |
| --- | --- | --- | --- | --- |
| Year | Team | Record | % | Postseason |
| 1946 | NY-A | 10–3–1 | .750 | 0–1 (Lost in AAFC championship game) |
| 1947 | NY-A | 11–2–1 | .821 | 0–1 (Lost in AAFC championship game) |
| 1948 | NY-A | 1–3–0 | .250 | 0–0 |
| 1949 | Ch-A | 4–8–0 | .333 | 0–0 |
| Totals | | 26–16–2 | .614 | 0–2 |

Joe Gibbs I and Joe Gibbs II

Gibbs is the most celebrated coach to ever lead the burgundy and gold. He's the only Redskins coach to win a Super Bowl—he has three rings, in fact—and has made nine playoff appearances in 15 seasons at the helm of the franchise. His winning percentages for the regular season (.625, 145–87) and postseason (.739, 17–6) are among the best in NFL history.

Gibbs achieved virtually all of his success in the 12-season period from 1981 to 1992, when the Redskins were one of the league's elite teams and showed traits of a dynasty. In addition to appearing in four Super Bowls, they won five NFC East titles and had 10 winning seasons.

By the time he stepped down, in March 1993, Gibbs was the most revered man in the nation's capital. He also was regarded as one of the greatest NFL coaches of all time largely by virtue of his unique ability to win three Super Bowls with three different quarterbacks, none of whom will ever make the Hall of Fame. He also won Super Bowls in two strike-shortened seasons, another monumental feat. Essentially, Gibbs was a model by which other NFL coaches were measured. He was enshrined in the Hall of Fame in 1996.

His coaching career in D.C. has been a tale of two vastly different periods, however. After an 11-year hiatus during which his racing team was busy capturing NASCAR championships, Gibbs returned in January 2004. In the past three seasons, though, he has experienced his two worst years ever, marks of 6–10 in 2004 and 5–11 in 2006 sandwiched around a 10–6 team that reached the second round of the playoffs in 2005.

Gibbs's goal on making his comeback was to return the Redskins to glory. They had posted only two winning seasons and one playoff appearance since he left, and people were saying if anyone could do it, he could. But he was not where he hoped to be, and where Redskins fans expected him to be, after three seasons back.

"You get upset when something like this happens," Gibbs said at a news conference to wrap up the 2006 season. "It's certainly a tough thing to go through. I have an obligation to our fans, our owner. As I said when I came here, I want to get us back to winning. None of us liked this year. But that's what it is. How far off are we, everybody's going to have their opinion. When you finish a year like this, there's going to be a lot of negative stuff to it. That's just part of the NFL. That's the life we live.

"Our fans kind of know where we are. They know we went 5–11. They're disappointed. For me, I'm determined to do what's best for the Redskins at all times. Not for one year, not for two years, not for five years. What would be the best thing for the Redskins in every situation."

One his long-time lieutenants, Joe Bugel, said that the situation has been very difficult for Gibbs "because he feels like he's letting the owner down and our great fans and the football team." Bugel, a member of the Gibbs-I staff who has assisted him for the past three seasons on offense, added that the issue of whether Gibbs may have tarnished his legacy never comes up. "The only thing we talk about is winning the next game," Bugel said. "If anybody can right this ship, it's Joe Gibbs."

More than four decades ago, a coach named Don Coryell also had lots of confidence in Joe Gibbs. After playing linebacker, tight end, and guard at San Diego State for three seasons in the early 1960s under Coryell, Gibbs was hired by him for his first assistant coaching job in 1964. Gibbs was a graduate assistant for two seasons before being promoted to offensive line coach in 1966, when the Aztecs finished 11–0 and captured the consensus Division II national championship.

"I saw he was going to be a really fine coach," said Coryell, who used the passing game to wreak havoc on offenses and later became known as "Air Coryell." "He had a way of talking to people, and he was so industrious and fired up that all these good traits you want in a player rubbed off on the fellows he had. He just did a terrific job, unbelievable for a young kid like that. I had a jewel in Joe Gibbs."

Gibbs later assisted on offense at Florida State, Southern California, and Arkansas, before reuniting with Coryell as the St. Louis Cardinals' offensive backfield coach in 1973, when "Air Coryell" first hit the NFL's radar screens. After five seasons there and a season as the offensive coordinator in Tampa Bay, Gibbs coached in San Diego under Coryell in 1979 and 1980, completing his 17-season assistant coaching apprenticeship.

As an assistant, Gibbs worked under a quartet of astute coaching minds: Coryell, John McKay (Southern Cal), and Frank Broyles (Arkansas)—all of whom are in the College Football Hall of Fame—and Bill Peterson (Florida State). He gleaned valuable direction from each one and assisted teams that had winning records in 14 of his 17 seasons.

In his last two seasons in San Diego, Gibbs called plays for one of the most explosive offenses in NFL history. So, on arriving in Washington in 1981, the 40-year-old man was being counted on to inject a similar excitement into an offense that often struggled under prior coach Jack Pardee. The Redskins opened the 1981 season 0–5, but Gibbs, thinking his job was on the line, made a memorable adjustment.

Having relied mostly on a pass-oriented attack, he balanced out the offense by calling for the single-back, two-tight end setup he had learned from his mentor, Coryell. The Redskins rebounded to finish 8–8 and rode their momentum in 1982 to capture Super Bowl XVII.

The Gibbs dynasty was born. He earned NFL Coach of the Year honors in 1982 and again in 1983, when the Redskins appeared in Super Bowl XVIII, becoming the first coach in two decades to receive that distinction two years in a row. Meanwhile, the master tactician implemented dazzling innovations and schemes. As then-Redskins quarterback Joe Theismann put it, Gibbs experimented with something new on offense week after week because he was always "curious about his own genius."

"He revealed a sort of offensive genius that I never saw coming," long-time *Sports Illustrated* pro football writer Paul Zimmerman said. "It wasn't so much with the Hogs or the ground attack. It was the 'bunch' formation they used to use, which was quite innovative. They had three receivers all running complicated patterns at the same time. All hell breaks loose, and they go every which way. It was quite a sophisticated passing system. After seeing him use it, I said this guy's really got a touch, he's really got some innovative ability. That's what put him over the top—his innovative ability."

Then-Redskins radio play-by-play man Frank Herzog found it fun to watch how Gibbs and his staff made deft adjustments at halftime that led to so many victories. "Teams would come out with the same approach offensively or defensively, while the Redskins would come out and, boom, they'd win the ball game," Herzog said. "It got to where you'd think at halftime what they were going to do to second-guess and adjust."

Two of Gibbs's fiercest coaching rivals at the time, the Giants' Bill Parcells and the Bears' Mike Ditka, described him as the best coach they ever faced. "He understood the game as well as anybody," said Ditka, who coached the Bears from 1982

Gibbs played guard, linebacker, and tight end in the early 1960s at San Diego State. His first assistant coaching stop was at San Diego State from 1964 to 1966. "I thought I had a jewel in Joe Gibbs," said Gibbs's mentor, Don Coryell, the Aztecs' head coach at the time. "He was a great coach and really, really helped the ball club."

to 1992 and went 1–2 against Gibbs in the playoffs. "When you watched what Joe Gibbs did on offense, he gave you a lot of icing and glitter and glamour, but it was basic. When it was all added up, he was going to block and protect the quarterback. He also had a core of good players, basic players that he loved and trusted, and they trusted him."

In addition to his cleverness with Xs and Os, Gibbs became synonymous with an indefatigable work ethic, meticulous game preparation, wily organizational, leadership and motivational skills, a fierce competitiveness, and a lust for perfection. In a reflection of their coach, his players were well-disciplined, unselfish, and rarely beat themselves with silly penalties, turnovers, and mental mistakes.

It all defined the Joe Gibbs's doctrine on winning.

"Coach Gibbs laid a foundation, and anytime you're going to have a championship in anything, you have to have a foundation," said Darryl Grant, a defensive tackle who played under Gibbs for 10 seasons. "He based his foundation on family. That was one of the principles that we had: We're a family, we're a unit, we're there to win games. Gibbs always preached that we stick together. We stood up for each other. Everybody didn't always love each other, but once we got on the field, we meant business. We were there to cover for each other. We were one."

"He was a great verbal leader, very charismatic, very smart," Grant added. "He's a guy who, with his words, could rile you up to move just about any mountain, and you respected that about him. We knew he was right, and we went out and did the things he said to do."

After retiring and spending more than a decade operating Joe Gibbs Racing, a period that included a stop at NBC as an NFL studio analyst, Gibbs signed on with the Redskins in 2004 as head coach and team president; he took charge of player-personnel decisions. But it's been a Herculean struggle at times, and he's been vilified in the media and by fans. During the 2004 and 2006 seasons, for example, he was criticized for waiting too long to bench aging and erratic quarterback Mark Brunell. Both times the delay may have cost the Redskins a legitimate shot at the playoffs.

Gibbs has also taken heat for a series of questionable player-personnel moves (general managers Bobby Beathard and Charley Casserly handled personnel issues during Gibbs-I), for being conservative with on-the-field decisions, for losing a host of games decided by three points or less (he's 6–10, compared with 31–13 during Gibbs-I), and for penalties and mental mistakes that have sometimes crippled his squad. In comparison, his teams in the 1980s and early 1990s rarely beat themselves.

Frustration in his voice and on his face has been noticeable. "It's been a tough year for him because he puts so much into it as far as wanting to be the best and taking the Redskins back to where they were in the past when they won all those titles," Redskins linebacker Marcus Washington said at the end of the 2006 season. "Sometimes he spends the night here. Not a lot of coaches around the league work that hard. He really inspires you because after a couple of tough losses he'll be fired up, and he'll be able to create some positives out of those negatives."

In Bugel's eyes, Gibbs is as intense as he always was. "You can describe Joe Gibbs in one word: passion," Bugel said. "He relays that to the players. I can see no difference back in the '80s and the 2000s right now. He's the same man. He coaches

the same way. He puts in 20 hours a day at the office. Nothing's changed."

Neither has his status in Canton. Hall of Fame officials say his spot is eternally secure and that only a note may be added to his bio about his coaching record in the twenty-first century. In the only other situation in which a Hall of Famer returned to the game after being inducted, when the great Cleveland Browns coach Paul Brown made a comeback as the Bengals' coach, a line that he later coached in Cincinnati was added to his bio..

"What I really like about him is he's a Hall of Fame coach, but he's not too proud to say, 'I made a mistake here, I should have done this or we need to do more of this,'" Marcus Washington said. "If you're willing to change a little and admit if you're wrong somewhere and learn from that . . . He lets you know, 'I'm not going to quit, I'm going to continue to work 'till we get to where we want to be.' I think he can get us there."

# KEN HOUSTON

## Hard-Hitting Safety Left Legacy as One of the Greatest Ever

S, No. 27, Prairie View A&M • 6–3, 197 • **NFL Career:** 1967–80 (14 seasons) • **Redskins Years:** 1973–80 (8) • **HOF Induction:** 1986 • NFL 1970s All-Decade Team and NFL 75th Anniversary Team • **Born:** November 12, 1944 (Lufkin, Tex.)

Upon hearing the news, Ken Houston said he felt a "numbness." It was May 1973, and the Houston Oilers' All-Pro safety just learned he had been traded. He was disappointed, to say the least.

"Nobody wants to be traded," he said. "You have fans and loyalty. I was living in Houston, and I didn't think at that particular time that they would trade me with the career I'd had in Houston. So I asked [general manager] Sid Gillman who he traded me to, and he told me the Redskins. I felt good about that because if you were not a Redskin, everybody watched them."

The Redskins were fresh off an appearance in Super Bowl VII, and with Houston anchoring the defensive backfield, they made the playoffs three more times in the 1970s. All the while, he fortified a distinguished career. A first-ballot inductee into the Pro Football Hall of Fame in 1986, he was named in 1994 to the NFL's 75th anniversary team as one of three greatest safeties to ever play the game, along with Larry Wilson and Ronnie Lott.

Houston's numbers support his recognition. In 14 seasons, six with the Oilers and his last eight with the Redskins, he was named to two all-star teams in the old American Football League, followed by 10 straight Pro Bowls. The perennial All-Pro intercepted 49 passes for 898 yards and returned nine for touchdowns, an all-time NFL record at the time that has since been broken. He's tied for first in most interceptions returned for touchdowns in one season (four) and in one game (two). He also scored on a fumble recovery, a blocked field goal and a punt return.

Houston is remembered, too, for his vicious hits that rattled a few running backs and wide receivers. Positioned mostly at strong safety, the 6–3, 200-pounder hunted opponents down with his long, fluid strides and popped them with a flying forearm, often corralling players around the neck. The clothesline tackle has since been outlawed.

## The Gibbs Years

| Year | Team | Record | % | Postseason |
|------|------|--------|------|------------|
| 1981 | Wash | 8–8 | .500 | 0–0 |
| 1982 | Wash | 8–1 | .889 | 4–0 (Won Super Bowl XVII) |
| 1983 | Wash | 14–2 | .875 | 2–1 (Lost Super Bowl XVIII) |
| 1984 | Wash | 11–5 | .688 | 0–1 |
| 1985 | Wash | 10–6 | .625 | 0–0 |
| 1986 | Wash | 12–4 | .750 | 2–1 |
| 1987 | Wash | 11–4 | .734 | 3–0 (Won Super Bowl XXII) |
| 1988 | Wash | 7–9 | .438 | 0–0 |
| 1989 | Wash | 10–6 | .625 | 0–0 |
| 1990 | Wash | 10–6 | .625 | 1–1 |
| 1991 | Wash | 14–2 | .875 | 3–0 (Won Super Bowl XXVI) |
| 1992 | Wash | 9–7 | .563 | 1–1 |
| 2004 | Wash | 6–10 | .375 | 0–0 |
| 2005 | Wash | 10–6 | .625 | 1–1 |
| 2006 | Wash | 5–11 | .313 | 0–0 |
| **Totals** | | **145–87** | **.625** | **17–6** |

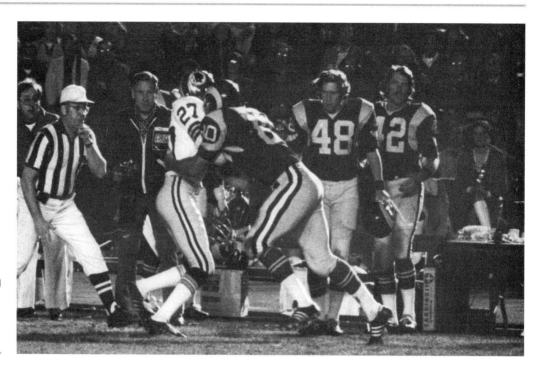

Houston, here intercepting a pass against the Rams in 1974, made the Pro Bowl seven straight times as a Redskin (1973–79).

"I just thought that was a more stunning blow," Houston said. "They called me dirty and everything else, but you definitely got the ball-carrier's attention. I wouldn't have made a dime in the NFL if I did that today, I would be fined every week. But I wasn't a dirty player."

In the eyes of Mark Murphy, a Redskin safety who played with Houston for four seasons, "Kenny had tremendous instincts and was a great hitter. He was kind of unorthodox because he tackled with his forearm. But he didn't miss many."

Houston said his hitting style was probably a carryover from when he played some offensive line in high school and college and was taught to block with his forearm. A native of Lufkin, Texas, he played his college ball at Prairie View A&M, a historically black college in Texas in the Southwestern Athletic Conference. He first played center—despite being so light for the position—before moving to linebacker once the coaches realized his combination of speed and quickness.

Houston became a two-time All-Conference and All-American linebacker and played on teams that twice won the black college national championship, as well as two conference titles.

The Oilers picked him in the ninth round of the 1967 AFL draft and converted him to safety. The rookie intercepted four passes and returned two for touchdowns. But there was a disconnect in his life. He said he left the game three times that season for personal reasons. "One is I was raised with a Christian background, and we didn't do a thing on Sunday but go to church," he said. "I was married, and I really didn't want to leave my family. And I'd graduated from college and wanted to be a teacher. Football just wasn't the first thing for me to do."

Houston credits Oilers coach Wally Lemm with talking him into staying each time he stepped away. And he soon became a superstar. In addition to racking up AFL all-star game and Pro Bowl appearances (he began playing in the Pro Bowl when the AFL merged with the NFL in 1970), he intercepted 25 passes in his first five seasons. He returned two of them for touchdowns in a 1971 clash with San Diego, after being knocked out of the game earlier.

Houston played at partial strength for most of the 1972 season owing to a dislocated toe and intercepted no passes. Nevertheless, Redskins coach George Allen, who had a keen eye for veteran talent, set his sights on acquiring the 28-year-old strong safety.

Allen traded five players to the Oilers for Houston: tackle Jim Snowden, wide receiver Clifton McNeil, tight end Mack Alston, defensive end Mike Fanucci, and defensive back Jeff Severson. The loss of five bodies, plus Houston's injury from the season before, triggered doubts about the practicality of the deal. A *Washington Star-Daily News* headline read: "A Houston From Houston Produces Guessing Game."

"I didn't quite understand the trade," said Rusty Tillman, a Redskins special teams star in the 1970s. "George gave up five players for him, and a lot of those guys were my friends because a lot of them were special teams guys: Mack Alston, Jeff Severson, Mike Fanucci. But after I was around Kenny Houston, I understood. He was a terrific football player, a tough guy. He was a big safety, and he could run."

The trade would go down as one of Allen's masterpieces. Houston, nearly 30 at the time, fit in perfectly with the "Over the Hill Gang," a wily group of veterans who fueled the Redskins' playoff run through the Allen era. He was a cornerstone on Washington's defense, earning All-Pro or All-NFC honors each season from 1973 to 1979. He called plays at times and saw action in 183 straight games before a broken arm sidelined him late in the 1979 season. And to the dismay of the Redskins' most despised rival, the Cowboys, he had a habit of producing gargantuan plays when the two teams collided:

- His tackle stopped running back Walt Garrison short of the goal line and preserved a 14–7 Monday night victory in 1973.
- He returned a punt 58 yards for a touchdown in a 28–21 Redskins win in 1974.
- His interception in overtime put the Redskins in position to score the winning points in a 30–24 victory in 1975.

- His interception helped preserve a 9–5 Redskins win in 1978.
- Dallas was on the Redskins' 3-yard line late in the first half of a 1979 game, but Houston blitzed and sacked quarterback Roger Staubach, forcing a fumble that a teammate recovered in a 34–20 Redskins victory.

Houston was often considered the best player on the Redskins, and teammates relished the opportunity to play with him. "Kenny and I knew each other so well and could count on each other being in a certain spot," said Redskins free safety Brig Owens, who played with Houston for five seasons. "We didn't have to communicate verbally. We just knew it. There were times we would switch positions. He would play free safety and I would play strong. During your career, you have the pleasure of playing with great players. Kenny was one of those players."

Mark Murphy echoed those thoughts. "Kenny Houston meant a lot to me in my career. I was very fortunate to learn from him as a backup safety my first two years and then play alongside him. He was a special person and a great role model."

Houston was a role model away from the game, too. With a soft-spoken, kind-hearted demeanor that belied his ferocity

## Houston Tackle Is Legend

Kenny Houston remembers the play like it was yesterday, only it was more than three decades ago on October 8, 1973.

With 24 seconds left in the Redskins-Cowboys Monday night duel, Dallas trailed, 14–7, and faced a fourth-and-goal at the 4. When fullback Walt Garrison caught quarterback Craig Morton's pass at the 1, virtually everyone among the 54,314 fans at RFK Stadium and the millions more watching on TV had to be thinking the Cowboys were about to pull within a point. But Houston appeared from his safety position, picked Garrison off his feet as he tried squirming toward the end zone, and bulldogged him to the ground short of the goal line. Ironically, the powerful Garrison was an off-season rodeo Cowboy who specialized in bulldogging steers.

For a few seconds, RFK Stadium went silent, then erupted into a deafening roar.

"That was probably the defining play of my career," Houston said. "There were other plays I thought were greater, like the back-to-back interceptions I returned for touchdowns in one game. But as far as one particular play that highlighted my career, that was it. Everywhere I go, people identify me with that play."

Redskins safety Brig Owens, who came over to help on the play, remembers it vividly: "After Garrison caught the ball, Kenny stuck him. He picked his feet up off the ground. That's one of the classic ways you're taught to tackle."

Houston's tackle stands as one of the most treasured moments in Redskins history.

Stopping Walt Garrison short of the goal line gave Houston a distinguished spot in Redskins lore. "Everywhere I go, people identify me with that play," he said.

on the field, he was immersed in civic, humanitarian, and charity endeavors during his football career: March of Dimes walk-a-thons, community youth groups, Athletes in Action, homes for the elderly, and church functions, to name a few. Plus, he was with a group of NFL players who in the early 1970s visited hospitals in the Far East caring for U.S. troops wounded in the Vietnam War.

Houston won many awards, including the Byron Whizzer White Award for Humanitarian Service and the Bart Starr Award, which goes to the player who best exemplifies outstanding character and leadership in the home, on the field, and in the community. The Ken Houston Humanitarian Award was named in his honor.

What influenced him to become involved in so many non-football-related activities? "To me, it was just a way of life," he said. "You've been given a gift, and it's just like giving something back. People enjoy you being there, and they get to know another side of a person, another side of a football player."

On the field, the Redskins honored the model citizen with Ken Houston Day at RFK Stadium on December 13, 1980, his next-to-last game in the NFL. After retirement, he coached defensive backs with the Houston Oilers (now the Tennessee Titans) and the University of Houston. He has a master's degree in counseling and has served for many years as a counselor in the Houston school system.

"I had eight of probably the most fun-filled years that I've ever had," Houston said of his playing days in Washington. "It was the epitome of what I thought football should be after football. We hung around for a few hours after practice, laughing, talking. I appreciated the opportunity to play with guys like Sonny Jurgensen, Charley Taylor, Billy Kilmer. That team had so many characters that will be remembered in football for a long, long time. You pretty much name it, and those guys went through there during my eight-year period."

## SAM HUFF

### Vicious Hitter Glamorized the Middle Linebacker Position

LB, No. 70, West Virginia • 6–1, 230 • **NFL Career:** 1956–67, 69 (13 seasons) • **Redskins Years:** 1964–67, 69 (5) • **HOF Induction:** 1982 • NFL 1950s All-Decade Team • **Born:** October 4, 1934 (Edna Gas, W.Va.)

He was mean. He was nasty. And, boy, could he lay a hit on a ball carrier. Welcome Sam Huff, one of the greatest middle linebackers in NFL history.

For 13 seasons, his first eight with the Giants and last five with the Redskins, Huff was one of the most feared defenders in the league. A field general equipped with razor-sharp instincts, he sniffed out runners and receivers like a hound dog and roamed the field like a hawk, intercepting 30 passes, one of the highest totals ever for a linebacker.

Huff achieved nearly all of his fame with the Giants, playing in four of his five Pro Bowls and earning all four of his All-Pro distinctions. With No. 70 manning the middle, the Giants made it to six NFL championship games, winning once. He was inducted in 1982 into the Pro Football Hall of Fame, which called him an "inspirational leader, brilliant diagnostician with great speed, tackling ability . . . noted for hard-

Huff was in the twilight of his career in 1969. But that didn't stop the nasty middle linebacker from corralling a few ball carriers.

hitting duels with premier running backs," Cleveland's Jim Brown and Green Bay's Jim Taylor to name a few.

Back when tackling rules were much more liberal than today, the middle linebacker downed opponents with clothesline hits that sent shivers through their bodies. Those hits would be illegal today. Other times, he grabbed ball carriers by an arm, a leg, or around the chest and wrestled them to the ground. "Sometimes, I twist their head a little, too, but most of them don't seem to mind," he once said of his graceful tackling style.

Such cold-bloodedness was a product of his childhood. Growing up poor in a coal mining camp in Edna Gas, West Virginia, with life simply a matter of day-to-day survival, Robert Lee "Sam" Huff developed a tough-guy demeanor.

"Everybody is just tougher," he said. "You learn to be independent, you learn to fight. If somebody says something bad about your dad or mom, you're going to knock the hell out of them. There are no negotiations. If a guy gives you a cheap shot, you have to hit him back. My dad was a little guy, but he was tough as hell. When he said something, you had to move. He didn't say it twice."

Although his dad and brother worked in the coal mines, Huff refused to do it for a living. And he had an out: He was an all-state football player in high school and doubled as a decent baseball player. Basketball was another story: "I couldn't play basketball because I was too mean to do that," he said. "The last basketball game I ever played, the guy went in for a lay-up, and I hit him and flipped him over, and he landed on his head. They had to call an ambulance and take him to the hospital. I can't play those kinds of sports. It's just not fun for me. So that's what I loved about football. Baseball, too, because I was a catcher, and nobody ever stole home against me. Some of them tried, but they didn't make it to home plate. It's just the way I am. I'm competitive now. That's why I'm not a good golfer. I grip the club too tight."

Huff won a football scholarship to West Virginia. He earned All-American honors playing guard and tackle on offense and defense, and made a slew of all-star teams. He was enshrined in the College Football Hall of Fame in 1980.

The Giants drafted Huff in the third round in 1956. But he was undersized at defensive tackle and discontent with coach Jim Lee Howell, walking out of training camp with fellow rookie Don Chandler. Both were talked back, and early in the season, Huff got the break that launched his star-studded career. When middle linebacker Ray Beck injured his ankle, defensive coach (and later famed Cowboys head coach) Tom Landry asked Huff if he would like to try the position.

"I said, 'I would love to do it,' Huff said. "Now, I could stand up and just see everything and key on running backs and take an angle of pursuit and take them down. I was always a good tackler. Ray Beck later told me after we finished playing, 'You know Sam, when I saw you play that first game when I was hurt, I went to Tom Landry and said, "I'm okay, now, I'm okay." Tom said, 'I want to take another look at Sam.'"

A lot of people focused on the eventual Rookie of the Year in 1956, when the Giants downed the Bears, 47–7, in the championship game. Playing behind a talented line consisting of ends Andy Robustelli and Jim Katcavage, and tackles Rosey Grier and Dick Modzelewski in the Giants' modern 4–3 scheme, Huff came to personify a ferocious defense that propelled the Giants to appearances in five more title games in the coming seasons.

Lenny Moore, a star running back for the Colts in those days who went on to Hall of Fame distinction, said Huff was "tenacious" and clever. "People who have talent are able to detect and determine what other teams are going to do in given situations regardless of what defense is called. He had that instinct. He used all of his innate ability."

Meanwhile, Huff was glamorizing the middle linebacker position. In 1959, when named the NFL's outstanding lineman (linebackers were then considered linemen), he appeared on the cover of *Time* magazine, which described him as "a confident, smiling fighter, fired with a devout desire to sink a thick shoulder into every ball carrier in the NFL." The next year, CBS aired a documentary narrated by celebrated anchorman Walter Cronkite, "The Violent World of Sam Huff." Huff was wired for sound, and viewers heard heavy breathing and grunts, dirty talk in the huddle, threatening banter among players, and crunching tackles.

Huff was a fan favorite in New York, where chants of "Huff, Huff, Huff, Huff" reverberated through Yankee Stadium. They sounded "very much like the chugging of a huge steam engine," Giants publicity director Don Smith once wrote. Huff's glory ride in the Big Apple ended in April 1964. Coach Allie Sherman, who was trading stars from the Giants' defense like shuffling a deck of cards, dealt him to the Redskins for talented halfback and punt returner Dick James, defensive end Andy Stynchula, and a draft pick. Huff was furious at Sherman—a feeling that exists to this day—and hinted at quitting football:

"I didn't want to be traded from a championship team, a championship organization.," said Huff, who arrived in Washington the same year as future Hall of Fame quarterback Sonny Jurgensen. "We had just lost to the Bears in the [1963] championship, and the head coach gets rid of five guys on the defensive unit. Allie Sherman was an offensive-oriented coach, and he didn't like us because we were Tom Landry's team that he put together defensively.

"I'll never forget that trade. I look at my life in Washington and with the Redskins and can't forget what I've accomplished here. But at the time, the trade was very, very upsetting."

Huff delayed signing with the Redskins for more than two months. He recalled that Redskins coach Bill McPeak enticed him into playing for Washington by coming to his home in New York and offering him his No. 70 jersey. He also said the Redskins doubled his salary to about $35,000 and inserted a no-trade clause in his contract. Said Huff, "I said, 'This is where it ends. Nobody will ever trade me again.'"

The trade did little to tarnish his standing as one of the NFL's fiercest players, as evidenced by this *Washington Post* headline on April 12, 1964: "Sam Huff Enjoys His Reputation As Villain Who Jolts Fullbacks." With Huff on board, the Redskins' defense improved to No. 2 in the league in 1965. He made the Pro Bowl for the last time that year and remained a steady presence on the field until an ankle injury in 1967

## An Inseparable Duo

Sam and Sonny, two names that have resonated for years among Redskins fans like none other. They're an institution in the nation's capital.

You see, the two Hall of Famers have been teaming in the broadcast booth for more than a quarter-century as Redskins radio analysts. They're both of the rah-rah type, openly voicing support for the Redskins, but they can also be critical. They are so respected that listeners will turn down the volume on their TV sets to hear them instead.

Their partnership has created a tight personal bond. "We are so close," Huff said. "To me, there's not a better person than Sonny. I'm closer to him than I am my own brothers. I see a lot more of Sonny Jurgensen. People don't know really what a wonderful person he is. They like to think of him when he was young and a lot of the carousing and stuff he did. But I tell you what, he's a great person."

Agreed Jurgensen, "I enjoy analyzing the games and watching the games. That's because of the people I work with. Sam was a roommate when I came here in 1964. He's like a brother."

After arriving in D.C. in separate trades in the spring of 1964, the two played together for five seasons and then entered broadcasting after retirement, Huff in 1973 as a Redskins radio analyst for D.C. station WMAL and Jurgensen in 1975 as an NFL color analyst for CBS. They coalesced in 1981 calling Redskin games with play-by-play man Frank Herzog, a trio that stayed together for 23 seasons until Larry Michael replaced Herzog starting in the 2004 season. Their broadcasts are now heard on the Redskins Radio Network.

halted his streak of 150 straight games played. He retired after that season. But when an assistant coach from his Giants years and one of his mentors, the legendary Vince Lombardi, signed on in 1969 to coach the Redskins, the 34-year-old linebacker returned as a player-coach. The Redskins posted a 7–5–2 mark under Lombardi, their first winning season in 14 years, and Huff, the defensive captain, picked off three passes, returning one 18 yards for a touchdown.

"I thought the world of Lombardi and Tom Landry, they were such great, great people in the sports world," Huff said. "They had a great influence on my life."

Although Huff failed to realize the same level of success with the Redskins as he did in New York, he said his enthusiasm for football never waned in D.C.: "When I came to Washington, it was like a rebuilding program almost every year. So it was very frustrating to try to pull this whole thing together. But the great part about it was [quarterback] Sonny Jurgensen coming at the same time. He basically took up the offense, and I took up the defense, and we worked together to make it exciting and to do the best we could with this team."

After retiring for good, Huff spent one season coaching the Redskins' linebackers in 1970. He has been working in the radio booth as a Redskins color analyst for more than 30 years.

In 1995, Huff launched the Middleburg (Virginia) Broadcasting Network, which produces radio programs on the thoroughbred racing industry. He and partner Carol Holden are the voices for the show *Trackside*, which is broadcast on Washington, Virginia, and West Virginia stations. Huff, who has had a lifelong interest in horses, breeds thoroughbreds on his 22-acre farm in Middleburg.

## SONNY JURGENSEN

### Extraordinary Passer Rewrote NFL Record Books

QB, No. 9, Duke • 6–0, 202 • **NFL Career:** 1957–74 (18 seasons) • **Redskins Years:** 1964–74 (11) • **HOF Induction:** 1983 • NFL 1960s All-Decade Team • **Born:** August 23, 1934 (Wilmington, N.C.)

Mention Sonny Jurgensen's name to his teammates, opponents, or others who saw him pick defenses apart with relative ease, and you get virtually the same reaction: The man possessed a lightning-quick release and the ability to throw tight spirals with touch, speed, and accuracy. "His arm was an absolute trigger," said one of his Eagles teammates, Hall of Fame receiver Tommy McDonald.

Fellow Hall of Famer Bobby Mitchell, one of Jurgensen's key targets in Washington, explained: "The redhead could fire it. He'd put a ball between two defenders that you just didn't think was going to get there. You'd learn pretty quickly to go with your pattern and get those hands out there because it's coming. He could put it where you want it. Based on the defense and where people were playing, he knew when to put some steam on it, he knew when to pull back, so it made it easier for you to catch. When you talk about the artistic part of it, it was just amazing what Sonny could do with that football."

As for a defender, Packers Hall of Fame cornerback Willie Wood said, "Once his passes were in the air, that ball would be

spotless. You wouldn't see any wrinkles on it. The balls were very soft, and his receivers rarely dropped them."

Jurgensen's talents made him one the greatest pure passers to ever play the game, and arguably the best ever to wear the burgundy and gold. In his 18-year career, he posted some of the most prodigious stats in NFL history, amassing more than 32,000 yards and 255 touchdown passes, and connecting on 2,433 of 4,262 passes (57.1 completion percentage). He rang up most of his numbers in the nation's capital, where he spent his final 11 seasons after playing seven years in Philly.

Jurgy was most lethal in the 1960s, serving as the point man for one of the most prolific offenses in NFL history. So much of the squad's offensive production stemmed from his golden right arm, which compensated for a nonproductive running game and kept the Redskins in games although their defense yielded lots of points. Despite lacking solid protection, the classic pocket passer evaded rushers who knew he was going to pass, stayed calm, and deftly spotted receivers in a way that seemed supernatural at times. Defenders found it maddening trying to sack him.

"We were scared to death of Sonny," said Cowboys Hall of Fame defensive tackle Bob Lilly, whose defense was picked apart by Jurgensen in some classic games in the 1960s. "You never could trap him, he threw the ball too quickly. He could think real fast. He couldn't run real fast, so we didn't have to worry about that. But he didn't wait around to let the ball go. When we got off the ground to see where the ball was, usually one of the Redskins had it somewhere downfield."

Jurgensen's feats are all the more amazing because he played on only one winning team in D.C., until coach George Allen arrived in 1971. Then, when the Redskins began winning big

---

### Still Zippin' It

How hard and accurately could Sonny Jurgensen throw a football? His radio broadcaster partner, Sam Huff, learned firsthand some two decades after Jurgy had retired from the game:

One time before a game we were broadcasting at RFK [right before the Redskins moved to FedEx-Field in 1997], I walked down on the field, and Sonny's standing there with footballs and says, "Where in the hell have you been? ESPN wants to do a show on us and nobody knows where in the hell you've been. Get over there, I've got to throw you some balls." I want to tell you, he put that damn ball right on my nose. I caught about 10 of them right in the same spot, same speed every time. He said, "I didn't think you'd catch that damn thing that good." I said, "I had to catch it, you're throwing it right in my face." He had zip on that ball.

Said Jurgensen, "I was just zipping balls into him, and he was like, 'Whoaa!'"

Jurgensen accepts congratulations from center Len Hauss after putting on a masterful performance in a 20–17 win over Miami in 1974. No. 9 led the NFC in passing that year, the last of his 18 seasons in the NFL.

under Allen, Jurgy was jinxed by injuries that stunted his playing time. He started sparingly and was out of action in five of the Redskins' six postseason games from the 1971 to 1974 seasons, including their 14–7 loss to Miami in Super Bowl VII. Dolphins Hall of Fame receiver Paul Warfield said Miami may have had a much tougher time winning had Jurgensen played quarterback instead of Billy Kilmer.

After capturing the NFC passing title at age 40 in 1974, his final season, Jurgy was forced into retirement by Allen. The coach packaged Jurgensen's uniform for delivery to the Pro Football Hall of Fame, where the great No. 9 was enshrined in 1983.

Christian Adolph "Sonny" Jurgensen, a North Carolina native, played his college ball at Duke University. He rarely threw for the run-oriented Blue Devils but was named an All-Atlantic Coast Conference quarterback as a junior. At the time, Duke backfield coach Ace Parker, a terrific quarterback in the NFL's early years, called him "the finest pro quarterback prospect I've seen in years."

After his senior season, Jurgensen played in an all-star bowl game against a team that included an Oklahoma halfback named Tommy McDonald, who was mesmerized by Jurgy's potential. "I knew right off the bat . . . this guy is going to be something else, something else!" McDonald roared. "His numbers were H-A-L-L OF F-A-M-E!"

Jurgensen started for the Eagles as a rookie in 1957 but became a backup when Philly traded for legendary quarterback Norm Van Brocklin in 1958. Van Brocklin retired after the Eagles won a championship in 1960, opening the door for Jurgensen, who blossomed into a star. He threw for NFL highs of 235 completions, 3,723 yards and 32 touchdowns in 1961,

as the Eagles finished 10–4. McDonald, his favorite receiver, remembered seeing Jurgensen once complete a 20-yard pass behind his back.

Jurgy set a few Eagles passing records. In the 1964 off-season, with new coach Joe Kuharich overhauling the Eagles' roster, he was dealt to Washington for fourth-year quarterback Norm Snead. (The Redskins' Claude Crabb and the Eagles' Jimmy Carr, both defensive backs, also swapped teams in the deal.) Jurgensen remembered thinking that he didn't want to be traded: "I was shocked. It happened on April Fool's Day. Somebody told me, and I thought they were kidding, putting me on. I'd just met Kuharich, and I didn't know anything about it. But it was the best thing to happen to me."

"To this day, I'll never understand why Kuharich traded Sonny to the Redskins," said McDonald, who was also traded at the time. "[Redskins coach] Bill McPeak must have been the happiest person on Earth when he got Sonny. The Philly fans absolutely loved him. Who doesn't want that type of quarterback, my gosh?"

The deal resulted in one of the most lopsided trades in NFL history. While Jurgy built a Hall of Fame career in D.C., Snead was above average at best, a distinction that long infuriated Eagles fans. "Snead was not exactly welcomed with open arms," said NFL Films producer Ray Didinger, a long-time Eagles beat reporter. "Then Jurgensen put up huge numbers in Washington, and the fans kept saying, 'Look at what he's doing down there.' Norm always seemed to suffer in comparison."

Jurgensen arrived in Washington with the image of a free spirit and a happy-go-lucky playboy who missed curfews. But the man who drove a Mercedes Benz with the license plate tag SJ-9 told the press his reputation was not warranted. "The

## Jurgy's All-Time NFL Career Totals

- An 82.8 passer rating
- 32,224 yards passing and 255 touchdown passes
- 2,433 of 4,262 passes completed (57.1 completion percentage)
- Five seasons of 3,000 yards or more passing
- Five seasons leading the NFL in passing yards
- 25 300-yard games
- At least one scoring passing in 23 straight games
- A 99-yard touchdown pass*
- Selected for five Pro Bowls and four All-Pro teams

*Tied for first in NFL history

## Some of Jurgy's Redskins Records at Retirement

- Most passing yards, career (22,585)
- Most passing yards, season (3,747)
- Most pass attempts, career (3,155)
- Most pass attempts, season (508)
- Most pass attempts, game (50)
- Most pass completions, career (1,831)
- Most pass completions, game (32)
- Most pass completions, season (288)
- Highest completion percentage, career (58.0)*,†
- Best passer rating, career (85.0)*,†
- Most touchdown passes, season (31)*
- Longest pass play, game (99 yards, three-way tie)*
- Most consecutive games, touchdown pass (23)*
- Lowest interception percentage, career (5.9)*

*Record still stands
†Minimum 1,000 attempts

skins finished 7–5–2 in their only season under legendary coach Vince Lombardi. Lombardi thought that Jurgensen was much more talented than Bart Starr, who quarterbacked the Packers during their glory years under Lombardi in the 1960s.

Sam Huff, the Redskins' starting middle linebacker in 1969, remembers Lombardi saying in a coaches meeting, "You know, if I had that red head [Jurgensen] in Green Bay, we would have been declared a monopoly" in the NFL.

Now, one could argue that Jurgensen had a marked advantage over his peers because he had such great receivers in Charley Taylor and Bobby Mitchell, both now in the Hall of Fame, and tight end Jerry Smith, who had Hall of Fame credentials. One could also say Jurgy made his receivers much better. "Sonny was the ultimate quarterback for me," Taylor said. "The NFL had other quarterbacks like Johnny Unitas and Bart Starr, but Sonny was the guy. He had a feel for the game, a feel for what was happening. He made things easier for you. When he was down and out, you just hung in there with him, and he made sure the ball got there."

"I don't think anybody has ever played with a quarterback as accurate as Sonny," said wide receiver Roy Jefferson, who played with Jurgy in his last four years in Washington. "They can talk about all these great quarterbacks, and it's just sad that he didn't play on a winning team because he would be the man they talk about the most. They don't take into consideration the amount of points this guy put up on the board on bad Redskins teams in the 1960s."

# PAUL KRAUSE

## Record-Setting Safety Played Centerfield "Like Willie Mays"

S, No. 26, No. 22, Iowa • 6–3, 200 • **NFL Career:** 1964–79 (16 seasons) • **Redskins Years:** 1964–67 (4) • **HOF Induction:** 1998 • **Born:** February 19, 1942 (Flint, Mich.)

Since retiring after the 1979 season, Paul Krause has held one of the most coveted defensive records in NFL history: He's No. 1 in all-time interceptions with 81. That achievement, combined with his Hall of Fame induction in 1998, is a source of embarrassment for the Redskins.

Krause played his first four seasons in D.C., a stretch that included a league-high 12 interceptions as a rookie in 1964 and two Pro Bowl appearances. But the 6–3, 200-pound safety was gone after the 1967 season. The Redskins strangely shipped him to Minnesota, where he played his final 12 seasons, for linebacker Marlin McKeever and a seventh-round draft choice.

Why did the trade take place?

Redskins' defensive backfield coach Ed Hughes didn't think much of Krause's playing ability and persuaded coach Otto Graham to make the trade, according to Sam Huff, a Redskins middle linebacker and defensive captain during Krause's stay in Washington. Plus, team president Edward Bennett Williams, who admired Krause's ability, was out of town when Graham pushed the eject button. When Williams returned, there was nothing he could do. At the time, Krause, who had averaged *seven* interceptions in his first four seasons, was bitter about the deal. "I didn't care for Otto Graham," he said.

trouble is that I'm red-haired and people notice me wherever I go," he once said. "If I'm at a party or having dinner out somewhere, somebody recognizes me, and the next thing you know the story is around that I was out having a ball."

Jurgy's protruding belly was also a topic of conversation. When Otto Graham became the Redskins' coach in 1966, he wanted Jurgensen to report to training camp without his paunch. Jurgy obliged, losing about 30 pounds before the season to get down to 190. But he didn't take kindly to Graham's orders. "I don't throw with my stomach," he once told the coach.

Meanwhile, Jurgensen almost single-handedly filled the seats at D.C. Stadium, orchestrating a series of record-breaking games and comebacks for the otherwise mediocre Redskins. He won his first NFL passing crown in 1967, completing 288 of 508 passes for 3,747 yards, NFL records that have since been broken, plus 31 touchdowns and 16 interceptions, and chalked up another passing title in 1969, when the Red-

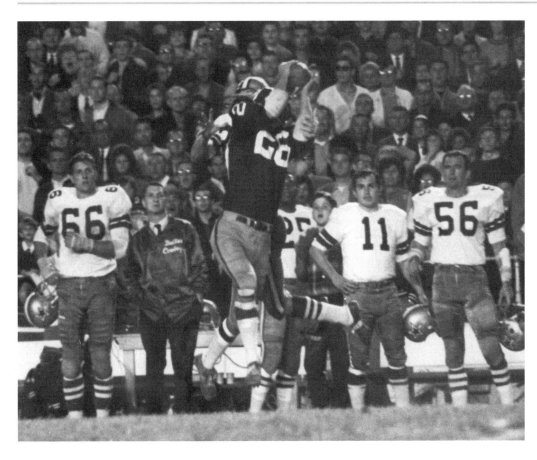

Krause leaps for an interception that preserved a 27–20 Redskin win over the Cowboys in 1967. Today, he holds the all-time NFL record for interceptions with 81.

"Graham listened to one of his defensive coaches who didn't know what he was doing. Then Graham traded me, so I don't think he knew what he was doing, either. He wasn't a great football coach."

The trade infuriated Huff, who had worked overtime to convince Graham to keep Krause. "I went to the coaching staff and said, 'Hey, I don't know what you guys have planned, but you don't ever want to trade a guy like Paul Krause,'" Huff said. "'He's a great football player. This guy can play weak-side safety like Willie Mays in centerfield.' They said he can't tackle and this and that. I said, 'I make all the tackles, that's what I get paid for.' They traded him anyway, and guess who has the most interceptions in the NFL. But what do coaches know."

Krause once played centerfield for real at the University of Iowa in the early 1960s, and he had a powerful throwing arm. "I remember one time playing Bradley University, I threw four guys out at home plate," he once said. Pro scouts drooled over his talents and tried luring him to the majors by offering lucrative contracts.

Krause, also a football star at Iowa, disdained the offers. But he badly damaged his shoulder in a football game against Michigan in his junior year. Unable to throw with the same velocity, he shelved his baseball aspirations and concentrated on football, developing into one of the best players in the Big Ten Conference. He picked off 12 passes combined in his junior and senior seasons (1962 and '63), and caught six touchdown passes as a senior to lead the Big Ten.

Drafted by the Redskins in the second round in 1964, he made an instant impact, showing soft hands and a keen sense of where quarterbacks place the ball. He picked off two passes in his first regular-season game and later that year recorded

interceptions in seven straight games, one of the longest such streaks in NFL history. It ended with two steals in a 36–31 win over the Giants on November 29, 1964, and gave him 12 with two games left. *Washington Post* sportswriter Byron Roberts wrote of Krause's sensational debut: "Like François Villon a prince of thieves," a reference to the French poet and thief from the 15th century.

Krause's 12 picks that year were two behind Dick "Night Train" Lane of the Los Angeles Rams (1952) and one behind Redskin Dan Sandifer (1948) in all-time single-season picks. He was named a consensus first-team All-Pro and a runner-up for NFL Rookie of the Year behind teammate Charley Taylor, and was selected to play in the Pro Bowl.

Krause, who made the Pro Bowl again in 1965 after intercepting six passes, said he liked playing for Redskins coach Bill McPeak. But McPeak was fired after the 1965 season and replaced by Graham, a Hall of Fame quarterback whose only head coaching experience was at the U.S. Coast Guard Academy. After two seasons under Graham, including a 1967 campaign when he picked off eight passes, Krause was traded to the Vikings.

"You throw that ball deep, Paul Krause was there," Huff said. "We used him to just play free safety, to just play the ball. To get as many turnovers as he did, that's what they drafted him for. Then they didn't like him. It doesn't take many moves like that before you say, 'What the hell's going on?'"

Krause played on mediocre teams in Washington. In Minnesota, he was a cornerstone on Vikings squads that made it to four Super Bowls (IV, VIII, IX, XI), losing each time. He manned the secondary on some of the best defenses in NFL history, including teams in the late 1960s and early 1970s that featured the "Purple People Eaters," the famed defensive line of Alan Page, Carl Eller, Gary Larsen, and Jim Marshall.

Krause was selected to play in six more Pro Bowls and intercepted another 53 passes in Minnesota, giving him a total of 81 by the time he retired after the 1979 season, two more than the former all-time leader, Giants great Emlen Tunnell. His 1,185 yards on interception returns is one of the highest totals in NFL history.

Krause said his key to intercepting so many throws rested with a combination of mental and physical prowess: "I knew what I could do, and I also knew the game very well. I also knew what the offense was trying to do to the defense. So I put myself in the positions I was supposed to be in to get the interceptions."

In hindsight, Krause would have liked to play for the Redskins his whole career. "But that's not the way it worked out," he said. "I had 12 good seasons with the Vikings, went to four Super Bowls, and had some great years. We had one of the best defenses ever to play football. That's why we won so many football games."

## WAYNE MILLNER

### "Money Player" Was One of NFL's First Great Receivers

E, No. 40, Notre Dame • 6–1, 189 • **NFL Career:** 1936–41, 45 (7 seasons) • **Redskins Years:** 1936–41, 45 (7) • **HOF Induction:** 1968 • NFL 1930s All-Decade Team • **Born:** January 31, 1913 (Roxbury, Mass.) • **Died:** November 19, 1976 (Arlington, Va.)

They called him the "Money Player." When the stakes were highest and the pressure the greatest, Wayne Millner had a knack for delivering.

Consider his two touchdown catches in the final two minutes of Notre Dame's come-from-behind 18–13 victory over Ohio State in 1935, a mythical "Game of the Century." Or his nine catches for 179 yards and two touchdowns in the Redskins' 28–21 win over Chicago in the 1937 championship, then the finest single-game receiving performance in NFL postseason history.

The win over the Bears was Millner's signature game in a seven-season NFL career that defined him as one of the league's first great receivers. He played end for the Redskins from 1936 to 1941 and, after a three-year break in the U.S. military during World War II, he returned for a final season in 1945. His totals of 124 catches for 1,578 yards and 12 touchdowns, paltry by today's standards, were all-time franchise records when he retired and helped propel Redskin squads that played in four NFL championship games, winning once.

Millner not only caught passes but also was a punishing blocker and tackler in the era of single-platoon football. The 6-foot, 190-pounder's diverse talents and feats earned him induction into the Pro Football Hall of Fame, which described him as a "great two-way player, a rock-'em, sock-'em performer on defense and a smooth, sure-fingered receiver when the Washington Redskins had the ball."

Millner was one of the favorite targets of the team's legendary passer of the era, Sammy Baugh. "He was not what you called a big end," Baugh once said. "[But] he was so quick, while he always was blocking his man. I always thought he did the best job of all the two-way ends of our time."

Wayne Millner and fellow Redskin great Cliff Battles were inducted into the Hall of Fame in 1968. Here, they hold a ball with the score of the game that decided the Eastern Division title in the Redskins' 1937 championship season. Millner caught two touchdown passes that day, and Battles rushed for 170 yards and scored two touchdowns of his own.

Redskins halfback Cliff Battles, who played with Millner in 1936 and 1937 and entered the Hall of Fame the same year as he, 1968, once said, "I always knew if I could get out into the open, Wayne would be there to throw a block for me. He would swing over from the weak side after making his initial block and hit a defensive back. Wayne's blocks determined whether or not I would get away for a long run."

Of course, Millner also had those big-play instincts, which were on display shortly after Notre Dame recruited him in 1933. That season, he blocked a punt and recovered it for a touchdown in the Fighting Irish's dramatic one-point victory over Army. Two years later, 5–0 Notre Dame trailed unbeaten and heavily favored Ohio State, 13–6, with less than two minutes left. After Millner's touchdown catch made it 13–12, the Irish recovered a Buckeyes fumble, and Notre Dame halfback Bill Shakespeare hit Millner in the end zone with 30 seconds left. The win helped build the Notre Dame mystique. Millner, a two-time All-American at Notre Dame, was voted into the College Football Hall of Fame in 1990.

The Boston Redskins selected Millner in the eighth round in 1936, allowing the Massachusetts native to play for a team close to home. Thrilled about acquiring him, Redskins coach Ray Flaherty sent a note to team owner George Preston Marshall that said, "With that big Yankee playing end, please accept my resignation if we do not win the championship this year!"

The Redskins fell short, losing to Green Bay in the 1936 championship game, before moving to Washington in 1937. Millner caught two touchdown passes in the Redskins' 49–14 rout of the Giants for the 1937 Eastern Division crown. In the championship game, the Bears built a 14–7 lead in the third period.

Welcome Millner time!

With the forward pass an evolving weapon in pro football, Millner caught a ball from Baugh in the flat and outraced defenders on Wrigley Field's frozen surface for a 55-yard touchdown play. Chicago regained the lead, 21–14. But Baugh connected with Millner on a similar play, and he outran the defense on a 77-yard play to tie the game. The Bears' defense began double- and triple-teaming Millner, so Baugh used him as a decoy and passed to fullback Ed Justice for the winning score in the fourth quarter. A sportswriter later asked Millner, who lacked blazing speed, how he ran so fast on his two scoring catches. "You'd run fast, too, if you had those big devils chasing you," he said, referring to Chicago's major size advantage.

Millner continued to be a key target for Baugh and other Redskin passers operating from the single-wing formation in the coming seasons. He posted career-highs of 294 receiving yards in 1939 and 22 catches in 1940. After the Redskins beat the Chicago Cardinals, 28–21, on October 13, 1940, one sports reporter wrote:

> Wayne Millner, all-professional end, played a marvelous game. His catching of Baugh's pass to tie the count was a masterful piece of work. Wayne cut to the far side of the gridiron, and then zig-zagged his course behind the Cardinals' defense to catch the ball in the "money-zone." But on receiving the leather, Wayne did the "Thurston the Magician" juggling act, and the spectators' hearts leaped every time the ball bounced, until he finally made the pay-off stab that tied the score.

After the 1941 season, his sixth in the league, Millner began serving in the U.S. Navy. He missed the next three seasons but returned in 1945 as a player-coach and then retired. In later years, he served as an assistant coach for the Redskins, the Eagles, the Baltimore Colts, Catholic University in D.C., and the University of Maryland. He was also the Eagles' head coach for the last 10 games of the 1951 season.

"He was one of the best," said Ace Parker, a Hall of Fame quarterback who played for the Brooklyn Dodgers during Millner's era. "He played offense and defense and could do everything. He was a good receiver."

## BOBBY MITCHELL

### Big-Play Threat Inflicted "Telling Damage" on Opponents

RB, WR, No. 49, Illinois • 6–0, 192 • **NFL Career:** 1958–68 (11 seasons) • **Redskins Years:** 1962–68 (7) • **HOF Induction:** 1983 • **Born:** June 6, 1935 (Hot Springs, Ark.)

Bobby Mitchell was in for a culture shock. A star running back for the Cleveland Browns in the late 1950s and early 1960s, he and his teammates would travel through Washington by bus when in D.C. to play the Redskins and see large numbers of black people in pockets of the city, thinking they would immediately embrace the first black player to join what was then the NFL's last all-white team. "We'd say, 'Man, this is super,'" he remembered.

It was anything but. Mitchell came to D.C. as part of a handful of black players to join the Redskins for the 1962 season after the U.S. government forced the Redskins to integrate. He found Washington to be a segregated city emblematic of the Old South, with many restaurants and other places that refused to admit blacks. His acceptance among both blacks and whites as a football player was not automatic, either:

> They hadn't had a black star here. So it was tough for everybody to accept that. Maybe it would have been a little better and easier for everybody if I'd come here as a Redskin draftee and then worked my way from there. But I came as a star, and a lot of people weren't ready for that. They didn't know how to handle it, both blacks and whites. I caught the devil from both sides. You can understand that blacks had been waiting for a black star for a long time, and they wanted me to be Superman. I couldn't do that. I made mistakes like everybody else out there.

Mitchell's exploits far outweighed his shortcomings. The veritable big-play threat, switched to flanker before the 1962 season, caught at least 58 passes in his first six years in Washington, once leading the league in catches and twice in receiving yardage. Blessed with exceptional speed and acceleration, uncanny faking ability, and terrific lateral moves and balance, he was twice named All-Pro and played in the Pro Bowl three times representing the burgundy and gold.

Mitchell's numbers were staggering by the time he retired in 1968 after 11 seasons. He gained 7,954 receiving and 2,735 rushing yards, plus 2,690 on kickoff returns and 699 on punt returns. His 14,078 combined yards were the third-highest total in NFL history at the time, and his 91 touchdowns ranked fifth. He was inducted in 1983 into the Pro Football Hall of Fame, which wrote, "Few offensive stars ever found more ways to inflict telling damage on a National Football League opponent than Bobby Mitchell."

"Bobby Mitchell was one of the greatest all-around ball players," said Baltimore Colts Hall of Famer Lenny Moore, who also switched from running back to receiver in the same era as Mitchell. "Anybody who can transition himself and be one of the best in the business at both positions, that's saying something, man."

Mitchell flourished after once feeling reluctant about pursuing a pro football career. After winning track honors at the University of Illinois, where he excelled in sprints, relays and hurdles, among other events, he considered training for the 1960 Olympics instead of playing in the NFL, although he had won Big Ten honors in his sophomore year as a running back. He played sparingly as a junior and senior due to injuries.

"I didn't care that much about football," he said. "I had loved it in high school, but my college career to me was disappointing. I was having such success in track that my track coach thought that once I turn my attention to it full time, we would do okay in the Olympics. The problem was it was 1958, and the Olympics weren't until 1960, so we had two years to train. Once I got convinced to try pro football, that was the end of that."

Mitchell was known in college as a fumbler, so Cleveland waited until the seventh round to draft him in 1958. Over the next four seasons he teamed with Jim Brown, perhaps the greatest running back in league history, and the two formed one of the finest backfield combinations ever. Brown dwarfed his teammate statistically, but the 6-foot, 195-pound Mitchell still averaged 574 yards rushing and 366 receiving during that four-year span, while returning three punts and three kickoffs for touchdowns. He tormented the Redskins, amassing 232

Mitchell was one of the favorite receiving targets of Redskin quarterbacks in the 1960s. He later served as a Redskins front-office executive for more than three decades.

yards rushing, five short of the NFL record held by Brown, and running for three scores in a 31–17 Cleveland win in 1959. He also rushed for three touchdowns in a 31–7 win over the Redskins in 1961.

But Cleveland coach Paul Brown yearned for another big back to pair with Jim Brown and eyed Ernie Davis, a bruising runner from Syracuse who won the Heisman Trophy in '61. The Redskins, who finished 1–12–1 in 1961, drafted Davis with the No. 1 pick and traded him to Cleveland for Mitchell and rookie running back Leroy Jackson, also an African American. "Ernie Davis didn't want to play for the Redskins because they didn't have any blacks," Mitchell said. "So Cleveland jumped on him thinking he was another Jim Brown. I was the commodity they had to give up in order to do that."

On December 15, 1961, the day after the trade, *Washington Post* sportswriter Shirley Povich wrote, "The Redskins' fascination for Mitchell, to the point of giving up the most publicized number one draft choice of the decade, is understandable. In the period since Mitchell abandoned his Olympic sprint ambitions and came into the league from U. of Illinois, he has wrecked the Washington team. The Redskins have scouted him mostly from the rear."

Shortly after the trade, Redskins coach Bill McPeak converted Mitchell to flanker, the position he desired to play coming out of college. The switch accelerated Mitchell's rise to stardom: "When I got here, we didn't have a good running attack, a good offensive line," Mitchell said. "But we did have a pretty good quarterback in Norm Snead, and [McPeak] brought this out to me, and we talked about it on my first day of training camp. I kind of pushed it a little bit, too. He asked me if I wanted to switch to outside, and I said yeah, although I didn't know if I could play it. I'd never played outside. After

several weeks Norm and I began to click and played real well together.

Mitchell thrived at the position, posting league-highs of 72 catches and 1,384 receiving yards in 1962, both franchise records, plus 11 touchdown catches. He also scored a team-high 72 points. In his first game as a Redskin, he zig-zagged through Cowboys defenders on a 92-yard kickoff return. The next week he showed his old buddies, the Browns, what they were missing. He didn't touch the ball for the first three quarters. But with Cleveland ahead, 16–10, and less than a minute to play, Snead hit him over the middle around midfield. Mitchell cut toward the sidelines, faked two defenders out of their shoes with a breathtaking stop-and-go move, and raced into the end zone. The Redskins won, 17–16.

"I'm running right at Paul Brown," Mitchell told NFL Films of the play. "It couldn't have been a better situation in life. I get to the sideline and, to this day when I see that film I say, 'God did that [fake] because I couldn't have done that. It is the most amazing move I've ever seen anyone do.'"

"He had all kinds of moves," said Don Bosseler, a great Redskins fullback at the time. "He could do all kinds of things out there, catch the ball, he was a good blocker, smart, had excellent speed. He was on top of me before I could get out of my stance, that's how quick he was." Redskins receiver Charley Taylor said Mitchell was "fast as lightning."

In 1963, Mitchell led the league in receiving yards with 1,436, breaking the Redskin record he set the year before. (Santana Moss broke his record in 2005.) He also caught a 99-yard touchdown pass, an NFL-long that has been accomplished several times over. In the coming years, Mitchell continued posting big numbers for the Redskins as part of one of the most lethal offensive attacks in NFL history. In one season, 1967, Taylor was first, tight end Jerry Smith second, and Mitchell fourth in receptions in the league.

Mitchell retired after the 1968 season, but legendary coach Vince Lombardi, hired by the Redskins before the 1969 campaign, influenced him to stay on in a front-office capacity. At the time, "Blacks weren't doing much of anything in the front office," Mitchell said.

He remained with the Redskins for another three-plus decades, a period when the Redskins went to five Super Bowls, winning three times. His titles ranged from director of pro scouting to assistant to the president to assistant general manager, a slot he accepted in 1981 and held until his retirement in 2003. He was also associated with many civic and charity groups in Washington. In 2000, a state-of-the-art football field in a disadvantaged neighborhood in D.C. was named Bobby Mitchell Field in recognition of his contributions to football and youth in the city.

"I'm very, very fortunate to have stayed with the same team for so many years," Mitchell said. "It's something that just doesn't happen. I consider it sort of my reward for staying and handling the tests and being the good guy, the whole works."

## JOHN RIGGINS

### Bruising Running Back Doubled as a Premier Entertainer

RB, No. 44, Kansas • 6–2, 235 • **NFL Career:** 1971–79, 81–85 (14 seasons) • **Redskins Years:** 1976–79, 81–85 (9) • **HOF Induction:** 1992 • NFL 1980s All-Decade Team • **Born:** August 4, 1949 (Seneca, Kan.)

John Riggins was more than a football player. He was an entertainer who relished the spotlight. Whether by graciously bowing to a cheering crowd at RFK Stadium after running for 185 yards in a playoff game, unexpectedly appearing in a tuxedo at a pre-Super Bowl party thrown by Redskins owner Jack Kent Cooke, or captivating the masses with his wit, sarcasm, charm, self-deprecating humor, and puckish smile, Riggins had a tremendous stage presence.

He specialized in amusing off-the-cuff remarks, such as his unforgettable line on returning to the Redskins after sitting out the 1980 season: "I'm bored, I'm broke, and I'm back." He also made the bold proclamation, "Ron may be President, but I'm the king," after President Reagan called to congratulate the Redskins for winning Super Bowl XVII, when Riggins earned MVP honors with a Super Bowl–record 166 yards rushing.

"John as an athlete had a great stage presence," said Joe Gibbs, who coached Riggins in Washington for five seasons. "He knew just when to say the right thing."

Some of Riggins's actions, though, irritated Redskins management and coaches. He publicly admitted being a "baaaddddd boy" after a 1985 off-season during which he was arrested on a drunk-in-public charge and, apparently intoxicated at another event, told Supreme Court Justice Sandra Day O'Connor to "loosen up, Sandy baby" and fell asleep on the floor while Vice President George Bush was giving a speech.

All along, Riggins marched to the beat of his own drum, as the saying goes, and did whatever pleased him at that very moment, no matter how ridiculous or inappropriate it might seem. After all, he was just being John Riggins.

"Everything I have done has been in fun," Riggins, who has pursued stage acting and sports broadcasting careers in his post-football life, once said. "I see myself as an entertainer, and the football field as my stage. If there wasn't anyone in the stadium, I wouldn't be there. What makes it fun is the cheering of the crowd, the fans."

"He was somehow a New Yorker who grew up in Kansas," said long-time *Sports Illustrated* NFL writer Paul Zimmerman, referring to Riggins's glibness. "I don't know how God did that."

Riggins's eccentricities aside, he was all business on the field. The 6–2, 240-pounder, a rare combination of size, speed, and power, proved to be one of the greatest backs in league history, specializing in running between the tackles. He stood in the top five in all-time NFL rushing yards (11,352), carries (2,916), and touchdowns (104) by the time he retired in 1985 after a 14-year career.

Riggo spent his first five seasons with the Jets and his last nine in Washington, where he set a series of team records. They include a 7,472-yard rushing total that is in no danger of being broken anytime soon, the most carries in team history (1,988), and the most 1,000-yard seasons (four). Amazingly, No. 44 rushed for more than half of his yards after turning 30, a time when most running backs are unable to produce at the pace they did in prior years.

"We had him toward the end of his career," Gibbs said. "I would surely liked to have coached him at 25–26–27. Of course, he might not be able to walk today because he'd have gotten the ball so many times. He was a star and a hallmark of what we did and made a lot of great plays for us. When he got his jaw set, he was something special."

"He was one of those old farm boys from Kansas," said Ron Saul, a Redskin guard who played with Riggins for six seasons. "He was one of those guys you'd hit over the head with a two-by-four, and he'd say, 'Why'd you do that?' And you'd go, 'Oh God.' John was a tough, tough guy. We all knew that when they called number 44, no matter how slow he got up from the play

The eccentric John Riggins

Riggins holds the Redskins' record for rushing yards with 7,472.

before, he was going to give you everything he had. When his number was called, he was going to give you six seconds of some hellacious adrenaline no matter what. He never took a play off. And if they asked him to block, he'd knock out a damn linebacker. He was the type of guy you wanted to be in a foxhole with."

Riggins was also a super-talented athlete as a kid. Reared on a farm in Centralia, Kansas, a town of about 500 people, he starred in football at Centralia High School, playing running back and other positions, and finished as a two-time state 100-yard dash champion, showing 9.8 speed with his 215-pound frame. His father, Gene Riggins, felt he was best at basketball.

At the same time, Riggins exhibited the clownish behavior that would become his trademark in future years. "I look back on those days," he said in *Sports Illustrated* on September 1, 1983, "and I think of the real me as a kind of jerk. Kick the basketball around and run around the court trying to pull a guy's pants down, throw the ball at the guy's head and yell 'Catch!' as it hits him in the nose. Hang around in the back of the huddle and chitchat, cause distractions, get my share of . . . laughs. I'm still that way."

Riggins played college football at the University of Kansas. He ran for 2,706 yards, including 1,131 as a senior, and topped most of the school rushing records set earlier in the 1960s by Gale Sayers, the "Kansas Comet," who went on to a Hall of Fame career with the Bears.

In 1971, the Jets made Riggins their No. 1 draft pick and the sixth overall selection. He led the squad in rushing and receiving as a rookie, although injuries slowed his progress in the coming years. But in 1975, he logged 1,005 rushing yards, caught 30 passes for 363 yards, and made the Pro Bowl for the first and only time in his career. He also attracted attention with his unorthodox hairstyles, one year sporting an afro and the next a Mohawk with an arrow down the middle of his scalp.

"Initially, you knew he was a character just by the way he carried himself," said Hall of Fame Jets quarterback Joe Namath, a free spirit in his own right. "I remember John from his Mohawk days and his motorcycle. He painted his toenails before a game. I thought that was cute. [Jets] Green, of course. He was eccentric, but as a teammate he was sensational. I never played a game with him when he wasn't prepared."

A free agent after the 1975 season, Riggins left New York and went south to the nation's capital, where Redskins coach George Allen signed him to a five-year, $1.5 million deal, an extraordinary contract at the time in the NFL. Washington's running game was halfback-oriented, and Riggins, used as a blocking back in the I-formation, gained 775 yards over the next two seasons. He played in only five games in 1977 because of a sprained knee.

Jack Pardee's entrance as Redskins coach in 1978 rejuvenated Riggins's career, and he posted 1,000-yard seasons in 1978, when he was named NFL Comeback Player of the Year, and in 1979. In the last game of the '79 season, Riggins outraced the entire Cowboys secondary for a career-long 66-yard touchdown run. "He was an incredibly fast man for his size," said Redskins quarterback Joe Theismann, who played with Riggo in his nine seasons in D.C.

After the season, Riggins wanted to negotiate for more money with a year left on his contract. But the Redskins balked, and he retired from the game just before the 1980 campaign. "I was tired and weary," Riggins told *Sports Illustrated* in 1983. "So why not pull your horns in? Why risk a broken neck? What was easy for everyone to understand was that here was Mr. Greedo asking for more money. Wants more, can't have it, must get out. I think now that what I was really doing was looking for an excuse to get out. If they'd said, 'O. K., you win, here's the money you want,' I think I'd have said, 'Ooooh, wait a second.'"

Leaving football stretched Riggins's pockets thin. So he returned for the 1981 season and gained 714 yards while splitting duties with halfback Joe Washington in Gibbs's single-back setup. But an injury to Washington in the 1982 preseason left Riggins as the primary back.

"The Diesel" grandly took his cue. In the 1982 postseason, he pieced together one of the most memorable stretches for a running back in NFL postseason history, carrying 136 times for 610 yards and four touchdowns in the four-game Super Bowl Tournament. He punctuated his feat by pulling off the most famous play in Redskins history, a 43-yard touchdown run on fourth-and-1 that gave Washington the lead for good in Super Bowl XVII. On the play, Riggo headed toward the left side behind the Hogs, Washington's powerful offensive line, and broke free en route to the end zone.

"It's great to go back and watch that play because people never thought John was fast, because he wasn't flashy," said offensive tackle Russ Grimm, the left guard on the play. "But they failed to realize he was a two-time, state 100-yard dash champ in high school. Straight ahead, he could run with anybody."

Riggins simply wore defenses down in the 1982 playoffs, gaining 253 of his yards in the fourth quarter. He earned the nickname "Mr. January."

"John was a horse," Theismann said. "His strength was his ability to get better and better with each game, with each carry."

Said Saul, "He'd just keep coming and coming at the same speed. In the first half, the other guys would stop him for 35 yards. But every time they hit him, it hurt. So all at once, they couldn't take the shots and would start ducking their heads, and he'd just start running right through those shoulder pads.

A lot of times, he'd get 35 yards in the first half and 80 in the second."

Riggins remained the primary engine of the Redskins' offense in the coming seasons, as opposing defenses got a regular dose of "Rigginomics." He enjoyed a banner season in 1983, rushing for a career-high 1,347 yards and an all-time NFL record 24 touchdowns, a mark since broken. He went 685 carries without a fumble until week 5 of the 1983 season. Following that season, he was named All-Pro for the first time in his career.

Riggo topped the 1,000-yard mark for the fifth time with 1,239 in 1984, when at age 35 he became the oldest player ever to rush for 1,000 yards. But his once indestructible body began to deteriorate, and back problems curtailed his playing time in 1985. He reluctantly retired after the season and was inducted into the Hall of Fame in 1992. He chose NFL Commissioner Paul Tagliabue, whom he barely knew, to present him in Canton.

As to why: "When you're getting married, you get a priest; when you're getting inducted, you get a commissioner," he said, noting that pop star Madonna had a headache and couldn't make the ceremony.

Sounds so Riggin-esque.

## CHARLEY TAYLOR

### Rugged Receiver, Great Open-Field Runner Tormented Defenses

RB, WR, No. 42, Arizona State • 6–3, 215 • **NFL Career:** 1964–77 (14 seasons) • **Redskins Years:** 1964–77 (14) • **HOF Induction:** 1984 • NFL 1960s All-Decade Team • **Born:** September 28, 1941 (Grand Prairie, Tex.)

Yes, Charley Taylor could catch passes. That he hauled in 649 in his 14-year career, once sitting No. 1 in the NFL record books, validates him as one of the best ever at doing so.

But what he did *after* catching the ball elevated him to an even loftier plane in NFL and Redskins lore. A running back for his first two and a half seasons, the 6–3, 215-pound Taylor was a great open-field runner who repeatedly converted short passes into long touchdown runs. He outhustled and outmuscled opponents and posted an assortment of dazzling moves that left defenders in disarray. He was often unstoppable.

"Once he caught the ball, nobody could tackle him," said Bobby Mitchell, a flanker who teamed with Taylor for five seasons. "He had quick movements and was shifty, and he'd just walk away from people once he got in the open."

Said NFL Films president Steve Sabol, "Charley Taylor was fantastic at taking a short pass over the middle and running with the ball through a broken field. He was maybe the best ever at gaining yards after the catch. He had some incredible runs. Tackler after tackler missed him. People forget he was once a running back. If they'd have kept the statistic of yards after the catch in his era, he would have some all-time records."

Taylor, who played his whole career in Washington, churned out 9,110 receiving yards, one of several accomplishments that rank him among the game's elite. He caught 79 touchdown passes, the No. 1 mark today in Redskins history, and is also first in total touchdowns (90). He earned first- or second-team

All-NFL honors six times and was selected to play in eight Pro Bowls. The Pro Football Hall of Fame honored him in 1984.

More than glitz and glamour, Taylor was a powerful blocker who manhandled defenders. He is remembered—albeit not too fondly by his victims—for perfecting the crackback block, which called for coming across the middle and blocking a linebacker or safety in hopes of eliminating them from the play and springing a ball carrier for a long run. Although the crackback was regarded at the time as a dirty below-the-waist block, Taylor said he never took cheap shots and always aimed for defenders in the chest.

"I'll tell you, man, he took down a lot of linebackers," said middle linebacker Sam Huff, a teammate of Taylor's in Washington for five seasons. "When he took them down, they went down. When Charley Taylor was out there, you looked to see who was there."

Huff, a bone-rattler in his own right, felt Taylor's toughness during the Redskins' training camp in 1964, Taylor's rookie year: "He went over the middle, and I decked him and said, 'Look, I could have really hurt you,'" Huff remembered. " 'You've got to look and see where those linebackers are so you can dodge them.' He was lying on his back and didn't say anything. When we scrimmaged a few days later, he hit me, and I flipped through the air. When I came down, I was lying on the ground, and he's standing over me saying, 'I've wanted to do that since high school.' I said, 'Okay, we're even.'"

Taylor, a Texas native, played his college ball at Arizona State and was an All-Western Athletic Conference halfback. The Redskins selected him with the No. 3 pick in the 1964 draft, and Taylor quickly showed signs of his pro potential. In a 28–17 loss in the College All-Star game to the defending NFL champion Chicago Bears, he rushed for more than 5 yards a carry, passed 14 yards for a TD, caught a 5-yard scoring pass, recovered two fumbles and, to top it off, was named the game's MVP.

He gave the amazing performance after his coach, Hall of Fame quarterback and U.S. Coast Guard Academy coach Otto Graham, made a pregame remark that the rookie was "very lazy."

"That was his excuse . . . he wanted to play me as a defensive back, not a running back," Taylor said of Graham. "A couple of running backs got knocked out. So I had to go in there."

At Taylor's inaugural training camp, Redskins coach Bill McPeak put him at defensive back. But when running back Tom "The Bomb" Tracy suffered an injury, Taylor replaced him in the backfield. He was an immediate hit, rushing for a team-high 755 yards that season and catching 53 passes—a record at the time for running backs—for another 814 yards. He was named NFL Rookie of the Year after becoming the first rookie in two decades to finish in the top 10 in rushing and receiving.

"When I got here, I was the best thing since sliced bread," Taylor said. "They had never seen anything like me before."

The Redskins, penning accolades about the rookie in their 1964 game programs, thought so, too:

- "The Arizona Kid, Charley Taylor, continues to blaze a trail through the National Football League unmatched by any rookie to ever wear the Redskins burgundy and gold."
- "Charley gives the Redskins' backfield something it has lacked for at least 15 years—a truly great running threat. This rookie from Arizona State is a big man in every way: He stands 6-feet-3, weighs 212 pounds and boasts the speed

Taylor was once the NFL's all-time leading receiver with 649 receptions. He also was a load for defenders to bring down. "Once he caught the ball, nobody could tackle him," one teammate said.

of a sprinter and an eel's elusiveness. He is Mr. Inside and Outside."

- "Except for kicking, Charley does about everything—he runs with a reckless abandon that has terrorized the (NFL) Eastern Division; he catches passes with the aplomb of a [Bobby] Mitchell; and when the occasion calls, he passes himself."

At the time, Taylor dreamed of becoming the next Jim Brown, then the league's premier running back and perhaps the best ever. "Every young player coming in during that time wanted to be like the man because he was awesome," Taylor said. "He was a fantastic player. Why not pattern yourself after him?"

It wasn't to be. Taylor's old adversary, Otto Graham, who became the Redskins' coach before the 1966 season, moved him to split end seven games into the year. Taylor said Graham was impressed that his star running back could find openings downfield as a receiver and gain lots of yardage after catching the ball. The coach also wanted a backfield featuring 225-pounders Joe Don Looney and Steve Thurlow, Taylor noted.

Taylor, who rushed for nearly 1,500 yards in his career, said he initially felt a "fear" of playing on the outside. Working one-on-one with Mitchell and watching game films of Colts great Lenny Moore, two players who made the same transition before him, eased the switch, he acknowledged.

The transition, in fact, was seamless for No. 42. With balls aimed his way from the accurate arm of quarterback Sonny Jurgensen, he led the NFL in receiving in 1966 (72 catches, 1,119 yards, 12 touchdowns) and 1967 (70 catches, 990 yards, nine touchdowns). In the latter year, he played in his fourth Pro Bowl in as many seasons.

"Charley was the go-to guy," said Steve Gilmartin, the Redskins' radio play-by-play man at the time. "In other words, if you want to pull out a ball game, 'Where's Charley, where's number 42?' He was a warrior, a tremendous player . . . big, fast, aware of everything on the field."

In the coming seasons, Taylor remained one of the league's premier receivers, despite enduring an assortment of injuries that short-circuited his playing time. He averaged 54 catches

on a mostly run-oriented offense from 1972 to 1975 and set the NFL's all-time reception record with his 634th catch on December 21, 1975, a mark that has been broken several times over. His 1975 season capped another string of four straight Pro Bowl appearances.

All the while, Taylor's rugged body allowed him to thrive in an era when defenders enjoyed wide latitude for hitting receivers, who could be jammed at the line or knocked off stride in the middle of a pattern, tactics that are illegal today. Taylor outwitted and outworked those covering him.

"I wasn't as fast as a lot of those guys," he said. "But I would say, 'We've got to play four quarters. In the fourth quarter, I'm going to be at the same speed as I was in the first. I'm going to wear that [defensive back] down to where we've both got the same speed.' That's the way I'd approach the game. 'Hey, you might run with me in the first quarter. But the fourth quarter is going to be mine.'"

Furthermore, Taylor said, a look into the defender's eyes signaled whether No. 42 would have a great game. "You lined up against [Hall of Famer] Lem Barney, and Lem is looking you dead in the eye, and you're going, 'This guy's got his mind made up. He's done his homework. He knows what he wants to do.' But you go up against a guy who looks in the backfield, looks back at you, looks over there. He's undecided about what the hell he wants to do on this play or the next play. Those kinds of guys you're sort of like, 'I got this guy.'"

After missing the 1976 season due to a shoulder injury, Taylor caught 14 passes in 1977 and called it quits. Two years later, he became a Redskins scout and helped spot Syracuse running back-receiver Art Monk, who was drafted by the Redskins in 1980 and eventually became the NFL all-time leader in total catches, a mark that has been broken. In addition to Monk, Taylor molded such receivers as Charlie Brown, Gary Clark, and Ricky Sanders into great players while coaching the Redskins' receivers from 1981 to 1993.

Today, Taylor leaves no doubt that he still bleeds burgundy and gold. "I had a wonderful relationship with the Redskins for almost 30 years," he said. "I took care of them, and they took care of me."

# 10

# Best of the Rest

SOME 1,400 PLAYERS have donned the burgundy and gold in the storied 75-year history of the Washington Redskins—men who have appeared in regular-season games or who have otherwise earned a spot on the official roster. Many others have made brief appearances in training camp and exhibition games, only to be cut.

They've come in all shapes and sizes, from all types of colleges, big and small, and from a cross-section of America, whether it's the coal- and steel-mining town of West Brownsville, Pennsylvania (Chuck Drazenovich), the mean streets of New York City (Vince Promuto), the Gulf city of Pascagoula, Mississippi (Diron Talbert), the California town of Palo Alto (Wilbur Wilkin), or even Alaska (Mark Schlereth). Some have hailed from other parts of the world, such as Canada, Sweden, American Samoa, Iran, and France.

In this chapter, you'll read about more than 100 Redskins who deserve special recognition for their achievements on the field. (Hall of Famers are featured in Chapter 9.) The careers of some have been much more celebrated than others, but in one way or another, they've all left their own unique mark on Redskins history.

## JOHN ADAMS

T, No. 42, Notre Dame • 6–7, 242 • **NFL Career:** 1945–49 (5 seasons) • **Redskins Years:** 1945–49 (5) • **Born:** September 22, 1921 (Charleston, Ark.) • **Died:** August 20, 1969 (Bethesda, Md.)

A Bunyanesque player competed for the Redskins in the 1940s. John "The Tree" Adams shined at tackle for five seasons, winning first- and second-team All-Pro honors in 1945 and 1946.

The towering man was a second-round draft pick of the Redskins in 1945 after starring at Notre Dame. In her 1947 book, *My Life with the Redskins,* Corrine Griffith wrote that she was in awe when he reported to the team. "The tallest gray suit I've ever seen walked in," wrote Griffith, wife of then-Redskins owner George Preston Marshall. "The suit, itself, was 5-feet-10 inches tall without a head or feet, and with its head and feet, it was 6-feet-7 inches—without shoes. The shoes added another inch, making it 6-feet-8 inches . . . 'Well, I'm back.' It was John 'The Tree' Adams from Ozark, Arkansas. He was named 'The Tree' because of his great height and terrific arm spread."

Adams possessed a distinct voice, too. In a press guide, the Redskins wrote that if he grew a beard, he would "out-Lincoln" Raymond Massey, a Canadian actor who could sound like President Abraham Lincoln.

Adams played in 55 games. A right tackle on offense, he opened holes for such runners as Dick Todd and Wilbur Moore, and gave quarterback Sammy Baugh time to pass.

## JOE AGUIRRE

OE-DE, No. 19, St. Mary's (California) • 6–4, 225 • **NFL Career:** 1941, 43–45 (4 seasons) • **Redskins Years:** 1941, 43–45 (4) • **Born:** October 17, 1918 (Rock Springs, Wyo.) • **Died:** July 13, 1985 (Grass Valley, Calif.)

Joe Aguirre is remembered most in Redskins lore for missing two late field goals in a one-point loss to Cleveland in the 1945 NFL championship game.

There was much more, however, to his four-year Redskin career. An end, he tallied 169 points on 13 touchdown receptions, 13 field goals, and 52 extra points, while catching 97 passes for 1,222 yards. He stood as one of the team's all-time leading scorers and receivers for some time.

Aguirre finished second in the league in receiving in 1943. He was a unanimous All-Pro in 1944, catching 34 passes for 210 yards and four touchdowns. Late that season, Al Costello of the *Washington Post* wrote that Aguirre was the best end in football at the time:

> Maybe [Green Bay's] Don Hutson is a better pass receiver; perhaps George Wilson of the Bears is a better blocker; possibly O'Neal Adams of the Giants is better defensively; but wrap all the requisites of a good football player—and end—into one package, and if it isn't Joe Aguirre, it's at least a reasonably exact facsimile.
>
> Take last Sunday, for instance, Joe scored the first 14 points to give the 'Skins a 14–0 lead at halftime. He took passes from [Frankie] Filchock to score and kicked both points. But it wasn't that so much as the way he eluded the Chi-Pitt defense both times with brilliant bits of deception that not only permitted himself to be as free as a bird but made himself an almost unmissable target for Filchock. He was, to put it mildly, terrific.

In 1945, Aguirre again earned All-Pro honors before leaving for the new All-America Football Conference, where he played four years with the Los Angeles Dons.

## 70 Greatest Redskins

In 2002, to honor the Redskins' 70th anniversary, a blue-ribbon panel selected the 70 greatest Redskins of all time, a group of players and coaches who were significant on-field contributors to the team's history.

| # | Name | Position | Redskins Years |
|---|------|----------|----------------|
| 21 | Terry Allen | RB | 1995–98 |
| 41 | Mike Bass | CB | 1969–75 |
| 20 | Cliff Battles | B | 1932–37 |
| 33 | Sammy Baugh | QB | 1937–52 |
| 31 | Don Bosseler | B | 1957–64 |
| 53 | Jeff Bostic | C | 1980–93 |
| 4 | Mike Bragg | P | 1968–79 |
| 80 | Gene Brito | DE | 1951–53, 55–58 |
| 43 | Larry Brown | RB | 1969–76 |
| 77 | Bill Brundige | DE | 1970–77 |
| 65 | Dave Butz | DT | 1975–88 |
| 21 | Earnest Byner | RB | 1989–93 |
| 84 | Gary Clark | WR | 1985–92 |
| 51 | Monte Coleman | LB | 1979–94 |
| 53 | Al DeMao | C | 1945–53 |
| 36 | Chuck Drazenovich | LB | 1950–59 |
| 35 | Bill Dudley | RB | 1950–51, 53 |
| 17 | Turk Edwards | T | 1932–40 |
| 44 | Andy Farkas | FB | 1938–44 |
| 37 | Pat Fischer | CB | 1968–77 |
| 28 | Darrell Green | CB | 1983–2002 |
| 68 | Russ Grimm | G | 1981–91 |
| 55 | Chris Hanburger | LB | 1965–78 |
| 57 | Ken Harvey | LB | 1994–98 |
| 56 | Len Hauss | C | 1964–77 |
| 27 | Ken Houston | S | 1973–80 |
| 70 | Sam Huff | LB | 1964–67, 69 |
| 66 | Joe Jacoby | T/G | 1981–93 |
| 47 | Dick James | RB | 1956–63 |
| 9 | Sonny Jurgensen | QB | 1964–74 |
| 22 | Charlie Justice | RB | 1950, 52–54 |
| 17 | Billy Kilmer | QB | 1971–78 |
| 26 | Paul Krause | DB | 1964–67 |
| 79 | Jim Lachey | T | 1988–95 |
| 14 | Eddie LeBaron | QB | 1952–53, 55–59 |

| # | Name | Position | Redskins Years |
|---|------|----------|----------------|
| 72 | Dexter Manley | DE | 1981–89 |
| 71 | Charles Mann | DE | 1983–93 |
| 58 | Wilbur Marshall | LB | 1988–92 |
| 73 | Mark May | T | 1981–89 |
| 79 | Ron McDole | DE | 1971–78 |
| 63 | Raleigh McKenzie | G | 1985–94 |
| 53 | Harold McLinton | LB | 1969–78 |
| 40 | Wayne Millner | E | 1936–41, 45 |
| 49 | Bobby Mitchell | FL | 1962–68 |
| 30 | Brian Mitchell | RB | 1990–99 |
| 81 | Art Monk | WR | 1980–93 |
| 3 | Mark Moseley | K | 1974–86 |
| 29 | Mark Murphy | S | 1977–84 |
| 21 | Mike Nelms | KR | 1980–84 |
| 52 | Neal Olkewicz | LB | 1979–89 |
| 23 | Brig Owens | DB | 1966–77 |
| 65 | Vince Promuto | G | 1960–70 |
| 44 | John Riggins | RB | 1976–79, 81–85 |
| 11 | Mark Rypien | QB | 1987–93 |
| 83 | Ricky Sanders | WR | 1986–93 |
| 76 | Ed Simmons | T | 1987–97 |
| 87 | Jerry Smith | TE | 1965–77 |
| 60 | Dick Stanfel | G | 1956–58 |
| 74 | George Starke | T | 1973–84 |
| 72 | Diron Talbert | DT | 1971–80 |
| 84 | Bones Taylor | E | 1947–54 |
| 42 | Charley Taylor | WR | 1964–77 |
| 7 | Joe Theismann | QB | 1974–85 |
| 67 | Rusty Tillman | LB | 1970–77 |
| 85 | Don Warren | TE | 1979–92 |
| 25 | Joe Washington | RB | 1981–84 |
| 17 | Doug Williams | QB | 1986–89 |
| | George Allen | Head Coach | 1971–77 |
| | Ray Flaherty | Head Coach | 1936–42 |
| | Joe Gibbs | Head Coach | 1981–92 |

## KI ALDRICH

C-LB, No. 55, Texas Christian • 6–0, 207 • **NFL Career:** 1939–42, 45–47 (7 seasons) • **Redskins Years:** 1941–42, 45–47 (5) • **Born:** June 1, 1916 (Rodgers, Tex.) • **Died:** March 12, 1983 (Temple, Tex.)

During Ki Aldrich's years in the NFL, there were centers who won more prestigious postseason honors, such as the Giants' Mel Hein, the Bears' Bulldog Turner, and the Packers' Charley Brock. Aldrich was outstanding in his own right, however. He was a rugged center and linebacker who averaged 50 minutes a game most seasons and never missed a game in his seven-year career, the last five with the Redskins.

"The Redskins have had some great centers in their 22-year history, but none better than Charles (Ki) Aldrich," Morris A. Bealle wrote in his book, *The Redskins: 1937–1958.*

Aldrich, who was Sammy Baugh's center for one season at Texas Christian, was an All-American in 1938 when the Horned Frogs finished 11–0 and won the national championship. He also played linebacker. TCU coach Dutch Meyer called him "the best man I've ever seen at sizing up plays." He was named to the College Football Hall of Fame in 1960.

The Chicago Cardinals drafted Aldrich in the first round in 1939, when the rookie received All-Pro recognition. He was traded to Washington in 1941, reunited with Baugh, and was a major contributor to the Redskins' 1942 NFL championship team. He missed the next two seasons while serving in the U.S. Navy during World War II but returned with six games left in the 1945 campaign and earned second-team All-Pro honors. He retired after the '47 season.

## TERRY ALLEN

RB, No. 21, Clemson • 5–11, 208 • **NFL Career:** 1991–2002 (12 seasons) • **Redskins Years:** 1995–98 (4) • **Born:** February 21, 1968 (Commerce, Ga.)

Terry Allen's story is one of fortitude: He recovered twice from major knee injuries to post 1,000-yard rushing seasons, a remarkable feat in the NFL. One reconstructive surgery was on his right knee, the other on his left knee, and both involved serious ligament tears. Doctors told him that his career might be over, but he refused to hang up his cleats, instead pursuing rigorous rehabilitation programs.

"I thought about [quitting] a lot of times," he said in *USA Today* in 1996. "My family wouldn't let me. It was like, 'You never quit anything before in your life. I don't know why you want to give up now.'"

Allen's resilience benefited the Redskins. The grind-it-out back rushed for 1,309 yards in 1995, his first season with the club, and a team-record 1,353 in 1996, when he made his only Pro Bowl appearance in a 12-year career. He led the Redskins in rushing in each of his four seasons in Washington and posted 4,086 yards, one of the highest totals in team history.

Allen also suffered knee damage at Clemson, and his health concerned NFL scouts. He lasted until the ninth round in 1990 and was drafted by the Vikings. He tore a knee ligament in the preseason and sat out the year but rushed for a Vikings-record 1,201 yards in 1992. He missed the following season after rupturing a knee ligament in training camp, only to pile up 1,031 yards in 1994.

The Vikings cut Allen, and he signed with the Redskins as an unrestricted free agent. The 5–11, 208-pounder sparked Washington's running attack. His 1,353 yards in 1996 snapped John Riggins's team record of 1,347 set in 1983. His 21 touchdowns that year led the NFL, and his 126 points were tops among nonkickers.

"His thing was just running people over," said Trent Green, a Redskin quarterback who teamed with Allen in Washington. "He was incredible at reading the blocks of his linemen and the timing he had at hitting the holes. His vision and his patience as a running back were outstanding. His legs were kind of his driving force, and the fact that everybody made such a big deal about his knees was kind of ironic."

Allen missed a chunk of games due to injuries in the next two seasons, and his numbers dipped. He played his last four seasons with New England (1999), New Orleans (2000), Baltimore (2001), and New Orleans (2002), never again topping the 1,000-yard mark.

## LAVAR ARRINGTON

LB, No. 56, Penn State • 6–3, 255 • **NFL Career:** 2000–2006 (7 seasons) • **Redskins Years:** 2000–05 (6) • **Born:** June 20, 1978 (Pittsburgh, Pa.)

LaVar Arrington set a towering bar for himself in pro football. On being taken by the Redskins as the No. 2 pick in the 2000 draft, Arrington chose No. 56, the number worn by the greatest outside linebacker in NFL history, Lawrence Taylor. Arrington was fresh off a celebrated career at Penn State, where he won the Bednarik Award as the nation's top defensive player and the Butkus Award as the nation's top linebacker, and comparisons of him to Taylor were everywhere.

"If you want to strive for greatness, you should pattern yourself after great people," Arrington said at the time. "Choosing 56 really gives me a head start."

Arrington never lived up to his personal barometer while wearing a Redskins uniform but still made three straight Pro Bowl appearances (2001, 2002, 2003). A package of power, speed and intensity, he either led or finished second on the Redskins in tackles during that period, proving to be a headache for ball carriers by hunting them down like a heat-seeking missile and delivering vicious hits. Redskins cornerback Fred Smoot once said Arrington "delivers the hardest blow" he's ever seen.

LaVar Arrington

"He's extremely quick, extremely fast, and he makes things happen," Norv Turner, the Redskins' head coach in Arrington's rookie season, once said.

By his second year, 2001, Arrington had evolved into one of the NFL's most feared outside linebackers. He posted a team-high 118 tackles and picked off three passes, including one of his most spectacular plays as a Redskin. With the team eyeing an 0–6 start, he returned an interception 67 yards for a touchdown to cut Carolina's fourth-quarter lead to 14–7. The Redskins proceeded to win, launching a five-game winning streak that put them in the playoff hunt. In addition to making the Pro Bowl, Arrington won The Quarterback Club Redskins Player of the Year award.

His frightening athletic skills were again on display in 2002. He recorded a team-high 11 sacks, plus four forced fumbles and three fumble recoveries. He frequently lined up at defensive end, a role he admittedly never felt comfortable with. In 2003, he forced seven fumbles to go with six sacks and two fumble recoveries.

All along, Arrington resembled an old-school linebacker, a player with the passion and intensity similar to someone like Sam Huff, the Giants' and Redskins' Hall of Fame middle linebacker from decades past. He credited Huff with his throwback mentality.

"I guess I look at pain differently than a lot of other people," Arrington once said. "Sam Huff always says, 'We linebackers play in pain.' It's just expected, maybe not so much from people, but from us as an elite corps of athletes. Linebackers take great pride in being able to perform under any circumstances. That's the attitude I have. I'm steel city, I'm blue collar, so the only way I probably wouldn't play is if something is hanging off or might come off. Anything short of death, I'm not going to miss a play."

As his stardom grew, Arrington became the face of the Redskins on and off the field. But his 2004 and 2005 seasons were mostly unproductive due to injuries, run-ins with management over contractual issues, and differences of opinion with coaches on how he should be used. A knee injury sidelined him for nearly all of the 2004 season, and he played sparingly early in the 2005 campaign while rumors swirled that he was too much of a freelancer and couldn't fit into the system of assistant head coach–defense Gregg Williams. He ended up starting 10 games but didn't produce a sack, interception, or fumble recovery until picking off a pass that set up a touchdown in the Redskins' win over Tampa Bay in the playoffs.

After the season, Arrington forfeited more than $4 million of a bonus owed to him so he could become a free agent. He played for the Giants in 2006 but was cut after the season.

## STEVE BAGARUS

HB-DB, No. 00, Notre Dame • 6–0, 173 • **NFL Career:** 1945–48 (4 seasons) • **Redskins Years:** 1945–46, 48 (3) • **Born:** June 19, 1919 (South Bend, Ind.) • **Died:** October 17, 1981 (Gaithersburg, Md.)

Only one Redskin has ever worn the numerals 00 on his jersey: Steve Bagarus. The exciting halfback wanted the double goose eggs in order to send a message to those watching him.

"I remember going through our films and seeing some guy wear number 00," NFL Films president Steve Sabol said. "I found out that it was Bagarus and went to interview him. He told me he wore 00 so the crowd, when it saw him coming off the bench, would say, 'Uh oh, look out, here comes Double-O.' That's one of my favorite Redskin stories."

Bagarus, a great receiver and open field runner, dazzled fans aplenty. He posted 1,150 receiving, 1,115 return and 328 rushing yards in three seasons in Washington in the 1940s. In his book, *The Redskins, 1937–1958,* Morris A. Bealle calls Bagarus "the slippery, shifty, sidestepping, pace-changing ghost of the gridiron. Bagarus was the scourge of the other teams' defenses in 1945 and 1946."

Fabled Redskin quarterback Sammy Baugh thought Bagarus was the best receiver out of the backfield he ever played with: "Bones [Taylor] is the best end for pass-catching the Redskins ever had," Baugh said in the *Washington Times-Herald* toward the end of his career in the early 1950s, "and Bugsy was the best of the lot among the backs, although we had a lot of good ones. I've thrown to such fine receivers as Charley Malone, Wayne Millner, Eddie Justice, Dick Todd, Wilbur Moore, Andy Farkas, Eddie Saenz, Bob Masterson, Joe Aguirre, Bob Seymour and a lot more. But I think Bones and Bugsy were the best."

After playing at Notre Dame, Bagarus spent time with the San Diego Bombers of the Pacific Coast Pro Football League. He thrilled crowds with breakaway runs and once returned an interception 100 yards for a touchdown. "Slippery Steve" signed with the Redskins in 1945 and showed how dangerous he was. He caught 35 passes for 623 yards and six scores, and returned punts for another 251 yards, as the Redskins reached the NFL championship game, in which he caught a 38-yard touchdown pass. He received first-team All-Pro recognition.

Bagarus was traded to Los Angeles before the 1947 season in a deal that angered Redskins fans. He broke his leg early in the season and sat out the whole year, then was waived early in the 1948 campaign. The Redskins re-signed him with six games to go.

Steve Bagarus

"All was love and kisses today at Griffith Stadium when the Redskins' prodigal son, Steve Bagarus, returned home after a rather disastrous year-and-a-half jaunt into the hinterlands," Dave Slattery of the *Washington Daily News* wrote on November 2, 1948. "Tanned and only two or three pounds above his best playing weight, the fancy dan of all Redskin halfbacks was supremely confident as he ran through warm-up exercises that his comeback would be successful."

Bagarus retired after the 1948 season. Except for Baugh's No. 33, he wore perhaps the most popular Redskin jersey number at the time: 00.

## CHAMP BAILEY

CB, No. 24, Georgia • 6–0, 192 • **NFL Career:** 1999–2006 (8 seasons) • **Redskins Years:** 1999–2003 (5) • **Born:** June 22, 1978 (Folkston, Ga.)

As one of the NFL's premier cornerbacks, Champ Bailey is often matched against a superstar wide receiver. He thrives on shutting them down. "I love it," he said in 2003, his final season with the Redskins. "That's what I dream about every night, matching up against the top guy, because I know that's going to drive me to be the best, and that's what I'm looking for—to be the best."

Champ Bailey

The 2002 campaign was perhaps his best all-around season in D.C. He picked off three passes and posted a then-career high 84 tackles, often sneaking up from his cornerback position to trip up ball carriers around the line of scrimmage. He also handled most of the team's punt-return duties, returning 24 for 238 yards (9.9-yard average).

"It's great to have the confidence to know he's going to shut somebody down no matter what," Redskins offensive tackle Jon Jansen said in 2003. "Everybody makes a mistake here or there, but he makes so few and covers so well, it's a huge boost to the whole team."

Bailey went to the Pro Bowl for the fourth straight time in 2003, becoming the first Redskin to do so since linebacker Ken Harvey (1994–97). In the 2004 offseason, the Redskins dealt him and a second-round pick to Denver for running back Clinton Portis. Bailey has since gone to three more Pro Bowls while wearing a Broncos uniform.

## SAM BAKER

K-FB, No. 45 (also wore No. 49), Oregon State • 6–2, 217 • **NFL Career:** 1953, 56–69 (15 seasons) • **Redskins Years:** 1953, 56–59 (5) • **Born:** November 12, 1929 (San Francisco, Calif.)

"Sugarfoot" Sam Baker gave the Redskins quite a kick in the 1950s. Baker's powerful right leg boomed placekicks and punts like few other players in the NFL at the time. He twice converted a then-Redskins-record 49-yard field goal and averaged an impressive 44 yards per punt in a four-season span. He led the league in field goals made, points, and punting average in different years. Plus, he kicked off.

Baker was an outstanding punter in college at Oregon State but never placekicked. He also was the greatest rusher at the time in school history with 1,947 career yards.

Drafted by the Los Angeles Rams, he was traded to the Redskins before the 1953 season. He mostly punted that year, averaging 36.1 yards, before departing to serve in the U.S. Army. After playing in the Canadian Football League, he returned to the Redskins in August 1956 and assumed kicking duties after halfback Vic Janowicz, who also handled field goals, got into a serious car accident.

Despite having never seriously worked on his field goals, Baker made a league-high 17 in 1956 with a 68 percent conversion clip (17–25). He booted his first 49-yarder and kicked a 21-yarder with seconds remaining in a two-point win over the Eagles. He also punted and rushed 25 times for a career-high 117 yards.

The next year, 1957, Baker won the NFL scoring title with 77 points, six of which came on a 20-yard run on a fake kick. At the time, he was considered the second-best field goal kicker in the NFL behind Cleveland's Lou Groza, a current Hall of Famer, and came to be called the "poor man's Groza." But "Baker can do one thing Groza can't—punt," the *Washington Daily News* pointed out.

Baker's punts were returned fewer yards than those of any other kicker in 1957, according to the *Daily News,* which noted that the Redskins gained more than 300 yards on the exchange of punts that season. "Baker has put the foot back in football for the Redskins," the *Daily News* wrote on September 19, 1958. "And he'll keep it there as long as he has one leg to stand on."

Quarterbacks have feared throwing to Bailey's side since he entered the NFL in 1999. He had an outstanding rookie season followed by four straight Pro Bowl years, starting every regular season game along the way, 80, plus two playoff contests. He intercepted 18 passes in five seasons as a Redskin.

The Redskins expected Bailey to become an elite cornerback when they drafted him with their No. 1 pick in 1999. He had a star-studded career at Georgia, winning the Bronko Nagurski Award as the nation's top defensive player as a junior in 1998. The multithreat also caught 59 passes for 978 yards and five touchdowns, in addition to returning punts and kickoffs and rushing.

Before his rookie season, Bailey accepted tutoring from Redskins superstar veteran cornerback Darrell Green. Green was impressed with how quickly Bailey, who was timed at 4.2 in the 40, picked up the system. "The things we've asked him to do, he's done like clockwork," Green said at the time. "I've told him, 'Obviously, we have to coach you and help you stay on top of things.' But generally speaking, the guy's pretty sharp."

Case in point: In his first preseason game, Bailey intercepted a pass and returned it 46 yards for a score. During the regular season, he was named NFC Defensive Player of the Week after intercepting three passes in a win over Arizona. He returned one of them 59 yards for a touchdown. He had other excellent games that month and was named NFL Rookie Defensive Player of the Month for October.

The following year, Bailey led the Redskins with five interceptions and 14 passes defensed, helping anchor the league's second-rated pass defense.

Baker continued booming 'em in 1958, recording a league-high 45.4-yard punting average. He also converted all 25 of his extra points but made only 13 of 26 field goals.

He had another disappointing season on the field goal front in 1959 (10–22), but one field goal was the most important one of his Redskins career. His 46-yarder with 12 seconds left lifted Washington to a 27–24 win over the defending-champion Baltimore Colts, arguably the greatest upset in Redskins history. A postgame newspaper headline read, "Baker's True Toe Sinks Baltimore."

But the Redskins, unhappy that he converted less than 50 percent of his field goals that season, traded him to Cleveland for lineman Fran O'Brien and Bob Khayat, a guard and placekicking specialist. He spent the next 10 seasons with three different teams, leading the NFL in field goal and extra point percentage while playing for the Eagles in 1966.

## MIKE BASS

CB, No. 41, Michigan • 6–0, 190 • **NFL Career:** 1967–75 (9 seasons) • **Redskins Years:** 1969–75 (7) • **Born:** March 31, 1945 (Ypsilanti, Mich.)

In Mike Bass's first two NFL seasons, two personally maddening years when the cornerback was on Detroit's practice squad nearly the whole time and appeared in only two games, he kept remembering something he'd been told by one of the league's all-time premier motivators, Vince Lombardi.

As a rookie, Bass was released on the final cut in the Packers' 1967 training camp, but Lombardi, then Green Bay's coach, assured him he had the talent to play in the NFL. When Bass became a free agent after his first two seasons and Lombardi signed on as the Redskins' coach in 1969, the cornerback seized the chance to play in Washington, where Lombardi's words rang true.

Manning the right side, No. 41 never missed a game over the next seven seasons. He intercepted 30 passes, one of the best marks in Redskins history, with 478 yards in returns and three touchdowns. He also returned a fumble for a score.

Despite playing for Lombardi for only one season, Bass considered him a great inspiration because the Hall of Fame coach had told him not to give up. "Coach Lombardi had that kind of an effect on you," Bass said. "If he said you could do something, you could do it. That remained in my mind the whole two years I was with the Lions."

Bass was also fortunate to have been coached for six seasons in D.C. by defensive mastermind George Allen, who "reaffirmed my ability to play in the league," as Bass put it. Under Allen, the Redskins played in Super Bowl VII, where Bass scored on one of the strangest plays in Super Bowl history. With the Redskins trailing, 14–0, and time running out, Miami kicker Garo Yepremian scooped up a blocked field goal and, appearing disoriented, batted it upward like a volleyball. Bass grabbed it and sprinted 49 yards down the sideline for a score.

Because the Redskins ultimately lost, Bass said that play isn't his most memorable one. Instead, he singled out a pass he intercepted and returned for a touchdown in a 1974 win over the Giants, plus games where he shut down the opponent's top receiver.

Bass considered himself slower than many receivers he covered (he ran a 4.5 40), but he overcame that with meticulous game preparation. He also laid hard hits on opponents, a skill

Mike Bass

he refined with help from two Redskins teammates: cornerback Pat Fischer and safety Kenny Houston.

"It was all technique, hitting and tackling, and it's all desire," he said. "In the beginning that wasn't one of my strong suits. My strong suit was the ability to cover. But after a few years and watching film and understanding the leverage aspect of tackling, and listening and speaking with Kenny and Pat, it became something I prided myself in."

Bass seriously injured his neck making a tackle in a 1975 game against the Giants. He started the last six games that season but retired during training camp the following summer.

"Mike did a great job, he was always prepared," Allen said at the time. "He doesn't make mental mistakes and has gotten everything out of himself as a player."

## VERLON BIGGS

DE, No. 89 (also wore No. 86), Jackson State • 6–4, 275 • **NFL Career:** 1965–74 (10 seasons) • **Redskins Years:** 1971–74 (4) • **Born:** March 16, 1943 (Moss Point, Miss.) • **Died:** June 7, 1994 (Moss Point, Miss.)

Verlon Biggs was a legend in the old American Football League. The Jets' defensive end appeared in three AFL all-star games and was reputed as a great pass rusher who made the big play. In Super Bowl III, he forced a fumble by Baltimore's Tom Matte in the Jets' monumental upset win.

In 1971, when Redskins coach George Allen traded a first-round draft pick for Biggs, then in his seventh season, no one in D.C. was frowning. "We couldn't draft a player as good as this," Allen said in the *Washington Star* on June 11, 1971.

Biggs never again achieved perennial superstar status, but he excelled at defensive end in four seasons in Washington as a member of Allen's "Over the Hill Gang." The 6-4, 275-pounder started all but one of a possible 62 games as a Redskin, including six playoff games, while bolstering the squad's bread and butter in those years: the defense. And he sometimes played like a superstar, as in a 24–10 win over St. Louis in 1972. Steve Guback of the *Washington Star* described Biggs's dominance that day: "Quick starts and power, that's his game on the football field. St. Louis offensive tackles Dan Dierdorf [a future Hall of Famer] and later Steve Wright couldn't control Biggs yesterday as he blocked a field goal, trapped the quarterback twice, helped force two interceptions and played a key role [on] a defense that stymied the Cardinals with only 79 yards rushing."

Redskin cornerback Mike Bass scooped up Biggs's blocked field goal and ran 32 yards for a score, and Washington's two interceptions led to touchdowns.

Later that season, Biggs, a second-team All-Pro in 1972, recovered a fumble of former Jets teammate Joe Namath and ran 16 yards for a score. He received a game ball that day. He also picked up a fumble in the 1973 season-opener against San Diego and ran 2 yards for a touchdown.

Biggs reported to training camp for an 11th season in 1975, but his delicate right knee wouldn't cooperate and he retired.

## DON BOSSELER

FB, No. 31, Miami • 6-1, 212 • **NFL Career:** 1957–64 (8 seasons) • **Redskins Years:** 1957–64 (8) • **Born:** January 24, 1936 (Weathersfield, N.Y.)

He was much lighter than most fullbacks of his day and a feather compared with today's glut of beefy running backs—but 207-pound Don Bosseler still pounded ahead with the best of them—and he had versatility, to boot.

Nicknamed the "Batavia Battering Ram," a take on his hometown of Batavia, New York, Bosseler ran for 3,112 yards and 22 touchdowns in eight NFL seasons, all with the Redskins. His yardage total stood as an all-time team record for nearly a decade. With a special flair for catching swing passes, Bosseler also amassed 1,083 yards and 23 touchdowns on 136 receptions. He made the Pro Bowl in 1960.

Bosseler is a member of the College Football Hall of Fame. He rushed for 1,642 yards at Miami (Florida), and the Redskins drafted him with the team's No. 1 pick in 1957. But he was slow in learning the coaches' schemes: "I was a little concerned I didn't pick up the system as fast as maybe the coaches wanted me to," he said. "But I started playing a little more as the exhibition season got toward the end, and [Redskins] coach Joe Kuharich said, 'You're our guy.' I was learning the system, trying to improve."

Redskins backfield coach Mike Nixon said in the *Washington Post* on November 13, 1957, that Bosseler had to be molded into a player who could fully exploit his skills. "He still had his mind fixed on those short gains when he came to us," Nixon said. "But we could tell the first few times he ran with the ball that his real potential hadn't been tapped. Here was a kid who could give the business of playing fullback a new and added twist. He didn't have to rely on power and heft and bull straight ahead. He had a dip and a sidestep like a halfback. We wanted to bring that talent out in him."

Bosseler improved and led the squad in rushing that season with a career-high 673 yards. That season, a couple of D.C. sportswriters touted Bosseler as clearly better than two of his contemporaries: Chicago's 225-pound Rick Casares and Baltimore's 217-pound Alan Ameche: "Bosseler, although he's the lightest of all the NFL fullbacks, is far and away the most versatile," Ev Gardner of the *Washington Daily News* wrote. "He can hit the line, run the ends, is a good pass receiver, is faster than many halfbacks and can block with the best of them. He makes Alan Ameche and Rick Casares look like sluggish trucks." Gardner added that Bosseler was a better blocker and

Don Bosseler

receiver than 232-pound Jim Brown, the legendary Cleveland Browns' running back.

Bosseler's next biggest season on the ground was 644 yards in 1959. His annual rushing totals gradually declined from then on, except for one year, although he posted a career-high 289 receiving yards in 1963. He also scored the first touchdown ever at D.C. Stadium (later RFK Stadium) on a 4-yard catch on October 1, 1961.

## JEFF BOSTIC

C, No. 53, Clemson • 6–2, 265 • **NFL Career:** 1980–93 (14 seasons) • **Redskins Years:** 1980–93 (14) • **Born:** September 18, 1958 (Greensboro, N.C.)

Jeff Bostic was undersized for his position. At 6–2, 265 pounds, the Redskins' 14-year center lined up against many nose guards and other linemen much bigger than him. He used that size deficiency to his advantage, relying on leverage and quickness to win battles in the trenches.

"I really liked playing guys who were a lot bigger than I was," he said. "I didn't like playing guys my size. I didn't like the 270- or 275-pound nose guards. I would have preferred a guy who was 310 or 320 because I could put my hands on them before they got out of their stance. Bigger guys just aren't as quick.

"Big is always a good commodity, but it's not the only commodity. There are other ways to skin a cat."

Bostic is one of the greatest centers in Redskins history. He was a fixture during the franchise's glory run in the 1980s and early 1990s, taking home three Super Bowl rings, and was a charter member of the Hogs, the Redskins' smash-mouth offensive line of his era. He played in 184 games, one of the highest all-time marks for a Redskin, and started 18 of 19 playoff games, including four Super Bowls. His 14-year career ties him with Len Hauss for the longest tenure as a pure Redskins center.

"Everybody said he was the small guy, undersized, but he played with great leverage," fellow Hog and long-time teammate Russ Grimm said. "He had good use of the hands and was a tenacious football player. He played against a lot of nose tackles that were 30 to 40 pounds heavier than him."

Having undergone five major operations in his career, including both knees, Bostic said he was fortunate to play as long as he did. He also acknowledged benefiting from breaks that opened doors for him to enter into and then rise to stardom in the NFL.

Bostic was a three-year starter on the offensive line at Clemson University, two years at center and one at guard, and earned All-Atlantic Coast Conference honors. Not drafted, he signed as a free agent with the Eagles but was cut in training camp, deflating his ambitions to play pro football. His father urged him to persevere:

"My dad really kind of begged me," Bostic said. "He said, 'You ought to go through Washington. They had a lot of interest in you before the draft.' I kind of blew it off. He said, 'You don't have anything else to do. You're going to come from [the Eagles camp in] West Chester, Pennsylvania through Washington to get to North Carolina.' I called their personnel guy, Mike Allman, and worked out for them, did some drills, running and snapping. That's when I learned that they had problems with their deep snapper, Ted Fritsch. Allman said,

'If we have a problem in our last preseason game, we're going to call you.'"

As fate would have it, Fritsch sent two snaps sailing over the punter's head. "Sure enough, the next day, they called," Bostic said.

The rookie played the 1980 season without any bad snaps and was solid on kick coverage units. Then, during training camp in the summer of 1981, he rose on the depth chart at center, challenging first-teamers Bob Kuziel and Dan Peiffer, and offensive line coach Joe Bugel tapped him to start. His transition to starter was largely a product of the firing of head coach Jack Pardee after the 1980 season and the arrival of Pardee's successor, Joe Gibbs.

"I was really glad to see Pardee gone," Bostic said. "He was a guy that loved veteran players. I needed an opportunity to show what I could do, and I'm not sure that would have happened. Gibbs came in and started everybody on a level ground."

Bostic started the next 56 games. In 1983, he made the Pro Bowl for the first and only time and won All-NFC honors on a Redskin squad that finished third in the NFL in rushing (164.1 yards per game). His starting streak came to an end on October 26, 1984, when he tore three ligaments in his right knee in a road loss to the St. Louis Cardinals, for whom his brother, Joe, played guard at the time.

"It was kind of ironic," Jeff Bostic said. "It was against my brother's team, it was on my mother's birthday, my mom and dad were at the game. It was the only game my wife went to on the road. It was a bad day."

The injury nearly forced Bostic to retire, but he rehabilitated himself after surgery and returned to play in the last 10 games of the 1985 season, starting six. He looked like his old self by the season finale, knocking defenders off the ball as George Rogers rushed for 206 yards. He won the Ed Block Courage Award as the team's comeback player of the year.

Bostic was a starter for virtually the rest of his career, including all 16 games in 1993, his 14th and final season. Shortly after, he underwent surgery on his right knee and was advised by a doctor to call it quits. He retired in March 1994 as the last original Hog to see playing time.

Bostic's Hog heritage lives on, for his house features a "Hog memorial" with all kinds of pig-related ornaments. They include a coconut painted in Redskin colors with a pig's face, and a pig riding the back of a dolphin, a reference to the Redskins' win over Miami in Super Bowl XVII. Professionally, has been a sideline reporter for CBS Radio-Westwood One, the network that broadcasts NFL games, and has provided TV color analysis on Redskins exhibition games for Comcast SportsNet.

## MIKE BRAGG

P, No. 4, Richmond • 5–11, 186 • **NFL Career:** 1968–80 (13 seasons) • **Redskins Years:** 1968–79 (12) • **Born:** September 26, 1946 (Richmond, Va.)

Next to Sammy Baugh, Mike Bragg is the greatest punter to ever don the burgundy and gold. Bragg set a Redskin record by punting 896 times, a mark in little danger of being broken (Matt Turk is next with 388), and never missed a game in his 13-year NFL career, playing in 188. All along, the crafty punter frustrated many opponents. A master at pinning offenses deep in their own territory, he was adept at angling the ball out of

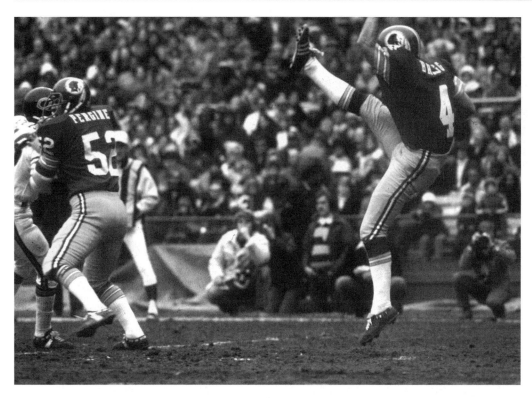

Mike Bragg

bounds into the "coffin corner," always aiming between the 5- and 10-yard lines. "Anytime we got around midfield, I was starting to think sideline," he said. "I'd tell everybody in the huddle I'm going left, so everybody knew they wanted to cover the left side of the field more, and when they got downfield they'd try to beat the guy who's trying to block them to that side. If I didn't get it out of bounds and it bounced, they were over there to down it."

Bragg was also superb at launching "pooch kicks" that were downed near the goal line. The goalposts were on the goal line in his first six seasons, and he used them as a visual guide to place the ball. In 1977, for example, he tallied a league-high 29 punts that were downed inside the 20. He compared the art to chipping a golf ball from the fairway onto the green. "It's like instead of hitting a nine-iron, I'm going to hit a gap wedge and just drop it in there and hope to get a good bounce," he said.

Unlike many other punters, Bragg often refrained from booming the ball downfield so as not to outkick his coverage team. He understood the importance of shorter punts with excellent hang time that allowed cover men to reach the punt returner faster and averaged a modest 39.8 yards in his career. His Redskin head coach for seven seasons, special teams pioneer George Allen, stressed the importance of posting a solid net average: punt distance minus return yardage.

"He'd say the best punter in the league doesn't always lead the league in gross average, but he will lead the league in net average and in downing the ball inside the 10," said Bragg, who aimed for up to 5.1 seconds of hang time and a 35-yard net average. "So that brought more of the team aspect into it because net average wasn't just purely kicking the ball. Somebody had to go down and make the tackle. You knew if you hit a frozen rope out there, 50 to 60 yards, it was going to come back 20 or 30 or all the way."

Bragg had only 10 punts blocked, once recording a string of 365 that weren't touched. He attributed such success mostly to quickness, saying he and his center worked to launch the punt in about two seconds and noting that anything above 2.2 put it at risk of being blocked.

Such skills were critical to conservative, defense-oriented Redskins teams that made the playoffs five times in the 1970s. Bragg welcomed his role, and he knew that simply having the chance to play for the Redskins was a dream come true. A diehard Redskins fan while growing up in the Richmond, Virginia, area, he later moved to Northern Virginia and attended J. E. B. Stuart High in Falls Church, Virginia, before punting and placekicking for three seasons at the University of Richmond. The Redskins drafted him in the fifth round in 1968.

"It was wonderful, what a great thing to have grown up in the area, and then to get drafted and come and play," he said. "I was in awe of everything. I was always a fan, then I became a Redskin. So how lucky and blessed am I?

"One year I'm going to a Redskins game [1967], and I'm watching Jerry Smith, Bobby Mitchell, Sonny Jurgensen, Charley Taylor, then less than a year later I'm in training camp. I'm like, 'This is so strange because these guys are now my teammates.'"

After 12 seasons in Washington, Bragg played his final year in 1980 for the Baltimore Colts.

## GENE BRITO

E, No. 80, Loyola Marymount • 6–1, 226 • **NFL Career:** 1951–53, 55–60 (9 seasons) • **Redskins Years:** 1951–53, 55–58 (7) • **Born:** October 23, 1925 (Huntington Park, Calif.) • **Died:** June 8, 1965 (Duarte, Calif.)

They called the Southern California native with Hollywood looks "Gentleman Gene." To opposing offenses, he was anything but.

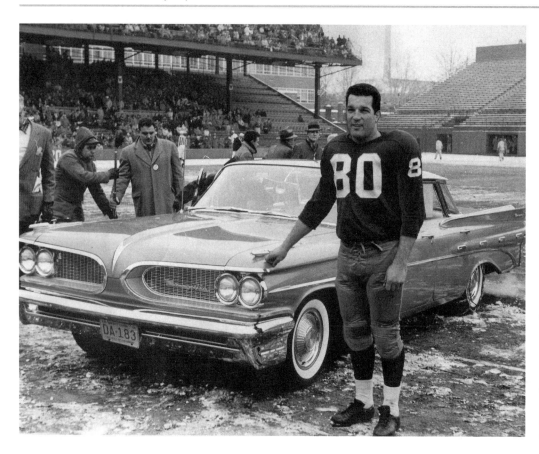

The popular Brito was honored in a pregame ceremony on Gene Brito Day at Griffith Stadium on December 14, 1958. Then-Vice President Richard Nixon presented him with the keys to a new car.

Gene Brito, one of the greatest defensive ends in Redskins history, was on the light side for his position at 6–2, 230 pounds, but he used quickness and deceptiveness, combined with an unmitigated ferocity, to overcome his lack of bulk and frequent double-teaming. Cleveland coach Paul Brown once wanted to put a Browns jersey on Brito because, as Brown put it, "Brito was more in my backfield than his own."

In seven seasons in Washington in the 1950s, Brito earned five trips to the Pro Bowl and first-team All-Pro honors four times. He never missed a game in a Redskins uniform, playing in 84 straight. (The NFL didn't keep official sack records until 1982, so it's unclear how many Brito had.)

"What a great defensive end," Baltimore Colts Hall of Fame running back-receiver Lenny Moore said. "I'll never forget Gene Brito. Very, very quick, very fast. He wasn't big by standards of a defensive end, but, man, you had to keep a back in the backfield to pick him up. He was as quick as a cat."

"The big, old, slow [offensive] linemen couldn't catch up with him," said Jim Ricca, a Redskins middle guard who played with Brito.

Brito was a true professional who never committed a personal foul while wearing a Redskins uniform. "I played as hard as I could, but I felt that anything dirty was uncalled for," he once said. He was also a class act off the field. After the career of Redskins halfback Vic Janowicz ended before the 1956 season due to a car crash, Brito organized a fund for him. Each week, 32 players chipped in at least $10 for Janowicz. Brito also dedicated himself to helping problem children.

A four-sport star at Loyola University (now Loyola Marymount) in Los Angeles, Brito came to the Redskins in 1951 as a 17th-round draft pick. He vied for one of six end berths on a squad that boasted six veterans at the position and three ballyhooed rookies with bigger physiques and fatter reputations.

Brito made the squad and was used mostly on offense, catching 24 passes for 313 yards. He tacked on 21 receptions for 270 yards and two touchdowns in 1952. In training camp in 1953, Redskins coach Curly Lambeau, knowing that Brito had made an impact on defense in college, moved him to defensive end, where his talents blossomed. He earned his first trip to the Pro Bowl that year. But he migrated to the Canadian Football League for a season.

On returning in 1955, he embarked on the greatest stretch of his career. He made the Pro Bowl in 1955, '56, '57, and '58, and received first-team All-Pro honors in three of those seasons.

How did he make such a smooth transition from offense to defense? "I just like to play football," he once said. "Offense or defense doesn't matter. Defense is just as much a part of football as offense. The prime requisite of a good defensive player is desire. You must want to play and want to win."

Brito was the Redskins' most beloved player in the 1950s. Among fans and teammates, his No. 80 was almost as revered as the No. 33 of Redskins long-time icon Sammy Baugh.

As the 1958 season wound down, it was rumored that Brito was nearing retirement, and the Redskins called their final home game that year "Gene Brito Day." Then-Vice President Richard Nixon honored him during pregame ceremonies: "You symbolize the Redskins' fighting spirit," Nixon told Brito.

Brito gave a classy reply to a hushed, admiring audience of more than 22,000 at Griffith Stadium: "I'll miss playing football very much. But I have this day to remind me of what a great honor it was to play football in Washington, D.C. Thank you for seven wonderful years."

Nixon gave Brito the keys to a new car, and the fans showed admiration for their star by carrying him off the field after the game.

"Seldom has a Washington player captured the imagination of the public the way the big guy has," Bob Addie of the *Washington Post* wrote on December 6, 1957. "He's played in more enemy backfields than any other man in Redskin history. Just before the start of every play, Gene crosses one foot over the other and puts his hands on his hips. He seems totally unconcerned, but he's a real bearcat once that ball is snapped."

Brito decided to keep playing, and after the 1958 season the Redskins traded him to Los Angeles, where he had two solid years. He was later stricken by a crippling muscular disease and died in 1965 at age 39.

## CHARLIE BROWN

WR, No. 87, South Carolina State • 5–10, 180 • **NFL Career:** 1982–87 (5 seasons) • **Redskins Years:** 1982–84 (3) • **Born:** October 29, 1958 (Charleston, S.C.)

In tweaking a line from the 1960s hit song "Downtown" by British singer Petula Clark, when the Redskins had no place to go, they could often go to "Downtown" Charlie Brown. The speedy wide receiver with long arms, long strides, and an excellent vertical leap was a highlight reel for two seasons in the early-1980s. He had a knack for maneuvering his way deep and catching bombs.

In 1982, Brown recorded a league-high 21.6-yard reception average and eight of the Redskins' top-10 gains: touchdown catches of 78, 65, 58, and 57 yards, plus receptions of 45, 43, 39, and 38 yards. In 1983, he became the first Redskin since Charley Taylor in 1966 to total more than 1,000 yards receiving (1,225) and caught 78 passes, a team record at the time. Both years, he made the Pro Bowl and received All-Pro recognition.

"You look at Charlie and his demeanor, nothing about Charlie said 'fast' except when he was catching the football," said Joe Washington, a Redskins wingback who teamed with Brown. "He was a very easy-going guy. He talked very softly, and he strolled around in a very non-intrusive manner . . . and he's out running and catching passes all over the field. Charlie would definitely be a guy most folks were probably a little surprised about."

Brown was indeed a surprise. A Redskins eighth-round draft pick in 1981 out of tiny South Carolina State, he spent his rookie season on injured reserve. He made a sudden impact in the 1982 season-opener, however, catching a 78-yard touchdown pass on a bomb from Joe Theismann. He hauled in 32 passes for 690 yards and eight touchdowns in the strike-shortened season and added 17 catches in the playoffs, including touchdowns in the NFC championship game and Super Bowl XVII, both Redskins wins.

That season, Brown was an original member of the Fun Bunch, players who gathered to slap high fives in the end zone after scoring catches, as well as the Smurfs, a trio of pint-sized receivers.

In 1983, Brown had six 100-yard receiving games and caught 14 passes for 401 yards and one touchdown in the playoffs, a 70-yarder in an NFC championship game win over San Francisco. In 1984, he spent four weeks on injured reserve and caught only 18 passes. He was traded after the season to Atlanta, where he played his last three seasons.

Brown returned to the Redskins as their AFC scouting coordinator in 2000. He later coached the Myrtle Beach Stingrays in the National Indoor Football League.

## EDDIE BROWN

S-KR, No. 25, Tennessee • 5–11, 190 • **NFL Career:** 1974–79 (6 seasons) • **Redskins Years:** 1975–77 (3) • **Born:** February 19, 1952 (Jasper, Tenn.)

Only $100. That's all the Redskins paid for Eddie Brown upon claiming him off waivers early in the 1975 season. The cheap investment rose to become one of the marquee kick returners of his era.

Brown led the NFL with 646 punt return yards in 1976, then the second-best total in NFL history and only a few yards from first. He made the Pro Bowl that year, as well as in 1977, when he returned a league-high 57 punts for 452 yards. His kickoff return numbers also were among the league-leaders both years.

"He wasn't very fast at all, but he had good instincts," said Roy Jefferson, a Redskins receiver who teamed with Brown. "When he caught the ball, he went wherever the open area was."

Brown played his 1974 rookie season and the first three games of 1975 in Cleveland. He was cut and signed by the Redskins, who had lost safety Ken Stone to injury and needed someone to fill in.

Brown saw action in the last 11 games as a "nickel back" and on special teams. An injury to kick return specialist Larry Jones before the 1976 season elevated him to the top return man. After six games, he led the NFL in kickoff returns. "He's second in punt returns and shows promise it won't be long before he breaks one all the way for a score," Redskins publicists wrote. "The sure-handed Brown has responded brilliantly to [Redskins coach] George Allen's faith in him."

Brown surely broke one, and it was spectacular! In a Monday night game against St. Louis on October 25, 1976, "steady" Eddie sloshed 71 yards through the mud and downpour at RFK Stadium in one of the most memorable plays in Redskins special teams history. A Redskins game program captured the excitement of the moment: "With the Cardinal special team streaming downfield to nail him, Eddie found a clearing block which put him past the initial wave of tacklers. Jetting toward the right sideline, Brown ran through, over and around Cardinals tacklers and headed for the end zone. The fans were on their feet, screaming encouragement and sensing a score . . . And they weren't disappointed. Stumbling twice as he got inside the 10, Brown righted himself and carried it in."

Brown's 13.46 punt return average in 1976 was then the second-best mark in Redskins history. He returned an NFL-record 11 punts in a game in 1977, and his 1,150 punt return yards were the most in Redskin history (a mark since broken) when he was traded to Los Angeles before the 1978 season. He played two seasons for the Rams and retired.

# LARRY BROWN

RB, No. 43, Kansas State • 5–11, 195 • **NFL Career:** 1969–76 (8 seasons) • **Redskins Years:** 1969–76 (8) • **Born:** September 19, 1947 (Clairton, Pa.)

Larry Brown epitomized toughness when he carried the Redskins' offense in the late 1960s and early 1970s. At 5–11 and with weight that fluctuated between 180 and 200 pounds, light for an NFL running back, he relied on power just as much as finesse. He played with injury after injury.

His fearless style made him one of the greatest rushers in Redskins history. He amassed 5,875 yards, now the team's second-highest all-time total, and impacted the Redskins' record books in other categories. He's tied with Dick James for the most single-game touchdowns (four) and points (24) in Redskins history.

His undersized body succumbed to the pounding. After gaining more than 5,000 yards in his first five seasons, then only the second player in NFL history to do so besides the great Jim Brown, an injury-plagued Larry Brown was little threat for the rest of his eight-year career.

Was Brown his own worst enemy? "Maybe, because I ran with such a reckless abandon," he said. "But the career span of a running back was so short, only three and a half years, regardless of the pounding you could take and despite whether you ran with a reckless abandon or not."

NFL Films president Steve Sabol hailed Brown's gritty style: "He's maybe the most underrated running back in NFL history. He literally left pieces of himself all over the field in every game he played. Talk about a reckless disregard for the consequences. A section of our Redskins highlights in 1972 was of him finishing his runs. He would get hit and spun and pinwheeled and helicoptered. He was only about 190 pounds and not very fast. But every step meant something for him."

Although he led Kansas State in rushing for two seasons, Brown wasn't expected to evolve into much when the Redskins chose him in the eighth round in 1969. First-year Redskins coach Vince Lombardi, however, saw Brown's potential, along with the fact that the rookie was slow getting off the ball. Lombardi learned that Brown was totally deaf in his right ear and had him fitted in training camp with a hearing aid so he could respond better to the quarterback's signals. As Brown tells the story:

He noticed while watching films in slow motion that I was getting off the ball seconds later than the rest of the offense. He questioned me about it, and I told him that I was having a great deal of difficulty [hearing the signals]. He nodded as if that satisfied his question. A few days later in the locker room, I saw two people walking toward me in these long white coats. My first reaction was, what did I do to deserve this kind of treatment? When you see people with long white coats, you think of hospitals or mental institutions. But shortly after, I found out they were there to give me a hearing examination, which confirmed the fact that I was totally deaf in my right ear.

Brown, equipped with big, powerful legs, began exploding into the line. He rushed for 888 yards, the league's fourth-highest total that season, and was runner-up in NFL Rookie of the Year voting. He followed in 1970 by leading the league in rushing with 1,125 yards, the first time a Redskins back had exceeded the 1,000-yard mark. After a 948-yard campaign in 1971, he tallied a career-high 1,216 in 1972, second in the league to Buffalo's O. J. Simpson. Brown was named NFL Player of the Year, as the Redskins reached Super Bowl VII.

Meanwhile, Brown's carries were piling up in the run-oriented offense of Redskins coach George Allen, who called his number over and over. The indefatigable running back, whom long-time D.C. sportswriter Morrie Siegel once tagged as "the greatest foot soldier in football today," welcomed Allen's intent to keep him as the focal point of the offense.

"If you don't touch the ball at all you're not recognized or respected as a running back," Brown said, "so you have to touch the ball to prove that you're the person who deserves to be in that position. [Allen] was very conservative about changing running backs and quarterbacks, and putting other people in the game, all of which could destroy the chemistry that exists at that particular time."

Brown's production plummeted after the 1972 season. He rushed for 860 yards in 1973, 430 in 1974 and 352 in 1975. He underwent surgery on his right knee after the 1975 season and returned as a blocking back in 1976, but he gained only 56 yards and called it quits.

# BILL BRUNDIGE

DT, No. 77, Colorado • 6–5, 270 • **NFL Career:** 1970–77 (8 seasons) • **Redskins Years:** 1970–77 (8) • **Born:** November 13, 1948 (Holyoke, Colo.)

Bill Brundige, a math major in college, rang up big numbers for the Redskins at the expense of opposing quarterbacks.

The 6–5, 270-pound tackle was a weapon on defenses that posted one of the highest sack totals in the NFL from 1971 to 1977, the seven-year coaching regime of defensive wizard George Allen. Brundige tallied 16 sacks alone in 1973, when the Redskins recorded 53, one of the best single-season marks in team history.

Brundige was once uncertain whether he would even have the chance to play college football, no less pro. Despite starring for a tiny high school in his home state, Colorado, he thought his chance of being noticed by recruiters was remote. But he excelled in an intrastate all-star game and was offered a scholarship to the University of Colorado, where he was an All-American defensive end and Big 8 Defensive Player of the Year as a senior.

Brundige was drafted in 1970 by the Redskins, who were then coached by the legendary Vince Lombardi. Soon after, Lombardi revealed a concern he had about the rookie who once combined physics, chemistry, and math into his studies at Colorado: "He has an IQ of 150, and it worries me," Lombardi told reporters. "He may be smarter than the coaches."

Lombardi died of cancer just before the 1970 season. Brundige has mixed feelings about not being able to play for the man who led the Packers to five NFL titles before coming to Washington:

"He was one of the greatest that ever lived," Brundige said. "But he was tough, and I was dreading it. I read about the things he did in training camp, and I said, 'Man, I don't want to play for this guy.' Then, when I got that phone call and the lady says, 'This is Pat Stone, confidential secretary for coach

Lombardi,' I said, 'Aaahhh.' He gets on the phone and says in his gruff voice, 'Bill, we drafted you in the second round.' I just said, 'Oh my God.'"

Brundige, who was a step slow to play end in the NFL, switched to defensive tackle before his rookie season. The next year, 1971, Allen arrived from Los Angeles and transformed the Redskins into an aging squad that became known as the Over the Hill Gang. Brundige said his "claim to fame" was being an honorary member of the Over the Hill Gang despite his status as one of the youngest Redskin players for nearly his first three seasons.

Known as a gentle giant, Brundige started consistently at tackle through the Allen era. In one of his most memorable plays, he sacked Jets quarterback Joe Namath in a 1972 game and forced a fumble that defensive end Verlon Biggs recovered and returned 16 yards for a score. "I've got a picture of that," Brundige said. "Namath, of course, had terrible knees and couldn't run . . . as crippled as he was. I flushed him out of the pocket, and he started running. I hit him in the back, and as I drove him into the ground, my helmet slipped, and I got up on my knees with my helmet down almost across my eyes. I walked off the field and said to [defensive coordinator Torgy Torgeson], 'What's going on?' He said Verlon Biggs just scored a touchdown, and I didn't even know I'd forced a fumble."

## DAVE BUTZ

DT, No. 65, Purdue • 6–7, 315 • **NFL Career:** 1973–88 (16 seasons) • **Redskins Years:** 1975–88 (14) • **Born:** June 23, 1950 (Lafayette, Ala.)

Dave Butz was an icon for 14 seasons on the Redskins' defense by virtue of his presence as an enforcer. He was a mountain of a man. The 6–7 Butz played at 315 pounds in the days before 300-pounders were commonplace in the NFL. His feet were a size 13 with a 7-E width. ("My dad said I'd be a foot taller if I didn't turn a foot under," he quipped.) He had a 19½-inch neck and wore a specially ordered 8-inch helmet. He was so colossal that Redskins safety Kenny Houston, who played with Butz for six seasons, thought he could seriously injure an opponent, albeit unintentionally.

Butz, an immovable object to many, used his size and skills to help anchor Washington's defensive line from 1975 to 1988. He ranks third in franchise history in sacks (59.5) and played in 203 games, fourth all-time in team history, missing only one from 1979 until retirement. He made the Pro Bowl once.

"Probably the best thing about Butzie is he played consistently all the time," said Diron Talbert, a defensive tackle who teamed with Butz for six seasons. "He was never up or down. His career was long because of that. That's hard for athletes to do. A lot of guys are up and down. They'll play a good game, then a bad game. That's what kills you."

Butz spent his first two seasons in St. Louis, then came to D.C. before the 1975 campaign in one of the most audacious trades in NFL history. Redskins coach George Allen gave the Cardinals two first-round picks and a second-rounder for the rights to Butz, a free agent. The Redskins also received fifth-, sixth-, and 15th-round picks, but Allen took widespread criticism given that Butz had missed nearly the entire 1974 season due to a knee injury. One NFL general manager called it a "terrible deal" for the Redskins.

Butz wore a gargantuan 8¼-inch helmet. "He had the biggest helmet in the world," NFL TV commentator John Madden said. "It wasn't polished at all. He had nicks on it. You could see the helmet colors of other teams on the helmet."

So much for the pessimism. None of the Cardinals' draft choices amounted to anything, while Butz proved to be worth the price. Twenty-five years old at the time, he joined a squad dotted by aging veterans and known as the Over the Hill Gang. He was stunned to learn how old the players were upon reporting for his first training camp at Dickinson College in Carlisle, Pennsylvania, in 1975:

"I was sitting with Timmy Temerario, the personnel manager for George Allen, and the doors opened at Dickinson College," he recalled. "All of a sudden, guys with gray hair, pot bellies, and sandals and shorts came out. I said, 'Damn, they've got a lot of old coaches.' Then I realized it was the players. It's amazing what the older group taught me. I had no kids, and they had kids going off to college. Then by the time I retired, I had kids getting ready for college. It was a whole cycle. I was able to experience both sides."

Butz improved steadily under Allen, but he disliked Allen's successor, Jack Pardee, with a passion. "I told general manager Bobby Beathard if Pardee comes back for a fourth year [in 1981] I'm going to retire," Butz said. "I didn't like the way he used spies. I wasn't going to play another year."

Joe Gibbs replaced Pardee in 1981, and Butz had his greatest year in 1983. He posted a career-high 11.5 sacks, forced a team-high five fumbles, and made 69 tackles, as the Redskins reached Super Bowl XVIII, one of the three Super Bowls Butz played in. (He earned two rings.) He was voted to nearly every All-Pro team and received second-team All-Pro recognition in 1984.

In the eyes of Danny White, the Cowboys' quarterback at the time, big No. 65 was a major impact player. "He was one of those guys who could turn a game around," White said. "Nobody realized how valuable he was to that team. He constantly collapsed the pocket on us. He'd knock the lineman back in my face. Of all the Redskins, he probably had more of an affect on us offensively than anybody on their team."

At the same time, Butz impersonated the Energizer Bunny. Despite myriad injuries and ailments, he just kept going and going and going. Case in point: He was hospitalized the day before a game in 1987 because of an intestinal parasite that prevented him from consuming food or liquids, including a glass of water, and forced his weight down to 275. He checked himself out of the hospital on the morning of the game and started, making seven tackles and a sack that preserved the Redskins' 17–16 win over the Jets. He returned to the hospital after the game.

Then there was the time that, when rushing the passer, he felt his left thumb hit the bottom of his wrist. "I said, 'Boy, that's unusual, I never felt that before.'" He left the field, the team doctor put a cast on his hand, and he returned to the game. He went to the hospital the next day, and doctors drilled holes in his hand and put pins in to set the broken bone.

Why in heaven's name did he play under such circumstances? "The thing I was put on this Earth to do was play pro football," he reasoned. "I could take it, I could dish it out."

## EARNEST BYNER

RB, No. 21, East Carolina • 5–10, 215 • **NFL Career:** 1984–97 (14 seasons) • **Redskins Years:** 1989–93 (5) • **Born:** September 15, 1962 (Milledgeville, Ga.)

In 14 NFL seasons, Earnest Byner amassed 8,251 rushing yards and 4,605 through the air, and combined six times for more than 1,000 yards rushing and receiving. He scored 71 touchdowns, 56 on the ground.

In the minds of many, however, one infamous moment defines his career. With a little more than a minute left in the 1987 AFC championship game and his Cleveland Browns trailing Denver, 38–31, Byner was running for what looked like a sure touchdown. But he fumbled the ball away, costing the Browns a trip to Super Bowl XXII. Four years later, when he caught a swing pass and dove into the corner of the end zone for the Redskins' first touchdown in their win in Super Bowl XXVI, did he feel vindicated?

"It was a crowning moment for me more so because we won the Super Bowl," he said. "Redemption for anything is not possible. You only learn from the experiences that you go through. That was a very tough learning experience for me, but I learned my lesson, graduated from it, kept growing and eventually got to be a champion."

After playing his first five seasons in Cleveland, Byner came to the Redskins in April 1989 in a trade for running back Mike Oliphant. Oliphant was out of the league in a few years, whereas Byner was a workhorse in Washington. He carried the ball a league-high 297 times in 1990 for a career-high 1,219 yards, followed by a 1,048-yard showing in 1991 that helped key the Redskins' march to Super Bowl XXVI. He made the Pro Bowl both years.

"We knew as soon as we traded for him it was the best thing that could happen to him and to us," said Jim Lachey, a Redskins offensive tackle who played with Byner. "Just a hard worker, there was no deficiency in his game. Could pass protect with the best of them, run with the best of them, and he was mentally sharp."

Byner tacked on a 998-yard rushing performance in 1992 and, after his numbers plummeted in 1993, his fifth and final year in Washington, he played two seasons in Cleveland and two in Baltimore. After retiring, he spent six years as the Ravens' director of player development and became the Redskins' running backs coach when Joe Gibbs returned in 2004, a position he holds today.

## JOHNNY CARSON

E, No. 82, Georgia • 6–3, 200 • **NFL Career:** 1954–60 (7 seasons) • **Redskins Years:** 1954–59 (6) • **Born:** January 31, 1930 (Atlanta, Ga.)

In the mid-1950s, Redskins quarterbacks benefited from a sure-handed go-to receiver named Johnny Carson. Carson led the Redskins in receiving in 1955, 1956, and 1957, averaging 32 catches, 510 yards (16.0 average) and three touchdowns during that span. He made the Pro Bowl in the '57 season.

Drafted by Cleveland in the 15th round in 1954, Carson was traded to the Redskins along with fullback Dale Atkeson before the season for halfback Don Paul. In his breakout game, he made two sensational touchdown catches in the Redskins' 27–17 upset in 1955 of the Browns, who were en route to winning their second straight NFL championship.

"He was an excellent pass receiver," said Joe Tereshinski, the Redskins' ends coach for nearly all of Carson's stay in Washington. "He had good speed and good moves."

Carson's numbers dipped after the 1957 season, and he was traded in 1960 to the Houston Oilers of the upstart American Football League. In his only season in Houston, he posted career-highs in receptions (45), yards (604) and touchdowns (four), as the Oilers won the AFL championship.

Carson played his college ball at Georgia, where he led the nation in receiving in 1953 with 46 catches and received All-American honors.

## GARY CLARK

WR, No. 84, James Madison • 5–9, 175 • **NFL Career:** 1985–95 (11 seasons) • **Redskins Years:** 1985–92 (8) • **Born:** May 1, 1962 (Radford, Va.)

The scene epitomized the passion that boiled inside Gary Clark: Late in the first half of a 1991 game against the Giants, the sure-handed receiver dropped what looked like a certain scoring pass. He proceeded to stew on the sidelines, his consternation visible to all. He redeemed himself in the second half with two touchdown catches in a 17–13 win that improved the Redskins to 8–0 in a season they capped with a Super Bowl victory.

It was not the only time Clark vented emotions during his 11-year career. In fact, he regularly used his fiery personality to will himself and his teammates to be the best. His numbers speak for themselves: 699 catches, 10,856 yards, 65 touchdowns. His greatest fame was during an eight-year span in Washington (1985–92), where he became one of the best Redskin receivers ever with 549 receptions for 8,742 yards, both third-best in team history, and 58 touchdowns. He made the Pro Bowl in 1986, 1987, 1990, and 1991.

"I was just a very emotional player," Clark said. "I wore my emotions on my sleeve. I pretty much told you how I felt. I didn't mince words so to speak. If I felt bad, I let you know I felt bad. If I felt you were playing sorry, I told you. If I was playing sorry, I told myself. I came from an era when losing sucks. I didn't see anything good about it."

"He was a pistol," said Doug Williams, a Redskin quarterback who played with Clark for four seasons. "He was probably one of the best and toughest competitors I've ever been around. He was one of those slippery-type guys who could get in cracks that a lot of other people couldn't get in."

Not bad for a 5–9, 173-pounder who played at Division I-AA James Madison and wasn't picked in the 1984 NFL draft despite finishing as the Dukes' all-time leading receiver. Clark instead signed with the Jacksonville Bulls of the United States Football League and caught 56 passes for 760 yards in the 1984 season. But the cash-strapped Bulls released some high-priced players, including Clark, and the Redskins, having received tapes of Clark from the Bulls, grabbed him in the NFL supplemental draft.

The Redskins were stacked at the position, so the coaches assigned him to return kicks. After all, he had finished second in the nation in punt returns one year in college. "I'll do anything they want me to do," Clark said at the time. "But I like catching a ball from a teammate's hand better than catching it from someone's foot."

He got his wish, becoming a starting receiver five games into the 1985 season. He quickly cemented his position, recording a breakout game with 11 catches for 193 yards against the Giants. Proving to be smart, tough and, as the Redskins' publicity staff called him, "faster than a speeding bullet," he caught 72 passes for 926 yards and a team-high five touchdowns that season.

It was the birth of a Redskins star who helped propel the franchise's dynasty of the 1980s and early 1990s. He posted many more glorious achievements:

- 11 catches for a team-record 241 yards (since broken) in 1986 against the Giants
- More than 1,000 yards receiving in five different seasons; tied with Art Monk for most seasons in Redskin history
- One of two Redskins receivers (Monk being the other one) ever to record three straight 1,000-yard and 70-plus catch seasons
- 28 100-yard games, second-most in team history

Clark also had a knack for making clutch receptions in high-stakes situations. His 38-yard scoring catch in overtime gave the Redskins a win over Minnesota in 1986. His 7-yard touchdown catch late in the 1987 NFC championship game lifted the Redskins over the Vikings. He caught a scoring pass in the Redskins' rout of Denver in Super Bowl XXII, plus seven passes for 114 yards and a touchdown in a win over Buffalo in Super Bowl XXVI.

Playing with two other great receivers, Monk and Ricky Sanders, a dangerous trio that formed "The Posse," Clark demanded the ball. He relied on his abrasive personality and ego to relay that desire. "He wanted nobody else to catch the ball," Williams said. "He felt like every football should be his football."

"When the game was on the line, he wanted the ball, and a lot of times he got the ball," said Charley Taylor, the great Redskins receiver who was Clark's position coach in Washington. "When it was third-and-9, he wanted the ball. If it was third-and-10 at the 10-yard line, he wanted the ball. He was a little guy with a very big heart."

Clark's fearlessness—the darting receiver welcomed running patterns over the middle—and his determination to succeed endeared him to long-time NFL TV color analyst John Madden. Madden put Clark on his prestigious All-Madden team year after year. "Gary Clark was one of my all-time favorites," Madden said. "He was a hell of a player, he was tough."

The 1991 season was perhaps Clark's finest. He caught 70 balls with career-highs of 1,340 yards, 10 touchdowns, and a 19.1-yard average. After his final season in Washington, 1992, he played two years with the Cardinals and one in Miami before retiring.

## MONTE COLEMAN

LB, No. 51, Central Arkansas • 6–2, 242 • **NFL Career:** 1979–94 (16 seasons) • **Redskins Years:** 1979–94 (16) • **Born:** November 4, 1957 (Pine Bluff, Ark.)

For Monte Coleman, it was all about responding to fear. The Redskins' outside linebacker subscribed to a rigorous year-round conditioning program to keep himself in peak physical shape. He spent countless hours in the weight room strengthening himself and did sprints and middle-distance running to improve his endurance. He knew that the more sweat that poured out, the crisper his performance would be by the fourth quarter of a game. His chiseled physique carried only 6 percent body fat.

Such an unwavering commitment was instrumental to Coleman playing 16 NFL seasons—all with the Redskins. "I was afraid of losing my job," he said. "I never got to the point of being complacent. I always wanted to stay one step ahead of anybody and everybody. It was something where, if I don't do what I need to do, it's very easy my career could be cut short or become premature."

Coleman is one of three Redskins to play at least 16 years with the franchise, along with Sammy Baugh (16) and Darrell Green (20), and saw action in 216 games, a team record until Green broke it in 1997. The Redskins brought in players to compete for Coleman's position but would have been foolish to part ways. He tallied 56.5 sacks, the team's fourth-highest total, and as one of the top coverage linebackers of his day, he intercepted 17 passes. He also had 15 fumble recoveries, the second-most in team history, 1,009 tackles, and four touchdowns.

"I was in the NFL for 30 years, and he's probably the best cover linebacker I was ever associated with and the best cover linebacker I've ever seen play the game," said Larry Peccatiello, the Redskins' linebacker coach for most of Coleman's tenure in D.C. "If they had a Hall of Fame for nickel linebackers, Monte Coleman would be in it. He had some injuries that held him out a little bit, but he wasn't an injury-prone guy. He was a great athlete, he was fast."

Coleman never dreamed he would play as long as he did. After not playing high school football, he walked on at an

NAIA college, Central Arkansas. The 6–2, 215-pounder played safety and cornerback in his first three years before switching to linebacker as a senior. He set a school record with 22 interceptions and received all-conference honors.

He became the first Central Arkansas player ever drafted in the NFL when the Redskins, who had never seen him play or practice, chose him in the 11th of 12 rounds in 1979. "I didn't go to that school, but we saw tapes of him," said Bobby Beathard, then the Redskins' general manager. [College scouting director] Dick Daniels raved about what an athlete he was and how fast he was. He was a dominant player at that level and, boy, could he run."

The Redskins guessed right. Coleman impressed the coaching staff with his strength, aggressiveness, quickness and instincts and was positioned as an outside linebacker. He played in all 16 games as a rookie and came to specialize in nickel pass coverage and blitzing. He also stood out on special teams. He intercepted a career-high three passes in both 1980 and 1981, and recorded a career-high 10.5 sacks in 1984 as part of a team-record 66-sack season.

Coleman, however, was dogged by injuries that forced him to miss chunks of playing time, despite the strenuous workout plan he followed to maintain his size, speed, and strength. He bulked up to 240 pounds and came to bench press 400 pounds, sporting a 53-inch chest and a 35-inch waist. At his best, he ran the 40 in 4.4 seconds.

Coaches and players were in awe of his vast physical ability. Peccatiello said that Coleman's nickname was "super" because he was "such a great specimen and a great athlete." In Beathard's eyes, he was probably faster than some of the squad's safeties.

"Monte Coleman may have been the most gifted athlete that I played with," said safety Mark Murphy, who played several years with Coleman. "He bulked up quickly, he didn't look like a safety when he got to us. He was so fast, I would not have wanted to race him."

"Monte was extremely strong," said defensive tackle Dave Butz, a long-time teammate of Coleman's. "Our weight coach would ride on his back up and down as he did push-ups."

After contributing to Redskins teams that played in four Super Bowls in the franchise's glory years of the 1980s and early 1990s, Coleman, who won three Super Bowl rings, was in the twilight of his career. Nevertheless, he recorded his finest performance ever in a 30–17 victory over Atlanta in 1993, his 15th season. His phenomenal day featured 15 tackles, two sacks, an interception and a forced fumble. He also recovered a fumble and ran 29 yards for a touchdown.

On retiring at age 37 at the end of the 1994 season, Coleman was one of four 1979 rookies who had lasted 16 seasons. None of the other three, quarterback Joe Montana, kicker Matt Bahr, and guard Max Montoya, were with the same team.

## STEPHEN DAVIS

RB, No. 48, Auburn • 6–0, 234 • **NFL Career:** 1996–2006 (11 seasons) • **Redskins Years:** 1996–2002 (7) • **Born:** March 1, 1974 (Spartanburg, S.C.)

For Redskins running back Stephen Davis, it was a case of waiting, watching, and learning. In his first three seasons, Davis bided his time while observing how two teammates,

running back Terry Allen and kick returner Brian Mitchell, carried the ball. He saw in both of them a toughness and a willingness to take on tacklers with reckless abandon, not to sidestep or dance around them as Davis had been prone to do. Davis was a reserve tailback in his first two seasons and played fullback in his third, rushing for 815 yards and five touchdowns.

Thus, when the time came for the 6–0, 234-pound Davis to carry the mantle as the Redskins' starting tailback, he was primed. In 1999, the bruising back rushed 290 times for a franchise-record 1,405 yards (NFL-high 4.8 average), despite missing the last two games because of injury. His yardage total was first in the NFC and third in the NFL. He also rushed for all of his touchdowns (17) and scored the most points in the league by a running back (104).

Davis, who made the Pro Bowl and was named The Quarterback Club Redskin Player of the Year, fueled a 10–6 squad that reached the second round of the playoffs. The Redskins adopted the mantra, "Believin' in Stephen."

"I learned from guys like Brian Mitchell and Terry Allen, seeing them run week in and week out," Davis said at the time. "Now, it's just paying off. I'm just utilizing what I've learned from them and making myself better."

The Redskins rewarded Davis with a nine-year, $90 million contract just before the 2000 season. "This is a big day," Redskin coach Norv Turner said at a press conference announcing the deal. "Stephen, to me, is one of the great stories I've been around. This has been a long ride for him. We felt he could be a great runner. He had to wait his turn."

Davis, a blend of power and speed, chalked up two more 1,000-yard campaigns in a Redskins uniform, 1,318 in 2000 behind an offensive line decimated by injuries and a new franchise record of 1,432 in 2001, becoming the first Redskin to rush for more than 1,000 yards in three straight seasons. He made the Pro Bowl again in 2000. "I'm downhill," he once told USA Today. "I want to get north-south, get in guys' faces. When you run at them, you're hard to stop."

Pretty good for a fourth-round pick in 1996 out of Auburn, where he placed high on the school's all-time rushing list (2,811 yards). He was a consensus Southeastern Conference first-team choice as a senior, when he tied Bo Jackson's single-season school record for touchdowns (17).

The workhorse's production tailed off in 2002 in coach Steve Spurrier's pass-happy offense; he rushed 207 times for 820 yards. Disgruntled, he signed as an unrestricted free agent with Carolina in February 2003, after piling up 5,790 rushing yards as a Redskin, 85 yards short of the team's all-time second-place mark held by Larry Brown.

Davis rushed for a career-high 1,444 yards for Carolina in 2003 and made his third Pro Bowl but experienced knee problems in the next two seasons and was released. He played with St. Louis in 2006.

## AL DEMAO

C-LB, No. 53, Duquesne • 6–2, 214 • **NFL Career:** 1945–53 (9 seasons) • **Redskins Years:** 1945–53 (9) • **Born:** February 29, 1920 (New Kensington, Pa.)

Al DeMao was one of the best centers in the NFL in the late 1940s and early 1950s. The 6–2, 215-pounder, who played

Al DeMao

when the Redskins hosted the Steelers at Griffith Stadium on November 2, 1952. Fans chipped in and bought him a new car that was presented during a halftime ceremony. The *Washington Evening Star* quoted Redskins owner George Preston Marshall as calling DeMao a "great athlete and a great citizen."

"DeMao was a good liaison man between the Redskins and the press, radio and public," wrote Lewis F. Atchison of the *Star.* "Sportswriters could rehash a game with him and come up with an intelligent and interesting story. He was at ease on television and radio, and no civic, club, or church meeting was too small for him to address. He never said, 'I can't make it,' even though there were times when it was inconvenient to attend."

DeMao played in all 60 games over his last five seasons, despite being banged up with injuries at times.

"From 1945 'till the last few weeks, DeMao has been the Redskins' No. 1 center, and no Washington player ever has given more of himself," Dave Slattery of the *Washington Daily News* wrote near the end of the 1952 season. "Throughout his career, Al has been a player's player."

## CHUCK DRAZENOVICH

LB-FB, No. 36, Penn State • 6–1, 225 • **NFL Career:** 1950–59 (10 seasons) • **Redskins Years:** 1950–59 (10) • **Born:** August 7, 1927 (Jere, W.Va.) • **Died:** February 27, 1992 (Annandale, Va.)

Nobody wants to mess with a college heavyweight boxing champ. Many opponents felt that way about Chuck Drazenovich.

The 6–1, 230-pound linebacker, described by Redskins publicists as a "tooth-jarring tackler," shook up many foes in his 10-year NFL career, all in Washington. He anchored the Redskins' defense and earned a litany of decorations, including multiple Pro Bowl and All-Pro honors.

Redskins running back Don Bosseler, a teammate of Drazenovich's for three seasons, compared him to another hard-hitting linebacker of that era: Eagles' Hall of Famer Chuck Bednarik. "He was tough as nails, almost like a Bednarik," Bosseler said. "He was a leader on defense and got the job done."

"Chuck Drazenovich was a great football player, a great linebacker," said Hall of Fame middle linebacker Sam Huff, whose first four NFL seasons were Drazenovich's last four.

Drazenovich's toughness was likely a product of his origins. He grew up in the coal-mining, steel-manufacturing town of West Brownsville, Pennsylvania, where "muscle is more prized than money" and where "the natives lift weights, squeeze bricks, pile up kegs of nails, and indulge in arm wrestling," Lewis F. Atchison of the *Washington Evening Star* once wrote in an article about Drazenovich. He starred in football and track in high school and played quarterback at Penn State. He was the 1950 college heavyweight boxing champ and established himself as the greatest shot putter in Penn State history at the time.

Detroit drafted Drazenovich in 1949 when he had another year of college eligibility. He played out his final season and was chosen by the Redskins in a special player pool in 1950. Positioned as a fullback and middle guard in the days of single-platoon football, he made an immediate impression.

"He has made everybody in camp, from coach Herman Ball to his teammates who have felt him rock and sock them both

when defenses regularly attacked offenses with six- and seven-man lines, often relied on his cleverness to block opponents and eliminate them from the play.

"Al was not that big, but he would out-fox you," said Jim Ricca, a Redskin middle guard who teamed with DeMao. "He'd lead-block in a certain direction, and the defense would think the runner was coming that way, but the runner was going the other way. He used your body to block you. Whatever direction you were going in, he took you. He was very smart, very intelligent."

DeMao also played linebacker, intercepting eight passes in his nine-year career—all with the Redskins.

The Redskins drafted DeMao, an All-American lineman at Duquesne, in the ninth round in 1942. He instead served in the Navy during World War II, rising to the rank of lieutenant, and commanded an amphibious landing ship during the historic Normandy invasion on June 6, 1944.

DeMao joined the Redskins in midseason 1945. He played in five games that year as part of a squad that reached the NFL championship game. He played in 11 games in 1946 and gradually took over as the starting center. That season marked the start of a long downward spiral for the Redskins, but snapping the ball to the man DeMao called the best quarterback ever—Sammy Baugh—offset the frustration. "I played with the great Sammy Baugh for eight years, so I couldn't have asked for anything more," he said.

DeMao, who was very popular with teammates, sportswriters and in the community, was honored with "Al DeMao Day"

Chuck Drazenovich

on offense and defense, feel his presence—some painfully," wrote Al Costello of the Washington Times-Herald.

Drazenovich, nicknamed "Charlie Cro" because of his Croatian ancestry, played on offense and defense in his first five seasons. He ran 117 times for 330 yards and eight touchdowns during that period, proving to be a "deadly yard-getter" in short yardage and goal-line situations, Redskin publicists wrote.

In 1955, Redskins coach Joe Kuharich made a move that transformed Drazenovich's career. Kuharich wanted to unveil a new alignment that would upgrade his defense, so he moved Drazenovich from middle guard, where he set up in a three-point stance, to a few feet deeper in a stand-up position. The switch helped Drazenovich better exploit his quickness and formed the basis for the 4–3 defense, which caught on in the NFL and remains a staple of the game today. At the same time, Drazenovich became perhaps the first middle linebacker as the position is currently known. "[Long-time Dallas coach] Tom Landry is credited with developing the four down linemen and three linebackers when he was the Giants' defensive coach in the late 1950s," NFL Films president Steve Sabol said. "But we saw this defense for the first time when Joe Kuharich coached the Redskins."

Drazenovich played middle linebacker exclusively for the rest of his career. He made the Pro Bowl in the 1955, 1956, 1957, and 1958 seasons and earned second-team All-Pro honors in three of those years. And he was a bright spot on a defense that struggled through a deplorable period in Redskins history. Charlotte News sportswriter Max Muhleman, who called Drazenovich an "ace linebacker and defensive signal caller," described how Washington's defense missed

him when he sat out a 21–0 loss to Green Bay in 1959: "This is nothing to be dogmatic about, but don't the Washington Redskins without Chuck Drazenovich somehow remind you of Rice Krispies with mufflers? No snap, no crackle, no defense."

Drazenovich retired after the 1959 season. Career-wise, he intercepted 15 passes and recovered seven fumbles, while playing in 113 of a possible 120 games, starting 60 straight in one stretch.

## BRAD DUSEK

LB, No. 59, Texas A&M • 6–2, 220 • **NFL Career:** 1974–81 (8 seasons) • **Redskins Years:** 1974–81 (8) • **Born:** December 13, 1950 (Temple, Tex.)

It's too bad Brad Dusek failed to get the full credit he was due. A very underrated player, No. 59 was one of the best outside linebackers in Redskins history.

In his eight-year NFL career, all in Washington, Dusek was a force on the left side and seemed to be always around the ball. He recovered 16 fumbles, intercepted four passes, and recorded 11 sacks. He had three fumble returns for touchdowns, second in NFL history at the time. Dusek posted more than 100 tackles in three straight seasons (1977–79) and led the Redskins twice during that period.

"Brad was a hell of a linebacker," said Rusty Tillman, a special teams ace and a teammate of Dusek's for four seasons. "He was a great special teams guy, too."

## Boxing Champ Gets Cold Feet

For three seasons in the mid-1960s, Chuck Drazenov-ich was a Redskins color analyst for WMAL radio in Washington. The play-by-play man at the time, Steve Gilmartin, remembers Drazenovich as a funny guy who came up with "things right off the top of his head that would internally bust me up." One of them was a story about a run-in Drazenovich had with Ed Neal, a 6–4, 285-pound lineman who played mostly for the Packers from 1945 to 1951. As Gilmartin tells it:

Drazenovich said they were playing a preseason game in Kansas City against the Packers. On a couple of kickoffs he had been cheap-shotted by this guy named Ed Neal, whose nickname was "The Blacksmith." So Drazenovich said to him, "I'm going to get your ass after this game." And the guy kind of looked at him and shrugged and walked away. So [Drazenovich] and some other Redskins went out to have a few beers after the game and went into a saloon. There was a lot of raucous yelling from the back room. Drazenovich said, "Let's see what's going on there." He went in and there's this guy sitting at a table, and he's breaking beer bottles over his arm. This is getting applause. Drazenovich said, "Who's that?" And someone said, "That's the guy you were going to fight." Drazenovich said, "Screw that." He went out and got himself a drink. He thought this thing isn't going to be that easy.

Dusek played a myriad of positions in college at Texas A&M. He rushed for 528 yards at fullback as a senior and was drafted in the third round as a linebacker by New England in 1973. The Patriots traded him before the season to the Redskins for defensive lineman Donnell Smith.

In the nation's capital, Dusek united with a coach who loved his veterans, George Allen. "It was kind of obvious that coach Allen didn't like rookies," Dusek said in the *Washington Star* in 1976. "I didn't know what to expect—if they made the trade because they wanted me, or just because they wanted to get rid of somebody."

The Dusek acquisition evolved into one of Allen's shrewdest deals among the many he made over the years: Smith was soon out of the league, but Dusek went on to an excellent NFL career. He spent the 1973 season on the taxi squad but appeared in every game in 1974, excelling on special teams and backing up outside linebacker Dave Robinson. When Robinson retired before the 1975 season, Dusek became the starter.

Dusek started 74 straight regular-season games at linebacker in the next five years. He was recognized as one of the best at his position and as a quiet and unassuming man who let his play do the talking. Savvy and a little undersized for his

position at 220 pounds, he was a "thinking man's linebacker, the type who uses finesse rather than sheer strength to play the position," Steve Guback of the *Star* once wrote.

Dusek gave All-Pro performances like the one in a 10–9 win over the Packers in 1977. He made 11 tackles and had a hand in three sacks. He was all over the place.

"People don't remember Brad hardly ever played linebacker before he came [to] us," Torgy Torgeson, the Redskins' defensive coordinator during Dusek's first four years in D.C., once said in the *Washington Post*. "He really does get better every week. His biggest attributes are his quickness and his toughness. He's got great intensity, and he hustles all over the field."

Dusek, who once received All-Pro recognition, played in every game from 1974 to 1980 (104). He missed six games in 1981 because of injuries and retired.

## HENRY ELLARD

WR, No.85, Fresno State • 5–11, 188 • **NFL Career:** 1983–98 (16 seasons) • **Redskins Years:** 1994–98 (5) • **Born:** July 21, 1961 (Fresno, Calif.)

Redskins coach Norv Turner knew the diligent, no-nonsense player he was getting when free agent receiver Henry Ellard signed with Washington in April 1994 in the twilight of a distinguished career.

Turner had been Ellard's position coach for six years with the Los Angeles Rams, where Ellard amassed nearly 10,000 yards receiving in his first 11 seasons and was a three-time Pro Bowler. He came to the Redskins as part of an offensive overhaul following a 4–12 campaign and the departure of star receivers Art Monk and Ricky Sanders.

"Henry is not only a veteran receiver, but one who is experienced working within our system," Turner said after a minicamp in the 1994 off-season. "The younger receivers have already learned a lot just from watching him."

Ellard led the Redskins in receiving for three straight seasons, becoming the first Redskin to do so since Charley Taylor in the 1970s. He averaged 61 catches, 1,139 yards and four touchdowns from 1994 to 1996 and topped the league in receiving average (19.5 yards) in 1996 at age 35.

Ellard lacked blazing speed but compensated for it by running impeccable routes. He also possessed a keen sense for finding the first-down marker. Of his 182 receptions in his first three seasons, 93 percent went for first downs. His nickname was "Grasshopper," for he was a top intercollegiate triple-jumper at Fresno State. He qualified for the 1992 Olympic Trials in the triple jump.

His receiving numbers slipped in 1997, and the Redskins didn't re-sign him. He kept himself in shape by running sprints at Cal State-Fullerton and signed with the Patriots during the 1998 campaign. He played five games in New England and ended his career by returning to Washington for the final three games that year.

Ellard retired ranked sixth in NFL history in catches (814) and third in receiving yards (13,777). He has been a preliminary nominee for induction into the Pro Football Hall of Fame.

# ANDY FARKAS

RB-WB-DB-KR, No. 44, Detroit • 5–10, 189 • **NFL Career:** 1938–45 (8 seasons) • **Redskins Years:** 1938–44 (7) • **Born:** May 2, 1916 (Clay Center, Ohio) • **Died:** April 10, 2001 (Traverse City, Mich.)

The loss of Hall of Fame running back Cliff Battles after the Redskins' 1937 championship season left a gaping hole in their backfield. "Handy" Andy Farkas filled the void.

Farkas, also known as "Anvil Andy," played in Washington during the next eight seasons, rushing for nearly 2,000 yards and leading the squad on the ground in 1938, 1939, 1942, and 1943. A great all-around player, he also tallied 1,086 receiving yards and intercepted 11 passes playing defensive back. He returned two kickoffs and a punt for touchdowns.

"He was an exceptionally good ballplayer," said Clyde Shugart, a Redskin lineman who teamed with Farkas. "He wasn't the fastest guy on the team, but he was very shifty when he ran the ball."

Farkas was a star runner at the University of Detroit, where he led the nation in scoring as a senior in 1937. The Redskins chose the 5–10, 190-pounder with their No. 1 choice in the 1938 draft, and early that season he made the home fans at Griffith Stadium forget about Battles, scoring on 1-, 7-, and 12-yard runs in a 37–13 rout of the Cleveland Rams. "If you were downtown at that moment, that tremendous roar you heard was 24,389 fans shouting their huzzahs for the little Hungarian from the University of Detroit," *Washington Post* columnist Shirley Povich wrote.

Farkas rushed for a league-high six touchdowns as a rookie, then produced his top season statistically in 1939, setting a then-NFL record with 11 touchdowns—five rushing, five receiving, and one on an interception return. One touchdown was on a 99-yard pass reception, the first of many times that play has happened in the NFL. His 68 points (he also kicked two extra points) were a league high that year.

Just before the 1940 season, Vincent X. Flaherty of the *Washington Times-Herald* wrote that Farkas was better than his childhood idol, legendary running back Red Grange: "Farkas made himself a great football player despite the fact you could never convince us he was cut out for the game," Flaherty wrote. "He made himself a great back simply through sheer determination to follow the touchdown trail of his idol. And though in years to come Andy's name may be long forgotten when Grange is yet riding the magic carpet of immortality . . . we firmly believe Grange never saw the day when he could carry Andy's shoes as a ball carrier. Perhaps Andy's touchdown record in professional football may support our argument."

Farkas missed nearly the whole 1940 season due to a knee injury and, after performing below expectations the next year, he was back at full speed in 1942. Mr. Everything rushed 125 times for 468 yards and three touchdowns, caught 11 passes for 143 yards and two scores, returned 16 punts for 219 yards (13.7 average), and intercepted three passes. He returned a kickoff 94 yards for a score.

Farkas was also key in a 14–6 win over Chicago in the NFL title game. With the Redskins up, 7–6, in the third quarter, he rushed 10 times on a 12-play, 44-yard drive in the third quarter, plunging into the end zone from the 1.

Farkas takes off on a run during a Redskins spring training practice in 1940 near the Washington Monument.

But on the ensuing kickoff, he took a shot in the head and nearly lost consciousness. As the *Washington Post* told it, he sat on the bench the rest of the game thinking he was in Detroit. He also wanted to notify his mother, whom he thought was in the stands but was really in Toledo, Ohio, that he was okay. Afterward, teammates congratulated Farkas for his fine performance, but he was too dazed to acknowledge anything. He sadly shook his head and muttered, "I sure hate to miss a game like that."

"Andy may not be able to remember his performance," the *Post* wrote, "but you can bet almost anything the Bears won't forget it."

# DICK FARMAN

G, No. 21, Washington State • 6–0, 219 • **NFL Career:** 1939–43 (5 seasons) • **Redskins Years:** 1939–43 (5) • **Born:** July 26, 1916 (Belmond, Iowa) • **Died:** May 5, 2002 (Seattle, Wash.)

Dick Farman was a standout guard for the Redskins during their glory days in the late 1930s and early 1940s. He played in 49 games over five seasons, receiving second-team All-Pro honors in 1940 and 1942 and near-consensus first-team All-Pro recognition in 1943. The Redskins reached the NFL championship game in each of those three seasons, winning once.

In college, Farman was an ironman guard for Washington State. He saw all but 11 of a possible 600 minutes of action in his final season. The Redskins drafted him in the 14th round in 1939.

According to the *Washington Post*, Farman and fellow Redskin Clyde Shugart formed perhaps the league's best pair of guards in 1940 and 1941.

# FRANKIE FILCHOCK

TB-QB-DB-HB, No. 30, Indiana • 5–11, 193 • **NFL Career:** 1938–41, 44–46, 50 (8 seasons) • **Redskins Years:** 1938–41, 44–45 (6) • **Born:** October 8, 1916 (Crucible, Pa.) • **Died:** June 20, 1994 (Lake Oswego, Okla.)

He was the Redskins' other great passer during their early years in Washington. Sammy Baugh was the best, but Frankie Filchock was darn good, too.

Filchock threw for 3,266 yards in five and a half seasons with the Redskins, with a 52 percent completion clip (224 of 431). He came close to winning the NFL passing title in 1939 and won it outright in 1944. He also rushed for 1,478 yards and seven touchdowns.

Born to Slovak parents in the coal-mining town of Crucible in western Pennsylvania, Filchock starred at Indiana University and was a second-round selection of the Pittsburgh Pirates in 1938. (The Pirates took future Supreme Court Justice Byron "Whizzer" White in the first round.) He played six games for Pittsburgh until the Redskins bought him as a replacement for the ailing Baugh. He was instrumental to Washington reaching the season finale in 1938 with a chance at winning the Eastern Division title.

The next year, Filchock recorded league highs in completion percentage (61.8) and touchdowns (11), plus 1,094 passing yards and a 111.6 quarterback rating. He also threw the first 99-yard touchdown pass in the NFL and rushed for a career-high 413 yards. He earned All-Pro recognition.

Filchock staged a contract holdout before the 1940 season and went to Kentucky to play pro baseball. While he was there, local media speculated that times could get tough for the Redskins without him. "Filchock, in case your memory is cloudy, [is] probably the best all-around back the Redskins' owned," Bob Ruark of the *Washington Daily News* wrote. "There isn't much he can't do on a gridiron, which includes a weekly fracture of his nose. Even a forward pass from his 1-yard line comes under the head of highly practicable and successful football with Filchock."

Filchock stayed with the Redskins through the 1941 season, after which he entered the U.S. Navy during World War II. He played for the Georgia Pre-Flight squad and was named to the United Press All-Service team as a tailback. He returned to the Redskins in 1944, the year they transitioned from a single-wing backfield to the T-formation, and edged Baugh as the league's best passer. He posted league highs in completions (84), completion percentage (57.1), and touchdown passes (13), in addition to 1,139 passing yards. He again received All-Pro honors.

Soon after putting up a valiant effort with two scoring passes in a one-point loss to Cleveland in the 1945 NFL championship game, Filchock, tired of being Baugh's backup, threatened to jump to the new All-America Football Conference if he wasn't traded, according to the *Washington Times-Herald*. The Redskins dealt him to the Giants, and he recorded big passing numbers as New York won the 1946 Eastern Division title.

NFL officials questioned Filchock and teammate Merle Hapes about an attempt by a man to fix the NFL championship game against the Bears. The league suspended Hapes but let Filchock play. He threw two touchdowns that day in a 24–14 loss to Chicago, but NFL Commissioner Bert Bell later suspended Filchock and Mapes indefinitely. (Filchock had also

been rumored to be involved in a possible gambling scandal with the Redskins in 1943.)

Filchock went to the Canadian Football League and coached and played two seasons each with Hamilton and Montreal. He was named league MVP in 1948 and played a key role in Montreal's Grey Cup championship win in 1949.

His NFL suspension was lifted in 1950, and he played one game for the expansion Baltimore Colts. In 1960, he became the first coach of the Denver Broncos in the upstart American Football League and compiled a 7–20–1 record in two seasons.

# PAT FISCHER

CB, No. 37, Nebraska • 5–9, 170 • **NFL Career:** 1961–77 (17 seasons) • **Redskins Years:** 1968–77 (10) • **Born:** January 2, 1940 (St. Edward, Neb.)

Pat Fischer was the type of player you would look at for the first time and say, "No way." No way could this pint-sized man start for nearly 17 seasons at cornerback and play at a high level game after game.

Fischer, listed at 5–9, 170 pounds, was really 169 pounds "soaking wet," according to one of his Redskin teammates, but he was fearless, never backing down from anyone. Whether it was covering much taller receivers or tackling a 230-pound running back head-on, the tenacious athlete got the job done. He is widely credited for inventing the bump-and-run defense.

By the time he retired after the 1977 season, Fischer had played cornerback in more games (213) than anyone in NFL history. He intercepted 56 passes, returning four for touchdowns, recovered 15 fumbles and earned multiple Pro Bowl and All-Pro honors. Redskin safety Kenny Houston, a teammate of Fischer's for five seasons, said that he has Hall of Fame credentials.

"He might be the toughest guy pound for pound I ever knew," said Rusty Tillman, a Redskins special teams star who played with Fischer for eight seasons: "He'd chew that stickum, that stuff you put on your hands to help catch the ball, and you couldn't even talk to him. If you tried, he was like a rabid dog, 'Raaaah.'

"I remember one time, we were playing St. Louis, and the Cardinals ran a sweep, and [offensive lineman] Conrad Dobler pulled out and tried to undercut him. Dobler was one of the dirtiest players in the league. Fischer came up with a handful of mud and just threw it in his face. He was setting the standard right from the get-go: Don't mess with me. He was afraid of nobody."

Such feistiness, as Fischer tells it, stemmed from the fact that he grew up with four older brothers who were very athletic and played football at the University of Nebraska. "It might have been that because I was smaller, you had to overcome that with more aggressiveness," he said. "They demonstrated that, and that's just how I played."

Fischer starred at quarterback and halfback at Nebraska, and was drafted in the 17th round by St. Louis in 1961. On the first day of training camp, the diminutive rookie learned there were no helmets or shoulder pads that fit him. "I just ran up and down the sidelines in shorts for the first few days," he said. "Then, I went over to the equipment manager at a

The diminutive Fischer takes an Eagles ball-carrier for a ride in 1968. "He might be the toughest guy pound for pound I ever knew," one of Fischer's Redskin teammates said.

nearby college, and he gave me a helmet and shoulder pads. Unfortunately, the helmet at the college was purple, and the Cardinals' helmet was white with a red bird. So I had distinguishing features when I went out on the field."

Fischer spent his first two seasons mostly returning kicks. But the coaches noticed his effectiveness at cornerback in stopping end runs and tapped him to start at the position in 1963, when he picked off eight passes. The next season, he intercepted a career-high 10 and returned two for touchdowns, earning Pro Bowl and consensus first-team All-Pro honors. He played three more years in St. Louis and signed with the Redskins as a free agent in June 1968.

The Redskins hoped Fischer would strengthen a defensive backfield that had just traded safety Paul Krause, now the all-time NFL interception leader. Fischer made the Pro Bowl for the third and final time in 1969 and in 1971 became a charter member of the veteran-dominated Over the Hill Gang under new coach George Allen.

Fischer was 31 at the time, the career twilight for many NFL players, and he had a disc removed from his back before the 1972 season. But he persevered on defensive-oriented squads that made the playoffs five times, anchoring the left side of the secondary in an era when defenders could hit receivers all over the field before the ball was in the air. Nicknamed "Mouse," he was a fan favorite in Washington largely because of his passion and ability to excel in a perceived underdog role. A *Washington Star-Daily News* headline read: "There's No Job Too Big For Little (5–9) Fischer."

Meanwhile, Fischer was busy shutting down receivers who towered over him, one being Eagles 6–8 wideout Harold Car-

michael. Fischer was matched against Carmichael whenever the NFC East foes met, and their battles were legendary, with Fischer holding his own against the man who caught 590 passes. "He hated Fischer," Tillman said of Carmichael.

"It doesn't matter how tall they are," Fischer reasoned. "You don't really have to do anything more than hit a hand or an arm. The question is, can he catch the ball with one hand?"

As for his keys to tackling, Fischer focused on leverage, proper positioning of his weight, and balance. Knowing that at his size he was weaker than many ball carriers, he tackled at angles where he made the greatest impact. "He may have been small," an NFL veteran once said, "but he hit like a son of a gun."

"Pat Fischer was a neat guy," NFL Films president Steve Sabol said. "I never knew a player who could explain the science of tackling in terms of geometry. We were doing a film on the hardest hits, and he got into an explanation of leveraging and angles and geometry. It was like being in a mechanical drawing class. When it comes to tackling, you think of putting your shoulder down and knocking some guy's helmet off. But he had a whole science about what angle, what degree you should hit the guy, how your legs would be bent, when you should explode into him. He wasn't one of the hardest tacklers but one of the deadliest. He rarely missed."

Said Kenny Houston, "He played 17 years, and that's kind of unheard of for a guy his size. He showed up every Sunday, and I'm thinking, 'How can this man do this?' He was just a tremendous competitor."

## ROB GOODE

FB-HB-LB-DB, No. 21 (also wore No. 39), Texas A&M • 6–4, 225 • **NFL Career:** 1949–51, 54–55 (5 seasons) • **Redskins Years:** 1949–51, 54–55 (5) • **Born:** June 5, 1927 (Roby, Tex.)

Rob Goode played less than five full seasons with the Redskins, but the bruising 6–4, 225-pound fullback was the team's all-time leading ground gainer when he departed early in the 1955 season.

Goode rushed 520 times for 2,257 yards (4.3 average) as a Redskin. He also set team records (since broken) with an 80-yard touchdown run, and 951 rushing yards and seven 100-yard games in one season. He was a decent receiver and linebacker—and tough.

"Rob takes a lot of punishment, and he seems to get over bruises quickly," Redskins coach Herman Ball said in the *Washington Evening Star* early in the 1951 season. "If he comes back after being out two days with a twisted ankle, he's usually ready to travel in high gear. Some of the others need two or three more days to get in shape, but not Goode. I think he'll do all right against the Giants."

Goode played in college at Texas A&M, where he was a one-man gang as a senior, leading his squad in passing, scoring, punt and kickoff returns, pass interceptions, and punting. He was the Redskins' top draft choice in 1949 and led the team in rushing for the next three seasons. His 951 yards in 1951 fell 20 yards shy of the league-leading mark, but he was No. 1 in rushing touchdowns (nine). In one game that year, he "ripped through and around the [Chicago] Cardinal line," as the *Washington Post* put it, for 104 of the Redskins' 232 rushing yards. He made the Pro Bowl that year.

He spent the next two years in the Marines and rejoined the Redskins in 1954 and went to the Pro Bowl for the second time. Injuries stunted his production early in the 1955 season, and the Redskins placed him on waivers after three games. He played the rest of the season for the Eagles and retired.

In addition to his rushing totals, Goode caught 43 passes for 503 yards and one touchdown as a Redskin. His dad once played semi-pro baseball with Redskins legend Sammy Baugh, Goode's teammate for three seasons in Washington.

## DARRYL GRANT

DT, No. 77, Rice • 6–1, 275 • **NFL Career:** 1981–91 (11 seasons) • **Redskins Years:** 1981–90 (10) • **Born:** Nov. 22, 1959 (San Antonio, Tex.)

Darryl Grant was a valuable Redskins defensive tackle during the 1980s. After playing his 1981 rookie season on the offensive line, he switched to the defensive side and averaged 68 tackles in his next nine seasons and twice posted more than 100, becoming the first Redskin ever to top the century mark in 1983. He also tallied 27 career sacks.

"We moved him to defensive tackle because he was so explosive," said Bobby Beathard, then the Redskins' general manager.

Grant's admirable statistics aside, he's indelibly linked with a play that is frozen in time in Redskins history: his interception of a tipped pass that he returned for a touchdown to secure a 31–17 victory over Dallas in the NFC championship game on January 17, 1983. The play catapulted Grant into the national limelight, for he was pictured on the cover of *Sports Illustrated* on Jan. 31, 1983, spiking the ball emphatically in the end zone. The cover read, "Wham! Bam! It's the Redskins! Darryl Grant Finishes off the Cowboys."

Grant said people remind him of the play all the time:

People walk up to me, some of whom I don't know from Adam, and say, "Hey, I just want to thank you for making that play." It's a great feeling, a very warming feeling because, when you think about it in the greater picture . . . as long as you have your memory, nobody can take that away. If people feel that strongly about those memories, it makes me feel good.

It just never goes away. It still sends chills down my spine.

## DARRELL GREEN

CB, No. 28, Texas A&I • 5–8, 170 • **NFL Career:** 1983–2002 (20 seasons) • **Redskins Years:** 1983–2002 (20) • **NFL 1990s All-Decade Team** • **Born:** February 15, 1960 (Houston, Tex.)

They called him "Mr. Redskin." For a man who played in more seasons and more games than anyone else to ever wear the burgundy and gold, and who represented the organization with utmost class, the title is fitting.

Darrell Green is an iconic figure in Redskin lore and one of the most celebrated cornerbacks in league history. In 20 seasons in Washington, the four-time NFL's Fastest Man and seven-time Pro Bowler intercepted a team-record 54 passes (Brig Owens is next with 36) and returned six of them for another team-record six touchdowns. He played in 295 games and started 258, other all-time team highs. His 20 seasons with one franchise, a phenomenal feat that may never be repeated in today's free-agency-driven NFL, tied the all-time NFL mark set by Los Angeles and St. Louis Rams offensive lineman Jackie Slater. Green, who retired at age 42 after avoiding any career-threatening injuries, was the oldest cornerback ever to play in the NFL. He is destined for the Pro Football Hall of Fame and becomes eligible for induction in 2008.

Who would have known that the 5–8, 170-pounder, a self-described "itty bitty" player, would last so long? Certainly not Darrell Green.

"I wanted to try to get a starting job and make the team," Green, speaking prior to his last game, said of his goals upon being drafted in 1983. "I don't know if you call those expectations, as much as hopes and dreams. The mindset of a kid 20 years ago was different. He wasn't thinking, 'Oh man, I know I'm here. I'm Darrell Green.' He was thinking, 'Man, I gotta try to hustle to make the team.'"

Then-Redskins general manager Bobby Beathard, who led efforts to draft Green in 1983, called him a "freak" because of his longevity. "It's not a surprise that he played so well," Beathard said. "But the surprising thing is that he matched up well against much bigger guys, and the other thing is, everybody's surprised that anybody can play 20 years. This guy stayed healthy for most of that time. He took care of himself, he was a strong guy. His athletic ability, agility and quickness probably were responsible for his survival. He would hit people, but he knew how to do it."

As much as Green is revered for his athletic feats, he is also one of the most popular and respected Redskins of all time—a model citizen to the fullest. A man who carried himself with dignity and humbleness, who was soft-spoken, friendly, and introspective when dealing with reporters, Green was the antithesis of the gaudiness and bombastic nature of so many pro athletes today. Case in point: He drove a Volkswagen bug with more than 100,000 miles on it. "He was not egotistical, just a level-headed person," one teammate said.

Green was also very active in local youth groups. In 1988, he founded the Darrell Green Youth Life Foundation, which provides financial, moral, and educational support for underprivileged D.C. youth. In 1996, he was named NFL Man of the Year and received the Bart Starr Award, which honors the player who best exemplifies outstanding character and leadership in the home, on the field, and in the community, and the Ken Houston Humanitarian Award, named after the Hall of Fame Redskins safety. A road near Redskins Park is named Darrell Green Boulevard, and he garnered the most votes in a 2006 *Washington Post* poll on the best Redskin of all time.

"What Darrell had which I've found that most of the great players have—the guys who are really and truly great, great team guys along with being great players—is great character," said Joe Gibbs, who coached Green in his first 10 seasons in Washington. "Darrell really cared for the team and was willing to sacrifice his own goals for the goals of the team. He also was a great athlete, and the Lord blessed him with a great body, and he took care of it. A speed corner who could play until he's [nearly 43] years old, that's unheard of.

"You normally let a guy play another few years if he's the right kind of guy. Darrell was the right kind of guy."

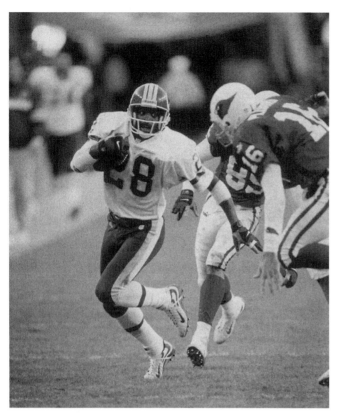

Green holds the Redskins record for interceptions (54) and most seasons played (20).

Green, a Houston native, first starred at Division II Texas A&I (now Texas A&M–Kingsville). In his senior season, 1982, the cornerback was named Lone Star Conference Defensive Player of the year after making 56 tackles and four interceptions. He was also an Associated Press 1st Team Little All-American that year, when he averaged an incredible 20.6 yards on 19 punt returns and returned two of them for touchdowns. He was inducted into the College Football Hall of Fame in 2003. But football was only half the story. He excelled in track, and his 100-meter time of 10.08 was at one point second in the country, behind famed Olympic sprinter Carl Lewis.

Many NFL scouts visited Texas A&I to check him out, including Beathard. "Darrell was a guy who, you could make one visit and look at tapes and in one practice tell what this guy was," Beathard said. "The only knock on him was that he was small. But if you're small, you have to be rare, and he was rare. It wasn't only his speed. It was his ability to recover. He could go from zero to full speed in two steps. That's really rare, and that's what you look for in corners even probably more than just out and out speed."

The 1983 NFL draft was stocked with blue-chip quarterback prospects, including John Elway, Dan Marino, and Jim Kelly, and Beathard said that the defending Super Bowl champion Redskins had their eyes on Marino and Green. When Miami selected Marino with the next-to-last pick in the first round at the time, the 27th, the Redskins swiped Green at No. 28. Green lasted until the final pick in the round because of his size, according to Beathard. "We had Dan Marino rated really high," he said. "We had a quarterback [Joe Theismann], so that wasn't our biggest need. But Dan kept slipping and slipping

and slipping. And we were worried about Darrell being taken. Miami took Marino, and we got Darrell."

The first time Green touched the ball, he returned a punt 61 yards in a 1983 preseason game. The Redskins were then in a contract dispute with cornerback Jeris White, and Green was tapped to start in the season opener against Dallas on September 5, 1983.

A packed house at RFK Stadium and millions watching on TV saw the rookie make one of the most spectacular plays ever in a Monday night game. In the second quarter, speedy Cowboys running back Tony Dorsett was off to the races down the left sideline and looked like a sure bet to reach the end zone. Green came out of nowhere as he sprinted past teammates and tackled Dorsett on the 6. The Cowboys had to settle for a field goal.

Washington lost the game, but the play stands out as one of Green's proudest moments as a Redskin. "The one that had the most national, eye-opening significance is chasing down Tony Dorsett on Monday night football," he said. "My class-

## Green's Greatest Moments

- Coming out of nowhere to chase down Cowboys speedster Tony Dorsett in his first regular-season game as a Redskin in 1983.
- A 72-yard interception return for a touchdown in a playoff game against the Rams on January 1, 1984, one of the longest postseason interception returns in Redskins history.
- Tackling the Rams' Eric Dickerson in a playoff game on December 28, 1986; Dickerson broke free and gained about a 10-yard lead in what looked like a certain touchdown, but Green accelerated and stopped him for a 65-yard gain.
- A career-high three interceptions in a 1987 game against Detroit.
- An acrobatic 52-yard punt return that accounted for the winning points in a 21–17 playoff win over the Bears on January 10, 1988. He fractured ribs on the return while hurdling a Bears player.
- Breaking up a pass at the goal line in the waning seconds of the NFC championship game on January 17, 1988. The play secured a 17–10 win over the Vikings and sent the Redskins to Super Bowl XXII.
- A team-record 78-yard fumble return for a touchdown in a 1993 game against Indianapolis.
- A 7-yard interception return for a score that clinched a 36–30 overtime win over Detroit in 1995. He also made a career-high 12 tackles.
- A career-high 83-yard interception return for a touchdown against the Eagles in 1997.
- Nine solo tackles in a 26–20 overtime win over San Francisco that clinched the NFC East title in 1999.

No. 28 waves goodbye to the crowd at FedExField on his final day as a Redskin, December 29, 2002.

mates and I talked about that in college just months before, thinking who could catch him. The world saw that: my first game, on Monday night."

Redskins defensive tackle Darryl Grant said he was out of position on the play: "It was a misdirection play, and Dorsett cut right up where I was supposed to be. Darrell ran him down from the back side and saved me and saved us. The whole stadium was just in awe. His speed was tremendous."

Green, a runner-up for AP NFL Defensive Rookie of the Year, would produce a slew of other amazing plays in the coming years (see list). He made the Pro Bowl for the first time in his second season (1984) and played in the all-star game twice more before the decade was out. By the 1990s, he showed no signs of slowing down—on the field and the track. In 1991, the year he played in his third Super Bowl and won his second ring, he was a unanimous All-Pro in a second straight season of all-league distinctions. That year he also captured the title of "World's Fastest Athlete" by winning a competition that included football, baseball, and track stars.

"I encouraged Darrell to try out for the Olympics, but he wouldn't do it," said Grant, a teammate of Green's for eight seasons. "I honestly believe he would have won the Gold Medal. Darrell was so fast, but I don't think he ever realized how fast he was. He was a tremendous player and a great teammate."

Green's seventh and final Pro Bowl season was 1997, leaving him two shy of the Redskins' all-time leader, Chris Hanburger. His 17th season, 1999, was a milestone year, for he surpassed Sammy Baugh and Monte Coleman for most seasons in a Redskins uniform. He was named to the NFL 1990s All-Decade Team, along with fellow cornerbacks Deion Sanders, Rod Woodson, and Aeneas Williams.

In addition to his greatness on the field, Green, a consummate professional, was a solid leader in the locker room. "You know why he had great leadership skills?" Charley Taylor, the Redskins' receivers coach from 1981 to 1993, asked rhetorically. "Because he didn't run his mouth a whole lot. When Darrell said something, it made sense. After a while, people said, 'This guy isn't just talking to be talking.' When he said something, it mattered. Darrell was the ultimate player. You wish you had 43 players like him."

Green became a mentor to younger players such as cornerback Champ Bailey. Green helped coach Bailey after the Redskins drafted him in the first round in 1999, providing tutoring and insight. "You play with the best, you pretty much draw a lot of good things from them," Bailey said during his first Redskins training camp. "Having him out there to tell me about the mistakes and things I do good is great. He's just an asset all around the team."

Green started in his first 17 seasons, but the Redskins signed Deion Sanders in 2000 and designated him to start in Green's place. Green being Green gracefully accepted a backup role. Never mind that he had regained his title in the off-season as the fastest Redskin, running a 4.24 in the 40-yard dash. He played his final three years mostly as a nickel cornerback and special teams player.

Green originally announced plans to retire after the 2001 season, his 19th. Late that year, he intercepted a pass by the Eagles' Donovan McNabb to mark the 19th straight season he had picked off at least one throw, an NFL record. McNabb was one of 41 quarterbacks Green intercepted in his career. The same game, a sign in the end zone at FedExField read, "Make it 20 years, No. 28."

The "ageless wonder" obliged. In his final game, a 20–14 win over Dallas on December 29, 2002, at FedExField, the Redskins honored him with a pregame retirement ceremony. With his typical touch of humility, he applauded the fans, and his claps were picked up by microphones and resonated through the stadium.

"It's been a great ride," the Redskins' elder statesman told the boisterous crowd of 80,000-plus. "I know I'm not going to be able to thank everyone. But the obvious thing is, there's no way I could be who I am without you." With that, the final chapter in a truly illustrious career was over. Darrell Green, though, will never be forgotten.

## RUSS GRIMM

G, No. 68, Pittsburgh • 6–3, 273 • **NFL Career:** 1981–91 (11 seasons) • **Redskins Years:** 1981–91 (11) • NFL 1980s All-Decade Team • **Born:** May 2, 1959 (Scottdale, Pa.)

A native of the working-class town of Scottdale, Pennsylvania, near Pittsburgh, Russ Grimm rooted for the dominant Steelers teams of the 1970s that won four Super Bowls. He liked that they were not flashy, just "good, hard-nosed blue collar players" with some great talent at the skill positions, as he put it. In college at Pittsburgh, he practiced at times with some of the Steelers, including Hall of Fame center Mike Webster, and gleaned from their approach to the game.

Grimm brought his own no-nonsense attitude to the NFL. Like a factory-line employee who punches his time card at the start and end of the day, he went about his work in yeoman fashion during an outstanding 11-year career with the Redskins, virtually all of it at left guard.

"I grew up in a small town," he said. "Dad worked at a paper factory, and mom did the books for a local clothing store. Hey, you have a job, you go to work, that's the bottom line. When work's over, have a cold beer, relax, and enjoy the evening."

Grimm's contributions are prominent in franchise lore. A pillar on the squad's overpowering offensive line of the 1980s and early 1990s, the Hogs, he made the Pro Bowl every year from 1983 to 1986, earning first team All-Pro honors in each of those seasons. He was named a starting guard on the NFL's All-Decade Team of the 1980s and has been a finalist for Hall of Fame induction several times.

When reflecting on Grimm, his Redskin teammates and coaches touch on his football savvy, among other attributes. "Russ was the consummate athlete, everything came easy to him," said Jim Hanifan, a Redskins offensive line coach who worked with Grimm for two seasons. "He was exceptionally quick, had great feet, very fine strength, and was a very, very smart player. Russ was a great puller, a great trapper, could make terrific adjustments in ball games. He had it all."

"Probably one of the smartest individuals as far as a football mind," said another ex-Hog, tackle Joe Jacoby. "As far as the intricacies of the game, figuring out something, blocking schemes, game plans."

Linebacker, not guard, was Grimm's dream position growing up. He idolized two nasty middle linebackers now in the Hall of Fame, the Steelers' Jack Lambert and the Bears' Dick Butkus, admiring the way they hit. He played quarterback and linebacker in high school, and was a linebacker in his first two years of college ball at Pitt.

"I wanted to play linebacker all the way," Grimm said. "You were in the middle of everything. It's not that you were playing one defensive end, and the [ball carrier] was running the other way. You had the chance to make all the plays."

After Grimm's sophomore year at Pitt, head coach Jackie Sherrill asked him how he felt about playing center. Grimm

Grimm, here protecting Mark Rypien in 1989, has been a finalist for Hall of Fame induction.

cringed. "I told him I'd never been in a three-point stance in my life, and that I was going to stay at linebacker. He informed me he wasn't asking me, he was telling me they were moving me. So I considered transferring." Grimm talked to West Virginia assistant coach Joe Pendry about playing linebacker, but Pendry was soon hired to coach at Pittsburgh, so Grimm stayed.

His transition to center was rough. "It was a rude awakening," Grimm said. "In spring ball, I'm still learning how to snap the ball and playing against Dave Logan, who went on to play nose tackle in the NFL. It took me a while to get adjusted, but I was stuck. All the other options were eliminated, so I had no other choice but to try to play the position."

Despite his ho-hum attitude, Grimm won the starting center job after bulking up from 240 to 255 pounds. He started for the next two seasons on Pitt teams that were 22–2, earning honorable mention All-American honors and playing in some college all-star games.

The Redskins drafted him in the third round in 1981. But the solid play in training camp of second-year center Jeff Bostic led the coaches to move Grimm to left guard. He made another smooth switch and was named to the NFL All-Rookie team despite playing the last seven games with torn knee cartilage.

In 1982, he played on his first of three NFL championship teams. That season in the Redskins' win in Super Bowl XVII, he helped clear a path that John Riggins used to run 43 yards for a touchdown in the most famous play in team history. The play was called "70 Chip." Grimm also opened holes over the years on "50 Gut," a run to the left side through the tackles. He became synonymous with the "Counter-Trey," a play that epitomized the dominance of the Hogs where he pulled to the right side like a freight train, often with left tackle Jacoby, to create running room.

Grimm, who played at about 275 pounds, said his legs were the strongest part of his body. "I felt if I could get underneath people, then I had a good chance of being successful." He also credited his offensive line coaches for his success, Joe Moore at Pitt and Joe Bugel and Hanifan with the Redskins.

Grimm once turned down a $1.2 million offer to play with the Pittsburgh Maulers of the United States Football League. He saw action in 79 straight games at one point, a streak that ended midway through the 1986 season due to a sprained neck. Other injuries in the coming seasons seriously curtailed his playing time, although when healthy he proved to be one of the most powerful offensive linemen in the league. In all, he played in 140 games before retiring after the 1991 season.

"The thing that impressed me about him is his toughness," said Redskin running back Joe Washington, who played with Grimm for four seasons. "This guy played with more things wrong with him, and a lot of people didn't know that especially when it came to his knees. And he did a good job. He was relentless."

Grimm later served as a Redskins assistant for nine seasons, the first five as tight ends coach and the last four as offensive line coach. He is credited with the early development of the Redskins' bookend offensive tackles of the 21st century, Chris Samuels, a four-time Pro Bowler, and Jon Jansen. He later coached the Steelers' offensive line for five seasons and won another ring when Pittsburgh captured Super Bowl XL. He became Arizona's assistant head coach and offensive line coach in January 2007.

## CHRIS HANBURGER

LB, No. 55, North Carolina • 6–2, 218 • **NFL Career:** 1965–78 (14 seasons) • **Redskins Years:** 1965–78 (14) • **Born:** August 13, 1941 (Fort Bragg, N.C.)

Chris Hanburger acted like a loner. He was very moody around the clubhouse and preferred not to socialize with teammates, and he barely uttered a word to reporters, often saying "no comment."

Hanburger was more sociable on the field, where he went out of his way to greet ball carriers—however unceremoniously. A featherweight of a linebacker, he specialized in brutalizing foes with vicious clothesline tackles. Instead of hitting ball carriers below the waist, textbook-style, the intimidator regularly tackled high, driving his powerful forearms into players to knock them off their feet. He took no mercy, hence his nicknames "The Hammer" and "The Hangman."

"He would go a whole game and not make a tackle below the jaw line," NFL Films president Steve Sabol said. "That was a legal move in the late 1960s and early 1970s. We have shots of him decapitating [Cowboys quarterback] Don Meredith. He would come in on a blitz and get you right around the throat. Few players in NFL history are so distinctive that a move or style of tackling is named after them, like Fred 'The Hammer' Williamson of the Chiefs."

Hanburger denied being especially ferocious: "I don't know that it was ferocity. If you can eliminate the guy and do it legally, then your day should be easier because whoever replaces him shouldn't be as good as he is. It was easier for me to come into somebody high because I had a little more leverage. My philosophy was if you don't hit anybody, you can play forever because you're never going to get hurt. I just tried to take ankles away from people, and I didn't get nailed head-on if I could avoid it."

Hanburger was one of the top outside linebackers of his era. In 14 seasons—all in Washington—he made the Pro Bowl nine times, the most in Redskins history. Positioned mostly on the weak side, he was a three-time All-NFL and four-time All-NFC player. He intercepted 19 passes and recovered 12 fumbles, and scored five touchdowns, two on interception returns and three off of fumble recoveries.

Aside from statistics, Hanburger possessed a brilliant football mind and phenomenal instincts for the game. He called the Redskins' defensive signals from 1973 to 1977 and was reputed as a defensive quarterback for head coach George Allen, a defensive genius himself. One teammate said that observing Hanburger's decisions during games "was like watching a great chess player making moves to counteract what the offense was doing."

"Chris Hanburger put us in more correct defenses than you could shake a stick at," said Dave Butz, a Redskin defensive tackle who played with him for several seasons. "He knew 125 different audibles. He knew all the defensive line calls, as well. He was the general."

"He was at that time the smartest player in the league," said John Hannah, a Hall of Fame offensive tackle for the New England Patriots from 1973 to 1985. "We did everything we could to try to eliminate him from the play. We knew if we didn't neutralize him, then we had less of a chance of winning."

The son of a career U.S. Army officer (perhaps the reason for his ornery personality), Hanburger spent two years in the army before starting his college career at North Carolina. He developed into an All-Atlantic Coast Conference linebacker and was an honorable mention All-American. With apparently little clue of the huge returns they would get from him, the Redskins drafted him in the 18th and final round in December 1964. He was the 244th player selected out of 252.

Hanburger was soon being touted as one of the best rookie linebackers to join the Redskins since Chuck Drazenovich in 1950. He excelled on special teams and broke into the starting lineup at linebacker in the sixth game of the 1965 season. Steve Gilmartin, the Redskins' radio play-by-play voice at the time, said the hard-hitting Jimmy Carr, then in his ninth season, taught Hanburger how to play weak-side linebacker.

Hanburger made the Pro Bowl for the first time in 1966, followed by appearances in the next three seasons. Redskins Hall of Fame linebacker Sam Huff, who played with him for four of his first five seasons, saw greatness in No. 55. "He was so quick off the ball, and he was a great blitzer who would go and get the quarterback," Huff said. "Nine Pro Bowls tells you that guy could play."

Hanburger returned to the Pro Bowl in 1972, probably the best season of his career. He intercepted four passes, scoring one touchdown, and was named NFC Defensive Player of the Year and a unanimous All-Pro, as the Redskins' dominant defense led the team's march to Super Bowl VII. That season kicked off a five-year streak of Pro Bowls for him.

All along, Hanburger proved to be rugged and durable. Beginning in 1968, he started 135 straight games, an amazing stretch that ended in 1977 after he had an appendicitis operation. He compensated for his size—the Redskins listed him

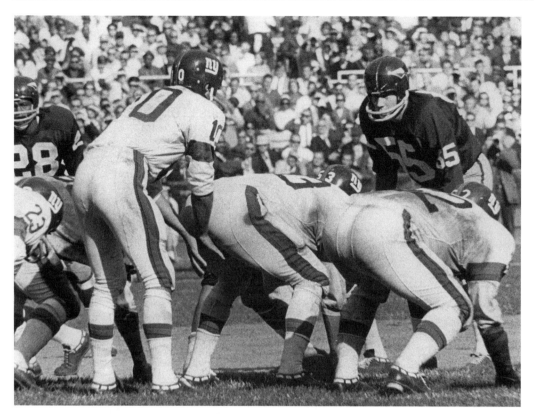

Hanburger eyes Giants quarterback Fran Tarkenton during a game in the late 1960s. Observing the wily linebacker "was like watching a great chess player making moves to counteract what the offense was doing," one of his Redskins teammates said.

at 218, but he dropped to as low as 200 at times—by being remarkably quick and agile. He specialized in blitzing because he was so fast at darting past offensive linemen and blocking backs, often leaving them flat-footed; one of his teammates called him "quick as a cat." In the Redskins' 1977 season-finale, he posted three solo sacks.

"Opponents never knew what he was going to do, where he was coming from," said Brig Owens, a Redskin safety who teamed with Hanburger for 12 seasons. "But they knew if he was coming, he was coming fast. Chris was very strong for his size. He could beat you with finesse or power, or he could throw you off-balance or roll back over you."

Owens is upset that Hanburger hasn't been inducted into the Hall of Fame. "His name should have been on the list of people selected to the Hall of Fame a long time ago," Owens said. "That's how good he was. He was a special player."

## CHARLEY HARRAWAY

RB, No. 31, San Jose State • 6–2, 215 • **NFL Career:** 1966–73 (8 seasons) • **Redskins Years:** 1969–73 (5) • **Born:** September 21, 1944 (Oklahoma City, Okla.)

If there's such a thing as the most devastating Redskins blocking back, Charley Harraway would get a lot of votes.

Harraway led the way for the great Larry Brown from 1969 to 1973, Harraway's five seasons with the Redskins. He averaged a modest 532 yards rushing during that period, but the real value of the 6–2, 215-pound fullback was in throwing crunching blocks that opened sizable holes for Brown, who posted two 1,000-yard seasons at the time.

"He was probably one of the best blocking backs I've ever been associated with," Brown said. "I was doing a lot of the

blocking when I was in college, so I could appreciate the kinds of blocks he made on the field."

In a 38–24 Monday night win over Los Angeles on December 13, 1971, Harraway threw a block that helped the Redskins clinch their first playoff spot in a quarter-century. On fourth-and-goal from the 2, Brown, sweeping wide to the right, cut behind Harraway's earth-shaking block on Rams safety Kermit Alexander and crossed the goal line, giving the Redskins a two-touchdown lead late in the first half.

Harraway played his first three years in Cleveland, and the Redskins paid $100 to sign him off waivers before the 1969 season. In addition to his rushing totals in Washington, he caught 146 passes for 1,142 yards and scored 26 touchdowns. He had 55 receptions alone in his rookie season. He left after the 1973 campaign for the new World Football League, where he played one year for the league-champion Birmingham Americans.

"Charlie Harraway was one of the most underrated team players in the history of the Redskins," said Ken Beatrice, a long-time D.C. radio sports commentator and a member of the panel that selected the 70 greatest Redskins of all time in 2002.

## RICKIE HARRIS

DB-KR, No. 46, Arizona • 5–11, 182 • **NFL Career:** 1965–72 (8 seasons) • **Redskins Years:** 1965–70 (6) • **Born:** May 15, 1943 (St. Louis, Mo.)

He was fearless, zig-zagging through traffic to outmaneuver bigger and stronger players flying at him from all directions. The whole time, speedy and elusive Rickie Harris was so determined to break a punt return for a touchdown. He did so three times in six seasons with the Redskins.

Harris averaged an impressive 8 yards per punt return from 1965 to 1970, as well as 23 yards per kickoff return. His body held up well despite the pounding a kick returner endures, for he played in all but one of a possible 84 games in his Redskin career. Dave Brady of the *Washington Post* praised him for his intrepidness in an article on September 27, 1970:

The Frisky Presence of Rickie Harris on the kick return teams almost guarantees that no Redskins game will be completely devoid of excitement. It may be negative, but it is always suspenseful.

Harris is the daring young man in the flying wedge, disdaining the dangers of a suicidal phase of the sport.

If his forward progress is stymied by headhunters with 20 to 80 pounds on him, 180-pound Harris still is not likely to cop out with a fair catch. He will give ground and risk censure in his enduring quest to break one all the way.

In the same article, Harris said, "I am always thinking of breaking a runback all the way on punts. If I cut to one side, I still keep my eye on the center. If I see any kind of a hole there, I change direction, because I know I will be going against the grain of the tacklers chasing me; they cannot turn back in time."

Harris, also a talented cornerback, signed with the Redskins as a rookie free agent in 1965 after playing at Arizona. He immediately established himself as one of the league's top punt returners, posting a career-high 12.2-yard average and running one back 57 yards for a score. He also returned an interception 34 yards for a touchdown.

In his other two punt returns for touchdowns, he ran 52 yards in the Redskins' 72–41 victory over the Giants in 1966 and 86 yards against the Giants in 1969. He played his last two seasons, 1971 and 1972, with New England.

# KEN HARVEY

LB, No. 57, California • 6–2, 237 • **NFL Career:** 1988–98 (11 seasons) • **Redskins Years:** 1994–98 (5) • **Born:** May 6, 1965 (Austin, Tex.)

Football, as Ken Harvey tells it, was a personal long shot. He played one year of high school ball in Texas, dropped out of school to flip burgers at McDonald's, and then returned for his senior year without rejoining the team. At that point, "football was dead for me," he recalled.

But Harvey refocused and played football at a California junior college before heading to the University of California, winning all-conference honors at linebacker as a senior. He went on to an outstanding 11-year NFL career, playing his last five seasons in Washington, where he was the most celebrated Redskins linebacker in the 1990s by virtue of his four straight Pro Bowl appearances.

Harvey called it a "big-time surprise" that he came so far after his football-related goals didn't exist at one point. "It wasn't something I thought was possible," he said. "To go that far and to last as long as I did is kind of amazing to me."

The 12th overall pick in the 1988 draft, Harvey played his first six seasons in Arizona, building a reputation as one of the league's best outside linebackers; he led the Cardinals in sacks from 1989 to 1993. His career took flight after he signed

Ken Harvey

with the Redskins as an unrestricted free agent in the 1994 off-season.

The 6–2, 237-pounder, a package of speed, quickness, and strength, made the Pro Bowl four straight times, the first Redskin to do so since offensive linemen Joe Jacoby and Russ Grimm (1983–86). Positioned as a linebacker on first and second downs and as a defensive end on third downs, he led the Redskins in sacks in his first four seasons in Washington, averaging 10, in addition to an average of 121 tackles.

His first year in Washington—1994—was perhaps the best season of his career. He posted a career-high 13.5 sacks, finishing tied for first in the NFC and second in the NFL. He also set a Redskins record for most single-season sacks by a linebacker, breaking the mark of 10.5 set by Monte Coleman in 1984. Harvey credited Coleman, who was in his final season in 1994, with improving his ability to play linebacker and defensive tackle Tim Johnson with helping him in rushing the passer.

Harvey missed only one game in his first four years in Washington, but he pulled a hamstring in the 1998 preseason and suffered a knee injury in the 11th game, forcing the Redskins to put him on injured reserve. He tried to rehabilitate himself, but his knee didn't cooperate, and he retired before the 1999 season. He later served as the president of the Redskins Alumni Association and has been a preliminary nominee for induction into the Pro Football Hall of Fame.

"Ken Harvey was just the consummate pro," said quarterback Trent Green, who played with Harvey for four seasons in Washington. "The way he took care of himself, the way he prepared himself in terms of workouts, he was always a guy who spent extra hours in the weight room. I used to watch Ken all the time in amazement in practices. He was a premier pass rusher . . . he did it while being quite a bit smaller than a lot of the tackles he was going up against."

# LEN HAUSS

LB, No. 56, Georgia • 6–2, 235 • **NFL Career:** 1964–77 (14 seasons) • **Redskins Years:** 1964–77 (14) • **Born:** July 11, 1942 (Jesup, Ga.)

In a 14-season span from 1964 to 1977, there was one constant on the Redskins' offensive line, an immovable object so to speak. Despite six off-season knee operations, one of which caused a blood clot that could have killed him, plus collarbone, rib, and elbow injuries, center Len Hauss played in all 196 games in his career—starting the last 192. Both marks are team records.

Hauss was darn good, too. He made the Pro Bowl five times and earned All-Pro or All-NFC honors in his last seven seasons. The 6–2, 235-pounder was one of the best centers of his era, holding his own against such dominant middle linebackers as Chicago's Dick Butkus, Green Bay's Ray Nitschke, and Atlanta's Tommy Nobis, among others.

"Len Hauss is one of the great offensive centers to ever play this game," said Redskins Hall of Fame linebacker Sam Huff, who teamed with Hauss for five seasons. "He has to be the best center that ever played for the Redskins. He was a very smart player, and he was all-heart. He was gutsy and played hurt. He never asked to come off the field."

Why not? "I tried to play every play," Hauss said. "I had a mindset that if that's your job, you're supposed to play, and if you don't play, there may be somebody out there better than you, and if you sit out half a game because you're injured, and somebody comes in, and he's better than you, adios. . . . I worked hard to keep my knee strong. Everybody has a lot of nagging injuries, but I didn't let the nagging injuries keep me from playing."

Prior to snapping balls, Hauss ran with them. He rushed for 1,500 yards, one of the top marks in the country, and scored 15 touchdowns as a senior in high school in Jesup, Georgia. He subsequently played fullback on the junior varsity team at Georgia, although he admittedly was "nothing outstanding." Before his sophomore season, Bulldogs varsity coach Johnny Griffith gave him an option. "He asked if I'd rather be a third-string fullback or a first-team center," Hauss recalled. "My decision was I want to play."

Hauss transitioned to center and earned All-Southeastern Conference honors as a sophomore. He underwent surgery for ligament damage in his left knee in the off-season, although he bounced back and played center regularly in his last two seasons at Georgia.

The Redskins chose Hauss in the ninth round in the 1964 draft, but his left knee gave him fits during training camp, and he considered quitting. Hauss said trainer Joe Kuczo convinced him to stick it out, noting that Kuczo went to Redskins coach Bill McPeak to set up a period of noncontact for Hauss that included running up steps and hills. "It gave me some time to get my knee worked on and back in the shape it needed to be," Hauss said.

Hauss was front and center on the Redskins' offensive line for 14 seasons. He holds the team record for most games played (196).

The rookie impressed McPeak, who once said that "in a one-on-one drill, [Hauss] knocked the devil out of Sam Huff." As Huff remembered, "He was a tough rookie from Georgia. The scrimmages I had against him were tougher than a lot of my regular-season games. I had a lot of respect for him."

Hauss began starting in the fifth game of the 1964 season and remained a fixture on the Redskins' O-line until retirement. Meantime, he was named to the Pro Bowl in four straight seasons, 1967 to 1970, along with 1972, when the Redskins appeared in Super Bowl VII. His pass protection helped quarterback Sonny Jurgensen gain the time he needed to throw for thousands of yards, and his blocking opened holes so Larry Brown could rush for thousands of yards.

In a November 11, 1970, article in the *Washington Evening Star,* Redskins middle linebacker Marlin McKeever compared Hauss to another standout center from that era, six-time Pro Bowler Mick Tingelhoff of the Vikings: "[Tingelhoff] is a good football player, no question about that. But Lennie's every bit as good. Mick is quick, and he blocks well, and he's a good pass blocker. Lennie, I think, is a better pass protector, and he fires out better because he's a lot stronger. And he doesn't give anything away in quickness."

Steve Gilmartin, the Redskins' radio play-by-play voice from 1964 to 1973, described Hauss as a "coach on the field." "He could handle anything," Gilmartin said. "If you put a guy on his nose, if you had gaps out there, he'd know instinctively who to pick up. He also called all the line signals."

Huff played with the same two quarterbacks for most of his career, Sonny Jurgensen and Billy Kilmer, and indicated that with "Sonny and Billy, I knew what both of them were going to do, I knew the feel of snapping the ball." Although offensive line positions have always been underappreciated, he felt it was a bonus to be out of the spotlight normally focused on the glamour players such as quarterbacks:

Billy, Sonny and I went out together a lot, we were really good friends. Did it bother me that I could eat and nobody asked me for an autograph, and people were coming up and shaking hands with [Jurgensen and Kilmer] wanting autographs, and they're getting upset? That's just life. But on the other hand, my buddies were home. The guys I played with at Georgia weren't out there being recognized because they had real jobs. I'm playing ball. Why should I be ungrateful just because I'm a center. There are a lot of guys who would give anything to be guards or centers or tackles.

Hauss said he'll always be a Redskin, and that he'll also cherish his most memorable moments on the field: "My most memorable moment is Sonny Jurgensen's most memorable moment and Billy Kilmer's most memorable moment and Bobby Mitchell's and Charley Taylor's and Larry Brown's and Jerry Smith's, because I snapped the ball for every one of their most memorable moments. I've got an edge that a lot of these people don't have because I was in on every one of those plays. I've got 10–12–15 moments that are really memorable."

## TERRY HERMELING

OT, No. 75, Nevada-Reno • 6–5, 255 • **NFL Career:** 1970–80 (11 seasons) • **Redskins Years:** 1970–80 (11) • **Born:** April 25, 1946 (Santa Maria, Calif.)

Terry Hermeling personified a warrior. He battled through many injuries and remained a Redskins fixture at left offensive tackle for a decade. The 1980 season, his final year, epitomized his toughness; he played in 14 games and started 11 despite a knee injury, a concussion, a sprained back, and torn ligaments and tendons in his hand.

"Hermeling is one of the last of a special breed on this club," Paul Attner of the *Washington Post* wrote toward the end of the 1980 campaign, "a man who played an entire Super Bowl with a knee so damaged it required surgery two days later, a man who considers it essential that he keeps playing despite his injuries; otherwise, he'd be letting down his teammates."

Hermeling told the *Post,* "I've had 11 great years of football, even with the injuries. I've enjoyed every second. I've been fortunate. I've always been able to overcome the injuries and still play. Maybe I've got a high tolerance of pain, I'm not sure. All I know is that if I was injured, I'd do anything I had to to get ready. In this business, I think you are expected to play hurt."

An all-conference lineman at Nevada-Reno, Hermeling signed with the Redskins as an undrafted free agent in 1970. He spent most of his rookie season on the taxi squad and performed well on special teams in 1971. He won the starting left tackle job in the 1972 preseason following an injury to Jim Snowden.

"Terry has good quickness, good speed and good strength," Redskins offensive line coach Mike McCormack said in the *Washington Star* at the time. "Everything you're looking for in a tackle. And he had a good exhibition season. That's why he got the job."

In 1972 and 1973, Hermeling missed all but one regular season game, but he seriously injured his right knee in the 1974 preseason and sat out the year, plus the first five games of 1975. But he showed no signs of rust in his first game back and received a game ball for playing a key role as the Redskins amassed 190 yards rushing in a 23–7 win over Cleveland.

Hermeling started the last nine games of the '75 season and missed only five games the rest of his career.

"Terry rises to the top in the 'big games' and has neutralized many defensive ends noted for their pass rush," Redskin publicists wrote late in his career.

## JOE JACOBY

OT-OG, No. 66, Louisville • 6–7, 320 • **NFL Career:** 1981–93 (13 seasons) • **Redskins Years:** 1981–93 (13) • NFL 1980s All-Decade Team • **Born:** July 6, 1959 (Louisville, Ky.)

It was the spring of 1981, and first-year Redskins coach Joe Gibbs was meeting separately with his rookie free agents. When 6–7, 300-pound Joe Jacoby sat down in his office, Gibbs goofed.

"Joe was going through his outlook on the team and what he was looking for and where I would fit on the roster," Jacoby said. "I remember he kept talking about my chances of making the team on the defensive line, not much as an end but as a defensive tackle. I just kind of agreed with him."

When Gibbs learned that Jacoby was really an offensive tackle, he directed his ire at offensive line coach Joe Bugel. "I walked out of my office and yelled for Joe Bugel," Gibbs once said. "I said, 'For cripes sake, Joe, why do we need another lineman? You've got 18 of them already. We can't coach that many. If we've signed him, can we get out of it?'"

The hulking Jacoby manhandled many players in his day.

The Redskins were smart to keep Jacoby, for he was one of the premier O-linemen in the NFL during the 1980s. He played left tackle, right tackle, and left guard in his 13-year career in Washington but made his greatest impact at left tackle, where he spent eight years protecting his quarterback's blind side. He earned four straight trips to the Pro Bowl as a left tackle (1983–86), plus multiple All-Pro honors.

The 6–7 Jacoby, whose weight fluctuated between 315 and 325 pounds, used his Herculean size and strength to overpower defenders and open gaping holes for such runners as John Riggins, George Rogers, and Earnest Byner. His signature play was the "Counter-Trey," in which he pulled with the guard next to him to the opposite side of the field. He also pulled on plays called "90 Truck" and "80 Truck." His nickname, appropriately, was "Route 66."

Jacoby was so massive—rivaling only 6–7, 315-pound defensive tackle Dave Butz as the Redskins' biggest player of the era—that defenders had trouble spotting pint-sized runners like Joe Washington trailing him.

"With 'Big Jake' being the size that he was," said the 5–10, 180-pound Washington, "I could easily hook on a little caboose ride with him and make sure that people had to come through him to get to me. Occasionally on the 'Counter-Trey,' I'd put my hand on his shirt and just let him be the eyes, and I just tried to stay behind and maneuver and see how much

yardage we can get. It was really a thrill to run behind a guy with that type of talent who seemed to really enjoy getting out there and throwing his body around."

Jacoby played left tackle in college at Louisville, where he co-captained the Cardinals as a senior. He was not drafted but, having been scouted by Redskins assistant general manager Charley Casserly, he was invited to try out for the squad. Then-general manager Bobby Beathard, impressed by the offensive lineman no other team wanted, signed the free agent in April 1981.

Jacoby hit the weight room and bulked up from 270 to 300 pounds by the start of training camp. He won a spot on the offensive line despite having to leave camp because of the death of his mother.

"Joe was not a terrific athlete," Beathard said. "He didn't have the good foot agility and foot movement and all that. But he had Joe Bugel as a line coach, who in my opinion was the best. He just did a great job with Jacoby, and Jacoby was sharp as a tack. And he is just as hard a worker as you could ever find. For him to turn into one of the great offensive tackles, that was really a plus for us, a lucky deal."

Jacoby started at left guard and right tackle early in the 1981 season and replaced Mark May, the Redskins' No. 1 draft pick that year and an Outland Trophy winner as the nation's

## Catchiest Redskin Nicknames

John "The Tree" Adams
"Sugarfoot" Sam Baker
"Slingin'" Sammy Baugh
Don Bosseler, "The Batavia Battering Ram"
Pete Cronan, "Cronan the Barbarian"
Dean Hamel, "The Tasmanian Devil"
Leon "Mule Train" Heath
Don "The Bull" Irwin
Charlie "Choo Choo" Justice
Billy Kilmer, "Furnace Face" or "Whisky"
Max "Bananas" Krause
Joe "The Bird" Lavender
Eddie LeBaron, "Little General," "Little Magician," or "Little Baron"
Charles Mann, "Mannster" or "C-Ment"
Ron McDole, "The Dancing Bear"
Harold McLinton, "Tank"
Bob "Blubber" Morgan
John Riggins, "The Diesel"
Mark Schlereth, "Stinky"
"Blackjack" Ben Scotti
Joe "Scooter" Scudero
Jim "Yazoo" Smith
Tom "The Bomb" Tracy
Wilbur "Wee Willie" Wilkin
And not to forget: Ed "Double-O" Boynton, a security guard at Redskin Park in the 1970s

best interior college lineman, as the starting left tackle in the ninth game. By the 1983 season, he had come into his own as one of the elites at his position. He was named a consensus first-team All-Pro, as the Redskins' machine-like offense set an NFL record for most points scored (541). He had also become a leader on the Redskins' smash-mouth offensive line of the era, the Hogs.

He remained at left tackle, once playing with a clublike cast on his hand during a Redskins' playoff win, but various injuries forced him to relinquish the position to All-Pro Jim Lachey midway through the 1988 campaign. He played mostly left guard and right tackle for the rest of his career until bulging disks in his back sidelined him for good during the 1993 season. He retired in July 1994.

To Jacoby, it was an honor being a Redskin during that era, when he played in four Super Bowls and won three rings. "It was a very special group, a very special time," he said.

"Jacoby was a force that I don't think too many people will ever see again in this league," said Jim Hanifan, the Redskins' offensive line coach from 1990 to 1996. "You've got a guy 6–7, 315 pounds, and there's not one ounce of fat on that body. The man has such great heart. He was really special."

## DICK JAMES

HB-DB, No. 47, Oregon • 5–9, 175 • **NFL Career:** 1956–65 (10 seasons) • **Redskins Years:** 1956–63 (8) • **Born:** May 22, 1934 (Grants Pass, Ore.) • **Died:** June 28, 2000 (Grants Pass, Ore.)

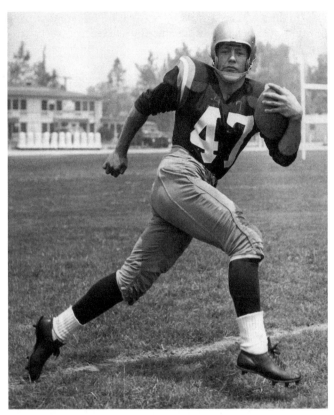

Dick James

The year was 1961. The 0–12–1 Redskins, hosting the Dallas Cowboys in the season-finale, were facing what would stand as the only winless season in team history. Washington had also gone without a win in 23 straight games. Somebody needed to step up.

Enter high-flying halfback Dick James. He scored a Redskins-record four touchdowns in their 34–24 win on 3-, 5-, and 39-yard runs, and on a 1-yard reception. He just missed a fifth touchdown. Today he is tied with Larry Brown for the Redskins' records for most single-game touchdowns (four) and points (24).

James's performance typified his stellar contributions over 10 NFL seasons, the first 8 with the Redskins. A versatile player, he rushed 502 times for 1,930 yards and 19 touchdowns while catching 104 passes for 1,669 yards and 15 scores. As one of the few remaining players who competed on both sides of the ball, he played safety and intercepted 12 passes. He returned punts and kickoffs to boot, regularly leading the Redskins in those categories.

"He could do all kinds of things," said Don Bosseler, a Redskins fullback who played with James for seven seasons. "He had all kinds of talent. If somebody went down offensively, and we were short on running backs, Dickie would go both ways. He'd run the ball from the line of scrimmage and turn around and start playing defensive back.

"He was a little guy, wiry, but he could block those big guys. He was tough, the gutsiest player. He saved a lot of games for us, too."

James's 5–9, 175-pound frame was no deterrence, for he would toss himself recklessly into a horde of tacklers while fighting for extra yardage. In the open field, he was like a jack-

rabbit—speedy and elusive. He was also durable, playing in 92 straight games from 1958 to 1964.

"Green Bay's fullback Jim Taylor is famous for gaining a couple of extra yards after he is hit, but as far as Redskins fans are concerned, no player steals more yardage on that second effort than Dick James," Redskin publicists wrote in 1963. "The littlest Redskin, James is like an Indian rubber ball once the enemy starts to lay hands on him. Dick bounces around all over the place, usually ending up with 6 or 7 yards no one thought or believed he could gain or steal."

James was also dangerous at the University of Oregon. He posted more than 1,400 yards rushing, 560 receiving, and more than 800 returning kicks. He also intercepted 10 passes and twice received all-conference honors. The Redskins drafted him in the eighth round in 1956, when he was named the team's Rookie of the Year.

Furthermore, James was one of the more popular players in Redskins history. Although Redskin fans had every reason to be frustrated with a squad that recorded some of the worst seasons in team history during his career in Washington, he was never booed at Griffith Stadium or D.C. Stadium (now RFK Stadium).

"There are good reasons for James' popularity," Jack Walsh of the *Washington Post* wrote on July 28, 1963. "Over a seven-year span, Dick has done many things especially well. He's given his full share of thrills as a broken field runner, pass receiver, punt and kickoff returner, and defensive back. There also is his skill as a holder for vital placekicks. This actually is an important talent, although generally minimized."

James was traded after the 1963 season to the Giants in the famous deal that brought future Hall of Fame linebacker Sam

Huff to the Redskins. He played one year in New York and one in Minnesota before retiring after the 1965 season.

## JON JANSEN

OT, No. 76, Michigan • 6–6, 310 • **NFL Career:** 1999–2006 (8 seasons) • **Redskins Years:** 1999–2006 (8) • **Born:** January 28, 1976 (Clawson, Mich.)

Jon Jansen loves to play football. You feel it when he talks about his vocation, and you sense the passion he has for the game.

On the field, he leaves no doubt where his heart is. In seven full seasons with the Redskins, Jansen has missed only one start in 116 possible games at offensive right tackle, including four playoff games. (He sat out the 2004 season with an Achilles tendon injury.) In 2005, he gave a Herculean effort by playing with soft casts protecting his two broken thumbs for nearly the first half of the season, and with a single cast for most of the rest of the year—and performed exceptionally.

When asked why he loves the game so much, Jansen responded, "I just like playing. It's fun. When it stops being fun, I'm going to get out of it. There are a lot of things in football that you don't love. Practice isn't necessarily something that you love. I'm not a body builder, so working out isn't necessarily something that you love, but it lets you do something that you do love better."

The Redskins' other book-end offensive tackle of the 21st century, Chris Samuels, called Jansen a leader. "The thing that stands out about Jon that I've always admired is that he's a tough guy," Samuels said. "Two broken thumbs [in 2005], kept slugging. He's a guy we definitely need and respect and love."

Jansen, who for some mystifying reason has been overlooked for the Pro Bowl, is justly nicknamed "Rock." The moniker stems from his college days at Michigan, where he started every game in four seasons at right tackle and earned first-team All-American honors.

On draft day 1999, the Redskins traded up to No. 37 in the second round and took Jansen. His impact in training camp and exhibition games was so strong that the coaches penned him as a starter for the season opener. Jansen has been "everything and more than what we expected," said the Redskins' offensive line coach at the time, Russ Grimm, a star from years past on the Hogs. "The guy is smart, he's tough, and he's a hard worker. He's also football smart."

Jansen was a key addition to a squad that reached the second round of the playoffs that year. (The 1999 O-line allowed 31 sacks, compared with a franchise-record 61 in 1998, and helped Stephen Davis rush for his first of three straight 1,000-yard seasons.) He started every game in his first five seasons—82 in all—and developed a fierce rival: Giants perennial All-Pro defensive end Michael Strahan. The two NFC East foes have had some classic battles. "I like beating up on him," Jansen has said of Strahan.

Jansen ruptured his Achilles in the 2004 exhibition-opener and was lost for the year. Not only was his absence conspicuous on an O-line that struggled in a 6–10 season, it was personally trying. He admitted to being dejected at times and said his wife, Martha, told him to stop feeling sorry for himself.

As Jansen made his comeback in 2005, the Redskins' offensive line enjoyed a resurgence on a team that reached the sec-

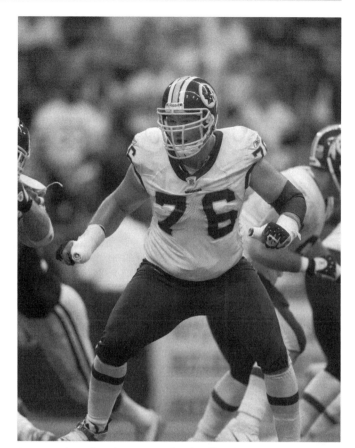

Jansen played with casts on both of his broken thumbs for the first half of the 2005 season.

ond round of the playoffs. When asked the reason behind the line's improved play, right guard Randy Thomas pointed at one man. "We got Jon Jansen back," Thomas said. "He brings a lot of heart and soul to the line, and he's my right-hand man."

That season, Jansen battled with casts on his broken thumbs, a rare feat for a lineman, while protecting the blind side of left-handed quarterback Mark Brunell. The 6–6, 310-pounder said he wanted to reinforce the notion that he can play despite a high level of discomfort. "I wanted to be the toughest son of a bitch out there, and I wanted everybody to know that I'm the toughest guy," he said. "I think I was able to prove that."

Jansen also showed signs of a warrior in 2006, playing about a third of the season with a nagging calf injury. He sat out one game. Redskins coach Joe Gibbs praised him for playing through the injury and putting forth some of his better games at the same time. Case in point: Jansen shut down Carolina superstar defensive end Julius Peppers, who had no sacks in a 17–13 Redskins win on November 26, after entering the game with a league-high 11. "He just refuses to come out of there," Gibbs said at the time of his rock at offensive tackle.

Another coach criticized Jansen for his play early in the season. In the November 2006 edition of the *New York Times* sports magazine, Cowboys coach Bill Parcells said that the tackle was getting pushed around and didn't look like the player he was earlier in his career. "You can't be in this business and not have thick skin," Jansen said when asked about Parcells's comments. "Second, you can't be in this business and not hear the things that are going around. You've got to take it for what it is."

In recent years, Jansen has become sort of a media celebrity. An Academic All-American at Michigan, he has spent several draft days as an ESPN analyst and has co-hosted a Redskins talk-show on Comcast SportsNet called *Monday Night Live.*

## ROY JEFFERSON

WR, No. 80, Utah • 6–2, 195 • **NFL Career:** 1965–76 (12 seasons) • **Redskins Years:** 1971–76 (6) • **Born:** November 9, 1943 (Texarkana, Ark.)

When ostentatious clothing was in vogue in the 1970s, Roy Jefferson was the Redskins' Mr. Flamboyance. The wide receiver wore pink, orange, and lavender jumpsuits, bell-bottom pants, colorful velvet hats, and a bag over his shoulder that resembled a purse. "He set the trend on the team," said Redskins receiver Charley Taylor, a teammate of Jefferson's for six seasons. "He was the fashion king in the mod style. He wore several outfits. You name it, he had it."

Jefferson also entertained on the field, where the sure-handed receiver with graceful strides made the Pro Bowl three times in his 11-year career. He played his first five seasons in Pittsburgh, leading the NFL in receiving yards in 1968 and setting a team record for catches the next year (67), before going to Baltimore, where he caught 45 passes in 1970.

Jefferson disliked Baltimore Colts owner Carroll Rosenbloom and requested a trade. The Redskins acquired him before the 1971 season in exchange for the team's top draft pick, receiver Cotton Speyrer, and two draft choices.

Playing in the run-oriented system of coach George Allen, Jefferson failed to match the monster numbers from earlier in his career, but he evolved into one of Allen's key veteran acquisitions, averaging 35 catches and 520 yards to accompany 16 scoring catches in six seasons in D.C. The 1971 season marked his best year statistically with the Redskins; he posted team highs of 47 catches and 701 receiving yards, while becoming the go-to receiver after Taylor suffered a season-ending injury in the fifth game. He made the Pro Bowl for the third and final time and earned All-NFC honors.

Jefferson was no stranger to clutch performances. In perhaps his greatest game ever, he caught eight passes for 137 yards and two touchdowns in a 38–24 win over the Rams on December 13, 1971. The victory clinched the Redskins' first playoff berth since 1945. His 32-yard scoring catch from Billy Kilmer in a 1972 playoff game lifted the Redskins to a 7–3 lead over Green Bay in their 16–3 win, the team's first postseason victory in nearly 30 years. Jefferson ran a quick post route on the play, a pattern he specialized in.

"Billy was very good at throwing that pass, and I felt that I made a very good cut on it," Jefferson said. "It's all a matter of taking the right angle. If the timing is right and if the guy is off of you, or even if he's in a bump-and-run, as long as you can get inside, there's really no way they can stop it unless they just sit somebody in a spot, and that would be somewhat ridiculous."

Jefferson snagged touchdowns in two other playoff games in Washington. Career-wise, he caught 451 passes for 7,539 yards (16.7 average) and 52 scores.

"He was a hard-nosed receiver whose only goal was to catch the ball no matter where it was," said Mike Bass, a Redskin cornerback who teamed with Jefferson for five seasons. "He was absolutely fantastic, and I don't think he ever got the credit he deserved."

## TRE' JOHNSON

OG-OT, No. 77, Temple • 6–2, 330 • **NFL Career:** 1994–2002 (9 seasons) • **Redskins Years:** 1994–2000, 2002 (8) • **Born:** August 30, 1971 (New York, N.Y.)

Eccentric and individualistic he was. With his wittiness, dreadlocks, and creative array of tattoos that included such sayings as "Might Makes Right" and "Fear No Man," Tre' Johnson had a uniqueness about him. "It's on your body for life, so you got to make it mean something," Johnson, speaking of his tattoos, once said in *Sport* magazine. "I designed them all, everything is custom. Nobody can duplicate my drawings."

Johnson was conspicuous on the field, too, where he flattened many defenders. The 300-plus-pound right guard, a self-proclaimed "Banga," was a punishing run blocker who could plow straight ahead or pull outside using his surprisingly quick feet. Among the strongest Redskins of his era, he could bench press about 600 pounds.

When healthy, Johnson was one of the best guards in the league. But from his rookie season, 1994, until 1998, he missed at least one game per year due to injury. (He was a Pro Bowl alternate in 1996). Toward the end of that five-year span, his weight climbed to nearly 350 pounds.

In 1999, after shedding 30 pounds, he started all 16 games for the first time, plus two playoff contests, and made the Pro Bowl. He threw blocks that opened holes for 1,405-yard rusher Stephen Davis and helped fortify an offensive line that allowed only 31 sacks, compared with a franchise-record 61 in 1998. He earned a game ball, along with the other offensive linemen, for helping overpower the Giants in a 50–21 win.

In 2000, however, Johnson tore up his knee four games into the season and missed the rest of the year. Released after the season, he signed with the Browns but played in only three games due to another knee injury. He returned to the Redskins in 2002 and played in the last 10 games before retiring.

In college, Johnson was a second-team All-American at Temple University. The Redskins drafted him in the second round in 1994.

## CHARLIE JUSTICE

HB, No. 22, North Carolina • 5–10, 170 • **NFL Career:** 1950, 52–54 (4 seasons) • **Redskins Years:** 1950, 52–54 (4) • **Born:** May 18, 1924 (Asheville, N.C.) • **Died:** October 17, 2003 (Cherryville, N.C.)

In the 1950s, the Redskins had a shifty, elusive runner who was electrifying at times. It's too bad the career of Charlie "Choo Choo" Justice was brief.

In four seasons in Washington, Justice carried the ball 266 times for 1,284 yards (4.8 average) and three touchdowns. He also caught 63 passes for 962 yards and seven scores, and punted 94 times (40.4 average). Al Costello of the *Washington Times-Herald* called him a "twisting, whirling dervish" after he ran for 120 yards in a win over the Chicago Cardinals in 1953.

"The little guy has everything," Curly Lambeau, the Redskins' coach in 1952 and 1953, once said in an article in the *Washington Daily-News*. "He has tremendous take-off speed and all the guts in the world. All he needs is a sliver of daylight, and he's gone. If he had a little more speed in the open, he'd be scoring touchdowns from any place on the field."

Justice was his most thrilling at the University of North Carolina. The 170-pound triple-threat (running, passing, kick returns) evolved into one of the premier college backs ever and finished as a two-time Heisman Trophy runner-up on some of the greatest teams in school history. He was inducted into the College Football Hall of Fame in 1961.

At the same time, Justice became a folk hero in North Carolina and gained national popularity. He was pictured in *Collier's, Life,* and *Pic,* among other national magazines. Famed bandleader Benny Goodman recorded a song about him titled, "All the way, Choo, Choo." (He got his nickname while playing football in the Navy when it was said he ran like a runaway locomotive.)

The Redskins, fascinated with star players from southern schools, drafted Justice in the 16th round in 1950, and he joined the team six games into the season. His best year was 1953, when he rushed for 616 yards, the fourth-best mark in the NFL, and caught 22 passes for 434 yards.

"His secret to picking up yardage is his ability to start at full speed and hit the intended hole a fraction of a second faster than some other backs," Al Costello of the *Times-Herald* wrote. "'Choo Choo' isn't too fast, but he isn't too slow, either. It is his ability to start at full speed that collects most of his yardage. An instinctive shiftiness helps, too."

## BILLY KILMER

QB, No. 17, UCLA • 6–0, 205 • **NFL Career:** 1961–62, 64–78 (17 seasons) • **Redskins Years:** 1971–78 (8) • **Born:** September 5, 1939 (Topeka, Kan.)

It's said that you can't measure heart, but it's obvious that Billy Kilmer's heart was big—really big.

The Redskins' quarterback was all grit and determination. Whether it was a busted nose, a separated shoulder, cracked ribs, or a gastrointestinal ailment that gave him terrible pains during a game, he kept on ticking. Even if Redskins fans who preferred having Sonny Jurgensen or Joe Theismann behind center showered him with boos, he remained unflappable. There was no quit in him.

"I was a competitor," Kilmer said. "I grew up as a little kid believing in playing hard, and it was just ingrained in me to play with a lot of injuries. You just played the game without thinking about anything else."

Kilmer said the harsh treatment by fans never bothered him. "It probably fired me up more than anything and made me tougher. When I heard that, I'd say, 'Screw these guys, I'll show them,' rather than sulking and worrying about my feelings. The more they booed, the better I got."

Kilmer's infectious will to win and uncanny leadership skills were critical to the Redskins' rise as one of the NFL's dominant teams of the 1970s. They made the playoffs five times in his first seven seasons in Washington (including an appearance in Super Bowl VII), a period when he quarterbacked the squad to 50 wins in 68 games. He was not the most athletically gifted

quarterback, as evidenced by his trademark wobbly passes, but he threw for 12,352 yards, one of the highest totals in Redskins history, completing 953 of 1,791 passes (53 completion percentage), with 103 touchdowns and 75 interceptions. Overall, he amassed nearly 21,000 passing yards and 148 touchdowns over 17 NFL seasons.

"Billy led by example," said Len Hauss, a Redskins center who teamed with Kilmer for seven seasons. "He was the first guy in the fight, the first guy out there to defend somebody else."

Ironically, Kilmer once heard he lacked the guts to play pro football. It was 1961, his rookie year in the NFL, when his San Francisco 49ers coach, Red Hickey, told him one of his coaches at UCLA had said he wasn't tough enough to make it in the NFL—this despite the fact that Kilmer had played with multiple injuries at UCLA, where as a senior the All-American led the nation in total offense with 1,889 yards (1,086 passing, 803 rushing) as one of the last of the single-wing halfbacks. He finished fifth in Heisman Trophy balloting that year and was inducted into the College Football Hall of Fame in 1999.

The 49ers drafted Kilmer in the first round in 1961. He played tailback in Hickey's exciting shotgun formation, rushing for nearly 1,000 yards and 15 scores and passing for another 477 up until the next-to-last game in the 1962 season, when he shattered his right leg in a car accident. The 49ers' doctor said his football career was probably over, even hinting at possible amputation. "He didn't make any bones about it," Kilmer said without pun. "He was 90 percent sure I would never play again."

In his mind, though, Kilmer was far from done. He underwent operations and months of agonizing rehabilitation, returning during the 1964 season as a reserve running back. He had lost a step due to the accident and switched to quarterback, remaining a third-stringer until being acquired by the expansion New Orleans Saints in 1967. He threw for nearly 7,500 yards in four seasons with the Saints, catching the eye of Los Angeles Rams coach George Allen; the two teams played each other several times during that period. "I never beat him," Kilmer said of Allen, "but I moved the ball against him and for some reason he liked something about me."

Allen loved Kilmer's smarts and competitiveness. Shortly after becoming the Redskins' coach in January 1971, Allen traded a reserve linebacker and two draft picks to the Saints for Kilmer to back up Sonny Jurgensen. Of Allen's 100-plus trades as an NFL coach, it would prove to be perhaps his best one, although Kilmer initially didn't want to play in Washington.

"I told George right away that I wanted to be traded, that I didn't want to play behind Sonny Jurgensen," he said. "That was like water over the duck's back. He didn't even listen to me. He said, 'You're going to be part of a winning organization. We're going to win here right away.'"

Allen was true to his word. When Jurgensen suffered a serious shoulder injury in an exhibition game, Kilmer took over and quarterbacked most of the 1971 season, leading the 9–4–1 Redskins to their first playoff appearance since 1945.

He followed with his best season ever in 1972. With Jurgensen again beset by injuries, Kilmer started most of the year, completing 120 of 225 passes for 1,648 yards and 19 touchdowns (career-high 84.6 quarterback rating). He earned Pro Bowl and All-NFC honors. In the high point of his career, he played a near-perfect game in the NFC championship against the Cowboys, completing 14 of 18 passes for 194 yards and

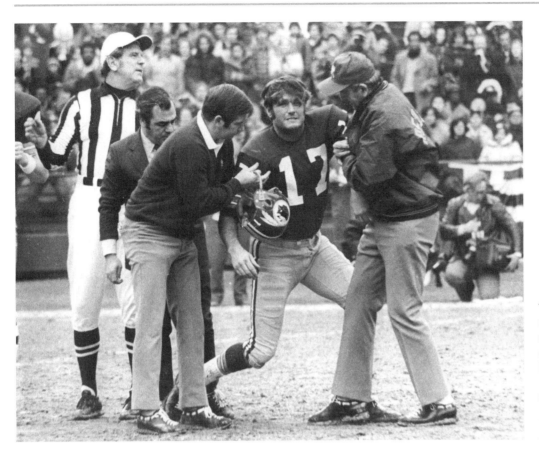

The gritty Kilmer is helped up after being knocked dizzy in the first quarter of a playoff game against the Packers on December 24, 1972. After regaining his senses on the sidelines, he played the rest of the way in a 16–7 Redskins win.

two scores in a 26–3 victory that hoisted the Redskins into Super Bowl VII.

Kilmer competed with Jurgy for playing time in the next two seasons and then with Joe Theismann for several years thereafter. He didn't have Jurgensen's grace, strong arm, or accuracy, calling himself the "No. 1 wobbly passer in the NFL." Media sometime questioned his talents—he once challenged two reporters to a fight in the locker room—and fans at RFK Stadium often became impatient with him. But his bulldog mentality and winning instincts endeared him to many, including *Washington Star* columnist Morrie Siegel, who compared him to an intense baseball competitor of the 1940s and 1950s, Eddie Stanky: "Billy the Kid does have his limitations," Siegel wrote on September 20, 1972. He is not a classic passer. On his long, go-for-broke attempts, the ball often flutters so lazily that the name of 'Pete Rozelle, Commissioner' sometimes can be read.

"On the other hand, Kilmer has a knack of sucking in his gut in adversity and exhaling a confidence that becomes contagious. He is professional football's Eddie Stanky. Critics said Stanky couldn't field, was a distinct liability as a hitter, and was not to be confused as an Olympic sprinter as a runner. They were right, but Stanky defied them. He was a winner who was not embarrassed by his shortcomings."

Meanwhile, Kilmer, who won awards for courage based on his ability to play with pain, specialized in gutsy performances:

- Despite an intestinal blockage that was rumored to be cancer and gave him violent pains, he threw four touchdowns in a 38–20 win over the Eagles that qualified the Redskins for the playoffs in 1973.

- He threw a career-high 23 touchdown passes despite playing much of the 1975 season with a separated right shoulder and a broken foot.
- Dazed from a blow that sent blood oozing out of his face, which looked like a "meat grinder" in the eyes of *Washington Star* sportswriter Steve Guback, he completed two fourth-down passes and a last-minute touchdown that decided a 19–17 win over the Giants in the 1976 season-opener.

### Kilmer Trivia

Before coming to the Redskins, Billy Kilmer had a hand in two of the more memorable plays in NFL history. In 1964, the 49ers' halfback fumbled a ball that Vikings defensive end Jim Marshall scooped up and took 66 yards into the *wrong end zone,* a gaffe that led to a 49ers safety.

While playing quarterback for New Orleans in 1970, Kilmer threw a 17-yard strike to Al Dodd in the final seconds to set up Tom Dempsey's NFL record-setting 63-yard field goal that gave the Saints a 19–17 win over Detroit. "It was one of the best passes I ever threw in my career," Kilmer said of his completion to Dodd. "I hit it right on the money."

"In another unbelievable display of valor, Billy came off the bench, bloodied and determined, to fashion a last-minute scoring drive," according to the Redskins' edition of *Pro!* magazine. "His nose and lip split wide open, Billy's only concern was to stop the flow of blood so his hands could grip the ball and throw."

By the 1978 campaign, Theismann was named the Redskins' undisputed starting quarterback, and Kilmer retired after the season. He later served as the commissioner of a semi-pro football league in Texas and a TV analyst for Redskins exhibition games.

In retrospect, Kilmer credits George Allen for reviving his NFL career by trading for him in 1971: "He gave me my second wind in football because I was basically almost at my retirement age at 31. Circumstances helped me. All I had to do was get in there, and when Sonny got hurt it gave me a chance to play. I just didn't make mistakes."

## JIM LACHEY

OT, No. 79, Ohio State • 6–6, 300 • **NFL Career:** 1985–95 (11 seasons) • **Redskins Years:** 1988–95 (8) • **Born:** June 4, 1963 (St. Henry, Ohio)

It's no secret that injuries can destroy an NFL career. In Jim Lachey's case, they prevented him from becoming one of the top offensive left tackles ever.

In a three-year span with the Redskins (1989–91), Lachey was the best left tackle in football. In addition to being a consensus first-team All-Pro each year, he made the Pro Bowl twice, earning the most votes at left tackle each time, and was named NFC Offensive Lineman of the Year in 1990.

Injuries in Lachey's last four seasons, however, forced him to miss 38 of 66 games, including nearly two full seasons. He has no regrets about the way his career ended, though: "I was very fortunate those injuries didn't happen the first three years of my career versus my last three, then I would have never been able to do what I did in my first eight," said Lachey, a member of the NFL's 1990s All-Decade Team set up to commemorate the league's 75th anniversary in 1994. "Sure, it would have been great to have another three or four years of domination, it just didn't happen. I know in my heart that when I played, the years I was on top of it I was on top of it. I can accept that and move on."

Lachey played left guard at Ohio State, where he earned All-American and All-Big-10 honors as a senior. San Diego picked him in the first round in 1985 (12th overall), and Chargers coach Don Coryell immediately said something that left him speechless: He was going to start at left tackle. "I about had a heart attack because I had never played left tackle," he said. "[But] I lined up at left tackle the next day and played there the rest of my career."

Lachey made multiple All-Rookie teams in 1985 and his first Pro Bowl in 1987. In the summer of 1988, he was traded to the Los Angeles Raiders, who after the opening game dealt him to the Redskins for quarterback Jay Schroeder. The 6–6, 300-pound baby Hog began at right tackle before replacing Joe Jacoby at left tackle.

In about a 60-game span from 1989 to 1992, Lachey said he yielded only two sacks. His finest season was 1991, when No. 79 allowed none as part of an offensive line that gave immobile

Jim Lachey

quarterback Mark Rypien airtight protection in the Redskins' Super Bowl–winning season.

Lachey had remarkably quick feet and an ability to gain excellent leverage on pass rushers, two skills he began to develop while competing in football, basketball, and track for the St. Henry (Ohio) High Redskins. In basketball, he learned how to shuffle his feet and as a shot putter, "I did the glide, power step, and throw, the same motion I used as a left tackle on every pass play."

"Jim had great feet, he was a great pass protector," said fellow Hog Russ Grimm, a teammate of Lachey's for four seasons. "That's when defenses were going to more of the nickel rush, the dime packages with faster linebackers on the tackles. Jimmy had the feet to handle it."

## JOE LAVENDER

CB, No. 20, San Diego State • 6–4, 185 • **NFL Career:** 1973–82 (10 seasons) • **Redskins Years:** 1976–82 (7) • **Born:** February 10, 1949 (Rayville, La.)

Quarterbacks hesitated to throw his way because of his blanket coverage. With a height of 6–4 and an enormous wingspan, hence his nickname "The Bird," cornerback Joe Lavender was intimidating.

Lavender was a cornerstone in the Redskins' defensive backfield for seven seasons in the 1970s and early 1980s. He intercepted 29 passes, one of the best marks in team history, and bolstered a secondary that year after year held opponents to less than a 50 percent completion rate. He earned a "big-play" reputation by intercepting a host of passes late in games.

A 12th-round draft pick of the Eagles in 1973, Lavender played three seasons in Philly, once scoring touchdowns in back-to-back weeks on a 96-yard fumble return and a 37-yard interception return. When Redskins cornerback Mike Bass announced his retirement just before the 1976 season, Lavender came to Washington in a trade for defensive tackle Manny Sistrunk and three draft picks.

Lavender, one of a small group of players in his era to wear eyeglasses during games, elevated his play upon arriving in D.C. He picked off a career-high eight passes in 1976, including two in the end zone in an overtime win over his former team, the Eagles, and earned second-team All-Pro honors. The Redskins went to the playoffs that year.

In his only Pro Bowl seasons, Lavender intercepted six passes in both 1979 and 1980 while playing a key role on a vaunted pass defense that finished No. 1 in the league in 1980. That year, he gave his best career performance with three picks in a 40–17 win over San Diego, one of which he returned 51 yards for a touchdown.

"If they throw at me, I feel I'll always be making some type of effort to destroy the play," Lavender once said in the *Washington Star*.

Lavender played in every game in his first six seasons in Washington, but he was slowed by a pulled hamstring in 1982 and missed several weeks of play. He retired after the season with 33 career interceptions, 434 return yards, and three touchdowns.

## EDDIE LEBARON

QB, No. 14, Pacific • 5–7, 165 • **NFL Career:** 1952–53, 55–63 (11 seasons) • **Redskins Years:** 1952–53, 55–59 (7) • **Born:** January 7, 1930 (San Rafael, Calif.)

Eddie LeBaron's size was often mentioned in the same breath as his ability to play quarterback. His array of nicknames included the "Little General," the "Little Magician," the "Little Baron" and simply "L'il Eddie." He played at 5–7, 165 pounds, but his diminutive frame was no impediment to his rising to great heights in the NFL.

"I never had a problem," said LeBaron, who threw for 13,399 yards and 104 touchdowns in 11 seasons, his first seven with the Redskins. "I didn't have balls knocked down. I released it high and quick. I went to four Pro Bowls and had a pretty good record throwing the ball."

In his day, no quarterback was better at hiding the ball after the snap, a skill that froze defenders and masked his lack of size. The technique, often used on play-action passes, allowed him to evade the rush before connecting with receivers using his rifle arm. He'd also fake to one runner and hand to another or roll out on bootlegs. One sportswriter said LeBaron showed "Houdini-like ball-handling." NFL Films president Steve Sabol called him one of the deftest ball handlers in league history.

"Eddie was a magician with the ball," said Jim Ricca, a Redskin lineman who played with LeBaron for two seasons. "You never knew who had the ball, he was so slick. That was his big claim to fame—his ball handling, faking to the different backs. I remember one time three players on the defensive line got

confused and all of a sudden Eddie's standing in the end zone with the ball. He rolled out and had the ball on his hip, and he was gone. He was elusive and tricky, and he was so short that people couldn't really see him."

True, with LeBaron in the pocket, it looked like David versus Goliath, for he was stared down by menacing rushers the likes of 6–6, 284-pound Gene "Big Daddy" Lipscomb and 6–4, 245-pound Gino Marchetti of the Baltimore Colts, and 6–5, 285-pound Roosevelt Grier of the Giants. Once, LeBaron threw a scoring pass that helped his East team beat the West in the Pro Bowl in January 1959. Winning players earned $300 apiece, a fortune in those days, and the West's Lipscomb was peeved. After the game, LeBaron was standing outside his locker room when Lipscomb issued a warning. "You little S. O. B.," Lipscomb barked. "I'll get you next year."

LeBaron, also a master at calling plays, was a great quarterback in college, too. A California native, he played at the College of the Pacific in Stockton, California, and was coached briefly by the "Grand Old Man of Football," the legendary Amos Alonzo Stagg, who once called him "one of the finest passers I've coached in 60 years." LeBaron, a three-time unanimous Little All-America, was awarded the Pop Warner Trophy as the Pacific Coast's outstanding player in his senior year, 1949. He also starred in three all-star bowl games. He was inducted into the College Football Hall of Fame in 1980.

Many NFL scouts questioned his lack of size. He lasted until the 10th round of the 1950 draft, when Redskins owner George Preston Marshall said enough is enough. "I ordered the drafting of LeBaron . . . " Marshall once said in the *Washington Post*. "I never had seen the boy play, but I knew his bowl record. I couldn't shake the feeling he was one of those overlooked players who would produce.

"Larry Siemering, his [Pacific] coach, was an old Redskin. Siemering said, 'Why do people worry about his size? He gets the job done, that's all that counts.'"

LeBaron signed with the Redskins in February 1950 but was called to serve as a U.S. Marine after the Korean War began that summer. A lieutenant, he fought in some of the war's bloodiest battles and was wounded twice. He won two Purple Hearts and received the Bronze Star and a letter of commendation for his heroism.

He returned to the Redskins in 1952 and played most of the year, completing 95 of 194 passes for 1,420 yards, with 14 touchdowns and 15 interceptions. The great Sammy Baugh was then in the last season of his 16-year career, and LeBaron said he didn't learn much from him because their styles were so distinct. But "Sam was great to be around and very good to talk to," he said. "He knew the game and the teams."

Just as LeBaron had established himself as the Redskins' quarterback of the future, coach Curly Lambeau questioned his skills and rotated him in the 1953 season with first-round draft pick Jack Scarbath. LeBaron thus bolted for the Canadian Football League, where he played one year with the Calgary Stampeders before re-signing with the Redskins and their new coach, Joe Kuharich, in 1955.

LeBaron made the Pro Bowl for the first time that year, followed by appearances in the 1957 and 1958 seasons. By the latter season, he was the league's best quarterback, in the eyes of Kuharich. "There are others who might be able to pass better than Eddie, others who can run better, others who can kick better," Kuharich wrote in a guest column in the *Atlanta*

*Journal* on September 24, 1958. "But there is no one who can do ALL of those things as well as LeBaron. And nobody executes a play better or analyzes a situation anywhere near as well as the Redskins' No. 14."

LeBaron still had his skeptics, but he had a stock response to those who thought he was too small: "I don't know how I'd play if I was bigger because I've never been bigger than I am." He said it was mostly the press that questioned his abilities. "The people I played against never said those things. It didn't bother me because it didn't come from anyone who I thought knew anything."

LeBaron retired after the 1959 season having thrown for 8,068 yards as a Redskin. But the expansion Dallas Cowboys coaxed him out of retirement and made a trade with the Redskins to acquire his rights. He made the Pro Bowl once as a Cowboy in 1962.

LeBaron, who attended law school during his playing days, later worked in the Atlanta Falcons' front office. He served as general manager (1977–82) and executive vice president (1983–85). He was named NFL Executive of the Year in 1980.

## PAUL LIPSCOMB

DT-OT, No. 76, Tennessee • 6–4, 260 • **NFL Career:** 1945–54 (10 seasons) • **Redskins Years:** 1950–54 (10) • **Born:** January 13, 1923 (Benton, Ill.) • **Died:** August 20, 1964 (Elm Grove, Tenn.)

For the last half of the 1940s, Green Bay tackle Paul Lipscomb gave opponents fits with his bruising style of play. The Redskins accused him of playing dirty after he smashed quarterback Sammy Baugh's mouth, splitting both lips, and hit center Clyde Ehrhardt so violently that he lost some teeth.

In 1950, the Redskins put a twist on the old saying, "If you can't beat 'em, join 'em," by saying, "If you can't beat him, get him to join you." They traded tackle Len Szafaryn straight up for Lipscomb, who crafted four straight Pro Bowl years while playing mostly on defense. He once received second-team All-Pro honors.

Herman Ball, who coached the Redskins in 1950, was certain that Lipscomb would be of immediate value. Ball's instincts were right. After a 27–17 loss to the Giants that season, Lipscomb was named Redskins Lineman of the Week.

"Lipscomb looked particularly good on three plays, two of them traps that failed to work when he blasted through to nail the ball handler," the *Washington Evening Star* wrote. "The third was a New York fumble which [Lipscomb] recovered on the 10-yard line, setting up the Redskins' second touchdown."

During Lipscomb's days in Washington, teams still complained about his brutal tactics on the field. He was ejected twice one season for rough play. He denied playing dirty. "I play the game hard, but not dirty," Lipscomb once said. "I got these playing that way," referring to scars above one eye and on the bridge of his nose. "It's a tough game. I've never accused anybody of trying to get me . . . and they shouldn't accuse me."

Lipscomb never missed a game in his first four seasons in Washington. He played one game in 1954 but was traded to Chicago, where he stayed the rest of the season to close out his career.

## CHIP LOHMILLER

K, No. 8, Minnesota • 6–3, 215 • **NFL Career:** 1988–96 (9 seasons) • **Redskins Years:** 1988–94 (7) • **Born:** July 16, 1966 (Woodbury, Minn.)

Chip Lohmiller was among the best kickers in the NFL in the early 1990s and is one of the most prolific to ever wear a Redskins uniform. With a muscular 6–3, 215-pound frame and a powerful right leg, Lohmiller led the NFC in field goals converted and points from 1990 to 1992; he tied the Saints' Morten Andersen for first in points in 1992.

His 149 points, 31 field goals, and 56 extra points were NFL highs in 1991 and played a key role in the Redskins' Super Bowl-winning season. He made the Pro Bowl that year and was named to several All-Pro teams. He kicked a league-best 30 field goals in 1992.

Lohmiller, a Redskins second-round draft pick in 1988 who set a series of kicking records at Minnesota, played seven seasons in Washington. He converted a field goal in 28 straight games, one of the best such marks in NFL history, and made 213 consecutive extra points, once the third-longest streak of all time. He kicked eight game-winning field goals.

Today, Lohmiller is second in Redskins history in total points (787) behind Mark Moseley (1,206), one of the team's most coveted records. He holds a lofty spot in nearly every other scoring and field goal-kicking category in the Redskins' record book.

## BILL MALINCHAK

WR, No. 24, Indiana • 6–1, 200 • **NFL Career:** 1966–74, 76 (10 seasons) • **Redskins Years:** 1970–74, 76 (6) • **Born:** April 2, 1944 (Charleroi, Pa.)

It is one of the most game-altering plays in football. A blocked punt can inject one team with waves of momentum while deflating another team to the point that it never recovers.

Bill Malinchak had the technique down to a science. A wide receiver, Malinchak blocked four punts for the Redskins in the 1970s. He deflected two in the first three games in 1972, including one that he scooped up and ran 16 yards for a score in a 24–21 Monday night win over Minnesota. Another Monday night audience saw him block one in a 14–7 victory over the Cowboys in 1973. He suspended his career on Wall Street to return to the Redskins for the final few weeks of the 1976 season, blocking a punt in a 27–14 season-ending win over the Cowboys that clinched a playoff berth.

In Washington, Malinchak starred on special teams units where blocking kicks was so common under head coach George Allen, the godfather of modern-day special teams. Malinchak also played two seasons in D.C. for a great special teams coach in Marv Levy, who called Malinchak and Steve Tasker the two best punt blockers ever. Levy was Buffalo's head coach when Tasker played there in the 1980s and 1990s and blocked seven punts.

Levy said he originally learned from Malinchak: "Bill Malinchak had a technique for blocking punts that made so much sense that others didn't use. It's a technique I've taught ever since to block a punt. Everybody comes in with their hands up. Bill split his hands out at the foot to block that ball

Malinchak flies through the air to block a punt against the Lions in 1973.

off the foot. His technique was not to raise his hands and block the kick, because the ball rises much faster than your hands, but to block it before it rises. That's what I taught, and that's how Steve Tasker became a fantastic punt blocker."

Malinchak, who set school receiving records at Indiana, played with Detroit from 1966 to 1969. He led Lions ends with 26 catches for 397 yards and four touchdowns one season. He played himself in the popular 1968 film, *Paper Lion*, a story about a journalist, George Plimpton (played by Alan Alda), who competes in a Lions training camp and chronicles his experiences.

Malinchak signed as a free agent with the Redskins early in the 1970 season. He was on the roster for five years, missed the 1975 campaign, but returned for the final three weeks plus a playoff game in 1976.

## CHARLEY MALONE

OE-DE, No. 19, Texas A&M • 6–4, 200 • **NFL Career:** 1934–40, 42 (8 seasons) • **Redskins Years:** 1934–40, 42 (8) • **Born:** June 18, 1910 (Hillsboro, Tex.) • **Died:** May 23, 1992 (Lake San Marcos, Calif.)

When the Redskins needed a wide target on the receiving end in their early years, Charley Malone was the man. The 6–4, 200-pound end led the squad in receiving in 1934, 1935, 1937, and 1938—a time when ball-movement was based primarily on the running game.

Signed in 1934 by Redskins owner George Preston Marshall out of Texas A&M, Malone caught 11 passes for 121 yards and two touchdowns as a rookie. In 1935, new coach Eddie Casey put added emphasis on the passing game, and Malone

responded with 22 receptions for a league-high 433 yards (19.7 average) and two scores.

Fellow end and future Hall of Famer Wayne Millner was the Redskins' top receiver in 1936. When Sammy Baugh arrived in 1937, however, Malone served as the great passer's favorite receiving target for two straight seasons. He caught 28 passes in 1937, when the Redskins won the NFL championship, and 24 in 1938. He finished among the league leaders both years.

Malone played six seasons before sitting out the 1941 campaign. He returned in 1942, played in five games and retired. Overall, he caught 137 passes for 1,932 yards (14.1 average) and 13 touchdowns in his eight-year career.

## DEXTER MANLEY

DE, No. 72, Oklahoma State • 6–3, 257 • **NFL Career:** 1981–91 (12 seasons) • **Redskins Years:** 1981–89 (9) • **Born:** February 2, 1959 (Houston, Tex.)

He could have gone down as one of the greatest defensive ends ever. A package of ferociousness combined with unmitigated speed and power, the 6–3, 257-pound Dexter Manley never took a play off as he brought a special passion to the game. He was one of the most feared pass rushers in the 1980s and posted the most sacks in the NFL (64) from 1982 to 1986.

Manley has been a preliminary nominee for Pro Football Hall of Fame induction, but he feels that he will never be enshrined in the prestigious body because of what he calls his "dark" history in pro football. He failed four drug tests and was banned for good from the NFL in his 12th season in 1991.

It's his top regret in life: "I grew up in Houston's third ward in the ghetto and fought guys older than me, I never lost a fight, I never lost a battle," he said, his emotions rising by the second. "But I lost this war to cocaine. I let drugs interfere and rob me and pimp me and prostitute me, and it took everything from me because I lost the desire to be the best football player. I lost focus. I had these great dreams, but my dreams were fading away because I was caught up in cocaine."

While he was on top of his game, there was never a dull moment with Manley. In addition to devouring quarterbacks—he holds the Redskins' all-time sack record (97.5)—he spewed outrageous comments and displayed a flamboyance that caused many an eye to roll. All along, he was modeling himself after another bombastic quote machine, boxing legend Muhammad Ali, and became a magnet for cameras and note pads.

- He predicted he would be the MVP of Super Bowl XVII, a distinction earned by John Riggins after the Redskins' win over Miami.
- He sported a Mohawk haircut (which Riggins once did, too) during training camp one year and called himself "Mr. D," a take on the popular actor, "Mr. T."
- Before a game against the 49ers, he vowed to "ring" the clock of quarterback Joe Montana, a metaphorical error.
- He once wore red- and electric-blue Spiderman practice tights, and dark Blues Brothers-style sunglasses during noncontact drills.
- He mocked General Alexander Haig by telling him, "I'm in charge, here." As secretary of state, Haig had incorrectly declared himself to be in charge of the White House after President Reagan was shot in 1981.

Manley admitted at times to having diarrhea of the mouth. Knowing his entertainment value, a number of Washington radio stations recruited the loquacious character to host shows. He interviewed such national figures as NFL Commissioner Pete Rozelle, famous sportscaster and *Monday Night Football* co-host Howard Cosell, boxing champ Sugar Ray Leonard, and late-night talk show host Jay Leno. He once asked Cosell, who himself was no stranger to controversy, if he had ever committed adultery.

"He told me, 'None of my fu . . . ing business,'" Manley said. "But Howard Cosell really liked me. He once pulled me aside and said, 'Manley, as long as you're controversial, you'll always make money.' I knew to make extra money, I needed to be talking off-the-wall stuff. I realized it's shock radio. I was making anywhere from $80,000 to 100 grand a year just on radio alone."

Fellow defensive end Charles Mann, a long-time teammate of Manley, said his headline-grabbing remarks made him who he was. "People loved Dexter Manley," Mann said. "And fans from other teams loved to hate Dexter Manley. It was a marketing ploy. He's selling his jerseys, and the mystique of Dexter Manley was alive and well."

The Redskins picked Manley in the fifth round in 1981 out of Oklahoma State. He played as a pass-rushing specialist in his first few games before breaking into the starting lineup, recording six sacks as a rookie. (The NFL started keeping official sack records in 1982.)

He grandly entered the lexicon of Redskin fans in the 1982 postseason, making what would go down as his signature sack: He knocked Cowboys quarterback Danny White out of the NFC championship game with a concussion. He later tipped a screen pass that fell into the hands of defensive tackle Darryl

Manley is the Redskins' all-time sack leader (97.5).

Grant, who took the ball into the end zone for the score that punched the Redskins' ticket to Super Bowl XVII—one of the most famous plays in Redskins history.

Manley's sack totals rose in each of the next four seasons, and he earned his first and only Pro Bowl appearance in 1986, his greatest year as a pro. He posted 18 sacks, second in the league to Giants linebacker Lawrence Taylor and a Redskins record that stands. Many news services selected him for their All-NFL teams, and the NFL Players Association named him NFC Defensive Lineman of the Year. U.S. Secretary of Defense Caspar Weinberger designated him the 1986 secretary of defense.

Offenses also showered him with respect, often double-teaming the right end by putting a tight end or H-back on his side. The only defensive end who came close to his speed and power at the time, Manley said, was the Eagles' 6–5, 300-pound Reggie White, who is now in the Hall of Fame.

"Most players don't have the speed and the power that I had," said Manley, who ran a 4.5 40, bench-pressed more than 500 pounds, and often played out of control, a formidable combination. I had the power to run right over a 300-pound

## Manley's Redskins Sack Records

- Most career (97.5)
- Most season (18)
- Most game (four, tied with Diron Talbert and Phillip Daniels)
- Most seasons leading Redskins (five)
- Most consecutive seasons with 10 or more (four)

lineman. I'd fire off the ball, run three or four steps, and hit him right in the face mask, catching him off guard. That makes them think, 'I don't know what's coming next from this guy.'"

"Dexter was in his own world," said Dave Butz, a Redskin defensive tackle who played with him for eight seasons. "He was very talented, very fast, had the ability to go one on one. Sometimes, he got too hyped up and forgot the play he was supposed to be doing, according to Darrell Grant, who was over on that side."

Said Grant, "It was chaotic playing with Dexter."

Manley, who specialized in talking trash during games, sometimes yelled at opposing head coaches to run the ball at him—Chicago's Mike Ditka, Dallas's Tom Landry, and Cincinnati's Forrest Gregg to name a few. Prior to Super Bowl XXII, he chewed out reporters and stormed out of a press conference after being peppered with questions about how the Redskins' were going to stop Broncos superstar quarterback John Elway. "Well, how are they going to stop Dexter Manley?" he shot back.

"I took that stuff personally because of the competitive part in me," said Manley, who had one and a half sacks that day in the Redskins' 42–10 win. "I had a great game. I destroyed Denver."

Life was good on the field for the prototype defensive end and money and fame were aplenty (he appeared on the cover of *Sports Illustrated* on November 23, 1987), but Manley was struggling personally. He began using cocaine and tested positive for drugs three times in the late 1980s. He said he never played while he was high on cocaine. After his third positive test midway through the 1989 season, he was banned from the NFL for a year.

After being reinstated, Manley signed with the Phoenix Cardinals and played four games in 1990. He spent the next season in Tampa Bay but tested positive a fourth time. His playing days ended with a short stint in the Canadian Football League in 1992.

Manley's retirement years have also been turbulent. He became addicted to crack cocaine, was arrested three times, and served two jail terms, the last of which ended in March 2004. He has since launched his own foundation called "Dexter's Team," which focuses on drug addiction, illiteracy, parenting, and education.

"Most great players get a chance to leave when they're ready," said Manley, who was illiterate until age 30. "But I left the game very disturbed because my whole life was about football. All of a sudden, I get there, I make it, I thought I'd arrived, I thought I was somebody. I thought I was invincible, bullet proof. But I was hit with reality."

## CHARLES MANN

DE, No. 71, Nevada–Reno • 6–6, 272 • **NFL Career:** 1983–94 (12 seasons) • **Redskins Years:** 1983–93 (11) • **Born:** April 12, 1961 (Sacramento, Calif.)

He was commonly known as the Redskins' other defensive end, the man on the side opposite his more boisterous and flamboyant teammate, Dexter Manley.

The quiet and unassuming Charles Mann built an identity all his own. He posted 82 sacks over 11 seasons with the Red-

Charles Mann

skins, the team's second-highest all-time mark behind Manley (97.5). He made the Pro Bowl four times, chalked up All-Pro honors, and was key to two Redskin Super Bowl-winning teams. He also won a Super Bowl playing for the 49ers in his last NFL season, 1994.

Mann said unequivocally that playing in Manley's shadow didn't bruise his ego: "My whole career I was overshadowed, but it wasn't a bad thing," he said. "I came in under the radar. People would game plan against us and say, 'Okay, these are the guys we've got to stop,' and they didn't think about me. So I'd have more sacks, more tackles than Dexter because they were double, triple-teaming him. Slowly but surely, even though in the media or with the common fan I may have been overshadowed, players know who players are, and they'd look at the film and say, "Okay, we've got to stop number 71. We know about Dexter, we hear about him, but 71 is making some stops. Seventy-one is a threat.'"

Mann's feats were pretty good for someone from a Division I-AA school, Nevada–Reno. He was voted Most Valuable Defensive Lineman in the Big Sky Conference in 1981 and 1982. In the latter year, as a senior, he led the conference in sacks (14) and was voted a Division I-AA All-American.

After the Redskins drafted him in the third round in 1983, the 6–6, 225-pound Mann wanted to play linebacker so he "could stand up and see the game," as he put it. He ran a 4.7 40 at the time and thought he had the speed to cover receivers. But Mann said the coaches "saw another version of a Dexter Manley," who was then in his third season, and positioned him at left defensive end behind Todd Liebenstein.

Mann's first start, a 42–20 win over the Los Angeles Rams on November 20, 1983, was memorable. On one play, he faked out future Hall of Fame offensive tackle Jackie Slater and sacked quarterback Vince Ferragamo for a safety.

"My family is from Sacramento, California, and I had a lot of family at that game," he said. "I was very excited, very nervous. Jackie Slater was an incredible player. I was scared to death, didn't sleep that night, but I beat him on the inside and got to Ferragamo for a safety."

After bulking up considerably in the off-season, Mann became an official starter in 1984 and recorded seven sacks, followed by a career-high 14.5 in 1985, certifying him as one of the league's elite pass rushers. He made the Pro Bowl for the first time in 1987, one of three seasons he led the Redskins in sacks, and turned in an outstanding three-sack, six-tackle performance in a 21–17 playoff win over Chicago in January 1988. "Skins' other end: Mann, what a year!" read a headline in the *Virginian-Pilot*.

Meanwhile, Mann stood as a hulk-like 275-pound end with quickness, strength, and smarts. His nicknames were "Mannster" and "C-Ment." All along, his goal was to sack quarterbacks and outperform Manley. "Dexter and I always competed," Mann said. "We had our own little inside match-ups going. I'd get to the quarterback, and I'd look to see where he was. I've got a bunch of pictures with me getting sacks, and Dexter's in the shadows getting handled or double-teamed or blocked out of the picture. And I'm sure he's got a bunch of pictures with him getting the sack and me standing out of the way. So it was a friendly competition, and I loved it. It made it all worth it. It wasn't just winning the game, it was about beating Dexter."

Personality-wise, Mann was the antithesis of Manley and gained respect for his professionalism. "Charles Mann was a good player who had strong character," said Manley, who had a nose for controversy. "He watched me and saw what not to do. So he was sort of like an ambassador as a player. Everybody liked him. He was no trash talker. He was quiet, humble. That's what I liked about him."

"Charles Mann was a good person on and off the field," said Dave Butz, a Redskins defensive tackle who played with Mann for six seasons and usually lined up next to him. "Very dedicated and worked very hard. He and I were good together. I had more strength and weight, he had the speed, which is a good combination."

Mann earned Pro Bowl honors again in 1988, 1989 and 1991, when he had 11.5 sacks in the Redskins' march to an eventual win in Super Bowl XXVI. A knee injury hobbled him for most of 1993, and he was cut after the season, a tremendous personal setback. "I was a Redskin until I died," he said. "I was not going to go to another team. That was unthinkable to me."

He acquiesced when the 49ers called with the 1994 season just under way, playing sparingly for a squad that captured Super Bowl XXIX. Mann said winning that Super Bowl wasn't nearly as gratifying as his championship years in Washington, but he appreciated playing with two franchises that won a combined eight Super Bowls in the 1980s and 1990s.

"That little five months in San Francisco was a great opportunity," said Mann, who officially retired as a Redskin in 1995. "I got to see two of the best organizations in the NFL and how they did it. The Redskins did it one way, and the 49ers did it another, and both thought they were doing it the best."

## WILBER MARSHALL

LB, No. 58, Florida • 6–1, 231 • **NFL Career:** 1984–95 (12 seasons) • **Redskins Years:** 1988–92 (5) • **Born:** April 18, 1962 (Titusville, Fla.)

In 1988, when Redskins owner Jack Kent Cooke doled out $6 million over five years for free agent linebacker Wilber Marshall, making him the highest-paid defensive player in NFL history at the time, it was hoped that Marshall would be the same destructive force he had been in Chicago. In the Windy City, he went to the Pro Bowl twice and starred on perhaps the greatest defense in NFL history, the 1985 Bears.

Maybe it was because the expectations were so high, but Marshall did not appear to terrorize offenses in his first three seasons in Washington, as he tried acclimating himself to the disciplined system of defensive coordinator Richie Petitbon. He made more than 100 tackles and averaged four sacks in 1988, 1989, and 1990 playing mostly on the weak side, nothing shabby. But when the Redskins moved the 6–1, 231-pounder to the strong side opposite the tight end before the 1991 season and allowed him to play more on third downs, he had the opportunity to make more plays.

The Redskins received a big return for their investment. Marshall, who possessed excellent athletic skills to go with a mean streak, returned to his menacing ways while posting arguably the greatest all-around season ever for a Redskins' defensive player in 1991. He tallied a career-high 135 tackles, including a team-high 11 for loss, plus five and a half sacks and five interceptions, one of which he returned 54 yards for a touchdown. He recovered two fumbles.

Those numbers were only appetizer for the postseason, when he was utterly devastating. He sneaked through undetected for three sacks in a 41–10 victory over the Lions in the NFC championship game and tormented Buffalo's offense in the Redskins' win in Super Bowl XXVI, recording a team-high 11 tackles and two forced fumbles. He received a number of postseason honors, including second-team All-Pro, although he was strangely excluded from the Pro Bowl.

Marshall received his just rewards in 1992 after posting six sacks, which tied him for the team-high, and two interceptions, returning one for a touchdown. He made the Pro Bowl for the third and final time and was chosen a first-team All-Pro. That was his final year in Washington. The former first round pick out of Florida played for Houston, Arizona, and the Jets before retiring after the 1995 season.

## MARK MAY

OL, No. 73, Pittsburgh • 6–6, 295 • **NFL Career:** 1981–89, 91–93 (12 seasons) • **Redskins Years:** 1981–89 (9) • **Born:** November 2, 1959 (Oneonta, N.Y.)

Nobody ever credited Mark May for congeniality on the field. He was as ornery and tenacious as they come, never avoiding a tussle when the opportunity was ripe.

His nastiness added another dimension to the Redskins' intimidating offensive line of the 1980s, the Hogs, of which he was a charter member. He played nine seasons for the Redskins that decade, making the Pro Bowl once, and had memorable skirmishes with such players as Cowboys Hall of Fame defensive lineman Randy White.

"Usually, I don't start anything, but if somebody starts out with a dirty shot at me, it's usually going to be a long day for him because I'll get him back sooner or later," May said in the *Washington Times* on December 19, 1986. "There will be a time in the game that he's not looking the right way, and the whistle hasn't blown, and I'll catch him."

Giants Hall of Fame linebacker Harry Carson called May a "cheap-shot artist." "I've never developed a relationship of hate with anybody—on or off the field," Carson wrote in his 1986 book, *Point of Attack: The Defense Strikes Back*. "There are certain players I have to keep an eye on, though. Like Mark May, a Redskins lineman. He's one of those guys who if you're standing around a pile, will knock you into it. He'll hit you when your back is turned."

May played his college ball at Pittsburgh. He starred at right tackle and did not allow a quarterback sack in his final two seasons, when the Panthers posted a combined 22–2 record. In 1980, "May Day" was a consensus first-team All-American as a senior and won the Outland Trophy, given to the top interior lineman in the country. He was inducted into the College Football Hall of Fame in 2005.

The Redskins drafted May in 1981 as a left tackle. He played there the first half of the season but moved to right guard to make room for rookie Joe Jacoby. In the coming years, he played every position on the offensive line except center, spending most of his time on the right side at guard and tackle. He was close to being one of the best offensive linemen in the game but was overlooked for postseason recognition perhaps because fellow Hogs like Jacoby and left guard Russ Grimm were perennial All-Pros. Jacoby said May's nickname was "Footsie" because he was slow compared with some of the other Hogs.

May started 50 straight games at one point. In 1988, he was the only offensive player to start every game, missing just four plays, and allowed only one sack while rotating between right guard and right tackle. He made his only Pro Bowl appearance.

The Redskins' offensive line coach at the time, Joe Bugel, knew the value of having a player like May. "You win football games with Mark Mays, believe me," Bugel said in the *Baltimore Sun* on January 10, 1987. "The funny thing is that he's improving with age [27]. That's a good sign. He's gotten better each year. I'm glad he's on our team. I really love coaching the guy. He's got a great attitude about the game. He gives you an honest day's work, plus a little bit more. You never have to worry about him showing up."

May suffered a season-ending knee injury midway through the 1989 campaign. He sat out the following season and played a year in San Diego and two with the Cardinals before retiring. After football, he broke into the broadcasting business and worked as a CBS color commentator for NFL games. He also worked for TNT and is now an analyst for ESPN college football studio shows, game telecasts and radio broadcasts.

# RON MCDOLE

DE, No. 79, Nebraska • 6–4, 265 • **NFL Career:** 1961–78 (18 seasons) • **Redskins Years:** 1971–78 (8) • **Born:** September 9, 1939 (Toledo, Ohio)

He was the exact opposite of a modern-day defensive end: protruding belly, a disdain for lifting weights, limited speed, and a user of the old double-bar face mask. His nickname was "The Dancing Bear."

No matter his appearance, physical limitations and practice habits, the Redskins' Ron McDole performed feats uncharacteristic for a defensive end. With quick reflexes and an amazing instinct for anticipating the direction of a pass, he intercepted 12 balls, perhaps the highest total for a defensive lineman in NFL history. His nimble feet enabled him to penetrate offensive lines and block an abundance of field goals and extra points, and he recovered seven fumbles. He also recorded three safeties and two in a season, placing him among the all-time NFL leaders in both categories.

His skills were a boon to Redskins coach George Allen's stingy defenses of the 1970s, as was his durability. McDole never missed a game in eight seasons as Washington's left defensive end and started all but one of a possible 121, including playoffs. In fact, he started nearly every one of the 250-plus games in his 18-year career.

Much was made in the media and among fans about McDole's rotund physique, but he said that never bothered him. His weight fluctuated from 180 pounds during his college playing days at Nebraska, to 300-plus during his time in the old American Football League in the 1960s, to about 265 with the Redskins.

"It didn't bother me as long as I could get the job done," he said. "With George, I had to weigh in at a certain weight every week, or I got fined. But I never got fined. George didn't really care what you looked like, as long as you got the job done. He said he never did have much luck with guys who looked like Greek Gods. I was in the right place."

Dan Dierdorf, a Hall of Fame offensive tackle for the old St. Louis Cardinals, came in contact with McDole's girth when the Redskins and Cardinals faced one another. "Playing against Ron McDole is like playing against a big pillow," he once said. "But it's amazing—he plays the run better than anybody I've ever faced."

At Nebraska, McDole earned All-American honors as an offensive end and tackle. He also played nose guard on defense. St. Louis picked him in the fourth round in 1961, but he was cut after the season. He played four games in 1962 with the AFL's Houston Oilers before being released again. The AFL's Buffalo Bills signed him before the 1963 season, and he soon became a starting end on dominant defenses that helped spark the Bills to AFL championships in 1964 and 1965.

McDole was a three-time All-Pro in his eight seasons in Buffalo and twice played in the league's all-star game. He was eventually named to the all-time AFL second team.

After the 1970 season, the Bills traded McDole to the Redskins for three draft choices. He thus became a charter member of the veteran-dominated "Over the Hill Gang" assembled by Allen and reacquainted himself with Redskins cornerback Pat Fischer. The two were teammates and co-captains at Nebraska, and both were drafted by the Cardinals in 1961. Today, Fischer is McDole's godfather because he once sponsored McDole for McDole's conversion to Catholicism.

Bill Brundige, a Redskins defensive tackle at the time, remembers his first encounter with McDole: "We're in the locker room, and all he's wearing is a jock strap. And you can hardly see the jock strap because of all the fat around him. He came from Buffalo in the winter and was just about as damn white as a polar bear. And I'm looking at this guy, whose fat is dripping over the sides of his jock strap and who's pale as a ghost, and I thought, 'This is the great Ron McDole, this is the guy coming in here? My God. George Allen is out of his mind.'"

McDole's talents defied his nonathletic appearance. In 1971, he intercepted a phenomenal three passes and rumbled 18 yards with one for a touchdown. He picked off three more as a Redskin, two in 1977, his 17th season. His ability to intercept balls hinged largely on his sense of whether the upcoming play was a run or a pass. "I could pretty much tell when the [offensive linemen] were going to let me come in and rush," he said. "So I'd bail out of there, and sure enough 99 percent of the time they would throw a screen. Being an ex-offensive end, I could catch."

As for his skill at blocking place kicks—he deflected three field goals and two extra points alone in 1975—McDole relied on his "uncanny balance and great, great feet," Brundige said. "The guys on the line when blocking for a kick interlock their feet, so you've got to be able to pick your feet up and get through there without tripping. McDole never tripped."

McDole possessed a lot of natural power but refused to lift weights to augment it. He didn't take part, for example, in a weightlifting program devised by a young coach hired by Allen. As McDole recalled: "George came to me and said, 'Why do you think we haven't had any injuries? It's that weight program.' I said, 'Oh God, here it comes.' He said, 'How come you haven't been doing your weights.' I said, 'George, look at this body. It took me 37 years to build this, you think I'm going to let a little kid ruin it?' He said, 'It is special.'"

Once when McDole was at a D.C. bar with quarterback Sonny Jurgensen and CBS sportscaster Tom Brookshier, he was twisting and turning on the dance floor with his burly body. Jurgensen thus nicknamed him "The Dancing Bear."

"That stayed with me for many years," said McDole, a past officer with the Redskins Alumni Association. "Everybody thought it was because of the way I looked and played on the field. It was quite a dance."

## RALEIGH MCKENZIE

OL, No. 63, Tennessee • 6–2, 280 • **NFL Career:** 1985–98 (14 seasons) • **Redskins Years:** 1985–94 (10) • **Born:** February 8, 1963 (Knoxville, Tenn.)

Raleigh McKenzie was the Redskins' version of a "sixth man." He could play any of the five down positions on the offensive line, whether for a few snaps, a full game, or major stretches. He was not a designated substitute, for he started 113 of 144 games in his 10 Redskins seasons, including 10 of 13 postseason games. Although it is impossible to list him at any one position, his versatility made him a vital member of the Redskins' dominant offensive line of his era, the Hogs.

McKenzie compared himself to Bobby Jones, the great Philadelphia 76ers forward who won the NBA's Sixth Man of the Year award in the 1982–83 season when the 76ers were league champions. "Bobby Jones was really a starter but the team was so talented he couldn't get on the court," he said. "That's the way I felt. I felt like we were so stacked at the line positions, it was tough to get in with the Hogs. But guys knew if they got hurt . . . when I came in I was like a starter. I didn't miss a beat."

"He's a guy who was a most valuable sixth man," said another Hog, tackle Joe Jacoby. "He filled in on the whole line,

Raleigh McKenzie

center, both guards, both tackles. He was a very gifted athlete and could pull in either direction."

There were many situations when "Rallo," who also saw time as a blocking tight end, proved to be ready and adaptable. Case in point: After playing left guard in the first eight (nonreplacement) games of the 1987 season, he moved to center to replace the injured Russ Grimm in the ninth game against Detroit. He returned to guard two weeks later against the Giants.

He started the next season, 1988, at left guard, moved to center two games later, then back to guard later in the year. In 1989, he filled in for four former Pro Bowlers at four different spots on the line. And when a series of injures depleted the offensive line in 1992, he started at center, left tackle, left guard, and back at center in a four-week stretch. In 1992 and 1993, he started at every offensive line position except right tackle.

The epitome of his flexibility was probably in a 1990 win over the Eagles. He played right guard, moved to center for the injured Jeff Bostic, and then switched to left guard for Russ Grimm, before returning to right guard. He started nine straight weeks at right guard and switched to the left side in a game against the Patriots.

McKenzie attributed his resourcefulness to his play at the University of Tennessee, where he started as a linebacker but moved to offensive line by the end of his first year. He played center and both guard positions for the Volunteers, and was chosen to play in the Japan Bowl all-star game. His head coach, Johnny Majors, once called him "one of the best offensive linemen I've ever been around." (His twin brother, Reggie, was a starting linebacker at Tennessee and went on to play five seasons in the NFL.)

The Redskins drafted McKenzie in the 11th round in 1985. "That wasn't a hard pick," then-Redskins general manager Bobby Beathard said. "He was a heck of a lineman at Tennessee. Our guys did a great job of scouting him. Raleigh was special. He fit a mold that we really liked, athletic, smart."

McKenzie began starting in his second season, 1986, and was the only Redskins offensive lineman to play every down in 1987 and to never miss a practice. He won United Press International All-NFC honors in the 1991 season. After a decade with the Redskins, he played two seasons in Philadelphia and two in San Diego before calling it quits. He officially retired as a Redskin in 2001.

"Rallo was a terrific pass protector with terrific upper-body strength," said Jim Hanifan, the Redskins' O-line coach from 1990 to 1996. "He used his hands exceptionally well and had really good feet."

## HAROLD MCLINTON

LB, No. 53, Southern • 6–2, 235 • **NFL Career:** 1969–78 (10 seasons) • **Redskins Years:** 1969–78 (10) • **Born:** July 1, 1947 (Fort Valley, Ga.) • **Died:** October 31, 1980 (Washington, D.C.)

Redskins training camps in the 1970s featured a constant theme, one that injected "fear" into Harold McLinton. Some-one always seemed to be in contention to take over his job as starting middle linebacker.

"Every year, you can count on certain things around this town," Steve Guback of the *Washington Star* wrote on August 13, 1978. "Federal taxes will be due in April, the summer will be hot and muggy, and just before the Redskins leave training camp, the word will make the rounds that middle linebacker Harold McLinton is going to be replaced."

"I go to camp every year scared," McLinton said in the *Washington Post* on September 7, 1978. "There isn't much difference in fear and respect, though. I respect the demands of the position, and I respect the people competing against me for it."

Yet, when all was said and done, No. 53 was in the starting lineup game after game. He started at middle linebacker for the Redskins through most of the 1970s, including all but one game over his last four seasons.

He was a very good linebacker, a smart player, and an unsung contributor to the great Redskin defenses of the era of coach George Allen. The 6–2, 235-pound McLinton specialized in delivering jarring hits. He was constantly around the ball, recovering seven fumbles and intercepting four passes. His nickname was "Tank" because of his layers of extra padding.

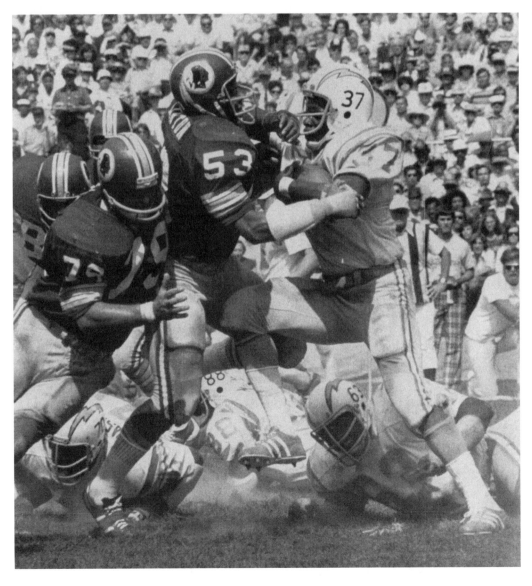

McLinton (53) plugged the middle for the Redskins' defense for a large part of the 1970s.

A Redskins sixth-round draft choice in 1969 out of Southern University in Baton Rouge, Louisiana, where he was one of the best linebackers in school history, McLinton was named Washington's starting left linebacker late in the 1969 season. He stayed on the left side until taking over as starting middle linebacker in the fourth game of the 1972 season. At the time, he was winning complements from a man who knew a thing or two about defenses, George Allen. "He [McLinton] has the attitude, intelligence and desire," Allen said in the *Post* on August 14, 1972. "He's making the mistakes all new middle linebackers make. But they're mistakes of over-aggressiveness. The same mistakes [Bears Hall of Famer] Dick Butkus made when he lacked experience."

McLinton helped key the Redskins' defensive-led run to Super Bowl VII that season but was benched midway through the 1973 campaign and placed on the taxi squad. He regained his starting role in 1974 and had his finest season to date on a defense that allowed 14 points per game, but he fractured his leg late in the year and missed the rest of the season.

McLinton, an overachiever who got little credit while playing with the All-Pros who dotted the Redskins' defense at the time, was an "extremely fiery, fiery guy who was never given his just due," said Mike Bass, a Redskin cornerback who teamed with him for seven seasons.

By 1977, McLinton felt as if he had emerged as one of the best middle linebackers in the NFL. He credited Vince Lombardi, who had coached him as a rookie, and Allen. "Playing football for the Washington Redskins for eight years has been the greatest experience of my life," McLinton said at the time. "I always wanted to play for winning coaches, and I've played for two of the best. Coach Allen has taught me more about football than I ever imagined, and it was Vince Lombardi who drafted me. I feel like a 15-year veteran with the knowledge that coach Allen has taught me."

McLinton was widely respected in the organization and the community, where he performed a lot of charity work. After shelving his pads, he maintained his ties to a youth program with Washington's public transit system. While coming home from a speaking engagement in October 1980, he exited his car on the side of a highway in Washington and was blindsided by a drunk driver, suffering massive injuries.

He underwent 19 hours of surgery and had his left leg amputated at the knee. More than 30 Redskins, including ex-teammates Brig Owens, Larry Brown, Roy Jefferson, Ray Schoenke, and Ted Vactor, were among 800 people who donated blood. McLinton passed away after a 30-day battle at age 33.

His son, Kevin, was eight years old at the time. "A lot of fans around here always tell me how great a guy he was, what he did for the community," Kevin said. "So when they tell me about the person he was, you can't help but feel proud of somebody in your family that accomplished so much."

## BRIAN MITCHELL

RB-KR, No. 30, S. W. Louisiana • 5–10, 220 • **NFL Career:** 1990–2003 (14 seasons) • **Redskins Years:** 1990–99 (10) • **Born:** August 18, 1968 (Fort Polk, La.)

He had an immeasurable quantity of heart and desire. He was hard-nosed, a throwback to the blue-collar NFL of the past,

Mitchell, one of the Redskins' most exciting players in the 1990s, holds the all-time NFL record for kick return yards (19,013).

and he was a true leader on and off the field. Such compliments are used loosely in sports today, but in the case of Brian Mitchell, they were oh so true.

Mitchell never took a play off in his 14-year NFL career, his first 10 with the Redskins. He discarded the welfare of his 5–10, 220-pound body every time he touched the ball, always seeking to make contact with defenders and even punish them. The multidimensional threat, a kickoff and punt returner, running back and receiver, used his bulldog mentality—which one Redskins teammate described as a "cocky aggressiveness"—to rack up chunks of real estate. He accumulated 23,330 all-purpose yards, today the second most in NFL history.

Running back kickoffs and punts was Mitchell's specialty, and he will be remembered as one of the most feared kick returners in league history. He amassed 19,013 return yards, one of the nine NFL special teams records he held on retirement. His return yardage record may never be challenged, for he is about 6,000 ahead of the retired Mel Gray. Mitchell retired holding 16 Redskins records for kick returns.

That Mitchell played with such a reckless abandon, instead of the finesse employed by many other kick returners, makes his accomplishments even more stunning. Kick returners in general don't last that long in the NFL, but Mitchell defied the law of averages and thrived.

His pugnacity, as he tells it, stemmed from his youth. "That's the way I was brought up, that's the way I've always been," he said. "My dad boxed in the army, and he would make me box with my older brothers. I never backed down. I would always feel I could accomplish something. He basically gave me the attitude that, 'If you think you can do it, you can. And if you do everything you possibly can to do it, you will.'"

Mitchell used that attitude in college, where he was dangerous whenever he touched the ball. As a quarterback at tiny Southwestern Louisiana, he became the first player in NCAA history to pass for more than 5,000 yards (5,447) and run for more than 3,000 (3,335). He also set the NCAA record for rushing touchdowns by a quarterback (47).

He joined the Redskins as a fifth-round draft pick in 1990 and raised eyebrows in training camp by engaging in fights, including a bout against 290-pound defensive end James "Jumpy" Geathers. That he never backed down in his career and even instigated a lot of friction held as a Brian Mitchell trademark. When there was jawing in a Redskin game, you could bet he was in the thick of it. He loved to talk trash. "I thought about everything out there that I did," he said. "I would pick the biggest guy on the team or the supposed baddest guy and get in his face and mess with him. And if I'm in his face, they're thinking, 'He's not that big, he has to be a little crazy.' So if you get them to think something's wrong with you, you can play mind games with people, and I did it all the time. It was more of a way of motivating myself. Somebody made the comment that football is 95 percent mental. I believed that because if you get guys thinking about something other than their jobs, that's half the battle."

As a rookie, Mitchell was positioned at running back but also returned punts and kickoffs. His explosiveness was in full view. The first time he touched the ball, he returned a kickoff 92 yards in a preseason game; he ended up leading the team in 1990 with a 26.3 kickoff return average. He also saw brief action at quarterback in a Monday night game at Philadelphia, completing three passes for 40 yards and rushing 1-yard for a touchdown.

In ensuing years, Mitchell proved to be one of the most versatile and talented all-around performers the NFL has ever seen. He set a single-season league record for most kick return yards with 1,930 in 1994, and he led the NFL in com-

bined yards from 1994 to 1996 and in 1998. Today, he and the great Jim Brown are the only players in NFL history to lead the league in combined yards at least four seasons. Mitchell received All-Pro honors in 1994 and '96 and made the Pro Bowl in 1995, his only invitation to the all-star game.

One of his greatest achievements occurred late in the 1999 season. He returned the opening kickoff 43 yards in a game against the 49ers, breaking Gray's all-time record for combined kickoff and punt return yards. Rumors were then swirling that Mitchell had lost a step, but he quieted his critics in a second-round playoff game against Tampa Bay, returning a kickoff 100 yards for a touchdown.

Mitchell said at the time that he was not ready to retire, and his teammates knew it would hurt to lose the veteran. "What is sometimes lost is Brian's leadership on the field," Redskins quarterback Brad Johnson said late in the 1999 season. "The leadership he brings to the table is phenomenal. Then, when you get him in there in a crucial situation, whether it's a two-minute drive or just in a big game, he's always making plays."

The Redskins released him in June 2000. He played three seasons with the Eagles and one with the Giants before calling it quits after the 2003 campaign. The 2004 season began with Mitchell holding the NFL all-time yardage record, although legendary 49ers wide receiver Jerry Rice surpassed him late in the year and retired after that season with 23,546. (Rice played 20 seasons, compared with 14 for Mitchell.)

Mitchell returned to the Redskins in February 2005 and signed a one-day contract that allowed him to officially retire as a member of the burgundy and gold. He has had his own talk show on one of the Washington area's all-sports radio stations, WTEM, and is a panelist on *Redskins Post Game Live* on Comcast SportsNet.

"I can honestly say this is one of the toughest guys I've ever been around," Redskins coach Joe Gibbs, who coached Mitchell in his first three seasons, said at his retirement press conference. "Football meant a lot to him, and he was very emotional."

## ART MONK

WR, No.81, Syracuse • 6–3, 210 • **NFL Career:** 1980–95 (16 seasons) • **Redskins Years:** 1980–93 (14) • NFL 1980s All-Decade Team • **Born:** December 5, 1957 (White Plains, N.Y.)

He was a quiet leader who played games in total silence. Trash talking and showboating were antithetical to his approach, for he embodied professionalism and carried himself with dignity on the field. Art Monk's goal was simple: Let his achievements do the talking.

And boy, did they. Monk is one of the premier wide receivers in NFL history. In 16 seasons, he caught 940 passes for 12,721 yards (13.5 average) and 68 touchdowns, retiring as the league's leader in total receptions; he has since been surpassed by a host of receivers. He set all-time NFL marks for most catches in one season (106 in 1984) and most consecutive games with receptions (183), both of which have been broken, and owns a slew of Redskin receiving records.

As Monk tells it, his silence was golden. "I've had guys say stuff to me and look me right in the eye and try to intimidate me," he told *Washingtonian* magazine in 1988. "But I just go back to the huddle and say, 'I'm going to catch this one, and

---

### Mitchell's NFL Special Teams Records

- Most combined kick return yards: kickoffs and punts (19,013)
- Most kick returns for touchdowns (13)
- Most kick returns (1,070)
- Most kickoff-return yards (14,014)
- Most kickoff returns (607)
- Most punt-return yards (4,999)
- Most punt returns (463)
- Most fair catches (231)
- Most single-season fair catches (33)

Monk retired as the NFL's all-time leader in catches (940). He barely uttered a peep during games, instead letting his play do the talking.

after I catch it maybe I can run over him.' I found that I excel more in those situations than when someone doesn't say anything to me."

Monk, a three-time Pro Bowler and two-time All-Pro, is a member of the NFL 1980s All-Decade Team. He has been a finalist for Hall of Fame induction seven times since becoming eligible in 2001 but keeps getting overlooked. "I don't think there's another guy who deserves it more than him," Don Warren, a Redskins tight end who teamed with Monk for 13 seasons, said of his Hall of Fame enshrinement. "He was a guy who helped the Redskins out tremendously."

"Everybody says he should be in, I don't know why he isn't," said another long-time Redskin teammate, guard Russ Grimm. "He'll get there."

Monk's art of pass catching was instrumental in propelling the Redskins' glory teams of the 1980s and early 1990s. He was on the roster for each of the squad's four Super Bowl appearances during the era, earning three rings. The legend also became one of the most beloved Redskins ever, as amplified by his selection as the best player in team history in the 50th anniversary "Greatest Redskins Poll" in 1986. He received 8,469 votes from fans, topping two Hall of Famers in running back John Riggins (8,154) and quarterback Sonny Jurgensen (8,069). Fans at RFK Stadium named a section after him called the "THE ART GALLERY."

When asked about his 16-year career, the modest and soft-spoken Monk replied, "I wouldn't have changed a thing. I came in not expecting anything and not even to really last very long in the NFL. I didn't think I was even talented enough to play on this level but ended up playing a long time and having a great career. I couldn't have asked for anything better."

Raised in the New York City suburb of White Plains, New York, Monk starred in track and football in high school and came to admire such dominant pro receivers as the Redskins' Charley Taylor, Otis Taylor, and Paul Warfield. He received a football scholarship to Syracuse, where he set school receiving

records with 102 catches for 1,644 yards and had more than 1,000 yards in both rushing and returning kicks.

Then-Redskins general manager Bobby Beathard was sold on Monk after scouting him. "He was a fabulous athlete, a very smart young guy," Beathard said. "He was a good worker, he had speed, he was smooth, great hands, he was a guy who loved to play pro football. I don't think Art Monk was a really hard guy to figure out or scout."

To Beathard, Monk was more of a receiver than a running back, and the Redskins took him in the first round in 1980 (18th overall), their first first-round pick since 1968. Monk, a starter by the fourth game, caught a team-high 58 passes for 797 yards and three touchdowns that season, breaking the club's rookie receiving record set in 1964 by none other than Charley Taylor. He was a unanimous All-Rookie selection.

At the same time, the 6–3, 210-pound Monk was drawing comparisons to Taylor, who had similar size and was just as physical. "People talked a lot about me falling in his footsteps when I got here, and that in itself was an honor," Monk said. "But really I just wanted to be myself. I didn't want to pattern myself after anybody. I had my own style and my own way of doing things. But he was an idol, and I looked up to him growing up."

Monk averaged 49 catches and 721 receiving yards and made 14 touchdown catches in his first four seasons, which were slightly abbreviated because of injuries. One injury forced him to miss the 1982 postseason that ended with the Redskins' win in Super Bowl XVII. (Monk had never missed a game or a practice because of injury in his four years at Syracuse.)

He crafted a historic season in his fifth year, 1984, catching an NFL-record 106 passes for a career-high 1,372 yards and seven touchdowns. He broke the record in the season finale against the Cardinals. Needing seven catches to top the record of 101 set by the Houston Oilers' Charlie Hennigan in 1964, Monk caught 11. His last reception, a 20-yarder on third-and-19, helped set up a field goal that gave the Redskins a 29–27 victory and the NFC East title. No wonder Monk's nickname was "money."

Monk was a consensus first-team All-Pro that year and received his first Pro Bowl invitation. He also made the Pro Bowl in 1985 and 1986. The latter year, he became the first Redskin receiver to record three straight 1,000-yard and 70-plus catch seasons.

All the while, No. 81 proved he was more substance than style, never one to be confused with his flashy teammate, receiver Gary Clark. His trademark pass pattern was the "dodge" route, a short route over the middle. Monk possessed the size, power, and toughness to execute the pattern, maneuvering through traffic and fending off linebackers and other defenders. He could also gain big yardage after the catch.

Monk rarely spoke to teammates or reporters, but when he spoke up in team meetings, other Redskins shut up in what coach Joe Gibbs once described as an "E. F. Hutton moment." His commitment to improve his strength and physical conditioning also spoke volumes, for he followed a rigorous workout plan that made his teammates envious. He filled his days with demanding combinations of weight lifting, wind sprints, distance running and racquetball. He often ran grueling sprints on a 45-degree, 15-yard hill, in one workout running 25 times uphill with straight leg-pumps, then 25 times backward, then 25 times in a stutter step. He added six 220-meter sprints and six 110-meter sprints.

Monk credited Terry Metcalf, a running back who played for the Redskins in 1981, with inspiring him to pursue such a grueling routine. "[Metcalf] was a fanatic with training and staying in shape," Monk said. "I just caught on and maintained that for the rest of my career. It wasn't just an in-season thing, it was during the off-season, a full-time thing: hills, biking, weights, track, agility, cardiovascular, just a combination of things."

As for Monk, "He was huge for a wide receiver, he could run, he had great hands, he was very physical, he had the talent, and he had the work ethic," Don Warren said. "I kind of molded myself a little after him, just watching the way he worked out. We spent many summers running sprints on the track. He's one of the hardest workers."

Said former Redskins quarterback Joe Theismann, "Art is as tough as any player I've ever played with and had every attribute you'd want to look for. If you were putting together a football team and fashioned it after a bunch of Art Monks, you'd win a lot of football games."

On October 12, 1992, Monk's became the league's all-time leading receiver in a Monday night game against Denver, making his 820th reception to top Seahawks great Steve Largent. By the end of the 1993 campaign, he had posted nine seasons of 50 or more catches and five with at least 1,000 yards.

But Monk and the Redskins fell into a contract dispute at the time, and he departed acrimoniously. In the next two years, he caught 46 passes for 581 yards and three touchdowns with the Jets, and six balls for 114 yards with the Eagles.

After failing to sign with a team for the 1996 season, Monk retired from the game in June 1997. The Redskins immediately announced plans to sign him to a ceremonial one-day contract so he could retire as a member of the burgundy and gold. "Nothing would delight us more than for Art Monk to officially retire as a Redskin," then-Redskins president John Kent Cooke said. "We look forward to signing Art one more time so he can go into the Hall of Fame as a Washington Redskin."

"I'll always consider myself a Redskin," Monk said.

## Monk's All-Time Redskin Records

- Most career receptions (888)
- Most career receiving yards (12,026)
- Most seasons, 1,000 or more receiving yards (5, tied with Gary Clark)
- Most games, 100 or more receiving yards (36)
- Most consecutive games, 100 or more receiving yards (three)
- Most receptions, game (13, tied with Kelvin Bryant)
- Most touchdowns, game (3, tied with multiple players)
- Most yards from scrimmage—rushing and receiving (12,358)

# WILBUR MOORE

DB-WB-HB-FB, No. 35, Minnesota • 5–11, 187 • **NFL Career:** 1939–46 (8 seasons) • **Redskins Years:** 1939–46 (8) • **Born:** April 22, 1916 (Austin, Minn.) • **Died:** August 9, 1965 (Takoma Park, Md.)

With Wilbur Moore, one need not worry about him punching his time card to leave early. He never took a play off.

Moore, an offensive and defensive back, played so vigorously and hit so hard that he broke 13 bones in his eight-year career with the Redskins, the most of any leading player in NFL history at the time. One play, his "spectacular man-on-a-trapeze tackle," epitomized his unwavering determination. In an exhibition game, no less, on September 23, 1945, he made a ridiculously high leap over three Packers players while aiming to make a tackle.

"What made Wilbur Moore a great football player was his fierce competitive spirit," Dutch Bergman, the Redskins' coach in 1943, once said in the *Washington Post*. "He gave everything he had, every minute."

Statistically, Moore was a great football player, too. The multipurpose threat rushed for 901 yards on 183 carries (4.9 average) and caught 91 passes for 1,224 yards (13.5 average). He was among the all-time Redskin leaders in rushing, receiving, and total points (144, 24 touchdowns) when he retired at the end of the 1946 season.

As brilliant as Moore was on offense, he was perhaps more valuable on pass defense. He tallied 13 interceptions and 167 return yards and was an intimidator in the backfield.

His talents and determination were on full display in the Redskins' 14–6 win over the Bears in the 1942 NFL championship game, one of his greatest days as a pro. A few plays after intercepting a pass, he made a breathtaking over-the-helmet catch in stride with a defender draped over his back while tumbling into the end zone for a 38-yard touchdown reception from Sammy Baugh.

In his book, *The Redskins, 1937–1958*, author Morris A. Bealle used Moore's appearance in a 42–20 win over Detroit midway through the 1943 season to point out that he was well respected by opponents: " . . . it was the first contest of 1943 that Wilbur Moore, the Galloping Gopher from [the

University of] Minnesota, failed to score a touchdown. The Lions put two and three men on him, allowing the other Redskin receivers to roam far and wide and pull down Slinging Sammy's buggywhip passes."

Moore, a part Indian who was nicknamed "Little Indian," was the Redskins' backfield coach from 1947 to 1950. He spent the 1951 season as the backfield coach at George Washington University in D.C. On August 9, 1965, he was shot to death outside his home in Prince George's County, Maryland.

# MARK MOSELEY

K, No. 3, Stephen F. Austin • 6–0, 205 • **NFL Career:** 1970–72, 74–86 (16 seasons) • **Redskins Years:** 1974–86 (13) • **Born:** March 12, 1948 (Laneville, Tex.)

When the game was on the line, it was Mark Moseley time. The Redskins' kicker yearned to perform under pressure and was as unflappable as concrete, characteristics he relied on to convert an abundance of clutch kicks that put the dagger in opponents. Whether with seconds left in the fourth quarter or in overtime, the regular season or the playoffs, Redskin coaches knew whose number to tap: No. 3.

Take his 54-yarder with 3:32 left that beat the Eagles in 1977, his 48-yarder 11:16 into overtime in 1981 that sent the Giants packing, or his crème de la crème of kicks, a 42-yarder in the snow with four seconds left that gave the Redskins a 15–14 win over the Giants in 1982 and put them in the playoffs, from which they advanced to win Super Bowl XVII.

"I wasn't one of these kickers that doubted myself," Moseley said. "I liked to be under the gun. I was always underneath the coaches' arms, begging them to let me go out and kick field goals. I wanted it to come down to me because I felt I was best prepared to go and win the game for us. I accepted the role of having the game on my shoulders."

"Mark was mentally tough," said Mike Bragg, a Redskins punter who played with him for six seasons. "He went through so many things that would derail the average guy. When they called time-out on him, I don't think it really mattered."

Moseley's clutch kicking is a cornerstone of his legacy as the greatest placekicker in Redskins history and one of the NFL's best ever. A two-time Pro Bowler, he rewrote the Redskins' record books with a boatload of all-time scoring and kicking marks that stand, including most career points (1,206). The franchise icon is also second in team history in most consecutive games played (170). He set NFL records, too.

To think the league nearly gave up on him. After scoring 67 points as a rookie in Philadelphia in 1970 (he beat ex-Redskins kicker Sam Baker out of a job before the season), he was cut during the 1971 training camp. He signed with Houston and scored 73 points that season but suffered an injury and was released after the first game in 1972.

Moseley sat out the rest of that season, as well as the entire 1973 campaign. The period was disillusioning for him. He wrote to every team and made calls hoping to get a tryout, but "nobody would even return a phone call," he remembered. He worked jobs in the Houston area that included installing septic tank systems.

But his self-confidence came in handy. To keep himself in shape in case he got another shot, he lifted weights feverishly

and put on 20 pounds of strength. Finally, a call came from Redskins coach George Allen, who had a nose for spotting great special teams players. Allen had been impressed that Moseley converted two field goals in soggy conditions in a 22–13 Redskins win over the Oilers in 1971 and offered him a contract over the phone, Moseley said.

In the summer of 1974, Moseley beat out several players, including veteran Redskins kicker Curt Knight, to win the starting job. Moseley, among the last of the straight-ahead, conventional-style kickers, gradually evolved into one of the best at his position while leading the Redskins in scoring for the next 12 seasons.

It helped that the 6–foot, 205-pounder was very strong for a kicker. He hauled hay while growing up on a farm in Texas and, during his college days, he worked a job where he lifted up to 700 pounds of pulpwood sticks on his shoulders. Combine that with his ability to squat up to 600 pounds in the weight room and his 4.3 time in the 40. "That's what helped to make me a really good kicker, that leg speed with the power that I had," he said. "I don't think too many kickers were like that at the time."

In 1977, Moseley's right leg converted 4 of 6 kicks past 50 yards, including his career-long and then-Redskins-record of 54. (He made 12 from 50 yards or greater in his career.) Such booming kicks triggered accusations from people like Cowboys general manager Tex Schramm and St. Louis Cardinals director of operations Joe Sullivan that Moseley had put lead in his right shoe to get more distance out of the ball. Sullivan once came on the field to observe Moseley kick in pregame warm-ups and ordered game officials to inspect his shoe. All of the charges over the years proved to be unfounded. "All of my coaches and teammates knew that that was not true," Moseley said. "It was easy to prove. That's why the officials always came back and said, 'Hey, this is ridiculous, this guy isn't cheating.'"

Between 1978 and 1984, Moseley was arguably the best kicker in the league. He made the Pro Bowl and several All-Pro teams in 1979, leading the NFL in field goals made for the third time. He fell into a slump in 1980, missing 10 of his first 14 in what he called a "terrible beginning for me, the worst I had ever seen." He bounced back, kicking a team-record-tying five field goals in one game that season, including 50- and 52-yarders.

He soon crafted one of the most outstanding kicking stretches in NFL history. Between the 1981 and 1982 seasons, Mr. Automatic set an NFL record with 23 straight field goals. His 21st straight, the indelible 42-yarder against the Giants on December 19, 1982, broke Garo Yepremian's NFL record of 20. The kick elevated him to celebrity status; he appeared the next day on ABC's *Good Morning America*. That year he also won the NFL's Most Valuable Player award, the first and only kicker ever to do so, and made his second Pro Bowl appearance.

In 1983, Moseley fueled a prolific offense that scored an NFL-record 541 points with a league-kicking-record 161 of his own. Except for a few blips, he remained solid in the coming years. But in the 11th game of the 1985 season, his holder of the previous decade, quarterback Joe Theismann, suffered a career-ending injury that also KO'ed Moseley's tenure in Washington. With Theismann's replacement, Jay Schroeder, doing the holding, Moseley endured a major slump that led the Redskins to release him after the sixth game of the 1986 season.

## Moseley's All-Time Redskins Marks

- Most seasons leading team in scoring (12)
- Most points, career (1,206)
- Most points, season (161, 1983)*
- Most consecutive games scoring (91)
- Most seasons leading NFL in field goals (4)
- Most field goal attempts, career (397)
- Most field goals, career (263)
- Most field goals, season (33, 1983)
- Most consecutive field goals (23)†
- Most consecutive field goals, season (20, 1982)
- Best field goal percentage, season (95.2%, 20 of 21, 1982)‡
- Most field goals, 50 yards or more, career (12)
- Most field goals, 50 yards or more, season (4, 1977)
- Most PATs attempted, career (442)
- Most PATs, career (417)
- Most PATs, season (62, 1983)

*An NFL record (since broken) for most points, no touchdowns, in a season.

†NFL record since broken.

‡Moseley set a Redskins record for best career field goal percentage (66.2%) that has since been broken.

Moseley said his release exemplified how coaches can easily lose confidence in a kicker. "It doesn't matter how good you are," he said. "I missed an extra point and a field goal against Dallas. . . . All of a sudden, I was falling apart. That's all it takes in a kicker."

Moseley resurfaced in Cleveland that year, his final one in the league. He made six of seven field goals in the regular season, plus a 22-yarder with seven seconds left that sent an AFC playoff game into overtime, followed by a 27-yarder that day for a 23–20 Browns win. He retired from the game as the fourth-leading scorer in NFL history with 1,382 points.

"To me, kicking is just a mindset," said Moseley, a former president of the Redskins Alumni Association. "If you want to be out there kicking, you've got to be ready to do it. I accepted that and enjoyed it. I had a lot of great moments with the Redskins."

# SANTANA MOSS

WR, No. 89, Miami • 5–10, 190 • **NFL Career:** 2001–2006 (6 seasons) • **Redskins Years:** 2005–2006 (2) • **Born:** June 1, 1979 (Miami, Fla.)

The Redskins struggled to produce home run pass plays in 2004, and coach Joe Gibbs insisted after the season that his offense needed to be more explosive, one consistently able to move the chains and keep defenses honest. A trade with the Jets brought a speedy wide receiver named Santana Moss, who caught a few long balls in 2005, his fifth year in the NFL.

He also proved to be the most electrifying wide receiver for the Redskins in a long time. That season, Moss amassed 1,483 receiving yards, snapping the team record set by Hall of Famer Bobby Mitchell in 1963 (1,436). Moss's yardage mark was second in the league. He also led the Redskins in receptions (84) and average per catch (17.7) and made the Pro Bowl for the first time.

Moss, sounding a bit modest, said that his thrilling season was largely a product of having "way more" opportunities to catch the ball than in his four years with the Jets. His 84 receptions were nearly 50 more than his seasonal average in New York.

"I had put up numbers, not as much, like that with the fewer opportunities I had with the Jets," he said. "It was just one of those years that I was giving back thanks to [the Redskins] for just giving me that chance, having the ball more and being a focal point of the offense more. When you get the opportunity, you can do those types of things."

In 2005, Moss was twice named NFC Offensive Player of the Week, the first time following a spectacular performance in which he caught 39- and 70-yard scoring passes in the final minutes of a 14–13 Monday night victory over the Cowboys at Texas Stadium. On the 70-yarder, quarterback Mark Brunell found No. 89 streaking down the middle of the field, and he caught a bomb in stride and ran into the end zone.

His breathtaking speed was on display many other times, too, like when he caught a screen pass against the Chiefs and took off down the sideline for a career-high 78-yard touchdown catch; he posted other career-bests of 10 receptions and 173 yards in that game. He also caught three touchdown passes, including 59- and 72-yard scores, in a win over the Giants. He posted five 100-yard receiving games in all.

As the 5–9 Moss gave defenses nothing but fits, he reminded many Redskin fans of a dynamic 5–9 receiver from the franchise's glory years in the 1980s and early 1990s: Gary Clark. Their similarities include eye-popping speed, fearlessness when running patterns, aggressiveness in attacking the ball, soft hands, and an unwavering competitiveness. Gibbs, who coached Clark in D.C., was reluctant to compare the two. "I don't like to compare because I've had so many great receivers when you think back on the history here," the coach said. "To me, what stands out about Santana is that he has phenomenal long-ball reaction. By that, I mean he can twist and turn his body and get the ball. And then he literally snatches it out of the air. He is extremely good when he hits the ground. When he hits the ground, you better watch it."

Said Redskins offensive tackle Chris Samuels, "If the ball is there, he'll attack it like he's 6–4. He's just an outstanding receiver."

Moss's numbers dipped in 2006, as the Redskins' passing game struggled early on, and he missed playing time due to a hamstring injury. He still finished second on the team in catches (55) and first in yards (790) and touchdowns (six, tied with tight end Chris Cooley).

He also produced big games. In a 36–30 win over Jacksonville in overtime, he caught three TD passes, including a 68-yarder that accounted for the winning points. On the game-winner, Brunell bulleted a risky 20-yard pass to Moss, who leaped to make the catch amid two defenders, turned upfield and raced into the end zone before jumping into the stands to celebrate with fans. He was named NFC Offensive Player of the Week.

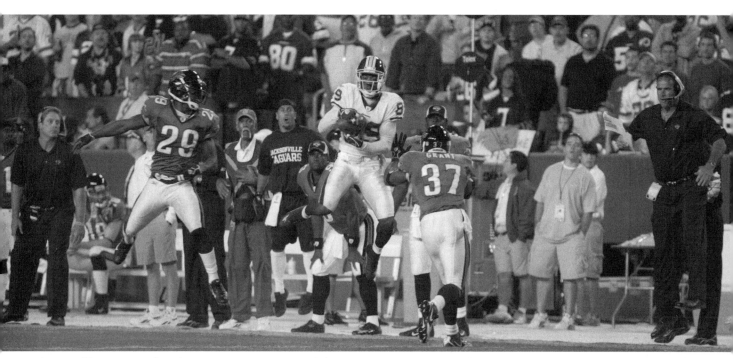

In one of his spectacular plays, Santana Moss turned this reception into a 68-yard catch-and-run that provided the winning points in a 36–30 overtime win over Jacksonville in 2006. He caught three touchdowns that day.

"Santana is amazing after the catch," Brunell said afterward. "There are a lot of good receivers out there, but he's certainly the best I've ever played with in running with the ball after the catch."

Moss, the older brother of current Giants receiver Sinorice Moss, traces his gift for catching long passes back to experiences in little league and high school ball: "They'd send me deep, and when you have so much repetition you get better at it. I just try to concentrate on the ball and not worry about what's around me and try to make adjustments all the time. When the ball gets up there, I just wait until the last minute and attack it."

After playing his college ball at Miami, Moss was the 16th player taken in the 2001 NFL draft. He caught 151 balls for 2,416 yards and 19 touchdowns with the Jets and returned two punts for scores, and the Redskins acquired him in a March 2005 trade for receiver Laveranues Coles. The deal appeared lopsided, for Coles had 90 catches in 2004, twice as many as Moss. It turned out to be one of the best trades the Redskins ever made.

Moss made no guarantees of what he could achieve, except to say he would give "150 percent" every time he steps on the field. "I'm never going to be that guy to talk," he said after catching two passes for 68 yards in a 2005 preseason game against the Steelers. "I go out there and put it on the field, and you tell me what I've done. I'm going to lay it on the line in practice, so when I get out there in the game, it comes naturally. I'm a hard-working guy who goes out and tries to take care of business every time I get a chance."

## HERB MUL-KEY

KR-RB, No. 28, no college • 6–0, 190 • **NFL Career:** 1972–74 (3 seasons) • **Redskins Years:** 1972–74 (3) • **Born:** November 15, 1949 (Atlanta, Ga.)

One of Hollywood's big hits around the start of the 2006 NFL season, *Invincible,* was the true story of a struggling bartender from south Philadelphia, Vince Papale, who overcomes unbelievable odds to make the Eagles' roster and plays on special teams in Philly for three seasons (1976–78).

Just prior, the Redskins had their own Vince Papale–type player in a man named Herb Mul-Key. Unlike Papale, who played in the World Football League before coming to the Eagles, Mul-Key had no pro experience, nor college for that matter, when he attended Redskins coach George Allen's free agent tryout camp before the 1972 season.

Just one player every three years. That's all Allen wanted for his free agent camps to be considered a success. He found a gem in Mul-Key, a 5–10, 180-pound speedster who played three seasons for the Redskins. The ex-Navy serviceman posted more than 1,500 kickoff return yards, including 1,011 with a 97-yard touchdown return in his only Pro Bowl season, 1973, when he also averaged nearly 10 yards on punt returns. He is second to Bobby Mitchell in the Redskins' record books with a 27.87 career kick return average.

His rags-to-riches story is rooted in the foresight of Redskins linebacker Harold McLinton. The late McLinton, an Atlanta native, encouraged Mul-Key to attend Allen's free-agent camp. Mul-Key, who rushed for more than 1,800 yards for an Atlanta semipro squad in 1970, borrowed money so he could fly to Washington. He and some 330 other no-names dreaming of NFL careers descended on the Georgetown University campus on April 14, 1972.

Mul-Key stood out among a motley bunch that included truck drivers and a refugee from Hungary. Then-Redskins special teams coach Marv Levy timed players on the wet field. "I happened to be where Mul-Key's group was running," Levy remembered. "I timed him in an amazing 4.35 [in the 40], which is like running 4.1 now. I told Tim Temerario, our director of player personnel, about Mul-Key's 4.35. He said, 'Oh, bullshit, let's time him again.' We did, and Tim says, 'What'd you get?' I said, '4.36.' Tim got 4.34."

Levy and Temerario were sold on Mul-Key, as was Allen. "He's the number one prospect," the coach told reporters. "He's good, that man's good."

Mul-Key signed a contract and made the roster but saw no action until the Redskins visited Dallas in the next-to-last game of the regular season. He made one of the most phenomenal debuts in NFL history. Mul-Key piled up 271 total yards: 173 on kickoff returns, 60 on eight rushes (7.5 average), and 38 on two catches. He almost single-handedly brought the Redskins back from a 25-point halftime deficit in their 34–24 loss. For those in disbelief, he gave an encore performance in the season-ending loss to Buffalo by accounting for 123 of the Redskins' 171 yards.

The "Mul-Key Way" was born, and it caught the attention of people coast to coast. A few days before the Redskins appeared that season in Super Bowl VII, a *Los Angeles Times* headline read: "Redskins' Herbert Mul-Key – He's One in a Million." Mul-Key played for the Redskins for two more years but was cut before the 1975 season, ending an experience that proved dreams really can come true.

"Everybody really enjoyed him because he survived something that no one else could," said Redskins cornerback Pat Fischer, one of his teammates. "You really appreciate a guy who comes from nowhere to make it. We all kind of adopted him."

## MARK MURPHY

S, No. 29, Colgate • 6–4, 210 • **NFL Career:** 1977–84 (8 seasons) • **Redskins Years:** 1977–84 (8) • **Born:** July 13, 1955 (Williamsville, N.Y.)

Redskins coach George Allen called him his "13th-round draft choice," but Mark Murphy really wasn't drafted. He signed with the Redskins as a free agent in 1977, the year the draft was reduced from 17 to 12 rounds.

The superstitious Allen believed that because he had had success with some of the Redskins' other 13th-round picks such as receiver Frank Grant and defensive tackle Dennis Johnson, then applying the tag to Murphy would yield similar results.

He was right. "Murph" enjoyed a solid career in Washington. After playing mainly special teams in his first two seasons, he started at free safety for the next six while calling defensive signals and contributing to Redskin teams that went to back-to-back Super Bowls in the early 1980s.

There were cries that Murphy was too slow for his position. Cowboys coach Tom Landry once said he thought he could outrun him, a remark that prompted a challenge from Murphy, who ran about a 4.7 40, for the two to race. "The funny thing is, he was a slow defensive back himself," Murphy said of Landry, who played for the Giants in the 1950s.

The 6-4, 210-pound Murphy compensated for a lack of speed with excellent range courtesy of his long strides, plus his height, long arms, and leaping ability. He also possessed keen instincts and field awareness. Such attributes helped him pick off 27 passes, including a league-high nine in 1983, when he earned Pro Bowl and consensus All-Pro honors. A fierce hitter, he averaged 153 tackles between 1979 and 1983, a period when he missed only one start out of a possible 80 games, including playoffs.

Mark Murphy

Murphy said that the references to his speed hardly bothered him: "I was a good athlete. I played basketball, baseball, and football at Colgate. An awful lot of good football players aren't necessarily great in the 40-yard dash. What helped me is I took over [linebacker] Chris Hanburger's role as the signal caller or field general. I was really involved in the strategy of our defense and understood what we were trying to do defensively. That helped me instinctively put myself in a position to make plays."

An all-conference safety at Colgate, Murphy also played outfield on the baseball team and received offers to sign coming out of college from such clubs as Pittsburgh and the New York Mets. Not wanting to risk spending years in the minors, he chose to pursue a football career.

The Redskins, who had scouted Murphy, didn't think he would be drafted but wanted to sign him as a free agent. They "hid" him during the 1977 draft in order to gain exclusive access to him as a free agent.

"There were about four or five of us they gambled wouldn't be drafted, and they put us up at a hotel out by Dulles Airport [in Northern Virginia]," Murphy said. "They drove us all around D.C. the second day of the draft, and as soon as the draft ended they brought us out to Redskin Park and said, 'You haven't been drafted. But we really like you, and we want to sign you as a free agent. Here's our offer. Take five minutes and think about it.'"

Murphy, who was pursued by other teams, including the Giants, signed a three-year deal with the Redskins worth up to $21,000. "The Redskins were the only team that wanted me to play safety, and that was pretty important to me," he said. "I felt I would be better staying at the same position that I played at Colgate rather than bulking up and becoming a linebacker."

An economics major at Colgate who earned an MBA during his playing days, Murphy was the Redskins' player representative to the National Football League Players Association for several years, including during the strike-shortened 1982 season. After retiring, he served as assistant executive director of the NFLPA and earned a law degree. He has been the athletic director at Northwestern University in Evanston, Illinois since 2003.

## JIM MUSICK

FB-DB, Southern California • 5–11, 205 • **NFL Career:** 1932–33, 35–36 (4 seasons) • **Redskins Years:** 1932–33, 35–36 (4) • **Born:** May 5, 1910 (Kirksville, Mo.) • **Died:** December 15, 1992 (Santa Ana, Calif.)

In 1932, Lud Wray, coach of the expansion Boston Braves, was acquiring talent for his new roster when he nabbed fullback Jim Musick out of Southern California. Musick had been key to the Trojans winning two Rose Bowls and a national championship, and he signed with the Braves for $150 a game. (No draft existed at the time.)

In an interview with the *Orange County Register* that appeared on May 11, 1986, Musick said that he wasn't guaranteed to make the team. By the start of training camp, about 75 players were competing for 23 roster spots, according to the newspaper. "I didn't even know if I had a job," Musick said. "It was during the Depression, and we didn't have much money."

Musick made the squad and rushed for 316 yards as a rookie. In 1933, the year the franchise changed its nickname to the Redskins, he carried 173 times for a league-high 809 yards (4.7 average) and five touchdowns. He received second-team All-Pro honors.

Musick sat out the 1934 season, preferring to work in the sheriff's department in Orange County, California. He returned to the Redskins but rushed for only 188 yards total in the 1935 and 1936 seasons, as knee injuries forced him to sit out a number of games. The Redskins released him, and he retired from the game.

In his four-year career, Musick ran 307 times for 1,313 yards (4.0 average) and eight touchdowns. He also caught three balls for 78 yards, completed 13 passes for 167 yards, and kicked 14 extra points.

## MIKE NELMS

KR, No. 21, Sam Houston State; Baylor • 6–1, 190 • **NFL Career:** 1980–84 (5 seasons) • **Redskins Years:** 1980–84 (5) • NFL 1980s All-Decade Team • **Born:** April 8, 1955 (Fort Worth, Tex.)

As in the certainty of having to pay taxes and death, one thing was guaranteed when a kickoff or punt floated in the direction of Redskins return specialist Mike Nelms: excitement.

Nelms was a threat whenever he touched the ball. Despite average speed for a return man, the 6–1, 190-pounder possessed the explosiveness to gain big yardage and the power, finesse, and smarts to break tackles, which he was adept at doing. You could never count him down even when he was boxed in, for he was remarkable at making something out of nothing. He gave 100 percent unbridled effort, and his legs moved until he was down.

Mike Nelms

Nelms's prowess and determination enabled him amass 6,067 combined return yards, one of many team records he set in five seasons in Washington. His marks have since been broken, except for his single-season kickoff return average, 29.7 yards in 1981. He made the Pro Bowl three times (1980, 1981, 1982) and was named to the NFL 1980s All-Decade Team.

Nelms relished the chance to return kicks. "I'm one of those sick guys, I'm one of the guys with the loose screw," he said. "I like contact. I like the physical aspect of football. I like knocking people out. Where else in the world can you go and get paid for knocking people out and releasing frustration."

Nelms's great hands were one of his trademarks; he rarely fumbled the ball. Another one was his refusal to fair catch on punts. He was charged with two fair catches as a Redskin, one of which was unintentional on his part. He thought raising his arm to signal fair catch was what he called a "selfish and coward's act" and preferred instead to throw his body in with the wolves. A 1983 *Washington Post* headline read, "A Fair Catch Is Foul Words for Mike Nelms." Then-Redskins general manager Bobby Beathard called him "tougher than nails."

Why was he so fearless? "If a wide receiver goes down the middle, and the quarterback throws the ball high, and the receiver pulls his arms down, everyone calls him a coward," Nelms said. "If it's fourth-and-1, a hole opens up for the running back and a linebacker is standing there, but the runner goes to the ground instead of burying his head and hitting the guy, you call him a coward. If a quarterback is getting ready to pass and knows he's going to get creamed by a defensive lineman and flinches and throws the ball away, what do you call him?

"I look at it the same way as a punt return man. Your job is to get your team the best field position possible. You can't do that by waving your hand or letting the ball hit the ground."

Nelms, a defensive back at Sam Houston State and later Baylor, was a seventh-round pick of the Bills in 1977. After being cut, he played nearly three seasons with the Ottawa Roughriders in the Canadian Football League. One year, he led his conference with 10 interceptions and topped the league in punt returns with 1,155 yards (10.9 average) and two touchdowns.

In the CFL, there was no fair catch rule and a 5-yard restraining area existed between the tacklers and the return man. The field was also 15 yards wider. Those factors helped prepare Nelms for returning punts in the NFL, psychologically and otherwise. "The fact that I had a chance to run with the ball on that great big old field, it's like running in a park, got me used to running in traffic," he said. "No fair catch got me accustomed to just never fair catching. The game is so fast up there. I liked that excitement, and I didn't want to give up the opportunity to run with the ball."

The Redskins scouted Nelms in the CFL, lured him away, and signed him in April 1980. "We brought him down as a free safety and punt returner," Beathard said. "It ended up that [free safety] Mark Murphy was calling all the defensive signals, and he had a lot of experience, so we used Nelms to return kicks. He turned out to be a Pro Bowl player. He was fantastic, probably the best hands I've ever seen to this day in catching punts."

Nelms gave the Redskins a new weapon while becoming the NFL's premier kick return man of the early-1980s. He gained at least 1,000 combined return yards in four of his five seasons in Washington, falling short only in the strike-shortened 1982 campaign. In 1981, he topped the NFL with his 29.7 kickoff return average and placed fourth in the NFC in punt returns (10.9 average), returning two for touchdowns. He earned All-Pro honors that season, as well as 1982 and 1983. He retired after the 1984 season.

## NEAL OLKEWICZ

LB, No. 52, Maryland • 6–0, 230 • **NFL Career:** 1979–89 (11 seasons) • **Redskins Years:** 1979–89 (11) • **Born:** January 30, 1957 (Phoenixville, Pa.)

Neal Olkewicz, a law enforcement major at the University of Maryland, wanted to be a police officer or an FBI agent coming out of college. His goal was to apprehend people and be "in the middle of the excitement," as he put it.

He instead played middle linebacker for 11 seasons in the NFL, all in Washington. An unheralded player who signed as a free agent in 1979, he was one of the Redskins' leading tacklers season after season and posted some 1,500 overall. Sporting a workmanlike attitude that stemmed from his upbringing in the steel town of Phoenixville, Pennsylvania—Redskin publicists described him as a "beer and pretzels guy"—he played in 150 games and started nearly every one, including 14 playoff games. He intercepted seven passes.

Olkewicz, slow and small for a linebacker at barely 6–0, 230 pounds, wasn't assured of a starting role every year, but

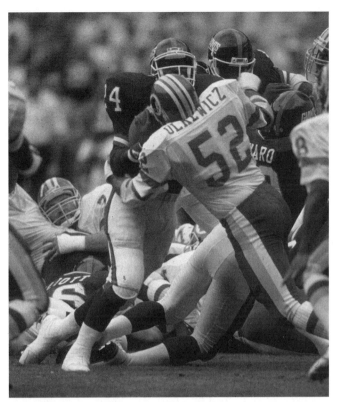

Olkewicz, here stopping the Giants' O. J. Anderson, was the Redskins' starting middle linebacker for most of the 1980s. He was one of general manager Bobby Beathard's prized free agent finds.

he fought to keep his position, singling out at least six seasons when the Redskins tried to replace him. He said it was good that his competitors were mostly lower-round draft picks and players the Redskins weren't paying big bucks. "I don't think I felt I was going to be cut all the time," he said. "But I was always aware that I wasn't too far from the outhouse. From the penthouse to the outhouse is a short walk."

"Neal played the game with a certain amount of uncertainty from year to year as to whether he'd be back playing," said Larry Pecciatello, Olkewicz's linebacker coach in Washington. "It comes from the fact that he was a free agent out of Maryland. He didn't have the fanfare and was never really granted the status of some of our other players. But Neal was a solid guy. We didn't have anybody tougher than Neal Olkewicz. I remember one game he dislocated his elbow and came back and played the next week. He wasn't the biggest or fastest guy, but he had other qualities that made him unique."

The Redskins got their first true look at Olkewicz when he was a senior at Maryland, a year when the 205-pound middle linebacker set a school single-season record for tackles (188). There was nothing outstanding about him, except his nose for the ball and terrific instincts, said then-Redskins general manager Bobby Beathard.

The Redskins worked him out before the 1979 draft and told him he might be picked late. Olkewicz wasn't optimistic. "I was not waiting to be drafted," he said. "Then they said they'd sign me as a free agent. I assumed it would be as a special teams player. I basically went in with the idea saying, 'Hey, I'll give it my best shot and see what happens.'"

Olkewicz exceeded his expectations. He replaced second-year man Don Hover as the starting middle linebacker midway through his rookie season and held the job the rest of the year. He earned a reputation as a fierce hitter and was nicknamed "Mole" or "Molekewicz" for his ability to battle through tackling piles and end up at the bottom near the ball carrier. He finished the season with 140 tackles, four forced fumbles, a sack, and an interception.

Two years later, in 1981, Olkewicz collected a career-high 187.5 stops and intercepted two passes. He returned one of them 10 yards for his only career touchdown, a key play that helped lift the Redskins to a 24–7 win over the Bears that halted an 0–5 start to the season. The Redskins went 8–8 that year before rising to become one of the league's elite teams.

Although No. 52 continued manning the middle and week after week recorded double digits in tackles—he started every game from 1982 to 1986—there were whispers he wasn't too talented. Such skepticism motivated him. "I knew I had to prove myself every time," he said. "In the long run, that helped me because a lot of guys are flashes in the pans for a couple of years and then they're gone, and I'd still be there."

Defensive end Dexter Manley, who played with Olky for nine seasons, called him an overachiever: "What I liked about Neal is he was a team player, and he had the heart of a lion. He wasn't very athletic, but Neal would show up on Sundays and play football."

Olkewicz continued producing late in his career. In 1988, his 10th season, he was named the Redskins' MVP on defense after posting 153 tackles despite coming out on passing downs. He was phased out in 1989 in favor of second-year player Greg Manusky and retired.

For someone who thought it was a long shot that he would start at middle linebacker in the pros, then went on to hold the position for a decade, Olkewicz felt privileged to have had the opportunity. "I was excited to be on the team to begin with, although once I got to training camp and started playing, I felt like I belonged," he said. "But I appreciated it, it wasn't like I took it for granted. I felt like I accomplished probably more than I should have. I was very happy to have played as long as I did and to be part of a winning team."

## JOHNNY OLSZEWSKI

FB, No. 0, California • 6–0, 205 • **NFL Career:** 1953–62 (10 seasons) • **Redskins Years:** 1958–60 (3) • **Born:** December 21, 1929 (Washington, D.C.) • **Died:** December 8, 1996 (Long Beach, Calif.)

When fullback Johnny Olszewski lowered his shoulder pads, pity the defender who challenged him one-on-one.

Olszewski (pronounced Ol-shoo-ski) could hit with the best of them. The 6–0, 205-pounder played three seasons in Washington, rushing for 1,164 yards. He averaged an outstanding 4.9 yards a carry and a league-high 6.6 in 1959. He also ran for a Redskins-record 190 yards in one game, a mark that stood for 13 years. He recorded a 165-yard day and a 136-yarder, as well.

"Johnny was a great fullback," said Joe Scudero, a teammate of Olszewski's for one season in Washington. "He was big, tough and strong. God, he was strong. He wasn't as big as the fullbacks today, but Johnny had great balance, great speed, great moves. He was tough as nails. He was fearless."

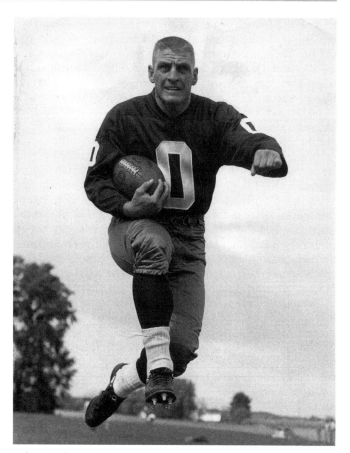

Johnny Olszewski

Olszewski, known affectionately as "Johnny O," was a unanimous All-American running back at California and a first-round pick of the Chicago Cardinals in 1953. He played there for five seasons, earning two-time Pro Bowl honors, and came to the Redskins in a trade before the 1958 season. The *Washington Evening Star* reported that the Redskins asked then-NFL Commissioner Bert Bell to waive the rule on players' numbers so Olszewski could wear the number 0. League rules at the time required that players wore numbers identifying their positions, such as 80s for ends and 70s for tackles.

Olszewski thus became the first Redskin to sport a goose egg on his jersey and remains the only player in team history to do so. He tallied 505 yards rushing in 1958, including 165 on 20 carries in a 37–21 win over Green Bay, a game in which he "not only gained ground but literally challenged and smashed into the ground anyone who got in his way," Dave Slattery of the *Washington Daily News* wrote.

"Not since Cinderella donned her glass slippers has a pair of shoes gained such fame," Slattery wrote. "Only these shoes which belong to a fullback named Johnny Olszewski are black, cleated, ungainly looking things. Nothing fancy about them all. But as far as the Redskins are concerned they are just as magical as Cinderella's. They were that deep, secret psychological weapon behind Washington's explosive 37–21 victory over Green Bay at Griffith Stadium yesterday."

Olszewski needed only 18 carries to crank out 190 yards in a 31–17 loss to Cleveland in 1959, the year he led the league in rushing average. He ran for 177 of those in the first half, including a 65-yard run.

After a 227-yard season in 1960, when he shared backfield duties with such players as fullback Don Bosseler, Olszewski left the Redskins. He played one year with the Lions and another with Denver in the American Football League before retiring.

## BRIG OWENS

S, No. 23, Cincinnati • 6–1, 190 • **NFL Career:** 1966–77 (12 seasons) • **Redskins Years:** 1966–77 (12) • **Born:** February 16, 1943 (Linden, Tex.)

The year was 1965, a time when it was taboo for blacks to play quarterback in the NFL. Brig Owens, the Cowboys' seventh-round draft pick that season, wanted to be a quarterback in the pros and thought he would get a chance. He had excelled at the position in college, finishing 12th in the nation one year in total offense in Cincinnati's multipronged system.

When Cowboys coach Tom Landry immediately moved him to defensive back, Owens was incredulous, although he didn't know at the time if Landry's decision was racially motivated. The same year, Dallas drafted Miami (of Ohio) quarterback Ernie Kellerman, who is white, and made him a defensive back.

"Landry told me I was a great athlete, and that he wanted to try to find a position for me," Owens said. "They already had Don Meredith playing quarterback, and they had [also] drafted Craig Morton, Jerry Rhome, and myself. In hindsight, [Landry] was correct. I was fortunate to play 12 years as a defensive back."

Owens was a Redskin for those 12 years, but he first spent the 1965 season on the Cowboys' taxi squad. During that period, Cowboys defensive backfield coach Dick Nolan taught Owens how to play safety, stressing such fundamentals as reading the pass versus the run and understanding how far receivers normally go before making their cuts. Just as important, Nolan instilled confidence in the rookie. "He told me, 'Don't ever forget that you can play this game,'" Owens said. "I always admired him for that. He's stood out in my memories."

Owens was frustrated, though, on the taxi squad. But before the 1966 season, the Cowboys shared some news that he singles out as the greatest thing to happen to him in his football career: "They told me I was going to be traded to the Redskins. I said, 'Thank you.'"

Owens's transition to the Redskins looked seamless. Playing strong safety, he intercepted seven passes in 1966. He picked off three alone in a 72–41 win over the Giants, returning one 60 yards for a touchdown, and scooped up a fumble and ran 62 yards for a score in the game.

Owens intercepted a career-high eight passes in 1968 and five in 1973, when the Redskins Alumni Association named him the team's defensive player of the year.

Such feats contributed to a career in which he made himself one of the greatest defensive backs in Redskins history. He set an all-time franchise record for interceptions (36) and is now in second place behind Darrell Green (54). He also amassed 686 interception return yards, a Redskins record to this day, and returned three passes for touchdowns, one of the best marks in team history.

Plus, Owens was a very heady player who called signals at times for the Redskins' sophisticated defenses of the 1970s

under George Allen, who often referred to Owens as one of his defensive generals. "[Owens] had great knowledge of the game, and he was always in position to make the play," said Hall of Fame linebacker Sam Huff, who played four seasons with him.

Hall of Fame safety Kenny Houston, a teammate of Owens's for five years, added, "He was never too high or too low. You could always depend on him. He was extremely smart, and he and [linebacker] Chris Hanburger were really good at calling signals."

Owens, who played both strong and free safety, was prepared every time he stepped on the field. He went so far as to compile notes on the tendencies of many starting wide receivers in the league, among other players, and he never missed a game in his first 11 seasons in Washington, playing in 154 straight. He attributed such durability largely to a rigorous year-round workout plan. He ran and practiced tai chi with the notion that it was much easier on his cardiovascular system if he always stayed in shape. "I prided myself on being the best-conditioned guy on the team," he said.

For everything Owens brought to the Redskins, though, it seemed that a newcomer was often challenging for his spot, whether it was four-time Pro Bowler Richie Petitbon in 1971, two-time Pro Bowler Roosevelt Taylor in 1972, or fourth-year man Bryant Salter in 1974. Owens was forced to rotate from free safety to strong safety, or vice versa, and was demoted at times to nickel back.

Owens said that it's possible he was jerked around because of his strong ties to the National Football League Players Association; he was the Redskins' representative to the NFLPA for seven seasons and lobbied for players' rights, including a higher percentage of the league's gross revenues, noting that "[management] called us communists back then."

"One thing coach Allen mentioned to me after he left the Redskins was that some of the things he did with me were not in his control," Owens said. "That sort of said enough."

Owens, whose brother, Marv, had a brief NFL career, earned a law degree during his playing days and served as assistant executive director of the NFLPA after retirement. He has since been a partner in law firms that have represented NFL players, including several Redskins.

## JOHN PALUCK

DE, No. 85 (also wore No. 86), Pittsburgh • 6–2, 245 • **NFL Career:** 1956, 59–65 (8 seasons) • **Redskins Years:** 1956, 59–65 (8) • **Born:** May 23, 1935 (Swoyersville, Pa.) • **Died:** April 22, 2003 (Fairfax, Va.)

His nicknames ranged from "Gentle John" to "Mean John." The latter seemed more appropriate, for ornery John Paluck was a very physical defensive end who harassed many quarterbacks in his day.

Consider this plug from Jack Walsh of the *Washington Post* on August 18, 1960, a few days after a Redskins exhibition game against the 49ers: "Paluck has all the physical equipment to be one of the top defensive ends, and he does enjoy knocking people down. In the 49er game, in which he bested [future Hall of Famer] Bob St. Clair, the agile 6–foot-9, 265-pounder, Paluck once moved in so fast he just breezed by quarterback John Brodie. Paluck thrust out his arm, and it amounted to a slap on Brodie's shoulder. And down he went. If Paluck had hit him head-on, chances are Brodie would have fumbled."

In eight seasons, all in Washington, Paluck made the Pro Bowl once (1964) and received scattered All-Pro recognition. He missed one game out of a possible 106. Nasty, powerful, and quick-footed, he posted a bevy of sacks, recovered 14 fumbles, and intercepted two passes.

Paluck played his college ball at Pittsburgh, where he received All-American honors and became known as one of the school's all-time great linemen. The Redskins drafted him in the second round in 1956. He recovered a league-high three fumbles that year, returning one 76 yards for the only touchdown he ever scored and the longest fumble return in Redskins history at the time.

Paluck credited one of the Redskins' best defensive ends ever, Gene Brito, with helping him get a roaring start in the NFL. Brito was in his fifth season when Paluck was a rookie. "Gene was very generous to me when I came up," Paluck once said in the *Washington Post.* "He tried to show me everything he knew about getting in at the passer."

After a two-year stint in the U.S. Army, Paluck returned to the Redskins in 1959 and started in the ensuing seasons at left defensive end. He was voted the team's MVP in 1960. He was traded after the 1965 season for the rights to Bears defensive tackle Stan Jones, a future Hall of Famer, and retired from the game.

Early in his career, Paluck was dubbed "Mean John." According to the *Post,* the nickname was a "trifle strong" for then-NFL Commissioner Bert Bell, and the Redskins began labeling him "Gentle John" in their media guide.

"He was quite a football player," said Pat Richter, a tight end who played with Paluck for three seasons. "Kind of unpredictable, so everybody kept their distance from 'Mean John.' He certainly was somebody that gave everything he had. He was tough. As a defensive player, he was exactly what you wanted out there. Whether it was practice or games, he just had kind of a mean streak in him. That's what made him a good player."

## LEMAR PARRISH

CB, No. 24, Lincoln University (Missouri) • 5–11, 185 • **NFL Career:** 1970–82 (13 seasons) • **Redskins Years:** 1978–81 (4) • **Born:** December 13, 1947 (West Palm Beach, Fla.)

Lemar Parrish is one of the best cornerbacks in NFL history. It's a mystery why he hasn't been enshrined in the Pro Football Hall of Fame since retiring from the game in 1982.

"Leapin' Lemar" intercepted 47 passes in his 13-year career and was an eight-time Pro Bowler. During his day, one could argue, he was the most dominant cornerback in the league. He spent four years in Washington and crafted two seasons at which one could only marvel:

- 1979: NFC-high nine interceptions, consensus first-team All-Pro, Pro Bowl
- 1980: seven interceptions (second in NFC), near-consensus first-team All-Pro, Pro Bowl

Parrish was also among the flashiest dressers in the league. His wardrobe included a mink coat, 45 pairs of shoes, and thousands of dollars worth of jewelry.

A seventh-round draft pick of the Bengals in 1970, Parrish stepped into the starting lineup as a rookie. Over the next seven seasons, he intercepted 25 passes and made the Pro Bowl six times. Equipped with blazing speed, he also returned punts and kickoffs, leading the league in punt return average in 1974 (18.8). That year, he scored on a 90-yard punt return and a 47-yard fumble return in a 28–17 win over the Redskins. He returned four punts, one kickoff, four interceptions and three fumbles for touchdowns as a Bengal.

When Redskins general manager Bobby Beathard traded a No. 1 draft pick to Cincinnati in 1978 for Parrish and defensive end Coy Bacon, many Redskins fans were probably feeling that if you can't beat him, then sign him.

In Washington, Parrish was relieved of his kick returning duties but took over the left cornerback spot vacated by longtime Redskins cornerback Pat Fischer. He made his presence known in the 1978 preseason, wrote Steve Guback of the *Washington Star:*

Funny thing, but since Parrish moved into the Redskins' secondary after recovering from a sprained foot, receivers everywhere seem to be almost spell-bound.

Maybe it's just a coincidence, but Redskins pass-grabbers had so many passes knocked down in practice by Parrish that they went out in the first exhibition against Minnesota and were so jittery they dropped a half-dozen.

Last week, with Parrish starting for the first time, Green Bay completed just eight paltry passes for the entire game. Packers receivers heard so many footsteps they flubbed another five.

Parrish picked off 22 passes as a Redskin and crafted a string of six straight games with an interception that ended in 1979, one of the longest such streaks in team history. In 1980, he had three games with two interceptions and was integral to the Redskins leading the NFL in pass defense.

The following year, Parrish suffered a series of injuries and picked off only one pass. He was traded to Buffalo, where he played in 1982 and retired. He has been a preliminary nominee for Hall of Fame induction.

## ERNY PINCKERT

BB-WB-DB-LB, No. 11, Southern California • 6–0, 197 • **NFL Career:** 1932–40 (9 seasons) • **Redskins Years:** 1932–40 (9) • **Born:** May 1, 1907 (Medford, Wis.) • **Died:** August 30, 1977 (Los Angeles, Calif.)

Redskins ball carriers of the 1930s such as stars Cliff Battles, Jim Musick, and Andy Farkas knew whom to depend on when they needed someone to run interference for them: Erny Pinckert.

Pinckert, a combination wingback and blocking back in the single-wing formation, was feared for his crushing blocks that wiped out defenders. He was perhaps the best blocking back of his day. In four of his nine NFL seasons, at least one runner for whom he blocked led the NFL in a major rushing category: Battles twice in yards and once in average, Musick once in yards, and Farkas once in touchdowns.

Pinckert used a simple philosophy: "Hit a guy hard three times and the fourth time he will get out of your way."

"He was a rough player," said Clyde Shugart, a Redskins lineman who played with Pinckert for two seasons. "He didn't mind if he cold-cocked somebody on the field. He was something else when he had that football uniform on. But he was like a Dr. Jekyll and Mr. Hyde. When he didn't have a football uniform on, he was a different person, a really nice guy. Everybody liked Erny."

Pinckert hit hard on defense, too. According to the Pro Football Researchers Association (PFRA), in a 1933 game, Boston Redskins coach William "Lone Star" Dietz assigned him to stop Bears ironman fullback Bronko Nagurski one on one—a rare bit of strategy in the NFL.

"Nagurski came through hard," PFRA wrote, "but Pinckert came from the other direction with a full head of steam and smashed into the Bears' fullback so hard [Nagurski] sat out the rest of the half on the bench. Early in the second half, Boston pulled the same trap when Nagurski again tried to run with the ball. This time, Nagurski was out for the rest of the game."

Pinckert first made a name for himself at Southern California. A two-time All-American, he ran for two touchdowns apiece in two Rose Bowl victories by the Trojans. The second one capped the 1931 season, when Pinckert was voted the best player in the country in a nationwide poll. He was inducted into the College Football Hall of Fame in 1957.

In 1932, Pinckert signed with the expansion Boston Braves (they became the Redskins in 1933). As a pro, he rushed 147 times for 536 yards and one touchdown, and caught 29 passes for 391 yards and one score. Off the field, Pinckert was a spiffy dresser and was voted best-dressed player in the NFL in 1937. He ran a successful clothing business after retiring from football.

## DICK POILLON

K-HB-DB-TB, No. 25, Canisius • 6–0, 197 • **NFL Career:** 1942, 46–49 (5 seasons) • **Redskins Years:** 1942, 46–49 (5) • **Born:** August 13, 1920 (Queens, N.Y.) • **Died:** November 14, 1994 (West Palm Beach, Fla.)

By the time he retired after the 1949 season, Dick Poillon stood as the Redskins' all-time leading scorer. Poillon, a kicking specialist, tallied 247 points, three-fourths of them on extra points and field goals. He also rushed for four touchdowns and caught five passes for scores, played defensive back, punted, and returned punts and kickoffs.

Poillon played for the semi-pro Long Island Indians of the American Association when the Redskins bought him in 1942. He saw action in seven games that year. He later served as a U.S. Army lieutenant during World War II with antiaircraft and antitank units in Europe. He rejoined the Redskins in 1946.

Poillon played in every game, 47 in all, over the next four seasons. In 1948, his 28-yard field goal with seconds remaining lifted the Redskins over the Steelers, 17–14. That season, he also used his powerful leg to post a league-high 2,697 punting yards. He finished with 5,804 in his career and a respectable 40.3 punting average.

He kicked three field goals to tie the NFL record in a 30–0 win over Green Bay in 1949.

## CLINTON PORTIS

RB, No. 26, Miami • 5–10, 212 • **NFL Career:** 2002–2006 (5 seasons) • **Redskins Years:** 2004–2006 (3) • **Born:** September 1, 1981 (Laurel, Miss.)

He wears goofy costumes that make him seem playful and meek. He comes across as soft-spoken and flashes a smile a mile wide. Hidden behind that façade, however, is one gritty football player.

In three seasons with the Redskins, Clinton Portis has rushed for 3,354 yards, one of the best marks in team history. That statistic is in black and white. It's not as well known that the 212-pound Portis is a devastating blocker who will take on anyone, anywhere, anytime. In fact, he's one of the premier backs in the NFL in pass protection, as Redskins offensive line coach Joe Bugel will tell you. "He's probably the toughest back we've ever coached without the football 'cause he's a heck of a blocker, a great pass blocker," Bugel said. "He has great hustle in getting downfield and blocking when we're throwing the football or somebody else has the ball, bar none."

Portis, a slippery runner who has great speed and vision, holds Redskin single-season records for rushing yards (1,516) and 100-yard rushing games (nine), both set in 2005. That year, he literally carried the team to a playoff berth by rushing for more than 100 yards each week during the Redskins' five-game, season-ending winning streak that clinched a postseason spot. He reeled off games of 136, 105, 112, 108, and 112 yards during the winning streak, averaging 27 carries per game, and earned the admiration of his coaches, teammates, and fans.

"Now, we're hanging our hats on the running game," Redskins offensive lineman Ray Brown said after Portis rushed for 108 yards in a 35–20 win over the Giants on December 24, 2005. "CP's playing some good football. I love the emotion he brings to the game. It's genuine, it's not fake, it's not flawed. The guy's really playing some good football. That sets up the passing game."

Portis's rushing yards in 2005 broke Stephen Davis's team mark of 1,432 set in 2001, while his 100-yard rushing game total broke Rob Goode's record of seven set in 1951. He is one of 10 players in NFL history to rush for 1,000 or more yards in his first four NFL seasons. A star in college at Miami who was selected in the second round by Denver in 2002, he rushed for 1,508 yards that season, a franchise rookie record for the Broncos, and was named NFL Rookie of the Year by the *Sporting News* and *Sports Illustrated*. He followed with a 1,591-yard season in 2003 and made the Pro Bowl.

In March 2004, the Redskins traded superstar cornerback Champ Bailey and a second-round pick to Denver for Portis. Portis's career in D.C. opened on a thrilling note, as he took his first Redskin handoff and ran 64 yards for a touchdown in the 2004 season opener against Tampa Bay. He rushed for 1,315 yards that season but wore down toward the end of the year after carrying the ball 343 times, the most to date in his career. He missed the final game with a pectoral injury.

Portis called it a "grind-it-out" season. He bulked up in 2005 and posted his third 1,500-yard rushing year. At the same time, he showed a wacky side of himself. During his weekly media sessions, he dressed up as self-developed fictional characters with such names as "Southeast Jerome," "Bro Sweet," "Dollar Bill," "Inspector 2-2" and "Sheriff Gonna

Getcha." The costumes consisted of outlandish glasses and wigs, among other colorful and bizarre attire. In addition to catching the eye of local media, Portis and his crazy identities were featured on the NFL Network, ESPN, and HBO's *Inside the NFL. Sports Illustrated* ran a feature on him.

Portis said his antics were all in the name of fun: "It's about coming together. Everyone around here is having fun. There's nobody who can be uptight when they see me like this."

Several teammates joined in one week with their own costumes, including tight end Chris Cooley and running back Rock Cartwright. Portis's costume parade just "created a little more humor, gave us a little personality," Cartwright said. "It was just something that Clinton does. He's a different guy. We're glad that he's part of our team."

But 2006 was a rough year for Portis. In the preseason opener, he separated his shoulder while making a tackle on an interception, an injury that lingered into the regular season and forced him to sit out a game. He later suffered an ankle injury. After fracturing his hand in the ninth game of the season, he was placed on injured reserve. He gained 523 yards on the year.

## VINCE PROMUTO

G, No. 65, Holy Cross • 6–1, 245 • **NFL Career:** 1960–70 (11 seasons) • **Redskins Years:** 1960–70 (11) • **Born:** June 8, 1938 (New York, N.Y.)

Growing up in New York's Bronx borough in the 1940s and 1950s, Vince Promuto was a student of how to act on the mean streets of his neighborhood: be tough. "The most interesting thing we did was see how tough you could be in fights," he said. "It wasn't about sports, it was about gangs in those days. Being tough was much more important than getting good marks. It was a cultural thing. Many people in the Italian neighborhoods at the time were not priests or lawyers."

Promuto was no saint, either, in his 11 seasons as a Redskin guard. Incorporating his tough-guy mentality, the 6–1, 245-pounder was super-physical, even brutal at times by today's standards. He would clothesline defenders and try to knock others out of games by aiming for their knees, two illegal techniques today. He said about the only thing one couldn't do then was leg-whip an opponent, which involved hitting someone on the shins with the back of your heel.

"That was my approach to the game, see how much you could punish someone," said Promuto, a two-time Pro Bowler. "I looked at football as a battleground. I'd always volunteer for the kickoff team, kickoff return, punt, punt return. The coach would say, 'You're starting.' I'd say, 'Yea, but I want to go break the wedge.' That was my attitude to football. It wasn't pretty."

Promuto's rough-and-tumble approach also stemmed from a need to compensate for his limited knowledge of the game's fundamentals. He didn't take up football until his junior year in high school and played under a small college coaching staff at Holy Cross, where he starred at offensive right tackle and linebacker.

He was quick and smart, though, and the Giants drafted him in the fourth round in 1960 and traded him to the Redskins for defensive back Dick Lynch. With a mindset that his Bronx neighborhood was the center of the universe, and the Giants being the only pro football team he knew anything about, Promuto was unaware that the Redskins even existed: "They called and said, 'This is the Washington Redskins. Will you play for us.' "I thought it was Washington state but the only question I asked was, [1960] being the first year of the American Football League, 'Is this an NFL team?' They said yes. And I said, 'Yeah, I'll play.' I had no idea it was Washington, D.C. I said, 'What the hell, it's the National Football League, I'll play wherever they want me to play.'"

Promuto initially thought he was getting royal treatment. He signed a $7,000 contract, and Redskins owner George Preston Marshall padded it by giving him five $100 bills. At that point, "I thought he was the greatest guy in the world," Pro-

Promuto leads the way for Larry Brown in 1969.

muto said of Marshall, normally tight with player salaries. "I later found out that the lowest you could give a player at the time was $7,500."

Promuto won the starting right guard position in training camp in 1960 and stayed there until injuries sidelined him for much of his 11th season, 1970. Along the way, he made the Pro Bowl in 1963 and 1964 and blocked for one of the league's most exciting offenses ever. He was also a personal bodyguard for the Redskins' prolific quarterback of the 1960s, Sonny Jurgensen.

Despite toiling on losing teams through most of his stay in Washington, including some of the worst in Redskins history, he rose to become a very popular player. A team captain year after year, he inspired teammates during games and helped some new players by letting them stay at his house until they got settled in the area.

"Vince was a leader," said Bobby Mitchell, a Redskins receiver who played with him for seven seasons. "Even on the days when we didn't play well and maybe he didn't play well himself, he was always sticking it to the guys. He thought if we didn't get it this time, we'll get it next time, do this better, do that better. He had a sincere attitude and cared about the team and the players."

Promuto was also a prankster. He would fold sheets so a teammate could get into a bed only halfway or put a hot gel that was normally used for warming up muscles into jock straps. "It burned," he said. "You'd put it on and get on the field and start sweating a little and scream." He would also mimic the bullhorn-voiced Vince Lombardi, who coached the Redskins in 1969. "He'd yell, 'What the hell is going on around here,'" Promuto said of the legendary Lombardi. "I could imitate him to a T. Once in a while he'd be near the locker room and hear me and look at me like, 'You son of a bitch, you.'"

Of the five Redskin head coaches Promuto played for, he admired Lombardi the most by far, but as the militaristic coach ran his players to exhaustion in practice before the 1969 season, Promuto nearly called it quits. "I went to see Lombardi one night in training camp," Promuto said. "I said, 'Coach, I'm no Mack truck or anything. I'm a human being. You're screaming and yelling, and I'm not going to take it.' What he said completely disarmed me. He went 'ha ha, ha. You Italians are all the same. You get too emotional.' Once I knew he had compassion, I could take anything he was willing to shove out."

Promuto yearned to play for George Allen, another championship-caliber coach who arrived in Washington in 1971, but he couldn't rehabilitate himself after a serious knee operation and retired.

## GEORGE ROGERS

RB, No. 38, South Carolina • 6–2, 230 • **NFL Career:** 1981–87 (7 seasons) • **Redskins Years:** 1985–87 (3) • **Born:** December 8, 1958 (Duluth, Ga.)

George Rogers rushed for more than 1,000 yards in two of his first four seasons, including an NFL-high 1,674 in 1981, a league record for a rookie. So when the Redskins acquired the two-time Pro Bowler in 1985 from the Saints for the 24th pick in that year's draft, it seemed like a steal. After all, Rogers was in his prime and still possessed the explosiveness to burst through holes and make sizable gains. He was pegged as the successor to aging Redskins legend John Riggins in the team's single-back offense.

Did Rogers live up to his billing? The 6–2, 230-pounder crafted two 1,000-yard seasons in three years with the Redskins and 10 100-yard games, including a 206-yard performance. But he was stricken with fumbleritis one year and beset with injuries another year, and some in the media argued that he failed to show up consistently in big games. The Redskins waived him after the 1987 season, ending a seven-year career in which he ran for 7,176 yards (4.2 average) and 54 touchdowns, and caught 55 passes for 368 yards. He has been a preliminary nominee for Pro Football Hall of Fame induction.

Rogers enjoyed a more celebrated career at South Carolina, becoming one of the top running backs in college history. He rushed for more than 5,200 yards and won the Heisman Trophy after a 1,781-yard senior season in 1980. He was inducted into the College Football Hall of Fame in 1997.

Rogers's arrival in the 1985 off-season triggered a buzz within the organization and around town. "George Rogers is a great running back," Redskins quarterback Joe Theismann told the press at the time. "He's a great worker. And I'll tell you, he's the quickest big back I've ever seen. If John's 'The Diesel,' I'd say George is somewhere in the BMW-Cadillac category."

Rogers alternated with Riggins most of that season and started the last five games, a stretch that included a 150-yard day against the Eagles and a 206-yarder against the Cardinals, one of the top rushing performances in Redskins history. He finished with 1,093 yards.

Riggins retired before the 1986 season, and Rogers took over as the Redskins' key runner. He rushed for 1,203 yards and an NFL-high 18 touchdowns, as the Redskins reached the NFC championship game. (Over the course of the 1985 and '86 seasons, he rushed for touchdowns in 13 straight games, a mark for which he and Riggins are tied for first in the Redskins' record books.)

Rogers was injury riddled in 1987 and gained 613 yards, a career low except for the strike-shortened 1982 season. He played sparingly in the Redskins' victory in Super Bowl XXII in January 1988.

## JOE RUTGENS

DT, No. 72, Illinois • 6–2, 255 • **NFL Career:** 1961–69 (9 seasons) • **Redskins Years:** 1961–69 (9) • **Born:** January 26, 1939 (Cedar Point, Ill.)

One look at the 6–2, 255-pound Joe Rutgens and you wouldn't think he had the body of an NFL defensive tackle: protruding belly, bird legs. But looks can be deceiving. In nine seasons with the Redskins, big No. 72 devoured ball carriers and made life miserable for many quarterbacks. The two-time Pro Bowler was one of the best defensive tackles in the league in the 1960s. He gave an old-school appearance by often playing with his shirttails hanging out and by using a double-crossbar face mask with a horseshoe to protect his nose.

"He probably had the worst body of anybody in the NFL," said Pat Richter, a tight end who played with Rutgens for seven seasons. "It was like taking an egg and putting two toothpicks in it, a big body and a couple of skinny round legs. But Joe probably got more out of his ability than anybody. He just gave everything he had and pushed himself to the limit."

After a star-studded college career at Illinois, Rutgens was a Redskin first-round draft pick in 1961. He missed the season-opener due to injury but started every game thereafter at right defensive tackle through the 1965 campaign, when his game was peaking. He made his second Pro Bowl and, by no coincidence, the Redskins sported one of the best defenses in the league. His other Pro Bowl was in 1963.

In his first few seasons, Rutgens concentrated more on stopping the run than anything else. With the guidance of assistant coach Ernie Stautner, a Hall of Fame defensive tackle for the Steelers who joined the Redskins' staff in 1965, he added finesse to his game and such techniques as the head slap, and turned into a fearsome pass rusher. The *Washington Daily News* noted that he twice threw quarterbacks for losses and participated in nearly a third of the Redskins' tackles in a 23–7 win over the Giants on November 7, 1965.

"When I first came up, I didn't know enough about rushing the passer," Rutgens once said in the *Washington Post*. "I was always too conscious about watching for runs. In the Big Ten, there wasn't much passing, and I never really learned how to rush a quarterback.

"Ernie has taught me a lot. He was the best when he played, and he looks like he could play now. It looks like he's in better shape than a lot of us—I won't mention names."

Rutgens considered dumping the quarterback to be his biggest thrill as a football player. "I get in everybody's way—the ball carrier's I hope—and I like to get my 'cotton-picking' hands on the passer," he said in the *Post*. "I will settle for beating my opponent two out of three times, to hurry the passer, or even getting by the guard cleanly just once."

Rutgens played the 1965 season with a back injury that caused nerve problems in his legs. The pain flared up again the next year, and he played in only five games. He turned in solid seasons in 1967 and 1968, but injuries limited him to nine games in 1969, and he was waived.

## MARK RYPIEN

QB, No. 11, Washington State • 6–4, 234 • **NFL Career:** 1987–97, 2001 (12 seasons) • **Redskins Years:** 1987–93 (7) • **Born:** October 2, 1962 (Calgary, Alberta, Canada)

By normal NFL standards, Mark Rypien posted dazzling numbers in his first three seasons as a Redskins starting quarterback: 57 percent completion rate, more than 7,500 passing yards, and 56 scoring passes. Rypien admits, however, that a quarterback who dons the burgundy and gold is judged foremost on whether he can win the big game. Two nonplayoff seasons, plus a third when the Redskins were eliminated from the playoffs after he threw three interceptions in a second-round loss, drew the wrath of Redskins fans spoiled by repeated dominance in the 1980s. He was pelted with boos, noting in jest that fans at times wanted to throw him into the Potomac River.

Toss in a contract holdout prior to the 1991 season, and Rypien was persona non grata in the nation's capital. A reader survey in *Washingtonian* magazine found him to be the "Athlete I'd Most Like to Trade."

Rypien deflected the criticism and crafted one of the best passing years in Redskins history. On a 1991 squad that romped through the regular season and captured Super Bowl XXVI, he

Mark Rypien

connected on 249 of 421 passes (59.1 completion percentage) for 3,564 yards and 28 touchdowns. His quarterback rating (97.9) was second in the league, and his touchdown-to-interception ratio (28–11) was tops in the NFL and stands as second-best ever for a Redskin behind Joe Theismann in 1983 (29–11). One week, he tied a team record by racking up six touchdown passes and threw for 442 yards, one of the highest marks in team history.

Plus, Rypien showed pinpoint accuracy on the long ball. He completed 17 passes of more than 45 yards and two of more than 75.

"Rypien was absolutely awesome throwing that ball downfield," then-offensive line coach Jim Hanifan said. "He was unbelievable. It wasn't just in games, it was in practice, too. He'd marvel us. We'd go, 'My God, did you see him throw that pass?' It was right on the money all the time. It was something else."

Rypien capped his dream season with an 18 of 33, 292-yard, two-touchdown performance in a 37–24 Super Bowl win over Buffalo and was named the game's MVP. He made All-Pro teams and played in the Pro Bowl for the second and final time.

How did he withstand the earlier pounding from fans and the press? "It didn't bother me," he said. "God, I wanted to win just as much as the next fan wanted me to win. It was just a matter of finding that scenario that said, 'Hey, no matter what, you're going to find a way to get it done.'"

The 6–4, 230-pound quarterback, a lumbering runner not to be confused with Gene Kelly for footwork or Carl Lewis for speed, functioned that season behind a brilliant offensive line that masked his lack of mobility. Intelligence and hard work helped him compensate for his athletic deficiencies, said one of the stars on that line, left tackle Jim Lachey. "He was on the same page with coach [Joe] Gibbs and the offensive coordinators and the quarterback coach," Lachey said. "He knew exactly what they wanted to do and went out there and executed it. He'd get introduced to a game plan a little bit probably on Tuesday, our off day. Wednesday morning, he'd have a heavy dose of that game plan and by the time we'd have a walk through at 11, he would have everything down, including checks."

Ryp went from being one of the league's hottest quarterbacks, however, to one who threw more interceptions than touchdowns in 1992 and 1993. After his stats took a precipitous fall in his injury-plagued 1993 campaign, he was waived. He was a journeyman quarterback for the rest of his career, playing in Cleveland (1994), St. Louis (1995 and 1997), Philadelphia (1996), and Indianapolis (2001). In all, he threw for nearly 16,000 yards in seven seasons in Washington and now stands high in the Redskins' record book in various categories:

- First in lowest percentage of passes intercepted in a career (33; minimum 1,000 throws)
- Second in highest career passer rating (80.2)
- Third in most yards passing in a season (3,768)

Rypien's years in D.C. included his marriage to a former Redskins cheerleader, Annette Hutcheson, whom he met shortly after being drafted by the team in the sixth round in 1986. "People were thinking I was a psychic" at the time of the marriage, said Rypien, who wrote in his high school yearbook that it was his dream to marry a Dallas Cowboys cheerleader.

The Canadian-born Rypien won all-state honors in football, baseball, and basketball as a high school senior in Spokane, Washington. He went on to post huge passing numbers at Washington State, then spent his first two seasons with the Redskins mostly on injured reserve. He beat out Jay Schroeder in the 1988 training camp for the No. 2 spot behind Doug Williams and debuted as the starter in the fourth game against Arizona with 26 of 41 passing for 303 yards and three touchdowns. He became the true starter in 1989.

Rypien found it a huge benefit to hold a clipboard in his first two seasons and observe. "I was able to learn the system, understand what it took to be a pro and do things in the weight room to get me prepared for the day when I did start," he said. "Quarterbacks are thrown right into the fire today."

## CHRIS SAMUELS

OT, No. 60, Alabama • 6–5, 310 • **NFL Career:** 2000–2006 (7 seasons) • **Redskins Years:** 2000–2006 (7) • **Born:** July 28, 1977 (Mobile, Ala.)

Chris Samuels has been to four Pro Bowls in seven seasons and is regarded as one of the best offensive left tackles in the NFL. There's nothing shabby about that, but he wants to also

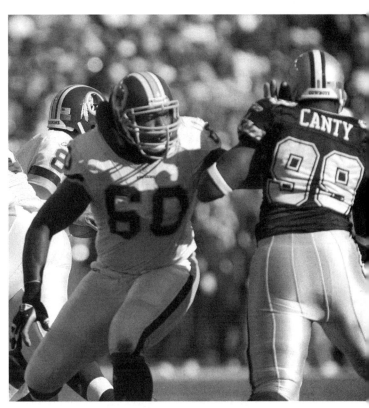

Chris Samuels (60)

be mentioned among the elite players at his position such as the Rams' Orlando Pace, Seattle's Walter Jones, Baltimore's Jonathan Ogden, and Cincinnati's Willie Anderson, all superstars as of the 2006 season.

Samuels is just about there. Redskins assistant head coach–offense Joe Bugel has compared the 6–5, 310-pounder to Jim Lachey, a perennial All-Pro left tackle for the Hogs in the late 1980s and early 1990s. Bugel has also found traces of "Gilligan," the fictional TV character from the 1960s who was stranded on an island, in Samuels. "Excellent athlete, good run man and pass blocker, and can run like a deer," Bugel said. "We isolate him one on one like we did with Lachey and leave him on the same guy the whole game. He's like Gilligan, he's got this guy the whole game."

The Redskins hoped for eventual stardom in Samuels when drafting him with the No. 3 overall pick in 2000. He didn't yield a sack in his last 47 games at Alabama and captured the Outland Trophy as the nation's best lineman as a senior.

As a Redskin, Samuels immediately showed the maturity and talent imperative for NFL success as a left tackle, which protects the blind side of a right-handed quarterback. He was positioned as the starting left tackle at the start of the 2000 exhibition season, and the Redskins' offensive line coach at the time, Russ Grimm, said that he had Pro Bowl honors awaiting him.

"He'll be one of the top tackles in the league soon," said Grimm, another famed player on the Hogs. "There will be some things he needs to learn and some mistakes may pop up. But he's been solid as far as assignments, and he's been good on pass protection. He's a physical player."

Early on, Samuels found it much more challenging lining up against pro defensive ends than those in college, whether it was the Eagles' Hugh Douglas or the Ravens' Michael McCrary, both established sack artists at the time. Samuels said NFL defensive linemen often resort to mind games in order to out-maneuver those on the opposite side of the ball: "Defensive linemen are much smarter in the NFL than in college. They'll set you up for a move later down the line."

Samuels made his first Pro Bowl in the 2001 season and followed up with an appearance in Honolulu in 2002. He missed out on a third straight trip to the all-star game in 2003, while losing confidence and struggling with his game, possibly because the Redskins had three different offensive line coaches in his first four seasons.

Things changed when Bugel, one of the greatest O-line coaches in NFL history, arrived in 2004. Samuels credits Bugel, the architect of the Hogs, with helping improve his fundamentals: "He's the best offensive line coach I've had on this level," Samuels said of Bugel after the Redskins piled up 481 yards in a 36–30 win over Jacksonville on October 1, 2006. "He's working on us every day. He's not satisfied with us just blocking a guy. He wants us to be perfect on technique and everything. Like today I thought I played pretty good but had a few plays where I got beat, and coach Bugel's going to be breathing down my neck when we watch film on the game."

Samuels, who battled ankle and knee injuries in 2004 and 2005 without missing a game, received Pro Bowl honors again in 2005 and 2006. He has missed only four starts in his career and has evolved into a true leader on the Redskins in his quiet, unassuming way. "Dancing and jaw-jacking and talking a lot of noise . . . that doesn't win games in my opinion," Samuels said. "I try to lead by example and with my play on the field."

Jon Jansen, the Redskins' other bookend offensive tackle of the 21st century, said Samuels has confronted teammates face to face in hopes of getting them motivated and focused. "Chris is a great person," Jansen said. "He's a good guy to have on the team because he's a quality individual. He's not going to go out and get in trouble and get other guys in trouble. He's a leader in that regard because he'll step up and say things that need to be said. The more guys you can have like that, especially as offensive linemen, the better chances you have of being successful."

"Chris cares about his teammates," Jansen added. "He cares about the offense and how we do. He doesn't want to go out and give a sub-par performance. That's why he's been to [four] Pro Bowls."

Samuels doesn't want his career to end like that of former Redskins defensive end Bruce Smith, an 11-time Pro Bowler who is destined for the Pro Football Hall of Fame—but failed to win a Super Bowl. "The Pro Bowls are great," Samuels said. "It's a blessing from God to make it there and stay healthy, but I want to win a Super Bowl. You look at one of my former teammates, [defensive end] Bruce Smith. Bruce went to so many Pro Bowls but didn't win a Super Bowl. That's the biggest thing that he misses. I want to win a Super Bowl."

## RICKY SANDERS

WR, No. 83, S. W. Texas State • 5–11, 180 • **NFL Career:** 1986–95 (10 seasons) • **Redskins Years:** 1986–93 (8) • **Born:** August 30, 1962 (Temple, Tex.)

His nickname was "Slick Rick." Graceful and with smooth strides, Ricky Sanders could run like a deer. He caught balls on all kinds of routes but electrified Redskins fans the most when hooking up with quarterbacks on the deep pass. He was gifted, too, at gaining chunks of yards after a reception.

A frequent guest on the highlight reels, Sanders caught 483 passes for 6,477 yards and 37 touchdowns in eight seasons in Washington, some of the best statistics in team history. Most of his production came when he was part of the Redskins' dangerous wide receiver trio of the late 1980s and early 1990s known as "The Posse."

Sanders was more fluid than his Posse comrades Art Monk and Gary Clark. He also was more of a finesse-oriented receiver than the other two and "brilliant at it," said Redskin Hall of Fame receiver Charley Taylor, Sander's position coach in Washington. "He was one of those guys who can run 60-yard patterns and their head never moves. I call them burners."

"He was a running back before he became a wide receiver, so he had a little more trickery in him," said Doug Williams, a Redskins quarterback who played with Sanders for four seasons.

Sanders played tailback at Southwest Texas State (now Texas State) and finished as the Bobcats' third all-time leading rusher (2,471 yards). He also displayed a talent at catching passes out of the backfield and from the slot position.

After college, he signed with the Houston Gamblers of the United States Football League, and head coach Jack Pardee (a former Redskins linebacker and head coach) and offensive coordinator Darrel "Mouse" Davis converted him to wide receiver. Sanders thrived in the Gamblers' innovative run-and-shoot offense. He caught 101 passes for 1,378 yards and 11 scores in two seasons in Houston while playing with quarterback Jim Kelly, who later crafted a Hall of Fame career in the NFL.

Meanwhile, the Redskins, who had first spotted Sanders at Southwest Texas State, focused on him in the USFL. After the league folded in 1986, he reported to New England, which had picked him in the 1984 supplemental NFL draft. Redskins general manager Bobby Beathard planned to swipe him away, though, and met with his New England counterpart, Dick Steinberg, hoping to acquire Sanders through a trade before he took the field for the Patriots.

"They hadn't started training camp yet, and we were hoping they wouldn't see him in uniform at their place," Beathard said. "We wanted to get him before any of that took place because if they see him and do everything with him, they won't want to trade him. They obviously scouted him in the USFL. I was willing to trade for him before they ever timed him."

The Redskins traded a third-round draft choice for Sanders, who saw limited action in the 1886 season, although he showed convincingly why Beathard was so interested in him; his first NFL catch was good for 71 yards. He really hit his stride after a torn knee ligament sidelined Monk for a few weeks late in the 1987 season.

Sanders caught eight passes for 164 yards, including 51- and 46-yard touchdowns, in a 27–24 win over Minnesota in the regular-season finale, sparking a memorable postseason climaxed by his sensational performance in Super Bowl XXII. On a day the Redskins destroyed Denver, 42–10, he inked his name in the Super Bowl record book, setting a new mark with 193 yards receiving and tying one with two scoring catches; both records have since been broken. His first touchdown reception, an 80-yard catch-and-run, ignited the Redskins' 35-point explosion in the second quarter. He scored on a

50-yard bomb later in the quarter and had nine catches on the day.

His receptions came off the arm of Williams. The two had formed a special connection while playing together on the Redskins' practice squad during the 1986 season. "The chemistry was instant," Sanders said. "He loved throwing the ball to me."

In the coming seasons, Sanders shined in the three-wide receiver setup implemented by Gibbs in the late 1980s. He averaged 61 catches over six seasons (1988–93), with career highs of 1,148 yards and 12 touchdowns in 1988, and 80 catches in 1989. He's now in a four-way tie for most Redskins touchdown catches in a season (12). After the 1993 campaign, he left the Redskins via free agency and signed with Atlanta, where he spent his final two seasons.

Looking back, Sanders said playing in the USFL in the run-and-shoot offense, where wide receivers are spread all over the field, helped him transition to the three-wide receiver alignment. "That was a great offense that Gibbs had, and it was pretty similar to the run-and-shoot," he said. "Some of the patterns were pretty similar, and you had an option on your routes. You could run a fade or a hook. It all depended on the coverage."

## DAN SANDIFER

DB-HB, No. 20, Louisiana State • 6–1, 190 • **NFL Career:** 1948–53 (6 seasons) • **Redskins Years:** 1948–49 (2) • **Born:** March 1, 1927 (Shreveport, La.) • **Died:** August 15, 1987 (Shreveport, La.)

## AND

## EDDIE SAENZ

HB-DB-KR, No. 99, Loyola of Los Angeles; Southern California • 5–11, 166 • **NFL Career:** 1946–51 (6 seasons) • **Redskins Years:** 1946–51 (6) • **Born:** September 21, 1922 (Santa Monica, Calif.) • **Died:** April 28, 1971 (Santa Monica, Calif.)

They had the potential to be electrifying with every touch of the ball. Eddie Saenz and Dan Sandifer—Redskin sparkplugs whose careers overlapped in the late 1940s.

Late that decade, there was no better kickoff-return tandem in the league. In 1947, Saenz (pronounced "signs") led the NFL in kickoff returns (29), yards (797), and touchdowns (2). His touchdown total is a Redskins single-season record and is tied with Brian Mitchell for a franchise career mark. He played in only four games in 1948 because of injury but Sandifer filled in by posting league-highs in kickoff returns (26), yards (594), and touchdowns (1). Then in 1949, the two tied for the most kickoff returns in the NFL (24), with Saenz gaining 465 yards and Sandifer 518.

They contributed mightily in other ways, too. The 5–11, 169-pound Saenz, a dangerous receiver out of the backfield, stood as the Redskins' fourth all-time leader in reception yards (1,318) by the time his six-year career in Washington ended after the 1951 season. He caught 83 passes and 10 touchdowns.

Saenz repeatedly turned in exciting performances, like when he caught two long touchdowns in a 1950 game against the Steelers. "Forbes Field was banked in snow, and the playing field ankle deep in mud," Morris A. Bealle wrote in his book, *The Redskins: 1937–1958.* "Ground work was impossible, so [Sammy] Baugh took to the air. He passed to Eddie Saenz for two touchdowns—63- and 75-yard pass plays."

The 6–1, 190-pound Sandifer, for his part, intercepted a league-record 13 passes as a rookie in 1948. (He now stands one behind Hall of Famer Dick "Night Train" Lane.) That season, he also tied Baugh's league record for the most picks in a game (four), a mark held by a host of players today. Plus, he became the first player to lead the NFL in interception return yards (258) and kickoff return yards (594) in the same season. (Detroit's Don Doll duplicated that feat in 1949.) In one 1948 game in which Sandifer had a "field day," Bealle wrote, the rookie intercepted two passes and ran a kickoff back 96 yards for a touchdown.

Sandifer was traded before the 1950 season to Pittsburgh for triple-threat Bill Dudley, a current Hall of Famer. He played for five other teams before retiring after the 1953 season.

## RON SAUL

OG, No. 64, Michigan State • 6–3, 254 • **NFL Career:** 1970–81 (12 seasons) • **Redskins Years:** 1976–81 (6) • **Born:** February 4, 1948 (Butler, Pa.)

Ron Saul was a "tough, hard-nosed battler," according to Redskin publicists, who started at left guard for the squad from 1976 to 1981. During that period, he helped Washington to four years of more than 2,000 yards rushing and the best passing yardage since the 1960s. Redskins backs ran behind him on the left side when they needed crucial gains.

Saul, a tireless worker in the weight room with tremendous upper body strength, overcame at least five knee operations in his career and an assortment of other injuries. To him, playing hurt was part of the job. "I hear guys today complain about 'turf toe,'" he once said in an article by the Pro Football Researchers Association. "What's that? I don't even know what that means. I had lots of cartilage torn, a broken nose, hip pointers. They would say, 'Shoot it up and play.'

"So we played. We prided ourselves on being tough. You had to be tough. There were always young guys coming out of college who wanted our jobs."

In college, Saul was an All-American at Michigan State and a first-team All-Big Ten player. The Houston Oilers drafted him in the fifth round in 1970. He played in 47 games over the next six seasons, missing the 1974 campaign with a knee injury. The Redskins traded third-, sixth-, and seventh-round picks to get him before the 1976 season.

Saul missed only a handful of games in his first five years in Washington. He was injured in the 1981 preseason and missed about a third of the year and banged up his knee again before the 1982 season. He spent the year on injured reserve but received a Super Bowl ring when the Redskins captured Super Bowl XVII. He retired from the game as an original member of the Redskins' famous offensive line of that era, the Hogs.

Saul's twin brother, Rich, was an offensive lineman for the Los Angeles Rams (1970–81). Another Saul brother, Bill, played linebacker for Baltimore, Pittsburgh, New Orleans, and Detroit (1962–70).

## Do You Know?

- That in the Redskins' 44–14 win over Pittsburgh on October 15, 1939, Redskins back Frankie Filchock threw a 99-yard touchdown pass to Andy Farkas, the longest pass play in NFL history at the time. With the Redskins backed up to their goal line on third down, Filchock stood in the end zone in punt formation. He had called for a fake punt with a screen pass to the right to Farkas. But Farkas thought the pass was to the left, where he ended up all by himself. Filchock flipped the ball to Farkas, who raced 97 yards to the end zone. There have since been nine other 99-yard pass plays in NFL history, including two more by the Redskins:

  - George Izo to Bobby Mitchell against Cleveland on September 15, 1963
  - Sonny Jurgensen to Gerry Allen against Chicago on September 15, 1968

- That Charlie Conerly, a quarterback drafted by the Redskins in 1945, became a "Marlboro Man," that rugged-looking cowboy once used in ads for Marlboro cigarettes, after retiring from football. Conerly waited until 1948 to sign with the Redskins and was immediately traded to the Giants in what would evolve into one of the worst deals in Redskins history. He had a solid 14-year career in New York.

- That Mel Allen, one of the most celebrated sportscasters ever and the voice of the Yankees for so many years, handled play-by-play on the Redskins' TV and radio networks in 1952 and 1953.

- That in 1957, the Redskins signed Pittsburgh All-American end Joe Walton, making him the first son of an NFL player to play in the league. His father, Frank "Tiger" Walton, was a ferocious lineman who played for the Redskins in the 1930s and 1940s. (Frank was a Redskins assistant coach in 1948, and Joe was a Redskins assistant from 1974 to 1980.) There is only one other known father-son combination in Redskins history. Joe Krakoski played defensive back in Washington in 1961 and his son, Joe, played linebacker in 1986.

- That the Redskins have had several brother-brother combos on the roster at the same time, including:

  - The Khayat brothers, offensive guard-kicker Bob and defensive end-tackle Ed, in 1962 and '63
  - The Turk brothers, punter Matt and center Dan, in 1997, '98, and '99
  - The Clemons brothers, linebacker Chris and defensive end Nic, in 2005

- That defensive back Johnny Sample played in Washington (1963–65) in between stints with teams that appeared in the two most famous games in NFL history. He played for the Baltimore Colts in their 23–17 win over the Giants in the 1958 NFL championship game, and for the Jets in their 16–7 win over the Colts in Super Bowl III in January 1969.

- That a host of Redskins who played during the 1960s rose to prominence in their post-NFL careers:

  - Ben Scotti, DB, 1959–61: founded a record label with his brother, Tony, called Scotti Brothers

## MARK SCHLERETH

OG, No. 69, Idaho • 6–3, 283 • **NFL Career:** 1989–2000 (12 seasons) • **Redskins Years:** 1989–94 (6) • **Born:** January 25, 1966 (Anchorage, Alaska)

With three Super Bowl rings to his name—one with the Redskins and two with the Broncos—Mark Schlereth had an NFL experience most football players can only dream of. Now, Schlereth is enjoying a postretirement career that also is the envy of many. He's an NFL in-studio analyst for ESPN and is one of the polished stars at the cable broadcasting network.

Schlereth joined ESPN in 2002, not long after retiring from football. A tough, hard-nosed competitor who played guard and appeared in 156 games, he saw action in his first six seasons in Washington, where he made the Pro Bowl once, and his last six in Denver. He also went under the knife for surgery nearly 30 times in his career, mostly to repair his banged-up knees, and suffered briefly from Guillain-Barré syndrome, a rare

neurological disease that can short-circuit the route between the impulses sent from the brain and the body's muscles.

The 6–3, 283-pounder refused to let ailments force him to retire prematurely. As he wrote on ESPN.com:

There were countless times when I'd play a game with torn cartilage in my knees. I'd be asked to "hang on for a few more weeks" before having surgery. I'll tell you what: In those moments, the negative feelings pile up—the exhaustion from ignoring the signals your body is sending you, the frustration from not being able to perform simple tasks—and you've got to dig deep into the recesses of your soul to remember why you continue to do it.

But I'd be back in the training room getting taped up for the next game. Why? Mostly because I loved the game. But also out of a sense of obligation to my teammates who relied on me. I could never let them down. Regardless of how beat up I'd get, I'd go out and play hard for them, because I know they'd do the same for me.

Records; later co-produced the TV lifeguard drama series "Baywatch"

- Tom Osborne, WR, 1960–61: University of Nebraska head football coach, 1973–97 (three national championships); U.S. congressman, 2001–2007
- Bob Khayat, K-OG-C, 1960, 1962–63: University of Mississippi chancellor, 1995–present
- Galen Hall, QB, 1962: University of Florida head football coach, 1984–89; later a head coach in the Arena Football League and in NFL Europe
- Pat Richter, TE-P, 1963–70: University of Wisconsin athletic director, 1989–2004
- Billy Hunter, WR-DB, 1965: Executive Director of the National Basketball Players Association, 1996–present
- Sid Williams, LB, 1967: U.S. ambassador to the Bahamas, 1994–98
- Bob Wade, DB, 1969: University of Maryland men's basketball coach, 1986–89
- Frank Ryan, QB, 69–70: Yale University athletic director, 1977–87

- That Frank Ryan also earned a doctorate (Ph.D.) in the realities of higher mathematics from Rice University.
- That John Wilbur, a Redskins guard in the early 1970s, was later a player, coach, and part owner of the World Football League's Hawaii Hawaiians—all at the same time.
- That former ABC *Monday Night Football* sportscaster Don Meredith referred to President Richard Nixon as "Tricky Dick," the president's less-than-flattering nickname from the ongoing Watergate scandal, in a tele-

cast of the Redskins-Steelers game on November 5, 1973. Meredith, known for his outrageous comments while in the broadcast booth, later publicly apologized for his remark.

- That guard Mark Schlereth, drafted by the Redskins in 1989, became the first native-born Alaskan to play in the NFL. His teammates nicknamed him "Stinky" after stinkheads, an Eskimo delicacy made from rotting fish heads.
- That Terry Crews, a linebacker who played for the Redskins in 1995, has since built a Hollywood career that has included roles in such films as *Starsky & Hutch, The Longest Yard,* and *The Benchwarmers.* He has starred in *Everybody Hates Chris,* a TV sitcom about a teenager growing up in the early 1980s in the Bedford-Stuyvesant neighborhood of Brooklyn, New York.
- That the Redskins had a defensive end who claims to have coined the term "sack," and another one who set the all-time NFL sack record. The menacing David "Deacon" Jones, a Redskin in 1974, said he conceived of the term "sack" during his years with the Los Angeles Rams in the 1960s, when he was a sack machine. Bruce Smith broke the sack record on December 7, 2003, No. 199 of his career total of 200. His victim was Giants quarterback Jesse Palmer, who starred in the reality television series *The Bachelor* in the spring of 2004.
- That the University of Southern California has produced the most players who have earned spots on the Redskins' active roster as of the 2006 season (38). A close second is Notre Dame (37), followed by Maryland (30), Penn State (27), Michigan State (23), and Georgia and Alabama (both with 20). Nine Redskins never played football in college.

---

Schlereth played his college ball at Division I-AA Idaho and joined the Redskins as a 10th-round draft pick in 1989. A latter-day Hog, he started six games as a rookie and seven in 1990 before enjoying a watershed season in 1991. While starting all 16 regular-season games, he won three Redskins Offensive Player of the Week honors and was a major reason they allowed a league-low nine sacks and had one of the best rushing attacks in the NFL. He also started all three postseason games, including a victory in Super Bowl XXVI, and was named to the Pro Bowl.

Schlereth crafted a 43-consecutive-game starting streak that ended in 1993 due to a knee injury. Soon after, he contracted Guillain-Barré syndrome and was sidelined for about the last half of the season. The Redskins' offensive line coach at the time, Jim Hanifan, praised his hard-nosed guard.

"They don't make them any tougher than Mark Schlereth," Hanifan said in a Redskins press guide. "He is *a muy malo hombre* [a very bad man], but only on the football field. No one admires Mark Schlereth more than I do."

Schlereth returned to play in every game in 1994 but signed as a free agent with Denver after the season. He started on Broncos teams that captured Super Bowls XXXII and XXXIII and made the Pro Bowl once more.

## RAY SCHOENKE

OG-OT, No. 62, Southern Methodist • 6–4, 250 • **NFL Career:** 1963–64, 66–75 (12 seasons) • **Redskins Years:** 1966–75 (10) • **Born:** September 10, 1941 (Wahiawa, Hawaii)

Before there was Hogs star Raleigh McKenzie, who could play any position on the offensive line, another king of versatility battled for the Redskins in the trenches: Ray Schoenke.

Schoenke floated from position to position on the O-line in his 10 seasons in Washington, starting or substituting wherever needed. He spent much time at the guard positions but also played tackle and center. Adaptability was his middle name.

He came to the rescue in two of the biggest wins in Redskins history. Against the Packers in the first round of the 1972 playoffs, he subbed at right guard for John Wilbur, who had a kidney injury. The next week in the NFC championship against Dallas, he subbed for Terry Hermeling at left guard for most of the game.

"Ray was one tough guy," said Billy Kilmer, the Redskins' quarterback at the time. "He played in our championship game against Dallas. He had his leg taped up. He was hurting really bad, but he gave it his all. Ray was like me. We didn't have a lot of talent, but we gave it our all and did a hell of a job. He didn't care if he was injured."

Schoenke was equally versatile at Southern Methodist, where he played fullback, guard, tackle, center, and linebacker. He received all-conference and All-American honors. Selected by the Cowboys in the 11th round in 1963, he played two seasons in Dallas but was cut. He sat out the 1965 campaign and became frustrated.

"It was terrible," he told the *Washington Star* in 1976. "For three days, I didn't come out of the bedroom in the house. I sold insurance and played touch football. On Sundays, I couldn't even watch the games. I would roam around town looking for pick-up touch games to play in."

Schoenke eventually signed with the Redskins as a free agent and won the starting left guard job early in the 1966 season. He continued rotating even into the latter years of his career, starting every game for the injured Hermeling at left tackle in 1974 and playing both guard positions in 1975, his final season. He was honored after a 23–7 win over Cleveland in 1975: "When injuries wiped out the left side of our offensive line," Redskins publicists wrote, "the SOS call went out to two veterans—Ray Schoenke, who can play guard, tackle or center, and Terry Hermeling, who had been sidelined for two seasons with a knee injury. Both played a super role as we rolled up 190 yards rushing against Cleveland, and each won a game ball."

## JOE SCUDERO

DB-HB-KR, No. 28, San Francisco • 5–9, 155 • **NFL Career:** 1954–58, 60 (6 seasons) • **Redskins Years:** 1954–58 (5) • **Born:** July 2, 1930 (San Francisco, Calif.)

He was an elusive little waterbug. In five seasons with the Redskins in the 1950s, Joe "Scooter" Scudero" churned out 1,738 yards on kickoff, punt, and interception returns. His 25.98-yard career kickoff return average is one of the best in Redskins history.

Scudero's best year by far was 1955, when he made his only Pro Bowl and received All-Pro honors. He gained exactly 1,000 yards and returned one kickoff and one punt for touchdowns. He also intercepted five passes and ran back two for scores. He was among the league leaders in kickoff return yards (699, 28.0 average) and punt return yards (241, 9.6 average). The "little scatback," as one sportswriter called him, helped the Redskins finish 8–4, their best record in the five-year coaching reign of Joe Kuharich.

Scudero, who played mostly defensive halfback with the Redskins, competed at about 155 pounds, about 20 less than the weight he was listed at. But he made up for his tiny frame with speed and shiftiness, noting that he ran a 9.6 in the 100-

yard dash. "The guys always kidded me in the locker room that I was too small," he said. "They'd say, 'The Little League field is on the other side of town.' I was always conscious of my weight because I wasn't very big. I never got hurt by contact."

An injury early in the 1956 season that Scudero described as a "devastating hamstring pull" never healed completely and prevented him from posting big numbers like he did in 1955. He was still dangerous at times, as in a 37–14 win over the Chicago Cardinals on October 6, 1957.

"Scudero was the busiest little man on the gridiron, playing much of the game on both offense and defense," Bus Ham wrote in the *Washington Post*. "He got loose for one run of 43 yards, ran back punts daringly, tackled his old San Francisco University teammate, Ollie Matson, time and again, and was Johnny-on-the-spot on forward passes."

Scudero was a star running back at San Francisco. He scored 16 touchdowns in the course of the 1950 and 1951 seasons while sharing ball-carrying duties with Matson, now a member of the Pro Football Hall of Fame.

After a year running track at San Francisco, Scudero played in the Canadian Football League in 1953 and led his conference with 950 rushing yards. In signing with the Redskins in 1954, he reunited with his college coach, Kuharich, who was in his first season in D.C. When Kuharich left the Redskins after the 1959 season to become head coach at Notre Dame, Scudero followed and served as an assistant coach with the Fighting Irish for one year. He returned to play in 1960 for the Steelers, but his hamstring injury forced him to retire.

During his career, Scudero pursued stage and screen acting in the off-season. In the 1950s, he guest-starred in two popular TV series, *Gunsmoke* and *Dragnet*.

## CLYDE SHUGART

G-LB-T, No. 51, Iowa State • 6–1, 230 • **NFL Career:** 1939–44 (5 seasons) • **Redskins Years:** 1939–44 (5) • **Born:** December 7, 1916 (Elberon, Ia.)

In five seasons in the NFL, Clyde Shugart earned his share of facial souvenirs and suffered some chipped teeth. Hardly anyone in his era wore facemasks on their leather helmets, which would seem like an especially perilous position to be in for a lineman like himself. "You didn't know any different," he said. "Even so, I worried about my teeth when I played pro ball. I didn't worry about breaking an arm or a leg, because I thought it would heal. But you don't grow new teeth, and that always bothered me."

Players then were less inclined to make helmet-to-helmet hits because they weren't protected by facemasks, he said, adding, "Now they use the head like a mallet sometimes."

The 6–1, 230-pound Shugart was a tough pulling guard who helped clear the way for runners like Wilbur Moore, Dick Todd, Andy Farkas, and Bob Seymour. Pulling was his specialty because he was fast for a lineman. Without that speed, he probably wouldn't have made it in pro football.

A track star in high school, Shugart was an all-conference tackle at Iowa State and came to the Redskins as a 15th-round pick in 1939. He was too small to play tackle in the NFL, and the Redskins switched him to guard. "In those days, we used the single-wing formation, and guards were leading a lot of plays, and you had to be fast enough to keep ahead of the backs," he said.

After the great Turk Edwards retired early in the 1940 season, Shugart became the fastest lineman on the team. He and Dick Farman formed perhaps the league's best pair of guards in 1940 and 1941, according to the *Washington Post*. Shugart, a second-team All-Pro in 1943 who also played linebacker, missed all but two of a possible 60 games in his career and played in three NFL championship games: 1940, 1942, and 1943.

Shugart had a near altercation with Bears Hall of Fame lineman George Musso in the 1942 championship, a 14–6 Redskins win. "Musso wasn't expecting me to block him, and I had a golden opportunity to let him have it," Shugart said. "Then he threatened to slug me, and we got into a discussion during a timeout. He said, 'You know what's going to happen?' I said, 'Yea, we'll both get thrown out of the game.' So we settled down and played football instead of throwing punches at each other."

## ED SIMMONS

OT, No. 76, Eastern Washington • 6–5, 330 • **NFL Career:** 1987–97 (11 seasons) • **Redskins Years:** 1987–97 (11) • **Born:** December 31, 1963 (Seattle, Wash.)

He could "dance on a light bulb." The Redskins' great offensive line coach of the 1980s, Joe Bugel, paid that complement to one of his Hogs, Ed Simmons, whose quickness and fluidity on his feet were remarkable for a 330-pound lineman.

"At first when he said it, I didn't understand it," said Simmons, who joined the Redskins in 1987. "I was like, 'I'm a little bit too heavy, what is he talking about, dancing on light bulbs?' He just liked the way I danced, the way the feet moved. Some guys look like they're walking in concrete. I was the opposite. My feet were real light. They were always ready to go in the opposite direction."

Big Ed was also known for his hustle. Bugel called him a "camera hog" because he always seemed to be around the ball, throwing that last block downfield to spring the runner for more yards or trying to peel defenders off a pile.

In his 11-year NFL career, all in Washington, Simmons played every position on the offensive line except for center and spent most of his time at right tackle. A series of knee injuries slowed his progress, and he missed a chunk of games at times.

When healthy, he was good. Take the 1995 season, when he played in all but three downs at right tackle (1,039 of 1,042) and was named to the *Sports Illustrated* All-NFC East team. The following year, he started the first 10 games and was having a Pro Bowl-caliber season until a knee injury sidelined him for five weeks. The Redskins averaged 65 yards rushing when he was out, compared with 142 in the 11 games he played that season. The Redskins Alumni Association named him Offensive Player of the Year. He retired after the 1997 campaign.

"If he could have stayed healthy without getting those knees hurt, then he had a chance of being a great one," said Jim Hanifan, the Redskins' offensive line coach from 1990 to 1996.

Simmons developed many of his athletic skills playing basketball at a Seattle high school. A center and power forward, he did slide drills for long stretches in practice with his arms up and knees bent; the aim was to improve his quickness. Eastern Washington University wanted to recruit Simmons

as a football player despite never seeing him play but couldn't find any quality film on him. An offensive line coach from the school thus attended one of his basketball games and, like so many others who would follow, was amazed at how light he was on his feet.

Simmons started at Eastern Washington for four years and was drafted by the Redskins in the sixth round in 1987. He got his first extended starting role in 1989.

## JERRY SMITH

TE, No. 87, Arizona State • 6–3, 208 • **NFL Career:** 1965–77 (13 seasons) • **Redskins Years:** 1965–77 (13) • **Born:** July 19, 1943 (Eugene, Ore.) • **Died:** October 15, 1986 (Silver Spring, Md.)

Shortly after the Redskins drafted Jerry Smith in the ninth round in 1965, skeptics downplayed the chances for the 6–3, 208-pounder with limited speed to make it in the NFL. One scout offered this dour assessment: "The trouble with Jerry Smith is that he's not quite big enough to be a tight end and not quite fast enough to be a wide end. He has great hands and a wonderful attitude, but he's the kind you just can't keep."

The Redskins were smart to latch onto Smith, for he became the best pass-catching tight end in team history. In his 13-year career, all in Washington, he hauled in 421 passes for 5,496 yards and 60 touchdowns, some of the greatest numbers for a tight end in NFL history upon his retirement in 1977. (His 60 touchdowns are third all-time in Redskins history.)

Smith's role as one of the dangerous playmakers on the squad's electrifying offense from the 1960s augments his lofty position in Redskins lore. In a five-season stretch (1966–70), he averaged 53 receptions, 684 receiving yards and eight

### A Special Bond

They came to the Redskins a season apart, Jerry Smith in 1965 and Brig Owens in 1966. Once their lives intersected, a tight friendship formed.

At a time when the practice was uncommon for blacks and whites in sports, the duo began to room together in training camp and on road trips—and continued to do so for more than a decade. Owens said that the two never realized their bond was unusual. He pointed out that they began rooming together several years before the popular 1971 movie, *Brian's Song*, about the strong friendship of Chicago Bears running backs Brian Piccolo, who was white, and Gale Sayers, who was black.

"When black and white were separate and unusually unequal in sports, Owens and Smith became fast friends—and roommates—for longer than all but the most special players even survive in the NFL," *Washington Post* columnist Ken Denlinger wrote on September 14, 1977.

Smith makes his second of three scoring catches in a 1967 game against the Rams. He earned the nickname "home run" for his propensity to come through in the clutch with touchdown receptions.

touchdowns, twice being named to the Pro Bowl and once a consensus first-team All-Pro.

It was hard to find a better pure receiving tight end at the time. "I'm very upset he's not in the Pro Football Hall of Fame, he was that good," said Bobby Mitchell, a teammate of Smith's and one of the Redskins' lethal receiving weapons in the 1960s. "Jerry Smith was an undersized player. He would be lucky if he weighed 180 pounds. But when it came to getting open and catching the football, he had no peers, and when it came to toughness he had no peers. He did it from his rookie season until his last year."

Smith lacked the size and speed of other great tight ends of his era such as 230-pounders John Mackey and Mike Ditka, but, like Baltimore Colts Hall of Fame receiver Raymond Berry, who was also not fleet of foot, he simply knew how to get open. He eluded defenders with deftness and savvy and then used his soft hands to secure the catch. An incredible amount of gritty determination and relentless effort also marked his game. Time after time, he made acrobatic catches while laying out his body and taking vicious hits. "The way he'd serve up his body was unbelievable," said Vince Promuto, a Redskins center who played with Smith for six seasons.

Smith was also a big-time player in college, first at Eastern Arizona Junior College and then at Arizona State, where in his senior year he won All-American honors after catching 42 passes for 618 yards and five touchdowns. In 1965, the Red-skins drafted the laid-back California native whose bangs, freckles and mischievous grin gave him the look of famous cartoon character Joe Palooka.

Smith was so good in the preseason that offensive ends coach George Wilson reportedly said he should have been a first-round pick. He started the last five games that year and caught 19 passes for 257 yards and two touchdowns. He also recovered two fumbles on special teams. He remained a split end until midway through the 1966 season, when Redskins coach Otto Graham pulled off the "great switch," moving Smith to tight end and Charley Taylor from running back to receiver. The move put their careers on a higher plane; Smith finished as the league's top receiving tight end that year with 54 catches for 686 yards and six scores, giving notice he had to be reckoned with.

"Jerry came in here as a wide receiver, but he didn't have blazing speed, plus he wasn't really the biggest guy," Taylor said. "Cornerbacks like [the Cowboys'] Cornell Green and [the Packers'] Herb Adderley kind of held him up a little bit. But you move him inside, where a linebacker had to cut him off the line, and he was quick enough to evade the guy. Then he was on the strong safety, and it was all over."

Smith's banner year was 1967, when he posted career-highs of 67 catches (second in the league), 849 yards and 12 touchdowns; the latter mark has him in a four-way tie for the most single-season scoring catches in Redskins history. In one game, a 28–28 tie with Los Angeles, Smith ran circles around Los Angeles' vaunted defense and caught three touch-downs, prompting Rams coach George Allen to shower him with praise: "Jerry Smith is the most underrated tight end in football," Allen said at the time. "He's fast, and he has all the moves. When he caught 54 passes last year, that was like a guy hitting 58 home runs. He's just great."

When none other than Allen began coaching the Redskins in 1971, Smith's reception numbers dipped sharply in the coach's conservative offense. Injuries also slowed him down, but he maintained his knack for clutch catches. He caught only

21 passes in 1972, for instance, but seven were for touchdowns, earning him the nickname "home run." In his last two productive seasons, he caught 44 passes in 1974 and 31 in 1975, before giving way to Jean Fugett as the starter.

Smith's stats may have waned, but his tenacity didn't. Safety Kenny Houston experienced it first-hand in practice, where the tight end showed no mercy on coverage men. "Every day, every play, it was a fight," said Houston, who played with Smith in the 1970s. "I've never seen a guy as competitive as Jerry Smith. He didn't have a lot of size, but he had a lot of moves. He could hold a pattern longer than a lot of other tight ends, meaning he had an ability with his body to make you think he was doing something else, then he would break away from you. So he was very good to work against. Covering a guy like him helped me become a better safety."

Smith was one of the most recognizable and popular Redskins of his era. He was selected by the NFL in 1971 to travel to U.S. military hospitals in the Far East and visit troops serving in the Vietnam War. He died of AIDs in 1986 at age 43.

"It is with great sadness that we learned of Jerry Smith's death last night," then-Redskins owner Jack Kent Cooke said in a statement on October 16, 1986. "He will sorely be missed by our community. Jerry was a great part of the tradition of the Washington Redskins for 13 seasons."

## RILEY SMITH

B-LB, No. 35, Alabama • 6–2, 200 • **NFL Career:** 1936–38 (3 seasons) • **Redskins Years:** 1936–38 (3) • **Born:** July 14, 1911 (Greenwood, Miss.) • **Died:** August 9, 1999 (Mobile, Ala.)

The name Riley "General" Smith may not immediately jump out at Redskins enthusiasts, but he's unique in franchise lore.

Smith was the Redskins' first draft pick. The all-everything back also scored all of Washington's points in a 13–3 win over the Giants on Thursday night, September 16, 1937, the Redskins' inaugural game in the nation's capital. He returned an interception 60 yards and kicked two field goals and an extra point, prompting *Washington Daily News* sportswriter Dick McCann to write a witty line that appeared in the Redskins' media guide for many years: "Reconstruction Finance Chairman Jesse Jones threw out the first ball, and Riley Smith played with it all night."

That night, with the Redskins clinging to a late 6–3 lead, Smith came through in the clutch. "When Giant passes were flooding the brilliantly-lighted field in a last desperate attempt to snatch victory away from the Redskins," Shirley Povich of the *Washington Post* wrote, "Riley Smith turned their own weapon against the New York behemoths, snatched a Giant pass on his own 40-yard line and streaked 60 yards down the sidelines for the only touchdown of the night. Sure, he kicked the point after that touchdown, too. He was something to see tonight, this quarterback who joined the Redskins fresh from his Rose Bowl triumphs."

Smith, primarily a blocking back, was so versatile in three seasons with the Redskins. Playing in the old single-wing formation, he

- completed 19 of 46 passes for 290 yards and three touchdowns
- caught 18 passes for 300 yards and three touchdowns
- rushed 45 times for 58 yards and two touchdowns

Smith also kicked field goals and extra points and scored a total of 108 points. There wasn't much he didn't do.

He was a multithreat at Alabama, too. The All-American quarterback passed, punted, and kicked extra points and field goals and starred on a Crimson Tide team that beat Stanford in the Rose Bowl. He even won an award for being the best blocker in the Southeastern Conference. He was enshrined in the College Football Hall of Fame in 1985.

The 1936 season marked the first year of the NFL draft. After the Eagles took University of Chicago back Jay Berwanger with the first pick, the Boston Redskins snatched Smith. In the *Boston Globe* on October 25, 1981, Smith told how easy it was for a first-round pick to sign at the time: "You know the big change between football now and then? The money: There just wasn't no money in the game then. I had about three or four conversations on the phone and, what the heck, I signed. I got $250 a game."

Smith started immediately and impressed the local media. After he kicked a field goal and two extra points in a 26–3 early season win over the Eagles, the *Globe* wrote the following before a game against the Brooklyn Dodgers: "Riley Smith, ex-Alabama star, will be at the signal-calling berth, and the demonstration which he gave at Philly proved that he's the answer to the Redskins' prayers for a capable field general. He's cool and calm under fire and has that football instinct which compels him to train his guns where they will do the most damage. Besides his sagacity, he also boasts of a placement toe which will ring up plenty of three pointers for the gridiron Tribe during the course of the ensuing campaign."

Smith had a hot toe in the 1937 NFL championship game, when he kicked four extra points on the frozen turf at Chicago's Wrigley Field in a 28–21 win over the Bears. He quit football after the 1938 season, telling the *Globe* in 1981 that he walked away because of his skimpy salary.

## DICK STANFEL

OG, No.60, San Francisco • 6–3, 230 • **NFL Career:** 1952–58 (7 seasons) • **Redskins Years:** 1956–58 (3) • NFL 1950s All-Decade Team • **Born:** July 20, 1927 (San Francisco, Calif.)

Dick Stanfel was ready to hang up his cleats. The Lions standout offensive guard had played in 1955 with three broken bones in his back and was aching all over. Then the phone rang. Redskins coach Joe Kuharich, Stanfel's college coach at San Francisco, called to ask if he'd come to the nation's capital via a trade. "I said, 'Yes, if you make a trade, I'll go," Stanfel recalled. Sure enough, in a deal that involved four teams, Stanfel signed on with the Redskins, who couldn't have asked for much more out of the powerful run blocker.

Stanfel made the Pro Bowl and earned unanimous first-team All-Pro honors in each of his three seasons in Washington. Combine that with two Pro Bowls and two consensus first-team All-Pro years in Detroit, and he was named to the NFL's All-Decade Team of the 1950s. He has been a finalist for enshrinement into the Pro Football Hall of Fame.

Stanfel's blocking was instrumental to the success in 1957 of the Redskins' "lollypop" backfield of rookies Don Bosseler, Jim Podoley, and Ed Sutton. The threesome combined that year for 1,522 rushing yards and 20 touchdowns, and often ran behind the 6–3, 230-pound Stanfel, who "blasts out holes for

Washington's fleet rookie running backs," United Press sportswriter Bob Serling wrote on October 30, 1957.

Serling quoted Redskins assistant coach Mike Nixon as saying that Stanfel's efficiency rating, or how he carried out his blocking assignments, was around 85 percent at the time, down from what Serling called an "almost unbelievable" 92 percent in 1956.

"He was super great," Bosseler said. "In my mind, he's one of the best guards who ever played the game. He could stop anybody, I don't care how big or strong they were. He was tough. There wasn't anybody better than Dick Stanfel at that time as a guard. Dick was strong and quick and would pull fast."

Stanfel, who played on the right side, was talented at blocking straight ahead and pulling to the outside. He mostly preferred the latter so he could lead a run "where a guy could go for 20 or 30 yards," he said. In his three seasons in Washington, he also provided pass protection for one of the most exciting Redskin quarterbacks ever, Eddie LeBaron.

Stanfel said that he learned many of his blocking techniques at San Francisco from Kuharich, a great guard at Notre Dame in the 1930s who later played for the Chicago Cardinals. After earning All-American honors, Stanfel was drafted in the second round in 1951 by the Lions, but a knee injury in a college all-star game forced him to miss the season. His first official year was 1952, when Detroit won its first of two straight NFL championships, followed by a Western Conference title.

After retiring from the game, Stanfel went to Notre Dame in 1959 to coach under his mentor, Kuharich, who had departed the Redskins at the same time. Stanfel established himself as an outstanding line coach and stayed with the Fighting Irish for four seasons, before coaching one year at California. He then followed Kuharich back to the NFL with the Eagles in 1964.

Stanfel later served as an assistant with the 49ers, Saints, and Bears; he had a 1–3 record as the Saints' interim head coach in 1980. In Chicago, where he was an assistant from 1981 to 1992, he built a great offensive line and won a Super Bowl ring in the 1985 season. In all, he coached for more than three decades.

## GEORGE STARKE

OT, No. 74, Columbia • 6–5, 260 • **NFL Career:** 1973–84 (12 seasons) • **Redskins Years:** 1973–84 (12) • **Born:** July 18, 1948 (New York, N.Y.)

When attending Ivy League Columbia University in New York City, George Starke didn't want to be a pro football player. After all, he had turned down full athletic scholarship offers from elite football programs such as Notre Dame, Ohio State, and Southern California. The math and physics major, who played on Columbia teams that went 4–14 in his two seasons there, wanted to be a physicist.

It's funny how career goals can get derailed. Starke played 12 seasons as an offensive right tackle for the Redskins, the last three as a member of the famed Hogs offensive line. "For a guy out of little Columbia University . . . to be able to go to the school I went to, get the education I got, at the same time come out of there, make it in pro football, then to captain the team for seven seasons, it's like a dream. Then to play with so

many great players, to be on the field with Sonny Jurgensen, John Riggins, Charley Taylor, Pat Fischer, Larry Brown, Chris Hanburger. That's glory."

Starke was in the twilight of his 12-year career when the Hogs were born in the early-1980s. He earned the title of "Head Hog" because of his seniority in the group, which included players who were about a decade younger than him. He served as a mentor to the young piglets. "I was doing for them what guys were doing for me when I came into the league," he said.

"[Starke] was a veteran when we were first formed," said Hog Russ Grimm, a rookie in 1981. "He was like the statesman. He wasn't at the tail end of his career but at the back end. George was a 260-pound tackle, and the younger guys coming in were getting bigger, stronger, faster every year. But George was a good player, a good technician."

Born and raised in New Rochelle, New York, Starke was a high school All-American and later played tight end and defensive end at Columbia, catching 35 passes for 478 yards. He also started as a 6–5 center and forward on Lions basketball teams ranked as high as fourth in the nation. He remembers receiving a call before the 1971 NFL draft from Redskins coach George Allen: "He said, 'Look, we're going to draft you. But I see you're a tight end. The Redskins already have a great tight end named Jerry Smith. Can you play anything else besides tight end?' I'm thinking off the top of my head. 'Probably tackle.'"

Starke went in the 11th round, but Allen traded him after training camp to Kansas City, which cut him before the 1971 season. He sat out the year and signed with Dallas the next summer, but the Cowboys released him after he lost out to rookie and Amherst grad Jean Fugett, a future Redskin, for a tight end spot. "It was kind of interesting that the Cowboys had a Columbia guy and an Amherst guy fighting for the same spot," Starke said. "Amherst isn't Ivy League, but it's close enough."

Washington immediately claimed Starke as a free agent, but he spent the 1972 season on the taxi squad. A Starke reality then set in: In a roller-coaster ride spanning two seasons, he had made four stops with three different teams without playing in a regular season game. "I wasn't sure I was going to make it," he said.

But when veteran right tackle Walter Rock was asked to sit out the fifth game of the 1973 season because of a bad ankle, Starke got a break. He was activated and started in Rock's place in a Redskins win over the Giants in New Haven, Connecticut, at the Yale Bowl, where he had also played in college. He saw more playing time that year and took over as the starting right tackle heading into the 1974 campaign.

Starke crafted a streak of 65 straight starts that ended due to injury in 1978. He soon regained his starting role and held it until he retired after the 1984 season. By then, he had gone from being what he called a "baby" on the Over the Hill Gang, which made the playoffs three times while he was on the active roster, to his senior citizen status on the Hogs, with whom he made three playoff appearances and won a Super Bowl ring.

Starke never realized his goal of becoming a physicist, but the eccentric fellow, who read newspaper editorial pages in the locker room before games, formed a number of businesses during his playing days, including film production and distribution companies that promoted Reggae music. He also dabbled in acting. A political activist, he dated the daughter of ex-Vice President Walter Mondale, a Democrat, and the daughter of billionaire minerals industrialist Charles Engelhard, Jr. He appeared as a sportscaster on several Washington television stations.

"I was just a different kind of cat," said Starke, whose nickname was "Silk." "My teammates accepted me for being a different kind of cat."

# DIRON TALBERT

DT, No. 72, Texas • 6–5, 255 • **NFL Career:** 1967–80 (14 seasons) • **Redskins Years:** 1971–80 (10) • **Born:** July 1, 1944 (Pascagoula, Miss.)

Diron Talbert looked like somebody you didn't want to mess with. He personified one menacing dude. "With a thick mustache, a tobacco chaw in his cheek and his sweaty cloth cap pulled down low over his brow, Talbert looks like a tough hombre even in practice," Steve Guback of the *Washington Star* once wrote.

Talbert was no pussycat in games, either, where the performance of the long-time Redskins defensive tackle was predicated largely on intimidation. The 6–5, 255-pounder with Goliath-size hands relied on the single- and double-head slap, which was legal through his first 10 seasons, and once in a while popped an opponent in the head with a forearm if nothing more than as a friendly greeting, although he stresses that he wasn't a dirty player.

Big ol' Diron also specialized in talking trash in his deep southern drawl in hopes of rattlin' and distracting his foes. After a sack, he would tell the quarterback, "Hey, I got you again," or "This is just too damn easy." Before the ball was snapped, he would ask an offensive lineman, "How's the family, how are the kids?"

"Anything silly," he said. "Sometimes, they'd think I'm crazy."

Talbert's tactics worked. He posted 56 sacks in 10 seasons as a Redskin, the fifth-highest total in franchise history, and helped anchor the imposing Redskins defenses of the 1970s that served as the backbone to five trips to the playoffs, including a Super Bowl appearance. He also recovered 10 fumbles. (Sacks became an official NFL statistic in 1982.)

"You look at Diron with his shirt off, he didn't have big, bulging muscles," said Bill Brundige, a Redskins defensive lineman who played with him for seven seasons. "In fact, he was kind of skinny. But he had tremendous hands and that natural strength you see in farmers. They don't have big, bulging muscles, but by God they can lift a bale of hay. And he was very quick and had a sense for the game. All great players have to have a sense for the game."

Talbert was raised on a farm in Mississippi before ending up in the oil refinery town of Texas City, Texas. He developed a much-needed toughness growing up the youngest of three brothers. "We didn't fight a lot, but we did a lot of pushing and shoving," he remembered. "I didn't have a choice."

Talbert's older brothers, Don and Charlie, starred in football at Texas, and Diron followed in line. (Don had a 10-year NFL career.) Playing under famed Longhorns coach Darrell Royal, he received honorable mention All-American honors as a defensive tackle in 1965, his junior year, and was drafted in the fifth round by the Los Angeles Rams. He remained at Texas as a senior and joined the Rams in 1967.

He missed most of his rookie year because of an injury but played in every game in 1968, rotating between tackle and end. He won a starting job the next year at defensive end and started at right tackle in 1970, remaining in that spot the rest of his career.

Talbert recorded 16 sacks in one of his four seasons in Los Angeles, a period when he played with future Hall of Famers in tackle Merlin Olsen and end David "Deacon" Jones, pillars on the Rams' intimidating defensive line known as the "Fearsome Foursome." Talbert learned the head slap from Jones, who is credited with patterning the technique.

When Talbert's coach in Los Angeles, George Allen, went to the Redskins after the 1970 season, Talbert wanted to follow the defensive mastermind to D.C. He got his wish on January 28, 1971, when Allen traded for six Rams who became known as the "Ramskins." Talbert liked the reunion. "I felt very comfortable to look up in the huddle and see some of the faces I already knew," he said. "We had about six or seven coaches that came over from L. A., too. It was fun."

Allen knew he had a great player in Talbert. "Talbert is one of the best 10 or 12 tackles in the league," the coach said in Bill Gildea's and Kenneth Turan's 1972 book, *The Future Is Now.* "He is more desirable than Deacon Jones or Merlin Olsen

---

## Diron's Quirks

In addition to serving as Redskins' defensive captain for a number of years, Diron Talbert took on some peripheral roles:

- In the early 1970s, he passed out caps that his buddies wore in practice; the caps promoted such companies as Goodyear, Miller, and Budweiser. The NFL ordered the "mad-hatter" to stop it. "The league did not like that at all," Talbert said emphatically. "You've got people paying big bucks for one-minute TV ads, then you get a 20-second up-close shot for free of a [Redskin] with one of those hats on."

- He nicknamed teammates. Linebacker Jack Pardee, for instance, was known as "Gabby" because he didn't talk a lot, and cornerback Pat Fischer took on the moniker "Dow Jones" because he worked as a stockbroker. Talbert, suspicious of the press, called Redskins who were quoted as unnamed sources in newspapers "stoolies."

- He made inflammatory remarks about the Cowboys, particularly quarterback Roger Staubach, as the marquee rivalry intensified to new heights in the 1970s.

- He launched the 5 O'clock Club, a group of players who met in a shack at Redskin Park after practice and drank cold beer. Charter members included Talbert, Ron McDole, Len Hauss, Billy Kilmer, and Sonny Jurgensen.

because his future is ahead of him. He sacked quarterbacks 16 times by himself last season. Think of that, 16 times."

Talbert made second-team All-Pro in 1973 and followed with his only Pro Bowl appearance in 1974. In a season-opening 49–13 win over the Giants in 1975, he sacked quarterback Craig Morton a team-record four times; two other Redskins have since tied that mark.

"Craig was a good friend of mine, and every time I sacked him he'd say something real nasty to me," Talbert said. "The last time I sacked him we were way ahead in the fourth quarter, and I told him, 'Craig, I got some bad news, they're not taking me out.'"

Meanwhile, the head slap remained a huge part of Talbert's game. Before the 1977 season, however, he learned that the NFL was planning to implement what became known as the "Deacon Jones rule." "I had a good sack record going," he said. "I had a lot of years where I'd get 10 or 12 sacks, 13. And George Allen called me that summer [of 1977] and said, 'Talbie, I've got some bad news.' I thought he was going to tell me he was firing me. He said, 'They're going to outlaw the head slap.' I said, 'You've got to be kidding me.' He said, 'No. It's going to happen this year. They're in meetings right now.' He said it's like taking a microphone away from an announcer."

Talbert competed in 154 straight games until a knee injury sidelined him late in the 1978 season. Overall, he saw action in 142 of 146 games as a Redskin, including seven playoff games.

"He was one of the good ol' boys who played very hard, played a long time," said fellow Redskins defensive tackle Dave Butz, a teammate of Talbert's for six seasons. "He was a cohesive piece of the defensive line."

## HUGH TAYLOR

E, No. 84 (also wore No. 28), Tulane; Oklahoma City • 6–4, 190 • **NFL Career:** 1947–54 (8 seasons) • **Redskins Years:** 1947–54 (8) • **Born:** July 6, 1923 (Wynne, Ark.) • **Died:** November 1, 1992 (Wynne, Ark.)

When Hugh Taylor debuted with the Redskins in 1947, he was a mere walk-on, a virtual unknown. He left the squad seven years later as the most prolific receiver in team history at the time.

He did it with a body that appeared vulnerable to cracking. With a wiry 6–4, 190-pound frame, hence his nickname "Bones," Taylor looked more like a basketball player than one of the NFL's finest receivers. But his physique was really a source of torment for defenders, for what he lacked in muscle he made up for in speed. He escaped those trying to catch him with beautiful fakes and long strides that made it seem he was galloping.

For every four of his catches, one was a touchdown—an amazing feat. "His secret is that he can clip off six yards in two steps," Jack Walsh of the *Washington Post* once wrote. "That means Bones has a stride of nine full feet. When you consider that a thoroughbred race horse has one of approximately 20 feet, you can see that Taylor is making the maximum use of those long legs of his."

"Bones was great," said Jim Ricca, a Redskin lineman who teamed with him for three seasons. "He was big, skinny, tall, and fast as greased lightning. We only had one wide receiver we threw to, and it was Bones."

Taylor set all-time Redskins marks of 272 receptions, 5,233 receiving yards, 58 touchdown catches, and 348 points, all of which have been broken. He holds the team records for career receiving average (19.2 yards) and single-season average (23.4), and is in a four-way tie for most single-season TD catches (12). He made the Pro Bowl twice.

An Arkansas native, Taylor attended Tulane University in New Orleans, where he was an all-conference basketball player. After serving almost four years in the navy, he went to Oklahoma City University and starred in baseball, basketball, and football. After his final season, 1946, he was not selected in the NFL draft and considered pursuing a baseball career, hoping to play for his favorite team, the Brooklyn Dodgers.

At the same time, the Redskins got lucky. Head coach Turk Edwards was browsing through a football magazine when he came across an item about Taylor catching nine touchdown passes in a 41-minute span at Oklahoma City. Taylor had not been picked as an All-American and no scouts had contacted him, but Edwards wrote to him with an enclosed contract. It came back signed in four days. "I was about to sign with another team," Taylor told Edwards, "but I'm signing with you because I always wanted to catch Sammy Baugh's passes."

Taylor got his wish and more, becoming the favorite target of the famous Redskins quarterback. The two hooked up right away. In Taylor's first game, on September 28, 1947, "the gangly newcomer," as the *Washington Post* called him, caught 62-, 36-, and 18-yard touchdown passes. Taylor also caught a 56-yard pass, as well as Baugh's 1,000th career completion. His 212 receiving yards that day set a league record for a player in his first game and held for 56 years.

What a smashing debut! "I just kept thinking at the time, man, this is so easy," Taylor told long-time *Washington Star* reporter Steve Guback in 1986.

Taylor proceeded to become one of the league's most dangerous receivers. He led the NFL with nine scoring catches in 1949 and a 21.4-yard reception average in 1950. But his best season was 1952, when he returned from knee surgery and set team records with 12 touchdown catches, 961 receiving yards, and a 23.4 average per reception.

There were no "wide receivers" during Taylor's era, and he was listed as an end. As he told Guback, the Redskins weren't that concerned with his blocking and began splitting him away from the offensive line about four yards. The move gave birth to the term "split end." "They tell me I was the first split end," Taylor said. "In fact, [legendary NFL forward passing authority] Sid Gillman still refers to the split end as the 'Taylor position.' Of course, it wasn't long before everybody was doing it."

The 1954 season, Taylor's last as a Redskin, marked the sixth straight year he led the squad in receptions, yards gained, and touchdown catches. And he went out, just as he had entered the league, in style, with a three-touchdown game—the fifth of his career—in a 37–20 win over the Chicago Cardinals on December 12, 1954. It was his 92nd straight game in a Redskins uniform.

Taylor fell into a contract dispute with Redskins owner George Preston Marshall after the season and went to play in Canada. After retiring from football, he made several coaching stops, including a stint as an assistant under Baugh for the New York Titans of the American Football League in the early1960s. He was head coach of the AFL's Houston Oilers in 1965, when they finished 4–10.

Taylor caught 58 scoring passes, a Redskins record when he departed after the 1954 season.

"He was probably as good a deep receiver as I ever played with," Eddie LeBaron, a great Redskins quarterback in the 1950s, said of Taylor. "He was as good as anyone in the league at that time."

## JOE TERESHINSKI

E-LB, No. 37 (also wore No. 89), Georgia • 6–2, 220 • **NFL Career:** 1947–54 (8 seasons) • **Redskins Years:** 1947–54 (8) • **Born:** December 7, 1923 (Glen Lyon, Pa.)

They didn't call him "Terrible Terry" for nothing. Joe Tereshinski was a rugged two-way end and linebacker who brought a special nastiness to the game. Opponents feared him. A Redskins game program story under the headline, "Enemies Have a Name for Joe Tereshinski—It's Terrible Terry," said it all:

> In the Bears-Redskins game of 1947, a news photographer overheard a Bears player shout, "Hey, that Redskins end, Tereshinski, just broke his arm!"
>
> The photog swears that Hunk Anderson, then Bears' line coach, rubbed his hands together gleefully and grunted, "Good!"
>
> All of which is not at all kindly, but it is definitely complimentary. It meant the Bears were glad to get Joe Tereshinski out of there and made no bones about it because the ex-Georgia wingman already in his first season had established himself as one of the roughest, toughest ends in the National Football League.

Tereshinski played end for about the first two-thirds of his eight-year Redskins career and spent his last two seasons mostly at linebacker. With receiver extraordinaire Bones Tay-

lor at the other end, Tereshinski focused mostly on blocking, and he was quite good at it, too. "I was a pretty good blocker, and I enjoyed it," said Tereshinski, who caught 43 passes for 451 yards and four touchdowns. "When we needed a few yards in the running game, the off-tackle play was usually called, and my job was to block the tackle in front of me. They usually outweighed me by quite a few pounds and were often the best defensive people on the field."

Tereshinski retired after the 1954 season and spent the next five seasons as the Redskins' ends coach. He was an offensive assistant at South Carolina in 1960.

In his college days, Tereshinski was an All-American end at Georgia. The Tereshinksi-Georgia connection has lived on. Both of his sons, Joe and Wally, played football for the Bulldogs, and a grandson, Joe, just finished his career at Georgia.

## JOE THEISMANN

QB, No. 7, Notre Dame • 6–0, 192 • **NFL Career:** 1974–85 (12 seasons) • **Redskins Years:** 1974–85 (12) • **Born:** September 9, 1949 (New Brunswick, N.J.)

From the time Joe Theismann first donned football pads as a 12-year-old, winning followed him everywhere. He quarterbacked Pop Warner and high school teams that went undefeated, a Notre Dame squad that played in back-to-back Cotton Bowls, and a Canadian Football League team that reached the Grey Cup, the league's championship.

The Redskins profited from his winning ways, too. He started under center on teams that made the playoffs four times in the 1980s and went to two Super Bowls, winning once. In fact, he is one of the best Redskins quarterbacks ever. In 12 seasons in D.C., he tallied 25,206 passing yards, 2,044

## Joe Theismann at Work

During his playing days, it seemed Joe Theismann never had a promotional opportunity he didn't like. He was extremely shrewd at marketing himself.

He owned restaurants. He endorsed shoes, cameras, and many other products. He published several editions of a book called *Quarterbacking*. He did motivational speaking. He co-hosted a morning TV talk show, *Good Morning Washington,* and a weekly TV show, *Joe Theismann's Redskin Report.* He worked as a disc jockey at a local radio station. "Hollywood Joe" also appeared in several movies, including *The Man with Bogart's Face* and *Cannonball Run II,* and played a part in the television series *BJ and the Bear.*

Theismann also was involved with a host of charities and stood on the corporate board of Children's Hospital. He was named NFL Man of the Year in 1982 for his work in the community. A superb all-around athlete, he went to the world finals in TV's "Superstars" competition.

The garrulous fellow was almost always accessible to reporters, mindful of a possible payoff down the road. "If I was respectful of the press, if a guy asked me for an interview, and I took the time to give it to him, maybe an endorser might say, 'Hey, let's take a chance on this guy,'" he said. "Back in the 1970s and 1980s, we didn't have the size of the contracts that exist today. You didn't have the car deals and apparel deals. I think I got $5,000 to wear shoes. That was phenomenal, it was huge money."

Former Redskins beat writer Steve Guback of the *Washington Star* knew to turn to the "king of the 30-second" sound bite when he needed a good quote. "There's the line that I've used that when Theismann opens the refrigerator and the light comes on, he'd start talking," Guback said. "Or put the pencil on the pad, and he'd start talking."

completions, and 3,602 attempts, all franchise records, plus 160 touchdown passes. He played in 163 straight games, third most in Redskins history.

Theismann leaves no doubt that he hates failure: "I got a taste of winning early, a taste of competition early in my life. People always told me I was too small, too fragile, too light. But I never adhered to or listened to what other people thought of me. And I always competed against people who were older or better than I was. The bar was always set so high for me. So I guess you could say my ego started a long, long time ago."

What an enormous ego it was. You see, Joe Theismann craved the spotlight. It was his world, his domain. A blend of flamboyance, charisma, and cockiness, and a man always dressed for success off the field, he used the media, product endorsements, entrepreneurial endeavors, corporate appearances, and Hollywood to mold himself into a thriving business that far exceeded his earnings from playing football. A 1980 *Washington Post* headline read, "Joe Theismann Incorporated."

Theismann's self-absorption rubbed some people the wrong way. He was loved, hated, castigated, and respected. He saw himself as a combination of egotism and self-confidence at the time. "There's absolutely no question I was a total egomaniac," he said. "Every way, any way I could promote myself, I tried. As I grew older, you understand that you have to have an ego, but you don't have to tell everyone you have one. Let your performance show your abilities."

One of his long-time Redskins teammates, offensive tackle George Starke, said Theismann's flair for self-promotion was a popular topic among people outside of football but never distracted his fellow Redskins. "It doesn't matter what your business is, whether you're a writer or a ditch digger or a football player or a policeman," Starke said. "What you want of your co-workers is that they give you a day's work for a day's pay. And Theismann always gave you a day's work for a day's pay. Always. I've been on the field when his nose was broken, his teeth knocked out. He never tried to go to the sideline."

Theismann exhibited an athlete's cockiness in his youth, when he was determined to someday become a pro quarterback. He admired several quarterbacks now in the Hall of Fame, including one who played a few miles from his home in northern New Jersey: the Jets' Joe Namath. The brash Namath recorded astronomical passing numbers and made the audacious prediction that his Jets would beat the heavily favored Baltimore Colts in Super Bowl III—and then backed it up with a win. Namath was who Theismann wanted to be.

"I thought he had a presence about him," Theismann said. "He had an aura about him that when he stepped on the field, the other team had to be thinking, 'Oh, crap.' And his teammates had to be saying, 'Let's go.' That was sort of what I wanted to aspire to. I wanted to be able to elicit those types of feelings from the men I played with and the men I competed against."

A three-sport athlete at South River High School in South River, N.J., the 5–10, 150-pound Theismann won football All-American honors as a senior. Many big-time college football programs recruited him, and he chose Notre Dame. He started at quarterback as a junior (1969) and senior (1970) and set a host of of school passing records. As a senior, he was a leading contender for the Heisman Trophy, and Notre Dame's sports information office changed the pronunciation of his name from "THEEZ-man" to "THIZE-man" to rhyme with Heisman. He finished second to Stanford's Jim Plunkett in Heisman Trophy voting and was inducted into the College Football Hall of Fame in 2003.

Theismann was drafted by the Miami Dolphins in the fourth round in 1971 and also received an offer to play shortstop for the Minnesota Twins. He discarded baseball, not wanting to play in a farm system, and came close to a deal with the Dolphins. He even proclaimed on a Miami television station, "Come hell or high water, I'll be a Miami Dolphin." But talks fell through, and he trekked north to play for the Toronto Argonauts of the CFL. He won the Eastern Conference passing title in 1971, when the Argonauts finished 10–4 and lost in the Grey Cup. In three seasons in Canada, he threw for 6,093 yards and used his scrambling ability to run for another 1,054.

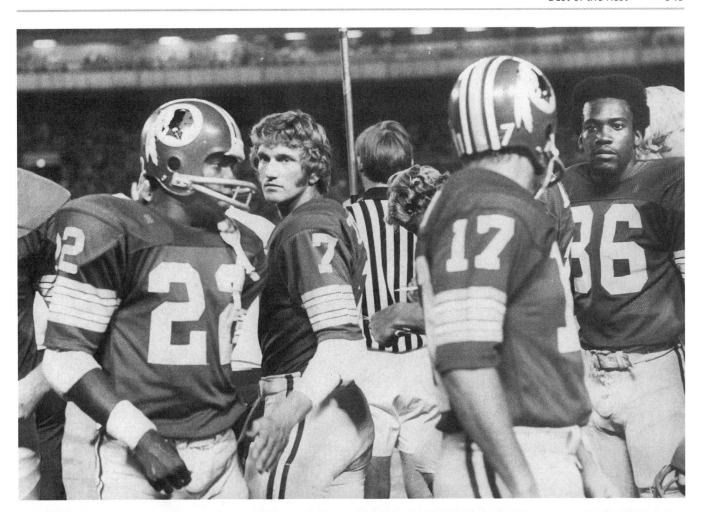

Theismann (7) didn't see eye to eye with veteran quarterbacks Billy Kilmer (17) and Sonny Jurgensen after arriving in Washington in 1974, and he eventually became uncertain about his NFL future. But by the early 1980s, he stood as one of the NFL's elite quarterbacks.

## The Snap Seen 'Round the World

Joe Theismann had one major injury in his 12 seasons in the NFL. That injury, suffered when Lawrence Taylor and his Giants teammates smashed Theismann's right leg on the night of November 18, 1985, ended his career.

"I can only relate to it this way," said Theismann, who had a compound fracture of the fibula and tibia. "If you were to take and lay your leg out over a curb and have a car run over it, that would be about the only way I guess you could imagine the pain. It was the most excruciating, intense pain I've ever felt in my life. That's about the best way to describe it. I wish it on no one.

"When I was laying on the field, coach [Joe] Gibbs knelt down next to me and said, 'This is a heck of a mess you've left me in.'"

After being carted off the field, Theismann was taken to a local hospital and had surgery that turned out to be successful. He remembers Taylor phoning him the day after the injury:

The nurse said, "Mr. Theismann, Mr. Taylor's on the phone, would you like to speak to him?" I said, "Give me the phone. LT, is that you?"

He said, "Joe, how are you doing?"

I said, "Not very well."

He asked why.

I said, "Because you broke both bones in my leg."

He said, "Joe, you have to understand something. I don't do things halfway. I've got to run now. Goodbye."

The injury came at a problematic juncture in Theismann's life. His reputation had deteriorated, a product of his enduring the worst season of his career and his antics off the field. Not long removed from a messy divorce, he was in a popular romance with actress Cathy Lee Crosby and had passed out "Get Hot With Cathy Lee" T-shirts to his teammates. Such behavior did little to endear him to the public or his teammates.

But *Washington Post* columnist Ken Denlinger touted Theismann as a phenomenal leader. "All Theismann eventually did was lead the Redskins to two more Super Bowls than [Sonny] Jurgensen and to one more Super Bowl victory than [Billy] Kilmer," Denlinger wrote shortly after the injury.

Meanwhile, Theismann underwent a long rehabilitation process and vowed to return for his 13th NFL season in 1986. Around the start of training camp, he worked out at Redskin Park before Redskins attorneys, a representative from his insurance company, Lloyd's of London, and his own attorney. He hoped to show he was able to continue playing.

"We were scheduled for about an hour workout," he said. "I rolled out to the right, and I could run and move pretty good. Then when I rolled out and tried to sprint left, I looked like Chester from *Gunsmoke* (a fictional TV character who walked with a noticeable limp). I was just dragging my right leg. This was about five to 10 minutes into the workout. I looked over toward the locker room where everybody had been standing and nobody was there. I went running over and said, 'Hey, guys, I'm not done.' One of them said to me, 'Oh yes you are.'"

Theismann's injury stunted a possible Hall of Fame career, but in hindsight he considers it a blessing. He has been a preliminary nominee for Hall of Fame induction but is a long shot to be enshrined. "I looked at it as an opportunity to go forward with my life and really work on myself as a person because, to be honest, I wasn't a very nice person," he said. "When doing lectures, I talk a lot about how that accident changed my life."

---

(In those three seasons, the Dolphins went to the Super Bowl three times, winning twice.)

At that point, Theismann wanted to test his skills in the NFL. The Redskins traded a first-round draft pick to the Dolphins for him before the 1974 season.

Theismann expected to start immediately, but he warmed the bench. The Redskins at the time were coached by George Allen, who loved his veterans, designating the aging Sonny Jurgensen and Billy Kilmer as his top two quarterbacks. Jurgensen and Kilmer became ticked off that Theismann, who wrote a book on quarterbacking before throwing his first pass in the NFL, voiced his desire to start. They mocked the rookie by calling him "THEEZ-man."

"One of his first statements when he came in was, 'God, if I can play in front of these two old men,'" Jurgensen said. "That kind of bonded Billy and me to say, 'We'll see, we'll make sure he stays on the bench, and we'll make him a punt returner,' which he ended up being. He had to wait his turn, but he wasn't ready."

Said Theismann, "My relationship with Billy and Sonny was always very strained. They had a relationship, and I was the odd man out. They had been together for a while, and I wanted what they had. All of us were very headstrong."

Theismann returned punts his first two seasons, averaging 10.5 yards one year, and threw only 33 passes. Disgruntled, he asked Allen to trade him. "I told George, 'Look, obviously, this is a very old football team, and I'm not an old person. Why don't you just trade me, and I'll come back in 10 years when I'm of the age when you want people around here?' He didn't do it. Thankfully, no one would listen to me at that time."

With Jurgy gone, Kilmer and Theismann rotated as starters for two seasons, while fans sounded cries of "We Want Joe" or "We Want Billy." The quarterback controversy got ugly at times. In a 1976 game against the Cardinals at RFK Stadium,

Theismann's career is about to end as Giants linebackers Harry Carson (53) and Lawrence Taylor (56) converge on No. 7. He was carted off the field a few minutes later. It was a "nasty-looking injury," said Redskin Jeff Bostic, who was in at guard on that play. "He was bleeding through his sock."

Theismann was banged up and left the field. After one play and with Allen's consent, he began returning to the huddle. Kilmer, already in the huddle, gave him the thumbs-out sign and stayed in for the rest of the game. Theismann felt humiliated. "I ran off the field, and George said, 'Well, I guess I didn't tell Billy that it was one play,'" Theismann remembered. "I'd earned the job, I won the job, I was the starting quarterback. But paybacks are hell. A few years later, I got knocked to the ground, and Billy came jogging out, and I gave him the thumb. What goes around comes around."

Theismann would see brighter days. After new Redskins coach Jack Pardee named him the undisputed starter for the 1978 campaign, he started each game but completed only 48 percent of his passes. He crafted a breakout year in 1979, however, posting then-career highs in a series of major passing categories, including completion percentage (59) and quarterback rating (83.9).

Washington's offensive coordinator at the time, Joe Walton, has been widely credited with Theismann's maturation as an NFL quarterback. Said Kirk Mee, a long-time Redskins scout and personnel expert:

You didn't know what Theismann would do when he first came up. He scared our team, and he scared the other team. Walton did a great job of getting him to play in a disciplined offense, and he made good decisions. Before, Joe Theismann would scramble, and he'd throw what he shouldn't throw. He'd try to do it all himself, try to make things happen, and many times it didn't happen. He'd throw an interception at an inopportune time. But when Theismann learned from Walton, it got to be where he wouldn't make those mistakes, and he was able to use the players around him better.

When the offensive-minded Joe Gibbs arrived as Redskins coach in 1981, Theismann elevated his game even more, this time to the elite level of NFL quarterbacks. He was the top-rated passer in the NFC in 1982, completing 64 percent of his regular-season throws and 68 percent in the playoffs, when he posted a remarkable 110.8 quarterback rating as the Redskins marched to a win over the Dolphins, the team that drafted Theismann in 1971, in Super Bowl XVII. He made his first Pro Bowl.

By then, he had become a bona fide leader on the Redskins, and he knew that even on bad days, he needed to do whatever it took to win. Case in point: In a late-season game against the Giants in 1982, he threw four interceptions. He also had two front teeth knocked out on a sack in the first half. But he made a play that epitomized his competitiveness and pugnacity. With the Giants up in the second half, 14–3, he sacrificed himself by throwing a crushing body block that allowed tailback Joe Washington to finish off a 22-yard touchdown run. The Redskins won, 15–14, qualifying for the playoffs for the first time since 1976.

Gibbs cringed when seeing Theismann with his teeth knocked out. "I'm looking at him saying, 'Man, if there's a time you take it to the house, it would be right now. Come back and find another day,'" the coach once told NFL Films. "Joe turned around and led us down the field for the [winning] score. That tells you, a tremendous competitor, wasn't coming out of there, wasn't giving somebody else the chance to take his job."

Said Joe Washington, "Joe was a leader as far as I was concerned. What showed toughness for me is that he wore a one-bar facemask his whole career. In pass situations, he stood in there just as strong as if he had a 280-pound back blocking for him as opposed to a 175-pound back. Joe was confident, and by having a confident quarterback who feels he can pull out anything, it really rolls off onto the rest of the players."

Theismann started in his second straight Pro Bowl in 1983, his best season statistically as a pro. In quarterbacking the Redskins to Super Bowl XVIII, he recorded a career-best 97.0 passer rating and threw 29 touchdowns and 11 interceptions, the best ratio in Redskins history. He was named league MVP and a consensus All-Pro.

He enjoyed another solid year in 1984 but fell off his game in 1985. He threw seven touchdowns and 16 interceptions through the first 10 games, acknowledging at the time that it was probably his worst year in football. Things got nastier in the 11th game. As he set up to pass, ferocious Giants linebacker Lawrence Taylor came charging through, leaped on his back, and bulldogged him down as other Giants converged on No. 7, shattering his right leg in several places. The horrific-looking play, seen by millions watching the Monday night game, ended Theismann's season. His career was over, too.

One career gone meant the start of another: network sportscasting. Equipped with a dynamic personality and polished public speaking skills, he became a CBS color commentator on NFL games. (He was an ABC color analyst for Super Bowl XIX.) He stayed with CBS for two years and provided color on Sunday night NFL games for ESPN for the next 18 seasons. When Monday night football moved to ESPN in 2006, he stayed on for one season as part of the network's No. 1 Monday night team. He has since been working as an analyst on ESPN Radio and ESPN.com.

## MIKE THOMAS

RB, No. 22, Oklahoma; Nevada–Las Vegas • 5–11, 190 • **NFL Career:** 1975–80 (6 seasons) • **Redskins Years:** 1975–78 (4) • **Born:** July 17, 1953 (Greenville, Tex.)

It was 1975, and the Redskins were in desperate need of a productive running back. The season before, Larry Brown had led an anemic running game with *430* yards, and the knees of the once great runner were shattered.

To top it off, the Redskins had no draft picks that year until the fifth round. Still, a running back was available, one who had rushed for more than 3,000 yards in two seasons at Nevada–Las Vegas: Mike Thomas.

"Prior to the draft, coach [George] Allen said something like, 'Wouldn't it be great if we could get another Larry Brown like we did [in] the eighth round in 1969,'" Mike Allman, then the Redskins' head of college scouting, once said in the *Washington Star*. "When the fifth round started, Roosevelt Leaks and Thomas were still there. I said, 'It'll be tough to pass up Leaks, even with the question about his knee. But I've got to check on Thomas. He should be picked by now."

The Redskins used their fifth-round pick (108th overall) on Thomas, who turned into the dynamic runner Allen was seeking. He rushed for 3,360 yards in four seasons as a Redskin, the second-most in team history at the time behind Brown. He also caught 192 passes for 2,011 yards and scored 30 touchdowns.

"When Larry Brown was kind of at the end of his career, Mike came in and played a few good years for us," said Redskins quarterback Billy Kilmer, who teamed with Thomas for four seasons. "Mike was a good, tough little back. He wasn't big, but he was very quick. He had good instincts and could catch the ball out of the backfield."

In college, Thomas originally enrolled at Oklahoma and ran 90 yards for a touchdown the first time he touched the ball. But an injury forced him out of the lineup, and he transferred to Nevada–Las Vegas. He gained 1,741 yards one year and was named an All-American.

Thomas burst onto the NFL scene early in the 1975 season, recording his first 100-yard game in a Monday night win over St. Louis. He started the last eight games, becoming one of the only rookies ever to start for Allen, who much-preferred veterans, and rushed for 919 yards. He was named NFL Rookie of the Year, the second Redskin to ever receive that distinction.

"As a rookie, Mike Thomas is a rarity," Morrie Siegel wrote in the *Star* during the 1975 season. "Allen's track record for hiring rookies is terrible. He almost regards them as persona non grata."

Despite his stellar season, Thomas felt he was void of the respect he deserved. "I had a great year, but there are a lot of people out there that think it was a fluke or something," he once said. "I gained almost 1,000 yards. Okay, now I've just got to do it again this year, or they'll never believe I'm for real. I guess I need to do it again just for myself, too."

Thomas defied the doubters. He rushed for 1,101 yards in 1976, including a workmanlike 31-carry, 195-yard day, as the Redskins made the playoffs. A hamstring injury bothered him in 1977, when his rushing total slipped to 806 yards. He gained only 533 in 1978, missing three games due to a mysterious sprained ankle while the Redskins were slumping en route to a .500 season.

The Redskins subsequently traded him to San Diego for a fifth-round draft choice. He rushed for 837 yards in two seasons there and retired due to an off-season knee injury. Thomas's brothers, Earl and Jimmy, also played in the NFL.

## RUSTY TILLMAN

LB, No. 67, Arizona; Northern Arizona • 6–2, 230 • **NFL Career:** 1970–77 (8 seasons) • **Redskins Years:** 1970–77 (8) • **Born:** February 27, 1946 (Beloit, Wis.)

He was the ultimate of wedge busters, a player who repeatedly sacrificed his body when motoring downfield to cover kickoffs and punts. A 6–2, 230-pound linebacker, Rusty Tillman saw action on every special teams unit in eight seasons with the Redskins in the 1970s. He enjoyed punt and kickoff coverage the most and used the age-old strategy of hard work to outperform his opponents.

"I always felt that I was an average guy athletically as far as how fast I was and how strong I was," he said. "But by giving 110 percent on special teams, I was able to beat the other guy a lot of times. As soon as I recognized that fact, that's probably when I started getting pretty good on special teams. I realized if you work harder, you try harder, and you give 110 percent all the time, you can be successful."

It was the nascent era of modern-day special teams, and Tillman said that many of his opponents failed to take them seriously. "You watch them on film, you can see they weren't running 100 percent, they weren't blocking 100 percent. You realized that all you had to do was give your best."

Tillman played his college ball at Arizona and Northern Arizona. He was not picked in the 1970 draft, although some teams, including St. Louis, Dallas, and Washington, were interested in signing him as a free agent. He said he picked the Redskins because he wanted to play for legendary coach Vince Lombardi, who was entering his second season in Washington. Tillman, a Wisconsin native, followed the Packers closely during their glory years in the 1960s under Lombardi.

Lombardi died of cancer just before the season and after Tillman's rookie season, along came a new coach who put a lot of stock in special teams: George Allen. Allen expected much from Tillman, a linebacker who evolved into a leader on special teams. "He used to come and talk to me before games, and we'd sit in the back of the locker room and share thoughts," Tillman said. "When we were done, I just felt like I had to win the game, it was all up to me. It wasn't until I quit playing and started talking to some of the other guys that I learned it happened to everybody. He had a way of making every guy feel like they were the most important guy on the team."

Tillman didn't play consistently at linebacker, but his love for special teams never wavered. He was very durable despite repeated injuries, playing in 107 of 122 games and 82 straight over his last six seasons; however, an injury just before the 1978 season sidelined him indefinitely. Another Redskin standout wedge buster of the era, Pete Wysocki, voiced concern about the loss of Tillman in the *Washington Star* on August 10, 1978:

> You just don't replace a guy like Rusty. I mean, they call him "The King of the Special Teams." You don't find in many guys that pride for the special teams.
>
> The guy is like a coach out there. He's made special teams into a science instead of it being just a bunch of young guys waiting around for the old guys to get hurt so they can play.
>
> I remember a game against Cleveland. He was the wedge buster. He leaped up in the air, threw his body across, and knocked down four guys—and then rolled over and made the tackle. I've never seen anything like that."

Tillman called it quits. He has since been an NFL assistant coach for the Seahawks (special teams, 1979–94), Buccaneers (defensive coordinator, 1995), Raiders (special teams, 1996–97), Colts (defensive coordinator, 1998–2000), and Vikings (special teams, 2003–2005). In 2001, he was the head coach of the New York-New Jersey Hitmen in the XFL league, which folded after one season.

"He was a good leader," said Diron Talbert, a Redskins defensive tackle who played with Tillman for seven years. "All the special teams guys liked to play with him. And he was a damn good middle linebacker. He just got stuck on a team where there was somebody a little better than him."

## DICK TODD

HB-DB, No. 41, Texas A&M • 5–11, 172 • **NFL Career:** 1939–42, 45–48 (8 seasons) • **Redskins Years:** 1939–42, 45–48 (8) • **Born:** October 2, 1914 (Thrall, Tex.) • **Died:** November 9, 1999 (Bryan, Tex.)

Dodgin' Dick Todd is one of the most sensational open-field runners to ever play for the Redskins. Loaded with finesse, speed, and amazing moves, he stood as the Redskins' all-time leader in rushing (1,573 yards) and receiving (119 catches, 1,826 yards, 20 touchdowns) on his retirement after the 1948

Dick Todd

season. He was No. 2 in total points (214). Redskins publicists referred to him as the "buzz-saw halfback of Sammy Baugh's era," an apparent reference to his ability to slice through defenders and make them miss. Equally dynamic on defense, Todd intercepted 16 passes. He also returned punts and kick-offs, punted, and kicked extra points.

You name it, Mr. Versatility did it. "He was a great athlete and an exceptional ballplayer," said Joe Tereshinski, a Redskins end who teamed with Todd for two seasons. "He was a very, very fierce competitor. He gave you 100 percent effort."

Todd, a Texas prep football legend, was also a multithreat at Texas A&M. He racked up 3,384 all-purpose yards, still one of the highest totals in school history. He captained the Aggies in football and basketball and competed on the track team. The Redskins drafted him in the third round in 1939.

In the coming seasons, Todd led the Redskins in major statistical categories and gave them a running, receiving, and scoring threat:

- Best rushing average in 1939 (4.7)
- Best receiving average in 1940 (20.1), with four touchdowns apiece on the ground and through the air
- Best receiving numbers in 1942 (23 catches, 328 yards, five touchdowns); played a key role in the Redskins' NFL championship season

From 1939 to 1941, Todd returned one punt each year for a touchdown. After he ran one back 71 yards for a score in a 1941 game against Cleveland, *Washington Post* sportswriter Merrell

Whittlesey wrote, "Early in the first period, the shifty 170-pound punt return specialist who, despite his stature, knows no peer in pro football, stalked under a Parker Hall punt on his own 29-yard line and was off like a shot. He quickly cut by the on-rushing Rams, outdistanced his interference and sped past midfield."

Todd spent two years in the U.S. Navy during World War II. He returned to the Redskins midway through the 1945 season and resorted to his old ways. He posted the team's top rushing averages in 1946 and 1947 and finished No. 1 in receiving in his final season, 1948.

It was no coincidence that Baugh was consistently one of the hottest passers in the league during Todd's tenure in D.C. The two formed a dangerous combo and were also close buddies. Baugh, a fellow Texan whose Texas Christian Hornfrogs played Todd's Texas A&M Aggies in 1936, named his son, Todd, after Dick Todd.

After retiring, Todd coached Texas A&M's backfield for two years. He became Washington's backfield coach in 1950 and was named interim head coach after Herman Ball was fired in 1951 with the Redskins at 0–3. They won five of their last nine games. Todd lost the "interim" label before the 1952 season, but he quit after two exhibition games.

## BOB TONEFF

DT, No. 79, Notre Dame • 6-3, 270 • **NFL Career:** 1952, 54–64 (12 seasons) • **Redskins Years:** 1959–64 (6) • **Born:** June 23, 1930 (Detroit)

Bob Toneff was a rock-solid, run-stopping defensive tackle in six seasons with the Redskins. In each of his first three years in Washington (1959–61), he made the Pro Bowl and received first-team All-Pro honors. He was the Redskins' regular left defensive tackle through the 1963 campaign and shared the position with Fred Williams in 1964, his last season in the NFL. He also played a little defensive end. He never missed a game as a Redskin, playing in 80.

At Notre Dame, Toneff was known to be among the fastest linemen in school history. One sportswriter called him a "one-man wrecking crew." Drafted by San Francisco in the second-round in 1952, he played for the 49ers for six seasons, showing his versatility by performing at defensive tackle, defensive end, corner linebacker, middle guard, and offensive guard. The ironman missed only one game with the 49ers and competed in five games in 1955 with his broken hand in a cast and still won consensus All-Pro defensive honors.

The Redskins traded a No. 2 draft pick for him in 1959. That year, he recovered a league-high five fumbles and shared the Redskins' MVP award with end Bill Anderson, the team's leading receiver that year.

## LAVERN TORGESON

LB-C, No. 53, Washington State • 6-0, 222 • **NFL Career:** 1951–57 (7 seasons) • **Redskins Years:** 1955–57 (3) • **Born:** February 28, 1929 (Lacrosse, Wash.)

LaVern "Torgy" Torgeson completed one of the longest player-coach tenures in Redskins history: 26 years. He spent the first three as a player and the next 23 as an assistant coach on defense.

Torgeson made the Pro Bowl twice and received two-time All-Pro honors as a Redskins linebacker from 1955 to 1957. He also played center.

A fifth-round draft choice of the Lions in 1951, Torgeson was part of an outstanding linebacker corps consisting of such players as future Hall of Famer Joe Schmidt during Detroit's three straight NFL championship game appearances from 1952 to 1954, two of which ended in victory. He showed tremendous instincts and range in pass coverage, intercepting 13 passes in four seasons in Detroit.

Torgeson earned Pro Bowl and All-Pro recognition in 1954 but was traded after the season to the Redskins for middle guard Jim Ricca and defensive end Walt Yowarsky.

"Torgeson, 24, is a key figure in the pro league," Jack Walsh of the *Washington Post* wrote on January 29, 1955. "There aren't many better linebackers than the four-year veteran who was co-captain of the Western Division champions [Detroit]. Most observers here felt that the 'Skins have the edge in the deal because of Torgeson."

Torgeson picked off another five passes in Washington. By the end of the 1957 season, he had played in 94 of 96 games in his career despite many injuries. He sat out the 1958 campaign to strengthen a damaged knee and signed again with the Redskins in 1959 but immediately retired for good.

In retirement, Torgeson had three coaching stints with the Redskins: 1959–61, 1971–77, and 1981–93. He was a member of five Redskin Super Bowl teams, including four in his final stint in D.C., and also coached with the Steelers and Los Angeles Rams. From the time he began playing until his last coaching season, 1993, he spent 43 consecutive years in the NFL.

# DON WARREN

TE, No. 85, San Diego State • 6–4, 240 • **NFL Career:** 1979–92 (14 seasons) • **Redskins Years:** 1979–82 (14) • **Born:** May 5, 1956 (Bellingham, Wash.)

The single-back, two-tight end set up was a staple of the Redskins' offense during their glory years of the 1980s and early 1990s. Year after year, running backs and wide receivers posted solid statistics in the innovative alignment.

Don Warren worked behind the scenes, relatively speaking, to make it click. A terrific blocking tight end and a charter member of the famed Hogs offensive line, the 6–4, 245-pounder was positioned on the line of scrimmage or in the backfield as an "H-back," and plowed ahead to grind out holes. He took on many linebackers and went shoulder-to-shoulder with much bigger linemen. He often stayed in on passing downs to give his quarterback more protection.

"Players such as Lawrence Taylor and Carl Banks [two Giants linebackers] knew the toughest afternoon they'd face would be against the Redskins because of Donnie Warren," Charley Casserly, a Redskins general manager and assistant GM during Warren's career, once said.

In 14 NFL seasons, all with the Redskins, Warren had 244 receptions for 2,536 yards. Starting in 1981, when first-year coach Joe Gibbs implemented the single-back, two-tight end system, his reception totals began to decline, as the Redskins

Don Warren

threw less and less to him but relied so much on his blocking. He averaged 16 catches in his final 12 seasons, with a career-low four in 1992, his last year.

It didn't bother Warren that he was often neglected in the Redskins' passing offense. "Gibbs once said to me, 'Sorry you're not catching a lot of balls, but I hope you understand, I hope you realize how important you are to this football team,'" Warren said. "'You basically have to stay in and help us out, so we can get big plays. Don't get frustrated about not catching a lot of balls.' I told him that if I can play, get Super Bowl rings, make a lot of money and be a part of this great team, I'm going to do whatever I can."

Warren accomplished all of the above, collecting three Super Bowl rings in the process. He's one of four Redskins to play for the franchise in three different decades and saw action in 193 regular season games, one of the highest totals in team history, plus four Super Bowls and all of a possible 19 postseason games.

All along, he was a warrior who insisted on playing with pain and injuries, although many of his contributions went unnoticed. He scraped and clawed with a hard-working, nononsense mentality and put in a rigorous day's work for 14 seasons. "He was just rock solid," said Mark Murphy, a Redskins safety who teamed with Warren for six seasons.

"A lot of the guys pretty much knew there's a difference between pain and injury," said Ed Simmons, a Redskins offensive lineman who also played with Warren for six seasons. "Donnie sometimes couldn't understand. We'd ask, 'Why aren't you coming out? You're still going to get paid.' That's what the buzz was about him. He just loved the game."

A Southern California native, Warren transferred from a junior college to play two seasons at San Diego State, where he caught 56 passes for 711 yards and six touchdowns and earned honorable mention All-American honors. The Redskins first saw him play when general manager Bobby Beathard attended a college all-star game after the 1978 season.

The Redskins took Warren in the fourth round in 1979. He made the roster after battling two fellow San Diego State players, Phil DuBois and Bill Helms, and pushed veteran Jean Fugett out of the starting spot several games into the season. He started 10 games, catching 26 passes, and followed up with a career-high 31 catches in 1980.

After the Redskins opened 0–5 in 1981, Gibbs switched from a pass-oriented system to more of a ground-based attack centered on the single-back, two-tight end setup, which he thought would help neutralize linebackers such as Lawrence Taylor. The two tight ends were Warren and rookie Clint Didier, a much more fluid receiver.

"That offense was fun because it gave you a lot of movement and flexibility," Warren said. "At times, I was a fullback in short-yardage and goal line situations. Sometimes, being the tight end in those situations, I couldn't hear the signals from the end of the line. So I liked lining up in the backfield, where I was basically a human battering ram. I had fun doing that. Teammates would say, 'We're going to take care of everybody except the middle linebacker, so he's yours.' I liked that aspect of football. Hey, either he wins or you win."

After the Redskins' maintained possession for 36 minutes in a playoff win over the Los Angeles Rams on December 28, 1986, Warren was named Redskins Offensive Player of the Game for his tremendous blocking in what was regarded as the team's best ball control job of the season. That year, he also received the Unsung Hero Award from the Redskins Alumni Association given to the Redskin who performs consistently well, often outstandingly, but somehow fails to get the full recognition his play merits.

Warren, nicknamed "Dutch" because of his Dutch-boy haircut, was named to the *Sports Illustrated* NFL All-Pro team in 1989 after catching only 15 passes, further confirming his excellence as a blocker. He didn't appreciate how other tight ends who caught lots of balls but blocked poorly sometimes earned postseason honors.

As much of a fighter as he was, Warren's body broke down in his final two seasons, first with a fractured right ankle that kept him out of six games in 1991 and then with a partially torn rotator cuff that forced him to go on injured reserve in the 1992 season, after which he called it quits. At his retirement press conference on July 16, 1993, an emotional Warren spoke of how the injuries had finally caught up with him: "After 14 years of being a human battering ram . . . it's definitely taken its toll," said Warren, who joined the Redskins as a scout in 2005. "I played 11 games last season on a partially torn rotator cuff, which didn't help. It's kind of ironic because playing while I was injured is the thing that kept me in the league so long. I wasn't going to change."

## JOE WASHINGTON

RB, No. 25, Oklahoma • 5–10, 180 • **NFL Career:** 1977–85 (9 seasons) • **Redskins Years:** 1981–84 (4) • **Born:** September 24, 1953 (Crockett, Tex.)

Joe Washington

They called him "Little Joe" or "Go-Go," a speedy pint-sized running back who was the master at improvisation when handling the ball. The quintessential all-purpose man amassed nearly 9,000 yards in nine NFL seasons, including 4,839 on the ground and 3,413 through the air. He also returned kickoffs and punts.

Joe Washington played four seasons in Washington, often thrilling the Redskins' faithful at RFK Stadium. Despite not playing a full season due to injuries, he rushed 455 times for 2,070 yards (4.6 average) and six touchdowns, and caught 149 passes for another 1,220 yards and 10 scores. "I was really fortunate I could play the way I did and have the kind of impact that I did in such a short period of time," he said.

After his rookie year in San Diego, Washington played three seasons with the Baltimore Colts and made the Pro Bowl for the only time in 1979. The Redskins traded a second-round draft choice to the Colts in April 1981 to acquire Washington, who provided much-needed quickness for an offense bereft of it the prior year. Rotating much of the year with John Riggins in a single-back offense, he led the Redskins in rushing and receiving, totaling 1,500 yards overall. He also caught 70 passes, two shy of the team record at the time.

"Joe Washington is unique," first-year Redskins coach Joe Gibbs said in a *Washington Post* article that season. "He's got that ability to go downfield from the backfield and run good deep patterns. And he knows how to lower his weight and shift his feet instinctively. Once he makes his cut, he really . . . scoots."

Injuries forced Washington to miss most of the 1982 campaign, when Riggins established himself as the team's premier back. He returned in 1983 to provide the perfect complement to Riggins as the speed back. On an offense that scored an NFL-record 541 points, he rushed for 772 yards on 145 carries (NFL-best 5.3-yard average), while catching 47 passes for 454 yards and six scores.

Washington was traded to Atlanta after the 1984 season. He saw action for one season and retired.

As productive as he was as a pro, Washington is best remembered by many for his celebrated college career at Oklahoma. He finished as the Sooners' all-time leading rusher with 3,995 yards and rang up nearly 6,000 overall. He finished third in Heisman Trophy balloting in his junior year, 1975, and was inducted into the College Football Hall of Fame in 2005.

# MARCUS WASHINGTON

LB, No. 53, Auburn • 6–3, 250 • **NFL Career:** 2000–2006 (7 seasons) • **Redskins Years:** 2004–2006 (3) • **Born:** October 17, 1977 (Auburn, Ala.)

Since signing with the Redskins as an unrestricted free agent in March 2004, outside linebacker Marcus Washington has emerged as one of the true leaders on the Redskins' defense. Very physical and equipped with great speed and instincts, he finished second on the team in tackles in 2004 and 2005, recording 130 and 125, respectively. It's no coincidence that the Redskins' defense finished third in the NFL in 2004 and ninth in 2005.

Washington made the Pro Bowl in 2004, when, in addition to tackles, he posted 4.5 sacks and a team-high 11 quarterback pressures. And many people will say he was robbed of a second straight trip to Honolulu in 2005, when he had arguably a better season than the previous year. He made a career-high 7.5 sacks and was named NFC Defensive Player of the Month for December after recording 35 tackles, four sacks, one interception, two forced fumbles, and two fumble recoveries in a five-game span. He was also tapped as The Quarterback Club Redskin Player of the Year.

Washington was a bit surprised that he was overlooked for the all-star game in 2005, but he appreciates that his teammates commend him for his work. "There are so many good players at each position in the NFL that sometimes it's hard to say who deserves to make it," he said. "But the biggest thing for me is when my teammates acknowledge me and say, 'Hey, Marcus, you had a good year. You deserve to make the Pro Bowl,' or 'You go hard every day in practice, it's really tough going against you.' That makes you feel good, my teammates saying that as opposed to other people who may be voting, fans who don't see what's going on here every day or how hard you work in the weight room."

Washington would certainly get the vote of Redskins assistant head coach–defense Gregg Williams. "Marcus Washington is a country-tough, hard-working, bring-your-lunch-bucket-to-work-every-single-day guy," Williams said. "He cares about every single snap, he loves to play the game. Marcus Washington is a leader of the whole Redskins team because of the way he practices."

The linebacker's brilliant performance in the final month of the 2005 season coincided with a five-game winning streak that clinched a playoff berth for the Redskins. In one win, a 35–7 demolition of Dallas, Washington delivered his best game as a Redskin.

No. 53 was all over the place. He sacked quarterback Drew Bledsoe twice, once forcing a fumble that set up a Redskins touchdown, and intercepted a pass that led to another seven points. He also made four tackles, two solo. Wherever the ball was, he pursued it like a shark eyeing its prey.

Washington, the king of enthusiasm, raised his emotional meter several levels during the game. He psyched himself and

Washington plows into Tampa Bay quarterback Chris Simms in a playoff game on January 7, 2006.

his teammates up with screams and aerial maneuvers, and often motioned for noise from the 90,000-plus at FedExField. "It was a huge game," Washington said. "I was just trying to bring the magic back around here. My enthusiasm spreads like wildfire, as you saw tonight. This was definitely Redskins football. Guys work so hard. It's nice to have something to show for it."

Said Redskins defensive tackle Joe Salave'a, "Marcus has the motor of a 12-year-old on a candy cane. It's something special. It's really a cancerous thing to have on your team because it rubs off on everybody else. I'm glad to be a teammate of his."

Washington, who played his first four seasons in Indianapolis, finished third on the Redskins in tackles in 2006, when he sat out the final two games due to injury. Without him, the defense yielded 579 yards to St. Louis and allowed Giants running back Tiki Barber to rush for a career-high 234.

Redskins coach Joe Gibbs was sorry to lose him. "What Marcus brings is just great excitement," the coach said at the time. "He loves to play. He's one of those guys, regardless of the situation, he goes 100 miles an hour. A lot of our players play off that."

# WILBUR WILKIN

T, No. 36, St. Mary's College (Calif.) • 6–4, 265 • **NFL Career:** 1938–43 (6 seasons) • **Redskins Years:** 1938–43 (6) • **Born:** April 21, 1916 (Bingham Canyon, Utah) • **Died:** May 16, 1973 (Palo Alto, Calif.)

Wilbur Wilkin is considered one of the most dominant tackles from the early years of the NFL. A Redskin for six seasons, he was a near-consensus first-team All-Pro in 1941 and 1942. Not only was the 6–4, 265-pounder gargantuan for his day, contrary to his nickname, "Wee Willie," but he possessed excellent speed for his size and tremendous strength. *Collier's* magazine, referring to biblical times, described him as being "just about as strong as Samson was reported to be—maybe stronger." In his book, *The Redskins: 1937–1958,* author Morris A. Bealle called him a "man mountain of bone, muscle and sinew."

A two-way lineman, Wilkin blocked straight ahead, pulled using his nimble feet, and tackled in a way that devastated opponents.

"Wilbur 'Wee Willie' Wilkin is the strongest and one of the fastest men on the Redskins' squad and is one of the greatest tackles in the National Football League," one newspaper wrote in 1940. "He is six-feet-four, weighs 265 and can do the hundred in less than 11 seconds. Is a veritable Gibraltar on defense and likes to block punts by crashing through, bodily picking up a protecting blocker and tossing him into the punter. Performed this feat against Detroit in 1938, setting up a touchdown that beat the Lions, 7–5, and again last year to give the 'Skins the break that led to the touchdown in the 9–7 (loss to) the Giants."

In college, Wilkin starred at tackle at St. Mary's in California but wasn't drafted. According to *Collier's,* Redskins coach Ray Flaherty spotted him in a boxing ring in San Francisco in January 1938 and became enamored of his size and athletic skills: "When 'Wee Willie' was introduced from the ring, Flaherty perked up as he watched the 21-year-old giant strip from his bathrobe. He was further impressed with the easy grace with which the boxer moved about. He didn't see much of 'Wee Willie' in action but what little he did see was impressive. 'Wee Willie' merely stuck out his left, feinted with his right, shifted easily and let go a crashing one-two that laid out his foe colder than a hunk of dry ice in less than a minute."

Flaherty learned about Wilkin's football exploits at St. Mary's and signed him before the 1938 season. Wilkin and another huge Redskin lineman at the time, future Hall of Famer Turk Edwards, formed an intimidating duo.

Meanwhile, Wilkin saw action in his first 57 games and 67 of 69 in his career, including three NFL championships. He was chosen the best lineman in the Redskins' humiliating 73–0 loss to the Bears in the 1940 title game. "But for Willie, the Bears would have run up more than 100 points," Bealle wrote. "It always took two and sometimes three blockers to keep him away from the ball carrier." In the 1942 title game, Wilkin made a critical tackle that contributed to a late goal-line stand in the Redskins' 14–6 win.

Wilkin left after the 1943 season to serve in the U.S. Marines during World War II. He returned to football in 1946, played briefly for the Chicago Rockets of the All-America Football Conference, and retired.

During his playing days, Wilkin was known to live a fast nightlife. He contracted stomach cancer in the early 1970s and died soon after. "Old timers remember blond 'Wee Willie' Wilkin among the first of the mobile big men," *Washington Post* sportswriter Bob Addie wrote shortly before Wilkin's death. "He was 6-foot-6 and weighed 270 pounds, give or take a few cocktails. Wilkin was a versatile man who could play equally well on or off the field."

# DOUG WILLIAMS

QB, No. 17, Grambling State • 6–4, 220 • **NFL Career:** 1978–82, 86–89 (9 seasons) • **Redskins Years:** 1986–89 (4) • **Born:** August 9, 1955 (Zachary, La.)

In four seasons as a Redskin, Doug Williams posted statistics that were pedestrian. He threw for 4,320 yards and 27 touchdown passes, never playing a complete season, mostly because of injuries.

Williams's legacy in Washington and his nine-year NFL career are based on much more than numbers, however. It comes down to this: He smashed the myth that a black quarterback couldn't lead his team to victory on the biggest stage in pro sports: the Super Bowl.

Williams threw for a Super Bowl-record 340 yards and four touchdowns in the Redskins' 42–10 rout of Denver in Super Bowl XXII in January 1988. Nearly all of his production keyed an awe-inspiring second quarter when the Redskins exploded for 35 points in less than six minutes. He was the unanimous choice as Super Bowl MVP.

Afterward, his coach at Grambling State, the fabled Eddie Robinson, called him the Jackie Robinson of his sport, a reference to the black player who broke down racial barriers in Major League baseball. Williams isn't convinced he should be credited with making NFL executives more receptive to signing black quarterbacks, though, saying those that dot the pro football landscape today are not all his doing.

"That's not something for me to say," he said, when asked whether he should be remembered as a pro football pioneer. "When Jackie Robinson came into baseball, I don't think he came in with the idea there would be more blacks, [although] I think he knew it was going to happen. He did what he needed to do because he had an opportunity to get it done. What I accomplished that day is because I was put in position to get it done. It was all about opportunity."

With further introspection, he added, "Now, I made a believer out of a lot of folks who probably never believed it would happen."

For years, Williams had heard that he was ill-suited, whether because of his perceived lack of quarterback skills or his race, to lead a team to an NFL championship. (His career completion percentage is less than 50.) Moreover, many pro football insiders had written him off not long before, pegging the tested veteran as a backup for the rest of his career. Toss in his personal hardships, including an assortment of injuries and the death of his first wife to a brain tumor.

What was he thinking after defying the skeptics and simultaneously reaching the pinnacle of his profession? "I had a lot on my mind," he said. "All the obstacles I had to overcome and a lot of the personal comments that had been made during my career about my ability to play the game, all the doubters. And now, just getting to the top of the game. Tomorrow didn't matter to me, yesterday was all history. In pro football, the

Doug Williams

## PETE WYSOCKI

LB, No. 50, Western Michigan • 6–2, 226 • **NFL Career:**
1975–80 (6 seasons) • **Redskins Years:** 1975–80 (6) • **Born:**
October 3, 1948 (Detroit, Mich) • **Died:** June 14, 2003
(Vienna, Va.)

Pete Wysocki was a wild man, as wild, in fact, as they come. A wedge buster on punt and kickoff coverage who showed a reckless disregard for his body, Wysocki was one of the top special teams players of his day in the NFL. His maniacal approach contributed to a cornucopia of injuries: stress fracture in the right foot, torn ankle ligaments, torn hamstring, cracked ribs, broken left hand, various finger dislocations, hyperextensions in both elbows, separations in both shoulders, chipped teeth, cervical neck injury, five concussions.

Through it all, No. 50 played with pain and never lost his drive to succeed. He missed two games in six seasons in Washington.

"Pete Wysocki was a passionate, gung-ho, dedicated guy, and he was tough," said Kirk Mee, a Redskins personnel executive from 1970 to 1995. "To play in the NFL, you've got to be tough, tough, tough. I'm not talking about tough. I'm talking about tough, tough, tough. Pete fit that bill."

Wysocki earned all-conference honors at Western Michigan, where he was a wide receiver, tight end, and linebacker. He spent four seasons in the Canadian Football League with several teams, once earning All-Pro honors, and signed as a free agent with the Redskins in June 1975.

Redskins coach George Allen, a fanatic about special teams, talked him into coming to Washington. Wysocki wanted to play outside linebacker, but Allen had other ideas. "Pete really thought he had a chance to be a starter in front of [nine-time Pro Bowl linebacker] Chris Hanburger," said Rusty Tillman, the Redskins' special teams captain at the time and another veritable wedge buster. "Anybody who was there knew that was a joke, except for Pete. So he was relegated to special teams."

Wysocki spent his first four Redskins seasons primarily on special teams, outmaneuvering blockers and wiping out return men. He got his first chance to start at linebacker in 1979 and manned the right side in the final nine games, recording 67 tackles and an interception, a sack, and a forced fumble. He was part of the "Pole Patrol," the Redskins' starting linebacker trio of Polish descent that included Brad Dusek and Neal Olkewicz. Wysocki also started at linebacker in 1980, his final season in the NFL.

In 2000, he was diagnosed with non-Hodgkin's lymphoma, a potentially fatal form of cancer, and he died in 2003. His loss hit the Redskins community hard. Wysocki was a very popular player, with a wit and sense of humor one could never forget. Tillman compared his personality to that of comedian and actor Robin Williams.

"Pete was one of my best friends on the team, and he was as funny a guy as I ever met," Tillman said. "Once, we were out at practice, and Pete was screwing up. So I laid it into him. I called him every name in the book for about two minutes. I just ripped him up one side and down the other. I got done, and he looked at me and said, 'Sticks and stones will break my bones, but names will never hurt me.' I thought that was the funniest thing I ever heard."

ultimate is winning the Super Bowl. You can't go any higher than that."

Williams, the No. 1 overall pick in the 1978 draft, was the first black quarterback ever drafted in the first round. He played his first five seasons with Tampa Bay, then two in the United States Football League, before becoming a Redskin before the 1986 season. He was designated a backup to Washington's starter and quarterback of the future, Jay Schroeder. Williams threw only one pass that season. But Schroeder was inconsistent and injury-plagued in 1987, and Williams replaced him in the season finale and paced the Redskins to playoff wins over Chicago and Minnesota. Then came Super Bowl XXII.

"I was happy for him," said cornerback Darrell Green, who played with Williams in Washington. "I know the racism he faced. There was no intention for Doug to play in any games that year. He was there as one of those older players [coach] Joe Gibbs has been known to have, the old guy in the corral to pinch hit or to help the young guys. We were all excited for Doug."

Williams retired after the 1989 season. He completed 1,240 of 2,507 passes with 100 touchdowns and 93 interceptions in his career.

"He was a leader, just an all-out good guy," said wide receiver Ricky Sanders, who caught two of Williams's four scoring passes in Super Bowl XXII and was one of his favorite targets in Washington. "Doug has the heart of a champion. Whatever it takes to win, he's going to do it."

# Appendix

## All-Time Records, Roster, Coaches, Results, Draft Picks, and Pro Bowl Players; Year-by-Year Results; Monday Night Lights; Ring of Fame

### TEAM RECORDS

#### GAMES WON

**Most Consecutive Games Won**

| | | |
|---|---|---|
| 14 | 1942–43 (includes playoffs) |
| 11 | 1991 |
| 11 | 1983 (includes playoffs) |

**Most Games Won, Season**

| | |
|---|---|
| 14 | 1983 |
| 14 | 1991 |
| 12 | 1986 |

**Most Games Won, Season (Including Playoffs)**

| | |
|---|---|
| 17 | 1991 |
| 16 | 1983 |
| 14 | 1997 |
| 14 | 1986 |

**Most Consecutive Games, Without Defeat**

17 (16 wins, 1 tie)...................1942–43 (includes playoffs)

#### GAMES LOST

**Most Consecutive Games Lost**

| | |
|---|---|
| 17 | 1960–61 |
| 8 | 1935 |
| 8 | 1950 |

**Most Games Lost, Season**

| | |
|---|---|
| 13 | 1994 |
| 12 | 1961 |
| 12 | 1993 |

**Most Consecutive Games Without Victory**

23 (20 losses, 3 ties)...................1960–61

#### SCORING

**Most Points, Season**

| | |
|---|---|
| 541 | 1983 |
| 485 | 1991 |
| 443 | 1999 |

**Fewest Points, Season**

| | |
|---|---|
| 55 | 1932 |
| 65 | 1935 |
| 103 | 1933 |

**Most Points, Game**

| | | |
|---|---|---|
| 72 | vs. Giants | 11/27/66 |
| 59 | vs. Yanks | 10/31/48 |
| 56 | vs. Falcons | 1/10/91 |

**Most Points, Both Teams, Game**

| | | |
|---|---|---|
| 113 | Redskins (72) vs. Giants (41) | 11/27/66* |
| 95 | Redskins (47) vs. Packers (48) | 10/17/83 |
| 87 | Redskins (42) vs. Eagles (45) | 9/28/47 |
| 87 | Redskins (42) vs. Cards (45) | 11/22/98 |

**Most Points Overcome to Win Game**

| | | |
|---|---|---|
| 21 | vs. Cowboys | 9/28/65 |
| (trailed 0–21, won 34–31) | | |
| 18 | vs. Giants | 12/2/73 |
| (trailed 3–21, won 27–24) | | |
| 17 | vs. Detroit | 11/4/90 |
| (trailed 21–38, won 41–38 in overtime) | | |
| 17 | vs. Falcons | 9/14/03 |
| (trailed 0–17, won 33–31) | | |

**Most Points Overcome to Tie Game**

| | | |
|---|---|---|
| 21 | vs. Eagles | 12/3/67 |
| (trailed 14–35, tied 35–35) | | |

**Most Points, Opponent, Overcome to win Game**

| | | |
|---|---|---|
| 24 | vs. Eagles | 10/27/46 |
| (led 24–0, lost 24–28) | | |
| 21 | vs. Cowboys | 9/12/99 |
| (led 35–14, lost 35–41) | | |
| 20 | vs. Cowboys | 9/5/83 |
| (led 23–3, lost 30–31) | | |
| 20 | vs. Eagles | 9/17/87 |
| (led 27–7, lost 37–42) | | |

**Most Points, One Half**

| | | |
|---|---|---|
| 43 | vs. Lions (2nd) | 11/14/48 |
| 38 | vs. Giants (2nd) | 11/27/66 |
| 38 | vs. Rams (1st) | 1/1/84† |
| 38 | vs. Cardinals (1st) | 11/9/58 |
| 36 | vs. Cardinals (2nd) | 11/22/98 |

**Most Points, Both Teams, One Half**

| | | |
|---|---|---|
| 65 | Redskins (38) vs. Giants (27) | 11/27/66 |
| 2nd Half | | |

| | | |
|---|---|---|
| 55 | Redskins (13) vs. Bears (42) | 10/26/47 |

2nd Half

| | | |
|---|---|---|
| 52 | Redskins (28) vs. Panthers (24) | 10/3/99 |

1st Half

| | | |
|---|---|---|
| 52 | Redskins (14) vs. Cardinals (38) | 10/22/50 |

1st Half

| | | |
|---|---|---|
| 52 | Redskins (31) vs. Eagles (21) | 10/1/55 |

2nd Half

## Most Points, One Quarter

| | | |
|---|---|---|
| 35 | vs. Broncos (2nd) | 1/31/88[†] |
| 28 | vs. Eagles (3rd) | 10/1/55 |
| 28 | vs. Giants (2nd) | 9/28/75 |
| 28 | vs. Falcons (2nd) | 11/3/85 |
| 28 | vs. Eagles (2nd) | 10/3/99 |
| 28 | vs. Cardinals (4th) | 11/6/83 |

## Most Points, Both Teams, One Quarter

| | | |
|---|---|---|
| 42 | Redskins (21) vs. Eagles (21) | 11/27/83 |

2nd Quarter

| | | |
|---|---|---|
| 42 | Redskins (28) vs. Eagles (14) | 10/1/55 |

3rd Quarter

| | | |
|---|---|---|
| 38 | Redskins (17) vs. Falcons (21) | 9/14/03 |

2nd Quarter

## Fewest Points, Both Teams, Game

| | |
|---|---|
| 0 | 4 times |

(Last Time vs. Giants 10/01/39)

## Largest Margin of Victory

| | | |
|---|---|---|
| 45 | vs. Lions | 9/1/91 |
| 44 | vs. Rams | 1/1/84[†] |
| 42 | vs. Bears | 12/15/74 |
| 42 | vs. Brooklyn | 11/21/39 |

## Largest Margin of Defeat

| | | |
|---|---|---|
| 73 | vs. Bears | 12/8/40[†] |
| 59 | vs. Browns | 11/7/54 |
| 53 | vs. Giants | 11/5/61 |

## Most Touchdowns, Season

| | |
|---|---|
| 63 | 1983 |
| 56 | 1991 |
| 54 | 1999 |

## Fewest Touchdowns, Season

| | |
|---|---|
| 6 | 1932 |

## Most Touchdowns, Game

| | | |
|---|---|---|
| 10 | vs. Giants | 11/27/66* |
| 8 | vs. Falcons | 11/10/91 |
| 8 | vs. Yanks | 10/31/48 |

## Most Touchdowns, Both Teams, Game

| | | |
|---|---|---|
| 16 | Redskins (10) vs. Giants (6) | 11/27/66* |
| 12 | Redskins (6) vs. Eagles (6) | 9/28/47 |
| 11 | Redskins (0) vs. Bears (11) | 12/8/40[†] |
| 11 | Redskins (6) vs. Packers (5) | 10/17/93 |
| 11 | Redskins (5) vs. Eagles (6) | 9/17/89 |

## POINTS AFTER TOUCHDOWNS

### Most PATs, Season

| | |
|---|---|
| 62 | 1983 |
| 56 | 1991 |
| 49 | 1999 |

### Most PATs, Game

| | | |
|---|---|---|
| 9 | vs. Giants | 11/27/66 |
| 8 | vs. Falcons | 11/10/91 |
| 8 | vs. Yanks | 10/31/48 |

### Most PATs, Both Teams, Game

| | | |
|---|---|---|
| 14 | Redskins (9) vs. Giants (5) | 11/27/66* |

## FIELD GOALS

### Seasons Leading League, Field Goals

| | |
|---|---|
| 8 | most recently 1992 |

### Most Field Goal Attempts, Season

| | |
|---|---|
| 49 | 1971* |
| 47 | 1983 |
| 43 | 1991 |

### Fewest Field Goal Attempts, Season

| | |
|---|---|
| 5 | 1940 |

### Most Field Goal Attempts, Game

| | | |
|---|---|---|
| 7 | vs. Oilers | 10/10/71 |
| 6, many times | (most recently vs. Eagles, 12/22/91) | |

### Most Field Goal Attempts, Both Teams, Game

| | | |
|---|---|---|
| 11 | Redskins (6) vs. Bears (5) | 11/14/71* |
| 11 | Redskins (6) vs. Giants (5) | 11/14/76* |

### Most Field Goals, Season

| | |
|---|---|
| 33 | 1983 |
| 31 | 1991 |
| 30 | 1990 |
| 30 | 1992 |

### Fewest Field Goals, Season

| | |
|---|---|
| 0 | 1932 |
| 0 | 1935 |

### Most Field Goals, Game

| | | |
|---|---|---|
| 5, many times | (most recently vs. Vikings, 10/25/92) | |

### Most Field Goals, Both Teams, Game

| | | |
|---|---|---|
| 8 | Redskins (5) vs. Bears (3) | 11/14/71 |

### Most Consecutive Games, Scoring Field Goals

| | |
|---|---|
| 28 | 1988–90 |

## SAFETIES

### Most Safeties, Season

| | |
|---|---|
| 3 | 1989 |

### Most Safeties, Game

| | | |
|---|---|---|
| 1, many times | (most recently vs. Cowboys, 11/5/06) | |

### Most Safeties Allowed, Game

| | | |
|---|---|---|
| 2 | vs. Giants | 11/5/61 |

## FIRST DOWNS

### Most First Downs, Season

| | |
|---|---|
| 353 | 1983 |
| 339 | 1984 |
| 338 | 1989 |
| 338 | 1999 |

### Fewest First Downs, Season

| | |
|---|---|
| 95 | 1935 |

### Most First Downs, Game

| | | |
|---|---|---|
| 39 | vs. Lions (14 rush/25 pass) | 11/4/90* |
| 35 | vs. Bears (9 rush/22 pass/ 4 pen) | 1/26/89 |
| 33 | vs. Packers (12 rush/21 pass) | 10/17/83 |
| 33 | vs. Browns (9 rush/22 pass/2 pen) | 11/26/67 |

### Fewest First Downs, Game

| | | |
|---|---|---|
| 4 | vs. Browns (2 rush/1 pass/1 pen) | 11/7/54 |

### Most First Downs, Both Teams, Game

| | | |
|---|---|---|
| 57 | Redskins (25) vs. Cardinals (32) | 11/10/96 |
| 56 | Redskins (33) vs. Packers (23) | 10/17/83 |
| 56 | Redskins (31) vs. Cardinals (25) | 11/22/98 |
| 55 | Redskins (25) vs. Cowboys (30) | 9/12/99 |

**Fewest First Downs, Both Teams, Game**
10....................Redskins (6) vs. Giants (4).....................12/11/60

**Most First Downs, Rushing, Season**
165..........................................................................1983
154..........................................................................1984
147..........................................................................1985

**Fewest First Downs, Rushing, Season**
55............................................................................1943
55............................................................................1961

**Fewest First Downs, Rushing, Game**
0.........................................vs. Saints.........................10/28/73
0.........................................vs. Dolphins......................10/13/74
0.........................................vs. Cowboys.........................9/6/81
0.........................................vs. Giants.........................12/13/97
1, many times.............................(most recently @ NYG, 10/30/05)

**Most First Downs, Rushing, Both Teams, Game**
36................Redskins (11) vs. Eagles (25)..............12/2/51*
31................Redskins (13) vs. Lions (18).................9/30/51

**Most First Downs, Passing, Season**
217..........................................................................1989
202..........................................................................1988
193..........................................................................1990

**Fewest First Downs, Passing, Season**
55............................................................................1961

**Most First Downs, Passing, Game**
25.........................................vs. Lions.........................11/4/90
22.........................................vs. Bears.......................11/26/89
22.........................................vs. Browns......................11/26/67

**Fewest First Downs, Passing, Game**
2...........................................vs. Cardinals......................9/19/71

**Most First Downs, Passing, Both Teams, Game**
38................Redskins (21) vs. Packers (17)............10/17/83
34................Redskins (11) vs. Cardinals (23)........11/10/96

**Most First Downs, Penalty, Season**
34............................................................................1999
31............................................................................2002
29............................................................................1987

**Fewest First Downs, Penalty, Season**
4............................................................................1944

**Most First Downs, Penalty, Game**
6.........................................vs. 49ers.........................11/12/67
6.........................................vs. Packers......................10/17/83
6.........................................vs. Eagles.......................11/26/00
6.........................................vs. Packers......................10/20/02

**Fewest First Downs, Penalty, Game**
0, many times.............................(most recently vs. Eagles, 12/27/03)

**Most First Downs, Penalty, Both Teams, Game**
12................Redskins (4) vs. Cowboys (8).............12/26/93
10................Redskins (6) vs. Packers (4)..............10/20/02

## NET YARDS GAINED
## RUSHING AND PASSING

**Most Yards Gained, Season**
6,253.........................................................................1989
6,139.........................................................................1983
5,965.........................................................................1999

**Fewest Yards Gained, Season**
2,015.........................................................................1935

**Most Yards Gained, Game**
676.........................................vs. Lions.........................11/4/90
625.........................................vs. Yanks.......................10/31/48
602.........................................vs. Broncos......................1/31/88†

**Fewest Yards Gained, Game**
64...........................................vs. Browns......................11/7/54
97...........................................vs. Colts.......................11/26/61

**Most Yards Gained, Both Teams, Game**
1,045...........Redskins (504) vs. Cowboys (541).................9/12/99
1,031...........Redskins (416) vs. Cardinals (615).............11/10/96
1,027...........Redskins (676) vs. Lions (351)..................11/4/90

**Fewest Yards Gained, Both Teams, Game**
154..............Redskins (103) vs. Giants (51)..................12/11/60

## RUSHING

## ATTEMPTS

**Most Rushing Attempts, Season**
629..........................................................................1983
609..........................................................................1979
588..........................................................................1984

**Fewest Rushing Attempts, Season**
320..........................................................................1943

**Most Rushing Attempts, Game**
64...........................................vs. Rams.......................12/25/51
62...........................................vs. Packers......................10/24/48

**Most Rushing Attempts, Both Teams, Game**
99................Redskins (62) vs. Packers (37).............10/24/48

**Fewest Rushing Attempts, Both Teams, Game**
36................Redskins (21) vs. Lions (15)...............12/5/99

## YARDS GAINED

**Most Yards Gained Rushing, Season**
2,625.........................................................................1983
2,523.........................................................................1985
2,328.........................................................................1979

**Fewest Yards Gained Rushing, Season**
904..........................................................................1944

**Most Yards Gained Rushing, Game**
420.........................................vs. Giants.........................10/8/33
352.........................................vs. Rams.......................11/25/51
307.........................................vs. Falcons......................11/3/85

**Fewest Yards Gained Rushing, Game**
5...........................................vs. Bears.......................12/8/40†
10..........................................vs. Buccaneers...................12/4/94
14..........................................vs. Eagles.......................9/28/47

**Most Yards Gained Rushing, Both Teams, Game**
558..............Redskins (420) vs. Giants (138)..................10/8/33
531..............Redskins (255) vs. Browns (276)...............11/15/59

**Highest Average Gain, Rushing, Season**
4.7...........................................................................1959
4.6...........................................................................1970
4.4...........................................................................1943
4.4...........................................................................1945

## TOUCHDOWNS

**Most Touchdowns, Rushing, Season**
30 .................................................................................................1983
27 .................................................................................................1996
23 .................................................................................................1986
23 .................................................................................................1999

**Fewest Touchdowns, Rushing, Season**
4 ...................................................................................................1977

**Most Touchdowns, Rushing, Game**
6 ........................................vs. Steelers ........................................10/14/34
5 ........................................vs. Browns .........................................10/13/91

## PASSING

### ATTEMPTS

**Most Passes Attempted, Season**
592 ................................................................................................1988
581 ................................................................................................1989
565 ................................................................................................1998

**Fewest Passes Attempted, Season**
113 ................................................................................................1933
152 ................................................................................................1934

**Most Passes Attempted, Game**
63 ...............................vs. Lions (43 comp) ...............................11/4/90
63 ...............................vs. Raiders (32) ..................................10/29/89
60 ...............................vs. Giants (28) ...................................11/23/97

**Fewest Passes Attempted, Game**
7, three times ..............................(last time vs. Giants, 12/11/60)
10 ...............................vs. Cowboys ....................................10/3/71

**Most Pass Attempts, Both Teams, Game**
100 .................Redskins (40) vs. 49ers (60) ...................11/17/86
95 .................Redskins (36) vs. Cardinals (59) ................11/10/96
94 .................Redskins (63) vs. Raiders (31) ...................10/29/89

### COMPLETIONS

**Most Passes Completed, Season**
337 ................................................................................................1989
327 ................................................................................................1988
324 ................................................................................................1999

**Fewest Passes Completed, Season**
34 .................................................................................................1933
44 .................................................................................................1934

**Most Passes Completed, Game**
43 ...............................vs. Lions ...........................................11/4/90
37 ...............................vs. Cardinals ...................................12/16/84
35 ...............................vs. Cardinals ...................................10/11/96

**Fewest Passes Completed, Game**
0 .................................vs. Giants .........................................12/11/60

**Most Passes Completed, Both Teams, Game**
57 .................Redskins (20) vs. Cardinals (37) ................12/16/84
56 .................Redskins (43) vs. Lions (13) .......................11/4/90
54 .................Redskins (17) vs. Colts (37) ........................11/7/93

**Highest Completion Percentage, Season**
64.0 (253 atts/162 comp) ..........................................1982
64.0 (228 atts/146 comp) ..........................................1945
61.9 (444 atts/275 comp) ..........................................1969

## YARDS GAINED

**Seasons Leading League, Passing Yardage**
8, most recently ..............................................................1989

**Most Net Yards Gained, Passing, Season**
4,349 .............................................................................1989
4,136 .............................................................................1988
3,926 .............................................................................1999

**Fewest Net Yards Gained, Passing, Season**
752 ................................................................................1935

**Most Net Yards Gained, Passing, Game**
501 ...............................vs. Yanks .........................................10/31/48
482 ...............................vs. Lions ...........................................11/4/90

**Fewest Yards Gained, Passing, Game**
−32 ...............................vs. Steelers ........................................11/27/55
−28 ...............................vs. Steelers ........................................12/7/58

**Most Yards Gained, Passing, Both Teams, Game**
849 .................Redskins (378) vs. Vikings (471) ...............11/2/86
821 .................Redskins (316) vs. Giants (505) ................10/28/62
771 .................Redskins (368) vs. Packers (403) ..............10/17/83

## TIMES SACKED

**Fewest Times Sacked, Season**
9 ...................................................................................1991
11 .................................................................................1972
17 .................................................................................1971

**Most Times Sacked, Season**
61 .................................................................................1998
52 .................................................................................1977
52 .................................................................................1985

**Most Times Sacked, Game**
9 ...............................vs. Cardinals ...................................10/4/64

## TOUCHDOWNS

**Most Touchdown Passes, Season**
33 .................................................................................1988
31 .................................................................................1967
30 .................................................................................1991

**Fewest Touchdowns Passes, Season**
1 ...................................................................................1933

**Most Touchdowns Passes, Game**
6 ...............................vs. Falcons .......................................11/10/91
6 ...............................vs. Cardinals ...................................11/23/47
6 ...............................vs. Brooklyn .....................................10/31/43

**Most Touchdowns Passes, Both Teams, Game**
11 .................Redskins (4) vs. Giants (7) .....................10/28/62
9 ...................Redskins (3) vs. Rams (6) .......................12/11/49
9 ...................Redskins (5) vs. Bears (4) .......................11/9/58

## PASSES HAD INTERCEPTED

**Fewest Passes Had Intercepted, Season**
9 (253 attempts) .............................................................1982
10 (228) ........................................................................1945
10 (342) ........................................................................1970
10 (470) ........................................................................2006

**Most Passes Had Intercepted, Season**
34 .................................................................................1963
32 .................................................................................1954

**Most Passes Had Intercepted, Game**

| | | |
|---|---|---|
| 8 | vs. Bears | 12/8/40† |
| 7 | vs. Steelers | 12/3/50 |
| 7 | vs. Giants | 12/8/63 |
| 7 | vs. Eagles | 12/21/75 |

**Most Passes Had Intercepted, Both Teams, Game**

| | | |
|---|---|---|
| 11 | Redskins (7) vs. Giants (4) | 12/8/63 |

## PUNTING

**Most Seasons Leading League (Average Distance)**

6, most recently ................................................................1958

**Most Consec. Seasons Leading League (Avg. Dist.)**

4 ...........................................................................1940–43*

**Most Punts, Season**

| | |
|---|---|
| 103 | 2004 |
| 103 | 1978 |
| 97 | 1998 |

**Fewest Punts, Season**

33 ...............................................................................1945

**Most Punts, Game**

| | | |
|---|---|---|
| 14 | vs. Eagles | 11/5/39 |
| 12 | vs. Eagles | 10/4/42 |

**Fewest Punts, Game**

0, many times .........................................(last time vs. Cardinals, 11/5/00)

**Most Punts, Both Teams, Game**

| | | |
|---|---|---|
| 28 | Redskins (14) vs. Eagles (14) | 11/5/39 |

**Fewest Punts, Both Teams, Game**

| | | |
|---|---|---|
| 2 | Redskins (1) vs. Packers (1) | 10/17/83 |
| 2 | Redskins (1) vs. Saints (1) | 11/18/90 |

## PUNT RETURNS

**Most Punt Returns, Season**

| | |
|---|---|
| 61 | 1975 |
| 57 | 1977 |
| 56 | 1987 |

**Fewest Punt Returns, Season**

15 ...............................................................................1960

**Most Punt Returns, Game**

| | | |
|---|---|---|
| 11 | vs. Buccaneers | 10/9/77 |
| 10 | vs. Saints | 12/26/82 |

**Most Punt Returns, Both Teams, Game**

| | | |
|---|---|---|
| 16 | Redskins (11) vs. Buccaneers (5) | 10/9/77 |
| 15 | Redskins (10) vs. Saints (5) | 12/26/82 |

**Most Yards, Punt Returns, Season**

| | |
|---|---|
| 688 | 1976 |
| 610 | 1991 |

**Fewest Yards, Punt Returns, Season**

45 ...............................................................................1970

**Most Yards, Punt Returns, Game**

| | | |
|---|---|---|
| 142 | vs. Giants | 10/11/87 |

**Fewest Yards, Punt Returns, Game**

| | | |
|---|---|---|
| −28 | vs. Cowboys | 12/11/66* |
| −10 | vs. Bills | 11/3/96 |

**Most Yards, Punt Returns, Both Teams, Game**

| | | |
|---|---|---|
| 177 | Redskins (55) vs. Packers (122) | 9/24/50 |

**Most Touchdowns, Punt Returns, Season**

3 .................................................................................1941

**Most Touchdowns, Punt Returns, Game**

1, many times .....................................(most recently vs. Colts, 10/22/06)

**Most Touchdowns, Punt Returns, Both Teams, Game**

| | | |
|---|---|---|
| 2 | Redskins (1) vs. Eagles (1) | 11/9/52* |

## KICKOFF RETURNS

**Seasons Leading League (Average Return)**

8 most recently .................................................................1995*

**Most Kickoff Returns, Season**

| | |
|---|---|
| 78 | 2003 |
| 74 | 1988 |
| 73 | 2006 |
| 71 | 1994 |

**Fewest Kickoff Returns, Season**

23 ...............................................................................1942

**Most Kickoff Returns, Game**

| | | |
|---|---|---|
| 9 | vs. Packers | 10/17/83 |
| 8 | vs. Saints | 9/22/68 |

**Most Kickoff Returns, Both Teams, Game**

| | | |
|---|---|---|
| 19 | Redskins (7) vs. Giants (12) | 11/27/66 |
| 17 | Redskins (9) vs. Packers (8) | 10/17/83 |

**Most Yards, Kickoff Returns, Season**

| | |
|---|---|
| 1,685 | 1994 |
| 1,673 | 1981 |
| 1,646 | 1995 |

**Most Yards, Kickoff Returns, Game**

| | | |
|---|---|---|
| 236 | vs. Browns | 10/15/63 |
| 236 | vs. Eagles | 9/28/47 |

**Most Yards, Kickoff Returns, Both Teams, Game**

| | | |
|---|---|---|
| 453 | Redskins (236) vs. Eagles (217) | 9/28/47 |
| 401 | Redskins (193) vs. Packers (208) | 10/17/83 |

**Highest Average, Kickoff Returns, Season**

28.2 (61 rets/1720 yds) .....................................................1962

**Most Touchdowns, Kickoff Returns, Game**

1, many times .....................................(last time vs. Cowboys, 9/17/06)

## FUMBLES

**Fewest Fumbles, Season**

| | |
|---|---|
| 13 | 1983 |
| 14 | 1990 |
| 15 | 1982 |

**Most Fumbles, Season**

| | |
|---|---|
| 36 | 1976 |
| 35 | 1980 |
| 34 | 2002 |
| 34 | 1988 |

**Most Fumbles, Game**

| | | |
|---|---|---|
| 8 | vs. Steelers | 11/14/37 |
| 8 | vs. Raiders | 10/29/89 |
| 7 | vs. Chargers | 9/9/01 |

**Most Fumbles, Both Teams, Game**

| | | |
|---|---|---|
| 13 | Redskins (8) vs. Steelers (5) | 11/14/37 |
| 13 | Redskins (6) vs. Giants (7) | 11/5/50 |
| 13 | Redskins (4) vs. Cardinals (9) | 10/25/76 |

**Fewest Fumbles Lost, Season**
6................................................................1990
7, many times...............................(most recently, 2006)

**Most Fumbles Lost, Season**
23..............................................................1976
21..............................................................1988

**Most Fumbles Lost, Game**
5.............................vs. Oilers....................10/30/88

**Most Fumbles Recovered, Season, Own and Opponents'**
40 (own 18, opponents 22)................................1984
35 (own 13, opponents 22)................................1976

**Fewest Fumbles Recovered, Season, Own and Opponents'**
12 (6 own, 6 opp).........................................1994

**Most Fumbles Recovered, Game, Own and Opponents'**
10................vs. Cardinals (2 own, 8 opp).........10/25/76

**Most Own Fumbles Recovered, Season**
26..............................................................1940

**Fewest Own Fumbles Recovered, Season**
2............................................................1958*

## TURNOVERS

**Fewest Turnovers, Season**
16..............................................................1982
17..............................................................2006
18..............................................................1996
18..............................................................1983

**Most Turnovers, Season**
46..............................................................1975
46..............................................................1988

**Fewest Turnovers, Game**
0, many times.......................(most recently @ Saints, 12/17/06)

**Most Turnovers, Game**
10.........................vs. Giants....................12/4/38
10.........................vs. Giants....................12/8/63
9..........................vs. Bears...................12/8/40†

**Most Turnovers, Both Teams, Game**
15.............Redskins (10) vs. Giants (5)............12/8/63

**Most Opponents' Touchdowns, Turnovers, Game**
3.............vs. Bears (3 ints)...................12/8/40†
3.............vs. Giants (2 ints/1 fum)...........12/8/63

## PENALTIES

**Fewest Penalties, Season**
40..............................................................1958

**Most Penalties, Season**
124.............................................................2003
122.............................................................1948
117.............................................................1978

**Fewest Penalties, Game**
0, many times....................(last time vs. Panthers, 11/16/03)

**Most Penalties, Game**
17.........................vs. Giants....................9/21/03
17.........................vs. Steelers.................10/10/48
16.........................vs. Yanks...................11/11/45
16.........................vs. Eagles...................11/2/47

16.........................vs. Giants....................10/3/48

**Most Penalties, Both Teams, Game**
32.............Redskins (17) vs. Giants (15)...........9/21/03

**Fewest Yards Penalized, Season**
332.............................................................1939

**Most Yards Penalized, Season**
1,110...........................................................1948
1,045...........................................................2004
1,038...........................................................2003

**Fewest Yards Penalized, Game**
0, many times....................(last time vs. Panthers, 11/16/03)

**Most Yards Penalized, Game**
160.........................vs. Steelers.................10/10/48
152.........................vs. Giants...................10/13/46
150.........................vs. Eagles...................11/24/46

# DEFENSIVE RECORDS

## SCORING

**Fewest Points Allowed, Season**
79..............................................................1932

**Most Points Allowed, Season**
432.............................................................1954
421.............................................................1998

**Fewest Points Allowed, Game**
0, many times....................(last time vs. Eagles, 9/30/91)

**Most Points Allowed, Game**
73.........................vs. Bears...................12/8/40†
62.........................vs. Browns..................11/7/54
56.........................vs. Bears...................10/26/47

**Most Points Allowed, One Half**
45.........................vs. Bears (2nd)............12/8/40†
42.........................vs. Bears (2nd)...........10/26/47
41.........................vs. Bears (1st)...........11/28/48

**Most Points Allowed, One Quarter**
31.........................vs. Bears (2nd)............9/29/85
28.........................vs. Chiefs (2nd)...........9/30/01
28.........................vs. Cardinals (2nd).......10/22/50

**Fewest Touchdowns Allowed, Season**
12..............................................................1939

**Most Touchdowns Allowed, Season**
57..............................................................1954
50..............................................................1998

**Fewest Touchdowns Allowed, Game**
0, many times....................(last time vs. Seahawks, 11/3/02)

**Most Touchdowns Allowed, Game**
11.........................vs. Bears...................12/8/40†
8..........................vs. Bears...................10/26/47

## POINTS AFTER TOUCHDOWNS

**Fewest PATs Allowed, Season**
7..............................................................1932

**Most PATs Allowed, Season**
49 ...................................................................1961

**Most PATs Allowed, Game**
8 .................................vs. Bears................................10/26/47
8 .................................vs. Browns..............................11/7/54

## FIELD GOALS

**Fewest Field Goals Allowed, Season**
2 ......................................................................1943

**Most Field Goals Allowed, Season**
31 ....................................................................2002

**Most Field Goals Allowed, Game**
5 .................................vs. Steelers.............................11/27/60
5 .................................vs. Giants..............................12/17/83
5 .................................vs. Giants..............................11/14/76

## FIRST DOWNS

**Fewest First Downs Allowed, Season**
82 ....................................................................1937

**Most First Downs Allowed, Season**
358 ...................................................................1996

**Fewest First Downs Allowed, Game**
0 .................................vs. Giants..............................9/27/42
3 .................................vs. Packers.............................11/4/34
4 .................................vs. Eagles..............................9/30/91

**Most First Downs Allowed, Game**
33 .................................vs. Browns..............................11/7/54
32 .................................vs. Eagles..............................9/17/89
32 .................................vs. Eagles..............................12/2/51
32 .................................vs. Cardinals...........................11/10/96

**Fewest First Downs Allowed, Rushing, Season**
46 ....................................................................1982
52 ....................................................................1942

**Most First Downs Allowed, Rushing, Season**
149 ...................................................................1969
146 ...................................................................1996

**Fewest First Downs Allowed, Rushing, Game**
0 .................................vs. Giants..............................9/27/42
0 .................................vs. Buccaneers..........................12/4/94
0 .................................vs. Eagles..............................9/30/91

**Most First Downs Allowed, Rushing, Game**
25 .................................vs. Eagles..............................12/2/51
21 .................................vs. Bills...............................11/3/96

**Fewest First Downs Allowed, Passing, Season**
34 ....................................................................1943

**Most First Downs Allowed, Passing, Season**
196 ...................................................................1983
194 ...................................................................1984
193 ...................................................................1999

**Fewest First Downs Allowed, Passing, Game**
0 .................................vs. Packers.............................11/4/34
0 .................................vs. Giants..............................9/28/42
1 .................................vs. Giants..............................12/19/43†

**Most First Downs Allowed, Passing, Game**
24 .................................vs. Eagles..............................9/17/89
24 .................................vs. Saints..............................9/11/94
23 .................................vs. Cardinals...........................11/10/96

**Fewest First Downs Allowed, Penalty, Season**
3 ......................................................................1957

**Most First Downs Allowed, Penalty, Season**
36 ....................................................................1965
32 ....................................................................1996

**Most First Downs Allowed, Penalty, Game**
8 .................................vs. Cowboys.............................12/26/93

## NET YARDS GAINED
## RUSHING AND PASSING

**Most Seasons Leading League, Fewest Yards Allowed**
5, most recently ........................................................1946

**Fewest Yards Allowed, Season**
1,950 .................................................................1943

**Most Yards Allowed, Season**
5,723 .................................................................1996

**Fewest Yards Allowed, Game**
51 (1 rush, 50 pass) ..................vs. Giants.............................9/27/42
51 (–1 rush, 52 pass) ................vs. Giants.............................12/11/60
61 .................................vs. Packers.............................11/4/34

**Most Yards Allowed, Game**
625 .................................vs. Yanks..............................10/31/48
615 .................................vs. Cardinals...........................11/10/96
602 .................................vs. Giants..............................10/28/62

## RUSHING

## ATTEMPTS

**Fewest Rushing Attempts Allowed, Season**
348 ...................................................................1991

**Most Rushing Attempts Allowed, Season**
625 ...................................................................1978
585 ...................................................................1980
556 ...................................................................1994

**Fewest Rushing Attempts Allowed, Game**
8 .................................vs. Seahawks............................12/23/89
10 .................................vs. Lions...............................1/8/00†
10 .................................vs. Dolphins............................12/2/90
10 .................................vs. Buccaneers..........................10/22/89
10 .................................vs. Bills...............................11/01/87

**Most Rushing Attempts Allowed, Game**
64 .................................vs. Steagles............................11/28/43
64 .................................vs. Eagles..............................12/2/51
64 .................................vs. Packers.............................12/1/46

## YARDS GAINED

**Fewest Rushing Yards Allowed, Season**
848 ...................................................................1942

**Most Rushing Yards Allowed, Season**
2,536 .................................................................1978

**Fewest Rushing Yards Allowed, Game**
–29 .................................vs. Rams...............................10/11/42
1 .................................vs. Buccaneers..........................10/22/89

**Most Rushing Yards Allowed, Game**
382 .................................vs. Bears...............................12/8/40

| | | |
|---|---|---|
| 376 | vs. Eagles | 11/21/48 |
| 351 | vs. Giants | 11/29/59 |

## TOUCHDOWNS

**Most Rushing Touchdowns Allowed, Game**

| | | |
|---|---|---|
| 5 | vs. Eagles | 10/17/48 |
| 5 | vs. Eagles | 10/23/49 |
| 5 | vs. Bills | 11/3/96 |
| 5 | vs. Colts | 11/2/69 |

## PASSING

### ATTEMPTS

**Fewest Pass Attempts Allowed, Season**

| | |
|---|---|
| 166 | 1935 |

**Most Pass Attempts Allowed, Season**

| | |
|---|---|
| 589 | 1999 |

**Fewest Pass Attempts Allowed, Game**

| | | |
|---|---|---|
| 1 | vs. Giants | 9/27/42 |
| 8 | vs. Cowboys | 12/10/00 |

**Most Pass Attempts Allowed, Game**

| | | |
|---|---|---|
| 63 | vs. Bears | 10/31/99 |
| 60 | vs. Eagles | 12/1/40 |
| 60 | vs. 49ers | 11/17/86 |

### COMPLETIONS

**Fewest Pass Completions Allowed, Season**

| | |
|---|---|
| 62 | 1936 |

**Most Pass Completions Allowed, Season**

| | |
|---|---|
| 338 | 1995 |

**Fewest Pass Completions Allowed, Game**

| | | |
|---|---|---|
| 0 | vs. Eagles | 10/18/36 |
| 1 | vs. Giants | 9/27/42 |
| 1 | vs. Giants | 10/1/39 |

**Most Pass Completions Allowed, Game**

| | | |
|---|---|---|
| 37 | vs. Cardinals | 12/16/84 |
| 37 | vs. Colts | 11/7/93 |
| 36 | vs. Bears | 10/31/99 |

### YARDS ALLOWED

**Seasons Leading League, Fewest Yards Allowed**

| | |
|---|---|
| 7 most recently | 1985 |

**Fewest Yards Allowed, Passing, Season**

| | |
|---|---|
| 1,026 | 1943 |

**Most Yards Allowed, Passing, Season**

| | |
|---|---|
| 3,975 | 1983 |

**Fewest Yards Allowed, Passing, Game**

| | | |
|---|---|---|
| −12 | vs. Cardinals | 12/21/80 |
| −3 | vs. Giants | 9/27/42 |
| 0 | vs. Eagles | 10/18/36 |

**Most Yards Allowed, Passing, Game**

| | | |
|---|---|---|
| 507 | vs. Cardinals | 11/10/96 |
| 505 | vs. Giants | 10/28/62 |
| 501 | vs. Yanks | 10/31/48 |

## TOUCHDOWNS

**Fewest Touchdowns Allowed, Passing, Season**

| | |
|---|---|
| 5 | 1942 |

**Most Touchdowns Allowed, Passing, Season**

| | |
|---|---|
| 37 | 1961 |

**Most Touchdowns Allowed, Passing, Game**

| | | |
|---|---|---|
| 7 | vs. Eagles | 10/17/54 |
| 7 | vs. Giants | 10/28/62 |

## SACKS

**Most Sacks, Season**

| | |
|---|---|
| 66 | 1984 |
| 55 | 1986 |
| 53 | 1973 |
| 53 | 1987 |

**Fewest Sacks, Season**

| | |
|---|---|
| 19 | 2006 |
| 25 | 2001 |
| 27 | 2003 |

**Most Sacks, Game**

| | | |
|---|---|---|
| 10 | vs. Buccaneers | 10/9/77 |
| 9 | vs. Cardinals | 12/21/80 |
| 8 | vs. Cowboys | 9/23/90 |
| 8 | vs. Vikings | 1/17/88[†] |

**Most Opponents Yards Lost Attempting to Pass, Season**

| | |
|---|---|
| 529 | 1984 |
| 424 | 1987 |
| 424 | 1986 |

**Fewest Opponents Yards Lost Attempting to Pass, Season**

| | |
|---|---|
| 135 | 1995 |
| 139 | 2001 |

**Most Opponents Yards Lost Attempting to Pass, Game**

| | | |
|---|---|---|
| 81 | vs. Browns | 10/30/60 |

## INTERCEPTIONS BY

**Most Passes Intercepted By, Season**

| | |
|---|---|
| 34 | 1966 |
| 34 | 1983 |
| 33 | 1980 |

**Fewest Passes Intercepted By, Season**

| | |
|---|---|
| 6 | 2006 |
| 11 | 1982 |
| 13 | 1998 |
| 13 | 1959 |

**Most Passes Intercepted By, Game**

| | | |
|---|---|---|
| 6 | vs. Chargers | 10/31/83 |

**Most Yards Returning Interceptions, Season**

| | |
|---|---|
| 598 | 1973 |
| 485 | 1992 |
| 480 | 1971 |

**Fewest Yards, Returning Interceptions, Season**

| | |
|---|---|
| 25 | 2006 |

**Most Touchdowns, Returning Interceptions, Season**

| | |
|---|---|
| 5 | 1971 |
| 4 | 1984 |
| 4 | 1973 |

**Most Touchdowns, Returning Interceptions, Game**

| | | |
|---|---|---|
| 2 | vs. Yanks | 10/31/48 |
| 2 | vs. Steelers | 12/19/65 |
| 2 | vs. Cowboys | 11/22/64 |

**Most Touchdowns, Returning Interceptions, Both Teams, Game**

| | | |
|---|---|---|
| 3 | Redskins (0) vs. Bears (3) | 12/8/40† |

## PUNTING

**Most Opponents' Punts, Game**

| | | |
|---|---|---|
| 14 | vs. Eagles | 11/5/39 |
| 13 | vs. Packers | 11/4/34 |

## PUNT RETURNS

**Fewest Opponents' Punt Returns, Season**

| | |
|---|---|
| 7 | 1962* |

**Fewest Yards Allowed, Punt Returns, Season**

| | |
|---|---|
| 34 | 1962 |

**Fewest Yards Allowed, Punt Returns, Game**

| | | |
|---|---|---|
| -16 | vs. Cowboys | 9/9/91 |
| -2 | vs. Seahawks | 9/19/76 |

**Most Touchdowns Allowed, Punt Returns, Season**

| | |
|---|---|
| 3 | 1952 |

## KICKOFF RETURNS

**Most Opponents' Kickoff Returns, Season**

| | |
|---|---|
| 91 | 1983 |

**Most Opponents' Kickoff Returns, Game**

| | | |
|---|---|---|
| 12 | vs. Giants | 11/27/66 |

## FUMBLES

**Most Opponents' Fumbles, Season**

| | |
|---|---|
| 46 | 1983 |

**Fewest Opponents' Fumbles, Season**

| | |
|---|---|
| 15 | 2006 |

**Most Opponents' Fumbles, Game**

| | | |
|---|---|---|
| 9 | vs. Cardinals | 10/25/76 |

**Most Opponents' Fumbles Recovered, Season**

| | |
|---|---|
| 27 | 1983 |

**Fewest Opponents' Fumbles Recovered, Season**

| | |
|---|---|
| 6 | 1994 |
| 6 | 2006 |
| 8 | 1988 |
| 8 | 1998 |

**Most Opponents' Fumbles Recovered, Game**

| | | |
|---|---|---|
| 8 | vs. Cardinals | 10/25/76 |
| 6 | vs. Eagles | 11/6/55 |

**Most Touchdown Returns, Fumbles Recovered, Game**

| | | |
|---|---|---|
| 2 | vs. Chargers | 9/16/73 |
| 2 | vs. Vikings | 11/29/84 |

## TURNOVERS

**Most Opponents Turnovers, Season**

| | |
|---|---|
| 61 | 1983 |

**Fewest Opponents Turnovers, Season**

| | |
|---|---|
| 12 | 2006* |

**Most Opponents Turnovers, Game**

| | | |
|---|---|---|
| 10 | vs. Cardinals (9 ints/1 fum) | 10/25/76 |
| 8 | vs. Chargers (6 ints/2 fum) | 10/31/83 |
| 7 | vs. Eagles (4 ints/3 fum) | 11/7/71 |
| 7 | vs. Chargers (4 ints/3 fum) | 09/16/73 |
| 7 | vs. Cardinals (4 ints/3 fum) | 9/19/71 |

**Most Defensive Touchdowns, Game**

| | | |
|---|---|---|
| 3 | vs. Steelers (2 ints/1 fum) | 12/19/65 |
| 2 | vs. Cowboys (2 ints) | 11/22/64 |
| 2 | vs. Pirates (1 int/1 fum) | 11/29/36 |
| 2 | vs. Yanks (2 ints) | 10/31/48 |
| 2 | vs. Giants (1 int/1 fum) | 11/27/66 |
| 2 | vs. Jets (1 int/1 fum) | 11/5/72 |
| 2 | vs. Chargers (2 fum) | 9/16/73 |
| 2 | vs. Cardinals (1 int/1 fum) | 9/6/83 |
| 2 | vs. Vikings (2 fum) | 11/29/84 |

**Most Defensive Touchdowns, Allowed, Game**

| | | |
|---|---|---|
| 3 | vs. Bears (3 ints) | 12/8/40† |
| 3 | vs. Giants (2 ints/1 fum) | 12/8/63 |

**Highest Turnover/Takeaway Ratio, Season**

| | |
|---|---|
| +43 | 1983* |

# INDIVIDUAL RECORDS

## SERVICE

**Most Seasons**

| | | |
|---|---|---|
| 20 | Darrell Green | 1983–2002 |
| 16 | Sammy Baugh | 1937–52 |
| 16 | Monte Coleman | 1979–94 |

**Most Games Played, Career**

| | | |
|---|---|---|
| 295 | Darrell Green | 1983–2002 |
| 216 | Monte Coleman | 1979–94 |
| 205 | Art Monk | 1980–93 |

**Most Consecutive Games Played, Career**

| | | |
|---|---|---|
| 196 | Len Hauss | 1964–77 |
| 170 | Mark Moseley | 1974–86 |
| 163 | Joe Theismann | 1974–85 |

**Most Consecutive Games Started, Career**

| | | |
|---|---|---|
| 192 | Len Hauss | 1964–77 |

## SCORING

**Most Seasons Leading Team (all consecutive)**

| | | |
|---|---|---|
| 12 | Mark Moseley | 1974–85 |
| 7 | Chip Lohmiller | 1988–94 |
| 5 | Curt Knight | 1969–73 |

## POINTS

**Most Points, Career**

| | | |
|---|---|---|
| 1,206 | Mark Moseley | 1974–86 |
| 787 | Chip Lohmiller | 1988–94 |
| 540 | Charley Taylor | 1964–77 |

**Most Points, Season**

| | | |
|---|---|---|
| 161 | Mark Moseley | 1983 |
| 149 | Chip Lohmiller | 1991 |
| 144 | John Riggins | 1983 |

**Most Points, No Touchdowns, Season**

| | | |
|---|---|---|
| 161 | Mark Moseley | 1983* |
| 149 | Chip Lohmiller | 1991 |
| 131 | Chip Lohmiller | 1990 |

**Most Seasons, 100 or More Points**

| | | |
|---|---|---|
| 4 | Chip Lohmiller | 1989–92 |
| 3 | Mark Moseley | 1979, 1983–84 |
| 2 | Curt Knight | 1971, 1973 |
| 2 | Brett Conway | 1999, 2001 |

**Most Points, Game**

| | | |
|---|---|---|
| 24 | Dick James vs. Cowboys (4 TDs) | 12/17/61 |
| 24 | Larry Brown vs. Eagles (4 TDs) | 12/16/73 |
| 20 | Andy Farkas vs. Rams (3 TDs, 2 PATs) | 9/25/38 |

**Most Consecutive Games Scoring**

| | | |
|---|---|---|
| 92 | Chip Lohmiller | 1988–93 |
| 91 | Mark Moseley | 1980–86 |
| 70 | Mark Moseley | 1974–78 |

## TOUCHDOWNS

**Most Seasons Leading Team**

| | | |
|---|---|---|
| 5 | Hugh Taylor | 1949–50, 52–54 |
| 5 | John Riggins | 1979, 1981, 83–85 |
| 4 | Andy Farkas | 1938–39, 1942–43 |
| 4 | Bobby Mitchell | 1962–65 |
| 4 | Charley Taylor | 1964–67 |
| 4 | Larry Brown | 1971–74 |
| 4 | Gary Clark | 1986–87, 89–90 |
| 4 | Stephen Davis | 1999–2002 |

**Most Consecutive Seasons Leading Team**

| | | |
|---|---|---|
| 4 | Bobby Mitchell | 1962–65 |
| 4 | Charley Taylor | 1964–67 |
| 4 | Larry Brown | 1971–74 |
| 4 | Stephen Davis | 1999–02 |

**Most Touchdowns, Career**

| | | |
|---|---|---|
| 90 | Charley Taylor | 1964–77 |
| 85 | John Riggins | 1976–79, 1981–85 |
| 65 | Art Monk | 1980–93 |

**Most Touchdowns, Season**

| | | |
|---|---|---|
| 24 | John Riggins | 1983 |
| 21 | Terry Allen | 1996 |
| 18 | George Rogers | 1986 |

**Most Touchdowns, Game**

| | | |
|---|---|---|
| 4 | Dick James vs. Cowboys | 12/17/61 |
| 4 | Larry Brown vs. Eagles | 12/16/73 |
| 3, many times | (last time by Stephen Davis vs. Rams, 11/24/2002) | |

**Most Consecutive Games Scoring Touchdowns**

| | | |
|---|---|---|
| 13 | John Riggins | 1982–83 |
| 13 | George Rogers | 1985–86 |

## POINTS AFTER TOUCHDOWN

**Most PATs Attempted, Career**

| | | |
|---|---|---|
| 442 | Mark Moseley | 1974–86 |
| 267 | Chip Lohmiller | 1988–94 |
| 175 | Curt Knight | 1969–73 |

**Most PATs Attempted, Season**

| | | |
|---|---|---|
| 63 | Mark Moseley | 1983 |
| 56 | Chip Lohmiller | 1991 |
| 51 | Mark Moseley | 1984 |

**Most PATs Attempted, Game**

| | | |
|---|---|---|
| 10 | Charlie Gogolak vs. Giants | 11/27/66* |

**Most PATs, Career**

| | | |
|---|---|---|
| 417 | Mark Moseley | 1974–86 |
| 262 | Chip Lohmiller | 1988–94 |
| 172 | Curt Knight | 1969–73 |

**Most PATs, Season**

| | | |
|---|---|---|
| 62 | Mark Moseley | 1983 |
| 56 | Chip Lohmiller | 1991 |
| 49 | Brett Conway | 1999 |

**Most PATs, Game**

| | | |
|---|---|---|
| 9 | Charlie Gogolak vs. Giants | 11/27/66* |
| 8 | Chip Lohmiller vs. Falcons | 11/10/91 |
| 8 | Dick Poillon vs. Yanks | 10/31/48 |

**Most Consecutive PATs**

| | | |
|---|---|---|
| 213 | Chip Lohmiller | 1988–94 |

## FIELD GOALS

**Most Seasons Leading League**

| | | |
|---|---|---|
| 4 | Mark Moseley | 1976–77, 79, 1982 |

**Most Consecutive Seasons Leading League**

| | | |
|---|---|---|
| 2 | Mark Moseley | 1976–77 |

**Most Seasons Leading Team (all consecutive)**

| | | |
|---|---|---|
| 12 | Mark Moseley | 1974–85 |
| 7 | Chip Lohmiller | 1988–94 |
| 5 | Curt Knight | 1969–73 |

**Most Field Goals Attempted, Career**

| | | |
|---|---|---|
| 397 | Mark Moseley | 1974–86 |
| 245 | Chip Lohmiller | 1988–94 |
| 175 | Curt Knight | 1969–73 |

**Most Field Goals Attempted, Season**

| | | |
|---|---|---|
| 49 | Curt Knight | 1971 |
| 47 | Mark Moseley | 1983 |
| 43 | Chip Lohmiller | 1991 |

**Most Field Goals Attempted, Game**

| | | |
|---|---|---|
| 7 | Curt Knight vs. Oilers | 10/10/71 |
| 6 | Curt Knight vs. Bears | 11/14/71 |
| 6 | Mark Moseley vs. Saints | 10/26/80 |
| 6 | Chip Lohmiller vs. Eagles | 10/21/90 |
| 6 | Chip Lohmiller vs. Eagles | 12/22/91 |
| 6 | Brett Conway vs. Giants | 11/21/99 |

**Most Field Goals, Career**

| | | |
|---|---|---|
| 263 | Mark Moseley | 1974–86 |
| 175 | Chip Lohmiller | 1988–94 |
| 101 | Curt Knight | 1969–73 |

**Most Field Goals, Season**

| | | |
|---|---|---|
| 33 | Mark Moseley | 1983 |
| 3 | Chip Lohmiller | 1991 |
| 30 | Chip Lohmiller | 1990 |
| 30 | Chip Lohmiller | 1992 |

**Most Field Goals, Game**

| | | |
|---|---|---|
| 5 | Curt Knight vs. Oilers | 10/10/71 |
| 5 | Curt Knight vs. Bears | 11/14/71 |
| 5 | Curt Knight vs. Colts | 11/18/73 |
| 5 | Mark Moseley vs. Saints | 10/26/80 |
| 5 | Chip Lohmiller vs. Bills | 12/30/90 |
| 5 | Chip Lohmiller vs. Eagles | 12/22/91 |
| 5 | Chip Lohmiller vs. Vikings | 10/25/92 |

**Most Field Goals, One Quarter**

| | | |
|---|---|---|
| 4 | Curt Knight vs. Giants (2nd) | 11/15/70 |

**Most Consecutive Games Scoring Field Goals**

| | | |
|---|---|---|
| 28 | Chip Lohmiller | 1988–90 |
| 15 | Mark Moseley | 1976–77 |

## Most Consecutive Field Goals
| | | |
|---|---|---|
| 23 | Mark Moseley | 1981–82 |
| 14 | Chip Lohmiller | 1990–91 |
| 11 | Curt Knight | 1969–70 |

## Longest Field Goal
| | | |
|---|---|---|
| 57 | Steve Cox vs. Seahawks | 9/28/86 |
| 56 | Chip Lohmiller vs. Colts | 12/22/90 |
| 55 | Steve Cox vs. Eagles | 9/7/86 |
| 55 | Chip Lohmiller vs. Cowboys | 9/23/90 |
| 55 | Brett Conway vs. Giants | 10/7/01 |

## Highest Field Goal Percentage, Career
(min 100 field goals)
| | | |
|---|---|---|
| 71.4 | Chip Lohmiller (175/245) | 1988–94 |
| 66.2 | Mark Moseley (263/397) | 1974–86 |
| 57.7 | Curt Knight (101/175) | 1969–73 |

## Highest Field Goal Percentage, Season
(min 20 field goals)
| | | |
|---|---|---|
| 95.2 | Mark Moseley (20/21) | 1982 |
| 81.2 | Scott Blanton (26/32) | 1996 |
| 78.8 | Brett Conway (26/33) | 2001 |

## Highest Field Goal Percentage, Game
(min 5 field goals)
| | | |
|---|---|---|
| 100 | Curt Knight vs. Colts | 11/18/73 (5–5) |
| 100 | Chip Lohmiller vs. Bills | 12/30/90 (5–5) |
| 100 | Chip Lohmiller vs. Vikings | 10/25/92 (5–5) |

## Most Field Goals, 50 or More Yards, Career
| | | |
|---|---|---|
| 12 | Mark Moseley | 1974–86 |
| 9 | Chip Lohmiller | 1988–94 |
| 5 | Brett Conway | 1998–2002 |

## Most Field Goals, 50 or More Yards, Season
| | | |
|---|---|---|
| 4 | Mark Moseley | 1977 |
| 3 | Chip Lohmiller | 1990 |
| 3 | Brett Conway | 1999 |

# RUSHING

## Most Seasons Leading Team
| | | |
|---|---|---|
| 6 | Larry Brown | 1969–74 |
| 5 | John Riggins | 1978–79, 1982–84 |
| 4 | Cliff Battles | 1932, 1934, 1936–37 |
| 4 | Andy Farkas | 1938–39, 1942–43 |
| 4 | Terry Allen | 1995–98 |
| 4 | Stephen Davis | 1999–2002 |

## Most Consecutive Seasons Leading Team
| | | |
|---|---|---|
| 6 | Larry Brown | 1969–74 |
| 4 | Terry Allen | 1995–98 |
| 4 | Stephen Davis | 1999–2002 |

# ATTEMPTS

## Most Attempts, Career
| | | |
|---|---|---|
| 1,988 | John Riggins | 1976–79, 1981–85 |
| 1,530 | Larry Brown | 1969–76 |
| 1,383 | Stephen Davis | 1996–2002 |

## Most Attempts, Season
| | | |
|---|---|---|
| 375 | John Riggins | 1983 |
| 356 | Stephen Davis | 2001 |
| 352 | Clinton Portis | 2005 |
| 347 | Terry Allen | 1996 |

## Most Attempts, Game
| | | |
|---|---|---|
| 45 | Jamie Morris vs. Bengals | 12/17/88 (OT)* |
| 39 | Earnest Byner vs. Patriots | 12/15/90 |
| 38 | Stephen Davis vs. Cardinals | 1/6/02 |
| 36 | Clinton Portis @ Chicago | 10/17/04 |

# YARDS GAINED

## Most Yards Gained, Career
| | | |
|---|---|---|
| 7,472 | John Riggins | 1976–79, 1981–85 |
| 5,875 | Larry Brown | 1969–76 |
| 5,790 | Stephen Davis | 1996–2002 |

## Most Seasons, 1,000 or More Yards Rushing
| | | |
|---|---|---|
| 4 | John Riggins | 1978–79, 1983–84 |
| 3 | Stephen Davis | 1999–2001 |

## Most Consecutive Seasons, 1,000 or More Yards Rushing
| | | |
|---|---|---|
| 3 | Stephen Davis | 1999–2001 |
| 2 | John Riggins | 1978–79 |
| 2 | John Riggins | 1983–84 |
| 2 | George Rogers | 1985–86 |
| 2 | Earnest Byner | 1990–91 |
| 2 | Terry Allen | 1995–96 |

## Most Yards Gained, Season
| | | |
|---|---|---|
| 1,516 | Clinton Portis | 2005 |
| 1,432 | Stephen Davis | 2001 |
| 1,405 | Stephen Davis | 1999 |
| 1,353 | Terry Allen | 1996 |

## Most Yards Gained, Game
| | | |
|---|---|---|
| 221 | Gerald Riggs vs. Eagles | 9/17/89 |
| 215 | Cliff Battles vs. NYG | 10/8/33 |
| 206 | George Rogers vs. Cardinals | 12/21/85 |
| 204 | Timmy Smith vs. Broncos | 1/31/88† |

## Most Games, 100 or More Yards Rushing, Career (Reg Season)
| | | |
|---|---|---|
| 19 | John Riggins | 1976–79, 81–85 |
| 19 | Larry Brown | 1969–76 |
| 18 | Stephen Davis | 1996–2002 |

## Most Games, 100 or More Yards Rushing, Season (Reg Season)
| | | |
|---|---|---|
| 9 | Clinton Portis | 2005 |
| 7 | Rob Goode | 1951 |
| 6 | Larry Brown | 1970 |
| 6 | Larry Brown | 1972 |
| 6 | Stephen Davis | 1999 |
| 6 | Stephen Davis | 2001 |
| 6 | Ladell Betts | 2006 |

## Most Consecutive Games, 100 or More Yards Rushing
| | | |
|---|---|---|
| 5 | Ladell Betts | 2006 |
| 5 | Clinton Portis | 2005 |
| 5 | Rob Goode | 1951 |

## Longest Run From Scrimmage (all TDs)
| | | |
|---|---|---|
| 88 | Billy Wells vs. Cardinals | 11/21/54 |
| 85 | Reggie Brooks vs. Eagle | 9/19/93 |
| 80 | Rob Goode vs. Packers | 9/24/50 |

# AVERAGE GAIN

## Highest Average Gain, Career (min 250 atts)
| | | |
|---|---|---|
| 5.1 | Joe Theismann | 1974–85 |
| 4.8 | Charlie Justice | 1950, 52–54 |
| 4.6 | Joe Washington | 1981–84 |

## Highest Average Gain, Season (min 100 atts)
| | | |
|---|---|---|
| 5.42 | Frank Atkins (147–797) | 1945 |
| 5.41 | Don Bosseler (119–644) | 1959 |
| 5.36 | Charlie Justice (115–616) | 1953 |

## Highest Average Gain, Game (10 attempts)
| | | |
|---|---|---|
| 11.9 | Stephen Davis (12–143) vs. Bears | 10/31/99 |
| 10.5 | J. Okszewski (18–190) vs. Browns | 11/15/59 |
| 10.3 | Keith Griffin (16–164) vs. Falcons | 11/3/85 |

## TOUCHDOWNS

### Most Seasons Leading Team
| | | |
|---|---|---|
| 7 | John Riggins | 1978–79, 81–85 |
| 4 | Larry Brown | 1970–73 |
| 4 | Stephen Davis | 1999–2002 |

### Most Consecutive Seasons Leading Team
| | | |
|---|---|---|
| 5 | John Riggins | 1981–85 |
| 4 | Larry Brown | 1970–73 |
| 4 | Stephen Davis | 1999–2002 |

### Most Touchdowns, Career
| | | |
|---|---|---|
| 79 | John Riggins | 1976–79, 81–85 |
| 45 | Stephen Davis | 1996–2002 |
| 37 | Terry Allen | 1995–98 |

### Most Touchdowns, Season
| | | |
|---|---|---|
| 24 | John Riggins | 1983 |
| 21 | Terry Allen | 1996 |
| 18 | George Rogers | 1986 |

### Most Touchdowns, Game
| | | |
|---|---|---|
| 3 | Cliff Battles vs. Giants | 10/17/37 |
| 3 | Andy Farkas vs. Rams | 9/25/38 |
| 3 | Andy Farkas vs. Dodgers | 11/12/39 |
| 3 | Andy Farkas vs. Bears | 12/19/43† |
| 3 | Don Bosseler vs. Eagles | 12/8/57 |
| 3 | Dick James vs. Cowboys | 12/17/61 |
| 3 | Ray McDonald vs. Saints | 9/24/67 |
| 3 | John Riggins vs. Cardinals | 10/9/83 |
| 3 | Reggie Evans vs. Lions | 10/23/83 |
| 3 | John Riggins vs. Rams | 1/1/84† |
| 3 | Otis Wonsley vs. Lions | 11/11/84 |
| 3 | John Riggins vs. Lions | 10/13/85 |
| 3 | Earnest Byner vs. Dolphins | 12/2/90 |
| 3 | Gerald Riggs vs. Bengals | 9/22/91 |
| 3 | Terry Allen vs. Giants | 10/20/96 |
| 3 | Terry Allen vs. Colts | 10/27/96 |
| 3 | Skip Hicks vs. Eagles | 11/15/98 |
| 3 | Stephen Davis vs. Giants | 9/19/99 |
| 3 | Stephen Davis vs. Jets | 9/26/99 |
| 3 | Stephen Davis vs. Rams | 11/24/02 |
| 3 | Clinton Portis vs. 49ers | 10/24/05 |

### Most Consecutive Games Rushing for Touchdowns
| | | |
|---|---|---|
| 13 | John Riggins | 1982–83* |
| 13 | George Rogers | 1985–86* |
| 10 | Terry Allen | 1995–96 |

## PASSING

### Most Seasons Leading League
| | | |
|---|---|---|
| 6 | Sammy Baugh | 1937, 40, 43, 45, 47, 49* |
| 2 | Sonny Jurgensen | 1967, 69 |

### Most Seasons Leading Team
| | | |
|---|---|---|
| 14 | Sammy Baugh | 1937–43, 45–51 |
| 8 | Sonny Jurgensen | 1964–70, 74 |
| 8 | Joe Theismann | 1978–85 |

### Most Consecutive Seasons Leading Team
| | | |
|---|---|---|
| 8 | Joe Theismann | 1978–85 |
| 7 | Sammy Baugh | 1937–43 |
| 7 | Sammy Baugh | 1945–51 |
| 7 | Sonny Jurgensen | 1964–70 |

## PASSER RATING

### Highest Passer Rating, Career
| | | |
|---|---|---|
| 85.0 | Sonny Jurgensen | 1964–74 |
| 80.2 | Mark Rypien | 1987–93 |
| 77.4 | Joe Theismann | 1974–85 |

### Highest Passer Rating, Season
| | | |
|---|---|---|
| 109.9 | Sammy Baugh | 1945 |
| 97.9 | Mark Rypien | 1991 |
| 97.0 | Joe Theismann | 1983 |

## ATTEMPTS

### Most Seasons Leading League
| | | |
|---|---|---|
| 4 | Sammy Baugh | 1937, 43, 47–48 |
| 3 | Sonny Jurgensen | 1966–67, 69 |

### Most Passes Attempted, Career
| | | |
|---|---|---|
| 3,602 | Joe Theismann | 1974–85 |
| 3,155 | Sonny Jurgensen | 1964–74 |
| 2,995 | Sammy Baugh | 1937–52 |

### Most Passes Attempted, Season
| | | |
|---|---|---|
| 541 | Jay Schroeder | 1986 |
| 519 | Brad Johnson | 1999 |
| 509 | Trent Green | 1998 |

### Most Passes Attempted, Game
| | | |
|---|---|---|
| 58 | Jay Schroeder vs. 49ers | 12/1/85 |
| 54 | Trent Green vs. Cardinals | 11/22/98 |
| 54 | Mark Rypien vs. Cowboys | 11/22/90 |

## COMPLETIONS

### Most Seasons Leading League
| | | |
|---|---|---|
| 5 | Sammy Baugh | 1937, 43, 45, 47–48 |
| 3 | Sonny Jurgensen | 1966–67, 69 |

### Most Passes Completed, Career
| | | |
|---|---|---|
| 2,044 | Joe Theismann | 1974–85 |
| 1,831 | Sonny Jurgensen | 1964–74 |
| 1,693 | Sammy Baugh | 1937–52 |

### Most Passes Completed, Season
| | | |
|---|---|---|
| 316 | Brad Johnson | 1999 |
| 293 | Joe Theismann | 1981 |
| 288 | Sonny Jurgensen | 1967 |

### Most Passes Completed, Game
| | | |
|---|---|---|
| 32 | Sonny Jurgensen vs. Browns | 11/26/67 |
| 32 | John Friesz vs. Giants | 9/18/94 |
| 32 | Brad Johnson vs. 49ers | 12/26/99 |

## COMPLETION PERCENTAGE

### Most Seasons Leading League
| | | |
|---|---|---|
| 7 | Sammy Baugh | 1940, 42–43, 45, 47–49 |

### Highest Completion Percentage, Career (min 1,000 atts)
| | | |
|---|---|---|
| 58.2 | Sonny Jurgensen | 1964–74 |
| 56.7 | Joe Theismann | 1974–85 |
| 56.5 | Sammy Baugh | 1937–52 |

### Highest Completion Percentage, Season (min 150 atts)
| | | |
|---|---|---|
| 70.3 | Sammy Baugh (128–182) | 1945 |
| 64.1 | Sonny Jurgensen (107–167) | 1974 |
| 63.9 | Joe Theismann (161–252) | 1982 |
| 62.1 | Patrick Ramsey (169–272) | 2004 |
| 62.1 | Mark Brunell (162–261) | 2006 |

### Highest Completion Percentage, Game (min 15 atts)
| | | |
|---|---|---|
| 88.9 | Mark Brunell vs. Texans (24–27) | 9/24/06 |

## YARDS GAINED

**Most Seasons Leading League**
4 ............... Sammy Baugh ........................ 1937, 40, 47–48
3 ............... Sonny Jurgensen ..................... 1966–67, 69

**Most Yards Gained, Career**
25,206 ............. Joe Theismann ................... 1974–85
22,585 ............. Sonny Jurgensen ................ 1964–74
21,886 ............. Sammy Baugh .................... 1937–52

**Most Yards Gained, Season**
4,109 .............. Jay Schroeder ..................... 1986
4,005 .............. Brad Johnson ..................... 1999
3,768 .............. Mark Rypien ...................... 1989

**Most Yards Gained, Game**
471 ............... Brad Johnson vs. 49ers ........... 12/26/99
446 ............... Sammy Baugh vs. Yanks .......... 10/31/48
442 ............... Mark Rypien vs. Falcons ......... 11/10/91

**Most Games, 300 or More Yards Passing, Career**
15 ............... Sonny Jurgensen ................... 1964–74
14 ............... Joe Theismann ..................... 1974–85
10 ............... Mark Rypien ....................... 1987–93

**Most Games, 300 or More Yards Passing, Season**
5 ................ Sonny Jurgensen ................... 1967
5 ................ Jay Schroeder ..................... 1986
5 ................ Mark Rypien ....................... 1989

**Most Consecutive Games, 300 or More Yards Passing, Season**
3 ................ Sonny Jurgensen ................... 1967

**Longest Pass Completion (all TDS)**
99 .......... Frank Filchock (to Farkas) vs. Steelers ... 10/15/39*
99 .......... George Izo (to Mitchell) vs. Browns ...... 9/15/63*
99 .......... Sonny Jurgensen (to Allen) vs. Bears ..... 9/15/68*

## AVERAGE GAIN

**Highest Average Gain, Career (1,000 atts)**
7.321 ............. Jay Schroeder .................... 1984–87
7.308 ............. Eddie LeBaron ................... 1952–53, 55–59
7.307 ............. Sammy Baugh .................... 1937–52

**Highest Average Gain, Season (150 atts)**
9.17 .............. Sammy Baugh .................... 1945
9.03 .............. Eddie LeBaron ................... 1957
8.47 .............. Mark Rypien ..................... 1991

**Highest Average Gain, Game (20 attempts)**
18.58 ............. Sammy Baugh vs. Yanks ......... 10/31/48*
   (24 atts–446 yards)

## TOUCHDOWNS

**Most Seasons Leading League**
2 ................ Frank Filchock .................... 1939, 44
2 ................ Sammy Baugh ..................... 1940, 47

**Most Seasons Leading Team**
13 ............... Sammy Baugh .............. 1937–38, 40–43, 45–51
8 ................ Sonny Jurgensen .................. 1964–70, 74
8 ................ Joe Theismann .................... 1978–85

**Most Consecutive Seasons Leading Team**
8 ................ Joe Theismann .................... 1978–85
7 ................ Sammy Baugh ..................... 1945–51
7 ................ Sonny Jurgensen .................. 1964–70

**Most Touchdown Passes, Career**
187 ............... Sammy Baugh ..................... 1937–52

179 ............... Sonny Jurgensen .................. 1964–74
160 ............... Joe Theismann .................... 1974–85

**Most Touchdown Passes, Season**
31 ............... Sonny Jurgensen .................. 1967
29 ............... Joe Theismann .................... 1983
28 ............... Sonny Jurgensen .................. 1966
28 ............... Mark Rypien ...................... 1991

**Most Touchdown Passes, Game**
6 ................ Sammy Baugh vs. Dodgers ......... 10/31/43
6 ................ Sammy Baugh vs. Cardinals ....... 11/23/47
6 ................ Mark Rypien vs. Falcons .......... 11/10/91

**Most Consecutive Games, Touchdown Passes**
23 ............... Sonny Jurgensen .................. 1966–68
15 ............... Joe Theismann .................... 1982–83

## HAD INTERCEPTED

**Most Consecutive Passes Attempted, None Intercepted**
162 ............... Joe Theismann .................... 1983
146 ............... Brad Johnson ..................... 1999

**Most Passes Had Intercepted, Career**
203 ............... Sammy Baugh ..................... 1937–52
138 ............... Joe Theismann .................... 1974–85
116 ............... Sonny Jurgensen .................. 1964–74

**Most Passes Had Intercepted, Season**
27 ............... Norm Snead ...................... 1963
23 ............... Sammy Baugh ..................... 1948
22 ............... Norm Snead ...................... 1961
22 ............... Norm Snead ...................... 1962
22 ............... Jay Schroeder .................... 1986

**Most Passes Had Intercepted, Game**
6 ................ Sammy Baugh vs. Giants .......... 11/11/51
6 ................ Jay Schroeder vs. Giants ......... 12/7/86

**Most Attempts, No Interceptions, Game**
50 ............... Doug Williams vs. Giants ......... 9/5/88

## LOWEST PERCENTAGE, PASSES HAD INTERCEPTED

**Most Seasons Leading League, Lowest Percentage, Passes Had Intercepted**
5 ................ Sammy Baugh ............. 1940, 42, 44–45, 47

**Lowest Percentage, Passes Had Intercepted, Career (min 1,000 atts)**
3.3 ............... Mark Rypien ...................... 1987–93
3.6 ............... Jay Schroeder .................... 1984–87
3.8 ............... Joe Theismann .................... 1974–85

**Lowest Percentage, Passes Had Intercepted, Season (min 150 atts)**
1.53 .............. Mark Brunell (4–261) ............ 2006
2.16 .............. Trent Green (11–509) ............ 1998
2.19 .............. Sammy Baugh (4–182) ........... 1945
2.34 .............. Gus Frerotte (11–470) ........... 1996

## TIMES SACKED

**Most Times Sacked, Career**
338 ............... Joe Theismann .................... 1974–85

**Most Times Sacked, Season**
49 ............... Trent Green ...................... 1998
48 ............... Joe Theismann .................... 1984

**Most Times Sacked, Game**

| 8 | Joe Theismann vs. Cowboys | 12/9/84 |

## RECEIVING

**Most Seasons Leading League**

| 2 | Charley Taylor | 1966–67 |

**Most Seasons Leading Team**

| 8 | Charley Taylor | 1966–69, 72–75 |
| 6 | Hugh Taylor | 1949–54 |
| 6 | Art Monk | 1980, 82, 84–85, 89,91 |

**Most Consecutive Seasons Leading Team**

| 6 | Hugh Taylor | 1949–54 |
| 4 | Bobby Mitchell | 1962–65 |
| 4 | Charley Taylor | 1966–69 |
| 4 | Charley Taylor | 1972–75 |

**Most Pass Receptions, Career**

| 888 | Art Monk | 1980–93 |
| 649 | Charley Taylor | 1964–77 |
| 549 | Gary Clark | 1985–92 |

**Most Seasons, 50 or More Pass Receptions**

| 9 | Art Monk | 1980–81, 84–86, 88–91 |
| 7 | Charley Taylor | 1964, 66–67, 69, 73–75 |
| 6 | Bobby Mitchell | 1962–67 |

**Most Pass Receptions, Season**

| 106 | Art Monk | 1984 |
| 91 | Art Monk | 1985 |
| 90 | Laveranues Coles | 2004 |

**Most Pass Receptions, Game**

| 13 | Art Monk vs. Lions (168 yds) | 11/4/90 |
| 13 | Art Monk vs. Bengals (230 yds) | 12/15/85 |
| 13 | Kelvin Bryant vs. Giants (130 yds) | 12/7/86 |

**Most Consecutive Games, Pass Receptions**

| 164 | Art Monk | 1983–93 |

## YARDS GAINED

**Most Yards Gained, Career**

| 12,026 | Art Monk | 1980–93 |
| 9,110 | Charley Taylor | 1964–77 |
| 8,742 | Gary Clark | 1985–92 |

**Most Seasons, 1,000 or More Yards, Pass Receiving**

| 5 | Art Monk | 1984–86, 89, 91 |
| 5 | Gary Clark | 1986–87, 89–91 |
| 3 | Henry Ellard | 1994–96 |

**Most Yards Gained, Season**

| 1,483 | Santana Moss | 2005 |
| 1,436 | Bobby Mitchell | 1963 |
| 1,397 | Henry Ellard | 1994 |

**Most Yards Gained, Game**

| 255 | Anthony Allen vs. Cardinals (7 rec) | 10/4/87 |
| 241 | Gary Clark vs. Giants (11) | 10/27/86 |
| 230 | Art Monk vs. Bengals (13) | 12/15/85 |

**Most Games, 100 or More Yards Pass Receiving, Career**

| 36 | Art Monk | 1980–93 |
| 28 | Gary Clark | 1985–92 |
| 23 | Bobby Mitchell | 1962–68 |
| 23 | Charley Taylor | 1964–77 |

**Most Games, 100 or More Yards Pass Receiving, Season**

| 7 | Bobby Mitchell | 1962 |

| 6 | Bobby Mitchell | 1963 |
| 6 | Art Monk | 1984 |
| 6 | Art Monk | 1985 |

**Most Consecutive Games, 100 or More Yards Pass Receiving**

| 3 | Santana Moss (wks 5–7) | 2005 |
| 3 | Art Monk (wks 9–11) | 1985 |
| 3 | Art Monk (wks 13–15) | 1985 |

**Longest Pass Reception (all TDS)**

| 99 | Andy Farkas (from Filchock) vs. Steelers | 10/15/39* |
| 99 | Bobby Mitchell (from Izo) vs. Browns | 9/15/63* |
| 99 | Gerry Allen (from Jurgensen) vs. Bears | 9/15/68* |

**Highest Average Gain, Career (min 200 receptions)**

| 19.24 | Hugh Taylor | 1947–54 |
| 18.19 | Henry Ellard | 1994–98 |
| 16.52 | Bobby Mitchell | 1962–68 |

**Highest Average Gain, Season (min 24 receptions)**

| 23.44 | Hugh Taylor | 1952 |
| 21.56 | Charlie Brown | 1982 |
| 21.36 | Hugh Taylor | 1950 |

**Highest Average Gain, Game (min 3 receptions)**

| 50.75 | Gary Clark vs. Falcons (4/208) | 11/10/91 |
| 49.33 | Charley Taylor vs. Rams (3/148) | 10/22/67 |
| 48.33 | Andy Farkas vs. Cardinals (3/145) | 11/19/39 |

## TOUCHDOWNS

**Most Seasons Leading Team**

| 8 | Charley Taylor | 1966–69, 71–74 |
| 7 | Hugh Taylor | 1947, 49–54 |
| 7 | Gary Clark | 1985–87, 89–92 |

**Most Consecutive Seasons Leading Team**

| 6 | Hugh Taylor | 1949–54 |
| 4 | Bobby Mitchell | 1962–65 |
| 4 | Charley Taylor | 1966–69 |
| 4 | Charley Taylor | 1971–74 |
| 4 | Gary Clark | 1989–92 |

**Most Touchdowns, Career**

| 79 | Charley Taylor | 1964–77 |
| 65 | Art Monk | 1980–93 |
| 60 | Jerry Smith | 1965–77 |

**Most Touchdowns, Season**

| 12 | Hugh Taylor | 1952 |
| 12 | Charley Taylor | 1966 |
| 12 | Jerry Smith | 1967 |
| 12 | Ricky Sanders | 1988 |

**Most Touchdowns, Game**

| 3 | Hugh Taylor vs. Eagles | 9/28/47 |
| 3 | Hal Crisler vs. Bulldogs | 10/16/49 |
| 3 | Hugh Taylor vs. Colts | 9/17/50 |
| 3 | Hugh Taylor vs. Cardinals | 10/22/50 |
| 3 | Hugh Taylor vs. Giants | 12/7/52 |
| 3 | Hugh Taylor vs. Cardinals | 12/12/54 |
| 3 | Jerry Smith vs. Rams | 10/22/67 |
| 3 | Pat Richter vs. Bears | 9/15/68 |
| 3 | Jerry Smith vs. Cowboys | 11/16/69 |
| 3 | Larry Brown vs. Eagles | 12/16/73 |
| 3 | Alvin Garrett vs. Lions | 1/8/83† |
| 3 | Art Monk vs. Colts | 10/7/84 |
| 3 | Anthony Allen vs. Cardinals | 10/4/87 |
| 3 | Gary Clark vs. Falcons | 11/10/91 |
| 3 | Michael Westbrook vs. Cardinals | 11/22/98 |
| 3 | Albert Connell vs. Jaguars | 10/22/00 |
| 3 | Santana Moss vs. Giants | 12/24/05 |
| 3 | Santana Moss vs. Jaguars | 10/1/06 |

## YARDS FROM SCRIMMAGE
### (Rushing and Receiving)

**Most Scrimmage Yards, Career**

| | | |
|---|---|---|
| 12,358 | Art Monk | 1980–93 |
| 10,628 | Charley Taylor | 1964–77 |
| 8,796 | Gary Clark | 1985–92 |

**Most Scrimmage Yards, Season**

| | | |
|---|---|---|
| 1,689 | Larry Brown | 1972 |
| 1,637 | Stephen Davis | 2001 |
| 1,631 | Stephen Davis | 2000 |

**Most Scrimmage Yards, Game**

| | | |
|---|---|---|
| 257 | Larry Brown vs. Eagles | 12/16/73 |
| 255 | Anthony Allen vs. Cardinals | 10/4/87 |
| 241 | Gary Clark vs. Giants | 10/27/86 |

## INTERCEPTIONS BY

**Most Seasons Leading Team**

| | | |
|---|---|---|
| 3 | Sammy Baugh | 1942–43, 45 |
| 3 | Norb Hecker | 1955–57 |
| 3 | Paul Krause | 1964–65, 67 |
| 3 | Brig Owens | 1966, 68, 70 |
| 3 | Ken Houston | 1973, 75, 77 |
| 3 | Vernon Dean | 1982, 84–85 |
| 3 | Darrell Green | 1986, 91, 98 |
| 3 | Tom Carter | 1993, 95–96 |
| 3 | Fred Smoot | 2001–03 |

**Most Consecutive Seasons Leading Team**

| | | |
|---|---|---|
| 3 | Norb Hecker | 1955–57 |
| 3 | Fred Smoot | 2001–03 |

**Most Interceptions By, Career**

| | | |
|---|---|---|
| 54 | Darrell Green | 1983–2002 |
| 36 | Brig Owens | 1966–72 |
| 31 | Sammy Baugh | 1937–52 |

**Most Interceptions By, Season**

| | | |
|---|---|---|
| 13 | Dan Sandifer | 1948 |
| 12 | Paul Krause | 1964 |
| 11 | Sammy Baugh | 1943 |

**Most Interceptions By, Game**

| | | |
|---|---|---|
| 4 | Sammy Baugh vs. Lions | 11/14/43* |
| 4 | Dan Sandifer vs. Yanks | 10/31/48* |

**Most Consecutive Games, Passes Intercepted By**

| | | |
|---|---|---|
| 7 | Paul Krause | 1964 |
| 6 | Lemar Parrish | 1978–79 |
| 6 | Barry Wilburn | 1987 |

## YARDS GAINED

**Most Yards Gained, Career**

| | | |
|---|---|---|
| 686 | Brig Owens | 1966–72 |
| 631 | Darrell Green | 1983–2002 |
| 491 | Sammy Baugh | 1937–52 |

**Most Yards Gained, Season**

| | | |
|---|---|---|
| 258 | Dan Sandifer | 1948 |
| 168 | George Cheverko | 1948 |
| 165 | Brig Owens | 1966 |

**Longest Return (All TDS)**

| | | |
|---|---|---|
| 100 | Barry Wilburn vs. Vikings | 12/26/87 |
| 93 | Dick Poillon vs. Eagles | 11/21/48 |
| 92 | Andre Collins vs. Buccaneers | 12/4/94 |

## TOUCHDOWNS

**Most Touchdowns, Career**

| | | |
|---|---|---|
| 6 | Darrell Green | 1983–2002 |
| 3 | Brig Owens | 1966–77 |
| 3 | Mike Bass | 1969–75 |
| 3 | Andre Collins | 1990–94 |

**Most Touchdowns, Season**

| | | |
|---|---|---|
| 2 | Dan Sandifer | 1948 |
| 2 | Dale Hackbart | 1961 |
| 2 | Vernon Dean | 1984 |
| 2 | Andre Collins | 1994 |

**Most Touchdowns, Game**

| | | |
|---|---|---|
| 2 | Dan Sandifer vs. Yanks | 10/31/48* |

## PUNTING

**Most Seasons Leading League**

| | | |
|---|---|---|
| 4 | Sammy Baugh | 1940–43* |

**Most Seasons Leading Team (all consecutive)**

| | | |
|---|---|---|
| 12 | Mike Bragg | 1968–79 |
| 9 | Sammy Baugh | 1939–47 |
| 5 | Pat Richter | 1963–67 |
| 5 | Matt Turk | 1995–99 |

## PUNTS

**Most Punts, Career**

| | | |
|---|---|---|
| 896 | Mike Bragg | 1968–79 |
| 388 | Matt Turk | 1995–99 |
| 338 | Sammy Baugh | 1937–52 |
| 338 | Pat Richter | 1963–70 |

**Most Punts, Season**

| | | |
|---|---|---|
| 104 | Tom Tupa | 2004 |
| 103 | Mike Bragg | 1978 |
| 93 | Matt Turk | 1998 |

**Most Punts, Game**

| | | |
|---|---|---|
| 14 | Sammy Baugh vs. Eagles | 11/5/39 |

**Longest Punt**

| | | |
|---|---|---|
| 85 | Sammy Baugh vs. Eagles | 12/1/40 |
| 81 | Sammy Baugh vs. Lions | 11/14/43 |
| 77 | Steve Cox vs. Bills | 11/1/87 |

## AVERAGE YARDAGE

**Highest Average, Punting, Career (min 300 punts)**

| | | |
|---|---|---|
| 45.10 | Sammy Baugh | 1937–52 |
| 43.77 | Matt Turk | 1995–99 |
| 41.96 | Pat Richter | 1963–70 |

**Highest Average, Punting, Season (min 30 punts)**

| | | |
|---|---|---|
| 51.40 | Sammy Baugh | 1940* |
| 48.73 | Sammy Baugh | 1941 |
| 46.59 | Sammy Baugh | 1942 |

**Highest Average, Punting, Game (min 4 punts)**

| | | |
|---|---|---|
| 59.40 | Sammy Baugh vs. Lions (5–297) | 10/27/40 |

## PUNT RETURNS

**Most Seasons Leading Team (all consecutive)**

| | | |
|---|---|---|
| 9 | Brian Mitchell | 1991–99 |
| 6 | Rickie Harris | 1965–70 |
| 5 | Dick James | 1959–63 |
| 5 | Mike Nelms | 1980–84 |

## Most Punt Returns, Career

| | | |
|---|---|---|
| 317 | Brian Mitchell | 1990–99 |
| 212 | Mike Nelms | 1980–84 |
| 119 | Ricky Harris | 1965–70 |

## Most Punt Returns, Season

| | | |
|---|---|---|
| 57 | Eddie Brown | 1977 |
| 53 | Larry Jones | 1975 |
| 49 | Mike Nelms | 1984 |

## Most Punt Returns, Game

| | | |
|---|---|---|
| 11 | Eddie Brown vs. Buccaneers | 10/9/77* |
| 10 | Mike Nelms vs. Saints | 12/26/82 |
| 9 | Mike Nelms vs. Cardinals | 12/21/80 |

# FAIR CATCHES

## Most Fair Catches, Career

| | | |
|---|---|---|
| 151 | Brian Mitchell | 1990–99 |

## Most Fair Catches, Season

| | | |
|---|---|---|
| 24 | Brian Mitchell | 1994 |
| 23 | Brian Mitchell | 1997 |
| 21 | Brian Mitchell | 1991 |

# YARDS GAINED

## Most Yards Gained, Career

| | | |
|---|---|---|
| 3,476 | Brian Mitchell | 1990–99 |
| 1,948 | Mike Nelms | 1980–84 |
| 1,150 | Eddie Brown | 1975–77 |

## Most Yards Gained, Season

| | | |
|---|---|---|
| 646 | Eddie Brown | 1976 |
| 600 | Brian Mitchell | 1991 |
| 506 | Brian Mitchell | 1998 |

## Longest Punt Return (All TDS)

| | | |
|---|---|---|
| 96 | Bill Dudley vs. Steelers | 12/3/50 |
| 90 | Jacquez Green vs. Eagles | 9/16/02 |
| 89 | Eric Metcalf vs. Giants | 10/28/01 |

# AVERAGE YARDAGE

## Highest Average, Career (min 40 returns)

| | | |
|---|---|---|
| 13.20 | Dick Todd | 1939–48 |
| 12.81 | John Williams | 1952–53 |
| 12.11 | Andy Farkas | 1938–44 |

## Highest Average, Season (min 20 returns)

| | | |
|---|---|---|
| 15.25 | John Williams | 1952 |
| 14.12 | Brian Mitchell | 1994 |
| 13.46 | Eddie Brown | 1976 |

# TOUCHDOWNS

## Most Touchdowns, Career

| | | |
|---|---|---|
| 7 | Brian Mitchell | 1990–99 |
| 3 | Dick Todd | 1939–44 |
| 3 | Rickie Harris | 1965–70 |
| 3 | Mike Nelms | 1980–84 |

## Most Touchdowns, Season

| | | |
|---|---|---|
| 2 | John Williams | 1952 |
| 2 | Bert Zagers | 1957 |
| 2 | Mike Nelms | 1981 |
| 2 | Brian Mitchell | 1991 |
| 2 | Brian Mitchell | 1994 |

# KICKOFF RETURNS

## Most Seasons Leading Team

| | | |
|---|---|---|
| 9 | Brian Mitchell | 1991–99 |
| 5 | Dick James | 1959–63 |
| 5 | Mike Nelms | 1980–84 |

## Most Kickoff Returns, Career

| | | |
|---|---|---|
| 421 | Brian Mitchell | 1990–99 |
| 174 | Mike Nelms | 1980–84 |
| 155 | Dick James | 1956–63 |

## Most Kickoff Returns, Season

| | | |
|---|---|---|
| 64 | Rock Cartwright | 2006 |
| 59 | Brian Mitchell | 1998 |
| 58 | Brian Mitchell | 1994 |
| 56 | Brian Mitchell | 1996 |

## Most Kickoff Returns, Game

| | | |
|---|---|---|
| 8 | Terry Metcalf vs. Cardinals | 9/20/81 |

# YARDS GAINED

## Most Yards Gained, Career

| | | |
|---|---|---|
| 9,586 | Brian Mitchell | 1990–99 |
| 4,128 | Mike Nelms | 1980–84 |
| 3,949 | Dick James | 1956–63 |

## Most Yards Gained, Season

| | | |
|---|---|---|
| 1,541 | Rock Cartwright | 2006 |
| 1,478 | Brian Mitchell | 1994 |
| 1,408 | Brian Mitchell | 1995 |
| 1,337 | Brian Mitchell | 1998 |

## Longest Kickoff Return (All TDS)

| | | |
|---|---|---|
| 102 | Larry Jones vs. Eagles | 11/24/74 |
| 101 | Brian Mitchell vs. Chargers | 12/6/98 |
| 100 | Rock Cartwright vs. Cowboys | 9/17/06 |
| 99 | Dale Atkeson vs. Eagles | 10/17/54 |
| 99 | Tony Green vs. Cardinals | 9/17/78 |
| 99 | Joe Johnson vs. Raiders | 10/29/89 |

# AVERAGE YARDAGE

## Highest Average, Career (min 40 returns)

| | | |
|---|---|---|
| 28.50 | Bobby Mitchell | 1962–68 |
| 27.87 | Herb Mul-key | 1972–74 |
| 25.98 | Joe Scudero | 1954–58 |

## Highest Average, Season (min 20 returns)

| | | |
|---|---|---|
| 29.70 | Mike Nelms | 1981 |
| 29.38 | Dick James | 1961 |
| 29.22 | Larry Jones | 1974 |

# TOUCHDOWNS

## Most Touchdowns, Career

| | | |
|---|---|---|
| 2 | Eddie Saenz | 1946–51 |
| 2 | Brian Mitchell | 1990–99 |

## Most Touchdowns, Season

| | | |
|---|---|---|
| 2 | Eddie Saenz | 1947 |

# COMBINED KICK RETURNS

## Most Combined Kick Returns, Career

| | | |
|---|---|---|
| 738 | Brian Mitchell | 1990–99 |
| 386 | Mike Nelms | 1980–84 |
| 253 | Dick James | 1956–63 |

**Most Combined Kick Returns, Season**
103 . . . . . . . . . . . . . . . . . . . . . . Brian Mitchell . . . . . . . . . . . . . . . . . . . . . . . 1998
100 . . . . . . . . . . . . . . . . . . . . . . Larry Jones . . . . . . . . . . . . . . . . . . . . . . . . . 1975
91 . . . . . . . . . . . . . . . . . . . . . . . Eddie Brown . . . . . . . . . . . . . . . . . . . . . . . . 1977
91 . . . . . . . . . . . . . . . . . . . . . . . Mike Nelms . . . . . . . . . . . . . . . . . . . . . . . . . 1984

**Most Combined Kick Returns, Game**
12 . . . . . . . . . . . . . . Larry Jones vs. Cowboys (p–6/ k–6) . . . . . . . . . 12/13/75
12 . . . . . . . . . . . . . . Eddie Brown vs. Buccaneers (11/1) . . . . . . . . . . 10/9/77
11 . . . . . . . . . . . . . . Larry Jones vs. Raiders (6/5) . . . . . . . . . . . . . . 11/23/75

## YARDS GAINED

**Most Yards Returned, Career**
13,062 . . . . . . . . . . . . . . . . . . . . Brian Mitchell . . . . . . . . . . . . . . . . . . . . . . . 1990–99
6,076 . . . . . . . . . . . . . . . . . . . . . Mike Nelms . . . . . . . . . . . . . . . . . . . . . . . . . 1980–84
4,743 . . . . . . . . . . . . . . . . . . . . . Dick James . . . . . . . . . . . . . . . . . . . . . . . . . 1956–63

**Most Yards Returned, Season**
1,930 . . . . . . . . . . . . . . . . . . . . . Brian Mitchell . . . . . . . . . . . . . . . . . . . . . . . 1994
1,843 . . . . . . . . . . . . . . . . . . . . . Brian Mitchell . . . . . . . . . . . . . . . . . . . . . . . 1998
1,723 . . . . . . . . . . . . . . . . . . . . . Brian Mitchell . . . . . . . . . . . . . . . . . . . . . . . 1995

## TOUCHDOWNS

**Most Touchdowns, Career**
9 . . . . . . . . . . . . . . . . . . . . . . . . Brian Mitchell . . . . . . . . . . . . . . . . . . . . . . . 1990–99
3 . . . . . . . . . . . . . . . . . . . . . . . . Dick Todd . . . . . . . . . . . . . . . . . . . . . . . . . . 1939–48
3 . . . . . . . . . . . . . . . . . . . . . . . . Rickie Harris . . . . . . . . . . . . . . . . . . . . . . . . 1965–70

**Most Touchdowns, Season**
2 . . . . . . . . . . . . . . . . . . . . . . . . Eddie Saenz . . . . . . . . . . . . . . . . . . . . . . . . . 1947
2 . . . . . . . . . . . . . . . . . . . . . . . . John Williams . . . . . . . . . . . . . . . . . . . . . . . . 1952
2 . . . . . . . . . . . . . . . . . . . . . . . . Bert Zagers . . . . . . . . . . . . . . . . . . . . . . . . . 1957
2 . . . . . . . . . . . . . . . . . . . . . . . . Tony Green . . . . . . . . . . . . . . . . . . . . . . . . . 1978
2 . . . . . . . . . . . . . . . . . . . . . . . . Mike Nelms . . . . . . . . . . . . . . . . . . . . . . . . . 1981
2 . . . . . . . . . . . . . . . . . . . . . . . . Brian Mitchell . . . . . . . . . . . . . . . . . . . . . . . 1991
2 . . . . . . . . . . . . . . . . . . . . . . . . Brian Mitchell . . . . . . . . . . . . . . . . . . . . . . . 1994

## FUMBLES

**Most Fumbles, Career**
47 . . . . . . . . . . . . . . . . . . . . . . . Sammy Baugh . . . . . . . . . . . . . . . . . . . . . . . 1937–52
42 . . . . . . . . . . . . . . . . . . . . . . . Joe Theismann . . . . . . . . . . . . . . . . . . . . . . 1974–85
42 . . . . . . . . . . . . . . . . . . . . . . . Mark Rypien . . . . . . . . . . . . . . . . . . . . . . . . 1987–93

**Most Fumbles, Season**
15 . . . . . . . . . . . . . . . . . . . . . . . Sammy Baugh . . . . . . . . . . . . . . . . . . . . . . . 1947
14 . . . . . . . . . . . . . . . . . . . . . . . Mark Rypien . . . . . . . . . . . . . . . . . . . . . . . . 1989
14 . . . . . . . . . . . . . . . . . . . . . . . Trent Green . . . . . . . . . . . . . . . . . . . . . . . . . 1998

**Most Fumbles, Game**
5 . . . . . . . . . . . . . . . . . . . Patrick Ramsey vs. Packers . . . . . . . . . . . . . . 10/20/02

## FUMBLES RECOVERED

**Most Fumbles Recovered, Career, Own and Opponents'**
21 . . . . . . . . . . . . . . . . . . . . . . . Sammy Baugh . . . . . . . . . . . . . . . . . . . . . . . 1937–52
16 . . . . . . . . . . . . . . . . . . . . . . . Brad Dusek . . . . . . . . . . . . . . . . . . . . . . . . . 1974–81
15 . . . . . . . . . . . . . . . . . . . . . . . Monte Coleman . . . . . . . . . . . . . . . . . . . . . . 1979–94

**Most Fumbles Recovered, Season, Own and Opponents'**
7 . . . . . . . . . . . . . . . . . . . . . . . . Sammy Baugh . . . . . . . . . . . . . . . . . . . . . . . 1947
6 . . . . . . . . . . . . . . . . . . . . . . . . Joe Theismann . . . . . . . . . . . . . . . . . . . . . . 1984

## OWN FUMBLES RECOVERED

**Most Own Fumbles Recovered, Season**
7 . . . . . . . . . . . . . . . . . . . . . . . . Sammy Baugh . . . . . . . . . . . . . . . . . . . . . . . 1947

6 . . . . . . . . . . . . . . . . . . . . . . . . Joe Theismann . . . . . . . . . . . . . . . . . . . . . . 1984

## OPPONENTS' FUMBLES RECOVERED

**Most Opponents' Fumbles Recovered, Career**
16 . . . . . . . . . . . . . . . . . . . . . . . Brad Dusek . . . . . . . . . . . . . . . . . . . . . . . . . 1974–81
15 . . . . . . . . . . . . . . . . . . . . . . . Monte Coleman . . . . . . . . . . . . . . . . . . . . . . 1979–94
14 . . . . . . . . . . . . . . . . . . . . . . . Chris Hanburger . . . . . . . . . . . . . . . . . . . . . 1965–78
14 . . . . . . . . . . . . . . . . . . . . . . . Neal Olkewicz . . . . . . . . . . . . . . . . . . . . . . . 1979–89

**Most Opponents' Fumbles Recovered, Season**
5 . . . . . . . . . . . . . . . . . . . . . . . . Paul Krause . . . . . . . . . . . . . . . . . . . . . . . . . 1965
4 . . . . . . . . . . . . . . . . . . . . . . . . Brad Dusek . . . . . . . . . . . . . . . . . . . . . . . . . 1975
4 . . . . . . . . . . . . . . . . . . . . . . . . Darryl Grant . . . . . . . . . . . . . . . . . . . . . . . . 1984
4 . . . . . . . . . . . . . . . . . . . . . . . . Fred Stokes . . . . . . . . . . . . . . . . . . . . . . . . . 1990
4 . . . . . . . . . . . . . . . . . . . . . . . . Sam Shade . . . . . . . . . . . . . . . . . . . . . . . . . . 2000

## YARDS RETURNING FUMBLES

**Longest Fumble Return (all TDS)**
78 . . . . . . . . . . . . . . . . . . Darrell Green vs. Colts . . . . . . . . . . . . . . . . . 10/7/93
76 . . . . . . . . . . . . . . . . . . John Paluck vs. Giants . . . . . . . . . . . . . . . . . . 12/2/56

## TOUCHDOWNS

**Most Touchdowns, Career**
3 . . . . . . . . . . . . . . . . . . . . . . . . Chris Hanburger . . . . . . . . . . . . . . . . . . . . . 1965–78
3 . . . . . . . . . . . . . . . . . . . . . . . . Brad Dusek . . . . . . . . . . . . . . . . . . . . . . . . . 1974–79

**Most Touchdowns, Season**
1, many times (last time by LaVar Arrington vs. Cowboys, 12/29/2002)

## COMBINED NET YARDS GAINED

**Rushing, Receiving, Interception Returns, Punt Returns, Kickoff Returns, Fumble Returns**

**Most Seasons Leading League**
4 . . . . . . . . . . . . . . . . . . . . . . . Brian Mitchell . . . . . . . . . . . . . . . . . . . . . . . 1994–96, 98

**Most Consecutive Seasons Leading League**
3 . . . . . . . . . . . . . . . . . . . . . . . Brian Mitchell . . . . . . . . . . . . . . . . . . . . . . . 1994–96

**Most Seasons Leading Team**
7 . . . . . . . . . . . . . . . . . . . . . . . Brian Mitchell . . . . . . . . . . . . . . . . . . . . . . . 1993–99
6 . . . . . . . . . . . . . . . . . . . . . . . Larry Brown . . . . . . . . . . . . . . . . . . . . . . . . 1969–74
3 . . . . . . . . . . . . . . . . . . . . . . . Bobby Mitchell . . . . . . . . . . . . . . . . . . . . . . 1962–63, 67
3 . . . . . . . . . . . . . . . . . . . . . . . Charley Taylor . . . . . . . . . . . . . . . . . . . . . . . 1964–66
3 . . . . . . . . . . . . . . . . . . . . . . . Earnest Byner . . . . . . . . . . . . . . . . . . . . . . . 1990–92

**Most Consecutive Seasons Leading Team**
7 . . . . . . . . . . . . . . . . . . . . . . . Brian Mitchell . . . . . . . . . . . . . . . . . . . . . . . 1993–99
6 . . . . . . . . . . . . . . . . . . . . . . . Larry Brown . . . . . . . . . . . . . . . . . . . . . . . . 1969–74
3 . . . . . . . . . . . . . . . . . . . . . . . Charley Taylor . . . . . . . . . . . . . . . . . . . . . . . 1964–66
3 . . . . . . . . . . . . . . . . . . . . . . . Earnest Byner . . . . . . . . . . . . . . . . . . . . . . . 1990–92

## ATTEMPTS

**Most Attempts, Career**
2,109 . . . . . . . . . . . . . . . . . . . . . John Riggins . . . . . . . . . . . . . . . . . . . . . . . . 1976–79, 81–85
1,768 . . . . . . . . . . . . . . . . . . . . . Larry Brown . . . . . . . . . . . . . . . . . . . . . . . . 1969–76
1,532 . . . . . . . . . . . . . . . . . . . . . Stephen Davis . . . . . . . . . . . . . . . . . . . . . . . 1996–2002

**Most Attempts, Season**
384 . . . . . . . . . . . . . . . . . . . . . . Stephen Davis . . . . . . . . . . . . . . . . . . . . . . . 2001
380 . . . . . . . . . . . . . . . . . . . . . . John Riggins . . . . . . . . . . . . . . . . . . . . . . . . 1983
379 . . . . . . . . . . . . . . . . . . . . . . Terry Allen . . . . . . . . . . . . . . . . . . . . . . . . . 1996

**Most Attempts, Game**

| | | |
|---|---|---|
| 45 | Jamie Morris vs. Bengals | 12/17/88 |
| 39 | Earnest Byner vs. Patriots | 12/15/90 |
| 39 | Stephen Davis vs. Cardinals | 1/6/02 |

## YARDS GAINED

**Most Yards Gained, Career**

| | | |
|---|---|---|
| 16,900 | Brian Mitchell | 1990–99 |
| 12,358 | Art Monk | 1980–93 |
| 10,803 | Charley Taylor | 1964–77 |

**Most Yards Gained, Season**

| | | |
|---|---|---|
| 2,477 | Brian Mitchell | 1994 |
| 2,357 | Brian Mitchell | 1998 |
| 2,348 | Brian Mitchell | 1995 |

## SACKS††

**Most Seasons Leading Team**

| | | |
|---|---|---|
| 5 | Dexter Manley | 1982, 84–86, 88 |
| 3 | Coy Bacon | 1978–80 |
| 3 | Charles Mann | 1987, 89, 91 |
| 3 | Ken Harvey | 1994–95, 97 |

**Most Sacks, Career**

| | | |
|---|---|---|
| 97.5 | Dexter Manley | 1981–89 |
| 82.0 | Charles Mann | 1982–93 |
| 59.5 | Dave Butz | 1975–88 |

**Most Sacks, Season**

| | | |
|---|---|---|
| 18.0 | Dexter Manley | 1986 |
| 15.0 | Coy Bacon | 1979 |
| 15.0 | Dexter Manley | 1985 |

**Most Sacks, Game**

| | | |
|---|---|---|
| 4.0 | Phillip Daniels vs. Cowboys | 12/18/05 |
| 4.0 | Diron Talbert vs. Giants | 9/28/75 |
| 4.0 | Dexter Manley vs. Giants | 10/2/88 |
| 3.5 | Rich Milot vs. Bears | 12/30/84† |

**Most Season, 10 or More Sacks**

| | | |
|---|---|---|
| 5 | Charles Mann | 1985–87, 89, 91 |
| 4 | Dexter Manley | 1983–86 |
| 3 | Coy Bacon | 1978–80 |

**Most Consecutive Seasons, 10 or More Sacks**

| | | |
|---|---|---|
| 4 | Dexter Manley | 1983–86 |
| 3 | Coy Bacon | 1978–80 |
| 3 | Charles Mann | 1985–87 |

††Sacks became an official statistic in 1982.

# OPPONENT INDIVIDUAL RECORDS

**Most Completions**

| | | |
|---|---|---|
| 37 | Jeff George (59 att), Colts | 11/7/93 |

**Most Touchdowns**

| | | |
|---|---|---|
| *7 | Adrian Burk, Eagles | 10/17/54 |
| *7 | Y. A. Tittle, Giants | 10/28/62 |

**Most Interceptions**

| | | |
|---|---|---|
| 6 | Ed Luther, Chargers | 10/31/83 |

**Longest Completion**

| | | |
|---|---|---|
| 99 | Jim Plunkett (to Cliff Branch), Raiders | 10/2/83 |

## RECEIVING

**Most Yards Gained**

| | | |
|---|---|---|
| 269 | Del Shofner, Giants (11 rec.) | 10/28/62 |

**Most Receptions**

| | | |
|---|---|---|
| 14 | Don Looney, Eagles | 12/1/40 |

**Most Touchdowns**

| | | |
|---|---|---|
| 4 | Bob Shaw, Rams | 12/11/49 |

**Longest Reception**

| | | |
|---|---|---|
| 99t | Jim Plunkett (to Cliff Branch), Raiders | 10/2/83 |

## INTERCEPTIONS

**Most Interceptions**

| | | |
|---|---|---|
| 4 | Jack Butler, Steelers | 12/13/53 |
| 4 | Jerry Norton, Cardinals | 11/20/60 |

**Most Yards Gained**

| | | |
|---|---|---|
| 121 | Mike Gaechter, Cowboys | 11/3/63 |

**Most Touchdowns**

| | | |
|---|---|---|
| 2 | Robert Massey, Cardinals | 10/4/92 |

**Longest Interception Return**

| | | |
|---|---|---|
| 96 | Dennis Thurman, Cowboys | 9/6/81 |
| 99 | George Buksar, Colts ran 18, lateralled to Ernie Zaleski who ran 81 yds | 11/26/50 |

## KICKOFF RETURNS

**Most KO Returns**

| | | |
|---|---|---|
| 8 | Harlan Huckleby, Packers | 10/17/83 |

**Most Yards Gained**

| | | |
|---|---|---|
| 208 | Harlan Huckleby, Packers | 10/17/83 |

**Longest KO Return**

| | | |
|---|---|---|
| 105t | Ollie Matson, Cardinals | 10/14/56 |

## PUNT RETURNS

**Most Punt Returns**

| | | |
|---|---|---|
| 8 | Stump Mitchell, Cardinals | 1/2/83 |
| 8 | Leon Bright, Giants | 9/13/81 |

**Most Yards Gained**

| | | |
|---|---|---|
| 107 | Charlie West, Vikings | 11/3/68 |

**Longest Punt Return**

| | | |
|---|---|---|
| 98t | Charlie West, Vikings | 11/3/68 |

## FUMBLE RETURNS

**Longest Returns**

| | | |
|---|---|---|
| 103t | Aeneus Williams, Cardinals | 12/24/00 |

## Redskins Championships

| | | | |
|---|---|---|---|
| NFC EAST: | 13 | | 1936, 1937, 1940, 1942, 1943, 1945, 1972, 1982, 1983, 1984, 1987, 1991, 1999 |
| NFC: | 5 | 1972 | Defeated Cowboys 26–3, Dec 31, 1972 (at RFK) |
| | | 1982 | Defeated Cowboys 31–17, Jan 22, 1983 (at RFK) |
| | | 1983 | Defeated 49ers 24–21, Jan 8, 1984 (at RFK) |
| | | 1987 | Defeated Vikings 17–10, Jan 17, 1988 (at RFK) |
| | | 1991 | Defeated Lions 41–10, Jan 12, 1992 (at RFK) |
| NFL: | 2 | 1937 (8–3 record) | Defeated Bears 28–21, in title game |
| | | 1942 (10–1 record) | Defeated Bears 14–6, in title game |
| SUPER BOWL: | 3 | 1982 | Defeated Dolphins 27–17 in Super Bowl XVII |
| | | 1987 | Defeated Broncos 42–10 in Super Bowl XXII |
| | | 1991 | Defeated Bills 37–24 in Super Bowl XXVI |
| PLAYOFF APPEARANCES: | 20 | | 1937, 1940, 1942, 1943, 1945, 1971, 1972, 1973, 1974, 1976, 1982, 1983, 1984, 1986, 1987, 1990, 1991, 1992, 1999, 2005 |

## Games

| | | |
|---|---|---|
| Regular Season: | 1932–2006 | Won 520, Lost 478, Tied 27 (.520) |
| Playoff Record: | 1937–2006 | Won 24, Lost 16 (.666) |
| Most Victories, Season: | 1991 | 17 (14–2 regular season, 3–0 playoffs, 17–2 overall) |
| Best Winning Pct., Season: | 1982 | .923 (8–1 regular season, 4–0 playoffs, 12–1 overall) |
| Worst Winning Pct., Season: | 1961 | 107 (1–12–1 regular season) |
| Most Consecutive Victories: | 14 | 10/4/42–11/7/43 |
| Most Consecutive Games Without Defeat: | 17 | 10/4/42–11/28/43 (16–0–1) |
| Most Consecutive Losses: | 17 | 10/30/60–11/19/61 |
| Most Consecutive Games Without Victory: | 23 | 10/16/60–12/17/61 (20 losses, 3 ties) |

## Attendance Records

**Largest Home Attendance:**
90,608 ......... 9/11/06 ............... vs. Minnesota Vikings at FedExField

**Largest Road Attendance:**
103,667 ............. 1/30/83 ................. Super Bowl XVII, Pasadena, CA, Miami Dolphins

## Washington Redskins Sellouts

The Washington Redskins have been sold out for every regular-season game since the beginning of the 1966 season.

The Redskins have sold out 310 consecutive home games, and with postseason contests, the total reaches 328 over the 40-year period.

## Postseason Records

The Washington Redskins have played in 38 postseason games in their history, earning a 23–15 record in those contests. They have reached the NFL's championship game 11 times, winning two World Championships and three Super Bowls. Along with Dallas and San Francisco, Washington ranks third among NFL teams for most Championship titles in the history of pro football.

Coach Joe Gibbs, who returned to the helm of the burgundy and gold in 2004, won three Super Bowls during his previous 12-year tenure from 1981 to 1992. His first came in Super Bowl XVII against Miami (following the 1982 season), the second in Super Bowl XII against Denver (following the 1987 season), and the third in Super Bowl XXVI against Buffalo (following the 1991 season).

## Most NFL Championships

| | |
|---|---|
| 12 | Green Bay Packers |
| 9 | Chicago Bears |
| 6 | New York Giants |
| 5 | Washington Redskins |
| | Dallas Cowboys |
| | San Francisco 49ers |
| 4 | Cleveland Browns |
| | Detroit Lions |
| | Pittsburgh Steelers |

The following is a complete list of the Redskins postseason games since their inception. Following the list is a postseason records section featuring team, individual offense and defense record for all playoff games and Super Bowls.

| Date | Playoff | Opponent | Result | Score | Attend. |
|---|---|---|---|---|---|
| Dec. 12, 1937 | 1937 NFL Championship | @ Chicago Bears | W | 28–21 | 15,870 |
| Dec. 8, 1940 | 1940 NFL Championship | Chicago Bears | L | 73–0 | 36,034 |
| Dec. 13, 1942 | 1942 NFL Championship | Chicago Bears | W | 14–6 | 36,006 |
| Dec. 19, 1943 | Eastern Division Playoff | @ New York Giants | W | 28–0 | 42,800 |
| Dec. 26, 1943 | NFL Championship | @ Chicago Bears | L | 41–21 | 34,320 |
| Dec. 16, 1945 | NFL Championship | @ Cleveland Browns | L | 15–14 | 32,178 |
| Dec. 26, 1971 | 1971 NFC Divisional Playoff | @ San Francisco | L | 24–20 | 45,327 |
| Dec. 24, 1972 | 1972 NFC Divisional Playoff | Green Bay | W | 16–3 | 53,140 |
| Dec. 31, 1972 | 1972 NFC Championship | Dallas | W | 26–3 | 53,189 |
| Jan. 14, 1973 | Super Bowl VII | Miami (@ Los Angeles) | L | 14–7 | 90,182 |
| Dec. 22, 1973 | 1973 NFC Divisional Playoff | @ Minnesota | L | 27–20 | 45,475 |
| Dec. 22, 1974 | 1974 NFC Divisional Playoff | @ LA Rams | L | 19–10 | 80,118 |

| Date | Playoff | Opponent | Result | Score | Attend. |
|---|---|---|---|---|---|
| Dec. 18, 1976 | 1976 NFC Divisional Playoff | @ Minnesota | L | 35–20 | 47,221 |
| Jan. 8, 1983 | 1982 NFC Wildcard Playoff | Detroit | W | 31–7 | 55,045 |
| Jan. 15, 1983 | 1982 NFC Divisional Playoff | Minnesota | W | 21–7 | 54,593 |
| Jan. 22, 1983 | 1982 NFC Championship | Dallas | W | 31–17 | 55,045 |
| Jan. 30, 1983 | Super Bowl XVII | Miami (@ Pasadena) | W | 27–17 | 103,667 |
| Jan. 1, 1984 | 1983 NFC Divisional Playoff | LA Rams | W | 51–7 | 55,363 |
| Jan. 8, 1984 | 1983 NFC Championship | San Francisco | W | 24–21 | 55,363 |
| Jan. 22, 1984 | Super Bowl XVIII | LA Raiders (@ Tampa) | L | 38–9 | 79,920 |
| Dec. 30, 1984 | 1984 NFC Divisional Playoff | Chicago | L | 23–19 | 55,431 |
| Dec. 28, 1986 | 1986 NFC Wildcard Playoff | LA Rams | W | 19–7 | 54,180 |
| Jan. 3, 1987 | 1986 NFC Divisional Playoff | @ Chicago | W | 27–13 | 65,141 |
| Jan. 11, 1987 | 1986 NFC Championship | @ NYG | L | 17–0 | 76,633 |
| Jan. 10, 1988 | 1987 NFC Divisional Playoff | @ Chicago | W | 21–17 | 58,153 |
| Jan. 17, 1988 | 1987 NFC Championship | Minnesota | W | 17–10 | 55,212 |
| Jan. 31, 1988 | Super Bowl XXII | Denver (@ San Diego) | W | 42–10 | 73,302 |
| Jan. 5, 1991 | 1990 NFC Wildcard Playoff | @ Philadelphia | W | 20–6 | 65,287 |
| Jan. 12, 1991 | 1990 NFC Divisional Playoff | @ San Francisco | L | 28–10 | 65,292 |
| Jan. 4, 1992 | 1991 NFC Divisional Playoff | Atlanta | W | 24–7 | 55,181 |
| Jan. 12, 1992 | 1991 NFC Championship | Detroit | W | 41–10 | 55,585 |
| Jan. 26, 1992 | Super Bowl XXVI | Buffalo (@ Minnesota) | W | 37–24 | 63,130 |
| Jan. 2, 1993 | 1992 NFC Wildcard Playoff | @ Minnesota | W | 24–7 | 57,353 |
| Jan. 9, 1993 | 1992 NFC Divisional Playoff | @ San Francisco | L | 20–13 | 64,991 |
| Jan. 8, 2000 | 1999 NFC Wildcard Playoff | Detroit | W | 27–13 | 79,441 |
| Jan. 15, 2000 | 1999 NFC Divisional Playoff | Tampa Bay | L | 14–13 | 65,835 |
| Jan. 7, 2006 | 2005 NFC Wildcard Playoff | @ Tampa Bay | W | 17–10 | 65,614 |
| Jan. 14, 2006 | 2005 NFC Divisional Playoff | @ Seattle | L | 2–10 | 67,551 |

# TEAM PLAYOFF RECORDS
# (ALL SINGLE GAME RECORDS)

## YARDS GAINED

**Most Net Yards Gained**
602 .................................................................vs. Denver, 1/31/88
445 ...................................................................vs. LA Rams, 1/1/84
441 ...............................................................@ San Francisco, 1/12/91

**Fewest Net Yards Gained**
157 ................................................................vs. Tampa Bay, 1/15/00
166 ...................................................................vs. Chicago, 12/13/42
190 ..........................................................@ New York Giants, 1/11/87

## FIRST DOWNS

**Most First Downs**
25 .................................................................@ San Francisco, 1/12/91
25 .......................................................................vs. Denver, 1/31/88
24 ........................................................4 times, last @ Minnesota, 1/12/93

**Fewest First Downs**
8 .......................................................................vs. Chicago, 12/13/42
8 .......................................................................vs. Chicago, 12/16/45
10 ...................................................................vs. Tampa Bay, 1/15/00
11 ...................................................................vs. Minnesota, 1/17/88

## RUSHING

**Most Yards Gained Rushing**
280 ....................................................................vs. Denver, 1/31/88
276 .....................................................................vs. Miami, 1/30/83
223 ....................................................................vs. Detroit, 1/8/00

**Fewest Yards Gained Rushing**
40 ...........................................................@ New York Giants, 1/11/87
46 ..................................................................vs. Tampa Bay, 1/15/00
49 ....................................................................@ LA Rams, 12/22/74

## Most Rushing Attempts
52 ......................................................................vs. Miami, 1/30/83
47 .....................................................................@ Minnesota, 1/2/93
45 ...............................................................vs. San Francisco, 1/8/84
45 .....................................................................vs. Atlanta, 1/4/92

**Fewest Rushing Attempts**
14 ....................................................................vs. Chicago, 12/ 8/40
16 ..........................................................@ New York Giants, 1/11/87
18 ...................................................................@ Minnesota, 12/18/76
21 ..............................................................@ San Francisco, 1/9193

## PASSING

**Most Passes Attempted**
51 ...................................................................vs. Chicago, 12/8/40
50 ...........................................................@ New York Giants, 1/11/87
49 ...................................................................@ Minnesota, 12/18/76
48 ...............................................................@ San Francisco, 1/12/91

**Fewest Passes Attempted**
13 ...................................................................vs. Chicago, 12/13/42
14 .................................................................vs. Green Bay, 12/24/72
17 ....................................................................vs. Detroit, 1/12/92
18 .....................................................................vs. Dallas, 12/31/72

**Most Passes Completed**
27 ...............................................................@ San Francisco, 1/12/91
26 .................................................................@ Minnesota , 12/18/76
22 ...................................................................vs. Chicago, 12/30/84
22 ...................................................................vs. Chicago, 12/12/37

**Fewest Passes Completed**
5 .......................................................................vs. Chicago, 12/13/42
7 .....................................................................vs. Green Bay, 12/24/72
9 .....................................................................vs. Minnesota, 1/17/88
11 ...............................................................@ San Francisco, 12/26/71

**Most Net Yards Passing**
371 ....................................................................vs. Chicago, 12/12/37
361 ...............................................................@ San Francisco, 1/12/91
322 ...................................................................vs. Denver, 1/31/88
315 ...................................................................vs. LA Rams, 1/1/84

**Fewest Net Yards Passing**

| | |
|---|---|
| 65 | vs. Chicago, 12/13/42 |
| 87 | vs. Miami, 1/14/73 |
| 90 | vs. LA Rams, 12/28/86 |
| 93 | @ San Francisco, 1/12/91 |

**Most Touchdown Passes**

| | |
|---|---|
| 4 | vs. Denver, 1/31/88 |
| 3 | vs. Detroit, 1/8/83 |
| 3 | vs. Chicago, 12/12/37 |
| 2 | 11 times, last vs. Buffalo, 12/26/92 |

**Most Passes Intercepted**

| | |
|---|---|
| 3 | 3 times, last @ San Francisco, 1/12/91 |

## SCORING

**Most Points Scored**

| | |
|---|---|
| 51 | vs. LA Rams, 1/1/84 |
| 42 | vs. Denver, 1/31/88 |
| 41 | vs. Detroit, 1/12/92 |

**Fewest Points Scored**

| | |
|---|---|
| 0 | vs. Chicago, 12/8/40 |
| 0 | @ New York Giants, 1/11/87 |
| 7 | vs. Miami, 1/14/73 |
| 9 | vs. LA Raiders, 1/22/84 |

**Largest Margins of Victory**

| | |
|---|---|
| 44 | vs. LA Rams, 1/1/84 (51–7) |
| 32 | vs. Denver, 1/31/88 (42–10) |
| 31 | vs. Detroit, 1/12/92 (41–10) |

**Most Touchdowns Scored**

| | |
|---|---|
| 6 | vs. LA Rams, 1/1/84 |
| 6 | vs. Denver, 1/31/88 |
| 5 | vs. Detroit, 1/12/92 |
| 4 | 3 times, last vs. Buffalo, 1/26/92 |

**Most Field Goals Scored**

| | |
|---|---|
| 4 | vs. Dallas, 12/31/72 |
| 4 | vs. LA Rams, 12/28/86 |
| 3 | 3 times, last vs. Buffalo, 1/26/92 |

**Most (One–Point) Points after Touchdown**

| | |
|---|---|
| 6 | vs. LA Rams, 1/1/84 |
| 6 | vs. Denver, 1/31/88 |
| 5 | vs. Detroit, 1/12/92 |

**Most Safeties**

| | |
|---|---|
| 1 | vs. Chicago, 12/30/84 |

## PENALTIES

**Most Penalties**

| | |
|---|---|
| 8 | @ Chicago, 1/3/87 |
| 7 | @ Minnesota, 12/18/76 |
| 7 | Chicago, 12/30/84 |

# INDIVIDUAL PLAYOFF RECORDS

## RUSHING

**Most Attempts, Game**

| | |
|---|---|
| 38 | John Riggins, vs. Miami, 1/30/83 |
| 37 | John Riggins, vs. Minnesota, 1/15/83 |
| 36 | John Riggins, vs. Dallas, 1/22/83 |
| 36 | John Riggins, vs. San Francisco, 1/8/84 |

**Most Yards Gained, Game**

| | |
|---|---|
| 204 | Timmy Smith, vs. Denver,1/31/88 |
| 185 | John Riggins, vs. Minnesota, 1/15/83 |
| 166 | John Riggins, vs. Miami, 1/30/83 |
| 140 | John Riggins, vs. Dallas, 1/22/83 |

**Longest Run from Scrimmage**

| | |
|---|---|
| 58t | Timmy Smith, vs. Denver, 1/31/88 |
| 58 | Stephen Davis, vs. Detroit, 1/8/00 |
| 43t | John Riggins, vs. Miami, 1/30/83 |
| 38 | Brian Mitchell, @ Minnesota, 1/2/93 |

**Most Consec. Games, 100 or More Yards Rushing**

| | |
|---|---|
| 6 | John Riggins (1982–1983 seasons) |

**Most Touchdowns, Game**

| | |
|---|---|
| 3 | John Riggins, vs. LA Rams, 1/1/84 |
| 2 | 8 times, last by Stephen Davis, 1/8/00 |

## PASSING

**Most Passes Completed, Game**

| | |
|---|---|
| 27 | Mark Rypien, @ San Francisco, 1/12/91 |
| 26 | Bill Kilmer, @ Minnesota, 12/18/76 |
| 22 | Joe Theismann, vs. Chicago, 12/30/84 |

**Most Passes Attempted, Game**

| | |
|---|---|
| 50 | Jay Schroeder, @ NY Giants, 1/11/87 |
| 49 | Bill Kilmer, @ Minnesota, 12/18/76 |
| 48 | Mark Rypien, @ San Francisco, 1/12/91 |

**Most Yards Gained on Passes, Game**

| | |
|---|---|
| 361 | Mark Rypien, @ San Francisco, 1/12/91 |
| 340 | Doug Williams, vs. Denver, 1/31/88 |
| 335 | Sammmy Baugh, vs. Chicago, 12/12/37 |
| 302 | Joe Theismann, vs. LA Rams, 1/1/84 |

**Most Touchdown Passes, Game**

| | |
|---|---|
| 4 | Doug Williams, vs. Denver, 1/31/88 |
| 3 | Joe Theismann, vs. Detroit, 1/8/83 |
| 3 | Sammy Baugh, vs. Chicago, 12/12/37 |
| 2 | 10 times, last by Mark Rypien, 1/26/92 |

**Most Passes Intercepted, Game**

| | |
|---|---|
| 5 | Frank Filchock, vs. Chicago,12/8/40 |
| 3 | 3 times, last by Mark Rypien, 1/12/91 |

**Longest Completed Passes**

| | |
|---|---|
| 80t | Doug Williams, vs. Denver, 1/31/88 |
| 78t | Sammy Baugh, vs. Chicago, 12/12/37 |
| 70t | Joe Theismann, vs. San Francisco, 1/8/84 |
| 60 | Joe Theismann, vs. LA Raiders, 1/22/84 |
| 51 | Bill Kilmer, vs. Dallas, 12/31/72 |

**Best Completion Percentage, Game (min. 15 attempts)**

| | |
|---|---|
| 78 | Joe Theismann, vs. LA Rams, 1/1/84 (18–23) |
| 76 | Sammy Baugh, vs. Chicago, 12/12/37 |
| 74 | Joe Theismann, vs. Minnesota, 1/15/83 (17–23) |
| 67 | Mark Rypien, @ Minnesota, 1/2/93 (16–24) |

## RECEIVING

**Most Passes Caught, Game**

| | |
|---|---|
| 10 | Art Monk, vs. Chicago, 12/30/84 |
| 10 | Art Monk, @ San Francisco, 1/12/91 |
| 9 | Ricky Sanders, vs. Denver, 1/31/88 |
| 9 | Wayne Millner, vs. Chicago, 12/12/37 |

**Most Yards Catching Passes, Game**

| | |
|---|---|
| 193 | Ricky Sanders, vs. Denver, 1/31/88 |
| 171 | Charlie Brown, vs. LA Rams, 1/1/84 |
| 163 | Art Monk, @ San Francisco, 1/12/91 |

160...............................................Wayne Millner, vs. Chicago, 12/12/37
146.................................................Charley Taylor, vs. Dallas, 12/31/72
137..............................................Charlie Brown, vs. San Francisco, 1/8/84

**Most Consec. Games, 100 or More Yards Receiving**
2...........................................................Charlie Brown (1983 season)

**Most Touchdown Receptions, Game**
3..................................................Alvin Garrett, vs. Detroit, 1/8/83
2..........................................4 times, last by Ricky Sanders, 1/31/88

## INTERCEPTIONS BY

**Most Interceptions, Game**
2..............................................3 times, last by Brad Edwards, 1/26/92

**Longest Interception Returns**
77t.................................................Jeris White, vs. Detroit, 1/8/83
72t.............................................Darrell Green, vs. LA Rams, 1/1/84
44.......................................Martin Mayhew, @ Minnesota, 1/2/93

## SCORING

**Most Field Goals Made, Game**
4...............................................Curt Knight, vs. Dallas, 1/31/72
4................................................Jess Atkinson, vs. LA Rams, 12/28/86
3............................................3 times, last by Chip Lohmiller, 1/26/92

**Longest Field Goals**
52.........................................Curt Knight, @ Minnesota, 12/22/73
48.........................................Brett Conway, vs. Tampa Bay, 1/15/00
47..........................................Mark Moseley, @ Minnesota, 12/18/76
46................................Curt Knight, twice, 12/24/72 and 12/31/72

## KICKOFF RETURNS

**Most Kickoff Returns, Game**
6............................................Eddie Brown, @ Minnesota, 12/18/76
5..............................................Alvin Garrett, vs. LA Raiders, 1/22/84
4.........................................3 times, last by Brian Mitchell, 1/15/00

**Most Yards Gained on Kickoff Returns, Game**
170............................Leslie Duncan, @ San Francisco, 12/26/71
136.........................................Eddie Brown, @ Minnesota, 12/18/76
128.............................................Mike Nelms, vs. Dallas, 1/22/83
100............................................Alvin Garrett, vs. LA Raiders, 1/22/84
100t.......................................Brian Mitchell, vs. Tampa Bay, 1/15/00

**Longest Kickoff Returns**
100t.......................................Brian Mitchell, vs. Tampa Bay, 1/15/00
76............................................Mike Nelms, vs. Dallas, 1/22/83
67.................................Leslie Duncan, @ San Francisco, 12/26/71

## PUNTING

**Best Gross Punting Average, Game (min. 4 punts)**
52.5.............................Sammy Baugh, vs. Chicago, 12/13/42 (6–315)
46.5.............................Mike Bragg, vs. Green Bay, 12/24/72 (6–279)
46.0.............................Mike Bragg, @ San Francisco, 12/26/71 (5–231)
45.2.............................Mike Bragg, @ LA Rams, 12/22/74 (5–226)

**Longest Punts**
66...........................Mike Bragg, @ San Francisco, 12/26/71
58.................................Mike Bragg, @ LA Rams, 12/22/74
57.............................Mike Bragg, vs. Green Bay, 12/24/72

## PUNT RETURNS

**Most Punt Returns, Game**
6................................Larry Brown, @ Minnesota, 12/18/76
6......................................Mike Nelms, vs. Miami, 1/30/83
5..............................Brian Mitchell, vs. Tampa Bay, 1/15/00

**Most Yards Gained on Punt Returns, Game**
70.............................Brian Mitchell, @ Minnesota, 1/2/93
60.................................Mike Nelms, vs. Detroit, 1/8/83
56...............................Nick Giaquinto, vs. LA Rams, 1/1/84

**Longest Punt Returns**
54.............................Brian Mitchell, @ Minnesota, 1/2/93
52t..........................Darrell Green, @ Chicago, 1/10/88
48...............................Nick Giaquinto, vs. LA Rams, 1/1/84

## SACKS

**Most Sacks, Career (since 1982)**
10..................................Charles Mann (15 games)
8.................................Dexter Manley (14 games)
7.......................................Fred Stokes (6 games)
5.5..............................Monte Coleman (20 games)
4.5.......................................Rich Milot (13 games)

**Most Sacks, Game (since 1982)**
3.5.........................Rich Milot, vs. Chicago, 12/30/84
3.................................Charles Mann, @ Chicago, 1/10/88
3.............................Wilber Marshall, vs. Detroit, 1/12/92

# DEFENSIVE PLAYOFF RECORDS

## TOTAL YARDS ALLOWED

**Most Net Yards Allowed**
425.......................................vs. San Francisco, 1/8/84
401........................................@ San Francisco, 1/9/93
385.......................................vs. LA Raiders, 1/22/84

**Fewest Net Yards Allowed**
148.........................................@ Minnesota, 1/2/93
169.............................................vs. Dallas, 12/31/72
176................................................vs. Miami, 1/30/83

## FIRST DOWNS

**Most First Downs Allowed**
25.........................................vs. Buffalo, 1/26/92
22.......................................@ San Francisco, 1/9/93
21...........................................@ Minnesota, 12/18/76
21................................................vs. Dallas, 1/22/83

**Fewest First Downs Allowed**
8.............................................vs. Dallas, 12/31/72
9.............................................vs. Miami, 1/10/83
9.........................................@ Minnesota, 1/2/93

## RUSHING

**Most Yards Allowed Rushing**
231.......................................vs. LA Raiders, 1/22/84
221..........................................@ Minnesota, 12/18/76
198...............................................vs. LA Rams, 12/28/86

**Fewest Yards Allowed Rushing**

| | |
|---|---|
| 43 | vs. Atlanta, 1/4/92 |
| 43 | vs. Buffalo, 1/26/92 |
| 44 | vs. Tampa Bay, 1/15/00 |

## PASSING

**Most Opponent Passes Attempted**

| | |
|---|---|
| 59 | vs. Buffalo, 1/26/92 |
| 48 | vs. San Francisco, 1/8/84 |
| 46 | vs. Detroit, 1/8/00 |

**Fewest Opponent Passes Attempted**

| | |
|---|---|
| 10 | vs. Chicago, 12/8/40 |
| 11 | vs. Miami, 1/14/73 |
| 14 | @ New York Giants, 1/11/87 |
| 17 | vs. Miami, 1/30/83 |
| 17 | vs. Chicago,12/30/84 |

**Most Opponent Passes Completed**

| | |
|---|---|
| 29 | vs. Buffalo, 1/26/92 |
| 27 | vs. San Francisco, 1/8/84 |
| 25 | vs. Detroit, 1/12/92 |

**Fewest Opponent Passes Completed**

| | |
|---|---|
| 4 | vs. Miami, 1/30/83 |
| 4 | vs. NY Giants, 12/19/43 |
| 6 | @ Minnesota, 1/2/93 |
| 7 | @ New York Giants, 1/11/87 |

**Most Opponent Net Yards Passing**

| | |
|---|---|
| 345 | vs. San Francisco, 1/8/84 |
| 292 | @ San Francisco, 1/12/91 |
| 286 | vs. Chicago, 12/26/43 |
| 275 | vs. Dallas, 1/22/83 |

**Fewest Opponent Net Passing Yards**

| | |
|---|---|
| 69 | vs. Miami, 1/14/73 |
| 73 | vs. Dallas, 12/31/72 |
| 75 | @ Minnesota, 1/2/93 |

## SCORING

**Most Opponent Points Scored**

| | |
|---|---|
| 73 | vs. Chicago, 12/8/40 |
| 41 | vs. Chicago, 12/26/43 |
| 38 | vs. LA Raiders, 1/22/84 |
| 35 | @ Minnesota, 12/18/76 |
| 28 | @ San Francisco, 1/12/91 |

**Fewest Opponent Points Scored**

| | |
|---|---|
| 3 | vs. Green Bay, 12/24/72 |
| 3 | vs. Dallas, 12/31/72 |
| 6 | @ Philadelphia, 1/5/91 |

**Opponent Largest Margins of Victory**

| | |
|---|---|
| 73 | vs. Chicago, 12/8/40 |
| 29 | vs. LA Raiders, 1/22/84 (38–9) |
| 18 | @ San Francisco, 1/12/91 (28–10) |
| 17 | @ New York Giants, 1/11/87 (17–0) |

**Most Opponent Touchdowns Scored**

| | |
|---|---|
| 11 | vs. Chicago, 12/8/40[†] |
| 5 | @ Minnesota, 12/18/86 |
| 5 | vs. LA Raiders, 1/22/84 |
| 4 | @ San Francisco, 1/12/91 |

**Most Opponent Field Goals Scored**

| | |
|---|---|
| 2 | 5 times, last @ San Francisco, 1/9/93 |

## PENALTIES

**Most Opponent Penalties**

| | |
|---|---|
| 12 | vs. Detroit, 1/8/00 |
| 8 | vs. LA Rams, 12/28/86 |
| 7 | 4 times, last @ Minnesota, 1/2/93 |

**Fewest Opponent Penalties**

| | |
|---|---|
| 2 | @ Minnesota, 12/22/73 |
| 2 | vs. Minnesota, 1/17/88 |
| 2 | vs. Tampa Bay, 1/15/00 |

# SINGLE GAME RECORDS

**From Scrimmage**

| | | | |
|---|---|---|---|
| by Redskins: | 88 | Billy Wells @ Cardinals | 1/21/54 |
| vs. Redskins: | 90 | Bobby Mitchell, Browns | 11/15/59 |
| in Washington: | 90 | Bobby Mitchell, Browns | 11/15/59 |

**Pass Play**

| | | | |
|---|---|---|---|
| by Redskins: | 99 | Andy Farkas vs. Steelers (pass from Frankie Filchock) | 10/15/39 |
| | 99 | Bobby Mitchell @ Browns (pass from George Izo) | 9/15/63 |
| | 99 | Gerry Allen @ Bears (pass from Sonny Jurgensen) | 9/15/68 |
| vs. Redskins: | 99 | Cliff Branch, Raiders (pass from Jim Plunkett) | 10/2/83 |
| in Washington: | 99 | Cliff Branch, Raiders (pass from Jim Plunkett) | 10/2/83 |
| | 99 | Andy Farkas, Redskins (pass from Frankie Filchock) | 10/22/39 |

**Punt Return**

| | | | |
|---|---|---|---|
| by Redskins: | 96 | Bill Dudley @ Steelers | 12/3/50 |
| vs. Redskins: | 98 | Charlie West, Vikings | 11/3/68 |
| in Washington: | 97 | Greg Pruitt, Raiders | 10/2/83 |

**Kickoff Return**

| | | | |
|---|---|---|---|
| by Redskins: | 102 | Larry Jones vs. Eagles | 11/24/74 |
| vs. Redskins: | 105 | Ollie Matson, Cardinals | 10/14/56 |
| in Washington: | 105 | Ollie Matson, Cardinals | 10/14/56 |

**Interception Return**

| | | | |
|---|---|---|---|
| by Redskins: | 100 | Barry Wilburn @ Vikings | 12/26/87 |
| vs. Redskins: | 99 | G. Buksar, Colts, ran 18 yds., lateralled to E. Zaleski who ran 81 yds | 11/26/50 |
| in Washington: | 99 | Buksar–Zaleski play above | 11/26/50 |

**Fumble Return**
by Redskins: ............................ 78t ............. Darrell Green vs. Colts ..................................................... 11/7/93
vs. Redskins: ........................... 77t ............. Jim Jeffcoat, Cowboys ..................................................... 9/24/89
in Washington: ........................ 78t ............. Darrell Green vs. Colts ..................................................... 11/7/93

**Field Goal**
by Redskins: ............................ 57 ............... Steve Cox vs. Seahawks ................................................... 9/28/86
vs. Redskins: ........................... 58 ............... Nick Lowery, Chiefs ......................................................... 9/18/83
in Washington: ........................ 58 ............... Nick Lowery, Chiefs ......................................................... 9/18/83

# The Last Time

**Overtime Game**
St. Louis Rams 37, Redskins 31 ............... 12/24/06 ............................................................ @ St. Louis

**Kickoff Returned for Touchdown**
by Redskins: ........................... 9/17/06 ................................... Rock Cartwright @ Cowboys (100 yards)
vs. Redskins: .......................... 12/5/04 ........................................ Derrick Ward, Giants (92 yards)

**Punt Returned for Touchdown**
by Redskins: ........................... 10/22/06 ................................. Antwaan Randle El @ Colts (87 yards)
vs. Redskins: .......................... 10/10/04 ...................................... B. J. Sams, Ravens (78 yards)

**Pass Interception for Touchdown**
by Redskins: ........................... 11/20/05 .......... Lemar Marshall vs. Oakland (17 yards) (pass from Kerry Collins )
vs. Redskins: .......................... 12/10/06 .......... Michael Lewis vs. Eagles (84 yards) (pass from Jason Campbell)

**Punt Blocked**
by Redskins: ........................... 12/24/06 ................................................ Vernon Fox @ St. Louis
vs. Redskins: .......................... 10/15/06 ............................................ Casey Cramer vs. Tennessee

**Field Goal Blocked**
by Redskins: ........................... 11/5/06 .................................................. Troy Vincent vs. Dallas
vs. Redskins: .......................... 10/9/05 ................................................... Trevor Pryce @ Denver

**Extra Point Blocked**
by Redskins ............................ 11/20/88 ......................................... Wilber Marshall @ San Francisco
vs. Redskins ........................... 11/2/03 ................................................. Flozell Adams @ Dallas

**Fake Field Goal Attempt**
by Redskins ............................ 9/15/96 ........................................ vs. Giants (Frerotte to Galbraith)
vs. Redskins ........................... 12/23/01 ........................................ vs. Bears (Maynard to Urlacher)

**Extra Point Missed**
by Redskins: ........................... 11/2/03 ..................................................... John Hall @ Dallas
vs. Redskins: .......................... 11/26/95 ............................................... Gary Anderson, Eagles

**40 Points**
by Redskins ............................ 10/23/05 ................................................. vs. San Francisco (52)
vs. Redskins ........................... 10/13/02 ................................................... @ New Orleans (43)

**Shutout**
by Redskins: ........................... 9/30/91 ............................................... Redskins 23 vs. Eagles 0
vs. Redskins: .......................... 10/30/05 ................................................ Redskins 0 @ NYG 36

**Fumble Returned for Touchdown**
by Redskins: ........................... 1/1/06 ............................................ Sean Taylor @ Philadelphia (39 yards)
vs. Redskins: .......................... 11/12/06 ............ Correll Buckhalter @ Philadelphia (37 yards, fumbled by teammate)

**Safety**
by Redskins: ........................... 11/5/06 .............................. Lemar Marshall vs. Cowboys (tackle in end zone)
vs. Redskins: .......................... 10/15/06 ............................ Casey Cramer vs. Tennessee (blocked punt;
                                                                                 Derrick Frost knocked ball out of end zone)

**500 Total Yards**
by Redskins ............................ 12/26/99 ................................................ @ San Francisco (511 yards)
vs. Redskins ........................... 12/24/06 .................................................... @ St. Louis (579 yards)

**400 Yards Passing**
by Redskins ............................ 12/26/99 ........................................ Brad Johnson @ 49ers (471 yards)
vs. Redskins ........................... 11/10/96 ................................... Boomer Esiason, Cardinals (522 yards)

**Four Touchdown Passes**
by Redskins: ........................... 12/18/05 ................................................ Mark Brunell vs. Dallas

vs. Redskins: ...................................................... 12/24/06 .................................................................. Marc Bulger @ Rams

**Five Touchdown Passes**
by Redskins: ...................................................... 10/11/64 ........................................................ Sonny Jurgensen vs. Eagles
vs. Redskins: ...................................................... 9/12/99 ............................................................. Troy Aikman, Cowboys

**Six Touchdown Passes**
by Redskins: ...................................................... 11/10/91 ............................................................ Mark Rypien vs. Falcons
vs. Redskins: .......................................................................................................................................................... Never

**200 Yards Receiving**
by Redskins: ...................................................... 10/21/01 ............................................. Rod Gardner vs. Panthers (208 yards)
vs. Redskins: ...................................................... 11/7/93 ............................................. Reggie Langhorne, Colts (203 yards)

**Three Touchdown Receptions**
by Redskins: ...................................................... 10/1/06 .......................................................... Santana Moss vs. Jaguars
vs. Redskins: ...................................................... 12/7/97 .............................................................. Rob Moore @ Cardinals

**200 Yards Rushing**
by Redskins: ...................................................... 9/17/89 ............................................. Gerald Riggs vs. Eagles (221 yards)
vs. Redskins: ...................................................... 12/30/06 ............................................. Tiki Barber vs. Giants (234 yards)

**Three Touchdowns Rushing**
by Redskins: ...................................................... 10/23/05 ....................................................... Clinton Portis vs. 49ers
vs. Redskins: ...................................................... 12/30/06 .............................................................. Tiki Barber vs. Giants

**Four Touchdowns Rushing**
by Redskins: .......................................................................................................................................................... Never
vs. Redskins: ...................................................... 11/21/54 ........................................................... Ollie Matson, Cardinals

**100–Yard Rusher, 200–Yard Passer**
by Redskins ............................... 12/17/06 @ New Orleans .................................. RB Ladell Betts (22–119), QB Jason Campbell (13–28, 204, 1 TD)
vs. Redskins ............................... 12/24/06 @ St. Louis .................................. RB Stephen Jackson (33–120), QB Marc Bulger (25–38, 388, 4 TD)

**Four Field Goals**
by Redskins: ...................................................... 12/10/06 ......................................................... Shaun Suisham vs. Eagles
vs. Redskins: ...................................................... 10/8/06 ................................................................ Jay Feeley @ Giants

**Five Field Goals**
by Redskins: ...................................................... 10/25/92 ......................................................... Chip Lohmiller @ Vikings
vs. Redskins: ...................................................... 10/30/05 ................................................................ Jay Feely @ Giants

**Three Interceptions**
by Redskins: ...................................................... 10/17/99 ........................................................ Champ Bailey @ Cardinals
vs. Redskins: ...................................................... 12/14/03 ........................................................ Terence Newman, Cowboys

## Redskins Super Bowl MVPs

John Riggins, Super Bowl XVII
Doug Williams, Super Bowl XXII
Mark Rypien, Super Bowl XXVI

*NFL record
†Playoffs

## ALL-TIME ROSTER

| Name | Position | College | Year |
|------|----------|---------|------|
| **A** | | | |
| Absher, Dick | LB | Maryland | 1967 |
| Adams, John | T | Notre Dame | 1945–49 |
| Adams, Willie | LB | New Mexico State | 1965–66 |
| Adickes, Mark | G | Baylor | 1990–91 |
| Aducci, Nick | B | Nebraska | 1954–55 |
| Aguirre, Joe | E | St. Mary's (Calif.) | 1941, 43–45 |
| Akers, David | K | Louisville | 1998–99 |
| Akins, Frank | B | Washington State | 1943–46 |
| Alban, Dick | B | Northwestern | 1952–55 |
| Albright, Ethan | LS | North Carolina | 2001–06 |
| Aldrich, Ki | C | TCU | 1941–43, 45–46 |
| Alexander, Patrise | LB | S. W. Louisiana | 1996–98 |
| Alexander, Stephen | TE | Oklahoma | 1998–01 |
| Alford, Bruce | K | TCU | 1967 |
| Allen, Gerry | B | Nebraska–Omaha | 1967–69 |
| Allen, Terry | RB | Clemson | 1995–98 |
| Allen, John | C | Purdue | 1955–58 |
| Alston, Mack | TE | Maryland State | 1970–72 |
| Ananis, Vito | B | Boston College | 1945 |
| Anderson, Bill | E | Tennessee | 1958–63 |
| Anderson, Bob | RB | Colorado | 1975 |
| Anderson, Bruce | E | Williamette | 1970 |
| Anderson, Erick | LB | Michigan | 1994–95 |
| Anderson, Gary | G | Stanford | 1980 |
| Anderson, Stuart | LB | Virginia | 1982–85 |
| Anderson, Terry | WR | Bethune–Cookman | 1978 |
| Anderson, Willie | WR | UCLA | 1996 |
| Andrako, Steve | C | Ohio State | 1940–41 |
| Apsit, Megs | B | USC | 1933 |
| Archer, David | QB | Iowa State | 1988 |
| Archuleta, Adam | S | Arizona State | 2006 |
| Arenz, Arnie | LB | St. Louis | 1934 |
| Ariri, Obed | K | Clemson | 1987 |
| Armstead, Jessie | LB | Miami | 2002–03 |
| Arneson, Jim | G | Arizona | 1975 |
| Arnold, Walt | TE | New Mexico | 1984 |
| Arrington, LaVar | LB | Penn State | 2000–05 |
| Artman, Corrie | T | Stanford | 1932 |
| Asher, Jamie | TE | Louisville | 1995–98 |
| Ashmore, Darryl | T | Northwestern | 1996–97 |
| Atkeson, Dale | B | No College | 1954–56 |
| Atkins, Pervis | RB | New Mexico State | 1964 |
| Atkinson, Jess | K | Maryland | 1986–87 |
| Audet, Earl | T | USC | 1945 |
| Aveni, John | K | Indiana | 1961 |
| Avery, Don | T | USC | 1946–47 |
| Avery, Jim | E | Northern Illinois | 1966 |
| **B** | | | |
| Bacon, Coy | DE | Jackson State | 1978–81 |
| Badaczewski, John | G | Western Reserve | 1949–51 |
| Badanjek, Rick | RB | Maryland | 1986 |
| Badger, Brad | G/T | Stanford | 1997–99 |
| Bagarus, Steve | RB | Notre Dame | 1945–46, 1948 |
| Bagdon, Ed | G | Michigan State | 1952 |
| Bailey, Champ | CB | Georgia | 1999–01 |
| Bailey, Robert | CB | Miami | 1995 |
| Baker, Sam | K | Oregon State | 1953, 1956–59 |
| Baltzell, Vic | DB | Southwestern (Kan.) | 19335 |
| Bandison, Romeo | DT | Oregon | 1995–96 |
| Bandy, Don | G | Tulsa | 1967–68 |
| Banks, Carl | LB | Michigan State | 1993 |
| Banks, Tony | QB | Michigan State | 2001 |
| Banks, Willie | G | Alcorn A&M | 1968–69 |
| Banta, Jack | RB | USC | 1941 |
| Barber, Ernie | C | San Francisco | 1945 |

| Name | Position | College | Year |
|------|----------|---------|------|
| Barber, Jim | T | San Francisco | 1935–41 |
| Barber, Shawn | LB | Richmond | 1998–01 |
| Barefoot, Ken | E | Virginia Tech | 1968 |
| Barfield, Ken | T | Mississippi | 1954 |
| Barker, Bryan | P | Santa Clara | 2001–03 |
| Barker, Ed | E | Washington State | 1954 |
| Barker, Tony | LB | Rice | 1992 |
| Barnes, Billy Ray | RB | Wake Forest | 1962–63 |
| Barnes, Brandon | LB | Missouri | 2004 |
| Barnes, Tomur | CB | North Texas | 1996 |
| Barnes, Walt | DT | Nebraska | 1966–68 |
| Barnett, Doug | DE | Azusa Pacific | 1985 |
| Barnett, Troy | DT | North Carolina | 1996 |
| Barnett, Steve | T | Oregon | 1964 |
| Barnhardt, Tom | P | North Carolina | 1988–00 |
| Barni, Roy | B | San Francisco | 1955–56 |
| Barnwell, Malcolm | WR | Virginia Union | 1985 |
| Barrington, Tom | B | Ohio State | 1966 |
| Barrow, Mike | LB | Miami | 2004 |
| Barry, Paul | B | Tulsa | 1953 |
| Bartkowski, Steve | QB | California | 1985 |
| Bartos, Hank | G | North Carolina | 1938 |
| Bartos, Joe | B | Navy | 1950 |
| Bass, Mike | CB | Michigan | 1969–75 |
| Bassi, Dick | G | Santa Clara | 1937 |
| Batiste, Michael | G | Tulane | 1998 |
| Bates, Michael | KR | Arizona | 2001 |
| Battaglia, Marco | TE | Rutgers | 2001 |
| Battles, Cliff | B | West Virginia Wesleyan | 1932–37 |
| Baugh, Sam | QB | TCU | 1937–52 |
| Bauman, Rashad | CB | Oregon | 2001 |
| Baughan, Maxie | LB | Georgia Tech | 1971 |
| Bausch, Frank (Pete) | C | Kansas | 1934–36 |
| Bayless, Martin | S | Bowling Green | 1994 |
| Beasley, Tom | G | No College | 1944 |
| Beatty, Ed | C | Mississippi | 1961 |
| Beban, Gary | QB | UCLA | 1968–69 |
| Bedell, Brad (IA–4) | OL | Colorado | 2003 |
| Bedore, Tom | G | No College | 1944 |
| Beinor, Ed | T | Notre Dame | 1942 |
| Bell, Coleman | TE | Miami | 1994–95 |
| Bell, William | RB | Georgia Tech | 1994–96 |
| Benish, Dan | DT | Clemson | 1987 |
| Benson, Cliff | TE | Purdue | 1987 |
| Bentley, Scott | K | Florida State | 2000 |
| Berrang, Ed | E | Villanova | 1949–52 |
| Berschet, Merve | G | Illinois | 1954–55 |
| Betts, Ladell | RB | Iowa | 2002–06 |
| Bigby, Keiron | WR | Brown | 1987 |
| Biggs, Verlon | DE | Jackson State | 1971–75 |
| Bingham, Guy | C | Montana | 1992–93 |
| Birlem, Keith | B | San Jose State | 1939 |
| Bishop, Harold | TE | LSU | 1996 |
| Blanchard, Cary | K | Oklahoma State | 1998 |
| Blanton, Scott | K | Oklahoma | 1996–98 |
| Boensch, Fred | G | Stanford | 1947–48 |
| Boll, Don | T | Nebraska | 1953–59 |
| Bond, Chuck | T | Washington | 1937–38 |
| Bond, Randal | B | Washington | 1938 |
| Bonner, Brian | LB | Minnesota | 1989 |
| Boose, Dorian | DE | Washington State | 2001 |
| Bosch, Frank | DT | Colorado | 1968–70 |
| Boschetti, Ryan | DL | UCLA | 2004–06 |
| Bosseler, Don | B | Miami | 1957–64 |
| Bostic, Jeff | C | Clemson | 1980–93 |
| Boswell, Ben | T | TCU | 1934 |
| Boutte, Marc | DT | LSU | 1994–99 |
| Bowen, Matt | S | Iowa | 2003–05 |
| Bowie, Larry | FB | Georgia | 1996–99 |
| Bowles, Todd | S | Temple | 1986–90, 92–93 |
| Boykin, Deral | S | Louisville | 1994 |
| Braatz, Tom | DE | Marquette | 1957–59 |

| Name | Position | College | Year |
|---|---|---|---|
| Bradley, Harold | E | Elon | 1938 |
| Bragg, Mike | P | Richmond | 1968–79 |
| Branch, Bruce | KR | Penn State | 2002 |
| Branch, Reggie | RB | East Carolina | 1985–89 |
| Brandes, John | TE | Cameron | 1990–92 |
| Brandt, David | OL | Michigan | 2001 |
| Brantley, John | LB | Georgia | 1992–93 |
| Breding, Ed | LB | Texas A&M | 1967–68 |
| Breedlove, Rod | LB | Maryland | 1960–64 |
| Brewer, Homer | B | Mississippi | 1960 |
| Briggs, Bill | DE | Iowa | 1966–67 |
| Briggs, Bob | B | Central Oklahoma State | 1965 |
| Brilz, Darrick | G | Oregon State | 1987 |
| Brito, Gene | DE | Loyola (Calif.) | 1951–53, 55–58 |
| Britt, Ed | B | Holy Cross | 1937 |
| Britt, Oscar | G | Mississippi | 1946 |
| Brohm, Jeff | QB | Louisville | 1995 |
| Brooks, Bill | WR | Boston University | 1996 |
| Brooks, Perry | DT | Southern | 1978–84 |
| Brooks, Reggie | RB | Notre Dame | 1993–95 |
| Broughton, Nehemiah | RB | The Citadel | 2005–06 |
| Brown, Antonio | WR | West Virginia | 2004–05 |
| Brown, Buddy | G | Arkansas | 1951–52 |
| Brown, Charlie | WR | South Carolina State | 1982–84 |
| Brown, Dan | E | Villanova | 1950 |
| Brown, Doug | DT | Simon Fraser | 1998–99 |
| Brown, Eddie | S | Tennessee | 1975–77 |
| Brown, Hardy | LB | Tulsa | 1950 |
| Brown, Jamie | T | Florida A&M | 1999 |
| Brown, Larry | RB | Kansas State | 1969–76 |
| Brown, Ray | G | Arkansas State | 1989–95, 2004–05 |
| Brown, Tom | DB | Maryland | 1969 |
| Brown, Wilbert | OL | Houston | 2002 |
| Brownlow, Darrick | LB | Illinois | 1995–96 |
| Brueckman, Charley | C | Pittsburgh | 1958 |
| Brundige, Bill | DE | Colorado | 1970–77 |
| Brunell, Mark | QB | Washington | 2004–06 |
| Brunet, Bob | RB | Louisiana Tech | 1968, 1970–77 |
| Bryant, Kelvin | RB | North Carolina | 1986–88, 1990 |
| Bryant, Trent | CB | Arkansas | 1981 |
| Buck, Jason | DE | BYU | 1991–93 |
| Buckley, Curtis | CB | East Texas State | 1999 |
| Buckley, Curtis | CB | East Texas State | 1999–2000 |
| Budd, Frank | WR | Villanova | 1963 |
| Buggs, Danny | WR | West Virginia | 1976–79 |
| Bukich, Rudy | QB | USC | 1957–58 |
| Buksar, George | B | Purdue | 1951–52 |
| Bunch, Derek | LB | Michigan State | 1987 |
| Burks, Shawn | LB | LSU | 1986 |
| Burkus, Carl | T | George Washington | 1948 |
| Burman, George | G | Northwestern | 1971–72 |
| Burmeister, Danny | S | North Carolina | 1987 |
| Burnett, Chester | LB | Arizona | 1998 |
| Burrell, John | WR | Rice | 1966–67 |
| Busich, Sam | E | Ohio State | 1936 |
| Butkus, Carl | T | George Washington | 1948 |
| Butsko, Harry | LB | Maryland | 1963 |
| Butz, Dave | DT | Purdue | 1975–88 |
| Byner, Earnest | RB | East Carolina | 1989–93 |

**C**

| Name | Position | College | Year |
|---|---|---|---|
| Cafego, George | QB | Tennessee | 1943 |
| Caldwell, Ravin | LB | Arkansas | 1987–92 |
| Campbell, Jason | QB | Auburn | 2005–06 |
| Campbell, Jesse | S | North Carolina State | 1997–98 |

| Name | Position | College | Year |
|---|---|---|---|
| Campbell, Khary | LB | Bowling Green | 2004–06 |
| Campbell, Matt | OL | South Carolina | 2001 |
| Campiglio, Bob | B | W. Liberty State | 1933 |
| Campofreda, Nick | C | Western Maryland | 1944 |
| Campora, Don | T | Pacific | 1953 |
| Canidate, Trung | RB | Arizona | 2003 |
| Caravello, Joe | TE | Tulane | 1987–88 |
| Carlson, Mark | T | S. Connecticut State | 1987 |
| Carpenter, Brian | CB | Michigan | 1983–84 |
| Carpenter, Preston | E | Arkansas | 1964–66 |
| Carr, Jim | LB | Morris Harvey | 1964–65 |
| Carrier, Mark | FS | USC | 2000 |
| Carroll, Jim | LB | Notre Dame | 1966–68 |
| Carroll, Leo | DE | San Diego State | 1969–70 |
| Carroll, Vic | T | Nevada | 1936–42 |
| Carson, John | E | Georgia | 1954–59 |
| Carter, Andre | DE | California | 2006 |
| Carter, Ki-Jana | RB | Penn State | 2001 |
| Carter, Tom | CB | Notre Dame | 1993–96 |
| Cartwright, Rock | FB | Kansas State | 2002–06 |
| Casares, Rick | RB | Florida | 1965 |
| Caster, Rich | TE | Jackson State | 1981–82 |
| Castiglia, Jim | B | Georgetown | 1947–48 |
| Catanho, Al | LB | Rutgers | 1996 |
| Centers, Larry | RB | Stephen F. Austin | 1999–00 |
| Chamberlain, Byron | TE | Wayne State | 2003 |
| Chandler, Jeff | K | Florida | 2004 |
| Chase, Martin | DT | Oklahoma | 2003 |
| Cherne, Hal | T | DePaul | 1933 |
| Cherry, Raphel | S | Hawaii | 1985 |
| Cheverko, George | B | Ohio State | 1948 |
| Christensen, Erik | E | Richmond | 1956 |
| Churchwell, Don | T | Mississippi | 1959 |
| Cichowski, Gene | B | Indiana | 1958–59 |
| Cifers, Ed | E | Tennessee | 1941–42, 1946 |
| Clair, Frank | E | Ohio State | 1941 |
| Claitt, Rickey | FB | Bethune–Cookman | 1980–81 |
| Clark, Algy | DB | Ohio State | 1932 |
| Clark, Gary | WR | James Madison | 1985–92 |
| Clark, Jim | G | Oregon | 1952–53 |
| Clark, Mike | DE | Florida | 1981 |
| Clark, Ryan | DB | LSU | 2004–05 |
| Clay, Billie | B | Mississippi | 1966 |
| Clay, Ozzie | B | Iowa State | 1964 |
| Clemens, Chris | LB | Georgia | 2003–06 |
| Clemons, Nic | DL | Georgia | 2005–06 |
| Clifton, Gregory | WR | Johnson C. Smith | 1993 |
| Cloud, John | B | William & Mary | 1952–53 |
| Cochran, Tom | B | Auburn | 1949 |
| Cofer, Joe | S | Tennessee | 1987 |
| Coffey, Ken | S | S. W. Texas State | 1983–86 |
| Coia, Angelo | WR | USC | 1964–65 |
| Coleman, Ben | OL | Wake Forest | 2001 |
| Coleman, Greg | P | Florida A&M | 1988 |
| Coleman, Marco | DE | Georgia Tech | 1999–01 |
| Coleman, Monte | LB | Central Arkansas | 1979–94 |
| Coles, Laveranues | WR | Florida State | 2003–04 |
| Collier, Jim | E | Arkansas | 1963 |
| Collins, Andre | LB | Penn State | 1990–94 |
| Collins, Paul (Rip) | E | Pittsburgh | 1932–35 |
| Collins, Shane | DE | Arizona State | 1992–94 |
| Collins, Todd | QB | Michigan | 2006 |
| Concannon, Rick | G | NYU | 1934–36 |
| Condit, Merle | B | Carnegie Tech | 1945 |
| Conklin, Cary | QB | Washington | 1990–93 |
| Conkright, Bill | C | Oklahoma | 1943 |
| Connell, Albert | WR | Texas A&M | 1997–00 |
| Connell, Mike | P | Cincinnati | 1980–81 |
| Conway, Brett | K | Penn State | 1998–02 |
| Cook, Anthony | DE | South Carolina State | 1999 |
| Cooley, Chris | HB | Utah State | 2004–06 |

| Name | Position | College | Year |
|------|----------|---------|------|
| Copeland, Danny | S | Eastern Kentucky | 1991–93 |
| Corbitt, Don | C | Arizona | 1948 |
| Cortez, Jose | K | Oregon State | 2002 |
| Coupee, Al | B | Iowa | 1946 |
| Cowne, John | C | Virginia Tech | 1987 |
| Cowsette, Del | DT | Maryland | 2001–02 |
| Cox, Bill | B | Duke | 1951–52, 1955 |
| Cox, Steve | P | Arkansas | 1985–88 |
| Coyle, Eric | C | Colorado | 1962–63 |
| Crabb, Claude | CB | Colorado | 1962–63 |
| Crane, Dennis | DT | USC | 1968–69 |
| Crews, Terry | LB | Western Michigan | 1995 |
| Crisler, Harold | E | San Jose State | 1948–49 |
| Crissy, Cris | WR | Princeton | 1981 |
| Croftcheck, Don | G | Indiana | 1965–66 |
| Cronan, Peter | LB | Boston College | 1981–85 |
| Cronin, Gene | DE | Pacific | 1961–62 |
| Crossan, Dave | C | Maryland | 1965–69 |
| Crotty, Jim | B | Notre Dame | 1960–61 |
| Crow, Orien | C | Haskell Indian School | 1933–34 |
| Crutchfield, Buddy | CB | N. Carolina Central | 1998 |
| Cudzik, Walt | C | Purdue | 1954 |
| Cunningham, Doug | RB | Mississippi | 1974 |
| Cunningham, Jim | RB | Pittsburgh | 1961–63 |
| Curtis, Bobby | LB | Savannah State | 1987 |
| Curtis, Mike | LB | Duke | 1977–78 |
| Curtis, Travis | S | West Virginia | 1988, 1991 |
| Cvercko, Andy | G | Northwestern | 1963 |

**D**

| Name | Position | College | Year |
|------|----------|---------|------|
| Dahl, Rob | G | Notre Dame | 1996–97 |
| Dale, Roland | E | Mississippi | 1950 |
| Daniels, Calvin | LB | North Carolina | 1986 |
| Daniels, Phillip | DL | Georgia | 2004–06 |
| Dalton, Lional | DT | Eastern Michigan | 2003 |
| Darre, Bernie | G | Tulane | 1961 |
| Davidson, Ben | DT | Washington | 1962–63 |
| Davis, Andy | B | George Washington | 1952 |
| Davis, Brian | CB | Nebraska | 1987–90 |
| Davis, Fred | T | Alabama | 1941–42, 1945 |
| Davis, Jack | G | Maryland | 1959 |
| Davis, Stephen | RB | Auburn | 1996–02 |
| Davis, Wayne | DB | Indiana State | 1989–90 |
| Davlin, Mike | T | San Francisco | 1955 |
| Day, Eagle | QB | Mississippi | 1959–60 |
| Deal, Rufus | B | Auburn | 1942 |
| Dean, Fred | G | Texas Southern | 1978–82 |
| Dean, Vernon | CB | San Diego State | 1982–87 |
| DeCarlo, Art | DB | Georgia | 1956–57 |
| DeCorrevont, Bill | B | Northwestern | 1945 |
| Dee, Bob | DE | Holy Cross | 1957–58 |
| Deeks, Don | T | Washington | 1947 |
| DeFrance, Chris | WR | Arizona State | 1979 |
| DeFruiter, Bob | B | Nebraska | 1945–47 |
| Dekker, Al | WR | Michigan State | 1953 |
| Deloplaine, Jack | RB | Salem College | 1978 |
| DeMao, Al | C | Duquesne | 1945–53 |
| Dennis, Pat | DB | Louisiana Monroe | 2004 |
| Dennison, Glenn | TE | Miami | 1987 |
| Denson, Moses | RB | MD Eastern Shore | 1974–75 |
| Denton, Tim | CB | Sam Houston State | 1998–99 |
| Dess, Darrell | G | North Carolina State | 1965–66 |
| Didier, Clint | TE | Portland State | 1982–87 |
| Didion, John | LB | Oregon State | 1969–70 |
| Dishman, Cris | CB | Purdue | 1997–98 |
| Dockery, Derrick | G | Texas | 2003–06 |
| Doering, Chris | WR | Florida | 2002 |
| Doering, Jason | S | Wisconsin | 2004 |
| Doll, Don | DE | USC | 1953 |

| Name | Position | College | Year |
|------|----------|---------|------|
| Donnalley, Rick | C | North Carolina | 1984–85 |
| Doolan, John | B | Georgetown | 1945 |
| Dorow, Al | QB | Michigan State | 1954–56 |
| Dotson, Santana | DL | Baylor (IR) | 2002 |
| Doughty, Reed | S | Northern Colorado | 2006 |
| Dow, Ken | B | Oregon State | 1941 |
| Dowda, Harry | DB | Wake Forest | 1949–53 |
| Dowler, Boyd | WR | Colorado | 1971 |
| Downey, Patrick | OL | New Hampshire | 2002 |
| Drake, Troy | T | Indiana | 1998 |
| Drakeford, Tyronne | CB | Virginia Tech | 2000 |
| Drazenovich, Chuck | LB | Penn State | 1950–59 |
| Dubinetz, Greg | G | Yale | 1979 |
| DuBois, Phil | TE | San Diego State | 1979–80 |
| Duckett, T. J. | RB | Michigan State | 2006 |
| Duckworth, Joe | E | Colgate | 1947 |
| Dudley, Bill | RB | Virginia | 1950–51, 1953 |
| Duff, Jamal | DE | San Diego State | 1997–98 |
| Dugan, Fred | WR | Dayton | 1961–63 |
| Duich, Steve | G | San Diego State | 1969 |
| Dukes, Chad | RB | Pittsburgh | 2000 |
| Duncan, Leslie | DB | Jackson State | 1971–73 |
| Dunn, Coye | B | USC | 1943 |
| Dunn, K. D. | TE | Clemson | 1987 |
| Dupard, Reggie | RB | SMU | 1989–90 |
| Dusek, Brad | LB | Texas A&M | 1974–81 |
| Dwyer, Jack | DB | Loyola (CA) | 1951 |
| Dye, Les | E | Syracuse | 1944–45 |
| Dyer, Henry | RB | Grambling | 1969–70 |

**E**

| Name | Position | College | Year |
|------|----------|---------|------|
| Ecker, Enrique | T | John Carroll | 1952 |
| Edwards, Brad | S | South Carolina | 1990–93 |
| Edwards, Turk | T | Washington State | 1932–40 |
| Edwards, Weldon | T | TCU | 1948 |
| Ellers, Pat | DB | Notre Dame | 1992–94 |
| Elewonibi, Moe | T | BYU | 1990–93 |
| Elisara, Pita (DNP–8) | OL | Indiana | 2003 |
| Ellard, Henry | WR | Fresno State | 1994–98 |
| Elliott, Matt | C | Michigan | 1992 |
| Ellis, Ed | T | Buffalo | 2000 |
| Ellstrom, Marv | B | Oklahoma | 1943 |
| Ellstrom, Swede | FB | Oklahoma | 1934 |
| Elmore, Doug | DB | Mississippi | 1962 |
| Elter, Leo | RB | Duquesne | 1955–57 |
| Emtman, Steve | DT | Washington | 1997 |
| Erhardt, Clyde | C | Georgia | 1946–49 |
| Erickson, Carl | C | Washington | 1938–39 |
| Ervins, Ricky | RB | USC | 1991–94 |
| Espy, Mike | WR | Mississippi | 2006 |
| Etherly, David | CB | Portland State | 1987 |
| Eubanks, John | CB | Southern Miss | 2006 |
| Evans, Charles | RB | USC | 1974 |
| Evans, Demetric | DL | Georgia | 2004–06 |
| Evans, Greg | S | TCU | 1998 |
| Evans, Leomont | S | Clemson | 1996–99 |
| Evans, Reggie | RB | Richmond | 1983 |

**F**

| Name | Position | College | Year |
|------|----------|---------|------|
| Fanucci, Mike | DE | Arizona State | 1972 |
| Farkas, Andy | FB | Detroit | 1938–44 |
| Farman, Dick | G | Washington State | 1939–43 |
| Farmer, Tom | B | Iowa | 1947–48 |
| Farris, Jimmy | WR | Montana | 2005–06 |
| Faulkner, Jeff | DE | Southern | 1993 |
| Fauria, Christian | TE | Colorado | 2006 |
| Feagin, Tom | G | Houston | 1963 |
| Felber, Nip | E | North Dakota | 1932 |
| Felton, Ralph | LB | Maryland | 1954–60 |
| Ferris, Neil | DB | Loyola (CA) | 1951–52 |
| Filchock, Frankie | QB | Indiana | 1938–41, 1944–45 |

| Name | Position | College | Year |
|------|----------|---------|------|
| Fiore, Dave | OL | Hofstra | 2003 |
| Fiorentino, Al | G | Boston College | 1943–44 |
| Fischer, Mark | C | Purdue | 1998–01 |
| Fischer, Pat | CB | Nebraska | 1968–77 |
| Fisher, Bob | T | USC | 1940 |
| Flemister, Zeron | TE | Iowa | 2000–03 |
| Fletcher, Derrick | G | Baylor | 2000 |
| Flick, Tom | QB | Washington | 1981 |
| Flores, Mike | DT | Louisville | 1995 |
| Flowers, Richmond | QB | Duke | 2002 |
| Foltz, Vernon | C | St. Vincent's | 1944 |
| Forte, Ike | RB | Arkansas | 1978–80 |
| Fox, Vernon | DB | Fresno State | 2006 |
| Foxx, Dion | LB | James Madison | 1995 |
| Frahm, Dick | B | Nebraska | 1935 |
| Frain, Todd | TE | Nebraska | 1986 |
| Francis, Dave | FB | Ohio State | 1963 |
| Francis, James | LB | Baylor | 1999 |
| Frankian, Ike | E | St. Mary's | 1933 |
| Franz, Todd | DB | Tulsa | 2002–04 |
| Frazier, Frank | G | Miami | 1987 |
| Freeman, Bob | DB | Auburn | 1962 |
| Frerrote, Gus | QB | Tulsa | 1994–98 |
| Friedman, Lennie | OL | Duke | 2003–04 |
| Friesz, John | QB | Idaho | 1994 |
| Frisch, Dave | TE | Colorado State | 1997 |
| Fritsch, Ted | C | St. Norbert | 1976–79 |
| Frost, Derrick | P | Northern Iowa | 2005–06 |
| Fryar, Irving | WR | Nebraska | 1999–00 |
| Fryer, Brian | WR | Alberta (Canada) | 1976–78 |
| Fugett, Jean | TE | Amherst | 1976–79 |
| Fulcher, Bill | G | Georgia Tech | 1956–58 |
| Fuller, Larry | B | No College | 1944–45 |
| **G** | | | |
| Gaffney, Jim | B | Tennessee | 1945–46 |
| Gage, Steve | S | Tulsa | 1987–88 |
| Gaines, William | DT | Florida | 1995–97 |
| Galbraith, Scott | TE | USC | 1995–96 |
| Gannon, Rich | QB | Delaware | 1993 |
| Gardener, Daryl | DT | Baylor | 2002 |
| Gardner, Rod | WR | Clemson | 2001–04 |
| Garner, Dwight | RB | California | 1986 |
| Garrett, Alvin | WR | Angelo State | 1981–84 |
| Garzoni, Mike | B | USC | 1947 |
| Geathers, James | DT | Wichita State | 1990–92 |
| Gentry, Lee | B | Tulsa | 1941 |
| George, Jeff | QB | Illinois | 2000–01 |
| German, Jim | QB | Centre College | 1939 |
| Gesek, John | C | Cal State Sacramento | 1994–95 |
| Giaquinto, Nick | RB | Connecticut | 1981–83 |
| Gibson, Alec | DT | Illinois | 1987 |
| Gibson, Joe | B | Tulsa | 1943 |
| Gilbert, Sean | DT | Pittsburgh | 1996 |
| Gillespie, Robert | RB | Florida | 2002 |
| Gilmer, Harry | QB | Alabama | 1948–52, 1954 |
| Givens, Reggie | LB | Penn State | 2000 |
| Glick, Gary | DB | Colorado A&M | 1959–61 |
| Gob, Art | E | Pittsburgh | 1959–60 |
| Gogolak, Charlie | K | Princeton | 1966–68 |
| Golston, Kedric | DT | Alabama | 2006 |
| Goodburn, Kelly | P | Emporia State | 1990–93 |
| Goode, Bob | RB | Texas A&M | 1949–51, 1954–55 |
| Goodnight, Clyde | E | Tulsa | 1949–50 |
| Goodyear, John | B | Marquette | 1942 |
| Goosby, Tom | G | Baldwin–Wallace | 1966 |
| Gouveia, Kurt | LB | BYU | 1987–94, 99 |
| Graf, Dave | LB | Penn State | 1981 |
| Graham, Don | LB | Penn State | 1989 |

| Name | Position | College | Year |
|------|----------|---------|------|
| Graham, Kent | QB | Ohio State | 2001 |
| Grant, Alan | CB | Stanford | 1994 |
| Grant, Bob | LB | Wake Forest | 1971 |
| Grant, Darryl | DT | Rice | 1981–90 |
| Grant, Frank | WR | S. Colorado State | 1973–78 |
| Grant, Orantes | LB | Georgia | 2002–03 |
| Gray, Bill | G | Oregon State | 1947–48 |
| Green, Darrell | CB | Texas A&M–Kingsville | 1983–02 |
| Green, Jacques | WR | Florida | 2002 |
| Green, Robert | RB | William & Mary | 1992 |
| Green, Tony | RB | Florida | 1978 |
| Green, Trent | QB | Indiana | 1995–98 |
| Greer, Donovan | CB | Texas A&M | 2001 |
| Griffin, Cornelius | DT | Alabama | 2004–06 |
| Griffin, Keith | RB | Miami | 1984–88 |
| Grimm, Dan | C | Colorado | 1969 |
| Grimm, Russ | G | Pittsburgh | 1981–91 |
| Guglielmi, Ralph | QB | Notre Dame | 1955, 1958–60 |
| Gulledge, David | FS | Jacksonville State | 1992 |
| Gundlach, Herman | G | Harvard | 1935 |
| **H** | | | |
| Hackbart, Dale | DB | Wisconsin | 1961–63 |
| Hageman, Fred | C | Kansas | 1961–64 |
| Haight, Mike | T | Iowa | 1992 |
| Haines, Kris | WR | Notre Dame | 1979 |
| Haji-Sheikh, Ali | K | Michigan | 1987 |
| Haley, Dick | DB | Pittsburgh | 1959–60 |
| Haley, Jermaine | DT | Butte College | 2003–04 |
| Hall, Galen | QB | Penn State | 1962 |
| Hall, John | K | Wisconsin | 2003–06 |
| Hall, Windlan | DB | Arizona State | 1977 |
| Ham, Derrick | DE | Miami | 2000 |
| Hamdan, Gibran | QB | Indiana | 2003 |
| Hamel, Dean | DT | Tulsa | 1985–88 |
| Hamilton, Malcolm | LB | Baylor | 1998–99 |
| Hamilton, Rick | LB | Central Florida | 1993–94 |
| Hamilton, Steve | DE | East Carolina | 1985–88 |
| Hamlin, Gene | C | Western Michigan | 1970 |
| Hammond, Bobby | RB | Morgan State | 1979–80 |
| Hanburger, Chris | LB | North Carolina | 1965–78 |
| Hancock, Mike | TE | Idaho State | 1973–75 |
| Hanna, Zip | G | South Carolina | 1945 |
| Hansen, Ron | G | Minnesota | 1954 |
| Harbour, Dave | C | Illinois | 1988–89 |
| Hardeman, Buddy | RB | Iowa State | 1979–80 |
| Hare, Cecil | FB | Gonzaga | 1941–42, 1945 |
| Hare, Ray | QB | Gonzaga | 1940–43 |
| Harlan, Jim | T | Howard Payne | 1978 |
| Harmon, Clarence | RB | Mississippi State | 1977–82 |
| Harold, George | B | Allen | 1968 |
| Harraway, Charley | RB | San Jose State | 1969–73 |
| Harris, Don | S | Rutgers | 1978–79 |
| Harris, Hank | G | Texas | 1947–48 |
| Harris, Jim | DB | Howard Payne | 1970 |
| Harris, Joe | LB | Georgia Tech | 1977 |
| Harris, Rickie | DB | Arizona | 1965–70 |
| Harris, Walt | CB | Mississippi State | 2004–05 |
| Harrison, Kenny | WR | SMU | 1980 |
| Harrison, Lloyd | CB | North Carolina State | 2000 |
| Harrison, Nolan | DE | Indiana | 2000 |
| Harry, Carl | WR | Utah | 1989, 1992 |
| Hart, Jim | QB | Southern Illinois | 1984 |
| Hartley, Howard | B | Duke | 1948 |
| Hartman, Bill | B | Georgia | 1938 |
| Harvey, Ken | LB | California | 1994–98 |
| Harvin, Allen | RB | Cincinnati | 1987 |
| Hasselbeck, Tim | QB | Boston College | 2003 |

| Name | Position | College | Year |
|---|---|---|---|
| Hatcher, Ron | FB | Michigan State | 1962 |
| Hauss, Len | C | Georgia | 1964–77 |
| Haws, Kurt | TE | Utah | 1994 |
| Hayden, Ken | C | Arkansas | 1943 |
| Hayes, Jeff | P | North Carolina | 1982–85 |
| Haymond, Alvin | DB | Southern | 1972 |
| Haynes, Hall | DB | Santa Clara | 1950, 1953–55 |
| Haynes, Reggie | TE | UNLV | 1978 |
| Hazelwood, Ted | T | North Carolina | 1953 |
| Heath, Leon | FB | Oklahoma | 1951–53 |
| Heck, Andy | T | Notre Dame | 1999–00 |
| Hecker, Norb | DB | Baldwin–Wallace | 1955–57 |
| Heenan, Pat | E | Notre Dame | 1960 |
| Hegarty, Bill | T | Villanova | 1960 |
| Heinz, Bob | DT | Pacific | 1978 |
| Hendershot, Larry | LB | Arizona State | 1967 |
| Henderson, Jon | WR | Colorado State | 1970 |
| Hendren, Bob | T | USC | 1949–51 |
| Hennessey, Jerry | DE | Santa Clara | 1952–53 |
| Hermeling, Terry | T | Nevada | 1970–80 |
| Hernandez, Joe | WR | Arizona | 1964 |
| Hickman, Dallas | DE | Califonia | 1976–81 |
| Hickman, Donnie | G | USC | 1978 |
| Hicks, Skip | RB | UCLA | 1998–00 |
| Hill, Calvin | RB | Yale | 1976–77 |
| Hill, Irv | B | Trinity | 1933 |
| Hill, Nate | DE | Auburn | 1989 |
| Hitchcock, Ray | C | Minnesota | 1987 |
| Hoage, Terry | S | Georgia | 1991 |
| Hobbs, Stephen | WR | North Alabama | 1990–92 |
| Hochertz, Martin | DE | Southern Illinois | 1993 |
| Hodgson, Pat | TE | Georgia | 1966 |
| Hoelscher, David | DT | Eastern Kentucky | 1998 |
| Hoffman, Bob | QB | USC | 1940–41 |
| Hoffman, John | DE | Hawaii | 1969–70 |
| Hogeboom, Gary | QB | Central Michigan | 1990 |
| Hokuf, Steve | B | Nebraska | 1933–35 |
| Holdman, Warrick | LB | Texas A&M | 2005–06 |
| Hollar, John | B | Appalachian State | 1948–49 |
| Hollinquest, Lamont | LB | USC | 1993–94 |
| Holloway, Derek | WR | Arkansas | 1986 |
| Holly, Bob | QB | Princeton | 1982–83 |
| Holman, Walter | RB | West Virginia State | 1987 |
| Holman, Willie | DE | South Carolina State | 1973 |
| Holmer, Walt | B | Northwestern | 1933 |
| Holsey, Bernard | DL | Duke | 2003 |
| Horner, Sam | B | VMI | 1960–61 |
| Horstmann, Roy | FB | Purdue | 1933 |
| Horton, Ethan | TE | North Carolina | 1994 |
| Hostetler, Jeff | QB | West Virginia | 1997 |
| Houghton, Jerry | T | Washington State | 1950 |
| Houston, Ken | S | Prairie View | 1973–80 |
| Houston, Walt | G | Purdue | 1955 |
| Hover, Don | LB | Washington State | 1978–79 |
| Howard, Desmond | WR | Michigan | 1992–94 |
| Howell, Dixie | B | Alabama | 1937 |
| Hudson, Bob | G | Clemson | 1959 |
| Huff, Ken | G | North Carolina | 1983–85 |
| Huff, Sam | LB | West Virginia | 1964–67, 1969 |
| Hughley, George | FB | Central Oklahoma State | 1965 |
| Hull, Mike | RB | USC | 1971–74 |
| Humphries, Stan | QB | NE Louisiana | 1989–91 |
| Huntington, Greg | C | Penn State | 1993 |
| Hunter, Bill | DB | Syracuse | 1965 |
| Hurley, George | G | Washington State | 1932–33 |
| Husak, Todd | QB | Stanford | 2000 |
| Husted, Michael | K | Virginia | 2000 |
| Hutson, Tony | G | NE Oklahoma | 2000 |
| Hyatt, Fred | WR | Auburn | 1973 |

| Name | Position | College | Year |
|---|---|---|---|
| **I** | | | |
| Imhof, Martin | DE | San Diego State | 1974 |
| Intrieri, Marne | G | Loyola (Md.) | 1933–34 |
| Irwin, Don | FB | Colgate | 1936–39 |
| Izo, George | QB | Notre Dame | 1961–64 |
| **J** | | | |
| Jackson, Benard | DL | Tennessee | 2002 |
| Jackson, Charles | S | Texas Tech | 1987 |
| Jackson, Ladairis | DE | Oregon State | 2002–03 |
| Jackson, Leroy | RB | Western Illinois | 1962–63 |
| Jackson, Steve | LB | Texas–Arlington | 1966–67 |
| Jackson, Trenton | WR | Illinois | 1967 |
| Jackson, Wilbur | FB | Alabama | 1980–82 |
| Jacobs, Jack | QB | Oklahoma | 1946 |
| Jacobs, Taylor | WR | Florida | 2003–05 |
| Jacoby, Joe | T/G | Louisville | 1981–93 |
| Jaffurs, John | G | Penn State | 1946 |
| Jagielski, Harry | T | Indiana | 1956 |
| James, Dick | RB | Oregon | 1956–63 |
| Janowicz, Vic | B | Ohio State | 1954–55 |
| Jansen, Jon | T | Michigan | 1999–02 |
| Jaqua, Jon | S | Lewis & Clark | 1970–72 |
| Jarrett, Craig | P | Michigan State | 2002 |
| Jefferson, Roy | WR | Utah | 1971–76 |
| Jencks, Bob | K/E | Miami (OH) | 1965 |
| Jenkins, Jacque | FB | Vanderbilt | 1943–46 |
| Jenkins, James | TE | Rutgers | 1991–00 |
| Jenkins, Ken | RB | Bucknell | 1985–86 |
| Jessie, Tim | RB | Auburn | 1987 |
| Jimoh, Adebola | DB | Utah State | 2003–06 |
| Johnson, A.J. | | S.W. Texas State | 1989–94 |
| Johnson, Andre | T | Penn State | 1996 |
| Johnson, Billy | WR | Widener | 1988 |
| Johnson, Brad | QB | Minnesota | 1999–00 |
| Johnson, Bryan | FB | Boise State | 2000–03 |
| Johnson, Dennis | DT | Delaware | 1974–77 |
| Johnson, Jimmie | TE | Howard | 1989–91 |
| Johnson, (Howard), Joe | WR | Notre Dame | 1989–91 |
| Johnson, Larry | C | Haskell Indian | 1933–35, 1944 |
| Johnson, Mitch | T | UCLA | 1966–68, 1972 |
| Johnson, Patrick | WR | Oregon | 2003 |
| Johnson, Randy | QB | Texas A&I | 1975–76 |
| Johnson, Richard | WR | Colorado | 1987 |
| Johnson, Rob | QB | USC | 2003 |
| Johnson, Robert | TE | Auburn | 2005 |
| Johnson, Sidney | CB | California | 1990–92 |
| Johnson, Tim | DT | Penn State | 1990–95 |
| Johnson, Tre | T | Temple | 1994–00, 02 |
| Johnston, Jim | B | Washington | 1939–40 |
| Jones, Aki | DL | Fordham | 2005 |
| Jones, Anthony | TE | Wichita State | 1984–88 |
| Jones, Chuck | E | George Washington | 1955 |
| Jones, David | C | Texas | 1987 |
| Jones, Deacon | DE | Mississippi Vocational | 1974 |
| Jones, Greg | LB | Colorado | 1997–00 |
| Jones, Harvey | B | Baylor | 1947 |
| Jones, Jimmie | DE | Wichita State | 1984–88 |
| Jones, Joe | DE | Tennessee State | 1979–80 |
| Jones, Kenyatta | OL | South Florida | 2003–04 |
| Jones, Larry | WR | N.E. Missouri State | 1974–77 |
| Jones, Larry | FB | Miami | 1995 |
| Jones, Melvin | G | Houston | 1981 |
| Jones, Robert | LB | East Carolina | 2001 |
| Jones, Rod | OL | Kansas | 2002 |
| Jones, Stan | DT | Maryland | 1966 |
| Jordan, Curtis | FS | Texas Tech | 1981–86 |
| Jordan, Jeff | RB | Washington | 1971–72 |
| Joseph, Ricot | DB | Central Florida | 2002 |
| Junker, Steve | E | Xavier | 1961–62 |

| Name | Position | College | Year |
|------|----------|---------|------|
| Junkin, Trey | LB | Louisiana Tech | 1984 |
| Jurgensen, Sonny | QB | Duke | 1964–74 |
| Justice, Charlie | RB | North Carolina | 1950, 1952–54 |
| Justice, Ed | B | Gonzaga | 1936–42 |
| Juzwik, Steve | B | Notre Dame | 1942 |
| **K** | | | |
| Kahn, Ed | G | North Carolina | 1935–37 |
| Kalaniuvalu, Alai | G | Oregon State | 1994 |
| Kau, Ndukwe | DE | Rice | 1998–00 |
| Kamp, Jim | T | Oklahoma City | 1933 |
| Kammerer, Carl | DE | Pacific | 1963–69 |
| Kane, Rick | RB | San Jose State | 1984 |
| Kantor, Joe | RB | Notre Dame | 1966 |
| Karamatic, George | B | Gonzaga | 1938 |
| Karas, Emil | E | Dayton | 1959 |
| Karcher, Jim | G | Ohio State | 1936–39 |
| Karras, Lou | T | Purdue | 1950–51 |
| Karras, Ted | DT | Northwestern | 1987 |
| Katrishen, Mike | T | Southern Mississippi | 1948–49 |
| Kaufman, Mel | LB | Cal Poly SLO | 1981–88 |
| Kawal, Ed | C | Illinois | 1937 |
| Keating, Chris | LB | Maine | 1985 |
| Keenan, Jack | T | South Carolina | 1944–45 |
| Kehr, Rick | G | Carthage | 1987–88 |
| Kelley, Gordon | LB | Georgia | 1962–63 |
| Kelly, John | T | Florida A&M | 1966–67 |
| Kenneally, Gus | E | St. Bonaventure | 1932 |
| Kerr, Jim | DB | Penn State | 1961–62 |
| Khayat, Bob | K | Mississippi | 1960, 1962–63 |
| Khayat, Ed | DT | Tulane | 1957, 1962–63 |
| Kick, Jim | RB | Wyoming | 1977 |
| Killings, Cedric | DL | Carson–Newman | 2005–06 |
| Kilmer, Bill | QB | UCLA | 1971–78 |
| Kimball, Bruce | G | Massachusetts | 1983–84 |
| Kimble, Garry | CB | Sam Houston State | 1987 |
| Kimmel, J. D. | T | Houston | 1955–56 |
| Kimmel, John | LB | Colgate | 1987 |
| Kimrin, Ola | K | Texas El Paso (5 games 04) | 2004 |
| Kincaid, Jim | B | South Carolina | 1954 |
| Kinney, Kelvin | DE | Virginia State | 1997–98 |
| Kirk, Randy | LB | San Diego State | 1990 |
| Kitts, Jim | FB | Ferrum | 1998 |
| Knight, Curt | K | Coast Guard | 1969–73 |
| Koch, Markus | DE | Boise State | 1986–91 |
| Koniszewski, John | T | George Washington | 1945–46, 1948 |
| Kopay, Dave | RB | Washington | 1969–70 |
| Kovatch, John | E | Notre Dame | 1942–46 |
| Kozlowski, Brian | TE | Connecticut | 2004–05 |
| Krakoski, Joe | B | Illinois | 1961 |
| Krakoski, Joe | LB | Washington | 1986 |
| Krause, Max | FB | Gonzaga | 1937–40 |
| Krause Paul | DB | Iowa | 1964–67 |
| Krause, Red | C | St. Louis | 1938 |
| Kresky, Joe (Mink) | G | Wisconsin | 1932 |
| Kreuger, Al | RB | USC | 1941–42 |
| Krouse, Ray | T | Maryland | 1960 |
| Kruczek, Mike | QB | Boston College | 1980 |
| Kubin, Larry | LB | Penn State | 1982–84 |
| Kuchta, Frank | C | Notre Dame | 1959 |
| Kuehl, Ryan | DT | Virginia | 1996–97 |
| Kupp, Jake | G | Washington | 1966 |
| Kuziel, Bob | G | Pittsburgh | 1975–80 |
| **L** | | | |
| Laaveg, Paul | G | Iowa | 1970–75 |

| Name | Position | College | Year |
|------|----------|---------|------|
| Lachey, Jim | T | Ohio State | 1988–95 |
| Lane, Skip | S | Mississippi | 1987 |
| Lang, Kenard | DE | Miami | 1997–01 |
| Lapka, Ted | E | St. Ambrose | 1943–44, 1946 |
| LaPresta, Benny | B | St. Louis | 1933 |
| Larson, Bill | TE | Colorado State | 1977 |
| Larson, Pete | RB | Cornell | 1967–68 |
| Lasse, Dick | LB | Syracuse | 1960–61 |
| Lathrop, Kit | DT | Arizona State | 1987 |
| Laster, Donald | T | Tennessee State | 1982–83 |
| Laufenberg Babe | QB | Indiana | 1983–85 |
| Lavender, Joe | CB | San Diego State | 1976–82 |
| Law, Dennis | WR | East Tennessee State | 1979 |
| Lawrence, don | T | Notre Dame | 1959–61 |
| LeBaron, Eddie | QB | Pacific | 1952–53, 1955–59 |
| Leeuwenberg, Jay | G | Colorado | 2000 |
| Lemek, Ray | T | Notre Dame | 1959–61 |
| Lennan, Reid | G | No College | 1945 |
| Leon, Tony | G | Alabama | 1943 |
| Lewis, Dan | RB | Wisconsin | 1965 |
| Lewis, Ron | G | Washington State | 1995 |
| Leverette, Otis | DE | UAB | 2001–02 |
| Liebenstein, Todd | DE | UNLV | 1982–85 |
| Lipscomb, Paul | T | Tennessee | 1950–54 |
| Livingston, Howie | B | Fullerton JC | 1948–50 |
| Lloyd, Brandon | WR | Illinois | 2006 |
| Lockett, J. W. | B | Central Oklahoma State | 1964 |
| Lockett, Kevin | WR | Kansas State | 2001–02 |
| Logan, Marc | FB | Kentucky | 1995–97 |
| Lohmiller, Chip | K | Minnesota | 1988–94 |
| Lolatai, Al | G | Weber State | 1945 |
| Long, Bob | WR | Wichita State | 1969 |
| Lookabaugh, John | E | Maryland | 1946–47 |
| Looney, Joe Don | RB | Oklahoma | 1966–67 |
| Lorch, Karl | DT | USC | 1976–81 |
| Lott, Andre | DB | Tennessee | 2002 |
| Love, John | WR | North Texas State | 1967 |
| Loverne, David | OL | San Jose State | 2002 |
| Lowe, Gary | B | Michigan State | 1956–57 |
| Lowry, Quentin | LB | Youngstown State | 1981–83 |
| Luce, Lew | B | Penn State | 1961 |
| Lynch, Dick | B | Notre Dame | 1958 |
| Lyle, Keith | S | Virginia | 2001 |
| **M** | | | |
| MacAfee, Ken | E | Alabama | 1959 |
| Macioszczck, Art | FB | Western Michigan | 1948 |
| MacMurdo, Jim | T | Pittsburgh | 1932–33 |
| Madarik, Elmer | B | Detroit | 1948 |
| Malinchak, Bill | WR | Indiana | 1970–74, 1976 |
| Malone, Benny | RB | Arizona State | 1978–79 |
| Malone, Charley | E | Texas A&M | 1934–40, 1942 |
| Mandeville, Chris | DB | Cal–Davis | 1989 |
| Manley, Dexter | DE | Oklahoma State | 1981–89 |
| Mann, Charles | DE | Nevada–Reno | 1983–93 |
| Manton, Tillie | FB | TXCU | 1938 |
| Manusky, Greg | LB | Colgate | 1988–90 |
| Marciniak, Ron | C | Kansas State | 1955 |
| Marcus, Pete | E | Kentucky | 1944 |
| Marshall, Lemar | LB | Michigan State | 2002–06 |
| Marshall, Leonard | DT | LSU | 1994 |
| Marshall, Rich | T | Stephen F. Austin | 1966 |
| Marshall, Wilber | LB | Florida | 1988–92 |
| Martin, Aaron | DB | North Carolina College | 1968 |
| Martin, Jamie | QB | Weber State | 1997 |
| Martin, Jim | K | Notre Dame | 1964 |
| Martin, Steve | DE | Jackson State | 1987 |

| Name | Position | College | Year |
|---|---|---|---|
| Mason, Eddie | LB | North Carolina | 1999–02 |
| Mason, Tommy | RB | Tulane | 1971–72 |
| Masterson, Bob | E | Miami | 1938–43 |
| Maston, Le'Shai | FB | Baylor | 1998 |
| Matich, Trevor | C | BYU | 1994–96 |
| Matthews, Shane | QB | Florida | 2002 |
| Mattson, Riley | T | Oregon | 1961–64 |
| Mauti, Rich | WR | Penn State | 1984 |
| May, Mark | T | Pittsburgh | 1981–89 |
| Mayhew, Martin | CB | Florida State | 1989–92 |
| Mays, Alvoid | CB | West Virginia | 1990–94 |
| Mays, Damon | WR | Missouri | 1996 |
| Mazurek, Fred | B | Pittsburgh | 1965–66 |
| McCabe, Dick | B | Pittsburgh | 1959 |
| McCants, Damerien | WR | Delaware State | 2002–04 |
| McChesney, Bob | E | UCLA | 1936–42 |
| McClellion, Central | CB | Ohio State | 2001 |
| McCrary, Greg | TE | Clark | 1978, 1981 |
| McCune, Robert | LB | Louisville | 2005–06 |
| McCullough, Sultan | RB | USC | 2003 |
| McDaniel, John | WR | Lincoln | 1978–80 |
| McDole, Ron | DE | Nebraska | 1971–78 |
| McDonald, Ray | RB | Idaho | 1967–68 |
| McEwen, Craig | TE | Utah | 1987–88 |
| McGee, Tim | WR | Tennessee | 1993 |
| McGee, Tony | DE | Bishop (Tex.) | 1982–84 |
| McGrath, Mark | WR | Montana State | 1983–85 |
| McGriff, Curtis | DT | Alabama | 1987 |
| McIntosh, Roger (Rocky) | LB | Miami | 2006 |
| McKee, Paul | E | Syracuse | 1947–48 |
| McKeever, Marlin | LB | USC | 1968–70 |
| McKenzie, Raleigh | G | Tennessee | 1985–94 |
| McKinney, Zion | WR | South Carolina | 1980 |
| McLinton, Harold | LB | Southern | 1969–78 |
| McMillan, Mark | CB | Alabama | 1999 |
| McNeil, Clifton | WR | Grambling | 1971–72 |
| McNeil, Nick | LB | Western Carolina | 2005 |
| McPhail, Hal | FB | Xavier | 1934–35 |
| McQuaid, Dan | T | UNLV | 1985–87 |
| McQuilken, Kim | QB | Lehigh | 1978–80 |
| McRae, Stan | E | Michigan State | 1946 |
| Meade, Jim | B | Maryland | 1939–40 |
| Meads, Johnny | LB | Nicholls State | 1992 |
| Meadows, Ed | DB | Duke | 1959 |
| Melinger, Steve | E | Kentucky | 1956–57 |
| Mendenhall, Mat | DE | BYU | 1981–82 |
| Merkle, Ed | G | Oklahoma A&M | 1944 |
| Mercein, Chuck | RB | Yale | 1969 |
| Metcalf, Terry | RB | San Diego State | 1981 |
| Michaels, Ed | G | Villanova | 1937 |
| Micka, Mike | FB | Colgate | 1944 |
| Mickles, Joe | RB | Mississippi | 1989 |
| Middleton, Ron | TE | Auburn | 1988, 1990–93 |
| Millen, Matt | LB | Penn State | 1991 |
| Miller, Allen | LB | Ohio | 1962–63 |
| Miller, Clark | DE | Utah State | 1969 |
| Miller, Dan | K | Florida | 1982 |
| Miller, Fred | T | Pacific | 1955 |
| Miller, John | T | Boston College | 1956, 1958–59 |
| Miller, Tom | B | Hampden–Sydney | 1945 |
| Milner, Wayne | E | Notre Dame | 1936–41, 1945 |
| Mills, Lamar | DT | Indiana | 1994 |
| Milot, Rich | LB | Penn State | 1979–87 |
| Misltead, Rod | G | Delaware State | 1998–99 |
| Mims, Chris | DT | Tennessee | 1997 |
| Mingo, Gene | K | No College | 1967 |
| Mitchell, Bobby | FL | Illinois | 1962–68 |
| Mitchell, Brian | RB | S.W. Louisiana | 1990–99 |
| Mitchell, Kevin | LB | Syracuse | 2000–03 |

| Name | Position | College | Year |
|---|---|---|---|
| Mitchell, Michael | CB | Howard Payne | 1987 |
| Modzelewski, Dick | DT | Maryland | 1953–54 |
| Mojsiejenko, Ralf | P | Michigan State | 1989–90 |
| Molinaro, Jim | OL | Notre Dame | 2004–06 |
| Momsen, Tony | C | Michigan | 1952 |
| Monachino, Jim | B | California | 1955 |
| Monaco, Ray | G | Holy Cross | 1944 |
| Monasco, Don | B | Texas | 1954 |
| Monk, Art | WR | Syracuse | 1980–93 |
| Mont, Tommy | QB | Maryland | 1947–49 |
| Montgomery, Anthony | DT | Minnesota | 2006 |
| Moore, Chuck | G | Arkansas | 1962 |
| Moore, Darryl | G | Texas–El Paso | 1992–93 |
| Moore, Jeff | RB | Jackson State | 1984 |
| Moore, Larry | C | BYU | 2002–03 |
| Moore, Michael | G | Troy State | 2000 |
| Moore, Wilbur | B | Minnesota | 1939–46 |
| Moran, Jim | G | Holy Cross | 1935–36 |
| Morgan, Bob | DT | Maryland | 1954 |
| Morgan, Boyd | S | USC | 1939–40 |
| Morgan, Mike | LB | LSU | 1968 |
| Morley, Sam | E | Stanford | 1954 |
| Morris, Jamie | RB | Michigan | 1988–89 |
| Morrison, Darryl | S | Arizona | 1993–96 |
| Morrison, Tim | CB | North Carolina | 1986–87 |
| Mortensen, Fred | QB | Arizona State | 1979 |
| Morton, Chad | RB | USC | 2003–04 |
| Morton, Christian | DB | Illinois | 2005–06 |
| Morton, Michael | RB | UNLV | 1985 |
| Moseley, Mark | K | Stephen F. Austin | 1974–86 |
| Moss, Eddie | RB | S.E. Missouri State | 1977 |
| Moss, Joe | T | Maryland | 1952 |
| Moss, Santana | WR | Miami | 2005–06 |
| Muhammad, Calvin | WR | Texas Southern | 1984–85 |
| Mul-Key, Herb | RB | No College | 1972–74 |
| Murphy, Mark | S | Colgate | 1977–84 |
| Murray, Eddie | K | Tulane | 1995 |
| Murray, Eddie | K | Tulane | 1995, 2000 |
| Murrell, Adrian | RB | West Virginia | 2000 |
| Musgrove, Spain | DT | Utah State | 1967–69 |
| Musick, Jim | FB | USC | 1932–33, 1935–36 |
| Myslinski, Tom | G | Tennessee | 1992 |
| **N** | | | |
| Natowich, Andy | B | Holy Cross | 1944 |
| Ndukwe, Ikechuku | OL | Northwestern | 2005 |
| Nelms, Mike | KR | Baylor | 1980–84 |
| Nelson, Ralph | RB | No College | 1975 |
| Niemi, Laurie | T | Washington State | 1949–53 |
| Nichols, Gerald | DT | Florida State | 1993 |
| Ninowski, Jim | QB | Michigan State | 1967–68 |
| Nisby, John | G | Pacific | 1962–64 |
| Nix, Doyle | B | SMU | 1958–59 |
| Nobile, Leo | G | Penn State | 1947 |
| Noble, Brandon | DL | Penn State | 2003–05 |
| Noble, James | WR | Stephen F. Austin | 1986 |
| Nock, George | RB | Morgan State | 1972 |
| Noga, Al | DE | Hawaii | 1993 |
| Norman, Jim | T | No College | 1955 |
| Norris, Hal | B | California | 1955–56 |
| North, Jim | T | Central Washington | 1944 |
| Norton, Jim | T | Washington | 1969 |
| Nott, Dug | B | Detroit | 1935 |
| Nottage, Dexter | DE | Florida A&M | 1994–96 |
| Novak, Nick | K | Maryland | 2005, 2006 |
| Nugent, Dan | G | Auburn | 1976–78, 1980 |
| Nussbaumer, Bob | E | Michigan | 1947–48 |
| **O** | | | |
| O'Brien, Fran | T | Michigan State | 1960–66 |

| Name | Position | College | Year |
|------|----------|---------|------|
| O'Brien, Gail | T | Nebraska | 1934–36 |
| O'Dell, Stu | LB | Indiana | 1974–76 |
| Ohalete, Ifeanyi | S | US | 2001–03 |
| Ogrin, Pat | DT | Wyoming | 1981–82 |
| Oliphant, Mike | RB | Puget Sound | 1988 |
| Oliver, Muhammad | CB | Oregon | 1995 |
| Olkewicz, Neal | LB | Maryland | 1979–89 |
| Olsson, Les | G | Mercer | 1934–38 |
| Olszewski, John | B | California | 1958–60 |
| Orr, Terry | TE | Texas | 1986–92 |
| Osborne, Tom | WR | Hastings (Neb.) | 1960–61 |
| Ostrowski, Chet | E | Notre Dame | 1954–59 |
| Owen, Tom | QB | Wichita State | 1982 |
| Owens, Brig | DB | Cincinnati | 1966–77 |
| Owens, Don | T | Southern Mississippi | 1957 |
| Owens, Rich | DE | Lehigh | 1995–97 |

**P**

| Name | Position | College | Year |
|------|----------|---------|------|
| Paine, Jeff | LB | San Jose State | 1986 |
| Paluck, John | DE | Pittsburgh | 1956, 1959–65 |
| Palmer, Sterling | DE | Florida State | 1993–96 |
| Papit, John | B | Virginia | 1951–53 |
| Pardee, Jack | LB | Texas A&M | 1971–72 |
| Parks, Mickey | C | Oklahoma | 1938–40 |
| Parrish, Lemar | CB | Lincoln | 1978–81 |
| Pasqua, Joe | T | SMU | 1943 |
| Paternoster, Angelo | G | Georgetown | 1943 |
| Patten, David | WR | Western Carolina | 2005–06 |
| Patterson, Dimitri | DB | Tuskegee | 2005 |
| Patton, Joe | T | Alabama A&M | 1994–98 |
| Patton, Marvcus | LB | UCLA | 1995–98 |
| Paul, Tito | CB | Ohio State | 1999 |
| Pebbles, Jim | E | Vanderbilt | 1946–49, 1951 |
| Peete, Rodney | QB | USC | 1999 |
| Peiffer, Dan | C | Southeast Missouri State | 1980 |
| Pellegrini, Bob | LB | Maryland | 1962–65 |
| Pepper, Gene | G | Missouri | 1950–53 |
| Pergine, John | LB | Notre Dame | 1973–75 |
| Perrin, Lonnie | RB | Illinois | 1979 |
| Peters, Floyd | T | San Francisco State | 1970 |
| Peters, Tony | S | Oklahoma | 1979–82, 1984–85 |
| Peters, Volney | T | USC | 1954–57 |
| Peterson, Nelson | RB | West Virginia Wesleyan | 1937 |
| Pettey, Phil | G | Missouri | 1987 |
| Petitbon, Richie | S | Tulane | 1971–72 |
| Phillips, Joe | WR | Kentucky | 1985–87 |
| Piasecky, Al | E | Duke | 1943–45 |
| Pierce, Antonio | LB | Arizona | 2001–04 |
| Pierce, Dan | RB | Memphis State | 1970 |
| Pinckert, Erny | FB | USC | 1932–40 |
| Planutis, Jerry | B | Michigan State | 1956 |
| Podoley, Jim | RB | Central Michigan | 1957–60 |
| Poillon, Dick | B | Canisius | 1942, 1946–49 |
| Polsfoot, Fran | E | Washington State | 1953 |
| Ponds, Antwaune | LB | Syracuse | 1998 |
| Portis, Clinton | RB | Miami | 2004–06 |
| Posey, Jeff | LB | Southern Mississippi | 2006 |
| Pottios, Myron | LB | Notre Dame | 1971–73 |
| Pounds, Darryl | CB | Nicholls State | 1995–99 |
| Pourdanish, Shar | T | Nevada | 1996–98 |
| Powell, Carl | DL | Louisville | 2002 |
| Presley, Leo | C | Oklahoma | 1945 |
| Prestel, Jim | T | Idaho | 1966–67 |

| Name | Position | College | Year |
|------|----------|---------|------|
| Prioleau, Pierson | S | Virginia Tech | 2005–06 |
| Promuto, Vince | G | Holy Cross | 1960–70 |
| Pucillo, Mike | OL | Auburn | 2006 |

**Q**

| Name | Position | College | Year |
|------|----------|---------|------|
| Query, Jeff | WR | Millikin | 1995 |
| Quinlan, Bill | DE | Michigan State | 1965 |
| Quirk, Ed | B | Missouri | 1948–51 |

**R**

| Name | Position | College | Year |
|------|----------|---------|------|
| Raab, Marc | C | USC | 1993 |
| Raba, Bob | TE | Maryland | 1981 |
| Rabach, Casey | OL | Wisconsin | 2005–06 |
| Rae, Mike | QB | USC | 1981 |
| Ramsey, Knox | G | William & Mary | 1952–53 |
| Ramsey, Patrick | QB | Tulane | 2002–05 |
| Randle El, Antwaan | WR | Indiana | 2006 |
| Rasby, Walter | TE | Wake Forest | 2001, 2004 |
| Raymer, Cory | C | Wisconsin | 1995–01, 2004–05 |
| Reaves, Willard | RB | Northern Arizona | 1989 |
| Rector, Ron | B | Northwestern | 1966 |
| Reed, Alvin | TE | Prairie View | 1973–75 |
| Reed, Andre | WR | Kutztown (Pa.) | 2000 |
| Reed, Bob | G | Tennessee State | 1965 |
| Reem, Matt | T | Minnesota | 1996 |
| Reger, John | LB | Pittsburgh | 1964–66 |
| Renfro, Will | T | Memphis State | 1957–59 |
| Reynolds, Mack | QB | LSU | 1960 |
| Ribar, Frank | G | Duke | 1943 |
| Ricca, Jim | C | Georgetown | 1951–54 |
| Richard, Stanley | S | Texas | 1995–98 |
| Richardson, Grady | TE | Cal State Fullerton | 1979–80 |
| Richardson, Huey | LB | Florida | 1992 |
| Richter, Pat | WR | Wisconsin | 1963–70 |
| Riggins, John | RB | Kansas | 1976–79, 1981–85 |
| Riggs, Gerald | RB | Arizona State | 1989–91 |
| Riggs, Jim | TE | Clemson | 1993 |
| Riley, Jack | T | Northwestern | 1933 |
| Riley, Karon | DE | Minnesota | 2006 |
| Roberts, Jack | B | Georgia | 1932 |
| Roberts, Walter | WR | San Jose State | 1969–70 |
| Robinson, Dave | LB | Penn State | 1973–74 |
| Robinson, Lybrant | DE | Delaware State | 1989 |
| Robinson, Tony | QB | Tennessee | 1987 |
| Roby, Reggie | P | Iowa | 1993–94 |
| Rock, Walter | T | Maryland | 1968–73 |
| Rocker, Tracy | DT | Auburn | 1989–90 |
| Roehnelt, Bill | LB | Bradley | 1960 |
| Rogers, Carlos | CB | Auburn | 2005–06 |
| Rogers, George | RB | South Carolina | 1985–87 |
| Rosato, Sal | B | Villanova | 1945–47 |
| Rose, Carlton | LB | Michigan | 1987 |
| Rosenfels, Sage | QB | Iowa State | 2001 |
| Rosso, George | B | Ohio State | 1954 |
| Roussel, Tom | LB | Southern Mississippi | 1968–70 |
| Roussos, Mike | T | Pittsburgh | 1948–49 |
| Rowe, Ray | TE | San Diego State | 1992 |
| Royal, Robert | TE | LSU | 2002–05 |
| Rubbert, Ed | QB | Louisville | 1987 |
| Rucker, Keith | DT | Ohio Wesleyan | 1997 |
| Rumph, Mike | DB | Miami | 2006 |
| Runnels, Tom | RB | North Texas State | 1956–57 |
| Rush, Tyrone | RB | North Alabama | 1994 |
| Russell, Bo | T | Auburn | 1939–40 |
| Russell, Cliff | WR | Utah | 2002–03 |
| Russell, Darrell | DT | USC | 2003 |
| Russell, Twan | LB | Miami | 1997–99 |
| Rutgens, Joe | DT | Illinois | 1961–69 |

| Name | Position | College | Year |
|------|----------|---------|------|
| Ruthstrom, Ralph | B | SMU | 1947 |
| Rutledge, Jeff | QB | Alabama | 1990–92 |
| Ryan, Frank | QB | Rice | 1969–70 |
| Ryczek, Dan | C | Virginia | 1973–75 |
| Rykovich, Jules | B | Illinois | 1952–53 |
| Rymkus, Lou | T | Notre Dame | 1943 |
| Rypien, Mark | QB | Washington State | 1987–93 |
| Rzempoluch, Ted | DB | Virginia | 1963 |
| | | | |
| **S** | | | |
| Saenz, Eddie | RB | USC | 1946–51 |
| Sagnella, Anthony | DT | Rutgers | 1987 |
| Salave'a, Joe | DL | Arizona | 2004–06 |
| Salem, Ed | B | Alabama | 1951 |
| Salter, Bryant | S | Pittsburgh | 1974–75 |
| Sample, Johnny | DB | Maryland State | 1963–65 |
| Samuels, Chris | T | Alabama | 2000–06 |
| Sanchez, John | T | San Francisco | 1947–49 |
| Sanders, Chris | TE | Texas A&M | 1997 |
| Sanders, Deion | CB | Florida State | 2000 |
| Sanders, Lonnie | DB | Michigan State | 1963–67 |
| Sanders, Ricky | WR | SW Texas State | 1986–93 |
| Sandifer, Dan | DB | LSU | 1948–49 |
| Sanford, Haywood | E | Alabama | 1940 |
| Sarboe, Phil | DB | Washington State | 1934 |
| Sardisco, Tony | G | Tulane | 1956 |
| Sasa, Don | DT | Washington State | 1997 |
| Saul, Ron | G | Michigan State | 1976–81 |
| Savage, Sebastian | CB | North Carolina State | 1995 |
| Sawyer, John | TE | Southern Mississippi | 1983 |
| Scafide, John | T | Tulane | 1933 |
| Scanlan, Jerry | T | Hawaii | 1980–81 |
| Scarbath, Jack | QB | Maryland | 1953–54 |
| Schick, Doyle | LB | Kansas | 1961 |
| Schilling, Ralph | E | Oklahoma City | 1946 |
| Schlereth, Mark | G | Idaho | 1989–94 |
| Schmidt, Kermit (Dutch) | E | Cal Poly–Pomona | 1932 |
| Schoenke, Ray | G | SMU | 1966–75 |
| Schrader, Jim | C | Notre Dame | 1954, 1956–61 |
| Schroeder, Jay | QB | UCLA | 1984–88 |
| Scissum, Williard | G | Alabama | 1987 |
| Scott, Greg | DE | Hampton | 2002 |
| Scott, Jake | S | Georgia | 1976–78 |
| Scotti, Ben | DB | Maryland | 1959–61 |
| Scudero, Joe | B | San Francisco | 1954–58 |
| Scully, Mike | C | Illinois | 1988 |
| Seals, George | G | Missouri | 1964 |
| Seay, Virgil | WR | Troy State | 1981–84 |
| Sebek, Nick | B | Indiana | 1950 |
| Sedoris, Chris | C | Purdue | 1996 |
| Seedborg, John | E | Arizona State | 1965 |
| Sellers, Mike | TE | Walla Walla | 1999–00, 2004–06 |
| Seno, Frank | B | George Washington | 1943–44, 1949 |
| Serwanga, Kato | CB | California | 2001–02 |
| Settles, Tony | LB | Elon | 1987 |
| Severson, Jeff | DB | Long Beach State | 1972 |
| Seymour, Bob | B | Oklahoma | 1940–45 |
| Shade, Sam | S | Alabama | 1999–02 |
| Sharp, Everett | T | California Tech | 1944–45 |
| Shedd, Kenny | WR | Northern Iowa | 2000 |
| Shepard, Derrick | WR | Oklahoma | 1987–88 |
| Shepherd, Bill | FB | Western Maryland | 1935 |
| Shepherd, Leslie | WR | Temple | 1994–98 |
| Shiner, Dick | QB | Maryland | 1964–66 |
| Shoener, Herb | E | Iowa | 1948–49 |
| Shorter, Jim | DB | Detroit | 1964–67 |
| Shugart, Clyde | G | Iowa State | 1933–43 |

| Name | Position | College | Year |
|------|----------|---------|------|
| Shula, Don | DB | John Carroll | 1957 |
| Shuler, Heath | QB | Tennessee | 1994–96 |
| Siano, Tony | C | Fordham | 1932 |
| Siegert, Herb | G | Illinois | 1949–51 |
| Siemering, Larry | C | San Francisco | 1935–36 |
| Siever, Paul | T | Penn State | 1992–93 |
| Simmons, Ed | T | Eastern Washington | 1987–97 |
| Simmons, Roy | G | Georgia Tech | 1983 |
| Simmons, Terrance | OL | Alabama State | 2001 |
| Simon, John | RB | Louisiana Tech | 2003 |
| Sims, Keith | G | Iowa State | 1997–00 |
| Sinko, Steve | T | Duquesne | 1934–36 |
| Sistrunk, Manny | DT | Arkansas AM&N | 1970–75 |
| Skaggs, Justin | WR | Evangel | 2002 |
| Slivinski, Steve | G | Washington | 1939–43 |
| Smith, Ben | E | Alabama | 1937 |
| Smith, Bruce | DE | Virginia Tech | 2000–03 |
| Smith, Cedric | FB | Florida | 1994–95 |
| Smith, Clifton | LB | Syracuse | 2003 |
| Smith, Derek M. | LB | Arizona State | 1997–00 |
| Smith, Dick | DB | Northwestern | 1967–68 |
| Smith, Ed | FB | NYU | 1936 |
| Smith, George | C | California | 1937, 1941–43 |
| Smith, Hugh | E | Kansas | 1962 |
| Smith, Jack | E | Stanford | 1943 |
| Smith, Jerry | TE | Arizona State | 1965–77 |
| Smith, Jim | DB | Oregon | 1968 |
| Smith, Jimmy | RB | Elon | 1984 |
| Smith, John | WR | North Texas State | 1978 |
| Smith, Larry | RB | Florida | 1974 |
| Smith, Paul | DE | New Mexico | 1979–80 |
| Smith, Ricky | CB | Alabama State | 1984 |
| Smith, Riley | QB | Alabama | 1936–38 |
| Smith, Timmy | RB | Texas Tech | 1987–88 |
| Smith, Vernice | G | Florida A&M | 1993–95 |
| Smoot, Fred | CB | Mississippi State | 2001–04 |
| Snead, Norm | QB | Wake Forest | 1961–63 |
| Sneddon, Bob | B | St. Mary's (Calif.) | 1944 |
| Snidow, Ron | DE | Oregon | 1963–67 |
| Snipes, Angelo | LB | West Georgia | 1986 |
| Snowden, Jim | T | Notre Dame | 1965–72 |
| Sobolenski, Joe | G | Michigan | 1949 |
| Sommer, Mike | B | George Washington | 1958–59, 1961 |
| Sommers, John | C | UCLA | 1947 |
| Spaniel, Frank | B | Notre Dame | 1950 |
| Sparks, Dave | G | South Carolina | 1954 |
| Spirida, John | E | St. Anselm's | 1939 |
| Springs, Shawn | CB | Ohio State | 2004–06 |
| Stacco, Ed | T | Colgate | 1948 |
| Stai, Brenden | G | Nebraska | 2002 |
| Stallings, Don | E | North Carolina | 1960 |
| Stanfel, Dick | G | San Francisco | 1956–58 |
| Stanley, Walter | WR | Mesa (Colo.) | 1990 |
| Starke, George | T | Columbia | 1973–84 |
| Stasica, Leo | B | Colorado | 1943 |
| Staton, Jim | T | Wake Forest | 1951 |
| Steber, John | G | Georgia Tech | 1946–50 |
| Steffen, Jim | DB | UCLA | 1961–65 |
| Stenn, Paul | T | Villanova | 1946 |
| Stensrud, Mike | DT | Iowa State | 1989 |
| Stephens, Leonard | TE | Howard | 2002 |
| Stephens, Louis | G | San Francisco | 1955–60 |
| Stephens, Rod | LB | Georgia Tech | 1995–96 |
| Steponovich, Mike | G | St. Mary's | 1933 |
| Stevens, Matt | S | Appalachian State | 1998–00 |
| Stief, Dave | WR | Portland State | 1983 |
| Stits, Bill | DB | UCLA | 1959 |
| Stock, Mark | WR | VMI | 1993 |
| Stokes, Fred | DE | Georgia Southern | 1989–92 |
| Stokes, Tim | T | Oregon | 1975–77 |
| Stone, Ken | S | Vanderbilt | 1973–75 |

| Name | Position | College | Year |
|---|---|---|---|
| Stout, Pete | B | TCU | 1949–50 |
| Stoutmire, Omar | S | Fresno State | 2005 |
| Stovall, Dick | C | Abilene Christian | 1949 |
| Stowe, Tyronne | LB | Rutgers | 1994 |
| Stralka, Clem | G | Georgetown | 1938–42, 1945–46 |
| Strickland, Fred | LB | Purdue | 1999 |
| Stuart, Jim | T | Oregon | 1938 |
| Stubblefield, Dana | DT | Kansas | 1998–00 |
| Sturt, Fred | G | Bowling Green | 1974 |
| Stynchula, Andy | DT | Penn State | 1960–63 |
| Suisham, Shaun | K | Bowling Green | 2006 |
| Sulsfsted, Alex | G | Miami (Ohio) | 2002 |
| Suminski, Dave | G | Wisconsin | 1953 |
| Sutton, Ed | B | North Carolina | 1957–59 |
| Sutton, Eric | CB | San Diego State | 1996 |
| Sweeney, Walt | G | Syracuse | 1974–75 |
| Sykes, Bob | B | San Jose State | 1952 |
| Sykes, Joe | DE | Southern | 2006 |
| Symonette, Josh | S | Tennessee Tech | 2000 |
| Szafaryn, Len | T | North Carolina | 1949 |
| Szott, Dave | OL | Penn State | 2001 |
| **T** | | | |
| Talbert, Diron | DT | Texas | 1971–80 |
| Tamm, Ralph | T | West Chester | 1991 |
| Tanner, Barron | DT | Oklahoma | 1999 |
| Taylor, Charley | WR | Arizona State | 1964–77 |
| Taylor, Hugh (Bones) | E | Oklahoma City | 1947–54 |
| Taylor, Keith | S | Illinois | 1994–96 |
| Taylor, Mike | T | USC | 1971 |
| Taylor, Roosevelt | DB | Grambling | 1972 |
| Taylor, Sean | S | Miami | 2004–06 |
| Temple, Mark | B | Oregon | 1936 |
| Tereshinski, Joe | E | Georgia | 1947–54 |
| Terrell, Daryl | OL | Southern Miss | 2003 |
| Terrell, David | CB | Texas–El Paso | 2000–03 |
| Theismann, Joe | QB | Notre Dame | 1974–85 |
| Theofiledes, Harry | QB | Waynesburg | 1968 |
| Thibodeauz, Keith | CB | NW Louisiana | 1997 |
| Thielemann, R. C. | G | Arkansas | 1985–88 |
| Thomas, Chris | WR | Cal Poly–San Luis Obis | 1997–99 |
| Thomas, Duane | RB | West Texas State | 1973–74 |
| Thomas, George | B | Oklahoma | 1950–51 |
| Thomas, Johnny | CB | Baylor | 1988–90, 92–94 |
| Thomas, Mike | RB | UNLV | 1975–78 |
| Thomas, Ralph | E | San Francisco | 1955–56 |
| Thomas, Randy | OL | Mississippi State | 2003–06 |
| Thomas, Spencer | S | Washburn | 1975 |
| Thompson, Derrius | WR | Baylor | 1999–02 |
| Thompson, Ricky | WR | Baylor | 1978–81 |
| Thompson, Steve | DT | Minnesota | 1987 |
| Thrash, James | WR | Missouri Southern | 1997–00, 2004–06 |
| Thure, Brian | T | California | 1995 |
| Thurlow, Steve | RB | Stanford | 1966–68 |
| Tice, Mike | TE | Maryland | 1989 |
| Tillman, Rusty | LB | Northern Arizona | 1970–77 |
| Tilton, Ron | G | Tulane | 1986 |
| Titchenal, Bob | C | San Jose State | 1940–42 |
| Todd, Dick | RB | Texas A&M | 1939–42, 1945–48 |
| Toibin, Brendan | K | Richmond | 1987 |
| Toneff, Bob | DT | Notre Dame | 1959–64 |
| Torgeson, LaVern | LB | Washington State | 1955–57 |
| Torrence, Leigh | CB | Stanford | 2006 |
| Tosi, Flavio | E | Boston College | 1934–36 |
| Towns, Morris | T | Missouri | 1984 |
| Tracy, Tom | B | Tennessee | 1963–64 |
| Trotter, Jeremiah | LB | Stephen F. Austin | 2002–03 |

| Name | Position | College | Year |
|---|---|---|---|
| Truitt, Dave | TE | North Carolina | 1987 |
| Truitt, Olanda | WR | Mississippi State | 1994–95 |
| Tucker, Ross | OL | Princeton | 2001 |
| Tuckey, Dick | FB | Manhattan | 1938 |
| Tupa, Tom | P | Ohio State | 2004–05 |
| Turk, Dan | C | Wisconsin | 1997–99 |
| Turk, Matt | P | Wisconsin–Whitewater | 1995–99 |
| Turley, Doug | E | Scranton | 1944–48 |
| Turner, J. T. | G | Duke | 1984 |
| Turner, Jay | B | George Washington | 1938–39 |
| Turner, Kevin | LB | Pacific | 1981 |
| Turner, Scott | CB | Illinois | 1995–97 |
| Tuthill, James | K | Cal Poly | 2002 |
| Tyrer, Jim | T | Ohio State | 1974 |
| **U** | | | |
| Ucovich, Mitchell | T | San Jose State | 1944 |
| Uhlenhake, Jeff | C | Ohio State | 1996–97 |
| Ulinski, Harry | C | Kentucky | 1950–51, 1953–56 |
| Ungerer, Joe | T | Fordham | 1944–45 |
| Upshaw, Regan | DE | California | 2003 |
| **V** | | | |
| Vactor, Ted | DB | Nebraska | 1969–74 |
| Vanderbeek, Matt | LB | Michigan State | 1995–96 |
| Varty, Mike | LB | Northwestern | 1974 |
| Vaughn, Clarence | S | Northern Illinois | 1987–91 |
| Venuto, Sam | B | Guilford | 1952 |
| Verdin, Clarence | WR | S.W. Louisiana | 1986–87 |
| Vereb, Ed | RB | Maryland | 1960 |
| Vickers, Kipp | T | Miami | 1999, 2002 |
| Vincent, Troy | DB | Wisconsin | 2006 |
| Vital, Lionel | RB | Nicholls State | 1987 |
| Voytek, Ed | G | Purdue | 1957–58 |
| **W** | | | |
| Waddy, Ray | CB | Texas A&I | 1979–80 |
| Wade, Bob | DB | Morgan State | 1969 |
| Wade, Todd | OL | Mississippi | 2006 |
| Ward, David (Nubbin) | E | Haskell Indian | 1933 |
| Ware, Kevin | TE | Washington | 2003 |
| Waechler, Henry | DT | Nebraska | 1987 |
| Wahler, Jim | DT | UCLA | 1992–93 |
| Walker, Brian | S | Washington State | 1996–97 |
| Walker, Marquis | CB | S.E. Missouri State | 1996 |
| Walker, Rick | TE | UCLA | 1980–85 |
| Walter, Tyson | OL | Ohio State | 2006 |
| Walters, Tom | DB | Southern Mississippi | 1964–67 |
| Walton, Alvin | S | Kansas | 1986–91 |
| Walton, Frank | G | Pittsburgh | 1944–45 |
| Walton, Joe | E | Pittsburgh | 1957–60 |
| Watters, Dale (Muddy) | T | Florida | 1932–33 |
| Ward, Bill | G | Washington State | 1946–47 |
| Warner, Ron | DE | Kansas | 2003–04 |
| Warren, Don | TE | San Diego State | 1979–92 |
| Washington, Anthony | CB | Fresno State | 1983–84 |
| Washington, Fred | T | North Texas State | 1968 |
| Washington, James | S | UCLA | 1995 |
| Washington, Joe | RB | Oklahoma | 1981–84 |
| Washington, Marcus | LB | Auburn | 2004–06 |
| Washington, Mickey | CB | Texas A&M | 1992 |
| Watson, Jim | C | Pacific | 1945 |
| Watson, Kenny | RB | Penn State | 2002 |
| Watson, Sid | B | Northwestern | 1958 |
| Watts, George | T | Appalachian State | 1942 |
| Weatherall, Jim | T | Oklahoma | 1958 |
| Weaver, Charlie | LB | USC | 1981 |
| Weil, Jack | P | Wyoming | 1989 |
| Weisenbaugh, Heinie | B | Pittsburgh | 1935–36 |

| Name | Position | College | Year |
|------|----------|---------|------|
| Welch, Herb | DB | UCLA | 1989 |
| Weldon, Casey | QB | Florida State | 1999 |
| Weldon, Larry | QB | Presbyterian | 1944–45 |
| Weller, Rabbit (Bub) | B | Haskell Indian | 1933 |
| Wells, Billy | B | Michigan State | 1954, 1956–57 |
| Westbrook, Michael | WR | Colorado | 1995–01 |
| Westfall, Ed | B | Ohio Wesleyan | 1932–33 |
| Whisenhunt, Ken | TE | Georgia Tech | 1990 |
| White, Jeris | CB | Hawaii | 1980–82 |
| White, Manuel | FB | UCLA | 2005–06 |
| Whited, Marvin | G | Oklahoma | 1942–45 |
| Whitfield, A.D. | RB | North Texas State | 1966–68 |
| Whitley, Taylor | OL | Texas A&M | 2006 |
| Whitlow, Bob | C | Arizona | 1960–61 |
| Wiggins, Paul | T | Oregon | 1998 |
| Wilbur, John | G | Stanford | 1971–73 |
| Wilburn, Barry | CB | Mississippi | 1985–89 |
| Wilde, George | B | Texas A&M | 1947 |
| Wilder, James | RB | Missouri | 1990 |
| Wilkerson, Basil | E | Oklahoma City | 1932 |
| Wilkin, Willie | T | St. Mary's (Calif.) | 1939–43 |
| Wilkins, Roy | LB | Georgia | 1960–61 |
| Wilkinson, Dan | DT | Ohio State | 1998–01 |
| Williams, Clarence | RB | South Carolina | 1982 |
| Williams, Doug | QB | Grambling | 1986–89 |
| Williams, Eric | DT | Washington State | 1990–93 |
| Williams, Fred | T | Arkansas | 1964–65 |
| Williams, Gerard | DB | Langston | 1976–78 |
| Williams, Greg | FS | Mississippi State | 1982–84 |
| Williams, Jamel | S | Nebraska | 1997–98 |
| Williams, Jeff | T | Rhode Island | 1978–80 |
| Williams, John | B | USC | 1952–53 |
| Williams, Kevin | CB | Iowa State | 1985, 1988 |
| Williams, Marvin | TE | Fullerton State | 1987 |
| Williams, Michael | TE | Alabama A&M | 1982–84 |
| Williams, Robert | CB | Baylor | 1993 |
| Williams, Sid | LB | Southern | 1967 |
| Williamson, Ernie | T | North Carolina | 1947 |
| Willis, Keith | DT | Northeastern | 1993 |
| Willis, Larry | S | Texas–El Paso | 1973 |
| Wilson, Bobby | DT | Michigan State | 1991–94 |
| Wilson, Eric | LB | Maryland | 1987 |
| Wilson, Mark | OL | California | 2004 |
| Wilson, Ted | WR | Central Florida | 1987 |
| Wilson, Wayne | RB | Shepard | 1987 |
| Winans, Tydus | WR | Fresno State | 1994–95 |
| Winey, Brandon | OT | LSU | 2003 |

| Name | Position | College | Year |
|------|----------|---------|------|
| Windham, David | LB | Jackson State | 1987 |
| Wingate, Heath | C | Bowling Green | 1967 |
| Winslow, Doug | WR | Drake | 1976–77 |
| Witucki, Casimir | G | Indiana | 1950–51, 1953–56 |
| Wonsley, Otis | RB | Alcorn State | 1981–85 |
| Woodberry, Dennis | CB | S. Arkansas | 1987–88 |
| Woodruff, Lee | FB | Mississippi | 1932 |
| Woods, Tony | DE | Pittsburgh | 1994–96 |
| Woodward, Dick | C | Iowa | 1952 |
| Wooten, John | G | Colorado | 1968 |
| Wright, Kenny | CB | Northwestern State | 2006 |
| Wright, Steve | T | Alabama | 1970 |
| Wright, Toby | CB | Nebraska | 1999 |
| Wrigth, Ted | B | North Texas State | 1934–35 |
| Wuerffel, Danny | QB | Florida | 2002 |
| Wulff, Jim | B | Michigan State | 1960–61 |
| Wyant, Fred | QB | West Virginia | 1956 |
| Wyche, Sam | QB | Furman | 1971–73 |
| Wycheck, Frank | TE–FB | Maryland | 1993–94 |
| Wycoff, Doug | FB | Georgia Tech | 1934 |
| Wynn, Renaldo | DL | Notre Dame | 2002–06 |
| Wynne, William | DE | Tennessee State | 1977 |
| Wysocki, Pete | LB | Western Michigan | 1975–80 |

**Y**

| Name | Position | College | Year |
|------|----------|---------|------|
| Yarber, Eric | WR | Idaho | 1986–87 |
| Yehobah–Kodie, Phil | LB | Penn State | 1995 |
| Yoder, Todd | TE | Vanderbilt | 2006 |
| Yonaker, John | E | Notre Dame | 1952 |
| Youel, Jim | B | Iowa | 1946–48 |
| Young, Bill | T | Alabama | 1937–42, 1946 |
| Young, Roy | T | Texas A&M | 1938 |
| Young, Wilburn | DE | William Penn | 1981 |
| Youngblood, Jim | LB | Tennessee Tech | 1984 |
| Yowarsky, Walt | E | Kentucky | 1951–54 |

**Z**

| Name | Position | College | Year |
|------|----------|---------|------|
| Zagers, Bert | B | Michigan State | 1955, 1957–58 |
| Zelenka, Joe | LS | Wake Forest | 2000 |
| Zellner, Peppi | DE | Fort Valley State | 2003 |
| Zendejas, Max | K | Arizona | 1986 |
| Zeno, Joe | G | Holy Cross | 1942–44 |
| Zorich, Chris | DT | Notre Dame | 1997 |
| Zimmerman, Roy | B | San Jose State | 1940–42 |

## ALL-TIME COACHING RECORDS

| Head Coach | Regular Season | | | | Playoffs | | |
| | W | L | T | Pct. | W | L | Yrs. |
|------------|---|---|---|------|---|---|------|
| Lud Wray | 4 | 4 | 2 | .500 | 0 | 0 | 1932 |
| Lone Star Dietz | 11 | 11 | 2 | .500 | 0 | 0 | 1933–34 |
| Eddie Casey | 2 | 8 | 1 | .227 | 0 | 0 | 1935 |
| Ray Flaherty | 54 | 21 | 3 | .712 | 2 | 2 | 1936–42 |
| Arthur "Dutch" Bergman | 6 | 3 | 1 | .650 | 1 | 1 | 1943 |
| Dud DeGroot | 14 | 5 | 1 | .725 | 0 | 1 | 1944–45 |
| A.G. "Turk" Edwards | 16 | 18 | 1 | .471 | 0 | 0 | 1946–48 |
| John Whelchel | 3 | 3 | 1 | .500 | 0 | 0 | 1949 |
| Herman Ball | 4 | 16 | 0 | .200 | 0 | 0 | 1949–51 |
| Dick Todd | 5 | 4 | 0 | .556 | 0 | 0 | 1951 |
| Earl "Curly" Lambeau | 10 | 13 | 1 | .438 | 0 | 0 | 1952–53 |
| Joe Kuharich | 26 | 32 | 2 | .450 | 0 | 0 | 1954–58 |
| Mike Nixon | 4 | 18 | 2 | .208 | 0 | 0 | 1959–60 |
| Bill McPeak | 21 | 46 | 3 | .321 | 0 | 0 | 1961–65 |
| Otto Graham | 17 | 22 | 3 | .440 | 0 | 0 | 1966–68 |

| Head Coach | Regular Season | | | | Playoffs | | |
|---|---|---|---|---|---|---|---|
| | W | L | T | Pct. | W | L | Yrs. |
| Vince Lombardi | 7 | 5 | 2 | .571 | 0 | 0 | 1969 |
| Bill Austin | 6 | 8 | 0 | .429 | 0 | 0 | 1970 |
| George Allen | 67 | 30 | 1 | .689 | 2 | 5 | 1971–77 |
| Jack Pardee | 24 | 24 | 0 | .500 | 0 | 0 | 1978–80 |
| Joe Gibbs | 145 | 87 | 0 | .625 | 17 | 6 | 1981–92/04–06 |
| Richie Petitbon | 4 | 12 | 0 | .250 | 0 | 0 | 1993 |
| Norv Turner | 49 | 59 | 1 | .450 | 1 | 1 | 1994-00 |
| Terry Robiskie | 1 | 2 | 0 | .333 | 0 | 0 | 2000 (interim) |
| Marty Schottenheimer | 8 | 8 | 0 | .500 | 0 | 0 | 2001 |
| Steve Spurrier | 12 | 20 | 0 | .375 | 0 | 0 | 2002 |
| **Total** | **520** | **479** | **27** | **.521** | **23** | **16** | **1932–2006** |

# ALL–TIME ASSISTANT COACHES

**A**
Aldrich, Charles "Ki" .................................................1947
Arapoff, Jason .................................................1992–00
Arnsparger, Bill .................................................2001
Austin, Bill .................................................1969–70, 1973–77

**B**
Baker, Ray .................................................1937–39
Ball, Herman .................................................1952–54
Bass, Marvin .................................................1952
Banker, Chuck .................................................1987–88
Bielski, Dick .................................................1973–76
Blache, Greg .................................................2004–06
Bowser, Bob .................................................1978–80
Breaux, Don .................................................1981–93, 2004–06
Brindise, Noah .................................................2002–03
Bugel, Joe .................................................1981–89, 2004–06
Burns, DeChon .................................................2002–03
Burns, Jack .................................................1989–91, 2004–06
Byner, Earnest .................................................2004–06

**C**
Cabrelli, Larry .................................................1951
Callahan, Ray .................................................1978–80
Cameron, Cam .................................................1994–96
Carpenter, Ken .................................................1968
Carpenter, Lew .................................................1969–70
Carmichael, Pete Jr. .................................................2001
Carter, Rubin .................................................1999–00
Catavolos, George .................................................2002–03
Cherundolo, Charles .................................................1964–65
Clarke, Ken .................................................2003
Collins, Jim .................................................2002–03
Crumpler, Bobby .................................................2003–06

**D**
DePaul, Bobby .................................................1989–93
Diange, Joe .................................................1987
Dickson, George .................................................1969–70, 1978–80
Doll, Don .................................................1966–70
Dowhower, Rod .................................................1990–93
Dowler, Boyd .................................................1971–72
Dudley, Bill .................................................1953
Dunn, John .................................................1984–86, 2004–05

**E**
Edwards, George .................................................2002–03
Edwards, Glenn "Turk" .................................................1940–45, 1949
Evans, Dick .................................................1955–58

**F**
Fazio, Foge .................................................2000
FitzGerald, Jeff .................................................1998–99
Flaherty, Pat .................................................2000

**G**
Gibbs, Coy .................................................2004–06
Gibron, Abe .................................................1960–64
Gray, Jerry .................................................2006
Grimm, Russ .................................................1992–00
Guenther, Paul .................................................2002–03

**H**
Haluchak, Mike .................................................1994–96
Hanifan, Jim .................................................1990–96
Hastings, John .................................................2002–06
Hayes, Tom .................................................1995–99
Hawkins, Ralph .................................................1972–77
Hefferle, Ernie .................................................1959
Helton, Kim .................................................2002–03
Henning, Dan .................................................1981–82, 1987–88
Hickman, Bill .................................................1973–77, 1981–88
Hilton, John .................................................1978–80
Hilyer, Jim .................................................1975–76
Hixon, Stan .................................................2004–06
Holland, Lawson .................................................2002–03
Holmes, Jerry .................................................2001
Horton, Ray .................................................1994–96
Huff, Sam .................................................1969–70
Hughes, Ed .................................................1964–67
Hunley, Ricky .................................................2002
Hunt, John .................................................2002–03

**J**
Jackson, Bobby .................................................1994–99
Jackson, Hue .................................................2001–03
Jackson, Steve .................................................2004–06

**K**
Karmelowicz, Bob .................................................1994–96
Kilroy, Frank .................................................1962–64
Kuharich, Joe .................................................1954

**L**
Lanham, Paul .................................................1973–77, 1987–88
Lazor, Bill .................................................2004–06
Leggett, Earl .................................................1997–99
Levy, Marv .................................................1971–72
Lewis, Marvin .................................................2002
Lindsey, Dale .................................................1997–98, 2004–06
Lynn, Ron .................................................1994–96

**M**
Mann, Richard .................................................2001
Manusky, Greg .................................................2001
Marchibroda, Ted .................................................1961–65, 1971–74
Martz, Mike .................................................1997–98
Mathews, Ray .................................................1968
Matuszak, Marv .................................................1977
McCormack, Mike .................................................1966–72
McCulley, Pete .................................................1977

## ALL–TIME RESULTS— WASHINGTON REDSKINS VS:

| Year | Game | Winner | Score | At |
|---|---|---|---|---|
| **Arizona Cardinals** | | | **Redskins lead RS 71–44–2** | |
| 1932 | 1 | Chicago Cardinals | 9–0 | Boston |
| | 2 | Boston Braves | 8–6 | Chicago |
| 1933 | 1 | Redskins | 10–0 | Chicago |
| | 2 | Tie | 0–0 | Boston |
| 1934 | 1 | Redskins | 9–0 | Boston |
| 1935 | 1 | Chicago Cardinals | 6–0 | Boston |
| 1936 | 1 | Redskins | 13–10 | Boston |
| 1937 | 1 | Chicago Cardinals | 21–14 | Wash |
| 1939 | 1 | Redskins | 28–7 | Wash |
| 1940 | 1 | Redskins | 28–21 | Wash |
| 1942 | 1 | Redskins | 28–0 | Wash |
| 1943 | 1 | Redskins | 13–7 | Wash |
| 1945 | 1 | Redskins | 24–21 | Wash |
| 1947 | 1 | Redskins | 45–21 | Wash |
| 1949 | 1 | Chicago Cardinals | 38–7 | Chicago |
| 1950 | 1 | Chicago Cardinals | 38–28 | Wash |
| 1951 | 1 | Redskins | 7–3 | Chicago |
| | 2 | Redskins | 20–17 | Wash |
| 1952 | 1 | Redskins | 23–7 | Chicago |
| | 2 | Chicago Cardinals | 17–6 | Wash |
| 1953 | 1 | Redskins | 24–13 | Chicago |
| | 2 | Redskins | 28–17 | Wash |
| 1954 | 1 | Chicago Cardinals | 38–16 | Chicago |
| | 2 | Redskins | 37–20 | Wash |
| 1955 | 1 | Chicago Cardinals | 24–10 | Wash |
| | 2 | Redskins | 31–0 | Chicago |
| 1956 | 1 | Chicago Cardinals | 31–3 | Wash |
| | 2 | Redskins | 17–14 | Chicago |
| 1957 | 1 | Redskins | 37–14 | Chicago |
| | 2 | Chicago Cardinals | 44–14 | Wash |
| 1958 | 1 | Chicago Cardinals | 37–10 | Chicago |
| | 2 | Redskins | 45–31 | Wash |
| 1959 | 1 | Chicago Cardinals | 49–21 | Chicago |
| | 2 | Redskins | 23–14 | Wash |
| 1960 | 1 | St. Louis Cardinals | 44–7 | St. Louis |
| | 2 | St. Louis Cardinals | 26–14 | Wash |
| 1961 | 1 | St. Louis Cardinals | 24–0 | Wash |
| | 2 | St. Louis Cardinals | 38–24 | St. Louis |
| 1962 | 1 | Redskins | 24–14 | Wash |
| | 2 | Tie | 17–17 | St. Louis |
| 1963 | 1 | St. Louis Cardinals | 21–7 | Wash |
| | 2 | St. Louis Cardinals | 24–20 | St. Louis |
| 1964 | 1 | St. Louis Cardinals | 23–7 | Wash |
| | 2 | St. Louis Cardinals | 38–24 | St. Louis |
| 1965 | 1 | St. Louis Cardinals | 37–16 | Wash |
| | 2 | Redskins | 24–20 | St. Louis |
| 1966 | 1 | St. Louis Cardinals | 23–7 | St. Louis |
| | 2 | Redskins | 26–20 | Wash |
| 1967 | 1 | St. Louis Cardinals | 27–21 | Wash |
| 1968 | 1 | St. Louis Cardinals | 41–14 | St. Louis |
| 1969 | 1 | Redskins | 33–17 | Wash |
| 1970 | 1 | St. Louis Cardinals | 27–17 | St. Louis |
| | 2 | Redskins | 28–27 | Wash |
| 1971 | 1 | Redskins | 24–17 | St. Louis |
| | 2 | Redskins | 20–0 | Wash |

| Year | Game | Winner | Score | At |
|------|------|--------|-------|-----|
| 1972 | 1 | Redskins | 24–10 | Wash |
|      | 2 | Redskins | 13–3 | St. Louis |
| 1973 | 1 | St. Louis Cardinals | 34–27 | St. Louis |
|      | 2 | Redskins | 31–13 | Wash |
| 1974 | 1 | St. Louis Cardinals | 17–10 | St. Louis |
|      | 2 | St. Louis Cardinals | 23–20 | Wash |
| 1975 | 1 | Redskins | 27–27 | Wash |
|      | 2 | St. Louis Cardinals | 27–17 (ot) | St. Louis |
| 1976 | 1 | Redskins | 20–10 | Wash |
|      | 2 | Redskins | 16–10 | St. Louis |
| 1977 | 1 | Redskins | 24–14 | Wash |
|      | 2 | Redskins | 26–20 | St. Louis |
| 1978 | 1 | Redskins | 28–10 | St. Louis |
|      | 2 | St. Louis Cardinals | 27–17 | Wash |
| 1979 | 1 | Redskins | 17–7 | St. Louis |
|      | 2 | Redskins | 30–28 | Wash |
| 1980 | 1 | Redskins | 23–0 | Wash |
|      | 2 | Redskins | 31–7 | St. Louis |
| 1981 | 1 | St. Louis Cardinals | 40–30 | St. Louis |
|      | 2 | Redskins | 42–21 | Wash |
| 1982 | 1 | Redskins | 12–7 | St. Louis |
|      | 2 | Redskins | 28–0 | Wash |
| 1983 | 1 | Redskins | 38–14 | St. Louis |
|      | 2 | Redskins | 45–7 | Wash |
| 1984 | 1 | St. Louis Cardinals | 26–24 | St. Louis |
|      | 2 | Redskins | 29–27 | Wash |
| 1985 | 1 | Redskins | 27–10 | Wash |
|      | 2 | Redskins | 27–16 | St. Louis |
| 1986 | 1 | Redskins | 28–21 | Wash |
|      | 2 | Redskins | 20–17 | St. Louis |
| 1987 | 1 | Redskins | 28–21 | Wash |
|      | 2 | Redskins | 34–17 | St. Louis |
| 1988 | 1 | Arizona Cardinals | 30–21 | Phoenix |
|      | 2 | Redskins | 33–17 | Wash |
| 1989 | 1 | Redskins | 30–28 | Wash |
|      | 2 | Redskins | 29–10 | Phoenix |
| 1990 | 1 | Redskins | 31–0 | Wash |
|      | 2 | Redskins | 38–10 | Phoenix |
| 1991 | 1 | Redskins | 34–0 | Wash |
|      | 2 | Redskins | 20–14 | Phoenix |
| 1992 | 1 | Phoenix Cardinals | 27–24 | Phoenix |
|      | 2 | Redskins | 41–3 | Wash |
| 1993 | 1 | Phoenix Cardinals | 17–10 | Wash |
|      | 2 | Phoenix Cardinals | 36–6 | Phoenix |
| 1994 | 1 | Phoenix Cardinals | 19–16 | Wash |
|      | 2 | Arizona Cardinals | 17–15 | Arizona |
| 1995 | 1 | Redskins | 27–7 | Wash |
|      | 2 | Arizona Cardinals | 24–20 | Arizona |
| 1996 | 1 | Arizona Cardinals | 37–34 | Wash |
|      | 2 | Arizona Cardinals | 27–26 | Arizona |
| 1997 | 1 | Redskins | 19–13 | Wash |
|      | 2 | Redskins | 38–28 | Arizona |
| 1998 | 1 | Arizona Cardinals | 29–27 | Arizona |
|      | 2 | Arizona Cardinals | 45–42 | Wash |
| 1999 | 1 | Redskins | 24–10 | Arizona |
|      | 2 | Redskins | 28–3 | Wash |
| 2000 | 1 | Arizona Cardinals | 16–15 | Arizona |
|      | 2 | Redskins | 20–3 | Wash |
| 2001 | 1 | Redskins | 20–10 | Arizona |
|      | 2 | Redskins | 20–17 | Wash |
| 2002 | 1 | Redskins | 31–23 | Wash |
| 2005 | 1 | Redskins | 17–13 | Arizona |

**Atlanta Falcons**          Redskins lead RS 14–5–1
                             Redskins lead PS 1-0

| Year | Game | Winner | Score | At |
|------|------|--------|-------|-----|
| 1966 | 1 | Redskins | 33–20 | Wash |
| 1967 | 1 | Tie | 20–20 | Atlanta |
| 1969 | 1 | Redskins | 27–20 | Wash |
| 1972 | 1 | Redskins | 24–13 | Wash |
| 1975 | 1 | Redskins | 30–27 | Atlanta |
| 1977 | 1 | Redskins | 10–6 | Wash |
| 1978 | 1 | Falcons | 20–17 | Atlanta |
| 1979 | 1 | Redskins | 16–7 | Atlanta |

| Year | Game | Winner | Score | At |
|------|------|--------|-------|-----|
| 1980 | 1 | Falcons | 10–6 | Atlanta |
| 1983 | 1 | Redskins | 37–21 | Wash |
| 1984 | 1 | Redskins | 27–14 | Wash |
| 1985 | 1 | Redskins | 44–10 | Atlanta |
| 1987 | 1 | Falcons | 21–20 | Atlanta |
| 1989 | 1 | Redskins | 31–30 | Atlanta |
| 1991 | 1 | Redskins | 56–17 | Wash |
|      | 2 | *Redskins | 24–7 | Wash |
| 1992 | 1 | Redskins | 24–17 | Wash |
| 1993 | 1 | Redskins | 30–17 | Wash |
| 1994 | 1 | Falcons | 27–20 | Wash |
| 2003 | 1 | Redskins | 33–31 | Atlanta |
| 2006 | 1 | Falcons | 24–14 | Wash |

*NFC Divisional Playoff

**Baltimore Ravens**          Ravens lead RS 2-1

| Year | Game | Winner | Score | At |
|------|------|--------|-------|-----|
| 1997 | 1 | Ravens | 20–17 | Wash |
| 2000 | 1 | Redskins | 10–3 | Wash |
| 2004 | 1 | Ravens | 17–10 | Wash |

**Buffalo Bills**          Bills lead RS 6-4
                           Redskins lead PS 1-0

| Year | Game | Winner | Score | At |
|------|------|--------|-------|-----|
| 1972 | 1 | Bills | 24–17 | Wash |
| 1977 | 1 | Redskins | 10–0 | Buffalo |
| 1981 | 1 | Bills | 21–14 | Buffalo |
| 1984 | 1 | Redskins | 41–14 | Wash |
| 1987 | 1 | Redskins | 27–7 | Buffalo |
| 1990 | 1 | Redskins | 29–14 | Wash |
| 1991 | 1 | *Redskins | 37–24 | Minneapolis |
| 1993 | 1 | Bills | 24–10 | Buffalo |
| 1996 | 1 | Bills | 38–13 | Buffalo |
| 1999 | 1 | Bills | 34–17 | Wash |
| 2003 | 1 | Bills | 24–7 | Buffalo |

*Super Bowl XXVI

**Carolina Panthers**          Redskins lead RS 7–1

| Year | Game | Winner | Score | At |
|------|------|--------|-------|-----|
| 1995 | 1 | Redskins | 20–17 | Wash |
| 1997 | 1 | Redskins | 24–10 | Carolina |
| 1998 | 1 | Redskins | 28–25 | Carolina |
| 1999 | 1 | Redskins | 38–36 | Wash |
| 2000 | 1 | Redskins | 20–17 | Wash |
| 2001 | 1 | Redskins | 17–14 | Wash (OT) |
| 2003 | 1 | Panthers | 20–17 | Carolina |
| 2006 | 1 | Redskins | 17–13 | Wash |

**Chicago Bears**          Bears lead RS 20–17–1
                           Redskins lead PS 4-3

| Year | Game | Winner | Score | At |
|------|------|--------|-------|-----|
| 1932 | 1 | Tie | 7–7 | Boston |
| 1933 | 1 | Bears | 7–0 | Chicago |
|      | 2 | Redskins | 10–0 | Boston |
| 1934 | 1 | Bears | 21–0 | Boston |
| 1935 | 1 | Bears | 30–14 | Boston |
| 1936 | 1 | Bears | 26–0 | Boston |
| 1937 | 1 | Redskins* | 28–21 | Chicago |
| 1938 | 1 | Bears | 31–7 | Chicago |
| 1940 | 1 | Redskins | 7–3 | Wash |
|      | 2 | Bears* | 73–0 | Wash |
| 1941 | 1 | Bears | 35–21 | Chicago |
| 1942 | 1 | Redskins* | 14–6 | Wash |
| 1943 | 1 | Redskins | 21–7 | Wash |
|      | 2 | Bears* | 41–21 | Chicago |
| 1945 | 1 | Redskins | 28–21 | Wash |
| 1946 | 1 | Bears | 24–20 | Chicago |
| 1947 | 1 | Bears | 56–20 | Wash |
| 1948 | 1 | Bears | 48–13 | Chicago |
| 1949 | 1 | Bears | 31–21 | Wash |
| 1951 | 1 | Bears | 27–0 | Wash |
| 1953 | 1 | Bears | 27–24 | Wash |
| 1957 | 1 | Redskins | 14–3 | Chicago |
| 1964 | 1 | Redskins | 27–20 | Wash |
| 1968 | 1 | Redskins | 38–28 | Chicago |
| 1971 | 1 | Bears | 16–15 | Chicago |

| Year | Game | Winner | Score | At |
|------|------|--------|-------|-----|
| 1974 | 1 | Redskins | 42–0 | Wash |
| 1976 | 1 | Bears | 33–7 | Chicago |
| 1978 | 1 | Bears | 14–10 | Wash |
| 1980 | 1 | Bears | 35–21 | Chicago |
| 1981 | 1 | Redskins | 24–7 | Chicago |
| 1984 | 1 | Bears‡ | 23–19 | Wash |
| 1985 | 1 | Bears | 45–10 | Chicago |
| 1986 | 1 | Redskins† | 27–13 | Chicago |
| 1987 | 1 | Redskins† | 21–17 | Chicago |
| 1988 | 1 | Bears | 34–14 | Wash |
| 1989 | 1 | Redskins | 38–14 | Wash |
| 1990 | 1 | Redskins | 10–9 | Wash |
| 1991 | 1 | Redskins | 20–7 | Chicago |
| 1996 | 1 | Redskins | 10–3 | Wash |
| 1997 | 1 | Redskins | 31–8 | Chicago |
| 1999 | 1 | Redskins | 48–22 | Wash |
| 2001 | 1 | Bears | 20–15 | Wash |
| 2003 | 1 | Bears | 27–24 | Chicago |
| 2004 | 1 | Redskins | 13–10 | Chicago |
| 2005 | 1 | Redskins | 9–7 | Wash |

*NFL Championship
†NFC Divisional Playoff
‡NFC First-Round Playoff

## Cincinnati Bengals — Redskins lead RS 4–3

| Year | Game | Winner | Score | At |
|------|------|--------|-------|-----|
| 1970 | 1 | Redskins | 20–0 | Wash |
| 1974 | 1 | Bengals | 28–17 | Cincinnati |
| 1979 | 1 | Redskins | 28–25 | Wash |
| 1985 | 1 | Redskins | 27–24 | Wash |
| 1988 | 1 | Bengals | 20–17 | Cincinnati (OT) |
| 1991 | 1 | Redskins | 34–27 | Cincinnati |
| 2004 | 1 | Bengals | 17–10 | Wash |

## Cleveland Browns — Browns lead RS 33–9–1

| Year | Game | Winner | Score | At |
|------|------|--------|-------|-----|
| 1950 | 1 | Browns | 20–14 | Cleveland |
|  | 2 | Browns | 45–21 | Wash |
| 1951 | 1 | Browns | 45–0 | Cleveland |
| 1952 | 1 | Browns | 19–15 | Cleveland |
|  | 2 | Browns | 48–24 | Wash |
| 1953 | 1 | Browns | 30–14 | Wash |
|  | 2 | Browns | 27–3 | Cleveland |
| 1954 | 1 | Browns | 62–3 | Cleveland |
|  | 2 | Browns | 34–14 | Wash |
| 1955 | 1 | Redskins | 27–17 | Cleveland |
|  | 2 | Browns | 24–14 | Wash |
| 1956 | 1 | Redskins | 20–9 | Wash |
|  | 2 | Redskins | 20–17 | Cleveland |
| 1957 | 1 | Browns | 21–17 | Cleveland |
|  | 2 | Tie | 30–30 | Wash |
| 1958 | 1 | Browns | 20–10 | Wash |
|  | 2 | Browns | 21–14 | Cleveland |
| 1959 | 1 | Browns | 34–7 | Cleveland |
|  | 2 | Browns | 31–17 | Wash |
| 1960 | 1 | Browns | 31–10 | Wash |
|  | 2 | Browns | 27–16 | Cleveland |
| 1961 | 1 | Browns | 31–7 | Cleveland |
|  | 2 | Browns | 17–6 | Wash |
| 1962 | 1 | Redskins | 17–16 | Cleveland |
|  | 2 | Redskins | 17–9 | Wash |
| 1963 | 1 | Browns | 37–14 | Cleveland |
|  | 2 | Browns | 27–20 | Wash |
| 1964 | 1 | Browns | 27–13 | Wash |
|  | 2 | Browns | 34–24 | Cleveland |
| 1965 | 1 | Browns | 17–7 | Wash |
|  | 2 | Browns | 24–16 | Cleveland |
| 1966 | 1 | Browns | 38–14 | Wash |
|  | 2 | Browns | 14–3 | Cleveland |
| 1967 | 1 | Browns | 42–37 | Cleveland |
| 1968 | 1 | Browns | 24–21 | Wash |
| 1969 | 1 | Browns | 27–23 | Cleveland |
| 1971 | 1 | Browns | 20–13 | Wash |
| 1975 | 1 | Redskins | 23–7 | Cleveland |
| 1979 | 1 | Redskins | 13–9 | Cleveland |
| 1985 | 1 | Redskins | 14–7 | Cleveland |
| 1988 | 1 | Browns | 17–13 | Wash |
| 1991 | 1 | Redskins | 42–17 | Wash |
| 2004 | 1 | Browns | 17–13 | Cleveland |

## Dallas Cowboys — Cowboys lead RS 55–35–2; Redskins lead PS 2–0

| Year | Game | Winner | Score | At |
|------|------|--------|-------|-----|
| 1960 | 1 | Redskins | 26–14 | Wash |
| 1961 | 1 | Tie | 28–28 | Dallas |
|  | 2 | Redskins | 34–24 | Wash |
| 1962 | 1 | Tie | 35–35 | Dallas |
|  | 2 | Cowboys | 38–10 | Wash |
| 1963 | 1 | Redskins | 21–17 | Wash |
|  | 2 | Cowboys | 35–20 | Dallas |
| 1964 | 1 | Cowboys | 24–18 | Dallas |
|  | 2 | Redskins | 28–16 | Wash |
| 1965 | 1 | Cowboys | 27–7 | Dallas |
|  | 2 | Redskins | 34–31 | Wash |
| 1966 | 1 | Cowboys | 31–30 | Wash |
|  | 2 | Redskins | 34–31 | Dallas |
| 1967 | 1 | Cowboys | 17–14 | Wash |
|  | 2 | Redskins | 27–20 | Dallas |
| 1968 | 1 | Cowboys | 44–24 | Wash |
|  | 2 | Cowboys | 29–20 | Dallas |
| 1969 | 1 | Cowboys | 41–28 | Wash |
|  | 2 | Cowboys | 20–10 | Dallas |
| 1970 | 1 | Cowboys | 45–21 | Wash |
|  | 2 | Cowboys | 34–0 | Dallas |
| 1971 | 1 | Redskins | 20–16 | Dallas |
|  | 2 | Cowboys | 13–0 | Wash |
| 1972 | 1 | Redskins | 24–20 | Wash |
|  | 2 | Cowboys | 34–24 | Dallas |
|  | 3 | Redskins* | 26–3 | Wash |
| 1973 | 1 | Redskins | 14–7 | Wash |
|  | 2 | Cowboys | 27–7 | Dallas |
| 1974 | 1 | Redskins | 28–21 | Wash |
|  | 2 | Cowboys | 24–23 | Dallas |
| 1975 | 1 | Redskins | 30–24OT | Wash |
|  | 2 | Cowboys | 31–10 | Dallas |
| 1976 | 1 | Cowboys | 20–7 | Wash |
|  | 2 | Redskins | 27–14 | Dallas |
| 1977 | 1 | Cowboys | 34–16 | Dallas |
|  | 2 | Cowboys | 14–7 | Wash |
| 1978 | 1 | Redskins | 9–5 | Wash |
|  | 2 | Cowboys | 37–10 | Dallas |
| 1979 | 1 | Redskins | 34–20 | Wash |
|  | 2 | Cowboys | 35–34 | Dallas |
| 1980 | 1 | Cowboys | 17–3 | Wash |
|  | 2 | Cowboys | 14–10 | Dallas |
| 1981 | 1 | Cowboys | 26–10 | Wash |
|  | 2 | Cowboys | 24–10 | Dallas |
| 1982 | 1 | Cowboys | 24–10 | Wash |
|  | 2 | Redskins* | 31–17 | Wash |
| 1983 | 1 | Cowboys | 31–30 | Wash |
|  | 2 | Redskins | 31–10 | Dallas |
| 1984 | 1 | Redskins | 34–14 | Wash |
|  | 2 | Redskins | 30–28 | Dallas |
| 1985 | 1 | Cowboys | 44–14 | Dallas |
|  | 2 | Cowboys | 13–7 | Wash |
| 1986 | 1 | Cowboys | 30–6 | Dallas |
|  | 2 | Redskins | 41–14 | Wash |
| 1987 | 1 | Redskins | 13–7 | Dallas |
|  | 2 | Redskins | 24–20 | Wash |
| 1988 | 1 | Redskins | 35–17 | Dallas |
|  | 2 | Cowboys | 24–17 | Wash |
| 1989 | 1 | Redskins | 30–7 | Dallas |
|  | 2 | Cowboys | 13–3 | Wash |
| 1990 | 1 | Redskins | 19–15 | Wash |
|  | 2 | Cowboys | 27–17 | Dallas |
| 1991 | 1 | Redskins | 33–31 | Dallas |
|  | 2 | Cowboys | 24–21 | Wash |
| 1992 | 1 | Cowboys | 23–10 | Dallas |
|  | 2 | Redskins | 20–17 | Wash |
| 1993 | 1 | Redskins | 35–16 | Wash |
|  | 2 | Cowboys | 38–3 | Dallas |

| Year | Game | Winner | Score | At |
|------|------|--------|-------|-----|
| 1994 | 1 | Cowboys | 34–7 | Wash |
|  | 2 | Cowboys | 31–7 | Dallas |
| 1995 | 1 | Redskins | 27–23 | Wash |
|  | 2 | Redskins | 24–17 | Dallas |
| 1996 | 1 | Cowboys | 21–10 | Dallas |
|  | 2 | Redskins | 37–10 | Wash |
| 1997 | 1 | Redskins | 21–16 | Wash |
|  | 2 | Cowboys | 17–14 | Dallas |
| 1998 | 1 | Cowboys | 31–10 | Wash |
|  | 2 | Cowboys | 23–7 | Dallas |
| 1999 | 1 | Cowboys | 41–35(OT) | Wash |
|  | 2 | Cowboys | 38–20 | Dallas |
| 2000 | 1 | Cowboys | 27–21 | Wash |
|  | 2 | Cowboys | 32–13 | Dallas |
| 2001 | 1 | Cowboys | 9–7 | Dallas |
|  | 2 | Cowboys | 20–14 | Wash |
| 2002 | 1 | Cowboys | 27–20 | Dallas |
|  | 2 | Redskins | 20–14 | Wash |
| 2003 | 1 | Cowboys | 21–14 | Dallas |
|  | 2 | Cowboys | 27–0 | Wash |
| 2004 | 1 | Cowboys | 21–18 | Wash |
|  | 2 | Cowboys | 13–10 | Dallas |
| 2005 | 1 | Redskins | 14–3 | Dallas |
|  | 2 | Redskins | 35–7 | Wash |
| 2006 | 1 | Cowboys | 27–10 | Dallas |
|  | 2 | Redskins | 22–19 | Wash |

*NFC Championship

### Denver Broncos

Broncos lead RS 6–4
Redskins lead PS 1–0

| Year | Game | Winner | Score | At |
|------|------|--------|-------|-----|
| 1970 | 1 | Redskins | 19–3 | Denver |
| 1974 | 1 | Redskins | 30–3 | Wash |
| 1980 | 1 | Broncos | 20–17 | Denver |
| 1986 | 1 | Broncos | 31–30 | Denver |
| 1987 | 1 | Redskins* | 42–10 | San Diego |
| 1989 | 1 | Broncos | 14–10 | Wash |
| 1992 | 1 | Redskins | 34–3 | Wash |
| 1995 | 1 | Broncos | 38–31 | Denver |
| 1998 | 1 | Broncos | 38–16 | Wash |
| 2001 | 1 | Redskins | 17–10 | Denver |
| 2005 | 1 | Broncos | 21–19 | Denver |

*Super Bowl XXII

### Detroit Lions

Redskins lead RS 25–10
Redskins lead PS 3–0

| Year | Game | Winner | Score | At |
|------|------|--------|-------|-----|
| 1932 | 1 | Spartans | 10–0 | Portsmouth |
| 1933 | 1 | Spartans | 13–0 | Boston |
| 1934 | 1 | Lions | 24–0 | Detroit |
| 1935 | 1 | Lions | 17–7 | Boston |
|  | 2 | Lions | 14–0 | Detroit |
| 1938 | 1 | Redskins | 7–5 | Detroit |
| 1939 | 1 | Redskins | 31–7 | Wash |
| 1940 | 1 | Redskins | 20–14 | Detroit |
| 1942 | 1 | Redskins | 15–3 | Detroit |
| 1943 | 1 | Redskins | 42–20 | Wash |
| 1946 | 1 | Redskins | 17–16 | Wash |
| 1947 | 1 | Lions | 38–21 | Detroit |
| 1948 | 1 | Redskins | 46–21 | Wash |
| 1951 | 1 | Lions | 35–17 | Detroit |
| 1956 | 1 | Redskins | 18–17 | Wash |
| 1965 | 1 | Lions | 14–10 | Detroit |
| 1968 | 1 | Redskins | 14–3 | Wash |
| 1970 | 1 | Redskins | 31–10 | Wash |
| 1973 | 1 | Redskins | 20–0 | Detroit |
| 1976 | 1 | Redskins | 20–7 | Wash |
| 1978 | 1 | Redskins | 21–19 | Detroit |
| 1979 | 1 | Redskins | 27–24 | Detroit |
| 1981 | 1 | Redskins | 33–31 | Wash |
| 1982 | 1 | Redskins* | 31–7 | Wash |
| 1983 | 1 | Redskins | 38–17 | Wash |
| 1984 | 1 | Redskins | 28–14 | Wash |
| 1985 | 1 | Redskins | 24–3 | Wash |
| 1987 | 1 | Redskins | 20–13 | Wash |
| 1990 | 1 | Redskins | 41–38 | Detroit |

| Year | Game | Winner | Score | At |
|------|------|--------|-------|-----|
| 1991 | 1 | Redskins | 45–0 | Wash |
|  | 2 | Redskins† | 41–10 | Wash |
| 1992 | 1 | Redskins | 13–10 | Wash |
| 1995 | 1 | Redskins | 36–30OT | Wash |
| 1997 | 1 | Redskins | 30–7 | Wash |
| 1999 | 1 | Lions | 33–17 | Detroit |
|  | 2 | Redskins* | 27–13 | Wash |
| 2000 | 1 | Lions | 15–10 | Detroit |
| 2004 | 1 | Redskins | 17–10 | Detroit |

*NFC First Round Playoff
†NFC Championship

### Green Bay Packers

Packers lead RS 16–12–1
PS tied 1–1

| Year | Game | Winner | Score | At |
|------|------|--------|-------|-----|
| 1932 | 1 | Packers | 21–0 | Boston |
| 1933 | 1 | Tie | 7–7 | Green Bay |
|  | 2 | Redskins | 20–7 | Boston |
| 1934 | 1 | Packers | 10–0 | Boston |
| 1936 | 1 | Packers | 31–2 | Green Bay |
|  | 2 | Packers | 7–3 | Boston |
|  | 3 | Packers† | 21–6 | New York |
| 1937 | 1 | Redskins | 14–6 | Wash |
| 1939 | 1 | Packers | 24–14 | Milwaukee |
| 1941 | 1 | Packers | 22–17 | Wash |
| 1943 | 1 | Redskins | 33–7 | Milwaukee |
| 1946 | 1 | Packers | 20–7 | Wash |
| 1947 | 1 | Packers | 27–10 | Milwaukee |
| 1948 | 1 | Redskins | 23–7 | Milwaukee |
| 1949 | 1 | Redskins | 30–0 | Wash |
| 1950 | 1 | Packers | 35–21 | Milwaukee |
| 1952 | 1 | Packers | 35–20 | Milwaukee |
| 1958 | 1 | Redskins | 37–21 | Wash |
| 1959 | 1 | Packers | 21–0 | Green Bay |
| 1968 | 1 | Packers | 27–7 | Wash |
| 1972 | 1 | Redskins | 21–16 | Wash |
|  | 2 | Redskins‡ | 16–3 | Wash |
| 1974 | 1 | Redskins | 17–6 | Green Bay |
| 1977 | 1 | Redskins | 10–9 | Wash |
| 1979 | 1 | Redskins | 38–21 | Wash |
| 1983 | 1 | Packers | 48–47 | Green Bay |
| 1986 | 1 | Redskins | 16–7 | Green Bay |
| 1988 | 1 | Redskins | 20–17 | Milwaukee |
| 2001 | 1 | Packers | 37–0 | Green Bay |
| 2002 | 1 | Packers | 30–9 | Green Bay |
| 2004 | 1 | Packers | 28–14 | Wash |

### Houston Texans

Redskins lead RS 2–0

| Year | Game | Winner | Score | At |
|------|------|--------|-------|-----|
| 2002 | 1 | Redskins | 26–10 | Wash |
| 2006 | 1 | Redskins | 31–15 | Houston |

### Indianapolis Colts

Colts lead RS 18–10

| Year | Game | Winner | Score | At |
|------|------|--------|-------|-----|
| 1953 | 1 | Colts | 27–17 | Baltimore |
| 1954 | 1 | Redskins | 24–21 | Wash |
| 1955 | 1 | Redskins | 14–13 | Baltimore |
| 1956 | 1 | Colts | 19–17 | Baltimore |
| 1957 | 1 | Colts | 21–17 | Wash |
| 1958 | 1 | Colts | 35–10 | Baltimore |
| 1959 | 1 | Redskins | 27–24 | Wash |
| 1960 | 1 | Colts | 20–0 | Baltimore |
| 1961 | 1 | Colts | 27–6 | Wash |
| 1962 | 1 | Colts | 34–21 | Baltimore |
| 1963 | 1 | Colts | 26–20 | Wash |
| 1964 | 1 | Colts | 45–17 | Baltimore |
| 1965 | 1 | Colts | 38–7 | Wash |
| 1966 | 1 | Colts | 37–10 | Baltimore |
| 1967 | 1 | Colts | 17–13 | Wash |
| 1969 | 1 | Colts | 41–17 | Baltimore |
| 1973 | 1 | Redskins | 22–14 | Wash |
| 1977 | 1 | Colts | 10–3 | Baltimore |
| 1978 | 1 | Colts | 21–17 | Baltimore |
| 1981 | 1 | Redskins | 38–14 | Wash |
| 1984 | 1 | Redskins | 35–7 | Indianapolis |
| 1990 | 1 | Colts | 35–28 | Indianapolis |
| 1993 | 1 | Redskins | 30–24 | Wash |

| Year | Game | Winner | Score | At |
|------|------|--------|-------|-----|
| 1994 | 1 | Redskins | 41–27 | Indianapolis |
| 1996 | 1 | Redskins | 31–16 | Wash |
| 1999 | 1 | Colts | 24–21 | Indianapolis |
| 2002 | 1 | Redskins | 26–21 | Wash |
| 2006 | 1 | Colts | 36–22 | Indianapolis |

**Jacksonville Jaguars** — Redskins lead RS 3–1

| Year | Game | Winner | Score | At |
|------|------|--------|-------|-----|
| 1997 | 1 | Redskins | 24–12 | Wash |
| 2000 | 1 | Redskins | 35–16 | Jacksonville |
| 2002 | 1 | Jaguars | 26–7 | Jacksonville |
| 2006 | 1 | Redskins | 36–30 | Wash |

**Kansas City Chiefs** — Redskins lead RS 6–1

| Year | Game | Winner | Score | At |
|------|------|--------|-------|-----|
| 1971 | 1 | Chiefs | 27–20 | KC |
| 1976 | 1 | Chiefs | 33–30 | Wash |
| 1983 | 1 | Redskins | 27–12 | Wash |
| 1992 | 1 | Chiefs | 35–16 | KC |
| 1995 | 1 | Chiefs | 24–3 | KC |
| 2001 | 1 | Chiefs | 45–13 | Wash |
| 2005 | 1 | Chiefs | 28–21 | Wash |

**Miami Dolphins** — Dolphins lead RS 6–3 / PS tied 1–1

| Year | Game | Winner | Score | At |
|------|------|--------|-------|-----|
| 1972 | 1 | Dolphins* | 14–7 | Los Angeles |
| 1974 | 1 | Redskins | 20–17 | Wash |
| 1978 | 1 | Dolphins | 16–0 | Wash |
| 1981 | 1 | Dolphins | 13–0 | Miami |
| 1982 | 1 | Redskins† | 27–17 | Pasadena |
| 1984 | 1 | Dolphins | 35–17 | Wash |
| 1987 | 1 | Dolphins | 23–21 | Miami |
| 1990 | 1 | Redskins | 42–20 | Wash |
| 1993 | 1 | Dolphins | 17–10 | Miami |
| 1999 | 1 | Redskins | 21–10 | Wash |
| 2003 | 1 | Dolphins | 24–23 | Miami |

*Super Bowl VII
†Super Bowl XVII

**Minnesota Vikings** — Redskins lead RS 7–6 / Redskins lead PS 3–2

| Year | Game | Winner | Score | At |
|------|------|--------|-------|-----|
| 1968 | 1 | Vikings | 27–14 | Minnesota |
| 1970 | 1 | Vikings | 19–10 | Wash |
| 1972 | 1 | Redskins | 24–21 | Minnesota |
| 1973 | 1 | Vikings* | 27–20 | Minnesota |
| 1975 | 1 | Redskins | 31–30 | Wash |
| 1976 | 1 | Vikings* | 35–20 | Minnesota |
| 1980 | 1 | Vikings | 39–14 | Wash |
| 1982 | 1 | Redskins† | 21–7 | Wash |
| 1984 | 1 | Redskins | 31–17 | Minnesota |
| 1986 | 1 | Redskins | 44–38OT | Wash |
| 1987 | 1 | Redskins | 27–24OT | Minnesota |
|  | 2 | Redskins‡ | 17–10 | Wash |
| 1992 | 1 | Redskins | 15–13 | Minnesota |
|  | 2 | Redskins¶ | 24–7 | Minnesota |
| 1993 | 1 | Vikings | 14–9 | Wash |
| 1998 | 1 | Vikings | 41–7 | Minnesota |
| 2004 | 1 | Redskins | 21–18 | Wash |
| 2006 | 1 | Vikings | 19–16 | Wash |

*NFC Divisional Playoff
†NFC Second–Round Playoff
‡NFC Championship
¶NFC First–Round Playoff

**New England Patriots** — Redskins lead RS 6–1

| Year | Game | Winner | Score | At |
|------|------|--------|-------|-----|
| 1972 | 1 | Patriots | 24–23 | NE |
| 1978 | 1 | Redskins | 16–14 | NE |
| 1981 | 1 | Redskins | 24–22 | Wash |
| 1984 | 1 | Redskins | 26–10 | NE |
| 1990 | 1 | Redskins | 25–10 | NE |
| 1996 | 1 | Redskins | 27–22 | NE |
| 2003 | 1 | Redskins | 20–17 | Wash |

**New Orleans Saints** — Redskins lead RS 14–7

| Year | Game | Winner | Score | At |
|------|------|--------|-------|-----|
| 1967 | 1 | Redskins | 31–10 | NO |
|  | 2 | Saints | 30–14 | Wash |

| Year | Game | Winner | Score | At |
|------|------|--------|-------|-----|
| 1968 | 1 | Saints | 37–17 | NO |
| 1969 | 1 | Redskins | 26–20 | NO |
|  | 2 | Redskins | 17–10 | Wash |
| 1971 | 1 | Redskins | 24–14 | Wash |
| 1973 | 1 | Saints | 19–3 | NO |
| 1975 | 1 | Redskins | 41–3 | Wash |
| 1979 | 1 | Saints | 14–10 | Wash |
| 1980 | 1 | Redskins | 22–14 | Wash |
| 1982 | 1 | Redskins | 27–10 | NO |
| 1986 | 1 | Redskins | 14–6 | NO |
| 1988 | 1 | Redskins | 27–24 | Wash |
| 1989 | 1 | Redskins | 16–14 | NO |
| 1990 | 1 | Redskins | 31–17 | Wash |
| 1992 | 1 | Saints | 20–3 | NO |
| 1994 | 1 | Redskins | 38–24 | NO |
| 2001 | 1 | Redskins | 40–10 | NO |
| 2002 | 1 | Saints | 43–27 | Wash |
| 2003 | 1 | Saints | 24–20 | Wash |
| 2006 | 1 | Redskins | 16–10 | Wash |

**New York Giants** — Giants lead RS 84–60–4 / PS tied 1–1

| Year | Game | Winner | Score | At |
|------|------|--------|-------|-----|
| 1932 | 1 | Braves | 14–6 | Boston |
|  | 2 | Tie | 0–0 | NY |
| 1933 | 1 | Redskins | 21–20 | Boston |
|  | 2 | Giants | 7–0 | NY |
| 1934 | 1 | Giants | 16–3 | Boston |
|  | 2 | Giants | 3–0 | NY |
| 1935 | 1 | Giants | 20–12 | Boston |
|  | 2 | Giants | 17–6 | NY |
| 1936 | 1 | Giants | 7–0 | Boston |
|  | 2 | Redskins | 14–0 | NY |
| 1937 | 1 | Redskins | 13–3 | Wash |
|  | 2 | Redskins | 49–14 | NY |
| 1938 | 1 | Giants | 10–7 | Wash |
|  | 2 | Giants | 36–0 | NY |
| 1939 | 1 | Tie | 0–0 | Wash |
|  | 2 | Giants | 9–7 | NY |
| 1940 | 1 | Redskins | 21–7 | Wash |
|  | 2 | Giants | 21–7 | NY |
| 1941 | 1 | Giants | 17–10 | Wash |
|  | 2 | Giants | 20–13 | NY |
| 1942 | 1 | Giants | 14–7 | Wash |
|  | 2 | Redskins | 14–7 | NY |
| 1943 | 1 | Giants | 14–10 | NY |
|  | 2 | Giants | 31–7 | Wash |
|  | 3 | Redskins* | 28–0 | NY |
| 1944 | 1 | Giants | 16–13 | NY |
|  | 2 | Giants | 31–0 | Wash |
| 1945 | 1 | Redskins | 21–14 | NY |
|  | 2 | Redskins | 17–0 | Wash |
| 1946 | 1 | Redskins | 24–14 | Wash |
|  | 2 | Giants | 31–0 | NY |
| 1947 | 1 | Redskins | 28–20 | Wash |
|  | 2 | Giants | 35–10 | NY |
| 1948 | 1 | Redskins | 41–10 | Wash |
|  | 2 | Redskins | 28–21 | NY |
| 1949 | 1 | Giants | 45–35 | Wash |
|  | 2 | Giants | 23–7 | NY |
| 1950 | 1 | Giants | 21–17 | Wash |
|  | 2 | Giants | 24–21 | NY |
| 1951 | 1 | Giants | 35–14 | Wash |
|  | 2 | Giants | 28–14 | NY |
| 1952 | 1 | Giants | 14–10 | Wash |
|  | 2 | Redskins | 27–17 | NY |
| 1953 | 1 | Redskins | 13–9 | Wash |
|  | 2 | Redskins | 24–21 | NY |
| 1954 | 1 | Giants | 51–21 | Wash |
|  | 2 | Giants | 24–7 | NY |
| 1955 | 1 | Giants | 35–7 | NY |
|  | 2 | Giants | 27–20 | Wash |
| 1956 | 1 | Redskins | 33–7 | Wash |
|  | 2 | Giants | 28–14 | NY |
| 1957 | 1 | Giants | 24–20 | Wash |
|  | 2 | Redskins | 31–14 | NY |

| Year | Game | Winner | Score | At |
|---|---|---|---|---|
| 1958 | 1 | Giants | 21–14 | Wash |
| | 2 | Giants | 30–0 | NY |
| 1959 | 1 | Giants | 45–14 | NY |
| | 2 | Giants | 24–10 | Wash |
| 1960 | 1 | Tie | 24–24 | NY |
| | 2 | Giants | 17–3 | Wash |
| 1961 | 1 | Giants | 24–21 | Wash |
| | 2 | Giants | 53–0 | NY |
| 1962 | 1 | Giants | 49–34 | NY |
| | 2 | Giants | 42–24 | Wash |
| 1963 | 1 | Giants | 24–14 | Wash |
| | 2 | Giants | 44–14 | NY |
| 1964 | 1 | Giants | 13–10 | NY |
| | 2 | Redskins | 36–21 | Wash |
| 1965 | 1 | Redskins | 23–7 | NY |
| | 2 | Giants | 27–10 | Wash |
| 1966 | 1 | Giants | 13–10 | NY |
| | 2 | Redskins | 72–41 | Wash |
| 1967 | 1 | Redskins | 38–34 | Wash |
| 1968 | 1 | Giants | 48–21 | NY |
| | 2 | Giants | 13–10 | Wash |
| 1969 | 1 | Redskins | 20–14 | Wash |
| 1970 | 1 | Giants | 35–33 | NY |
| | 2 | Giants | 27–24 | Wash |
| 1971 | 1 | Redskins | 30–3 | NY |
| | 2 | Redskins | 23–7 | Wash |
| 1972 | 1 | Redskins | 23–16 | NY |
| | 2 | Redskins | 27–13 | Wash |
| 1973 | 1 | Redskins | 21–3 | New Haven, Conn. |
| | 2 | Redskins | 27–24 | Wash |
| 1974 | 1 | Redskins | 13–10 | New Haven, Conn. |
| | 2 | Redskins | 24–3 | Wash |
| 1975 | 1 | Redskins | 49–13 | Wash |
| | 2 | Redskins | 21–13 | NY |
| 1976 | 1 | Redskins | 19–17 | Wash |
| | 2 | Giants | 12–9 | NY |
| 1977 | 1 | Giants | 20–17 | NY |
| | 2 | Giants | 17–6 | Wash |
| 1978 | 1 | Giants | 17–6 | NY |
| | 2 | Redskins | 16–13OT | Wash |
| 1979 | 1 | Redskins | 27–0 | Wash |
| | 2 | Giants | 14–6 | NY |
| 1980 | 1 | Redskins | 23–21 | NY |
| | 2 | Redskins | 16–13 | Wash |
| 1981 | 1 | Giants | 17–7 | Wash |
| | 2 | Redskins | 30–27OT | NY |
| 1982 | 1 | Redskins | 27–17 | NY |
| | 2 | Redskins | 15–14 | Wash |
| 1983 | 1 | Redskins | 33–17 | NY |
| | 2 | Redskins | 31–22 | Wash |
| 1984 | 1 | Redskins | 30–14 | Wash |
| | 2 | Giants | 37–13 | NY |
| 1985 | 1 | Giants | 17–3 | NY |
| | 2 | Redskins | 23–21 | Wash |
| 1986 | 1 | Giants | 27–20 | NY |
| | 2 | Giants | 24–14 | Wash |
| | 3 | Giants[†] | 17–0 | NY |
| 1987 | 1 | Redskins | 38–12 | NY |
| | 2 | Redskins | 23–19 | Wash |
| 1988 | 1 | Giants | 27–20 | NY |
| | 2 | Giants | 24–23 | Wash |
| 1989 | 1 | Giants | 27–24 | Wash |
| | 2 | Giants | 20–17 | NY |
| 1990 | 1 | Giants | 24–20 | Wash |
| | 2 | Giants | 21–10 | NY |
| 1991 | 1 | Redskins | 17–13 | NY |
| | 2 | Redskins | 34–17 | Wash |
| 1992 | 1 | Giants | 24–7 | Wash |
| | 2 | Redskins | 28–10 | NY |
| 1993 | 1 | Giants | 41–7 | Wash |
| | 2 | Giants | 20–6 | NY |
| 1994 | 1 | Giants | 31–23 | NY |
| | 2 | Giants | 21–19 | Wash |

| Year | Game | Winner | Score | At |
|---|---|---|---|---|
| 1995 | 1 | Giants | 24–15 | Wash |
| | 2 | Giants | 20–13 | NY |
| 1996 | 1 | Redskins | 31–10 | NY |
| | 2 | Redskins | 31–21 | Wash |
| 1997 | 1 | Tie | 7–7OT | Wash |
| | 2 | Giants | 30–10 | NY |
| 1998 | 1 | Giants | 31–24 | NY |
| | 2 | Redskins | 21–14 | Wash |
| 1999 | 1 | Redskins | 50–21 | NY |
| | 2 | Redskins | 23–13 | Wash |
| 2000 | 1 | Redskins | 16–6 | NY |
| | 2 | Giants | 9–7 | Wash |
| 2001 | 1 | Giants | 23–9 | NY |
| | 2 | Redskins | 35–21 | Wash |
| 2002 | 1 | Giants | 19–17 | NY |
| | 2 | Giants | 27–21 | Wash |
| 2003 | 1 | Giants | 24–21OT | Wash |
| | 2 | Redskins | 20–7 | NY |
| 2004 | 1 | Giants | 20–14 | NY |
| | 2 | Redskins | 31–7 | Wash |
| 2005 | 1 | Giants | 36–0 | NY |
| | 2 | Redskins | 35–20 | Wash |
| 2006 | 1 | Giants | 19–3 | NY |
| | 2 | Giants | 34–28 | Wash |

*Division Playoff
†NFC Championship

**New York Jets**                                 Redskins lead RS 7–1

| Year | Game | Winner | Score | At |
|---|---|---|---|---|
| 1972 | 1 | Redskins | 35–17 | NY |
| 1976 | 1 | Redskins | 37–16 | NY |
| 1978 | 1 | Redskins | 23–3 | Wash |
| 1987 | 1 | Redskins | 17–6 | Wash |
| 1993 | 1 | Jets | 3–0 | Wash |
| 1996 | 1 | Redskins | 31–16 | Wash |
| 1999 | 1 | Redskins | 27–20 | NY |
| 2003 | 1 | Redskins | 16–3 | Wash |

**Oakland Raiders**                               Raiders lead RS 7–3
                                                  Raiders lead PS 1–0

| Year | Game | Winner | Score | At |
|---|---|---|---|---|
| 1970 | 1 | Raiders | 34–20 | Oakland |
| 1975 | 1 | Raiders | 26–23 OT | Wash |
| 1980 | 1 | Raiders | 24–21 | Oakland |
| 1983 | 1 | Redskins | 37–35 | Wash |
| | 2 | Raiders* | 38–9 | Tampa |
| 1986 | 1 | Redskins | 10–6 | Wash |
| 1989 | 1 | Raiders | 37–24 | LA |
| 1992 | 1 | Raiders | 21–20 | Wash |
| 1995 | 1 | Raiders | 20–8 | Wash |
| 1998 | 1 | Redskins | 29–19 | Oakland |
| 2005 | 1 | Raiders | 16–13 | Wash |

*Super Bowl XVIII

**Philadelphia Eagles**                           Redskins lead RS 74–64–5
                                                  Redskins lead PS 1–0

| Year | Game | Winner | Score | At |
|---|---|---|---|---|
| 1934 | 1 | Redskins | 6–0 | Boston |
| | 2 | Redskins | 14–7 | Philadelphia |
| 1935 | 1 | Eagles | 7–6 | Boston |
| 1936 | 1 | Redskins | 26–3 | Philadelphia |
| | 2 | Redskins | 17–7 | Boston |
| 1937 | 1 | Eagles | 14–0 | Wash |
| | 2 | Redskins | 10–7 | Philadelphia |
| 1938 | 1 | Redskins | 26–23 | Philadelphia |
| | 2 | Redskins | 20–14 | Wash |
| 1939 | 1 | Redskins | 7–0 | Philadelphia |
| | 2 | Redskins | 7–6 | Wash |
| 1940 | 1 | Redskins | 34–17 | Philadelphia |
| | 2 | Redskins | 13–6 | Wash |
| 1941 | 1 | Redskins | 21–17 | Philadelphia |
| | 2 | Redskins | 20–14 | Wash |
| 1942 | 1 | Redskins | 14–10 | Philadelphia |
| | 2 | Redskins | 30–27 | Wash |
| 1944 | 1 | Tie | 31–31 | Philadelphia |
| | 2 | Eagles | 37–7 | Wash |

| Year | Game | Winner | Score | At |
|------|------|--------|-------|-----|
| 1945 | 1 | Redskins | 24–14 | Wash |
| | 2 | Eagles | 16–0 | Philadelphia |
| 1946 | 1 | Eagles | 28–24 | Wash |
| | 2 | Redskins | 27–10 | Philadelphia |
| 1947 | 1 | Eagles | 45–42 | Philadelphia |
| | 2 | Eagles | 38–14 | Wash |
| 1948 | 1 | Eagles | 45–0 | Wash |
| | 2 | Eagles | 42–21 | Philadelphia |
| 1949 | 1 | Eagles | 49–14 | Philadelphia |
| | 2 | Eagles | 44–21 | Wash |
| 1950 | 1 | Eagles | 35–3 | Philadelphia |
| | 2 | Eagles | 33–0 | Wash |
| 1951 | 1 | Redskins | 27–23 | Philadelphia |
| | 2 | Eagles | 35–21 | Wash |
| 1952 | 1 | Eagles | 38–20 | Philadelphia |
| | 2 | Redskins | 27–21 | Wash |
| 1953 | 1 | Tie | 21–21 | Philadelphia |
| | 2 | Redskins | 10–0 | Wash |
| 1954 | 1 | Eagles | 49–21 | Wash |
| | 2 | Eagles | 41–33 | Philadelphia |
| 1955 | 1 | Redskins | 31–30 | Philadelphia |
| | 2 | Redskins | 34–21 | Wash |
| 1956 | 1 | Eagles | 13–9 | Philadelphia |
| | 2 | Redskins | 19–17 | Wash |
| 1957 | 1 | Eagles | 21–12 | Philadelphia |
| | 2 | Redskins | 42–7 | Wash |
| 1958 | 1 | Redskins | 24–14 | Philadelphia |
| | 2 | Redskins | 20–0 | Wash |
| 1959 | 1 | Eagles | 30–23 | Philadelphia |
| | 2 | Eagles | 34–14 | Wash |
| 1960 | 1 | Eagles | 19–13 | Philadelphia |
| | 2 | Eagles | 38–28 | Wash |
| 1961 | 1 | Eagles | 14–7 | Philadelphia |
| | 2 | Eagles | 27–24 | Wash |
| 1962 | 1 | Redskins | 27–21 | Philadelphia |
| | 2 | Eagles | 37–14 | Wash |
| 1963 | 1 | Eagles | 37–24 | Wash |
| | 2 | Redskins | 13–10 | Philadelphia |
| 1964 | 1 | Redskins | 35–20 | Wash |
| | 2 | Redskins | 21–10 | Philadelphia |
| 1965 | 1 | Redskins | 23–21 | Wash |
| | 2 | Eagles | 21–14 | Philadelphia |
| 1966 | 1 | Redskins | 27–13 | Philadelphia |
| | 2 | Eagles | 37–28 | Wash |
| 1967 | 1 | Eagles | 35–24 | Philadelphia |
| | 2 | Tie | 35–35 | Wash |
| 1968 | 1 | Redskins | 17–14 | Wash |
| | 2 | Redskins | 16–10 | Philadelphia |
| 1969 | 1 | Tie | 28–28 | Wash |
| | 2 | Redskins | 34–29 | Philadelphia |
| 1970 | 1 | Redskins | 33–21 | Philadelphia |
| | 2 | Redskins | 24–6 | Wash |
| 1971 | 1 | Tie | 7–7 | Wash |
| | 2 | Redskins | 20–13 | Philadelphia |
| 1972 | 1 | Redskins | 14–0 | Wash |
| | 2 | Redskins | 23–7 | Philadelphia |
| 1973 | 1 | Redskins | 28–7 | Philadelphia |
| | 2 | Redskins | 38–20 | Wash |
| 1974 | 1 | Redskins | 27–20 | Philadelphia |
| | 2 | Redskins | 26–7 | Wash |
| 1975 | 1 | Eagles | 26–10 | Philadelphia |
| | 2 | Eagles | 26–3 | Wash |
| 1976 | 1 | Redskins | 20–17OT | Philadelphia |
| | 2 | Redskins | 24–0 | Wash |
| 1977 | 1 | Redskins | 23–17 | Wash |
| | 2 | Redskins | 17–14 | Philadelphia |
| 1978 | 1 | Redskins | 35–30 | Wash |
| | 2 | Eagles | 17–10 | Philadelphia |
| 1979 | 1 | Eagles | 28–17 | Philadelphia |
| | 2 | Redskins | 17–7 | Wash |
| 1980 | 1 | Eagles | 24–14 | Philadelphia |
| | 2 | Eagles | 24–0 | Wash |
| 1981 | 1 | Eagles | 36–13 | Philadelphia |
| | 2 | Redskins | 15–13 | Wash |

| Year | Game | Winner | Score | At |
|------|------|--------|-------|-----|
| 1982 | 1 | Redskins | 37–34 OT | Philadelphia |
| | 2 | Redskins | 13–9 | Wash |
| 1983 | 1 | Redskins | 23–13 | Philadelphia |
| | 2 | Redskins | 28–24 | Wash |
| 1984 | 1 | Redskins | 20–0 | Wash |
| | 2 | Eagles | 16–10 | Philadelphia |
| 1985 | 1 | Eagles | 19–6 | Wash |
| | 2 | Redskins | 17–12 | Philadelphia |
| 1986 | 1 | Redskins | 41–14 | Wash |
| | 2 | Redskins | 21–14 | Philadelphia |
| 1987 | 1 | Redskins | 34–24 | Wash |
| | 2 | Eagles | 31–27 | Philadelphia |
| 1988 | 1 | Redskins | 17–10 | Wash |
| | 2 | Redskins | 20–19 | Philadelphia |
| 1989 | 1 | Eagles | 42–37 | Wash |
| | 2 | Redskins | 10–3 | Philadelphia |
| 1990 | 1 | Redskins | 13–7 | Wash |
| | 2 | Eagles | 28–14 | Philadelphia |
| | 3 | Redskins* | 20–6 | Philadelphia |
| 1991 | 1 | Redskins | 23–0 | Wash |
| | 2 | Eagles | 24–22 | Philadelphia |
| 1992 | 1 | Redskins | 16–12 | Wash |
| | 2 | Eagles | 17–13 | Philadelphia |
| 1993 | 1 | Eagles | 34–31 | Philadelphia |
| | 2 | Eagles | 17–14 | Wash |
| 1994 | 1 | Eagles | 21–17 | Philadelphia |
| | 2 | Eagles | 31–29 | Wash |
| 1995 | 1 | Eagles | 37–34OT | Philadelphia |
| | 2 | Eagles | 14–7 | Wash |
| 1996 | 1 | Eagles | 17–14 | Wash |
| | 2 | Redskins | 26–21 | Philadelphia |
| 1997 | 1 | Eagles | 24–10 | Philadelphia |
| | 2 | Redskins | 35–32 | Wash |
| 1998 | 1 | Eagles | 17–12 | Philadelphia |
| | 2 | Redskins | 28–3 | Wash |
| 1999 | 1 | Eagles | 35–28 | Philadelphia |
| | 2 | Redskins | 20–17OT | Wash |
| 2000 | 1 | Redskins | 17–14 | Philadelphia |
| | 2 | Eagles | 23–20 | Wash |
| 2001 | 1 | Redskins | 13–3 | Philadelphia |
| | 2 | Eagles | 20–6 | Wash |
| 2002 | 1 | Eagles | 37–7 | Wash |
| | 2 | Eagles | 34–21 | Philadelphia |
| 2003 | 1 | Eagles | 27–25 | Philadelphia |
| | 2 | Eagles | 31–7 | Wash |
| 2004 | 1 | Eagles | 28–6 | Philadelphia |
| | 2 | Eagles | 17–14 | Wash |
| 2005 | 1 | Redskins | 17–10 | Wash |
| | 2 | Redskins | 31–20 | Philadelphia |
| 2006 | 1 | Eagles | 27–3 | Philadelphia |
| | 2 | Eagles | 21–19 | Wash |

*NFC First–Round Playoff

| Pittsburgh Steelers | | | Redskins lead RS 42–30–3 | |
|------|------|--------|-------|-----|
| 1933 | 1 | Redskins | 21–6 | Pittsburgh |
| | 2 | Pirates | 16–14 | Boston |
| 1934 | 1 | Redskins | 7–0 | Pittsburgh |
| | 2 | Redskins | 39–0 | Boston |
| 1935 | 1 | Pirates | 6–0 | Pittsburgh |
| | 2 | Redskins | 13–3 | Boston |
| 1936 | 1 | Pirates | 10–0 | Pittsburgh |
| | 2 | Redskins | 30–0 | Boston |
| 1937 | 1 | Redskins | 34–20 | Wash |
| | 2 | Pirates | 21–13 | Pittsburgh |
| 1938 | 1 | Redskins | 7–0 | Pittsburgh |
| | 2 | Redskins | 15–0 | Wash |
| 1939 | 1 | Redskins | 44–14 | Wash |
| | 2 | Redskins | 21–14 | Pittsburgh |
| 1940 | 1 | Redskins | 40–10 | Pittsburgh |
| | 2 | Redskins | 37–10 | Wash |
| 1941 | 1 | Redskins | 24–20 | Pittsburgh |
| | 2 | Redskins | 23–3 | Wash |
| 1942 | 1 | Redskins | 28–14 | Wash |
| | 2 | Redskins | 14–0 | Pittsburgh |

| Year | Game | Winner | Score | At |
|---|---|---|---|---|
| 1945 | 1 | Redskins | 14–0 | Pittsburgh |
| | 2 | Redskins | 24–0 | Wash |
| 1946 | 1 | Tie | 14–14 | Wash |
| | 2 | Steelers | 14–7 | Pittsburgh |
| 1947 | 1 | Redskins | 27–26 | Wash |
| | 2 | Steelers | 21–14 | Pittsburgh |
| 1948 | 1 | Redskins | 17–14 | Wash |
| | 2 | Steelers | 10–7 | Pittsburgh |
| 1949 | 1 | Redskins | 27–14 | Pittsburgh |
| | 2 | Redskins | 27–14 | Wash |
| 1950 | 1 | Steelers | 26–7 | Wash |
| | 2 | Redskins | 24–7 | Pittsburgh |
| 1951 | 1 | Redskins | 22–7 | Pittsburgh |
| | 2 | Steelers | 20–10 | Wash |
| 1952 | 1 | Redskins | 28–24 | Pittsburgh |
| | 2 | Steelers | 24–23 | Wash |
| 1953 | 1 | Redskins | 17–9 | Pittsburgh |
| | 2 | Steelers | 14–13 | Wash |
| 1954 | 1 | Steelers | 37–7 | Pittsburgh |
| | 2 | Redskins | 17–14 | Wash |
| 1955 | 1 | Redskins | 23–14 | Pittsburgh |
| | 2 | Redskins | 28–17 | Wash |
| 1956 | 1 | Steelers | 30–13 | Pittsburgh |
| | 2 | Steelers | 23–0 | Wash |
| 1957 | 1 | Steelers | 28–7 | Pittsburgh |
| | 2 | Redskins | 10–3 | Wash |
| 1958 | 1 | Steelers | 24–16 | Pittsburgh |
| | 2 | Tie | 14–14 | Wash |
| 1959 | 1 | Redskins | 23–17 | Pittsburgh |
| | 2 | Steelers | 27–6 | Wash |
| 1960 | 1 | Tie | 27–27 | Wash |
| | 2 | Steelers | 22–10 | Pittsburgh |
| 1961 | 1 | Steelers | 20–0 | Pittsburgh |
| | 2 | Steelers | 30–14 | Wash |
| 1962 | 1 | Steelers | 23–21 | Pittsburgh |
| | 2 | Steelers | 27–24 | Wash |
| 1963 | 1 | Steelers | 38–27 | Pittsburgh |
| | 2 | Steelers | 34–28 | Wash |
| 1964 | 1 | Redskins | 30–0 | Pittsburgh |
| | 2 | Steelers | 14–7 | Wash |
| 1965 | 1 | Redskins | 31–3 | Pittsburgh |
| | 2 | Redskins | 35–14 | Wash |
| 1966 | 1 | Redskins | 33–27 | Pittsburgh |
| | | Redskins | 24–10 | Wash |
| 1967 | 1 | Redskins | 15–10 | Pittsburgh |
| 1968 | 1 | Redskins | 16–13 | Wash |
| 1969 | 1 | Redskins | 14–7 | Pittsburgh |
| 1973 | 1 | Steelers | 21–16 | Pittsburgh |
| 1979 | 1 | Steelers | 38–7 | Pittsburgh |
| 1985 | 1 | Redskins | 30–23 | Pittsburgh |
| 1988 | 1 | Redskins | 30–29 | Wash |
| 1991 | 1 | Redskins | 41–14 | Pittsburgh |
| 1997 | 1 | Steelers | 14–13 | Pittsburgh |
| 2000 | 1 | Steelers | 24–3 | Pittsburgh |
| 2004 | 1 | Steelers | 16–7 | Pittsburgh |

## St. Louis Rams — Redskins lead RS 20–7–1, PS tied 2–2

| Year | Game | Winner | Score | At |
|---|---|---|---|---|
| 1937 | 1 | Redskins | 16–7 | Cleveland |
| 1938 | 1 | Redskins | 37–13 | Wash |
| 1941 | 1 | Redskins | 17–13 | Wash |
| 1942 | 1 | Redskins | 33–14 | Wash |
| 1944 | 1 | Redskins | 14–10 | Wash |
| 1945 | 1 | Rams* | 15–14 | Cleveland |
| 1948 | 1 | Rams | 41–13 | Wash |
| 1949 | 1 | Rams | 53–27 | LA |
| 1951 | 1 | Redskins | 31–21 | Wash |
| 1962 | 1 | Redskins | 20–14 | Wash |
| 1963 | 1 | Redskins | 37–14 | LA |
| 1967 | 1 | Tie | 28–28 | LA |
| 1969 | 1 | Rams | 24–13 | Wash |
| 1971 | 1 | Redskins | 38–24 | LA |
| 1974 | 1 | Redskins | 23–17 | LA |
| | 2 | Rams† | 19–10 | LA |
| 1977 | 1 | Redskins | 17–14 | Wash |
| 1981 | 1 | Redskins | 30–7 | LA |
| 1983 | 1 | Redskins | 42–20 | LA |
| | 2 | Redskins† | 51–7 | Wash |
| 1986 | 1 | Redskins‡ | 19–7 | Wash |
| 1987 | 1 | Rams | 30–26 | Wash |
| 1991 | 1 | Redskins | 27–6 | LA |
| 1993 | 1 | Rams | 10–6 | LA |
| 1994 | 1 | Redskins | 24–21 | LA |
| 1995 | 1 | Redskins | 35–23 | St. Louis |
| 1996 | 1 | Redskins | 17–10 | St. Louis |
| 1997 | 1 | Rams | 23–20 | Wash |
| 2000 | 1 | Redskins | 33–20 | St. Louis |
| 2002 | 1 | Redskins | 20–17 | Wash |
| 2005 | 1 | Redskins | 24–9 | St. Louis |
| 2006 | 1 | Rams | 37–31 | St. Louis |

*NFL Championship
†NFC Divisional Playoff
‡NFC First–Round Playoff

## San Diego Chargers — Redskins lead RS 6–2

| Year | Game | Winner | Score | At |
|---|---|---|---|---|
| 1973 | 1 | Redskins | 38–0 | Wash |
| 1980 | 1 | Redskins | 40–17 | Wash |
| 1983 | 1 | Redskins | 27–24 | San Diego |
| 1986 | 1 | Redskins | 30–27 | San Diego |
| 1989 | 1 | Redskins | 26–21 | Wash |
| 1998 | 1 | Redskins | 24–20 | Wash |
| 2001 | 1 | Chargers | 30–3 | San Diego |
| 2005 | 1 | Chargers | 23–17OT | Wash |

## San Francisco 49ers — 49ers lead RS 13–9–1, 49ers lead PS 3–1

| Year | Game | Winner | Score | At |
|---|---|---|---|---|
| 1952 | 1 | 49ers | 23–27 | Wash |
| 1954 | 1 | 49ers | 41–7 | SF |
| 1955 | 1 | Redskins | 7–0 | Wash |
| 1961 | 1 | 49ers | 35–3 | SF |
| 1967 | 1 | Redskins | 31–28 | Wash |
| 1969 | 1 | Tie | 17–17 | SF |
| 1970 | 1 | 49ers | 26–17 | SF |
| 1971 | 1 | 49ers* | 24–20 | SF |
| 1973 | 1 | Redskins | 33–9 | Wash |
| 1976 | 1 | Redskins | 24–21 | SF |
| 1978 | 1 | Redskins | 38–20 | Wash |
| 1981 | 1 | 49ers | 30–17 | Wash |
| 1983 | 1 | Redskins† | 24–21 | Wash |
| 1984 | 1 | 49ers | 37–31 | SF |
| 1985 | 1 | 49ers | 35–8 | Wash |
| 1986 | 1 | Redskins | 14–6 | Wash |
| 1988 | 1 | 49ers | 37–21 | SF |
| 1990 | 1 | 49ers | 26–13 | SF |
| | 2 | 49ers* | 28–10 | SF |
| 1992 | 1 | 49ers* | 20–13 | SF |
| 1994 | 1 | 49ers | 37–22 | Wash |
| 1996 | 1 | 49ers | 19–16OT | Wash |
| 1998 | 1 | 49ers | 45–10 | Wash |
| 1999 | 1 | Redskins | 26–20OT | SF |
| 2002 | 1 | 49ers | 20–10 | SF |
| 2004 | 1 | Redskins | 26–16 | SF |
| 2005 | 1 | Redskins | 52–17 | Wash |

*NFC Divisional Playoff
†NFC Championship

## Seattle Seahawks — Redskins lead RS 9–4, Seahawks lead PS 1–0

| Year | Game | Winner | Score | At |
|---|---|---|---|---|
| 1976 | 1 | Redskins | 31–7 | Wash |
| 1980 | 1 | Seahawks | 14–0 | Wash |
| 1983 | 1 | Redskins | 27–17 | Seattle |
| 1986 | 1 | Redskins | 19–14 | Wash |
| 1989 | 1 | Redskins | 29–0 | Seattle |
| 1992 | 1 | Redskins | 16–3 | Seattle |
| 1994 | 1 | Seahawks | 28–7 | Wash |
| 1995 | 1 | Seahawks | 27–20 | Wash |
| 1998 | 1 | Seahawks | 24–14 | Seattle |

| Year | Game | Winner | Score | At |
|---|---|---|---|---|
| 2001 | 1 | Redskins | 27–14 | Wash |
| 2002 | 1 | Redskins | 14–3 | Seattle |
| 2003 | 1 | Redskins | 27–20 | Wash |
| 2005 | 1 | Redskins | 20–17OT | Wash |
| | 2 | Seahawks* | 20–10 | Seattle |

*NFC Divisional Playoff

**Tampa Bay Buccaneers**  RS tied 7–7
PS tied 1–1

| Year | Game | Winner | Score | At |
|---|---|---|---|---|
| 1977 | 1 | Redskins | 10–0 | Tampa Bay |
| 1982 | 1 | Redskins | 21–13 | Tampa Bay |
| 1989 | 1 | Redskins | 32–28 | Wash |
| 1993 | 1 | Redskins | 23–17 | Tampa Bay |
| 1994 | 1 | Buccaneers | 26–21 | Tampa Bay |
| | 2 | Buccaneers | 17–14 | Wash |
| 1995 | 1 | Buccaneers | 14–6 | Tampa Bay |
| 1996 | 1 | Buccaneers | 24–10 | Tampa Bay |
| 1998 | 1 | Redskins | 20–16 | Wash |
| 1999 | 1 | Buccaneers* | 14–13 | Tampa Bay |
| 2000 | 1 | Redskins | 20–17OT | Wash |
| 2003 | 1 | Buccaneers | 35–13 | Wash |
| 2004 | 1 | Redskins | 16–10 | Wash |
| 2005 | 1 | Buccaneers | 36–35 | Tampa Bay |
| | 2 | Redskins† | 17–10 | Tampa Bay |
| 2006 | 1 | Buccaneers | 20–17 | Tampa Bay |

*NFC Divisional Playoff
†NFC First–Round Playoff

**Tennessee Titans**  Titans lead RS 6–4

| Year | Game | Winner | Score | At |
|---|---|---|---|---|
| 1971 | 1 | Redskins | 22–13 | Wash |
| 1975 | 1 | Oilers | 13–10 | Houston |
| 1979 | 1 | Redskins | 29–27 | Wash |
| 1985 | 1 | Redskins | 16–13 | Wash |
| 1988 | 1 | Oilers | 41–17 | Houston |
| 1991 | 1 | Redskins | 16–13OT | Wash |
| 1997 | 1 | Oilers | 28–14 | Tennessee |
| 2000 | 1 | Titans | 27–21 | Wash |
| 2002 | 1 | Redskins | 31–14 | Tennessee |
| 2006 | 1 | Titans | 25–22 | Wash |

# ALL-TIME TOP DRAFT PICKS
## (1936–2007)

| Year | Rd | Pos | Player | College |
|---|---|---|---|---|
| 1936 | 1 | QB | Riley Smith | Alabama |
| 1937 | 1 | QB | Sammy Baugh | TCU |
| 1938 | 1 | B | Andy Farkas | Detroit |
| 1939 | 1 | T | I.B. Hale | TCU |
| 1940 | 1 | B | Ed Boell | NYU |
| 1941 | 1 | B | Forrest Evanshevski | Michigan |
| 1942 | 1 | B | Ordan Sanders | Texas |
| 1943 | 1 | B | Jack Jenkins | Missouri |
| 1944 | 1 | B | Mike Micka | Colgate |
| 1945 | 1 | B | Jim Hardy | USC |
| 1946 | 1 | B | Cal Ross | UCLA |
| 1947 | 1 | B | Cal Rossi | UCLA |
| 1948 | 1 | B | Harry Gilmer | Alabama |
| 1949 | 1 | FB | Rob Goode | Texas A&M |
| 1950 | 1 | HB | George Thomas | Oklahoma |
| 1951 | 1 | FB | Leon Heath | Oklahoma |
| 1952 | 1 | QB | Larry Isbell | Baylor |
| 1953 | 1 | QB | Jack Scarbath | Maryland |
| 1954 | 1 | TE | Steve Melinge | Kentucky |
| 1955 | 1 | QB | Ralph Guglielmi | Notre Dame |
| 1956 | 1 | RB | Ed Vereb | Maryland |
| 1957 | 1 | FB | Don Bosseler | Miami |
| 1958 | 2 | RB | Mike Sommer | George Washington |

| Year | Rd | Pos | Player | College |
|---|---|---|---|---|
| 1959 | 1 | QB | Don Allard | Boston College |
| 1960 | 1 | QB | Richie Lucas | Penn State |
| 1961 | 1 | QB | Norm Snead | Wake Forest |
| 1962 | 1 | RB | Ernie Davis | Syracuse |
| 1963 | 1 | TE | Pat Richter | Wisconsin |
| 1964 | 1 | RB | Charley Taylor | Arizona State |
| 1965 | 2 | T | Bob Breitenstein | Tulsa |
| 1966 | 1 | K | Charlie Gogolak | Princeton |
| 1967 | 1 | FB | Ray McDonald | Idaho |
| 1968 | 1 | DB | Jim Smith | Oregon |
| 1969 | 2 | DB | Eugene Epps | UTEP |
| 1970 | 2 | DE | Bill Brundige | Colorado |
| 1971 | 2 | WR | Cotton Speyrer | Texas |
| 1972 | 8 | RB | Moses Denson | Maryland State |
| 1973 | 5 | G | Charles Cantrell | Lamar |
| 1974 | 6 | TE | Jon Keyworth | Colorado |
| 1975 | 5 | RB | Mike Thomas | UNLV |
| 1976 | 5 | T | Mike Hughes | Baylor |
| 1977 | 4 | DE | Duncan McColl | Stanford |
| 1978 | 6 | RB | Tony Green | Florida |
| 1979 | 4 | TE | Don Warren | San Diego State |
| 1980 | 1 | WR | Art Monk | Syracuse |
| 1981 | 1 | T | Mark May | Pittsburgh |
| 1982 | 2 | CB | Vernon Dean | San Diego State |
| 1983 | 1 | CB | Darrell Green | Texas A&I |
| 1984 | 2 | DT | Bob Slater | Oklahoma |
| 1985 | 2 | CB | Tory Nixon | San Diego State |
| 1986 | 2 | DE | Markus Koch | Boise State |
| 1987 | 2 | CB | Brian Davis | Nebraska |
| 1988 | 2 | K | Chip Lohmiller | Minnesota |
| 1989 | 3 | DT | Tracy Rocker | Auburn |
| 1990 | 2 | LB | Andre Collins | Penn State |
| 1991 | 1 | DT | Bobby Wilson | Michigan State |
| 1992 | 1 | WR | Desmond Howard | Michigan |
| 1993 | 1 | CB | Tom Carter | Notre Dame |
| 1994 | 1 | QB | Heath Shuler | Tennessee |
| 1995 | 1 | WR | Michael Westbrook | Colorado |
| 1996 | 1 | T | Andre Johnson | Penn State |
| 1997 | 1 | DE | Kenard Lang | Miami |
| 1998 | 2 | TE | Stephen Alexander | Oklahoma |
| 1999 | 1 | CB | Champ Bailey | Georgia |
| 2000 | 1 | LB | LaVar Arrington | Penn State |
| 2001 | 1 | WR | Rod Gardner | Clemson |
| 2002 | 1 | QB | Patrick Ramsey | Tulane |
| 2003 | 2 | WR | Taylor Jacobs | Florida |
| 2004 | 1 | S | Sean Taylor | Miami |
| 2005 | 1 | CB | Carlos Rogers | Auburn |
| 2005 | 1 | QB | Jason Campbell | Auburn |
| 2006 | 2 | LB | Rocky McIntosh | Miami |
| 2007 | 1 | S | LaRon Landry | LSU |

# REDSKINS DRAFT HISTORY

| Round | Selection No. | Name | Position | College |
|---|---|---|---|---|
| **1936** | | | | |
| 1 | 2 | Riley Smith | B | Alabama |
| 2 | 11 | Keith Topping | E | Stanford |
| 3 | 20 | Ed Smith | B | NYU |
| 4 | 29 | Paul Tangora | G | Northwestern |
| 5 | 38 | Wilson Groseclose | T | TCU |
| 6 | 47 | Larry Lutz | T | California |
| 7 | 56 | Don Irwin | B | Colgate |
| 8 | 65 | Wayne Millner | E | Notre Dame |
| 9 | 74 | Marcel Saunders | G | Loyola (CA) |
| **1937** | | | | |
| 1 | 6 | Sammy Baugh | B | TCU |
| 2 | 16 | Nello Falaschi | B | Santa Clara |
| 3 | 26 | Maurice Eldar | B | Kansas State |
| 4 | 36 | Dick Bassi | G | Santa Clara |

| | Selection | | | |
|---|---|---|---|---|
| Round | No. | Name | Position | College |
| 5 | 46 | Chuck Bond | T | Washington |
| 6 | 56 | Jimmie Cain | B | Washington |
| 7 | 66 | Rotta Holland | G | Kansas State |
| 8 | 76 | Joel Eaves | E | Auburn |
| 8 | 86 | Bill Docherty | T | Temple |
| 10 | 96 | Dom MacCara | E | NC State |

**1938**

| Round | No. | Name | Position | College |
|---|---|---|---|---|
| 1 | 9 | Andy Farkas | B | Detroit |
| 2 | 24 | Sam Chapman | B | California |
| 3 | 39 | Dave Price | C | Mississippi |
| 4 | 49 | Elmer Dohrmann | E | Nebraska |
| 5 | 59 | Roy Young | T | Texas A&M |
| 6 | 69 | Bill Hartman | B | Georgia |
| 7 | 79 | Ed Parks | C | Oklahoma |
| 8 | 89 | Jack Abbitt | B | Elon |
| 9 | 99 | Dick Johnson | E | Washington |
| 10 | 109 | Henry Bartos | G | North Carolina |

**1939**

| Round | No. | Name | Position | College |
|---|---|---|---|---|
| 1 | 8 | I. B. Hale | T | TCU |
| 2 | 18 | Charley Holm | B | Alabama |
| 3 | 28 | Dick Todd | B | Texas A&M |
| 4 | 38 | Dave Anderson | B | California |
| 5 | 48 | Quinton Lumpkin | C | Georgia |
| 6 | 58 | Bo Russell | T | Auburn |
| 7 | 68 | Wilbur Moore | B | Minnesota |
| 8 | 78 | Jimmy Johnson | B | Washington |
| 9 | 88 | Jim German | B | Centre |
| 10 | 98 | Bob O'Mara | B | Duke |
| 11 | 108 | Steve Silvinski | G | Washington |
| 12 | 118 | Bob Hoffman | B | USC |
| 13 | 128 | Eric Tipton | B | Duke |
| 14 | 138 | Dick Farman | T | Washington State |
| 15 | 148 | Clyde Shugart | T | Iowa State |
| 16 | 158 | Boyd Morgan | B | USC |
| 17 | 168 | Phil Smith | T | St. Benedict's |
| 18 | 178 | Paul Coop | T | Centre |
| 19 | 188 | Matt Kuber | G | Villanova |
| 20 | 189 | Al Cruver | B | Washington |

**1940**

| Round | No. | Name | Position | College |
|---|---|---|---|---|
| 1 | 8 | Ed Boell | B | NYU |
| 2 | 18 | Buddy Banker | B | Tulane |
| 3 | 28 | Bill Kirchem | T | Tulane |
| 4 | 38 | Joe Boyd | T | Texas A&M |
| 5 | 48 | Roy Zimmerman | B | San Jose State |
| 6 | 58 | Bud Orf | E | Missouri |
| 7 | 68 | Bob Hoffman | B | USC |
| 8 | 78 | Bob Seymour | B | Oklahoma |
| 9 | 88 | Howard Stoecker | T | USC |
| 10 | 98 | Allen Johnson | G | Duke |
| 11 | 108 | Sam Bartholomew | B | Tennessee |
| 12 | 118 | Ernie Lain | B | Rice |
| 13 | 128 | Hayward Sanford | E | Alabama |
| 14 | 138 | Bolo Perdue | E | Duke |
| 15 | 148 | Steve Andrako | C | Ohio State |
| 16 | 158 | Jay Graybeal | B | Oregon |
| 17 | 168 | Charley Slagle | B | North Carolina |
| 18 | 178 | Buck Murphy | B | Georgia Tech |
| 19 | 188 | Mel Wetzel | T | Missouri |
| 20 | 198 | Steve Sitko | B | Notre Dame |

**1941**

| Round | No. | Name | Position | College |
|---|---|---|---|---|
| 1 | 10 | Forest Evashevski | B | Michigan |
| 3 | 25 | Fred Davis | T | Alabama |
| 5 | 40 | Jim Stuart | T | Oregon |
| 6 | 50 | Ed Cifers | E | Tennessee |
| 7 | 60 | Al Krueger | E | USC |
| 8 | 70 | Henry Wilder | B | Iowa State |
| 9 | 80 | Bill Grimmett | E | Tulsa |
| 10 | 90 | Ed Hickerson | G | Alabama |
| 11 | 100 | Joe Aguirre | E | St. Mary's (Calif.) |
| 12 | 110 | Jack Banta | B | USC |

| | Selection | | | |
|---|---|---|---|---|
| Round | No. | Name | Position | College |
| 13 | 120 | Roy Conn | T | Arizona |
| 14 | 130 | Deward Tornell | B | San Jose State |
| 15 | 140 | Morris Buckingham | C | San Jose State |
| 16 | 150 | Ken Dow | B | Oregon State |
| 17 | 160 | Stan McRae | E | Michigan State |
| 18 | 170 | Joe Osmanski | B | Holy Cross |
| 19 | 180 | Earl Fullilove | T | Georgetown |
| 20 | 190 | Ed Hiestand | E | Vanderbilt |
| 21 | 197 | Tom Riggs | T | Illinois |
| 22 | 204 | Lee Gentry | B | Tulsa |

**1942**

| Round | No. | Name | Position | College |
|---|---|---|---|---|
| 1 | 6 | Spec Sanders | B | Texas |
| 2 | 21 | Rufus Deal | B | Auburn |
| 3 | 36 | Joe Zeno | G | Holy Cross |
| 4 | 46 | Harley McCollum | T | Tulane |
| 5 | 56 | Bob Fitch | E | Minnesota |
| 6 | 66 | George Peters | B | Oregon State |
| 7 | 76 | Frank Swiger | B | Duke |
| 8 | 86 | Johnny Goodyear | B | Marquette |
| 9 | 96 | Al DeMao | C | Duquesne |
| 10 | 106 | Phil Ahwesh | B | Duquesne |
| 11 | 116 | John Kovatch | E | Notre Dame |
| 12 | 126 | Bill deCorrevont | B | Northwestern |
| 13 | 136 | Marvin Whited | B | Oklahoma |
| 14 | 146 | Dee Chipman | B | BYU |
| 15 | 156 | George Watts | T | Appalachian State |
| 16 | 166 | Gene Stewart | B | Willamette |
| 17 | 176 | Charlie Timmons | B | Clemson |
| 18 | 186 | Tiny Croft | T | Ripon |
| 19 | 191 | Steve Juzwik | B | Notre Dame |
| 20 | 196 | Al Couppee | B | Iowa |

**1943**

| Round | No. | Name | Position | College |
|---|---|---|---|---|
| 1 | 10 | Jack Jenkins | B | Vanderbilt |
| 2 | 25 | Bill Dutton | B | Pittsburgh |
| 3 | 40 | Bob Dove | E | Notre Dame |
| 4 | 50 | Wally Ziemba | C | Notre Dame |
| 5 | 60 | Lou Rymkus | T | Notre Dame |
| 6 | 70 | Tony Leon | G | Alabama |
| 7 | 80 | Bob Motl | E | Northwestern |
| 8 | 90 | Walt McDonald | B | Tulane |
| 9 | 100 | George Perpich | T | Georgetown |
| 10 | 110 | Can Wood | C | Mississippi |
| 11 | 120 | Harry Wright | G | Notre Dame |
| 12 | 130 | Oscar Britt | G | Mississippi |
| 13 | 140 | Dick Weber | G | Syracuse |
| 14 | 150 | Joe Day | B | Oregon State |
| 15 | 160 | Frank Dornfield | B | Georgetown |
| 16 | 170 | John Baklarz | T | Arizona State |
| 17 | 180 | Leo Mogus | E | Youngstown State |
| 18 | 190 | Dick Secrest | B | Rochester |
| 19 | 200 | Don Nolander | C | Minnesota |
| 20 | 210 | Johnny Barrett | B | Georgetown |
| 21 | 220 | Tom Vohs | T | Colgate |
| 22 | 230 | Charlie Yancey | B | Mississippi State |
| 23 | 240 | Roman Bentz | T | Tulane |
| 24 | 250 | Swifty Berthold | E | Syracuse |
| 25 | 260 | Vince Pacewic | B | Loyola (Calif.) |
| 26 | 270 | Joe Riccardi | T | Ohio |
| 27 | 280 | Johnny Jafurs | G | Penn State |
| 28 | 290 | Frank Akins | B | Washington State |
| 29 | 295 | Bill Corry | B | Florida |
| 30 | 300 | Bo Bogovich | G | Delaware |

**1944**

| Round | No. | Name | Position | College |
|---|---|---|---|---|
| 1 | 8 | Mike Micka | B | Colgate |
| 2 | 23 | Earl Audet | T | USC |
| 3 | 39 | Ed Doherty | B | Boston College |
| 4 | 50 | Jackie Fellows | B | Fresno State |
| 5 | 61 | Hal Fischer | G | Texas |
| 6 | 72 | Cliff White | T | Murray State |
| 7 | 83 | Ted Ogdahl | | Williamette |

| Round | Selection No. | Name | Position | College |
|---|---|---|---|---|
| 8 | 94 | Bob Sneddon | B | St. Mary's (Ca.) |
| 9 | 105 | Bill Aldworth | T | Minnesota |
| 10 | 116 | Bill Joslyn | B | Stanford |
| 11 | 127 | Charley Walker | C | Kentucky |
| 12 | 138 | Boyd Clement | C | Oregon State |
| 13 | 149 | Jim Gaffney | B | Tennessee |
| 14 | 160 | Ted Ossowski | T | Oregon State |
| 15 | 171 | Tom Davis | B | Duke |
| 16 | 182 | John Batorski | E | Colgate |
| 17 | 193 | Clyde Ehrhardt | C | Georgia |
| 18 | 204 | Dave Brown | E | UCLA |
| 19 | 215 | Bill Ivy | T | Northwestern |
| 20 | 226 | Bruce Babcock | B | Rochester |
| 21 | 237 | Bill Reinhard | B | California |
| 22 | 248 | Ed Bauer | G | South Carolina |
| 23 | 259 | Smokey Martin | B | Cornell |
| 24 | 270 | Lee Gustafson | B | Oregon State |
| 25 | 281 | Nick Pappas | T | Utah |
| 26 | 292 | Lindsey Bowen | E | Rice |
| 27 | 303 | Bill Gustafson | T | Washington State |
| 28 | 314 | Bill Yablonski | C | Holy Cross |
| 29 | 320 | Buster Hollingbery | C | Washington State |
| 30 | 326 | Willard Sheller | B | Stanford |

**1945**

| Round | Selection No. | Name | Position | College |
|---|---|---|---|---|
| 1 | 8 | Jim Hardy | QB | USC |
| 2 | 23 | Tree Adams | T | Notre Dame |
| 3 | 38 | George Bujan | C | Oregon |
| 4 | 51 | Johnny North | E | Vanderbilt |
| 5 | 61 | John Steber | G | Georgia Tech |
| 6 | 71 | Art Porter | E | Tulane |
| 7 | 84 | Carl Kuykendall | B | Auburn |
| 8 | 94 | Frank Brogger | E | Michigan State |
| 9 | 104 | Mack Creger | B | Northwestern |
| 10 | 117 | Paul McKee | E | Syracuse |
| 11 | 127 | Charlie Conerly | QB | Mississippi |
| 12 | 147 | John Putnik | E | Utah State |
| 13 | 150 | Eddie Saenz | B | USC |
| 14 | 160 | Dom Fusci | T | South Carolina |
| 15 | 170 | Bobby Jenkins | B | Alabama |
| 16 | 183 | Ed Stacco | T | Colgate |
| 17 | 193 | Jim Bradshaw | C | Auburn |
| 18 | 203 | Bill Shipkey | B | Stanford |
| 19 | 216 | Sid Halliday | T | SMU |
| 20 | 226 | Chick Davidson | T | Cornell |
| 21 | 236 | Gabby Martin | E | SMU |
| 22 | 249 | Jim McCurdy | C | Stanford |
| 23 | 259 | Cy Souders | E | Ohio State |
| 24 | 269 | Ben Wall | B | Western Michigan |
| 25 | 282 | George Hillery | E | UTEP |
| 26 | 292 | Milford Dreblow | B | USC |
| 27 | 302 | Frank Irwin | T | Duke |
| 28 | 315 | Leon Diner | E | Denver |
| 29 | 320 | Bob Cummings | C | Vanderbilt |
| 30 | 325 | Don Nolander | T | Minnesota |

**1946**

| Round | Selection No. | Name | Position | College |
|---|---|---|---|---|
| 1 | 9 | Cal Rossi | B | UCLA |
| 2 | 19 | Stan Koslowski | B | Holy Cross |
| 3 | 29 | Gay Adelt | B | Utah |
| 4 | 39 | Walt Trojanowski | B | Connecticut |
| 5 | 49 | Bob Hendren | T | USC |
| 6 | 59 | George Callanan | B | USC |
| 7 | 69 | Bob Skoglund | E | Notre Dame |
| 8 | 79 | Jake Leicht | B | Oregon |
| 9 | 89 | Chick Maggioli | B | Illinois |
| 10 | 99 | Monte Moncrief | T | Texas A&M |
| 11 | 109 | Joe Tereshinski | E | Georgia |
| 12 | 119 | Stan Sprague | E | Illinois |
| 13 | 129 | Harry Adelman | E | USC |
| 14 | 139 | Bof Butchofsky | B | Texas A&M |
| 15 | 149 | Mike Prashaw | T | Michigan |
| 16 | 159 | Ed Robnett | B | Texas Tech |
| 17 | 169 | LeMar Dykstra | B | Colorado |

| Round | Selection No. | Name | Position | College |
|---|---|---|---|---|
| 18 | 179 | Bob Ward | B | San Jose State |
| 19 | 189 | John Pehar | T | USC |
| 20 | 199 | Roger Robinson | B | Syracuse |
| 21 | 209 | Charley Cadenhead | C | Mississippi State |
| 22 | 219 | Bob Rodas | G | Santa Clara |
| 23 | 229 | Charlie Webb | E | LSU |
| 24 | 239 | Marion Flanagan | B | Texas A&M |
| 25 | 249 | Roland Phillips | T | Georgia Tech |
| 26 | 259 | Jim Hallmark | B | Texas A&M |
| 27 | 269 | Fay Mills | T | Alabama |
| 28 | 279 | William Ritter | B | Georgia Tech |
| 29 | 289 | Sarkis Takesian | B | California |
| 30 | 299 | Mike Campbell | E | Mississippi |

**1947**

| Round | Selection No. | Name | Position | College |
|---|---|---|---|---|
| 1 | 3 | Carl Rossi | B | UCLA |
| 2 | 16 | Red Knight | B | LSU |
| 3 | 27 | Hank Foldberg | E | Army |
| 4 | 38 | Mike Garzoni | G | USC |
| 5 | 58 | Hank Harris | T | Texas |
| 7 | 67 | Roy Karrasch | E | UCLA |
| 8 | 78 | Ernie Williamson | T | North Carolina |
| 9 | 87 | L. G. Carmody | B | C. Washington |
| 10 | 98 | U.S. Savage | E | Richmond |
| 11 | 107 | Bob Steckroth | E | William & Mary |
| 12 | 118 | Weldon Edwards | T | TCU |
| 13 | 127 | Earl Wheeler | C | Arkansas |
| 14 | 138 | Billy Gold | B | Tennessee |
| 15 | 147 | Jack Hart | T | Detroit |
| 16 | 158 | Tom Nichols | B | Richmond |
| 17 | 167 | Harry Dowda | B | Wake Forest |
| 18 | 178 | Charlie Webb | E | LSU |
| 19 | 187 | Elmo Bond | T | Washington State |
| 20 | 198 | Jim Hefti | B | St. Lawrence |
| 21 | 207 | Tom Dudley | E | Virginia |
| 22 | 218 | Jim Smith | B | Iowa |
| 23 | 227 | Hal Mullins | T | Duke |
| 24 | 238 | Francis Bocoka | E | Washington State |
| 25 | 247 | Otis Sacrinty | B | Wake Forest |
| 26 | 258 | Milt Dropo | C | Connecticut |
| 27 | 267 | Lynn Brownson | B | Stanford |
| 28 | 278 | Joe Colone | B | Penn State |
| 29 | 285 | Herb Schoener | E | Iowa |
| 30 | 294 | Bob Pievo | T | Purdue |

**1948**

| Round | Selection No. | Name | Position | College |
|---|---|---|---|---|
| Bonus Choice | 1 | Harry Gilmer | B | Alabama |
| 1 | 4 | Lowell Tew | B | Alabama |
| 2 | 16 | Tommy Thompson | C | William & Mary |
| 3 | 28 | Don Sandifer | B | LSU |
| 4 | 38 | Jack Weisenberger | B | Michigan |
| 5 | 48 | Jack Kurkowski | B | Detroit |
| 6 | 58 | Jerry Cady | T | Gustavus Adolphus |
| 7 | 68 | Bob Anderson | B | Stanford |
| 8 | 78 | Mike Katrishen | T | Southern Miss. |
| 9 | 88 | Ed Marshall | T | Pennsylvania |
| 10 | 98 | Ted Andrus | G | S. W. Louisiana |
| 11 | 108 | Carl Russ | B | Rice |
| 12 | 118 | Chick Jagade | B | Indiana |
| 13 | 128 | Eddie Quirk | B | Missouri |
| 14 | 138 | Art Pollard | B | Arizona |
| 15 | 148 | Chuck Newman | E | Louisiana Tech |
| 15 | 151 | Dale Schwartzkopf | E | Texas Tech |
| 16 | 158 | Ray Pearcy | C | Oklahoma |
| 17 | 168 | Gene Veilela | T | Scranton |
| 18 | 178 | Cloyce Box | B | West Texas State |
| 19 | 188 | Bryan Bell | B | Washington & Lee |
| 20 | 198 | Joel Williams | C | Texas |
| 21 | 208 | Lou Hoitsma | E | William & Mary |
| 22 | 218 | Floyd Lawhorn | G | Texas Tech |
| 23 | 228 | Dick West | B | Princeton |
| 24 | 238 | Roland Oakes | E | Missouri |
| 25 | 248 | Ed Watkins | T | Idaho |
| 26 | 258 | Don Corbitt | C | Arizona |

| Round | Selection No. | Name | Position | College |
|---|---|---|---|---|
| 27 | 268 | Buddy Bowen | B | Mississippi |
| 28 | 278 | Vic Paulson | E | Cal-Santa Barbara |
| 29 | 286 | Barney Welch | B | Texas A&M |
| **1949** | | | | |
| 1 | 8 | Rob Goode | B | Texas A&M |
| 2 | 18 | Laurie Niemi | T | Washington State |
| 3 | 28 | Len Szafaryn | T | North Carolina |
| 4 | 38 | Mike DeNoia | B | Scranton |
| 5 | 48 | Eddie Berrang | E | Villanova |
| 7 | 68 | Chet Fritz | G | Missouri |
| 8 | 78 | Bob Kennedy | B | North Carolina |
| 9 | 88 | Ed McNeil | E | Michigan |
| 10 | 98 | Vic Vasicek | G | Texas |
| 11 | 108 | Homer Hobbs | G | Georgia |
| 12 | 118 | Harry Varner | T | Arizona |
| 13 | 128 | Ed Henke | T | USC |
| 14 | 138 | Pat Haggerty | E | William & Mary |
| 15 | 148 | Gene Frassetto | T | California |
| 16 | 158 | Dick Flowers | T | Alabama |
| 17 | 168 | Ross Pritchard | B | Arkansas |
| 18 | 178 | Herb Siegert | G | Illinois |
| 19 | 188 | Bob Hainlen | B | Colorado State |
| 20 | 198 | Ollie Fletcher | E | USC |
| 21 | 208 | Tommy Hughes | B | Duke |
| 22 | 218 | Bill Clements | E | UCLA |
| 23 | 228 | Frank Pattee | B | Kansas |
| 24 | 238 | Jim Cullom | G | California |
| 25 | 248 | Nick Sebek | B | Indiana |
| **1950** | | | | |
| 1 | 5 | George Thomas | B | Oklahoma |
| 2 | 18 | Hally Haynes | B | Santa Clara |
| 3 | 31 | Lou Karras | T | Purdue |
| 4 | 44 | Harry Ulinski | C | Kentucky |
| 5 | 57 | Frank Spaniel | B | Notre Dame |
| 6 | 70 | Gene Pepper | G | Missouri |
| 7 | 83 | Jerry Houghton | T | Washington State |
| 8 | 96 | John Rohde | E | Pacific |
| 9 | 109 | Don Winslow | T | Iowa |
| 10 | 122 | Eddie LeBaron | QB | Pacific |
| 11 | 135 | Dan Brown | E | Villanova |
| 12 | 148 | Bill Chauncey | B | Iowa State |
| 13 | 161 | Clay Davis | C | Oklahoma State |
| 14 | 174 | Lyle Button | T | Illinois |
| 15 | 187 | Alex Lloyd | E | Oklahoma State |
| 16 | 200 | Charlie Justice | B | North Carolina |
| 17 | 213 | Jim Cullom | G | California |
| 18 | 226 | Alvin Duke | B | Arkansas |
| 19 | 239 | Ed White | E | Alabama |
| 20 | 252 | George Bayer | T | Washington |
| 21 | 265 | Cas Witucki | G | Indiana |
| 22 | 278 | John deLaurentis | T | Waynesburg |
| 23 | 291 | Joe Zuravieff | E | Northwestern |
| 24 | 304 | Dick Tilton | T | Nevada |
| 25 | 317 | Art Stewart | B | S. E. Oklahoma |
| 26 | 330 | Earl Roth | B | Maryland |
| 27 | 343 | Ed Lee | T | Kansas |
| 28 | 356 | Ralph Shoaf | B | West Virginia |
| 29 | 369 | Johnny Lundin | G | Minnesota |
| 30 | 382 | Bob Noppinger | E | Georgetown |
| **1951** | | | | |
| 1 | 3 | Leon Heath | B | Oklahoma |
| 2 | 14 | Eddie Salem | B | Alabama |
| 2 | 20 | Jim Staton | T | Wake Forest |
| 3 | 28 | Walt Yowarsky | T | Kentucky |
| 4 | 39 | Paul Giroski | T | Rice |
| 6 | 64 | Jonn Martinkovic | E | Xavier |
| 7 | 75 | Jonny Papit | B | Virginia |
| 8 | 86 | Billy Cox | B | Duke |
| 9 | 100 | Jake Rowden | C | Maryland |
| 10 | 111 | Bob Jensen | E | Iowa State |
| 11 | 122 | Bill DeChard | B | Holy Cross |

| Round | Selection No. | Name | Position | College |
|---|---|---|---|---|
| 12 | 136 | Al Applegate | G | Scranton |
| 13 | 147 | Dick Campbell | B | Wyoming |
| 14 | 158 | Adrian Burk | QB | Baylor |
| 15 | 172 | Vic Thomas | T | Colorado |
| 16 | 183 | Bob Bates | C | Texas A&M |
| 17 | 194 | Gene Brito | E | Loyola (Calif.) |
| 18 | 208 | Dom Fucci | B | Kentucky |
| 19 | 219 | Buddy Brown | G | Arkansas |
| 20 | 230 | John Krestes | B | Purdue |
| 21 | 244 | Clarence Marable | T | TCU |
| 22 | 255 | Elliot Speed | C | Alabama |
| 23 | 266 | Cecil Martin | B | N. Texas State |
| 24 | 280 | Tom Powers | B | Duke |
| 25 | 291 | Bob Chubb | E | Shippensburg |
| 26 | 32 | Johnny Williams | B | USC |
| 27 | 316 | Bill Johnson | B | Stetson |
| 28 | 327 | John Kadiec | G | Missouri |
| 29 | 338 | Bart Stewart | B | S. E. Oklahoma |
| 30 | | Nick Bolkovac | T | Pittsburgh |
| **1952** | | | | |
| 1 | 6 | Larry Isbell | B | Baylor |
| 2 | 18 | Andy Davis | B | George Washington |
| 3 | 30 | Al Dorow | B | Michigan State |
| 4 | 42 | Dick Hightower | C | SMU |
| 5 | 54 | Jim Clark | G | Oregon State |
| 6 | 66 | Ed Kensler | G | Maryland |
| 7 | 78 | Vic Janowicz | B | Ohio State |
| 8 | 90 | Hubert Johnston | T | Iowa |
| 9 | 102 | Dick Alban | B | Northwestern |
| 10 | 114 | Chet Ostrowski | E | Notre Dame |
| 11 | 126 | Orlanda Mazza | E | Michigan State |
| 12 | 138 | Frank Middendorf | C | Cincinnati |
| 13 | 150 | Ray Potter | T | LSU |
| 14 | 162 | Doug Conway | T | TCU |
| 15 | 174 | Julius Wittman | T | Ohio State |
| 16 | 186 | Marv Berschet | T | Illinois |
| 17 | 198 | Bill Bocetti | B | Washington & Lee |
| 18 | 210 | Ed Bartlett | E | California |
| 19 | 222 | Joe Marvin | B | UCLA |
| 20 | 234 | Roger Kinson | C | Missouri |
| 21 | 246 | Dick Jenkins | T | Illinois |
| 22 | 258 | Jim O'Rourke | B | N.C. State |
| 23 | 270 | Ken Barfield | T | Mississippi |
| 24 | 282 | Ted Kirkland | T | Vanderbilt |
| 25 | 294 | Sal Gero | T | Elon |
| 26 | 306 | Danny Goode | B | Hardin-Simmons |
| 27 | 318 | Ben White | E | SMU |
| 28 | 330 | Ron Engel | B | Minnesota |
| 29 | 342 | John Pappa | B | California |
| 30 | 354 | Bob Linn | B | Case Western |
| **1953** | | | | |
| 1 | 3 | Jack Scarbath | B | Maryland |
| 2 | 16 | Dick Modzelewski | T | Maryland |
| 3 | 27 | Paul Dekker | E | Michigan State |
| 4 | 40 | Don Boll | G | Nebraska |
| 5 | 51 | Nick Carras | B | Missouri |
| 8 | 88 | Lew Weidensaul | E | Maryland |
| 11 | 123 | Alex Webster | B | N.C. State |
| 12 | 136 | Buzz Nutter | C | Virginia Tech |
| 14 | 160 | Ed Timmerman | B | Michigan State |
| 15 | 171 | Dave Suminski | T | Wisconsin |
| 16 | 184 | Jim Slay | E | Mississippi |
| 17 | 195 | Bob Haner | B | Villanova |
| 18 | 208 | Jim Turner | B | Texas Tech |
| 19 | 219 | Tom Flyzik | T | George Washington |
| 20 | 232 | Bill Link | G | Wake Forest |
| 21 | 243 | Jim Dublinski | C | Utah |
| 22 | 256 | Ed Pucci | G | USC |
| 23 | 267 | Ed Bierne | E | Detroit |
| 24 | 280 | Stan Butterworth | B | Bucknell |
| 25 | 291 | Art Hurd | G | Maryland |
| 26 | 304 | Walt Ashcraft | T | USC |

| Round | Selection No. | Name | Position | College |
|---|---|---|---|---|
| 27 | 315 | John Zanetti | T | John Carroll |
| 28 | 328 | Bob Buckley | B | USC |
| 29 | 339 | Pat Shires | B | Tennessee |
| 30 | 352 | Bob Mathias | B | Stanford |
| **1954** | | | | |
| 1 | 7 | Steve Mellinger | E | Kentucky |
| 2 | 19 | Jim Schrader | C | Notre Dame |
| 4 | 38 | Ralph Felton | B | Maryland |
| 5 | 55 | Billy Wells | B | Michigan State |
| 6 | 67 | Bill McHenry | C | Washington & Lee |
| 7 | 79 | Harry Jagielski | T | Indiana |
| 8 | 91 | Bill Marker | E | West Virginia |
| 9 | 103 | Jerry Minnick | T | Nebraska |
| 10 | 115 | Merrill Green | B | Oklahoma |
| 11 | 127 | Gene Wilson | B | South Carolina |
| 12 | 139 | Ben Dunkerly | T | West Virginia |
| 13 | 151 | Roger Dornburg | B | Wisconsin |
| 14 | 163 | Roger Nelson | T | Oklahoma |
| 15 | 175 | Hugh Merck | T | South Carolina |
| 16 | 187 | Gilmer Spring | E | Texas |
| 17 | 199 | Jerry Coody | B | Baylor |
| 18 | 211 | Walt Cudzik | C | Purdue |
| 19 | 223 | Jerry Witt | B | Wisconsin |
| 20 | 235 | Sam Morley | E | Stanford |
| 21 | 247 | John Cavaglieri | T | N. Texas St. |
| 22 | 259 | Max Schmaling | B | Purdue |
| 23 | 271 | Pete Carrieri | G | Villanova |
| 24 | 283 | Will Renfro | E | Memphis State |
| 25 | 295 | George Rosso | G | Ohio State |
| 26 | 307 | Dorsey Gibson | B | Oklahoma State |
| 27 | 319 | Ken Yarborough | E | North Carolina |
| 28 | 331 | Ron Hansen | T | Minnesota |
| 29 | 343 | Ted Kress | B | Michigan |
| 30 | 355 | Don Rondou | B | Northwestern |
| **1955** | | | | |
| 1 | 3 | Ralph Guglielmi | QB | Notre Dame |
| 3 | 27 | Ray Perkins | B | Syracuse |
| 5 | 51 | Don Glantz | T | Nebraska |
| 7 | 75 | Eric Christensen | E | Richmond |
| 7 | 79 | Ron Marciniak | G | Kansas State |
| 8 | 86 | Johnny Allen | C | Purdue |
| 9 | 99 | John Miller | T | Boston College |
| 10 | 110 | Tom Louderback | G | San Jose State |
| 11 | 123 | Larry Parker | B | North Carolina |
| 12 | 134 | John Barish | T | Waynesburg |
| 13 | 147 | Len Oniskey | T | Cornell |
| 14 | 158 | Tom Braatz | E | Marquette |
| 15 | 171 | Charley Horton | B | Vanderbilt |
| 16 | 182 | Hal Norris | B | California |
| 17 | 195 | Don Shea | G | Georgia |
| 18 | 206 | Don Bailey | B | Penn State |
| 19 | 219 | Bob Dee | E | Holy Cross |
| 20 | 230 | Ron Geyer | T | Michigan |
| 21 | 243 | Buck George | B | Clemson |
| 22 | 254 | Joe Boland | B | George Washington |
| 23 | 267 | Chick Donaldson | C | West Virginia |
| 24 | 278 | Bob Ready | T | Notre Dame |
| 25 | 291 | Frank Radella | C | Wyoming |
| 26 | 302 | Walt Houston | G | Purdue |
| 27 | 316 | A.J. Baker | B | Arkansas |
| 28 | 326 | Arch Cassidy | T | Florida |
| 29 | 339 | Bing Bordier | E | USC |
| 30 | 350 | Tom Petty | E | Virginia Tech |
| **1956** | | | | |
| 1 | 11 | Ed Vereb | B | Maryland |
| 2 | 23 | John Paluck | E | Pittsburgh |
| 3 | 35 | Fred Wyant | B | West Virginia |
| 4 | 40 | Fran Machinsky | T | Ohio State |
| 5 | 58 | Gary Lowe | B | Michigan State |
| 7 | 82 | Donnie Caraway | B | Houston |
| 8 | 93 | Dick James | B | Oregon |

| Round | Selection No. | Name | Position | College |
|---|---|---|---|---|
| 9 | 106 | Whitey Rouviere | B | Miami |
| 11 | 130 | Tom Powell | G | Colgate |
| 12 | 140 | Gerry Planutis | B | Michigan State |
| 13 | 154 | Jerry Ward | G | Dayton |
| 14 | 165 | Pat Uebel | B | Army |
| 16 | 189 | Wells Gray | G | Wisconsin |
| 17 | 22 | Eagle Day | QB | Mississippi |
| 18 | 213 | Jim Pyburn | E | Auburn |
| 19 | 226 | Ray Lemak | G | Notre Dame |
| 20 | 237 | Vince Gonzalez | B | LSU |
| 21 | 250 | Howard Schnellenberger | E | Kentucky |
| 22 | 261 | George Nicula | T | Notre Dame |
| 23 | 274 | Don St. John | B | Xavier |
| 24 | 285 | Johnny Tatum | C | Texas |
| 25 | 298 | Franklin Brooks | G | Georgia Tech |
| 26 | 309 | Dave Burnham | B | Wheaton |
| 27 | 322 | Royce Flippin | B | Princeton |
| 28 | 333 | Billy Hicks | B | Alabama |
| 29 | 346 | Pat Bisceglia | G | Notre Dame |
| 30 | 356 | Buck Mystrom | G | Michigan State |
| **1957** | | | | |
| 1 | 8 | Don Bosseler | B | Miami |
| 2 | 20 | Joe Walton | E | Pittsburgh |
| 3 | 32 | Eddie Sutton | B | North Carolina |
| 4 | 39 | Jim Podoley | B | Central Michigan |
| 6 | 68 | J.T. Frankenberger | T | Kentucky |
| 7 | 80 | Wally Merz | T | Colorado |
| 8 | 92 | Paul Lopata | B | Central Michigan |
| 9 | 104 | Galen Laack | G | Pacific |
| 10 | 116 | Don Dobrino | B | Iowa |
| 11 | 138 | Dick Foster | T | Idaho |
| 12 | 140 | Wade Mitchell | QB | Georgia Tech |
| 13 | 152 | Claude Austin | B | George Washington |
| 14 | 164 | George Rice | T | Wofford |
| 15 | 176 | Brad Bomba | E | Indiana |
| 16 | 188 | Joe Brodsky | B | Florida |
| 17 | 200 | Fred Brock | B | Wheaton |
| 18 | 212 | Ed Sakach | G | George Washington |
| 19 | 224 | John Bauer | B | Villanova |
| 20 | 236 | Buddy Frick | E | South Carolina |
| 21 | 248 | Sam Owen | B | Georgia Tech |
| 22 | 260 | Ed Voytek | G | Purdue |
| 23 | 272 | Al Viola | G | Northwestern |
| 24 | 284 | Bob Jennings | C | Furman |
| 25 | 296 | Dick Sassels | T | Catawba |
| 26 | 308 | Paul Rotenberry | B | Georgia Tech |
| 27 | 320 | Ormand Anderson | T | Georgia Tech |
| 28 | 332 | Guy Martin | B | Colgate |
| 29 | 344 | George Benedict | E | Springfield |
| 30 | 356 | Art Luppino | B | Arizona |
| **1958** | | | | |
| 2 | 15 | Mike Sommer | B | George Washington |
| 3 | 27 | Stan Flowers | B | Georgia Tech |
| 3 | 30 | Bill Anderson | B | Tennessee |
| 4 | 39 | Dan Nolan | QB | Lehigh |
| 5 | 53 | Jim Van Pelt | QB | Michigan |
| 6 | 65 | Dick Lynch | B | Notre Dame |
| 7 | 77 | Leon Bennett | T | Boston College |
| 8 | 89 | Buddy Payne | E | North Carolina |
| 9 | 101 | Frank Kuchta | C | Notre Dame |
| 10 | 113 | Ben Preston | T | Auburn |
| 11 | 125 | Darrell Dess | T | N.C. State |
| 12 | 137 | Eddie Michaels | G | Villanova |
| 13 | 149 | Ken Ford | QB | Hardin-Simmons |
| 14 | 161 | Jack Faris | E | Penn State |
| 15 | 173 | Jack Davis | T | Arizona |
| 16 | 185 | Fred Polzer | E | Virginia |
| 17 | 197 | Fred Wilt | T | Richmond |
| 18 | 209 | Lennie King | B | Connecticut |
| 19 | 221 | Don Stephenson | C | Georgia Tech |
| 20 | 233 | Lou Pelham | E | Florida |

| Round | Selection No. | Name | Position | College |
|---|---|---|---|---|
| 21 | 245 | Jackie Simpson | G | Mississippi |
| 22 | 257 | Charley Sanders | B | W. Texas State |
| 23 | 269 | Ron Schomburger | E | Florida State |
| 24 | 282 | Rod Hanson | E | Illinois |
| 25 | 293 | John Groom | G | TCU |
| 26 | 305 | Frank Bloomquist | G | Iowa |
| 27 | 317 | Perry Gehring | E | Minnesota |
| 28 | 329 | Joe Biggs | G | Hardin-Simmons |
| 29 | 341 | Ed Coffin | B | Syracuse |
| 30 | 353 | Ted Smith | E | Georgia Tech |
| **1959** | | | | |
| 1 | 4 | Don Allard | QB | Boston College |
| 3 | 28 | Emil Karas | T | Dayton |
| 4 | 40 | Jim Wood | E | Oklahoma State |
| 5 | 49 | Bob Wetoska | T | Notre Dame |
| 6 | 65 | Jim McFalls | T | VMI |
| 7 | 76 | Don Lawrence | T | Notre Dame |
| 7 | 79 | Mitch Ogiego | QB | Iowa |
| 7 | 81 | Jim Kenney | E | Boston |
| 8 | 89 | Gene O'Pella | E | Villanova |
| 9 | 100 | Dick Haley | B | Pittsburgh |
| 10 | 113 | Ron Togh | B | Notre Dame |
| 11 | 124 | Gerry Marciniak | G | Michigan |
| 12 | 137 | Roger Wypyszynski | T | St. Norbert |
| 13 | 148 | Billy Shoemake | E | LSU |
| 14 | 161 | Kurt Schwarz | G | Maryland |
| 15 | 172 | Fred Hood | E | N.E. Oklahoma |
| 16 | 185 | Dick Splain | T | New Haven |
| 17 | 196 | Jim Healy | G | Holy Cross |
| 18 | 209 | Joe Kapp | QB | California |
| 19 | 220 | Bobby Lauder | B | Auburn |
| 20 | 233 | Billy Brewer | B | Mississippi |
| 21 | 244 | Mel Reight | B | West Virginia |
| 22 | 257 | Art Gob | E | Pittsburgh |
| 23 | 268 | Clarence Alexander | B | S.E. Louisiana |
| 24 | 281 | George Darrah | B | F&M |
| 25 | 292 | Bob Sargent | T | Colby |
| 26 | 305 | Gene Grabosky | T | Syracuse |
| 27 | 316 | Norm Odyniec | B | Notre Dame |
| 28 | 329 | Billy Austin | B | Rutgers |
| 29 | 340 | Don Lockwood | G | Tulane |
| 30 | 353 | Jim Colclough | B | Boston College |
| **1960** | | | | |
| 1 | 4 | Richie Lucas | QB | Penn State |
| 2 | 21 | Sam Homer | HB | VMI |
| 3 | 28 | Andy Stynchula | T | Penn State |
| 4 | 48 | Vince Promuto | G | Holy Cross |
| 5 | 52 | Don Stallings | T | North Carolina |
| 6 | 64 | Dave Hudson | E | Florida |
| 8 | 87 | Earl Kohlhaas | G | Penn State |
| 9 | 100 | Dwight Bumgarner | E | Duke |
| 11 | 124 | Jim Elfrid | C | Colorado State |
| 12 | 136 | Jim Crotty | HB | Notre Dame |
| 13 | 148 | Bill Herron | E | Georgia |
| 14 | 160 | Charley Milstead | B | Texas A&M |
| 15 | 172 | Bernie Darre | G | Tulane |
| 16 | 184 | Joe Kulbacki | B | Purdue |
| 17 | 196 | Billy Roland | G | Georgia |
| 18 | 208 | John Lawrence | G | N.C. State |
| 19 | 220 | Ron Maltony | G | Purdue |
| 20 | 232 | Jimmy Wolf | HB | Panhandle State |
| **1961** | | | | |
| 1 | 2 | Norm Snead | QB | Wake Forest |
| 1 | 3 | Joe Rutgens | T | Illinois |
| 3 | 39 | Jim Cunningham | B | Pittsburgh |
| 6 | 72 | Joe Krakoski | B | Illinois |
| 6 | 73 | John O'Day | T | Miami |
| 7 | 87 | Jim Kerr | B | Penn State |
| 8 | 101 | Charley Barnes | E | N.E. Louisiana |
| 9 | 115 | Joel Arrington | B | Duke |
| 11 | 143 | Riley Mattson | T | Oregon |

| Round | Selection No. | Name | Position | College |
|---|---|---|---|---|
| 12 | 157 | Bob Coolbaugh | E | Richmond |
| 13 | 171 | Doug Emore | B | Mississippi |
| 14 | 185 | Doyle Schick | B | Kansas |
| 15 | 199 | Bob Jonson | E | Michigan |
| 16 | 213 | Ron Petty | T | Louisville |
| 17 | 227 | Joe Bellino | B | Navy |
| 18 | 241 | George Tolford | T | Ohio State |
| 19 | 255 | Tony Romeo | E | Florida State |
| 20 | 269 | Mike Ingram | G | Ohio State |
| **1962** | | | | |
| 1 | 1 | Ernie Davis | B | Syracuse |
| 2 | 15 | Joe Hernandez | B | Arizona |
| 3 | 29 | Bob Mitinger | E | Penn State |
| 4 | 43 | Billy Neighbors | T | Alabama |
| 7 | 85 | Bert Coan | HB | Kansas |
| 8 | 99 | Ron Hatcher | FB | Michigan State |
| 9 | 113 | Dave Viti | E | Boston |
| 10 | 127 | John Childress | G | Arkansas |
| 11 | 141 | Carl Palazzo | T | Adams State |
| 12 | 155 | Terry Terrebonne | HB | Tulane |
| 13 | 169 | Bill Whisler | E | Iowa |
| 14 | 183 | Jim Costen | HB | South Carolina |
| 15 | 197 | Len Velia | T | Georgia |
| 16 | 211 | Tommy Brooker | E | Alabama |
| 17 | 225 | Alan Miller | G | Ohio |
| 18 | 239 | Carl Charon | B | Michigan State |
| 19 | 253 | Claude Crabb | B | Colorado |
| 20 | 267 | Ed Trancygier | QB | Florida State |
| **1963** | | | | |
| 1 | 7 | Pat Richter | E | Wisconsin |
| 2 | 22 | Lonnie Sanders | B | Michigan State |
| 3 | 35 | Ron Snidow | T | Oregon |
| 6 | 78 | Charley Nickoson | T | Ohio |
| 7 | 91 | Dave Francis | B | Ohio State |
| 9 | 119 | Billy Joe | B | Villanova |
| 10 | 134 | Rod Foster | G | Ohio State |
| 11 | 147 | Allen Schau | E | Western Michigan |
| 12 | 162 | Bob Caldwell | C | Georgia Tech |
| 13 | 175 | John Greiner | E | Purdue |
| 14 | 190 | Tom Winingder | B | Georgia Tech |
| 15 | 203 | Harry Butsko | LB | Maryland |
| 16 | 218 | Dave Adams | G | Arkansas |
| 17 | 231 | Ron Whaley | HB | Tenn.-Chattanooga |
| 18 | 246 | Drew Roberts | E | Cal State-Humboldt |
| 19 | 259 | Jim Turner | QB | Utah State |
| 20 | 274 | Joe Baughan | T | Auburn |
| **1964** | | | | |
| 1 | 3 | Charley Taylor | HB | Arizona State |
| 2 | 18 | Paul Krause | DB | Iowa |
| 5 | 59 | Jim Snowden | FB | Notre Dame |
| 6 | 74 | Russ Brown | E | Florida |
| 7 | 87 | Dick Shiner | QB | Maryland |
| 9 | 115 | Len Hauss | C | Georgia |
| 10 | 130 | Rick Leeson | B | Pittsburgh |
| 11 | 143 | Gene Donaldson | LB | Purdue |
| 12 | 158 | Bob Avolerin | T | Tennessee |
| 13 | 171 | Tom McDonald | B | Notre Dame |
| 14 | 186 | Tom Urbanik | B | Penn State |
| 15 | 199 | Dick Evers | T | Colorado State |
| 16 | 214 | Tommy Walters | S | Mississippi |
| 17 | 227 | Ozzie Clay | B | Iowa State |
| 18 | 242 | Bob Jones | G | Nebraska |
| 19 | 255 | John Seedborg | G | Arizona State |
| 20 | 270 | Fordon Guest | B | Arkansas |
| **1965** | | | | |
| 2 | 21 | Bob Breitenstein | T | Tulsa |
| 3 | 34 | Kent McCloughan | B | Nebraska |
| 8 | 105 | Don Croftcheck | G-LB | Indiana |
| 9 | 118 | Jerry Smith | E | Arizona State |
| 10 | 133 | Bob Briggs | FB | Central State |

| Round | Selection No. | Name | Position | College |
|---|---|---|---|---|
| 11 | 146 | Willie Adams | G | New Mexico State |
| 12 | 160 | John Strohmeyer | T | Michigan |
| 13 | 174 | Biff Bracy | HB | Duke |
| 14 | 189 | Dave Estrada | HB | Arizona State |
| 15 | 202 | Ben Baldwin | B | Vanderbilt |
| 16 | 217 | Robert Reed | G | Tennessee A&I |
| 17 | 230 | Gary Hard | E | Vanderbilt |
| 18 | 245 | Chris Hanburger | LB | North Carolina |
| 19 | 258 | Roosevelt Ellerbe | B | Iowa State |
| **1966** | | | | |
| 1 | 6 | Charlie Gogolak | K | Princeton |
| 2 | 21 | Walter Barnes | T | Nebraska |
| 3 | 38 | Tom Barrington | FB | Ohio State |
| 4 | 53 | Bill Clay | DB | Mississippi |
| 5 | 70 | Dick Lemay | T | Vanderbilt |
| 6 | 94 | Earl Yates | T | Duke |
| 7 | 101 | George Patton | T | Georgia |
| 8 | 115 | Stan Mitchell | FB | Tennessee |
| 9 | 131 | Jack Shinholser | LB | Florida State |
| 10 | 145 | Caesar Belser | DB | Ark-Monticello |
| 11 | 161 | Dick Reding | | Northwestern State |
| 12 | 175 | John Stipech | LB | Utah |
| 13 | 191 | Heath Wingate | C | Bowling Green |
| 14 | 205 | Jerry Lovelace | RB | Texas Tech |
| 15 | 221 | Hal Seymour | K-RB | Florida |
| 16 | 235 | Hal Wantland | RB | Tennessee |
| 17 | 251 | Mitch Zalnasky | E | Pittsburgh |
| 18 | 265 | Joe Burson | RB | Georgia |
| 19 | 281 | Andre White | E | Florida A&M |
| 20 | 295 | John Kelly | C | Florida A&M |
| **1967** | | | | |
| 1 | 13 | Ray McDonald | FB | Idaho |
| 2 | 39 | Spain Musgrove | DT | Utah State |
| 3 | 64 | Curg Belcher | DB | BYU |
| 6 | 135 | Don Bandy | T | Tulsa |
| 7 | 168 | Bruce Matte | QB-RB | Miami (Ohio) |
| 7 | 172 | John Love | FL | North Texas State |
| 8 | 190 | Larry Hendershot | G-LB | Arizona State |
| 9 | 222 | Pete Larsen | HB | Cornell |
| 10 | 247 | Tim Houlton | DT | St. Norbert |
| 10 | 250 | Bruce Sullivan | DB | Illinois |
| 11 | 275 | Bill Brown | C | UTEP |
| 12 | 300 | Ron Sepic | E | Ohio State |
| 13 | 328 | Bob Rodwell | LB | Eastern Michigan |
| 14 | 353 | Andy Socha | HB | Marshall |
| 15 | 378 | Ed Breding | G | Texas A&M |
| 16 | 406 | Alfredo Avila | DB | Sul Ross |
| 17 | 431 | Lyle Baucom | T | Cal St.-San Fran. |
| **1968** | | | | |
| 1 | 12 | Yazoo Smith | DB | Oregon |
| 2 | 38 | Tom Roussel | LB | Southern Miss. |
| 4 | 94 | Dennis Crane | DT | USC |
| 5 | 113 | Ken Barefoot | TE | Virginia Tech |
| 5 | 117 | Mike Bragg | K | Richmond |
| 6 | 149 | Willie Banks | G | Alcorn State |
| 7 | 176 | Bob Brunet | RB | LSU |
| 8 | 203 | Brian Magnuson | RB | Montana |
| 9 | 230 | Frank Liberatore | DB | Clemson |
| 11 | 284 | Tom Garretson | DB | Northwestern |
| 12 | 311 | Dave Weedman | DT | W. Washington |
| 13 | 338 | Mike St. Louis | T | Central Missouri |
| 14 | 365 | Dave Zivich | T | Cal-Santa Barbara |
| 15 | 392 | Coger Coverson | G | Texas Southern |
| 16 | 419 | Willie Turner | RB | Jackson State |
| 17 | 446 | Frank Bosch | DT | Colorado |
| **1969** | | | | |
| 2 | 46 | Eugene Epps | DB | UTEP |
| 3 | 62 | Ed Cross | RB | Arkansas-Pine Bluff |
| 5 | 114 | Bill Kishman | DB | Colorado State |
| 6 | 139 | Harold McClinton | LB | Southern |

| Round | Selection No. | Name | Position | College |
|---|---|---|---|---|
| 7 | 166 | Jeff Anderson | RB | Virginia |
| 7 | 173 | John Didion | C | Oregon State |
| 8 | 191 | Larry Brown | RB | Kansas State |
| 11 | 269 | Eric Norri | DT | Notre Dame |
| 12 | 295 | Bob Shannon | DB | Tennessee State |
| 13 | 322 | Mike Shook | DB | North Texas State |
| 14 | 347 | Rick Brand | DT | Virginia |
| 15 | 374 | Paul Rogers | T | Virginia |
| 16 | 399 | Mike Washington | LB | Southern |
| 17 | 426 | Rich Dobbert | DE | Springfield |
| **1970** | | | | |
| 2 | 43 | Bill Brundige | DE | Colorado |
| 4 | 103 | Paul Laaveg | T | Iowa |
| 5 | 114 | Manny Sistrunk | DT | Arkansas A&M |
| 5 | 121 | Danny Pierce | RB | Memphis State |
| 7 | 173 | Roland Merritt | WR | Maryland |
| 7 | 178 | James Harris | DT | Howard Payne |
| 8 | 200 | Paul Johnson | DB | Penn St. |
| 9 | 225 | Ralph Sonntag | T | Maryland |
| 11 | 277 | Mack Alston | TE | Maryland State |
| 12 | 303 | James Kates | LB | Penn State |
| 13 | 339 | Joe Patterson | T | Lawrence |
| 14 | 355 | Tony Moro | RB | Dayton |
| 15 | 381 | Vic Lewandowsky | C | Holy Cross |
| 16 | 407 | Steve Bushore | WR | Emporia State |
| 17 | 433 | Earl Maxfield | DT | Baylor |
| **1971** | | | | |
| 2 | 38 | Cotton Speyrer | WR | Texas |
| 6 | 141 | Conway Hayman | G | Delaware |
| 7 | 161 | Willie Germany | DB | Morgan State |
| 9 | 219 | Mike Fanucci | DE | Arizona State |
| 10 | 244 | Jesse Taylor | RB | Cincinnati |
| 11 | 272 | George Starke | T | Columbia |
| 12 | 297 | Jeff Severson | DB | Long Beach |
| 13 | 322 | Dan Ryczek | C | Virginia |
| 14 | 349 | Bill Bynum | QB | W. New Mexico |
| 15 | 375 | Tony Christnovich | G | Lacrosse |
| 16 | 500 | Glenn Tucker | LB | North Texas Stte |
| **1972** | | | | |
| 8 | 203 | Moses Denson | RB | Maryland State |
| 9 | 229 | Steve Boekholder | DE | Drake |
| 10 | 255 | Mike Oldham | WR | Michigan |
| 11 | 281 | Jeff Welch | DB | Arkansas State |
| 12 | 307 | Don Bunce | QB | Stanford |
| 13 | 332 | Frank Grant | WR | S. Colorado |
| 14 | 365 | Mike O'Quinn | G | McNeese State |
| 15 | 385 | Carl Taibi | DE | Colorado |
| 16 | 411 | Steve Higginbotham | DB | Alabama |
| 17 | 437 | Kevin Clemente | LB | Boston College |
| **1973** | | | | |
| 5 | 117 | Charles Cantrell | G | Lamar |
| 8 | 193 | Mike Hancock | TE | Idaho State |
| 9 | 218 | Rich Galbos | RB | Ohio State |
| 9 | 233 | Eddie Sheats | LB | Kansas |
| 10 | 245 | Ken Stone | DB | Vanderbilt |
| 12 | 311 | Ernie Webster | G | Pittsburgh |
| 13 | 337 | Dennis Johnson | DT | Delaware |
| 14 | 363 | Herb Marshall | DB | Cameron |
| 16 | 415 | Mike Wedman | K | Colorado |
| 17 | 441 | Jeff Davis | RB | Mars Hill |
| **1974** | | | | |
| 6 | 144 | Jon Keyworth | TE | Colorado |
| 7 | 180 | Mike Varty | LB | Northwestern |
| 8 | 196 | Darwin Robinson | RB | Dakota State |
| 9 | 2118 | Mark Sens | DE | Colorado |
| 9 | 228 | Mike Flater | K | Colorado School of Mines |
| 9 | 233 | Jim Kennedy | TE | Colorado State |
| 10 | 258 | Johnny Vann | DB | South Dakota |

| Round | Selection No. | Name | Position | College |
|---|---|---|---|---|
| 11 | 282 | Joe Miller | T | Villanova |
| 13 | 332 | Stu O'Dell | LB | Indiana |
| 14 | 361 | Don Van Galder | QB | Utah |
| 16 | 411 | Nate Anderson | RB | Eastern Illinois |
| **1975** | | | | |
| 5 | 108 | Mike Thomas | RB | UNLV |
| 6 | 147 | Mark Doak | T | Nebraska |
| 9 | 228 | Dallas Hickman | DE | California |
| 11 | 277 | Ardell Johnson | DB | Nebraska |
| 11 | 282 | Jerry Hackenbruck | DE | Oregon State |
| 13 | 344 | Morris McKie | DB | North Carolina State |
| 14 | 359 | Dave Benson | LB | Weber State |
| 15 | 384 | Art Kuehn | C | UCLA |
| 16 | 412 | Dennis Pavelka | G | Nebraska |
| 17 | 437 | Carl Taylor | DE | Memphis State |
| **1976** | | | | |
| 5 | 148 | Mike Hughes | G | Baylor |
| 6 | 179 | Tom Marvaso | DB | Cincinnati |
| 8 | 234 | Bryan Fryer | WR | Alberta |
| 9 | 254 | Curtis Akins | G | Hawaii |
| 10 | 272 | Paul Strohmeier | LB | Washington |
| 11 | 308 | Dean Gissler | DE | Nebraska |
| 12 | 342 | Walter Tullis | DB | Delaware State |
| 13 | 364 | Waymon Britt | DB | Michigan |
| 14 | 393 | Quinn Buckner | DB | Indiana |
| 15 | 426 | John Monroe | RB | Bluefield State |
| 17 | 476 | Chuck Willis | DB | Oregon |
| **1977** | | | | |
| 4 | 97 | Duncan McColl | DE | Stanford |
| 7 | 198 | Reggie Haynes | TE | UNLV |
| 9 | 246 | Mike Northington | RB | Purdue |
| 10 | 273 | James Sykes | RB | Rice |
| 11 | 300 | Don Harris | DB | Rutgers |
| 12 | 327 | Curtis Kirkland | DE | Missouri |
| **1978** | | | | |
| 6 | 159 | Tony Green | RB | Florida |
| 8 | 202 | Walker Lee | WR | North Carolina |
| 8 | 219 | Don Hover | LB | Washington State |
| 9 | 243 | John Hurley | QB | Santa Clara |
| 10 | 270 | Scott Hertenstein | DE | Azusa Pacific |
| 11 | 297 | Mike Williams | DE | Texas A&M |
| 12 | 324 | Steve McCabe | G | Bowdoin |
| **1979** | | | | |
| 4 | 103 | Don Warren | TE | San Diego State |
| 7 | 182 | Rich Milot | LB | Penn State |
| 9 | 233 | Kris Haines | WR | Notre Dame |
| 11 | 289 | Monte Coleman | LB | Arkansas State |
| 11 | 300 | Tony Hall | WR | Knoxville |
| **1980** | | | | |
| 1 | 18 | Art Monk | WR | Syracuse |
| 2 | 55 | Matt Mendenhall | DE | BYU |
| 6 | 155 | Farley Bell | LB | Cincinnati |
| 7 | 187 | Melvin Jones | G | Houston |
| 9 | 241 | Lawrence McCullough | WR | Illinois |
| 10 | 268 | Lewis Walker | RB | Utah |
| 11 | 295 | Mike Matocha | DE | Texas-Arlington |
| 12 | 327 | Marcene Emmett | DE | Northern Alabama |
| **1981** | | | | |
| 1 | 20 | Mark May | T | Pittsburgh |
| 3 | 69 | Russ Grimm | G | Pittsburgh |
| 4 | 90 | Tom Flick | QB | Washington |
| 5 | 119 | Dexter Manley | DE | Oklahoma State |
| 5 | 132 | Gary Sayre | G | Clemson |
| 6 | 148 | Larry Kubin | LB | Penn State |
| 8 | 201 | Charlie Brown | WR | South Carolina State |

| Round | Selection No. | Name | Position | College |
|---|---|---|---|---|
| 9 | 231 | Darryl Grant | G | Rice |
| 10 | 257 | Phil Kessel | QB | Northern Michigan |
| 10 | 267 | Allan Kennedy | T | Washington State |
| 11 | 284 | Jerry Hill | WR | Northern Alabama |
| 12 | 314 | Clint Didier | WR | Portland State |
| **1982** | | | | |
| 2 | 49 | Vernon Dean | CB | San Diego State |
| 3 | 61 | Carl Powell | WR | Jackson State |
| 4 | 99 | Todd Liebenstein | DE | UNLV |
| 5 | 133 | Michael Williams | TE | Alabama A&M |
| 6 | 153 | Lamont Jeffers | LB | Tennessee |
| 7 | 180 | John Schactner | LB | Northern Arizona |
| 8 | 223 | Ralph Warthen | DT. | G. Webb |
| 9 | 226 | Ken Coffey | DB | S. W. Texas State |
| 9 | 238 | Randy Trautman | DT | Boise St. |
| 10 | 254 | Harold Smith | DE | Kentucky State |
| 10 | 265 | Terry Daniels | DB | Tennessee |
| 11 | 281 | Dan Miller | K | Miami |
| 11 | 291 | Bob Holly | QB | Princeton |
| 12 | 309 | Dan Laster | T | Tennessee State |
| 12 | 322 | Jeff Goff | LB | Arkansas |
| **1983** | | | | |
| 1 | 28 | Darrell Green | CB | Texas A&I |
| 2 | 56 | Richard Williams | RB | Memphis State |
| 3 | 84 | Charles Mann | DE | Nevada |
| 6 | 166 | Bob Winckler | T | Wisconsin |
| 6 | 168 | Babe Laufenberg | QB | Indiana |
| 7 | 196 | Kelvin Bryant | RB | North Carolina |
| 8 | 224 | Todd Hallstrom | T | Minnesota |
| 9 | 251 | Marcus Gilbert | RB | TCU |
| 10 | 279 | Geff Gandy | K | Baylor |
| **1984** | | | | |
| 2 | 31 | Bob Slater | DT | Oklahoma |
| 2 | 55 | Steve Hamilton | DE | East Carolina |
| 3 | 83 | Jay Schroeder | QB | UCLA |
| 4 | 102 | Jimmy Smith | RB | Elon |
| 5 | 125 | Jeff Pegues | LB | East Carolina |
| 6 | 167 | Curt Singer | T | Tennessee |
| 7 | 195 | Mark Smith | WR | North Carolina |
| 8 | 223 | Jeff Smith | DB | Missouri |
| 10 | 279 | Keith Griffin | LB | Miami |
| 11 | 306 | Anthony Jones | TE | Wichita State |
| 12 | 335 | Curtland Thomas | WR | Missouri |
| **1985** | | | | |
| 2 | 33 | Tory Nixon | DB | San Diego State |
| 5 | 122 | Raphel Cherry | RB | Hawaii |
| 6 | 162 | Danzell Lee | TE | Lamar |
| 7 | 177 | Jamie Harris | KR | Oklahoma State |
| 7 | 185 | Lionel Vitel | RB | Nicholls State |
| 8 | 219 | Barry Wilburn | CB | Mississippi |
| 9 | 247 | Mitch Geier | G | Troy State |
| 10 | 263 | Terry Orr | RB | Texas |
| 11 | 290 | Raleigh McKenzie | G | Tennessee |
| 11 | 304 | Garry Kimble | DB | Sam Houston State |
| 12 | 309 | Dean Hamel | DT | Tulsa |
| 12 | 331 | Bryan Winn | LB | Houston |
| **1986** | | | | |
| 2 | 30 | Marcus Koch | DE | Boise State |
| 2 | 45 | Walter Murray | WR | Hawaii |
| 3 | 75 | Alvin Walton | DB | Kansas |
| 5 | 113 | Ravin Caldwell | LB | Arkansas |
| 6 | 146 | Mark Rypien | QB | Washington State |
| 6 | 156 | Jim Huddleston | G | Virginia |
| 7 | 186 | Rick Badanjek | RB | Maryland |
| 8 | 213 | Kurt Gouveia | LB | BYU |
| 9 | 239 | Wayne Asberry | DB | Texas A&M |
| 11 | 297 | Kenny Fells | RB | Henderson State |
| 12 | 323 | Eric Yarber | WR | Idaho |

| Round | Selection No. | Name | Position | College |
|---|---|---|---|---|
| **1987** | | | | |
| 2 | 30 | Brian Davis | DB | Nebraska |
| 2 | 48 | Wally Kleine | T | Notre Dame |
| 5 | 117 | Timmy Smith | RB | Texas Tech |
| 6 | 144 | Steve Gage | DB | Tulsa |
| 7 | 164 | Johnny Thomas | DB | Baylor |
| 8 | 192 | Clarence Vaughn | DB | N. Illinois |
| 9 | 219 | Alfred Jenkins | RB | Arizona |
| 10 | 248 | Ted Wilson | WR | Central Florida |
| 11 | 304 | Laron Brown | WR | Texas |
| 12 | 331 | Ray Hitchcock | C | Minnesota |
| **1988** | | | | |
| 2 | 55 | Chip Lohmiller | K | Minnesota |
| 3 | 66 | Mike Oliphant | KR | Puget Sound |
| 4 | 109 | Jamie Morris | RB | Michigan |
| 5 | 127 | Carl Mims | DB | Sam Houston State |
| 6 | 159 | Stan Humphries | QB | N.E. Louisiana |
| 7 | 193 | Harold Hicks | DB | San Diego State |
| 8 | 221 | Darryl McGill | RB | Wake Forest |
| 9 | 249 | Blake Peterson | LB | Mesa College |
| 10 | 277 | Henry Brown | T | Ohio State |
| 11 | 305 | Curt Koch | DE | Colorado |
| 12 | 315 | Wayne Ross | P | San Diego State |
| **1989** | | | | |
| 3 | 66 | Tracy Rocker | DT | Auburn |
| 4 | 110 | Erik Affholter | WR | USC |
| 5 | 129 | Tim Smiley | DB | Arkansas State |
| 5 | 139 | Lybrant Robinson | DE | Delaware State |
| 6 | 149 | Al Johnson | DB | S.W. Texas State |
| 7 | 179 | Kevin Hendrix | LB | South Carolina |
| 9 | 233 | Charles Darrington | TE | Kentucky |
| 10 | 263 | Mark Schlereth | C | Idaho |
| 12 | 316 | Jimmy Johnson | TE | Howard |
| 12 | 317 | Joe Mickles | RB | Mississippi |
| **1990** | | | | |
| 2 | 46 | Andre Collins | LB | Penn State |
| 3 | 76 | Moe Elewonibi | G | BYU |
| 4 | 86 | Cary Conklin | QB | Washington |
| 4 | 109 | Rocco Labbe | DB | Boston College |
| 5 | 130 | Brian Mitchell | RB | S.W. Louisiana |
| 6 | 160 | Kent Walls | DT | Nebraska |
| 9 | 243 | Tim Moxley | G | Ohio State |
| 10 | 262 | D'Juan Francisco | DB | North Dakota |
| 10 | 270 | Thomas Rayam | DT | Alabama |
| 11 | 297 | Jon Leverenz | LB | Minnesota |
| **1991** | | | | |
| 1 | 17 | Bobby Wilson | DT | Michigan State |
| 3 | 76 | Ricky Ervins | RB | USC |
| 6 | 159 | Dennis Ransom | TE | Texas A&M |
| 7 | 188 | Keith Cash | WR | Texas |
| 8 | 215 | Jimmy Spencer | DB | Florida |
| 9 | 43 | Charles Bell | DB | Baylor |
| 10 | 270 | Cris Shale | P | Bowling Green |
| 11 | 299 | David Gulledge | S | Jacksonville State |
| 12 | 326 | Keenan McCardell | WR | UNLV |
| **1992** | | | | |
| 1 | 4 | Desmond Howard | WR | Michigan |
| 2 | 47 | Shane Collins | DE | Arizona State |
| 3 | 74 | Paul Siever | G | Penn State |
| 4 | 112 | Chris Hakel | QB | William & Mary |
| 6 | 168 | Ray Rowe | TE | San Diego State |
| 7 | 196 | Calvin Holmes | DB | USC |
| 8 | 224 | Darryl Moore | G | UTEP |
| 9 | 252 | Boone Powell | LB | Texas |
| 10 | 280 | Tony Barker | LB | Rice |
| 11 | 308 | Terry Smith | WR | Penn State |
| 12 | 336 | Matt Elliott | C | Michigan |

| Round | Selection No. | Name | Position | College |
|---|---|---|---|---|
| **1993** | | | | |
| 1 | 17 | Tom Carter | CB | Notre Dame |
| 2 | 45 | Reggie Brooks | RB | Notre Dame |
| 3 | 71 | Rick Hamilton | LB | Central Florida |
| 3 | 80 | Ed Bunn | P | UTEP |
| 4 | 101 | Sterling Palmer | DE | Florida State |
| 5 | 128 | Greg Huntington | C | Penn State |
| 6 | 155 | Darryl Morrison | CB | Arizona |
| 6 | 160 | Frank Wycheck | TE | Maryland |
| 8 | 212 | Lamont Hollinquest | LB | USC |
| **1994** | | | | |
| 1 | 3 | Heath Shuler | QB | Tennessee |
| 2 | 31 | Tre Johnson | T | Temple |
| 3 | 67 | Tydus Winans | WR | Fresno State |
| 3 | 97 | Joe Patton | T | Alabama A&M |
| 4 | 105 | Kurt Haws | TE | Utah |
| 6 | 164 | Dexter Nottage | DE | Florida A&M |
| 7 | 197 | Gus Frerotte | QB | Tulsa |
| **1995** | | | | |
| 1 | 4 | Michael Westbrook | WR | Colorado |
| 2 | 37 | Cory Raymer | C | Wisconsin |
| 3 | 68 | Daryl Pounds | CB | Nicholls State |
| 4 | 103 | Larry Jones | RB | Miami |
| 5 | 137 | Jamie Asher | TE | Louisville |
| 5 | 152 | Rich Owens | DE | Lehigh |
| 6 | 176 | Brian Thure | T | California |
| 7 | 226 | Scott Turner | CB | Illinois |
| **1996** | | | | |
| 1 | 30 | Andre Johnson | T | Penn State |
| 4 | 102 | Stephen Davis | RB | Auburn |
| 5 | 138 | Leomont Evans | S | Clemson |
| 6 | 174 | Kelvin Kinney | DE | Virginia State |
| 7 | 215 | Jeremy Asher | LB | Oregon |
| 7 | 250 | Deandre Maxwell | WR | San Diego State |
| **1997** | | | | |
| 1 | 17 | Kenard Lang | DE | Miami |
| 2 | 51 | Greg Jones | LB | Colorado |
| 3 | 80 | Derek Smith | LB | Arizona State |
| 4 | 115 | Albert Connell | WR | Texas A&M |
| 5 | 132 | Jamel Williams | S | Nebraska |
| 5 | 140 | Keith Thibodeaux | CB | N.W. Louisiana |
| 5 | 148 | Twan Russell | LB | Miami |
| 5 | 162 | Brad Badger | G | Stanford |
| **1998** | | | | |
| 2 | 48 | Stephen Alexander | TE | Oklahoma |
| 3 | 69 | Skip Hicks | RB | UCLA |
| 4 | 113 | Shawn Barber | LB | Richmond |
| 5 | 140 | Mark Fischer | C | Purdue |
| 6 | 170 | Pat Palmer | WR | Northwestern State |
| 7 | 191 | David Terrell | CB | UTEP |
| 7 | 206 | Antwaune Ponds | LB | Syracuse |
| **1999** | | | | |
| 1 | 7 | Champ Bailey | CB | Georgia |
| 2 | 37 | Jon Jansen | T | Michigan |
| 4 | 107 | Nate Stimson | LB | Georgia Tech |
| 5 | 165 | Derek Smith | OL | Virginia Tech |
| 6 | 181 | Jeff Hall | K | Tennessee |
| 7 | 217 | Tim Alexander | WR | Oregon State |
| **2000** | | | | |
| 1 | 2 | LaVar Arrington | LB | Penn State |
| 1 | 3 | Chris Samuels | T | Alabama |
| 3 | 62 | Lloyd Harrison | CB | N.C. State |
| 4 | 129 | Michael Moore | G | Troy State |
| 5 | 155 | Quincy Sanders | S | UNLV |
| 6 | 202 | Todd Husak | QB | Stanford |
| 7 | 216 | Del Cowsette | DT | Maryland |
| 7 | 250 | Ethan Howell | WR | Oklahoma State |

| Round | Selection No. | Name | Position | College |
|---|---|---|---|---|
| **2001** | | | | |
| 1 | 15 | Rod Gardner | WR | Clemson |
| 2 | 45 | Fred Smoot | CB | Mississippi State |
| 4 | 109 | Sage Rosenfels | QB | Iowa State |
| 5 | 154 | Darnerien McCants | WR | Delaware State |
| 6 | 186 | Mario Monds | DT | Cincinnati |
| **2002** | | | | |
| 1 | 32 | Patrick Ramsey | QB | Tulane |
| 2 | 56 | Ladell Betts | RB | Iowa |
| 3 | 79 | Rashad Bauman | CB | Oregon |
| 3 | 87 | Cliff Russell | WR | Utah |
| 5 | 159 | Andre Lott | S | Tennessee |
| 5 | 160 | Robert Royal | TE | LSU |
| 6 | 192 | Reggie Coleman | T | Tennessee |
| 7 | 230 | Jeff Grau | LS | UCLA |
| 7 | 234 | Greg Scott | DE | Hampton |
| 7 | 257 | Rock Cartwright | FB | Kansas State |
| **2003** | | | | |
| 2 | 44 | Taylor Jacobs | WR | Florida |
| 3 | 81 | Derrick Dockery | G | Texas |
| 7 | 232 | Gibran Hamdan | QB | Indiana |
| **2004** | | | | |
| 1 | 5 | Sean Taylor | S | Miami (Fla.) |
| 3 | 81 | Chris Cooley | TE | Utah State |
| 5 | 151 | Mark Wilson | OL | California |
| 6 | 180 | Jim Molinaro | OL | Notre Dame |
| **2005** | | | | |
| 1 | 9 | Carlos Rogers | CB | Auburn |
| 1 | 25 | Jason Campbell | QB | Auburn |
| 4 | 120 | Manuel White | RB | UCLA |
| 5 | 154 | Robert McCune | LB | Louisville |
| 6 | 183 | Jared Newberry | LB | Stanford |
| 7 | 222 | Nehemiah Broughton | RB | The Citadel |
| **2006** | | | | |
| 2 | 35 | Rocky McIntosh | OLB | Miami |
| 5 | 153 | Anthony Montgomery | DT | Minnesota |
| 6 | 173 | Reed Doughty | S | Northern Colorado |
| 6 | 196 | Kedrick Golston | DT | Georgia |
| 7 | 230 | Kili Lefotu | OG | Arizona |
| 7 | 250 | Kevin Simon | ILB | Tennessee |
| **2007** | | | | |
| 1 | 6 | LaRon Landry | S | LSU |
| 5 | 143 | Dallas Sartz | LB | Southern California |
| 6 | 179 | H.B. Blades | LB | Pittsburgh |
| 6 | 205 | Jordan Palmer | QB | UTEP |
| 7 | 216 | Tyler Ecker | TE | Michigan |

## ALL-TIME PRO BOWL PLAYERS

| Year | Name | Position |
|---|---|---|
| 1950 | Bill Dudley | HB |
| | Harry Gilmer | QB |
| | Paul Lipscomb | T |
| 1951 | Sammy Baugh | QB |
| | Bill Dudley | RB |
| | Rob Goode | FB |
| | Paul Lipscomb | T |
| | Laurie Niemi | T |
| 1952 | Harry Gilmer | QB |
| | Paul Lipscomb | T |
| | Laurie Niemi | T |
| | Hugh Taylor | E |
| | John Williams | HB |

| Year | Name | Position |
|---|---|---|
| 1953 | Gene Brito | E |
| | Don Boll | T |
| | Paul Lipscomb | T |
| 1954 | Dick Alban | HB |
| | Rob Goode | FB |
| | Hugh Taylor | E |
| | Bill Wells | HB |
| 1955 | Gene Brito | E |
| | Chuck Drazenovich | LB |
| | Eddie LeBaron | QB |
| | Volney Peters | T |
| | Joe Scudero | HB |
| | Torgy Torgeson | LB |
| | Harry Ulinski | C |
| 1956 | Sam Baker | P |
| | Gene Brito | E |
| | Al Dorow | QB |
| | Chuck Drazenovich | LB |
| | Leo Elter | RB |
| | Dick Stanfel | G |
| | Torgy Torgeson | LB |
| 1957 | Gene Brito | E |
| | John Carson | E |
| | Chuck Drazenovich | LB |
| | Eddie LeBaron | QB |
| | Jim Podoley | RB |
| | Dick Stanfel | G |
| 1958 | Gene Brito | E |
| | Chuck Drazenovich | LB |
| | Eddie LeBaron | QB |
| | Jim Schrader | C |
| | Dick Stanfel | G |
| 1959 | Bill Anderson | E |
| | Don Bosseler | RB |
| | Jim Schrader | C |
| | Bob Toneff | DT |
| 1960 | Bill Anderson | E |
| | Bob Khayat | DT |
| | Bob Toneff | DT |
| 1961 | Dickie James | RB |
| | Ray Lemek | T |
| | Jim Schrader | C |
| | Bob Toneff | DT |
| 1962 | Rod Breedlove | LB |
| | Bobby Mitchell | FL |
| | John Nisby | G |
| 1963 | Bobby Mitchell | FL |
| | Vince Promuto | G |
| | Joe Rutgens | DT |
| | Norm Snead | QB |
| 1964 | Sam Huff | LB |
| | Sonny Jurgensen | QB |
| | Paul Krause | DB |
| | Bobby Mitchell | FL |
| | John Paluck | DE |
| | Vince Promuto | G |
| | Charley Taylor | RB |
| 1965 | Paul Krause | DB |
| | Joe Rutgens | DT |
| | Charley Taylor | RB |
| 1966 | Chris Hanburger | LB |
| | Sonny Jurgensen | QB |
| | Charley Taylor | WR |
| 1967 | Chris Hanburger | LB |
| | Len Hauss | C |
| | Sonny Jurgensen | QB |
| | Jerry Smith | TE |
| | Charley Taylor | WR |
| 1968 | Chris Hanburger | LB |
| | Len Hauss | C |
| 1969 | Larry Brown | RB |
| | Pat Fischer | CB |
| | Chris Hanburger | LB |

| Year | Name | Position |
|------|------|----------|
| | Len Hauss | C |
| | Sonny Jurgensen | QB |
| | Jerry Smith | TE |
| 1970 | Larry Brown | RB |
| | Len Hauss | C |
| 1971 | Larry Brown | RB |
| | Len Hauss | C |
| | Roy Jefferson | WR |
| | Curt Knight | K |
| 1972 | Larry Brown | RB |
| | Speedy Duncan | PR |
| | Chris Hanburger | LB |
| | Len Hauss | C |
| | Billy Kilmer | QB |
| | Charley Taylor | WR |
| 1973 | Chris Hanburger | LB |
| | Ken Houston | FS |
| | Herb Mul-Key | PR |
| | Charley Taylor | WR |
| 1974 | Chris Hanburger | LB |
| | Ken Houston | SS |
| | Diron Talbert | DT |
| | Charley Taylor | WR |
| 1975 | Chris Hanburger | LB |
| | Ken Houston | SS |
| | Charley Taylor | WR |
| 1976 | Eddie Brown | PR |
| | Chris Hanburger | LB |
| | Ken Houston | SS |
| | Mike Thomas | RB |
| 1977 | Eddie Brown | PR |
| | Jean Fugett | TE |
| | Ken Houston | SS |
| 1978 | Tony Green | PR |
| | Ken Houston | SS |
| 1979 | Ken Houston | SS |
| | Mark Moseley | K |
| | Lemar Parrish | CB |
| 1980 | Mike Nelms | PR |
| | Lemar Parrish | CB |
| 1981 | Mike Nelms | PR |
| 1982 | Charlie Brown | WR |
| | Mark Moseley | K |
| | Mike Nelms | PR |
| | Tony Peters | SS |
| | Joe Theismann | QB |
| 1983 | Jeff Bostic | C |
| | Charlie Brown | WR |
| | Dave Butz | DT |
| | Russ Grimm | G |
| | Joe Jacoby | T |
| | Mark Murphy | FS |
| | Joe Theismann | QB |
| 1984 | Darrell Green | CB |
| | Russ Grimm | G |
| | Joe Jacoby | T |
| | Art Monk | WR |
| 1985 | Russ Grimm | G |
| | Joe Jacoby | T |
| | Art Monk | WR |
| 1986 | Gary Clark | WR |
| | Darrell Green | CB |
| | Russ Grimm | G |
| | Joe Jacoby | T |
| | Dexter Manley | DE |
| | Art Monk | WR |
| | Jay Schroeder | QB |
| 1987 | Gary Clark | WR |
| | Darrell Green | CB |
| | Charles Mann | DE |
| 1988 | Charles Mann | DE |
| | Mark May | T |
| 1989 | Charles Mann | DE |
| | Mark Rypien | QB |
| 1990 | Earnest Byner | RB |

| Year | Name | Position |
|------|------|----------|
| | Gary Clark | WR |
| | Darrell Green | CB |
| | Jim Lachey | T |
| 1991 | Earnest Byner | RB |
| | Gary Clark | WR |
| | Darrell Green | CB |
| | Jim Lachey | T |
| | Chp Lohmiller | K |
| | Charles Mann | DE |
| | Mark Rypien | QB |
| | Mark Schlereth | G |
| 1992 | Wilber Marshall | LB |
| 1994 | Ken Harvey | LB |
| | Reggie Roby | P |
| 1995 | Ken Harvey | LB |
| | Brian Mitchell | KR/PR |
| 1996 | Terry Allen | RB |
| | Gus Frerotte | QB |
| | Darrell Green | CB |
| | Ken Harvey | LB |
| | Matt Turk | P |
| 1997 | Cris Dishman | CB |
| | Darrell Green | CB |
| | Ken Harvey | LB |
| | Matt Turk | P |
| 1998 | Matt Turk | P |
| 1999 | Stephen Davis | RB |
| | Brad Johnson | QB |
| | Tre Johnson | G |
| 2000 | Stephen Alexander | TE |
| | Champ Bailey | CB |
| | Marco Coleman | DE |
| | Stephen Davis | RB |
| 2001 | LaVar Arrington | LB |
| | Chris Samuels | OT |
| | Champ Bailey | CB |
| 2002 | LaVar Arrington | LB |
| | Champ Bailey | CB |
| | Chris Samuels | OT |
| 2003 | LaVar Arrington | LB |
| | Champ Bailey | CB |
| | Laveranues Coles | WR |
| 2004 | Marcus Washington | LB |
| 2005 | Santana Moss | WR |
| | Chris Samuels | OT |
| 2006 | Chris Samuels | OT |

# YEAR-BY-YEAR RESULTS

| 1932 | | | | 4–4–2 |
|------|---|---|---|-------|
| Oct. 2 | L | | 0–14 | Brooklyn |
| Oct. 9 | W | | 14–6 | NY Giants |
| Oct. 16 | L | | 0–9 | Chi. Cardinals |
| Oct. 23 | T | | 0–0 | at NY Giants |
| Oct. 30 | T | | 7–7 | Chicago Bears |
| Nov. 6 | W | | 19–6 | Staten Island |
| Nov. 13 | L | | 0–21 | Green Bay |
| Nov. 20 | L | | 0–10 | at Portsmouth |
| Nov. 27 | W | | 8–6 | at Chi. Cardinals |
| Dec. 4 | W | | 7–0 | at Brooklyn |
| | | | | |
| **1933** | | | | **5–5–2** |
| Sept. 17 | T | | 7–7 | at Green Bay |
| Sept. 24 | L | | 0–7 | at Chicago Bears |
| Oct. 1 | W | | 21–6 | at Pittsburgh |
| Oct. 8 | W | | 21–20 | NY Giants |
| Oct. 15 | L | | 0–13 | Portsmouth |
| Oct. 22 | W | | 10–0 | Chi. Cardinals |
| Oct. 29 | L | | 14–16 | Pittsburgh |
| Nov. 5 | W | | 10–0 | Chicago Bears |
| Nov. 12 | L | | 0–7 | at NY Giants |
| Nov. 19 | W | | 20–7 | Green Bay |

| Date | Result | Score | Opponent |
|---|---|---|---|
| Nov. 26 | L | 0–14 | at Brooklyn |
| Dec. 3 | T | 0–0 | at Chi. Cardinals |

**1934** — 6–6

| Date | Result | Score | Opponent |
|---|---|---|---|
| Sept. 16 | W | 7–0 | at Pittsburgh |
| Sept. 30 | L | 6–10 | at Brooklyn |
| Oct. 7 | L | 13–16 | at NY Giants |
| Oct. 14 | W | 39–0 | Pittsburgh |
| Oct. 17 | L | 0–24 | at Detroit |
| Oct. 21 | W | 6–0 | Philadelphia |
| Oct. 28 | W | 9–0 | Chi. Cardinals |
| Nov. 4 | L | 0–10 | Green Bay |
| Nov. 11 | L | 0–21 | Chicago |
| Nov. 18 | W | 14–7 | at Philadelphia |
| Nov. 25 | L | 0–3 | at NY Giants |
| Dec. 2 | W | 13–3 | Brooklyn |

**1935** — 2–8–1

| Date | Result | Score | Opponent |
|---|---|---|---|
| Sept. 9 | W | 7–3 | Brooklyn |
| Oct. 6 | L | 12–20 | NY Giants |
| Oct. 13 | L | 7–17 | Detroit |
| Oct. 20 | L | 6–17 | at NY Giants |
| Oct. 27 | L | 0–6 | at Pittsburgh |
| Oct. 30 | L | 0–14 | at Detroit |
| Nov. 3 | L | 6–7 | Philadelphia |
| Nov. 10 | L | 14–30 | Chicago Bears |
| Nov. 17 | Cancelled | | at Philadelphia |
| Nov. 24 | L | 0–6 | Chi. Cardinals |
| Dec. 1 | W | 13–3 | Pittsburgh |
| Dec. 8 | T | 0–0 | at Brooklyn |

**1936** — 7–5

| Date | Result | Score | Opponent |
|---|---|---|---|
| Sept. 13 | L | 0–10 | at Pittsburgh |
| Sept. 20 | W | 26–3 | at Philadelphia |
| Sept. 27 | W | 14–3 | at Brooklyn |
| Oct. 4 | L | 0–7 | NY Giants |
| Oct. 11 | L | 2–31 | at Green Bay |
| Oct. 18 | W | 17–7 | Philadelphia |
| Nov. 1 | W | 13–10 | Chi. Cardinals |
| Nov. 8 | L | 3–7 | Green Bay |
| Nov. 15 | L | 0–26 | Chicago Bears |
| Nov. 22 | W | 30–6 | Brooklyn |
| Nov. 29 | W | 30–0 | Pittsburgh |
| Dec. 6 | W | 14–0 | at NY Giants |
| *World Championship* | | | |
| Dec. 13 | L | 6–21 | Green Bay |

**1937** — 8–3

| Date | Result | Score | Opponent |
|---|---|---|---|
| Sept. 15 | W | 13–3 | NY Giants |
| Sept. 24 | L | 14–21 | Chi. Cardinals |
| Oct. 3 | W | 11–7 | at Brooklyn |
| Oct. 10 | L | 0–14 | Philadelphia |
| Oct. 17 | W | 34–20 | Pittsburgh |
| Oct. 24 | W | 10–7 | at Philadelphia |
| Oct. 31 | W | 21–0 | Brooklyn |
| Nov. 14 | L | 13–21 | at Pittsburgh |
| Nov. 21 | W | 16–7 | at Cleveland Rams |
| Nov. 28 | W | 14–6 | Green Bay |
| Dec. 5 | W | 49–14 | at NY Giants |
| *World Championship* | | | |
| Dec. 12 | W | 28–21 | at Chicago Bears |

**1938** — 6–3–2

| Date | Result | Score | Opponent |
|---|---|---|---|
| Sept. 11 | W | 26–23 | at Philadelphia |
| Sept. 18 | T | 16–16 | Brooklyn |
| Sept. 25 | W | 37–13 | Cleveland Rams |
| Oct. 9 | L | 7–10 | NY Giants |
| Oct. 16 | W | 7–5 | at Detroit |
| Oct. 23 | W | 20–14 | Philadelphia |
| Oct. 30 | T | 6–6 | at Brooklyn |
| Nov. 6 | W | 7–0 | at Pittsburgh |
| Nov. 13 | L | 7–31 | at Chicago Bears |
| Nov. 27 | W | 15–0 | Pittsburgh |
| Dec. 4 | L | 0–36 | at NY Giants |

**1939** — 8–2–1

| Date | Result | Score | Opponent |
|---|---|---|---|
| Sept. 17 | W | 7–0 | at Philadelphia |
| Oct. 1 | T | 0–0 | NY Giants |
| Oct. 8 | W | 41–13 | Brooklyn |
| Oct. 15 | W | 44–14 | Pittsburgh |
| Oct. 22 | W | 21–14 | at Pittsburgh |
| Oct. 29 | L | 14–24 | at Green Bay |
| Nov. 5 | W | 7–6 | Philadelphia |
| Nov. 12 | W | 42–0 | at Brooklyn |
| Nov. 19 | W | 28–7 | Chi. Cardinals |
| Nov. 26 | W | 31–7 | Detroit |
| Dec. 3 | L | 7–9 | at NY Giants |

**1940** — 9–2

| Date | Result | Score | Opponent |
|---|---|---|---|
| Sept. 15 | W | 24–17 | Brooklyn |
| Sept. 22 | W | 21–7 | NY Giants |
| Oct. 6 | W | 40–10 | at Pittsburgh |
| Oct. 13 | W | 28–21 | Chi. Cardinals |
| Oct. 20 | W | 34–17 | Philadelphia |
| Oct. 27 | W | 20–14 | at Detroit |
| Nov. 3 | W | 37–10 | Pittsburgh |
| Nov. 10 | L | 14–16 | at Brooklyn |
| Nov. 17 | W | 7–3 | Chicago Bears |
| Nov. 24 | L | 7–21 | at NY Giants |
| Dec. 1 | W | 13–6 | Philadelphia |
| *World Championship* | | | |
| Dec. 8 | L | 0–73 | Chicago Bears |

**1941** — 6–5

| Date | Result | Score | Opponent |
|---|---|---|---|
| Sept. 28 | L | 10–17 | NY Giants |
| Oct. 5 | W | 3–0 | at Brooklyn |
| Oct. 12 | W | 24–20 | at Pittsburgh |
| Oct. 19 | W | 21–17 | at Philadelphia |
| Oct. 26 | W | 17–13 | Cleveland Rams |
| Nov. 2 | W | 23–3 | Pittsburgh |
| Nov. 9 | L | 7–13 | at Brooklyn |
| Nov. 16 | L | 21–35 | at Chicago Bears |
| Nov. 23 | L | 13–20 | at NY Giants |
| Nov. 30 | L | 17–22 | Green Bay |
| Dec. 7 | W | 20–14 | Philadelphia |

**1942** — 10–1

| Date | Result | Score | Opponent |
|---|---|---|---|
| Sept. 20 | W | 28–14 | Pittsburgh |
| Sept. 27 | L | 7–14 | NY Giants |
| Oct. 4 | W | 14–10 | at Philadelphia |
| Oct. 11 | W | 33–14 | Cleveland Rams |
| Oct. 18 | W | 21–10 | at Brooklyn |
| Oct. 25 | W | 14–0 | at Pittsburgh |
| Nov. 1 | W | 30–27 | Philadelphia |
| Nov. 8 | W | 28–0 | Chi. Cardinals |
| Nov. 15 | W | 14–7 | at NY Giants |
| Nov. 22 | W | 23–3 | Brooklyn |
| Nov. 29 | W | 15–3 | at Detroit |
| *World Championship* | | | |
| Dec. 13 | W | 14–6 | Chicago |

**1943** — 6–3–1

| Date | Result | Score | Opponent |
|---|---|---|---|
| Oct. 10 | W | 27–0 | Brooklyn |
| Oct. 17 | W | 33–7 | at Green Bay |
| Oct. 24 | W | 13–7 | Chi. Cardinals |
| Oct. 31 | W | 48–10 | at Brooklyn |
| Nov. 7 | T | 14–14 | at Phil–Pitt |
| Nov. 14 | W | 42–20 | Detroit |
| Nov. 21 | W | 21–7 | Chicago |
| Nov. 28 | L | 14–27 | Phil–Pitt |
| Dec. 5 | L | 10–14 | at NY Giants |
| Dec. 12 | L | 7–31 | NY Giants |
| *Eastern Title Playoff* | | | |
| Dec. 19 | W | 28–0 | at NY Giants |
| *World Championship* | | | |
| Dec. 26 | L | 21–41 | at Chicago Bears |

**1944** — 6–3–1

| Date | Result | Score | Opponent |
|---|---|---|---|
| Oct. 8 | T | 31–31 | at Philadelphia |
| Oct. 15 | W | 21–14 | at Boston Yanks |
| Oct. 22 | W | 17–14 | Brooklyn Tigers |
| Oct. 29 | W | 42–20 | Chi–Pitt |
| Nov. 5 | W | 14–10 | Cleveland Rams |
| Nov. 12 | W | 10–0 | at Brooklyn Tigers |

| Date | | Score | Opponent |
|---|---|---|---|
| Nov. 19 | L | 7–37 | Philadelphia |
| Nov. 26 | W | 14–7 | Boston Yanks |
| Dec. 3 | L | 13–16 | at NY Giants |
| Dec. 10 | L | 0–31 | NY Giants |

## 1945 (8–2)

| Date | | Score | Opponent |
|---|---|---|---|
| Oct. 7 | L | 20–28 | at Boston Yanks |
| Oct. 14 | W | 14–0 | at Pittsburgh |
| Oct. 21 | W | 24–14 | Philadelphia |
| Oct. 28 | W | 24–14 | at NY Giants |
| Nov. 4 | W | 24–21 | Chi. Cardinals |
| Nov. 11 | W | 34–7 | Boston Yanks |
| Nov. 18 | W | 28–21 | Chicago Bears |
| Nov. 25 | L | 0–16 | at Philadelphia |
| Dec. 2 | W | 24–0 | Pittsburgh |
| Dec. 9 | W | 17–0 | NY Giants |
| | | World Championship | |
| Dec. 16 | L | 14–15 | at Cleveland Rams |

## 1946 (5–5–1)

| Date | | Score | Opponent |
|---|---|---|---|
| Sept. 29 | T | 14–14 | Pittsburgh |
| Oct. 6 | W | 17–16 | Detroit |
| Oct. 13 | W | 24–14 | NY Giants |
| Oct. 20 | W | 14–6 | at Boston Yanks |
| Oct. 27 | L | 24–28 | Philadelphia |
| Nov. 3 | L | 7–14 | at Pittsburgh |
| Nov. 10 | W | 17–14 | Boston Yanks |
| Nov. 17 | L | 20–24 | at Chicago Bears |
| Nov. 24 | W | 27–10 | at Philadelphia |
| Dec. 1 | L | 7–20 | Green Bay |
| Dec. 8 | L | 0–31 | at NY Giants |

## 1947 (4–8)

| Date | | Score | Opponent |
|---|---|---|---|
| Sept. 28 | L | 42–45 | at Philadelphia |
| Oct. 5 | W | 27–26 | Pittsburgh |
| Oct. 12 | W | 28–20 | NY Giants |
| Oct. 19 | L | 10–27 | at Green Bay |
| Oct. 26 | L | 20–56 | Chicago Bears |
| Nov. 2 | L | 14–38 | Philadelphia |
| Nov. 9 | L | 14–21 | at Pittsburgh |
| Nov. 16 | L | 21–38 | at Detroit |
| Nov. 23 | W | 45–21 | Chi. Cardinals |
| Nov. 30 | L | 24–27 | at Boston Yanks |
| Dec. 7 | L | 10–35 | at NY Giants |
| Dec. 14 | W | 40–13 | Boston Yanks |

## 1948 (7–5)

| Date | | Score | Opponent |
|---|---|---|---|
| Sept. 26 | W | 17–14 | Pittsburgh |
| Oct. 3 | W | 41–10 | NY Giants |
| Oct. 10 | L | 7–10 | at Pittsburgh |
| Oct. 17 | L | 0–45 | Philadelphia |
| Oct. 24 | W | 23–7 | at Green Bay |
| Oct. 31 | W | 59–21 | Boston Yanks |
| Nov. 7 | W | 23–7 | at Boston Yanks |
| Nov. 14 | W | 46–21 | Detroit |
| Nov. 21 | L | 21–42 | at Philadelphia |
| Nov. 28 | L | 13–48 | at Chicago Bears |
| Dec. 5 | L | 13–41 | Los Angeles |
| Dec. 12 | W | 28–21 | at NY Giants |

## 1949 (4–7–1)

| Date | | Score | Opponent |
|---|---|---|---|
| Sept. 26 | L | 7–38 | at Chi. Cardinals |
| Oct. 3 | W | 27–14 | at Pittsburgh |
| Oct. 9 | L | 35–45 | NY Giants |
| Oct. 16 | W | 38–14 | NY Bulldogs |
| Oct. 23 | L | 14–49 | at Philadelphia |
| Oct. 30 | T | 14–14 | at NY Bulldogs |
| Nov. 6 | W | 27–14 | Pittsburgh |
| Nov. 13 | L | 21–44 | Philadelphia |
| Nov. 20 | L | 21–31 | Chicago Bears |
| Nov. 27 | L | 7–23 | at NY Giants |
| Dec. 4 | W | 30–0 | Green Bay |
| Dec. 11 | L | 27–53 | at Los Angeles |

## 1950 (3–9)

| Date | | Score | Opponent |
|---|---|---|---|
| Sept. 17 | W | 38–14 | at Baltimore |
| Sept. 24 | L | 21–35 | at Green Bay |
| Oct. 1 | L | 7–26 | Pittsburgh |
| Oct. 8 | L | 17–21 | NY Giants |
| Oct. 22 | L | 28–38 | Chi. Cardinals |
| Oct. 29 | L | 3–35 | at Philadelphia |
| Nov. 5 | L | 21–24 | at NY Giants |
| Nov. 12 | L | 0–33 | Philadelphia |
| Nov. 19 | L | 14–20 | at Cleveland |
| Nov. 26 | W | 38–28 | Baltimore |
| Dec. 3 | W | 24–7 | at Pittsburgh |
| Dec. 10 | L | 21–45 | Cleveland |

## 1951 (5–7)

| Date | | Score | Opponent |
|---|---|---|---|
| Sept. 30 | L | 17–35 | at Detroit |
| Oct. 7 | L | 14–35 | NY Giants |
| Oct. 14 | L | 0–45 | at Cleveland |
| Oct. 21 | W | 7–3 | Chi. Cardinals |
| Oct. 28 | W | 27–23 | at Philadelphia |
| Nov. 4 | L | 0–27 | Chicago Bears |
| Nov. 11 | L | 14–28 | at NY Giants |
| Nov. 18 | W | 22–7 | at Pittsburgh |
| Nov. 25 | W | 31–21 | Los Angeles |
| Dec. 2 | L | 21–35 | Philadelphia |
| Dec. 9 | W | 20–17 | at Chi. Cardinals |
| Dec. 16 | L | 10–20 | Pittsburgh |

## 1952 (4–8)

| Date | | Score | Opponent |
|---|---|---|---|
| Sept. 28 | W | 23–7 | at Chi. Cardinals |
| Oct. 5 | L | 20–35 | at Green Bay |
| Oct. 12 | L | 6–17 | Chi. Cardinals |
| Oct. 19 | W | 28–24 | at Pittsburgh |
| Oct. 26 | L | 15–19 | at Cleveland |
| Nov. 2 | L | 23–24 | Pittsburgh |
| Nov. 9 | L | 20–38 | at Philadelphia |
| Nov. 16 | L | 17–23 | San Francisco |
| Nov. 23 | L | 10–14 | NY Giants |
| Nov. 30 | L | 24–48 | Cleveland |
| Dec. 7 | W | 27–17 | at NY Giants |
| Dec. 14 | W | 27–21 | Philadelphia |

## 1953 (6–5–1)

| Date | | Score | Opponent |
|---|---|---|---|
| Sept. 27 | W | 24–13 | at Chi. Cardinals |
| Oct. 2 | T | 21–21 | at Philadelphia |
| Oct. 11 | W | 13–9 | NY Giants |
| Oct. 18 | L | 14–30 | Cleveland |
| Oct. 25 | L | 17–27 | at Baltimore |
| Nov. 1 | L | 3–27 | at Cleveland |
| Nov. 8 | W | 28–17 | Chi. Cardinals |
| Nov. 15 | L | 24–27 | Chicago Bears |
| Nov. 22 | W | 24–21 | at NY Giants |
| Nov. 29 | W | 17–9 | at Pittsburgh |
| Dec. 6 | W | 10–0 | Philadelphia |
| Dec. 13 | L | 13–14 | Pittsburgh |

## 1954 (3–9)

| Date | | Score | Opponent |
|---|---|---|---|
| Sept. 26 | L | 7–41 | at San Francisco |
| Oct. 2 | L | 7–37 | at Pittsburgh |
| Oct. 10 | L | 21–51 | NY Giants |
| Oct .17 | L | 21–49 | Philadelphia |
| Oct. 24 | L | 7–24 | at NY Giants |
| Oct. 31 | W | 24–21 | Baltimore |
| Nov. 7 | L | 3–62 | at Cleveland |
| Nov. 14 | W | 17–14 | Pittsburgh |
| Nov. 21 | L | 16–38 | at Chi. Cardinals |
| Nov. 28 | L | 33–41 | at Philadelphia |
| Dec. 5 | L | 14–34 | Cleveland |
| Dec. 12 | W | 37–20 | Chi. Cardinals |

## 1955 (8–4)

| Date | | Score | Opponent |
|---|---|---|---|
| Sept. 25 | W | 27–17 | at Cleveland |
| Oct. 1 | W | 31–30 | at Philadelphia |
| Oct. 9 | L | 10–24 | Chi. Cardinals |
| Oct. 16 | L | 14–24 | Cleveland |
| Oct. 23 | W | 14–13 | at Baltimore |
| Oct. 30 | L | 7–35 | at NY Giants |
| Nov. 6 | W | 34–21 | Philadelphia |

| Date | | Score | Opponent |
|---|---|---|---|
| Nov. 13 | W | 7–0 | San Francisco |
| Nov. 20 | W | 31–0 | at Chi. Cardinals |
| Nov. 27 | W | 23–14 | at Pittsburgh |
| Dec. 4 | L | 20–27 | NY Giants |
| Dec. 11 | W | 28–17 | Pittsburgh |

**1956** — 6–6

| Date | | Score | Opponent |
|---|---|---|---|
| Sept. 30 | L | 13–30 | at Pittsburgh |
| Oct. 6 | L | 9–13 | at Philadelphia |
| Oct. 14 | L | 3–31 | Chi. Cardinals |
| Oct. 21 | W | 20–9 | Cleveland |
| Oct. 28 | W | 17–14 | at Chi. Cardinals |
| Nov. 11 | W | 18–17 | Detroit |
| Nov. 18 | W | 33–17 | NY Giants |
| Nov. 25 | W | 20–17 | at Cleveland |
| Dec. 2 | L | 14–28 | at NY Giants |
| Dec. 9 | W | 19–17 | Philadelphia |
| Dec. 16 | L | 0–23 | Pittsburgh |
| Dec. 23 | L | 17–19 | at Baltimore |

**1957** — 5–6–1

| Date | | Score | Opponent |
|---|---|---|---|
| Sept. 29 | L | 7–28 | at Pittsburgh |
| Oct. 6 | W | 37–14 | at Chi. Cardinals |
| Oct. 13 | L | 20–24 | NY Giants |
| Oct. 20 | L | 14–44 | Chi. Cardinals |
| Oct. 27 | W | 31–14 | at NY Giants |
| Nov. 3 | L | 17–21 | at Cleveland |
| Nov. 10 | L | 17–21 | Baltimore |
| Nov. 17 | T | 30–30 | Cleveland |
| Nov. 24 | L | 12–21 | at Philadelphia |
| Dec. 1 | W | 14–3 | at Chicago Bears |
| Dec. 8 | W | 42–7 | Philadelphia |
| Dec. 15 | W | 10–3 | Pittsburgh |

**1958** — 4–7–1

| Date | | Score | Opponent |
|---|---|---|---|
| Sept. 18 | W | 24–14 | at Philadelphia |
| Oct. 4 | L | 10–37 | at Chi. Cardinals |
| Oct. 12 | L | 14–21 | NY Giants |
| Oct. 19 | W | 37–21 | Green Bay |
| Oct. 26 | L | 10–35 | at Baltimore |
| Nov. 2 | L | 16–24 | at Pittsburgh |
| Nov. 9 | W | 45–31 | Chi. Cardinals |
| Nov. 16 | L | 10–20 | Cleveland |
| Nov. 23 | L | 0–30 | at NY Giants |
| Nov. 30 | L | 14–21 | at Cleveland |
| Dec. 7 | T | 14–14 | Pittsburgh |
| Dec. 14 | W | 20–0 | Philadelphia |

**1959** — 3–9

| Date | | Score | Opponent |
|---|---|---|---|
| Sept. 17 | L | 21–49 | at Chi. Cardinals |
| Oct. 4 | W | 23–17 | at Pittsburgh |
| Oct. 11 | W | 23–14 | Chi. Cardinals |
| Oct. 18 | L | 6–27 | Pittsburgh |
| Oct. 25 | L | 7–34 | at Cleveland |
| Nov. 1 | L | 23–30 | at Philadelphia |
| Nov. 8 | W | 27–24 | Baltimore |
| Nov. 15 | L | 17–31 | Cleveland |
| Nov. 22 | L | 0–21 | at Green Bay |
| Nov. 29 | L | 14–45 | at NY Giants |
| Dec. 6 | L | 14–34 | Philadelphia |
| Dec. 13 | L | 10–24 | NY Giants |

**1960** — 1–9–2

| Date | | Score | Opponent |
|---|---|---|---|
| Sept. 25 | L | 0–20 | at Baltimore |
| Oct. 9 | W | 26–14 | Dallas |
| Oct. 16 | T | 24–24 | at NY Giants |
| Oct. 23 | T | 27–27 | at Pittsburgh |
| Oct. 30 | L | 10–31 | Cleveland |
| Nov. 6 | L | 7–44 | at St. Louis |
| Nov. 13 | L | 13–19 | at Philadelphia |
| Nov. 20 | L | 14–26 | St. Louis |
| Nov. 27 | L | 10–22 | at Pittsburgh |
| Dec. 4 | L | 16–27 | at Cleveland |
| Dec. 11 | L | 3–17 | NY Giants |
| Dec. 18 | L | 28–38 | Philadelphia |

**1961** — 1–12–1

| Date | | Score | Opponent |
|---|---|---|---|
| Sept. 17 | L | 3–35 | at San Francisco |
| Sept. 24 | L | 7–14 | at Philadelphia |
| Oct. 1 | L | 21–24 | NY Giants |
| Oct. 8 | L | 7–31 | at Cleveland |
| Oct. 15 | L | 0–20 | at Pittsburgh |
| Oct. 22 | L | 0–24 | St. Louis |
| Oct. 29 | L | 24–27 | Philadelphia |
| Nov. 5 | L | 0–53 | at NY Giants |
| Nov. 12 | L | 6–17 | Cleveland |
| Nov. 19 | T | 28–28 | at Dallas |
| Nov. 26 | L | 6–27 | Baltimore |
| Dec. 3 | L | 24–38 | at St. Louis |
| Dec. 10 | L | 14–30 | Pittsburgh |
| Dec. 17 | W | 34–24 | Dallas |

**1962** — 5–7–2

| Date | | Score | Opponent |
|---|---|---|---|
| Sept. 16 | T | 35–35 | at Dallas |
| Sept. 23 | W | 17–16 | at Cleveland |
| Sept. 30 | W | 24–14 | St. Louis |
| Oct. 8 | W | 20–14 | Los Angeles |
| Oct. 14 | T | 17–17 | at St. Louis |
| Oct. 21 | W | 27–21 | at Philadelphia |
| Oct. 28 | L | 34–49 | at NY Giants |
| Nov. 4 | L | 10–38 | Dallas |
| Nov. 11 | W | 17–9 | Cleveland |
| Nov. 18 | L | 21–23 | at Pittsburgh |
| Nov. 25 | L | 24–42 | NY Giants |
| Dec. 2 | L | 14–37 | Philadelphia |
| Dec. 8 | L | 21–34 | at Baltimore |
| Dec. 15 | L | 24–27 | Pittsburgh |

**1963** — 3–11

| Date | | Score | Opponent |
|---|---|---|---|
| Sept. 15 | L | 14–37 | at Cleveland |
| Sept. 21 | W | 37–14 | at Los Angeles |
| Sept. 29 | W | 21–17 | Dallas |
| Oct. 6 | L | 14–24 | NY Giants |
| Oct. 13 | L | 24–37 | Philadelphia |
| Oct. 20 | L | 27–38 | at Pittsburgh |
| Oct. 27 | L | 7–21 | St. Louis |
| Nov. 3 | L | 20–35 | at Dallas |
| Nov. 10 | L | 20–24 | at St. Louis |
| Nov. 17 | L | 28–34 | Pittsburgh |
| Nov. 24 | W | 13–10 | at Philadelphia |
| Dec. 1 | L | 20–36 | Baltimore |
| Dec. 8 | L | 14–44 | at NY Giants |
| Dec. 15 | L | 20–27 | Cleveland |

**1964** — 6–8

| Date | | Score | Opponent |
|---|---|---|---|
| Sept. 13 | L | 13–27 | Cleveland |
| Sept. 20 | L | 18–24 | at Dallas |
| Sept. 25 | L | 10–13 | at NY Giants |
| Oct. 4 | L | 17–23 | St. Louis |
| Oct. 11 | W | 35–20 | Philadelphia |
| Oct. 18 | L | 24–38 | at St. Louis |
| Oct. 25 | W | 27–20 | Chicago |
| Nov. 1 | W | 21–10 | at Philadelphia |
| Nov. 8 | L | 24–34 | at Cleveland |
| Nov. 15 | W | 30–0 | Pittsburgh |
| Nov. 22 | W | 28–16 | Dallas |
| Nov. 29 | W | 36–21 | NY Giants |
| Dec. 6 | L | 7–14 | Pittsburgh |
| Dec. 13 | L | 17–45 | at Baltimore |

**1965** — 6–8

| Date | | Score | Opponent |
|---|---|---|---|
| Sept. 19 | L | 7–17 | Cleveland |
| Sept. 26 | L | 7–27 | at Dallas |
| Oct. 3 | L | 10–14 | at Detroit |
| Oct. 10 | L | 16–37 | St. Louis |
| Oct. 17 | L | 7–38 | Baltimore |
| Oct. 24 | W | 24–20 | at St. Louis |
| Oct. 31 | W | 23–21 | Philadelphia |
| Nov. 7 | W | 23–7 | at NY Giants |
| Nov. 14 | L | 14–21 | at Philadelphia |
| Nov. 21 | W | 31–3 | at Pittsburgh |
| Nov. 28 | W | 34–31 | Dallas |

| Dec. 5 | L | 16–24 | at Cleveland |
| Dec. 12 | L | 10–27 | NY Giants |
| Dec. 19 | W | 35–14 | Pittsburgh |
| | | | |
| **1966** | | | **7–7** |
| Sept. 11 | L | 14–38 | Cleveland |
| Sept. 18 | L | 7–23 | at St. Louis |
| Sept. 25 | W | 33–27 | at Pittsburgh |
| Oct. 2 | W | 24–10 | Pittsburgh |
| Oct. 9 | W | 33–20 | Atlanta |
| Oct. 16 | L | 10–13 | at NY Giants |
| Oct. 23 | W | 26–20 | St. Louis |
| Oct. 30 | W | 27–13 | at Philadelphia |
| Nov. 6 | L | 10–37 | at Baltimore |
| Nov. 13 | L | 30–31 | Dallas |
| Nov. 20 | L | 3–14 | at Cleveland |
| Nov. 27 | W | 72–41 | NY Giants |
| Dec. 11 | W | 34–31 | at Dallas |
| Dec. 18 | L | 28–37 | Philadelphia |
| | | | |
| **1967** | | | **5–6–3** |
| Sept. 17 | L | 24–35 | at Philadelphia |
| Sept. 24 | W | 30–10 | at New Orleans |
| Oct. 1 | W | 38–34 | NY Giants |
| Oct. 8 | L | 14–17 | Dallas |
| Oct. 15 | T | 20–20 | at Atlanta |
| Oct. 22 | T | 28–28 | at Los Angeles |
| Oct. 29 | L | 13–17 | Baltimore |
| Nov. 5 | L | 21–27 | St. Louis |
| Nov. 12 | W | 31–28 | San Francisco |
| Nov. 19 | W | 27–20 | at Dallas |
| Nov. 26 | L | 37–42 | at Cleveland |
| Dec. 3 | T | 35–35 | Philadelphia |
| Dec. 10 | W | 15–10 | at Pittsburgh |
| Dec. 17 | L | 14–30 | New Orleans |
| | | | |
| **1968** | | | **5–9** |
| Sept. 15 | W | 38–28 | at Chicago |
| Sept. 22 | L | 17–37 | at New Orleans |
| Sept. 29 | L | 21–48 | at NY Giants |
| Oct. 6 | W | 17–14 | Philadelphia |
| Oct. 13 | W | 16–13 | Pittsburgh |
| Oct. 20 | L | 14–41 | at St. Louis |
| Oct. 27 | L | 10–13 | NY Giants |
| Nov. 3 | L | 14–27 | at Minnesota |
| Nov. 10 | W | 16–10 | at Philadelphia |
| Nov. 17 | L | 24–44 | Dallas |
| Nov. 24 | L | 7–27 | Green Bay |
| Nov. 28 | L | 20–29 | at Dallas |
| Dec. 8 | L | 21–24 | Cleveland |
| Dec. 15 | W | 14–3 | Detroit |
| | | | |
| **1969** | | | **7–5–2** |
| Sept. 21 | W | 26–20 | at New Orleans |
| Sept. 28 | L | 23–27 | at Cleveland |
| Oct. 5 | T | 17–17 | at San Francisco |
| Oct. 12 | W | 33–17 | St. Louis |
| Oct. 19 | W | 20–14 | NY Giants |
| Oct. 26 | W | 14–7 | at Pittsburgh |
| Nov. 2 | L | 17–41 | at Baltimore |
| Nov. 9 | T | 28–28 | Philadelphia |
| Nov. 16 | L | 28–41 | Dallas |
| Nov. 23 | W | 27–20 | Atlanta |
| Nov. 30 | L | 13–24 | Los Angeles |
| Dec. 7 | W | 34–29 | at Philadelphia |
| Dec. 14 | W | 17–14 | New Orleans |
| Dec. 21 | L | 10–20 | at Dallas |
| | | | |
| **1970** | | | **6–8** |
| Sept. 20 | L | 17–26 | at San Francisco |
| Sept. 27 | L | 17–27 | at St. Louis |
| Oct. 4 | W | 33–21 | at Philadelphia |
| Oct. 11 | W | 31–10 | Detroit |
| Oct. 19 | L | 20–34 | at Oakland |
| Oct. 25 | W | 20–0 | Cincinnati |
| Nov. 1 | W | 19–3 | at Denver |
| Nov. 8 | L | 10–19 | Minnesota |

| Nov. 15 | L | 33–35 | at NY Giants |
| Nov. 22 | L | 21–45 | Dallas |
| Nov. 29 | L | 24–27 | NY Giants |
| Dec. 6 | L | 0–34 | at Dallas |
| Dec. 13 | W | 24–6 | Philadelphia |
| Dec. 20 | W | 28–27 | St. Louis |
| | | | |
| **1971** | | | **9–4–1** |
| Sept. 19 | W | 24–17 | at St. Louis |
| Sept. 26 | W | 30–3 | at NY Giants |
| Oct. 3 | W | 20–16 | at Dallas |
| Oct. 10 | W | 22–13 | Houston |
| Oct. 17 | W | 20–0 | St. Louis |
| Oct. 24 | L | 20–27 | at Kansas City |
| Oct. 31 | W | 24–14 | New Orleans |
| Nov. 7 | T | 7–7 | Philadelphia |
| Nov. 14 | L | 15–16 | at Chicago |
| Nov. 21 | L | 0–13 | Dallas |
| Nov. 28 | W | 20–13 | at Philadelphia |
| Dec. 5 | W | 23–7 | NY Giants |
| Dec. 13 | W | 38–24 | at Los Angeles |
| Dec. 19 | L | 13–20 | Cleveland |
| | | *Playoffs* | |
| Dec. 26 | L | 20–24 | at San Francisco |
| | | | |
| **1972** | | | **11–3** |
| Sept. 18 | W | 24–21 | at Minnesota |
| Sept. 24 | W | 24–10 | St. Louis |
| Oct. 1 | L | 23–24 | at New England |
| Oct. 8 | W | 14–0 | Philadelphia |
| Oct. 15 | W | 33–3 | at St. Louis |
| Oct. 22 | W | 24–20 | Dallas |
| Oct. 29 | W | 23–16 | at NY Giants |
| Nov. 5 | W | 35–17 | at NY Jets |
| Nov. 12 | W | 27–13 | NY Giants |
| Nov. 20 | W | 24–13 | Atlanta |
| Nov. 26 | W | 21–16 | Green Bay |
| Dec. 3 | W | 23–7 | at Philadelphia |
| Dec. 9 | L | 24–34 | at Dallas |
| Dec. 17 | L | 17–24 | Buffalo |
| | | *Playoffs* | |
| Dec. 24 | W | 16–3 | Green Bay |
| Dec. 31 | W | 26–3 | Dallas |
| | | *Super Bowl VII, Los Angeles, Calif.* | |
| Jan. 14 | L | 7–14 | Miami |
| | | | |
| **1973** | | | **10–4** |
| Sept. 16 | W | 38–0 | San Diego |
| Sept. 23 | L | 27–34 | at St. Louis |
| Sept. 30 | W | 28–7 | at Philadelphia |
| Oct. 8 | W | 14–7 | Dallas |
| Oct. 14 | W | 21–3 | at NY Giants |
| Oct. 21 | W | 31–13 | St. Louis |
| Oct. 28 | L | 3–19 | at New Orleans |
| Nov. 5 | L | 16–21 | at Pittsburgh |
| Nov. 11 | W | 33–9 | San Francisco |
| Nov. 18 | W | 22–14 | Baltimore |
| Nov. 22 | W | 20–0 | at Detroit |
| Dec. 2 | W | 27–24 | NY Giants |
| Dec. 9 | L | 7–27 | at Dallas |
| Dec. 16 | W | 38–20 | Philadelphia |
| | | *Playoffs* | |
| Dec. 22 | L | 20–27 | at Minnesota |
| | | | |
| **1974** | | | **10–4** |
| Sept. 15 | W | 13–10 | at NY Giants |
| Sept. 22 | L | 10–17 | St. Louis |
| Sept. 30 | W | 30–3 | Denver |
| Oct. 6 | L | 17–28 | at Cincinnati |
| Oct. 13 | W | 20–17 | Miami |
| Oct. 20 | W | 24–3 | NY Giants |
| Oct. 27 | L | 20–23 | at St. Louis |
| Nov. 3 | W | 17–6 | at Green Bay |
| Nov. 10 | W | 27–20 | at Philadelphia |
| Nov. 17 | W | 28–21 | Dallas |
| Nov. 24 | W | 26–7 | Philadelphia |
| Nov. 28 | L | 23–24 | at Dallas |

| | | | |
|---|---|---|---|
| Dec. 9 | W | 23–17 | at Los Angeles |
| Dec. 15 | W | 42–0 | Chicago |
| Playoffs | | | |
| Dec. 22 | L | 10–19 | at Los Angeles |

**1975** **8–6**

| | | | |
|---|---|---|---|
| Sept. 21 | W | 41–3 | New Orleans |
| Sept. 28 | W | 49–13 | NY Giants |
| Oct. 5 | L | 10–26 | at Philadelphia |
| Oct. 13 | W | 27–17 | St. Louis |
| Oct. 19 | L | 10–13 | at Houston |
| Oct. 26 | W | 23–7 | at Cleveland |
| Nov. 2 | W | 30–24 | Dallas |
| Nov. 9 | W | 21–13 | at NY Giants |
| Nov. 16 | L | 17–20 | at St. Louis |
| Nov. 23 | L | 23–26 | Oakland |
| Nov. 30 | W | 31–30 | Minnesota |
| Dec. 7 | W | 30–27 | at Atlanta |
| Dec. 13 | L | 10–31 | at Dallas |
| Dec. 21 | L | 3–26 | Philadelphia |

**1976** **10–4**

| | | | |
|---|---|---|---|
| Sept. 12 | W | 19–17 | NY Giants |
| Sept. 19 | W | 31–7 | Seattle |
| Sept. 27 | W | 20–17 | at Philadelphia |
| Oct. 3 | L | 7–33 | at Chicago |
| Oct. 10 | L | 30–33 | Kansas City |
| Oct. 17 | W | 20–7 | Detroit |
| Oct. 25 | W | 20–10 | St. Louis |
| Oct. 31 | L | 7–20 | Dallas |
| Nov. 7 | W | 24–21 | at San Francisco |
| Nov. 14 | L | 9–12 | at NY Giants |
| Nov. 21 | W | 16–10 | at St. Louis |
| Nov. 28 | W | 24–0 | Philadelphia |
| Dec. 5 | W | 37–16 | at NY Jets |
| Dec. 12 | W | 27–14 | at Dallas |
| Playoffs | | | |
| Dec. 18 | L | 20–35 | at Minnesota |

**1977** **9–5**

| | | | |
|---|---|---|---|
| Sept. 18 | L | 17–20 | at NY Giants |
| Sept. 25 | W | 10–6 | Atlanta |
| Oct. 2 | W | 24–14 | St. Louis |
| Oct. 9 | W | 10–0 | at Tampa Bay |
| Oct. 16 | L | 16–34 | at Dallas |
| Oct. 23 | L | 6–17 | NY Giants |
| Oct. 30 | W | 23–17 | Philadelphia |
| Nov. 7 | L | 3–10 | at Baltimore |
| Nov. 13 | W | 17–14 | at Philadelphia |
| Nov. 21 | W | 10–9 | Green Bay |
| Nov. 27 | L | 7–14 | Dallas |
| Dec. 4 | W | 10–0 | at Buffalo |
| Dec. 10 | W | 26–20 | at St. Louis |
| Dec. 17 | W | 17–14 | LA Rams |

**1978** **8–8**

| | | | |
|---|---|---|---|
| Sept. 3 | W | 16–14 | at New England |
| Sept. 10 | W | 35–30 | Philadelphia |
| Sept. 17 | W | 28–10 | at St. Louis |
| Sept. 24 | W | 23–3 | NY Jets |
| Oct. 2 | W | 9–5 | Dallas |
| Oct. 8 | W | 21–19 | at Detroit |
| Oct. 15 | L | 10–17 | at Philadelphia |
| Oct. 22 | L | 6–17 | at NY Giants |
| Oct. 29 | W | 38–20 | San Francisco |
| Nov. 6 | L | 17–21 | at Baltimore |
| Nov. 12 | W | 16–13 | NY Giants |
| Nov. 19 | L | 17–27 | St. Louis |
| Nov. 23 | L | 10–37 | at Dallas |
| Dec. 3 | L | 0–16 | Miami |
| Dec. 10 | L | 17–20 | at Atlanta |
| Dec. 16 | L | 10–14 | Chicago |

**1979** **10–6**

| | | | |
|---|---|---|---|
| Sept. 2 | L | 27–29 | Houston |
| Sept. 9 | W | 27–24 | at Detroit |
| Sept. 17 | W | 27–0 | NY Giants |
| Sept. 23 | W | 17–7 | at St. Louis |
| Sept. 30 | W | 16–7 | at Atlanta |
| Oct. 7 | L | 17–28 | at Philadelphia |
| Oct. 14 | W | 13–9 | at Cleveland |
| Oct. 21 | W | 17–7 | Philadelphia |
| Oct. 28 | L | 10–14 | New Orleans |
| Nov. 4 | L | 7–38 | at Pittsburgh |
| Nov. 11 | W | 30–28 | St. Louis |
| Nov. 18 | W | 34–20 | Dallas |
| Nov. 25 | L | 6–14 | at NY Giants |
| Dec. 2 | W | 38–21 | Green Bay |
| Dec. 9 | W | 28–14 | Cincinnati |
| Dec. 16 | L | 34–35 | at Dallas |

**1980** **6–10**

| | | | |
|---|---|---|---|
| Sept. 8 | L | 3–17 | Dallas |
| Sept. 14 | W | 23–21 | at NY Giants |
| Sept. 21 | L | 21–24 | at Oakland |
| Sept. 28 | L | 0–14 | Seattle |
| Oct. 5 | L | 14–24 | at Philadelphia |
| Oct. 13 | L | 17–20 | at Denver |
| Oct. 19 | W | 23–0 | St. Louis |
| Oct. 26 | W | 22–14 | New Orleans |
| Nov. 2 | L | 14–39 | Minnesota |
| Nov. 9 | L | 21–35 | at Chicago |
| Nov. 15 | L | 0–34 | Philadelphia |
| Nov. 23 | L | 10–14 | at Dallas |
| Nov. 30 | L | 6–10 | at Atlanta |
| Dec. 7 | W | 40–17 | San Diego |
| Dec. 13 | W | 16–13 | NY Giants |
| Dec. 21 | W | 31–7 | at St. Louis |

**1981** **8–8**

| | | | |
|---|---|---|---|
| Sept. 6 | L | 10–26 | Dallas |
| Sept. 13 | L | 7–17 | NY Giants |
| Sept. 20 | L | 30–40 | at St. Louis Cardinals |
| Sept. 27 | L | 13–36 | at Philadelphia |
| Oct. 4 | L | 17–30 | San Francisco |
| Oct. 11 | W | 24–7 | Chicago |
| Oct. 18 | L | 10–13 | at Miami |
| Oct. 25 | W | 24–22 | New England |
| Nov. 1 | W | 42–21 | St. Louis |
| Nov. 8 | W | 33–31 | Detroit |
| Nov. 15 | W | 30–27 | at NY Giants |
| Nov. 22 | L | 10–24 | at Dallas |
| Nov. 29 | L | 14–21 | at Buffalo |
| Dec. 6 | W | 15–13 | Philadelphia |
| Dec. 13 | W | 38–14 | Baltimore |
| Dec. 20 | W | 30–7 | at LA Rams |

**1982** **8–1**

| | | | |
|---|---|---|---|
| Sept. 12 | W | 37–34 | at Philadelphia |
| Sept. 19 | W | 21–13 | at Buccaneers |
| Nov. 21 | W | 27–17 | at NY Giants |
| Nov. 28 | W | 13–9 | Philadelphia |
| Dec. 5 | L | 10–24 | Dallas |
| Dec. 12 | W | 12–7 | at St. Louis |
| Dec. 19 | W | 15–14 | NY Giants |
| Dec. 26 | W | 27–10 | at New Orleans |
| Jan. 2 | W | 28–0 | St. Louis |

DNP: (Home): Cleveland, Pittsburgh, San Francisco, Minnesota
DNP: (Away): Dallas, Houston, Cincinnati
Playoffs

| | | | |
|---|---|---|---|
| Jan. 8 | W | 31–7 | Detroit |
| Jan. 15 | W | 21–7 | Minnesota |
| Jan. 22 | W | 31–17 | Dallas |

Super Bowl XVII, Pasadena, Calif.

| | | | |
|---|---|---|---|
| Jan. 30 | W | 27–17 | Miami |

**1983** **14–2**

| | | | |
|---|---|---|---|
| Sept. 5 | L | 30–31 | Dallas |
| Sept. 11 | W | 23–13 | at Philadelphia |
| Sept. 18 | W | 27–12 | Kansas City |
| Sept. 25 | W | 27–17 | at Seattle |
| Oct. 2 | W | 37–35 | Los Angeles Raiders |
| Oct. 9 | W | 38–14 | at St. Louis |
| Oct. 17 | L | 47–48 | at Green Bay |

| Date | Result | Score | Opponent |
|---|---|---|---|
| Oct. 23 | W | 38–17 | Detroit |
| Oct. 31 | W | 27–24 | at San Diego |
| Nov. 6 | W | 45–7 | St. Louis |
| Nov. 13 | W | 33–17 | at NY Giants |
| Nov. 20 | W | 42–20 | at LA Rams |
| Nov. 27 | W | 28–24 | Philadelphia |
| Dec. 4 | W | 37–21 | Atlanta Falcons |
| Dec. 11 | W | 31–10 | at Dallas |
| Dec. 17 | W | 31–22 | NY Giants |
| Playoffs | | | |
| Jan. 1 | W | 51–7 | LA Rams |
| Jan. 8 | W | 24–21 | San Francisco |
| Super Bowl XVIII, Tampa, Fla. | | | |
| Jan. 22 | L | 9–38 | LA Raiders |

**1984 — 11–5**

| Date | Result | Score | Opponent |
|---|---|---|---|
| Sept. 2 | L | 17–35 | Miami |
| Sept. 10 | L | 31–37 | at San Francisco |
| Sept. 16 | W | 30–14 | NY Giants |
| Sept. 23 | W | 26–10 | at New England |
| Sept. 30 | W | 20–0 | Philadelphia |
| Oct. 7 | W | 35–7 | at Indianapolis |
| Oct. 14 | W | 34–14 | Dallas |
| Oct. 21 | L | 24–26 | at St. Louis |
| Oct. 28 | L | 13–37 | at NY Giants |
| Nov. 5 | W | 27–14 | Atlanta |
| Nov. 11 | W | 28–14 | Detroit |
| Nov. 18 | L | 10–16 | at Philadelphia |
| Nov. 25 | W | 41–14 | Buffalo |
| Nov. 29 | W | 31–17 | at Minnesota |
| Dec. 9 | W | 30–28 | at Dallas |
| Dec. 16 | W | 29–27 | St. Louis |
| Playoffs | | | |
| Dec. 30 | L | 19–23 | Chicago |

**1985 — 10–6**

| Date | Result | Score | Opponent |
|---|---|---|---|
| Sept. 9 | L | 14–44 | at Dallas |
| Sept. 15 | W | 16–13 | Houston |
| Sept. 22 | L | 6–19 | Philadelphia |
| Sept. 29 | L | 10–45 | at Chicago |
| Oct. 7 | W | 27–10 | St. Louis |
| Oct. 13 | W | 24–3 | Detroit |
| Oct. 20 | L | 3–17 | at NY Giants |
| Oct. 27 | W | 14–7 | at Cleveland |
| Nov. 3 | W | 44–10 | at Atlanta |
| Nov. 10 | L | 7–13 | Dallas |
| Nov. 18 | W | 23–21 | New York |
| Nov. 24 | W | 30–23 | at Pittsburgh |
| Dec. 1 | L | 8–35 | San Francisco |
| Dec. 8 | W | 17–12 | at Philadelphia |
| Dec. 15 | W | 27–24 | Cincinnati |
| Dec. 21 | W | 27–16 | at St. Louis |

**1986 — 12–4**

| Date | Result | Score | Opponent |
|---|---|---|---|
| Sept. 7 | W | 41–14 | Philadelphia |
| Sept. 14 | W | 10–6 | LA Raiders |
| Sept. 21 | W | 30–27 | at San Diego |
| Sept. 28 | W | 19–14 | Seattle |
| Oct. 5 | W | 14–6 | at New Orleans |
| Oct. 12 | L | 6–30 | at Dallas |
| Oct. 19 | W | 28–21 | St. Louis |
| Oct. 27 | L | 20–27 | at NY Giants |
| Nov. 2 | W | 44–38 | Minnesota |
| Nov. 9 | W | 16–7 | at Green Bay |
| Nov. 17 | W | 14–6 | San Francisco |
| Nov. 23 | W | 41–14 | Dallas |
| Nov. 30 | W | 20–17 | at St. Louis |
| Dec. 7 | L | 14–24 | NY Giants |
| Dec. 13 | L | 30–31 | at Denver |
| Dec. 21 | W | 21–14 | at Philadelphia |
| Playoffs | | | |
| Dec. 28 | W | 19–7 | LA Rams |
| Jan. 3 | W | 27–13 | at Chicago |
| Jan. 11 | L | 0–17 | at NY Giants |

**1987 — 11–4**

| Date | Result | Score | Opponent |
|---|---|---|---|
| Sept. 13 | W | 34–24 | Philadelphia |
| Sept. 20 | L | 20–21 | at Atlanta |
| Sept. 27 | Cancelled | | New England |
| Oct. 4 | W | 28–21 | St. Louis |
| Oct. 11 | W | 38–12 | at NY Giants |
| Oct. 19 | W | 13–7 | at Dallas |
| Oct. 25 | W | 17–16 | NY Jets |
| Nov. 1 | W | 27–7 | at Buffalo |
| Nov. 8 | L | 27–31 | at Philadelphia |
| Nov. 15 | W | 20–13 | Detroit |
| Nov. 23 | L | 26–30 | LA Rams |
| Nov. 29 | W | 23–19 | NY Giants |
| Dec. 6 | W | 34–17 | at St. Louis |
| Dec. 13 | W | 24–20 | Dallas |
| Dec. 20 | L | 21–23 | at Miami |
| Dec. 26 | W | 27–24 | at Minnesota |
| Playoffs | | | |
| Jan. 10 | W | 21–17 | at Chicago |
| Jan. 17 | W | 17–10 | Minnesota |
| Super Bowl XXII San Diego, Calif. | | | |
| Jan. 31 | W | 42–10 | Denver |

**1988 — 7–9**

| Date | Result | Score | Opponent |
|---|---|---|---|
| Sept. 5 | L | 20–27 | at NY Giants |
| Sept. 11 | W | 30–29 | Pittsburgh |
| Sept. 18 | W | 17–10 | Philadelphia |
| Sept. 25 | L | 21–30 | at Phoenix |
| Oct. 2 | L | 23–24 | NY Giants |
| Oct. 9 | W | 35–17 | at Dallas |
| Oct. 16 | W | 33–17 | Phoenix |
| Oct. 23 | W | 20–17 | at Green Bay |
| Oct. 30 | L | 17–41 | at Houston |
| Nov. 6 | W | 27–24 | New Orleans |
| Nov. 13 | L | 14–34 | Chicago |
| Nov. 21 | L | 21–37 | at San Francisco |
| Nov. 27 | L | 13–17 | Cleveland |
| Dec. 4 | W | 20–19 | at Philadelphia |
| Dec. 11 | L | 17–24 | Dallas |
| Dec. 17 | L | 17–20 | at Cincinnati |

**1989 — 10–6**

| Date | Result | Score | Opponent |
|---|---|---|---|
| Sept. 11 | L | 24–27 | NY Giants |
| Sept. 17 | L | 37–42 | Philadelphia |
| Sept. 24 | W | 30–7 | at Dallas |
| Oct. 1 | W | 16–14 | at New Orleans |
| Oct. 8 | W | 30–28 | Phoenix |
| Oct. 15 | L | 17–20 | at NY Giants |
| Oct. 22 | W | 32–28 | Tampa Bay |
| Oct. 29 | L | 24–37 | LA Raiders |
| Nov. 5 | L | 3–13 | Dallas |
| Nov. 12 | W | 10–3 | at Philadelphia |
| Nov. 20 | L | 10–14 | Denver |
| Nov. 26 | W | 38–14 | Chicago |
| Dec. 3 | W | 29–10 | at Phoenix |
| Dec. 10 | W | 26–21 | San Diego |
| Dec. 17 | W | 31–30 | at Atlanta |
| Dec. 23 | W | 29–0 | at Seattle |

**1990 — 10–6**

| Date | Result | Score | Opponent |
|---|---|---|---|
| Sept. 9 | W | 31–0 | Phoenix |
| Sept. 16 | L | 13–26 | at San Francisco |
| Sept. 23 | W | 19–15 | Dallas |
| Sept. 30 | W | 38–10 | at Phoenix |
| Oct. 14 | L | 20–24 | NY Giants |
| Oct. 21 | W | 13–7 | Philadelphia |
| Oct. 28 | L | 10–21 | at NY Giants |
| Nov. 4 | W | 41–38 | at Detroit |
| Nov. 12 | L | 14–28 | at Philadelphia |
| Nov. 18 | W | 31–17 | New Orleans |
| Nov. 22 | L | 17–27 | at Dallas |
| Dec. 2 | W | 42–20 | Miami |
| Dec. 9 | W | 10–9 | Chicago |
| Dec. 15 | W | 25–10 | at New England |
| Dec. 22 | L | 28–35 | at Indianapolis |
| Dec. 30 | W | 29–14 | Buffalo |
| Playoffs | | | |
| Jan. 4 | W | 20–6 | at Philadelphia |
| Jan. 12 | L | 10–28 | at San Francisco |

## 1991 — 14–2

| Date | | Score | Opponent |
|---|---|---|---|
| Sept. 1 | W | 45–0 | Detroit |
| Sept. 9 | W | 33–31 | at Dallas |
| Sept. 15 | W | 34–0 | Phoenix |
| Sept. 22 | W | 34–27 | at Cincinnati |
| Sept. 30 | W | 23–0 | Philadelphia |
| Oct. 6 | W | 20–7 | at Chicago |
| Oct. 13 | W | 42–17 | Cleveland |
| Oct. 27 | W | 17–13 | at NY Giants |
| Nov. 3 | W | 16–13 | Houston |
| Nov. 10 | W | 56–17 | Atlanta |
| Nov. 17 | W | 41–14 | at Pittsburgh |
| Nov. 24 | L | 21–24 | Dallas |
| Dec. 1 | W | 27–6 | at LA Rams |
| Dec. 8 | W | 20–14 | at Phoenix |
| Dec. 15 | W | 34–17 | NY Giants |
| Dec. 22 | L | 22–24 | at Philadelphia |
| Playoffs | | | |
| Jan. 4 | W | 24–7 | Atlanta |
| Jan. 12 | W | 41–10 | Detroit |
| Super Bowl XXVI, Minneapolis, Minn. | | | |
| Jan. 26 | W | 37–24 | Buffalo |

## 1992 — 9–7

| Date | | Score | Opponent |
|---|---|---|---|
| Sept. 7 | L | 10–23 | at Dallas |
| Sept. 13 | W | 24–17 | Atlanta |
| Sept. 20 | W | 13–10 | Detroit |
| Oct. 4 | L | 24–27 | at Phoenix |
| Oct. 12 | W | 34–3 | Denver |
| Oct. 18 | W | 16–12 | Philadelphia |
| Oct. 25 | W | 15–13 | at Minnesota |
| Nov. 1 | L | 7–24 | NY Giants |
| Nov. 8 | W | 16–3 | at Seattle |
| Nov. 15 | L | 15–35 | at Kansas City |
| Nov. 23 | L | 3–20 | at New Orleans |
| Nov. 29 | W | 41–3 | Phoenix |
| Dec. 6 | W | 28–10 | at NY Giants |
| Dec. 13 | W | 20–17 | Dallas |
| Dec. 20 | L | 13–17 | at Philadelphia |
| Dec. 26 | L | 20–21 | LA Rams |
| Playoffs | | | |
| Jan. 2 | W | 24–7 | at Minnesota |
| Jan. 9 | L | 13–20 | at San Francisco |

## 1993 — 4–12

| Date | | Score | Opponent |
|---|---|---|---|
| Sept. 6 | W | 35–16 | Dallas |
| Sept. 12 | L | 10–17 | Phoenix |
| Sept. 19 | L | 31–34 | at Philadelphia |
| Oct. 4 | L | 10–17 | at Miami |
| Oct. 10 | L | 7–41 | NY Giants |
| Oct. 17 | L | 6–36 | at Phoenix |
| Nov. 1 | L | 10–24 | at Buffalo |
| Nov. 7 | W | 30–24 | Indianapolis |
| Nov. 14 | L | 6–20 | at NY Giants |
| Nov. 21 | L | 6–10 | at LA Rams |
| Nov. 28 | L | 14–17 | Philadelphia |
| Dec. 5 | W | 23–17 | at Tampa Bay |
| Dec. 11 | L | 0–3 | NY Jets |
| Dec. 19 | W | 30–17 | Atlanta |
| Dec. 26 | L | 3–38 | at Dallas |
| Dec. 31 | L | 9–14 | Minnesota |

## 1994 — 3–13

| Date | | Score | Opponent |
|---|---|---|---|
| Sept. 4 | L | 7–28 | Seattle |
| Sept. 11 | W | 38–24 | at New Orleans |
| Sept. 18 | L | 23–31 | at NY Giants |
| Sept. 25 | L | 20–27 | Atlanta |
| Oct. 2 | L | 7–34 | Dallas |
| Oct. 9 | L | 17–21 | at Philadelphia |
| Oct. 16 | L | 16–19 | Arizona |
| Oct. 23 | W | 41–27 | at Indianapolis |
| Oct. 30 | L | 29–31 | Philadelphia |
| Nov. 6 | L | 22–37 | San Francisco |
| Nov. 20 | L | 7–31 | at Dallas |
| Nov. 27 | L | 19–21 | NY Giants |
| Dec. 4 | L | 21–26 | at Tampa Bay |
| Dec. 11 | L | 15–17 | at Arizona |
| Dec. 18 | L | 14–17 | Tampa Bay |
| Dec. 24 | W | 24–21 | at LA Rams |

## 1995 — 6–10

| Date | | Score | Opponent |
|---|---|---|---|
| Sept. 3 | W | 27–7 | Arizona |
| Sept. 10 | L | 8–20 | Oakland |
| Sept. 17 | L | 31–38 | at Denver |
| Sept. 24 | L | 6–14 | at Tampa Bay |
| Oct. 1 | W | 27–23 | Dallas |
| Oct. 8 | L | 34–37 | at Philadelphia |
| Oct. 15 | L | 20–24 | at Arizona |
| Oct. 22 | W | 36–30 | Detroit |
| Oct. 29 | L | 15–24 | NY Giants |
| Nov. 5 | L | 3–24 | at Kansas City |
| Nov. 19 | L | 20–27 | Seattle |
| Nov. 26 | L | 7–14 | Philadelphia |
| Dec. 3 | W | 24–17 | at Dallas |
| Dec. 10 | L | 13–20 | at NY Giants |
| Dec. 17 | W | 35–23 | at St. Louis |
| Dec. 24 | W | 20–17 | Carolina |

## 1996 — 9–7

| Date | | Score | Opponent |
|---|---|---|---|
| Sept. 1 | L | 14–17 | Philadelphia |
| Sept. 8 | W | 10–3 | Chicago |
| Sept. 15 | W | 31–10 | at NY Giants |
| Sept. 22 | W | 17–10 | at St. Louis |
| Sept. 29 | W | 31–16 | NY Jets |
| Oct. 13 | W | 27–22 | at New England |
| Oct. 20 | W | 31–21 | NY Giants |
| Oct. 27 | W | 31–16 | Indianapolis |
| Nov. 3 | L | 13–38 | at Buffalo |
| Nov. 10 | L | 34–37 | Arizona |
| Nov. 17 | W | 26–21 | at Philadelphia |
| Nov. 24 | L | 16–19 | San Francisco |
| Nov. 28 | L | 10–21 | at Dallas |
| Dec. 8 | L | 10–24 | at Tampa Bay |
| Dec. 15 | L | 26–27 | at Arizona |
| Dec. 22 | W | 37–10 | Dallas |

## 1997 — 8–7–1

| Date | | Score | Opponent |
|---|---|---|---|
| Aug. 31 | W | 24–10 | at Carolina |
| Sept. 7 | L | 13–14 | at Pittsburgh |
| Sept. 14 | W | 19–13 | Arizona |
| Sept. 28 | W | 24–13 | Jacksonville |
| Oct. 5 | L | 10–24 | at Philadelphia |
| Oct. 13 | W | 21–16 | Dallas |
| Oct. 19 | L | 14–28 | at Tennessee |
| Oct. 26 | L | 17–20 | Baltimore |
| Nov. 2 | W | 31–8 | at Chicago |
| Nov. 9 | W | 30–7 | Detroit |
| Nov. 16 | L | 14–17 | at Dallas |
| Nov. 23 | T | 7–7 | NY Giants |
| Nov. 30 | L | 20–23 | St. Louis |
| Dec. 7 | W | 38–28 | at Arizona |
| Dec. 13 | L | 10–30 | at NY Giants |
| Dec. 21 | W | 35–32 | Philadelphia |

## 1998 — 6–10

| Date | | Score | Opponent |
|---|---|---|---|
| Sept. 6 | L | 24–31 | at NY Giants |
| Sept. 14 | L | 10–45 | San Francisco |
| Sept. 20 | L | 14–24 | at Seattle |
| Sept. 27 | L | 16–38 | Denver |
| Oct. 4 | L | 10–31 | Dallas |
| Oct. 11 | L | 12–17 | at Philadelphia |
| Oct. 18 | L | 7–41 | at Minnesota |
| Nov. 1 | W | 21–14 | NY Giants |
| Nov. 8 | L | 27–29 | at Arizona |
| Nov. 15 | W | 28–3 | Philadelphia |
| Nov. 22 | L | 42–45 | Arizona |
| Nov. 29 | W | 29–19 | at Oakland |
| Dec. 6 | W | 24–20 | San Diego |
| Dec. 13 | W | 28–25 | at Carolina |
| Dec. 19 | W | 20–16 | Tampa Bay |
| Dec. 27 | L | 7–23 | at Dallas |

## 1999

| | | | |
|---|---|---|---|
| Sept. 12 | L | 35–41 | Dallas |
| Sept. 19 | W | 50–21 | at NY Giants |
| Sept. 26 | W | 27–20 | at NY Jets |
| Oct. 3 | W | 38–36 | Carolina |
| Oct. 17 | W | 24–10 | at Arizona |
| Oct. 24 | L | 20–38 | at Dallas |
| Oct. 31 | W | 48–22 | Chicago |
| Nov. 7 | L | 17–34 | Buffalo |
| Nov. 14 | L | 28–35 | at Philadelphia |
| Nov. 21 | W | 23–13 | NY Giants |
| Nov. 28 | W | 20–17 | Philadelphia |
| Dec. 5 | L | 17–33 | at Detroit |
| Dec. 12 | W | 28–3 | Arizona |
| Dec. 19 | L | 21–24 | at Indianapolis |
| Dec. 26 | W | 26–20 | at San Francisco |
| Jan. 2 | W | 21–10 | Miami |

**Playoffs**

| | | | |
|---|---|---|---|
| Jan. 8 | W | 27–13 | Detroit |
| Jan. 15 | L | 13–14 | at Tampa Bay |

## 2000

**8–8**

| | | | |
|---|---|---|---|
| Sept. 3 | W | 20–17 | Carolina |
| Sept. 10 | L | 10–15 | at Detroit |
| Sept. 18 | L | 21–27 | Dallas |
| Sept. 24 | W | 16–6 | at NY Giants |
| Oct. 1 | W | 20–17 | Tampa Bay |
| Oct. 8 | W | 17–14 | at Philadelphia |
| Oct. 15 | W | 10–3 | Baltimore |
| Oct. 22 | W | 35–16 | at Jacksonville |
| Oct. 30 | L | 21–27 | Tennessee |
| Nov. 5 | L | 15–16 | at Arizona |
| Nov. 20 | W | 33–20 | at St. Louis |
| Nov. 26 | L | 20–23 | Philadelphia |
| Dec. 3 | L | 7–9 | NY Giants |
| Dec. 10 | L | 13–32 | at Dallas |
| Dec. 16 | L | 3–24 | at Pittsburgh |
| Dec. 24 | W | 20–3 | Arizona |

## 2001

**8–8**

| | | | |
|---|---|---|---|
| Sept. 9 | L | 3–30 | at San Diego |
| Sept. 24 | L | 0–37 | at Green Bay |
| Sept. 30 | L | 13–45 | Kansas City |
| Oct. 7 | L | 9–23 | at NY Giants |
| Oct. 15 | L | 7–9 | at Dallas |
| Oct. 21 | W | 17–14 (OT) | Carolina |
| Oct. 28 | W | 35–21 | NY Giants |
| Nov. 4 | W | 27–14 | Seattle |
| Nov. 18 | W | 17–10 | at Denver |
| Nov. 25 | W | 13–3 | at Philadelphia |
| Dec. 2 | L | 14–20 | Dallas |
| Dec. 9 | W | 20–10 | at Arizona |
| Dec. 16 | L | 6–20 | Philadelphia |
| Dec. 23 | L | 15–20 | Chicago |
| Dec. 30 | W | 40–10 | at New Orleans |
| Jan. 6 | W | 20–17 | Arizona |

## 2002

**7–9**

| | | | |
|---|---|---|---|
| Sept. 8 | W | 31–23 | Arizona |
| Sept. 16 | L | 7–37 | Philadelphia |
| Sept. 22 | L | 10–20 | at San Francisco |
| Oct. 6 | W | 31–14 | at Tennessee |
| Oct. 13 | L | 27–43 | New Orleans |
| Oct. 20 | L | 9–30 | at Green Bay |
| Oct. 27 | W | 26–21 | Indianapolis |
| Nov. 3 | W | 14–3 | at Seattle |
| Nov. 10 | L | 7–26 | at Jacksonville |
| Nov. 17 | L | 17–19 | at NY Giants |
| Nov. 24 | W | 20–17 | St. Louis |
| Nov. 28 | L | 20–27 | at Dallas |
| Dec. 8 | L | 21–27 | NY Giants |
| Dec. 15 | L | 21–34 | at Philadelphia |
| Dec. 22 | W | 26–10 | Houston |
| Dec. 29 | W | 20–14 | Dallas |

## 2003

**10–6**

| | | | |
|---|---|---|---|
| Sept. 4 | W | 16–13 | NY Jets |
| Sept. 14 | W | 33–31 | at Atlanta |
| Sept. 21 | L | 21–24 (OT) | NY Giants |
| Sept. 28 | W | 20–17 | New England |
| Oct. 5 | L | 25–27 | at Philadelphia |
| Oct. 12 | L | 13–35 | Tampa Bay |
| Oct. 19 | L | 7–24 | at Buffalo |
| Nov. 2 | L | 14–21 | at Dallas |
| Nov. 9 | W | 27–20 | Seattle |
| Nov. 16 | L | 17–20 | at Carolina |
| Nov. 23 | L | 23–24 | at Miami |
| Nov. 30 | L | 20–24 | New Orleans |
| Dec. 7 | W | 20–7 | at NY Giants |
| Dec. 14 | L | 0–27 | Dallas |
| Dec. 21 | L | 24–27 | at Chicago |
| Dec. 29 | L | 7–31 | Philadelphia |

## 2004

**6–10**

| | | | |
|---|---|---|---|
| Sept. 12 | W | 16–10 | Tampa Bay |
| Sept. 19 | L | 14–20 | at NY Giants |
| Sept. 27 | L | 18–21 | Dallas |
| Oct. 3 | L | 13–17 | at Cleveland |
| Oct. 10 | L | 0–17 | Baltimore |
| Oct. 17 | W | 13–10 | at Chicago |
| Oct. 31 | L | 14–28 | Green Bay |
| Nov. 7 | W | 17–10 | at Detroit |
| Nov. 14 | L | 10–17 | Cincinnati |
| Nov. 21 | L | 6–28 | at Philadelphia |
| Nov. 28 | L | 7–16 | at Pittsburgh |
| Dec. 5 | W | 31–7 | NY Giants |
| Dec. 12 | L | 14–17 | Philadelphia |
| Dec. 18 | W | 26–16 | at San Francisco |
| Dec. 26 | L | 10–13 | at Dallas |
| Jan. 2 | W | 21–18 | Minnesota |

## 2005

**10–6**

| | | | |
|---|---|---|---|
| Sept. 11 | W | 9–7 | Chicago |
| Sept. 19 | W | 14–13 | at Dallas |
| Oct. 2 | W | 20–17 | Seattle |
| Oct. 9 | L | 19–21 | at Denver |
| Oct. 16 | L | 21–28 | at Kansas City |
| Oct. 23 | W | 52–17 | San Francisco |
| Oct. 30 | L | 0–36 | at NY Giants |
| Nov. 6 | W | 17–10 | Philadelphia |
| Nov. 13 | L | 35–36 | at Tampa Bay |
| Nov. 20 | L | 13–16 | Oakland |
| Nov. 27 | L | 17–23 | San Diego |
| Dec. 4 | W | 24–9 | at St. Louis |
| Dec. 11 | W | 17–13 | at Arizona |
| Dec. 18 | W | 35–7 | Dallas |
| Dec. 24 | W | 35–17 | NY Giants |
| Jan. 1 | W | 31–20 | at Philadelphia |

**Playoffs**

| | | | |
|---|---|---|---|
| Jan. 7 | W | 17–10 | at Tampa Bay |
| Jan. 14 | L | 10–20 | at Seattle |

## 2006

**5–11**

| | | | |
|---|---|---|---|
| Sept. 11 | L | 16–19 | Minnesota |
| Sept. 17 | L | 10–27 | at Dallas |
| Sept. 24 | W | 31–15 | at Houston |
| Oct. 1 | W | 36–30 | Jacksonville |
| Oct. 8 | L | 3–19 | at NY Giants |
| Oct. 15 | L | 22–25 | Tennessee |
| Oct. 22 | L | 22–36 | at Indianapolis |
| Nov. 5 | W | 22–19 | Dallas |
| Nov. 12 | L | 3–27 | at Philadelphia |
| Nov. 19 | L | 17–20 | at Tampa Bay |
| Nov. 26 | W | 17–13 | Carolina |
| Dec. 3 | L | 14–24 | Atlanta |
| Dec. 10 | L | 19–21 | Philadelphia |
| Dec. 17 | W | 16–10 | at New Orleans |
| Dec. 24 | L | 31–37 | at St. Louis |
| Jan. 1 | L | 28–34 | NY Giants |

**5–11**

NY Jets
at Atlanta
NY Giants
New England
at Philadelphia
Tampa Bay
at Buffalo
at Dallas
Seattle
at Carolina
at Miami
New Orleans
at NY Giants
Dallas
at Chicago
Philadelphia

## MONDAY NIGHT LIGHTS

| | |
|---|---|
| Oct. 19, 1970 | Oakland 34, Washington 20 |
| Dec. 13, 1971 | Washington 38, Los Angeles 24 |
| Sept. 18, 1972 | Washington 24, Minnesota 21 |
| Nov. 20, 1972 | Washington 24, Atlanta 13 |
| Oct. 8, 1973 | Washington 14, Dallas 7 |
| Nov. 5, 1973 | Pittsburgh 21, Washington 16 |
| Sept. 30, 1974 | Washington 30, Denver 3 |
| Dec. 9, 1974 | Washington 23, Los Angeles 17 |
| Oct. 13, 1975 | Washington 27, St. Louis 17 |
| Sept. 27, 1976 | Washington 20, Philadelphia 17 (OT) |
| Oct. 25, 1976 | Washington 20, St. Louis 10 |
| Nov. 7, 1977 | Baltimore 10, Washington 3 |
| Nov. 21, 1977 | Washington 10, Green Bay 9 |
| Oct. 2, 1978 | Washington 9, Dallas 5 |
| Nov. 6, 1978 | Baltimore 21, Washington 17 |
| Sept. 17, 1979 | Washington 27, NY Giants 0 |
| Sept. 8, 1980 | Dallas 17, Washington 3 |
| Oct. 13, 1980 | Denver 20, Washington 17 |
| Sept. 5, 1983 | Dallas 31, Washington 30 |
| Oct. 17, 1983 | Green Bay 48, Washington 47 |
| Oct. 31, 1983 | Washington 27, San Diego 24 |
| Sept. 10, 1984 | San Francisco 37, Washington 31 |
| Nov. 5, 1984 | Washington 27, Atlanta 14 |
| Sept. 9, 1985 | Dallas 44, Washington 14 |
| Oct. 7, 1985 | Washington 27, St. Louis 10 |
| Nov. 18, 1985 | Washington 23, NY Giants 21 |
| Oct. 27, 1986 | NY Giants 27, Washington 20 |
| Nov. 17, 1986 | Washington 14, San Francisco 6 |
| Oct. 19, 1987 | Washington 13, Dallas 7 |
| Nov. 23, 1987 | LA Rams 30, Washington 26 |
| Sept. 5, 1988 | NY Giants 27, Washington 20 |
| Nov. 21, 1988 | San Francisco 37, Washington 21 |
| Sept. 11, 1989 | NY Giants 27, Washington 24 |
| Nov. 20, 1989 | Denver 14, Washington 10 |
| Nov. 12, 1990 | Philadelphia 28, Washington 14 |
| Sept. 9, 1991 | Washington 33, Dallas 31 |
| Sept. 30, 1991 | Washington 23, Philadelphia 0 |
| Sept. 7, 1992 | Dallas 23, Washington 10 |
| Oct. 12, 1992 | Washington 34, Denver 3 |
| Nov. 23, 1992 | New Orleans 20, Washington 3 |
| Sept. 6, 1993 | Washington 35, Dallas 16 |
| Oct. 4, 1993 | Miami 17, Washington 10 |
| Nov. 1, 1993 | Buffalo 24, Washington 10 |
| Oct. 13, 1997 | Washington 21, Dallas 16 |
| Sept. 14, 1998 | San Francisco 45, Washington 10 |
| Sept. 18, 2000 | Dallas 27, Washington 21 |
| Oct. 30, 2000 | Tennessee 27, Washington 21 |
| Nov. 20, 2000 | Washington 33, St. Louis 20 |
| Sept. 24, 2001 | Green Bay 37, Washington 0 |
| Oct. 15, 2001 | Dallas 9, Washington 7 |
| Sept. 16, 2002 | Philadelphia 37, Washington 7 |
| Sept. 27, 2004 | Dallas 21, Washington 18 |
| Sept. 19, 2005 | Washington 14, Dallas 13 |
| Sept. 11, 2006 | Minnesota 19, Washington 16 |

Overall record: 25–29

## RING OF FAME

The upper deck at FedExField bears white plaques honoring those who have made distinguished contributions to the Redskins. Named the Ring of Fame, there are now 41 honorees on the stadium wall.

| | | |
|---|---|---|
| George Allen | Len Hauss | Bobby Mitchell |
| Cliff Battles | Phil Hochberg | Art Monk |
| Sammy Baugh | Ken Houston | Mark Moseley |
| Gene Brito | Sam Huff | Brig Owens |
| Larry Brown | Joe Jacoby | Vince Promuto |
| Dave Butz | Dick James | John Riggins |
| Jack Kent Cooke | Sonny Jurgensen | Jerry Smith |
| Wayne Curry | Charlie Justice | Charley Taylor |
| Bill Dudley | Billy Kilmer | Joe Theismann |
| Pat Fischer | Eddie LeBaron | Lamar "Bubba" Tyer |
| Joe Gibbs | Vince Lombardi | Doug Williams |
| Darrell Green | Dexter Manley | |
| Russ Grimm | Charles Mann | |
| Chris Hanburger | George Preston Marshall | |
| Ken Harvey | Wayne Millner | |

## Photo Credits

The author wishes to thank the following sources for permission to reprint the photographs that appear in this book: Washington Redskins, Samu Quereshi, Ron Sachs of Consolidated News Photos, Mark Greek of the Washingtoniana Division at the D.C. Public Library, John Kent Cooke and the Jack Kent Cooke Foundation, United Press International, Oakland Raiders, Miami Dolphins, Dallas Cowboys, San Diego State University, Washington State University, and the Washington Redskins Cheerleaders Alumni Association.

CHAPTER 2
p. 4, top: Jack Kent Cooke Foundation. Courtesy John Kent Cooke.
p. 6, top: Jack Kent Cooke Foundation. Courtesy John Kent Cooke.

CHAPTER 3
p. 7, bottom: Jack Kent Cooke Foundation. Courtesy John Kent Cooke.
p. 9, bottom: Jack Kent Cooke Foundation. Courtesy John Kent Cooke.
p. 10, top: From the collection of Samu Quereshi.
p. 13, top: Jack Kent Cooke Foundation. Courtesy John Kent Cooke.
p. 14, bottom: From the collection of Samu Quereshi.
p. 15, bottom: Jack Kent Cooke Foundation. Courtesy John Kent Cooke.
p. 25, top: Jack Kent Cooke Foundation. Courtesy John Kent Cooke.

CHAPTER 4
p. 36, top: Copyright *Washington Post.* Reprinted by permission of the D.C. Public Library.
p. 39, top: Copyright *Washington Post.* Reprinted by permission of the D.C. Public Library.
p. 41, top: Copyright *Washington Post.* Reprinted by permission of the D.C. Public Library.
p. 46, bottom: From the collection of Samu Quereshi.
p. 50, top: Copyright *Washington Post.* Reprinted by permission of the D.C. Public Library.

CHAPTER 5
p. 56, top: Photo by Malcolm W. Emmons. From the collection of Samu Quereshi.
p. 57, top: Photo courtesy of Washington Redskins Cheerleaders Alumni Association.
p. 67, top: Jack Kent Cooke Foundation. Courtesy John Kent Cooke.

CHAPTER 6
p. 76, top: Copyright *Washington Post.* Reprinted by permission of the D.C. Public Library.
p. 80, bottom: Jack Kent Cooke Foundation. Courtesy John Kent Cooke.
p. 83, bottom: Copyright *Washington Post.* Reprinted by permission of the D.C. Public Library.
p. 86, top: Photo by Paul Fine. From the collection of Samu Quereshi.
p. 90, top: Arnie Sachs–Consolidated News Photos.
p. 91, bottom: Photo by United Press International. From the collection of Samu Quereshi.
p. 92, top: Photo by Malcolm W. Emmons. From the collection of Samu Quereshi.

p. 93, top: Photo courtesy of Miami Dolphins.
p. 100, bottom: Copyright *Washington Post.* Reprinted by permission of the D.C. Public Library.
p. 101: Copyright *Washington Post.* Reprinted by permission of the D.C. Public Library.

REDSKINS-COWBOYS RIVALRY
p. 115, bottom: Photo courtesy of Dallas Cowboys.

CHAPTER 7
p. 128, top: Jack Kent Cooke Foundation. Courtesy John Kent Cooke.
p. 130, top: Jack Kent Cooke Foundation. Courtesy John Kent Cooke.
p. 131: Arnie Sachs-Consolidated News Photos.
p. 133, bottom: Photo by United Press International. From the collection of Samu Quereshi.
p. 134, top: Photo by United Press International. From the collection of Samu Quereshi.
p. 135, top: Jack Kent Cooke Foundation. Courtesy John Kent Cooke.
p. 141, top: Photo courtesy of Oakland Raiders.
p. 142, top: Photo courtesy of Oakland Raiders.
p. 149, top: Arnie Sachs-Consolidated News Photos.
p. 151, top: Arnie Sachs-Consolidated News Photos.
p. 164, bottom: Jack Kent Cooke Foundation. Courtesy John Kent Cooke.
p. 178, top: Arnie Sachs–Consolidated News Photos.
p. 179, top: Arnie Sachs–Consolidated News Photos.

CHAPTER 8
p. 193, top: Ron Sachs–Consolidated News Photos.
p. 198, top left: Ron Sachs–Consolidated News Photos.
p. 202, top: Arnie Sachs–Consolidated News Photos.

CHAPTER 9
p. 240, top: From the collection of Samu Quereshi.
p. 241, bottom: Copyright *Washington Post.* Reprinted by permission of the D.C. Public Library.
p. 244, top: Photo courtesy of Washington State University.
p. 246, top: Copyright *Washington Post.* Reprinted by permission of the D.C. Public Library.
p. 248, top: Photo courtesy of San Diego State University.
p. 251, bottom: Copyright *Washington Post.* Reprinted by permission of the D.C. Public Library.
p. 252, top: Photo by Paul Fine. From the collection of Samu Quereshi.
p. 258, top: Copyright *Washington Post.* Reprinted by permission of the D.C. Public Library.
p. 261, bottom: Jack Kent Cooke Foundation. Courtesy John Kent Cooke.

CHAPTER 10
p. 274, top: Copyright *Washington Post.* Reprinted by permission of the D.C. Public Library.
p. 284, top: Copyright *Washington Post.* Reprinted by permission of the D.C. Public Library.
p. 297, top: Copyright *Washington Post.* Reprinted by permission of the D.C. Public Library.
p. 322, top: Copyright *Washington Post.* Reprinted by permission of the D.C. Public Library.
p. 343, top: Copyright *Washington Post.* Reprinted by permission of the D.C. Public Library.
p. 345: Arnie Sachs-Consolidated News Photos.

MICHAEL RICHMAN is a veteran journalist who has covered sports for more than two decades. His articles on Redskins nostalgia have appeared in Sports Illustrated magazine and Redskins team media outlets, and he has contributed to many other publications. In 2003, he received an award from the Pro Football Researchers Association for feature writing. He works at the Voice of America in Washington, D.C.